PAGE 58

ON THE ROAD

YOUR COMPLETE DESTINATION GUIDE
In-depth reviews, detailed listings and insider tips

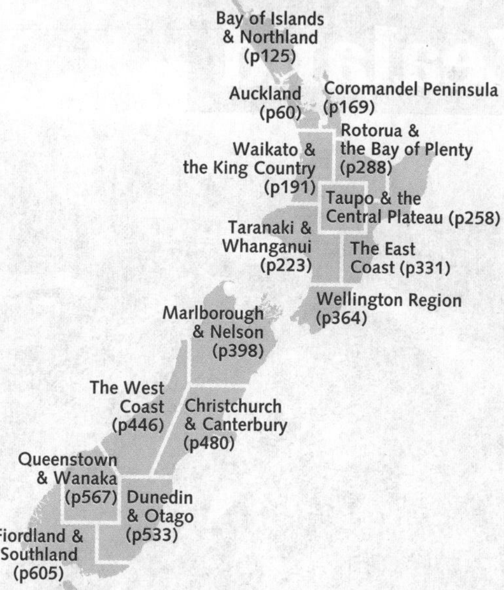

PAGE 675

SURVIVAL GUIDE

VITAL PRACTICAL INFORMATION TO HELP YOU HAVE A SMOOTH TRIP

Directory A–Z 676
Transport 690
Language 699
Index 706
Map Legend 718

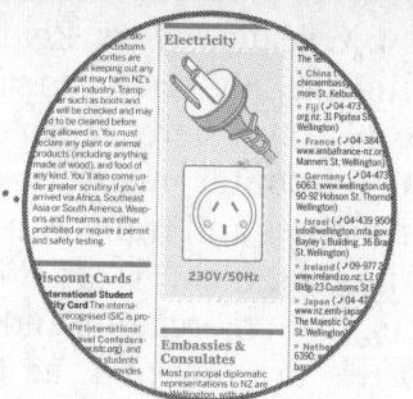

THIS EDITION WRITTEN AND RESEARCHED BY

Charles Rawlings-Way

Brett Atkinson, Sarah Bennett, Peter Dragicevich, Lee Slater

welcome to New Zealand

The New 'Big Easy'

Forget New Orleans... New Zealand can rightly claim the 'Big Easy' crown for the sheer ease of travel here. It isn't a place where you encounter many on-the-road frustrations: buses and trains run on time; roads are in good nick; ATMs proliferate; pickpockets, scam merchants and bedbug-ridden hostels are few and far between; and the food is unlikely to send you running for the nearest public toilets (which are usually clean and stocked with the requisite paper). And there are no snakes, and only one poisonous spider – the rare katipo – sightings of which are considered lucky. This decent nation is a place where you can relax and enjoy (rather than endure) your holiday.

Walk on the Wild Side

There are just 4.36 million New Zealanders, scattered across 268,680 sq km: bigger than the UK with one-fourteenth the population. Filling in the gaps are the sublime forests, mountains, lakes, beaches and fiords that have made NZ one of the best hiking (locals call it 'tramping') destinations on the planet. Tackle one of nine epic 'Great Walks' – you've probably heard of the Heaphy and Milford Tracks – or just spend a few dreamy hours wandering through some easily accessible wilderness.

SCOTT DARSNEY / LONELY PLANET IMAGES ©

Plucked straight from a film set or a coffee-table book of picture-perfect scenery, New Zealand is jaw-droppingly gorgeous. 'Wow!' will escape from your lips at least once a day.

(left) Runner along ridge near the summit of Roy's Peak (p597), Wanaka. (below) Detail of Maori carving, Tongariro National Park (p275), Central Plateau.

RICHARD I'ANSON / LONELY PLANET IMAGES ©

Food, Wine & Beer

Kiwi food was once a bland echo of a British Sunday dinner, but these days NZ chefs find inspiration in new-world culinary oceans, especially the Pacific with its abundant seafood and encircling cuisines. And don't go home without trying some Maori faves: paua (abalone), kina (sea urchin) and kumara (sweet potato) make regular menu appearances. Thirsty? NZ's cool-climate wineries have been collecting wine-award trophies for decades now, but the country's booming craft-beer scene also deserves your serious scrutiny. And with coffee culture firmly entrenched, you can usually slake your craving for a decent double-shot.

Maori Culture

If you're even remotely interested in rugby, you'll have heard of the all-conquering All Blacks, NZ's national team, who would never have become world-beaters without their awesome Maori players. But this is just one example of how Maori culture impresses itself on contemporary Kiwi life: across NZ you can hear Maori language, watch Maori TV, see main-street *marae* (meeting houses), join in a *hangi* (Maori feast) or catch a cultural performance with traditional Maori song, dance and usually a blood-curdling *haka* (war dance). And don't let us stop you from considering *ta moko*, traditional Maori tattooing (often applied to the face).

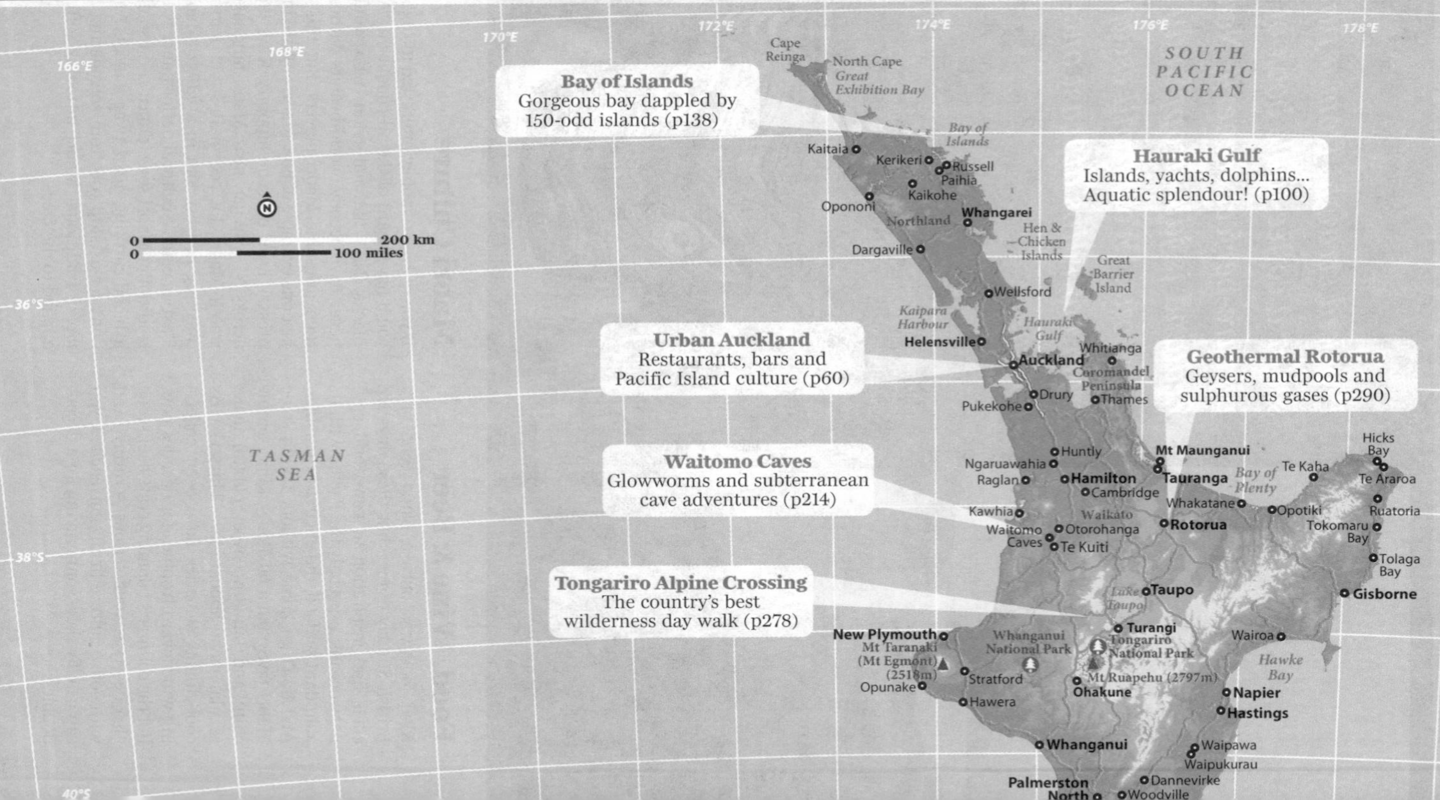
Bay of Islands
Gorgeous bay dappled by 150-odd islands (p138)
Hauraki Gulf
Islands, yachts, dolphins... Aquatic splendour! (p100)
Urban Auckland
Restaurants, bars and Pacific Island culture (p60)
Geothermal Rotorua
Geysers, mudpools and sulphurous gases (p290)
Waitomo Caves
Glowworms and subterranean cave adventures (p214)
Tongariro Alpine Crossing
The country's best wilderness day walk (p278)
SOUTH PACIFIC OCEAN
TASMAN SEA
0 200 km
0 100 miles
166°E
168°E
170°E
172°E
174°E
176°E
178°E
36°S
38°S
40°S
Cape Reinga
North Cape
Great Exhibition Bay
Bay of Islands
Kaitaia
Kerikeri
Russell
Paihia
Kaikohe
Opononi
Whangarei
Northland
Hen & Chicken Islands
Dargaville
Great Barrier Island
Wellsford
Kaipara Harbour
Hauraki Gulf
Helensville
Auckland
Whitianga
Coromandel Peninsula
Drury
Thames
Pukekohe
Huntly
Ngaruawahia
Raglan
Hamilton
Cambridge
Mt Maunganui
Tauranga
Bay of Plenty
Te Kaha
Hicks Bay
Te Araroa
Ruatoria
Whakatane
Opotiki
Tokomaru Bay
Tolaga Bay
Kawhia
Waikato
Waitomo Caves
Otorohanga
Te Kuiti
Rotorua
Lake Taupo
Taupo
Gisborne
New Plymouth
Mt Taranaki (Mt Egmont) (2518m)
Opunake
Stratford
Hawera
Whanganui National Park
Turangi
Tongariro National Park
Mt Ruapehu (2797m)
Ohakune
Wairoa
Hawke Bay
Napier
Hastings
Whanganui
Waipawa
Waipukurau
Palmerston North
Dannevirke
Woodville

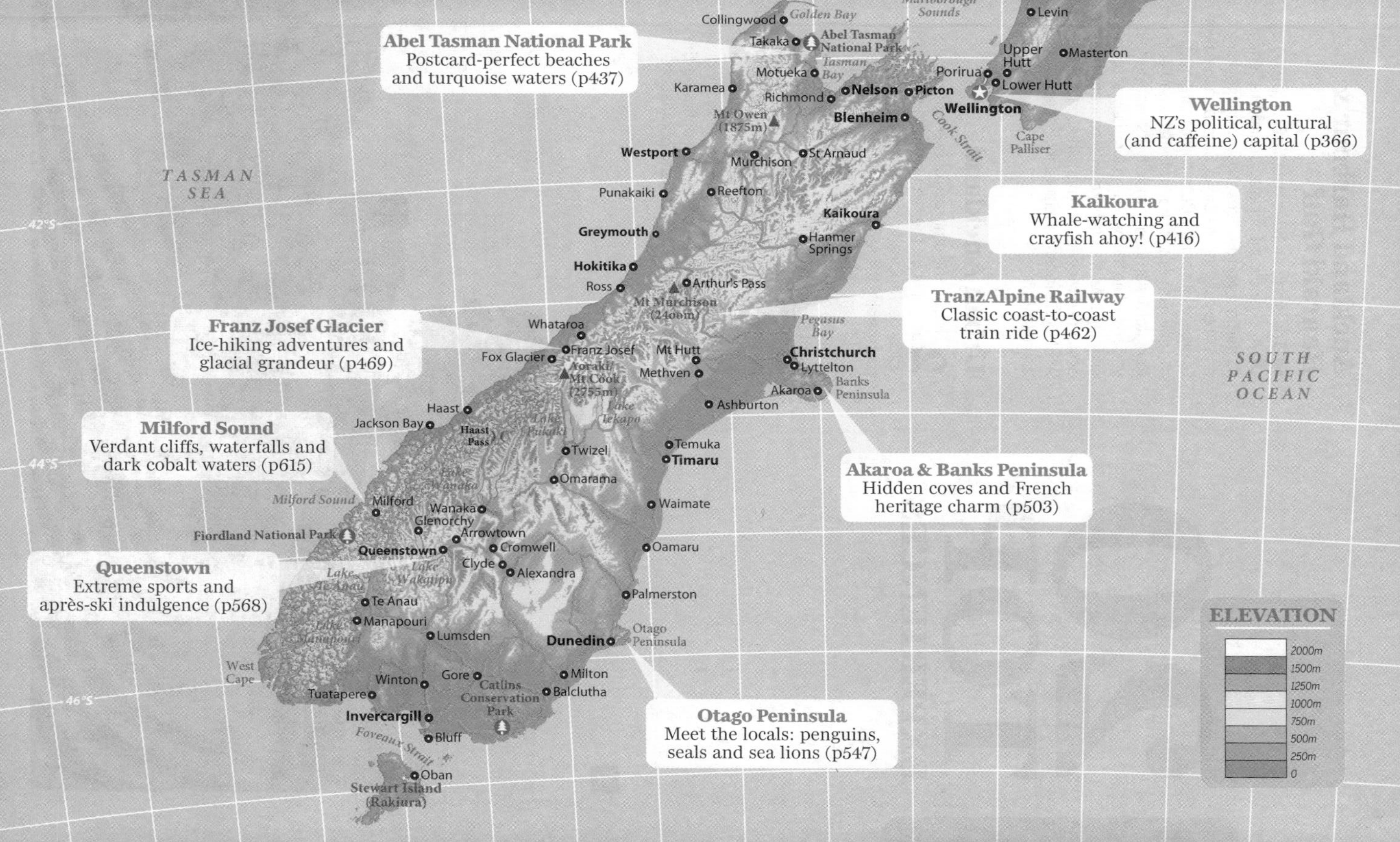
Abel Tasman National Park
Postcard-perfect beaches and turquoise waters (p437)
Wellington
NZ's political, cultural (and caffeine) capital (p366)
Kaikoura
Whale-watching and crayfish ahoy! (p416)
TranzAlpine Railway
Classic coast-to-coast train ride (p462)
Franz Josef Glacier
Ice-hiking adventures and glacial grandeur (p469)
Milford Sound
Verdant cliffs, waterfalls and dark cobalt waters (p615)
Akaroa & Banks Peninsula
Hidden coves and French heritage charm (p503)
Queenstown
Extreme sports and après-ski indulgence (p568)
Otago Peninsula
Meet the locals: penguins, seals and sea lions (p547)
TASMAN SEA
SOUTH PACIFIC OCEAN
42°S
44°S
46°S
Collingwood
Golden Bay
Takaka
Abel Tasman National Park
Motueka
Tasman Bay
Karamea
Richmond
Nelson
Picton
Blenheim
Mt Owen (1875m)
Westport
Murchison
St Arnaud
Punakaiki
Reefton
Greymouth
Kaikoura
Hanmer Springs
Hokitika
Ross
Arthur's Pass
Mt Murchison (2400m)
Pegasus Bay
Whataroa
Franz Josef
Fox Glacier
Mt Hutt
Methven
Christchurch
Lyttelton
Banks Peninsula
Akaroa
Aoraki/Mt Cook (2755m)
Haast
Jackson Bay
Haast Pass
Lake Pukaki
Lake Tekapo
Ashburton
Temuka
Timaru
Twizel
Omarama
Lake Wanaka
Milford Sound
Milford
Wanaka
Glenorchy
Arrowtown
Fiordland National Park
Queenstown
Cromwell
Clyde
Alexandra
Lake Wakatipu
Lake Te Anau
Te Anau
Manapouri
Lake Manapouri
Lumsden
Waimate
Oamaru
Palmerston
Dunedin
Otago Peninsula
Milton
Balclutha
West Cape
Winton
Gore
Catlins Conservation Park
Tuatapere
Invercargill
Bluff
Foveaux Strait
Oban
Stewart Island (Rakiura)
Levin
Masterton
Upper Hutt
Lower Hutt
Porirua
Wellington
Cook Strait
Cape Palliser
ELEVATION
2000m
1500m
1250m
1000m
750m
500m
250m
0

20 TOP EXPERIENCES

Auckland Harbour & Hauraki Gulf

1 The island-studded Hauraki Gulf (p100) is Auckland's aquatic playground, sheltering its harbour and east-coast bays and providing ample excuse for the City of Sails' pleasure fleet to breeze into action. Despite the maritime traffic, the gulf has resident pods of whales and dolphins. Rangitoto is an icon of the city, its near-perfect volcanic cone the backdrop for many a tourist snapshot. Yet it's Waiheke, with beautiful beaches, acclaimed wineries and upmarket eateries, that is Auckland's most popular island escape. Waiheke Island (p103)

Urban Auckland

2 Held in the embrace of two harbours and built on the remnants of long-extinct volcanoes, Auckland (p60) isn't your average metropolis. It's regularly rated one of the world's most liveable cities, and while it's never going to challenge NYC or London in the excitement stakes, it's blessed with good beaches, is flanked by wine regions and has a large enough population to support a thriving dining, drinking and live-music scene. Cultural festivals are celebrated with gusto in this ethnically diverse city, which has the distinction of having the world's largest Pacific Island population.

1

OLIVER STREWE / LONELY PLANET IMAGES ©

2

AMOS CHAPPLE / LONELY PLANET IMAGES ©

Geothermal Rotorua

3 The first thing you'll notice about Rotorua (p290) is the sulphur smell – this geothermal hot spot whiffs like old socks. But as the locals point out, volcanic by-products are what everyone is here to see: gushing geysers, bubbling mud, steaming cracks in the ground, boiling pools of mineral-rich water... Rotorua is unique, a fact exploited by some fairly commercial local businesses. But you don't have to spend a fortune – there are plenty of affordable (and free) volcanic encounters to be had in parks, Maori villages or just along the roadside. Wai-O-Tapu Thermal Wonderland (p307)

Wellington

4 Voted the 'coolest little capital in the world' by Lonely Planet in 2011, windy Wellington (p366) lives up to the mantle by keeping things fresh and dynamic. It's long famed for a vibrant arts and music scene, fuelled by excellent espresso and more restaurants per head than New York, but a host of craft-beer bars have now elbowed in on the action. Edgy yet sociable, colourful yet often dressed in black, Wellington is big on the unexpected and unconventional. Erratic weather only adds to the excitement.

3

4

OLIVER STREWE / LONELY PLANET IMAGES ©

5

DAVID WALL / LONELY PLANET IMAGES ©

Kaikoura

5 First settled by Maori with their keen nose for seafood, Kaikoura (p416) is now NZ's best spot for both consuming and communing with marine life. When it comes to 'seafood and eat it', crayfish is still king, but on fishing tours you can hook into other edible wonders of the unique Kaikoura deep. Whales are definitely off the menu, but you're almost guaranteed a good gander at Moby's mates on a whale-watching tour, or there's swimming with seals and dolphins, or spotting some of the many birds – including albatross – that wheel around the shore.

Franz Josef & Fox Glaciers

6 The spectacular glaciers of Franz Josef (p469) and Fox (p474) are remarkable for many reasons, including their rates of accumulation and descent, and their proximity to both the loftiest peaks of the Southern Alps and the Tasman Sea around 10km away. Several short walks meander towards the glaciers' fractured faces (close enough for you to feel insignificant!), or you can take a hike on the ice with Franz Josef Glacier Guides or Fox Glacier Guiding. The ultimate encounter is on a scenic flight, which often also provides grandstand views of Mt Cook, Westland forest and a seemingly endless ocean.
Franz Josef Glacier (p469)

Waitomo Caves

7 Waitomo (p214) is a must-see: an astonishing maze of subterranean caves, canyons and rivers perforating the northern King Country limestone. Black-water rafting is the big lure here (like white-water rafting but through a dark cave), plus glowworm grottoes, underground abseiling and more stalactites and stalagmites than you'll ever see in one place again. Above ground, Waitomo township is a quaint collaboration of businesses: a pub, a cafe, a holiday park and some decent B&Bs. But don't linger in the sunlight – it's party time downstairs!

Bay of Islands

8 Turquoise waters lapping in pretty bays, dolphins frolicking at the bows of boats, pods of orcas gliding gracefully by: chances are these are the kind of images that drew you to New Zealand in the first place, and these are exactly the kind of experiences that the Bay of Islands (p138) delivers so well. Whether you're a hardened sea dog or a confirmed landlubber, there are myriad options to tempt you out on the water to explore the 150-odd islands that dot this beautiful bay.
Urupukapuka Island (p150)

7

8

9

10

GARETH MCCORMACK / LONELY PLANET IMAGES ©

Tongariro Alpine Crossing

9 At the centre of the North Island, Tongariro National Park (p275) presents an alien landscape of alpine desert punctuated by three smoking and smouldering volcanoes. This track offers the perfect taste of what the park has to offer, skirting the base of two of the mountains and providing views of craters, brightly coloured lakes and the vast Central Plateau stretching out beyond. It's for these reasons that it's often rated as one of the world's best single-day wilderness walks. Emerald Lakes (p278)

Rugby

10 Rugby Union is NZ's national game and governing preoccupation. If your timing's good you might catch the revered national team (and reigning world champions), the All Blacks, in action. The 'ABs' are resident gods: mention Richie McCaw or Dan Carter in any conversation and you'll win friends for life. Or just watch some kids chasing a ball around a suburban field on a Saturday morning, or yell along with the locals in a small-town pub as the big men collide on the big screen.

Abel Tasman National Park

11 Here's nature at its most seductive: lush green hills fringed with golden sandy coves, slipping gently into warm shallows before meeting a crystal-clear sea of cerulean blue. Abel Tasman National Park (p437) is the quintessential postcard paradise, where you can put yourself in the picture assuming an endless number of poses: tramping, kayaking, swimming, sunbathing, or even makin' whoopee in the woods. This sweet-as corner of NZ raises the bar and keeps it there. Abel Tasman Coast Track (p437)

11

DAVID WALL / LONELY PLANET IMAGES ©

Maori Culture

12 NZ's indigenous Maori culture (p657) is accessible and engaging: join in a *haka* (war dance); chow down at a traditional *hangi* (Maori feast cooked in the ground); carve a pendant from bone or *pounamu* (jade); learn some Maori language; or check out an authentic cultural performance with song, dance, legends, arts and crafts. Big-city and regional museums around NZ are crammed with Maori artefacts and historical items, but this is also a living culture: vibrant, potent and contemporary.

12

PETER BENNETTS / LONELY PLANET IMAGES ©

Otago Peninsula

13 The Otago Peninsula (p547) is stunning proof there's more to the South Island's outdoor thrills than heart-stopping alpine and lake scenery. Amid a backdrop of coastal vistas combining rugged, hidden beaches with an expansive South Pacific horizon, it's very easy to come face to face with penguins, seals and sea lions. Beyond the rare yellow-eyed penguin (hoiho), other fascinating avian residents include the royal albatross. The peninsula's Taiaroa Head is the world's only mainland royal albatross colony: visit in January or February to see these magnificent ocean-spanning birds.

Heaphy Track

14 Beloved of NZ trampers, and now mountain bikers in winter, the four- to six-day Heaphy Track (p444) is the jewel of Kahurangi National Park, the great wilderness spanning the South Island's northwest corner. Highlights include the mystical Gouland Downs and surreal nikau palm coast, while the townships at either end – at Golden Bay and Karamea – will bring you back down to earth with the most laid-back of landings.

13

14

ANDREW BAIN / LONELY PLANET IMAGES ©

WILL SALTER / LONELY PLANET IMAGES ©

Central Otago

15 Here's your chance to balance virtue and vice, all against a backdrop of some of NZ's most starkly beautiful landscapes. Take to two wheels to negotiate the easygoing Otago Central Rail Trail (p551), cycling into heritage South Island towns such as Clyde and Naseby. Tuck into well-earned beers in laid-back country pubs, or linger for a classy lunch in the vineyard restaurants of Bannockburn. Other foodie diversions include Cromwell's weekly farmers market, and the summer stone-fruit harvest of the country's best orchards.

Skiing & Snowboarding

16 NZ is studded with some massive mountains (p42), and you're guaranteed of finding decent snow right through the winter season (June to October). Most of the famous slopes are on the South Island: hip Queenstown and hippie Wanaka are where you want to be, with iconic ski runs like Coronet Peak, the Remarkables and Treble Cone close at hand. There are also dedicated snowboarding and cross-country (Nordic) snow parks here. And on the North Island, Mt Ruapehu offers the chance to ski down a volcano. Coronet Peak (p45)

Queenstown

17 Queenstown (p568) may be renowned as the birthplace of bungy jumping, but there's more to NZ's adventure hub than leaping off a bridge attached to a giant rubber band. Against the utterly scenic backdrop of the jagged indigo profile of the Remarkables mountain range, travellers can spend days skiing, hiking or mountain biking, before dining in cosmopolitan restaurants or partying in some of NZ's best bars. Next-day options include hang gliding, kayaking or river rafting, or easing into your NZ holiday with sleepier detours to Arrowtown or Glenorchy. View over Lake Wakatipu (p593)

Milford Sound

18 Fingers crossed you'll be lucky enough to see Milford Sound (p615) on a clear, sunny day. That's definitely when the world-beating collage of waterfalls, verdant cliffs and peaks, and dark cobalt waters is at its best. More likely though is the classic Fiordland combination of mist and drizzle, with the iconic profile of Mitre Peak revealed slowly through shimmering sheets of precipitation. Either way, keep your eyes peeled for seals and dolphins, especially if you're exploring NZ's most famous fiord by kayak.

18

CHRISTOPHER GROENHOUT / LONELY PLANET IMAGES ©

19

DAVID WALL / LONELY PLANET IMAGES ©

20

DAVID WALL / LONELY PLANET IMAGES ©

TranzAlpine

19 In less than five hours the *TranzAlpine* (p462) crosses from the Pacific Ocean to the Tasman Sea. Leaving Christchurch, the train speeds across the Canterbury Plains to the foothills of the Southern Alps. After a cavalcade of tunnels and viaducts, it enters the broad expanse of the Waimakariri Valley. A stop at Arthur's Pass village is followed by the 8.5km Otira tunnel, burrowing right through the bedrock of NZ's alpine spine. Then it's all downhill: through the Taramakau River valley, past Lake Brunner, and finally into sleepy Greymouth.

Akaroa & Banks Peninsula

20 Infused with a healthy dash of Gallic ambience, French-themed Akaroa (p503) bends languidly around one of the prettiest harbours on the Banks Peninsula. Sleek dolphins and plump penguins inhabit clear waters perfect for sailing and exploring. Elsewhere on the peninsula, the spidery Summit Rd prescribes the rim of an ancient volcano while winding roads descend to hidden bays and coves. Spend your days tramping and kayaking amid the improbable landscape and seascape, while relaxing at night in chic bistros or cosy B&B accommodation.

need to know

Currency
» New Zealand dollars ($)

Language
» English, Maori and New Zealand Sign Language

When to Go

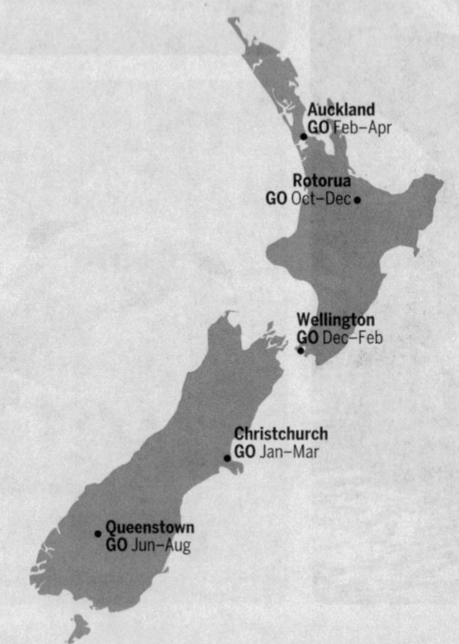

High Season (Dec–Feb)
» Summer: busy beaches, outdoor explorations, festivals, sporting events.

» Big-city accommodation prices rise.

» High season in the ski towns is winter (Jun–Aug).

Shoulder (Mar–Apr)
» Prime travelling time: fine weather, short queues, kids in school, warm(ish) ocean.

» Long evenings supping Kiwi wines and craft beers.

» Spring (Sep–Nov) is shoulder season too.

Low Season (May-Aug)
» Head for the Southern Alps for some brilliant southern-hemisphere skiing

» No crowds, good accommodation deals and a seat in any restaurant.

» Warm-weather beach towns might be half asleep.

Your Daily Budget

Budget less than $130
» Dorm beds or campsites: $25–35 per night

» City food markets for self-catering bargains

» Explore NZ with a money-saving bus pass

Midrange $130–250
» Double room in a midrange hotel/motel: $100–180

» Midrange restaurants, a movie or a live band, and a few beers at the pub

» Hire a car and explore further

Top end more than $250
» Double room in a top-end hotel: from $180

» Three-course meal in a classy restaurant: $70

» Take a guided tour, go shopping or hit some ritzy bars

Money

» ATMs are widely available, especially in larger cities and towns. Credit cards accepted in most hotels and restaurants.

Visas

» Citizens of Australia, the UK and 56 other countries don't need visas for NZ (length-of-stay allowances vary). See www.immigration.govt.nz.

Mobile Phones

» European phones will work on NZ's network, but not most American or Japanese phones. Use global roaming or a local SIM card and prepaid account.

Driving

» Drive on the left; the steering wheel is on the right side of the car (...in case you can't find it).

Websites

» **100% Pure New Zealand** (www.newzealand.com) Official tourism site.

» **Department of Conservation** (www.doc.govt.nz) DOC parks and camping info.

» **Lonely Planet** (www.lonelyplanet.com/new-zealand) Advice from travellers who've actually been there.

» **Destination New Zealand** (www.destination-nz.com) Slick tourism site.

» **Living Landscapes** (www.livinglandscapes.co.nz) Maori tourism operators.

» **DineOut** (www.dineout.co.nz) Restaurant reviews.

Exchange Rates

Australia	A$1	NZ$1.30
Canada	C$1	NZ$1.23
China	Y10	NZ$1.98
Euro zone	€1	NZ$1.59
Japan	¥100	NZ$1.62
Singapore	S$1	NZ$0.97
UK	UK£1	NZ$1.92
US	US$1	NZ$1.25

For current exchange rates see www.xe.com.

Important Numbers

Regular NZ phone numbers have a two-digit area code followed by a seven-digit number. Within a region, the area code is still required. Drop the initial 0 if dialling from abroad.

NZ country code	64
International access code from NZ	00
Emergency (ambulance, fire, police)	111
Directory assistance	018
International directory	0172

Arriving in NZ

» **Auckland International Airport**
Airbus Express – 24-hour
Shuttle Bus – 24-hour door-to-door services
Taxi – around $70; 45 minutes to the city
See also p99

» **Wellington Airport**
Bus – Airport Flyer from 6am to 9.30pm
Shuttle Bus – 24-hour door-to-door services
Taxi – around $30; 20 minutes to the city
See also p388

» **Christchurch Airport**
Bus – City Flyer from 7.15am to 9.15pm
Shuttle Bus – 24-hour door-to-door services
Taxi – around $50; 25 minutes to the city
See also p501

Driving Around New Zealand

There are extensive bus networks and a couple of handy train lines criss-crossing NZ, but for the best scenery, flexibility and pure freedom it's hard to beat piling into a campervan or rent-a-car and hitting the open road. Scanning the map you might think that driving from A to B won't take long, but remember that many of the roads here are two-lane country byways, traversing hilly landscape in curves, crests and convolutions: always allow plenty of time to get wherever you're going. And who's in a hurry anyway? Slow down and see more of the country: explore little end-of-the-line towns, stop for a swim/surf/beer, and pack a Swiss Army knife for impromptu picnics at roadside produce stalls.

what's new

For this new edition of New Zealand, our authors have hunted down the fresh, the transformed, the hot and the happening. These are some of our favourites. For up-to-the-minute recommendations, see lonelyplanet.com/new-zealand.

Mountain Biking, Queenstown

1 With new trails and the opening of the gondola-assisted Queenstown Bike Park, the South Island's adventure capital is now a southern-hemisphere hub for two-wheeled downhill thrills (p575).

Auckland Art Gallery

2 This wonderful gallery – housing more than 15,000 works – has just reopened after a major refurbishment, with a sexy new wing emerging from the original heritage building (p62).

Wallace Arts Centre, Auckland

3 A brilliant new (and free!) contemporary art gallery in a historic mansion in Hillsborough, a few kilometres south of the city centre (p74).

Addington, Christchurch

4 Welcome to Christchurch's funkiest and most exciting post-earthquake neighbourhood. Previously sleepy Addington is now being transformed with new cafes, restaurants, theatres and live-music venues (p495).

Don Stafford Wing, Rotorua Museum

5 Named after a former curator, this amazing new museum extension houses eight intricate, interactive galleries dedicated to Rotorua's Te Arawa people (p292).

Craft Beer Trail, Nelson

6 Sunny Nelson claims the crown of NZ Brewing Capital, and summons its subjects with a Craft Beer Trail that hops around the region (p429).

Hawke's Bay Coastal Cycle Trail

7 What Hawke's Bay lacks in golden sand it now makes up for with new cycle trails, including a coastal run from Bayview to Clifton (p352).

Wynyard Quarter, Auckland

8 Formerly the 'Western Reclamation', this waterside precinct has been reinvented as the far hipper Wynyard Quarter, with bars, cafes and public spaces, linking up with the Viaduct (p65).

Steampunk HQ, Oamaru

9 Forging an eccentric combination of Victoriana and an industrial future, Oamaru's new Steampunk HQ gallery adds a quirky layer to the town's fascinating heritage ambience (p560).

New Zealand Rugby Museum

10 Yeah, we know, this museum has been a Palmerston North fixture for years, but the shiny new premises are really worth barracking for (p252).

West Coast Wildlife Centre, Franz Josef

11 Get up close to a kiwi (a bird, not a person) and see conservation in action in the amazing hatchery and nursery (p469).

Te Manuka Tutahi Marae, Whakatane

12 Laid-back Whakatane has a beautiful new *marae* (meeting house), right on the main street. Actually, it dates from 1875 but travelled for many years to get here (p322)!

if you like...

Cities

New Zealand is urbanised: 72% of Kiwis reside in the 16 biggest towns, and one-in-three New Zealanders lives in Auckland. It follows that cities here are great fun. Coffeeshops, restaurants, bars, boutiques, bookshops, museums, galleries... You're never far from a live gig or an espresso.

Auckland Sydney for beginners? We prefer 'Seattle minus the rain', infused with vibrant South Pacific culture (p62)

Wellington All the lures you'd expect in a capital city, packed into what is really just a very big town. Is San Francisco this pretty? (p366)

Christchurch Re-emerging from recent earthquakes with energy and verve, largely due to the determination and resilience of proud locals (p482)

Dunedin Exuding artsy, boozy ambience (so many students!) and close to superb wildlife-viewing opportunities on the Otago Peninsula (p535)

Hamilton NZ's fourth-largest town doesn't raise much of a blip on the tourist radar, but the bar scene, restaurants, museum and Waikato River deserve a second look (p195)

Extreme Activities

We're not sure if it's something that has evolved to lure tourists, or if it's something innate in the Kiwi psyche, but extreme activities (skydiving, bungy jumping, jetboating, zorbing, white-water rafting etc) are part and parcel of today's NZ experience.

Queenstown Bungy Strap yourself into the astonishing Shotover Canyon Swing or Nevis Highwire Bungy and propel yourself into the void (p570)

Sky Walk & Sky Jump, Sky Tower NZ's adrenaline-pumping extreme scene permeates even downtown Auckland (p75)

Franz Josef skydive If you're really up for some super-human thrills, this is the highest skydiving in NZ, at 18,000ft (p472)

Waitomo black-water rafting Don a wetsuit, a life vest and a helmet with a torch attached and rampage along an underground river – wild times! (p215)

U-fly Extreme Yes, YOU fly – a stunt plane, no less – across the clear blue skies above Motueka (p433)

History

White NZ history goes back just a couple of hundred years, but Maori have lived here since at least AD 1200.

Waitangi Treaty Grounds In the Bay of Islands, where the contentious Treaty of Waitangi was first signed by Maori chiefs and the British Crown (p146)

Dunedin Railway Station More than 100 years old, trimmed with mosaic tiles and stained-glass windows; one of NZ's most photographed buildings (p536)

Oamaru Historic Precinct Beautifully restored whitestone buildings and warehouses, now housing eclectic galleries, restaurants and artisan workshops (p559)

Te Papa Wellington's vibrant treasure-trove museum, where history – both Maori and Pakeha – speaks, sparkles, shakes...and is even shaped like a squid (p374)

Whanganui River Road Drive alongside the slow-curling Whanganui River past Maori towns and stands of deciduous trees, remnants of failed Pakeha farms (p247)

RICHARD CUMMINS / LONELY PLANET IMAGES ©

» Te Papa (p374; Wellington), designed by Jasmax Architects

Maori Culture

After you touch down in NZ it won't take you long to notice how prominent, potent and accessible indigenous Maori culture is in contemporary society: language, music, arts and crafts, performance, tattoos and, of course, rugby.

Rotorua Catch a cultural performance at one of several venues: experience a *haka* (war dance) and a *hangi* (Maori feast), with traditional song, dance, folklore and storytelling (p294)

Shark Nett Gallery Hidden away in Havelock, this is NZ's largest private collection of Maori carvings (p410)

Footprints Waipoua Explore the staggeringly beautiful Waipoua Kauri Forest on Northland's west coast with a Maori guide (p164)

Te Ana Maori Rock Art Centre Learn about traditional Maori rock art in Timaru before exploring remote sites around South Canterbury (p518)

Kotuku Gallery In Whataroa on the South Island's West Coast: greenstone and bone, done the right way, by the right people – carving as storytelling (p468)

Museums

Take time out from the wineries, beaches and bars and spend a few hours meandering through a museum: it's good for the soul.

Auckland Museum A classical Greek-temple design housing a superb collection of Maori and Pacific Islander artefacts, with wonderful guided tours (p67)

Canterbury Museum One of the few heritage buildings to survive the Christchurch earthquakes unscathed: a fascinating showcase of Maori culture and natural history (p483)

Te Papa The country's biggest and best is in Wellington – brilliant by any measure (p374)

Puke Ariki New Plymouth's snazzy waterfront museum is dappled with Maori, colonial and wildlife exhibits...and a great cafe (p226)

World of WearableArt & Classic Cars Museum Nelson's WOW remains as popular as ever, with the added (and more than a little incongruous) bonus of a classic-cars display out the back (p427)

Tramping

NZealand has a world-wide reputation for hiking, with nine epic 'Great Walks' managed by the Department of Conservation (DOC). But you needn't be Sir Edmund Hillary: short walks can also deliver a taste of wilderness.

Milford Track Justifiably famous, Milford is our pick of the Great Walks: 53.5km of gorgeous fiords, sounds, peaks and raindrops (p613)

Cape Reinga Coastal Walkway A 53km Northland long-haul, easily bitten off as a series of short, scenic strolls (p158)

Banks Peninsula Track A 35km four-day meander (or two-day dash) around the perforated Banks Peninsula, southeast of Christchurch (p505)

Mt Taranaki short walks You can loop around the mountain or bag the summit, but a couple of hours spent strolling on its photogenic flanks is equally rewarding (p235)

Robert Ridge & Lake Angelus In Nelson Lakes National Park; an achievable summit and a magical mountain lake (p430)

If you like... mountain biking,
don't miss a rampaging run through the superb Redwoods Whakarewarewa Forest just outside Rotorua (p305)

If you like... surfing,
wax your longboard and head for Surf Hwy 45 south of New Plymouth (p238)

Pubs, Bars & Beer

Sometimes it's the simple things you encounter on holiday that stay with you: a sunset, a conversation, a splash in the sea, a cold beer at the end of a long day on the road...

Wellington craft-beer scene Malthouse and Hashigo Zake, just two of nearly a dozen craft-beer bars in the capital – something to do with thirsty politicians? (p383)

Hood St Precinct Hamilton's Hood St and Victoria St offer up more pubs, beer barns and bars than you have nights left on your holiday (p199)

Dunedin bars Eureka, Albar, Tonic and Inch Bar: four great bars in NZ's best university town (p543)

Mussel Inn Lose an evening in tiny Takaka with live music and a host of home brews (p444)

Moutere Inn Dating back to 1850, this is reputedly the oldest pub in the land – surely that alone is enough of an excuse to visit (p432)

Foodie Experiences

NZ is no longer the land of meat and three veg: eating here these days can be as simple or sophisticated as you like, with the emphasis squarely on fresh regional produce (without a boiled turnip in sight).

Eating out in Auckland When it comes to fine dining, cafes and delicatessens, Auckland no only takes the cake, it takes the bouillabaisse, the lamb rack, the fish pie... (p88)

Central Otago vineyard restaurants Eye-popping scenery combined with the best of NZ food and wine (p552)

Bay of Plenty kiwifruit Pick up a dozen fuzzy, ripe and delicious kiwifruit from roadside stalls for as little as $1 per dozen (p320)

Hokitika Wildfoods Festival You're a big baby, Bear Grylls – eating insects can be lots of fun! (p465)

Original Kaikoura Seafood BBQ Swing by this fabulous outdoor fish shack for some whitebait, mussels, paua (abalone) or crayfish, cooked hot and fresh (p420)

Wine Regions

If you haven't been down to your local liquor store in the last decade, you might have missed the phenomenon that is NZ wine: a pristine environment, abundant sunshine, volcanic soils and passionate wine-makers have been busy bottling world-beating cool-climate drops.

Marlborough The country's biggest and best wine region just keeps on turning out superb sauvignon blanc: don't be picky, just drink some (p414)

Martinborough A small-but-sweet wine region a day trip from Wellington: easy cycling and easy-drinking pinot noir (p392)

Waiheke Island Auckland's favourite weekend playground has a hot, dry microclimate: perfect for Bordeaux-style reds and rosés (p103)

Gibbston Valley Negotiate a tasty pathway through the vineyards of this meandering river valley near Queenstown (p585)

Waipara Valley A short hop north of Christchurch are some spectacular vineyards producing equally spectacular riesling (p510)

MICHAEL GEBICKI / LONELY PLANET IMAGES ©

» Cathedral Cove (p183), Hahei, Coromandel Peninsula

Markets

Weekend markets are big business in NZ – the national appetite for organic, locally grown and artisan produce is seemingly bottomless. They're also great places to eat breakfast, drink coffee, watch buskers, meet friends and generally unwind.

Dunedin Farmers Market Organic fruit and veg, Dunedin's own Green Man beer, robust coffee and homemade pies; stock up for life on the road (p543)

Nelson Market A big, busy weekly market featuring everything from Doris' traditional bratwursts to new-age clothing (p423)

Otara Market Multicultural and edgy, Auckland's Saturday-morning Otara Market brims with buskers, arts and crafts, fashions and food. The city's Polynesian community is particularly present (p97)

River Traders Market Whanganui's riverside market is a Saturday-morning fixture: up to 100 stalls, with a particularly good farmers market section (p245)

Harbourside Market Wellington's obligatory fruit-and-veg pit stop, complemented by fancy artisan produce in the adjacent City Market (p379)

Beaches

NZ has a heckuva lot of coastline: plenty of sun, surf and sand (much of which is volcanic, coloured black or brown). Top tip: book your trip for summer, or you might find the water a little cooler than you bargained for...

Karekare Classic black-sand beach west of Auckland, with wild surf (Eddie Vedder nearly drowned here). Look, but don't touch (p115)

Hahei Iconic Kiwi beach experience on the Coromandel Peninsula, with mandatory side trip to Cathedral Cove (p183)

Wainui On the North Island's East Coast: surfing, sandcastles, sunshine... The quintessential beach-bum beach (p340)

Wharariki Beach No car park, no ice-cream van, no swimsuits... This isolated stretch near Farewell Spit is for wanderers and ponderers (p443)

Manu Bay NZ's most famous surf break (seen *Endless Summer*?) peels ashore south of Raglan. There's not much sand, but the point break is what you're here for (p204)

Skiing

Snowbunny? Powderhound? Downhill deity? Whatever your snowy persuasion, if you're here to ski you won't be disappointed. The South Island offers hundreds of world-class runs, and there are a few good ones on the North Island too.

Treble Cone Everything from challenging downhill terrain to snowboard half-pipes and cross-country skiing at the nearby Cadrona Snow Farm, 26km from Wanaka (p45)

Whakapapa & Turoa The North Island's best ski fields wind down Mt Ruapehu in Tongariro National Park, easily accessible from Taupo (p276)

Canterbury From Mt Hutt and Methven's après-ski buzz, to smaller fields like Ohau, Round Hill, Porters and Broken River (p46)

Coronet Peak The Queenstown area's oldest ski field, just 18km from town; night skiing on Friday and Saturday (p45)

Snowpark NZ This dedicated snowboard park 36km from Wanaka has more rails than the *Orient Express* (p604)

month by month

Top Events

1. **National Jazz Festival,** April
2. **New Zealand International Sevens,** February
3. **World of WearableArt Award Show,** September
4. **Marlborough Wine Festival,** February
5. **World Buskers Festival,** January

January

New Zealand peels its eyes open after New Year's Eve, gathers its wits and gets set for another year. Great weather, cricket season in full swing and happy holidays for the locals.

Festival of Lights

New Plymouth's Pukekura Park (p226) is regularly plastered with adjectives like 'jewel' and 'gem', but the gardens really sparkle during this festival. It's a magical scene: pathways glow and trees are impressively lit with thousands of lights. Live music, dance and kids' performances too.

World Buskers Festival

Christchurch could use a little cheering up: jugglers, musos, tricksters, puppeteers, mime artists and dancers perform throughout the festival (www.worldbuskersfestival.com) at various venues. Shoulder into the crowd, see who's performing in the middle and maybe leave a few dollars. Avoid if you're scared of audience participation...

February

The sun is shining, the kids are still on holidays, and the sav blanc is chillin' in the fridge: this is prime party time across NZ. Book your festival tickets (and beds) in advance.

Waitangi Day

On 6 February 1840, the Treaty of Waitangi was first signed between Maori and the British Crown. The day remains a public holiday across NZ, but in Waitangi itself (the Bay of Islands) there's a lot happening: guided tours, concerts, market stalls and family entertainment.

Marlborough Wine Festival

NZ's biggest and best wine festival (www.wine-marlborough-festival.co.nz) features tastings from around 50 Marlborough wineries (also NZ's biggest and best), plus fine food and entertainment. It's mandatory over-indulgence (usually on a Saturday early in the month). Keep quiet if you don't like sauvignon blanc...

New Zealand International Arts Festival

Feeling artsy? This month-long spectacular (www.festival.co.nz) happens in Wellington in February–March every even-numbered year, and is sure to spark your imagination. NZ's cultural capital exudes artistic enthusiasm with theatre, dance, music and visual arts. International acts aplenty (National Theatre of Scotland, Hofesh Shechter, Bon Iver).

Te Matatini National Kapa Haka Festival

This engrossing Maori *haka* (war dance) competition happens in February in odd-numbered years: much gesticulation, eye-bulging and tongue extension. Venues vary (see www.tematatini.co.nz): 2013 will be Rotorua. And it's not just the *haka:* expect traditional song, dance, storytelling and other performing arts.

Fringe NZ

Music, theatre, comedy, dance, visual arts... but not the mainstream stuff that makes it into the New Zealand International Arts Festival. These are the fringe-dwelling, unusual, emerging, controversial, low-budget and/or downright weird acts that don't seem to fit in anywhere else (www.fringe.org.nz). Great stuff!

Splore

Explore Splore (www.splore.net), a cutting-edge outdoor summer fest in Tapapakanga Regional Park on the Coromandel Peninsula, southeast of Auckland. Contemporary live music, performance, visual arts, safe swimming, pohutukawa trees… If we were feeling parental, we'd tell you to take sunscreen, a hat and a water bottle.

New Zealand International Sevens

Yeah, we know, it's not rugby season, but February sees the world's top seven-a-side rugby teams crack heads in Wellington (www.sevens.co.nz): everyone from stalwarts like Australia, Wales and South Africa to minnows like the Cook Islands, Kenya and Canada. A great excuse for a party.

March

March brings a hint of autumn, harvest time in the vineyards and orchards (great if you're looking for work), long dusky evenings and plenty of festivals plumping out the calendar. Locals unwind post-tourist season.

Wildfoods Festival

Eat some worms, hare testicles or crabs at Hokitika's comfort-zone-challenging food fest (p465). Not for the mild-mannered or weak-stomached… But even if you are, it's still fun to watch! There are usually plenty of quality NZ brews available, too, which help subdue any difficult tastes.

WOMAD

Local and international music, arts and dance performances fill New Plymouth's Bowl of Brooklands to overflowing (www.womad.co.nz). An evolution of the original world-music festival dreamed-up by Peter Gabriel, who launched the innaugural UK concert in 1990. Perfect for families (usually not too loud).

Pasifika Festival

With around 140,000 Maori and notable communities of Tongans, Samoans, Cook Islanders, Niueans, Fijians and other South Pacific Islanders, Auckland has the largest Polynesian community in the world. These vibrant island cultures come together at this annual fiesta (www.aucklandcouncil.govt.nz) in Western Springs Park.

April

April is when canny travellers hit NZ: the ocean is still swimmable and the weather still mild, with nary a tourist or queue in sight. Easter equals pricey accommodation everywhere.

National Jazz Festival

Every Easter, Tauranga hosts the longest-running jazz fest (www.jazz.org.nz) in the southern hemisphere. The line up is invariably impressive (Kurt Elling, Keb Mo), and there's plenty of fine NZ food and wine to accompany the finger-snappin' sonics.

May

The nostalgia of autumn runs deep: party nights are long gone and another chilly Kiwi winter beckons. Thank goodness for the Comedy Festival! Last chance to explore Fiordland and Southland in reasonable weather. Farmers markets overflow.

New Zealand International Comedy Festival

Three-week laugh-fest (www.comedyfestival.co.nz) with venues across Auckland, Wellington and various regional centres: Whangarei to Invercargill with all the mid-sized cities in between. International gag-merchants (Arj Barker, Danny Bhoy) line up next to home-grown talent (anyone seen that Jermaine Clement guy lately?).

June

Time to head south: it's ski season! Queenstown and Wanaka hit their stride. For everyone else, head north: the Bay of Plenty is always sunny, and is it just us, or is Northland underrated?

Matariki

Maori New Year is heralded by the rise of Matariki (aka Pleiades star cluster) in May and the sighting of the new moon in June. Remembrance, education, music, film, commu-

PAUL KENNEDY / LONELY PLANET IMAGES ©

(Above) Maori women performing the *kapa haka* (cultural dance) during Waitangi Day celebrations
(Below) Members of a Polynesian group representing Tonga shelter from the rain during the Pasifika Festival

PAUL KENNEDY / LONELY PLANET IMAGES ©

nity days and tree planting take place, mainly around Auckland and Northland (www.tepapa.govt.nz).

New Zealand Gold Guitar Awards

We like both kinds of music: country and western! These awards (www.goldguitars.co.nz) in Gore cap off a week of ever-lovin' country twang and boot-scootin' good times, with plenty of concerts and buskers.

July

Wellington's good citizens clutch collars, shiver and hang out in bookshops: Auckland doesn't seem so bad now, eh? Ski season slides on: hit Mt Ruapehu on the North Island if Queenstown is overcrowded.

Queenstown Winter Festival

This southern snow-fest (www.winterfestival.co.nz) has been running since 1975, and now attracts around 45,000 snow-bunnies. It's a 10-day party, studded with fireworks, jazz, street parades, comedy, a Mardi Gras, a masquerade ball and lots of snow-centric activities on the mountain slopes.

New Zealand International Film Festival

After separate film festivals (www.nzff.co.nz) in Wellington, Auckland, Dunedin and Christchurch, a selection of flicks hits the road for screenings in regional towns from July to November (film buffs in

Greymouth and Masterton get positively orgasmic at the prospect).

Russell Birdman

Birdman rallies are just so '80s...but they sure are funny. This one in Russell (www.russellbirdman.co.nz) features the usual cast of costumed contenders propelling themselves off a jetty in pursuit of weightlessness. Bonus points if your name is Russell.

August

Land a good deal on accommodation pretty much anywhere except the ski towns. Winter is almost spent, but there's still not much happening outside: music and art are your saviours...or watch some rugby!

Taranaki International Arts Festival

Beneath the snowy slopes of Mt Taranaki, August used to be a time of quiet repose and reconstitution. Not anymore: this whizz-bang arts festival (www.taft.co.nz/artsfest) now shakes the winter from the city (New Plymouth) with music, theatre, dance, visual arts and parades.

Jazz & Blues Festival

You might think that the Bay of Islands is all about sunning yourself on a yacht while dolphins splash saltwater on your stomach. And you'd be right. But in the depths of winter, this jazzy little festival (www.jazz-blues.co.nz) will give you something else to do.

(Above) The crimson November blossom of the pohutukawa tree
(Below) Cycling through a vineyard near Martinborough, in the Waiarapa region

September

Spring is sprung. The amazing and surprising World of WearableArt Award Show is always a hit. And will someone please beat Canterbury in the annual ITM rugby cup final?

World of WearableArt Award Show

A bizarre (in the best possible way) two-week Wellington event (www.worldofwearableart.com) featuring amazing hand-crafted garments. Entries from the show are displayed at the World of WearableArt & Classic Cars Museum in Nelson after the event (Cadillacs and corsetry?).

Auckland International Boat Show

Auckland harbour blooms with sails and churns with outboard motors (www.auckland-boatshow.com). It doesn't command the instant nautical recognition of Sydney or San Diego, but Auckland really is one of the world's great sailing cities. And here's proof.

October

Post-rugby and pre-cricket, sports fans twiddle their thumbs: a trip to Kaikoura, perhaps? Around the rest of NZ October is 'shoulder season' – reasonable accommodation rates, minimal crowds and no competition for the good campsites.

Kaikoura Seafest

Kaikoura is a town built on crayfish. Well, not literally, but there sure are plenty of crustaceans in the sea here, many of which find themsleves on plates at Seafest (www.seafest.co.nz; also a great excuse to drink a lot and dance around).

November

Across Northland, the Coromandel Peninsula, the Bay of Plenty and the East Coast, NZ's iconic pohutukawa trees erupt with brilliant crimson blooms. The weather is picking up, and a few tourists are starting to arrive.

Toast Martinborough

Bound for a day of boozy indulgence, wine-swilling Wellingtonians head over Rimutaka Hill and roll into upmarket Martinborough (p394). The Wairarapa region produces some seriously good pinot noir: don't go home without trying some (...as if you'd be so silly).

Pohutukawa Festival

Markets, picnics, live music, kite-flying, cruises, snorkelling, poetry... It's all very clean-living and above-board, but not everything has to be about drinking, dancing and decadence. And just look at those pohutukawa trees (www.pohutukawafestival.co.nz).

BikeFest & Lake Taupo Cycle Challenge

Feeling fit? Try cycling 160km around Lake Taupo and then come and talk to us... In the week prior to the big race, BikeFest (www.bikefest.co.nz) celebrates all things bicycular: BMX, mountain bike, unicycle, tandem – whatever your preferred conveyance, you'll find someone else who's into it too.

Oamaru Victorian Heritage Celebrations

Ahhh, the good old days... When Queen Vic sat dourly on the throne, when hems were low, collars were high, and civic decency was a matter of course. Old Oamaru thoroughly enjoys this tongue-in-cheek historic homage (www.historicoamaru.co.nz): dress-ups, penny-farthing races, choirs, guided tours etc.

December

Summertime! The crack of leather on willow resounds across the nation's cricket pitches, and office workers surge towards the finish line. Everyone gears up for Christmas: avoid shopping centres like the plague.

Rhythm & Vines

Wine, music and song (all the good things) in sunny east-coast Gisborne on New Year's Eve (www.rhythmandvines.co.nz). Top DJs, hip-hop acts, bands and singer-songwriters compete for your attention. Or maybe you'd rather just drink some chardonnay and kiss someone on the beach.

itineraries

Whether you've got 13 days or 30, these itineraries provide a starting point for the trip of a lifetime. Want more inspiration? Head online to lonelyplanet.com/thorntree to chat with other travellers.

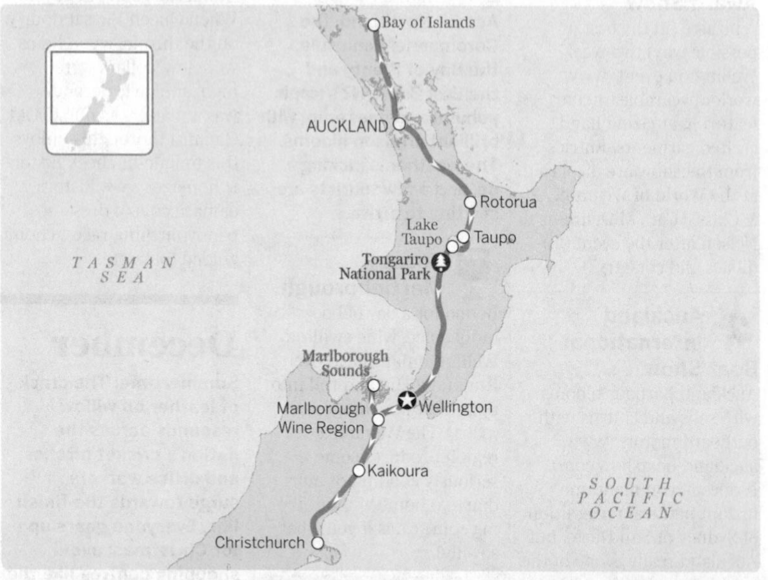

Two Weeks
North & South

From top to bottom (almost), this tour gives you a taste of the best of New Zealand.

Kick off your holiday in **Auckland**: it's NZ's biggest city, with awesome restaurants and bars, galleries and boutiques, beaches and bays. Not an urbanite? Head north to the salt-licked **Bay of Islands** for a couple of days R&R.

Tracking south, **Rotorua** is a unique geothermal hot spot: geysers, mud pools, steaming volcanic vents and accessible Maori culture make for an otherworldly experience. Further south, progressive **Taupo** has the staggeringly beautiful **Lake Taupo** and **Tongariro National Park** on its doorstep. Try some tramping, mountain biking or skydiving, then hoof it down to **Wellington**, a hip little city with an irrepressible arts scene.

Cross Cook Strait on the ferry (an adventure in itself) and see what all the fuss is about in the **Marlborough Wine Region**. The hypnotically hushed inlets, ranges and waterways of the **Marlborough Sounds** are nearby. Swinging southeast, spend a day in **Kaikoura**, a whale-watching paradise, then cruise into **Christchurch** for some southern culture and hospitality.

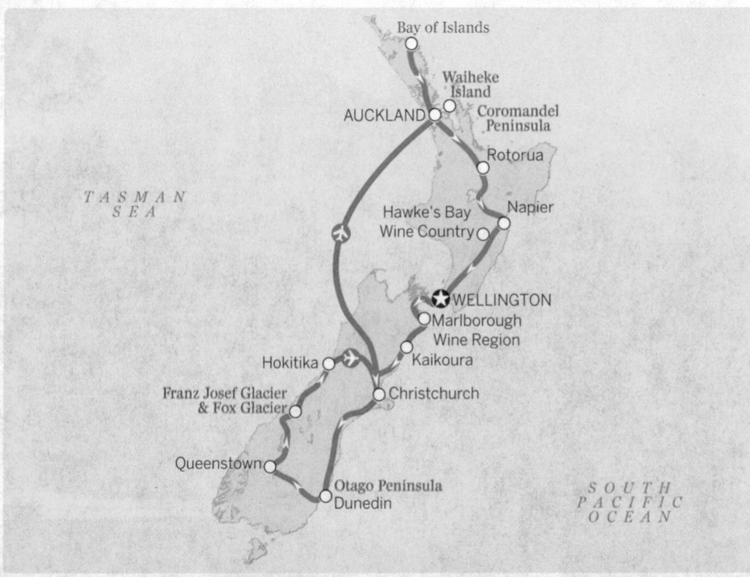

One Month

Kiwi Classics

Classy cities, geothermal eruptions, fantastic wine, Maori culture, glaciers, extreme activities, isolated beaches and forests: these are a few of NZ's favourite things, and what you'll want to see if you're a first-time visitor to Aotearoa.

Aka the 'City of Sails', **Auckland** is a South Pacific melting pot. Spend a few days shopping, eating, drinking and pinging between cafes: this is NZ at its most cosmopolitan. Make sure you get out onto the harbour on a ferry or a yacht, and find half a day to explore the beaches and wineries on **Waiheke Island**. Truck north to the **Bay of Islands** for a dose of aquatic adventure (dolphins, sailing, sunning yourself on deck), then scoot back south-east to check out the forests and beaches on the **Coromandel Peninsula**. Further south in **Rotorua**, get a nose full of egg gas, ogle a 30ft geyser, giggle at volcanic mud bubbles and experience a Maori cultural performance (work your *haka* into shape). Get your skates on and cruise down to **Napier** on the East Coast, NZ's archetypal art-deco sun city. While you're here, don't miss the bottled offerings of the **Hawke's Bay Wine Country** (...ohh, the chardonnay). Down in **Wellington**, the coffee's hot, the beer's cold and wind from the politicians generates its own low-pressure system. This is NZ's arts capital: catch a live band, a poetry slam, a gallery opening or some theatre.

Swan over to the South Island for a few days to experience the best the south has to offer. Start with a tour through the **Marlborough Wine Region** (sauvignon blanc heartland), then jump on a boat/plane/helicopter for a close encounter with a massive marine mammal in **Kaikoura**. Next stop is **Christchurch** – the southern capital is finding its feet again after the earthquakes – followed by the coast road south to the wildlife-rich **Otago Peninsula**, jutting abstractly away from the Victorian facades of student-soaked **Dunedin**. Try to catch some live music while you're in town.

Head inland via SH8 to bungy-obsessed **Queenstown**. If you have time, detour over to the West Coast for an unforgettable encounter with **Franz Josef Glacier** and **Fox Glacier**. From here you can keep driving back north or play airport hopscotch from Hokitika to Christchurch then back to Auckland.

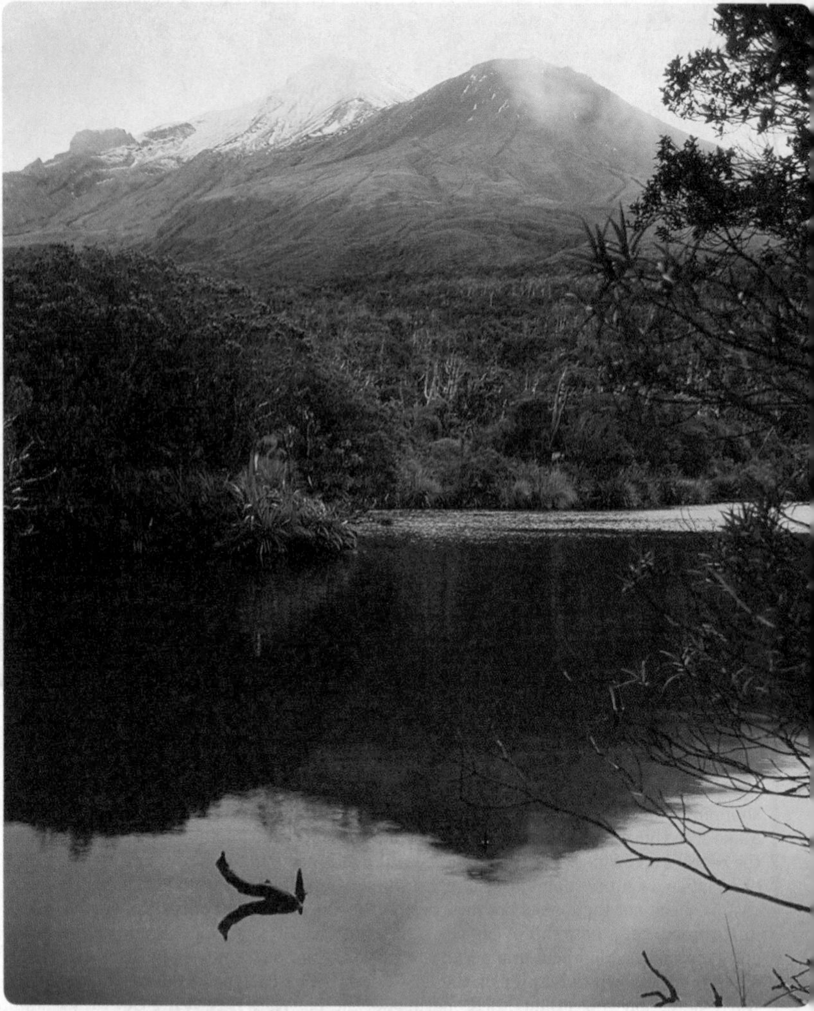

OLIVER STREWE / LONELY PLANET IMAGES ©

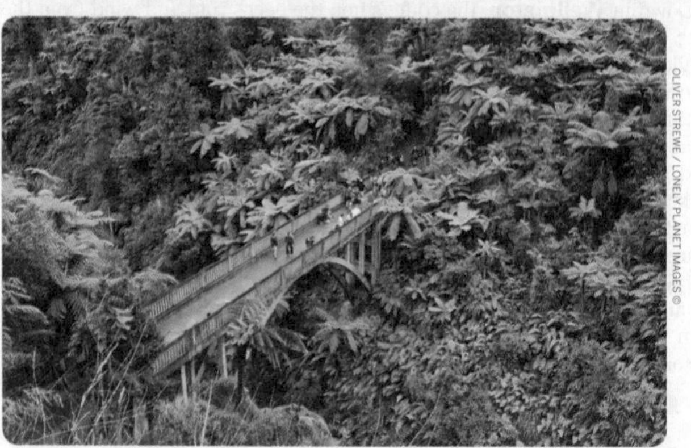

» (above) Mt Taranaki (Egmont National Park; p234), Taranaki.
» (left) Bridge to Nowhere (p248), Whanganui National Park.

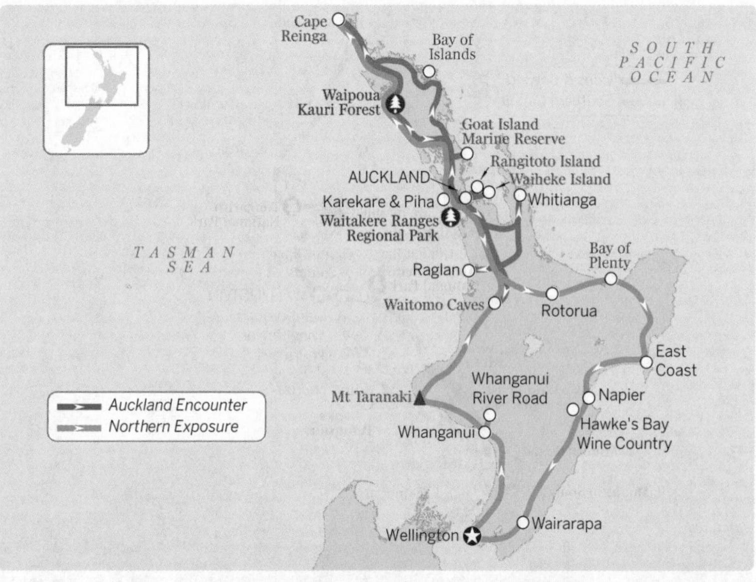

Three Weeks
Northern Exposure

Three-quarters of New Zealanders live on the North Island – find out why!

Begin in **Auckland**, NZ's biggest city. Eat streets abound: our faves are **Ponsonby Rd** in Ponsonby, **K Rd** in Newton, and **New North Rd** in Kingsland. Hike up **One Tree Hill (Maungakiekie)** to burn off resultant calories, and don't miss **Auckland Art Gallery** and **Auckland Museum**.

Heading north, the amazing **Waipoua Kauri Forest** is home to some seriously tall (and wide) timber. The rugged tip of the far north is **Cape Reinga**, shrouded in solitude and Maori lore.

Venture back south through geothermal **Rotorua** then around the **Bay of Plenty** to the sunny beaches of the **East Coast**. Art-deco **Napier** is surrounded by the chardonnay vines of **Hawke's Bay Wine Country**. Follow SH2 south into the sheepy/winey **Wairarapa** before soaring over the cloud-wrapped Rimutaka Range into hip **Wellington**.

The northwesterly route back to Auckland passes through **Whanganui** (detour up the joyously scenic **Whanagnui River Road**), and beyond to epic **Mt Taranaki**. Hit the point breaks near **Raglan** if you're into surfing, or go underground at **Waitomo Caves** for glorious glowworms.

Two Weeks
Auckland Encounter

Is there another 1.4-million-strong city with access to *two* oceans and such vibrant Polynesian culture? **Auckland** – one of the world's great nautical cities – also offers stellar bars and restaurants, museums, islands and beaches.

Don't-miss list: check out the Maori and South Pacific Islander exhibits at **Auckland Museum**, then wander across the **Domain** to **K Rd** for lunch. Pay a visit to the grand **Auckland Art Gallery** (with the new extension) and the iconic **Sky Tower**. **Ponsonby** is the ideal enclave for dinner and drinks.

Take the ferry over to **Rangitoto Island**, then chug into **Devonport** for a meal. Have a look at the **Waitakere Ranges Regional Park**, **Karekare** and **Piha**, then hit the **Kingsland** restaurants. Have breakfast in **Mt Eden**, climb **Maungawhau** then ferry-hop to **Waiheke Island** for some wineries and beaches.

Take your pick from activities within easy reach of the big smoke: snorkelling at **Goat Island Marine Reserve**, sailing the much-photographed **Bay of Islands**, ocean-gazing at **Cape Reinga**, ogling giant trees at **Waipoua Kauri Forest**, delving into **Waitomo Caves**, surfing at **Raglan** or beaching yourself at **Whitianga**.

Four to Six Weeks
Icons & Beyond

Virgin visitors to NZ will want to check out NZ's tourist icons, and maybe throw in some active wilderness experiences for good measure.

Cruise sail-dappled **Auckland** harbour, then take SH1 north to the winterless **Bay of Islands**: surfboards, kayaks, scuba gear – your choice. Heading south, hold your nose through the sulphurous sweats of **Rotorua**, then hook into idyllic **Taupo** and some tramping in the volcanic wilderness of **Tongariro National Park**. Take SH43 west to New Plymouth for photogenic **Mt Taranaki**, then stay up late in caffeinated **Wellington** and watch the nocturnal freak show pass onwards to oblivion.

Across Cook Strait, launch into some sea-kayaking in **Abel Tasman National Park** or disappear into the **Marlborough Sounds**. Track down the rain-swept West Coast with its iconic **glaciers**, then head over to adrenaline-addicted **Queenstown**. Mix and match highways to Te Anau for the side road to **Milford Sound**, then backtrack to SH6 and head north, swapping over to SH8 for cloud-piercing **Aoraki/Mt Cook**, before veering east back to **Christchurch**, a city on the mend. Don't miss an afternoon exploring the **Banks Peninsula**, southeast of town.

Three Weeks
Southern Circuit

Winging into **Christchurch** with three weeks at your disposal, there'll be plenty to keep you entertained, both urban and wild.

'ChCh' continues to rebuild post-earthquakes. Grab a kick-ass coffee at a **cafe** (try Addington Coffee Co-op), then visit the excellent **Canterbury Museum** or **International Antarctic Centre**. The **Avon River** cuts lazily through town – check its flow in the **Botanic Gardens**.

City saturated? Drive out to see eccentric **Banks Peninsula** and its wildlife-rich harbour, then head north for some whale-watching in **Kaikoura**. Continue through the famous **Marlborough Wine Region** and pretty harbour town **Picton**, and lose a day in the **Marlborough Sounds** waterways.

Detour west past artsy **Nelson** to eco-friendly **Golden Bay** (more paintbrushes than people). Southbound, check out the **West Coast glaciers** and continue through ski central **Queenstown**. Desolate **Doubtful Sound** is mesmerising, while the overgrown **Catlins** are perfectly chilled out.

Back up the east coast, check out Scottish-flavoured **Dunedin** then detour to the snowy heights of **Aoraki/Mt Cook** and **Lake Tekapo**, before rolling back into Christchurch.

Trekking in New Zealand

Top Five Long Tramps

Lake Waikaremoana Track, Te Urewera National Park
Heaphy Track, Kahurangi National Park
Abel Tasman Coast Track, Abel Tasman National Park
Cape Reinga Coastal Walkway, Northland
Milford Track, Fiordland

Top Five Short Tramps

Tongariro Alpine Crossing, Tongariro National Park
Kohi Point Walkway, Whakatane
Mangawhai Cliff Top Walkway, Northland
Pinnacles, Coromandel Peninsula
St Arnaud Ridge Track, Nelson Lakes National Park

Top Five Wildlife Encounters

Birdlife Okarito Three Mile Lagoon Walk, West Coast
Seals Cape Foulwind Walkway, West Coast
Gannets Cape Kidnappers Walkway, East Coast
Yellow-eyed penguins Graves Trail, Oamaru
Tuatara and birdlife Tiritiri Matangi Island, Hauraki Gulf

Trekking (aka bushwalking, hiking or tramping, as Kiwis call it) is the perfect vehicle for a close encounter with New Zealand's natural beauty. There are thousands of kilometres of tracks here – some well marked (including the nine 'Great Walks'), some barely a line on a map – plus an excellent network of huts enabling trampers to avoid lugging tents and (in some cases) cooking gear. Before plodding off into the forest, get up-to-date information from the appropriate authority – usually the Department of Conservation (p677) or regional i-SITE visitor information centres.

Planning Your Tramp

When to Go

» **Mid-December–late January** Tramping high season is during the school summer holidays, starting a couple of weeks before Christmas – avoid it if you can.

» **January–March** The summer weather lingers into March: wait until February if you can, when tracks are (marginally) less crowded. Most nonalpine tracks can be walked enjoyably at any time from about October through to April.

» **June–August** Winter is not the time to be out in the wild, especially at altitude – some paths close in winter because of avalanche danger and reduced facilities and services.

TRACK SAFETY

Thousands of people tramp across NZ without incident, but every year a few folks meet their maker in the mountains. Some trails are only for the experienced, fit and well equipped – don't attempt these if you don't fit the bill. Ensure you are healthy and feel comfortable walking for sustained periods.

NZ's climatic changeability subjects high-altitude walks to snow and ice, even in summer: always check weather and track conditions before setting off, and be ready for them to change rapidly. Consult a Department of Conservation (p677) visitor centre and share your intentions with a responsible person before starting longer walks.

See also www.mountainsafety.org.nz, and www.metservice.co.nz for weather updates.

What to Bring

Primary considerations: your feet and your shoulders. Make sure your footwear is tough and your pack isn't too heavy. Wet-weather gear is essential, especially on the South Island's waterlogged West Coast. If you're camping or staying in huts without stoves, bring a camping stove. Also bring insect repellent to keep sandflies away, and don't forget your scroggin – a mixture of dried fruit and nuts (and sometimes chocolate) for munching en route.

Books

DOC publishes detailed books on the flora, fauna, geology and history of NZ's national parks, plus leaflets (50c to $2) detailing hundreds of NZ walking tracks.

Lonely Planet's *Tramping in New Zealand* describes around 50 walks of various lengths and degrees of difficulty. Mark Pickering and Rodney Smith's *101 Great Tramps* has suggestions for two- to six-day tramps around the country. The companion guide, *202 Great Walks: The Best Day Walks in New Zealand,* by Mark Pickering, is handy for shorter, family-friendly excursions. *Accessible Walks,* by Anna and Andrew Jameson, is an excellent guide for elderly, disabled and family trampers, with detailed access information on more than 100 South Island walks.

New trampers should check out *Don't Forget Your Scroggin* by Sarah Bennett and Lee Slater – all about being safe and happy on the track. The *Birdseye Tramping Guides* from Craig Potton Publishing have fab topographical maps, and there are countless books covering tramps and short urban walks around NZ – scan the bookshops.

Maps

The topographical maps produced by **Land Information New Zealand** (LINZ; www.linz.govt.nz) are a safe bet. Bookshops don't often have a good selection of these, but LINZ has map-sales offices in major cities and towns, and DOC offices often sell LINZ maps for local tracks. Outdoor stores also stock them. LINZ' map series includes park maps (national, state and forest parks), dedicated walking-track maps, and detailed 'Topo50' maps (you may need two or three of these per track).

Websites

» **www.trampingtracks.co.nz** Descriptions, maps and photos of long and short tramps all over NZ.

» **www.tramper.co.nz** Articles, photos, forums and excellent track and hut information.

» **www.trampingnz.com** Region-by-region track info with readable trip reports.

» **www.peakbagging.org.nz** Find a summit and get up on top of it.

» **www.topomap.co.nz** Online topographic map of the whole country.

Track Classification

Tracks in NZ are classified according to various features, including level of difficulty. We loosely refer to the level of difficulty as easy, medium, hard or difficult. The widely used track classification system is as follows:

» **Short Walk** Well formed; allows for wheelchair access or constructed to 'shoe' standard (ie walking boots not required). Suitable for people of all ages and fitness levels.

» **Walking Track** Easy and well-formed longer walks; constructed to 'shoe' standard. Suitable for people of most ages and fitness levels.

» **Easy Tramping Track** or **Great Walk** Well formed; major water crossings have bridges and track junctions have signs. Light walking boots required.

» **Tramping Track** Requires skill and experience; constructed to 'boot' standard. Suitable for people of average physical fitness. Water crossings may not have bridges.

» **Route** Requires a high degree of skill, experience and navigation skills. Well-equipped trampers only.

Great Walks

NZ's nine official 'Great Walks' (one of which is actually a river trip!) are the country's most popular tracks. Natural beauty abounds, but prepare yourself for crowds, especially over summer.

All nine Great Walks are described in Lonely Planet's *Tramping in New Zealand,* and are detailed in pamphlets provided by DOC visitor centres.

To tramp these tracks you'll need to buy **Great Walk Tickets** before setting out. These track-specific tickets cover you for hut accommodation (from $22 to $54 per adult per night, depending on the track and season) and/or camping ($6 to $18 per adult per night). You can camp only at designated camping grounds; note there's no camping on the Milford Track. In the

Great Walks

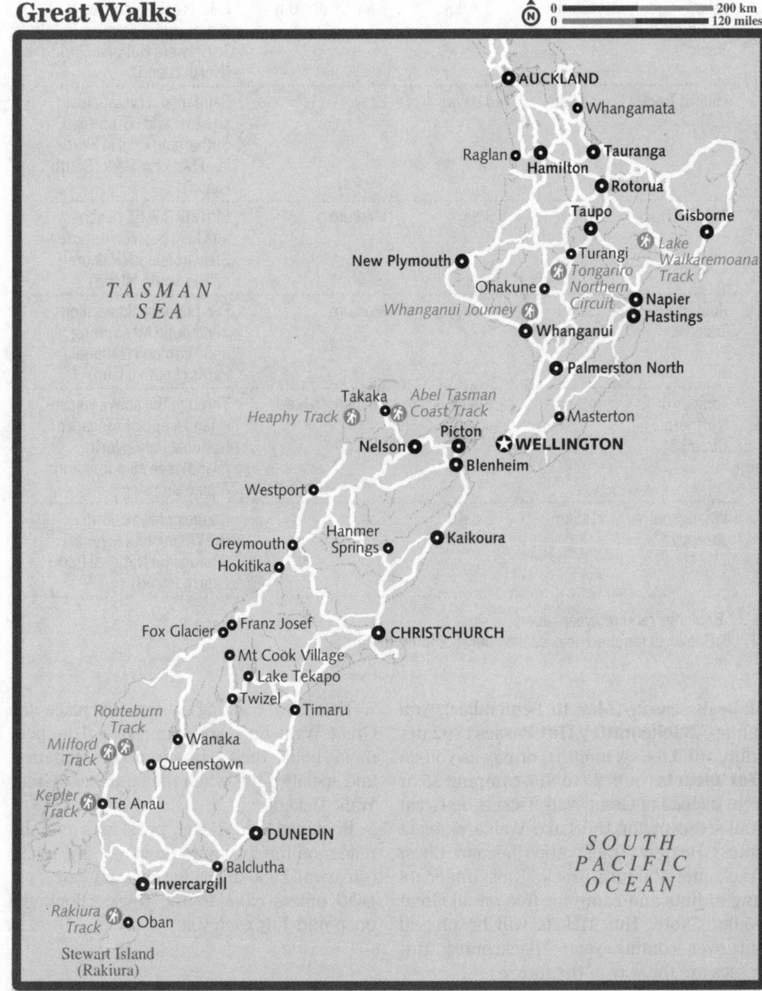

NEW ZEALAND'S NINE 'GREAT WALKS'

WALK	DISTANCE	DURATION	DIFFICULTY	DESCRIPTION
Abel Tasman Coast Track *	51km	3-5 days	Easy to medium	NZ's most popular walk (or sea kayak); beaches and bays in Abel Tasman National Park (South Island)
Heaphy Track *	82km	4-6 days	Medium to hard	Forests, beaches and karst landscapes in Kahurangi National Park (South Island)
Kepler Track **	60km	3-4 days	Easy to medium	Lakes, rivers, gorges, glacial valleys and beech forest in Fiordland National Park (South Island)
Lake Waikaremoana Track *	46km	3-4 days	Easy to medium	Lake views, bush-clad slopes and swimming in Te Urewera National Park (North Island)
Milford Track **	53.5km	4 days	Easy	Rainforest, crystal-clear streams and 630m-high Sutherland Falls in Fiordland National Park (South Island)
Rakiura Track *	36km	3 days	Medium	Bird life (kiwi!), beaches and lush bush on remote Stewart Island (Rakiura; off the South Island)
Routeburn Track **	32km	3 days	Medium	Eye-popping alpine scenery around Mt Aspiring and Fiordland National Parks (South Island)
Tongariro Northern Circuit **	41km	3-4 days	Medium to hard	Through the active volcanic landscape of Tongariro National Park (North Island); see also Tongariro Alpine Crossing
Whanganui Journey **	145km	5 days	Easy	Canoe or kayak down the Whanganui River in Whanganui National Park (North Island)

* Bookings required year-round
** Bookings required peak season only (October to April)

off-peak season (May to September), you can use **Backcountry Hut Passes** ($92 per adult, valid for six months) or pay-as-you-go **Hut Tickets** (huts $5 to $15, camping $5 or free) instead of Great Walk Tickets on Great Walks except for the Lake Waikaremoana Track, Heaphy Track, Abel Tasman Coast Track and Rakiura Track. Kids under 18 stay in huts and camp for free on all Great Walks. (Note: Hut Tickets will be phased out over coming years; Backcounty Hut Passes are the way of the future.)

There's a booking system in place for Great Walk huts and campsites. Trampers must book their chosen accommodation and specify dates when they purchase Great Walk Tickets.

Bookings and ticket purchases can be made online (www.doc.govt.nz), by email (greatwalksbooking@doc.govt.nz) or via DOC offices close to the tracks. Bookings open mid-July each year.

» (above) Taking in views over Clinton Valley, Milford Track (p613), Fiordland.
» (left) Tramping the Lake Waikaremoana Track (p345), Te Urewera National Park.

Other Tracks

Of course, there are a lot more walks in NZ than just the Great ones.

North Island

» **Cape Reinga Coastal Walkway** A 53km, three- to four-day, easy beach tramp (camping only) in Northland. A 132km six- to eight-day route is also possible.

» **Mt Holdsworth–Jumbo Circuit** A 25km, medium-to-hard, two- to three-day tramp in Holdsworth Forest Park, out of Masterton, scaling alpine Mt Holdsworth.

» **Pouakai Circuit** A 25km, two- to three-day loop passing lowland rainforest, cliffs and subalpine forest at the foot of Mt Taranaki in Egmont National Park.

» **Tongariro Alpine Crossing** A brilliant 18km, one-day, medium tramp through Tongariro National Park.

South Island

» **Banks Peninsula Track** A 35km, two-day (medium) or four-day (easy) walk over the hills and along the coast of Banks Peninsula.

» **Tuatapere Hump Ridge Track** An excellent three-day, 53km circuit beginning and ending at Bluecliffs Beach on Te Waewae Bay, 20km from Tuatapere.

» **Kaikoura Coast Track** An easy three-day, 40km walk over private and public land along the spectacular coastline 43km south of Kaikoura.

» **Queen Charlotte Track** A 71km, three- to five-day medium walk in the Marlborough Sounds, affording great water views. Top-notch accommodation and water transport available.

TE ARAROA

After a lengthy planning and construction period, **Te Araroa** (The Long Pathway; www.teararoa.org.nz) finally opened in December 2011. A 3000km tramping trail from Cape Reinga in New Zealand's north to Bluff in the south (or the other way around), the route links existing tracks with new sections. Built over a decade, mostly by volunteers, it's one of the longest hikes in the world: check the website for maps and track notes, plus blogs and videos from hardy types who have completed the end-to-end epic.

» **Rees-Dart Track** A 70km, four- to five-day hard tramping track in Mt Aspiring National Park, through river valleys and traversing an alpine pass.

Backcountry Huts & Conservation Campsites

Huts

DOC maintains more than 950 backcountry huts in NZ's national and forest parks. Hut categories are as follows:

» **Basic Huts** Just a shed.

» **Standard Huts** No cooking equipment and sometimes no heating, but mattresses, water supply and toilets.

» **Serviced Huts** Mattress-equipped bunks or sleeping platforms, water supply, heating, toilets and sometimes cooking facilities.

Details about the huts can be found on the DOC website. Backcountry hut fees per adult per night range from free to $54, with tickets bought in advance at DOC visitor centres (some huts can also be booked online at www.doc.govt.nz). Children under 10 can use huts for free; 11- to 17-year-olds are charged half-price. If you do a lot of tramping, DOC sells a six-month **Backcountry Hut Pass** (adult/child $92/46), applicable to most huts except Great Walk huts in peak season (October to April, during which time you'll need Great Walk Tickets). In the low season (May to September), backcountry hut tickets and passes can also be used to procure a bunk or campsite on some Great Walks.

Depending on the hut category, a night's stay may use one or two tickets. Date your tickets and put them in the boxes provided at huts. Accommodation is on a first-come, first-served basis.

Campsites

DOC also manages 250 'Conservation Campsites' (usually vehicle-accessible) with categories as follows:

» **Basic Campsites** Basic toilets and water; free on a first-come, first-served basis.

» **Standard Campsites** Toilets and water supply, and perhaps barbecues and picnic tables; $6 to $10 on a first-come, first-served basis.

» **Serviced Campsites** Full facilities: flush toilets, tap water, showers and picnic tables. They may also have barbecues, a kitchen and a laundry. Costs $15; bookable via DOC visitor centres.

RESPONSIBLE TRAMPING

If you went straight from the cradle into a pair of hiking boots, some of these tramping tips will seem ridiculously obvious; others you mightn't have considered. Online, www.lnt.org is a great resource for low-impact hiking, and the Department of Conservation (DOC) site www.camping.org.nz has plenty more responsible camping tips. When in doubt, ask DOC or i-SITE staff.

The ridiculously obvious:

» Time your tramp to avoid peak season: less people = less stress on the environment and fewer snorers in the huts.

» Carry out *all* your rubbish. Burying rubbish disturbs soil and vegetation, encourages erosion, and animals will probably dig it up anyway.

» Don't use detergents, shampoo or toothpaste in or near watercourses (even if they're biodegradable).

» Use lightweight kerosene, alcohol or Shellite (white gas) stoves for cooking; avoid disposable butane gas canisters.

» Where there's a toilet, use it. Where there isn't one, dig a hole and bury your by-product (at least 15cm deep, 100m from any watercourse).

» If a track passes through a muddy patch, just plough straight on through – skirting around the outside increases the size of the bog.

You mightn't have considered:

» Wash your dishes 50m from watercourses; use a scourer, sand or snow instead of detergent.

» If you *really* need to scrub your bod, use biodegradable soap and a bucket, at least 50m from any watercourse. Spread the waste water around widely to help the soil filter it.

» If open fires are allowed, use only dead, fallen wood in existing fireplaces. Leave any extra wood for the next happy camper.

» Keep food-storage bags out of reach of scavengers by tying them to rafters or trees.

» Feeding wildlife can lead to unbalanced populations, diseases and animals becoming dependent on handouts. Keep your dried apricots to yourself.

Kids aged five to 17 pay half-price for Conservation Campsites; kids four and under stay free.

Guided Walks

If you're new to tramping or just want a more comfortable experience than the DIY alternative, several companies can escort you through the wilds, usually staying in comfortable huts (showers!), with meals cooked and equipment carried for you.

Places on the North Island where you can sign up for a guided walk include Mt Taranaki, Lake Waikaremoana and Tongariro National Park. On the South Island try Kaikoura, the Milford Track, Heaphy Track or Hollyford Track. Prices for a four-night guided walk start at around $1500, and rise towards $2000 for deluxe guided experiences.

Getting To & From Trailheads

Getting to and from trailheads can be problematic, except for popular trails serviced by public and dedicated trampers' transport. Having a vehicle only helps with getting to one end of the track (you still have to collect your car afterwards). If the track starts or ends down a dead-end road, hitching will be difficult.

Of course, tracks accessible by public transport (eg Abel Tasman Coast Track) are also the most crowded. An alternative is to arrange private transport, either with a friend or by chartering a vehicle to drop you at one end then pick you up at the other. If you intend to leave a vehicle at a trailhead, don't leave anything valuable inside – theft from cars in isolated areas is a significant problem.

Skiing & Snowboarding in New Zealand

Best Extreme Skiing

Heliskiing on the South Island is big fun (and big money): if you can afford it, spin your rotor blades up to the high, pristine slopes of Coronet Peak, Cardrona, Mt Hutt, Treble Cone or Mt Potts.

Best for Beginners or with Kids

Coronet Peak Queenstown
Mt Hutt Central Canterbury
Mt Dobson South Canterbury
Roundhill South Canterbury
The Remarkables Queenstown

Best Snowboarding

Mt Hutt Central Canterbury
Treble Cone Wanaka
Snow Park NZ Wanaka
Ohau South Canterbury
Whakapapa & Turoa,Tongariro National Park

Top Five Après-Ski Watering Holes

Powderkeg Ohakune
Blue Pub Methven
Cardrona Hotel Cardrona
Atlas Beer Cafe Queenstown
Monty's Queenstown

Global warming is triggering a worldwide melt, but New Zealand remains an essential southern-hemisphere destination for snow bunnies, with downhill skiing, cross-country (Nordic) skiing and snowboarding all passionately pursued. Heliskiing, where choppers lift skiers to the top of long, isolated stretches of virgin snow, also has its fans. The NZ ski season is generally June to October, though it varies considerably from one ski area to another, and can run as late as November.

Planning

Where to Go

The variety of locations and conditions makes it difficult to rate NZ's ski fields in any particular order. Some people like to be near Queenstown's party scene or Mt Ruapehu's volcanic landscapes; others prefer the quality high-altitude runs on Mt Hutt, uncrowded Rainbow or less-stressed club skiing areas. Club areas are publicly accessible and usually less crowded and cheaper than commercial fields, even though nonmembers pay a higher fee.

Practicalities

NZ's ski areas aren't generally set up as 'resorts' with chalets, lodges or hotels. Accommodation and après-ski carousing are often in

» (above) Skier dropping off a cliff at Treble Cone (p45), Wanaka.
» (left) Snowboarding at Coronet Peak (p45), Wanaka.

Skiing & Snowboarding Areas

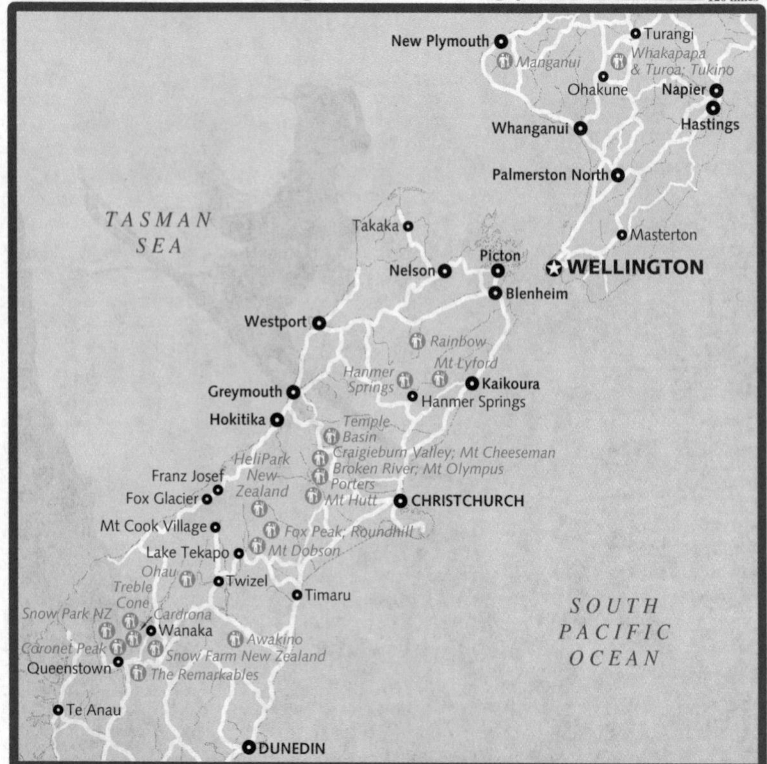

surrounding towns, connected with the slopes via daily shuttles. Many club areas have lodges you can stay at, subject to availability.

Visitor information centres in NZ, and Tourism New Zealand (p687) internationally, have info on the various ski areas and can make bookings and organise packages. Lift passes cost anywhere from $40 to $95 per adult per day (half-price for kids). Lesson-and-lift packages are available at most areas. Ski and snowboard equipment rental starts at around $40 a day (cheaper for multiday hire).

Websites

» **www.brownbear.co.nz/ski** Brilliant reference detailing all of NZ's ski areas.

» **www.snow.co.nz** Reports, cams and ski info across the country.

» **www.nzski.com** Reports, employment, passes and webcams for Mt Hutt, Coronet Peak and the Remarkables.

» **www.chillout.co.nz** Info on Mt Lyford, Hanmer Springs, Mt Cheeseman, Roundhill, Temple Basin, Fox Peak, Mt Dobson, Mt Olympus, Porters, Craigieburn Valley and Broken River ski areas.

» **www.newzealandsnowtours.com** Snowboarding and skiing tours, north and south.

North Island

Tongariro National Park

» **Whakapapa & Turoa** (☎Turoa 06-385 8456, Whakapapa 07-892 4000; www.mtruapehu.com; daily lift pass adult/child $95/57, valid at both resorts) On either side of Mt Ruapehu, these twin resorts comprise NZ's largest ski area. **Whakapapa** has 30 intermediate groomed runs, plus snowboarding, cross-country, downhill, a terrain park and the highest lift in NZ. Drive from Whakapapa Village (6km; free parking) or bus in from National Park Village, Taupo, Turangi or Whakapapa Village. Smaller

Turoa has a beginners' lift, plus snowboarding, downhill and cross-country. There's free parking or a shuttle from Ohakune (17km) which has the North Island's liveliest après-ski scene.

» **Tukino** (☎06-387 6294; www.tukino.co.nz; daily lift pass adult/child $50/30) Club-operated Tukino is on Mt Ruapehu's east, 46km from Turangi. It's 14km down a gravel road from the sealed Desert Rd (SH1), and you need a 4WD to get in. It's uncrowded, with mostly beginner and intermediate runs.

Taranaki

» **Manganui** (☎027 280 0860, snow-phone 06-759 1119; www.skitaranaki.co.nz; daily lift pass adult/child $40/25) Offers volcano-slope, club-run skiing on the eastern slopes of spectacular Mt Taranaki in Egmont National Park, 22km from Stratford (and a 20-minute walk from the car park). Ski off the summit when conditions permit: it's a sweaty two-hour climb to the crater, but the exhilarating 1300m descent compensates.

South Island

Queenstown & Wanaka

» **Coronet Peak** (☎03-450 1970, snow-phone 03-442 4620; www.nzski.com; daily lift pass adult/child $95/52) At the region's oldest ski field, snow-making systems and treeless slopes provide excellent skiing and snowboarding for all levels. There's night skiing Friday and Saturday, July to September. Shuttles run from Queenstown (18km).

» **The Remarkables** (☎03-450 1970, snow-phone 03-442 4615; www.nzski.com; daily lift pass adult/child $91/49) Visually remarkable, this ski field is also near Queenstown (28km), with shuttle buses during ski season. It has a good smattering of intermediate and advanced runs (only 10% beginner). Look for the sweeping 'Homeward Bound' run.

» **Treble Cone** (☎03-443 7443; www.treblecone.com; daily lift pass adult/child $95/48) The highest and largest of the southern lakes ski areas is in a spectacular location 26km from Wanaka, with steep slopes suitable for intermediate to advanced skiers. There are also half-pipes and a terrain park for boarders.

» **Cardrona** (☎03-443 7341, snow-phone 03-443 7007; www.cardrona.com; daily lift pass adult/child $94/46) Around 34km from Wanaka, with several high-capacity chairlifts, beginners tows and extreme snowboard terrain (including the 'Heavy Metal' snowboard park). Buses run from Wanaka and Queenstown during ski season. Good services for skiers with disabilities, plus an on-field crèche.

» **Snow Farm New Zealand** (☎03-443 7542; www.snowfarmnz.com; daily trail pass adult/child $40/20) NZ's only commercial Nordic (cross-country) ski area is 35km from Wanaka on the Pisa Range, high above Lake Wanaka. There are 50km of groomed trails, huts with facilities, and thousands of hectares of open snow.

» **Snow Park NZ** (☎03-443 9991; www.snowparknz.com; daily lift pass adult/child $88/41) NZ's only dedicated freestyle ski and snowboard area, with a plethora of pipes, terrain parks, boxes and rails and snow-making facilities. Backpacker-style accommodation, restaurant and bar; 34km from Wanaka, 58km from Queenstown.

South Canterbury

» **Ohau** (☎03-438 9885; www.ohau.co.nz; daily lift pass adult/child $75/30) This ski area on Mt Sutton, 42km from Twizel, has intermediate and advanced runs, excellent snowboarding/cross-country terrain, and a ski lodge.

HELISKIING

New Zealand's remote heights are tailor-made for heliskiing, with operators covering a wide off-piste area along the Southern Alps. Costs range from $800 to $1200 for three to eight runs. HeliPark New Zealand at Mt Potts is a dedicated heliski park. Heliskiing is also available at Coronet Peak, Treble Cone, Cardrona, Mt Hutt, Mt Lyford, Ohau and Hanmer Springs. Alternatively, independent operators include the following:

» **Alpine Heli-Ski** (☎03-441 2300; www.alpineheliski.com; Queenstown)

» **Backcountry Helicopters NZ** (☎03-443 9032; www.heliskinz.com; Wanaka)

» **Harris Mountains Heli-ski** (☎03-442 6722; www.heliski.co.nz; Queenstown & Wanaka)

» **Heli Ski Queenstown** (☎03-442 7733, 0800 123 4354; www.flynz.co.nz; Queenstown)

» **Methven Heliski** (☎03-302 8108; www.methvenheli.co.nz; Methven)

» **Southern Lakes Heliski** (☎03-442 6222; www.southernlakesheliski.co.nz; Queenstown)

» **Wilderness Heliski** (☎03-435 1834; www.wildernessheli.co.nz; Aoraki/Mt Cook)

» **Mt Dobson** (☎03-685 8039; www.dobson.co.nz; daily lift pass adult/child $72/28) The 3km-wide basin here, 26km from Fairlie, caters for learners and intermediates, and has a terrain park and famously dry powder. On a clear day you can see Mt Cook and the ocean from the summit.

» **Fox Peak** (☎03-685 8539, snow-phone 03-688 0044; www.foxpeak.co.nz; daily lift pass adult/child $50/10) A club ski area 40km from Fairlie in the Two Thumb Range. Expect rope tows, good cross-country skiing and dorm-style accommodation.

» **Roundhill** (☎021 680 694, snow-phone 03-680 6977; www.roundhill.co.nz; daily lift pass adult/child $72/36) A small field with wide, gentle slopes, perfect for beginners and intermediates. It's 32km from Lake Tekapo village.

Central Canterbury

» **Mt Hutt** (☎03-302 8811, snow-phone 03-308 5074; www.nzski.com; daily lift pass adult/child $87/48) One of the highest ski areas in the southern hemisphere, as well as one of NZ's best. It's close to Methven; Christchurch is 118km to the west – ski shuttles service both towns. Road access is rough – be extremely cautious in lousy weather. Plenty of beginner, intermediate and advanced slopes, with chairlifts, heliskiing and wide-open faces that are good for learning to snowboard.

» **HeliPark New Zealand** (☎03-303 9060; www.helipark.co.nz; access incl 1st run $325, per subsequent run $75) A snow-white gem, sitting on Mt Potts above the headwaters of the Rangitata River, 75km from Methven. It offers helicopter-accessed skiing. Accommodation and meals are available at a lodge 8km from the ski area.

» **Porters** (☎03-318 4002; www.skiporters.co.nz; daily lift pass adult/child $82/42) The closest commercial ski area to Christchurch (96km away on the Arthur's Pass road). 'Big Mama', at 620m, is one of the steepest runs in NZ, but there are wider, gentler slopes, too. There's a half-pipe for snowboarders, good cross-country runs along the ridge, and lodge accommodation.

» **Temple Basin** (☎03-377 7788; www.templebasin.co.nz; daily lift pass adult/child $68/37) A club field 4km from Arthur's Pass township. It's a 50-minute walk uphill from the car park to the ski-area lodges. There's floodlit skiing at night and backcountry runs for snowboarders.

» **Craigieburn Valley** (☎03-318 8711; www.craigieburn.co.nz; daily lift pass adult/child $68/45) Centred on Hamilton Peak, Craigieburn Valley is 40km from Arthur's Pass. It's one of NZ's most challenging club areas, with intermediate and advanced runs (no beginners). Accommmodation in please-do-a-chore lodges.

» **Broken River** (☎03-318 8713, snow-phone 03-383 8888; www.brokenriver.co.nz; daily lift pass adult/child $65/35) Not far from Craigieburn Valley is another club field, with a 15- to 20-minute walk from the car park and a real sense of isolation. Reliable snow; laid-back vibe. Catered or self-catered lodge accommodation available.

» **Mt Cheeseman** (☎03-344 3247, snow-phone 03-318 8794; www.mtcheeseman.co.nz; daily lift pass adult/child $70/35) Another cool club area in the Craigieburn Range, this family-friendly operation is 112km from Christchurch (the closest club to the city). Based on Mt Cockayne, it's a wide, sheltered basin with drive-to-the-snow road access. Lodge accommodation available.

» **Mt Olympus** (☎03-318 5840; www.mtolympus.co.nz; daily lift pass adult/child $70/35) Difficult to find (but worth it), 2096m Mt Olympus is 58km from Methven, 12km from Lake Ida. This club area has intermediate and advanced runs, and solid cross-country trails to other areas. Access is sometimes 4WD-only, depending on conditions. Lodge accommodation available.

Northern South Island

» **Hanmer Springs** (☎027 434 1806; www.skihanmer.co.nz; daily lift pass adult/child $60/30) A commercial field based on Mt St Patrick, 17km from Hanmer Springs township, with mostly intermediate and advanced runs. There are pipe-rides for snowboarders, and a new beginners' tow was installed in 2012.

» **Mt Lyford** (☎03-315 6178, snow-phone 03-366 1220; www.mtlyford.co.nz; daily lift pass adult/child $70/35) Around 60km from both Hanmer Springs and Kaikoura, and 4km from Mt Lyford village, this is more of a 'resort' than most NZ ski fields, with accommodation and eating options. There's a good mix of runs and a terrain park.

» **Rainbow** (☎03-521 1861, snow-phone 0832 226 05; www.skirainbow.co.nz; daily lift pass adult/child $70/35) Borders Nelson Lakes National Park (100km from Nelson, a similar distance from Blenheim), with varied terrain, minimal crowds and good cross-country skiing. Chains are often required. St Arnaud is the closest town (32km).

Otago

» **Awakino** (☎03-434 9497; www.skiawakino.com; daily lift pass adult/child $45/20) A small player in North Otago, but worth a visit for intermediate skiers. Oamaru is 45km away; Omarama is 66km inland. Weekend lodge-and-ski packages available.

Extreme New Zealand

Best Anti-Gravity Action

Bungy Jumping There are plenty of places in New Zealand where you can hurl yourself into oblivion attached to a giant rubber band, but why mess around: head straight to Queenstown for the biggest and the best.

Top Five White-Water Rafting Trips

Buller Gorge Murchison
Tongariro River Taupo
Kawarau River Queenstown
Kaituna River Rotorua
Shotover Canyon Queenstown

Top Five Surfing Spots

Manu Bay Raglan
Tauranga Bay Westport
Waikanae Beach Gisborne
St Clair Beach Dunedin
Mount Beach Mt Maunganui

Top Five Mountain-Biking Tracks

Makara Peak Mountain Bike Park Wellington
Redwoods Whakarewarewa Forest Rotorua
Queenstown Bike Park Queenstown
Otago Central Rail Trail Otago
42 Traverse Central Plateau

New Zealand's astounding natural assets encourage even the laziest lounge lizards to drag themselves outside and get active. 'Extreme' sports are abundant and supremely well organised here. Mountaineering is part of the national psych; skydivin g, mountain biking, jetboating and rock climbing are well established; and pant-wetting, illogical activities like bungy jumping have become everyday pursuits. Adrenaline-pumping activities obviously have an element of risk, but the perception of danger is part of the thrill (...but make sure you have travel insurance anyway).

Bungy Jumping

Bungy jumping was made famous by Kiwi AJ Hackett's 1986 plunge from the Eiffel Tower, after which he teamed up with champion NZ skier Henry van Asch to turn the endeavour into a profitable enterprise. And now you can get crazy too!

Queenstown is a spiderweb of bungy cords, including a 43m jump off the Kawarau Bridge, a 47m leap from a ledge at the top of a gondola, and the big daddy, the 134m Nevis Highwire. Other South Island bungy jumps include Waiau River (near Hanmer Springs) and Mt Hutt ski field. On the North Island, try Taupo, Taihape, Auckland and Rotorua. Varying the theme, try the 109m-high Shotover Canyon Swing or Nevis Arc in Queenstown, both seriously high rope swings: *swooosh...*

Caving

Caving (aka spelunking) opportunities abound in NZ's honeycombed karst (limestone) regions. You'll find local clubs and organised tours around Auckland, Waitomo, Whangarei, Westport and Karamea. Golden Bay also has some mammoth caves. Useful resources:

» **Auckland Speleo Group** (www.asg.org.nz)

» **New Zealand Speleological Society** (www.caves.org.nz)

» **Wellington Caving Group** (www.caving.wellington.net.nz)

Horse Trekking

Unlike some other parts of the world where beginners get led by the nose around a paddock, horse trekking in NZ lets you really get out into the countryside, on a farm, in the forest or along a beach. Rides range from one-hour jaunts (from around $50) to week-long, fully catered treks.

On the North Island, Taupo, the Coromandel Peninsula, Waitomo, Pakiri, Ninety Mile Beach, Rotorua, the Bay of Plenty and East Cape are top places for an equine encounter.

On the South Island, all-day horseback adventures happen around Kaikoura, Nelson, Mt Cook, Lake Tekapo, Hanmer Springs, Queenstown, Glenorchy, Methven, Mt Hutt, Cardrona, Te Anau and Dunedin. Treks are also offered alongside Paparoa National Park on the West Coast. For info and operator listings, check out the following:

» **100% Pure New Zealand** (www.newzealand.com)

» **Auckland SPCA Horse Welfare Auxiliary Inc** (www.horsetalk.co.nz)

» **True NZ Horse Trekking** (www.truenz.co.nz/horsetrekking)

Jetboating

Hold onto your breakfast: passenger-drenching 360-degree spins ahoy! On the South Island, the Shotover and Kawarau Rivers (Queenstown) and the Buller River (Westport) have fab jetboating. The Dart River (Queenstown) is less travelled but also good, while the Waiatoto River (Haast) and Wilkin River (Mt Aspiring National Park) are superb wilderness experiences. Try also the Kawarau River (Cromwell), Waiau River (Te Anau) and Wairahurahiri River (Tuatapere).

On the North Island, the Whanganui, Motu, Rangitaiki and Waikato Rivers are excellent for jetboating, and there are sprint jets at the Agrodome in Rotorua. Jetboating around the Bay of Islands in Northland is also de rigueur.

Paragliding & Kiteboarding

Paragliding (dangling from a modified parachute that glides over the water while being pulled along by a speedboat or jet ski) is perhaps the easiest way for humans to achieve assisted flight. After a half-day of instruction you should be able to do limited solo flights. Tandem flights happen in Queenstown, Wanaka, Nelson and Te Mata Peak in Hawke's Bay. The **New Zealand Hang Gliding and Paragliding Association** (www.nzhgpa.org.nz) rules the roost.

Kiteboarding (aka kitesurfing), where a mini parachute drags you across the ocean on a mini surfboard, can be attempted at Paihia, Tauranga, Mt Maunganui, Raglan, Wellington and Nelson. You can tee up lessons at most of these places, too. Karikari Peninsula near Cape Reinga on NZ's northern tip is a kiteboarding mecca.

Mountain Biking

NZ is laced with quality mountain-biking opportunities. Mountain bikes can be hired in major towns or adventure-sports centres like Queenstown, Wanaka, Nelson, Picton, Taupo and Rotorua, which also have repair shops.

Various companies will take you up to the tops of mountains and volcanoes (eg Mt Ruapehu, Christchurch's Port Hills, Cardrona and the Remarkables) so you can hurtle down without the grunt-work of getting to the top first. Rotorua's Redwoods Whakarewarewa Forest offers famously good mountain biking, as does the 42 Traverse near National Park Village (close to Tongariro National Park), the Alexandra goldfield trails in Central Otago, the new Queenstown Bike Park, and Twizel near Mt Cook. Other North Island options include Woodhill Forest, Waihi, Te Aroha, Te Mata Peak and Makara Peak in Wellington; down south try Waitati Valley and Hayward Point near Dunedin, Canaan Downs near

» (above) Jetboating along the Shotover River, Queenstown region (p571).
» (left) Surf instruction at Raglan (p201), Waikato.

CYCLE TOURING

OK, so cruising around the country on a bicycle isn't necessarily 'extreme', but it is super-popular in New Zealand, especially during summer. Most towns offer bike hire, at either backpacker hostels or specialist bike shops, with bike repair shops in bigger towns.

If you're not after altitude, the **Otago Central Rail Trail** between Middlemarch and Clyde is a winner. The **Little River Rail Trail** in Canterbury (en route to Banks Peninsula) is also fabulous. For an off-the-beaten-highway option, try the **Southern Scenic Route** from Invercargill round Tuatapere to Te Anau. For more detailed touring info, see Lonely Planet's *Cycling New Zealand*.

The $50-million Nga Haerenga, New Zealand Cycle Trail (p693) – a national bike path from Kaitaia to Bluff – is a network of bike trails featuring 18 'Great Rides' (a similar concept to tramping's 'Great Walks'). Some sections/trails are still in the developmental stages, but some stages are open; see the website for updates.

Online resources:

» **Independent Cycle Tours** (www.cyclehire.co.nz)

» **Paradise Press** (www.paradise-press.co.nz) *Pedallers' Paradise* booklets by Nigel Rushton.

Abel Tasman National Park, Mt Hutt, Methven and the Banks Peninsula.

Some traditional tramping tracks are open to mountain bikes, but the Department of Conservation (p677) has restricted access in many cases due to track damage and the inconvenience to walkers, especially at busy times. Never cycle on walking tracks in national parks unless it's permissible (check with DOC), or risk heavy fines and the unfathomable ire of hikers. The Queen Charlotte Track is a good one to cycle, but part of it is closed in summer. Resources include the following:

» **Classic New Zealand Mountain Bike Rides** (www.kennett.co.nz) Details short and long rides all over NZ.

» **New Zealand Mountain Biker** (www.nzmtbr.co.nz) A mag that comes out every two months.

Mountaineering

NZ has a proud mountaineering history – this was, after all, the home of Sir Edmund Hillary (1919–2008), who, along with Tenzing Norgay, was the first to reach the summit of Mt Everest. When he came back down, Sir Ed famously uttered to friend George Lowe, 'Well, George, we knocked the bastard off!'

The Southern Alps are studded with impressive peaks and challenging climbs. The Aoraki/Mt Cook region is outstanding; other mountaineering areas extend along the spine of the South Island from Tapuaenuku (in the Kaikoura Ranges) and the Nelson Lakes peaks in the north to the rugged southern mountains of Fiordland. Another area with climbs for all levels is Mt Aspiring National Park. To the south in the Forbes Mountains is Mt Earnslaw, flanked by the Rees and Dart Rivers.

The Christchurch-based **New Zealand Alpine Club** (NZAC; www.alpineclub.org.nz) proffers professional information and produces the annual *NZAC Alpine Journal* and the quarterly *The Climber* magazine. Professional outfits for training, guiding and advice can be found at Wanaka, Aoraki/Mt Cook, Lake Tekapo, and Fox and Franz Josef Glaciers.

Rock Climbing

Time to chalk up your fingers and don some natty little rubber shoes. On the North Island, popular rock-climbing areas include Auckland's Mt Eden Quarry; Whanganui Bay, Kinloch, Kawakawa Bay and Motuoapa near Lake Taupo; Mangatepopo Valley and Whakapapa Gorge on the Central Plateau; Humphries Castle and Warwick Castle on Mt Taranaki; and Piarere and Wharepapa South in the Waikato.

On the South Island, try the Port Hills area above Christchurch or Castle Hill on the road to Arthur's Pass. West of Nelson, the marble and limestone mountains of

Golden Bay and Takaka Hill provide prime climbing. Other options are Long Beach (north of Dunedin), and Mihiwaka and Lovers Leap on the Otago Peninsula.

Climb New Zealand (www.climb.co.nz) has the low-down on the gnarliest overhangs around NZ, plus access and instruction info.

Sea Kayaking

Sea kayaking is a fantastic way to see the coast, and get close to wildlife you'd otherwise never see.

Highly rated sea kayaking areas in NZ's north include the Hauraki Gulf (particularly off Waiheke and Great Barrier Islands), the Bay of Islands and Coromandel Peninsula; in the south, try the Marlborough Sounds (Picton) and along the coast of Abel Tasman National Park. Fiordland is also a hot spot, with a heap of tour operators in Te Anau, Milford, Doubtful Sound and Manapouri. Also try the Otago Peninsula, Stewart Island and Kaikoura down south; or Waitemata Harbour, Hahei, Raglan and East Cape up north. Useful resources:

» **Kiwi Association of Sea Kayakers** (KASK; www.kask.org.nz)

» **Sea Kayak Operators Association of New Zealand** (www.skoanz.org.nz)

Scuba Diving

NZ is prime scuba territory, with warm waters up north, brilliant sea life and plenty of interesting sites.

Up north, get wet at the Bay of Islands Maritime and Historic Park, Hauraki Gulf Maritime Park, the Bay of Plenty, Great Barrier Island, Goat Island Marine Reserve, the Alderman Islands, Te Tapuwae o Rongokako Marine Reserve near Gisborne, and Sugar Loaf Islands Marine Park near New Plymouth. The Poor Knights Islands near Whangarei are reputed to have the best diving in NZ (with the diveable wreck of the Greenpeace flagship *Rainbow Warrior* nearby). Stay tuned to see whether the MV *Rena,* grounded off Tauranga in 2011, will become a dive site.

Down south, the Marlborough Sounds Maritime Park hosts the *Mikhail Lermontov,* the largest diveable cruise-ship wreck in the world. In Fiordland head for Dusky Sound, Milford Sound and Doubtful Sound, which offer amazingly clear pseudo-deep-water conditions not far below the surface. Invercargill, with its Antarctic waters, also has a diving club.

Expect to pay anywhere from $180 for a short, introductory, pool-based scuba course, and around $600 for a four-day, PADI-approved, ocean dive course. One-off organised boat- and land-based dives start at around $170. Useful resources include:

» **Dive New Zealand** (www.divenewzealand.com)

» **New Zealand Underwater Association** (www.nzunderwater.org.nz)

Skydiving

Feeling confident? For most first-time skydivers, a tandem skydive will help you make the leap, even if common sense starts to get the better of you. Tandem jumps involve training with a qualified instructor, then experiencing up to 45 seconds of free fall before your chute opens. The thrill is worth every dollar (around $250/300/350 for a 8000/10,000/12,000ft jump; extra for a DVD/photograph). The **New Zealand Parachute Federation** (www.nzpf.org) is the governing body.

At the time of writing, safety concerns had sparked a wholesale review of skydiving in NZ, operators having to comply with stringent new Civil Aviation Authority regulations. Ask your operator if they have CAA accreditation before you take the plunge.

White-Water Rafting, Kayaking & Canoeing

There are almost as many white-water rafting and kayaking possibilities as there are rivers in the country, and there's no shortage of companies to get you into the rapids. Rivers are graded from I to VI, with VI meaning 'unraftable'. On the rougher stretches there's usually a minimum age limit of 12 or 13 years.

Popular South Island rafting rivers include the Shotover and Kawarau Rivers (Queenstown), Rangitata River (Christchurch), Buller River (Murchison), Karamea River (Westport) and the Arnold and Waiho

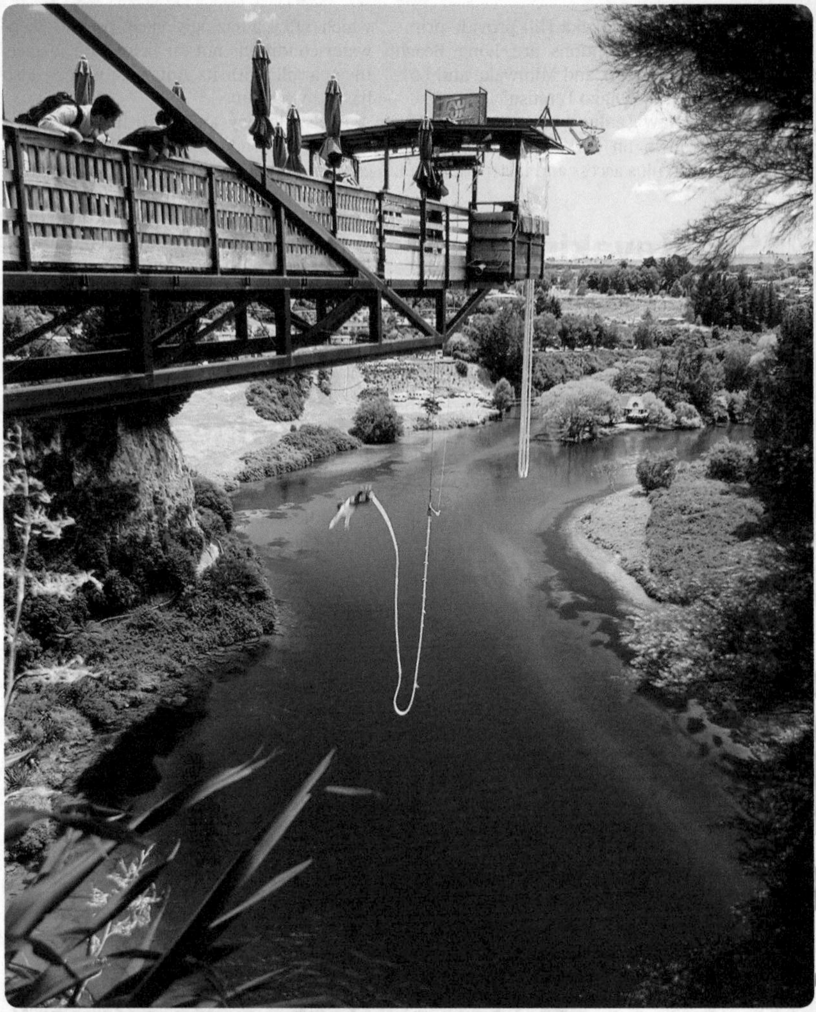

DAVID WALL / LONELY PLANET IMAGES ©

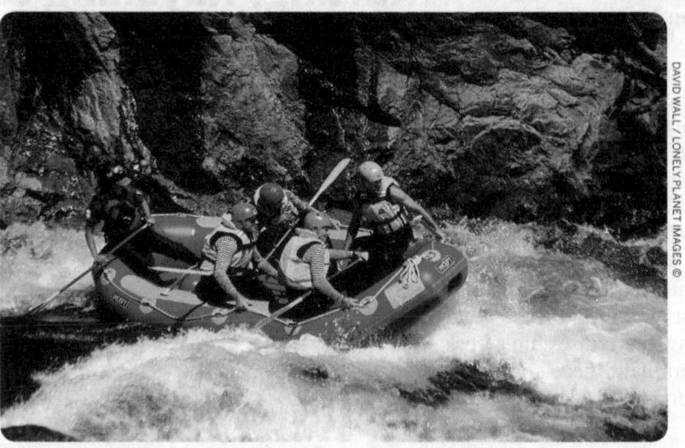

» (above) Bungy jumping over the Waikato River (p267), Taupo.
» (left) Rafting along the Buller River, Buller Gorge (p448), West Coast.

SURFING IN NEW ZEALAND *JOSH KRONFELD*

As a surfer I feel particularly guilty in letting the reader in on a local secret – New Zealand has a sensational mix of quality waves perfect for beginners and experienced surfers. As long as you're willing to travel off the beaten track, you can score some great, uncrowded waves. The islands of NZ are hit with swells from all points of the compass throughout the year. So, with a little weather knowledge and a little effort, numerous options present themselves. Point breaks, reefs, rocky shelves and hollow sandy beach breaks can all be found – take your pick!

Surfing has become increasingly popular in NZ and today there are surf schools up and running at most premier surf beaches. It's worth doing a bit of research before you arrive: **Surfing New Zealand** (www.surfingnz.co.nz) recommends a number of surf schools on its website. If you're on a surf holiday in NZ, consider purchasing a copy of the *New Zealand Surfing Guide* by Mike Bhana.

Surf.co.nz (www.surf.co.nz) provides information on many great surf spots, but most NZ beaches hold good rideable breaks. Some of the ones I particularly enjoy:

» **Waikato** Raglan, NZ's most famous surf break and usually the first stop for overseas surfies

» **Coromandel** Whangamata

» **Bay of Plenty** Mt Maunganui, now with a 250m artificial reef that creates huge waves, and Matakana Island

» **Taranaki** Fitzroy Beach, Stent Rd and Greenmeadows Point all lie along the 'Surf Highway'

» **East Coast** Hicks Bay, Gisborne city beaches and Mahia Peninsula

» **Wellington Region** Beaches such as Lyall Bay, Castlepoint and Tora

» **Marlborough & Nelson** Kaikoura Peninsula, Mangamaunu and Meatworks

» **Canterbury** Taylors Mistake and Sumner Bar

» **Otago** Dunedin is a good base for surfing on the South Island, with access to a number of superb breaks, such as St Clair Beach

» **West Coast** Punakaiki and Tauranga Bay

» **Southland** Porridge and Centre Island

NZ water temperatures and climate vary greatly from north to south. For comfort while surfing, wear a wetsuit. In summer on the North Island you can get away with a spring suit and boardies; on the South Island, a 2mm–3mm steamer. In winter on the North Island use a 2mm–3mm steamer, and on the South Island a 3mm–5mm with all the extras.

Josh Kronfeld, surfer & former All Black.

Rivers on the West Coast. The grading of the Shotover Canyon varies from III to V+, depending on the time of year. The Kawarau River is rated IV; the Rangitata River has everything from I to V.

On the North Island try the Rangitaiki, Wairoa, Motu, Mokau, Mohaka, Waitomo, Tongariro and Rangitikei Rivers. There are also the Kaituna Cascades near Rotorua, the highlight of which is the 7m drop at Okere Falls.

Canoeing is so popular on the North Island's Whanganui River that it's been designated one of NZ's 'Great Walks'! You can also dip your paddle into northern lakes like Lake Taupo and Lake Rotorua, as well as freshwater lakes on the South Island. Many backpacker hostels close to canoe-friendly waters have Canadian canoes and kayaks for hire (or free loan), and loads of commercial operators run guided trips.

Resources include:

» **New Zealand Rafting Association** (NZRA; www.nz-rafting.co.nz)

» **Whitewater NZ** (www.rivers.org.nz)

» **New Zealand Kayak** (www.canoeandkayak.co.nz) NZ's premier kayaking magazine.

regions at a glance

Auckland

Beaches
Food & Drink
Volcanoes

Beaches

From the calm, child-friendly bays facing the Hauraki Gulf to the black-sand surf beaches of the west coast, to the breathtaking coastline of the offshore islands, water lovers really are spoilt for choice.

Food & Drink

As well as having the lion's share of the nation's best restaurants, Auckland has excellent markets, a plethora of cheap Asian eateries, a lively cafe and bar scene, and wine regions on three of its flanks. And coffee culture is booming (don't tell anyone from Wellington...)

Volcanoes

Auckland is, quite literally, a global hot spot: over 50 separate volcanoes have formed this unique topography – and the next one could pop up at any time. Take a hike up one of the dormant cones dotting the landscape for a high, wide and handsome city panorama.

p60

Bay of Islands & Northland

Beaches
Forests
History

Beaches

Bay after beautiful bay lines Northland's east coast, making it a favourite destination for families, surfers and fishing enthusiasts. To the west, windswept beaches stretch for dozens of kilometres, in places forming towering sand dunes.

Forests

Kauri forests once blanketed the entire north, and in the pockets where the giants remain, particularly in the Waipoua Forest, they're an imposing sight.

History

New Zealand was settled top down by both Maori and Europeans, with missionaries erecting the country's oldest surviving buildings in Kerikeri. In nearby Waitangi, the treaty that founded the modern nation was first signed.

p125

Coromandel Peninsula

Beaches
Forests
Mining Towns

Beaches

Some of the country's most beautiful beaches are dotted around this compact peninsula, and while they're extremely popular in summer, splendid isolation can still be found.

Forests

Dense bushland shrouds the ranges at the heart of the peninsula, much of which is protected by the Coromandel Forest Park and is accessible via well-maintained walking tracks.

Mining Towns

The gold-rush roots of Thames and Coromandel Town are displayed through cutesy streets lined with historic wooden buildings, while at the base of the peninsula, Waihi teeters on the edge of a giant opencast mine.

p169

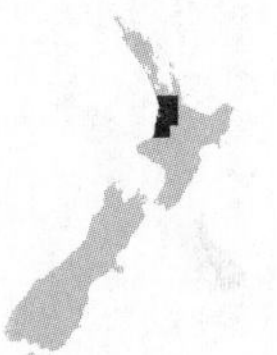

Waikato & the King Country

Caves
Beaches
Small Towns

Caves

Don't miss a visit to Waitomo Caves, NZ's most staggering cave site. Black-water rafting (through underground rivers) is almost mandatory, or you can just float lazily through amazing grottoes of glow worms.

Beaches

Around Raglan you'll find safe swimming and world-class surf beaches, including legendary Manu Bay. Further south are wild, isolated Tasman Sea beaches where your footprints are the only ones within miles.

Small Towns

Hamilton is the big smoke here, but far more charming are small towns such as Te Aroha, Cambridge, Matamata, Raglan and Waitomo: great pubs, cafes, restaurants and friendly locals.

p191

Taranaki & Whanganui

National Parks
Friendly Cities
Beaches

National Parks

Steeped in Maori lore, Whanganui National Park is one of NZ's most isolated, interesting parks. Lording over New Plymouth, Mt Taranaki (Egmont National Park) is picture perfect with fabulous tramping.

Friendly Cities

New Plymouth, Whanganui and Palmerston North are mid-sized cities usually overlooked by travellers. But stay a day. You'll find fantastic restaurants, hip bars, great coffee, wonderful museums and friendly folk.

Beaches

Hit Surf Hwy 45 south of New Plymouth for black-sand beaches and gnarly breaks. Whanganui offers remote and storm-buffered beaches; the Horowhenua District has acres of empty brown sand.

p223

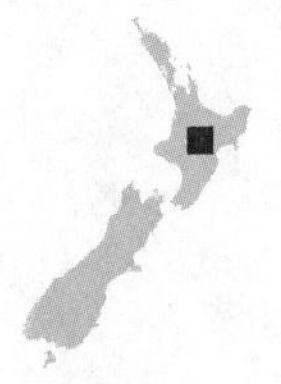

Taupo & the Central Plateau

Lake & Rivers
Mountains
Adrenaline

Lake & Rivers

NZ's mightiest river is born from NZ's greatest lake: aquatic pursuits in picturesque settings abound (kayaking, sailing, fishing). The water is famously chilly, but hot springs bubble up on the lakeside and riverbank.

Mountains

The three steaming, smoking, occasionally erupting volcanoes at the heart of the North Island are an imposing sight, the focus of skiing in winter and tramping at other times.

Adrenaline

Skydiving, bungy jumping, white-water rafting, jetboating, mountain biking, wakeboarding, parasailing, skiing – you want thrills, you got 'em.

p258

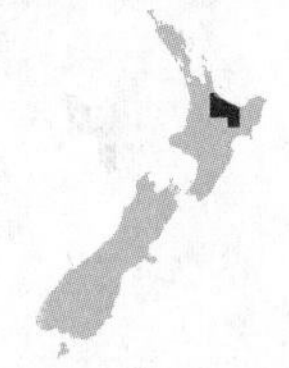

Rotorua & the Bay of Plenty

Active Earth
Maori Culture
Outdoor Action

Active Earth

The Rotorua landscape is littered with geysers, steaming geothermal vents, hot mineral springs and boiling mud pools. NZ's only active volcano, Whakaari (White Island), is 48km off the coast of Whakatane.

Maori Culture

Engage with Maori culture in Rotorua: a slew of companies offer cultural experiences for travellers, most involving traditional dance and musical performance, a *haka* (war dance) and a *hangi* (Maori feast).

Outdoor Action

Try paragliding, surfing, skydiving, zorbing, jetboating, blokarting, white-water rafting, mountain biking, kayaking…or just have a swim at the beach.

p288

The East Coast

Coastal Scenery
Wine & Food
Architecture

Coastal Scenery

Follow in the footsteps (or rather wake) of early Maori and James Cook along this stretch of coastline, home to the East Cape Lighthouse and Cape Kidnappers' gaggling gannet colony.

Wine & Food

Sip your way through Gisborne's bright chardonnays or head to Hawke's Bay for seriously good Bordeaux-style reds and some excellent winery dining.

Architecture

Napier's art-deco town centre is a magnet for architecture lovers, the keenest of whom time their visit for the annual Art Deco Weekend, an extravaganza of music, wine, cars and costume.

p331

Wellington Region

Museums
Cafe Culture
Nightlife

Museums

Crow-barred into the city centre is a significant collection of quality display spaces, including the highly interactive Te Papa museum and internationally flavoured City Gallery.

Cafe Culture

With more than a dozen roasters and scores of hip cafes, Wellington remains the coffee capital of NZ. Get a hit from one of the best: Midnight Espresso or Caffe L'Affare.

Nightlife

Between the boho bars around Cuba St and Courtenay Pl's glitzy drinking dens, you should find enough to keep you entertained until sun-up.

p364

Marlborough & Nelson

National Parks
Wineries
Wildlife

National Parks

Not satisfied with just one national park, the Nelson region has three – Nelson Lakes, Kahurangi and the Abel Tasman. You could tramp in all three over a week.

Wineries

Bobbing in Marlborough's sea of sauvignon blanc, riesling, pinot noir and bubbly are barrel loads of quality cellar-door experiences and some fine regional food.

Wildlife

The top of the South Island is home to myriad creatures, both in the water and on the wing. Kaikoura is a great one-stop shop: spot a whale or swim with dolphins and seals.

p398

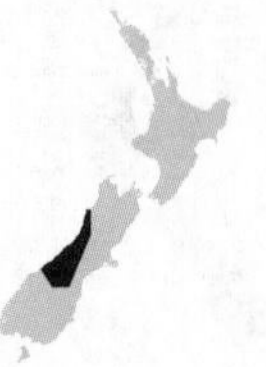

The West Coast

Natural Wonders
Tramping
History

Natural Wonders

With around 90% of its land lying within the conservation estate, the West Coast has abundant natural wonders. Don't miss Oparara's famous arch and Punakaiki's Pancake Rocks.

Tramping

The West Coast offers tracks from an easy hour through to hard-core epics. Old mining and milling routes like Charming Creek Walkway and Mahinapua Walkway entice beginners and history buffs.

History

The coast's pioneering history comes vividly to life at places like Denniston, Shanty Town, Reefton and Jackson's Bay.

p446

Christchurch & Canterbury

Heritage
Outdoor Action
Epic Scenery

Heritage
Earthquakes have damaged Christchurch's architectural heritage, but the Canterbury Museum, Botanic Gardens and Avon River still showcase the city's history. Nearby, Akaroa proudly celebrates its French heritage.

Outdoor Action
Tramp the alpine valleys around Arthur's Pass, kayak with dolphins on pristine Akaroa Harbour, or head inland for tramping and kayaking amid the glacial lakes of the Aoraki/Mt Cook National Park.

Epic Scenery
Descend from Banks Peninsula's Summit Rd to explore hidden bays and coves, and experience nature's grand scale: the river valleys, soaring peaks and glaciers of the Southern Alps.

p480

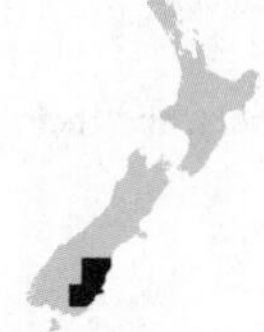

Dunedin & Otago

Wildlife
Wineries
History

Wildlife
Otago Peninsula's wild menagerie – seals, sea lions and penguins – patrol the rugged coastline; while rocky Taiaroa Head is the planet's only mainland breeding location for the magnificent royal albatross.

Wineries
Barrel into the craggy valleys of Bannockburn for excellent vineyard restaurants and the world's best pinot noir, or delve into the up-and-coming Waitaki Valley wine scene for riesling and pinot gris.

History
Explore the arty and storied streets of Dunedin, or escape by foot or penny-farthing bicycle into the heritage Victorian ambience of Oamaru's restored Harbour-Tyne Historic Precinct.

p533

Queenstown & Wanaka

Outdoor Action
Epic Scenery
Wineries

Outdoor Action
Nowhere else on earth offers so many adventurous activities: bungy jumping, river rafting and mountain biking only scratch Queenstown's adrenaline-fuelled surface.

Epic Scenery
Queenstown's photogenic combination of Lake Wakatipu and the soaring Remarkables is a real jaw-dropper. Or venture into prime NZ wilderness around Glenorchy and Mt Aspiring National Park.

Wineries
Start with lunch at Amisfield Winery's award-winning restaurant, then explore the Gibbston Valley: cottage accommodation, artisan cheeses and excellent pinot noir concealed in a meandering river valley.

p567

Fiordland & Southland

Epic Scenery
National Parks
Outdoor Action

Epic Scenery
The star of the show is remarkable Milford Sound, but take time to explore the rugged Catlins coast or experience the remote, end-of-the-world appeal of Stewart Island.

National Parks
Fiordland National Park comprises much of NZ's precious Te Wahipounamu Southwest New Zealand World Heritage area. Further south, Rakiura National Park showcases Stewart Island's beauty.

Outdoor Action
Test yourself by tramping the Milford or Tuatapere Hump Ridge Tracks, or negotiate a sea kayak around glorious Doubtful Sound.

p605

❯ **Every listing is recommended by our authors, and their favourite places are listed first**

❯ **Look out for these icons:**

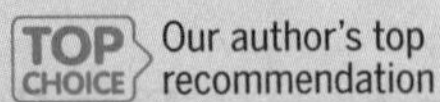

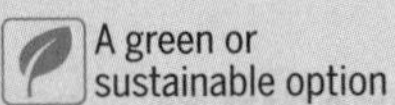

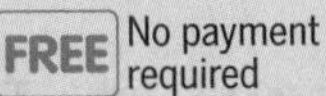

AUCKLAND 60

AUCKLAND 62
HAURAKI GULF ISLANDS . . 100
Waiheke Island 103
Great Barrier Island......109
WEST AUCKLAND 113
NORTH AUCKLAND 118
Goat Island Marine Reserve 123

BAY OF ISLANDS & NORTHLAND.......125

WHANGAREI DISTRICT... 128
Mangawhai 128
Whangarei 130
Tutukaka Coast & the Poor Knights Islands.....135
BAY OF ISLANDS 138
Russell 142
Paihia & Waitangi........146
Kerikeri.................150
THE FAR NORTH......... 153
Doubtless Bay...........156
Karikari Peninsula 157
Cape Reinga & Ninety Mile Beach 158
Ahipara.................160
HOKIANGA 162
Opononi & Omapere 164
KAURI COAST 165
Waipoua Forest.......... 165

COROMANDEL PENINSULA........169

Thames 173
Coromandel Town 176
Far North Coromandel ...179
Whitianga...............180
Hot Water Beach 184
Tairua 185
Whangamata............186
Waihi & Waihi Beach 187
Karangahake Gorge......189

WAIKATO & THE KING COUNTRY...........191

WAIKATO 194
Hamilton 195
Raglan 201
Te Awamutu............ 205
Cambridge............. 206
Matamata 209
Te Aroha................210
THE KING COUNTRY......211
Kawhia 211
Otorohanga 212
Waitomo Caves......... 214
Te Kuiti.................219
Taumarunui............ 220
Owhango 221

TARANAKI & WHANGANUI.......223

New Plymouth 226
Mt Taranaki (Egmont National Park)...........234
Surf Highway 45.........238
Whanganui............. 240
Whanganui National Park... 246
Palmerston North 252

TAUPO & THE CENTRAL PLATEAU.............258

LAKE TAUPO REGION 260
Taupo 260
Turangi & Around........273
THE CENTRAL PLATEAU... 275
Tongariro National Park ..275
National Park Village.....282
Ohakune................283

ROTORUA & THE BAY OF PLENTY 288

ROTORUA...............290
AROUND ROTORUA......304
BAY OF PLENTY 308
Tauranga 308
Mt Maunganui...........315
Katikati............... 320
Whakatane 322
Whakaari (White Island) ..326
Ohope..................327
Opotiki 328

THE EAST COAST...331

EAST CAPE 334
Pacific Coast Hwy 334
Gisborne 338
Te Urewera National Park..344
HAWKE'S BAY 347
Napier................. 348
Hastings & Around.......356
Cape Kidnappers 361
Central Hawke's Bay 362

See the Index for a full list of destinations covered in this book.

On the Road

WELLINGTON REGION 364
WELLINGTON 366
KAPITI COAST 389
Paekakariki 389
Paraparaumu 390
THE WAIRARAPA 391
Martinborough 392
Greytown 395

MARLBOROUGH & NELSON 398
MARLBOROUGH REGION ... 400
Picton 400
Queen Charlotte Track 407
Kenepuru & Pelorus Sounds .. 409
Blenheim 411
Kaikoura 416
NELSON REGION 423
Nelson 423
Motueka 432
Motueka to Abel Tasman ... 435
Golden Bay 440
Kahurangi National Park .. 444

THE WEST COAST ... 446
MURCHISON & BULLER GORGE 448
WESTPORT & AROUND 450
WESTPORT TO KARAMEA .. 452
KARAMEA & AROUND 452
WESTPORT TO GREYMOUTH 455
Punakaiki & Paparoa National Park 455
REEFTON & GREY VALLEY 457
GREYMOUTH 459
HOKITIKA 463
HOKITIKA TO WESTLAND TAI POUTINI NATIONAL PARK 467
WESTLAND TAI POUTINI NATIONAL PARK 469
Franz Josef Glacier 469
Fox Glacier 474
SOUTH TO HAAST 477
HAAST REGION 477

CHRISTCHURCH & CANTERBURY 480
CHRISTCHURCH 482
AROUND CHRISTCHURCH .. 502
Akaroa & Banks Peninsula .. 503
NORTH CANTERBURY 510
Hanmer Springs 510
CENTRAL CANTERBURY ... 514
Arthur's Pass 515
Methven 516
SOUTH CANTERBURY 518
Timaru 518
Inland & Mackenzie Country 521
Aoraki/Mt Cook National Park 528

DUNEDIN & OTAGO .. 533
DUNEDIN & THE OTAGO PENINSULA .. 535
Dunedin 535
Otago Peninsula 547
CENTRAL OTAGO 551
Cromwell 551
Alexandra 554
Alexandra to Palmerston .. 555
NORTH OTAGO & WAITAKI 558
Oamaru 559
Waitaki Valley 564

QUEENSTOWN & WANAKA 567
QUEENSTOWN REGION ... 568
Queenstown 568
Arrowtown 587
Glenorchy 591
Lake Wakatipu Region 593
WANAKA REGION 595
Wanaka 595

FIORDLAND & SOUTHLAND 605
FIORDLAND 607
Te Anau 607
Te Anau–Milford Hwy 612
Milford Sound 615
Doubtful Sound 618
SOUTHERN SCENIC ROUTE 619
Tuatapere 619
CENTRAL SOUTHLAND .. 621
Invercargill 621
THE CATLINS 625
Invercargill to Papatowai .. 627
Papatowai to Balcutha .. 629
Stewart Island 630

Auckland

POPULATION: 1.4 MILLION

Includes »

Auckland 62
Sights 62
Activities......................... 75
Tours.............................. 79
Festivals & Events 80
Sleeping.......................... 82
Eating 88
Drinking.......................... 92
Entertainment................ 94
Shopping 96
Hauraki Gulf Islands 100
West Auckland............... 113
North Auckland 118
Goat Island Marine Reserve......................... 123

Best Places to Eat

» Grove (p88)
» La Cigale market (p91)
» Depot (p88)
» Clooney (p89)
» MooChowChow (p89)

Best Places to Stay

» Hotel de Brett (p83)
» Auckland Takapuna Oaks (p87)
» Verandahs (p84)
» 23 Hepburn (p84)
» Waldorf Celestion (p83)

Why Go?

Paris may be the city of love, but Auckland is the city of many lovers, according to its Maori name, Tamaki Makaurau. Those lovers so desired this place that they fought over it for centuries.

It's hard to imagine a more geographically blessed city. Its two harbours frame a narrow isthmus punctuated by volcanic cones and surrounded by fertile farmland. From any of its numerous vantage points you'll be astounded by how close the Tasman Sea and Pacific Ocean come to kissing and forming a new island.

As a result, water's never far away – whether it's the ruggedly beautiful west-coast surf beaches or the glistening Hauraki Gulf with its myriad islands. And within an hour's drive from the high-rise heart of the city there are dense tracts of rainforest, thermal springs, wineries and wildlife reserves. No wonder Auckland's rated as offering the third-best quality of life of any major city.

When to Go

Auckland has a mild climate, with the occasional frost in winter and high humidity in summer. Summer months have an average of eight days of rain, but the weather is famously fickle, with 'four seasons in one day' possible at any time of the year. If you're after a big-city buzz, don't come between Christmas and New Year, when Aucklanders desert the city for the beach en masse. The sights remain open but many cafes and restaurants close, some not surfacing again until well into January.

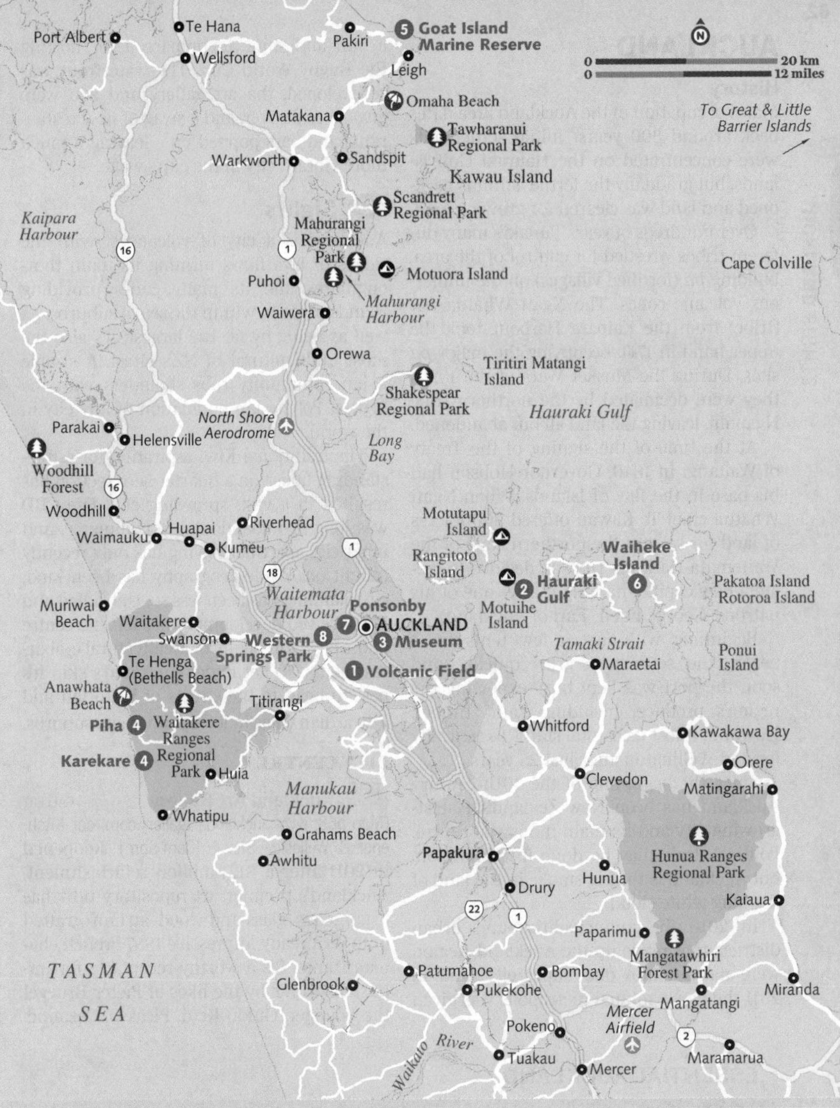

Auckland Highlights

1 Going with the flows, exploring Auckland's fascinating **volcanic field** (p71)

2 Getting back to nature on the island sanctuaries of the beautiful **Hauraki Gulf** (p100)

3 Being awed by the Maori *taonga* (treasures) of the **Auckland Museum** (p67)

4 Going west to the mystical and treacherous black sands of **Karekare** and **Piha** (p115)

5 Swimming with the fishes at **Goat Island Marine Reserve** (p123)

6 Schlepping around world-class wineries and beaches on **Waiheke Island** (p103)

7 Buzzing around the cafes, restaurants and bars of **Ponsonby** (p89)

8 Soaking up the Polynesian vibe at the **Pasifika Festival** (p81), held in March at Western Springs Park

AUCKLAND

History

Maori occupation in the Auckland area dates back around 800 years. Initial settlements were concentrated on the Hauraki Gulf islands, but gradually the fertile isthmus beckoned and land was cleared for growing food.

Over hundreds of years Tamaki's many different tribes wrestled for control of the area, building *pa* (fortified villages) on the numerous volcanic cones. The Ngati Whatua *iwi* (tribe) from the Kaipara Harbour took the upper hand in 1741, occupying the major *pa* sites. During the Musket Wars of the 1820s they were decimated by the northern tribe Ngapuhi, leaving the land all but abandoned.

At the time of the signing of the Treaty of Waitangi in 1840, Governor Hobson had his base in the Bay of Islands. When Ngati Whatua chief Te Kawau offered 3000 acres of land for sale on the northern edge of the Waitemata Harbour, Hobson decided to create a new capital, naming it after one of his patrons, George Eden (Earl of Auckland).

Beginning with just a few tents on a beach, the settlement grew quickly, and soon the port was kept busy exporting the region's produce, including kauri timber. However, it lost its capital status to centrally located Wellington after just 25 years.

Since the beginning of the 20th century Auckland has been New Zealand's fastest-growing city and its main industrial centre. Political deals may be done in Wellington, but Auckland is the big smoke in the land of the long white cloud.

In 2010 the municipalities and urban districts that made up the Auckland Region were merged into one 'super city', and in 2011 the newly minted metropolis was given a buff and shine to prepare it for hosting the Rugby World Cup. The waterfront was redeveloped, the art gallery and zoo were given a makeover, and a swag of new restaurants and bars popped up – leaving a much more vibrant city in the cup's wake.

Sights

Auckland is a city of volcanoes, with the ridges of lava flows forming its main thoroughfares and its many cones providing islands of green within the sea of suburbs. As well as being by far the largest, it's also the most multicultural of NZ's cities. A sizable Asian community rubs shoulders with the biggest Polynesian population of any city in the world.

The traditional Kiwi aspiration for a free-standing house on a quarter-acre section has resulted in a vast, sprawling city. The CBD was long ago abandoned to commerce, and inner-city apartment living has only recently caught on. While geography has been kind, city planning has been less so. Unbridled and ill-conceived development has left the centre of the city with plenty of architectural embarrassments. To get under Auckland's skin it's best to head to the streets of Victorian and Edwardian villas in its hip inner-city suburbs.

CITY CENTRE

TOP CHOICE **Auckland Art Gallery** GALLERY

(Map p68; www.aucklandartgallery.com; cnr Kitchener & Wellesley Sts; ⌚10am-5pm) Reopened in 2011 after a $121-million refurbishment, Auckland's premier art repository now has a gorgeous glass-and-wood atrium grafted onto its already impressive 1887 French chateau frame. It's a worthy receptacle for important works by the likes of Pieter Bruegel the Younger, Guido Reni, Picasso, Cezanne,

ESSENTIAL AUCKLAND

» **Eat** Multiculturally, at one of the city's food halls

» **Drink** Cold Waiheke Island rosé on a hot summer's day

» **Read** *Under the Mountain* (1979) – Maurice Gee's teenage tale of slimy things lurking under Auckland's volcanoes

» **Listen to** *One Tree Hill* (1987) – U2's elegy to their Kiwi roadie is no less poignant now that the tree is gone

» **Watch** *Sione's Wedding* (2006) – comedy set in Grey Lynn and central Auckland

» **Festival** Pasifika

» **Online** www.aucklandnz.com; www.aucklandcouncil.govt.nz; www.lonelyplanet.com/new-zealand/auckland

» **Area code** ☎09

AUCKLAND IN...

Two Days

Start by acquainting yourself with the inner city. Take our walking tour from Karangahape Rd (K Rd) to the Wynyard Quarter, stopping along the way to have at least a quick whiz around the NZ section of the Auckland Art Gallery. Catch a ferry to **Devonport**, head up North Head and cool down at **Cheltenham Beach** (weather and tide permitting), before ferrying back to the city for dinner.

On day two, head up **One Tree Hill**, wander around **Cornwall Park** and then visit the **Auckland Museum** and **Domain**. Take a trip along **Tamaki Drive**, stopping at **Bastion** or **Achilles Point** to enjoy the harbour views. Spend the evening dining and bar hopping in **Ponsonby**.

Four Days

On the third day, get out on the **Hauraki Gulf**. Catch the ferry to **Waiheke Island** and divide your time between the beaches and the wineries.

For your final day, head west. Grab breakfast in **Titirangi** before exploring the **Waitakere Ranges Regional Park**, **Karekare** and **Piha**. Freshen up for a night on the town on **K Rd** or **Britomart**.

Gauguin and Matisse. It also showcases the best of NZ art, from the intimate 19th-century portraits of tattooed Maori subjects by Charles Goldie, to the text-scrawled canvasses of Colin McCahon, and beyond.

Free tours depart from the main entrance at 11.30am, 12.30pm and 1.30pm.

Albert Park & Auckland University PARK, UNIVERSITY

(Map p68) Hugging the hill on the city's eastern flank, Albert Park is a charming Victorian formal garden overrun by students during term time, the more radical of whom have been known to deface the statues of Governor Grey and Queen Victoria. Auckland University's campus stretches over several streets and incorporates a row of stately Victorian merchant houses (Princes St) and **Old Government House** (Waterloo Quadrant). The latter was the colony's seat of power from 1856 until 1865, when Wellington became the capital.

The **University Clock Tower** (22 Princes St) is Auckland's architectural triumph. The stately 'ivory tower' (1926) tips its hat towards art nouveau (the incorporation of NZ flora and fauna into the decoration) and the Chicago School (the way it's rooted into the earth). It's usually open, so wander inside.

At the centre of the campus is a wall of the **Albert Barracks** (1847), a fortification that enclosed 9 hectares, including Albert Park, during the New Zealand Wars.

Sky Tower LANDMARK

(Map p68; www.skycityauckland.co.nz; cnr Federal & Victoria Sts; adult/child $25/8; ⌚8.30am-10.30pm) The impossible-to-miss Sky Tower looks like a giant hypodermic giving a fix to the heavens. Spectacular lighting renders it space-age at night and the colours change for special events. At 328m it is the tallest structure in the southern hemisphere. A lift takes you up to the observation decks in 40 stomach-lurching seconds; look down through the glass floor panels if you're after an extra kick. It costs $3 extra to catch the skyway lift to the ultimate viewing level. Late afternoon is a good time to go up: you can sip a beverage in the Sky Lounge as the sun sets. Sky Tower is also home to the SkyWalk (p75) and SkyJump (p75). The tower is the best part of the SkyCity complex, a tacky 24-hour casino with ritzy restaurants, cafes, bars, theatres and hotels.

Civic Theatre ARCHITECTURE

(Map p68; www.civictheatre.co.nz; cnr Queen & Wellesley Sts) The 'mighty Civic' (1929) is one of seven 'atmospheric theatres' remaining in the world and a fine survivor from cinema's Golden Age. The auditorium has lavish Moorish decoration and a starlit southern-hemisphere sky in the ceiling, complete with cloud projections. The foyer is an Indian indulgence, with elephants and monkeys hanging from every conceivable fixture. Buddhas were planned to decorate the street frontage but were considered too

Central Auckland

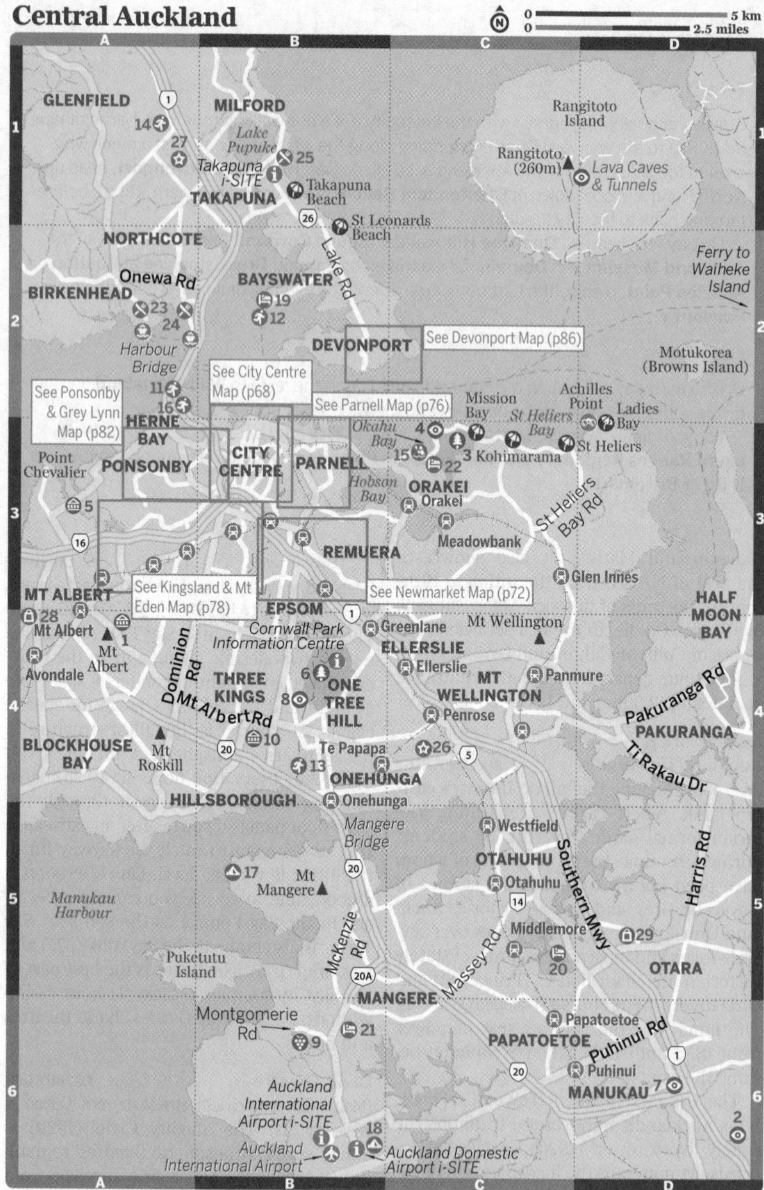

risqué at the time – they chose neoclassical naked boys instead!

If at all possible, try to attend a performance here. It's mainly used for touring musicals, big premieres and Film Festival (p81) screenings.

St Patrick's Cathedral CHURCH
(Map p68; www.stpatricks.org.nz; 43 Wyndham St; ⌚7am-7pm) Auckland's Catholic cathedral is one of its loveliest buildings. Polished wood and Belgian stained glass lend warmth to the interior of this majestic Gothic Revival

Central Auckland

Sights

1	Alberton	A4
2	Auckland Botanic Gardens	D6
3	Bastion Point	C3
4	Kelly Tarlton's	C3
5	MOTAT 2	A3
6	One Tree Hill	B4
7	Rainbow's End	D6
8	Stardome Observatory	B4
9	Villa Maria Estate	B6
10	Wallace Arts Centre	B4

Activities, Courses & Tours

11	Auckland Bridge Climb & Bungy	A2
12	CharterLink	B2
13	Coast to Coast Walkway	B4
14	Dive Centre	A1
15	Fergs Kayaks	C3
16	Gulfwind	A2
	Penny Whiting Sailing School	(see 16)

Sleeping

17	Ambury Regional Park	B5
18	Auckland Airport Campervan Park	B6
19	Auckland Takapuna Oaks	B2
20	Grange Lodge	C5
21	Jet Park	B6
22	Nautical Nook	C3

Eating

23	Eight.Two	A2
24	Engine Room	A2
25	Takapuna Beach Cafe	B1

Entertainment

26	Mt Smart Stadium	C4
27	North Shore Events Centre	A1

Shopping

28	Avondale Sunday Market	A4
29	Otara Market	D5

church (1907). There's a historical display in the old confessional on the left-hand side.

BRITOMART, VIADUCT HARBOUR & WYNYARD QUARTER

Stretching for only a small grid of blocks above the train station, Britomart is a tiny enclave of historic buildings and new developments that has been transformed into one of the city's best eating, drinking and, increasingly, shopping precincts.

Once a busy commercial port, the Viaduct Harbour was given a major makeover for the 1999/2000 and 2003 America's Cup tournaments. It's now a fancy dining and boozing precinct, and guaranteed to have at least a slight buzz any night of the week. Historical plaques, public sculpture and the chance to gawk at millionaires' yachts make it a diverting place for a stroll.

Connected to the Viaduct by a raiseable bridge, Wynyard Quarter opened in advance of another sporting tournament, 2011's Rugby World Cup. With its public plazas, waterfront cafes, events centre, fish market and children's playground, it has quickly become Auckland's favourite new place to promenade.

The precinct is something of a work-in-progress, with plans to tart up the scrappy surrounds. Still, things have gotten off to a good start and we hope that the free outdoor movies and night markets become summertime institutions.

Voyager – New Zealand Maritime Museum MUSEUM

(Map p68; ☎09-373 0800; www.maritimemuseum.co.nz; 149-159 Quay St; adult/child $17/9; ⏲9am-5pm) This well-presented museum traces NZ's seafaring history from Maori voyaging canoes to the America's Cup. Recreations include a tilting 19th-century steerage-class cabin and a fab 1950s beach store and bach (holiday home). The *Blue Water Black Magic* exhibition is a tribute to Sir Peter Blake, the Whitbread-Round-the-World and America's Cup–winning yachtsman who was murdered in 2001 while on an environmental monitoring trip on the Amazon.

Check the website for details of regular historic steam-tug and sailing-ship cruises.

HAVE YOUR SAY

Found a fantastic restaurant that you're longing to share with the world? Disagree with our recommendations? Or just want to talk about your most recent trip?

Whatever your reason, head to lonelyplanet.com, where you can post a review, ask or answer a question on the Thorntree forum, comment on a blog, or share your photos and tips on Groups. Or you can simply spend time chatting with like-minded travellers. So go on, have your say.

START ST KEVIN'S ARCADE, KARANGAHAPE RD
FINISH WYNYARD QUARTER
DISTANCE 4.5KM
DURATION AROUND THREE HOURS

Walking Tour
City Centre Ramble

Auckland's CBD can seem scrappy, so this walk aims to show you some hidden nooks and architectural treats.

Start among the second hand boutiques of 1 **St Kevin's Arcade** and take the stairs down to Myers Park. Look out for the reproduction of 2 **Michelangelo's Moses** at the bottom of the stairs. Continue through the park, taking the stairs on the right just before the overpass to head up to street level.

Heading down Queen St, you'll pass the 3 **Auckland Town Hall** and 4 **Aotea Sq**, the civic heart of the city. On the next corner is the wonderful 5 **Civic Theatre**. Turn right on Wellesley St and then left onto Lorne St. Immediately to your right is 6 **Khartoum Pl**, a pretty little square with tiling celebrating the suffragettes; NZ women were the first in the world to win the vote. Head up the stairs to the 7 **Auckland Art Gallery**.

Behind the gallery is 8 **Albert Park**. Cross through it and turn left into Princes St, where a row of 9 **Victorian merchants' houses** faces the 10 **University Clock Tower**. Cut around behind the clock tower to 11 **Old Government House** and then follow the diagonal path back to Princes St. The attractive building on the corner of Princes St and Bowen Ave was once the city's main 12 **synagogue**.

Head down Bowen Ave and cut through the park to the 15 **Chancery precinct**, an upmarket area of designer stores and cafes. A small square connects it to 14 **High St**, Auckland's main fashion strip. Take a left onto 15 **Vulcan Lane**, lined with historic pubs. Turn right onto Queen St and follow it down to the 16 **Britomart Train Station**, housed in the former central post office. You're now standing on reclaimed land – the original shoreline was at Fort St.

Turn left on Quay St and head to 17 **Viaduct Harbour**, bustling with bars and cafes, and then continue over the bridge to the rejuvenated 18 **Wynyard Quarter**.

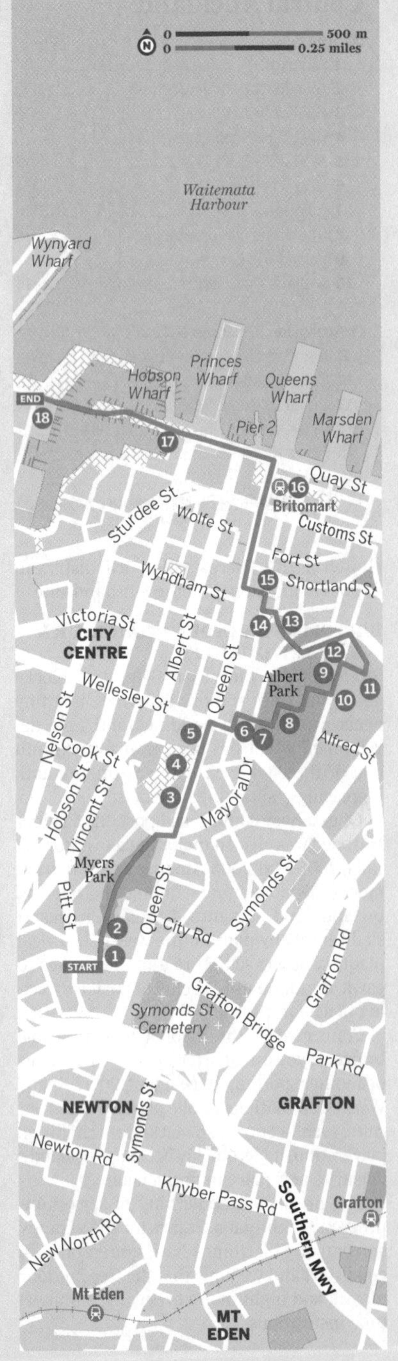

Auckland Fish Market MARKET
(Map p68; www.aucklandfishmarket.co.nz; 22-32 Jellicoe St; ⏲6am-7pm) No self-respecting city with a position like this should be without a fish market. Auckland's has a boisterous early-morning auction, retail fish shops, eateries and a seafood-cooking school.

Dockline Tram TRAM
(www.aucklandtram.co.nz; adult/child $5/1; ⏲9am-7.30pm Dec-Feb, 10am-5pm Mar-Nov) A dose of nostalgia is offered by this heritage tram, but the 15-minute loop won't take you anywhere very interesting.

MT EDEN

Mt Eden (Maungawhau) VOLCANO
(Map p78; ⏲road access 7am-11pm) From the top of Auckland's highest volcanic cone (196m) the entire isthmus and both harbours are laid bare. The symmetrical crater (50m deep) is known as *Te Ipu Kai a Mataaho* (the Food Bowl of Mataaho, the god of things hidden in the ground) and is highly *tapu* (sacred); do not enter it, but feel free to explore the remainder of the mountain. The remains of *pa* terraces and storage pits are clearly visible.

You can drive to the very top or you can join the legions of fitness freaks jogging or trudging up. Tour buses are banned from the summit, but shuttles will transport infirm passengers to the top from the car park on the lower slopes.

Eden Garden GARDENS
(Map p72; www.edengarden.co.nz; 24 Omana Ave; adult/child $8/6; ⏲9am-4pm) On the eastern slopes of Mt Eden, this horticultural showpiece is noted for its collections of camellias, rhododendrons and azaleas.

PARNELL & NEWMARKET

Parnell likes to think of itself as a village, although the only tractors to be seen here are the SUVs driven by the affluent suburb's soccer mums. This is one of Auckland's oldest areas and has retained several heritage buildings. Inexplicably, it also has an excellent selection of budget accommodation, although it's doubtful that backpackers will be frequenting the pricey eateries of the main strip. Neighbouring Newmarket is a busy shopping precinct known for its boutiques.

TOP CHOICE **Auckland Museum** MUSEUM
(Map p76; ☎09-309 0443; www.aucklandmuseum.com; adult/child $10/free; ⏲10am-5pm) Dominating the Domain is this imposing neoclassical temple (1929), capped with an impressive copper-and-glass dome (2007). Its comprehensive display of Pacific Island and Maori artefacts on the ground floor deserves to be on your 'must see' list. Highlights include a 25m war canoe and an extant carved meeting house (remove your shoes before entering). There's also an Egyptian mummy (a sure-fire hit with the kids) and a fascinating display on the volcanic field, including an eruption simulation.

The upper floors are given over to military displays, fulfilling the building's dual role as a war memorial. Auckland's main ANZAC commemorations take place at dawn on 25 April at the cenotaph in the museum's forecourt.

Hour-long museum highlights tours (adult/child $20/8) are held daily at 10.30am, 12.30pm and 2pm. Half-hour Maori cultural performances (adult/child $25/13) take place at 11am and 1.30pm, with Maori gallery tours (adult/child $10/5) departing immediately afterwards.

Auckland Domain PARK
(Map p76) Covering about 80 hectares, this green swathe contains sports fields, interesting sculpture, formal gardens, wild corners and the **Wintergarden** (admission free; ⏲9am-5.30pm Mon-Sat, 9am-7.30pm Sun Nov-Mar, 9am-4.30pm Apr-Oct), with its fernery, tropical house, cool house, cute cat statue and neighbouring cafe. The mound in the centre of the park is all that remains of Pukekaroa, one of Auckland's volcanoes. At its humble peak, a totara surrounded by a palisade honours the first Maori king.

Holy Trinity Cathedral CHURCH
(Map p76; www.holy-trinity.org.nz; Parnell Rd; ⏲10am-3pm) Auckland's Anglican cathedral is a hodgepodge of architectural styles, especially compared to **St Mary's** (1886) next door, a wonderful wooden Gothic Revival church with a burnished interior and interesting stained-glass windows. The cathedral's windows are also notable, especially

City Centre

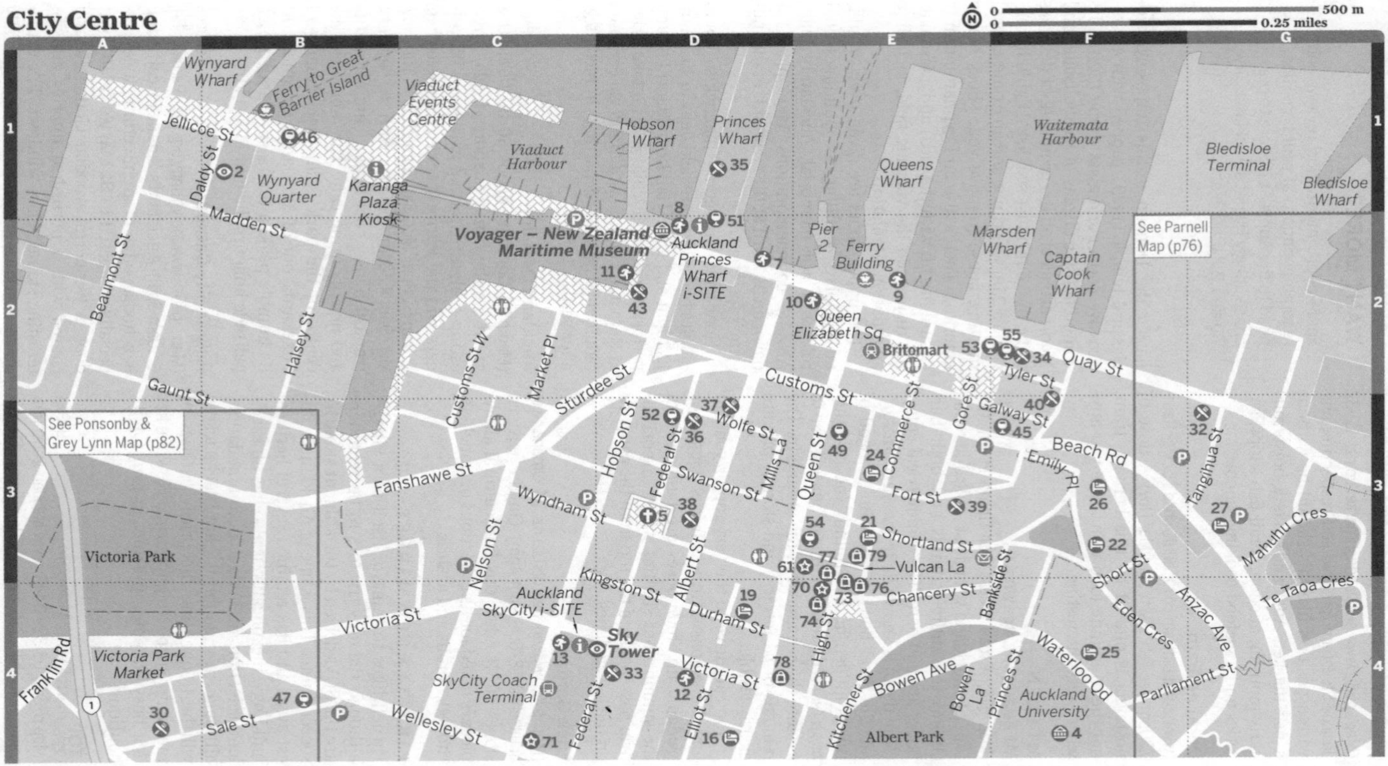

0 500 m
0 0.25 miles

Wynyard Wharf
Ferry to Great Barrier Island
Viaduct Events Centre
Jellicoe St
46
Daldy St
2
Wynyard Quarter
Karanga Plaza Kiosk
Madden St
Viaduct Harbour
Hobson Wharf
Princes Wharf
35
8
51
Voyager – New Zealand Maritime Museum
Auckland Princes Wharf i-SITE
7
11
43
Queens Wharf
Pier 2
Ferry Building
9
10
Queen Elizabeth Sq
Waitemata Harbour
Marsden Wharf
Captain Cook Wharf
Bledisloe Terminal
Bledisloe Wharf
See Parnell Map (p76)
Beaumont St
Halsey St
Gaunt St
Customs St W
Market Pl
Sturdee St
Britomart
53
55
34
Quay St
Tyler St
Customs St
Commerce St
Gore St
Galway St
40
45
32
Tangihua St
See Ponsonby & Grey Lynn Map (p82)
Hobson St
52
36
37
Wolfe St
Federal St
Mills La
Queen St
49
24
Beach Rd
Emily Pl
26
Fanshawe St
Swanson St
Fort St
39
27
Mahuhu Cres
Victoria Park
Wyndham St
38
5
54
21
Shortland St
22
Nelson St
Albert St
61
77
79
Vulcan La
Short St
Kingston St
70
73
76
Chancery St
Bankside St
Anzac Ave
Te Taoa Cres
Auckland SkyCity i-SITE
19
74
Eden Cres
Victoria St
Durham St
High St
Franklin Rd
Victoria Park Market
13
Sky Tower
33
Victoria St
12
78
Waterloo Qd
25
Bowen Ave
Bowen La
Princes St
Kitchener St
Parliament St
SkyCity Coach Terminal
47
30
Sale St
Wellesley St
Federal St
Elliot St
16
71
Albert Park
Auckland University
4

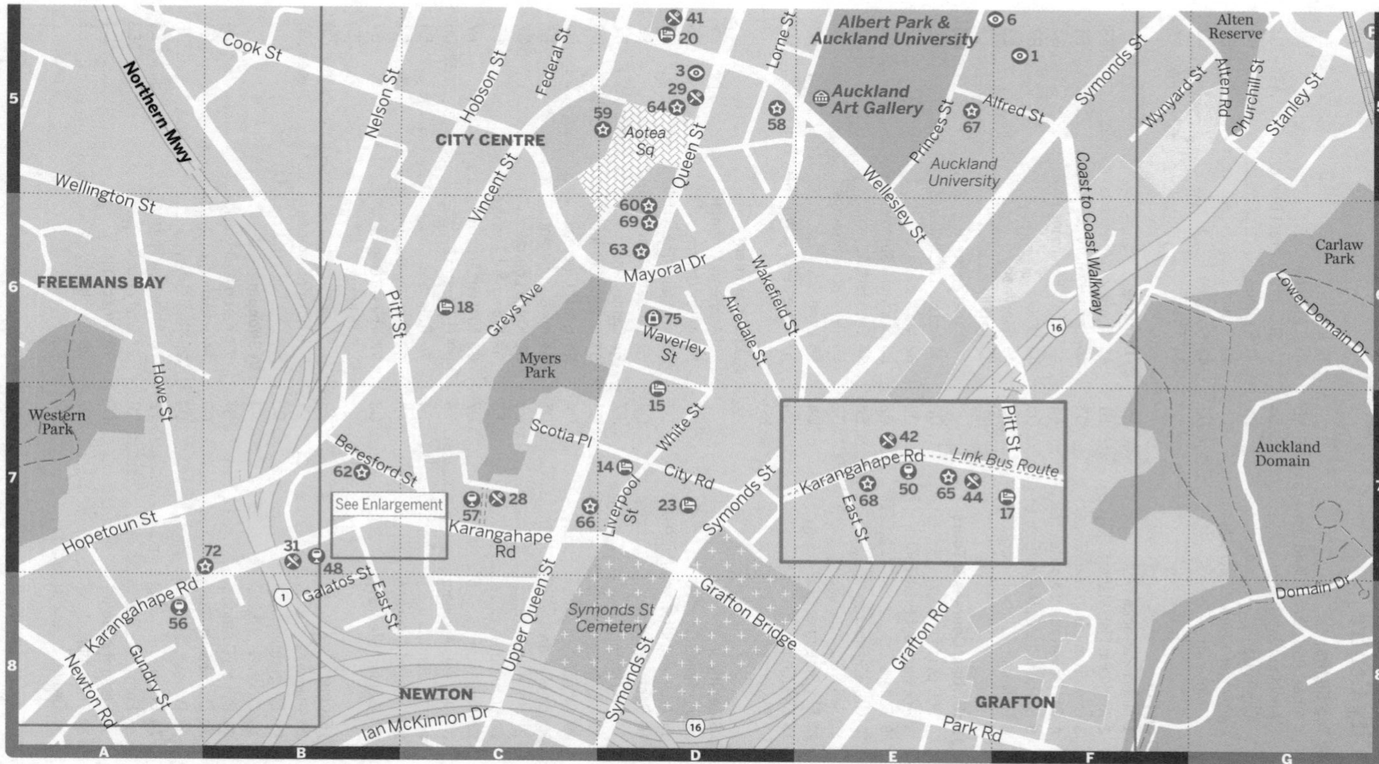

Albert Park & Auckland University
Auckland Art Gallery
Auckland University
Alten Reserve
Carlaw Park
Auckland Domain
Myers Park
Western Park
Symonds St Cemetery
Aotea Sq
CITY CENTRE
FREEMANS BAY
NEWTON
GRAFTON
Cook St
Northern Mwy
Nelson St
Hobson St
Federal St
Lorne St
Queen St
Princes St
Alfred St
Symonds St
Wynyard St
Alten Rd
Churchill St
Stanley St
Wellington St
Vincent St
Wellesley St
Coast to Coast Walkway
Mayoral Dr
Wakefield St
Airedale St
Lower Domain Dr
Pitt St
Greys Ave
Waverley St
Howe St
White St
Scotia Pl
Beresford St
City Rd
Liverpool St
Karangahape Rd
Link Bus Route
East St
See Enlargement
Hopetoun St
Galatos St
Upper Queen St
Grafton Bridge
Grafton Rd
Domain Dr
Newton Rd
Gundry St
Ian McKinnon Dr
Park Rd

City Centre

Top Sights

Albert Park & Auckland University........E5
Auckland Art Gallery E5
Sky Tower D4
Voyager – New Zealand Maritime Museum D2

Sights

1 Albert Barracks Wall........F5
2 Auckland Fish Market........B1
3 Civic Theatre D5
4 Old Government House F4
5 St Patrick's Cathedral........D3
6 University Clock Tower........F5

Activities, Courses & Tours

7 360 Discovery D2
8 Auckland Jet Boat Tours D2
9 Fullers........E2
10 GreatSights........E2
11 Sail NZ D2
12 Sky Screamer........D4
13 SkyJump C4
SkyWalk ....(see 13)

Sleeping

14 Auckland City YHA........D7
15 Auckland International YHA........D7
16 Base Auckland D4
17 BK Hostel........F7
18 City Lodge........C6
19 CityLife D4
20 Elliott Hotel D5
21 Hotel de Brett........E3
22 Jucy Hotel F3
23 Langham D7
24 Nomads Auckland E3
25 Quadrant........F4
26 Waldorf Celestion F3
27 Waldorf Stadium........G3

Eating

28 Alleluya........C7
29 Burgerfuel........D5
30 Clooney A4
31 Coco's Cantina B7
32 Countdown G3
33 Depot........D4
34 Ebisu........F2
35 Euro D1
36 Federal & Wolfe........D3
37 Food Alley D3
38 Grove D3
39 Ima........E3
40 L'Assiette........F3
O'Connell Street Bistro........(see 21)
41 Reslau D5
42 Satya E7
43 Soul Bar D2
44 Theatre E7

Drinking

45 Agents & Merchants/Racket........F3
46 Conservatory B1
47 Dida's Freemans Bay........B4
48 DOC........B7
49 Everybody's........E3
50 Family........E7
Hotel de Brett........(see 21)
51 Ice House........D2
52 Mo's........D3
53 Northern Steamship Co. E2
54 Occidental E3
55 Tyler Street Garage........F2
56 Urge........A8
57 Wine Cellar & Whammy Bar........C7

Entertainment

58 Academy Cinemas........D5
59 Aotea Centre........D5
60 Auckland Town Hall D6
61 Cassette Nine E3
62 Centurian........B7
63 Classic Comedy Club........D6
64 Event Cinemas........D5
65 Ink & Coherent........E7
66 Khuja Lounge........C7
67 Maidment Theatre........E5
68 NZ Film Archives E7
69 Q Theatre........D6
70 Rakinos E4
71 SkyCity Theatre........C4
72 Thirsty Dog........B7
Ticketek ....(see 75)
Ticketmaster........(see 75)
Ticketmaster........(see 59)

Shopping

73 Karen Walker........E4
74 Pauanesia........E4
75 Real Groovy........D6
76 Strangely Normal E4
77 Unity Books........E3
78 Whitcoulls........D4
79 Zambesi........E3

DON'T MISS

AUCKLAND VOLCANIC FIELD

Some cities think they're tough just by living in the shadow of a volcano. Auckland's built on 50 of them and, no, they're not all extinct. The last one to erupt was Rangitoto about 600 years ago and no one can predict when the next eruption will occur. Auckland's quite literally a hot spot – with a reservoir of magma 100km below, waiting to bubble to the surface. But relax: this has only happened 19 times in the last 20,000 years.

Some of Auckland's volcanoes are cones, some are filled with water and some have been completely quarried away. Moves are afoot to register the field as a World Heritage site and protect what remains. Most of the surviving cones show evidence of terracing from when they formed a formidable series of Maori *pa*. The most interesting to explore are Mt Eden (p67), One Tree Hill (p74) and Rangitoto, but Mt Wellington (Maungarei), Mt Albert (Owairaka), Mt Roskill (Puketapapa), Lake Pupuke, Mt Mangere and Mt Hobson (Remuwera) are all worth a visit.

the rose window by English artist Carl Edwards, which is particularly striking above the simple kauri altar.

Parnell Rose Gardens GARDENS
(Map p76; 85-87 Gladstone Rd; ⌚7am-7pm) These formal gardens are blooming excellent from November to March. A stroll through the park leads to peaceful **Judges Bay** and tiny **St Stephen's Chapel** (Judge St), built for the signing of the constitution of NZ's Anglican Church (1857).

Highwic HISTORIC BUILDING
(Map p72; www.historic.org.nz; 40 Gillies Ave; adult/child $9/free; ⌚10.30am-4.30pm Wed-Sun) A marvellous example of a Carpenter Gothic house (1862), sitting amid lush, landscaped grounds.

Kinder House HISTORIC BUILDING
(Map p76; www.kinder.org.nz; 2 Ayr St; entry by donation; ⌚noon-3pm Wed-Sun; 📶) Built of volcanic stone, this 1857 home displays the subtle but skilful watercolours and memorabilia of the Reverend Dr John Kinder (1819–1903), who was the headmaster of the Church of England Grammar School.

Ewelme Cottage HISTORIC BUILDING
(Map p76; www.historic.org.nz; 14 Ayr St; adult/child $8.50/free; ⌚10.30am-4.30pm Sun) Built in 1864 for a clergyman who clearly didn't throw wild parties, this storybook cottage has been left in exceptionally good condition.

TAMAKI DRIVE

This scenic, pohutukawa-lined road heads east from the city, hugging the waterfront. In summer it's a jogging/cycling/rollerblading blur.

A succession of child-friendly, peaceful swimming beaches starts at Ohaku Bay. Around the headland is Mission Bay, a popular beach with an iconic art-deco fountain, historic mission house, restaurants and bars. Safe swimming beaches Kohimarama and St Heliers follow. Further east along Cliff Rd, the Achilles Point lookout offers panoramic views. At its base is Ladies Bay, where nudists put up with mud and shells for the sake of relative seclusion.

Buses 745 to 769 from Britomart follow this route.

Kelly Tarlton's AQUARIUM
(Map p64; ☎09-531 5065; www.kellytarltons.co.nz; 23 Tamaki Dr; adult/child $34/17; ⌚9.30am-5.30pm) In the **Underwater World**, sharks and stingrays swim around and over you as you're shunted on a conveyor belt through transparent tunnels in what were once stormwater and sewage holding tanks. If you want to get even closer, you can enter the tanks in a shark cage ($79; 12.30pm, 1.30pm and 3pm), and if that doesn't sound terrifying enough, you can dive directly into the tanks ($129; 10am).

In a post-*Happy Feet* world, Kelly Tarlton's biggest attraction is the permanent winter wonderland known as **Antarctic Encounter**. It includes a walk through a replica of Robert Falcon Scott's 1911 Antarctic hut, and a ride aboard a heated snowcat through a frozen environment where a colony of king and Gentoo penguins lives. New owners with big plans took over the aquarium in March 2012, so there may be some new attractions in place by the time you visit.

Book online for a shorter wait (queues can be horrendous) and a 10% discount. There's

Newmarket

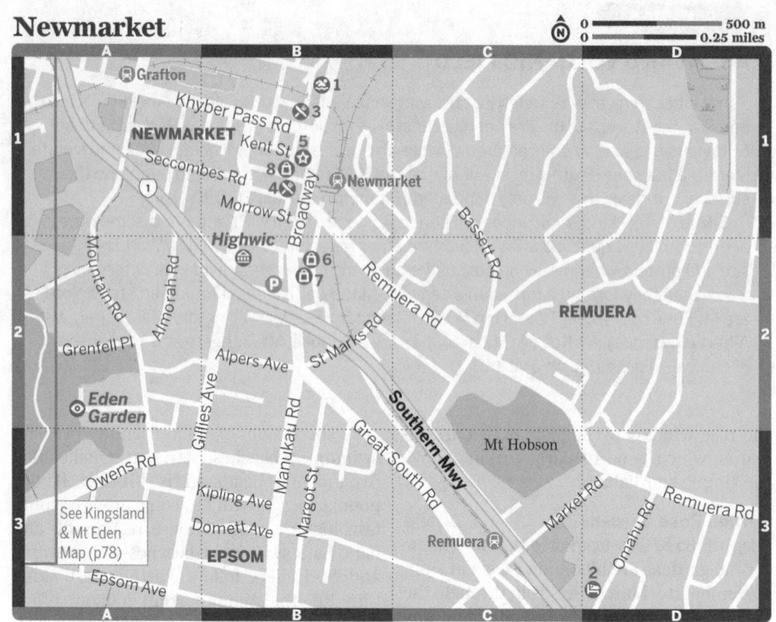

Newmarket

Top Sights
Eden Garden....A2
Highwic....B2

Activities, Courses & Tours
1 Olympic Pools & Fitness Centre....B1

Sleeping
2 Omahu Lodge....D3

Eating
3 Basque Kitchen Bar....B1
4 Teed St Larder....B1

Entertainment
5 Rialto....B1

Shopping
6 Karen Walker....B2
7 Texan Art Schools....B2
8 Zambesi....B1

a free shark-shaped shuttle bus that departs from 172 Quay St (opposite the ferry terminal) on the hour between 9am and 4pm.

Bastion Point PARK
(Map p64; Hapimana St) Politics, harbour views and lush lawns combine on this pretty headland with a chequered history. An elaborate cliff-top garden mausoleum honours Michael Joseph Savage (1872–1940), the country's first Labour prime minister, whose socialist reforms left him adored by the populace. Follow the lawn to a WWII gun embankment – one of many that line the harbour.

DEVONPORT

Nestling at the bottom of the North Shore, Devonport is a short ferry trip from the city. Quaint without being sickeningly twee, it retains a village atmosphere, with many well-preserved Victorian and Edwardian buildings and loads of cafes. If your interests are less genteel, there are two volcanic cones and easy access to the first of the North Shore's beaches.

For a self-guided tour of historic buildings, pick up the *Old Devonport Walk* pamphlet from the i-SITE. Bikes can be hired from the ferry terminal, making a pedal-powered exploration of the lower North Shore beaches an enticing possibility.

Ferries to Devonport (adult/child return $11/5.80, 12 minutes) depart from the Auckland Ferry Building every 30 minutes (hourly after 8pm) from 6.15am to 11.15pm Monday to Thursday (until 1am Friday and Saturday), and from 7.15am to 10pm on Sundays and public holidays. Some Waiheke Island and Rangitoto ferries also stop here.

Mt Victoria & North Head VOLCANO

Mt Victoria (Takarunga; Map p86; Victoria Rd) and **North Head** (Maungauika; Map p86; Takarunga Rd; ⌚6am-10pm) were Maori *pa* and they remain fortresses of sorts, with the navy maintaining a presence. Both have gun embankments and North Head is riddled with tunnels, dug at the end of the 19th century in response to the Russian threat, and extended during WWI and WWII. The gates are locked at night, but that's never stopped teenagers from jumping the fence and terrifying themselves on subterranean explorations. Between the two, **Cambria Reserve** stands on the remains of a third volcanic cone that was largely quarried away.

FREE **Navy Museum** MUSEUM

(Map p86; www.navymuseum.mil.nz; Torpedo Bay; ⌚10am-5pm) The navy has been in Devonport since the earliest days of the colony. Its history is on display at this well-presented and often moving museum, focussing on the stories of the sailors themselves.

WESTERN SPRINGS

Auckland Zoo ZOO

(Map p78; www.aucklandzoo.co.nz; Motions Rd; adult/child $21/11; ⌚9.30am-5pm, last entry 4.15pm) At this modern, spacious zoo, the big foreigners tend to steal the attention from the timid natives, but if you can wrestle the kids away from the tigers and orang-utans, there's a well-presented NZ section. Called *Te Wao Nui*, it's divided into six ecological zones: Coast (seals, penguins), Islands (mainly lizards, including NZ's pint-sized dinosaur, the tuatara), Wetlands (ducks, herons, eels), Night (kiwi, naturally, along with frogs, native owls and weta), Forest (birds) and High Country (cheekier birds and lizards).

Western Springs PARK

(Map p78; Great North Rd) Parents bring their children to this picturesque park to be traumatised by pushy, bread-fattened geese and to partake of the popular adventure playground. It's a great spot for a picnic and to get acquainted with playful pukeko (swamp hens). Formed by a confluence of lava flows, more than 4 million litres bubble up into the central lake daily. Until 1902 this was Auckland's main water supply.

From the city, catch any bus heading west via Great North Rd (adult/child $3.40/2). By car, take the Western Springs exit from the North Western Motorway.

MOTAT MUSEUM

(Museum of Transport & Technology; Map p78; www.motat.org.nz; 805 Great North Rd; adult/child $14/8; ⌚10am-5pm) This trainspotter's and technology boffin's paradise is spread over two sites and 19 hectares. In **MOTAT 1** look out for Helen Clark's Honda 50 motorbike and the cutesy pioneer village. **MOTAT 2** (Map p64) is an aircraft graveyard, featuring rare military and commercial planes. The two sites are linked by a vintage tram (free with admission, $1 otherwise), which passes the park and zoo. It's a fun kids' ride whether you visit MOTAT or not.

WHAT BECAME OF NGATI WHATUA?

By the end of the 1840s Maori were already a minority in the Auckland area, and eventually the Ngati Whatua o Orakei *hapu* (subtribe) was reduced to a small block of land in the vicinity of Okahu Bay and Bastion Point. In 1886 Bastion Point was confiscated by the government for military use, and then in 1908 more land was taken to build a sewage pipe that pumped raw effluent into the water in front of the *hapu*'s last remaining village at Okahu Bay. All but the cemetery was confiscated in 1951, with the people removed from their homes and the village destroyed to 'clean up' the area before the royal visit of Queen Elizabeth II.

When the government decided to sell the prime real estate on Bastion Point in 1977, the *hapu* staged a peaceful occupation that lasted for 507 days before they were once again taken into custody. It was a seminal moment in the Maori protest movement. During the next decade the government apologised and returned the land where the *marae* now stands. At the time of research, further negotiations between the government and *hapu* were progressing, with several of the volcanic cones likely to be part of the final settlement. The former railway land on which the Vector Arena now sits has already been returned.

DON'T MISS

NORTH SHORE BEACHES

A succession of fine swimming beaches stretches from North Head to Long Bay. The gulf islands provide a picturesque backdrop and shelter them from strong surf, making them safe for supervised children. Aim for high tide unless you fancy a lengthy walk to waist-deep water. **Cheltenham Beach** is a short walk from Devonport. **Takapuna Beach**, closest to the Harbour Bridge, is Auckland's answer to Bondi and the most built up. Nearby **St Leonards Beach**, popular with gay men, requires clambering over rocks at high tide.

OTHER SUBURBS

One Tree Hill PARK

(Maungakiekie; Map p64; www.cornwallpark.co.nz) This volcanic cone was the isthmus' key *pa* and the greatest fortress in the country. It's easy to see why: a drive or walk to the top (182m) offers 360-degree views. At the summit is the grave of John Logan Campbell, who when gifting the land to the city in 1901 requested that a memorial (the imposing obelisk and statue above the grave) be built to the Maori people. Nearby is the stump of the last 'one tree'.

Allow plenty of time to explore the craters and surrounding **Cornwall Park**, with its impressive mature trees and **Acacia Cottage** (1841), Auckland's oldest wooden building. The information centre (p97) has fascinating interactive displays illustrating what the *pa* would have looked like when 5000 people lived here.

Near the excellent **children's playground**, the **Stardome Observatory** (☎09-624 1246; www.stardome.org.nz; 670 Manukau Rd; exhibits free, shows adult/child $10/8; ⏲10am-3pm Mon, 9.30am-4.30pm & 6.30-9.30pm Tue-Fri) offers stargazing and planetarium shows that aren't dependent on Auckland's fickle weather (usually 8pm Wednesday to Saturday; phone ahead).

To get here from the city, take a train to Greenlane and walk 1km along Green Lane West. By car, take the Greenlane exit of the Southern Motorway and turn right into Green Lane West.

FREE **Wallace Arts Centre** GALLERY

(Map p64; www.tsbbankwallaceartscentre.org.nz; Pah Homestead, 72 Hillsborough Rd, Hillsborough; ⏲10am-3pm Tue-Fri, 10am-5pm Sat & Sun) Housed in a gorgeous 1879 mansion with views to One Tree Hill and the Manakau Harbour, the Wallace Arts Centre is lavishly endowed with contemporary NZ art from a private collection, generously offered for free public viewing. The collection is so extensive that the works are changed every four to six weeks. Even if you're not much of a culture vulture, it's worth the trip to explore the house, pick which room you'd have as your bedroom, have lunch on the veranda and wander among the magnificent trees in the park (collect a map from the homestead's reception). And the art is very accessible, ranging from a life-size skeletal rugby ruck to a vibrant Ziggy Stardust painted on glass.

Bus 299 (Lynfield) departs every 15 minutes from Wellesley St in the city (near the Civic Theatre) and heads to Hillsborough Rd ($4.50, about 40 minutes).

FREE **Auckland Botanic Gardens** GARDENS

(Map p64; www.aucklandbotanicgardens.co.nz; 102 Hill Rd, Manurewa; ⏲8am-6pm mid-Mar–mid-Oct, 8am-8pm mid-Oct–mid-Mar) This 64-hectare park has over 10,000 plants (including threatened species), dozens of themed gardens and an infestation of wedding parties. By car, take the Southern Motorway, exit at Manurewa and follow the signs. Otherwise take the train to Manurewa ($5.70, 40 minutes) and then walk along Hill Rd (1.5km).

Alberton HISTORIC BUILDING

(Map p64; www.historic.org.nz; 100 Mt Albert Rd; adult/child $9/free; ⏲10.30am-4.30pm Wed-Sun) A classic colonial mansion (1863), Alberton featured as a backdrop for some scenes in *The Piano*. It's a 1km walk from Mt Albert train station.

Spookers AMUSEMENT PARK

(☎09-291 9002; www.spookers.co.nz; 833 Kingseat Rd, Karaka; 1/2 attractions $20/35; ⏲8pm-late Fri & Sat) If walking around an old mental hospital in the dark wasn't scary enough, try it with freaks dripping blood and wielding chainsaws chasing you. Attractions include the *Haunted House*, the *Freaky Forest of Fear*, *Disturbia* and, perhaps freakiest of all, the summer-only *Cornevil* set in a real corn maze. It's rated R16, but there are some R8 daytime *Creepers* shows.

Take the Southern Motorway to the Papakura off-ramp (about 32km), turn left and drive 14km towards impending doom.

Rainbow's End AMUSEMENT PARK
(Map p64; www.rainbowsend.co.nz; 2 Clist Cres; superpass adult/child $49/39; ⌚10am-5pm) It's a bit lame by international standards but Rainbow's End has enough rides (including a corkscrew rollercoaster) to keep the kids happy all day, plus plenty of sugary snacks to fuel it all. Admission includes unlimited rides.

Activities

Hey, this is the 'City of Sails' and nothing gets you closer to the heart and soul of Auckland than sailing on the gulf. If you can't afford a yacht cruise, catch a ferry instead.

Visitors centres and public libraries stock the city council's *Auckland City's Walkways* pamphlet, which has a good selection of urban walks, including the Coast to Coast Walkway (p77).

Trading on the country's action-packed reputation, Auckland has sprouted its own set of insanely frightening activities. Look around for backpacker reductions or special offers before booking anything.

Sailing

Sail NZ SAILING
(Map p68; ☎0800 397 567; www.explorenz.co.nz; Viaduct Harbour) Shoot the breeze on a genuine America's Cup yacht (adult/child $160/115) or head out on a Whale & Dolphin Safari (adult/child $160/105); dolphins are spotted 90% of the time and whales 75%. The *Pride of Auckland* fleet of glamorous large yachts offers 90-minute Harbour Sailing Cruises (adult/child $75/55), 2½-hour Dinner Cruises ($120/85) and full-day Sailing Adventures ($165/125).

CharterLink SAILING
(Map p64; ☎09-445 7114; www.charterlink.co.nz; Bayswater Marina; per day $345-1125) Charters a fleet of well-maintained older yachts, luxury yachts and catamarans.

Gulfwind SAILING
(Map p64; ☎09-521 1564; www.gulfwind.co.nz; Westhaven Marina) Offers charters (half-/full day $395/795) and small-group sailing courses; a two-day Start Yachting course costs $595.

Penny Whiting Sailing School SAILING
(Map p64; ☎09-376 1322; www.pennywhiting.com; Westhaven Marina; course $700) Runs 15-hour learners' courses either as five afternoon lessons or over two weekends.

Extreme Sports

SkyWalk EXTREME SPORTS
(Map p68; ☎0800 759 925; www.skywalk.co.nz; Sky Tower, cnr Federal & Victoria Sts; adult/child $145/115; ⌚10am-4.30pm) The Sky Tower offers an ever-expanding selection of pant-wetting activities. If you thought the observation deck was for pussies, SkyWalk involves circling the 192m-high, 1.2m-wide outside halo of the tower without rails or a balcony – but with a safety harness (they're not completely crazy).

SkyJump EXTREME SPORTS
(Map p68; ☎0800 759 586; www.skyjump.co.nz; Sky Tower, cnr Federal & Victoria Sts; adult/child $225/175; ⌚10am-5pm) This 11-second, 85km/h base wire leap from the observation deck of the Sky Tower is more like a parachute jump than a bungy and it's a rush and a half. Combine it with the SkyWalk in the Look 'n' Leap package ($290).

Auckland Bridge Climb & Bungy BUNGY
(Map p64; ☎09-360 7748; www.bungy.co.nz; Curran St, Herne Bay; climb adult/child $120/80, bungy $150/120) Bungy originators, AJ Hackett, offer the chance to climb up or jump off the Auckland Harbour Bridge.

ONE TREE TO RULE THEM ALL

Looking at One Tree Hill, your first thought will probably be 'Where's the bloody tree?'. Good question. Up until 2000 a Monterey pine stood at the top of the hill. This was a replacement for a sacred totara that was chopped down by British settlers in 1852. Maori activists first attacked the foreign usurper in 1994, finishing the job in 2000. It's unlikely that another tree will be planted until local land claims have moved closer to resolution, but you can bet your boots that this time around it'll be a native.

Auckland's most beloved landmark achieved international recognition in 1987 when U2 released the song 'One Tree Hill' on their acclaimed *The Joshua Tree* album. It was only released as a single in NZ, where it went to number one.

Parnell

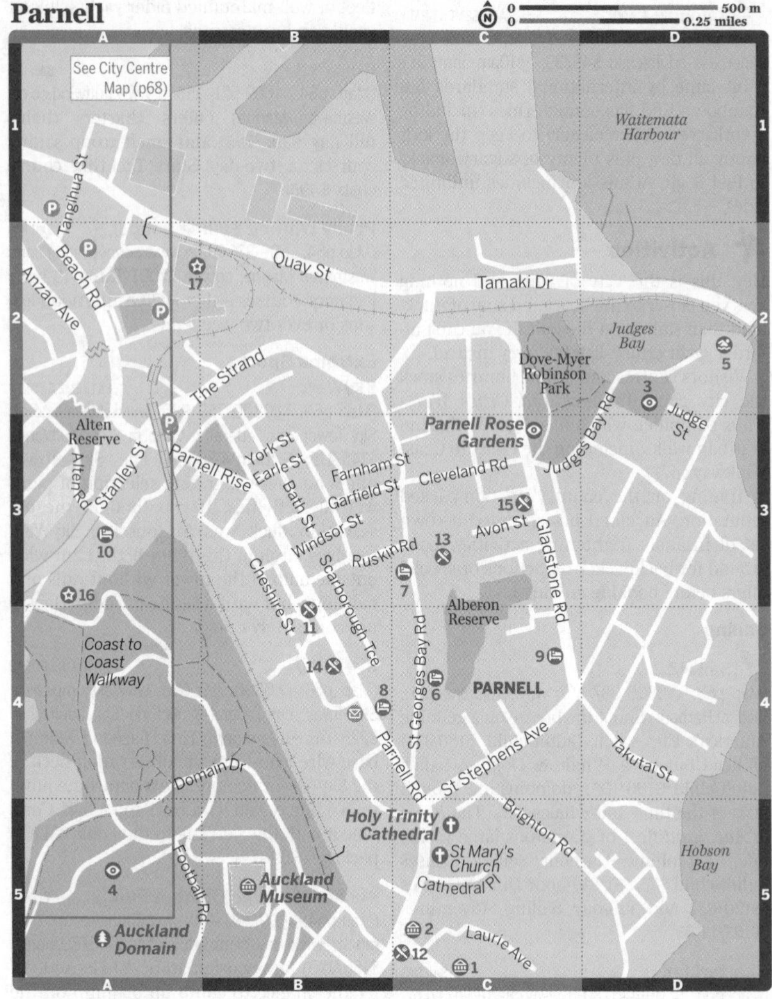

NZ Skydive SKYDIVING

(☎0800 865 867; www.nzskydive.co.nz; 9000/12,000ft $245/295) Offers tandem skydives from Mercer airfield, 55km south of Auckland; capture your excitement/terror on DVD for $165.

Sky Screamer BUNGY

(Map p68; ☎09-377 1328; www.skyscreamer.co.nz; cnr Albert & Victoria Sts; ride $40; ⏰9am-10pm Sun-Thu, 10am-2am Fri & Sat) Imagine a giant slingshot with yourself as the projectile. Rest assured, once you're strapped in and reverse-bungyed 60m up in the air, the whole city will hear you scream.

Diving

Dive Centre DIVING

(Map p64; ☎09-444 7698; www.divecentre.co.nz; 97 Wairau Rd, Takapuna; PADI Open Water $599) Runs PADI courses and books diving charters.

Kayaking

Fergs Kayaks KAYAKING

(Map p64; ☎09-529 2230; www.fergskayaks.co.nz; 12 Tamaki Dr, Okahu Bay; ⏰10am-5pm) Hires out kayaks and paddleboards (per hour/day from $15/50), bikes ($20/120) and inline skates $15/30). Day and night guided kayak trips are available to Devonport (three

Parnell

Top Sights
Auckland Domain ... A5
Auckland Museum ... B5
Holy Trinity Cathedral ... C5
Parnell Rose Gardens ... C3

Sights
1 Ewelme Cottage ... C5
2 Kinder House ... C5
3 St Stephen's Chapel ... D2
4 Wintergarden ... A5

Activities, Courses & Tours
5 Parnell Baths ... D2

Sleeping
6 City Garden Lodge ... C4
7 Lantana Lodge ... C3
8 Parnell Inn ... B4
9 Quality Hotel Barrycourt ... C4
10 Quest Carlaw Park ... A3

Eating
11 Burgerfuel ... B4
12 Domain & Ayr ... C5
13 La Cigale ... C3
14 Non Solo Pizza ... B4
15 Rosehip Cafe ... C3

Entertainment
16 ASB Tennis Centre ... A3
Ticketmaster ... (see 17)
17 Vector Arena ... A2

hours, 8km, $95) or Rangitoto Island (six hours, 13km, $120).

Auckland Sea Kayaks KAYAKING
(☎0800 999 089; www.aucklandseakayaks.co.nz) Takes guided trips (including lunch) to Rangitoto ($225, 10 hours) and Browns Island/Motukorea ($175, six hours). Multiday excursions also available.

Other Water Activities

Auckland Jet Boat Tours JETBOATING
(Map p68; ☎0508 255 382; www.aucklandjetboattours.co.nz; Princes Wharf; adult/child incl museum $65/45) Take a 40-minute blast around the harbour and then peruse the Maritime Museum at a more leisurely pace.

New Zealand Surf'n'Snow Tours SURFING
(☎09-828 0426; www.newzealandsurftours.com; 5-/12-day tour $799/1699) Runs day-long surfing courses that include transport, gear and two two-hour lessons ($120). Day tours usually head to Piha (with/without own gear $50/99; year-round), while five- and twelve-day tours include accommodation in Ahipara (October to May only).

Parnell Baths SWIMMING
(Map p76; www.parnellbaths.co.nz; Judges Bay Rd; adult/child $6.30/4.20; ⏲6am-8pm Mon-Fri, 8am-8pm Sat & Sun Nov-Apr) Outdoor saltwater pools with an awesome 1950s mural.

Olympic Pools & Fitness Centre SWIMMING
(Map p72; www.theolympic.co.nz; 77 Broadway; adult/child $7.50/5; ⏲5.30am-9.30pm Mon-Fri, 7am-8pm Sat & Sun) Pools, gym, sauna, steam room and crèche.

Ballooning

Balloon Expeditions BALLOONING
(☎09-416 8590; www.balloonexpeditions.co.nz; flight $340) Offers hour-long flights in a hot-air balloon at sunrise, including breakfast and a bottle of bubbles.

Balloon Safaris BALLOONING
(☎09-415 8289; www.balloonsafaris.co.nz; flight $345) Allow four hours for these early morning flights (including one hour in the air), which include snacks and sparkling wine.

Tramping

Coast to Coast Walkway WALKING
(Map p64; www.aucklandcity.govt.nz) Heading clear across the country from the Tasman to the Pacific (actually, that's only 16km), this walk encompasses One Tree Hill, Mt Eden, the Domain and the University, keeping as much as possible to reserves rather than city streets. You can do it in either direction: starting from the Viaduct Basin and heading south, it's marked by yellow markers and milestones; heading north from Onehunga there are blue markers. We recommend catching the train to Onehunga, the least

AUCKLAND FOR CHILDREN

All of the east coast beaches (St Heliers, Kohimarama, Mission Bay, Okahu Bay, Cheltenham, Narrow Neck, Takapuna, Milford, Long Bay) are safe for supervised kids, while sights such as Rainbow's End, Kelly Tarlton's, Auckland Museum and Auckland Zoo are all firm favourites. Parnell Baths has a children's pool, but on wintry days, head to the thermal pools at Parakai or Waiwera.

Kingsland & Mt Eden

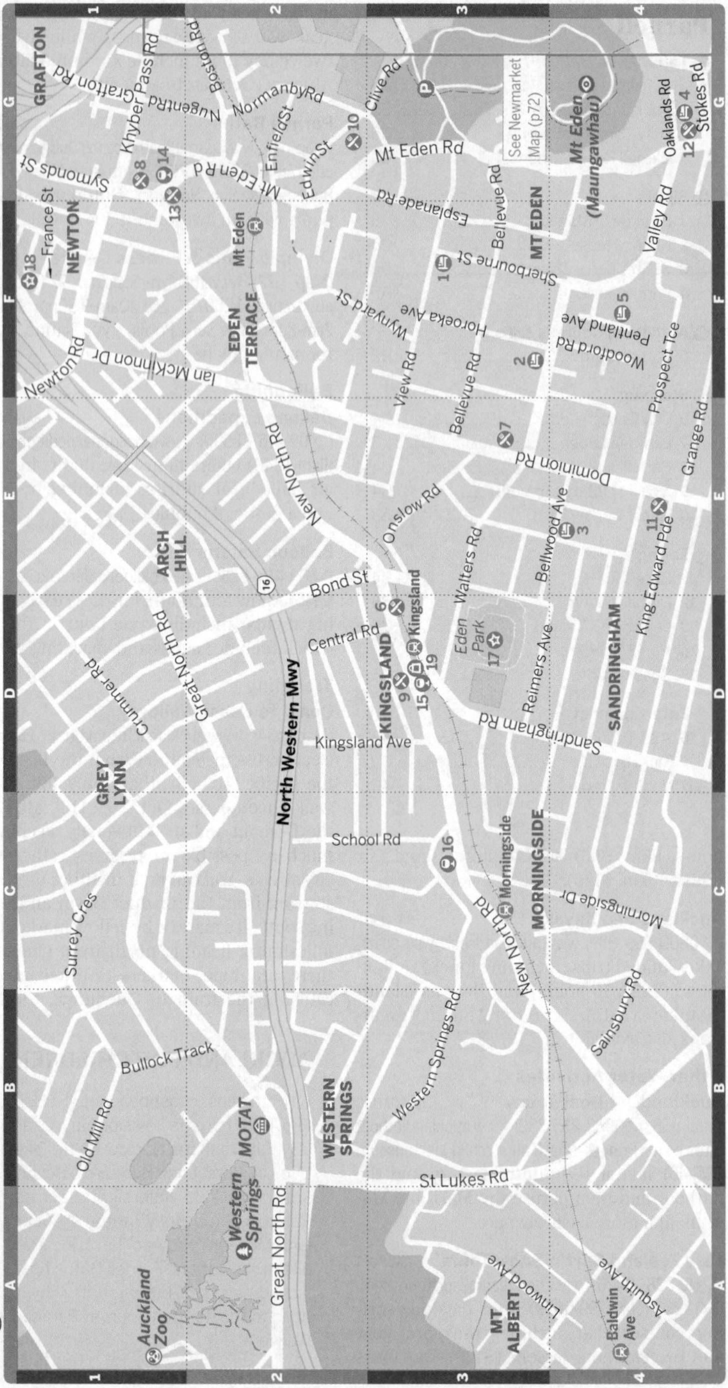

Kingsland & Mt Eden

Top Sights

Auckland Zoo ... A1
MOTAT ... B2
Mt Eden (Maungawhau) ... G4
Western Springs ... A2

Sleeping

1 Bamber House ... F3
2 Bavaria ... F3
3 Eden Park B&B ... E4
4 Oaklands Lodge ... G4
5 Pentlands ... F4

Eating

6 Atomic Roastery ... D3
7 Burgerfuel ... E3
8 French Cafe ... G1
9 Fridge ... D3
10 Gala ... G2
11 Merediths ... E4
12 Molten ... G4
13 O'Sarracino ... G1
Shaky Isles ... (see 19)

Drinking

14 Galbraith's Alehouse ... G1
15 Neighbourhood ... D3
16 Winehot ... C3

Entertainment

17 Eden Park ... D3
18 Kings Arms Tavern ... F1

Shopping

19 Royal Jewellery Studio ... D3

impressive trailhead, and finishing up at one of the Viaduct's bars. From Onehunga Station, take Onehunga Mall up to Princes St, turn left and pick up the track at the inauspicious park by the motorway.

Tours

Cultural Tours

TIME Unlimited CULTURAL TOUR
(09-446 6677; www.newzealandtours.travel) To Integrate Maori Experiences (TIME) is the motto. A hefty set of cultural, fishing, kayaking, trekking and sightseeing tours are outlined on their website, including excellent kayak-fishing excursions (full day $295)

Toru Tours CULTURAL TOUR
(027 457 0011; www.torutours.com; with/without performance $213/178) Maori cultural tours stopping in at a *marae*, Auckland Museum (with an optional cultural show), the native critter section of the zoo, Mt Eden, One Tree Hill and Bastion Point. Three-hour Express Tours ($69) are also available.

Tamaki Hikoi CULTURAL TOUR
(0800 282 552; www.tamakihikoi.co.nz; 1/3 hr $40/95) Ngati Whatua guides lead these Maori cultural tours, including an hour's walk around the Domain; a three-hour tour including a walk and a cultural performance; and a three-hour walking tour from Mt Eden (Maungawhau) to the Domain (transfers from the city included).

Wineries

NZ Winepro WINE TASTING
(09-575 1958; www.nzwinepro.co.nz; tours $119-325) Offers a range of highly rated tours to all of Auckland's wine regions, combining tastings with sightseeing.

Wine Trail Tours WINE TASTING
(09-630 1540; www.winetrailtours.co.nz) Small-group tours around West Auckland wineries and the Waitakere Ranges (half-/full day $115/245); further afield to Matakana ($255); or a combo of the two ($255).

Fine Wine Tours WINE TASTING
(0800 023 111; www.insidertouring.co.nz) Tours of Kumeu, Matakana and Waiheke wineries including four-hour Kumeu tour ($169), with cheese ($189); six-hour tour including Muriwai Beach ($245); food-and-wine tour with stops at city providores ($245).

Walking

Waitakere Tours TRAMPING
(0800 492 482; www.waitakeretours.co.nz; per day $150) Lifelong Westies (West Aucklanders) offering guided tours of the west coast beaches, as well as guided walks in the Waitakeres.

Bush & Beach TRAMPING, WINE TASTING
(09-837 4130; www.bushandbeach.co.nz) Guided walks in the Waitakere Ranges and along west coast beaches (half-/full day $140/225, including transfers); half-day city minibus

tours ($140); and food, wine and art tours in either Matakana or Kumeu (half-/full day $179/295).

Auckland Ghost Tours WALKING TOUR
(☎09-630 5721; www.aucklandghosttours.com; adult/child $50/25) Stories of Auckland's scary side – and we don't just mean the architecture – shared on a two-hour walking tour of the central city.

Hiking NZ TRAMPING
(☎0800 697 232; www.hikingnewzealand.com) Runs 'hiking safaris' leaving from Auckland, including Far North ($995, six days); and Volcanoes & Rainforest ($1880, 10 days).

Bus Tours

Explorer Bus BUS TOUR
(☎0800 439 756; www.explorerbus.co.nz; adult/child $40/20) This hop-on, hop-off service departs from the Ferry Building every hour from 10am to 3pm (more frequently in summer), heading to 14 tourist sites around the central city.

Gray Line BUS TOUR
(☎0800 698 687; www.graylinetours.co.nz; tour $74; ⏲9.15am) Three-hour bus tour taking in the Harbour Bridge, Wynyard Quarter, Queen St, university, museum, Domain and Tamaki Dr.

GreatSights BUS TOUR
(Map p68; ☎0800 744 487; www.greatsights.co.nz; adult/child $74/37; ⏲8.45am) Three-hour bus tours, including the Harbour Bridge, Viaduct, Queen St, Domain, Parnell and Tamaki Dr.

Cruises

Riverhead Ferry CRUISE
(☎09-376 0819; www.riverheadferry.co.nz; adult/child $38/20) Offers harbour and gulf cruises including a 90-minute jaunt up the inner harbour to Riverhead (p117), returning after two hours' pub time.

Fullers CRUISE
(Map p68; ☎09-367 9111; www.fullers.co.nz; Ferry Building, 99 Quay St; adult/child $38/19; ⏲10.30am & 1.30pm) As well as ferry services, Fullers has daily 1½-hour harbour cruises which include a stop on Rangitoto, a complimentary cuppa and a free return ticket to Devonport.

360 Discovery CRUISE
(Map p68; ☎0800 360 3472; www.360discovery.co.nz; Pier 4, 139 Quay St; cruise adult/child $27/17, 3-day pass $35/21; ⏲10am, noon & 2.30pm) Apart from their regular ferries, 360 has an Auckland Harbour cruise that stops at Devonport's Torpedo Bay, Rangitoto, Motuihe and Orakei Wharf (for Kelly Tarlton's). You can either stay onboard for the full 1½ hours or hop on and off as many times as you like over the course of three days.

Other Tours

Paradise Motorcycle Tours MOTORCYCLE TOUR
(☎09-473 9404; www.paradisemotorcycletours.co.nz) See the sights on a guided motorcycle tour or hire a bike for a self-guided trip. Tours range from a two-hour pillion ride around the city ($199) to a 21-day guided ride on a 1200cc BMW bike ($19,904).

Red Carpet Tours MOVIE LOCATIONS
(☎09-410 6561; www.redcarpet-tours.com) This brave fellowship will run a gauntlet of orcs to get you safely there (to Hobbiton/Matamata) and back again in one day ($245), or show you all of Middle Earth over 12 days ($6320).

Festivals & Events

Check www.aucklandnz.com for full details of what's on in the city.

Auckland Anniversary Day Regatta SPORTS
(www.regatta.org.nz) The 'City of Sails' lives up to its name; Monday of last weekend in January.

MAORI NZ: AUCKLAND

Evidence of Maori occupation is literally carved into Auckland's volcanic cones. The dominant *iwi* (tribe) of the isthmus was Ngati Whatua, but these days there are Maori from almost all of NZ's *iwi* living here.

For an initial taste of Maori culture, start at Auckland Museum (p67), where there's a wonderful Maori collection and a culture show. For a more personalised experience, take a tour with TIME Unlimited (p79), Toru Tours (p79) or Ngati Whatua's Tamaki Hikoi (p79), or visit the *marae* and recreated village at Te Hana (p122).

LOCAL KNOWLEDGE

URBAN PASIFIKA *SHIMPAL LELISI*

To try Pacific Island food in Auckland, head to the markets at Otara, Avondale or Mangere, or to a festival day put on by the community – Pasifika (p81) and Polyfest (p81) are always good. Polyfest is in March, and it's the biggest PI cultural festival in the world. It's been going on since the early '70s and it's enormous, with thousands of people coming through. I was in the Niuean group when I was at school, and it was when I first got the buzz for performing. It's amazing now watching the calibre of the performances.

The students take it really seriously, and there are new moves every year - it's like *Strictly Ballroom*! At its core Polyfest is still about teaching the young people all of the old songs, but it's really exciting to see change.'

Shimpal Lelisi, actor (bro'Town, Sione's Wedding)

Laneway Festival MUSIC
(www.lanewayfestival.com.au) Presents the latest batch of international indie wunderkinds to an adoring crowd in a one-day festival on Anniversary Day.

Music In Parks MUSIC
(www.musicinparks.co.nz) A series of free gigs in parks around the city; runs from January until March.

Movies In Parks FILM
(www.moviesinparks.co.nz) Just like it sounds: free movies in parks in February and March.

Lantern Festival CULTURAL
(www.asianz.org.nz) Three days of Asian food and culture in Albert Park to welcome the lunar New Year (usually held in early February).

Devonport Food & Wine Festival FOOD & WINE
(www.devonportwinefestival.co.nz; admission $30) Sip and sup with the smart set at this two-day festival in mid-February.

Big Gay Out GAY & LESBIAN
(www.biggayout.co.nz) The big event on the gay and lesbian calendar; 12,000 people descend on Coyle Park, Pt Chevalier on a Sunday afternoon in mid-February.

Splore MUSIC
(www.splore.net; Tapapakanga Regional Park) Three days of camping and music (generally of the dancy and soulful variety), held by the beach in mid-February. The headliners always include big-name international acts.

Auckland Cup Week SPORTS
(www.ellerslie.co.nz; Ellerslie Racecourse) Back a winner at the biggest horse race of the year; early March.

Auckland Arts Festival ARTS
(www.aucklandfestival.co.nz) Held over three weeks in March in odd-numbered years, this is Auckland's biggest celebration of the arts.

Pasifika Festival CULTURAL
(www.aucklandcouncil.govt.nz) Western Springs Park hosts this giant Polynesian party with cultural performances, food and craft stalls; held early to mid-March.

Polyfest CULTURAL
(www.asbpolyfest.co.nz; Sports Bowl, Manukau) Massive Auckland secondary schools' Maori and Pacific Islands cultural festival.

Royal Easter Show AGRICULTURAL
(www.royaleastershow.co.nz; ASB Showgrounds, 217 Green Lane West) It's supposedly agricultural but people descend in their droves for the funfair rides.

NZ International Comedy Festival COMEDY
(www.comedyfestival.co.nz) Three-week laughfest with local and international comedians; held late April to early May.

Out Takes FILM, GAY & LESBIAN
(www.outtakes.org.nz; Rialto Cinemas) Gay and lesbian film festival, running from late May to early June.

NZ International Film Festival FILM
(www.nzff.co.nz) Auckland goes crazy for art-house films from mid-July.

Auckland Art Fair ARTS
(www.artfair.co.nz; Viaduct Events Centre) Art for sale (lots of it), in August in odd-numbered years.

Ponsonby & Grey Lynn

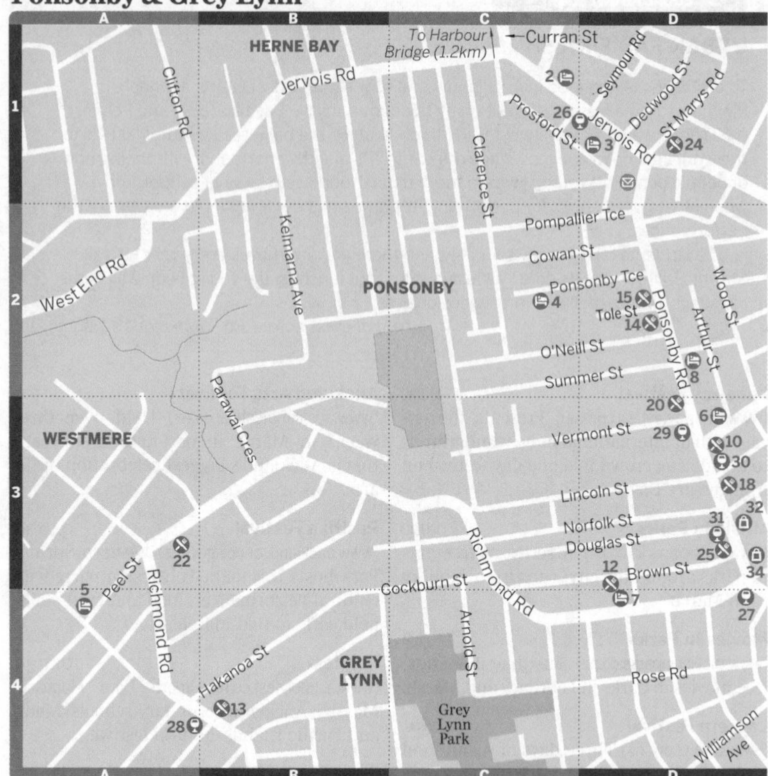

NZ Fashion Week FASHION
(www.nzfashionweek.com) Is any country better qualified to show what you can do with merino wool and a sense of imagination? Held in early September.

Auckland International Boat Show SPORTS
(www.auckland-boatshow.com) It doesn't command the instant nautical recognition of Sydney or San Diego, but Auckland really is one of the world's great sailing cities. And here's proof; held in September.

Heritage Festival CULTURAL
(www.aucklandcouncil.govt.nz) Two weeks of fabulous (mainly free) tours of Auckland's neighbourhoods and historic buildings; mid-September.

Diwali Festival of Lights CULTURAL
(www.asianz.org.nz) Auckland's Indian community lights up the city with an explosion of colour, music and dance; held in mid-October.

Grey Lynn Park Festival CULTURAL
(www.greylynnparkfestival.org) Join Grey Lynn's students, Pacific Islanders, lesbians, urban bohemians, hipsters and hippies in the park on the third Saturday in November for a free festival of craft and food stalls, and live music.

Santa Parade PARADE
(www.santaparade.co.nz) Santa gets an early start proceeding with his minions along Queen St before partying in Aotea Sq on the last Sunday of November.

Christmas in the Park FAMILY
(www.christmasinthepark.co.nz) A party so big it has to be held in the Auckland Domain.

Sleeping

CITY CENTRE

Auckland has plenty of luxury hotels, with many of the international chains taking up

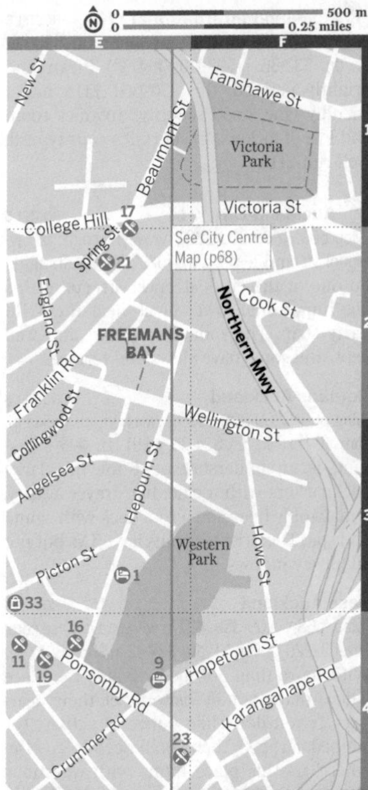

inner-city real estate. At the other extreme, any backpackers who leave with a bad impression of Auckland have invariably stayed in crummy, noisy digs in the city centre. Not all of the cheap city accommodation is bad but you'll generally find better in the inner suburbs.

TOP CHOICE Hotel de Brett BOUTIQUE HOTEL **$$$**
(Map p68; ☎09-925 9000; www.hoteldebrett.com; 2 High St; r $300-600; @☏) Supremely hip, this lavishly refurbished historic hotel has been zooshed up with stripy carpets and clever designer touches in every nook of the extremely comfortable rooms. Prices include breakfast, free broadband and a pre-dinner drink.

Waldorf Celestion APARTMENT **$$**
(Map p68; ☎09-280 2200; www.celestion-waldorf.co.nz; 19-23 Anzac Ave; apt $137-239) A rash of Waldorfs have opened in recent years, all presenting a similar set of symptoms: affordable, modern, inner-city apartments in city fringe locations. We prefer the Waldorf Celestioin for its stylish red, black and grey colour palate, and the sumptuous velvet curtains in reception.

Ponsonby & Grey Lynn

Sleeping

1	23 Hepburn	E3
2	Abaco on Jervois	C1
3	Brown Kiwi	D1
4	Great Ponsonby Arthotel	C2
5	Henry's	A4
6	Ponsonby Backpackers	D3
7	Red Monkey	D4
8	Uenuku Lodge	D2
9	Verandahs	E4

Eating

10	Agnes Curran	D3
11	Burgerfuel	E4
12	Cocoro	D3
13	Delicious	B4
14	Dizengoff	D2
15	Landreth & Co	D2
16	MooChowChow	E4
17	New World	E1
18	Ponsonby Road Bistro	D3
19	Ponsonby Village International Food Court	E4
20	Prego	D3
21	Queenie's Lunchroom	E2
22	Richmond Rd Cafe	A3
23	Satya	E4
24	Soto	D1
25	SPQR	D3

Drinking

26	Dida's Wine Lounge & Tapas Bar	D1
27	Golden Dawn	D4
28	Gypsy Tea Room	A4
29	Lolabar	D3
30	Mea Culpa	D3
31	Ponsonby Social Club	D3

Shopping

	Karen Walker	(see 30)
32	Marvel	D3
33	Texan Art Schools	E3
34	Women's Bookshop	D3
	Zambesi	(see 18)

Elliott Hotel APARTMENT $$
(Map p68; ☎09-308 9334; www.theelliotthotel.com; cnr Elliott & Wellesley Sts; apt $139-219; P) Housed in a grand historic building (1880s), this apartment-style hotel is much plusher than the price implies. Rooms may not be huge but the high ceilings let your spirits rise.

Quadrant HOTEL $$
(Map p68; ☎09-984 6000; www.thequadrant.com; 10 Waterloo Quadrant; apt $165-600;) Slick, central and full of all the whiz-bang gadgets, this apartment-style complex is an excellent option. The only catch is that the units are tiny and the bathrooms beyond small.

Waldorf Stadium APARTMENT
(Map p68; ☎09-337 5300; www.stadium-apartments-hotel.co.nz; 40 Beach Rd; apt $162-357) Another of the Waldorf chain, this large newish block has spacious (if generic) family-friendly apartments with double-glazing to keep out the road noise.

CityLife HOTEL $$
(Map p68; ☎09-379 9222; www.heritagehotels.co.nz/citylife-auckland; Durham St; apt $169-850; P@) A worthy tower-block hotel offering numerous apartments over dozens of floors, ranging from studios to three-bedroom suites. Facilities include a heated lap pool, gym, valet parking and a babysitting service.

Jucy Hotel HOTEL $
(Map p68; ☎09-379 6633; www.jucyhotel.com; 62 Emily Pl; hostel s/d $49/69, hotel r $99; P@) The Jucy car-rental company has taken over this long-standing hostel, repainted everything in their trademark lurid green and purple, and converted it into a zippy budget hotel. Rooms in the main section have en suites, and there's a hostel wing for those who don't mind bunks and shared bathrooms.

City Lodge HOTEL $
(Map p68; ☎09-379 6183; www.citylodge.co.nz; 150 Vincent St; s $75, d $99-115; @) City Lodge is a YMCA-run, purpose-built tower for the budget market. The tiny rooms and stamp-sized bathrooms may be plain, but they make a clean and secure resting place. There's a fantastic industrial-style kitchen and a comfy lounge.

Auckland International YHA HOSTEL $
(Map p68; ☎09-302 8200; www.yha.co.nz; 5 Turner St; dm $32-36, r $98-110; P@) Clean and brightly painted, this 170-bed YHA has a friendly vibe, good security, a games room and lots of lockers. In short, it's your typical, well-run YHA.

Auckland City YHA HOSTEL $
(Map p68; ☎09-309 2802; www.yha.co.nz; 18 Liverpool St; dm $29-49, s/d $76/92; @) Struggle up one of the city's steepest streets to this big, impersonal tower block near the K Rd party strip. The rooms are clean and well kept, and some have views and terraces.

Nomads Auckland HOSTEL $
(Map p68; ☎09-300 9999; www.nomadsauckland.com; 16 Fort St; dm $24-36, r $91-111; @) Bustling is an understatement for this large backpackers with a cafe, bar, travel agency, female-only floor and a roof deck with sauna and spa. The private rooms have TVs but not all have windows.

Base Auckland HOSTEL $
(Map p68; ☎09-358 4877; www.stayatbase.com; Level 3, 229 Queen St; dm $27-32, r $65-93; @) With more than 500 beds, this is the place where many young visitors get their bearings. If you don't like a hive of activity (or stained carpets), then you'll need to go elsewhere, as this place hums with questions about who's got work where, whether bungy jumping's worth it and where the cute guys/girls are. There's a bar to aid this last quest.

FREEMAN'S BAY

Verandahs HOSTEL $
(Map p82; ☎09-360 4180; www.verandahs.co.nz; 6 Hopetoun St; dm $27-31, s $55, d $72-88, tr $92; P@) Ponsonby Rd, K Rd and the city are an easy walk from this grand hostel, housed in two neighbouring villas overlooking the mature trees of Western Park. It's easily Auckland's best backpackers.

23 Hepburn B&B $$$
(Map p82; ☎09-376 0622; www.23hepburn.co.nz; 23 Hepburn St; r $210-250; P) The three boutique rooms are a symphony in muted whites and creams, inducing the pleasant sensation of waking up inside an extremely chic pavlova. Continental breakfast is left in your fridge the previous evening to enjoy at your leisure.

PONSONBY & GREY LYNN

Henry's B&B $$$
(Map p82; ☎09-360 2700; www.henrysonpeel.co.nz; 33 Peel St; r/apt $220/275; @☜☘) These beautiful wooden villas are what Auckland's inner suburbs are all about. Henry's has been stylishly renovated, adding en suites to the downstairs rooms and a self-contained harbour-view apartment above.

Great Ponsonby Arthotel B&B $$$
(Map p82; ☎09-376 5989; www.greatpons.co.nz; 30 Ponsonby Tce; r $245-400; P@) This deceptively spacious Victorian villa has gregarious hosts, impressive sustainability practices, great breakfasts and it's located a stone's throw from Ponsonby Rd in a quiet cul-de-sac. Studio apartments open onto an attractive rear courtyard.

Abaco on Jervois MOTEL $$
(Map p82; ☎09-360 6850; www.abaco.co.nz; 57 Jervois Rd; r $125-165, ste $184-205; P) A neutral-toned motel, with a contemporary fit-out, including slick stainless-steel kitchenettes (with dish drawers and proper ovens) and fluffy white towels for use in the spa. The darker rooms downstairs are priced accordingly.

Red Monkey GUESTHOUSE $
(Map p82; ☎09-360 7977; www.theredmonkey.co.nz; 49 Richmond Rd; weekly s $240-280, d $360-480; @) If you're planning to stay for a week or longer, make one of these two renovated villas your home away from home. There are lamps, bedside tables and built-in wardrobes in all the smartly decorated rooms, most of which share bathrooms. Book well ahead.

Brown Kiwi HOSTEL $
(Map p82; ☎09-378 0191; www.brownkiwi.co.nz; 7 Prosford St; dm $27-30, r $72; @☜) As unassuming as its namesake, this gay-friendly hostel is tucked away in a busy-by-day commercial strip, a stone's throw from all the good shopping and grazing opportunities. The garden courtyard is made for mooching.

Uenuku Lodge HOSTEL $
(Map p82; ☎09-378 8990; www.uenukulodge.co.nz; 217 Ponsonby Rd; dm $26-33, s $48, d $62-80; P@☜) It could do with a freshen up, but this hostel is well located and some of the rooms afford city views. There's a decent lounge, a large kitchen, good security and a courtyard.

Ponsonby Backpackers HOSTEL $
(Map p82; ☎09-360 1311; www.ponsonby-backpackers.co.nz; 2 Franklin Rd; dm $26-28, s/d $45/62; P@☜) The interiors don't live up to the imposing exterior of this turreted wooden villa, commanding a corner site on tree-lined Franklin Rd. Yet it's kept reasonably clean and is superbly located.

NEWTON

Langham HOTEL $$$
(Map p68; ☎09-379 5132; www.auckland.langhamhotels.co.nz; 83 Symonds St; r $220-390, ste $510-2430; P@☜☘) The glamour of the giant chandelier in reception dissipates somewhat once you reach the low-ceilinged guest floors. Still, the Langham's service is typically faultless, the beds are heavenly, and its day spa is reputedly the best in Auckland.

BK Hostel HOSTEL $
(Map p68; ☎09-307 0052; www.bkhostel.co.nz; 3 Mercury Lane; s $45-49, d $58-66; @☜☘) Prices are cheaper for windowless rooms, but if you're planning to be partying in the neighbourhood's all-night clubs, that might be an advantage. The hostel is housed in a 1910 building with high ceilings and good security.

MT EDEN

Eden Park B&B B&B $$$
(Map p78; ☎09-630 5721; www.bedandbreakfastnz.com; 20 Bellwood Ave; s $135-150, d $235-250; ☜) If you know any rugby fans who require chandeliers in their bathrooms, send them here. The hallowed turf of Auckland's legendary rugby ground is only a block away and while the rooms aren't overly large for the prices, they mirror the Edwardian elegance of this fine wooden villa.

Bamber House HOSTEL $
(Map p78; ☎09-623 4267; www.hostelbackpacker.com; 22 View Rd; dm $28-30, d $70-90; P@☜) The original house here is a mansion of sorts, with some nicely maintained period trimmings and large grounds. The new prefab cabins have less character but come with en suites.

Pentlands HOSTEL $
(Map p78; ☎09-638 7031; www.pentlands.co.nz; 22 Pentland Ave; dm $25-28, s/d $46/68; P@☜) Set down a peaceful tree-lined cul-de-sac, this powder-blue villa offers recently renovated rooms, a sunny deck with a BBQ, and quiet tables on the lawn. It's an altogether chilled-out environment.

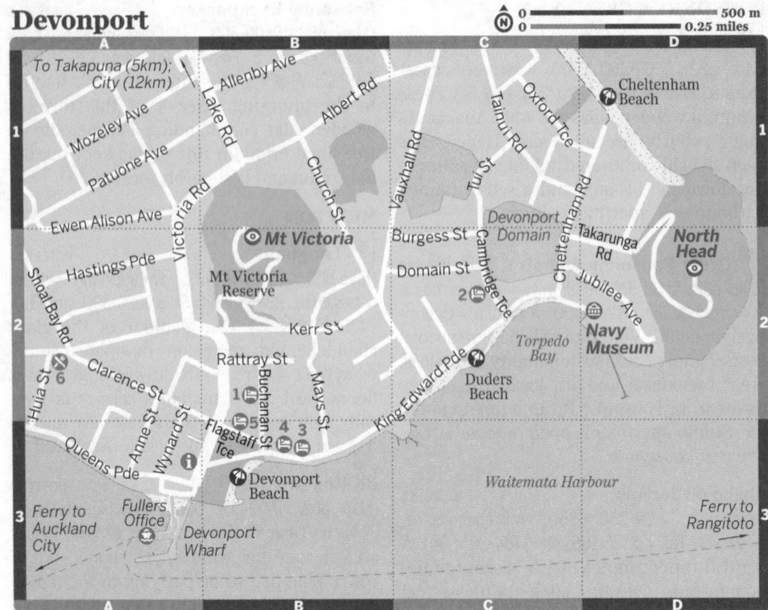

Devonport

Top Sights

Mt Victoria B2
Navy Museum D2
North Head D2

Sleeping

1 Devonport Motel B2
2 Devonport Sea Cottage C2
3 Hampton Beach House B3
4 Parituhu B3
5 Peace & Plenty Inn B3

Eating

6 Calliope Road Cafe A2

Oaklands Lodge HOSTEL $
(Map p78; ☎09-638 6545; www.oaklands.co.nz; 5a Oaklands Rd; dm $25-27, s $48, d $64-74; @ wi-fi) At the foot of the mountain in a leafy cul-de-sac, this bright, well-kept hostel is close to Mt Eden village and city buses. The communal facilities are in good nick.

Bavaria GUESTHOUSE $$
(Map p78; ☎09-638 9641; www.bavariabandbhotel.co.nz; 83 Valley Rd; s $95-110, d $145-175; P @ wi-fi) Sitting somewhere between a B&B and a small hotel, this spacious villa offers large, airy rooms and a buffet breakfast. The communal TV lounge, dining room and deck all encourage mixing and mingling.

PARNELL & NEWMARKET

City Garden Lodge HOSTEL $
(Map p76; ☎09-302 0880; www.citygardenlodge.co.nz; 25 St Georges Bay Rd; dm $30-32, s/d $54/70; P @ wi-fi) Occupying a character-filled, two-storey house built for Tongan royalty, this friendly and well-run backpackers has a lovely garden and high-ceilinged rooms. If you need to unwind, there's yoga on the front lawn.

Quest Carlaw Park APARTMENT $$
(Map p76; ☎09-304 0521; www.questcarlawpark.co.nz; 15 Nicholls Lane; apt $130-320; @ wi-fi) It's in an odd spot but this set of smart, modern apartments is handy for Parnell, the city and the Domain, and if you've got a car you're practically on the motorway.

Parnell Inn MOTEL $$
(Map p76; ☎09-358 0642; www.parnellinn.co.nz; 320 Parnell Rd; r $105-140; P @ wi-fi) You'll get a chipper welcome from the friendly folks at this good-looking, revamped motel with local photography on the walls. Rooms 3 and 4 have great harbour views and some rooms have kitchenettes.

Quality Hotel Barrycourt HOTEL $$
(Map p76; ☎09-303 3789; www.barrycourt.co.nz; 20 Gladstone Rd; units $113-283, r $131-179, ste $188-283; P) A mixed bag of more than 100 motel rooms and units are available in this large, well-maintained complex with friendly multilingual staff. The newer north wing has some fantastic harbour views.

Lantana Lodge HOSTEL $
(Map p76; ☎09-373 4546; www.lantanalodge.co.nz; 60 St Georges Bay Rd; dm $27-30, s/d $59/70; P) There are only eight rooms available in this cosy villa on a quiet street with an instantly welcoming, social vibe. It's not flash by any means, but it's clean enough to be homely.

DEVONPORT

Devonport has masses of beautiful Edwardian B&Bs within a relaxing ferry ride of the city.

Peace & Plenty Inn B&B $$$
(Map p86; ☎09-445 2925; www.peaceandplenty.co.nz; 6 Flagstaff Tce; s $195-265, d $265-465; P) This perfectly located, five-star Victorian house is stocked with antique furnishings and a thousand conversation pieces. The romantic, luxurious rooms have en suites, TVs, flowers, free sherry/port and local chocolates.

Hampton Beach House B&B $$$
(Map p86; ☎09-445 1358; www.hamptonbeachhouse.co.nz; 4 King Edward Pde; s $195, r $235-305; @) One of a fine strip of waterside mansions, this upmarket, gay-friendly, Edwardian B&B has rooms opening onto the rear garden. It's all very tastefully done; expect quality linen and gourmet breakfasts.

Devonport Motel MOTEL $$
(Map p86; ☎09-445 1010; www.devonportmotel.co.nz; 11 Buchanan St; r $150;) This minimotel has just two units in the tidy back garden. They're modern, clean, self-contained and in a nice quiet location that's still close to Devonport's action (such as it may be).

Parituhu B&B $$
(Map p86; ☎09-445 6559; www.parituhu.co.nz; 3 King Edward Pde; r $125-185;) There's only one double bedroom (with its own adjoining bathroom) available in this cute Edwardian waterfront bungalow. It's a relaxing and welcoming place, and gay- and lesbian-friendly too.

Devonport Sea Cottage COTTAGE $$
(Map p86; ☎09-445 7117; www.devonportseacottage.nz.com; 3a Cambridge Tce; s/d $110/130;) Head up the garden path to your own self-contained cottage, which has everything you'll need for a relaxing stay near the sea. Excellent weekly rates are available in summer.

OTHER AREAS

TOP CHOICE **Auckland Takapuna Oaks** HOTEL $$
(Map p64; ☎09-445 7100; www.aucklandtakapunaoaks.co.nz; 1 Beresford St, Bayswater; apt $129-349; P @) It sounds almost too good to be true: affordable spacious apartments (with full kitchens and laundry facilities) situated at the end of a peaceful peninsula that's close to beaches and a short ferry ride from the city. But wait, there's more: harbour and city views, breakfast included and ample parking... There may not be a free set of steak knives but they do chuck in a return ferry ticket each day.

Omahu Lodge B&B $$$
(Map p72; ☎09-524 5648; www.omahulodge.co.nz; 33 Omahu Rd, Remuera; s $170-200, d $230-325;) Art and family photos cover the walls at this cheerful, deluxe B&B. The three en-suite rooms in the main house all have neighbourhood views, but the spacious suite opens straight onto the solar-heated pool.

Jet Park HOTEL $$
(Map p64; ☎09-275 4100; www.jetpark.co.nz; 63 Westney Rd, Mangere; r $153-310, ste $220-430; @) Friendly Jet Park has comfortable rooms, a decent vibe (unusual for an airport hotel), and a pool straight out of *Hawaii 5-0*. Departure screens in the lobby and free airport shuttles mean there's no excuse for missing your flight.

Grange Lodge MOTEL $$
(Map p64; ☎09-277 8280; www.grangelodge.co.nz; cnr Grange & Great South Rds, Papatoetoe; units $115-190;) If you've driven up from the south and can't face crossing the city, consider staying at this friendly little suburban motel, offering reasonable rates, free wi-fi and a teddy bear in every room. It's hardly a salubrious location but it is handy for the airport. From the Southern Motorway, take the East Tamaki Rd exit, turn right and right again onto Great South Rd.

Nautical Nook B&B $$
(Map p64; ☎09-521 2544; www.nauticalnook.com; 23b Watene Cres, Orakei; s/d $108/162; 📶) If you're a sailing buff you'll find a kindred spirit in Keith, who runs this cosy homestay with his wife Trish. The lounge and terrace have views over the harbour, and the beach is close at hand.

Auckland Airport Campervan Park CAMPERVAN PARK
(Map p64; ☎09-256 8527; www.aucklandairport.co.nz; Jimmy Ward Crescent, Mangere; sites from $29; 📶) The world's first airport-run campervan park offers 54 powered spaces with toilets and showers, all within 1km of the terminals. It's a great option for those wanting to park-up after a long flight before hitting the road.

Ambury Regional Park CAMPSITE $
(Map p64; ☎09-366 2000; www.arc.govt.nz; Ambury Rd, Mangere; sites per adult/child $10/5) A slice of country in the middle of suburbia, this regional park is also a working farm. Facilities are limited (a vault toilet, warm showers and not much shade) but it's handy to the airport, right on the water and dirt cheap.

Eating

Because of its size and ethnic diversity, Auckland tops the country when it comes to dining options and quality. Lively eateries have sprung up to cater to the numerous Asian students, offering inexpensive Japanese, Chinese and Korean staples. If you're on a budget, you'll fall in love with the city's food halls.

Aucklanders demand good coffee, so you never have to walk too far to find a decent cafe. Suburbs such as Ponsonby, Grey Lynn and Kingsland are teeming with them. Some double as wine bars or have gourmet aspirations, while others are content to fill their counters with fresh, reasonably priced snacks.

The 2011 Rugby World Cup brought with it a flurry of restaurant and bar openings, shifting the locus of gastronomic activity back to the city centre. Nowadays the hippest new foodie enclaves are Britomart (the blocks above the train station) and Federal St (under the Sky Tower) – although Ponsonby still stands out for the quality and variety of its eateries.

You'll find large supermarkets in most neighbourhoods; there's a particularly handy **Countdown** (Map p68; www.countdown.co.nz; 76 Quay St; ⏲24hr) at the bottom of town and a **New World** (Map p82; www.newworld.co.nz; 2 College Hill, Freemans Bay; ⏲7am-midnight) by Victoria Park. Self-caterers should consider the Otara Market (p97) and Avondale Sunday Market (p97) for cheap, fresh vegetables and La Cigale (p91) for fancier fare.

CITY CENTRE

TOP CHOICE **Grove** MODERN NZ $$$
(Map p68; ☎09-368 4129; www.thegroverestaurant.co.nz; St Patrick's Sq, Wyndham St; mains $43; ⏲lunch Mon-Fri, dinner Mon-Sat) Romantic fine dining at its best: the room is cosy and moodily lit, the menu encourages sensual experimentation and the service is effortless. If you can't find anything to break the ice from the extensive wine list, give it up mate – it's never going to happen.

Depot MODERN NZ $$
(Map p68; www.eatatdepot.co.nz; 86 Federal St; dishes $14-32; ⏲7am-late) Opened to instant acclaim in 2011, TV chef Al Brown's first Auckland eatery offers first-rate comfort food in informal surrounds (communal tables, butcher tiles and a constant buzz). Dishes are divided into 'small' and 'a little bigger' and are designed to be shared. A pair of clever shuckers are kept busy serving up the city's freshest oysters.

Food Alley FOOD HALL $
(Map p68; 9 Albert St; mains $7-13; ⏲10.30am-10pm) There's Chinese, Indian, Thai, Vietnamese, Turkish, Malaysian, Korean and Japanese on offer at this large, no-frills (but plenty of thrills) food hall. Our pick of the bunch is Wardani, hidden in the back corner, serving first-rate Indonesian fare.

O'Connell Street Bistro FRENCH $$$
(Map p68; ☎09-377 1884; www.oconnellstbistro.com; 3 O'Connell St; lunch $28-38, dinner $34-45; ⏲lunch Mon-Fri, dinner Mon-Sat) O'Connell St is a grown-up treat, with elegant decor and truly wonderful food and wine, satisfying lunchtime powerbrokers and dinnertime daters alike. If you're dining before 7.30pm, a fixed-price menu is available (two-/three-courses $33/40).

Federal & Wolfe CAFE $$
(Map p68; 10 Federal St; mains $12-21; ⏲7am-3pm Mon-Sat; 📶) Packing crates and mismatched chairs (some seemingly liberated from a high school) lend an air of recycled chic to

this corner cafe. Yet the be-suited swarm here for the first-rate coffee, delicious food (much of it organic and free range) and a quick dose of cool to get them through their working day.

Ima MIDDLE EASTERN **$$**
(Map p68; ☎09-300 7252; www.imacuisine.co.nz; 57 Fort St; lunch $15-23, dinner $26-34; ⏲lunch Mon-Fri, dinner Tue-Sat) Named after the Hebrew word for mother, the menu is a harmonious blend of Israeli, Palestinian, Yemenite and Lebanese dishes. Excellent coffee, too.

Reslau CAFE **$**
(Map p68; 39 Elliott St; mains $7.50-11; ⏲7.30am-7.30pm Mon-Wed, 7.30am-9.30pm Thu-Sat) Spilling into the Elliott Stables laneway, this tiny cafe–wine bar literally has a trolley-load of delicious snacks and light meals, not to mention excellent coffee.

BRITOMART, VIADUCT HARBOUR & WYNYARD QUARTER

Soul Bar MODERN NZ **$$**
(Map p68; ☎09-356 7249; www.soulbar.co.nz; Viaduct Harbour; mains $20-42; ⏲11am-late) Eating seafood by the water is a must in Auckland and this modernist gastrodome boasts an unbeatable see-and-be-seen location (Jay-Z and Beyoncé dined not-at-all-inconspicuously on the deck) and some of the best seafood in town.

Euro MODERN NZ **$$**
(Map p68; ☎09-309 9866; www.eurobar.co.nz; Shed 22, Princes Wharf; mains $28-45; ⏲lunch & dinner) Euro is a thoroughly slick package of imaginative cuisine, good-looking wait staff and sexy surrounds. The dishes are always as pretty as a picture and the relaxed atmosphere gets decidedly more bar-like as the night progresses.

Ebisu JAPANESE **$$**
(Map p68; www.ebisu.co.nz; 116-118 Quay St; large plates $28-35; ⏲lunch Mon-Fri, dinner daily) Auckland's food-lovers are in the midst of a minicraze for *izakaya*, a style of drinking and eating that eschews Japanese formality, yet doesn't involve food being flung around the room or chugging along on a conveyor belt. This large bar gets it exactly right, serving exquisite plates, large and small, designed to be shared.

L'Assiette FRENCH **$$**
(Map p68; www.lassiette.co.nz; 9 Britomart Pl, Britomart; breakfast & lunch $10-19, dinner $28-33; ⏲breakfast & lunch daily, dinner Thu-Sat) Fresh and bright, this little cafe is a popular coffee-and-pastry stop for harried office workers. By night it morphs into a fully fledged bistro, serving a delicious but limited menu of French classics at reasonable prices.

FREEMANS BAY

Clooney MODERN NZ **$$$**
(Map p68; ☎09-358 1702; www.clooney.co.nz; 33 Sale St; mains $42-45; ⏲dinner) Like the Hollywood actor of the same name, Clooney is suave, stylish and extremely sophisticated, suited up in basic black. While the taste combinations are complex, the results are faultless – which coupled with impeccable service puts Clooney firmly in the pricy-but-worth-it category.

Queenie's Lunchroom CAFE **$$**
(Map p82; www.queenieslunchroom.co.nz; 24a Spring St; mains $11-22; ⏲8am-3.30pm) Kiwiana reigns supreme at this eccentric corner cafe with one wall devoted to a 1950s paint-by-numbers Maori maiden mural. The food is a step up from standard cafe fare, with an adventurous menu justifying the prices.

PONSONBY & GREY LYNN

Auckland's busiest restaurant-cafe-bar strip is so damn cool it has its own website (www.ponsonbyroad.co.nz).

TOP CHOICE **MooChowChow** THAI **$$**
(Map p82; ☎09-360 6262; www.moochowchow.co.nz; 23 Ponsonby Rd; dishes $18-30; ⏲lunch Tue-Fri, dinner Tue-Sat) It's Thai, Nahm Jim, but not as we know it. Bangkok's street food has been channelled into this supremely Ponsonby mooching spot without missing a piquant note. We haven't had a bad dish here, and we've sampled most of the menu.

SPQR ITALIAN **$$**
(Map p82; www.spqrnz.co.nz; 150 Ponsonby Rd; mains $25-39; ⏲noon-late) This Ponsonby Rd hot spot is well known for Roman-style, thin, crusty pizzas and excellent Italian-influenced mains. The surrounds are a stylish blend of the industrial and the chic, the lights are *low* (bring your reading glasses!), the buzz constant and the smooth staff aren't beyond camping it up.

Cocoro JAPANESE **$$$**
(Map p82; ☎09-360 0927; www.cocoro.co.nz; 56a Brown St; dishes $5-25, degustation $80; ⏲lunch & dinner Tue-Sat) Japanese elegance infuses everything about this excellent restaurant,

from the soft lighting and chic decor, to the professional staff and the delicate flavours of the artistically arranged food. Dishes are designed to be shared, tapas-style – or more correctly *izakaya*-style.

Richmond Rd Cafe CAFE **$$**
(Map p82; www.richmondrdcafe.co.nz; 318 Richmond Rd; mains $14-25; ⊙7am-4pm) The location is a little odd – anchored to a small island of industry in a sea of suburbia – but this is one of Auckland's 'it' cafes regardless. If you're suffering from breakfast boredom, you're bound to find the antidote within its creative menu.

Ponsonby Road Bistro INTERNATIONAL **$$**
(Map p82; ☎09-360 1611; www.ponsonbyroadbistro.co.nz; 165 Ponsonby Rd; mains $23-36; ⊙lunch Mon-Fri, dinner Mon-Sat) Portions are large at this modern, upmarket restaurant with an Italian/French sensibility and first-rate service. Imported cheese and wine are a highlight, and the crispy-based pizzas make a delicious shared snack.

Ponsonby Village International Food Court FOOD HALL **$**
(Map p82; www.ponsonbyfoodcourt.co.nz; 106 Ponsonby Rd; mains $8-20; ⊙10am-10pm;) The city's best food hall, only partly due to its location at the heart of the Ponsonby strip. There's Italian, Japanese, Malaysian, Chinese, Turkish, Thai, Lao and Indian on offer but we rarely go past the excellent Vietnamese and Indonesian.

Prego ITALIAN **$$**
(Map p82; ☎09-376 3095; www.prego.co.nz; 226 Ponsonby Rd; mains $23-37; ⊙noon-midnight) This friendly and stylish Italian restaurant covers all the bases, with a fireplace in winter and a courtyard in summer. And on the subject of bases, the pizza is pretty damn fine, as are the inventive Italian mains.

Dizengoff CAFE **$**
(Map p82; 256 Ponsonby Rd; mains $7-19; ⊙6.30am-5pm) This stylish shoebox crams in a mixed crowd of corporate and fashion types, gay guys, Jewish families and Ponsonby denizens, as well as travellers. Mouth-watering scrambled eggs, tempting counter food and heart-starting coffee are on offer, plus a great stack of reading material if you tire of eavesdropping and people-watching.

Burgerfuel BURGERS **$**
(www.burgerfuel.com; burgers $6-13;) Ponsonby (Map p83; 114 Ponsonby Rd); City (Map p68; 291 Queen St); Parnell (Map p76; 187 Parnell Rd); Mt Eden (Map p78; 214 Dominion Rd) Kiwis love their gourmet burgers, so much that they've taken the concept to the world; you can find Kiwi-run chains from Auckland to Edinburgh, by way of Oman and Athens. Burgerfuel are exemplars of the art, filling their buns with high-quality, fresh ingredients and giving them petrolhead names like Studnut Stilton and V8 Vegan.

Landreth & Co CAFE **$$**
(Map p82; www.landrethandco.co.nz; 272 Ponsonby Rd; mains $14-25; ⊙6.30am-4pm;) A popular brunch spot with a sunny rear courtyard and free wi-fi. It's fully licensed, just in case you feel the urge for a beer with your truffled eggs.

Soto JAPANESE **$$**
(Map p82; ☎09-360 0021; www.soto.co.nz; 13 St Marys Rd; mains $29-33; ⊙lunch Tue-Fri, dinner Tue-Sat) Auckland has a surfeit of excellent Japanese restaurants but this is one of the best. The staff glide by efficiently, leaving a trail of exquisitely presented dishes in their wake – including sushi, sashimi and *zensai* (Japanese tapas).

Agnes Curran CAFE **$**
(Map p82; 181 Ponsonby Rd (enter Franklin Rd); snacks $7-9) It may sound like someone's maiden aunt but this cute little cafe is much more hipster than spinster. Still Aunt Agnes would appreciate the cake selection and fresh baguettes, although the super-strong coffee might set her heart aflutter.

Delicious ITALIAN **$$**
(Map p82; www.delicious.co.nz; 472 Richmond Rd; mains $28-34; ⊙lunch Wed-Fri, dinner Tue-Sat) The name doesn't lie. Foodies flock to this neighbourhood eatery for simple but first-rate pasta, risotto and gnocchi. They don't take bookings so expect to wait – it's usually busy.

Satya INDIAN **$$**
(www.satya.co.nz; mains $11-26;); 17 Great North Rd (Map p82; ☎09-361 3612; ⊙lunch Mon-Sat, dinner daily); 271 Karangahape Rd (Map p68; ☎09-377 0027; ⊙lunch & dinner) Hugely popular, this humble-looking and humbly priced eatery has the best *dahi puri* (chickpea, potato and yoghurt on a pappadam) and masala dosa (crêpe filled with potato-and-onion curry) in town.

NEWTON

K Rd is known for its late-night clubs, but cafes and plenty of inexpensive ethnic restaurants are mixed in with the second hand boutiques, tattooists and adult shops.

French Cafe FRENCH $$$

(Map p78; ☎09-377 1911; www.thefrenchcafe.co.nz; 210 Symonds St; mains $45; ⏰lunch Fri, dinner Tue-Sat) The legendary French Cafe has been rated as one of Auckland's top restaurants for around 20 years now and it still continues to excel. The cuisine is (unsurprisingly) French, but chef Simon Wright sneaks in some Pacific Rim touches.

Coco's Cantina ITALIAN $$

(Map p68; www.cocoscantina.co.nz; 376 Karangahape Rd; mains $27-31; ⏰5pm-late Tue-Sat) Rub shoulders with Auckland's hipsters and foodsters at this bustling cantina where the wait for a table is part of the experience. Propping up the bar is hardly a hardship: the ambience and drinks list see to that. The rustic menu is narrowly focussed, seasonal and invariably delicious.

Alleluya CAFE $

(Map p68; St Kevin's Arcade, Karangahape Rd; mains $10-19; ⏰8am-3pm; 📶🖉) To the bohemian denizens of K Rd, Alleluya means good coffee, moreish cakes and lots of vegetarian options. It's situated at the end of the city's hippest arcade, with windows offering a wonderful snapshot of the city skyline.

Theatre CAFE $

(Map p68; www.theatrecoffee.co.nz; 256 Karangahape Rd; ⏰7am-3pm) Once the grand entrance to a long-gone theatre, this narrow vaulted corridor has been transformed into a supremely cool licensed cafe serving excellent coffee, cooked breakfasts and made-to-order sandwiches and bagels.

O'Sarracino ITALIAN $$

(Map p78; ☎09-309 3740; www.osarracino.co.nz; 3 Mt Eden Rd; mains $22-38; ⏰dinner Tue-Sat) A delicious reminder that Neapolitan cuisine offers so much more than pizza, this excellent restaurant serves generous antipasti, light and simple pasta, and delectable seafood *secondi*. The somewhat grand surroundings were once the chapel of a funeral parlour.

KINGSLAND

Atomic Roastery CAFE $

(Map p78; www.atomiccoffee.co.nz; 420c New North Rd; snacks $9-10; ⏰8am-3pm) Coffee hounds should follow their noses to this, one of the country's best-known coffee roasters. Tasty accompaniments include pies served in mini-frypans, rolls, salads and cakes.

Shaky Isles CAFE $

(Map p78; 492 New North Rd; mains $10-21; ⏰8am-4pm; 📶) Kingsland's coolest cafe has cute cartoons on the wall, free wi-fi and serves delicious cooked breakfasts and super-food salads.

Fridge CAFE $

(Map p78; 507 New North Rd; mains $8-20; ⏰breakfast & lunch) Serves excellent coffee, gourmet pies, healthy salads and wraps, and drool-inducing cakes.

MT EDEN

Merediths MODERN NZ $$$

(Map p78; ☎09-623 3140; www.merediths.co.nz; 365 Dominion Rd; 6-9 course degustation $90-130; ⏰lunch Fri, dinner Tue-Sat) Dining at Merediths is the culinary equivalent of blackwater rafting – tastes surprise you at every turn, you never know what's coming next and you're left with a sense of breathless exhilaration.

Molten MODERN NZ $$$

(Map p78; ☎09-638 7236; www.molten.co.nz; 422 Mt Eden Rd; mains $32-35; ⏰lunch Tue-Sat, dinner Mon-Sat) Under the volcano's shadow, Molten oozes neighbourhood charm and erupts with flavour. The consistently excellent menu is extremely well crafted, taking advantage of the latest seasonal produce to create innovative, beautifully presented meals.

Gala CAFE $

(Map p78; www.galacafe.co.nz; Zone 23, 23 Edwin St; mains $11-20; ⏰breakfast & lunch) Mixing modern architecture and antique silver tea services, this bright cafe brings sophistication to the prison precinct. The whiteboard menu is crammed with interesting options: try My Mother-in-law's North Indian Eggs for a fragrant version of eggs on toast.

PARNELL & NEWMARKET

TOP CHOICE **La Cigale** FRENCH $$

(Map p76; ☎09-366 9361; www.lacigale.co.nz; 69 St Georges Bay Rd; cafe $8-18, bistro $30; ⏰cafe 9am-4pm Mon-Fri, bistro dinner Wed-Fri, market 9am-1.30pm Sat & Sun) Catering to Francophiles, foodies and homesick Gauls, this warehouse stocks French imports (wine, cheese, tinned snails etc) and has a patisserie-laden cafe.

Yet it's during the weekend farmers markets that this *cigale* (cicada) really chirps, with stalls laden with produce and all manner of tasty eats. Three nights a week the space is converted into a quirky bistro, where mains are ordered three days in advance and served in large communal bowls.

Basque Kitchen Bar TAPAS $$
(Map p72; ☎09-523 1057; 61 Davies Cres; tapas $7-15; ⏲4pm-late Mon-Thu & Sat, noon-late Fri) It doesn't look like much but this dark little bar serves delectable tapas accompanied by a large range of Spanish wine and sherry. The stuffed squid is sublime.

Teed St Larder CAFE $
(Map p72; www.teedstreetlarder.co.nz; 7 Teed St; ⏲8am-4pm) Polished concrete floors, beer crate tables and colourful oversized lampshades set the scene at Newmarket's best cafe. There are plenty of enticing cooked items on the menu but it's hard to go past the delicious sandwiches and tarts beckoning from the counter.

Rosehip Cafe CAFE $$
(Map p76; 82 Gladstone Rd; mains $15-27; ⏲7am-4pm) The name fits: it's near the Rose Gardens and it's pretty darn hip. The cooked meals are a tad pricey but the food is delicious.

Domain & Ayr CAFE $
(Map p76; 492 Parnell Rd; mains $9-19; ⏲8am-3.30pm; ✎) Fair-trade and organic delights that won't unduly strain the bank balance await in this light-filled cafe. There's a good selection of counter food as well as delicious cooked breakfasts, salads and plenty of options for vegetarians.

Non Solo Pizza ITALIAN $$
(Map p76; ☎09-379 5358; www.nonsolopizza.co.nz; 259 Parnell Rd; mains $23-39; ⏲lunch & dinner) Like the name says, there's not only pizza on offer here – delicious though that is. NSP has a large menu of classic Italian antipasti, pasta and grills and a cool street-facing bar with a chandelier made of Peroni bottles.

DEVONPORT

Calliope Road Cafe CAFE $
(Map p86; 33 Calliope Rd; mains $6-17; ⏲8am-3pm) Devonport's best cafe is at a short remove from the main tourist strip, serving a tasty mix of cafe classics and Southeast Asian dishes to locals in the know.

OTHER AREAS

TOP CHOICE **Takapuna Beach Cafe** CAFE $$
(Map p64; www.takapunabeachcafe.co.nz; 22 The Promenade; mains $15-25; ⏲7am-5pm) With a menu that reads like a travel magazine (Moroccan eggs, Berkshire pork, Central Otago muesli) and absolute beach views, it's no wonder this cafe is constantly buzzing. If you can't snaffle a table you can always grab an award-winning ice cream or snack from the attached shop.

Engine Room MODERN NZ $$$
(Map p64; ☎09-480 9502; www.engineroom.net.nz; 115 Queen St, Northcote; meals $32-35; ⏲dinner Tue-Sat) One of Auckland's best restaurants, this informal eatery serves up lighter-than-air goat's cheese soufflés, inventive whiteboard mains and oh-my-God chocolate truffles. It's worth booking ahead and catching the ferry.

Eight.Two MODERN NZ $$$
(Map p64; ☎09-419 9082; www.eightpointtwo.co.nz; 82 Hinemoa St, Birkenhead; mains $34-35; ⏲dinner Mon-Sat) Hollowed out of an old villa, this dazzlingly white dining room offers a similarly breezy menu and a great wine list. Catch the Birkenhead ferry from the city for a memorable night out.

Drinking

Auckland's nightlife tends to be quiet during the week – if you're looking for some vital signs, head to Ponsonby Rd, Britomart or the Viaduct. K Rd wakes up late on Friday and Saturday; don't even bother staggering this way before 11pm.

CITY CENTRE

Hotel de Brett BAR
(Map p68; www.hoteldebrett.com; 2 High St; ⏲noon-late) Grab a beer in the cornerbar, a cocktail in the chic art-deco housebar or nab a spot by the fire in the atrium, an interesting covered space fashioned from the alleyway between the old buildings.

Mo's BAR
(Map p68; www.mosbar.co.nz; cnr Wolfe & Federal Sts; ⏲4pm-3am Mon-Fri, 6pm-3am Sat) There is something about this tiny corner bar that makes you want to invent problems just so the barperson can solve them with soothing words and an expertly poured martini. It's just that kind of place.

GAY & LESBIAN AUCKLAND

The Queen City (as it's known for completely coincidental reasons) has by far the country's biggest gay population. While the bright lights attract gays and lesbians from all over the country, the even brighter lights of Sydney eventually steal many of the 30- to 40-somethings, leaving a gap in the demographic. There are a handful of gay venues but they only really kick off on the weekends.

To find out what's going on, grab a copy of the fortnightly newspaper *Express* (available from gay venues) or log on to www.gaynz.com. The big events on the calendar are the Big Gay Out (p81) and the Out Takes (p81) film festival.

Venues change with alarming regularity, but these ones, along with straight-friendly SPQR, were the stayers at the time of research:

Family (Map p68; www.familybar.co.nz; 270 Karangahape Rd, Newton) Trashy, brash and young, this bar can be a lot of fun, with dancing into the wee hours.

Urge (Map p68; www.urgebar.co.nz; 490 Karangahape Rd, Newton; ⌚9pm-late Thu-Sat) Older and hairier than Family, this black-painted pocket-sized venue has DJs on Friday and Saturday nights.

Lolabar (Map p82; www.lolabar.co.nz; 212 Ponsonby Rd, Ponsonby; ⌚5pm-late Tue-Sat) Upmarket cocktail-style bar with regular drag shows.

Centurian (Map p68; www.centuriansauna.co.nz; 18 Beresford St, Newton; before/after 3pm $23/28; ⌚11am-2am Sun-Thu, 11am-6am Fri & Sat) Gay men's sauna.

Everybody's BAR
(Map p68; www.everybodys.co.nz; 44 Queen St) Part of the transformation of a forgotten cinema complex, Everybody's sprawls through various stylish spaces, including a mezzanine with couches and discreet banquettes.

Occidental PUB
(Map p68; www.occidentalbar.co.nz; 6 Vulcan Lane; ⌚7.30am-late Mon-Fri, 9am-late Sat & Sun) Belgian beer, Belgian food (plenty of *moules* and *frites* – mussels and chips) and live music are on offer at this historic 1870 pub.

BRITOMART, VIADUCT HARBOUR & WYNYARD QUARTER

Tyler Street Garage BAR
(Map p68; www.tylerstreetgarage.co.nz; 120 Quay St; ⌚11.30am-late) Just in case you were in any doubt that this was actually a garage, they've left the parking lines painted on the concrete floor. It's still an excellent place to get well lubricated, with on-to-it staff and a little roof terrace facing over the wharves.

Agents & Merchants/Racket BAR
(Map p68; www.agentsandmerchants.co.nz; Roukai Lane, 50 Customs St; ⌚11am-late Mon-Sat) Tucked into their own covered lane with an outdoor fireplace and sofas, this duo conjures an old-world yet thoroughly modern atmosphere. A&M serves excellent tapas and wine while Racket makes one well into the morning once the DJs kick in.

Northern Steamship Co. PUB
(Map p68; www.northernsteamship.co.nz; 122 Quay St) Standard lamps hang upside down from the ceiling while the mural behind the bar dreams of NZ summer holidays in this good-looking large pub by the train station.

Conservatory BAR
(Map p68; www.theconservatory.co.nz; North Wharf, 1-17 Jellicoe St) The coolest of the new Wynyard Quarter hang-outs is this liquored up greenhouse sprouting a living wall of greenery and a profusion of cocktails.

Ice House THEME BAR
(Map p68; Princes Wharf; before/after 6pm $25/30; ⌚noon-midnight Sun-Thu, noon-2am Fri & Sat) Put on special clothing and sip a complimentary vodka-based cocktail in this gimmicky bar where everything from the seats to your glass is made of ice. You can only stay inside the shimmering ice world for 30 minutes, making it a quick way to blow your cold hard cash.

PONSONBY & GREY LYNN

Along Ponsonby Rd, the line between cafe, restaurant, bar and club gets blurred. A lot of eateries also have live music or become clubs later on.

Golden Dawn BAR
(Map p82; http://thegoldendawntavernofpower.blogspot.com/; 134b Ponsonby Rd (enter Richmond Rd);

⌚4pm-late Tue-Sun) Here be where Ponsonby's hipsters hide. Occupying an old shopfront and an inviting stables yard, this late-night drinking den regularly hosts random happenings: live bands, burlesque, drag and the like.

Gypsy Tea Room COCKTAIL BAR
(Map p82; www.gypsytearoom.co.nz; 455 Richmond Rd; ⌚4-11.30pm Sun-Thu, 3pm-2am Fri & Sat) No one comes here for tea. This cute wine/cocktail bar has dishevelled charm in bucketloads.

Mea Culpa COCKTAIL BAR
(Map p82; 3/175 Ponsonby Rd; ⌚5pm-1am Sun-Wed, Thu-Sat 5pm-3am) If you can't find a cocktail to your taste at this small but perfectly formed bar, it's nobody's fault but your own.

Ponsonby Social Club BAR
(Map p82; www.ponsonbysocialclub.com; 152 Ponsonby Rd; ⌚5pm-late) Half-and-half alleyway and bar, the back end of this long, narrow space heaves on the weekends when the DJs crank out classic funk and hip-hop.

Dida's Wine Lounge & Tapas Bar WINE BAR
(Map p82; www.glengarrywines.co.nz; 54 Jervois Rd; ⌚11.30am-midnight) Great food and an even better wine list attract a grown-up crowd. There's an associated wine store, providore and cafe next door and another, more food-focussed branch in **Freemans Bay** (Map p68; cnr Sale & Wellesley Sts; tapas $7-12; ⌚8am-6pm Sun & Mon, 7am-8pm Tue-Sat).

NEWTON

Wine Cellar & Whammy Bar BAR
(Map p68; St Kevin's Arcade, Karangahape Rd; ⌚5pm-midnight Mon-Thu, 5.30pm-2am Fri & Sat) Secreted down some stairs in an arcade, this is the kind of bar that Buffy the Vampire Slayer would have hung out in on Auckland-based assignments. It's dark, grungy and very cool, with regular live music in the neighbouring Whammy Bar.

DOC BAR
(Map p68; 352 Karangahape Rd; ⌚5pm-late) This little bar's endemic critters are indie kids who have been known to dance on tables to sugary pop later in the night. The only endangered species here are healthy livers, so we doubt it's got anything whatsoever to do with the Department of Conservation.

Galbraith's Alehouse BREWERY, PUB
(Map p78; www.alehouse.co.nz; 2 Mt Eden Rd; ⌚noon-11pm) Brewing up real ales and lagers on-site, this English-style pub offers bliss on tap. The back-door beer garden trumps the brightly lit bar.

KINGSLAND

Winehot WINE BAR
(Map p78; www.winehot.co.nz; 605 New North Rd, Morningside; ⌚5pm-late Tue-Sat) Behind an unlikely-looking doorway, this tiny black-painted and chandelier-festooned hideaway serves an impressive selection of both beer and wine along with delicious platters of French goodies (terrines, pâtés, baguettes).

Neighbourhood BAR
(Map p78; www.neighbourhood.co.nz; 498 New North Rd; 📶) With picture windows overlooking Eden Park and a front terrace that's pick-up central after dark, this upmarket pub is the place to be either side of rugby fixtures. DJs play on weekends.

☆ Entertainment

The *NZ Herald* has an in-depth rundown of the coming week's happenings in its *Time Out* magazine on Thursday and again in its Saturday edition. If you're planning a big night along K Rd, then visit www.kroad.co.nz for a detailed list of bars and clubs.

Tickets for most major events can be bought from the following:

Ticketek TICKETING AGENCY
(☎0800 842 538; www.ticketek.co.nz) Outlets include Real Groovy (p96) and **SkyCity Theatre** (Map p68; ☎09-363 6000; www.skycity.co.nz; cnr Victoria & Federal Sts).

Ticketmaster TICKETING AGENCY
(☎09-970 9700; www.ticketmaster.co.nz) Outlets at Real Groovy (p96), **Vector Arena** (Map p76; ☎09-358 1250; www.vectorarena.co.nz; Mahuhu Cres), Aotea Centre (p95) and Britomart Train Station (p99).

Live Music & Nightclubs

The Viaduct, Britomart and K Rd are the main late-night hang-outs, but some of the Ponsonby Rd bars continue into the wee smalls. Cover charges vary depending on the night and the event. See also Whammy Bar (above) for live indie music and Ponsonby Social Club (above) for a boogie.

TOP CHOICE **Rakinos** DJ
(Map p68; www.rakinos.com; Level 1, 35 High St) By day it's a cafe but we only head here after dark, when the DJs are spinning old-school hip-hop, funk, Motown and R'n'B like it's, well, anytime between 1968 and the present.

When the mood takes, it's hands-down our favourite place to bust a move.

Cassette Nine CLUB

(Map p68; www.cassettenine.com; 9 Vulcan Lane, City; ⌚noon-late Tue-Sat) Auckland's most out-there hipsters gravitate to this eccentric bar/club where swishy boys rub shoulders with beardy dudes and girls in very short dresses, and the music ranges from live indie to international DJ sets.

Kings Arms Tavern LIVE MUSIC

(Map p78; www.kingsarms.co.nz; 59 France St, Newton) Auckland's leading small venue for local and international bands, which play four or five nights per week. It's a rite of passage if you want to get your band noticed.

Ink & Coherent CLUB

(Map p68; www.inkcoherent.co.nz; 268 & 262 Karangahape Rd, Newton) Neighbouring venues for serious dance aficionados, sometimes hosting big-name DJs.

Khuja Lounge DJ

(Map p68; www.khuja.co.nz; 536 Queen St, Newton; ⌚8pm-late Wed-Sat) Above the Westpac building, this laid-back bar has a lively roster of DJs and jazz/soul/hip-hop bands.

Thirsty Dog LIVE MUSIC

(Map p68; www.thirstydog.co.nz; 469 Karangahape Rd, Newton) This dog's both thirsty and noisy, with a booming sound system and a regular roster of local musos.

AUCKLAND TOP 10 PLAYLIST

Download these Auckland songs to your MP3 player for cruising the city's streets:

» 'Grey Lynn Park' – The Veils (2011)

» 'Auckland CBD Part Two' – Lawrence Arabia (2009)

» 'Forever Thursday' – Tim Finn (2008)

» 'Riverhead' – Goldenhorse (2004)

» 'A Brief Reflection' – Nesian Mystik (2002)

» 'Hopetown Bridge' – Dave Dobbyn (2000)

» 'New Tattoo' – Hello Sailor (1994)

» 'Dominion Road' – The Mutton Birds (1992)

» 'Andy' – The Front Lawn (1989)

» 'One Tree Hill' – U2 (1987)

Cinema

Most offer cheaper rates on weekdays before 5pm; Tuesday is usually bargain day.

Rialto CINEMA

(Map p72; ☎09-369 2417; www.rialto.co.nz; 167 Broadway, Newmarket; adult/child $16.50/10) Screens art-house and international films, plus some of the better mainstream fare.

Academy Cinemas CINEMA

(Map p68; ☎09-373 2761; www.academycinemas.co.nz; 44 Lorne St, City; adult/child $14/8) Screens independent foreign and art-house films in the basement of the Central Library.

Event Cinemas CINEMA

(Map p68; ☎09-369 2400; www.eventcinemas.co.nz; Level 3, 297 Queen St, City; adult/child $16.50/10.50) Part of Aotea Sq's futuristic Metro mall, which also includes bars and a food court.

NZ Film Archives CINEMA

(Map p68; ☎09-379 0688; www.filmarchive.org.nz; 300 Karangahape Rd, Newton; ⌚11am-5pm Mon-Sat) A wonderful resource of more than 150,000 Kiwi feature films, documentaries and TV shows, which you can watch for free on a TV screen.

Theatre, Classical Music & Comedy

Auckland's main arts and entertainment complex is grouped around Aotea Sq. Branded **The Edge** (☎09-357 3355; www.the-edge.co.nz), it comprises the Town Hall, Civic Theatre (p63) and Aotea Centre.

Auckland Town Hall CLASSICAL MUSIC

(Map p68; 305 Queen St) This elegant Edwardian venue (1911) hosts concert performances by the likes of the NZ Symphony Orchestra (www.nzso.co.nz) and Auckland Philharmonia (www.apo.co.nz).

Aotea Centre THEATRE

(Map p68; 50 Mayoral Dr) Auckland's largest venue for theatre, dance, ballet and opera, with two main stages: the cavernous ASB Auditorium and the tiny Herald Theatre. NZ Opera (www.nzopera.com) regularly performs here.

Q Theatre THEATRE

(Map p68; ☎09-309 9771; www.qtheatre.co.nz; 305 Queen St) The city's newest theatre showcases works by various companies as well as intimate live music events. Silo Theatre (www.silotheatre.co.nz) often performs here.

Classic Comedy Club COMEDY
(Map p68; ☎09-373 4321; www.comedy.co.nz; 321 Queen St; tickets $5-27) Auckland's top venue for comedy, with performances from Wednesday through to Saturday.

Maidment Theatre THEATRE
(Map p68; ☎09-308 2383; www.maidment.auckland.ac.nz; 8 Alfred St) The University's theatre often stages Auckland Theatre Company (www.atc.co.nz) productions.

Sport

Eden Park RUGBY, CRICKET
(Map p78; www.edenpark.co.nz; Reimers Ave, Kingsland) Fresh from its Rugby World Cup makeover, this is the stadium for top rugby (winter) and cricket (summer) tests by the All Blacks (www.allblacks.com) and the Black Caps (www.blackcaps.co.nz), as well as the home ground for Auckland Rugby (www.aucklandrugby.co.nz), the Blues Super Rugby team (www.theblues.co.nz), and Auckland Cricket (www.aucklandcricket.co.nz). To get here, take the train from Britomart to Kingsland Station.

Mt Smart Stadium RUGBY, FOOTBALL
(Map p64; www.mtsmartstadium.co.nz; Maurice Rd, Penrose) The venue of choice for the Warriors rugby league team (www.warriors.co.nz), Auckland Football Federation (www.aucklandfootball.org.nz), Athletics Auckland (www.athleticsauckland.co.nz) and *really* big concerts.

North Shore Events Centre BASKETBALL
(Map p64; ☎09-443 8199; www.nseventscentre.co.nz; Argus Pl, Wairau Valley) The home ground of the NZ Breakers basketball team (www.nzbreakers.co.nz) and an occasional concert venue.

ASB Tennis Centre TENNIS
(Map p76; www.aucklandtennis.co.nz; 1 Tennis Lane, Parnell) In January the women's ASB Classic (www.asbclassic.co.nz) is held here, followed by the men's Heineken Open (www.heinekenopen.co.nz).

Shopping

Followers of fashion should head to High St in the city, Newmarket's Teed and Nuffield Sts, and Ponsonby Rd. For secondhand boutiques try K Rd or Ponsonby Rd.

CITY CENTRE

Real Groovy MUSIC
(Map p68; www.realgroovy.co.nz; 438 Queen St; ⌚9am-7pm Sat-Wed, 9am-9pm Thu & Fri) A music-lovers' nirvana, this huge store has masses of new, second hand and rare releases, as well as concert tickets, giant posters, DVDs, books, magazines and clothes.

Pauanesia GIFTS
(Map p68; www.pauanesia.co.nz; 35 High St; ⌚9.30am-6.30pm Mon-Fri, 10am-4.30pm Sat & Sun) A treasure-trove of homewares and gifts with a pronounced Polynesian influence.

Unity Books BOOKS
(Map p68; www.unitybooks.co.nz; 19 High St; ⌚8.30am-7pm Mon-Thu, 8.30am-9pm Fri, 9am-6pm Sat, 11am-6pm Sun) Excellent independent bookshop with knowledgeable staff.

Strangely Normal CLOTHING
(Map p68; www.strangelynormal.com; 19 O'Connell St) Quality, NZ-made, men's tailored shirts straight out of *Blue Hawaii* sit alongside hipster hats, sharp shoes and cufflinks.

Karen Walker CLOTHING
(www.karenwalker.com) City (Map p68; 15 O'Connell St); Ponsonby (Map p82; 171 Ponsonby Rd); Newmarket (Map p72; 6 Balm St) Join Madonna and Kirsten Dunst in wearing Walker's cool (but pricey) threads.

Zambesi CLOTHING
(www.zambesi.co.nz) City (Map p68; cnr Vulcan Lane & O'Connell St); Ponsonby (Map p82; 169 Ponsonby Rd); Newmarket (Map p72; 38 Osborne St) The most famous fashion label to come out of NZ, and much sought after by local and international celebs.

Whitcoulls BOOKS
(Map p68; www.whitcoulls.co.nz; 210 Queen St) The mothership of the biggest local chain, with good travel and fiction sections.

PONSONBY & GREY LYNN

Women's Bookshop BOOKS
(Map p82; www.womensbookshop.co.nz; 105 Ponsonby Rd; ⌚10am-6pm) An excellent independent bookshop that's a community resource in its own right.

Marvel CLOTHING
(Map p82; www.marvelmenswear.co.nz; 143 Ponsonby Rd) Smart, tailored shirts and trousers in interesting fabrics and quirky partywear are the mainstays of this local menswear designer.

Texan Art Schools ARTS & CRAFTS
(www.texanartschools.co.nz; ⌚9.30am-5.30pm) Ponsonby (Map p82; 95 Ponsonby Rd); Newmarket (Map p72; 366 Broadway) Despite the name, it's

AUCKLAND, THE BIG TARO

There are nearly 180,000 Pacific Islanders (PI) living in Auckland, making it the world's principal Polynesian city. Samoans are by far the largest group, followed by Cook Islanders, Tongans, Niueans, Fijians, Tokelauans and Tuvaluans. The biggest PI communities can be found in South Auckland and pockets of West and Central Auckland.

Like the Maori renaissance of recent decades, Pasifika has become a hot commodity for Auckland hipsters. You'll find PI motifs everywhere: in art, architecture, fashion, homewares, movies and especially in music.

got nothing to do with the Lone Star State. A collective of 200 local artists sell their wares here.

KINGSLAND

Royal Jewellery Studio JEWELLERY
(Map p78; www.royaljewellerystudio.com; 486 New North Rd; ⏲10am-5pm) Displaying interesting work by local artisans, including some beautiful Maori designs, this is a great place to pick up authentic *pounamu* (greenstone) jewellery.

OTHER AREAS

Otara Market MARKET
(Map p64; Newbury St; ⏲6am-noon Sat) Held in the car park between the Manukau Polytech and the Otara town centre, this market has a palpable Polynesian atmosphere and is a good place to stock up on South Pacific food, music and fashions. Take bus 497 from Britomart ($6.80, 50 minutes).

Avondale Sunday Market MARKET
(Map p64; www.avondalesundaymarkets.co.nz; Avondale Racecourse, Ash St; ⏲6am-noon Sun) Easier to get to than the Otara Markets, Avondale also has a distinctly Polynesian atmosphere and is particularly good for fresh produce. Take the train to Avondale station.

ℹ Information

Internet Access

Auckland Council has set up free wi-fi in parts of the city centre, Newton, Ponsonby, Kingsland, Mt Eden and Parnell, but at the time of writing, its future was up in the air, pending sponsorship. Public libraries are a safe bet for computers with free internet access and, often, wi-fi. Internet cafes catering mainly to gaming junkies are scattered about the inner city.

Media

Metro Glossy monthly magazine covering Auckland issues in depth.

New Zealand Herald (www.nzherald.co.nz) The country's biggest daily newspaper.

Medical Services

Auckland City Hospital (☎09-367 0000; www.adhb.govt.nz; Park Rd, Grafton; ⏲24hr) The city's main hospital has a dedicated accident and emergency (A&E) service.

Auckland Metro Doctors & Travelcare (☎09-373 4621; www.aucklandmetrodoctors.co.nz; 17 Emily Pl, City; ⏲9am-5.30pm Mon-Fri, 10am-2pm Sat) Specialises in health care for travellers, such as vaccinations and travel consultations.

Starship Children's Hospital (☎09-367 0000; www.adhb.govt.nz; Park Rd, Grafton; ⏲24hr) Has its own A&E department.

Tourist Information

Auckland Domestic Airport i-SITE (☎09-256 8480; ⏲7am-9pm) In the Air New Zealand terminal.

Auckland International Airport i-SITE (☎09-275 6467; ⏲24hr) Located on your left as you exit the customs hall.

Auckland Princes Wharf i-SITE (☎09-307 0612; www.aucklandnz.com; 137 Quay St; ⏲9am-5.30pm)

Auckland SkyCity i-SITE (☎09-363 7182; www.aucklanμdnz.com; SkyCity Atrium, cnr Victoria & Federal Sts; ⏲8am-8pm)

Cornwall Park Information Centre (☎09-630 8485; www.cornwallpark.co.nz; Huia Lodge; ⏲10am-4pm)

Devonport i-SITE (☎09-446 0677; www.northshorenz.com; 3 Victoria Rd; ⏲8.30am-5pm; @📶)

DOC Information Centre (☎09-379 6476; www.doc.govt.nz; Auckland Princes Wharf i-SITE, 137 Quay St; ⏲9am-5pm Mon-Sat)

Karanga Plaza Kiosk (www.waterfrontauckland.co.nz; Wynyard Quarter; ⏲10am-5.30pm) What looks like a haphazardly stacked set of shipping containers is actually Wynyard Quarter's striking little visitor centre.

Takapuna i-SITE (☎09-486 8670; 34-36 Hurstmere Rd; ⏲8.30am-5pm Mon-Fri, 10am-3pm Sat & Sun)

PLANE DELAYED? TIME FOR A TIPPLE!

Clearly the roar of jets doesn't bother grapes, as NZ's most awarded winery is just 4km from the airport. The parklike grounds of **Villa Maria Estate** (Map p64; www.villamaria.co.nz; 118 Montgomerie Rd; ⌚9am-6pm Mon-Fri, 9am-4pm Sat & Sun) are a green oasis in the encircling industrial zone. A series of concerts is held here every January and February featuring big international artists popular with the 40- to 50-something wine-swilling demographic.

Short tours ($5) take place at 11am and 3pm. There's a charge for tastings ($5), but lingering over wine and cheese on the terrace sure beats hanging around the departure lounge.

ℹ Getting There & Away

Air

Auckland is the main gateway to NZ (see the Transport chapter for flights into NZ), and a hub for domestic flights. **Auckland International Airport** (AKL; ☎09-275 0789; www.aucklandairport.co.nz; Ray Emery Dr, Mangere) is 21km south of the city centre. It has separate international and domestic terminals, each with a tourist information centre. A free shuttle service operates every 15 minutes (5am to 10.30pm) between the terminals and there's also a sign-posted footpath (about a 10-minute walk). Both terminals have left-luggage facilities, ATMs and car-rental desks, although you may get better rates from companies in town.

For flights to Great Barrier Island, see Great Barrier Island's Getting There & Away information. The following are the other domestic airlines flying from Auckland and the destinations they serve:

Air New Zealand (☎09-357 3000; www.airnewzealand.co.nz) Flys to Kaitaia, Kerikeri, Whangarei, Hamilton, Tauranga, Whakatane, Gisborne, Rotorua, Taupo, New Plymouth, Napier, Whanganui, Palmerston North, Masterton, Wellington, Nelson, Blenheim, Christchurch, Queenstown and Dunedin.

Jetstar (☎0800 800 995; www.jetstar.com) Flies to Wellington, Christchurch, Queenstown and Dunedin.

Sunair (☎0800 786 847; www.sunair.co.nz; one way $160) Flies to Whitianga twice daily.

Bus

Coaches depart from 172 Quay St, opposite the Ferry Building, except for InterCity services, which depart from **SkyCity Coach Terminal** (☎09-913 6220; 102 Hobson St). Many south-bound services also stop at the airport.

Dalroy Express (☎0508 465 622; www.dalroytours.co.nz) Operates a daily coach between Auckland and New Plymouth ($60, six hours).

Go Kiwi (☎07-866 0336; www.go-kiwi.co.nz) Has daily Auckland City–International Airport–Thames–Tairua–Whitianga shuttles.

InterCity (☎09-583 5780; www.intercity.co.nz)

Main Coachline (☎09-278 8070; www.maincoachline.co.nz) Has a bus most days between Auckland and Dargaville (three hours) via Orewa, Warkworth and Matakohe.

Naked Bus (☎0900 62533; www.nakedbus.com) Naked Buses travel along SH1 as far north as Kerikeri (four hours) and as far south as Wellington (12 hours), as well as heading to Tauranga (3½ hours) and Napier (12 hours). The cost of calling their helpline is $1.99 per minute.

Car, Caravan & Campervan

HIRE Auckland has the biggest selection of hire agencies, with a swag of them conveniently grouped together along Beach Rd and Stanley St close to the city centre. The major companies have offices at the airport.

A2B (☎09-254 4670; www.a2b-car-rental.co.nz; 167 Beach Rd) Cheap older cars with no visible hire-car branding, making them less of a thief-magnet.

Apex Car Rentals (☎09-307 1063; www.apexrentals.co.nz; 156 Beach Rd)

Budget (☎09-976 2270; www.budget.co.nz; 163 Beach Rd)

Escape (☎0800 216 171; www.escaperentals.co.nz; 39 Beach Rd) Eccentrically painted campervans.

Explore More, Maui & Britz (☎09-255 3910; www.maui.co.nz; 36 Richard Pearse Dr, Mangere)

Gateway 2 NZ (☎0508 225 587; www.gateway2nz.co.nz; 50 Ascot Rd, Mangere)

Gateway Motor Home Hire (☎09-296 1652; www.motorhomehire.co.nz)

Go Rentals (☎09-257 5142; www.gorentals.co.nz; Auckland Airport)

Hertz (☎09-367 6350; www.hertz.co.nz; 154 Victoria St)

Jucy (☎0800 399 736; www.jucy.co.nz)

Kea Campers (☎09-448 8800; www.keacampers.com)

NZ Frontiers (☎09-299 6705; www.newzealandfrontiers.com) Campervans.

Omega (☎09-377 5573; www.omegarentals.com; 75 Beach Rd)

Quality Rentals (☎0800 680 123; www.qualityrental.co.nz; 8 Andrew Baxter Dr, Mangere)

Thrifty (☎09-309 0111; www.thrifty.co.nz; 150 Khyber Pass Rd)

Wilderness Motorhomes (☎09-255 5300; www.wilderness.co.nz; 21 Rennie Drive, Mangere)

PURCHASE Mechanical inspection services are on hand at the following second hand car fairs, where sellers pay to display their cars:

Auckland Car Fair (☎09-529 2233; www.carfair.co.nz; Ellerslie Racecourse, Green Lane East; display fee $35; ⌚9am-noon Sun) Auckland's largest car fair.

City Car Fair (☎09-837 7817; www.aucklandcitycarfair.co.nz; 27 Alten Rd; display fee $25; ⌚8am-1pm Sat)

Motorcycle

See also Paradise Motorcycle Tours (p80).

NZ Motorcycle Rentals (☎09-486 2472; www.nzbike.com; 72 Barrys Point Rd, Takapuna; per day $145-360) Guided tours also available.

Train

Overlander (☎0800 872 467; www.tranzscenic.co.nz) trains depart from **Britomart station** (Queen St), the largest underground diesel train station in the world. They depart from Auckland at 7.25am (daily late September to April, Friday to Sunday otherwise) and arrive in Wellington at 7.25pm (the return train from Wellington departs and arrives at the same time). Useful stops include Hamilton (2½ hours), Otorohanga (three hours), Te Kuiti (3¼ hours), Taumarunui (4½ hours), National Park (5½ hours), Ohakune (6½ hours), Palmerston North (9½ hours) and Paraparaumu (11 hours). A standard fare to Wellington is $129, but a limited number of discounted seats are available for each journey at $79 and $99 (first in, first served).

Getting Around

To & From the Airport

A taxi between the airport and the city usually costs between $60 and $80, more if you strike traffic snarls.

Airbus Express (☎09-366 6400; www.airbus.co.nz; one-way/return adult $16/26, child $6/12) Runs between the terminals and the city, every 10 minutes from 7am to 7pm and at least hourly through the night. Stops include Mt Eden Rd or Dominion Rd (on request), Symonds St, Queen St and the Ferry Building. Reservations are not required; buy a ticket from the driver or online. The trip usually takes less than an hour (longer during peak times).

Super Shuttle (☎0800 748 885; www.supershuttle.co.nz) This convenient door-to-door shuttle charges $28 for one person heading between the airport and a city hotel; the price increases for outlying suburbs. You'll save money if you share a shuttle.

Bicycle

Maxx Regional Transport (see below) publishes free cycle maps, available from public buildings such as stations, libraries and i-SITEs. Bikes can be taken on ferries (free) and trains ($1), but only folding bikes are allowed on buses.

Adventure Cycles (☎09-940 2453; www.adventure-auckland.co.nz/adventurecycles; 9 Premier Ave, Western Springs; per day $25-40, per week $100-150, per month $230-300; ⌚7.30am-7pm Thu-Mon) Hires out road, mountain and long-term touring bikes, runs a buy-back scheme and does repairs.

Car & Motorcycle

Auckland's motorways jam up badly at peak times, particularly the Northern and Southern Motorways. It's best to avoid them between 7am and 9am, and from 4pm to 7pm. Things also get tight around 3pm during term time, which is the end of the school day.

Expect to pay for parking in central Auckland during the day, from Monday to Saturday. Most parking meters are pay-and-display; follow the instructions, collect your ticket and display it inside your windscreen. You usually don't have to pay between 6pm and 8am or on Sunday – check the meters and parking signs carefully.

Prices can be steep at parking buildings. Better value are the council-run open-air parks near the old train station on Beach Rd ($8 per day) and on Ngaoho Pl, off The Strand ($6 per day).

Public Transport

Due to rampant privatisation during the 1980s, Auckland's public transport system is run by a hodgepodge of different operators and as a result there are few integrated public transport passes. The Auckland Council is trying to sort out the mess with their HOP smartcard (www.myhop.co.nz), but until it's bedded down it's probably not worth your while. They also run the **Maxx** (☎09-366 6400; www.maxx.co.nz) information service, covering buses, trains and ferries, which has an excellent trip-planning feature. The Discovery Pass provides a day's transport on most trains and buses and on North Shore ferries ($15); buy it on the bus or train or at Fullers offices.

BUS Bus routes spread their tentacles throughout the city and you can purchase a ticket from the driver. Many services terminate around Britomart station. Some bus stops have electronic displays giving an estimate of waiting times; be warned: they lie.

Single-ride fares in the inner city are 50c for an adult and 30c for a child (free for HOP users). If you're travelling further afield there are fare stages from $1.80/1 (adult/child) to $10.30/6.10.

Perhaps the most useful services are the environmentally friendly Link Buses that loop in both directions around three routes (taking in many of the major sights) from 7am to 11pm:

» City Link (50c, every seven to 10 minutes) – Britomart, Queen St, Karangahape Rd, with some buses connecting to Wynyard Quarter.

» Inner Link (maximum $1.80, every 10 to 15 minutes) – Queen St, SkyCity, Victoria Park, Ponsonby Rd, Karangahape Rd, Museum, Newmarket, Parnell and Britomart.

» Outer Link (maximum $3.40, every 15 minutes) – Art Gallery, Ponsonby, Herne Bay, Westmere, MOTAT 2, Pt Chevalier, Mt Albert, St Lukes Mall, Mt Eden, Newmarket, Museum, Parnell, University.

FERRY Auckland's Edwardian baroque **Ferry Building** (Quay St) sits grandly at the end of Queen St. Fullers (p80) ferries (to Bayswater, Birkenhead, Devonport, Great Barrier Island, Half Moon Bay, Northcote, Motutapu, Rangitoto and Waiheke) leave direcly behind the building, while 360 Discovery (p80) ferries (to Coromandel, Gulf Harbour, Motuihe, Rotoroa and Tiritiri Matangi) leave from adjacent piers.

Sealink (p107) ferries to Great Barrier Island leave from Wynyard Wharf, along with some car ferries to Waiheke, but most of the ferries to Waiheke leave from Half Moon Bay which is in East Auckland.

TRAIN Auckland's train services are limited and infrequent but the trains are generally clean, cheap and on time – although any hiccup on the lines can bring down the entire network.

Impressive Britomart station (p99) has food retailers, foreign-exchange facilities and a ticket office. Downstairs are plush toilets and left-luggage lockers.

There are just four train routes: one runs west to Waitakere, one runs south to Onehunga, and two run south to Pukekohe. Services are at least hourly from around 6am to 8pm (later on the weekends). Pay the conductor on the train (one stage $1.70); they'll come to you. All trains have wheelchair ramps.

Taxi

Auckland's many taxis usually operate from ranks, but they also cruise popular areas. **Auckland Co-op Taxis** (☎09-300 3000; www.3003000.co.nz) is one of the biggest companies. There's a surcharge for transport to and from the airport and cruise ships, and for phone orders.

HAURAKI GULF ISLANDS

The Hauraki Gulf, stretching between Auckland and the Coromandel Peninsula, is dotted with *motu* (islands) and gives the Bay of Islands stiff competition in the beauty stakes. Some islands are only minutes from the city and make excellent day trips: wine-soaked Waiheke and volcanic Rangitoto really shouldn't be missed. Great Barrier requires more effort (and cash) to get to, but provides an idyllic escape from modern life.

There are 47 islands in the Hauraki Gulf Maritime Park, administered by DOC. Some are good-sized islands, others are no more than rocks jutting out of the sea. They're loosely put into two categories: recreation and conservation. The recreation islands can easily be visited and their harbours are dotted with yachts in summer. The conservation islands, however, have restricted access. Permits are required to visit some, while others are closed refuges for the preservation of rare plants and animals, especially birds.

The gulf is a busy highway for marine mammals. Sei, minke and Bryde's whales are regularly seen in its outer reaches, along with orcas and bottlenose dolphins. You might even spy a passing humpback.

Rangitoto & Motutapu Islands

POP 75

Sloping elegantly from the waters of the gulf, 259m **Rangitoto** (www.rangitoto.org), the largest and youngest of Auckland's volcanic cones, provides a picturesque backdrop to all of the city's activities. As recently as 600 years ago it erupted from the sea and was probably active for several years before settling down. Maori living on **Motutapu** (Sacred Island; www.motutapu.org.nz), to which Rangitoto is now joined by a causeway, certainly witnessed the eruptions, as footprints have been found embedded in ash and oral history details several generations living here before the eruption.

The island makes for a great day trip. Its harsh scoria slopes hold a surprising amount of flora (including the world's largest pohutukawa forest) and there are excellent walks, but you'll need sturdy shoes and plenty of water. Although it looks steep, up

BATTLE OF THE BACHES

During the 1920s a dinky set of simple baches started to sprout on Rangitoto on land leased from the council, forming a thriving community of holiday-makers. In the 1930s prison labour was used to construct roads, public toilets, tennis courts and a swimming pool out of the scoria. It was back-breaking work, but the men weren't locked up and by all accounts enjoyed island life. The threat of fire was a constant danger for the bach-holders, as it is today – the baking scoria keeps the leaf litter tinder-dry.

During the 1970s and '80s the bach community itself came under threat – a significant number of houses were removed when their leases expired, with the plan to remove them all. Following a public outcry, the remaining communities were listed as Historic Areas by the Historic Places Trust in 1997. Just left of the wharf, a 1929 bach has been fully restored and opened as a museum of sorts; the hours are sporadic but it's most likely to be open on summer weekends.

close it's shaped more like an egg sizzling in a pan. The walk to the summit only takes an hour and is rewarded with sublime views. At the top a loop walk goes around the crater's rim. A walk to lava caves branches off the summit walk and takes 30 min utes return. There's an information board with walk maps at the wharf.

Motutapu, in contrast to Rangitoto, is mainly covered in grassland, which is grazed by sheep and cattle. Archaeologically, this is a very significant island, with the traces of centuries of continuous human habitation etched into its landscape.

At Home Bay there's a **DOC campsite** (www.doc.govt.nz; adult/child $6/3) with only basic facilities (running water and a flush toilet). Bring cooking equipment, as open fires are forbidden, and book online. It's a three-hour walk from **Rangitoto wharf**; Fullers run a weekend-only service to Home Bay in the summer months.

In 2011 both islands were officially declared predator-free after an extensive eradication program. Endangered birds such as takahe and tieke (saddleback) have been released and others such as kakariki and bellbirds have returned of their own volition; listen for their chiming calls while you're exploring.

Getting There & Around

Fullers (09-367 9111; www.fullers.co.nz; adult/child return $27/14) Has 20-minute ferry services to Rangitoto from Auckland's Ferry Building (three daily on weekdays, four on weekends) and Devonport (two daily). They also offer the Volcanic Explorer (adult/child $59/30), a guided tour around the island in a canopied 'road train'.

Motuihe Island

Between Rangitoto and Waiheke Islands, 176-hectare Motuihe has a lovely white-sand beach and a fascinating history. There are three *pa* sites, last occupied by the Ngati Paoa tribe. The island was sold in 1840 (for a heifer, blankets, frocks, garden tools, pots and pans) and from 1872 to 1941 served as a quarantine station. During WWI the dashing swashbuckler Count von Luckner launched a daring escape from the island (where he was interned with other German and Austrian nationals), making it 1000km to the Kermadec Islands before being recaptured.

Motuihe has been rendered pest-free and is now subject to a vigorous reforestation project by enthusiastic volunteers. As a result, endangered birds have returned, including the loquacious tieke. Contact the **Motuihe Trust** (0800 668 844; www.motuihe.org.nz) if you want to get involved. On weekends in January the trust runs heritage- and restoration-themed guided tours ($5); book through 360 Discovery.

Apart from the trust's headquarters, the only accommodation on the island is a basic **DOC campsite** (www.doc.govt.nz; adult/child $6/3); only toilets and water are provided. There are no permanent residents or shops, except for a lunchtime kiosk during January.

Getting There & Away

360 Discovery (0800 360 3472; www.360discovery.co.nz; adult/child return $27/17) Three ferries make the hour-long journey from Auckland every day.

Waiheke Island

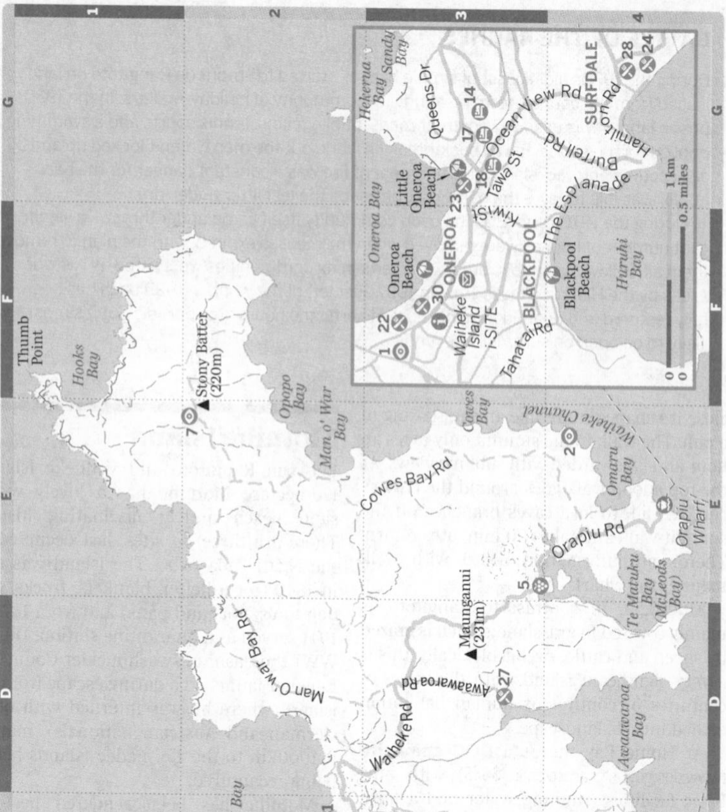

0 4 km
0 2 miles

HAURAKI GULF
Thumb Point
Hooks Bay
Stony Batter (220m)
Fossil Bay
Onetangi Bay
Matiatia Wharf
Matiatia Bay
Palm Beach
PALM BEACH
ONEROA
See Enlargement
Onetangi Beach
ONETANGI
OSTEND
Ostend Rd
Man O' war Bay Rd
Opopo Bay
Man o' War Bay
Waiheke Rd
Awaawaroa Rd
Cowes Bay Rd
Maunganui (231m)
Cowes Bay
Car Ferry Wharf
Kennedy Point
Te Whau Point
Te Whau Dr
OMIHA
Carsons Rd
Rocky Bay
Gordons Rd
Awaawaroa Bay
Te Matuku Bay (McLeods Bay)
Orapiu Rd
Orapiu Wharf
Omaru Bay
Waiheke Channel
To Auckland (18km)
Tamaki Strait

Oneroa Bay
Hekerua Bay
Sandy Bay
Oneroa Beach
Little Oneroa Beach
Queens Dr
ONEROA
Waiheke Island i-SITE
Kiwi St
Tawa St
Ocean View Rd
Tahatai Rd
BLACKPOOL
Blackpool Beach
The Esplanade
Burrell Rd
SURFDALE
Hamilton Rd
Huruhi Bay
0 1 km
0 0.5 miles

Waiheke Island

POP 7700

Waiheke is 93 sq km of island bliss only a 35-minute ferry ride from the CBD. Once they could hardly give land away here; nowadays multimillionaires rub shoulders with the old-time hippies and bohemian artists who gave the island its green repute. Auckland office workers fantasise about swapping the daily motorway crawl for a watery commute and a warm, dry microclimate.

On Waiheke's city side, emerald waters lap at rocky bays, while its ocean flank has some of the region's best sandy beaches. While beaches are the big drawcard, wine is a close second. There are 19 boutique wineries to visit, many with swanky restaurants and breathtaking city views. On top of that, the island boasts dozens of galleries and craft stores.

Waiheke has been inhabited since at least the 14th century, most recently by Ngati Paoa, and there are more than 40 *pa* sites scattered around the island. Europeans arrived with the missionary Samuel Marsden in the early 1800s and the island was soon stripped of its kauri forest.

There are petrol stations in Oneroa, Ostend and Onetangi, ATMs in Oneroa and Ostend, and a supermarket in Ostend.

Sights & Activities

Beaches

Waiheke's two best beaches are **Onetangi**, a long stretch of white sand at the centre of the island, and **Palm Beach**, a pretty little horseshoe bay between Oneroa and Onetangi. Both have nudist sections; head west just past some rocks in both cases. **Oneroa** and neighbouring **Little Oneroa** are also excellent, but you'll be sharing the waters with moored yachts in summer.

Wineries

Waiheke's hot, dry microclimate has proved excellent for bordeaux reds, syrah and some superb rosés. Because of an emphasis on quality rather than quantity, the premium wine produced here is relatively expensive. And be warned: most of the wineries charge for tastings (from $3 to $10; sometimes refunded if you make a purchase). Some are spectacularly located and worth a visit for that reason alone. Over summer many extend their hours, some even sprouting temporary restaurants.

Waiheke Island

Sights
- Art Gallery .... (see 1)
- 1 Artworks Complex F3
- 2 Connells Bay E4
- 3 Dead Dog Bay B3
- 4 Goldie Vineyard B3
- 5 Passage Rock E3
- 6 Saratoga Estate C3
- 7 Stony Batter Historic Reserve E2
- 8 Stonyridge C3
- 9 Waiheke Museum & Historic Village C3
- Whittaker's Musical Museum .... (see 1)
- Wild On Waiheke .... (see 8)

Activities, Courses & Tours
- 10 Ross Adventures A2

Sleeping
- 11 Crescent Valley Eco Lodge C2
- 12 Enclosure Bay B2
- 13 Fossil Bay Lodge A2
- 14 Hekerua Lodge G3
- 15 Kina C2
- 16 Onetangi Beach Apartments C2
- 17 Punga Lodge G3
- 18 Tawa Lodge G3
- 19 Whakanewha Regional Park Campsite C4

Eating
- 20 Cable Bay A2
- 21 Casita Miro C2
- 22 Delight F3
- 23 Dragonfired G3
- 24 Island Thyme & Thymes Tables G4
- 25 Mudbrick A3
- 26 Ostend Market B3
- 27 Poderi Crisci D3
- 28 Stefano's G4
- 29 Te Whau B3
- 30 Wai Kitchen F3

Drinking
- 31 Charlie Farley's C2

Entertainment
- Art-House Cinema .... (see 1)
- Community Theatre .... (see 1)

Pick up the *Waiheke Island of Wine* map for a complete list of vinyards on the island.

Goldie Vineyard WINERY
(www.goldieroom.co.nz; 18 Causeway Rd; tastings $5-10, refundable with purchase; noon-4pm Wed-Sun Mar-Nov, daily Dec-Feb) Founded as Goldwater Estate in 1978, this is Waiheke's pioneering vineyard. The tasting room sells well-stocked baskets for a picnic among the vines (for two people $55).

Passage Rock WINERY
(09-372 7257; www.passagerockwines.co.nz; 438 Orapiu Rd; noon-4pm Sat & Sun Aug-Dec, daily Jan, Wed-Sun Feb-Apr) Excellent pizza among the vines.

Saratoga Estate WINERY, BREWERY
(09-372 6450; www.saratogaestate.com; 72 Onetangi Rd; 11am-4pm) Has a cafe and microbrewery on site.

Stonyridge WINERY
(09-372 8822; www.stonyridge.com; 80 Onetangi Rd; tastings per wine $3-15; 11.30am-5pm) Famous organic reds, an atmospheric cafe, tours ($10, 35 minutes, 11.30am Saturday and Sunday) and the occasional dance party.

Wild On Waiheke WINERY, BREWERY
(09-372 3434; www.wildonwaiheke.co.nz; 82 Onetangi Rd; tastings per beer or wine $2; 11am-4pm Thu-Sun, daily in summer) If you like to shoot stuff after a few drinks, this winery and microbrewery offers tastings, archery, laser clay shooting, *pètanque*, a sandpit and a giant chess board.

Art & Culture

The *Waiheke Art Map* brochure, free from the i-SITE, lists 37 galleries and craft stores.

Artworks Complex ARTS CENTRE
(2 Korora Rd; @) The Artworks complex houses a **community theatre** (09-372 2941; www.artworkstheatre.org.nz), an **art-house cinema** (09-372 4240; www.wicc.co.nz; adult/child $14/7), an attention-grabbing **art gallery** (09-372 9907; www.waiheke artgallery.org.nz; admission free; 10am-4pm) and **Whittaker's Musical Museum** (09-372 5573; www.musical-museum.org; adult/child $5/free; 1-4pm), a collection of antique concert instruments. This is also the place for free internet access, either on a terminal at the **library** (9am-5.30pm Mon-Fri, 10am-4pm Sat; @) or in the allocated wi-fi room.

Stony Batter Historic Reserve HISTORIC SITE
(www.fortstonybatter.org.nz; Stony Batter Rd; adult/child $8/5; 10am-3.30pm) At the bottom end of the island, Stony Batter has WWII tunnels and gun emplacements that were built in 1941 to defend Auckland's harbour. The walk leads through private farmland and derives its name from the boulder-strewn fields. Bring a torch and cash.

Waiheke Museum & Historic Village MUSEUM
(www.waihekemuseum.org.nz; 165 Onetangi Rd; admission by donation; noon-4pm Wed, Sat & Sun) Displays Islander artefacts in six restored buildings.

Dead Dog Bay GARDENS
(www.deaddogbay.co.nz; Margaret Reeve Lane; adult/child $10/free; 10am-5pm) Wander steep pathways through rainforest, wetlands and gardens scattered with sculpture in this jealousy-inducing private property.

Connells Bay GARDENS
(09-372 8957; www.connellsbay.co.nz; Cowes Bay Rd; adult/child $30/15; by appointment, late Oct-late Apr) A pricey but excellent private sculpture park featuring a stellar roster of NZ artists. Admission is by way of a two-hour guided tour; book ahead.

Walks

Ask at the i-SITE about the island's beautiful coastal walks (ranging from one to three hours) and the 3km Cross Island Walkway (from Onetangi to Rocky Bay). Other tracks traverse **Whakanewha Regional Park**, a haven for rare coastal birds and geckos, and the Royal Forest & Bird Protection Society's three reserves: **Onetangi** (Waiheke Rd), **Te Haahi-Goodwin** (Orapiu Rd) and **Atawhai Whenua** (Ocean View Rd).

Kayaking

Ross Adventures KAYAKING
(09-372 5550; www.kayakwaiheke.co.nz; Matiatia beach; half-/full-day trips $85/145, per hr hire from $25) It's the fervently held opinion of Ross that Waiheke offers kayaking every bit as good as the legendary Abel Tasman National Park. He should know – he's been offering guided kayak trips for over 20 years. Experienced sea kayakers can comfortably circumnavigate the island in four days, exploring hidden coves and sand spits inaccessible by land.

LOCAL KNOWLEDGE

WAIHEKE ISLAND *ZOË BELL*

Thirty years ago, Waiheke Island was home to an eclectic mix of outlaws who could not (or chose not to) live in 'normal' society: hippies and hermits, alternative healers and writers, potters and pot growers, and everything in between. Sometime in the late '80s, Waiheke was 'discovered', and it's quite a different place now. But even with all the changes – fine dining, vineyards and luxury holiday homes – Waiheke Island's identity and spirit are still undeniable. The beautiful weather remains the same, as do the phenomenal vistas, the lush bush and native birds, the chooks in your neighbours' backyards, the feeling that everything deserves to move a little slower (we call it 'Waiheke time'), the smell of honeysuckle, the crystal waters, the best fish and chips ever, the house I was born in and, probably, still a few pot growers. Waiheke was, and remains, like nowhere else on the planet.

Zoë Bell, stuntwoman & actor

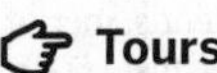

Tours

Ananda Tours FOOD & WINE
(☎09-372 7530; www.ananda.co.nz) Offers a gourmet wine and food tour ($110) and a wine connoisseurs' tour ($210). Small-group, informal tours can be customised, including visits to artists' studios.

Fullers FOOD & WINE
(☎09-367 9111; www.fullers.co.nz) Runs a Wine on Waiheke Tour (adult $115, 4½ hours, departs Auckland 1pm) that visits three of the island's top wineries and includes a platter of nibbles. Taste of Waiheke (adult $125, 5½ hours, departs Auckland 11am) also includes three wineries plus an olive grove and light lunch. There's also a 1½-hour Explorer Tour (adult/child $49/25, departs Auckland 10am, 11am and noon). All prices include the ferry and an all-day bus pass.

Waiheke Island Adventures FOOD & WINE
(☎09-372 6127; www.waihekeislandadventures.com) Scenic tours ($25), vineyard tours ($25), or Stony Batter tours ($35) in a 15-seater bus. Art and beach tours also available.

Waiheke Executive Transport WINE, CULTURAL
(☎0800 372 200; www.waiheketransport.co.nz) Highlights tours (from $15), wine tours (standard/premium $89/115) and art tours ($115).

Festivals & Events

Sculpture on the Gulf ARTS
(www.sculptureonthegulf.co.nz) A wacky 2km cliff-top sculpture walk, held every January in odd-numbered years.

Waiheke Blues Festival MUSIC
(www.waihekeblues.co.nz) Live blues played in various venues on the last weekend in August.

Sleeping

Waiheke is so popular in the summer holidays that many locals rent out their houses and bugger off elsewhere. You'll need to book ahead and even then there are very few bargains. Prices drop considerably in winter, especially midweek.

Tawa Lodge GUESTHOUSE **$$**
(☎09-372 9434; www.pungalodge.co.nz; 15 Tawa St; r $120, apt $175-240;) Between the self-contained cottage at the front and the apartment at the rear are three reasonably priced loft rooms sharing a small kitchen and bathroom. On a hot day there's a wonderfully languid vibe as guests spill out onto the deck.

Fossil Bay Lodge CABIN **$**
(☎09-372 8371; www.fossilbay.webs.com; 58 Korora Rd; s $45, d $75-120;) Three cutesy cabins open onto a courtyard facing the main building, which houses the toilets, a communal kitchen and living area and, on the other side, a Steiner kindergarten. Apart from the occasional squawking duck (or toddler), it's a peaceful place.

Punga Lodge B&B **$$**
(☎09-372 6675; www.pungalodge.co.nz; 223 Ocean View Rd; r $145-165, apt $140-200; @) Both the colourful en-suite rooms in the house and the self-contained garden units have access to decks looking onto a lush tropical garden. There's a spa, and prices include home-made breakfast, afternoon tea and wharf transfers.

Enclosure Bay B&B **$$$**
(☎09-372 8882; www.enclosurebay.co.nz; 9 Great Barrier Rd; r $325, ste $450) If you're going to shell out for a luxury B&B you're going to want something a little special, and that's certainly what's offered here. Each of the three guest rooms have sumptuous views and balconies, and the owners subscribe to the nothing's-too-much-trouble school of Kiwi hospitality.

Crescent Valley Eco Lodge GUESTHOUSE **$$**
(☎09-372 4321; www.waihekeecolodge.co.nz; 50 Crescent Rd East; r $145;) Surrounded by bush and peaceful gardens this little eco-retreat has only two tidy rooms, affable hosts and a spa pool under the stars. Bathrooms are private but not en suite.

Onetangi Beach Apartments APARTMENT **$$$**
(☎09-372 0003; www.onetangi.co.nz; 27 The Strand; apt $189-410;) Three different blocks of townhouses are clumped together, all offering modern, perfectly located, well-managed accommodation, along with a spa and sauna. Best (and priciest) are the Strand Apartments, with large decks overlooking the sea.

Hekerua Lodge HOSTEL **$**
(☎09-372 8990; www.hekerualodge.co.nz; 11 Hekerua Rd; sites from $18, dm $32-36, s $55, d $86-120; @) This secluded hostel is surrounded by native bush and has a barbecue, stone-tiled pool, sunny deck, casual lounge area and its own walking track. It's far from luxurious, but it has a laid-back feel, no doubt assisted by the serene images of Buddha scattered about.

Kina HOSTEL **$**
(☎09-372 8971; www.kinabackpackers.co.nz; 421 Seaview Rd; dm $27-31, s/tw $55/68, d $70-90; @) This old-style, well-positioned hostel has a large garden overlooking Onetangi Beach. The rooms are a little cell-like but the dorms have only two bunk beds and linen is provided.

Whakanewha Regional Park Campsite CAMPSITE **$**
(☎09-366 2000; www.arc.govt.nz; Gordons Rd; sites per adult/child $10/5) A pretty but basic campsite with toilets, gas barbecues and drinking water. Self-contained campervans can park in the neighbouring car park for a single night only (per adult/child $5/3).

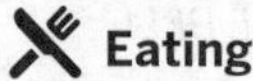

Eating

Priding itself on the finer things in life, Waiheke has some excellent eateries and, if you're lucky, the views will be enough to distract from the hole being bored into your hip pocket.

Te Whau WINERY **$$$**
(☎09-372 7191; www.tewhau.com; 218 Te Whau Dr; mains $42-44; ⊙lunch Fri-Sun, dinner Sat, extended summer) Perched on the end of Te Whau peninsula, this winery restaurant has exceptional views, food and service, and one of the finest wine lists you'll see in the country. Try its own impressive bordeaux blends, merlot, chardonnay and rosé for $3 per taste (11am to 5pm).

Dragonfired PIZZERIA **$**
(Little Oneroa Beach; mains $8-12; ⊙11am-8pm;) Specialising in what they describe as 'artisan woodfired food', this black caravan by the beach serves the three Ps: pizza, polenta plates and pocket bread. It's easily the best place for cheap eats on the island.

Island Thyme & Thymes Tables CAFE, RESTAURANT **$**
(☎09-372 3400; www.islandthyme.co.nz; 8 Miami Ave, Surfdale; Island Thyme light meals $9, Thymes Tables mains $36; ⊙Island Thyme breakfast & lunch, Thymes Tables dinner Tue-Sat) For pre-packaged gourmet meals, deli goodies, tempting pastries and excellent coffee, clock in on Island Thyme, downstairs. Thymes Tables, upstairs, is an elegant '*plat du jour*' restaurant offering only one or two dishes per evening, posted daily on the blackboard outside.

Wai Kitchen CAFE **$$**
(www.waikitchen.co.nz; 1/149 Ocean View Rd, Oneroa; mains $17-23; ⊙9am-4pm, extended summer) Why? Well firstly there's the lively menu abounding in Mediterranean and Asian flavours. Then there's the charming service and the breezy ambience of this glassed-in wedge, facing the *wai* (water).

Casita Miro SPANISH **$$**
(☎09-372 7854; www.mirovineyard.co.nz; 3 Brown St, Onetangi; dishes $19-40; ⊙lunch Wed-Sun, dinner Sat) A wrought-iron and glass pavilion backed with a Gaudi-esque mosaic garden

is the stage for a very entertaining troupe of servers who will guide you through the menu of delectable *racion tapas* – dishes bigger than regular tapas, designed to be shared.

Cable Bay WINERY **$$$**
(☎09-372 5889; www.cablebayvineyards.co.nz; 12 Nick Johnstone Dr; mains $42-45; ⌚lunch daily, dinner Thu-Sun, extended summer) Impressive ubermodern architecture, sculpture and beautiful views set the scene for this acclaimed restaurant. The food is sublime but if the budget won't stretch to a meal, stop in for a wine tasting (from $8) or a snack on the terrace.

Poderi Crisci ITALIAN **$$$**
(☎09-372 2148; www.podericrisci.co.nz; 205 Awaawaroa Rd; mains $32; ⌚lunch Fri-Sun) Owned by the Italian-born patriarch behind Parnell's Non Solo Pizza, Poderi Crisci has quickly gained a sterling reputation for its food, particularly its four-hour Sunday long lunches. Italian varietals and olives have been planted alongside the existing vines.

Delight TURKISH **$$**
(☎09-372 9035; www.delightcafe.co.nz; 29 Waikare Rd, Oneroa; mains $14-23, mezze $10-19; ⌚8am-3pm daily year-round, dinner Fri-Sun Nov-Mar) If you're bored with eggs Benedict, try one of the piquant breakfast tagines at this stylish cafe/mezze bar. Paninis, wraps and salads are served along with more traditional mezze, and the views are just as delicious.

Mudbrick WINERY **$$$**
(☎09-372 9050; www.mudbrick.co.nz; 126 Church Bay Rd; mains $41-49; ⌚lunch & dinner) Auckland and the gulf are at their glistening best when viewed from Mudbrick's picturesque veranda. The winery also offers tours and tastings (from $10, 10am to 5pm).

Stefano's PIZZERIA **$$**
(☎09-372 5309; www.stef.co.nz; 18 Hamilton Rd, Surfdale; mains $16-31; ⌚5.30-9.30pm Tue-Sun, extended summer) The best-smelling joint on Waiheke, serving pasta and pizza in the presence of a dodgy mural. It also does takeaways.

Ostend Market MARKET
(www.ostendmarketwaiheke.co.nz; War Memorial Hall, Belgium St; ⌚7.30am-1pm Sat) Stock up on fresh local produce and peruse local craft and second hand knick-knacks.

Drinking

Apart from the wineries, you'll find bars in Oneroa and pubs in Surfdale and Ostend.

Charlie Farley's BAR
(www.charliefarleys.co.nz; 21 The Strand, Onetangi; ⌚8.30am-late) Supping on a Waiheke wine or beer under the pohutukawas on the beach-gazing deck, it's easy to see why the locals love this place.

Information

Waiheke Island i-SITE (☎09-372 1234; www.waihekenz.com; 118 Ocean View Rd; ⌚9am-5pm) As well as the very helpful main office, there's a (usually unstaffed) counter in the ferry terminal at Matiatia Wharf.

Getting There & Away

Fullers (☎09-367 9111; www.fullers.co.nz; return adult/child $35/18; ⌚5.20am-11.45pm Mon-Fri, 6.25am-11.45pm Sat, 7am-9.30pm Sun) Has frequent passenger ferries from Auckland to Matiatia Wharf (on the hour from 9am to 5pm), some via Devonport.

Sealink (☎09-300 5900; www.sealink.co.nz; adult/child/car/motorcycle return $30/17/130/48; ⌚4.30am-6.30pm Mon-Thu, 4.30am-8pm Fri, 6am-6.30pm Sat & Sun) Runs car ferries to Kennedy Point, mainly from Half Moon Bay (east Auckland) but some leave from Wynyard Wharf in the city. The ferry runs at least every two hours and takes 45 minutes (booking essential).

360 Discovery (☎0800 360 3472; www.360discovery.co.nz) You can pick up the 360 Discovery tourist ferry at Orapiu on its journey between Auckland and Coromandel Town. However Orapiu is quite remote and not served by buses.

Getting Around

Bike

Various bicycle routes are outlined in the *Bike Waiheke!* brochure, available from the wharf and the i-SITE; be prepared for a lot of hills.

Waiheke Bike Hire (☎09-372 7937; Matiatia Wharf) Hires mountain bikes (half-/full day $25/35) from their base near the wharf and at the Oneroa i-SITE.

Bus

The island has regular bus services, starting from Matiatia Wharf and heading through Oneroa (adult/child $1.50/80c, five minutes) on their way to all the main settlements, as far west as Onetangi (adult/child $4.20/2.40, 30 minutes); see **MAXX** (☎09-366 6400; www.maxx.co.nz) for timetables. A day pass (adult/child $8.20/5) is available from the Fullers counter at Matiatia Wharf.

Car, Motorbike & Scooter

Fun Rentals (☎09-372 8001; www.funrentals.co.nz; 14a Belgium St, Ostend; per day car/scooter/4WD from $59/49/59) If you're staying overnight, this company has the advantage of offering 24-hour rental periods (as opposed to a calendar day); transfers from the ferry are included. They offer unlimited kilometres and an insurance excess of $1500, falling to $1000 for over 25-year-olds.

Rent Me Waiheke (☎09-372 3339; www.rentmewaiheke.co.nz; 14 Ocean View Rd, Matiatia; per calendar day cars/scooters $59/49) Unlimited kilometres; excess $3000, dropping to $2500 for over 25s.

Waiheke Auto Rentals (☎09-372 8998; www.waihekerentals.co.nz; Matiatia Wharf; per calendar day car & scooter from $59, motorbike & 4WD from $79) Excess $1500, dropping to $1000 if you're over 25 years old. There's an additional charge of 65c per kilometre for cars or 4WDs.

Waiheke Rental Cars (☎09-372 8635; www.waihekerentalcars.co.nz; Matiatia Wharf; per calendar day car/4WD from $59/79) Unlimited kilometres; excess $3000, dropping to $2500 for over 25s.

Taxi

Waiheke Independent Taxis (☎0800 300 372)
Waiheke Taxi Co-op (☎09-372 8038)
Waiheke Taxis (☎09-372 3000)

Rotoroa Island

From 1911 to 2005 the only people to have access to this blissful little island on the far side of Waiheke were the alcoholics and drug addicts who came (or were sentenced) here to dry out – and the Salvation Army staff who cared for them. In 2011, after 100 years, 82-hectare **Rotoroa** (☎0800 76 86 76; www.rotoroa.org.nz; access fee $5) opened to the public, giving visitors access to three sandy swimming beaches and the social history and art displays in the restored buildings of the former treatment centre. There are also three well-appointed, wildly retro holiday homes for rent ($250 to $500).

ℹ Getting There & Away

360 Discovery (☎0800 360 3472; www.360discovery.co.nz; adult/child from Auckland $55/30, from Orapiu $21/13) From Auckland the ferry takes 75 minutes, stopping at Orapiu on Waiheke Island en route. There are four boats per week from Labour Day to Easter (daily in January) and two boats per week over the cooler months.

Tiritiri Matangi Island

This magical, 220-hectare, predator-free **island** (www.tiritirimatangi.org.nz) is home to the tuatara (a prehistoric lizard) and lots of endangered native birds, including the very rare and colourful takahe. Other birds that can be seen here include the bellbird, stitchbird, saddleback, whitehead, kakariki, kokako, little spotted kiwi, brown teal, NZ robin, fernbird and penguins; 78 different species have been sighted in total. The saddleback was once close to extinction with just 150 left, but now there are more than 600 on Tiritiri alone. To experience the dawn chorus in full flight, stay overnight at the **DOC bunkhouse** (☎09-425 7812; www.doc.govt.nz; adult/child $30/20); book well ahead and ensure there's room on the ferry.

The island was sold to the Crown in 1841, deforested and farmed until the 1970s. Since 1984 hundreds of volunteers have planted 250,000 native trees and the forest cover has regenerated. An 1864 lighthouse stands on the eastern end of the island.

ℹ Getting There & Away

360 Discovery (☎0800 360 3472; www.360discovery.co.nz; return Auckland/Gulf Harbour $66/49; ⏲Wed-Sun) Book a guided walk ($5) with your ferry ticket; the guides know where all the really cool birds hang out.

Motuora Island

Halfway between Tiritiri Matangi and Kawau, Motuora has 80 predator-free hectares and is used as a kiwi 'crèche'. There's a wharf on the west coast of the island, but you'll need your own boat to get here. The **DOC campsite** (☎027-492 8586; www.doc.govt.nz; adult/child $6/3) requires bookings and provides toilets, cold showers and water. There's also a bach that sleeps five ($52); bring your own linen and food.

Kawau Island

POP 300

Kawau Island lies 50km north of Auckland off the Mahurangi Peninsula. There are few proper roads through the island, the residents relying mainly on boats. The main attraction is **Mansion House** (adult/child $4/2;

noon-2pm), an impressive wooden manor extended from an 1845 structure by Governor George Grey, who purchased the island in 1862. It houses a fine collection of Victoriana, including some of Grey's effects, and is surrounded by the original exotic gardens. A set of short walks (10 minutes to two hours) are signposted from Mansion House, leading to beaches, the old copper mine and a lookout; download DOC's *Kawau Island Historic Reserve map* (www.doc.govt.nz).

Sleeping & Eating

Kawau Lodge B&B $$$
(09-422 8831; www.kawaulodge.co.nz; North Cove; s $160, d $210-245) This eco-conscious boutique hotel has its own jetty, wraparound decks and views. Meals ($10 to $60) can be arranged, as can excursions.

Mansion House Cafe Restaurant
(09-422 8903; lunch $12-18, dinner $18-28; hrs vary) If you haven't packed a picnic, this idyllically situated eatery will be a welcome relief, serving all-day breakfasts, sandwiches and hearty evening meals. It's also your only option for stocking up on bread, milk, ice and pre-ordered newspapers.

Getting There & Away

Kawau Water Taxis (0800 111 616; www.kawauwatertaxis.co.nz) Daily ferries from Sandspit to Kawau (adult/child return $50/26) and a water-taxi service (minimum charge $130). The Super Cruise (adult/child $68/30, barbecue lunch $22/11) departs Sandspit at 10.30am and circles the island, delivering the post to 75 different wharves.

Great Barrier Island

POP 860

Named Aotea (meaning cloud) by the Maori and Great Barrier (due to its position at the edge of the Hauraki Gulf) by James Cook, this rugged and exceptionally beautiful place falls in behind South, North and Stewart as NZ's fourth-largest island (285 sq km). It closely resembles the Coromandel Peninsula to which it was once joined, and like the Coromandel it was once a mining, logging and whaling centre. Those industries have long gone and today two-thirds of the island is publicly owned and managed by DOC.

Great Barrier has unspoilt beaches, hot springs, old kauri dams, a forest sanctuary and a network of tramping tracks. Because there are no possums on the island, the native bush is lush.

Although only 88km from Auckland, Great Barrier seems a world – and a good many years – away. The island has no supermarket, no electricity supply (only private solar, wind and diesel generators) and no main drainage (only septic tanks). Many roads are unsealed and petrol costs are high. Mobile-phone reception is very limited and there are no banks, ATMs or street lights.

From around mid-December to mid-January is the peak season, so make sure you book transport, accommodation and activities well in advance.

Tryphena is the main settlement, 4km from the ferry wharf at Shoal Bay. Strung out along several kilometres of coastal road, it consists of a few dozen houses and a handful of shops and accommodation places. From the wharf it's 3km to Mulberry Grove, and then another 1km over the headland to Pa Beach and the Stonewall Store.

The airport is at **Claris**, 12km north of Tryphena, a small settlement with a general store, bottle shop, laundrette, garage, pharmacy and cafe.

Whangaparapara is an old timber town and the site of the island's 19th-century whaling activities. **Port Fitzroy** is the other main harbour on the west coast, a one-hour drive from Tryphena. These four main settlements have fuel available.

Activities

Water Sports

The beaches on the west coast are safe, but care needs to be taken on the surf-pounded eastern beaches. **Medlands Beach**, with its wide sweep of white sand, is one of the most beautiful and accessible beaches on the island. Remote **Whangapoua**, in the north-east, requires more effort to get to, while **Kaitoke**, **Awana Bay** and **Harataonga** on the east coast are also worth a visit.

Okiwi Bar has an excellent right-hand break, while Awana has both left- and right-hand breaks. Pohutukawa trees shelter the pretty bays around Tryphena.

Diving is excellent, with shipwrecks, pinnacles, lots of fish and more than 33m visibility at some times of the year.

Hooked on Barrier DIVING, FISHING
(09-429 0740; www.hookedonbarrier.co.nz; 89 Hector-Sanderson Rd; half-/full-day charter $700/1200) Hooked on Barrier hires out diving, snorkelling, fishing, surfing and

Great Barrier Island

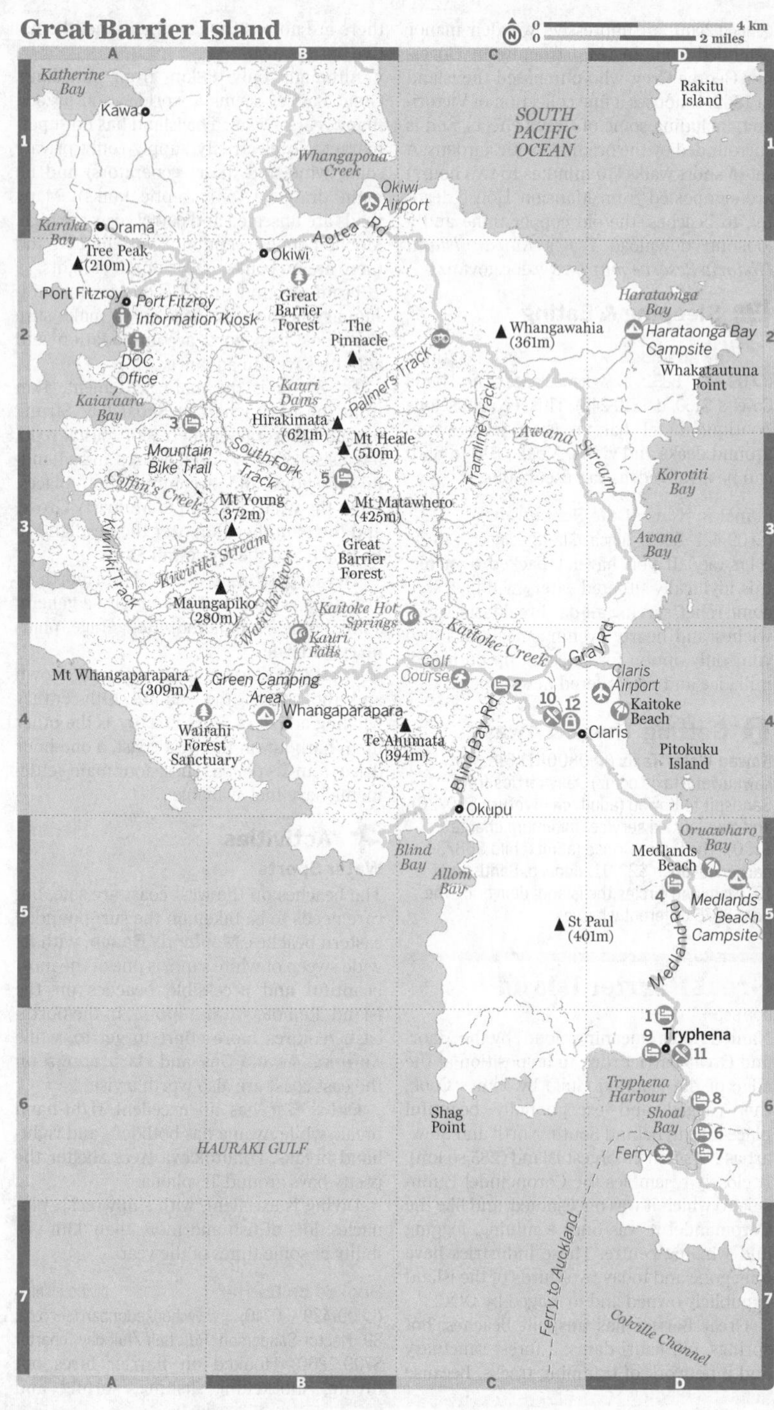

Great Barrier Island

Activities, Courses & Tours

Hooked on Barrier .... (see 12)

Sleeping

1 Aotea Lodge D6
2 Crossroads Lodge C4
3 Kaiaraara Hut A2
4 Medlands Beach Backpackers & Villas D5
5 Mt Heale Hut B3
6 Pigeons Lodge D6
7 Shoal Bay Lodge D6
8 Sunset Waterfront Lodge D6
9 Tipi & Bob's Waterfront Lodge D6

Eating

10 Claris Texas C4
Currach Irish Pub .... (see 11)
Tipi & Bob's Waterfront Lodge ... (see 9)
11 Wild Rose D6

Shopping

12 Aotea Community Art Gallery C4

kayaking gear, as well as running fishing, diving and sightseeing charters.

Mountain Biking

With rugged scenery and relatively little traffic on the roads, mountain biking is a popular activity here. There's a designated 25km ride beginning on Blind Bay Rd, Okupu, winding beneath the Ahumata cliffs before crossing Whangaparapara Rd and beginning the 15km Forest Rd ride through beautiful forest to Port Fitzroy. Cycling on other DOC walking tracks is prohibited.

Tramping

The island's very popular walking tracks are outlined in DOC's free *Great Barrier Island (Aotea Island)* booklet. Before setting out, make sure you're properly equipped with water and food, and be prepared for both sunny and wet weather.

The most popular easy walk is the 45-minute **Kaitoke Hot Springs Track**, starting from Whangaparapara Rd and leading to natural hot springs in a bush stream. Check the temperature before getting in and don't put your head under the water.

Windy Canyon, which is only a 15-minute walk from Aotea Rd, has spectacular rock outcrops and affords great views of the island. From Windy Canyon, an excellent trail continues for another two to three hours through scrubby forest to Hirakimata (Mt Hobson, 621m), the highest point on the island, with views across the Hauraki Gulf and Coromandel. Near the top of the mountain are lush forests and a few mature kauri trees that survived the logging days. From Hirakimata it is 40 minutes south to Mt Heale Hut or two hours west through forest and past a kauri driving dam to Kaiaraara Hut, where it's another 45 minutes on to Port Fitzroy.

A more challenging tramp is the hilly **Tramline Track** (five hours), which starts on Aotea Rd and follows old logging tramlines to Whangaparapara Harbour. The initial stages of this track are not maintained and in some parts the clay becomes slippery after rain.

Of a similar length, but flatter and easier walking, is the 11km **Harataonga Coastal Walk** (five hours), which heads from Harataonga Bay to Whangapoua.

Many other trails traverse the forest, taking between 30 minutes and five hours. The **Aotea Track** combines bits of other paths into a three-day walk, staying overnight in each of the huts.

See Great Barrier Island's Getting Around information for details of shuttle buses to and from the trailheads.

Sleeping

Unless you're camping, Great Barrier isn't a cheap place to stay. At pretty much every price point you'll pay more than you would for a similar place elsewhere. Rates drop considerably, however, in the off-season. **Island Accommodation** (☎09-429 0995; www.islandaccommodation.co.nz) offers a booking service, which is particularly handy for finding self-contained houses for longer stays.

Aotea Lodge APARTMENT **$$**
(☎09-429 0628; www.aotealodge.com; 41 Medland Rd; units $120-210) A well-tended, sunny garden surrounds these reasonably priced units, perched on the hill just above Tryphena. They range from a two-bedroom house to an unusual mezzanine unit loaded with bunks, but each has its own cooking facilities.

Shoal Bay Lodge APARTMENT **$$**
(☎09-429 0890; www.shoalbaylodge.co.nz; 145 Shoal Bay Rd; apt $150-240) Hidden among the trees these comfy self-contained apartments offer sea views, bird song, solar power and environmentally friendly cleaning products. Best is the three-bedroom lodge with its sunset-guzzling deck.

Sunset Waterfront Lodge MOTEL $$$
(☎09-429 0051; www.sunsetlodge.co.nz; Mulberry Grove; apt $195-300) Gaze across the lawn to the sea from the attractive studio units, or fight over who's going to get the pointy room in the two-bedroom A-frame villas. There's a small shop and cafe next door.

Pigeons Lodge APARTMENT $$
(☎09-429 0437; www.pigeonslodge.co.nz; 179 Shoal Bay Rd; apt $135) Above the water, south of Tryphena, Pigeons has two tidy self-contained units near the top of the drive, sharing a deck and a barbecue. The owners lead a double life as real-estate agents, which is handy if you fall in love with the island and fancy staying.

Medlands Beach Backpackers & Villas HOSTEL $
(☎09-429 0320; www.medlandsbeach.com; 9 Mason Rd; dm $35, d/units from $70/120) Chill out in the garden of this house on the hill, overlooking beautiful Medlands Beach. The backpackers' area is simple, with a little double cabin for romantic budgeteers at a slight remove from the rest. The self-contained houses sleep up to six.

Tipi & Bob's Waterfront Lodge MOTEL $$$
(☎09-429 0550; www.waterfrontlodge.co.nz; 38 Puriri Bay Rd; units $195-350) West of Tryphena, these smart but overpriced motel-style units have some wonderful sea views and very helpful owners. The complex includes a restaurant and bar.

Crossroads Lodge HOSTEL $
(☎09-429 0889; www.xroadslodge.com; 1 Blind Bay Rd; dm/s/d $30/50/75; @ 📶) This low-key backpackers is 2km from the airfield and close to forest walks and hot springs. Mountain bikes can be hired, and golf clubs can be borrowed to play on the nearby nine-hole golf course.

Kaiaraara & Mt Heale Huts HUT $
(www.doc.govt.nz; dm per adult/child $15/5) These DOC huts in the Great Barrier Forest have bunk beds, cold running water, chemical toilets and a kitchen/dining area. Bring your own sleeping bag and cooking/eating equipment and book online. Mt Heale Hut sleeps 20 people and has a gas cooker, but Kaiaraara Hut (which sleeps 28) doesn't.

DOC Campsites CAMPSITE $
(☎09-379 6476; www.doc.govt.nz; site per adult/child $10/5) There are campsites at Harataonga Bay, Medlands Beach, Akapoua Bay, Whangapoua, The Green (Whangaparapara) and Awana Bay. All have basic facilities, including water, cold showers (none at The Green), toilets and a food preparation shelter. You need to bring your own gas cooking stove as open fires are prohibited. Book in advance online as the sites are not staffed.

Eating & Drinking

In summer, most places are open daily but for the rest of the year the hours can be sporadic. There's a monthly guide as to what's open when posted on www.thebarrier.co.nz but it still pays to call ahead for an evening meal.

Self-caterers will find small stores in Tryphena, Claris, Whangaparapara and Port Fitzroy.

Wild Rose CAFE $
(☎09-429 0905; Blackwell Dr; mains $5-18; ⏲8.30am-4pm) Wild Rose does the best impersonation of an Auckland cafe on the island, albeit with the addition of local crowd-pleasers such as toasted sandwiches and burgers. It uses free-range, organic and local produce whenever possible.

Claris Texas CAFE $
(129 Hector Sanderson Rd; mains $5-13; ⏲8am-4pm; @ 📶) While it doesn't live up to the promise of its quirky name, this is the best gap-filler in the centre of the island, serving cooked breakfasts, nachos, salads and pies.

Tipi & Bob's Waterfront Lodge RESTAURANT $$$
(☎09-429 0550; www.waterfrontlodge.co.nz; 38 Puriri Bay Rd; mains $32-33; ⏲breakfast & dinner) Serving simple but satisfying meals in large portions, this popular haunt has an inviting deck overlooking the harbour. There's a cheaper pub menu in the bar.

Currach Irish Pub PUB $$
(☎09-429 0211; Blackwell Dr; mains $14-28; ⏲from 4pm) This lively, child-friendly pub has a changing menu of seafood, steak and burgers, and is the island's social centre. Rub shoulders with local musos on jam nights.

Shopping

Aotea Community Art Gallery ARTS & CRAFTS
(80 Hector Sanderson Rd; ⏲10.30am-3.30pm) Nothing if not eclectic, this showcase for

the island's artsy fraternity sells everything from paintings to handmade soap, to baby booties, to cross-stitched Virgin Marys.

Information

There's an information kiosk at the GBI Rent-A-Car office in Claris. Claris Texas cafe has internet access.

DOC Office (☎09-429 0044; www.doc.govt.nz; ⏲8am-4.30pm Mon-Fri) Call in for brochures, maps, weather information and to sign the intentions book for longer walks.

Great Barrier Island i-SITE (www.greatbarriernz.com; Claris Airport; ⏲11am-noon Mon, Wed & Fri, 8am-2.30pm Sat, extended in summer) Stocks brochures including their own *Great Barrier Island* pamphlet, which is full of useful information and has a handy map.

Port Fitzroy Information Kiosk (☎09-429 0848; www.thebarrier.co.nz; ⏲9.30am-3pm Mon-Sat) Privately run kiosk that publishes the *Great Barrier Island Visitor Information Guide*.

Getting There & Away

Air

Fly My Sky (☎09-256 7026; www.flymysky.co.nz; one way adult/child $104/79) Flies at least three times a day from Auckland. Cheaper flights are available if you travel to the island on a Sunday or leave on a Friday ($76), and there's a special return fare for flying one way and ferrying the other (adult/child $179/159).

Great Barrier Airlines (☎09-275 9120; www.greatbarrierairlines.co.nz; one way standard/advance $124/99) Departs from Auckland Domestic Airport (at least twice daily) and North Shore Aerodrome (at least daily) for the 30-minute flight to Claris. In summer they also stop at Okiwi, as well as offering on-demand flights to Whangarei and Whitianga.

Sunair (☎0800 786 847; www.sunair.co.nz; one way $160) Flies from Whitianga twice daily.

Boat

Fullers (☎09-367 9111; www.fullers.co.nz; adult/child one way $75/45) Runs the fastest services (2½ hours) from Auckland's Ferry Building to Shoal Bay and Port Fitzroy from mid-December to the end of January, as well as on the Easter long weekend.

Sealink (☎09-300 5900; www.sealink.co.nz; return adult/child/car/motorcycle $120/79/370/100) The main provider, running car ferries from three to five days a week from Wynyard Wharf in Auckland to Tryphena's Shoal Bay (six hours).

Getting Around

Most roads are narrow and windy but even small hire cars can handle the unsealed sections. Many of the accommodation places will pick you up from the airport or wharf if notified in advance.

Aotea Car Rentals (☎0800 426 832; www.aoteacarrentals.co.nz; Mulberry Grove) Hires out cars (from $60), 4WDs (from $75) and vans (from $99). Rental clients get to use the associated Great Barrier Travel trampers' shuttles for free.

GBI Rent-A-Car (☎09-429 0062; www.greatbarrierisland.co.nz; 67 Hector Sanderson Rd) Has a somewhat battered fleet of cars starting at $55 and 4WDs from $85. They also operate shuttle services from Claris to Tryphena ($20), Medlands ($15), Whangaparapara ($20) and Port Fitzroy ($30, minimum four passengers), as well as trampers' shuttles. There's a $5 flagfall for solo passengers; call ahead to book.

Great Barrier Travel (☎09-429 0474; www.greatbarriertravel.co.nz; tickets from $10) Runs shuttles between Tryphena and Claris (timed to meet all the planes and boats), a daily shuttle from Claris to Port Fitzroy, and transfers to and from the walking tracks. Call ahead to confirm times and to book.

WEST AUCKLAND

West Auckland epitomises rugged: wild black-sand beaches, bush-shrouded ranges, and mullet-haired, black-T-shirt-wearing 'Westies'. The latter is just one of several stereotypes of the area's denizens. Others include the back-to-nature hippie, the eccentric bohemian artist and the dope-smoking surfer dude, all attracted to a simple life at the edge of the bush.

Add to the mix Croatian immigrants, earning the fertile fields at the base of the Waitakere Ranges the nickname 'Dallie Valley' after the Dalmatian coast where many hailed from. These pioneering families planted grapes and made wine, founding one of NZ's major industries.

Titirangi

POP 3200

This little village marks the end of Auckland's suburban sprawl and is a good place to spot all of the stereotypes mentioned above over a caffe latte, fine wine or cold beer. Once home to NZ's greatest modern painter, Colin McCahon, there remains an artsy feel to the place. Titirangi means

'Fringe of Heaven' – an apt name for the gateway to the Waitakere Ranges, or indeed a hair salon. This is the last stop for petrol and ATMs on your way west.

Sights

McCahon House MUSEUM
(www.mccahonhouse.org.nz; 67 Otitori Bay Rd; admission $5; ⏱10am-2pm Wed, Sat & Sun) It's a mark of the esteem in which Colin McCahon is held that the house he lived and painted in during the 1950s has been opened to the public as a minimuseum. The swish pad next door is home to the artist lucky enough to win the McCahon Arts Residency. Look for the signposts pointing down Park Rd, just before you reach Titirangi village.

FREE **Lopdell House Gallery** GALLERY
(www.lopdell.org.nz; 418 Titirangi Rd; ⏱10am-4.30pm) An excellent modern art gallery housed in the former Hotel Titirangi (1930), on the edge of the village, with a theatre and Italian bakehouse attached.

Sleeping & Eating

Fringe of Heaven B&B **$$$**
(☎09-817 8682; www.fringeofheaven.com; 4 Otitori Bay Rd; r $225-265) Surrounded by native bush, this Frank Lloyd Wright–inspired house offers glorious views over Manukau Harbour, an outdoor bath, glowworms in the garden and a songbird choir – all within 20 minutes of the city centre.

Hardware Cafe CAFE **$$**
(404 Titirangi Rd; brunch $10-18, dinner $22-28; ⏱6am-4.30pm Sun-Tue, 6am-late Wed-Sat) Great for Westie-watching, this popular licensed cafe serves delicious, reasonably priced cooked breakfasts and lunches along with a tempting array of counter food. More substantial evening meals start from $22.

Waitakere Ranges

This 160-sq-km wilderness was covered in kauri until the mid-19th century, when logging claimed most of the giant trees. A few stands of ancient kauri and other mature natives survive amid the dense bush of the regenerating rainforest, which is now protected inside the Waitakere Ranges Regional Park. Bordered to the west by wildly beautiful beaches on the Tasman Sea, the park's rugged terrain makes an excellent day trip from Auckland.

Sights & Activities

Arataki VISITORS CENTRE
(☎09-817 0077; www.arc.govt.nz; Scenic Dr; ⏱9am-5pm) As well as providing information on the 250km of trails within the park, this impressive, child-friendly centre, with its Maori carvings (some prodigiously well hung) and spectacular views, is an attraction in its own right. The carvings that greet visitors at the entrance depict the ancestors of the Kawerau *iwi*. You can also book here for several basic campsites (adult/child $5/3) within the park – toilets are provided but nothing much else.

A 1.6km nature trail opposite the centre leads visitors past labelled native species, including mature kauri.

Hillary Trail & other tracks TRAMPING
(www.arc.govt.nz/hillarytrail) Arataki Vistor Centre is the starting point for this 70km trail, opened in 2010 to honour NZ's most famous son, Everest-conqueror Sir Edmund Hillary. It can be tackled in stages or in its four-day entirety, staying at campsites along the way. Walkers head to the coast at Huia then tick off all the iconic Westie beaches: Whatipu, Karekare, Piha and, Sir Ed's favourite, remote Anawhata. From here you can continue up the coast through Te Henga to Muriwai or head through bush to the Cascades Kauri area to end at Swanson train station.

Other noted walks in the park include the **Kitekite Track** (1.8km, 30 minutes one way), the **Fairy Falls Track** (5.6km, 2½-hour loop) and the **Auckland City Walk** (1.5km, one-hour loop).

Rain Forest Express NARROW-GAUGE RAILWAY
(☎09-302 8028; www.watercare.co.nz; 280 Scenic Dr; 2.5hr trip adult/child $25/12) Departs from Jacobsons' Depot and follows an old logging track through several tunnels deep into the bush. You'll need to book well ahead; check the website for the schedule. Less regular are the 3½-hour twilight trips (adult/child $28/14), offering glimpses of glowworms and cave weta.

Waitakere Tramline Society NARROW-GAUGE RAILWAY
(☎09-818 4946; www.waitakeretramline.org.nz; adult/child $15/5) Runs four scenic trips every Sunday that pass through a glowworm tunnel en route to the Waitakere Falls and Dam. Trips start from the end of Christian Rd, which runs south of Swanson station.

LOCAL KNOWLEDGE

HILLARY TRAIL *PETER HILLARY*

My family grew up loving Auckland's wild west coast, where the Tasman Sea pounds the black-sand beaches and black-back gulls ride the westerlies. Our family has walked and explored and lived out here for nearly a century and this is also where we came to grieve after my mother and sister were killed in 1975, where the invigorating salty air and the marvellous wild vistas to the Tasman Sea worked like a balm for our broken hearts. My father would come here to dream up and then prepare for new expeditionary challenges. It seemed the right sort of environment for someone like him: not a passive coastline, but active and exciting, with huge cliffs, crashing waves, thick bush and a tantalising far-away horizon.

Peter Hillary, mountaineer & explorer

AWOL Canyoning Adventures CANYONING (☎09-834 0501; www.awoladventures.co.nz; ⊙half-/full day $145/175) Offers plenty of slippery, slidey, wet fun in Piha Canyon, including glowworm-illuminated night trips ($165); transfers from Auckland are included.

Canyonz CANYONING (☎0800 422 696; www.canyonz.co.nz; trips $195) Runs canyoning trips from Auckland to the Blue Canyon, which has a series of 18 waterfalls ranging from 2m to 25m in height.

Karekare

Few stretches of sand have more personality than Karekare. Those prone to metaphysical musings inevitably settle on descriptions such as 'spiritual' and 'brooding'. Perhaps history has left its imprint: in 1825 it was the site of a ruthless massacre of the local Kawerau *iwi* by Ngapuhi invaders. Wild and gorgeously undeveloped, this famous beach has been the setting for onscreen moments both high- and lowbrow, from Oscar-winner *The Piano* to *Xena, Warrior Princess*.

From the car park the quickest route to the black-sand beach involves wading through a stream. Karekare rates as one of the most dangerous beaches in the country, with strong surf and ever-present rips, so don't even think about swimming unless the beach is being patrolled by lifeguards (usually only in summer). Pearl Jam singer Eddie Vedder nearly drowned here while visiting Neil Finn's Karekare pad.

Follow the road over the bridge and up along Lone Kauri Rd for 100m, where a short track leads to the pretty **Karekare Falls**. This leafy picnic spot is the start of several walking tracks.

Karekare has no shops of any description and no public transport. To get here take Scenic Dr and Piha Rd until you reach the well-signposted turn-off to Karekare Rd.

Piha

If you notice an Auckland surfer dude with a faraway look, chances are they're day-dreaming about Piha... or just stoned. This beautifully rugged, iron-sand beach has long been a favourite for refugees from the city's stresses – whether for day trips, weekend teenage parties or family holidays.

Although Piha is popular, it's also incredibly dangerous, with wild surf and strong undercurrents; so much so that it's spawned its own popular reality TV show, *Piha Rescue*. If you don't want to inadvertently star in it, always swim between the flags, where lifeguards can provide help if you get into trouble.

Piha may be bigger and more populated than Karekare, but there's still no supermarket, liquor shop, bank or petrol station, although there is a small general store that doubles as a cafe, takeaway shop and post office.

Sights & Activities

The view of the coast as you drive down Piha Rd is spectacular. Perched on its haunches near the centre of the beach is **Lion Rock** (101m), whose 'mane' glows golden in the evening light. It's actually the eroded core of an ancient volcano and a Maori *pa* site. A path at the south end of the beach takes you to some great lookouts. At low tide you can walk south along the beach and watch the surf shooting through a ravine in another large rock known as the **Camel**. A little further along, the waves crash through the **Gap** and form a safe swimming hole. A small colony of blue penguins nests at the beach's north end.

For surfboard hire, refer to the Piha Store and Piha Surf Shop listings.

Sleeping & Eating

TOP CHOICE Piha Beachstay – Jandal Palace HOSTEL $
(☎09-812 8381; www.pihabeachstay.co.nz; 38 Glenesk Rd; dm $33, r $86-120; @📶) Attractive and ecofriendly, just like the surf lifesaver who runs it, this wood-and-glass lodge has extremely smart facilities. It's 1km from the beach but there's a little stream at the bottom of the property and bushwalks nearby. In winter an open fire warms the large communal lounge.

Black Sands Lodge APARTMENT $$
(☎021 969 924; www.pihabeach.co.nz/Black-Sands-Lodge.htm; Beach Valley Rd; cabin $130, apt $180-220; 📶) These two modern conjoined apartments with private decks match their prime location with attractive touches such as stereos and DVD players. The cabin is kitted out in a 1950s Kiwiana bach style and shares a bathroom with the main house. Bikes and wi-fi are free for guests, and in-room massage and lavish dinners can be arranged on request. It's gay-friendly too.

Piha Domain Motor Camp CAMPSITE $
(☎09-812 8815; www.pihabeach.co.nz; 21 Seaview Rd; sites from $15, s/d cabin $50/60; 📶) Smack-bang on the beach, this well-kept campsite is great for those seeking an old-fashioned, cheap-as-chips, no-frills, family holiday. To keep unruly teens at bay, under 20s must be accompanied by parents. The cabins are tiny.

Piha Surf Accommodation CABIN $
(☎09-812 8723; www.pihasurf.co.nz; 122 Seaview Rd; caravans & cabins $60-90) Each basic but charmingly tatty caravan has its own linen, TV, fridge, cooker and long-drop toilet, and they share a very simple shower. The private cabins have the same rudimentary bathroom arrangement but are a more comfortable option.

Piha Cafe CAFE $$
(www.thepihacafe.co.nz; 20 Seaview Rd; mains $13-23; ⏲9am-4pm Wed & Thu, 9am-7pm Fri-Sun) Big-city standards mesh seamlessly with sand-between-toes informality at this attractive ecofriendly cafe. Cooked breakfasts and crispy pizzas provide sustenance for a hard day's surfing – then afterwards, head back here for a cold beverage on the deck.

Piha Store BAKERY $
(www.pihastore.co.nz; Seaview Rd; snacks $2-10) Call in for pies and other baked goods, groceries and ice creams. The attached Lion Rock Surf Shop rents surfboards (two hours/half-day/day $15/25/35) and body boards ($10/20/25).

Shopping

West Coast Gallery ARTS & CRAFTS
(www.westcoastgallery.co.nz; Seaview Rd; ⏲10am-5pm Wed-Sun) The work of more than 180 local artists is sold from this small not-for-profit gallery next to the Piha fire station.

Piha Surf Shop OUTDOOR EQUIPMENT
(www.pihasurf.co.nz; 122 Seaview Rd; ⏲8am-5pm) A family-run venture, with well-known surfboard designer Mike Jolly selling his wares and wife Pam selling a small range of crafts. Surfboards (three hours/day $25/35), wet suits ($8/15) and boogie boards ($15/25) can be hired and private surfing lessons can be arranged.

Getting There & Away

There's no public transport to Piha, but **NZ Surf'n'Snow Tours** (☎09-828 0426; www.newzealandsurftours.com; one way $25, return trip incl surfing gear $99) provides shuttles when the surf's up.

Te Henga (Bethells Beach)

Breathtaking Bethells Beach is reached by taking Te Henga Rd at the northern end of Scenic Dr. It's another raw, black-sand beach with surf, windswept dunes and walks, such as the popular one over giant sand dunes to Lake Wainamu (starting near the bridge on the approach to the beach).

Kumeu & Around

West Auckland's main wine-producing area still has some vineyards owned by the original Croatian families who kick-started NZ's wine industry. The fancy eateries that have mushroomed in recent years have done little to dint the relaxed farmland feel to the region, but everything to encourage an afternoon's indulgence on the way back from the beach or the hot pools. And unlike Waiheke Island, most cellars here offer free tastings.

Eating & Drinking

Tasting Room TAPAS $$
(☎09-412 6454; www.thetastingshed.com; 609 SH16; dishes $5-24; ⊙4-9pm Wed & Thu, noon-10pm Fri-Sun) Complementing its rural aspect with rustic chic decor, this slick eatery conjures up delicious dishes designed to be shared. It's not exactly tapas as the menu strays from Spain, appropriating flavours from Asia, the Middle East, Croatia, Serbia, Italy and France.

Dante's PIZZERIA $$
(www.dantespizza.co.nz; 316 Main Rd, Huapai; pizza $16-24; ⊙from 3.30pm Wed-Sun;) Widely regarded as Auckland's best pizzeria, this tiny takeaway is the only one in NZ to carry an official accreditation with the True Neapolitan Pizza Association.

Bees Online CAFE $$
(☎09-411 7953; www.beesonline.co.nz; 791 SH16, Waimauku; mains $19-32; ⊙10am-5pm Wed-Sun) At this architecturally impressive facility you can watch the busy bees at work, safely behind glass, and then taste the results in the store. The cafe showcases honey and native bush ingredients. Mum and dad might even get a coffee in peace while the kids play spot-the-queen in the hive.

Soljans Estate WINERY
(www.soljans.co.nz; 366 SH16; mains $19-33; ⊙tastings 9am-5.30pm, cafe 9.30am-3pm) One of the pioneering Croat-Kiwi family vineyards, Soljans has a wonderful (albeit atmosphere-deficient) cafe offering brunch, Dalmatian-style squid and Vintner's platters crammed with Mediterranean treats.

Hallertau BREWERY
(☎09-412 5555; www.hallertau.co.nz; 1171 Coatesville-Riverhead Hwy, Riverhead; mains $22-37; ⊙11am-midnight) If you'd rather hit the hops than Kumeu's wines, Hallertau offers tasting paddles of five of its microbrews ($14), served on a vine-covered terrace edging the restaurant.

Riverhead PUB
(www.theriverhead.co.nz; cnr Queen & York Sts, Riverhead; mains $15-36; ⊙11am-late Mon-Sat, 9am-late Sun) A blissful terrace, shaded by oak trees and overlooking the river, makes this 1857 hotel a memorable drink stop, even if the menu doesn't quite live up to its gastropub ambitions. Make a day of it, with a boat cruise (p80) from the city to the pub's own jetty.

Kumeu River WINERY
(www.kumeuriver.co.nz; 550 SH16; ⊙9am-5pm Mon-Fri, 11am-5pm Sat) Owned by the Brajkovich family, this winery produces one of NZ's best chardonnays, among other things.

Coopers Creek WINERY
(www.cooperscreek.co.nz; 601 SH16, Huapai; ⊙10.30am-5.30pm) Buy a bottle, spread out a picnic in the attractive gardens and, from January to Easter, enjoy Sunday afternoon jazz sessions.

Getting There & Away

From central Auckland, Kumeu is 25km up the Northwestern Motorway (SH16). Helensville-bound buses head here from Lower Albert St (adult/child $7.90/4.50, 50 minutes), but you'll really need a car or bike to get around.

Muriwai Beach

Yet another rugged black-sand surf beach, stretching 60km, Muriwai Beach's main claim to fame is the **Takapu Refuge gannet colony**, spread over the southern headland and outlying rock stacks. Viewing platforms get you close enough to watch (and smell) these fascinating seabirds. Every August hundreds of adult birds return to this spot to hook up with their regular partners and get busy – expect lots of outrageously cute neck-rubbing, bill-touching and general snuggling. The net result is a single chick per season; December and January are the best times to see the little fellas testing their wings before embarking on an impressive odyssey.

Nearby, a couple of short tracks will take you through beautiful native bush to a lookout that offers views along the length of the beach. Wild surf and treacherous rips mean that swimming is safe only when the beach is patrolled (and you must always swim between the flags). Apart from surfing, Muriwai Beach is a popular spot for hang gliding, parapunting, kiteboarding and horse riding. There are also tennis courts, a golf course and a cafe that doubles as a takeaway chippie.

THE GREAT GANNET OE

After honing their flying skills, young gannets get the ultimate chance to test them – a 2000km journey to Australia. They usually hang out there for several years before returning home, never to attempt the journey again. Once back in the homeland they spend a few years waiting for a piece of waterfront property to become available in the colony, before settling down with a regular partner to nest – returning to the same patch of dirt every year. In other words, they're your typical New Zealander on their OE (Overseas Experience). Why are they called Kiwis again?

Helensville

POP 2600

A smattering of heritage buildings, antique shops and cafes makes village-like Helensville a good whistle-stop for those taking SH16 north.

Activities

Parakai Springs THERMAL POOLS
(www.parakaisprings.co.nz; 150 Parkhurst Rd; adult/child $16/8; ⏲10am-9pm) Aucklanders bring their bored children to Parakai, 2km northwest of Helensville, on wet wintry days as a cheaper alternative to Waiwera. It has large thermally heated swimming pools, private spas ($8 per hour) and a couple of hydroslides.

Woodhill Mountain Bike Park MOUNTAIN BIKING
(☎027 278 0949; www.bikepark.co.nz; Restall Rd, Woodhill; adult/child $7/2, bike hire per hr $25-30; ⏲9am-4pm Thu-Tue, 10am-10pm Wed) Maintains many challenging tracks (including jumps and beams) within Woodhill Forest, 14km south of Helensville.

Tree Adventures ROPES COURSE
(☎0800 827 926; www.treeadventures.co.nz; Restall Rd, Woodhill; 1/4/8/10 courses $16/34/38/40; ⏲9.30am-5.30pm) A set of high-ropes courses within Woodhill Forest, consisting of swinging logs, nets, balance beams, Tarzan swings and a flying fox.

4 Track Adventures QUAD BIKES
(☎09-420 8104; www.4trackadventures.co.nz; Restall Rd, Woodhill; 1½/2½/3½hr tours $155/236/275) Rattle through Woodhill Forest (and along Muriwai Beach on the longer tours) on a quad bike. Pick up from Auckland is available at $50 per person.

Sleeping

Malolo House B&B $
(☎09-420 7262; www.malolohouse.co.nz; 110 Commercial Rd; r $70-120) Housed in a beautifully refurbished kauri villa that served for a time as the town's hospital, Malolo offers a range of restful accommodation, including two luxury en-suite doubles and cheaper ones with shared bathrooms.

Information

Helensville Library (Commercial Rd; @)
Visitor Information Centre (☎09-420 8060; www.helensville.co.nz; 87 Commercial Rd; ⏲10am-4pm Mon-Sat) Pick up free brochures detailing the *Helensville Heritage Trail* and *Helensville Riverside Walkway*.

Getting There & Away

Bus 60 heads from Lower Albert St (near Britomart) to Helensville ($10.30, 1½ hours).

NORTH AUCKLAND

The Auckland super-city sprawls 90km north of the CBD to just past the point where SH16 and SH1 converge at Wellsford. Beaches, regional parks, tramping trails, quaint villages, wine, kayaking and snorkelling are the main drawcards.

Long Bay Regional Park

The northernmost of Auckland's East Coast Bays, Long Bay is a popular family picnic and swimming spot, attracting over a million visitors a year. A three-hour-return coastal walk heads north from the sandy beach to the Okura River, taking in secluded Grannys Bay and Pohutukawa Bay (which attracts nude bathers).

Regular buses head to Long Bay from Albert St in the city (adult/child $6.80/4, one hour); the $10 day pass works out cheapest. If you're driving, leave the Northern Motorway at the Oteha Valley Rd exit, head towards Browns Bay and follow the signs.

Shakespear Regional Park

Shooting out eastward just before Orewa, the Whangaparaoa Peninsula is a heavily developed spit of land with a sizable South African expat community. At its tip is this gorgeous 376-hectare regional park, it's native wildlife protected by a 1.7km pest-proof fence.

Sheep, cows, peacocks and pukeko ramble over the grassy headland, while pohutukawa-lined **Te Haruhi Bay** provides great views of the gulf islands and the city. Walking tracks take between 40 minutes and two hours, exploring native forest, WWII gun embankments, Maori sites and lookouts. If you can't bear to leave, there's an idyllic beachfront **campsite** (☎09-301 0101; www.arc.govt.nz; adult/child $10/5) with flush toilets and cold showers.

It's possible to get here via a torturous two-hour bus trip from Albert St. The one-way fare is $10.30, so it's best to buy a $10 day pass. An alternative is to take the **360 Discovery** (☎0800 360 3472; www.360discovery.co.nz; adult/child $14/8.20) ferry service to **Gulf Harbour**, a Noddy-town development of matching townhouses, a marina, country club and golf course. Enquire at the ferry office about picking up a bus or taxi from here. Alternatively, walk or cycle the remaining 3km to the park. The ferry is a good option for cyclists wanting to skip the boring road trip out of Auckland; carry-on bikes are free.

Orewa

POP 7400

Locals have fears that Orewa is turning into NZ's equivalent of Queensland's Gold Coast, but until they start exporting retirees and replacing them with bikini-clad parking wardens that's unlikely to happen. It is, however, very built-up and high-rise apartment towers have begun to sprout.

Sights & Activities

Orewa Beach BEACH

Orewa's 3km-long stretch of sand is its main drawcard. Being in the gulf, it's sheltered from the surf but is still patrolled by lifeguards in the peak season.

Alice Eaves Scenic Reserve FOREST

(Old North Rd) Ten hectares of native bush with labelled trees, a *pa* site, a lookout and easy short walks.

WHICH HIGHWAY?

From Auckland, the multilane Northern Motorway (SH1) bypasses Orewa and Waiwera on a **tolled section** (☎0800 40 20 20; www.tollroad.govt.nz; per car/motorbike $4/2). It will save you about 10 minutes, provided you pay online or by phone (in advance or within five days of your journey) rather than stopping to queue at the toll booths.

Between Christmas and New Year SH1 can be terribly gridlocked heading north between the toll road and Wellsford; SH16 through Kumeu and Helensville is a sensible alternative. The same is true if heading south in the first few days of the New Year.

Millennium Walkway WALKING

Starting from South Bridge this 8km route loops through various parks before returning along the beach; follow the blue route markers.

Snowplanet SNOW SPORTS

(www.snowplanet.co.nz; 91 Small Rd, Silverdale; day pass adult/child $59/39; ⏲10am-10pm Sat-Thu, 10am-midnight Fri) A winter wonderland that allows every day to be a snowy one, Snowplanet offers indoor skiing, tobogganing and snowboarding. It's just off SH1, 8km south of Orewa.

Sleeping

Waves APARTMENT $$$

(☎09-427 0888; www.waves.co.nz; cnr Hibiscus Coast Hwy & Kohu St; units $180-299; 📶) Like a motel only much flasher, this complex offers spacious, self-contained apartments with double glazing and smart furnishings. The downstairs units have gardens and most have spa baths. Best of all, it's only a few metres from the beach.

Orewa Motor Lodge MOTEL $$

(☎09-426 4027; www.orewamotorlodge.co.nz; 290 Hibiscus Coast Hwy; units $155-195; 📶) One of a string of motels that line Orewa's main road, this complex has scrupulously clean wooden units that are prettied up with hanging flower baskets. There's also a spa pool.

Orewa Beach Top 10 HOLIDAY PARK $

(☎09-426 5832; www.orewaholidaypark.co.nz; 265 Hibiscus Coast Hwy; sites from $19, units $57-142; @) Taking up a large chunk of the beach's south end, this well-kept park has excellent facilities but road noise can be a problem. The prefab 'tourist flats' even have art on the walls and bedside lamps.

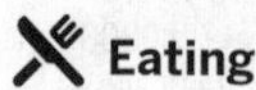

Eating

Mozaik CAFE $
(www.mozaik.co.nz; 350 Hibiscus Coast Hwy; mains $11-23; ⏲7am-5.30pm) Spilling out onto the pavement in the middle of the main drag, this licensed cafe offers an appealing array of counter food and a crowd-pleasing menu including pasta and burgers.

Asahi JAPANESE
(6 Bakehouse Lane; mains $11-20; ⏲9am-3pm Mon, 9am-9pm Tue-Sat) A handy little option for a sushi fix, with excellent *bento* boxes ($21.50).

Information

Hibiscus Coast i-SITE (☎09-426 0076; www.orewabeach.co.nz; 214a Hibiscus Coast Hwy; ⏲9am-5pm Mon-Fri, 10am-4pm Sat & Sun)

Getting There & Away

Direct buses run between Orewa and Albert St in the city (adult/child $11/6.10, 1¼ hours), as well as Shakespear Regional Park (adult/child $3.40/2, 35 minutes) and Waiwera (adult/child $1.80/1, 10 minutes).

Waiwera

This pleasant river-mouth village has a great beach, but it's the *wai wera* (hot waters) that people come here for. Warm mineral water bubbles up from 1500m below the surface to fill the 19 pools of the **Waiwera Thermal Resort** (☎09-427 8800; www.waiwera.co.nz; 21 Main Rd; adult/child $26/15; ⏲9am-9pm). There's a movie pool, 10 big slides, barbecues, private tubs ($50) and a health spa. If you can't face driving afterwards, luxuriously appointed modern houses have been built nearby (doubles $250); enquire about indulgence packages.

Squeezed between the Waiwera and Puhoi Rivers, the exquisite 134-hectare **Wenderholm Regional Park** (☎accommodation 09-366 2000; www.arc.govt.nz; sites per adult/child $10/5, house $128-170) has a diverse ecology, abundant bird life, beaches and walks (30 minutes to 2½ hours). **Couldrey House** (adult/child $3/free; ⏲1-4pm Sat & Sun, daily Jan), the original homestead (1860s), is now a museum. The campsite provides only tap water and long-drop toilets, and the council also rents two comfortable self-contained houses.

Bus 895 from Auckland's Albert St heads to Waiwera (adult/child $11/6.10, one hour) via Orewa.

Puhoi

POP 450

Forget dingy cafes and earnest poets – this quaint village is a slice of the real Bohemia. In 1863 around 200 immigrants from the present-day Czech Republic settled in what was then dense bush.

Sights & Activities

Church of Sts Peter & Paul CHURCH
(www.holyname.org.nz; Puhoi Rd) The village's pretty Catholic church dates from 1881 and has an interesting tabernacle painting (a copy of one in Bohemia), stained glass and statues.

Bohemian Museum MUSEUM
(www.puhoihistoricalsociety.org.nz; Puhoi Rd; adult/child $3/free; ⏲1-4pm Sat & Sun, daily Christmas-Easter) Tells the story of the hardship and perseverance of the original Bohemian pioneers.

Puhoi River Canoe Hire CANOEING
(☎09-422 0891; www.puhoirivercanoes.co.nz; 84 Puhoi Rd) Hires kayaks and Canadian canoes, either by the hour (kayak/canoe $25/50) or for an excellent 8km downstream journey from the village to Wenderholm Regional Park (single/double kayak $50/100, including return transport). Bookings are essential.

Eating & Drinking

Puhoi Valley CAFE $$
(www.puhoivalley.co.nz; 275 Ahuroa Rd; mains $13-22; ⏲10am-4pm) You'll find Puhoi Valley cheese in supermarkets nationwide but this blissful location is where it originates. It features heavily on the menu of their upmarket cheese-shop cafe, set alongside a lake, fountain and children's playground. In the summer there's music on the lawn.

Puhoi Hotel PUB
(www.puhoipub.co.nz; cnr Saleyards & Puhoi Rds; ⏲10am-7pm) There's character and then some in this 1879 pub, with walls completely covered in old photos, animal heads and vintage household goods.

Puhoi Cottage TEAHOUSE
(www.puhoicottage.co.nz; 50 Ahuroa Rd; ⏲10am-4pm Thu-Tue) Drop in for a Devonshire cream tea ($11).

Getting There & Away

Puhoi is 1km west of SH1. The turn-off is 2km past the Johnstone Hills tunnel.

Mahurangi & Scandrett Regional Parks

Straddling the head of Mahurangi Harbour, **Mahurangi Regional Park** (☎09-366 2000; www.arc.govt.nz; sites from $5, baches $106-128) has three distinct fingers: Mahurangi West, accessed from a turn-off 3km north of Puhoi; Scott Point on the eastern side, with road access 16km southeast of Warkworth; and isolated Mahurangi East, which can only be reached by boat. This boaties' paradise incorporates areas of coastal forest, *pa* sites and a historic homestead and cemetery. Its sheltered beaches offer prime sandy spots for a dip or picnic and there are loop walks ranging from 1½ to 2½ hours. Accommodation is available in four basic campsites and four baches sleeping six to eight.

On the way to Mahurangi West you'll pass **Zealandia Sculpture Garden** (☎09-422 0099; www.zealandiasculpturegarden.co.nz; 138 Mahurangi West Rd; admission $10; ⏲by appointment Nov-Mar only), where the work of Terry Stringer is showcased within impressive architecture and grounds.

On the ocean side of the Mahurangi Peninsula, **Scandrett Regional Park** (☎09-366 2000; www.arc.govt.nz; bach $128) has a sandy beach, walking tracks, patches of regenerating forest, another historic homestead, more *pa* sites and great views towards Kawau Island. Three baches (sleeping six to eight) are available for rent.

Warkworth

POP 3300

River-hugging Warkworth makes a pleasant pit stop, its dinky main street retaining a village atmosphere.

Sights

Dome Forest FOREST
(SH1) Two kilometres north of Warkworth, a track leads through this regenerating forest to the Dome summit (336m). On a fine day you can see the Sky Tower from a lookout near the top. The summit walk takes about 1½ hours return, or you can continue for a gruelling seven-hour one-way tramp through the Totora Peak Scenic Reserve, exiting on Govan Wilson Rd.

Sheepworld FARM
(www.sheepworldfarm.co.nz; SH1; adult/child $15/8, incl show $26/10; ⏲9am-5pm) The paddock of florescent sheep says all you need to know about this agricultural attraction, which offers farm experiences for little city slickers (pony rides, lamb feeding) and the ubiquitous sheep and dog show, including a shearing demonstration (showtimes 11am and 2pm).

Warkworth & District Museum MUSEUM
(www.wwmuseum.orcon.net.nz; Tudor Collins Dr; adult/child $8/2; ⏲9am-3pm) Pioneer-era detritus is displayed at this small local museum. Of more interest is the surrounding **Parry Kauri Park**, which harbours a couple of giant kauri trees, including the 800-year-old McKinney kauri (girth 7.6m).

FREE **Honey Centre** STORE
(www.honeycentre.co.nz; cnr SH1 & Perry Rd; ⏲8.30am-5pm) About 5km south of Warkworth, the Honey Centre makes a diverting pit stop, with its cafe, free honey tasting and glass-fronted hives. The shop sells all sorts of bee-related products, from candles to mead.

Sleeping & Eating

Bridgehouse Lodge MOTEL $$
(☎09-425 8351; www.bridgehouse.co.nz; 16 Elizabeth St; r $85-150; ⏲11am-late) Right by the river, this local institution has a mixed bag of rooms – some newer and nicer than others. The refurbished bar is downright swanky, dishing up fancy pub grub including burgers, pastas and pizzas (mains $15 to $30).

Ransom Wines WINERY
(www.ransomwines.co.nz; Valerie Close; tasting with purchase free, otherwise donation to Tawharanui Open Sanctuary of $5 ; ⏲10am-5pm Tue-Sun) Well signposted from SH1, about 3km south of Warkworth, Ransom produces great food wines and showcases them with matching tapas ($17 for five) and tasting platters (per person $17 to $19).

WORTH A TRIP

TE HANA TE AO MARAMA

You'll see the terraces of a lot of historic *pa* (fortified village) sites etched into hillsides all around NZ, but if you want to get an idea of how these fortified villages actually looked, take a guided tour of the re-created *pa* at **Te Hana Te Ao Marama** (www.tehana.co.nz; 307-308 SH1, Te Hana). Tours leave on the hour from 10am to 3pm daily (adult/child $25/13). The daytime tours can be combined with a *powhiri* (formal welcome) on to the very real *marae* (Maori temple) next door, with some packages including a meal and a cultural concert.

For the most atmospheric experience, take one of the Friday night *Starlight Tours* (adult/child $100/50, bus from Auckland $25 extra), where you'll be on the receiving end of a *powhiri*, have a meal within the *marae* complex and then proceed into the dramatically lit village for a guided tour and concert.

Information

Warkworth i-SITE (☎09-425 9081; www.warkworthnz.com; 1 Baxter St; ⊙8.30am-5pm Mon-Fri, 9am-3pm Sat & Sun)

Getting There & Away

InterCity and Naked Bus services both pass through town, en route between Auckland and the Bay of Islands; see Northland's Getting There & Away section.

Matakana & Around

Matakana suffers from reverse alcoholism – the more wine gets poured into it, the more genteel it becomes. A decade ago it was a nondescript rural village with a handful of heritage buildings and an old-fashioned country pub. Now the locals watch bemused as Auckland's chattering classes idle away the hours in stylish wine bars and cafes. The most striking symbol of the transition is the fantastical **Matakana Cinemas** (☎09-422 9833; www.matakanacinemas.co.nz; 2 Matakana Valley Rd) complex, its domed roof reminiscent of an Ottoman bathhouse. The humble **Farmers Market** (www.matakanavillage.co.nz; ⊙8am-1pm Sat) is held in its shadow – or should that be Farmers Upmarket?

The reason for this epicurean ecstasy is the success of the area's boutique wineries, which are developing a name for pinot gris, merlot, syrah and a host of obscure varietals. Local vineyards are detailed in the free *Matakana Coast Wine Country* (www.matakanacoast.com) and *Matakana Wine Trail* (www.matakanawine.com) brochures. Both are available from the Matakana Information Centre in the foyer of the cinema.

Sights

TOP CHOICE **Tawharanui Regional Park** BEACH
(☎09-366 2000; www.arc.govt.nz; Takatu Rd) A partly unsealed road leads to this 588-hectare reserve at the end of a peninsula. This special place is an open sanctuary for native birds, protected by a pest-proof fence, while the northern coast is a marine park (bring a snorkel). There are plenty of walking tracks (1½ to four hours) but the main attraction is **Anchor Bay**, one of the region's finest white-sand beaches. Camping is allowed at a basic site near the beach (adult/child $10/5) and there's a six-person bach for hire ($128).

Omaha BEACH
The nearest swimming beach to Matakana, Omaha has a long stretch of white sand, good surf and plenty of ritzy holiday homes.

Brick Bay Sculpture Trail SCULPTURE PARK
(www.brickbaysculpture.co.nz; Arabella Lane, Snells Beach; adult/child $12/8; ⊙10am-5pm) After taking an hour-long artistic ramble through the beautiful grounds of Brick Bay Wines, recuperate with a wine tasting at the architecturally impressive cafe.

FREE **Morris & James** STORE
(www.morrisandjames.co.nz; 48 Tongue Farm Rd; ⊙9am-5pm) Watch the potters at work during the free daily tour (11.30am) or just call in to check out the colourful finished products and the courtyard cafe.

Sleeping

Sandspit Holiday Park PARK $
(☎09-425 8610; www.sandspitholidaypark.co.nz; 1334 Sandspit Rd; sites from $16, units $60-152; @☎) A campsite masquerading as a pioneer village, this quirky place incorporates his-

toric buildings and faux shopfronts into its facilities. It's right by the water at Sandspit.

Matakana Country Lodge B&B $$$
(☎09-422 3553; www.matakanacountry.co.nz; 149 Anderson Rd; r $275-375;) It's only five minutes from Matakana by way of an unsealed road and a very long driveway, but this lodge offers tranquillity in bucketloads and expansive views over the countryside. The three guest rooms have the run of the entire villa, including the kitchen, pool and spa.

Eating & Drinking

Plume WINERY $$
(☎09-422 7915; www.plumerestaurant.co.nz; 49a Sharp Rd; mains $20-32; ⊙lunch Tue-Sun, dinner Fri & Sat) The best of the winery restaurants, Plume has rural views from its terrace and an adventurous menu that jumps from China to Spain by way of Thaliand and India.

Vintry WINE BAR
(☎09-423 0251; www.thevintry.co.nz; 2 Matakana Valley Rd; tastings from $8.50; ⊙10am-10pm) In the Matakana Cinemas complex, this wine bar serves as a one-stop cellar door for all the local producers.

Matakana House PUB
(☎09-422 9770; 11 Matakana Valley Rd; ⊙3pm-late Mon-Fri, noon-late Sat & Sun) A real local pub, this 1903 wooden hotel has taxidermied animals everywhere, a beer garden out front and occasional live music and DJs. It's an affectation-free zone.

Information

Matakana Information Centre (☎09-422 7433; www.matakanainfo.org.nz; 2 Matakana Valley Rd; ⊙10am-1pm) In the foyer of the cinema complex.

Getting There & Away

Matakana village is a 10km drive northeast of Warkworth along Matakana Rd; there's no public transport. Ferries for Kawau Island leave from Sandspit, 8km east of Warkworth along Sandspit Rd.

Leigh

POP 390

Appealing little Leigh (www.leighbythesea.co.nz) has a picturesque harbour dotted with fishing boats, and a decent swimming beach at **Matheson Bay**. Longstanding **Goat Island Dive & Snorkel** (☎0800 348 369; www.goatislanddive.co.nz; 142a Pakiri Rd; mask, snorkel & fin hire $18, dive trips incl equipment $100-260, PADI Open Water $600) offers PADI courses and boat dive trips in the Hauraki Gulf, throughout the year.

Apart from its proximity to Goat Island, the town's other claim to fame is the legendary **Leigh Sawmill** (☎09-422 6019; www.sawmillcafe.co.nz; 142 Pakiri Rd; mains $12-32; ⊙10am-late daily Jan–mid-Feb, noon-late Thu, 10am-late Fri-Sun mid-Feb–Dec), a spunky little pub and beer garden that's a regular stop on the summer rock circuit, sometimes attracting surprisingly big names. If you imbibe too much at the on-site **microbrewery** (⊙1.30-5pm Fri & Sat), there's accommodation inside the old sawmill shed, including basic backpacker rooms (from $25) and massive doubles with en suites (from $125). Alternatively, you can rent the Cosy Sawmill Family Cottage (from $300, sleeps 10).

Goat Island Marine Reserve

Only 3km from Leigh, this 547-hectare aquatic area was established in 1975 as the country's first marine reserve. In less than 40 years the sea has reverted to a giant aquarium, giving an impression of what the NZ coast must have been like before humans arrived. You only need step knee-deep into the water to see snapper (the big fish with blue dots and fins), blue maomao and stripy parore swimming around. There are dive areas all round Goat Island, which sits just offshore, or you can snorkel or dive directly from the beach.

Excellent interpretive panels explain the area's Maori significance (it was the landing place of one of the ancestral canoes) and provide pictures of the species you're likely to encounter. Colourful sponges, forests of seaweed, boarfish, crayfish and stingrays are common sights, and if you're very lucky you may see orcas and bottle-nosed dolphins. Visibility is claimed to be at least 10m, 75% of the time.

A **glass-bottomed boat** (☎09-422 6334; www.glassbottomboat.co.nz; adult/child $25/13) provides an opportunity to see the underwater life while staying dry. Trips last 45 minutes and run from the beach all year round, weather permitting; ring to check conditions and to book.

You can usually rent kayaks and snorkelling gear right from the beach. Snorkelling gear (from $15), wetsuits (from $18) and underwater cameras ($45) can also be hired at **Seafriends** (☎09-422 6212;

www.seafriends.org.nz; 7 Goat Island Rd; ⌚9am-7pm), further up the road, which also has saltwater aquariums and a cafe.

Pakiri

Blissful Pakiri Beach, 12km past Goat Island (4km of the road is unsealed), is an unspoilt expanse of white sand and rolling surf – a large chunk of which is protected as a regional park.

Right by the water, **Pakiri Beach Holiday Park** (☎09-422 6199; www.pakiriholidaypark.co.nz; 261 Pakiri River Rd; sites from $46, units $60-310) has a shop and tidy units of varying degrees of luxury in a secure setting under the shade of pohutukawas.

Just 6km on from Pakiri is **Pakiri Horse Riding** (☎09-422 6275; www.horseride-nz.co.nz; Rahuikiri Rd), which has more than 80 horses available for superb bush-and-beach rides, ranging from one hour ($65) to multiday 'safaris'. Accommodation is provided in basic but spectacularly situated beachside cabins (dorm/cabin $30/150) or in a comfortable four-bedroom house ($500) secluded among the dunes.

Bay of Islands & Northland

Includes »

Mangawhai 128
Waipu & Bream Bay 129
Whangarei 130
Tutukaka Coast & the Poor Knights Islands 135
Bay of Islands 138
Paihia & Waitangi 146
Kerikeri 150
Whangaroa Harbour 155
Doubtless Bay 156
Karikari Peninsula 157
Cape Reinga & Ninety Mile Beach 158
Opononi & Omapere 164
Waipoua Forest 165
Trounson Kauri Park 166

Best Places to Eat

» à Deco (p134)
» Acorn Bar & Bistro (p156)
» Bennetts (p129)
» Food at Wharepuke (p152)

Best Places to Stay

» Kahoe Farms Hostel (p155)
» Endless Summer Lodge (p161)
» Little Earth Lodge (p133)
» Tree House (p162)

Why Go?

For many New Zealanders, the phrase 'up north' conjures up sepia-toned images of family fun in the sun, pohutukawa in bloom and dolphins frolicking in pretty bays. From school playgrounds to work cafeterias, owning a bach (holiday house) 'up north' is a passport to popularity.

Beaches are the main drawcard and they're present in profusion. Visitors from more crowded countries are flummoxed to wander onto beaches without a scrap of development or another human being in sight. The west coast shelters the most spectacular remnants of the ancient kauri forests that once blanketed the top of the country. The remaining giant trees are an awe-inspiring sight and one of the nation's treasures.

It's not just natural attractions that are on offer: history hangs heavily here as well. The site of the earliest settlements of both Maori and Europeans, Northland is unquestionably the birthplace of the nation.

When to Go

The 'winterless north' boasts a subtropical climate, which is most noticeable from Kerikeri upwards. It averages seven rainy days per month in summer but 16 in winter. Temperatures are often a degree or two warmer than Auckland, especially on the east coast. Like all the nation's beach hotspots, Northland's beaches go crazy at New Year and remain busy throughout the January school holidays. Don't fret, as the long lazy days of summer usually continue into February and March. Even in winter the average highs hover around 16°C and the average lows around 7°C.

Bay of Islands & Northland Highlights

1. Splashing about, body surfing, sunbathing and strolling at any of the abundant beaches on either coast
2. Watching oceans collide while souls depart at **Cape Reinga** (p158)
3. Paying homage to the ancient kauri giants of the **Waipoua Forest** (p165)
4. Diving at one of the world's top spots, the **Poor Knights Islands** (p135)
5. Frolicking with dolphins and claiming your own island paradise among the many in the **Bay of Islands** (p138)
6. Surfing the sand dunes at **Ninety Mile Beach** (p158) or Hokianga's **North Head** (p162)
7. Delving into history and culture at the **Waitangi Treaty Grounds** (p146)

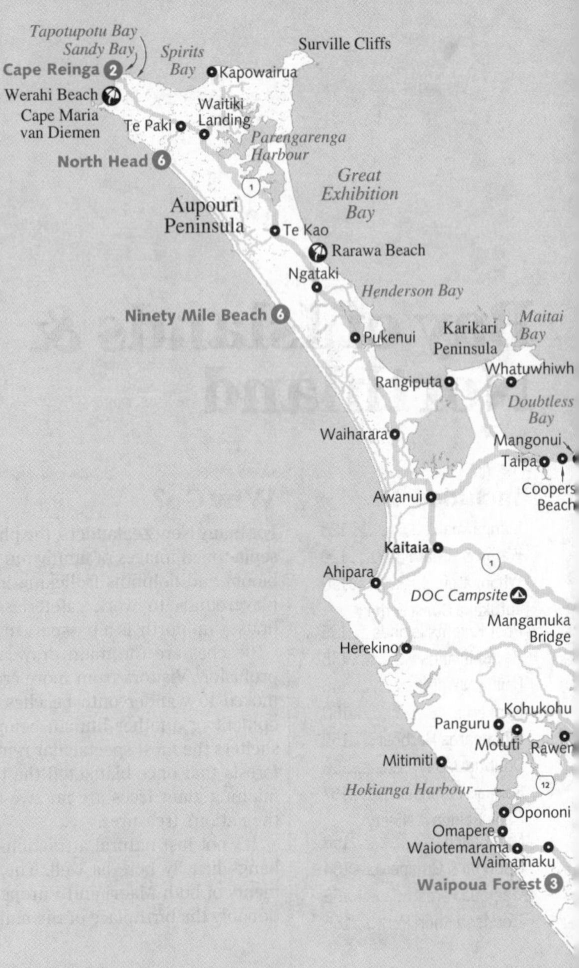

0 50 km
0 30 miles

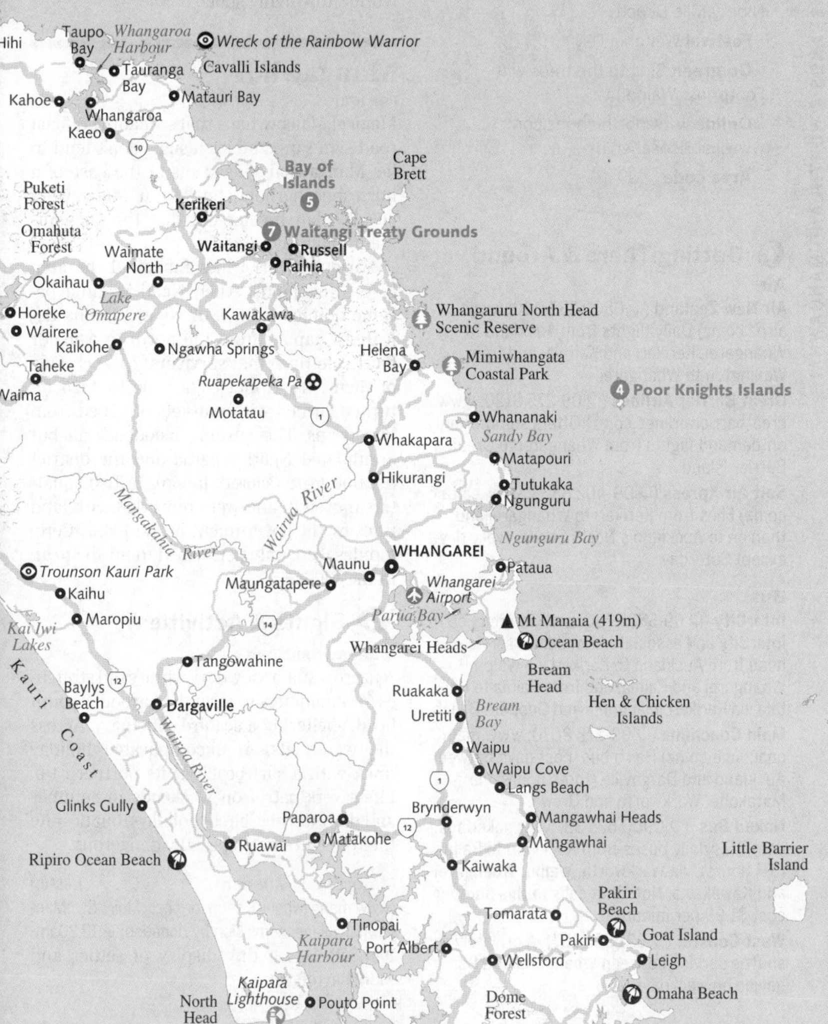

ESSENTIAL NORTHLAND

» **Eat** Kumara, Dargaville's knobbly claim to fame

» **Drink** Orange juice, Kerikeri's signature squeeze

» **Read** *The House of Strife* (1993), Maurice Shadbolt's riveting novel set during the Northland War

» **Listen to** *Cape Reinga Way* (2011) by The Nukes, ukeleles heading to the afterlife

» **Watch** *Land of the Long White Cloud* (2009) – fishing philosophers on Ninety Mile Beach

» **Festival** Waitangi Day

» **Go green** Sing to the trees with Footprints Waipoua

» **Online** www.northlandnz.com; www.kauricoast.co.nz

» **Area code** ☎09

Getting There & Around

Air

Air New Zealand (☎0800 737 000; www.airnz.co.nz) Daily flights from Auckland to Whangarei, Kerikeri and Kaitaia, and from Wellington to Whangarei.

Great Barrier Airlines (☎09-275 9120; www.greatbarrierairlines.co.nz) Offers summer-only, on-demand flights from Whangarei to Great Barrier Island.

Salt Air Xpress (☎09-402 8338; www.saltair.co.nz) Flies from Kerikeri to Whangarei and then on to Auckland's North Shore, every day except Saturday.

Bus

InterCity (☎09-583 5780; www.intercity.co.nz) InterCity and associated Northliner services head from Auckland to Kerikeri via Waipu, Whangarei and Paihia; and from Paihia to Kaitaia via Kerikeri, Mangonui and Coopers Beach.

Main Coachline (☎09-278 8070; www.maincoachline.co.nz) Has a bus most days between Auckland and Dargaville (three hours) via Matakohe, Warkworth and Orewa.

Naked Bus (☎0900 625 33; www.nakedbus.com) Has daily buses from Auckland to Paihia (3¾ hours), via Warkworth, Waipu, Whangarei and Kawakawa. Note that calls to this number cost $1.99 per minute.

West Coaster (☎021 380 187) A privately run shuttle service between Whangarei and Dargaville on weekdays.

WHANGAREI DISTRICT

To truly experience this area you have to be prepared to get wet. Beach after clear-watered beach offers munificent opportunities for swimming, surfing, splashing about or just wading in the shallows. Consequently the hot spots heave with Kiwi holidaymakers at peak times, but even then it's possible to find isolated stretches of sand where your footprints are the only ones.

If you're reading this and you're a diving fanatic, drop everything and head to Tutukaka immediately. The neighbouring Poor Knights Islands are considered one of the world's top diving spots.

Mangawhai

POP 1670

Magical Mangawhai – that's what the official road sign says, and such signs don't tend to lie. Mangawhai Village sits at the base of a horseshoe harbour, but it's at Mangawhai Heads, 5km further on, that the enchantment really takes hold.

Various Maori tribes inhabited the area before the 1660s, when Ngati Whatua became dominant. In 1807 Ngati Whatua defeated Ngapuhi from the north in a major battle, letting the survivors escape. One of them was Hongi Hika, who in 1825 returned, armed with muskets obtained from Europeans. The ensuing bloodbath all but annihilated Ngati Whatua and the district became *tapu* (sacred, taboo). British squatters moved in and were rewarded with land titles by the government in the 1850s. Ceremonies were only performed to lift the *tapu* in the 1990s.

Sights & Activities

Mangawhai Heads BEACH

A narrow spit of powdery white sand stretches for kilometres to form the harbour's south head, sheltering a seabird sanctuary. Across the water sits an uncomplicated holiday town with a surf beach at its northern tip. Life-savers patrol on weekends in summer and daily during school holidays, but despite the rollers it's not especially dangerous.

Mangawhai Museum MUSEUM

(www.mangawhai-museum.org.nz; Moir St, Mangawhai Village; admission by donation; ⏲10.30am-1pm Sat) Has a tiny display of settler and Maori artefacts.

Mangawhai Cliff Top Walkway TRAMPING
Starting at Mangawhai Heads, this track affords extensive views of sea and land. It takes two to three hours, provided you time it with a return down the beach at low tide. This is part of Te Araroa, the national walking track.

Sleeping

Milestone Cottages COTTAGES $$
(09-431 4018; www.milestonecottages.co.nz; 27 Moir Pt Rd, Mangawhai Heads; cottages $125-260;) A Pasifika paradise with lush tropical gardens and five self-contained cottages (sleeping up to five). At the time of research the owners were planning to sell off the front three cottages, including the pool; check before booking.

Mangawhai Lodge B&B $$$
(09-431 5311; www.seaviewlodge.co.nz; 4 Heather St, Mangawhai Heads; s $185, d $190-195, unit $220-280;) The comfortable, smartly furnished rooms have access to the picture-perfect wraparound veranda at this boutique B&B, with a commanding position and great views.

Eating

TOP CHOICE **Bennetts** CAFE $
(09-431 5072; www.bennettsofmangawhai.com; 52 Moir St, Mangawhai Village; mains $13-22; shop 9.30am-4pm, cafe breakfast & lunch, dinner seasonally) Rural France comes to the village in the form of this atmospheric chocolaterie, gelateria and cafe, where you can sit by the fountain in the courtyard listening to Edith Piaf while pigging out on delectable truffles and sipping a glass of wine.

Sail Rock Cafe CAFE $
(12a Wood St, Mangawhai Heads; mains $13-32; 9.30am-late) At the tail end of a day's surfing, this is the place to chat about the break that got away over an ice-cold beer and a serving of salt-and-pepper squid.

Smashed Pipi CAFE, BAR $
(www.smashedpipi.com; 40 Moir St, Mangawhai Village; mains $12-20) An eclectic combination, with counter food and a blackboard menu in the cafe, occasional live music in the bar, and vibrant ceramics and glassware in the neighbouring gallery.

Mangawhai Market MARKET $
(Moir St; 9am-1pm Sat) Held in the library hall in Mangawhai Village, this is a good place to stock up on organic produce (including wine and olive oil) and peruse local craft. Another market is held on Sunday mornings in the Domain, Mangawhai Heads, from mid-October to Easter.

Information

Visitor Information Centre (09-431 5090; www.mangawhai.co.nz) It's only staffed sporadically (mainly on weekends and in high summer), but there are information boards outside.

Waipu & Bream Bay

POP 1491

Generations of Kiwi kids have giggled over the name 'Waipu'; the makers of Imodium missed a golden opportunity by failing to adopt it as their product's brand name for the NZ market. Be that as it may, Waipu and neighbouring **Waipu Cove** are bonny wee places.

MAORI NZ: NORTHLAND

Known to Maori as Te Tai Tokerau, this region has a long and proud Maori history and today has one of the country's highest percentages of Maori people. Along with East Cape, it's a place where you might hear Maori being spoken. In mythology the region is known as the tail of the fish of Maui.

Maori sites of particular significance include Cape Reinga, the Waitangi Treaty Grounds, Ruapekapeka Pa Historic Reserve and, in the Waipoua Forest, Tane Mahuta.

Maori cultural experiences are offered by many local operators, including Footprints Waipoua, Sandtrails Hokianga, Motuti Marae, Ahikaa Adventures, Sand Safaris, Terenga Paraoa, Native Nature Tours, Taiamai Tours, Tiki Tours, Rewa's Village and Culture North. Many businesses catering to travellers are owned or run by Maori individuals or *hapu* (subtribal) groups. **Tai Tokerau Tourism** (www.taitokerau.co.nz) lists dozens of them on its website.

The original 934 British settlers came from Scotland via Nova Scotia (Canada) between 1853 and 1860. These dour Scots at least had the good sense to eschew frigid Otago, where so many of their kindred settled, for sunnier northern climes. Their story comes to life through holograms, a short film and interactive displays at the **Waipu Museum** (36 The Centre; adult/child $8/3; ⌚9.30am-4.30pm; @).

Only 10% of current residents are direct descendants, but there's a big get-together on 1 January every year, when the **Highland Games** (www.waipugames.co.nz; adult/child $15/5), established in 1871, take place in Caledonian Park.

There are excellent walks in the area, including the **Waipu Coastal Trail**, which heads south from Waipu Cove to Langs Beach, passing the **Pancake Rocks** on the way. The 2km **Waipu Caves Walking Track** starts at Ormiston Rd and passes through farmland and a scenic reserve en route to a large cave containing glowworms and limestone formations; bring a torch, a compass and sturdy footwear to delve the depths.

Bream Bay has miles of blissfully deserted beach, blighted only slightly by a giant oil refinery at the north end. At **Uretiti**, a stretch of beach south of a **Department of Conservation (DOC) campsite** (www.doc.govt.nz; SH1; sites per adult/child $8/4) is unofficially considered 'clothing optional'. Over New Year the crowd is evenly split between Kiwi families, serious European nudists and gay guys.

Sleeping

Stonehouse GUESTHOUSE $
(☎09-432 0432; www.stonehousewaipu.co.nz; 641 Cove Rd; apt $80-220; 📶) Nestled between the road to Waipu Cove and a saltwater lagoon, this unique Cornish-style house built of huge stone slabs offers three self-contained units decorated in bright, fresh colours. They range from the budget-orientated 'cutesy' (with a double sofa bed downstairs and six bunks above) to more comfortable rooms in the main house, which can be rented either individually or as a three-room apartment with a spacious living area.

Waipu Wanderers Backpackers HOSTEL $
(☎09-432 0532; waipu.wanderers@xtra.co.nz; 25 St Marys Rd; dm/s/d $30/45/66; 📶) There are only three rooms at this bright and friendly backpackers in Waipu township – a real home away from home – with free fruit in season.

Ruakaka Reserve Motor Camp HOLIDAY PARK $
(☎09-432 7590; www.motorcamp.co.nz; 21 Ruakaka Beach Rd; sites from $22, units $46-112; 📶) Priced and positioned somewhere between a DOC campsite and a holiday park, this ginormous motor camp offers simple facilities on a grassy area fronting the beach and rivermouth at Ruakaka.

Eating

Cafe Deli CAFE $
(29 The Centre; mains $8-19; ⌚9am-4pm) Enticing salads, pasta, muffins and organic, fair-trade coffee are served at this attractive little cafe on the Waipu strip.

Pizza Barn ITALIAN $
(2 Cove Rd; mains $12-25; ⌚11.30am-late Wed-Sun Apr-Nov, daily Dec-Mar) In Waipu even the pizza place has a tartan logo (and a cool ladies' loo). Pizza Barn has popular platters, light fare and hunger-assuaging pizzas that go well with cold beer as this cool place morphs into a bar.

Beach House MODERN NZ $$
(891 Cove Rd; mains $20-35; ⌚5pm-late Wed-Sat, 9am-late Sun) Attached to the Waipu Cove Resort, this little restaurant offers hearty meals in a distinctive courtyard enclosed by *ponga* (tree fern) logs.

Information

Tourist brochures and internet access are available at the museum.

Getting There & Away

Waipu Cove can be reached by a particularly scenic route heading from Mangawhai Heads through Langs Beach. Otherwise turn off SH1 38km south of Whangarei.

InterCity (p128) and Naked Bus (p128) both operate bus services.

Whangarei

POP 52,200

Northland's only city is surrounded by natural beauty and its compact town centre offers plenty of rainy-day diversions. It's hardly NZ's most thrilling city but you may be pleasantly surprised by the thriving artistic community and the interesting selection of cafes and bars.

Sights

TOWN BASIN

Whangarei's tourist centrepiece, this attractive riverside marina is home to museums, cafes, shops, interesting public art, an information centre and an ever-expanding fleet of flash yachts. It's a great place for a stroll, with a marked **Art Walk** and **Heritage Trail** to guide you on your way. An **artisans' market** is held on Saturdays from October to April under the shade of the spiky new canopy on the pedestrian bridge.

Whangarei Art Museum GALLERY
(www.whangareiartmuseum.co.nz; The Hub, Town Basin; admission by donation; ⏲10am-4pm) With its brand new home, accessed through the Hub information centre (p135), Whangarei's public gallery has an interesting permanent collection, the star of which is a 1904 portrait by Goldie (p674).

Clapham's Clocks MUSEUM
(www.claphamsclocks.com; Town Basin; adult/child $8/4; ⏲9am-5pm) Far more interesting than it sounds, this collection of 1400 ticking, gonging and cuckoo-ing timepieces constitutes the National Clock Museum.

CITY CENTRE

FREE **Old Library Arts Centre** GALLERY
(www.apt.org.nz; 7 Rust Ave; ⏲10am-4pm Tue-Fri, 9am-noon Sat) Local artists are exhibited in this wonderful art-deco building and a night market is held here on the last Friday of each month, selling art, craft, antiques and second-hand goods. Set between the old and new libraries is **Pou**, an intriguing sculpture consisting of 10 large poles carved with Maori, Polynesian, Celtic, Croatian and Korean motifs. Grab an interpretive pamphlet from the library.

FREE **Botanica & Cafler Park** GARDENS
(First Ave & Water St; ⏲10am-4pm) Native ferns, tropical plants and cacti are displayed in this little council-run fernery, set on the edge of cute Cafler Park. The park encloses the Waiarohia Stream and includes a rose garden and a scented garden.

SURROUNDS

FREE **Abbey Caves** CAVES
(Abbey Caves Rd) The budget traveller's answer to Waitomo, Abbey Caves is an undeveloped network of three caverns full of glowworms and limestone formations, 4km east of town. Grab a torch, strong shoes and a mate (you wouldn't want to be stuck down here alone if things go pear-shaped) and prepare to get wet. The surrounding reserve is a forest of crazily shaped rock extrusions. If you're staying at neighbouring Little Earth Lodge, you can borrow helmets and hire head torches.

Kiwi North MUSEUM, WILDLIFE
(www.kiwinorth.co.nz; 500 SH14, Maunu; adult/child $10/5; ⏲10am-3pm) Five kilometres west of Whangarei, this complex includes a veritable village of 19th-century buildings and a museum displaying an impressive collection of Maori and colonial artefacts. A new gecko and kiwi house offers a rare chance to see the country's feathery fave in a darkened nocturnal house.

Native Bird RecoveryCentre WILDLIFE CENTRE
(www.whangareinativebirdrecovery.org.nz; 500 SH14, Maunu; admission free; ⏲10.30am-4.30pm Mon-Fri) Next to Kiwi North, this avian hospital nurses sick and injured birds back to health. Say hi to the talking tuis.

Whangarei Falls WATERFALL
(Otuihau; Ngunguru Rd) These 26m-high falls are the Kim Kardashian of NZ waterfalls – not the most impressive but reputedly the most photographed. Short walks provide views of the water cascading over the edge of an old basalt lava flow. The falls can be reached on the Tikipunga bus ($3, no service on Sundays), leaving from Rose St in the city.

SAH Reed Memorial Kauri Park FOREST
(Whareora Rd) A grove of immense 500-year-old kauri trees has been preserved in this lush tract of native bush, where a cleverly designed boardwalk leads you effortlessly up into the canopy. To get here, head north on Bank St and turn right into Whareora Rd.

Quarry Gardens GARDENS
(www.whangareiquarrygardens.org.nz; Russell Rd; admission by donation; ⏲8am-5pm) Green-fingered volunteers have transformed this old quarry into a blissful park with a lake, waterfalls, pungent floral aromas, wild bits, orderly bits and lots of positive energy.

FREE **Quarry Arts Centre** ARTS CENTRE
(www.quarryarts.org; 21 Selwyn Ave; ⏲9.30am-4.30pm) An eccentric village of artists'

Whangarei

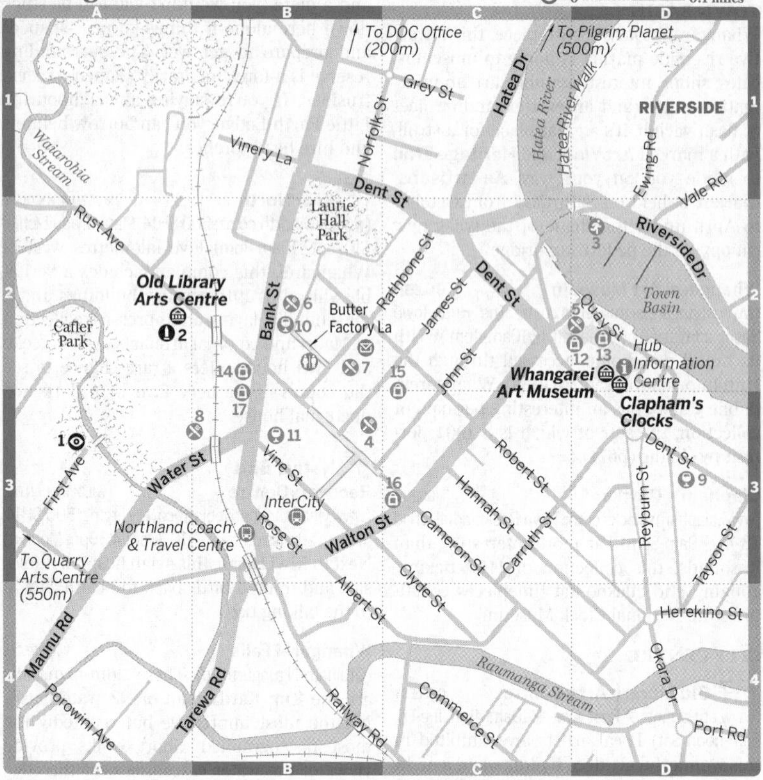

studios and co-operative galleries where you can often pick up well-priced art and craft. To get here, take Rust Ave, turn right into Western Hills Dr and then left into Russell Rd.

Activities

The free *Whangarei Walks* brochure, available from the i-SITE, has maps and detailed descriptions of some excellent local tracks. The **Hatea River Walk** follows the river from the Town Basin to the falls (three hours return). Longer tracks head through **Parihaka Reserve**, which is just east of the Hatea River and encompasses the remnants of a volcanic cone (241m) and a major *pa* (fortified village) site. The city is spread out for inspection from the lookout at the top, which is equally accessible by car. Other tracks head through **Coronation Scenic Reserve**, an expanse of bush immediately west of the centre that includes two *pa* sites and abandoned quarries.

Skydive Ballistic Blondes SKYDIVING
(☎0800 695 867; www.skydiveballisticblondes.co.nz; 12,000ft tandem $340) Not only is this the oddest-named skydiving outfit in the country, it's also the only one licensed to land on the beach (Ocean Beach or Paihia).

Pacific Coast Kayaks KAYAKING
(☎09-436 1947; www.nzseakayaking.co.nz; kayak hire 2½/4/8hr $40/60/80, tours $40-120) Hires kayaks and offers a range of guided paddles to various locations in the vicinity and beyond.

Tours

Pupurangi Hire & Tour CULTURAL TOUR
(☎09-438 8117; www.hirentour.co.nz; Jetty 1, Riverside Dr; ⏲10.30am-5.30pm) Offers a suite of

Whangarei

Top Sights

Clapham's Clocks ... D2
Old Library Arts Centre ... A2
Whangarei Art Museum ... D2

Sights

1 Botanica & Cafler Park ... A3
2 Pou ... A2

Activities, Courses & Tours

3 Pupurangi Hire & Tour ... D2

Eating

4 Fresh ... B3
5 Mokaba ... D2
6 Nectar ... B2
7 Pimarn Thai ... B2
8 Whangarei Growers' Market ... B3

Drinking

9 Brauhaus Frings ... D3
10 Butterbank ... B2
11 McMorrissey's ... B3

Shopping

12 Bach ... D2
13 Burning Issues ... D2
14 Classics ... B2
15 Kathmandu ... C2
16 Market Books ... C3
17 Tuatara ... B3

hour-long tours of Whangarei, all with a Maori flavour, including *waka* (canoe) trips on the river ($35). It also hires kayaks (per hour $17), *waka* ($25), aquacycles ($17) and bikes ($15).

Terenga Paraoa CULTURAL TOUR
(09-430 3083; departs Town Basin; adult/child morning $55/30, afternoon $32/20; 9.30am & 1pm) Guided Maori cultural tours taking in Whangarei Harbour, Mt Manaia, the Kauri Park and, in the mornings, Parihaka *pa*. By the time you're reading this, *waka* (canoe) journeys should also be offered.

Tiki Tours CULTURAL TOUR
(09-437 2955; Charmaine.tiki@xtra.co.nz; 2hr tour $35; 11am & 2pm Mon-Sat) Departing from the Hub, this well-priced tour takes in the Falls and Parihaka before heading to the Tikipunga Tavern for a traditional Maori meal.

Sleeping

TOP CHOICE **Little Earth Lodge** HOSTEL $
(09-430 6562; www.littleearthlodge.co.nz; 85 Abbey Caves Rd; dm/s/d/tr $30/67/70/90; @) Set on a farm 4km from town and right next to Abbey Caves, Little Earth's standards are so high that most other hostels look shabby in comparison. Forget dorm rooms crammed with nasty spongy bunks: settle down in a proper cosy bed with nice linen and a maximum of two roommates. Resident critters include miniature horses Tom and Jerry, and the lovable pooch Muttley.

Pilgrim Planet GUESTHOUSE $$
(09-459 1099; www.pilgrimplanet.co.nz; 63 Hatea Dr; r $115-145; @) Upmarket rooms open onto a shared kitchen and lounge, giving this smart place the sociability of a hostel but without the German teenagers living off rice and canned corn (not that there's anything wrong with that!).

Whangarei Views B&B $$
(09-437 6238; www.whangareiviews.co.nz; 5 Kensington Heights Rise; s/d $99/120, apt $169-229; @) The name clearly articulates its prime proposition: views over the city and then some. Modern and peaceful, it has a self-contained two-bedroom flat downstairs and a B&B room in the main part of the house. To get here, follow the directions to Quarry Gardens. Kensington Heights Rise is off Russell Rd.

Lodge Bordeaux MOTEL $$$
(09-438 0404; www.lodgebordeaux.co.nz; 361 Western Hills Dr; apt $195-540; @) Sitting somewhere between a super-schmick motel and an apartment hotel, Lodge Bordeaux has tasteful units with stellar kitchens and bathrooms (most with spa baths), private balconies and access to excellent wine. To get here, take Rust Ave and turn left into Western Hills Dr.

BK's Pohutukawa Lodge MOTEL $$
(09-430 8634; www.pohutukawalodge.co.nz; 362 Western Hills Dr; units $125-190; @) Just west of town, this straightforward, nicely furnished motel has 14 units with well-kept facilities and ample parking. Thoughtful extras include plunger coffee and ironing equipment.

YHA Manaakitanga HOSTEL $
(09-438 8954; www.yha.co.nz; 52 Punga Grove Ave; dm/r $30/90; @) This small hostel has

only a handful of rooms on a quiet hillside overlooking the river. It has a covered deck and barbecue area, and a short walk leads through the bush to glowworms. To get here, head east on Riverside Dr and look for Punga Grove Ave, heading uphill on the left.

Whangarei Top 10 HOLIDAY PARK $
(09-437 6856; www.whangareitop10.co.nz; 24 Mair St; sites from $20, units $67-253;) This centrally located riverside holiday park has friendly owners, a better-than-average set of units and supershiny stainless-steel surfaces. Mair St is off Hatea Dr, north of the city centre.

Eating

TOP CHOICE à Deco MODERN NZ $$$
(09-459 4957; 70 Kamo Rd; mains $37-39; lunch Fri, dinner Tue-Sat) Northland's best restaurant offers an inventive menu that prominently features local produce, including plenty of seafood. Art-deco fans will adore the setting – a wonderfully curvaceous marine-style villa with original fixtures. To get here, head north on Bank St and veer left into Kamo Rd.

Pimarn Thai THAI $$
(12 Rathbone St; mains $16-22; lunch Mon-Sat, dinner daily;) As gaudy as every good Thai restaurant should be (lots of gold and coloured glass), Pimarn has a lengthy menu featuring all of Thailand's blockbuster dishes, including a tasty *pad thai*.

Nectar CAFE $
(www.nectarcafe.co.nz; 88 Bank St; mains $10-18; breakfast & lunch Mon-Sat) Nectar offers the winning combination of fair-trade coffee, generous serves from a menu full of Northland produce, friendly staff (some drawn from a youth development program) and urban views from the back windows.

Fresh CAFE $
(12 James St; mains $10-22; 7.30am-4pm Sat-Wed, 7.30am-7pm Thu & Fri) Fresh as a daisy, and with supersized flower photography on the walls, this chic cafe serves up great coffee and interesting breakfasts. It's open later for after-work drinkies on Thursday and Friday.

Mokaba CAFE $
(Town Basin; mains $8-18) The best of the Town Basin's cafes has outdoor tables overlooking the forest of yacht masts, and indoor seating bleeding into a gallery. The usual cooked-breakfast suspects are on offer along with a fresh selection of counter food.

Stumpy's FISH & CHIPS $
(121 Riverside Dr; meals $4-20; 10am-7pm Mon-Thu, 10am-8pm Fri-Sun) A legendary chippie with a seafood basket ($14) that could leave you stumped.

Whangarei Growers' Market MARKET
(Water St; 6.30-10.30am Sat) Early birds get the best local produce at this long-standing farmers market.

Drinking & Entertainment

Brauhaus Frings BREWERY
(www.frings.co.nz; 104 Dent St; 10am-late) This popular microbrewery has a range of chemical-free beers, a terrace, board games and live music on Wednesday (jam night), Friday and every second Sunday. It's usually closed by 10pm earlier in the week but can push on to 3am.

Butterbank BAR
(www.butterfactory.co.nz; 84 Bank St; 4pm-late Tue-Sat) Occupying a converted bank building, this tapas and cocktail bar hosts live musicians on Fridays. As the hours dissolve, DJs kick in.

McMorrissey's IRISH PUB
(www.mcmorrisseys.co.nz; 7 Vine St; noon-late) A better-than-average Irish pub with cosy old-world decor and live music (trad Irish, rock and jam sessions).

Shopping

See also Quarry Arts Centre (p131).

Tuatara ARTS & CRAFTS
(www.tuataradesignstore.co.nz; 29 Bank St) A primo spot for funky Maori and Pasifika design, art and craft.

Bach ARTS & CRAFTS
(www.thebach.org.nz; Town Basin) You'll often find well-priced gifts and souvenirs at this excellent co-op store representing over 100 Northland artisans.

Burning Issues ARTS & CRAFTS
(www.burningissuesgallery.co.nz; Town Basin; 10am-5pm) Exquisite high-end arty stuff, especially glasswear, ceramics and jewellery.

Market Books BOOKS
(www.marketbooks.co.nz; 85 Cameron St) Search the shelves for a rare collectable treasure or

grab something trashy and secondhand for the beach.

Classics GIFTS
(www.classics.net.nz; 41 Bank St) Interesting eclectica, from Rubik's cubes to literature.

Kathmandu OUTDOOR EQUIPMENT
(www.kathmandu.co.nz; 22 James St; 9am-5.30pm Mon-Fri, 9am-4pm Sat, 10am-3pm Sun) A branch of the outdoor and travel supplies empire, selling everything from tents to plug adapters.

Information

DOC Office (09-470 3300; www.doc.govt.nz; 149 Bank St; 8.30am-4pm Mon-Fri)

Hub Information Centre (09-430 1188; Town Basin; 9am-5.30pm;) Branch of the i-SITE, in the foyer of the Art Museum.

Whangarei i-SITE (09-438 1079; www.whangareinz.com; 92 Otaika Rd (SH1); 8.30am-5pm Mon-Fri, 9am-4pm Sat & Sun;) Information, cafe, toilets and internet access.

Getting There & Around

Air

Whangarei Airport (WRE; 09-436 0047; www.whangareiairport.co.nz; Handforth St) Whangarei Airport is at Onerahi, 6km southeast of the centre. Air New Zealand, Salt Air Xpress and Great Barrier Airlines flights (p128) all service Whangarei. Taxis into town cost around $25. A city bus stops 400m away on Church St ($3, 18 buses on weekdays, seven on Saturdays).

Bus

Bus services (p128) to Whangarei are run by InterCity, whose buses stop outside the **Northland Coach & Travel Centre** (09-438 3206; 3 Bank St; 8am-5pm Mon-Fri, 8.30am-2.30pm Sat & Sun) and Naked Buses, whose buses stop at the Hub, in the Town Basin. West Coaster shuttles also service Whangarei.

Taxi

A1 Cabs (0800 438 3377)

Whangarei Heads

Whangarei Heads Rd winds 35km along the northern reaches of the harbour to its entrance, passing mangroves and picturesque pohutukawa-lined bays. Holiday homes, B&Bs and galleries are dotted around the water-hugging small settlements. There are great views from the top of **Mt Manaia** (419m), a sheer rock outcrop above McLeod Bay, but prepare for a lung- and leg-busting 1½-hour climb.

Bream Head caps off the craggy finger of land. A five-hour one-way walking track from **Urquharts Bay** to **Ocean Beach** passes through the **Bream Head Scenic Reserve** and lovely **Smugglers Bay** and **Peach Cove**.

Magnificent **Ocean Beach** stretches for miles on the other side of the headland. There's decent surfing to be had and lifeguards patrol the beach in summer. A detour from **Parua Bay** takes you to glorious **Pataua**, a small settlement that lies on a shallow inlet linked to a surf beach by a footbridge.

Sleeping & Eating

Kauri Villas B&B $$
(09-436 1797; www.kaurivillas.com; 73 Owhiwa Rd, Parua Bay; r $125-175;) Perched on a hill with views back over the harbour to Whangarei, this pretty blue-trimmed villa has an old world feel due in part to some very chintzy wallpaper. The decor's more restrained in the self-contained lodge and annex rooms.

Parua Bay Tavern PUB $$
(www.paruabaytavern.co.nz; 1034 Whangarei Heads Rd; meals $15-24; 11.30am-late) A magical spot on a summer's day, this friendly pub is set on a thumb-shaped peninsula, with a sole pohutukawa blazing red against the green water. Grab a seat on the deck, a cold beverage and a decent pub meal.

Tutukaka Coast & the Poor Knights Islands

If Goat Island Marine Reserve whetted your appetite, diving at the Poor Knights is the feast followed by a wafer-thin mint that might cause your stomach to explode. Apart from the natural underwater scenery, two decommissioned navy ships have been sunk nearby for divers to explore.

Following the road northeast of Whangarei for 26km, you'll first come to the sweet village of **Ngunguru** near the mouth of a broad river. **Tutukaka** is 1km further on, its marina bustling with yachts, dive crews and game-fishing boats.

From Tutukaka the road heads slightly inland, popping out 10km later at the golden sands of **Matapouri**. A blissful 20-minute coastal walk leads from here to **Whale Bay**, fringed with giant pohutukawa trees.

MARINE RICHES AT THE POOR KNIGHTS

Established in 1981, this marine reserve is rated as one of the world's top-10 diving spots. The islands are bathed in a subtropical current from the Coral Sea, so varieties of tropical and subtropical fish not seen in other NZ waters can be observed here. The waters are clear, with no sediment or pollution problems. The 40m to 60m underwater cliffs drop steeply to the sandy bottom and are a labyrinth of archways, caves, tunnels and fissures that attract a wide variety of sponges and colourful underwater vegetation. Schooling fish, eels and rays are common (including manta rays in season).

The two main volcanic islands, Tawhiti Rahi and Aorangi, were home to the Ngai Wai tribe, but since a raiding-party massacre in the early 1800s the islands have been *tapu* (forbidden). Even today the public is barred from the islands, in order to protect their pristine environment. Not only do tuatara and Butler's shearwater breed here, but there are unique species of flora, such as the Poor Knights lily.

Continuing north from Matapouri, the wide expanse of **Sandy Bay**, one of Northland's premier surf beaches, comes into view. Long-boarding competitions are held here in summer. The road then loops back to join SH1 at Hikurangi. A branch leading off from this road doubles back north to the coast at **Whananaki**, where there are more glorious beaches and the **Otamure Bay DOC campsite** (☎09-433 8402; www.doc.govt.nz; sites per adult/child $8/4).

Activities

Dive trips leave from Tutukaka and cater for both first-timers and experts. There are some excellent walks along the coast. Pick up a copy of the *Tutukaka Coast Tracks & Walks* brochure from the Whangarei i-SITE (p135).

Dive! Tutukaka DIVING
(☎0800 288 882; www.diving.co.nz; Marina Rd; 2 dives with gear $249) Deservedly Tutukaka's main operator, Dive! has won an array of tourism, business and environmental awards. It offers a variety of dive courses and excursions, including a five-day PADI open-water course ($799). Perhaps the jewel in its crown is the much-raved-about Perfect Day Ocean Cruise ($149), which includes a commentary, lunch and snacks, snorkelling from a platform in the middle of the marine reserve, kayaking through caves and arches, paddle-boarding, and sightings of dolphins (usually) and whales (occasionally). Cruises run from November to April, departing at 11am and returning at 4.15pm. In the off months, snorkellers can tag along on the dive boats.

Dive! Tutukaka has daily shuttles from Whangarei for its customers ($20).

Yukon Dive DIVING
(☎09-434 4506; www.yukon.co.nz; 2 dives with full gear $235) An owner-operator offering dive trips for a maximum of 12 people at a time.

Tutukaka Surf Experience SURFING
(☎09-434 4135; www.tutukakasurf.co.nz; Marina Rd; 2hr lesson $75) If you've got the bushy blond hair-do and baggy boardies but need credibility to pull off the look, these guys run regular surf lessons at 9am most days in summer and on the weekends otherwise, operating from whichever beach has the best beginner breaks that day. If you've already got the skills, you can buy or hire a board here (per day $45).

Sleeping

Lupton Lodge B&B $$
(☎09-437 2989; www.luptonlodge.co.nz; 555 Ngunguru Rd; s $118-150, d $165-210; @☎≋) The rooms are spacious, luxurious and full of character in this historic homestead (1896), peacefully positioned in farmland halfway between Whangarei and Ngunguru. Wander the orchard, splash around the pool or shoot some snooker in the guest lounge.

Pacific Rendezvous MOTEL $$
(☎09-434 3847; www.pacificrendezvous.co.nz; Motel Rd; apt $180-245) Perfectly situated for spectacular views on the south head of Tutukaka harbour, this is a great choice for families and small groups. Most of the units are 1960s duplexes with multiple bedrooms, but they're all individually owned and decorated. Some are smart and some are a little tired, but they're all kept shipshape by the friendly managers.

Eating & Drinking

Schnappa Rock CAFE, BAR $$
(www.schnapparock.co.nz; cnr Marina Rd & Marlin Pl; breakfast & lunch $10-22, dinner $26-35; breakfast, lunch & dinner) Filled with expectant divers in the morning and those capping off their Perfect Days in the evening, this cafe-restaurant-bar is often buzzing – not least because of the excellent coffee. Top NZ bands play on summer weekends.

Whangarei Deep Sea Anglers Club PUB $
(www.sportfishing.co.nz; Tutukaka Marina; mains $9-23; from 4pm) The club plays host to the nicely named Moocha's, where standard eats (burgers, fish and chips, ham steaks) and a good children's menu mingle with mounted fish and garrulous locals.

Marina Pizzeria PIZZERIA $$
(www.marinapizzeria.co.nz; Tutukaka Marina; pizzas $15-29; lunch & dinner Thu-Sun) Everything is homemade at this excellent takeaway joint and restaurant – the bread, the pasta, the pizza and the ice cream.

Russell Rd

The quickest route to Russell takes SH1 to Opua and then crosses by ferry. The old Russell Rd is a snaking scenic route that adds about half an hour to the trip.

The turn-off is easy to miss, 6km north of Hikurangi at Whakapara (look for the sign to Oakura). It's worth a stop after 13km at the **Gallery & Cafe** (www.galleryhelenabay.co.nz; mains $14-18; 10am-5pm) high above Helena Bay for excellent organic fair-trade coffee, scrummy cake, amazing views and a gander at some interesting Kiwiana art and craft. Is there anything that corrugated iron can't do?

At Helena Bay an unsealed detour leads 8km to **Mimiwhangata Coastal Park**, a gorgeous part of the coastline with sand dunes, pohutukawa trees, jutting headlands and picturesque beaches. DOC manages a range of accommodation options in the reserve, including a well-appointed **lodge** (per week $512-2045 per week) and a simpler but comfortable **cottage** and **beach house** (per week $358-1534); each sleeps seven to eight people. Basic **camping** (per adult/child $8/4) is available at secluded Waikahoa Bay.

Back on Russell Rd, you'll find the **Farm** (09-433 6894; www.thefarm.co.nz; 3632 Russell Rd; sites from $13, dm/s $20/30, d $60-100), a rough-and-ready backpackers rambling through various buildings, including an old woolshed fitted out with a mirror ball. The rooms are basic and its popular with bikers during the summer holidays, but off-season it's a chilled-out rustic escape. Best of all, you can arrange a **horse trek** (2hr $50) or **motorbike ride** (1hr $60) through the 1000-acre working farm.

At an intersection shortly after the Farm, Russell Rd branches off to the left for an unsealed, winding section traversing the **Ngaiotonga Scenic Reserve**. Unless you're planning to explore the forest (there are two short walks: the 20-minute **Kauri Grove Nature Walk** and the 10-minute **Twin Bole Kauri Walk**), you're better off veering right onto the sealed Rawhiti Rd.

After 2.6km, a side road leads to the **Whangaruru North Head Scenic Reserve**, which has beaches, walking tracks and fine scenery. A loop route from DOC's **Puriri Bay Campsite** (09-433 6160; www.doc.govt.nz; sites per adult/child $7/4) leads up to a ridge, offering a remarkable coastal panorama.

If you want to head directly to Russell, continue along Rawhiti Rd for another 7km before veering left onto Manawaora Rd, which skirts a succession of tiny idyllic bays before reconnecting with Russell Rd.

Otherwise take a detour to isolated **Rawhiti**, a small Ngapuhi settlement where life still revolves around the *marae*. Rawhiti is the starting point for the tramp to Cape Brett, a tiring eight-hour, 16.3km walk to the top of the peninsula, where overnight stays are possible in DOC's **Cape Brett Hut** (dm $13). An access fee is charged for crossing private land (adult/child $30/15), which you can pay at the Paihia i-SITE (p149). Another option is to take a water taxi to Cape Brett lighthouse from Russell or Paihia and walk back.

A shorter one-hour walk leads through Maori land and the **Whangamumu Scenic Reserve** to **Whangamumu Harbour**. There are more than 40 ancient Maori sites on the peninsula and the remains of an unusual whaling station. A net fastened between the mainland and Net Rock was used to ensnare or slow down whales so the harpooners could get in an easy shot.

BAY OF ISLANDS

Undeniably pretty, the Bay of Islands ranks as one of NZ's top drawcards. The footage that made you want to come to NZ in the first place no doubt featured lingering shots of lazy, sun-filled days on a yacht floating atop these turquoise waters punctuated by around 150 undeveloped islands. The reality is that NZ has many beautiful spots and this bay, while wonderful, could be a teensy bit overhyped.

What sets it apart from the rest is its fascinating history and substantial tourist infrastructure. Paihia has one of the best selections of budget accommodation of anywhere in the country. After that the budget goes out the window as a bewildering array of boat trips clamour to wrestle money out of your wallet. There's no point coming here if you don't head out on the water, so be prepared to fork out.

The Bay of Islands is a place of enormous historical significance. Maori knew it as Pewhairangi and settled here early in their migrations. As the site of NZ's first permanent British settlement (at Russell), it is the birthplace of European colonisation. It was here that the Treaty of Waitangi was drawn up and first signed in 1840; the treaty remains the linchpin of race relations in NZ today.

Activities

The Bay of Islands offers some fine subtropical diving, made even better by the sinking of the 113m navy frigate HMNZS *Canterbury* in Deep Water Cove near Cape Brett. Local operators also head to the wreck of the *Rainbow Warrior* off the Cavalli Islands, about an hour from Paihia by boat. Both offer a colourful feast of pink anemones, yellow sponges and abundant fish life.

There are plenty of opportunities for kayaking or sailing around the bay, either on a guided tour or by renting and going it alone. Cruises and dolphin-swimming are also available.

Dive North DIVING
(☎09-402 5369; www.divenorth.co.nz; reef & wreck $220) Experienced operators based in Kerikeri but offering free pick-ups from Paihia. They cover all the local dive sites and offer PADI courses.

Paihia Dive DIVING
(☎09-402 7551; www.divenz.com; Williams Rd, Paihia; reef & wreck $229) Offers combined reef and wreck trips to either the *Canterbury* or the *Rainbow Warrior*. Various PADI courses are available and gear can be hired.

Bay of Islands

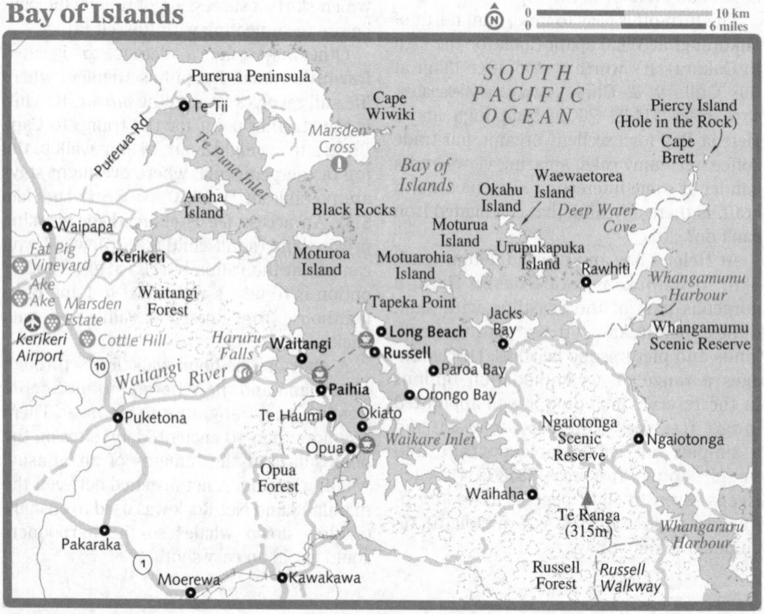

Dive Ops DIVING
(☎09-402 5454; www.diveops.co.nz; 2 dives incl equipment $230-280) Family-run diving operators, based out of Paihia.

Island Kayaks & Bay Beach Hire KAYAKING, BOATING
(☎09-402 6078; www.baybeachhire.co.nz; Marsden Rd, Paihia; half-day kayaking tour $69; ⊙9am-5.30pm) Hires kayaks (from $15 per hour), sailing catamarans ($50 first hour, $40 per additional), motor boats ($85 first hour, $25 per additional), mountain bikes ($35 per day), boogie boards ($25 per day), fishing rods ($10 per day), wetsuits and snorkelling gear (both $20 per day).

Coastal Kayakers KAYAKING
(☎0800 334 661; www.coastalkayakers.co.nz; Te Karuwha Pde, Paihia) Runs guided tours (half-/full day $75/95, minimum two people) and multiday adventures. Kayaks (per hour/half-/full day $15/40/50) and snorkelling gear (per day $15) can also be rented.

Skydive Zone SKYDIVING
(☎09-407 7057; www.skydivezoneboi.co.nz; Kerikeri Airport; tandem jump from 16,000/12,000/8000ft $395/325/265) At the time of research, this operator offered the highest tandem jump in the North Island and one of the most scenic.

Flying Kiwi Parasail PARASAILING
(☎09-402 6068; www.parasail-nz.co.nz; solo $99, tandem $89) Departs from both Paihia and Russell wharves for NZ's highest parasail (1200ft).

Great Escape Yacht Charters SAILING
(☎09-402 7143; www.greatescape.co.nz) Offers sailing lessons (two-day course $445) and yacht hire (per day $120 to $780).

Northland Paddleboarding PADDLEBOARDING
(☎027 777 1035; www.northlandpaddleboarding.co.nz; beginner lessons per hr $50) If you've been lured by all the talk of toning your tummy while blatting around on the water, these guys will get you standing up on a board and paddling around the bay in no time.

Horse Trek'n HORSE RIDING
(☎027 233 3490; www.horsetrekn.co.nz; 2hr ride $95) Offers treks through the Waitangi Forest.

Jet Ski Adventure Tours JET SKIING
(☎027 435 4497; www.jetskikayak.co.nz; Te Ti Bay, Paihia) While we must confess to finding jet skis incrediby annoying, they can be a really fun way of exploring the bay. These guys set themselves up on the beach during summer and take tours all the way out to the Hole in the Rock.

POU HERENGA TAI TWIN COAST CYCLE TRAIL

Eventually this cycle route will stretch from the Bay of Islands clear across the country to the Hokianga Harbour. OK, so that's only 84km, but as far as we're concerned that still gives you boasting rights when you get home. The final route will head from Opua to Kawakawa, Ngawha Springs, Kaikohe and finish up in Horeke.

At the time of research, the 13km section from **Kaikohe** to **Okaihau** had been completed, starting from a rest area immediately west of Kaikohe on SH12 and passing through an abandoned rail tunnel before skirting **Lake Omapere**. A 7km section from Kawakawa to Otiria has also opened, starting near the train station. For maps, tips and updates, visit www.nzcycletrail.com/twin-coast-cycle-trail-pou-herenga-tai.

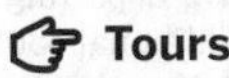

Tours

Where do you start? First by praying for good weather, as torrential rain or choppy seas could literally put a dampener on some options. The Paihia i-SITE (p149) is extremely helpful and can book tours. Some of the hostels can arrange cheap deals and several of the main operators offer backpacker specials.

Boat

You can't leave the Bay of Islands without taking some sort of cruise, and there are plenty of vessels keen to get you onboard, including sailing boats, jetboats and large launches. Boats leave from either Paihia or Russell, calling into the other town as their first stop.

Of all the bay's islands, perhaps the most striking is **Piercy Island (Motukokako)** off Cape Brett, at the bay's eastern edge. This steep-walled rock fortress is rent by a vast natural arch – the famous **Hole in the Rock**. Provided the conditions are right, most boat tours will pass right through the heart of the island. En route it's likely you'll encounter

SWIMMING WITH DOLPHINS

Cruises offering the opportunity to interact with wild dolphins operate all year round and are one of the bay's big drawcards. They have a high success rate and you're generally offered a free trip if dolphins aren't sighted. Dolphin swims are subject to weather and sea conditions, with restrictions if calves are present.

It's totally up to the dolphins as to whether they chose to swim with you or not. There's no point timidly floating around the boat; you're more likely to attract cetacean attention if you're prepared to muck around, duck and dive, make dolphin noises and generally act like you're a good-time-human. You'll need to be a strong swimmer to keep abreast with them – even when they're humouring you by cruising along at half-speed.

Only three operators are licensed for dolphin-swimming: Explore NZ, Fullers and the yacht Carino. All pay a portion of the cost towards marine research, via DOC.

bottlenose and common dolphins, and you may see orcas, other whales and penguins.

The best way to explore the bay is under sail. In most cases you can either help crew the boat (no experience required), or just spend the afternoon island-hopping, sunbathing, swimming, snorkelling, kayaking and fishing.

Explore NZ CRUISES, SAILING
(☎09-402 8234; www.explorenz.co.nz; cnr Marsden & Williams Rds, Paihia) This was the first outfit to offer dolphin-swimming trips in the bay. Their Swim with the Dolphins Cruise (adult/child $89/45) is a four-hour trip departing at 8am and 12.30pm, with an additional $30 payable if you choose to swim. If you'd like to see dolphins but prefer to stay dry, the four-hour Discover the Bay Cruise (adult/child $95/48) departs at 9am and 1.30pm, heading to the Hole in the Rock and stopping at Urupukapuka Island. This cruise is combined with a trip to Kerikeri Basin in the seven-hour Day Discovery Cruise (adult/child $109/45).

Other options include a day sail on *Lion NZ* (adult/child $110/70), the 80ft maxi yacht used by the late Sir Peter Blake on two Whitbread round-the-world races and his winning Sydney-to-Hobart entry in 1984. If you've a taste for speed, Ocean Adventure (adult/child $95/48) is a 2½ hour blast on a rigid-hulled inflatable to the Hole in the Rock.

Fullers Great Sights CRUISES
(☎0800 653 339; www.dolphincruises.co.nz; Paihia Wharf) The four-hour Dolphin Cruise (adult/child $95/48) departs daily at 9am and 1.30pm, actively seeking out dolphins and any other marine mammals en route to the Hole in the Rock, stopping at Urupukapuka Island on the way back.

You won't visit the Hole in the Rock on the four-hour Dolphin Eco Experience (adult/child $105/53, departs 8am and 12.30pm), rather the focus is finding pods of dolphins you can swim with.

The full-day Cream Trip (adult/child $109/55) follows the old supply and mail route around the whole of the bay and includes dolphin-swimming and boom-netting (where you can get close to the critters while being dragged through the water in a net).

A glamorous option for an overnight cruise is the launch **Ipipiri** (www.overnightcruise.co.nz; s/d $563/750). On this floating hotel the accommodation is by way of en-suite state rooms. All meals are included, and if you get sick of lazing around the bar on the sundeck, you can partake in kayaking, snorkelling or island walks.

R Tucker Thompson SAILING
(☎09-402 8430; www.tucker.co.nz) There's sailing and then there's this... Run by a charitable trust with an education focus, the *Tucker* is a majestic tall ship offering day sails (adult/child $145/73, including a barbecue lunch) and late-afternoon cruises (adult/child $69/35). It also partners with the Historic Places Trust and DOC for special sailings. Talking like a pirate is optional.

Rock OVERNIGHT CRUISE
(☎0800 762 527; www.rocktheboat.co.nz; dm/s/d $178/356/396) A former vehicle ferry that's now a floating hostel, the Rock has six-bed dorms, twin, double and family rooms, and (of course) a bar. The cruise departs at 5pm and includes a barbecue and seafood dinner with live music, then a full day spent island-hopping, fishing, kayaking, snorkelling and swimming.

Carino SAILING, DOLPHIN-SWIMMING
(☎09-402 8040; www.sailingdolphins.co.nz; adult/child $114/69) This 50ft catamaran is the only yacht licensed for swimming with dolphins. A barbecue lunch is available for $6.

Ecocruz SAILING
(☎0800 432 627; www.ecocruz.co.nz; dm/d $595/1350) A highly recommended three-day/two-night sailing cruise aboard the 72ft ocean-going yacht *Manawanui*, with an emphasis on the marine environment. Prices include accommodation, food, fishing, kayaking and snorkelling.

She's a Lady SAILING
(☎0800 724 584; www.bay-of-islands.com; day sail $97) On the day sails you can try your hand at snorkelling or paddling about in a see-through-bottomed kayak. The operator also charters boats for longer trips and runs a sailing school.

Phantom SAILING
(☎0800 224 421; www.yachtphantom.com; adult/child $110/60) A fast 50ft racing sloop, known for its wonderful food (10 people maximum, BYO allowed).

Gungha II SAILING
(☎0800 478 900; www.bayofislandssailing.co.nz; day sail $90) A beautiful 65ft ocean yacht with a friendly crew; lunch included.

Mack Attack JETBOATING
(☎0800 622 528; www.mackattack.co.nz; 9 Williams Rd, Paihia; adult/child $89/40) Fasten your seatbelt for a high-speed 1½-hour Hole in the Rock trip on board a jetboat – good fun and handy if you're short on time.

Bus

It's cheaper and quicker to take trips to Cape Reinga from Ahipara, Kaitaia or Doubtless Bay, but if you're short on time, several long day trips (10 to 12 hours) leave from the Bay of Islands. They all drive one way along Ninety Mile Beach, stopping to sandboard on the dunes.

Fullers (see opposite) runs regular bus tours and backpacker-oriented versions, both stopping at Puketi Forest. The standard, child-friendly version (adult/child $129/65) includes an optional lunch at Houhora (lunch $23). It also runs **Awesome NZ** (☎0800 653 339; www.awesomenz.com; tour $115) tours, with louder music, more time sandboarding and stops to chuck a Frisbee around at Taputaputa Beach and devour fish and chips at Mangonui.

Explore NZ's Dune Rider (adult/child $145/110) also samples Mangonui's feted fish and chips and includes a stop at Gumdiggers Park.

Transport options to the Hokianga and Waipoua Forest are limited, so a day trip makes sense if you don't have your own car or if you're time starved. Fullers' Discover Hokianga (adult/child $105/61) takes in Tane Mahuta and Wairere Boulders in an eight-hour tour with local Maori guides.

Maori

Native Nature Tours CULTURAL, TRAMPING
(☎0800 668 873; www.nativenaturetours.co.nz; 581 Tipene Rd, Motatau; day treks $185-195, overnight $375) A local couple formally welcome you to their *marae* (temple) and and lead you on treks into their ancestral lands, including visits to sacred sites and an introduction to Maori food and medicine. Overnight stays include a traditional *hangi* (earth-cooked meal) and glowworm spotting.

Taiamai Tours Heritage Journeys CULTURAL, CANOEING
(☎09-405 9990; www.taiamaitours.co.nz; 2½hr tour $135; ⊙10am & 1pm Oct-Apr) For a hands-on experience of Maori culture, paddle a traditional 50ft carved *waka* from the Waitangi bridge to the Haruru Falls. The Ngapuhi hosts wear traditional garb and perform the proper *karakia* (incantations) and share stories.

Other

Salt Air SCENIC FLIGHTS
(☎09-402 8338; www.saltair.co.nz; Marsden Rd, Paihia) Offers a range of scenic flights, including a five-hour light aircraft and 4WD tour to Cape Reinga and Ninety Mile Beach ($425) and helicopter flights out to the Hole in the Rock ($220).

Total Tours FOOD & WINE
(☎0800 264 868; www.totaltours.co.nz) Head to the countryside around Kerikeri on a full-day Food, Wine and Craft tour ($99), half-day wine tour ($75) or an evening Wine & Dine tour ($120), departing from Paihia's Maritime Building.

WORTH A TRIP

HOLD ON UNTIL KAWAKAWA

Kawakawa is just an ordinary Kiwi town, located on SH1 south of Paihia, but the public toilets (60 Gillies St) are anything but. They were designed by Austrian-born artist and ecoarchitect Friedensreich Hundertwasser who lived near Kawakawa in an isolated house without electricity from 1973 until his death in 2000. The most photographed toilets in NZ are typical Hundertwasser – lots of wavy lines decorated with ceramic mosaics and brightly coloured bottles, and with grass and plants on the roof. Other examples of his work can be seen in Vienna and Osaka.

Kawakawa's other claim to fame is the railway line running through the centre of the main street, on which you can take a 45-minute spin pulled by **Gabriel the steam engine** (☎021 171 2697; www.bayofislandsvintagerailway.org.nz; adult/child $10/3; ⊙10.45am, noon, 1.15pm, 2.30pm Fri-Sun, daily school holidays).

South of town, a signpost from SH1 points to **Kawiti Glowworm Caves** (☎09-404 0583; 49 Waiomio Rd; adult/child $15/7.50; ⊙8.30am-4.30pm). Explore the insect-illuminated caverns with a 30-minute subterranean tour.

Festivals & Events

Tall Ship Race SPORTS
Held in Russell on the first Saturday after New Year's Day.

Waitangi Day COMMEMORATION
Various ceremonial events at Waitangi on 6 February.

Country Rock Festival MUSIC
(www.country-rock.co.nz; festival pass $50) Second weekend in May.

Russell Birdman LUNACY
(www.russellbirdman.co.nz) Where a bunch of lunatics with flying contraptions jump off the wharf into the frigid (July) waters to the amusement of all.

Jazz & Blues Festival MUSIC
(www.jazz-blues.co.nz; festival pass $50) Second weekend in August.

Weekend Coastal Classic SPORTS
(www.coastalclassic.co.nz) NZ's largest yacht race, from Auckland to the Bay of Islands, held on Labour Weekend in October.

Russell

POP 820

Although it was once known prosaically as 'the hellhole of the Pacific', those coming to Russell for debauchery will be sadly disappointed: they've missed the orgies on the beach by 170 years. Instead they'll find a sweetly historic town that is a bastion of gift shops and B&Bs. In summer, you can often rent kayaks or dinghies from the water's edge along the Strand.

Before it was known as a hellhole, or even as Russell, it was Kororareka (Sweet Penguin), a fortified Ngapuhi village. In the early 19th century the tribe permitted it to become Aotearoa's first European settlement. It quickly became a magnet for rough elements such as fleeing convicts, whalers and drunken sailors. By the 1830s dozens of whaling ships at a time were anchored in the harbour. Charles Darwin described it in 1835 as full of 'the refuse of society'.

In 1830 the settlement was the scene of the so-called Girls' War, when two pairs of Maori women were vying for the attention of a whaling captain called Brind. A chance meeting between the rivals on the beach led to verbal abuse and fighting. This minor conflict quickly escalated as family members rallied around to avenge the insult and harm done to their respective relatives. Hundreds were killed and injured over a two-week period before missionaries managed to broker a peace agreement.

After the signing of the Treaty of Waitangi in 1840, Okiato (where the car ferry now leaves from) was the residence of the governor and the temporary capital. The capital was officially moved to Auckland in 1841 and Okiato, which was by then known as Russell, was eventually abandoned. The name Russell ultimately passed to Kororareka – a marginally better choice than Bruce or Barry.

Sights

Pompallier Mission HISTORIC BUILDING
(www.pompallier.co.nz; The Strand; tours adult/child $10/free; ⊙10am-4pm) Built in 1842 to house the Catholic mission's printing press, this

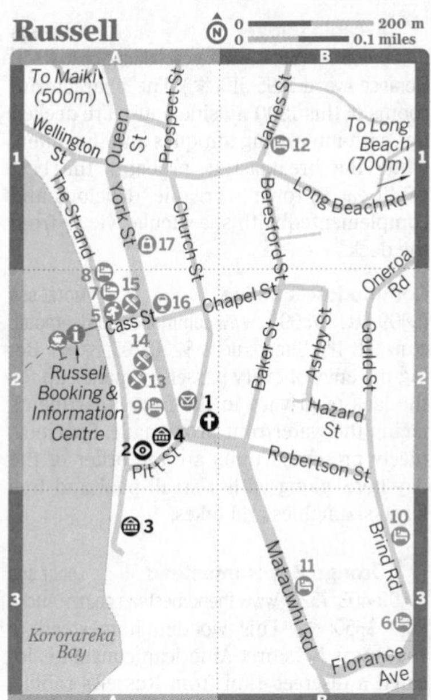

rammed earth building is the mission's last remaining building in the Western Pacific. A staggering 40,000 books were printed here in Maori. In the 1870s it was converted into a private home, but it has been restored to its original state, complete with tannery and printing workshop. On the excellent guided tour you get to play with the tools and learn how to 'skive off' and become a 'dab hand'.

ChristChurch CHURCH

(Church St) Creationists may be surprised to learn that Charles Darwin made a donation towards the cost of the construction of this, the country's oldest church (1836). The biggest memorial in the graveyard commemorates Tamati Waka Nene, a powerful Ngapuhi chief from the Hokianga who sided against Hone Heke in the Northland War. If you look closely at the church's exterior, you'll see musket and cannonball holes dating from the 1845 battle.

Maiki HILL

(Flagstaff Rd) Overlooking Russell, this is the hill where Hone Heke chopped down the flagpole four times. You can drive up but the view justifies a climb. Take the track west from the boat ramp along the beach at low tide, or up Wellington St otherwise.

Russell

Sights
1 ChristChurch A2
2 Haratu A2
3 Pompallier Mission A3
4 Russell Museum A2

Activities, Courses & Tours
5 Russell Mini Tours A2

Sleeping
6 Arcadia Lodge B3
7 Commodore's Lodge A2
8 Duke of Marlborough A2
9 Hananui Lodge & Apartments A2
10 Pukeko Cottage B3
11 Russell Motel B3
12 Russell Top 10 .... B1

Eating
Duke of Marlborough .... (see 8)
13 Gables A2
14 Hone's A2
15 Pizza Port A2
Tuk Tuk .... (see 16)

Drinking
16 Pub 'round the Corner A2

Shopping
17 Just Imagine A1

Tapeka Point LOOKOUT, BEACH

(www.tapeka.com) North of Russell, on the other side of Maiki hill, Tapeka Rd heads down to a quiet, sandy beach in the shadow of a craggy headland. A *pa* once stood at the top of the hill, and you need only follow the pathway to realise that the position was strategic as well as scenic, with views stretching to the far northern reaches of the Bay of Islands.

Long Beach BEACH

(Long Beach Rd) About 1.5km behind Russell (an easy walk or cycle) is this placid, child-friendly beach. Turn left (facing the sea) to visit Donkey Bay, a small cove that is an unofficial nudist beach.

Russell Museum MUSEUM

(www.russellmuseum.org.nz; 2 York St; adult/child $7.50/2; ⌚10am-4pm) This small, modern museum has a well-presented Maori section, a large 1:5-scale model of Captain Cook's *Endeavour* and a 10-minute video on the town's history.

Haratu CULTURAL BUILDING
(www.kororarekanz.com; cnr The Strand & Pitt St; ⊙10am-5pm Tue-Sat Sep-Apr) Run by the local *marae* society, Haratu brings authentic Maori art and craft to the Russell waterfront, most of which is available for purchase. There are also audiovisual displays and information boards.

Tours

Russell Mini Tours MINIBUS
(☎0800 64 64 86; www.dolphincruises.co.nz; cnr The Strand & Cass St; adult/child $29/14; ⊙10am, 11am, 1pm, 2pm, 3pm & 4pm) Minibus tour with commentary.

Sleeping

Being a tourist trap, Russell has few decent midrange options. There are several tiny budget lodges, but you'll need to book ahead at busy times. If budget is not a consideration, Russell does luxury very well.

TOP CHOICE **Wainui** HOSTEL $
(☎09-403 8278; www.pelnet.org/wainui; 92d Te Wahapu Rd; dm/r $27/64;) Hard to find but well worth the effort, this modern bush retreat with direct beach access has only two rooms sharing a pleasant communal space. It's 5km from Russell on the way to the car ferry. Take Te Wahapu Rd and then turn right into Waiaruhe Way.

Arcadia Lodge B&B $$$
(☎09-403 7756; www.arcadialodge.co.nz; 10 Florance Ave; d $195-310;) The characterful rooms of this 1890 hillside house are decked out with interesting antiques and fine linen, while the breakfast is probably the best you'll eat in town – organic, delicious and complemented with spectacular views from the deck.

Commodore's Lodge MOTEL $$$
(☎09-403 7899; www.commodoreslodgemotel.co.nz; 28 The Strand; units $200-295;) Being the envy of every passer-by makes up for the lack of privacy in the front apartments facing the waterfront promenade. Spacious, nicely presented units are the order of the day here, along with a small pool and free kayaks, dinghies and bikes.

Orongo Bay Homestead LODGE $$$
(☎09-403 7527; www.thehomestead.co.nz; Aucks Rd; r $650;) This wooden homestead (c 1860) was NZ's first American consulate, located a discreet 4km from Russell's rabble. Accommodation is by way of three stylishly plush rooms in the converted barn facing a chocolate-box lake. When one of the charming hosts is an acclaimed food critic, you can be assured that the breakfast will be memorable (dinners by arrangement).

HONE HEKE & THE NORTHLAND WAR

Just five years after he had been the first signatory to the treaty, Ngapuhi chief Hone Heke was so disaffected that he was planning to chop down Kororareka's flagstaff, a symbol of British authority, for the fourth time. Governor FitzRoy was determined not to let that happen and garrisoned the town with soldiers and marines.

On 11 March 1845 the Ngapuhi staged a diversionary siege of the town. It was a great tactical success, with Chief Kawiti attacking from the south and another party attacking from Long Beach. While the troops rushed off to protect the township, Hone Heke felled the Union Jack on Maiki (Flagstaff Hill) for the fourth and final time. The British were forced to evacuate to ships lying at anchor. The captain of the HMS *Hazard* was wounded severely in the battle and his replacement ordered the ships' cannons to be fired on the town; most of the buildings were razed. The first of the New Zealand Wars had begun.

In the months that followed, British troops (united with Hokianga-based Ngapuhi) fought Heke and Kawiti in several battles. During this time the modern *pa* (fortified village) was born, effectively the world's first sophisticated system of trench warfare. It's worth stopping at **Ruapekapeka Pa Historic Reserve** (Ruapekapeka Rd), off SH1 south of Kawakawa, to see how impressive these fortifications were. Here you can wander the site of the last battle of the Northland War, brought to life through detailed information boards. Eventually Heke, Kawiti and George Grey (the new governor) made their peace, with no side the clear winner.

Hananui Lodge & Apartments MOTEL $$$
(09-403 7875; www.hananui.co.nz; 4 York St; units $190-320;) Choose between sparkling motel-style units in the trim waterside lodge or apartments in the newer block across the road. Pick of the bunch are the upstairs waterfront units with views straight over the beach.

Ferry Landing Backpackers HOSTEL $
(09-403 7985; www.ferrylandingrussell.co.nz; 395 Aucks Rd, Okiato Pt; dm/s/d $28/50/60;) More like a homestay than a hostel, with only two rooms on offer within the owners' house. It sits on the hill directly above the ferry landing in Okiato – you'll need a car to stay here.

Duke of Marlborough HISTORIC HOTEL $$
(09-403 7829; www.theduke.co.nz; 35 The Strand; r $165-360;) Holding NZ's oldest pub license, the Duke boasts about 'serving rascals and reprobates since 1827', although the building has burnt down twice since then. The upstairs accommodation ranges from small, bright rooms in a 1930s extension to snazzy, spacious doubles facing the water.

Russell Top 10 HOLIDAY PARK $
(09-403 7826; www.russelltop10.co.nz; 1 James St; sites/units from $39/80;) This leafy park has a small store, good facilities, wonderful hydrangeas, tidy cabins and nice units. Showers are clean, but metered.

Russell Motel MOTEL $$
(09-403 7854; www.motelrussell.co.nz; 16 Matauwhi Bay Rd; units $125-199;) Sitting amid well-tended gardens, this old-fashioned motel offers a good range of units and a kidney-shaped pool that the kids will love. The studios are a little dark but you really can't quibble for this price in central Russell.

Pukeko Cottage HOSTEL $
(09-403 8498; www.pukekocottagebackpackers.co.nz; 14 Brind Rd; s/d $25/50;) More like staying at a mate's place than a hostel, this homely house has just two bedrooms for rent and a caravan in the back garden. It's certainly not dirty, but the cleanliness is bloke-standard. Barry, the artist owner, is always up for a chat.

Eating & Drinking

For a country so hooked on cafe culture and a town so touristy, it's disappointing that Russell doesn't have more on offer.

Gables MODERN NZ $$
(09-403 7670; www.thegablesrestaurant.co.nz; 19 The Strand; mains $27-42) Serving an imaginative take on Kiwi classics (lamb, beef and lots of seafood), the Gables occupies an 1847 building on the waterfront, built using whale vertebrae for foundations. Ask for a table by the windows for watery views.

Duke of Marlborough PUB $$
(www.theduke.co.nz; 35 The Strand; lunch $18-29, dinner $24-40) There's no better spot in Russell to while away a few hours, glass in hand, than the Duke's sunny deck. Thankfully the upmarket pub grub matches the views.

Tuk Tuk THAI
(19 York St; mains $15-24; 10.30am-11pm;) Thai fabrics adorn the tables and Thai favourites fill the menu. In clement weather grab a table out front and watch Russell's little world go by.

Pizza Port PIZZERIA $
(Cass St; pizza $11-20; lunch & dinner) There are a couple of tables, but you're better off grabbing one of the gourmet wood-fired pizzas and battling the seagulls at the beach.

Hone's PIZZERIA, BAR $$
(York St; pizza $19-27) Head out to the pebbled courtyard behind the Gables restaurant for wood-fired pizza, cold beer and a good vibe.

Pub 'round the Corner PUB
(www.pubroundthecorner.co.nz; 19 York St; noon-late) A cool, cosy tavern with a beer garden and pool tables.

Shopping

Just Imagine... ARTS & CRAFTS
(www.justimagine.co.nz; 25 York St; 10am-5pm) Full of gorgeous glassware and paintings, this gallery also offers art junkies a caffeine fix.

Information

Russell Booking & Information Centre (09-403 8020; www.russellinfo.co.nz; Russell Pier; 8am-5pm, later in summer)

Getting There & Away

The quickest way to reach Russell by car is via the car ferry (car/motorcycle/passenger $11/5.50/1), which runs every 10 minutes from Opua (5km from Paihia) to Okiato (8km from Russell), between 6.40am and 10pm. Buy your tickets on board. If you're travelling from the south, a scenic alternative is Russell Rd.

On foot, the quickest and easiest way to reach Russell is on one of the regular passenger ferries from Paihia (adult/child one way $7/3, return $12/5). They run from 7am to 7pm (until 10pm October to May), generally every 20 minutes but hourly in the evenings. Buy your tickets on board or at the i-SITE in Paihia.

Paihia & Waitangi

POP 1800

The birthplace of NZ (as opposed to Aotearoa), Waitangi inhabits a special, somewhat complex place in the national psyche – aptly demonstrated by the mixture of celebration, commemoration, protest and apathy that accompanies the nation's birthday (Waitangi Day, 6 February).

It was here that the long-neglected and much-contested Treaty of Waitangi was first signed between Maori chiefs and the British Crown, establishing British sovereignty or something a bit like it, depending on whether you're reading the English or Maori version of the document. If you're interested in coming to grips with NZ's history and race relations, this is the place to start.

Joined to Waitangi by a bridge, Paihia would be a fairly nondescript coastal town if it wasn't the main entry point to the Bay of Islands. If you're not on a tight budget, do yourself a favour, get on a ferry and get thee to Russell, which is far nicer.

There are some good walks in the area, including an easy 5km track that follows the coast from Opua to Paihia.

Sights & Activities

Waitangi Treaty Grounds HISTORIC SITE
(09-402 7437; www.waitangi.net.nz; 1 Tau Henare Dr; adult/child $25/12; 9am-5pm Apr-Sep, 9am-7pm Oct-Mar) Occupying a headland draped in manicured lawns and native bush, this is the most significant site in NZ's history (and as such entry is free to NZ citizens upon presentation of a passport or drivers' license). It was here on 6 February 1840 that the first 43 Maori chiefs, after much discussion, signed the Treaty of Waitangi with the British Crown (eventually over 500 would sign it).

The **Treaty House** was built in 1832 as the four-room home of British resident James Busby. It's now preserved as a memorial and museum containing displays, which include a copy of the treaty. Just across the lawn, the magnificently detailed **whare runanga** (meeting house) was completed in 1940 to mark the centenary of the treaty.

Paihia

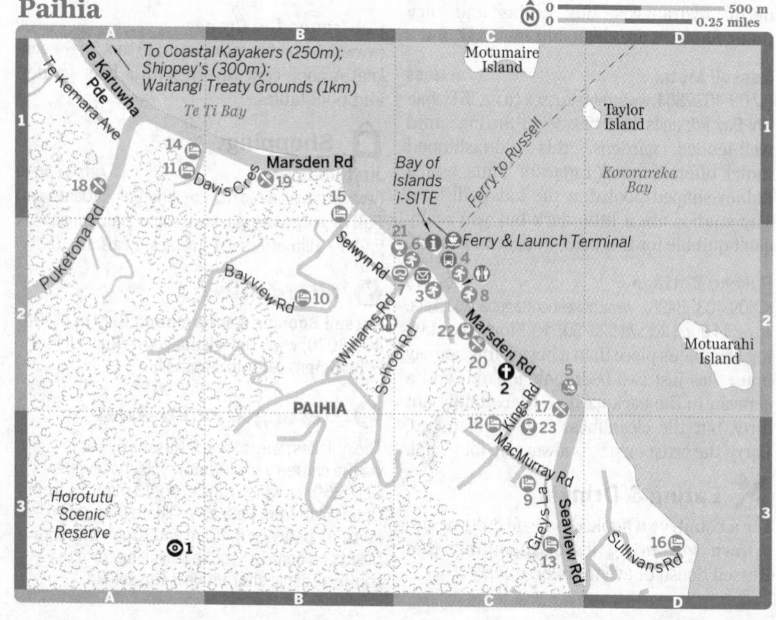

The fine carvings represent the major Maori tribes. Near the cove is the 35m **waka taua** (war canoe), which was also built for the centenary; a photographic exhibit details how it was fashioned from gigantic kauri logs.

The importance of the treaty is well understood by a NZ audience, but visitors might find it surprising that there's not more information displayed here about the role it has played in the nation's history: the long litany of breaches by the Crown, the wars and land confiscations that followed, and the protest movement that led to the current process of redress for historic injustices.

International visitors will get more out of what is already quite a pricy admission fee if they pay extra for a guided tour or cultural performance (adult/child $18/10 for each; check the website or call for times). The 30-minute performance demonstrates traditional Maori song and dance, including that ultimate crowd-pleaser, the *haka* (war dance). The Ultimate Waitangi Experience (adult/child $30/15) is a combined ticket including a tour and a performance. In summer, a 45-minute twilight show (adult/child $25/8) is staged at 6pm.

Finally, the two-hour **Culture North Night Show** (☎09-402 5990; www.culturenorth.co.nz; admission $65; ⏰7.30pm when numbers allow) is a dramatisation of Maori history held in the *whare runanga*. It begins with a traditional Maori welcome and heads into an atmospheric theatrical performance accompanied by a sound-and-light show. Free transfers from Paihia are included in the price.

Paihia

Sights

1	Opua Forest	A3
2	St Paul's Church	C2

Activities, Courses & Tours

3	Explore NZ	C2
4	Fullers Great Sights	C2
5	Island Kayaks & Bay Beach Hire	C2
6	Mack Attack	C2
7	Paihia Dive	C2
8	Salt Air	C2

Sleeping

9	Admiral's View Lodge	C3
10	Allegra House	B2
11	Cap'n Bob's Beachhouse	A1
12	Peppertree Lodge	C3
13	Pickled Parrot	C3
14	Seabeds	A1
15	Swiss Chalet	B1
16	Tarlton's Lodge	D3

Eating

17	Alfresco's	C2
18	Countdown	A1
	Paihia Farmers' Market	(see 3)
19	Pure Tastes	B1
20	Swiss Cafe & Grill	C2

Drinking

21	Bay of Islands Swordfish Club	C2
22	Mako Beach Bar	C2
23	Pipi Patch Bar	C3

Haruru Falls WATERFALL

(Haruru Falls Rd) A walking track (1½ hours one way, 5km) leads from the Treaty Grounds along the Waitangi River to these attractive horseshoe falls, which are lit up at night. Part of the path follows a boardwalk through the mangroves. Otherwise you can drive here, turning right off Puketona Rd onto Haruru Falls Rd.

St Paul's Church CHURCH

(Marsden Rd) St Paul's isn't particularly old (1925), but it stands on the site of NZ's first church – a simple raupo (bulrush) hut constructed in 1823. It's an altogether charming building, built from Kawakawa stone. Look for the native birds in the stained glass above the altar – the kotare (kingfisher) represents Jesus (the king plus 'fisher of men'), while the tui (parson bird) and kereru (wood pigeon) portray the personalities of the Williams brothers (one scholarly, one forceful), who set up the mission station here.

Opua Forest FOREST

Just behind Paihia, this regenerating forest has walking trails ranging from 10 minutes to five hours. A few large trees have escaped axe and fire, including some big kauri. If you walk up from School Rd for about 30 minutes, you'll find a couple of good lookouts. Pamphlets with details on all the Opua Forest walks are available from the i-SITE. You can drive into the forest by taking Oromahoe Rd west from Opua.

Sleeping

What makes Paihia such a desirable base for backpackers is the high standard and wide range of hostels. Kings Rd is the main 'backpackers' row'; if you can't find a bed in one of our favourite places (reviewed below), there are several other reputable places on this strip.

If your budget is more flexible, Russell has more atmosphere, but Paihia is more convenient and has a wider selection of motels, apartments and B&Bs lining the waterfront and scattered about the surrounding hills.

TOP CHOICE Seabeds HOSTEL $

(09-402 5567; www.seabeds.co.nz; 46 Davis Cres; dm/s/d/apt $26/59/85/95; @) Offering comfortable, friendly and quietly stylish budget digs in a converted motel, this newcomer has raised the already high bar on the Paihia scene. Of course, it helps that all the furnishings are brand new, but the little design touches suggest that it hasn't skimped on quality.

Tarlton's Lodge B&B $$

(09-402 6711; www.tarltonslodge.co.nz; 11 Sullivans Rd; r $160-270;) Striking architecture combines with up-to-the-minute decor in this hilltop B&B with expansive bay views. Of the three luxurious suites in the main building, two have their own outdoor spa. The mid-priced rooms are in an older building across the lane, but they share the same aesthetic, pleasing panoramas and breakfast.

Peppertree Lodge HOSTEL $

(09-402 6122; www.peppertree.co.nz; 15 Kings Rd; dm $25-28, r $69-86; @) Simple, clean rooms with high ceilings and good linen. Plus there's a stash of bikes, racquets, kayaks and two barbecues for guests' use, making this a sociable choice.

Pickled Parrot HOSTEL $

(09-402 6222; www.pickledparrot.co.nz; Greys Lane; sites per person $19, dm $26, s/d $60/70; @) Surrounded by tropical plants, this friendly, well-maintained backpackers' stalwart has cute cabins, free bikes, free breakfast and a good vibe.

Baystay B&B B&B $$

(09-402 7511; www.baystay.co.nz; 93a Yorke Rd, Haruru Falls; r $145-185; @) Probably the only accommodation in NZ to have a Johnny Mnemonic pinball machine in the lounge room, this isn't your average B&B. Enjoy valley views from the spa pool of this slick, gay-friendly establishment. Yorke Rd is off Puketona Rd, just before you reach the falls.

Bay of Islands Holiday Park HOLIDAY PARK $

(09-402 7646; www.bayofislandsholidaypark.co.nz; 678 Puketona Rd; site/unit from $38/70; @) Picturesquely placed under tall trees by a set of shallow rapids on the Waitangi River, 7km down Puketona Rd, this wonderful holiday park has excellent units and shady campsites.

Allegra House B&B $$$

(09-402 7932; www.allegra.co.nz; 39 Bayview Rd; r/apt $245/275; @) Offering astonishing views of the bay from an eyrie high above the township, Allegra has three handsome B&B rooms and a spacious self-contained apartment.

Cook's Lookout MOTEL $$$

(09-402 7409; www.cookslookout.co.nz; Causeway Rd; apt $195-295;) Named after an All Black ex-owner rather than the good captain, Cook's is an old-fashioned motel with dated decor made creditable through a winning combination of friendly owners, breathtaking views and a solar-heated swimming pool. To get here, take Puketona Rd towards Haruru Falls, turn right into Yorke St and then take the second right into Causeway Rd.

Cap'n Bob's Beachhouse HOSTEL $

(09-402 8668; www.capnbobs.co.nz; 44 Davis Cres; dm/s/tw/d $25/49/64/86; @) The captain's out at sea but this small backpackers has a new first mate keeping things shipshape. Its a homely place, with sea views from the veranda and more than a touch of charm.

Te Haumi HOMESTAY $$

(09-402 6818; joshlefi@xtra.co.nz; 41b Te Haumi Dr; s/d $145/165) At this proper homestay, you'll join Te Haumi's hospitable hosts for breakfast in the morning and wine and nibbles in the evening – yet once you're in your comfy downstairs room, you'll have all the privacy you'll need. The house backs on to a nature reserve and has bay views. Listen for kiwi at night. Te Haumi Dr heads inland from the main road, about halfway between Opua and Paihia.

Beachside Holiday Park HOLIDAY PARK $
(09-402 7678; www.beachsideholiday.co.nz; 1290 SH11; sites/units from $18/60;) Wake up at the water's edge at this sheltered camping ground, south of the township. The angular lemon cabins have 1970s charm, and there are kayaks for hire.

Admiral's View Lodge MOTEL $$
(09-402 6236; www.admiralsviewlodge.co.nz; 2 MacMurray Rd; apt $120-270;) This hillside lodge offers natty units with balconies just begging for a relaxed sunset gin and tonic. Some have spa baths and bay views.

Swiss Chalet MOTEL $$
(09-402 7615; www.swisschalet.co.nz; 3 Bayview Rd; units $175-380;) This motel has a spa, barbecue, Sky TV and a wide range of good clean rooms with balconies. There's a slight (Swiss) cheese factor but you can't accuse it of looking anonymous.

Eating

TOP CHOICE **Shippey's** FISH & CHIPS $
(www.shippeys.com; Waitangi Bridge; mains $6-12; 10am-late) Our favourite spot for a feed in Paihia is also one of the cheapest. Tuck into fresh fish and chips served as the good lord intended them – in newspaper with a cold beverage in hand – onboard a permanently moored 19th-century tall ship. The views over the inlet and bay are magical, particularly at sunset.

Waikokopu Cafe CAFE $
(www.waikokopu.co.nz; Waitangi Treaty Grounds; mains $13-21; 9am-5pm) The setting is a cracking start – by a pond, backed by bush and overlooking the Treaty Grounds. The locale is matched by Kiwi icons on the menu: the ever popular 'fush and chups' and the Rainbow Warrior, 'French toast sunk in maple syrup, bacon and banana'.

Pure Tastes MODERN NZ $$
(09-402 0003; www.puretastes.co.nz; 116 Marsden Rd; breakfast $16-19, mains $30-34; breakfast, lunch & dinner) Occupying a small canvas-and-glass corner of the Paihia Beach Resort, this first-rate restaurant serves interesting, beautifully presented food using mainly Northland ingredients.

Alfresco's PUB $$
(09-402 6797; 6 Marsden Rd; mains $23-32; 7.30am-late) It doesn't look like much but there's a reason why the locals flock to this casual restaurant/cafe/bar: great food (including plenty of local seafood), reasonable prices and a warm welcome being chief among them. Settle in for live music from 3pm to 6pm every Sunday afternoon.

Swiss Cafe & Grill SWISS $$
(48 Marsden Rd; mains $20-32; dinner) Unpretentious but excellent, this waterfront restaurant has a wide-ranging and eclectic menu, which includes pasta, nicely prepared fish dishes and Swiss comfort food such as schnitzel and homemade strudel.

Paihia Farmers' Market MARKET
(www.bayofislandsfarmersmarket.org.nz; Village Green; 2-5.30pm) Stock up on local fruit, vegetables, pickles, preserves, honey, fish, smallgoods, eggs, cheese, bread, wine and oil, straight from the producer.

Countdown SUPERMARKET
(6 Puketona Rd; 7am-10pm) The main place to stock up on provisions.

Drinking

God bless backpackers: they certainly keep the bars buzzing. There are plenty of places along Kings Rd and in the town centre to explore, so don't feel hemmed in by our list.

Pipi Patch Bar BAR
(18 Kings Rd; 5pm-late) The party hostel has the party bar: a popular spot with large video screens and a decent terrace. You'll be shuffled inside at midnight to keep the neighbours happy – although most of them are backpackers who'll be here anyway.

Mako Beach Bar BAR
(50 Marsden Rd; noon-late) If you get sick of hanging around with other travellers, head to this rough-edged locals' hang-out, where you might catch some live music on the weekends.

Bay of Islands Swordfish Club BAR
(Swordy; www.swordfish.co.nz; upstairs, 96 Marsden Rd; 4pm-late) Great views, cold beer and tall tales abound at this brightly lit club bar where creatures from the deep protrude from every available surface.

Information

Bay of Islands i-SITE (09-402 7345; www.visitnorthland.co.nz; Marsden Rd; 8am-5pm Mar–mid-Dec, 8am-7pm mid-Dec–Feb;) Information and internet access.

Getting There & Around

All buses serving Paihia, such as InterCity and Naked Bus, stop at the Maritime Building by the wharf.

The only buses heading to the west coast are Fullers' *Discover Hokianga* tour (p140) and the Paihia–Auckland leg of the **Magic Travellers Network** (☎09-358 5600; www.magicbus.co.nz) hop-on, hop-off service. The fare ($69, three buses weekly) includes unlimited stops and pick-ups anywhere along the route, including Opononi, Waipoua Forest, Dargaville and Matakohe. There are also tours (p141) to Cape Reinga and the Hokianga.

Ferries depart regularly for Russell.

For bikes, visit Bay Beach Hire (p139).

Urupukapuka Island

The largest of the bay's islands, Urupukapuka is a tranquil place crisscrossed with walking trails and surrounded by aquamarine waters. Native birds are plentiful thanks to a conservation initiative that has rendered this and all of the neighbouring islands predator-free; check that there aren't any rats, mice or ants stowing away on your boat or in your gear before leaving the mainland.

Most of the regular boat tours moor at Otehei Bay for a little island time; if you want to stay over, you can usually arrange to split the trip up and return at a later date. There are **DOC campsites** (www.doc.govt.nz; sites per adult/child $8.10/2) at Cable, Sunset and Urupukapuka Bays. They have water supplies, cold showers (except Sunset Bay) and composting toilets; bring food, a stove and fuel.

The **Waterfront Bar & Cafe** (www.oteheibay.co.nz; Otehei Bay; mains $15-24) serves light meals (hot chips, sandwiches, burgers, fish and chips) to passengers arriving on the boat tours, and in the height of summer also offers evening meals. Kayaks can be rented from **Bay of Islands Kayaking** (☎021 272 3353; www.bayofislandskayaking.co.nz; hire from $10, island transfer & guided paddle $120), based here.

Kerikeri

POP 5900

Kerikeri means 'dig dig', which is apt, as a lot of digging goes on in the fertile farmland that surrounds the town. Famous for its oranges, Kerikeri also produces plenty of kiwifruit (don't call them kiwis unless you want to offend Kiwis), vegetables and, increasingly, wine. If you're looking for some back-breaking, poorly paid work that Kiwis (the people, as opposed to kiwifruit) aren't keen to do, your working holiday starts here.

A snapshot of early Maori and Pakeha (European New Zealander) interaction is offered by a cluster of historic sites centred on the picturesque river basin. In 1819 the powerful Ngapuhi chief Hongi Hika allowed Rev Samuel Marsden to start a mission under the shadow of his Kororipo Pa. There's an ongoing campaign to have the area recognised as a Unesco World Heritage Site.

Sights & Activities

Stone Store & Mission House HISTORIC BUILDINGS
(www.historic.org.nz; 246 Kerikeri Rd; ⏲10am-4pm) Sitting pretty at Kerikeri Basin, the country's most venerable architectural coupling represents the oldest of their kind in the country. Dating from 1836, the Stone Store is NZ's oldest stone building. It sells interesting gifts as well as the type of goods that used to be sold in the store – although these days you'll have a hard time bartering pigs for muskets. Tours ($10) of the wooden Mission House, NZ's oldest building (1822), depart from here and include entry to *The Soul Trade* exhibition on the 1st floor of the store.

Just up the hill is a marked historical walk, which leads to the site of **Kororipo Pa**. Huge war parties led by Hika once departed from here, terrorising much of the North Island and slaughtering thousands during the Musket Wars. The role of missionaries in arming Ngapuhi remains controversial. The walk emerges near the cute wooden **St James Anglican Church** (1878).

Rewa's Village MUSEUM
(Landing Rd; adult/child $5/1; ⏲9.30am-4.30pm) If you had a hard time imagining Kororipo Pa in its original state, take the footbridge across the river to this fascinating mock-up of a traditional Maori fishing village.

Aroha Island WILDLIFE RESERVE
(www.arohaisland.co.nz; 177 Rangitane Rd; admission free; ⏲9.30am-5.30pm Thu-Tue) Reached via a permanent causeway through the mangroves, this 5-hectare island provides a haven for the North Island brown kiwi and other native birds, as well as a pleasant picnic spot

Kerikeri

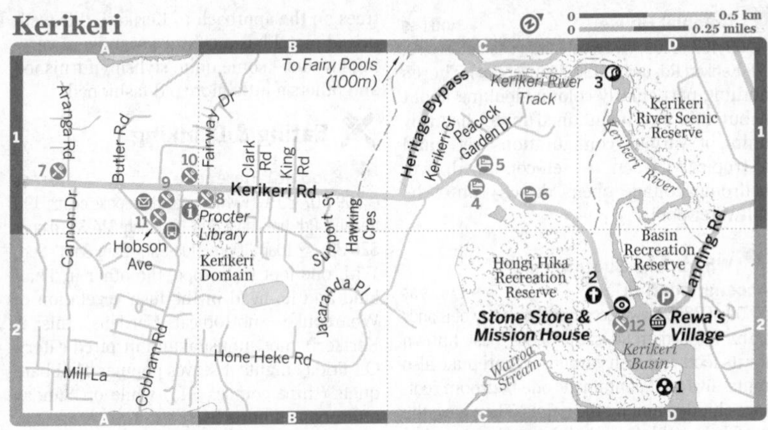

for their nonfeathered admirers. It has a visitor centre and kayaks for rent (from $18).

Kerikeri River Track WALKING
Starting from Kerikeri Basin, this 4km-long track leads past **Wharepuke Falls** and the **Fairy Pools** to the **Rainbow Falls**, where the sheet of water encloses a moss-covered cavern. Alternatively, you can reach the Rainbow Falls from Rainbow Falls Rd, in which case it's only a 10-minute walk.

Kerikeri

Top Sights
- Rewa's Village ... D2
- Stone Store & Mission House ... D2

Sights
- 1 Kororipo Pa ... D2
- 2 St James Anglican Church ... D2
- 3 Wharepuke Falls ... D1

Sleeping
- 4 Bed of Roses ... C1
- 5 Colonial House ... C1
- 6 Wharepuke Subtropical Accommodation ... C1

Eating
- 7 Black Olive ... A1
- 8 Cafe Jerusalem ... B1
- 9 Cafe Zest ... A1
- 10 Fishbone ... A1
- Food at Wharepuke ... (see 6)
- 11 Kerikeri Farmers' Market ... A1
- 12 Pear Tree ... D2

Sleeping

Pagoda Lodge LODGE, CAMPSITE $
(☎09-407 8617; www.pagoda.co.nz; 81 Pa Rd; sites/safari tent from $32/100, apt $80-300; wi-fi) Built in the 1930s by an oddball Scotsman with an Asian fetish, this lodge features pagoda-shaped roofs grafted onto wooden cottages. The property descends to the river and is dotted with Buddhas, gypsy caravans and safari tents with proper beds, or you can pitch your own. To get here, take Cobham Rd, turn left into Kerikeri Inlet Rd and then left into Pa Rd.

Kerikeri Farm Hostel HOSTEL $
(☎09-407 6989; www.farmhostel.co.nz; 1574 Springbank Rd (SH10); dm/s/d $24/50/56; @ wi-fi) Less a farm, more an orange grove, this quiet rural house 4km out of town sleeps only 12. It's a homely place, with a sole chandelier adding a bit of bling to the cosy lounge.

Bed of Roses B&B $$$
(☎09-407 4666; www.bedofroses.co.nz; 165 Kerikeri Rd; r $225-350; @) It's all petals and no thorns at this stylish B&B, furnished with French antiques, luxe linens and comfy beds. The house has an art-deco ambience and awesome views.

Aroha Island CAMPSITE $
(☎09-407 5243; www.arohaisland.co.nz; 177 Rangitane Rd; sites/units from $18/86) Kip among the kiwi on the eco island of love *(aroha)*. There's a wide range of reasonably priced options, from the peaceful campsites with basic facilities by the shelly beach to a whole house. The entire island, indoors and out, is nonsmoking.

Colonial House MOTEL $$
(☎09-407 9106; www.colonialhousemotel.co.nz; 178 Kerikeri Rd; units $130-245; @☎) There's nothing particularly colonial-looking about it but this well-maintained motel has tidy units of various configurations set amid a tropical garden. A self-contained two-bedroom cottage opens directly onto the saltwater pool.

Wharepuke Subtropical Accommodation CABINS $$
(☎09-4078933; www.accommodation-bay-of-islands.co.nz; 190 Kerikeri Rd; cabins $180) Best known for its food and lush gardens, Wharepuke also rents five self-contained one-bedroom cottages hidden among the palms. They have the prefabricated look of holiday-park cabins but are a step up in terms of fixtures and space.

Kauri Park MOTEL $$
(☎09-407 7629; www.kauripark.co.nz; 512 Kerikeri Rd; units $130-170; @☎) Hidden behind tall trees on the approach to Kerikeri, this well-priced motel has a mixture of units of varying layouts – some quite stylishly furnished and others a little more old-fashioned.

Eating & Drinking

Food at Wharepuke CAFE $$
(☎09-407 8936; www.foodatwharepuke.co.nz; 190 Kerikeri Rd; breakfast $14-16, lunch $14-35, dinner $26-35; ⊙10am-10pm Tue-Sat, 9am-3pm Sun) With one foot in Europe, the other in Thailand and its head in the lush vegetation of Wharepuke Subtropical Gardens, this is Kerikeri's most unusual and inspired eatery. On Friday nights it serves popular Thai banquets (three courses $45) while on Sunday afternoons it hosts live jazz.

Fishbone CAFE $
(88 Kerikeri Rd; mains $7-15; ⊙breakfast & lunch) Kerikeri's best brekkie spot serves excellent coffee and food. Dr Seuss fans should try the green (pesto) eggs and ham.

KERIKERI COTTAGE INDUSTRIES

You'd be forgiven for thinking that everyone in Kerikeri is involved in some small-scale artisanal enterprise or other, as the bombardment of craft shops on the way into town attests.

While Northland isn't known for its wine, a handful of vineyards near Kerikeri are doing their best to change that. The little-known red grape chambourcin has proved particularly suited to the region's subtropical humidity, along with pinotage and syrah.

Look out for the *Art & Craft Trail* and *Wine Trail* brochures for helpful maps and additional places to vist.

Kerikeri Farmers' Market (www.boifm.org.nz; Hobson Ave; ⊙8.30am-noon Sun) An excellent place to sample a range of what the region has to offer, from sausages to *limoncello*.

Get Fudged & Keriblue (www.getfudged.co.nz; 560 Kerikeri Rd; ⊙9am-5pm) An unusual pairing of ceramics and big, decadent slabs of fudge.

Makana Confections (www.makana.co.nz; 504 Kerikeri Rd; ⊙9am-5.30pm) If you're a recovering sugar junkie, you may need to drive into town with your eyes closed to avoid this boutique chocolate factory, where you can watch production through a window in the shop.

Marsden Estate (www.marsdenestate.co.nz; 56 Wiroa Rd; mains $19-22; ⊙10am-4pm) A lovely stop for tasting the area's best wine and eating lunch on the deck.

Ake Ake (www.akeakevineyard.co.nz; 165 Waimate North Rd; tastings $5, tour $5, mains $26-34; ⊙10am-6pm Tue-Sun summer, Wed-Sun winter) Offers vineyard tours (11.30am) and tastings, both of which are free if you order lunch or buy a bottle. The swanky restaurant is open for lunch and dinner on the days the cellar door is open.

Cottle Hill (www.cottlehill.co.nz; Cottle Hill Dr; tastings $5, free with purchase; ⊙10am-5pm Nov-Mar, 10am-5pm Wed-Sun Apr-Oct) Makes wine, port and grappa and has some interesting old cars kicking about.

Fat Pig Vineyard (www.fatpig.co.nz; 177 Puketotara Rd; ⊙11am-6pm) Wines and port.

WORTH A TRIP

PUKETI & OMAHUTA FORESTS

Inland from Kerikeri, the Puketi and Omahuta Forests form a continuous expanse of native rainforest. Logging in Puketi was stopped in 1951 to protect not only the remaining kauri but also the endangered kokako bird. Keep an eye out for this rare charmer (grey with a blue wattle) on your wanders.

The forests are reached by several entrances and contain a network of walking tracks varying in length from 15 minutes (the wheelchair-accessible Manginangina Kauri Walk) to two days (the challenging Waipapa River Track); see the DOC website for other walks.

You'll find a **DOC campsite** (☎09-407 0300; www.doc.govt.nz; Waiare Rd; sites per adult/child $7/3.50), two three-person cabins ($21) and a 18-bunk hut (exclusive use $62) at the Puketi Recreation Area on the forests' eastern fringe. The hut has hot showers, a kitchen and a flush toilet, while the cabins and campsite make do with cold showers.

Adventure Puketi (www.forestwalks.com; tours $75-155) leads guided eco-walks through the forest, including night-time tours to seek out the nocturnal wildlife.

Pear Tree RESTAURANT, BAR $$
(☎09-407 8479; www.thepeartree.co.nz; 215 Kerikeri Rd; mains $18-33; ⊙lunch & dinner) Kerikeri's best located and most upmarket restaurant occupies an old homestead right on the basin (book ahead for a table on the veranda). Mains run the gamut of bistro favourites, along with the occasional Asian dish.

Cafe Jerusalem MIDDLE EASTERN $$
(Village Mall, Kerikeri Rd; mains $17-20; ⊙11am-late) Northland's best falafels, served with a smile and a social vibe.

Cafe Blue CAFE
(582 Kerikeri Rd; mains $8-20; ⊙9am-3pm) It may be on the main road into town but this garden cafe is a peaceful oasis, serving sandwiches, salads, renowned Cornish pasties, pancakes and sub-$20 grills.

Cafe Zest CAFE, BAR $
(73 Kerikeri Rd; mains $10-19; ⊙7.30am-4pm Mon-Wed, 7.30am-8.30pm Thu-Sat, 7.30am-2pm Sun) Bathed in Kerikeri's orange glow, cute little Zest serves cafe fare during the day and tapas in the evening, but the main reason to drop by is to sample wines from all of the local producers.

Black Olive ITALIAN $$
(☎09-407 9693; www.theblackolive.net; 308 Kerikeri Rd; mains $12-36; ⊙dinner Tue-Sun) Call ahead for popular pasta and pizza take aways, or grab a seat in the restaurant or garden.

Information

Procter Library (Cobham Rd; ⊙8am-5pm Mon-Fri, 9am-2pm Sat, 9am-1pm Sun; @☎) Drop by for tourist brochures and free internet access.

Getting There & Away

Air

Bay of Islands (Kerikeri) Airport (☎09-407 7147; www.bayofislandsairport.co.nz; 218 Wiroa Rd) 8km southwest of town. Air New Zealand and Salt Air Xpress both run flights (p128) to Kerikeri.

Dial-a-Ride (☎0508 342 527; www.dial-a-ride.co.nz) Operates a shuttle service from the airport to Kerikeri, Paihia, Opua and Kawakawa.

Bus

InterCity (p128) and partner buses leave from a stop at 9 Cobham Rd, opposite the library.

THE FAR NORTH

If it sounds remote, that's because it is. Here's your chance to get off the beaten track, although that often means onto unsealed roads. The far-flung Far North is always playing second fiddle to the Bay of Islands for attention and funding, yet the subtropical tip of the North Island has more breathtaking coastline per square kilometre than anywhere but the offshore islands. Parts of the Far North are noticeably economically depressed and in places could best be described as gritty. While the 'winterless north' may be a popular misnomer, summers here are long and leisurely.

Matauri & Tauranga Bays

It's a short detour from SH10, but the exceptionally scenic loop route leading inland to these awesome beaches is a world away from the glitzy face presented for tourists in the Bay of Islands.

Matauri Bay is a long sandy surf beach, 18km off SH10, with the 17 Cavalli Islands scattered offshore. **Matauri Bay Holiday Park** (☎09-405 0525; www.matauribayholidaypark.co.nz; sites from $20, units $130-180) takes up the north end of the beach and has a shop selling groceries, booze and petrol. On top of the headland above the park is a monument to the *Rainbow Warrior*; the Greenpeace ship's underwater resting place among the Cavalli Islands is a popular dive site.

DOC maintains a 12-person **hut** (☎09-407 0300; www.doc.govt.nz; sites per adult/child $13/6.10) on Motukawanui Island, but you'll need a boat or kayak to reach it and you'll need to book ahead. Only water, mattresses and a composting toilet are provided; bring everything else.

Back on the main road, the route heads west, passing through pleasant Te Ngaere village and a succession of little bays before the turn-off to Tauranga Bay, a smaller beach where the sand is a peachy pink colour. **Tauranga Bay Holiday Park** (☎09-405 0436; www.taurangabay.co.nz; sites from $18, cabins $97-170; @📶) has campsites and log cabins on the picturesque beachfront, but it lacks trees and bears the brunt of the weather. A minimum $59 charge per night for campsites and a seven-night minimum stay apply in January.

Down a private road leading from Tauranga Bay, **Northland Sea Kayaking** (☎09-405 0381; www.northlandseakayaking.co.nz; half-/full day tours $75/95) leads kayak explorations of this magical coastline of coves, sea caves and islands. Accommodation is available in conjunction with tours for $20 extra per person.

There's no public transport to these parts or to neighbouring Whangaroa.

THE BOMBING OF THE RAINBOW WARRIOR

On the morning of 10 July 1985, New Zealanders awoke to news reporting that a terrorist attack had killed a man in Auckland Harbour. The Greenpeace flagship *Rainbow Warrior* had been sunk at its anchorage at Marsden Wharf, where it was preparing to sail to Moruroa Atoll near Tahiti to protest against French nuclear testing.

It took some time to find out exactly what had happened, but a tip-off from a Neighbourhood Watch group lead to the arrest of two French foreign intelligence service (DGSE) agents, posing as tourists. The agents had detonated two mines on the boat in staggered explosions – the first designed to cause the crew to evacuate and the second to sink her. However, after the initial evacuation, some of the crew returned to the vessel to investigate and document the attack. Greenpeace photographer Fernando Pereira was drowned below decks following the second explosion.

The arrested agents pleaded guilty to manslaughter and were sentenced to 10 years' imprisonment. In response, the French government threatened to embargo NZ goods from entering the European Economic Community – which would have crippled NZ's economy. A deal was struck whereby France paid $13 million to NZ and apologised, in return for the agents being delivered into French custody on a South Pacific atoll for three years. France eventually paid over $8 million to Greenpeace in reparation – and the bombers were quietly freed before their sentence was served.

Initially French President Mitterrand denied any government involvement in the attack, but following an inquiry he eventually sacked his Defence Minister and the head of the DGSE, Admiral Pierre Lacoste. On the 20th anniversary of the attack, *Le Monde* newspaper published a report from Lacoste dating from 1986 declaring that the president had personally authorised the operation.

The bombing left a lasting impact on NZ, and French nuclear testing at Moruroa ceased for good in 1996. The wreck of the *Rainbow Warrior* was re-sunk near Northland's Cavalli Islands, where it can be explored by divers. The masts were bought by the Dargaville Museum and overlook the town. The memory of Fernando Pereira endures in a peaceful bird hide in Thames. A memorial to the boat sits atop a Maori *pa* site at Matauri Bay, north of the Bay of Islands.

Whangaroa Harbour

Just around the headland from Tauranga Bay is the narrow entrance to Whangaroa Harbour. The small fishing village of Whangaroa is 6km from SH10 and calls itself the 'Marlin Capital of NZ'.

There are plenty of charter boats for game-fishing (December to April); prices start at around $1200 a day. If you're planning to hook a monster, insist on it being released once caught – striped marlin and swordfish are among NZ's least-sustainable fishing options.

An excellent 20-minute hike starts from the car park at the end of Old Hospital Rd and goes up **St Paul's Rock** (213m), which dominates the village. At the top you have to use a wire cable to pull yourself up, but the views make it worth the effort.

The **Wairakau Stream Track**, heading north to Pekapeka Bay, begins near the church hall on Campbell Rd in Totara North on the other side of the bay. It's an extremely beautiful, undeveloped stretch and you can cool off in swimming holes along the way. The two-hour hike passes through forest, an abandoned farm and around a steep-walled estuary before arriving at DOC's **Lane Cove Hut** (☎09-407 0300; www.doc.govt.nz; sole occupancy $164), which has 16 beds and composting toilets. Bring everything else and book well ahead; it's usually booked out by Kiwi families over summer.

Duke's Nose Track (1¼ hours return) starts behind the cottage and leads up Kairara Rocks; look for the Duke of Wellington's aquiline profile in the rock face. You'll need to haul yourself up a chain for the last 10m but the views are worth it.

If you don't fancy walking back – or if you don't fancy walking at all – **Bushmansfriend** (☎09405 1844; www.bushmansfriend.co.nz) arranges water taxis from Lane Cove ($20), one-hour boat tours ($40) and guided walks, returning by boat ($105).

On the other side of the harbour's north head is **Taupo Bay**, a surf beach that attracts a loyal Kiwi contingent in summer. On easterly swells, there are quality right-handers to surf at the southern end of the bay, by the rivermouth. It's reached by an 11km sealed road signposted from SH10.

FISH FOR THE FUTURE

While NZ's fisheries are more tightly controlled than most, conservation groups note that most fishing is still unsustainable at present levels. **Forest & Bird** (www.forestandbird.org.nz) publishes a *Best Fish Guide*, which is downloadable from its website. The following are the best and worst choices if you're hankering for a seafood chow-down.

Ten best Anchovy, pilchard, sprats, cockles, garfish, kina, skipjack tuna, kahawai, blue cod, yellow-eyed mullet

Ten worst Orange roughy, shark (porbeagle, mako, blue, lemonfish/rig), oreo (deepwater dory), southern bluefin tuna, snapper, bluenose, jack mackerel, arrow squid, skate, striped marlin

Sleeping & Eating

TOP CHOICE **Kahoe Farms Hostel** HOSTEL $
(☎09-405 1804; www.kahoefarms.co.nz; dm $30, r $76-96) On SH10, 10km north of the turn-off to Whangaroa, this hostel has a deservedly great reputation – for its comfortable accommodation, for its bucolic setting, for its home-cooked Italian food, but mostly for its welcoming owners. The backpackers' cottage is great, but slightly up the hill there's an even more impressive villa with excellent-value en-suite rooms.

Sunseeker Lodge HOSTEL $
(☎09-405 0496; www.sunseekerlodge.co.nz; Old Hospital Rd; dm/s/d/tr $25/50/66/90, units $120-150; @☎) Up the hill in Whangaroa, this friendly lodge has a sublime spa with a jaw-dropping view, hires out kayaks and motor boats, and will pick you up from Kaeo on SH10.

Marlin PUB
(Whangaroa Rd; mains $15-20; ⊙lunch & dinner) A friendly local pub with good honest tucker served from the attached cafe.

Information

Boyd Gallery (☎09-405 0230; Whangaroa Rd; ⊙8am-7pm) The general store, but also acts as a tourist information office.

Doubtless Bay

POP 6030

The bay gets its unusual name from an entry in Cook's logbook, where he wrote that the body of water was 'doubtless a bay'. No kidding, Cap'n. It's a bloody big bay at that, with a string of pretty swimming beaches heading towards the Karikari Peninsula.

The main centre, Mangonui (meaning 'Big Shark'), retains a fishing-port feel, despite cafes and gift shops now infesting its well-labelled line of historical waterfront buildings. They were constructed in the days when Mangonui was a centre of the whaling industry (1792–1850) and exported flax, kauri wood and gum.

The popular holiday settlements of Coopers Beach, Cable Bay and Taipa are restful pockets of beachside gentrification.

Sights & Activities

Grab the free *Heritage Trail* brochure from the information centre for a 3km self-guided walk taking in 22 historic sites. Other walks lead to attractive **Mill Bay**, west of Mangonui, and **Rangikapiti Pa Historic Reserve**, which has ancient Maori terracing and a spectacular view of Doubtless Bay – particularly at sunrise and sunset. A walkway runs from Mill Bay to the *pa*, but you can also drive nearly to the top.

Butler Point Whaling Museum MUSEUM
(www.butlerpoint.co.nz; Marchant Rd; adult/child $12/2; ⌚by appointment) At Hihi, 15km northeast of Mangonui, is this small private museum and Victorian homestead (1843) set in lovely gardens. Its first owner, Captain Butler, left Dorset when he was 14 and at 24 was captain of a whaling ship. He settled here in 1839, had 13 children and became a trader, farmer, magistrate and Member of Parliament.

Sleeping

There's plenty of accommodation around the bay but most is horribly overpriced in summer. Outside the peak months things settle down considerably.

TOP CHOICE **Old Oak** BOUTIQUE HOTEL $$
(☎09-406 1250; www.theoldoak.co.nz; 66 Waterfront Dr, Mangonui; s $125, d $175-225, ste $295; 📶) A snazzy renovation has transformed this atmospheric 1861 kauri inn into an elegant boutique hotel with contemporary design and top-notch furnishings. It oozes character, not least because the building is reputedly haunted.

Mangonui Waterfront Apartments Motel APARTMENTS $$
(☎09-406 0347; www.mangonuiwaterfront.co.nz; 88 Waterfront Dr; apt $120-225; @📶) Sleeping two to eight people, these historic apartments on the Mangonui waterfront have loads of character, each one different but all with balconies, a sense of space and their own barbecue. Try to book 100-year-old Tahi.

Puketiti Lodge HOSTEL $
(☎09-406 0369; www.puketitilodge.co.nz; 10 Puketiti Dr; dm/r $40/150; @📶) If this is what they mean by flashpacking, bring it on. For $40 you get a comfy bunk in a spacious six-person dorm opening on to a large deck with awesome views, a locker big enough for the burliest backpack and, perhaps most surprisingly, breakfast. Turn inland at Midgley Rd, 6km south of Mangonui village, just after the Hihi turn-off.

By The Bay APARTMENTS $$$
(www.beachfrontapartments.co.nz; 16 Braemar Ave; apt $200-400; 📶) Long, lovely Coopers Beach beckons from the bottom of the lawn at this upmarket set of apartments. The owners operate a day spa, offering in-house massage and beauty treatments.

Eating

There are a few cafes, takeaways and stores scattered around the other beaches, but Mangonui has the best eating options – and they're actually pretty great.

TOP CHOICE **Acorn Bar & Bistro** MODERN NZ $$
(☎09-406 0896; 66 Waterfront Dr, Mangonui; mains $26-33; ⌚dinner Wed-Mon) A fitting companion piece to its neighbour, the Old Oak, this handsome little restaurant serves a concise, seasonal menu taking advantage of the freshest seafood, straight off the wharf, and the best of the local farm produce.

Waterfront Cafe & Bar CAFE $
(Waterfront Dr, Mangonui; brunch $11-18, dinner $14-29; ⌚8.30am-late) The best cafe in the Far North, Waterfront has water views, friendly service and old-world charm. A pizza menu kicks in at lunch and extends into dinner, where it supplements bistro dishes.

Thai Chef THAI $$
(☎09-406 1220; www.thaichef.co.nz; 80 Waterfront Dr, Mangonui; mains $18-26; ⊙dinner Tue-Sun) The best Thai restaurant in Northland serves piquant dishes with names such as *The 3 Alcoholics*, *Spice Girls* and *Bangkok Showtime*. The *Sexy Little Duck* is irresistible.

Mangonui Fish Shop FISH & CHIPS $
(137 Waterfront Dr; fish & chips $8.80; ⊙10am-8pm; 📶) You can eat outdoors over the water at this famous chippie, which also sells smoked fish and seafood salads. Grab a crayfish salad and a cold beer, and all will be right with the world. If the queues are too long, the other fish and chip shop across the road is also good.

Shopping

Far North Wine Centre WINE
(60 Waterfront Dr, Mangonui; ⊙10.30am-4.30pm Tue-Sun) Sample and purchase wine from the local Lava Rock and Manaia ranges.

Flax Bush ART & CRAFT
(www.flaxbush.co.nz; 50 Waterfront Dr, Mangonui) Seashells, Pasifika and Maori knick-knacks.

Information

Doubtless Bay Visitor Information Centre
(☎09-406 2046; www.doubtlessbay.co.nz; 118 Waterfront Dr, Mangonui; ⊙10am-4pm Mon-Sat; @)

Getting There & Away

InterCity buses stop at the BP service station on Waterfront Dr in Mangonui, outside the wholesalers in Coopers Beach, opposite the shop in Cable Bay and outside the Shell station in Taipa. **Busabout Kaitaia** (☎09-408 1092; www.cbec.co.nz) has services to Kaitaia ($5, one hour).

Karikari Peninsula

The oddly shaped Karikari Peninsula bends into a near-perfect right angle. The result is beaches facing north, south, east and west in close proximity; if the wind's annoying you or you want to catch some surf, a sunrise or a sunset, just swap beaches. Despite its natural assets, the sun-baked peninsula is blissfully undeveloped, with farmers well outnumbering tourist operators. There's no public transport and you won't find a lot of shops or eateries either.

Sights & Activities

Tokerau Beach is the long, sandy stretch forming the western edge of Doubtless Bay. Neighbouring Whatuwhiwhi is smaller and more built-up, facing back across the bay. Maitai Bay, with its tiny twin coves, is the loveliest of them all, at the lonely end of the peninsula down an unsealed road. It's a great spot for swimming – the waters sheltered enough for the kids but with enough swell to body surf.

Rangiputa faces west at the elbow of the peninsula; the pure white sand and crystal-clear sheltered waters come straight from a Pacific Island daydream. A turn-off on the road to Rangiputa takes you to remote Puheke Beach, a long, windswept stretch of snow-white sand dunes forming Karikari's northern edge.

Various local watersports operators can be contacted under the umbrella of **Watersports Paradise** (☎0508 727 234; www.watersportsparadise.co.nz).

Karikari Estate WINERY
(www.karikariestate.co.nz; Maitai Bay Rd; tastings $12; ⊙11am-4pm) An ominous sign of creeping gentrification is the luxury golf club and winery on the way to Maitai Bay. Impressive Karikari Estate produces acclaimed red wines and has a cafe attached - and while the wine tastings are shamelessly overpriced, at least the sublime views are free.

Airzone Kitesurfing School KITESURFING
(☎021 202 7949; www.kitesurfnz.com; 1-/2-/3-day course $195/350/485) The unique set-up of Karikari Peninsula makes it one of the world's premium spots for kiteboarding, or at least that's the opinion of this experienced crew. Learners get to hone their skills on flat water before heading to the surf, while the more experienced can chase the wind around the peninsula.

A to Z Diving DIVING
(☎09-408 3336; www.atozdiving.co.nz; 13-15 Whatuwhiwhi Rd; 2 dives incl equipment $160-230) Offers PADI courses and dive trips in Doubtless Bay and at the *Rainbow Warrior*.

Karikari Kayaks KAYAKING
(☎09-4087575; www.karikari-kayaking.co.nz) Hires kayaks from the northern end of Tokerau Beach.

Sleeping

Whatuwhiwhi Top 10 Holiday Park HOLIDAY PARK $
(09-408 7202; www.whatuwhiwhitop10.co.nz; 17 Whatuwhiwhi Rd; sites from $62, units $82-385) Sheltered by hills and overlooking the beach, this friendly complex has a great location, good facilities, free barbecues and kayaks for hire. They also offer dive fills and PADI diving instruction.

Maitai Bay DOC Campsite CAMPSITE $
(www.doc.govt.nz; Maitai Bay Rd; sites per adult/child $8/4) A large first-in, first-served (no bookings) camping ground at the peninsula's most beautiful beach, with chemical toilets, drinking water and cold showers.

Carrington Resort RESORT $$$
(09-408 7222; www.heritagehotels.co.nz; r $429-476, villa $580; @) There's something very Australian-looking about this hilltop lodge, with its wide verandas and gum trees, tempered by Maori and Pacific design in the spacious rooms and villas. The view over the golf course to the dazzling white beach is exquisite.

Cape Reinga & Ninety Mile Beach

Maori consider Cape Reinga (Te Rerenga-Wairua) the jumping-off point for souls as they depart on the journey to their spiritual homeland. That makes the Aupouri Peninsula a giant diving board, and it even resembles one – long and thin, it reaches 108km to form NZ's northern extremity. On its west coast Ninety Mile Beach (Ninety Kilometre Beach would be more accurate) is a continuous stretch lined with high sand dunes, flanked by the Aupouri Forest.

Sights & Activities

Cape Reinga CAPE
Standing at windswept **Cape Reinga Lighthouse** (a 1km walk from the car park) and looking out over the ocean engenders a real end-of-the-world feeling. This is where the waters of the Tasman Sea and Pacific Ocean meet, breaking together into waves up to 10m high in stormy weather. Little tufts of cloud often cling to the ridges, giving sudden spooky chills even on hot days.

Visible on a promontory slightly to the east is a spiritually significant 800-year-old pohutukawa tree; souls are believed to slide down its roots. Out of respect to the most sacred site in Maoridom, don't go near the tree and refrain from eating or drinking anywhere in the area.

Cape Reinga Coastal Walkway TRAMPING
Contrary to expectation, Cape Reinga isn't actually the northernmost point of the country; that honour belongs to Surville Cliffs further to the east. A walk along Te Werahi Beach to Cape Maria van Diemen (five hours loop) takes you to the westernmost point. This is one of many sections of the three- to four-day, 53km Cape Reinga Coastal Walkway (from Kapowairua to Te Paki Stream) that can be tackled individually. Beautiful **Tapotupotu Bay** is a two-hour walk east of Cape Reinga, via Sandy Bay and the cliffs. From Tapotupotu Bay it's an eight-hour walk to **Spirits Bay**, one of NZ's most beautiful beaches. Both bays are also accessible by road.

Te Paki Recreation Reserve NATURE RESERVE
A large chunk of the land around Cape Reinga is part of the Te Paki Recreation Reserve managed by DOC. It's public land with free access; leave the gates as you found them and don't disturb the animals. There are 7 sq km of giant sand dunes on either side of the mouth of Te Paki Stream. Clamber up to take flying leaps off the dunes or to toboggan down them.

Great Exhibition Bay BEACH
On the east coast, Great Exhibition Bay has dazzling snow-white silica dunes. There's no public road access, but some tours pay a *koha* (donation) to cross Maori farmland or approach the sand by kayak from Parengarenga Harbour.

Nga-Tapuwae-o-te-Mangai TEMPLE
(6576 Far North Rd) With its two domed towers (Arepa and Omeka, alpha and omega) and the Ratana emblem of the star and crescent moon, you could be forgiven for mistaking this temple for a mosque. Ratana is a Maori Christian sect with more than 50,000 adherents, formed in 1925 by Tahupotiki Wiremu Ratana, who was known as 'the mouthpiece of God'. The temple is built on land where Ratana once stood; the name translates as 'the sacred steps of the mouthpiece'. You'll pass it at Te Kao, 46km south of Cape Reinga.

Gumdiggers Park OUTDOOR MUSEUM
(www.gumdiggerspark.co.nz; 171 Heath Rd, Waiharara; adult/child $12/6; ⏲9am-5pm) Kauri forests covered this area for over 100,000 years, leaving ancient logs and the much-prized gum (used for making varnish and linoleum) buried beneath. Digging it out of the mud was the region's main industry from the 1870s to the 1920s. In 1900, some 7000 gumdiggers (wearing rubber gumboots – the NZ name for Wellingtons) were digging holes all over Northland, including at this site. Start with the 15-minute video telling the story of the trees, their mysterious destruction and the gum industry. Rope paths head through the bush, leading past reproductions of gumdiggers' huts, ancient kauri stumps and holes left by the diggers. It was a hard life for the workers, who used jute sacks for their tents, bedding and clothing.

Ancient Kauri Kingdom WOODTURNERS
(www.ancientkauri.co.nz; 229 Far North Rd, Awanui; ⏲8.30am-5pm; @📶) It's tacky and overpriced, but Ancient Kauri Kingdom is still worth a stop. Here 50,000-year-old kauri stumps dragged out of swamps are fashioned into furniture, woodcraft products and a fair bit of tourist tat. The large complex includes a cafe, gift shop and workshop. A huge kauri log has an impressive spiral staircase carved into it that leads to the mezzanine level.

Tours

Bus tours go to Cape Reinga from Kaitaia, Ahipara, Doubtless Bay and the Bay of Islands; there's no other public transport up here.

Cape Reinga Adventures 4WD
(☎09-409 8445; www.capereingaadventures.co.nz; half-/full-day 4WD trips $75/135) Real action men who offer 4WD tours (including sunset visits to the cape after the crowds have gone), fishing, kayaking and sandboarding as day activities or as part of overnight camping trips.

Far North Outback Adventures 4WD
(☎09-408 0927; www.farnorthtours.co.nz; price on application) Flexible, day-long tours from Kaitaia and Ahipara, including morning tea and lunch. Options include visits to remote areas such as Great Exhibition Bay.

Harrison's Cape Runner BUS
(☎0800 227 373; www.harrisonscapereingatours.co.nz; 123 North Rd, Kaitaia; adult/child $50/25) Day trips from Kaitaia along Ninety Mile Beach that include sandboarding and a picnic lunch.

Paradise 4x4 4WD
(☎0800 494 392; www.paradisenz.co.nz; price on application) Operates flexible 4WD tours from Doubtless Bay up Ninety Mile Beach to Cape Reinga, including a seafood lunch with local wine. Hokianga, Doubtless Bay beaches, wine and golf tours are also available.

Sand Safaris BUS
(☎0800 869 090; www.sandsafaris.co.nz; adult/child $60/35) A family-owned operation running coach trips from Ahipara and Kaitaia, including a Maori welcome, sandboarding and a picnic lunch.

Ahikaa Adventures CULTURAL
(☎09-409 8228; www.ahikaa-adventures.co.nz; tours $70-190) Maori culture permeates these tours, which can include sand-surfing, kayaking, fishing and pigging out on traditional *kai* (food).

SEED FOR THE FUTURE

The local Ngati Kuri, guardians of the sacred spaces around the Cape, have come up with a unique way of funding reforestation. For $20 you can assuage your carbon guilt by planting a native tree or bush of your choice – or, if you don't want to break a nail, letting the staff plant it for you; contact **Natives** (☎09-409 8482; www.natives.co.nz).

Sleeping & Eating

Unless you're a happy camper you won't find much decent accommodation up here. Pukenui – literally 'Big Stomach' – is the best place to fill yours; there's a cafe, takeaways and grocery store. The only other options are unremarkable eateries at Ancient Kauri Kingdom and Houhora Heads.

North Wind Lodge Backpackers HOSTEL $
(☎09-409 8515; www.northwind.co.nz; 88 Otaipango Rd, Henderson Bay; dm/s/tw/d $30/60/66/80) Six kilometres down an unsealed road on the peninsula's east side, this unusual turreted house offers a homely environment and plenty of quiet spots on the lawn to sit with a beer and a book.

DOC campsites CAMPSITES $
(www.doc.govt.nz; sites per adult/child $7.60/3.50) There are spectacularly positioned sites at Kapowairua, Tapotupotu Bay and Rarawa Beach. Only water, composting toilets and cold showers are provided. Bring a cooker, as fires are not allowed, and plenty of repellent to ward off the evil mosquitoes and sandflies. 'Freedom/Leave No Trace' camping is allowed along the Cape Reinga Coastal Walkway.

Getting There & Around

Apart from numerous tours, there's no public transport past Pukenui, which is linked to Kaitaia ($5, 45 minutes) by **Busabout Kaitaia** (☎09-408 1092; www.cbec.co.nz).

As well as Far North Rd (SH1), rugged vehicles can travel along Ninety Mile Beach itself. However, cars have been known to hit soft sand and be swallowed by the tides – look out for unfortunate vehicles poking through the sands. Check tide times before setting out; avoid it 2½ hours either side of high tide. Watch out for 'quicksand' at Te Paki Stream – keep moving. Many car-rental companies prohibit driving on the sands; if you get stuck, your insurance won't cover you.

Fill up with petrol before hitting the Aupouri Peninsula.

Kaitaia

POP 5200

Nobody comes to the Far North to hang out in this provincial town, but it's a handy stop if you're after a supermarket, a post office or an ATM. It's also a jumping-off point for tours to Cape Reinga and Ninety Mile Beach.

Sights

Te Ahu Centre ARTS CENTRE
(www.teahu.org.nz; Matthews Ave) At the time of research, the cinema was the only part of this striking, multi-million-dollar new civic centrepiece that had opened. By the time you're reading this, the eclectic local-history exhibits of the Far North Regional Museum will be on display; check the website for details.

Okahu Estate Winery WINERY
(www.okahuestate.co.nz; 520 Okahu Rd; ⌚noon-4pm Mon-Fri, extended summer) Just south of town, off the road to Ahipara, Kaitaia's only winery offers free tastings and sells local produce, including the famous Kaitaia Fire chilli sauce. Enquire about tours ($5).

Sleeping & Eating

Mainstreet Lodge HOSTEL $
(☎09-408 1275; www.mainstreetlodge.co.nz; 235 Commerce St; dm $27-34, s $55-70, d $64-78; @ wi-fi) Maori carvings abound at this groovy old cottage, which has a modern purpose-built wing facing the rear courtyard. The friendly owners know the area inside-out.

Loredo Motel MOTEL $$
(☎09-408 3200; www.loredomotel.co.nz; 25 North Rd; units $130-210; wi-fi pool) Opting for a breezy Spanish style (think stucco walls and terracotta tiles), this tidy motel has well-kept units set among palm trees and lawns. It's not quite Benidorm, but there is a swimming pool.

Beachcomber RESTAURANT $$
(www.beachcomber.net.nz; 222 Commerce St; lunch $17-33, dinner $27-35; ⌚lunch & dinner Mon-Sat) Easily the best place to eat in town, with a wide range of seafood and meatier fare, all deftly prepared, and a well-stocked salad bar.

Information

Far North i-SITE (☎09-408 0879; www.topofnz.co.nz; South Rd; ⌚8.30am-5pm; @)

Getting There & Away

Kaitaia Airport (www.bayofislandsairport.co.nz; Quarry Rd) is 6km north of town. **Busabout Kaitaia** (☎09-408 1092; www.cbec.co.nz) has services to Doubtless Bay ($5, one hour), Pukenui ($5, 45 minutes) and Ahipara ($3.50, 15 minutes). Both Air New Zealand (p128) and InterCity (p128) operate services to Kaitaia.

Ahipara

POP 1130

All good things must come to an end, and Ninety Mile Beach does it at this spunky beach town. A few holiday mansions have snuck in, but mostly it's just the locals keeping it real, rubbing shoulders with visiting surfers.

The area is known for its huge sand dunes and massive gum field, where 2000 people once worked. Sandboarding and quad-bike rides are popular activities on the dunes above Ahipara and further around the Tauroa Peninsula.

NGATI TARARA

As you're travelling around the north you might notice the preponderance of road names ending in '-ich'. *Haere mai, dobro došli* and welcome (as the sign leading into Kaitaia proclaims) to one of the more peculiar ethnic conjunctions in the country.

From the end of the 19th century, men from the Dalmatian coast of what is now Croatia started arriving in NZ looking for work. Many ended up in Northland's gum fields. Pakeha society wasn't particularly welcoming to the new immigrants, particularly during WWI – they were on Austrian passports. Not so the small Maori communities of the north. Here they found an echo of Dalmatian village life, with its emphasis on extended family and hospitality, not to mention a shared history of injustice at the hands of colonial powers.

The Maori jokingly named them Tarara, as their rapid conversation in their native tongue sounded like 'ta-ra-ra-ra-ra' to Maori ears. Many Croatian men married local *wahine* (women), founding clans that have left several of today's famous Maori with Croatian surnames, like singer Margaret Urlich and former All Black Frano Botica. You'll find large Tarara communities in the Far North, Dargaville and West Auckland.

Sights

Shipwreck Bay BEACH

(Wreck Bay Rd) The best surf is to be had at this small cove at the western end of the beach, so named for the shipwrecks that are still visible at low tide.

Ahipara Viewpoint LOOKOUT

(Gumfields Rd) Views stretch to eternity and beyond from this lookout on the bluff behind Ahipara. It's reached by an extremely rough road leading off the unsealed Gumfields Rd, which starts at the western end of Foreshore Dr.

Activities

Ahipara Adventure Centre EQUIPMENT RENTAL

(☎09-409 2055; www.ahiparaadventure.co.nz; 15 Takahe St) Ahipara Adventure Centre hires out sandboards ($10 per half day), surfboards ($20 per hour), mountain bikes ($50 per day), kayaks ($25 per hour), blokarts for sand yachting ($65 per hour) and quad bikes ($85 per hour).

Tua Tua Tours QUAD BIKES

(☎0800 494 288; www.ahipara.co.nz/tuatuatours/; 250 Ahipara Rd; 2hr ride per person $135, 2 people $150) This local outfit gets great word-of-mouth for its reef- and dune-rider tours and Ultimate Sand Dune Safaris (three hours including sand tobogganing, per one/two people $185/200).

Ahipara Treks HORSE RIDING

(☎09-409 4122; ahiparahorsetreks@xtra.co.nz) Offers beach canters (from $70), including some farm and ocean riding (when the surf permits).

Sleeping

TOP CHOICE **Endless Summer Lodge** HOSTEL $

(☎09-409 4181; www.endlesssummer.co.nz; 245 Foreshore Rd; dm $28, d $70-85; @) Across from the beach, this superb kauri villa (1880) has been beautifully restored and converted into an exceptional hostel. There's no TV, which encourages bonding around the long table on the vine-covered back terrace. Body boards and sandboards can be borrowed and surfboards can be hired.

Beach Abode APARTMENTS $$

(☎09-409 4070; www.beachabode.co.nz; 11 Korora St; apt $145-190; wi-fi) Wander through the subtropical garden to the beach from your self-contained studio or two-bedroom apartment, or just lie in bed and lose yourself in the view.

90 Mile Beach Ahipara Holiday Park HOLIDAY PARK $

(☎09-409 4864; www.ahiparaholidaypark.co.nz; 168 Takahe St; sites from $20, dm/r $28/95, units $95-310; @ wi-fi) There's a large range of accommodation on offer at this holiday park, including cabins, motel units and a worn but perfectly presentable YHA-affiliated backpackers' lodge. The communal hall has an open fire and colourful murals.

Beachfront APARTMENTS $$

(☎09-409 4007; www.beachfront.net.nz; 14 Kotare St; apt $175-310; wi-fi) Who cares if it's a bit bourgeois for Ahipara? These two upmarket, self-contained apartments have watery views and there's direct access to the beach.

Eating

Gumdiggers Cafe CAFE
(3 Ahipara Rd; mains $10-16; 7am-2pm) Good coffee and huge portions are the hallmarks of this friendly little cafe, serving cooked breakfasts, nachos, burgers and platters that would polish off your average ploughman.

Bidz Takeaways FISH & CHIPS
(Takahe St; meals $6-12; 9am-8pm) You'll need a flip-top head to fit Bidz' seafood burger into your mouth – it's jam-packed with battered oysters, scallops, mussels and fish. There's a grocery store attached.

Getting There & Around

Busabout Kaitaia (09-408 1092; www.cbec.co.nz) runs services from Kaitaia ($3.50, 15 minutes).

HOKIANGA

The Hokianga Harbour stretches out its skinny tentacles to become the fourth-biggest in the country. Its ruggedly beautiful landscape is painted in every shade of green and brown. The water itself is rendered the colour of ginger ale by the bush streams that feed it.

Of all the remote parts of Northland, this is the pocket that feels the most removed from the mainstream. Pretension has no place here. Isolated, predominantly Maori communities nestle around the harbour's many inlets, as they have done for centuries. Discovered by legendary explorer Kupe, it's been settled by Ngapuhi since the 14th century. Hippies arrived in the late 1960s and their legacy is a thriving little artistic scene.

Many of the roads remain unsealed and in poor repair after decades of neglect from government bodies. Tourism dollars are channelled eastward to the Bay of Islands, leaving this truly fascinating corner of the country remarkably undeveloped, which is the way many of the locals like it.

Mitimiti

The tiny community at Mitimiti, which consists of only 30 families and not even a shop, has the unspoilt 20km stretch of coast between the Hokianga and Whangape Harbours all to itself. The 40km drive from Kohukohu via Panguru (14km of it unsealed) is quite an experience: prepare to dodge cows, sheep, potholes and kids.

Sandtrails Hokianga (09-409 5035; www.sandtrailshokianga.co.nz; 32 Paparangi Dr) offers an inside perspective on Mitimiti's tight-knit Maori community, with two-hour Sandscapes dune-buggy tours, which head 12km along the beach to the giant dunes that form the harbour's north head ($155), or personally tailored tours staying overnight in the guide's house ($665 for two people).

Motuti

It's worth taking a short detour from the road to Mitimiti to visit **St Mary's Church** (Hata Maria; www.hokiangapompallier.org.nz; Motuti Rd), where NZ's first Catholic bishop is buried beneath the altar. Jean Baptiste Pompallier arrived in the Hokianga in 1838, celebrating NZ's first Mass at Totara Point. He was interred here in 2002 after an emotional 14-week pilgrimage full of Maori ceremony brought his remains back from France.

The nearby **Motuti Marae** (09-409 5545; www.motuti.co.nz; 318 Motuti Rd; tours 90min/day $30/60, stay $180) offers *marae* tours and stays, including a traditional Maori welcome and, on the longer tours, the opportunity to take part in flax-weaving, carving and stick games.

Kohukohu

POP 190

Quick, someone slap a preservation order on Kohukohu before it's too late. There can be few places in NZ where a Victorian village full of interesting kauri buildings has been so completely preserved with hardly a modern monstrosity to be seen. During the height of the kauri industry it was a busy town with a sawmill, shipyard, two newspapers and banks. These days it's a very quiet backwater on the north side of Hokianga Harbour, 4km from the Rawene car ferry (p164). There are no regular bus services and the only place to eat (or check your email) is the local pub. It does, however, have **Village Arts** (www.villagearts.co.nz; 1376 Kohukohu Rd; 10am-4pm), an excellent little commercial art gallery.

Tree House (09-405 5855; www.treehouse.co.nz; 168 West Coast Rd; sites/dm $18/31, s $60-68, tw & d $80, ;) is the best place to stay in the Hokianga, with helpful hosts and brightly painted little cottages set among exotic fruit and nut trees. This quiet retreat is 2km from the ferry terminus (turn sharp left as you come off the ferry).

WORTH A TRIP

NGAWHA SPRINGS

Near Kaikohe, these hot springs have been used by Ngapuhi for their curative powers since the 17th century. Hone Heke brought his injured warriors here during the Northland War.

Unlike many of NZ's thermal resorts, there are no hydroslides or big pools for the kids to splash about in. There aren't even any showers. Here it's all about stewing in the murky water in small pools of varying temperatures. Ngawha has two complexes, the better of which is **Ngawha Springs Pools** (☎09-405 2245; adult/child $4/2; ⏱9am-9pm).

Hidden Walks (☎021 277 7301; www.hiddenwalks.com; adult/child $28/20) offers guided walks through the thermal area taking in the remains of a historic mercury mine.

Horeke & Around

Tiny Horeke was NZ's second European settlement after Russell. A Wesleyan mission operated here from 1828 to 1855. In 1840, 3000 Ngapuhi gathered here for what was the single biggest signing of the Treaty of Waitangi.

Sights & Activities

Mangungu Mission House HISTORIC BUILDING
(www.historic.org.nz; Motukiore Rd; adult/child $3/1; ⏱noon-4pm Sat & Sun) Completed in 1839, this sweet wooden cottage contains relics of the missionaries who once inhabited it and of Horeke's shipbuilding past. In the grounds there's a large stone cross and a simple wooden church. Mangungu is 1km down the unsealed road leading along the harbour from Horeke village.

Wairere Boulders Nature Park NATURE PARK
(www.wairereboulders.co.nz; McDonnell Rd; adult/child $10/5; ⏱daylight) At Wairere, massive basalt rock formations have been eroded into odd fluted shapes by the acidity of ancient kauri forests, creating a Zen-garden effect. Allow an hour for the main loop track, which follows a burbling Coca-Cola-coloured stream. It's a good path, but wear sensible shoes and expect a few ducks and climbs. An additional track leads through rainforest to a platform at the end of the boulder valley (allow 1½ hours).

The park is signposted from SH1 and Horeke; the last 3km are unsealed. If you don't have your own transport, the only way to get here is on Fullers' Discover Hokianga tour (p141), departing from Paihia.

Quad Safaris QUAD BIKES
(☎09-401 9544; www.wairerevalley.com; 20 McDonnell Rd; 1½hr-tour $90) Offers quad bike tours through bush to the Wairere boulder valley.

Rawene

POP 440

Founded shortly after Horeke, Rawene was NZ's third European settlement. A surprising number of historic buildings (including six churches!) remain from a time when the harbour was considerably busier than it is now. Information boards outline a heritage trail of the main sights.

There aren't any ATMs or banks, but you can get petrol here.

Sights

Clendon House HISTORIC BUILDING
(www.historic.org.nz; Clendon Esplanade; adult/child $7/3.50; ⏱10am-4pm Sun May-Oct, Sat & Sun Nov-Apr) Clendon House was built in the bustling 1860s by James Clendon, a trader, shipowner and magistrate. After his death, his 34-year-old half-Maori widow Jane was left with a brood of kids and a whopping £5000 debt. She managed to clear the debt and her descendants remained in the house until 1972, when it passed to the Historic Places Trust along with many of its original chattels.

Hokianga Art Gallery GALLERY
(2 Parnell St; ⏱10am-3pm) Sells interesting contemporary art with a local focus.

Sleeping & Eating

Rawene Holiday Park HOLIDAY PARK $
(☎09-405 7720; www.raweneholidaypark.co.nz; 1 Marmon St; dm $20, sites/units from $30/45; @📶🏊) Tent sites shelter in the bush at this nicely managed park. The cabins are simple, with one converted into a bunkroom for backpackers (linen costs extra).

Boatshed Cafe CAFE $
(8 Clendon Esplanade; mains $8-17; ⏱8.30am-4pm) You can eat overlooking the water at

LOCAL KNOWLEDGE

HOKIANGA *ANIKA MOA*

I love the north of the north island, the beaten, bloody and beautiful landscape and *wairua* (spirit). The small towns up north, where I grew up, reach out all along the moody west coast. As kids, my brother and I would sneak in to Ngawha Springs and have our mud baths in the morning – smelling of rotten eggs for the rest of the day. In Opononi we'd go crab hunting on the rocks with Uncle Rata, then take the car ferry from Rawene home. At Pawarenga – a dusty old Maori town – we'd go horse riding with the cuzzies, learn Maori with my Grandpa, eat *karahu* and oysters, and, as we grew up, drink with the aunties and uncles. We'd drive to Kaitaia to buy all our food for the next week, and hang at the local pubs. Then further north for the Mangonui fish 'n' chip shop, the best *kai* (food) in Aotearoa. When we were tired, we'd drive to Ahipara and sleep on the beach.

Anika Moa, singer/songwriter

this excellent cafe, a cute place with heart-warming food and a gift shop selling local art and crafts.

Getting There & Away

There are no regular bus services to Rawene. From the centre of town a **car ferry** (09-405 2602; car & driver one way/return $16/24, passenger $2/4; 7.30am-7.30pm) heads to the northern side of the Hokianga, docking 4km south of Kohukohu at least hourly. You can buy your ticket for this 15-minute ride on board. It usually leaves Rawene on the half-hour and the north side on the hour.

Opononi & Omapere

POP 480

These tranquil settlements near the south head of Hokianga Harbour more or less run into one another. The water's much clearer here and good for swimming. Views are dominated by the mountainous sand dunes across the water at North Head. If you're approaching Omapere from the south, the view of the harbour is nothing short of spectacular.

Activities

Hokianga Express SANDBOARDING
(09-405 8872; adult/child $25/15) A boat departs from Opononi Jetty and takes you across the harbour to the large golden sand dunes, where you can sandboard down a 30m slope and skim over the water. Boats leave on the hour, on demand; call ahead or book at the i-SITE.

Arai te Uru Heritage Walk WALKING
Starting at the car park at the end of Signal Station Rd, this short walk (30 minutes return) follows the cliffs and passes through a tall stand of manuka before opening out to the grassy southern headland of the Hokianga and the remains of an old signal station. Built to assist ships making the treacherous passage through the harbour mouth, the station was closed in 1951 due to the decline in shipping in the harbour.

Six Foot Track TRAMPING
The Six Foot Track at the end of Mountain Rd gives access to many Waima Forest walks.

Tours

Footprints Waipoua CULTURAL
(09-405 8207; www.footprintswaipoua.co.nz; adult/child $95/35) Led by Maori guides, this four-hour twilight tour into Waipoua Forest is a fantastic introduction to both the culture and the forest giants. Tribal history and stories are shared, and mesmerising *karakia* (prayer, incantation) recited before the gargantuan trees.

Sandtrails Hokianga DUNE BUGGY
(09-409 5035; www.sandtrailshokianga.co.nz) Jump off the Hokianga Express boat (included in the price) and into a dune buggy for a sandy ride to Mitimiti ($185, 3¾ hours) or a 70-minute Sandsecrets tour ($95).

Sleeping & Eating

Each of these neighbouring villages has its own grocery store and takeaways.

GlobeTrekkers Lodge HOSTEL $
(09-405 8183; www.globetrekkerslodge.com; SH12, Omapere; dm/s/d $26/50/65; @) Unwind in casual style at this home-style hostel with harbour views and bright dorms. Private rooms have plenty of thoughtful touches, such as writing desks, mirrors, art and fluffy

towels. There's a stereo but no TV, encouraging plenty of schmoozing in the grapevine-draped BBQ area.

Hokianga Haven B&B $$
(☎09-405 8285; www.hokiangahaven.co.nz; 226 SH12, Omapere; r $160) This modern house with original Kiwi art on the walls offers spacious accommodation on the harbour's edge and glorious views of the sand dunes. Alternative healing therapies can be arranged.

Copthorne Hotel & Resort HOTEL $$
(☎09-405 8737; www.omapere.co.nz; 336 SH12, Omapere; r $145-260;) Despite the original grand Victorian villa having been violated by aluminium joinery, this waterside complex remains an attractive spot for a summer's drink or bistro meal ($19 to $36). The more expensive rooms in the newer accommodation block have terraces and water views.

Opononi Hotel HOTEL $$
(☎09-405 8858; www.opononihotel.com; 19 SH12; r $129) The rooms at the old Opononi pub aren't huge but the white-paint and blond-wood makeover has left them quietly stylish. Try to grab one of the front two – they're a bit bigger and have the best views. Otherwise aim for those facing away from the pub for a quieter stay.

Opononi Lighthouse Motel MOTEL $$
(☎09-405 8824; www.lighthousemotel.co.nz; 45 SH12; units $125-210; @) Scrupulously clean, this refurbished motel has very comfortable harbourside units, plus a communal barbecue, a spa pool, and a cutesy lighthouse and water feature in the front garden.

Information

Hokianga i-SITE (☎09-405 8869; 29 SH12; 9am-5pm; @)

Getting There & Away

There's no regular public transport to these parts but Magic Travellers Network (p150) and Crossings Hokianga are options.

Waiotemarama & Waimamaku

These neighbouring villages, nestled between the Hokianga Harbour and the Waipoua Forest, are the first of many tiny rural communities scattered along this underpopulated stretch of SH16.

Activities

Labyrinth Woodworks MAZE
(www.nzanity.co.nz; 647 Waiotemarama Gorge Rd; maze $4; 9am-5pm) An Aladdin's cave of handmade puzzles and games. Crack the code in the outdoor maze by collecting letters to form a word.

Fern River Horse Trekking HORSE RIDING
(☎09-405 8344; www.fernriver.co.nz; 953 Waiotemarama Gorge Rd, Waimamaku; 1/2/3/4hr trek $40/75/110/120) Leads horse treks through farmland and along deserted beaches.

Eating

Morrell's Cafe CAFE
(7235 SH12, Waimamaku; mains $9-16; 9am-4pm) Painted the colour of a block of cheddar, this cafe and craft shop occupies a former cheese factory. It's the last good eatery before Baylys Beach, so drop in for coffee or an eggy breakfast.

KAURI COAST

Apart from the odd bluff and river, this coast is basically unbroken and undeveloped for the 110km between the Hokianga and Kaipara Harbours. The main reason for coming here is to marvel at the kauri forests, one of the great natural highlights of NZ. This is one for the chubby chasers of the tree-hugging fraternity – you'd need 8m arms to get them around some of the big boys here. At the time of writing discussions were underway with a view to protecting all of the remaining forests in a new Kauri National Park; watch this space.

There are few stores or eateries and no ATMs north of Dargaville, so stock up beforehand if you're planning to spend any time here. Trampers should check DOC's website for walks in the area (www.doc.govt.nz).

Waipoua Forest

The highlight of Northland's west coast, this superb forest sanctuary – proclaimed in 1952 after much public pressure – is the largest remnant of the once-extensive kauri forests of northern NZ. The forest road (SH12) stretches for 18km and passes some huge trees – a kauri can reach 60m in height and have a trunk more than 5m in diameter.

Control of the forest has been returned to Te Roroa, the local *iwi* (tribe), as part of a settlement for Crown breaches of the Treaty of Waitangi. Te Roroa runs the **Waipoua Forest visitor centre** (☎09-439 6445; www.teroroa.iwi.nz; 1 Waipoua River Rd; ⌚9am-6.30pm summer, 9am-4.30pm winter), cafe and camping ground near the south end of the park.

Sights & Activities

Tane Mahuta TREE

Near the north end of the park, not far from the road, stands mighty Tane Mahuta, named for the Maori forest god. At 51.5m, with a 13.8m girth and wood mass of 244.5 cubic metres, he's the largest kauri alive. You don't so much look at Tane Mahuta; it's as if you're granted an audience to his hushed presence. He's been holding court here for somewhere between 1200 and 2000 years.

Te Matua Ngahere, Four Sisters & Yakas TREES

From the Kauri Walks car park, a 20-minute (each way) walk leads past the Four Sisters, a graceful stand of four tall trees that have fused together at the base, to Te Matua Ngahere (the Father of the Forest). Even the most ardent tree-hugger wouldn't consider rushing forward to throw their arms around him and call him 'Daddy', even if there wasn't a fence. At 30m he's shorter than Tane Mahuta, but he has the same noble presence, reinforced by a substantial girth – he's the fattest living kauri (16.4m). He presides over a clearing surrounded by mature trees that look like matchsticks in comparison.

A 30-minute (each way) path leads from near the Four Sisters to Yakas, the seventh-largest kauri.

Lookout LOOKOUT

For a bird's-eye view over the canopy, head to the forest lookout, near the very south end of the park. You can either drive to it (the road is well signposted but not suitable for campervans) or take the 2.5km Lookout Track from the visitor centre.

Sleeping & Eating

Waipoua Lodge B&B $$$

(☎09-439 0422; www.waipoualodge.co.nz; SH12; r $583) This fine old villa at the southern edge of the forest has four luxurious, spacious suites, which were originally the stables, the woolshed and the calf-rearing pen! Decadent dinners ($70) are available.

Waipoua Forest Campground CAMPSITE $

(☎09-439 6445; www.teroroa.iwi.nz; 1 Waipoua River Rd; site/unit/house from $15/20/175) Situated next to the Waipoua River and the visitor centre, this peaceful camping ground offers hot showers, flush toilets and a kitchen. The cabins are extremely spartan, with unmade swab beds (bring your own linen or hire it). There are also whole houses for rent, sleeping 10.

Trounson Kauri Park

The 450-hectare Trounson Kauri Park has an easy half-hour loop walk leading from the picnic area by the road. It passes through beautiful forest with streams, some fine kauri stands, a couple of fallen trees and another Four Sisters – two pairs of trees with conjoined trunks. DOC operates a **campsite** (www.doc.govt.nz; sites per adult/child $11/5.10) at the edge of the park, which has a communal kitchen and hot showers.

Just 2km from SH12, **Kauri Coast Top 10 Holiday Park** (☎09-439 0621; www.kauricoasttop10.co.nz; Trounson Park Rd; dm/site/unit from $30/40/110; @) is an attractive riverside camping ground with good facilities and a small shop. It also organises night-time **nature walks** (adult/child $25/15), which explain the flora and nocturnal wildlife that thrives here. This is a rare chance to see a kiwi in the wild. Trounson has a predator-eradication program and has become a mainland refuge for threatened native bird species, so you should at least hear a morepork (a native owl) or a brown kiwi.

If you're approaching from the north, it's easier to take the second turn-off to the park, near Kaihu, which avoids a rough unsealed road.

Kai Iwi Lakes

These three trout-filled freshwater lakes nestle together near the coast, 12km off SH12. The largest, Taharoa, has blue water fringed with sandy patches. Lake Waikere is popular with water-skiers, while Lake Kai Iwi is relatively untouched. A half-hour walk leads from the lakes to the coast and it's another two hours to reach the base of volcanic **Maunganui Bluff** (460m); the hike up and down it takes five hours.

Camping (☎09-439 0986; lakes@kaipara.govt.nz; adult/child $10/5) is permitted at the side of Lake Taharoa; cold showers, drinking water and flush toilets are provided.

Baylys Beach

A village of brightly coloured baches and a few new holiday mansions, Baylys Beach is 12km from Dargaville, off SH12. It lies on 100km-long Ripiro Ocean Beach, a surf-pounded stretch of coast that has been the site of many shipwrecks. The beach is a gazetted highway: you can drive along its hard sand at low tide, although it is primarily for 4WDs. Despite being NZ's longest drivable beach, it's less well known and hence less travelled than Ninety Mile Beach. Ask locals about conditions and check your hire-car agreement before venturing onto the sand. Quad bikes (single/double $75/95) can be hired at the holiday park.

It's pretty kooky, but **Skydome Observatory** (☎09-439 1856; www.skydome.org.nz; 28 Seaview Rd; stargazing $20-40) is a massive, technologically advanced telescope and it's located on the front lawn of someone's house. Call ahead for bookings.

Sleeping

Sunset View Lodge B&B $$
(☎09-439 4342; www.sunsetviewlodge.co.nz; 7 Alcemene Lane; r $175-190; @) If gin-in-hand sunset-gazing is your thing, this large, modern B&B fits the bill. The upstairs rooms have terrific sea views and there's a self-service bar with an honesty box in the guest lounge.

Baylys Beach Holiday Park HOLIDAY PARK $
(☎09-439 6349; www.baylysbeach.co.nz; 24 Seaview Rd; site/unit from $16/50; @) Circled by pohutukawa trees, this midsized camping ground has tidy facilities and attractive cream and green units ranging from basic cabins to a cottage that sleeps six.

Eating

Funky Fish CAFE, BAR $$
(☎09-439 8883; www.thefunkyfish.co.nz; 34 Seaview Rd; lunch $14-20, dinner $22-28; lunch Thu-Sun, dinner Tue-Sun) Brightly decorated with murals and mosaics, this highly popular cafe, restaurant and bar has a wonderful back garden and a wide-ranging menu, including lots of seafood. Bookings are advisable in summer.

Sharky's FISH & CHIPS
(1 Seaview Rd; mains $6-20; 8.30am-8pm) A handy combination of bottle shop, general store, bar and takeaway, serving all-day breakfasts.

Dargaville

POP 4500

When a town proclaims itself the 'kumara capital of NZ' (it produces two-thirds of the country's sweet potatoes), you should know not to expect too much. Founded in 1872 by timber merchant Joseph Dargaville, this once-important river port thrived on the export of kauri timber and gum. As the forests were decimated, it declined and today is a quiet backwater servicing the agricultural Northern Wairoa area.

Sights & Activities

Dargaville Museum MUSEUM
(www.dargavillemuseum.co.nz; adult/child $12/2; 9am-4pm) Perched on top of a hill, the Dargaville Museum is more interesting than most regional museums. There's a large gumdigging display, plus maritime, Maori and musical-instrument sections and a neat model railway. Outside, the masts of the *Rainbow Warrior* are mounted at a lookout near a *pa* site and there's a recreation of a gumdiggers' camp.

Kumara Box AGRICULTURAL
(www.kumarabox.co.nz; 503 Pouto Rd; tours $20) If you want to learn about the district's knobbly purple claim-to-fame, book ahead for Kumara Ernie's show. It's surprisingly entertaining, usually involving a journey by home-built tractor-train through the fields to 'NZ's smallest church'.

Sleeping & Eating

Campervans can enjoy the views from the Dargaville Museum car park for $10 per night.

Greenhouse Backpackers HOSTEL $
(☎09-439 6342; greenhousebackpackers@ihug.co.nz; 15 Gordon St; dm/s/d $28/45/70; @) This converted 1921 schoolhouse has classrooms partitioned into a large dorm and a communal lounge, both painted with colourful murals. Better still are the cosy units in the back garden, decked out with heated towel rails and electric blankets.

Blah, Blah, Blah... CAFE, BAR $
(101 Victoria St; breakfast $6-20, lunch $8-28, dinner $20-28; breakfast & lunch daily, dinner Tue-Sat) The number-one eatery in Dargaville (admittedly that's not saying much) has a garden area, hip music, deli-style snacks, a global menu (dukkha, confit duck, steak) and cocktails.

Riverside Produce Market MARKET
(Kapia St; ⏲2.30-5.30pm Thu) Selling local produce and craft, it's as good a place as anywhere to stock up on kumara.

Information

DOC Kauri Coast Area Office (☎09-439 3450; www.doc.govt.nz; 150 Colville Rd; ⏲8am-4.30pm Mon-Fri)

Visitor Information Centre (☎09-439 4975; www.kauriinfocentre.co.nz; 4 Murdoch St; ⏲9am-6pm; 📶) Operates out of the interesting Woodturners Kauri Gallery & Studio. Books accommodation and tours.

Getting There & Away

The main bus stop is in Kapia St. Main Coachline (p128) buses and West Coaster (p128) shuttles offer services.

Pouto Point

A narrow spit descends south of Dargaville, bordered by the Tasman Sea and Wairoa River, and comes to an abrupt halt at the entrance of NZ's biggest harbour, the Kaipara. It's an incredibly remote headland, punctuated by dozens of petite dune lakes and the lonely Kaipara Lighthouse (built from kauri in 1884). Less than 10km separates Kaipara Harbour's north and south heads, but if you were to drive between the two you'd cover 267km.

A 4WD can be put to its proper use on the ocean-hugging 71km stretch of beach from Dargaville. DOC's *Pouto Hidden Treasures* is a helpful guide for motorists, with tips for protecting both your car and the fragile ecosystem. It can be downloaded at www.doc.govt.nz.

Matakohe

POP 400

Apart from the rural charms of this village, the reason for visiting is the superb **Kauri Museum** (www.kaurimuseum.com; 5 Church Rd; adult/child $25/8; ⏲9am-5pm). The giant cross-sections of trees are astounding in themselves but the entire industry is brought to life through video kiosks, artefacts, fabulous furniture and marquetry, and reproductions of a pioneer sawmill, boarding house, gumdigger's hut and Victorian home. The Gum Room holds a weird and wonderful collection of kauri gum, the amber substance that can be carved, sculpted and polished to a jewel-like quality. The museum shop stocks mementoes crafted from kauri wood and gum.

Facing the museum is the tiny kauri-built **Matakohe Pioneer Church** (1867), which served both Methodists and Anglicans, and acted as the community's hall and school. Nearby, you can wander through a historic **schoolhouse** (1878) and **post office/telephone exchange** (1909).

Sleeping & Eating

Matakohe Holiday Park HOLIDAY PARK $
(☎09-431 6431; www.matakoheholidaypark.co.nz; 66 Church Rd; site/unit from $19/55; @📶🏊) With perhaps the cosiest lounge you'll find in a camping ground, this little park has modern amenities, plenty of space and good views of Kaipara Harbour.

Matakohe House B&B
(☎09-431 7091; www.matakohehouse.co.nz; 24 Church Rd; s/d $135/160; @📶) A short walk from the Kauri museum, this B&B occupies a pretty villa with a cafe attached. The simply furnished rooms open out onto a veranda and offer winning touches like complimentary port and chocolates. It was for sale when we visited, so call ahead.

Petite Provence B&B $$
(☎09-431 7552; www.petiteprovence.co.nz; 703c Tinopai Rd; s/d $110/150) This attractive, French-influenced B&B is a popular weekender for Aucklanders, so it pays to book ahead. Excellent dinners can be arranged for $45 per person.

Getting There & Away

Main Coachline services operate.

Coromandel Peninsula

Includes »

Miranda 173
Thames 173
Coromandel Town 176
Far North Coromandel 179
Whitianga 180
Coroglen & Whenuakite 183
Hahei 183
Hot Water Beach 184
Tairua 185
Puketui Valley 186
Opoutere 186
Whangamata 186
Waihi & Waihi Beach 187
Karangahake Gorge 189
Paeroa 190

Best Beaches

» New Chum's Beach (p180)
» Hahei Beach (p184)
» Cathedral Cove (p183)
» Otama Beach (p180)
» Hot Water Beach (p184)

Best Places to Stay

» Black Jack Lodge (p180)
» Driving Creek Villas (p177)
» Cotswold Cottage (p175)
» Bowentown Beach Holiday Park (p188)

Why Go?

The Coromandel Peninsula juts into the Pacific east of Auckland, forming the eastern boundary of the Hauraki Gulf. Although relatively close to the metropolis, the Coromandel offers easy access to splendid isolation. Its dramatic, mountainous spine bisects it into two very distinct parts.

The east coast has some of the North Island's best white-sand beaches. When Auckland shuts up shop for Christmas/ New Year, this is where it heads. The cutesy historic gold-mining towns on the west side escape the worst of the influx, their muddy wetlands and picturesque stony bays holding less appeal for the masses. This coast has long been a refuge for alternative lifestylers. Down the middle, the mountains are criss-crossed with walking tracks, allowing trampers to explore large tracts of untamed bush where kauri trees once towered and are starting to do so again.

When to Go

With the beaches playing the starring role here, summer is the best time to visit. When the pohutukawa trees put on their pre-Christmas display, the entire peninsula is edged in crimson. The population explodes during the summer school holidays (from Christmas until the end of January) and things can go a little nuts on New Year's Eve. Balmy February and March are slightly quieter. Being mountainous, the region attracts more rainfall than elsewhere on the east coast (3000mm or even 4500mm a year) – peaking from May to September.

Coromandel Peninsula Highlights

1 Travelling remote gravel roads under a crimson canopy of ancient pohutukawa trees in **Far North Coromandel** (p179)

2 Staking out your own patch of footprint-free sand at **New Chum's Beach** (p180)

3 Kayaking around the hidden islands, caves and bays of **Te Whanganui-A-Hei Marine Reserve** (p182)

4 Burning your butt in a freshly dug thermal pool in the sands of **Hot Water Beach** (p184)

5 Pigging out on smoked mussels in **Coromandel Town** (p176)

6 Penetrating the mystical depths of the dense bush of

Coromandel Forest Park (p177) and **Karangahake Gorge** (p189)

7 Watching the offshore islands glow in the dying haze of a summer sunset from **Hahei Beach** (p184)

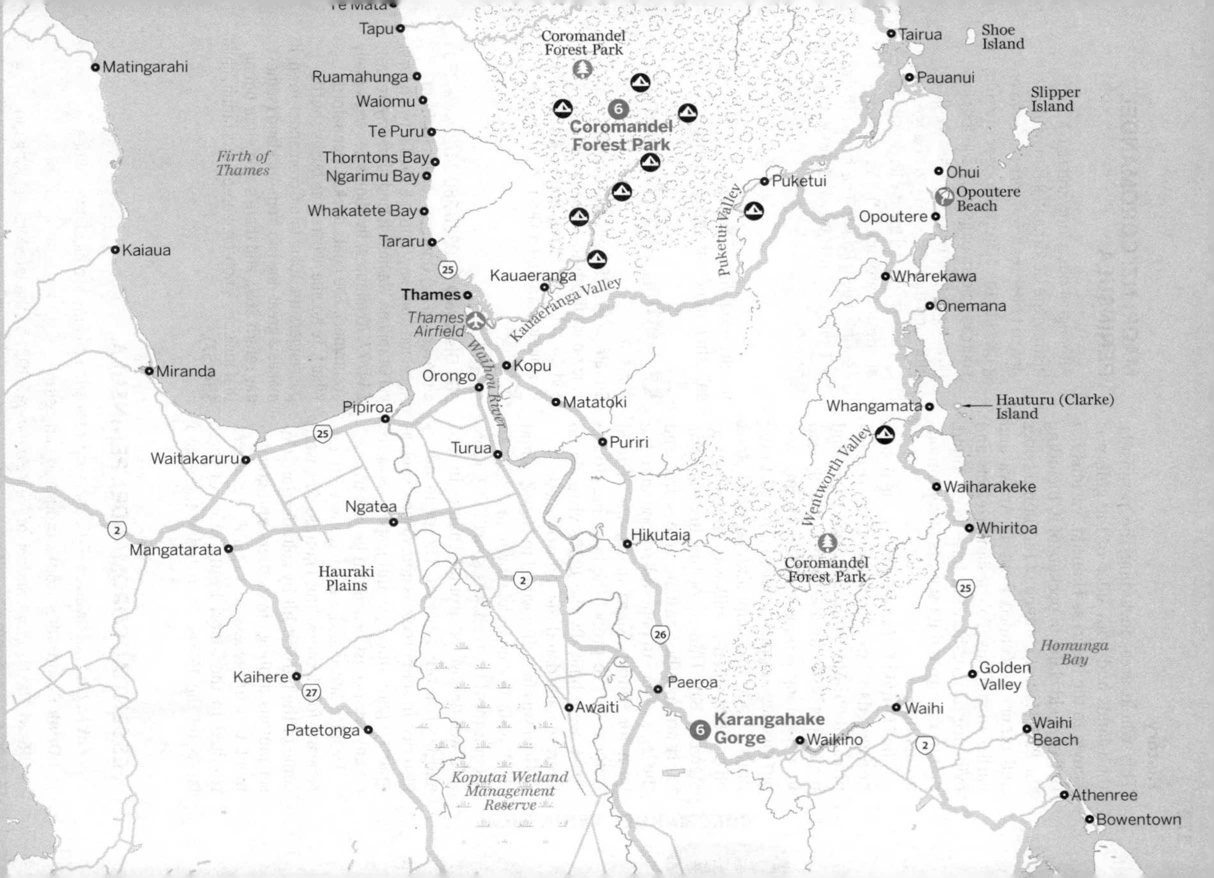

History

This whole area, including the peninsula, the islands and both sides of the gulf, was known to the Maori as Hauraki. Various *iwi* (tribes) held claim to pockets of it, including the Pare Hauraki branch of the Tainui tribes and others descended from Te Arawa and earlier migrations. Polynesian artefacts and evidence of moa-hunting have been found, pointing to around 1000 years of continuous occupation.

The Hauraki *iwi* were some of the first to be exposed to European traders. The region's proximity to Auckland, safe anchorages and ready supply of valuable timber initially lead to a booming economy. Kauri logging was big business on the peninsula. Allied to the timber trade was shipbuilding, which took off in 1832 when a mill was established at Mercury Bay. Things got tougher once the kauri around the coast became scarce and the loggers had to penetrate deeper into the bush for timber. Kauri dams, which used water power to propel the huge logs to the coast, were built. By the 1930s virtually no kauri remained and the industry died.

Gold was first discovered in New Zealand (NZ) near Coromandel Town in 1852. Although this first rush was short-lived, more gold was discovered around Thames in 1867 and later in other places. The peninsula is also rich in semiprecious gemstones, such as quartz, agate, amethyst and jasper. A fossick on any west-coast beach can be rewarding.

Despite successful interactions with Europeans for decades, the Hauraki *iwi* were some of the hardest hit by colonisation. Unscrupulous dealings by settlers and government to gain access to valuable resources resulted in the Maori losing most of their lands by the 1880s. Even today there is a much lower Maori presence on the peninsula than in neighbouring districts.

MAORI NZ: COROMANDEL PENINSULA

Although it has a long and rich Maori history, the Coromandel Peninsula doesn't offer many opportunities to engage with the culture. Pioneer pursuits such as gold-mining and kauri logging have been given much more attention, although this is starting to change.

Historic *pa* (fortified village) sites are dotted around, with the most accessible being Paaku. There are others at Opito Beach, Hahei and Hot Water Beach.

Getting There & Around

Air

Sunair (07-575 7799; www.sunair.co.nz) Twice-daily flights to Whitianga from Auckland and Great Barrier Island, and weekday flights to Whitianga from Hamilton, Rotorua and Tauranga.

Boat

360 Discovery (0800 360 3472; www.360discovery.co.nz) Operates ferries to/from Auckland (one-way/return $55/88, two hours) via Orapiu on Waiheke Island (one-way/return $44/77, 70 minutes) five times per week (daily in summer). The boats dock at Hannafords Wharf, Te Kouma, where free buses shuttle passengers the 10km into Coromandel Town. It makes a great day trip from Auckland (same-day return $69), and there's a day-tour option that includes a hop-on, hop-off bus (adult/child $94/57).

ESSENTIAL COROMANDEL PENINSULA

» **Eat** Buckets of bivalves – mussels, oysters and scallops are local specialities

» **Drink** Boiled water from a mountain campsite

» **Read** *The Penguin History of New Zealand* (2003) by the late Michael King, an Opoutere resident

» **Listen to** Top Kiwi bands at the Coromandel Gold New Year's Eve festival (p182)

» **Watch** The birds in the Firth of Thames

» **Festival** The peninsula-wide Pohutukawa Festival (www.pohutukawafestival.co.nz)

» **Go green** Witness forest regeneration at the Driving Creek Railway (p177)

» **Online** www.thecoromandel.com

» **Area code** 07

Bus

Go Kiwi (☎07-866 0336; www.go-kiwi.co.nz) Has daily Auckland City–International Airport–Thames–Tairua–Whitianga shuttles year-round, with a connection to Opoutere and Whangamata. From mid-December to Easter it also runs Rotorua–Tauranga–Waihi–Whangamata–Whitianga and Coromandel Town–Whitianga shuttles.

InterCity (www.intercity.co.nz) Has two routes to/from the peninsula: Auckland–Thames–Paeroa–Waihi–Tauranga and Hamilton–Te Aroha–Paeroa–Thames–Coromandel Town. Local routes include Thames–Coromandel Town–Whitianga and Whitianga–Tairua–Thames.

Naked Bus (www.nakedbus.com) Buses on the Auckland–Tauranga–Mt Maunganui–Rotorua–Gisborne route stop at Ngatea, where local associate Tairua Bus Company continues on to Whitianga.

Tairua Bus Company (TBC; ☎07-864 7194; www.tairuabus.co.nz) As well as local buses on the Thames–Tairua–Hahei–Whitianga–Coromandel Town route, TBC has a Hamilton–Cambridge–Te Aroha–Thames–Tairua service.

Car

Car is the only option for accessing some of the more remote areas, but be careful to check hire agreements as there are plenty of gravel roads and a few streams to ford. Most of them are in good condition and even a small car can cope unless the weather's been particularly wet.

Miranda

It's a pretty name for a settlement on the swampy Firth of Thames, just an hour's drive from Auckland. The two reasons to come here are splashing around in the thermal pools and birdwatching – but doing both at the same time might be considered impolite.

This is one of the most accessible spots for studying waders or shorebirds all year round. The vast mudflat is teeming with aquatic worms and crustaceans, which attract thousands of Arctic-nesting shorebirds over the winter – 43 species of wader have been spotted here. The two main species are the bar-tailed godwit and the lesser or red knot, but it isn't unusual to see turnstones, sandpipers and the odd vagrant red-necked stint. One godwit tagged here was tracked making an 11,570km nonstop flight from Alaska. Short-haul travellers include the pied oystercatcher and the threatened wrybill from the South Island, and banded dotterels and pied stilts.

The **Miranda Shorebird Centre** (☎09-232 2781; www.miranda-shorebird.org.nz; 283 East Coast Rd; ⏲9am-5pm) has bird-life displays, hires out binoculars and sells useful bird-watching pamphlets ($2). Nearby are a hide and several walks (30 minutes to two hours). The centre offers clean bunk-style accommodation (dorm beds/rooms $25/85) with a kitchen.

Miranda Hot Springs (www.mirandahotsprings.co.nz; Front Miranda Rd; adult/child $13/6; ⏲9am-9.30pm), 5km south, has a large thermal swimming pool (reputedly the largest in the southern hemisphere), a toasty sauna pool and private spas ($10 extra).

Next door is **Miranda Holiday Park** (☎07-867 3205; www.mirandaholidaypark.co.nz; 595 Front Miranda Rd; sites per adult/child $21/11, dm $34, units $145-311; @), which has excellent sparkling-clean units and facilities, its own thermally heated pool and a floodlit tennis court.

Thames

POP 6800

Dinky wooden buildings from the 19th-century gold rush still dominate Thames, but grizzly prospectors have long been replaced by alternative lifestylers. If you're a vegetarian ecowarrior you'll feel right at home. It's a good base for tramping or canyoning in the nearby Kauaeranga Valley.

Captain Cook arrived here in 1769, naming the Waihou River the 'Thames' 'on account of its bearing some resemblance to that river in England'; you may well think otherwise. This area belonged to Ngati Maru, a tribe of Tainui descent. Their spectacular meeting house, Hotunui (1878), holds pride of place in the Auckland Museum.

After opening Thames to gold-miners in 1867, Ngati Maru were swamped by 10,000 European settlers within a year. When the initial boom turned to bust, a dubious system of government advances resulted in Maori debt and forced land sales.

Sights

Goldmine Experience MINE

(www.goldmine-experience.co.nz; cnr Moanataiari Rd & Pollen St; adult/child $15/5; ⏲ 10am-4pm daily Jan-Mar, 10am-1pm Apr, May, Sep & Dec) Walk through a mine tunnel, watch a stamper battery crush rock, learn about the history of the Cornish miners and try your hand at panning for gold ($2 extra).

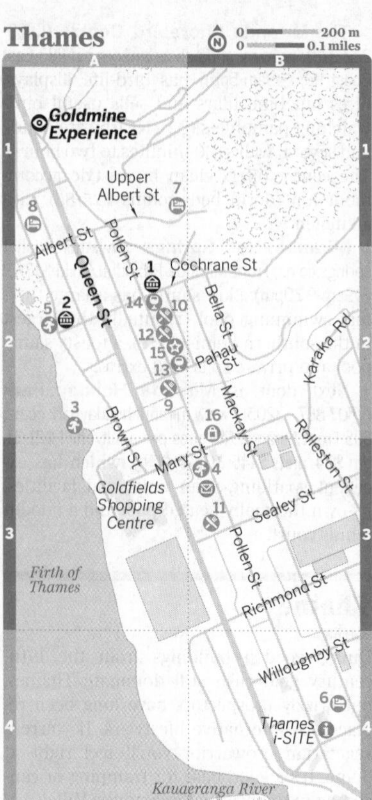

Thames

Top Sights
Goldmine Experience A1

Sights
1 Historical Museum A2
2 School of Mines & Mineralogical Museum A2

Activities, Courses & Tours
3 Karaka Bird Hide A2
4 Paki Paki Bike Shop B3
5 Thames Small Gauge Railway A2

Sleeping
6 Gateway Backpackers B4
7 Ocean View on Thames A1
8 Sunkist A1

Eating
9 Coco Espresso A2
10 Nakontong A2
Organic Co-op .... (see 10)
11 Rocco B3
12 Sola Cafe A2

Drinking
13 Junction Hotel A2
14 Speak Easy A2

Entertainment
15 Multiplex Cinemas A2

Shopping
16 Grahamstown Market B2

School of Mines & Mineralogical Museum MUSEUM
(www.historicplaces.org.nz; 101 Cochrane St; adult/child $5/free; 11am-3pm Wed-Sun) The Historic Places Trust runs tours of these buildings, which house an extensive collection of NZ rocks, minerals and fossils. The oldest section (1868) was part of a Methodist Sunday school, situated on a Maori burial ground. The Trust also distributes a free self-tour pamphlet taking in Thames' significant buildings.

Butterfly & Orchid Garden GARDENS
(www.butterfly.co.nz; Victoria St; adult/child $11/6; 9.30am-4pm) Anyone with a fairy complex will adore the Butterfly & Orchid Garden, 3km north of town within the Dickson Holiday Park. It's an enclosed jungle full of hundreds of exotic flappers.

Historical Museum MUSEUM
(cnr Cochrane & Pollen Sts; adult/child $5/2; 1-4pm) Pioneer relics, rocks and old photographs of the town.

Activities

Hauraki Rail Trail CYCLING
(www.haurakirailtrail.co.nz) This two-day cycle route connects Thames to Te Aroha via Paihia. Enquire at the i-SITE for more details.

Karaka Bird Hide BIRDWATCHING
(admission free) Built with compensation funds from the *Rainbow Warrior* bombing, this hide can be reached by a boardwalk through the mangroves just off Brown St.

Thames Small Gauge Railway NARROW-GAUGE RAILWAY
(Brown St; tickets $2; 11am-3pm Sun) Young 'uns will enjoy the 900m loop ride on this cute-as-a-button train.

Canyonz CANYONING
(☎0800 422 696; www.canyonz.co.nz; trips $290) This outfit runs canyoning trips to the Sleeping God Canyon in the Kauaeranga Valley. Expect a vertical descent of over 300m, requiring abseiling, water-sliding and jumping.

Eyez Open CYCLING
(☎07-868 9018; www.eyezopen.co.nz) Rents out bikes ($30 per day) and organises small-group cycling tours of the Coromandel Peninsula (one- to four-day tours from $150 to $770).

Paki Paki Bike Shop CYCLING
(☎07-867 9026; 535 Pollen St) Rents out bikes ($25 per day) and performs repairs.

Sleeping

Cotswold Cottage B&B $$
(☎07-868 6306; www.cotswoldcottage.co.nz; 36 Maramarahi Rd; r $165-205; 📶) Looking over the river and racecourse, 3km southeast of town, this pretty villa has had a modern makeover with luxuriant linen and an outdoor spa pool. The comfy rooms all open onto a deck.

Ocean View on Thames B&B $$
(☎07-868 3588; www.retreat4u.co.nz; 509 Upper Albert St; ste $160, apt $180-250; 📶) Aside from the expansive views, it's the little touches that make this place so special – such as fresh flowers and, in the two-bedroom apartment downstairs, a fridge stocked with cost-price beverages offered on an honesty system.

Gateway Backpackers HOSTEL $
(☎07-868 6339; overend@xtra.co.nz; 209 Mackay St; dm $25-27, s $50, d $62-72; @) Generations of Kiwis grew up in state houses just like this, giving this relaxed, friendly hostel a homely feel. Bathrooms are in short supply but there are pleasant rooms, a nice garden and free laundry facilities.

Coastal Motor Lodge MOTEL $$
(☎07-868 6843; www.stayatcoastal.co.nz; 608 Tararu Rd; units $135-175; 📶) Motel and chalet-style accommodation is provided at this smart, welcoming place, 2km north of Thames. It overlooks the sea, making it a popular choice, especially in the summer months.

Grafton Cottage & Chalets CHALET $$
(☎07-868 9971; www.graftoncottage.co.nz; 304 Grafton Rd; units $150-220; @📶🏊) Perched on a hill, most of these attractive wooden chalets have decks with awesome views. The hospitable hosts provide free internet access and breakfast, as well as use of the pool, spa and barbecue areas.

Brunton House B&B B&B $$
(☎07-868 5160; www.bruntonhouse.co.nz; 210 Parawai Rd; r $160-180, tr $195; @📶🏊) Renovations of this impressive two-storey kauri villa (1875) have upgraded the kitchen and bathrooms, while staying true to the building's historic credentials (there are no en suites). Guests can relax in the grounds, by the pool, in the designated lounge or on the upstairs terrace.

Sunkist HOSTEL $
(☎07-868 8808; www.sunkistbackpackers.com; 506 Brown St; sites from $19, dm $25-29, r $66; @📶) It's not the friendliest place, but this hostel in a character-filled 1860s heritage building has spacious dorms, a garden and free bikes. It also offers 4WD hire and shuttles to the Kauaeranga Valley ($35 return).

Eating

Rocco MODERN NZ $$
(☎07-868 8641; 109 Sealey St; mains $23-34; ⏲dinner Tue-Sun) Housed in one of Thames' gorgeous kauri villas, Rocco serves tapas and more substantial mains, making good use of local ingredients such as mussels and fish. In clement weather, take a seat among the crushed-shell and swirling brick paths outside.

Nakontong THAI $$
(☎07-868 6821; 728 Pollen St; mains $16-20; ⏲lunch Mon-Fri, dinner daily; 🥕) This is the most popular restaurant in Thames by a country mile. Although the bright lighting may not induce romance, the tangy Thai dishes will provide a warm glow.

Sola Cafe VEGETARIAN $
(720b Pollen St; mains $9-13; ⏲8am-4pm; @📶🥕) Bright and friendly, this meat-free cafe is first rate. Expect excellent coffee and a range of vegan, dairy-free and gluten-free options that include heavenly salads.

Coco Espresso CAFE $
(661 Pollen St; snacks $4.50; ⏲8am-2.30pm Tue-Fri, 8am-noon Sat) Occupying a corner of an old villa, this chic little cafe, decked out all in white, serves excellent coffee and enticing pastries and cakes.

Organic Co-op SELF-CATERING
(736 Pollen St; ⊙9am-5pm Mon-Fri, 9am-noon Sat; ✎) A good source of planet-friendly vegetables, nuts, bread, eggs and meat.

Drinking & Entertainment

Speak Easy WINE BAR
(746 Pollen St; ⊙Wed-Sun) The cutest little bar on the Coromandel Peninsula, with art-deco chandeliers, zany wallpaper and regular live music. It's the sort of place where a solo traveller of any gender can chill out over a glass of wine.

Junction Hotel PUB
(www.thejunction.net.nz; 700 Pollen St) Serving thirsty gold-diggers since 1869, the Junction is the archetypal slightly rough-around-the-edges, historic, small-town pub. Live music attracts a younger crowd on the weekends, while families head to the corner-facing Grahamstown Bar & Diner for hearty pub grub.

Multiplex Cinemas CINEMA
(www.cinemathames.co.nz; 708 Pollen St) Screening recent blockbusters in poorly sound-insulated cinemas.

Shopping

Pollen St has a good selection of gift and homeware stores selling local art and craft.

Grahamstown Market MARKET
(Pollen St; ⊙8am-noon Sat) On Saturday mornings the Grahamstown Market fills the street with organic produce and handicrafts.

Information

Thames i-SITE (☎07-868 7284; www.thamesinfo.co.nz; 206 Pollen St; ⊙9am-5pm)

Getting There & Around

InterCity, Tairua Bus Company and Go Kiwi all run bus services (p173) to Thames.

Thames to Coromandel Town

Narrow SH25 snakes along the coast past pretty little bays and rocky beaches. Sea birds are plentiful, and you can fish, dig for shellfish and fossick for quartz, jasper and even gold-bearing rocks on the beaches. The landscape turns crimson when the pohutukawa (often referred to as the 'New Zealand Christmas tree') blooms in December.

A handful of stores, motels, B&Bs and camping grounds are scattered around the tiny settlements that front the picturesque bays. Backpackers can make themselves at home in **Wolfie's Lair** (☎07-868 2777; www.wolfieslair.co.nz; 11 Firth View Rd, Te Puru; dm/r $27/54), a tidy house in a Te Puru cul-de-sac with three rooms to rent. The wolf in question is less big and bad, more little and yappy.

At Tapu you can turn inland for a mainly sealed 6km drive to the **Rapaura Water Gardens** (☎07-868 4821; www.rapaura.com; 586 Tapu-Coroglen Rd; adult/child $15/6; ⊙9am-5pm), a marriage of water, greenery, sculpture and platitudes. There's accommodation on-site (cottage/lodge $165/275) and a well-regarded cafe (mains $14 to $29).

From Wilsons Bay the road heads away from the coast and climbs over several hills and valleys before dropping down to Coromandel Town, 55km from Thames. The view looking towards the island-studded Coromandel Harbour is exquisite.

Coromandel Town

POP 1480

Crammed with heritage buildings, Coromandel Town is a thoroughly quaint little place. Its natty cafes, interesting art stores, excellent sleeping options and delicious smoked mussels could keep you here longer than you expected.

Gold was discovered at Driving Creek in 1852. Initially the local Patukirikiri *iwi* kept control of the land and received money from digging licences. After initial financial success the same fate befell them as the Ngati Maru in Thames. By 1871, debt had forced them to sell all but 778 mountainous acres of their land. Today, fewer than 100 people remain who identify as part of this *iwi*.

Sights

Heritage buffs can tour around 29 historic sites featured in the Historic Places Trust's *Coromandel Town* pamphlet (free from the i-SITE).

Coromandel Goldfield Centre & Stamper Battery HISTORIC BUILDING
(☎07-866 8758; 360 Buffalo Rd; adult/child $10/5) The rock-crushing machine clatters into life during the informative one-hour tours of this 1899 plant; call ahead for times. You can also try panning for gold ($5). Outside of the

DON'T MISS

COROMANDEL FOREST PARK

More than 30 walks crisscross the Coromandel Forest Park, spread over several major blocks throughout the centre of the Coromandel Peninsula. The most popular hike is the challenging six- to eight-hour return journey up to the **Pinnacles** (759m) in the Kauaeranga Valley behind Thames. Other outstanding tramps include the **Coromandel Coastal Walkway** in Far North Coromandel, from Fletcher Bay to Stony Bay, and the **Puketui Valley** walk to abandoned gold mines.

The **Department of Conservation (DOC) Kauaeranga Visitor Centre** (07-867 9080; www.doc.govt.nz; Kauaeranga Valley Rd; 8.30am-4pm) has interesting displays about the kauri forest and its history. Its staff sell maps and conservation resources and dispense advice. The centre is 14km off SH25; it's a further 9km along a gravel road to the start of the trails. Enquire at the Thames hostels about shuttles.

The DOC **Pinnacles Hut** (adult/child $15/7.50) has 80 beds, gas cookers, heating, toilets and cold showers. The 10-bunk **Crosbies Hut** (adult/child $15/7.50) is a four- to six-hour tramp from Thames or the Kauaeranga Valley. There are also four basic **back-country campsites** (adult/child $6/3) in this part of the park: one near each hut and others at Moss Creek and Billygoat Basin; expect only a toilet. A further eight **conservation campsites** (adult/child $10/5) are accessible from Kauaeranga Valley Rd. Bookings must be made online for the huts and some of the campsites.

tours it's worth stopping for a gander at NZ's largest working waterwheel.

Coromandel Mining & Historic Museum MUSEUM
(841 Rings Rd; adult/child $3/50c; 10am-1pm Sat & Sun Feb–mid-Dec, 10am-4pm daily mid-Dec–Jan) This small museum provides a glimpse of pioneer life.

Activities

Driving Creek Railway & Potteries NARROW-GAUGE RAILWAY
(07-866 8703; www.drivingcreekrailway.co.nz; 380 Driving Creek Rd; adult/child $25/10; departures 10.15am & 2pm) A lifelong labour of love for its conservationist owner, this unique train runs up steep grades, across four trestle bridges, along two spirals and a double switchback, and through two tunnels, finishing at the 'Eye-full Tower'. The hour-long trip passes artworks and regenerating native forest – more than 17,000 natives have been planted, including 9000 kauri. It's worth lingering for the video about the extraordinary guy behind it all, well-known potter Barry Brickell.

Coromandel Kayak Adventures KAYAKING
(07-866 7466; www.kayakadventures.co.nz) Offers paddle-powered tours ranging from half-day ecotours (from $200) to fishing trips (half/full day $200/385). Also rents kayaks (from $25/65 per hour/day).

Mussel Barge Snapper Safaris FISHING
(07-866 7667; www.musselbargesafaris.co.nz; adult/child $50/25) Fishing trips with a uniquely local flavour and lots of laughs.

Tours

Tri Sail Charters SAILING
(0800 024 874; www.trisailcharters.co.nz; half/full day $50/110) Cruise the Coromandel Harbour with your mates (a minimum of four) on an 11.2m trimaran (three-hulled yacht).

Argo Tours DRIVING
(07-868 6633; www.argotoursnz.wordpress.com) Explore native bush and old gold workings in a mini 8WD. If you can muster a posse (up to five people), prices drop as low as $39 per person.

Coromandel Adventures DRIVING
(07-866 7014; www.coromandeladventures.co.nz; adult/child $25/15) Offers various trips including a hop-on, hop-off service around Coromandel Town and a transfer to Whangapoua Beach.

Sleeping

Driving Creek Villas COTTAGES $$$
(07-866 7755; www.drivingcreekvillas.com; 21a Colville Rd; villas $295-415;) This is the posh, grown-up's choice – three spacious, self-contained, modern, wooden villas with plenty of privacy. The Polynesian-influenced interior design is slick and the bush setting, complete with bubbling creek, sublime.

Anchor Lodge MOTEL, HOSTEL $
(07-866 7992; www.anchorlodgecoromandel.co.nz; 448 Wharf Rd; dm $25-26, r $55-75, units $165-350;) Not many places can boast their own gold mine and glowworm cave, but this upmarket backpacker-motel combo has them, and a small heated swimming pool and spa to boot. The 2nd-floor units have harbour views.

Little Farm APARTMENT $$
(07-866 8427; www.thelittlefarmcoromandel.co.nz; 750 Tiki Rd; r $115-130;) Overlooking a private wetland reserve at the rear of a fair-dinkum farm, these three comfortable units offer plenty of peace and quiet. The largest has a full kitchen and superb sunset views.

Green House B&B $$
(07-866 7303; www.greenhousebandb.co.nz; 505 Tiki Rd; r $150-165;) Good old-fashioned hospitality and smartly furnished rooms are on offer here. The downstairs room opens onto the host's lounge, so it's worth paying $15 more for an upstairs room with a view.

Jacaranda Lodge B&B $$
(07-866 8002; www.jacarandalodge.co.nz; 3195 Tiki Rd; s $80, d $135-165;) Located among 6 hectares of farmland and rose gardens, this two-storey cottage offers a bucolic retreat. Some rooms share bathrooms but expect fluffy towels and personalised soap in mini *kete* (woven flax bags).

Coromandel Motel & Holiday Park HOLIDAY PARK $
(07-866 8830; www.coromandelholidaypark.co.nz; 636 Rings Rd; sites from $40, units $80-220;) Well kept and welcoming, with nicely painted cabins and manicured lawns, this large park includes the semi-separate Coromandel Town Backpackers. It gets busy in summer, so book ahead. Also hires bikes ($30 per day).

Tui Lodge HOSTEL $
(07-866 8237; www.coromandeltuilodge.co.nz; 60 Whangapoua Rd; sites from $15, dm $25, r $60-80;) Pleasantly rural, this cheery backpackers has plenty of trees, a sauna ($5), free bikes, fruit (in season) and straight-up rooms. The pricier ones have en suites.

Lion's Den HOSTEL $
(07-866 8157; www.lionsdenhostel.co.nz; 126 Te Tiki St; dm/r $26/60;) Chill out to the hippy vibe in this magical place. A tranquil garden with fish pond, fairy lights and wisteria, and a relaxed collection of comfy rooms (dotted with African bits and bobs), make for a soothing spot to rest your bones.

Eating & Drinking

Umu CAFE $
(22 Wharf Rd; breakfast $11-18, lunch $12-25, dinner $14-32; breakfast, lunch & dinner;) Umu serves classy cafe fare, including excellent pizza, mouth-watering counter food (tarts and quiches around $7), superb coffee and tummy-taming breakfasts.

Pepper Tree MODERN NZ $$
(07-866 8211; www.peppertreerestaurant.co.nz; 31 Kapanga Rd; lunch $22-26, dinner $26-36; lunch & dinner;) Coromandel Town's most upmarket option dishes up generously proportioned meals with an emphasis on local seafood. On a summer's evening, the courtyard tables under the shady tree are the place to be.

Mussel Kitchen SEAFOOD $$
(www.musselkitchen.co.nz; cnr SH25 & 309 Rd; mains $15-20; lunch year-round, dinner Dec-Mar) Designed to look like a historic store, this cool cafe-bar sits among fields 3km south of town. Mussels are served in a multitude of ways alongside an eclectic globetrotting menu (laksa, barbecued pork ribs, pasta). In summer, the garden bar is irresistible.

Driving Creek Cafe VEGETARIAN $
(180 Driving Creek Rd; mains $12-17; 9.30am-5pm;) A large selection of vegetarian, vegan, gluten-free, organic and fair-trade delights awaits at this funky mud-brick cafe. The food is beautifully presented, fresh and healthy. Once sated, the kids can play in the sandpit while the adults check their email.

Coromandel Smoking Co SEAFOOD
(www.corosmoke.co.nz; 70 Tiki Rd; 9am-5pm) For a delicious snack or cooking supplies, Coromandel Smoking Co has a wonderful range of smoked fish and seafood. You can't leave town without trying the extremely addictive smoked mussels.

Coromandel Oyster Company SEAFOOD
(1611 Tiki Rd; 9am-5pm) If you prefer your bivalves au naturel, this is the place for newly landed mussels, scallops, cooked crayfish and, of course, oysters.

Star & Garter Hotel PUB
(www.starandgarter.co.nz; 5 Kapanga Rd;) Making the most of the simple kauri interior of an 1873 building, this smart pub has pool tables, decent sounds and a roster of live music and DJs on the weekends. The beer garden is smartly clad in corrugated iron.

Information

Coromandel Town i-SITE (07-866 8598; www.coromandeltown.co.nz; 355 Kapanga Rd; 9am-5pm; @)

Getting There & Away

By far the nicest way to travel to Coromandel Town from Auckland is on a 360 Discovery (p172) ferry. The town is also serviced by InterCity, Tairua Bus Company and Go Kiwi buses (p173).

SENSIBLE CYCLISTS' LEAPFROG

There's no charge for carrying your bike on a 360 Discovery (p172) ferry. Touring cyclists can avoid Auckland's traffic fumes and treacherous roads completely by catching the ferry at Gulf Harbour to Auckland's ferry terminal, and then leapfrogging directly to Coromandel Town.

Far North Coromandel

Supremely isolated and gobsmackingly beautiful, the rugged tip of the Coromandel Peninsula is well worth the effort required to reach it. The best time to visit is summer, when the gravel roads are dry, the pohutukawa trees are in their crimson glory and camping's an option (there isn't a lot of accommodation up here).

The 1260-hectare **Colville Farm** (07-866 6820; www.colvillefarmholidays.co.nz; 2140 Colville Rd; sites/units from $10/70, dm/s/d $25/38/66; @) has a range of interesting accommodation, including bare-basics bush lodges and self-contained houses. Guests can try their hands at farm work (including milking) or go on horse treks ($40 to $150, one to five hours).

The nearby **Mahamudra Centre** (07-866 6851; www.mahamudra.org.nz; site/dm/s/tw $15/23/45/70) is a serene Tibetan Buddhist retreat that has a stupa, a meditation hall and regular meditation courses. It offers simple accommodation in a parklike setting.

Another 1km brings you to the tiny settlement of **Colville** (25km north of Coromandel Town). It's a remote rural community by a muddy bay and a magnet for alternative lifestylers. There's not much here except for the **Green Snapper Cafe** (07-866 6697; 2312 Colville Rd; mains $8-16; 9am-3pm Wed, Thu, Sat & Sun, 9am-late Fri, extended in summer) and the quaint **Colville General Store** (07-866 6805; Colville Rd; 8.30am-5pm), selling just about everything from organic food to petrol (warning: this is your last option for either).

Three kilometres north of Colville the sealed road turns to gravel and splits to straddle each side of the peninsula. Following the west coast, ancient pohutukawa spread overhead as you pass turquoise waters and stony beaches. The small DOC-run **Fantail Bay campsite** (adult/child $9.20/2), 23km north of Colville, has running water and a couple of long-drop toilets under the shade of puriri trees. Another 7km brings you to the **Port Jackson campsite** (adult/child $9.20/2), a larger DOC site right on the beach.

There's a spectacular lookout about 4km further on, where a metal dish identifies the various islands on the horizon. Great Barrier Island is only 20km away, looking every part the extension of the Coromandel Peninsula that it once was.

The road stops at **Fletcher Bay** – a magical land's end. Although it's only 37km from Colville, allow an hour for the drive. There's another **DOC campsite** (adult/child $10/5) here, as well as **Fletcher Bay Backpackers** (07-866 6685; www.doc.govt.nz; dm $26) – a simple affair that has four rooms with four bunks in each. Bring sheets and food.

The **Coromandel Coastal Walkway** is a scenic, 3½-hour one-way hike between Fletcher Bay and **Stony Bay**. It's a relatively easy walk with great coastal views and an ambling section across farmland. If you're not keen on walking all the way back, **Coromandel Discovery** (07-866 8175; www.coromandeldiscovery.co.nz; adult/child $110/65) will drive you from Coromandel Town up to Fletcher Bay and pick you up from Stony Bay four hours later.

At Stony Bay, where the east coast road terminates, there's another **DOC campsite** (adult/child $9.20/2) and a small DOC-run bach (holiday home) that sleeps five ($77). Heading south there are a couple of nice beaches peppered with baches on the way to the slightly larger settlement of Port Charles.

Tangiaro Kiwi Retreat (07-866 6614; www.kiwiretreat.co.nz; 1299 Port Charles Rd; units $225-325;) offers eight brand-new one- or two-bedroom self-contained wooden cottages, each pair sharing a barbecue. There's a bush-fringed spa, an in-house masseuse ($70 per hour) and, in summer, a cafe and licensed restaurant.

Another 8km brings you to the turn-off leading back to Colville, or you can continue south to Waikawau Bay, where there's a large **DOC campsite** (☎07-866 1106; adult/child $9.20/2) which has a summer-only store. The road then winds its way south past Kennedy Bay before cutting back to come out near the Driving Creek Railway.

All of the DOC campsites should be booked online at www.doc.govt.nz.

Coromandel Town to Whitianga

There are two routes from Coromandel Town southeast to Whitianga. The main road is the slightly longer but quicker SH25, which enjoys sea views and has short detours to pristine sandy beaches. The other is the less-travelled but legendary 309 Rd, an unsealed, untamed route through deep bush.

STATE HIGHWAY 25

SH25 starts by climbing sharply to an incredible lookout before heading steeply down. The turn-off at Te Rerenga follows the harbour to **Whangapoua**. There's not much at this beach except for generic holiday homes, but you can walk along the rocky foreshore to the remote, beautiful and often-deserted **New Chum's Beach** (30 minutes), regarded as one of the most beautiful in the country due, in part, to its complete lack of development.

Continuing east on SH25 you soon reach **Kuaotunu**, a more interesting holiday village on a beautiful stretch of white-sand beach, with a cafe-gallery, a store and an ancient petrol pump. **Black Jack Lodge** (☎07-866 2988; www.black-jack.co.nz; 201 SH25; dm $33, s/tw/d from $53/76/86; 📶) has a prime position directly across from the beach. It's a lovely little hostel with smart facilities and bikes and kayaks for hire.

For a touch more luxury, head back along the beach and up the hill to **Kuaotunu Bay Lodge** (☎07-866 4396; www.kuaotunubay.co.nz; SH25; s/d $270/295), an elegant B&B set among manicured gardens, offering a small set of spacious sea-gazing rooms.

Heading off the highway at Kuaotunu takes you (via an unsealed road) to one of Coromandel's best-kept secrets. First the long stretch of **Otama Beach** comes into view, deserted but for a few houses and farms. There's extremely basic camping (think long-drop toilet in a corrugated shack) in a farmer's field at **Otama Beach Camp** (☎07-866 2362; www.otamabeachcamp.co.nz; 400 Blackjack Rd; sites per adult/child $10/5, cottages $150-260). Down by the beach they've recently built a couple of self-contained, ecofriendly cottages (sleeping four to six), with solar power, a composting waste-water system and ocean views.

Continue along the road and you'll be in for a shock. Just when you think you're about to fall off the end of the earth, the seal starts again and you reach **Opito** – a hidden-away enclave of 250 flash properties (too smart to be called baches), of which only 16 have permanent residents. It's more than a little weird, but it is a magical beach. You can walk to a Ngati Hei *pa* (fortified village) site at the far end.

One of the 'real' residences houses the delightful folks of **Leighton Lodge** (☎07-866 0756; www.leightonlodge.co.nz; 17 Stewart Pl; s $135-145, d $170-190; @). This smart B&B has a self-contained flat downstairs and an upstairs room with a view-hungry balcony.

309 ROAD

Starting 3km south of Coromandel Town, the 309 cuts through the Coromandel Range for 21km (most of which is unsealed but well maintained), rejoining SH25 7km south of Whitianga. The **Waterworks** (www.thewaterworks.co.nz; 471 309 Rd; adult/child $18/12; ⏲9am-6pm Nov-Apr, 10am-4pm May-Oct), 5km from SH25, is a wonderfully bizarre park filled with whimsical water-powered amusements made from old kitchen knives, washing machines, bikes and toilets.

Two kilometres later there's a two-minute walk through a pretty patch of bush to the 10m-high **Waiau Falls**. Stop again after another 500m for an easy 10-minute walk through peaceful native bush to an amazing kauri grove. This stand of 600-year-old giants escaped the carnage of the 19th century, giving a majestic reminder of what the peninsula once looked like. The biggest tree has a 6m circumference.

If you enjoy the remoteness and decide to linger, **Wairua Lodge** (☎07-866 0304; www.wairualodge.co.nz; 251 Old Coach Rd; r $145-235) is a peaceful B&B with charming hosts, nestled in the bush towards the Whitianga end of the 309. There's a riverside swimming hole on the property, a barbecue, a spa and a romantic outdoor bathtub.

Whitianga

POP 3800

Whitianga's big attractions are the sandy beaches of Mercury Bay and the diving, boating and kayaking opportunities afforded by the craggy coast and nearby Te Whanganui-A-Hei Marine Reserve. The pretty harbour is a renowned base for game-fishing (especially marlin and tuna, particularly between January and March). There are numerous charters on offer for would-be boaties, starting at around $500 and heading into the thousands. If you snag an overfished species, consider releasing your catch (p155).

A genuine nautical hero, the legendary Polynesian explorer and seafarer Kupe, is believed to have landed near here sometime around AD 950. The name Whitianga is a contraction of Te Whitianga a Kupe (the Crossing Place of Kupe).

Sights & Activities

Beaches SWIMMING, WALKING

Buffalo Beach stretches along Mercury Bay, north of Whitianga Harbour. A five-minute passenger ferry ride will take you across the harbour to Whitianga Rock Scenic & Historical Reserve, Flaxmill Bay, **Shakespeare Cliff Lookout**, Lonely Bay, Cooks Beach and **Captain Cook's Memorial**, all within walking distance. Further afield are Hahei Beach (13km), Cathedral Cove (15km) and Hot Water Beach (18km, one hour by bike).

Lost Spring SPA

(www.thelostspring.co.nz; 121a Cook Dr; per hr/day $28/60; ⌚11am-6pm Sun-Fri, 11am-8pm Sat) This expensive but intriguing Disney-meets-Rotorua thermal complex comprises a series of hot pools in a lush junglelike setting, complete with an erupting volcano. Yet this is an adult's indulgence (children under 14 not permitted), leaving the grown-ups to marinate themselves in tropical tranquillity, cocktail in hand. There's also a day spa and cafe.

Mercury Bay Museum MUSEUM

(www.mercurybaymuseum.co.nz; 11a The Esplanade; adult/child $5/50c; ⌚10am-4pm) A small but interesting museum focusing on local history – especially Whitianga's most famous visitors, Kupe and Cook.

Dive Zone DIVING

(☎07-867 1580; www.divethecoromandel.co.nz; 7 Blacksmith Lane; trips $150-225) A PADI five-star accredited dive facility offering a range of shore, kayak and boat dives.

Seafari Windsurfing WINDSURFING

(☎07-866 0677; Brophy's Beach) Based at Brophy's Beach, 4km north of central Whitianga, Seafari hires out sailboards (from $25 per hour) and kayaks (from $15 per hour), and provides windsurfing lessons (from $40 including gear).

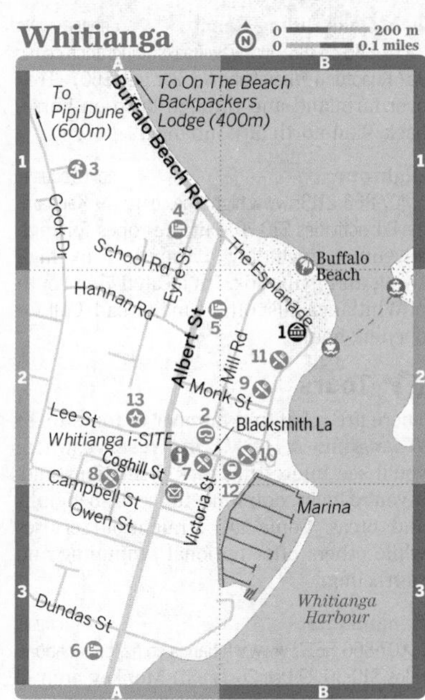

Whitianga

Sights
1 Mercury Bay Museum B2

Activities, Courses & Tours
2 Dive Zone A2
3 Lost Spring A1

Sleeping
4 Beachside Resort A1
5 Cat's Pyjamas A2
6 Mercury Bay Holiday Park A3

Eating
7 Cafe Nina A2
8 Coghill House A2
9 Monk St Market B2
10 Squids B2
11 Wild Hogs B2

Drinking
12 Blacksmith Bar B2

Entertainment
13 Mercury Twin Cinemas A2

Twin Oaks Riding Ranch HORSE RIDING
(☎07-866 5388; www.twinoaksridingranch.co.nz; 927 Kuaotunu-Wharekaho Rd; 2hr trek $60) Trek over farmland and through bush on horseback, 9km north of Whitianga.

Highzone ROPES COURSE
(☎07-866 2113; www.highzone.co.nz; 49 Kaimarama Rd; activities $10-70) Hit the ropes for high adventure, including a trapeze leap, high swing and flying fox. It's located 7km south of Whitianga, just off the main road. Call for opening hours.

Tours

There are a baffling number of tours to **Te Whanganui-A-Hei Marine Reserve**, where you'll see interesting rock formations and, if you're lucky, dolphins, fur seals, penguins and orcas. Some are straight-out cruises while others offer optional swimming and snorkeling.

Banana Boat CRUISE
(☎07-866 5617; www.whitianga.co.nz/bananaboat; rides $10-30; ⏲Dec 26-Jan 31) Monkey around in Mercury Bay on the bright-yellow (naturally), motorised Banana Boat – or split to Cathedral Cove.

Cave Cruzer CRUISE
(☎07-866 0611; www.cavecruzer.co.nz) A rigid-hull inflatable offering a one-hour (adult/child $50/30) or two-hour (adult/child $75/40) tour.

Glass Bottom Boat CRUISE
(☎07-867 1962; www.glassbottomboatwhitianga.co.nz; adult/child $85/50) Two-hour bottom-gazing tours.

Whitianga Adventures CRUISE
(☎0800 806 060; www.whitianga-adventures.co.nz; adult/child $65/40) Offers a two-hour Sea Cave Adventure in an inflatable.

Windborne SAILING
(☎027 475 2411; www.windborne.co.nz; day sail $95) Day sails in a 19m 1928 schooner.

Festivals & Events

Coromandel Gold Festival MUSIC
(www.coromandelgold.co.nz; Ohuka Farm, Buffalo Beach Rd; 2-day pass $169) Top NZ and international bands \ to the stage for a two-day festival culminating in the early hours of New Year's Day.

Sleeping

Pipi Dune B&B B&B $$
(☎07-869 5375; www.pipidune.co.nz; 5 Pipi Dune; r $160; wi-fi) You'll be as snug as a pipi in its shell in this attractive B&B in a quiet cul-de-sac, and you'll have a lot more room to move: pipi shells don't tend to come with guest lounges, kitchenettes, laundries and free wi-fi. To get here, head north on Cook Dr, turn left onto Surf St and then first right.

Beachside Resort MOTEL $$
(☎07-867 1356; www.beachsideresort.co.nz; 20 Eyre St; units $175-225; wi-fi, pool) Attached to the sprawling Oceans Resort, this modern motel has tidy units with kitchenettes and, on the upper level, balconies. Despite the name, it's set back from the beach but it does have a heated pool.

Within the Bays B&B $$$
(☎07-866 2848; www.withinthebays.co.nz; 49 Tarapatiki Dr; r $295; @) It's the combination of charming hosts and incredible views that make this B&B set on a hill overlooking Mercury Bay worth considering. It's extremely well set up for guests with restricted mobility – there's even a wheelchair-accessible bush track on the property.

On the Beach Backpackers Lodge HOSTEL $
(☎07-866 5380; www.coromandelbackpackers.com; 46 Buffalo Beach Rd; dm $25-27, s $38, d $70-96; @) Brightly painted and beachside, this large YHA-affiliate has a wide range of rooms, including some with sea views and en suites. It provides free kayaks, boogie boards and spades (for Hot Water Beach).

Cat's Pyjamas HOSTEL $
(☎07-866 4663; www.cats-pyjamas.co.nz; 12 Albert St; dm $25, d $60-70; @ wi-fi) Perfectly positioned between the pubs and the beach, this converted house offers bunk-filled dorms as well as private rooms, some with their own bathroom. There's a large lounge and a sunny courtyard for mooching about in.

Mercury Bay Holiday Park HOLIDAY PARK $
(☎07-866 5579; www.mercurybayholidaypark.co.nz; 121 Albert St; sites from $25, units $85-255; @ wi-fi, pool) Strangely planted in a suburban neighbourhood, this small holiday park is comfortable and clean, with playgrounds, trampoline, swimming pool and pool table.

Eating & Drinking

Cafe Nina CAFE $

(20 Victoria St; mains $9-19; ⏲8am-3pm) Barbecue for breakfast? Why the hell not. Too cool to be constricted to four walls, the kitchen grills bacon and eggs on an outdoor hotplate while the punters spill out onto tables in the park.

Squids SEAFOOD $$

(☎07-867 1710; www.squids.co.nz; 15/1 Blacksmith Lane; mains $17-25; ⏲lunch & dinner Mon-Sat) On a corner facing the harbour, this informal restaurant offers that rarest of conjunctions: good-value seafood meals in a prime location. If you don't fancy the steamed mussels, smoked seafood platter, chowder or catch of the day, steak's an option.

Wild Hogs PUB $$

(www.wildhogswhitianga.wordpress.com; 9 The Esplanade; mains $18-33; ⏲11am-late) While the name may conjure up images of hirsute, leather-clad bikers, the reality is much more genteel. The food's excellent, including juicy burgers and crispy pizzas laden with fancy toppings – best enjoyed on the shady deck.

Coghill House CAFE $

(www.thecog.co.nz; 10 Coghill St; mains $8-17; ⏲8am-3pm) Get an early start to the day on the sunny terrace of this side-street cafe, where the counter food beckons enticingly and the toasted sandwiches have gourmet aspirations.

Monk St Market DELI

(1 Monk St; ⏲10am-6pm Mon-Sat) Self-catering foodies should head here for deli goods, imported chocolate and organic produce.

Blacksmith Bar PUB

(www.blacksmithbar.co.nz; 1 Blacksmith Lane; ⏲10.30am-late) On the weekends, live bands keep the punters pumping until the wee hours (well, 1am). It's the kind of small-town pub that attracts all ages, styles and dancing abilities. There's a large beer garden out the back.

Entertainment

Mercury Twin Cinemas CINEMA

(☎07-867 1001; www.flicks.co.nz; Lee St) Latest-release mainstream and independent films.

Information

Whitianga i-SITE (☎07-866 5555; www.whitianga.co.nz; 66 Albert St; ⏲9am-5pm Mon-Fri, 9am-4pm Sat & Sun, extended in summer) Information and internet access ($3 per 15 minutes).

Getting There & Around

Sunair (p172) operates flights to Whitianga from Auckland, Great Barrier Island, Hamilton, Rotorua and Tauranga. Bus services are offered by InterCity, Tairua Bus Company and Go Kiwi.

Coroglen & Whenuakite

The blink-and-you'll-miss-them villages of Coroglen and Whenuakite are on SH25, south of Whitianga and west of Hot Water Beach. The legendary **Coroglen Tavern** (www.coroglentavern.com; 1937 SH25) is the archetypal middle-of-nowhere country pub that attracts big-name Kiwi bands in the summer.

Running from Labour Day (late October) to Queen's Birthday (early June), **Coroglen Farmers Market** (SH25; ⏲9am-1pm Sun) sells a bit of everything produced in the local area, from vegetables to compost.

Nearby, the folks at **Rangihau Ranch** (☎07-866 3875; www.rangihauranch.co.nz; Rangihau Rd; rides per hr $40) will lead you on horseback up a historic packhorse track, through beautiful bush to spectacular views.

Better than your average highway stop, **Colenso** (www.colensocafe.co.nz; SH25, Whenuakite; mains $7-14; ⏲10am-5pm) has excellent fair-trade coffee, scones, cakes and light snacks, as well as a shop selling homewares and gifts.

Hahei

POP 270 (7000 IN SUMMER)

A legendary Kiwi beach town, little Hahei balloons to bursting in summer but is nearly abandoned otherwise – apart from the busloads of tourists doing the obligatory stop-off at Cathedral Cove. It's a charming spot and a great place to unwind for a few days, especially in the quieter months. It takes its name from Hei, the eponymous ancestor of the Ngati Hei people, who arrived in the 14th century on the *Te Arawa* canoe.

Sights

Cathedral Cove BEACH

Beautiful Cathedral Cove, with its famous gigantic stone arch and natural waterfall shower, is best enjoyed early or late in the day – avoiding the worst of the hordes. At the time of research the arch was roped off due to rock falls, but it's still worth taking the coastal walk to the cove regardless.

At the car park, 1km north of Hahei, the signs suggest that the walk will take 45 minutes, but anyone who's not on a ventilator will do it in 30. On the way there's rocky **Gemstone Bay** (which has a snorkelling trail where you're likely to see big snapper, crayfish and stingrays) and sandy **Stingray Bay**. The walk from Hahei Beach to Cathedral Cove takes about 70 minutes.

Hahei Beach BEACH

Long, lovely Hahei Beach is made more magical by the view to the craggy islands in the distance. From the southern end of Hahei Beach, it's a 15-minute walk up to Te Pare, a *pa* site with splendid coastal views.

Activities

Cathedral Cove Sea Kayaking KAYAKING

(☎07-866 3877; www.seakayaktours.co.nz; 88 Hahei Beach Rd; half/full day $95/150; ⏲tours 9am & 2pm) This outfit runs guided kayaking trips around the rock arches, caves and islands in the Cathedral Cove area. The Remote Coast Tour heads the other way when conditions permit, visiting caves, blowholes and a long tunnel.

Cathedral Cove Dive & Snorkel DIVING

(☎07-866 3955; www.hahei.co.nz/diving; 48 Hahei Beach Rd; dives from $80) Takes daily dive trips and rents out scuba gear, snorkelling gear ($20), bikes ($20) and boogie boards ($20). A Discover Scuba half-day beginners' course costs $190 including all the gear.

Hahei Explorer BOAT TOUR

(☎07-866 3910; www.haheiexplorer.co.nz; adult/child $70/40) Hour-long jetboat rides touring the coast.

Sleeping & Eating

Hahei really does have a 'gone fishing' feel in the off-season. The local store remains open and the eateries take it in turns so that there's usually one option open every evening.

Tatahi Lodge HOSTEL, MOTEL $

(☎07-866 3992; www.tatahilodge.co.nz; Grange Rd; dm $29, r $86-123, units $150-400; @📶) A wonderful place where backpackers are treated with at least as much care and respect as the lush bromeliad-filled garden. The dorm rooms and excellent communal facilities are just as attractive as the pricier motel units.

Church COTTAGE $$

(☎07-866 3533; www.thechurchhahei.co.nz; 87 Hahei Beach Rd; cottages $135-230; @📶) Set within a subtropical garden, these beautifully kitted-out, rustic timber cottages have plenty of character. The ultracharming wooden church at the top of the drive is Hahei's swankiest eatery (mains $33 to $37), offering an ambitious (if overpriced) menu of adventurous country-style cooking.

Getting There & Around

Tairua Bus Company (p173) has bus connections to Hahei. In the height of summer the council runs a bus service from the Cooks Beach side of the ferry landing to Hot Water Beach, stopping at Hahei (adult/child $3/2). Another option on the same route is the **Cathedral Cove Shuttle** (☎027 422 5899; www.cathedralcoveshuttles.co.nz; up to 5 passengers $30).

Hot Water Beach

Justifiably famous, Hot Water Beach is quite extraordinary. For two hours either side of low tide, you can access an area of sand in front of a rocky outcrop at the middle of the beach where hot water oozes up from beneath the surface. Bring a spade, dig a hole and voila, you've got a personal spa pool. Surfers stop off before the main beach to access some decent breaks. The headland between the two beaches still has traces of a Ngati Hei *pa*.

Spades ($5) can be hired from the **Hot Water Beach Store** (Pye Pl), which has a cafe attached, while surfboards ($20 per hour) and body boards ($15) can be hired from the neighbouring surf shop.

Near the beach, **Moko** (www.moko.co.nz; 24 Pye Pl; ⏲10am-5pm) is full of beautiful things – art, sculpture, jewellery – with a modern Pasifika/Maori bent.

Sleeping & Eating

Hot Water Beach Top 10 Holiday Park HOLIDAY PARK $

(☎07-866 3116; www.hotwaterbeachholidaypark.com; 790 Hot Water Beach Rd; sites from $23, units $70-250; @📶) Bordered by tall bamboo and gum trees, this is a smallish, newish, well-run camping ground with a modern shower and toilet block and good, simple cabins.

Hot Water Beach B&B B&B $$$

(☎07-866 3991; www.hotwaterbedandbreakfast.co.nz; 48 Pye Pl; r $260) This hillside pad has priceless views (which go only part of the way towards justifying the hefty rates), a spa bath on the deck and attractive living quarters.

Hot Waves CAFE $
(8 Pye Pl; mains $10-18; ⏲8.30am-4pm) In summer everyone wants a garden table at this excellent cafe – sometimes there are queues stretching out the door. It also hires spades for the beach ($5).

Getting There & Away

The Hahei bus services stop here, but usually only on prebooked requests.

Tairua

POP 1270

Tairua and its twin town **Pauanui** sit either side of a river estuary that's perfect for windsurfing or for little kids to splash about in. Both have excellent surf beaches (Pauanui's is probably a shade better), but that's where the similarity stops. Where Tairua is a functioning residential town (with shops, ATMs and a choice of eateries), Pauanui is an upmarket refuge for over-wealthy Aucklanders – the kind who jet in and park their private planes by their grandiose beach houses before knocking out a round of golf. Friendly Tairua knows how to keep it real. Both are ridiculously popular in the summertime.

Sights & Activities

Various operators offer fishing charters and sightseeing trips, including **Waipae Magic** (☎021 632 024; dewy@slingshot.co.nz), **Taranui Charters** (☎07-864 8511; www.tairua.info/taranui), **Pauanui Charters** (☎07-864 9262; www.pauanuicharters.co.nz) and **Epic Adventures** (☎07-864 8193; www.epicadventures.co.nz).

Paaku MOUNTAIN
Around seven million years ago Paaku was a volcanic island, but now it forms the north head of Tairua's harbour. Ngati Hei had a *pa* here before being invaded by Ngati Maru in the 17th century. It's a steep 15-minute walk to the summit from the top of Paku Dr, with the pay-off being amazing views over Tairua, Pauanui and the Alderman Islands. Plaques along the way detail Tairua's colonial history, with only one rather dismissive one devoted to its long Maori occupation.

Dive Zone DIVING
(☎07-864 8800; www.divezone.co.nz; 307 Main Rd; boat dives from $150, PADI $595; ⏲7.30am-5pm) A new operator making a name for itself with reliable service, including regular opening hours. Also hires snorkelling gear ($20).

SAFETY

Hot Water Beach has dangerous rips, especially directly in front of the main thermal section. It's one of the four most dangerous beaches in NZ in terms of drowning numbers, although this may be skewed by the huge number of tourists that flock here. Regardless, swimming here is *not* safe if the lifeguards aren't on patrol.

Tairua Dive & Fishinn DIVING
(☎07-864 8054; www.divetairua.co.nz; The Esplanade) Tairua Dive & Fishinn hires out kayaks (some with glass bottoms), plus scuba, snorkel and fishing gear. It also runs fishing charters, dive trips out to the Alderman Islands (including full gear $199) and PADI courses.

Sleeping

Dell Cote B&B $$$
(☎07-864 8142; www.dellcote.com; Rewarewa Valley Rd; s/d $235/260; @) Nontoxic mud bricks and macrocarpa timber give this place an organic feel, and the swooping gardens add a dose of tranquillity. The loft room is particularly lovely.

Pacific Harbour Lodge HOTEL $$
(☎07-864 8581; www.pacificharbour.co.nz; 223 Main Rd; chalets $169-229; @) This 'island-style' resort in the town centre has spacious self-contained chalets, with natural wood and Gauguin decor inside and a South Seas garden outside. Discount packages are usually available.

Tairua Beach Villa Backpackers HOSTEL $
(☎07-864 8345; www.tairuabackpackers.co.nz; 200 Main Rd; dm $25-28, s $55-72, d $65-85; @) Rooms are homely and casual at this estuary-edge hostel in a converted house, and the dorm scores great views. Guests can help themselves to fishing rods, kayaks, sailboards and bikes.

Eating & Drinking

Manaia Cafe & Bar CAFE $$
(☎07-864 9050; 228 Main Rd; breakfast $11-19, lunch $14-23, dinner $20-32; ⏲8.30am-4pm Mon,

8.30am-late Wed-Sun) With courtyard seating for lazy summer brunches and a burnished copper bar to prop up later in the night, Manaia is a slick addition to the Tairua strip. The dinner menu features bistro faves with some artful twists.

Old Mill Cafe CAFE $
(www.theoldmillcafe.co.nz; 1 The Esplanade; mains $8-19; ⏲8am-8pm Thu-Sat, 8am-4pm Sun) There's nothing run-of-the-mill about this old dear. Zooshed up with bright-pink feature walls and elegant veranda furniture, it serves interesting cafe fare, as well as tapas from 4pm.

Punters Bar & Grill PUB $$
(Main Rd; mains $17-19; ⏲11am-late Tue-Sun) The local pub serves decent burgers and fish and chips.

Information

Tairua Information Centre (☎07-864 7575; www.tairua.info; 223 Main Rd; ⏲9am-5pm)

Getting There & Around

InterCity, Tairua Bus Company and Go Kiwi all run bus services (p173) to Tairua.

Tairua and Pauanui are connected by a **passenger ferry** (☎027-497 0316; one-way/return $3/5; ⏲daily Dec & Jan), which departs every two hours from 9am to 5pm (until 11pm in January). In other months the ferry offers a water-taxi service.

Puketui Valley

Located 12km south of Tairua is the turn-off to Puketui Valley and the historic **Broken Hills gold-mine workings**, which are 8km from the main road along a mainly gravel road. There are short walks up to the sites of stamper batteries, but the best hike is through the 500m-long Collins Drive mine tunnel. After the tunnel, keep an eye out for the short 'lookout' side trail, which affords panoramic views. It takes about three hours return; remember to take a torch and a jacket with you.

There's a basic **DOC campsite** (www.doc.govt.nz; adult/child $10/5) located in a pretty spot by the river. This is a wilderness area so take care and be properly prepared. Water from the river should be boiled before drinking.

Opoutere

File this one under best-kept secrets. Maybe it's a local conspiracy to keep at bay the hordes of Aucklanders who seasonally invade Pauanui and Whangamata, as this unspoilt long sandy expanse has been kept very quiet. Apart from a cluster of houses there's nothing for miles around. Swimming can be dangerous, especially near Hikinui Islet, which is close to the beach. On the sand spit is the Wharekawa Wildlife Refuge, a breeding ground for the endangered NZ dotterel.

Sleeping

Copsefield B&B $$
(☎07-865 9555; www.copsefield.co.nz; 1055 SH25; r $100-180) On SH25 but closer to Opoutere than it is to Whangamata, Copsefield is a peaceful country-style villa set in attractive, lush gardens with a spa and a riverside swimming hole. The main house has three attractive B&B rooms, while cheaper accommodation is offered in a separate bach-style cottage.

Opoutere YHA HOSTEL $
(☎07-865 9072; www.yha.co.nz; 389 Opoutere Rd; dm $27-30, r $80-116) Housed partly in the historic Opoutere Native School, this wonderful get-away-from-it-all hostel resounds with birdsong. Kayaks, hot-water bottles, alarm clocks, stilts and hula hoops can all be borrowed.

Getting There & Away

The **Go Kiwi** (☎0800 446 549; www.go-kiwi.co.nz) seasonal Auckland–Whitianga shuttle stops in Opoutere on request.

Whangamata

POP 3560

When Auckland's socially ambitious flock to Pauanui, the city's young and horny head to Whangamata to surf, get stoned and hook up. It can be a raucous spot over New Year, when the population swells to more than 40,000. It's a true summer holiday town, but in the off-season there may as well be tumbleweeds rolling down the main street.

Activities

Besides fishing (game-fishing runs from January to April), snorkelling near Hauturu

(Clarke) Island, surfing, kayaking, orienteering and mountain biking, there are excellent walks.

The **Wentworh Falls walk** takes 2½ hours (return); it starts 3km south of the town and 4km down the unsealed Wentworth Valley Rd. A further 3km south of Wentworth Valley Rd is Parakiwai Quarry Rd, at the end of which is the **Wharekirauponga walk**., a sometimes muddy 10km return track (allow 3½ to four hours) to a mining camp, battery and waterfall that passes unusual hexagonal lava columns and loquacious bird life.

Kiwi Dundee Adventures TRAMPING
(07-865 8809; www.kiwidundee.co.nz) Styling himself as a local version of Crocodile Dundee, Doug Johansen offers informative one- to 16-day wilderness walks in the Coromandel Peninsula and countrywide.

Sleeping

Marine Reserved APARTMENT $$$
(07-865 9096; www.marinereservedapartments.co.nz; cnr Ocean Rd & Lowe St; units $330;) It's a peculiar name but the other strange thing about this excellent townhouse complex is that up to six of you can stay here in considerable comfort for $330. Units have secure ground-floor parking, full modern kitchens and barbecues on the decks.

Southpacific Accommodation MOTEL, HOSTEL $
(07-865 9580; www.thesouthpacific.co.nz; 249 Port Rd; dm $27-29, s/d $70/90, units $147-168; @) This hard-to-miss corner-hogging complex consists of a big barn for backpackers and self-contained motel units. Facilities are clean and modern; bikes and kayaks are available for hire.

Wentworth Valley Campsite CAMPSITE $
(07-865 7032; www.doc.govt.nz; 474 Wentworth Valley Rd; adult/child $10/5) More upmarket than most DOC camping grounds, this campsite is accessed from the Wentworth Falls walk and has toilets, showers and gas barbecues.

Breakers MOTEL $$
(07-865 8464; www.breakersmotel.co.nz; 324 Hetherington Rd; units $175-195;) Facing the marina on the Tairua approach to Whangamata, this newish motel compensates for saggy beds with an enticing swimming pool and spa pools on the decks of the upstairs units.

Eating

Lazy Lizard CAFE $
(427 Port Rd; mains $10-17; 7.30am-3.30pm Tue-Sun) Winning points for its bizarre hand-shaped stools, this funky lizard does delicious counter food, cooked breakfasts, bagels and salads. The fair-trade organic coffee is first rate.

Craig's Traditional Fish & Chips FISH & CHIPS $
(701 Port Rd; mains $5-10; lunch & dinner Wed-Mon) All you could ask for in a chippie, Craig's scoops out pieces of grilled fresh fish and fat, salted chips. The service is friendly, and there's a TV and a stack of trashy mags to speed up the wait.

Soul Burger BURGERS $
(www.soulburger.co.nz; 441 Port Rd; burgers $10-15; 5-9pm Thu, 8am-9pm Fri-Sun winter, daily summer) Serving audacious burgers with names like Soul Blues Brother and Vegan Vibe, this hip corner joint has branched out into cooked breakfasts on the weekend.

Information

Whangamata i-SITE (07-865 8340; www.whangamatainfo.co.nz; 616 Port Rd; 9am-5pm Mon-Fri, 9.30am-3.30pm Sat & Sun)

Getting There & Away

Go Kiwi (0800 446 549; www.go-kiwi.co.nz) has a shuttle service to Whangamata.

Waihi & Waihi Beach

POP 4500 & 1800

Where most towns have hole-in-the-wall ATMs for people to access their riches, Waihi has a giant hole in the ground, right next to its main street. They've been dragging gold and silver out of Martha Mine, NZ's richest, since 1878. The town formed quickly thereafter and blinged itself up with grand buildings and a show-offy avenue of phoenix palms, now magnificently mature.

After closing down in 1952, open-cast mining restarted in 1988. The mine is still productive, but only just – it takes a tonne of rock to yield 3g to 6g of gold. It's expected to run out soon, and when it does, plans are afoot to convert the town's gaping wound into a major tourist attraction. Watch this space.

While Waihi is interesting for a brief visit, it's Waihi Beach where you'll want to linger. The two places are as dissimilar as surfing is from mining, separated by 11km of farmland. The long sandy beach stretches 9km to Bowentown, on the northern limits of Tauranga Harbour, where you'll find sheltered harbour beaches such as beautiful **Anzac Bay**. There's a very popular 45-minute walk north through bush to pristine **Orokawa Bay**, which has no road access.

Sights

Seddon St STREET

Waihi's main drag has interesting sculptures, information panels about Waihi's golden past and roundabouts that look like squashed daleks. Opposite the visitor centre, the skeleton of a derelict **Cornish Pumphouse** (1904) is the town's main landmark, atmospherically lit at night. From here the **Pit Rim Walkway** has fascinating views into the 250m-deep Martha Mine. If you want to get down into it, the mining company runs 1½-hour **Waihi Gold Mine Tours** (www.waihigoldminetours.co.nz; adult/child $28/14; 10am & 12.30pm Mon-Sat).

The *Historic Hauraki Gold Towns* pamphlet (free from the visitor centre) outlines walking tours of both Waihi and Paeroa.

Athenree Hot Springs THERMAL POOLS

(www.athenreehotsprings.co.nz; 1 Athenree Rd, Athenree; adult/child $7/4.50; 10am-7.30pm) In those months when the waters of Waihi Beach aren't inviting, retreat to these two small but blissful outdoor hot pools, hidden within a holiday park.

Heritage Museum MUSEUM

(www.waihimuseum.co.nz; 54 Kenny St, Waihi; adult/child $5/3; 10am-3pm Thu & Fri, noon-3pm Sat-Mon) The Heritage Museum has an art gallery and displays focusing on the region's gold-mining history. Prepare to squirm before the collection of miners' chopped-off thumbs preserved in glass jars.

Waihi Waterlily Gardens GARDENS

(www.waterlily.co.nz; 441 Pukekauri Rd, Waihi; adult/child $8.50/free; 11am-3pm Wed-Sun Oct-Apr) Seven hectares of ponds, peacocks and pretty things, 7km southwest of Waihi. There's a cafe on-site.

Activities

Goldfields Railway RAILWAY

(07-863 8251; www.waihirail.co.nz; 30 Wrigley St, Waihi; adult/child return $15/8; Fri-Mon Apr-Aug, daily Sep-Mar) Vintage trains depart Waihi for a 7km, 25-minute scenic journey to Waikino.

Sunshine Surf Coaching SURFING

(07-863 4857; www.sunshinesurfcoaching.co.nz; private lesson $120) Takes advantage of Waihi Beach's relatively gentle breaks to offer all-age surf instruction.

Over the Top Adventures DIRT BIKING

(021 205 7266; www.overthetopadventures.co.nz; 1 Surrey St, Waihi; tours $90-400) Offers on-/off-road dirt-bike tours, rents mountain bikes ($35 to $55 per day) and provides cycling transfers.

Dirtboard Waihi DIRTBOARDING

(021 244 1646; www.dirtboard.co.nz; per hr $30) Hit the slopes on a mutant snowboard-skateboard.

Bularangi Motorbikes MOTORBIKE TOURS

(07-863 6069; www.motorbikesnz.co.nz) Based in Waihi, Bularangi Motorbikes offers Harley Davidson rentals and one- to 21-day guided tours throughout the country.

Sleeping

TOP CHOICE **Bowentown Beach Holiday Park** HOLIDAY PARK $

(07-863 5381; www.bowentown.co.nz; 510 Seaforth Rd, Waihi Beach; sites from $25, units $95-374; @) Having nabbed a stunning stretch of sand this impressively maintained holiday park makes the most of it with first-rate motel units and campers' facilities. The barbecue area even has a water feature.

Athenree Hot Springs & Holiday Park HOLIDAY PARK $

(07-863 5600; www.athenreehotsprings.co.nz; 1 Athenree Rd, Athenree; sites from $24, units $70-200; @) Harbour-hugging Athenree has smart accommodation and friendly owners. Entry to the thermal pools is free for guests, making this a top choice for the winter months.

Waihi Waterlily Gardens COTTAGE $$$

(07-863 8267; www.waterlily.co.nz; 441 Pukekauri Rd, Waihi; cottages $250) After-hours you get the gardens all to yourself if you're staying in one of these two cottages. They're beautifully decked out with comfy beds, quality linen, polished concrete floors and interesting art.

Manawa Ridge LODGE $$$

(☎07-863 9400; www.manawaridge.co.nz; 267 Ngatitangata Rd, Waihi; r $850) The views from this castle-like ecoretreat, perched on a 310m ridge 6km northeast of Waihi, take in the entire Bay of Plenty. Made of recycled railway timber, mud brick and lime-plastered straw walls, the rooms marry earthiness with sheer luxury.

Beachfront B&B B&B $$

(☎07-863 5393; www.beachfrontbandb.co.nz; 3 Shaw Rd, Waihi Beach; r $130) True to its name with absolute beachfront and spectacular sea views, this comfortable downstairs flat has a TV, fridge and direct access to the surf.

Waihi Beach Top 10 Holiday Resort HOLIDAY PARK $

(☎07-863 5504; www.waihibeach.com; 15 Beach Rd, Waihi Beach; sites from $29, units $85-265; @☎≋) This massive, resort-style holiday park is pretty darn flash, with a pool, gym, spa, beautiful kitchen and a smorgasbord of sleeping options.

Eating & Drinking

Porch CAFE, BAR $$

(www.theporch.co.nz; 23 Wilson Rd, Waihi Beach; brunch $14-20, dinner $29-36; ⏲breakfast & lunch daily, dinner Wed-Sat) Waihi Beach's coolest chow-down spot, serving sophisticated, substantial mains.

Flatwhite CAFE $$

(www.flatwhitecafe.co.nz; 21 Shaw Rd, Waihi Beach; brunch $14-20, dinner $20-27; ⏲breakfast, lunch & dinner; ☎) Funky, licensed and right by the beach, Flatwhite has a lively brunch menu and serves decent pizzas.

Ti-Tree Cafe CAFE $

(14 Haszard St, Waihi; brunch $11-18, pizza $17-24; ⏲breakfast & lunch daily, dinner Thu-Sat; ☎) Housed in a cute little wooden building with punga-shaded outdoor seating, Ti-Tree serves fair-trade organic coffee, cooked breakfasts and wood-fired pizza.

Shopping

Artmarket ARTS & CRAFTS

(www.artmarket.co.nz; 65 Seddon St, Waihi; ⏲10am-5pm) Stocks a first-rate selection of local arts and crafts.

Information

Waihi Visitor Centre (☎07-863 6715; www.waihi.org.nz; 126 Seddon St, Waihi; ⏲9am-5pm; @)

Getting There & Away

Waihi is serviced by InterCity buses and seasonal Go Kiwi (p187) shuttles.

Karangahake Gorge

The road between Waihi and Paeroa, through the bush-lined ramparts of the Karangahake Gorge, is one of the best short drives in the country. Walking and biking tracks take in old Maori trails, historic mining and rail detritus, and spookily dense bush. In Maori legend the area is said to be protected by a *taniwha*, a supernatural creature. The local *iwi* managed to keep this area closed to miners until 1875, aligning themselves with the militant Te Kooti.

The very worthwhile 4.5km **Karangahake Gorge Historic Walkway** takes 1½ hours (each way) and starts from the car park 14km west of Waihi. It follows the disused railway line and the Ohinemuri River to Owharoa Falls and Waikino station, where you can pick up the vintage train to Waihi, stopping in at **Waikino Station Cafe** (SH2; mains $10-18; ⏲9.30am-3pm) while you wait.

There are a range of shorter walks and loop tracks leading from the car park; bring a torch as some pass through tunnels. A two-hour tramp will bring you to Dickey's Flat, where there's a free **DOC campsite** (Dickey's Flat Rd) and a decent swimming hole. River water will need to be boiled for drinking. You'll find DOC information boards about the walks and the area's history at both the station and the main car park. A spectacular offshoot of the Hauraki Rail Trail (p174) cycling route also passes through here.

Across from the car park, **Golden Owl Lodge** (☎07-862 7994; www.goldenowl.co.nz; 3 Moresby St; dm $29, r $62-75; @☎) is a homely, handy tramping base, sleeping only 12. Allow $5 extra for linen in the dorm rooms.

Further up the same road, **Ohinemuri Estate Winery** (☎07-862 8874; www.ohinemuri.co.nz; Moresby St; mains $19-25; ⏲10am-5pm Wed-Sun, daily summer) has Latvian-influenced architecture and serves excellent lunches. You'd be right if you thought it was an unusual site for growing grapes – the fruit is imported from other regions. Tastings are $5, refundable with purchase. If you imbibe too much, snaffle the chalet-style hut ($115 to $145 per night) and revel in the charming atmosphere of this secluded place.

Paeroa

POP 3980

If you find yourself scratching your head in Paeroa, don't worry too much about it. The whole town is an elaborate Kiwi in-joke. It's the birthplace of Lemon & Paeroa (L&P), an icon of Kiwiana that markets itself as 'world famous in NZ'. The fact that the beloved fizzy drink is now owned by global monster Coca-Cola Amatil and produced in Auckland only serves to make the ubiquitous L&P branding even more darkly ironic. Still, generations of Kiwi kids have pestered their parents to take this route just to catch a glimpse of the giant L&P bottles.

The small **museum** (37 Belmont Rd; adult/child $2/1; ⏲noon-3pm Mon-Fri) has a grand selection of Royal Albert porcelain and other pioneer and Maori artefacts – look in the drawers. If pretty crockery is your thing, Paeroa is known for its antique stores.

L&P Cafe & Bar (SH2; mains $7-20; ⏲breakfast & lunch daily, dinner Fri-Sun) has a truck-stop ambience, but is as good a place as any to find out what all the fuss is about. You can order L&P fish and chips or an L&P brekkie, washed down with the lemony lolly water itself. The cafe shares the space with the **information centre** (☎07-862 8636; www.paeroa.org.nz; ⏲9am-3pm).

Waikato & the King Country

Includes »

Waikato 194
Hamilton 195
Raglan 201
Te Awamutu 205
Cambridge 206
Matamata 209
Te Aroha 210
The King Country 211
Kawhia 211
Otorohanga 212
Waitomo Caves 214
Te Kuiti 219
Taumarunui 220
Owhango 221

Best Outdoors

- Surfing at Manu Bay (p204)
- Waitomo Caves rafting (p214)
- Ngarupupu Point (p218)
- City Bridges River Tour (p197)
- Te Toto Gorge (p204)

Best Places to Stay

- Raglan Backpackers (p202)
- Solscape (p204)
- Aroha Mountain Lodge (p210)
- Abseil Inn (p216)

Why Go?

If the colour green had a homeland, this would be it. Here, verdant fields and rolling hills line New Zealand's mightiest river, the Waikato. Visitors from England might wonder why they bothered leaving home, especially in quaint towns like Cambridge where every effort has been made to replicate the 'mother country'.

But this veneer disguises another reality: this is Tainui country. In the 1850s this powerful tribal coalition elected a king to resist the loss of land and sovereignty. The fertile Waikato was forcibly taken from them, but they retained control of the limestone crags and forests of the King Country to within a whisper of the 20th century.

These days visitors can experience first-hand the region's genteel/wild dichotomy. Adrenaline junkies can hurl themsleves into Raglan's legendary surf, or into extreme underground pursuits in the extraordinary Waitomo Caves. Others will warm to the more sedate delights of Te Aroha's Edwardian thermal complex or Hamilton's gardens.

When to Go

The southern area around Taumarunui is wetter and colder than the rest of this region, which can suffer summer droughts. But either way, you're guaranteed to see a lot of green, green grass. Crowd-wise, if you avoid summer you'll avoid any accommodation shortfalls, but without the extra people around this region can seem a just a bit *too* agricultural. Raglan's surf breaks are always busy, regardless of the season (they didn't call the surf movie *The Endless Summer* for nothing).

Waikato & the King Country Highlights

1. Seeking subterranean stimulation in the **Waitomo Caves** (p214) (this is your chance to try black-water rafting)
2. Hitting the surf (and then the pub) in unhurried **Raglan** (p201)
3. Discovering your own bush-framed black-sand beach on the rugged **west coast** (p218)
4. Soaking up 'the love' in the thermal waters of **Te Aroha** (p210), an utterly seductive little town
5. Plotting a pub crawl around Hood and Victoria Sts in surprisingly buzzy **Hamilton** (p195)
6. Tramping through an inland

island paradise at **Maungatautari Ecological Island** (p207)

7 Indulging in Maori culture at Kawhia's **Kai Festival** (p212): and don't miss a soak at nearby **Te Puia Hot Springs** (p211)

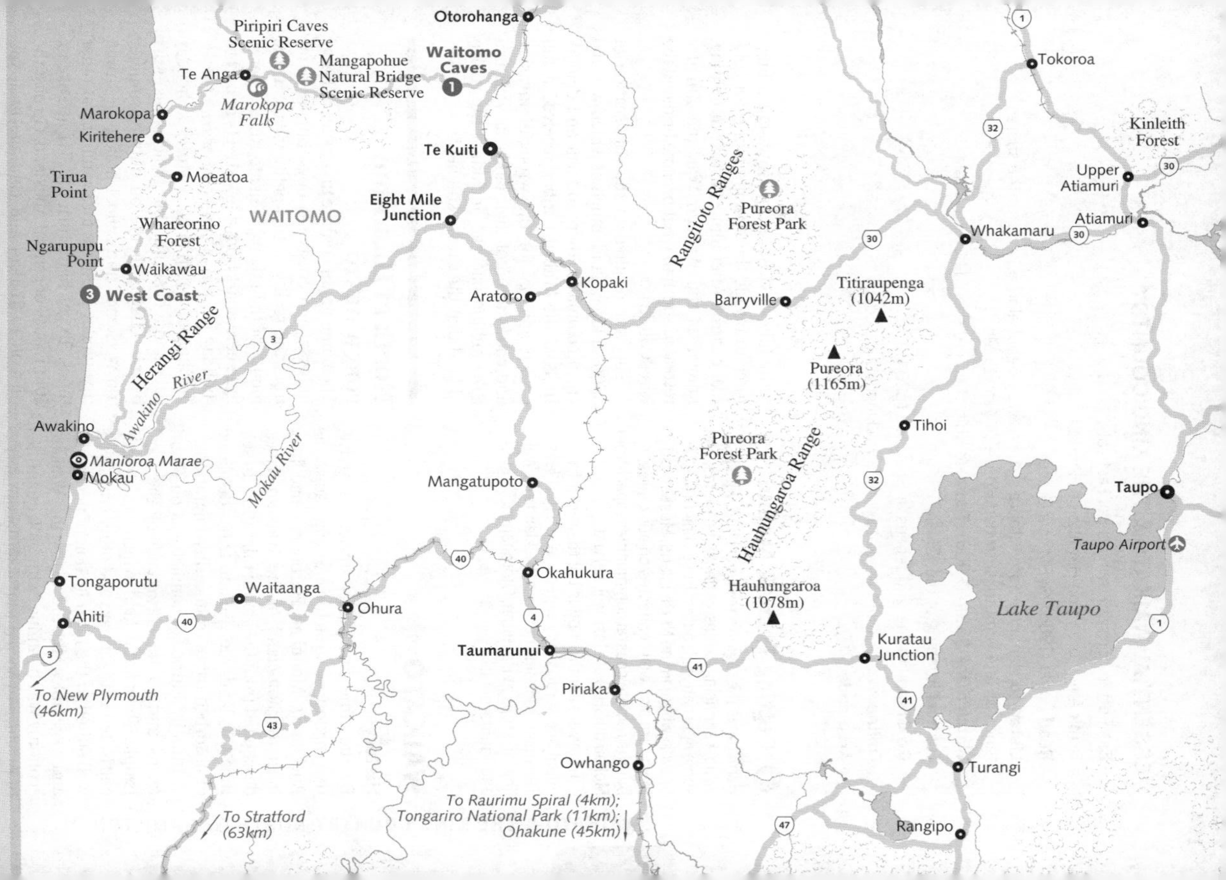

ESSENTIAL WAIKATO & THE KING COUNTRY

» **Eat** Rotten corn at Kawhia's Kai Festival

» **Drink** A few brews on Hamilton's Hood St

» **Read** *Potiki* (1986) by Patricia Grace

» **Listen to** Hamilton-born Kimbra's snaky/sexy debut album *Vows*, or the sacred sounds of Te Awamutu: Crowded House's 'Mean to Me'

» **Watch** *Black Sheep* (2006). Those Te Kuiti shearers should be very afraid

» **Festival** Running of the Sheep, Te Kuiti

» **Go Green** Off-the-grid tepees at Solscape (p204)

» **Online** www.hamiltonwaikato.com, www.kingcountry.co.nz

» **Area code** ☎07

Getting There & Around

Hamilton is the region's transport hub, with its airport servicing extensive domestic routes, and some international routes. Buses link the city to everywhere in the North Island. Most inland towns are also well connected on bus routes, but the remote coastal communities (apart from Mokau on SH3) are less well served.

Trains are another option but they are infrequent and surprisingly expensive on short legs. The main trunk-line between Auckland and Wellington stops at Hamilton, Otorohanga, Te Kuiti and Taumarunui.

WAIKATO

History

By the time Europeans started to arrive, this region – stretching as far north as Auckland's Manukau Harbour – had long been the homeland of the Waikato tribes, descended from the Tainui migration. In settling this land, the Waikato tribes displaced or absorbed tribes from earlier migrations.

Initially European contact was on Maori terms and to the advantage of the local people. Their fertile land, which was already cultivated with kumara and other crops, was well suited to the introduction of new fruits and vegetables. By the 1840s the Waikato economy was booming, with bulk quantities of produce exported to the settlers in Auckland and beyond.

Relations between the two cultures soured during the 1850s, largely due to the colonists' pressure to purchase Maori land. In response, a confederation of tribes united to elect a king to safeguard their interests, forming what became known as the Kingitanga (King Movement).

In July 1863 Governor Grey sent a huge force to invade the Waikato and exert colonial control. After almost a year of fighting, known as the Waikato War, the Kingites retreated south to what became branded the King Country.

The war resulted in the confiscation of 3600 sq km of land, much of which was given to colonial soldiers to farm and defend. In 1995 the Waikato tribes received a full Crown apology for the wrongful invasion and confiscation of their lands, as well as a $170 million package, including the return of land that the Crown still held.

North of Hamilton

PORT WAIKATO

The name might conjure up images of heavy industry and crusty sea dogs, but that's far from the reality of this petite village at the mouth of the mighty Waikato River. There's little here apart from a few streets of baches (holiday homes), a couple of *marae* (meeting house) complexes, a store, a holiday park and a beautiful (but treacherous) **surf beach**. Lifeguards are on duty in summer (on weekends and school holidays); strong rips render it unsafe for swimming at other times. To get here, turn off SH1 at Pokeno, 50km south of central Auckland. Go past the turn-off to Tuakau and continue until you see the Port Waikato signs.

Waikatoa Beach Lodge (☎09-232 9961; www.sunsetbeach.co.nz; 8 Centreway Rd; sites from $18, dm/s/d/f from $27/40/65/80) spoils visiting beach bums with smart rooms, decent linen, a garden scattered with seashells and a sleepy tabby cat. There's a welcoming kitchen/lounge area with gas cooking.

Continue south of Port Waikato for 28km and you'll reach **Nikau Cave** (☎09-233 3199; www.nikaucave.co.nz; 1770 Waikaretu Rd; adult/child $35/18; ⏲by appointment), where a tour (minimum two people) will take you through tight, wet squeezes to glowworms, limestone formations and subterranean streams. There's a cafe here, too.

RANGIRI

Following SH1 south you're retracing the route of the colonial army in the spectacular land grab that was the Waikato War. On 20 November 1863, 1500 British troops (some say it was 850 – either way, there was a lot of 'em), backed by gunboats and artillery, attacked the substantial fortifications erected by the Maori king's warriors at Rangiriri. They were repulsed a number of times and lost 49 men, but overnight many of the 500 Maori defenders retreated; the remaining 183 were taken prisoner the next day after the British gained entry to the *pa* (fortified village) by conveniently misunderstanding a flag of truce.

The **Rangiriri Heritage Centre** (☎07-826 3663; www.nzmuseums.co.nz; 12 Rangiriri Rd; admission free, film $5; ⏲7.30am-5pm) screens a short documentary about the battle, and across the road the **Maori War & Early Settlers Cemetery** (Rangiriri Rd; ⏲24hr) houses the soldiers' graves and a mound covering the mass grave of 36 Maori warriors.

Next to the heritage centre is the historic, elaborately wallpapered **Rangiriri Hotel** (☎07-826 3467; 8 Talbot St; lunch mains $11-19, dinner $17-28; ⏲11am-11pm), a cheery spot for lunch (try the scallops) or a beer at sunny outdoor tables.

NGARUAWAHIA & AROUND

The headquarters of the Maori King movement, Ngaruawahia (population 4940) is 19km north of Hamilton on SH1. The impressive fences of **Turangawaewae Marae** (☎07-824 5189; www.wakamaori.co.nz/maori-culture/marae/turangawaewae-marae; 29 River Rd) maintain the privacy of this important place, but twice a year visitors are welcomed. **Regatta Day** is held in mid-March, with *waka* (canoe) races and all manner of Maori cultural activities. For a week from 15 August the *marae* is open to celebrate **Koroniehana**, the anniversary of the coronation of the current king, Tuheitia.

Ask at the **post office** (3 Jesmond St) for directions

Hamilton

POP 206,400

Landlocked cities in an island nation will never have the glamorous appeal of their coastal cousins. Rotorua compensates with boiling mud and Taupo has its lake, but Hamilton and Palmerston North, despite majestic rivers, are left clutching short straws.

However, something strange has happened in Hamilton recently. The city's main street has sprouted a sophisticated and vibrant stretch of bars and eateries around Hood and Victoria Sts that – on the weekend at least – leaves Auckland's Viaduct Harbour for dead in the boozy fun stakes.

Oddly, the great grey-green greasy Waikato River rolls right through town, but the city's layout largely ignores its presence: unless you're driving across a bridge you'll hardly know it's there.

MAORI NZ: WAIKATO & THE KING COUNTRY

The Waikato/King Country region remains one of the strongest pockets of Maori influence in NZ. This is the heartland of the Tainui tribes, descended from those who disembarked from the *Tainui waka* (canoe) in Kawhia in the 14th century. Split into four main tribal divisions (Waikato, Hauraki, Ngati Maniapoto and Ngati Raukawa), Tainui are inextricably linked with the Kingitanga (King Movement), which has its base in Ngaruawahia.

The best opportunities to interact with Maori culture are the Kawhia Kai Festival, and Ngaruawahia's Regatta Day and Koroneihana celebrations. Interesting *taonga* (treasures) are displayed at museums in Hamilton and Te Awamutu. Reminders of the Waikato Land War can be found at Rangiriri, Rangiaowhia and Orakau.

Dozens of *marae* (meeting house) complexes are dotted around the countryside – including at Awakino, and at Kawhia, where the *Tainui waka* is buried. You won't be able to visit these without permission but you can get decent views from the gates. Some regional tours include an element of Maori culture, including Ruakuri Cave and Kawhia Harbour Cruises.

Hamilton

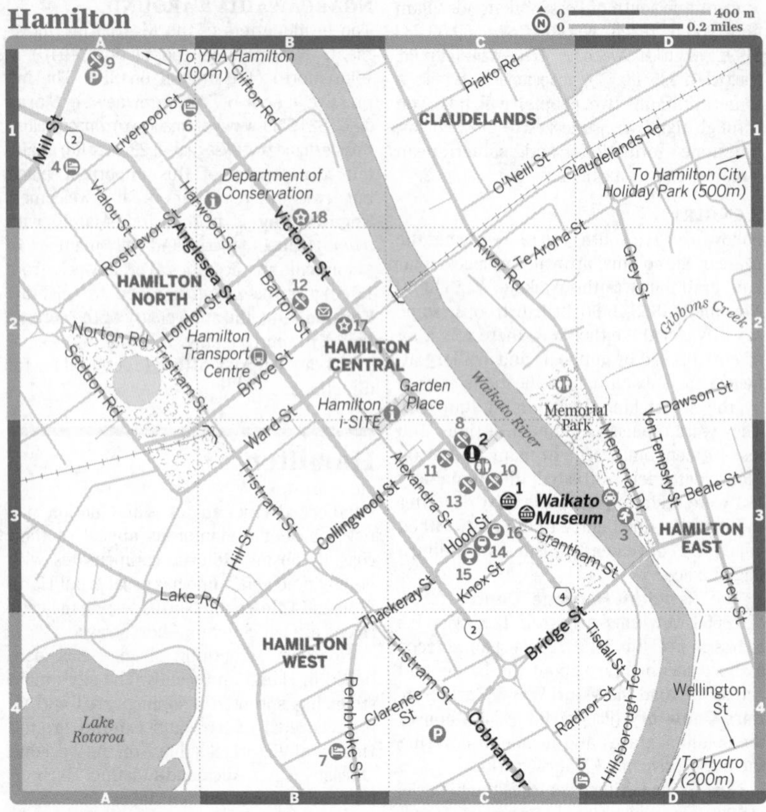

Sights

Waikato Museum MUSEUM

(www.waikatomuseum.co.nz; 1 Grantham St; admission free-$6.50; ⏲10am-4.30pm) The excellent Waikato Museum has five main areas: an art gallery; interactive science galleries; Tainui galleries housing Maori treasures, including the magnificently carved *waka taua* (war canoe), *Te Winikawaka*; a Hamilton history exhibition entitled 'Never a Dull Moment'; and a Waikato River exhibition. The museum also runs a rigorous program of public events. Admission is charged for some exhibits.

FREE **Hamilton Gardens** GARDENS

(www.hamiltongardens.co.nz; Cobham Dr; ⏲enclosed sector 7am-6pm, info centre 9am-5pm) Hamilton Gardens, spread over 50 hectares, incorporates a large park, cafe, restaurant and extravagant themed enclosed gardens. There are separate Italian Renaissance, Chinese, Japanese, English, American and Indian gardens complete with colonnades, pagodas and a mini Taj Mahal. Equally interesting are the sustainable Productive Garden Collection, a fragrant herb garden and the precolonisation Maori Te Parapara garden. Look for the impressive *Nga Uri O Hinetuparimaunga* (Earth Blanket) sculpture at the main gates. The gardens are southeast of Hamilton city centre.

Waikato River RIVER, PARK

The strong-flowing Waikato River is well worth investigating. Bush-covered riverside walkways run along both sides of the river and provide the city's green belt. Jogging paths continue to the boardwalk circling Lake Rotoroa, west of the centre. Memorial Park is closer to town, and has the remains of the *PS Rangiriri* – an iron-clad, steam-powered gunboat from the Waikato War – embedded in the riverbank (under restoration when we visited).

Hamilton

Top Sights
Waikato Museum ... C3

Sights
1 ArtsPost ... C3
2 Riff Raff ... C3

Activities, Courses & Tours
3 Cruise Waikato ... D3

Sleeping
4 Anglesea Motel ... A1
5 City Centre B&B ... D4
6 Eagles Nest Backpackers ... A1
7 YWCA ... B4

Eating
8 Chim-Choo-Ree ... C3
9 Pak 'n Save ... A1
10 Palate ... C3
11 River Kitchen ... C3
12 Rocket Coffee ... B2
13 Scott's Epicurean ... C3

Drinking
14 Diggers Bar ... C3
15 House on Hood ... C3
16 Limestone ... C3

Entertainment
17 Lido Cinema ... B2
18 Victoria Cinema ... B1

See Activities for some more options for exploring the river.

Riff Raff MONUMENT
(www.riffraffstatue.org; Victoria St;) One of Hamilton's more unusual public artworks is a life-size statue of *Rocky Horror Picture Show* writer Richard O'Brien aka Riff Raff, the time-warping alien from the planet Transsexual. It looks over a small park on the site of the former Embassy Theatre where O'Brien worked as a hairdresser, though it's hard to imagine 1960s Hamilton inspired the tale of bisexual alien decadence. Free wi-fi emanates from Riff Raff's three-pronged stun gun.

FREE **ArtsPost** GALLERY
(www.artspost.co.nz; 120 Victoria St; 10am-4.30pm) ArtsPost, near the Waikato Museum, is a contemporary gallery and gift shop housed in a grand, former post office. It focuses on the best of local art: paintings, glass, prints, textiles and photography. Check out the awesome floorboards.

Hamilton Zoo ZOO
(www.hamiltonzoo.co.nz; 183 Brymer Rd; adult/child/family $16/8/42, tours extra; 9am-5pm, last entry 3.30pm) Hamilton Zoo houses 500-plus species (including NZ's only tapir) and takes part in conservation breeding projects. There are various guided-tour options available, plus daily 'Meet the Keeper' talks for interesting insights from the critters' care-givers. The zoo is 8km from Hamilton city centre: take Norton Rd off Tristram St, then SH23 west towards Raglan, turn right at Newcastle Rd and then left onto Brymer Rd.

Activities

City Bridges River Tour KAYAKING
(07-847 5565; www.canoeandkayak.co.nz; 2hr trip adult/child $60/35) An interesting way to check out the Waikato River is on a City Bridges River Tour, a guided kayak tour through the city. No experience necessary; minimum three people.

Cruise Waikato BOAT TOUR
(0508 426 458; www.cruise-waikato.co.nz; Memorial Park Jetty, Memorial Dr; cruises adult/child from $25/10) Runs a range of river cruises, focused variously on sightseeing, history or your belly (coffee and muffins, *hangi* – a feast of maori food – or picnics). See the city from the river, rather than the other way around!

Extreme Edge ROCK CLIMBING
(07-847 5858; www.extremeedge.co.nz; 90 Greenwood St; day pass incl harness adult/child $17.50/13; noon-9.30pm Mon-Fri, 10am-7pm Sat & Sun) This airy hangar near the Frankton train station contains an array of hypercoloured climbing walls, 14m of which is overhanging. There's a dedicated kids'

TAUPIRI

About 26km north of Hamilton on SH1 is Taupiri (287m), the sacred mountain of the Tainui people. You'll recognise it by the cemetery on its slopes and the honking of passing car horns – locals saying hi to their loved ones as they pass by. In August 2006 thousands gathered here as the much-loved Maori queen, Dame Te Atairangikaahu, was transported upriver by *waka* (canoe) to her final resting place, an unmarked grave on the summit.

climbing zone, and free safety lessons for vert virgins.

Wiseway Canoe Adventures CANOEING
(☎021 988 335; www.wisewayadventures.com; 2hr trip adult/child $50/20) Wiseway Canoe Adventures offers guided trips through the city along the river, or offers freedom hire if you'd rather take things at your own pace. One- and three-hour trips also available.

Kiwi Balloon Company BALLOONING
(☎07-843 8538, 021 912 679; www.kiwiballoon company.co.nz; flights per person $320) A hot-air ballon flight is a lovely (and surprisingly unscary) option for gazing down on the lush Waikato countryside. The whole experience takes about four hours and includes a champagne breakfast and an hour's flying time.

Festivals & Events

Balloons Over Waikato SPORTS
(www.balloonsoverwaikato.co.nz) In March, get a legal high with Balloons over Waikato, a colourful hot-air balloon fest.

Hamilton 400 SPORTS
(www.hamilton.v8supercars.com.au) In April revheads flock to town for the Hamilton 400 V8 Supercar street race, part of the Australian V8 Supercars Championship. Vroom, vroom...

Hamilton River Festival CULTURAL, SPORTS
(www.hamiltonriverfestival.co.nz) In September/October, this month-long festival focuses on the mighty, moiling Waikato River, including a Cambridge-to-Hamilton kayak and a chilly 'Spring Dip' swim, plus food and cultural events around town.

Sleeping

The road into town from Auckland (Ulster St) is lined with dozens of unremarkable, traffic-noisy motels: passable for short stays.

Anglesea Motel MOTEL $$
(☎07-834 0010, 0800 426 453; www.anglesea motel.co.nz; 36 Liverpool St; d/2-/3-br units from $138/265/310; @ 📶 🏊) Getting great feedback from travellers and a far preferable option to anything on Ulster St's 'motel row', the Anglesea has plenty of space, friendly managers, free wi-fi, pool and squash and tennis courts, and not un-stylish decor. Hard to beat.

J's Backpackers HOSTEL $
(☎07-856 8934; www.jsbackpackers.co.nz; 8 Grey St; dm/s/d/tr $28/60/66/82; @ 📶) A homely hostel occupying a characterful house near Hamilton Gardens, friendly J's offers good security, a newly renovated (but small) kitchen, free bikes and bright, tidy rooms. There's a barbecue out the back and a Mongolian yurt lounge-space on the front lawn: sip a beer, strum a guitar and hope Ghengis Khan doesn't show up.

City Centre B&B B&B $$
(☎07-838 1671; www.citycentrebnb.co.nz; 3 Anglesea St; r $90-150, extra person $30; @ 📶 🏊) At the quiet riverside end of a central city street (five minutes' walk to the Victoria/Hood St action), this sparkling self-contained apartment opens on to a swimming pool. There's also a bedroom available in a wing of the main house. Self-catering breakfast provided.

YWCA HOSTEL $
(☎07-838 2219; www.ywcahamilton.org.nz; cnr Pembroke & Clarence Sts; s/d $30/60; @) You don't have to be young or female to stay at this four-storey apartment-block hostel. The rooms are cell-like but they're spotless, cheap and private. Each floor has shared bathroom facilities, good security, a kitchen and TV lounge. Weekly rates available.

Eagles Nest Backpackers HOSTEL $
(☎07-838 2704; www.eaglesbackpackers.co.nz; 937 Victoria St; dm/d $25/60; @ 📶) This laid-back 1st-floor eyrie has windowless internal rooms (with skylights) but they're clean and mercifully quiet given the hostel's busy position. The roomy (and reasonably funky) communal lounge opens onto a wee balcony overlooking the Victoria St fray, with a barbecue to sizzle a few snags.

YHA Hamilton HOSTEL $
(☎07-957 1848; www.yha.co.nz; 140 Ulster St; dm/s $29/49, d $59-69; @ 📶) Super-clean, quality linen, Sky TV, chilled-out lounge space, laundry, supermarket across the street...what's the catch? Well, the hostel occupies a former 'micro hotel', so the rooms and kitchen are tiny. If you're over 6ft tall you might struggle.

Hamilton City Holiday Park HOLIDAY PARK $
(☎07-855 8255; www.hamiltoncityholidaypark.co.nz; 14 Ruakura Rd; sites/units from $35/45; @ 📶) Simple cabins and leafy sites are the rule at this shady park. The amenities block and some of the older cabins are starting to feel a bit weary, but it's reasonably close to town (2km east of the centre) and very affordable.

Eating

River Kitchen CAFE $

(www.theriverkitchen.co.nz; 237 Victoria St; mains $7-16; ⏰7am-4pm Mon-Fri, 8am-4pm Sat & Sun; 🖉) Hip River Kitchen does things with simple style: cakes, gourmet breakfasts and fresh seasonal lunches (angle for the salmon hash), and a barista who knows his beans. It's the kind of place you visit for breakfast, come back to for lunch, then consider for breakfast the next day.

Chim-Choo-Ree MODERN NZ $$$

(☎07-839 4329; www.chimchooree.co.nz; 244 Victoria St; mains $30-34; ⏰4.30pm-late Tue-Sat) Hip little Chim-Choo-Ree, with its clackety bentwood chairs, concrete floor and kitsch art, is a casual fine-dining option that's been wowing the critics. Launch into the five-course tasting menu ($125/85 with/without wine), or mains like manuka-smoked eel and Canadian scallops with apple-and-radish salad. Footpath tables cop some noise from the bar next door: compete with choruses of *Mary Poppins* classics.

Scott's Epicurean INTERNATIONAL $

(☎07-839 6680; 181 Victoria St; mains $11-20; ⏰7am-4pm Mon-Fri, 8.30am-4pm Sat & Sun) This gorgeous joint features swanky leather banquettes, pressed-tin ceilings, great coffee and an interesting and affordable menu: try the *pytti panna* (Swedish bubble-and-squeak) or the ever-popular *spaghetti aglio e olio* (there'd be a riot if it ever dropped off the menu). Friendly service; fully licensed.

Rocket Coffee CAFE $

(www.rocketcoffee.co.nz; 302 Barton St; coffees from $4; ⏰8am-4pm Mon-Fri) Duck down Barton St for what some locals say is the coolest thing about Hamilton (other than perhaps the Riff Raff statue). Rocket Coffee is a warehouse-like bean barn, roasting on-site and enticing caffeine fiends to the communal table strewn with newspapers. Staff spin old-school vinyl (and take requests) in between playing barista and packaging up sacks of beans for shipment.

Palate MODERN NZ, FUSION $$$

(☎07-834 2921; www.palaterestaurant.co.nz; 170 Victoria St; mains $32-39; ⏰dinner Mon-Sat) Simple, sophisticated Palate has a well-deserved rep for lifting the culinary bar across regional NZ. Chef-owner Mat McLean delivers an innovative mod-NZ menu with highlights like honey-spiced duck with kumara and coconut puree, citrus couscous, orange salad and Cointreau jus.

Hydro CAFE $

(www.hydrocafe.co.nz; 33 Jellicoe Dr; mains $9-21; ⏰9am-3pm Mon-Thu, 8am-3.30pm Fri-Sun; 📶🖉) On the east side of the river (walk here along the water), Hydro is a fun cafe occupying an old block of neighbourhood shops, with tables spilling across the pavement. Great for brunch and light meals with novel taste combinations (the scallop salad with mango chilli is awesome). Wi-fi and by-the-glass NZ wines available.

Pak 'n Save SUPERMARKET

(Mill St; ⏰8am-10pm) Just north of downtown Hamilton.

Drinking

The blocks around Victoria and Hood Sts make for a boozy bar-hop, with weekend live music and DJs.

House on Hood BAR, CRAFT BEER

(www.houseonhood.co.nz; 27 Hood St) A crafty place for a craft beer or four, House on Hood is a 1915 barn with lots of drops to slake your thirst. Beer specials, tasting sessions and meal deals abound, plus Saturday-night bands and Sunday-afternoon DJs. Beer nirvana.

Diggers Bar BAR

(www.diggersbar.co.nz; 17b Hood St; ⏰3pm-late Tue-Sun) This funky good-time bar has outlasted plenty of come-and-go Hood St bars, with a wealth of liquid bread on tap and nightly live music in a huge room out the back. Buy four beers on a Wednesday night and score yourself a gourmet pizza.

Limestone BAR

(15 Hood St; ⏰8pm-late Wed, 7pm-late Thu & Sat, 4pm-late Fri) Inside Hamilton's oldest stone buliding – a former habardashery – moody Limestone offers respite from Hood St's otherwise raucous boozy nocturnal parade. An excellent range of bottled beers, a dazzling selection of spirits, and cigars to puff street-side.

Entertainment

Victoria Cinema CINEMA

(www.victoriacinema.co.nz; 690 Victoria St; adult/child $15.50/13.50; ⏰5pm-late) Watch art-house and international films while sipping on a fine wine or cold beer at 'Hamilton's home of fine movies'. Very bohemian. Tickets are $2 cheaper on weekdays.

Lido Cinema CINEMA (www.lidocinema.co.nz; Level 1, Centre Place, 501 Victoria St; adult/child $15/9; ⏲10am-late) Sassy Lido – all black carpet, chandeliers and gold fleurs-de-lis – offers an upmarket art-house movie experience in three 100-seat cinemas with comfy chairs and drinks to smooth the mood.

Information

Anglesea Clinic (☎07-858 0800; www.angleseamedical.co.nz; cnr Anglesea & Thackeray Sts; ⏲24hr) For accidents and urgent medical assistance.

Department of Conservation (DOC; ☎07-858 1000; www.doc.govt.nz; Level 5, 73 Rostrevor St; ⏲8am-4.30pm Mon-Fri)

Hamilton i-SITE (☎07-958 5960; www.visithamilton.co.nz; 5 Garden Pl; ⏲9am-5pm Mon-Fri, 9.30am-3.30pm Sat & Sun; 📶) Accommodation, activities and transport bookings, plus free wi-fi right across Garden Pl.

Post Office (36 Bryce St) Currency exchange available.

Waikato Hospital (☎07-839 8899; www.waikatodhb.govt.nz; Pembroke St; ⏲24hr)

Getting There & Away

Air

Air New Zealand (☎0800 737 000; www.airnewzealand.co.nz) Regular direct flights from Hamilton to Auckland, Christchurch, Palmerston North and Wellington.

Pacific Blue (☎0800 670 000; www.pacificblue.com.au) International flights between Hamilton and Sydney and Brisbane.

Sunair (☎07-575 7799, 0800 786 247; www.sunair.co.nz) Direct flights to Gisborne, Napier, Great Barrier Island and Whitianga.

Bus

All buses arrive and depart from the **Hamilton Transport Centre** (☎07-834 3457; www.hamilton.co.nz; cnr Anglesea & Bryce Sts).

Waikato Regional Council's Busit! (p201) coaches serve the region, including Ngaruawahia ($3.80, 25 minutes), Cambridge ($5.40, 40 minutes), Te Awamutu ($6.40, 50 minutes) and Raglan ($7.50, one hour).

Dalroy Express (☎06-759 0197, 0508 465 622; www.dalroytours.co.nz) operates a daily both-directions service between Auckland ($23, two hours) and New Plymouth ($41, four hours) via Hamilton, stopping at most towns, including Te Kuiti ($19, 1¾ hours) and Te Awamutu ($13, 20 minutes).

InterCity (☎09-583 5780; www.intercity.co.nz) services numerous destinations:

DESTINATION	PRICE	DURATION	FREQUENCY
Auckland	$30	2hr	11 daily
Cambridge	$23	25min	9 daily
Matamata	$27	50min	3 daily
Ngaruawahia	$17	20min	9 daily
Rotorua	$35	1½hr	5 daily
Te Aroha	$10	1hr	2 daily
Te Awamutu	$22	35min	3 daily
Wellington	$55	5hr	3 daily

Naked Bus (☎0900 625 33; www.nakedbus.com) services run to the following destinations (among many others).

DESTINATION	PRICE	DURATION	FREQUENCY
Auckland	$15	2hr	5 daily
Cambridge	$20	30min	5-7 daily
Matamata	$20	1hr	1 daily
Ngaruawahia	$20	30min	5 daily
Rotorua	$15	1½hr	4-5 daily
Wellington	$40	9½hr	1-2 daily

SHUTTLE BUSES

Minibus Express (☎07-856 3191, 0800 646 428; www.minibus.co.nz) Runs a shuttle between Hamilton and Auckland Airport (one way $75).

Raglan Scenic Tours (☎07-825 0507, 021 0274 7014; www.raglanscenictours.co.nz) Runs a shuttle linking Hamilton with Raglan (one way $30). Auckland airport service also available.

Train

Hamilton is on the **Overlander** (☎0800 872 467; www.tranzscenic.co.nz; ⏲daily Oct-Apr, Fri-Sun May-Sep) route between Auckland ($68, 2½ hours) and Wellington ($129, 9½ hours) via Otorohanga ($68, 45 minutes). Trains stop at Hamilton's **Frankton train station** (Fraser St), 1km west of the city centre; there are no ticket sales here – see the website for ticketing details.

Getting Around

To & From Airport

Hamilton International Airport (HIA; ☎07-848 9027; www.hamiltonairport.co.nz; Airport Rd) is 12km south of the city. International departure tax is $25 for those 12 years and over. The **Super Shuttle** (☎07-843 7778, 0800 748 885; www.supershuttle.co.nz; one way $23) offers a door-to-door service into the city. A taxi costs around $40.

Bus

Hamilton's **Busit!** (☎0800 4287 5463; www.busit.co.nz; city routes adult/child $3.10/2.10) network services the city-centre and suburbs daily from around 7am to 7.30pm (later on Friday). All buses pass through Hamilton Transport Centre. Busit! also runs a free No 51 CBD shuttle looping around Victoria, Liverpool, Anglesea and Bridge Sts every 10 minutes (7am to 6pm weekdays, 9am to 1pm Saturday)

Car

Rent-a-Dent (☎07-839 1049; www.rentadent.co.nz; 383 Anglesea St; ⌚7.30am-5pm Mon-Fri, 8am-noon Sat)

Taxi & Water taxi

Discovery River Taxis (☎0800 420 8294; www.discoveryrivercruises.co.nz; Memorial Park Jetty, Memorial Dr; trips from $10) Short trips to anywhere you like, up or down the river.
Hamilton Taxis (☎07-8477 477, 0800 477 477; www.hamiltontaxis.co.nz)

Raglan

POP 2640

Laid-back Raglan may well be NZ's perfect surfing town. It's small enough to have escaped mass development, but it's big enough to exhibit signs of life (good eateries, and a bar that attracts big-name bands in summer).

The nearby surf spots – Indicators, Whale Bay and Manu Bay – are internationally famous for their point breaks. Bruce Brown's classic 1964 wave-chaser film *The Endless Summer* features Manu Bay. Closer to town, the harbour just begs to be kayaked upon. This all serves to attract fit guys and gals from around the planet; Raglan may also be NZ's best-looking town!

Sights & Activities

FREE Old School Arts Centre ARTS CENTRE, GALLERY
(www.raglanartscentre.co.nz; Stewart St; ⌚10am-2pm Mon & Wed, exhibition hours vary) A community hub, the Old School Arts Centre has changing exhibitions and workshops, including weaving, carving, yoga and story-telling. Movies screen here regularly through summer ($11): grab a curry and a beer to complete the experience. The hippie/artsy **Raglan Creative Market** happens out the front on the second Sunday of the month (9am to 2pm).

Raglan Surf School SURFING
(☎07-825 7873; www.raglansurfingschool.co.nz; 5b Whaanga Rd, Whale Bay; 3hr lesson incl transport $89) The instructors at Raglan Surf School pride themselves on getting 95% of first-timers standing during their first lesson. Experienced wave hounds can rent surfboards (from $20 per hour), body boards ($5 per hour) and wet suits ($5 per hour). It's based at Karioi Lodge in Whale Bay.

Solscape SURFING
(☎07-825 8268; www.solscape.co.nz; 611 Wainui Rd, Manu Bay) Super-sustainable Solscape offers 2½-hour surfing lessons ($85), as well as board and wet-suit hire (per half-day $35).

Raglan Kayak KAYAKING
(☎07-825 8862; www.raglaneco.co.nz; Wallis St Wharf) Raglan Harbour is great for kayaking. This outfit runs three-hour guided harbour paddles (per person $70) and rents out kayaks (single/double per half-day $40/60). Learn the basics on the gentle Opotoru River, or paddle out to investigate the nooks and crannies of the pancake rocks on the harbour's northern edge.

Raglan Bone Carving Studio BONE CARVING
(☎07-825 7147, 021 0223 7233; www.maoribonecarving.com; 6 Snowden Pl; workshops $69, private lessons per hr $25) Carve your own bone pendant (now *that's* a souvenir!) with Rangi Wills, a reformed 'troubled teenager' who found out he was actually really good at carving things. Workshops run for three to four hours, or you can book a private lesson.

Tours

Raglan Scenic Tours GUIDED TOUR
(☎07-825 0507; www.raglanscenictours.co.nz) These guys run an array of sightseeing tours, including one hour around Raglan (adult/child $30/10), 3½ to four hours around Mount Karioi including Bridal Veil Falls and Te Toto Gorge ($90/40), and three to four hours to Kawhia ($70/40).

Cruise Raglan CRUISE
(☎07-825 7873; www.raglanboatcharters.co.nz; adult/child $40/29) Cruise Raglan offers atwo-hour sunset cruises around Raglan Harbour on the *Wahine Moe*, with a sausage sizzle and a few drinks.

Raglan

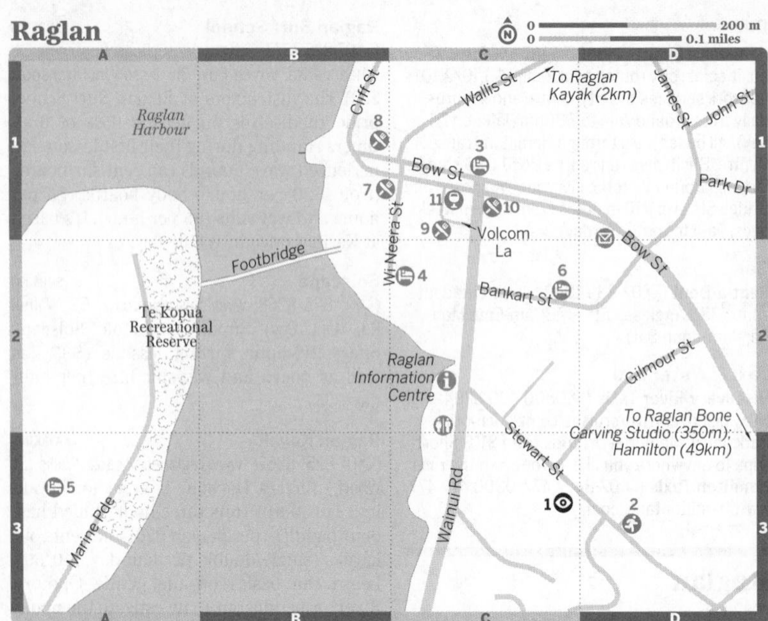

Raglan

Sights
1 Old School Arts Centre C3

Activities, Courses & Tours
2 Bike2Bay D3

Sleeping
3 Harbour View Hotel C1
4 Raglan Backpackers C2
5 Raglan Kopua Holiday Park A3
6 Raglan Sunset Motel C2

Eating
7 Aloha Market Place B1
8 Orca B1
9 Raglan Roast C1
10 The Shack C1

Drinking
11 Yot Club C1

Sleeping

TOP CHOICE **Raglan Backpackers** HOSTEL $
(07-825 0515; www.raglanbackpackers.co.nz; 6 Wi Neera St; dm $28, s $57, tw & d $72-82; @) This chipper, purpose-built hostel has a laid-back holiday-house mood. It's right on the water, with sea views from some rooms. Other rooms are arranged around a garden courtyard. There's also a separate self-contained wing that accomodates eight people. There are free bikes and kayaks/surfboards for hire (from $30/25per half-day), or take a yoga class, snooze in a hammock, strum a guitar or drip in the sauna. No wi-fi – it 'ruins the vibe'.

Journey's End B&B B&B, APARTMENT $$
(07-825 6727; www.raglanaccommodation.co.nz; 49 Lily St; s/d $100/140, exclusive use $200; wi-fi) These two attractive en-suite rooms share a central modern lounge with a kitchenette and a lovely deck overlooking the wharf and harbour. You can book out the whole place, or just one of the rooms and risk/enjoy the (potential) company of others. Fifteen minutes' walk from town.

Harbour View Hotel HISTORIC HOTEL $
(07-825 8010; harbourviewhotel@vodafone.co.nz; 14 Bow St; s from $70, tw & d from $90, f from $105) If you think that going to bed before the party's over is for the faint and feeble, then this two-storey, 106-year-old pub, with sunny verandas and kauri trimmings, is for you. Rooms are clean but you'll be sharing bathrooms (and there are no harbour views to speak of). Pub meals, live bands and big-screen rugby downstairs.

Raglan Kopua Holiday Park HOLIDAY PARK $
(☎07-825 8283; www.raglanholidaypark.co.nz; Marine Pde; sites from $34, dm/units from $56/85; @📶) A neatly maintained outfit with lots of sleeping options, on the spit across the inlet from town (there's a footbridge, or drive the long way around). No shade, but there's beach swimming and plenty of room to run amok.

Raglan Sunset Motel MOTEL $$
(☎07-825 0050; www.raglansunsetmotel.co.nz; 7 Bankart St; d $140; 📶) A block back from the action, this two-storey motel with faux shutters randomly adhered to the facade isn't quite a decade old. As you'd hope, everything's in good nick. The owners also have self-contained apartments (doubles from $150) and beach houses (four people from $250) available around town. Bike and kayak hire available (per half-day $30 and $45 respectively).

Eating

The Shack CAFE, INTERNATIONAL $
(19 Bow St; mains $9-18; ⏰8.30am-5pm Sat-Thu, 8.30am-late Fri; 🖉) Burgers, wraps, veggie fry-ups, curries, Middle Eastern plates, tapas... This shack ain't no hack when it comes to cafe fare. A longboard strapped to the wall, wobbly old floorboards, up-tempo tunes and international staff complete a very pretty picture.

Orca CAFE, MODERN NZ $$
(☎07-825 6543; www.orcarestaurant.co.nz; 2 Wallis St; breakfast $11-18, mains $19-33; ⏰9am-late Mon-Fri, 8am-late Sat & Sun) A day started at an Orca window seat, looking over the water, with some eggs Benedict and a superb coffee is a day well launched. Come back in the evening for rabbit pie, wine-appreciation nights and live music.

Raglan Roast CAFE $
(www.raglanroast.co.nz; Volcom La; coffee & biscuit $5; ⏰7.30am-5pm, reduced winter hours) This hole-in-the-wall coffee roaster with a fold-up front wall does the best brew in town, and that's about all (there's not much room for anything else). Stop by for a cup, a cookie and a conversation.

Aloha Market Place JAPANESE $
(5 Bow St; sushi $1.20-2.20, mains $10-13; ⏰11am-5pm, reduced winter hours; 🖉) It's takeaway without the grease, Japanese surfer-style. Grab some delicious rolled-to-order sushi, some udon noodles or a donburi rice bowl and head for the harbour. 'No rice, no life'.

Drinking & Entertainment

Orca and the Harbour View Hotel both host live music, usually on summer weekends.

Yot Club BAR, LIVE MUSIC
(www.mukuna.co.nz/waikato/raglan/yot-club.htm; 9 Bow St; admission free-$25; ⏰9pm-late) This raucous, nocturnal bar is where everyone goes to dance, with visiting DJs and bands (Harmonica Lewinsky were playing when we visted), a pool table and imported beers.

Information

Raglan Information Centre (☎07-825 0556; www.raglan.org.nz; 13 Wainui Rd; ⏰9.30am-5pm Mon-Fri, 10am-5pm Sat, 10am-4pm Sun) DOC brochures plus information about local accommodation and activities. Reduced winter hours.

West Coast Health Centre (☎07-825 0114; wchc@wave.co.nz; 12 Wallis St; ⏰9am-5pm Mon-Fri) General medical assistance.

Getting There & Around

From Hamilton, Raglan is 48km west along SH23. Unsealed back roads connect Raglan to Kawhia, 50km south; they're slow, winding and prone to rockslides, but scenic and certainly off the beaten track. Head back towards Hamilton for 7km and take the Te Mata/Kawhia turn-off and follow the signs; allow at least an hour.

Waikato District Council's **Busit!** (☎0800 4287 5463; www.busit.co.nz; adult/child $7.50/3.80) heads between Hamilton and Raglan (one hour) three times daily on weekdays and twice daily on weekends.

Raglan Scenic Tours (p201) runs a Raglan–Hamilton shuttle bus (one way $30). **Raglan Shuttle Co** (☎0800 8873 2 7873; www.raglanshuttle.co.nz) offers a parallel service.

Bike2Bay (☎07-825 0309; www.bike2bay.com; 24b Stewart St; hire per hr/half/full day $8/22/33; ⏰9.30am-5pm) has mountain bikes for hire, does repairs and runs bike tours around Raglan.

If you need a cab call **Raglan Taxi** (☎07-825 0506).

South of Raglan

OCEAN BEACH

Ocean Beach sits at the mouth of the harbour, 4kms southwest of Raglan down Riria Kereopa Memorial Dr. It's popular with windsurfers and kitesurfers, but strong currents make it extremely treacherous for swimmers.

WORTH A TRIP

RUAPEKE BEACH

Whale Bay marks the end of the sealed road, but a gravel road continues to the wild spans of Ruapuke Beach, 22km from Raglan, passing a couple of rusty, abandoned buses en route. It's dangerous for swimmers here, but popular with surf-casting fisherfolk. The gravel road continues to Mt Karioi and rejoins the inland road at Te Mata.

NGARUNUI BEACH

Less than 1km south of Ocean Beach, Ngarunui Beach is a great for grommets learning to surf. On the cliff-top is a clubhouse for the volunteer lifeguards who patrol part of the black-sand beach from late October until April. This is the only beach with lifeguards, and is the best ocean beach for swimming.

MANU BAY

A 2.5km journey from Ngarunui Beach will bring you to Manu Bay, a legendary surf spot said to have the longest left-hand break in the world. The elongated uniform waves are created by the angle at which the Tasman Sea swell meets the coastline (it works best in a southwesterly swell).

Sleeping

TOP CHOICE **Solscape** HOSTEL, CABINS $
(07-825 8268; www.solscape.co.nz; 611 Wainui Rd, Manu Bay; sites from $16, caboose dm/d $26/68, tepees per person $34, cottages d $115-180; @) This hippie hilltop hostel has dorms in old train carriages. It's the ultimate greenie experience: chilling in a tepee (surprisingly comfortable, available December to April), surrounded by native bush, knowing that you're completely 'off grid' – while not sacrificing hot showers (solar) and decent toilets (composting). Self-contained sea-view cottages (try for the 'Ivy'), surf lessons and massage ($65 per hour) complete a bewildering array of services.

WHALE BAY

Whale Bay is a renowned surf spot (p201) 1km west of Manu Bay. It's usually less crowded than Manu Bay, but from the bottom of Calvert Rd you have to clamber 600m over the rocks to get to the break.

Sleeping

Karioi Lodge HOSTEL $
(07-825 7873; www.karioilodge.co.nz; 5b Whaanga Rd, Whale Bay; dm/d $30/75; @) Deep in native bush, Karioi Lodge offers a sauna, a flying fox, mountain bikes, bush and beach walks, sustainable gardening, tree planting and the Raglan Surf School. There are no en suites but the rooms are clean and cosy. These friendly folks also run **Sleeping Lady Lodging** (07-825 7873; www.sleepinglady.co.nz; 5b Whaanga Rd, Whale Bay; lodges $165-570), a collection of seven luxury self-contained houses nearby, all with ocean views.

MT KARIOI

In legend, Mt Karioi (756m), the Sleeping Lady (check out that profile), is the sister to Mt Pirongia. At its base (8km south of Whale Bay) **Te Toto Gorge** is a steep cleft in the mountainside, with a vertigo-inducing lookout perched high over the chasm.

Starting from Te Toto Gorge car park, a strenuous but scenic track goes up the western slope. It takes 2½ hours to reach a lookout point, followed by an easier hour up to the summit. From the east side, the Wairake Track is a steeper 2½-hour climb to the summit, where it meets the Te Toto Track.

WAIREINGA (BRIDAL VEIL FALLS)

Just past Te Mata (a short drive south of the main Raglan–Hamilton road) is the turn-off to the 55m Waireinga (Bridal Veil Falls), 4km from the main road. From the car park, it's an easy 10-minute walk through mossy native bush to the top of the falls. It's a magical place, the effect compounded by the dancing rainbows swirling around the khaki-coloured pool far below (not suitable for swimming). A further 10-minute walk leads down to the bottom. Lock your car: theft is a problem here.

Magic Mountain Horse Treks (07-825 6892; www.magicmountain.co.nz; 334 Houtchen Rd, Te Mata; rides 1/2hr $50/70) runs horse treks around the hills, plus a ride to Waireinga (Bridal Veil Falls, $90).

PIRONGIA FOREST PARK

The main attraction of this 170-sq-km forest park is **Mt Pirongia** (www.mtpirongia.org.nz), its 959m summit clearly visible from much of the Waikato. The mountain is usually climbed from Corcoran Rd (three to five hours, one way) with tracks to other lookout points. Interestingly, NZ's tallest known kahikatea tree (66.5m) grows on the mountainside. There's a six-bunk DOC hut near the summit if you need to spend the night: maps and information are available from Hamilton DOC.

Te Awamutu

POP 9800

Deep into dairy-farming country, Te Awamutu (which means 'The River Cut Short'; the Waikato beyond this point was unsuitable for large canoes) is a real working town with real working people living in it – agrarian integrity by the bucketload! With a blossom-treed main street and a good museum, TA (aka Rose Town) makes a decent overnighter. (Finn fans might need longer.)

Sights

Te Awamutu Museum MUSEUM
(www.tamuseum.org.nz; 135 Roche St; admission by donation; ⌚10am-4pm Mon-Fri, 10am-1pm Sat, 1-4pm Sun) Te Awamutu Museum, 'where history never repeats', has a *True Colours*–painted shrine to local heroes Tim and Neil Finn. There are gold records, original lyrics, Finn memorabilia and oddities such as Neil's form-two exercise book. There's also a fine collection of Maori *taonga* (treasures), including the revered 'Uenuku', and an excellent display on the Waikato War. A great little museum.

FREE **Rose Garden** GARDEN
(cnr Gorst Ave & Arawata St; ⌚24hr) The Rose Garden is next to the i-SITE and has 2500 bushes and 51 varieties with fabulously fruity names like Big Daddy, Disco Dancer, Lady Gay and Sexy Rexy. The roses usually bloom from November to May.

Sleeping

Cloverdale House B&B $$
(☎07-872 1702; www.cloverdalehouse.co.nz; 141 Long Rd; d/q $140/200) Indulge your farmer fantasies at this smart new place in the dairy heartland, 8km east of Cambridge Rd. Two double rooms with en suites share a common lounge and kitchen (breakfast ingredients provided).

Rosetown Motel MOTEL $$
(☎0800 767 386, 07-871 5779; www.rosetownmotel.co.nz; 844 Kihikihi Rd; d/f from $115/140;) The older-style units at Rosetown (the new owners are weeding out the last of the teak veneer and yellow faux-marble) have kitchens, new linen and TVs, and share a spa. A solid choice if you're hankering for straight-up small-town sleeps.

Eating & Drinking

Redoubt Bar & Eatery PUB $$
(www.redoubtbarandeateryta.co.nz; cnr Rewi & Alexandra Sts; mains $16-34; ⌚10am-late) A relaxed little place to eat or drink, with cheap-but-potent cocktails, old photos on the walls and a decent menu stretching from pasta to curry. Watch tractors roll along the main street through fold-back windows.

Farenheight MODERN NZ, TAPAS $$
(☎07-871 5429; www.fahrenheitrestaurant.co.nz; Level 1, 13 Roche St; mains $15-36; ⌚lunch & dinner Tue-Sun) Bright as a button, this new upstairs bar/restaurant on the main drag is a classy place for a drink when the sun goes down on TA. No great menu surprises (chowder, lamb rump, pork belly, steaks) but this is surely

TE AWAMUTU'S SACRED SOUND

In the opening lines of Crowded House's first single *Mean to Me*, Neil Finn single-handedly raised his sleepy hometown, Te Awamutu, to international attention. It wasn't the first time it had provided inspiration – Split Enz songs *Haul Away* and *Kia Kaha*, with big bro Tim, include similar references.

Despite NZ's brilliant songwriting brothers being far from the height of their fame, Finn devotees continue to make the pilgrimage to Te Awamutu – just ask the staff at the i-SITE. They do a brisk trade in Finn T-shirts, Finn stamps and walking-tour brochures of sites from Finn history (their childhood home at 588 Teasdale St, their school, even Neil's piano tutor's house). It's NZ's version of Graceland!

If you're hoping for a close encounter with greatness, it's unlikely: the boys skipped town decades ago.

the only place within miles that does tapas! Bee-line for the balcony.

Indian Aroma INDIAN
(☎07-871 5555; www.indianaroma.co.nz; 23 Arawata St; mains $13-17; ⏰lunch Wed-Fri, dinner daily;) Brightening up the town with a saffron-yellow glow, this attractive restaurant with orderly glass-topped tables serves all the fragrant favourites. The roses on the tables are fake (a sin in Rose Town?).

☆ Entertainment

Regent Theatre CINEMA
(www.regent3.itgo.com; 235 Alexandra St; adult/child $15.50/9.50; ⏰10am-late) Built in 1932, this art-deco cinema has five screens and fabulous movie memorabilia in the foyer. It's *deathly* serious about turning off your mobile phone.

ℹ Information

Te Awamutu i-SITE (☎07-871 3259; www.teawamutuinfo.com; 1 Gorst Ave; ⏰9am-5pm Mon-Fri, 10am-4pm Sat & Sun) Oodles of local information.

ℹ Getting There & Away

Te Awamutu is on SH3, halfway between Hamilton and Otorohanga (29km either way). The regional bus service **Busit!** (☎0800 4287 5463; www.busit.co.nz) is the cheapest option for Hamilton (adult/child $6.40/4.30, 50 minutes, eight daily weekdays, three daily weekends).

Three daily **InterCity** (☎09-583 5780; www.intercity.co.nz) services connect Te Awamutu with Auckland ($29, 2½ hours), Hamilton ($22, 35 minutes) and Otorohanga ($22, 25 minutes).

The **Dalroy Express** (☎0508 465 622; www.dalroytours.co.nz) bus runs daily (in each direction) between Auckland ($29, 2½ hours) and New Plymouth ($40, 3½ hours), leaving from the i-SITE. Stops include Hamilton ($13, 25 minutes) and Otorohanga ($12, 20 minutes).

Around Te Awamutu

RANGIAOWHIA

Before the Waikato invasion, Rangiaowhia (located 5km east of Te Awamutu on Rangiaowhia Rd; ask at the i-SITE for directions) was a thriving Maori farming town, exporting wheat, maize, potatoes and fruit as far afield as Australia. It was home to thousands of inhabitants, two churches, a flour mill and a racecourse, and was the perfect model of what NZ under the Maori version of the Treaty of Waitangi had desired – two sovereign peoples interacting to mutual advantage.

In February 1864 the settlement was left undefended while King Tawhiao's warriors held fortified positions further north. In a key tactical move, General Cameron outflanked them and took the town, killing women, children and the elderly. This was a turning point in the campaign, demoralising the Maori and drawing the warriors out of their near impregnable *pa* fortifications.

Sadly, all that remains of the town is the cute 1854 Anglican **St Paul's Church** (☎07-871 5568; Rangiaowhia Rd; ⏰services 9am 1st & 3rd Sun of the month) and the Catholic mission's **cemetery**, standing in the midst of rich farming land – confiscated from the Maori and distributed to colonial soldiers.

The war ended further south at **Orakau**, where a roadside obelisk marks the site where 300 Maori, led by Rewi Maniapoto, repulsed three days of attacks against an unfinished *pa* by 1500 troops, before breaking out and retreating to what is now known as the King Country (losing 70 warriors).

WHAREPAPA SOUTH

A surreal landscape of craggy limestone provides some of the best **rock climbing** in the North Island. This isn't the best place for wannabe Spidermen (or women) to don their lycra bodysuits for the first time, but if you have the basic skills get ready to let your inner superhero shine.

Bryce's Rockclimbing (☎07-872 2533; www.rockclimb.co.nz; 1424 Owairaka Valley Rd; 1-day instruction for 1-2 people $440) is suited to the serious climber. On-site is NZ's largest retail climbing store, selling and hiring out a full range of gear. It also has an indoor bouldering cave, free to those staying out back in the ship-shape accommodation (dorm/double $25/66). There's a licensed cafe (open 8am to 5pm Friday to Monday, light meals $6 to $16).

Cambridge

POP 15,200

The name says it all. Despite the rambunctious Waikato River looking nothing like the Cam, the good people of Cambridge have done all they can to assume an air of English gentility: village greens, avenues of decidu-

WORTH A TRIP

MAUNGATAUTARI

Can a landlocked volcano become an island paradise? Inspired by the success of pest eradication and native species reintroduction in the Hauraki Gulf, a community trust has erected 47km of pest-proof fencing around the triple peaks of Maungatautari (797m) to create the impressive **Maungatautari Ecological Island** (www.maungatrust.org). This atoll of rainforest dominates the skyline between Te Awamutu and Karapiro and is now home to its first kiwi chicks in 100 years. The shortest route to the peak (1¾ hours) is from the northern side, while the entire north–south walk will take around six hours. Take Maungatautari Rd then Hicks Rd if coming from Karapiro, or Arapuni Rd then Tari Rd from Te Awamutu.

Out In The Styx (☎07-872 4505; www.styx.co.nz; 2117 Arapuni Rd, Pukeatua; dm/s/d $95/130/260), near the south end of the Maungatautari, provides a drop-off service to the northern entrance ($10 per person, minimum four), plus guided day- and night-walk options. The three stylishly furnished themed rooms (Polynesian, African or Maori) are especially nice, plus there are bunk rooms and a spa for soothing weary legs. Prices include a four-course dinner and breakfast.

ous trees, faux-Tudor houses... Even the public toilet looks like a Victorian cottage.

Famous for breeding and training thoroughbred horses, you can almost smell the wealth along the main street. Equine references are rife in public sculpture, and plaques boast of Melbourne Cup winners.

Sights & Activities

FREE Cambridge Museum MUSEUM
(www.cambridgemuseum.org.nz; 24 Victoria St; ⏲10am-4pm) In a former courthouse, the quirky Cambridge Museum has plenty of pioneer relics, a military history room and a small display on the local Te Totara Pa before it was wiped out. Oh, and there's a stuffed kiwi if you haven't managed to see a real one.

Jubilee Gardens GARDEN, MONUMENT
(Victoria St; ⏲24hr) Apart from its Spanish Mission town clock, Jubilee Gardens is a wholehearted tribute to the 'mother country'. A British lion guards the cenotaph, with a plaque that reads, 'Tell Britain ye who mark this monument faithful to her we fell and rest content'. Outmoded sentiment or awkward grammar – either way, the soldier statue looks confused.

Lake Karapiro LAKE
(www.waipadc.govt.nz/district/lake+karapiro; Maungatautari Rd) Eight kilometres southeast of Cambridge, Karapiro is the furthest downstream of a chain of eight hydroelectric power stations on the Waikato River. It's an impressive sight, especially when driving across the top of the 1947 dam. The 21km-long lake is also a world-class rowing venue. The **Boatshed Cafe** (www.theboatshed.net.nz; 21 Amber La, off Gorton Rd; ⏲10am-4pm Wed-Fri, 9am-4pm Sat & Sun) hires out basic kayaks (from $20 per half day); you can paddle to a couple of waterfalls in around an hour.

Waikato River Trails CYCLING, TRAMPING
(www.waikatorivertrails.com) Winding east from Cambridge, the 100km Waikato River Trails track was ascribed 'Quick Start' status as part of the Nga Haerenga, New Zealand Cycle Trail project (www.nzcycletrail.com), and opened in late 2011. You can walk or cycle the five combined trails (or parts thereof), with lots of history and local landscape en route.

Heritage & Tree Trail WALKING TOUR
Whether you're hip to history or tantalised by trees, this trail covers all the sights, including the Waikato River, the 1881 St Andrew's Anglican Church (look for the Gallipoli window) and leafy Lake Ko Utu. Grab a map at the Cambridge i-SITE.

Camjet JETBOATING
(☎0800 226 538; www.camjet.co.nz; trips adult/child $75/50) Can help adrenaline junkies shake off the cobwebs with a 35-minute spin to Karapiro dam on a jetboat. A 15-minute spin costs $45. Minimum four people.

Cambridge Thoroughbred Lodge GUIDED TOUR
(☎07-827 8118; www.cambridgethoroughbredlodge.co.nz; tours adult/child $12/5, show $12/5; ⏲tours

10am-2pm by arrangement) Cambridge Thoroughbred Lodge, 6km south of town on SH1, is a top-notch horse stud. Book ahead for 90-minute tours, or 'NZ Horse Magic' shows which get galloping several times a week.

Sleeping

Birches B&B $$
(☎07-827 6556; www.birches.co.nz; 263 Maungatautari Rd; s/d $100/150;) You're in luck! There's a pool, spa and tennis court at this picturesque 1930s weatherboard farmhouse, in farmland southeast of Cambridge. Sleep in the main house or self-contained cottage. Sheep and daffodils line the driveway.

Lofthouse APARTMENT $$
(☎07-827 3693; www.lofthouse.co.nz; 17 Dunning Rd; apt from $130) If you're travelling with friends, this self-contained rural retreat is an absolute steal – sleeping four people for the price of the apartment. Jump in the spa and enjoy the awesome views. It's 3km off SH1, near the top of Karapiro, and 11km from Cambridge.

House Boat Holidays HOUSEBOAT $$
(☎07-827 2195; www.houseboatescape.co.nz; Lake Karapiro; 2 nights $600) Humming 'Proud Mary' is acceptable as Lake Karapiro is technically still a river, but you're more likely to be relaxing than rolling. Load up this smart houseboat (sleeping eight) with kayaks and fishing gear and sail away for a splashy weekend.

Cambridge Coach House B&B, CABIN $$
(☎07-823 7922; www.cambridgecoachhouse.co.nz; 3796 Cambridge Rd, Leamington; d from $150, cottage $195) This farmhouse accommodation is a wee bit chintzy, but if you can forgive a chandelier or two it's a beaut spot to chill out, in the thick of Waikato's bucolic splendour. There's a double in the main building, two separate doubles and a self-contained cottage. It's a couple of kilometres south of town on the way to Te Awamutu.

Cambridge Mews MOTEL $$
(☎07-827 7166; www.cambridgemews.co.nz; 20 Hamilton Rd; apt from $155;) All the spacious units in this chalet-style motel have double spa baths, decent kitchens and are immaculately maintained. The architect did a great job...the interior decorator less so. A 10-minute walk to town.

Cambridge Motor Park HOLIDAY PARK $
(☎07-827 5649; www.cambridgemotorpark.co.nz; 32 Scott St; sites from $16, units $42-$105;) A quiet, well-maintained camping ground with lots of green, green grass. The emphasis is on tents and vans here, but the cabins and units are fine. Drive over the skinny Victoria Bridge from the Cambridge town centre.

Eating

TOP CHOICE **Red Cherry** CAFE $$
(☎07-823 1515; www.redcherrycoffee.co.nz; cnr SH1 & Forrest Rd; meals $7-21; breakfast & lunch daily, dinner Fri & Sat;) With happy staff and a cherry-red espresso machine working overtime, barn-like Red Cherry offers coffee roasted on-site, delicious counter food and impressive cooked breakfasts (oh those corn-and-pumpkin fritters). It's Cambridge's best cafe by a country mile (it's actually a country 4km out of Cambridge on the way to Hamilton).

Nash MODERN NZ, WINE BAR $$$
(☎07-827 5596; www.thenash.net.nz; 47 Alpha St; mains $28-34; lunch & dinner) All white/grey/black paint and dapper, quick-moving staff, sexy Nash has transformed the old National Hotel, sinking the boot firmly into Ye Olde Cambridge. We hope it lasts: the braised lamb shoulder with roast-garlic mash and pea puree is sublime, and the streetside terrace is just made for people-watching while quaffing Kiwi wine.

Onyx CAFE, RESTAURANT $$
(☎07-827 7740; 70 Alpha St; mains $20-39; breakfast, lunch & dinner) All-day Onyx occupies a lofty space, with onyx-black furnishings and warm-toned timber floors. Wood-fired pizzas are the mainstay, plus salads, tortillas, sandwiches, steaks, cakes, organic coffee and 95% NZ wines. At night it's almost urbane.

Information

Cambridge i-SITE (☎07-823 3456; www.cambridge.co.nz; cnr Victoria & Queen Sts; 9am-5pm Mon-Fri, 10am-4pm Sat & Sun; @) Free Heritage & Tree Trail and town maps, and internet access.

Getting There & Away

Being on SH1, 22km southeast of Hamilton, Cambridge is well connected by bus. Environment Waikato's **Busit!** (☎0800 4287 5463; www.busit.co.nz) heads to Hamilton ($6.40, 40 minutes, seven daily weekdays, three daily weekends).

InterCity (☎09-583 5780; www.intercity.co.nz) services numerous destinations:

DESTINATION	PRICE	DURATION	FREQUENCY
Auckland	$40	2½hr	12 daily
Hamilton	$24	30min	8 daily
Matamata	$22	30min	2 daily
Rotorua	$33	1¼hr	5 daily
Wellington	$75	8½hr	3 daily

Naked Bus (☎0900 625 33; www.nakedbus.com) services to the same destinations are as follows.

DESTINATION	PRICE	DURATION	FREQUENCY
Auckland	$13	2½hr	6 daily
Hamilton	$20	30min	5 daily
Matamata	$24	2¼hr	1 daily
Rotorua	$15	1¼hr	4 daily
Wellington	$33	9½hr	1 daily

Matamata

POP 7800

Matamata was just one of those pleasant, horsey country towns you drove through until Peter Jackson's epic film trilogy *Lord of the Rings* put it on the map. During filming 300 locals got work as extras (hairy feet weren't a prerequisite). And now Jackson's *The Hobbit* is being filmed here – hobbits ahoy!

Most tourists who come to Matamata are dedicated hobbit-botherers: for everyone else there's a great cafe, avenues of mature trees and undulating green hills.

Sights & Activities

Hobbiton Movie Set & Farm Tours MOVIE LOCATION
(☎07-888 1505; www.hobbitontours.com; 501 Buckland Rd, Hinuera; adult/child $66/5; ⏲tours 9.50am, 10.45am, noon, 1.15pm, 2.30pm, 3.45pm, 5pm) This is NZ's top attraction for *LOTR* boffins, and pretty interesting even if you haven't seen the movies. Due to copyright, all the intricately constructed movie sets around the country were dismantled after filming, but Hobbiton's owners negotiated to keep their hobbit holes, which have been completely rebuilt for the filming of *The Hobbit*. Also on offer is a hands-on Sheep Farm Experience (adult/child $16/5), explaining all things woolly. Free transfers leave from the Matamata i-SITE. Otherwise, head towards Cambridge and turn right into Puketutu Rd and then left into Buckland Rd, stopping at the Shire's Rest Cafe. All manner of combined tour/accommodation packages also available.

Wairere Falls WATERFALL
About 15km northeast of Matamata are the spectacular 153m-high Wairere Falls (the highest on the North Island). From the car park it's a 45-minute walk through native bush to the lookout or a steep 90-minute climb to the summit.

Firth Tower MUSEUM, HISTORIC BUILDING
(www.firthtower.co.nz; Tower Rd; grounds free, tours adult/child $5/1; ⏲10am-4pm) Firth Tower was built by Auckland businessman Josiah Firth in 1882. The 18m concrete tower was a fashionable status symbol, and is now filled with Maori and pioneer artefacts. Around it are 10 other historic buildings (closed Tuesday and Wednesday), including a schoolroom, a church and a jail. It's located 3km east of town.

Opal Hot Springs SWIMMING
(www.opalhotsprings.co.nz; 257 Okauia Springs Rd; adult/child $8/4, 30min private spas $10/5; ⏲9am-9pm) Opal Hot Springs isn't nearly as glamorous as it sounds but it does have three large thermal pools. Turn off just north of Firth Tower and follow the road for 2km. There's a holiday park here too.

Skydive Waikato SKYDIVING
(☎07-888 8763; www.freefall.co.nz; tandem $245-310) Skydive Waikato offers thrilling gravity-powered plummets above Matamata Airfield, 10km north of Matamata on SH27.

Sleeping

Broadway Motel & Miro Court Villas MOTEL **$$**
(☎07-888 8482; www.broadwaymatamata.co.nz; 128 Broadway; s $86-135, d $96-159, apt $250; @) This sprawling family-run motel complex has spread from a well-maintained older-style block to progressively newer and flasher blocks set back from the street (with

cool light fittings and funky panels of wallpaper). The nicest are the chic apartment-style Miro Court villas. There's a fun kids' play area in the centre.

Southern Belle APARTMENT **$$**
(☎07-888 5518; www.southernbelle.co.nz; 101 Firth St; r $120, extra person $40; 📶) Taking over the top floor of a grand old house (a transported vision from Savannah or Baton Rouge), this suite has three elegant bedrooms, a comfortable lounge and a kitchenette (just a microwave for cooking, but there's a barbecue downstairs that guests can use).

Eating & Drinking

TOP CHOICE **Workman's Cafe Bar** CAFE
(www.matamata-info.co.nz/workmans; 52 Broadway; lunch $15, dinner $28-32; ⏲breakfast & lunch Wed-Sun, dinner Tue-Sun) Truly eccentric (old transistor radios dangling from the ceiling; a wall-full of art-deco mirrors; Johnny Cash on the stereo), this funky eatery has built itself a reputation that extends beyond Matamata. The poached salmon Benedict is a showstopper!

Redoubt Bar & Eatery PUB **$$**
(www.facebook.com/redoubtmatamata; 48 Broadway; lunch $12-20, dinner $26-34; ⏲11am-late Mon-Fri, 9.30am-late Sat & Sun) The sister establishment of Te Awamutu's Redoubt, Matamata's version is just as good: thin-crust pizzas, chowder, steaks, a winning hash stack (or 'hesh steck' in Kiwi accent), and live music every Friday. Oh, and plenty of Monteiths!

Information

Matamata i-SITE (☎07-888 7260; www.matamatanz.co.nz; 45 Broadway; ⏲9am-5pm Mon-Fri, 9am-3pm Sat & Sun) The super-helpful Matamata i-SITE has free town maps, all the guff on local attractions and extended summer hours. Hobbiton tours leave from here.

Getting There & Away

Matamata is on SH27, 20km north of Tirau.

InterCity (☎09-583 5780; www.intercity.co.nz) runs to Cambridge ($22, 40 minutes, two daily), Hamilton ($27, one hour, three daily), Rotorua ($27, one hour, one daily) and Tauranga ($23, one hour, two daily).

Naked Bus (☎0900 625 33; www.nakedbus.com) runs to Auckland ($27, 3½ hours, two daily), Cambridge ($20, two hours, one daily), Hamilton ($20, 3½ hours, two daily) and Tauranga ($14, one hour, one daily).

Te Aroha

POP 3800

Te Aroha has a great vibe. You could even say that it's got 'the love', which is the literal meaning of the name. Tucked under the elbow of the bush-clad Mt Te Aroha (952m), it's a good base for tramping or 'taking the waters' in the town's therapeutic thermal springs.

Sights & Activities

Te Aroha Mineral Spas SPA
(☎07-884 8717; www.tearohapools.co.nz; Boundary St, Te Aroha Domain; 30min session adult/child $18/11; ⏲10.30am-9pm Mon-Fri, 10.30am-10pm Sat & Sun) In the quaint Edwardian Hot Springs Domain behind the Te Aroha i-SITE, this spa offers relaxing private tubs, massage, beauty therapies and aromatherapy. Also here is the temperamental Mokena Geyser – the world's only known soda geyser – which blows its top every 40 minutes or so, shooting water 3m into the air (the most ardent eruptions are between noon and 2pm).

Te Aroha Leisure Pools SWIMMING, BATHHOUSE
(www.tearohapools.co.nz; Boundary St, Te Aroha Domain; adult/child $6.50/4.50; ⏲10am-5.45pm Mon-Fri, to 6.45pm Sat & Sun) The Leisure Pools have outdoor heated freshwater pools for splashing about in. There's also a thermal bathhouse and a toddlers' pool.

Te Aroha Museum MUSEUM
(www.tearoha-museum.com; Te Aroha Domain; adult/child $4/2; ⏲11am-4pm Nov-Mar, noon-3pm Apr-Oct) Te Aroha's lovely museum is in the town's ornate former thermal sanatorium (aka the 'Treasure of Te Aroha'). Displays include quirky ceramics, old spa-water bottles, historic photos and an amazing old printing press from the *Te Aroha News*.

Mt Te Aroha TRAMPING
Trails up Mt Te Aroha start at the top of the domain. It's a 45-minute climb to Bald Spur/Whakapipi Lookout (350m), then another 2.7km (two hours) to the summit.

Sleeping

TOP CHOICE **Aroha Mountain Lodge** LODGE, B&B **$$**
(☎07-884 8134; www.arohamountainlodge.co.nz; 5 Boundary St; s/d/ste/cottage $115/135/155/250) Spread over two *aroha*-ly Edwardian villas on the hillside above town, the plush Mountain Lodge offers affordable luxury (*sooo* much nicer than a regulation motel) and op-

tional breakfast ($20 per person). The self-contained Gold Miner's Cottage sleeps six.

Te Aroha YHA HOSTEL $
(☎07-884 8739, 0800 278 299; www.yha.co.nz; Miro St; dm/tr $23/56) This top-of-the-town YHA is a homely, TV-free, three-bedroom cottage with welcoming management, a well-stocked herb rack, a pile of *National Geographics* and an old nylon-string guitar leaning in the corner. A 10km mountain-bike track wheels away from the back door. Call in advance (it's closed sometimes in winter).

Te Aroha Motel MOTEL $$
(☎07-884 9417; www.tearohamotel.co.nz; 108 Whitaker St; s/d/tr/q $85/100/120/150;) Welcome to the love-town motel (with a couple of palm trees out the front, this could almost be Vegas!). Inside are old-fashioned but reasonably priced and tidy units with kitchenettes, right in the centre of town. And what a lavish lawn!

Te Aroha Holiday Park HOLIDAY PARK $
(☎07-884 9567; www.tearohaholidaypark.co.nz; 217 Stanley Rd; sites from $15, units $32-75; @) Wake up to a bird orchestra among the oaks at this site – possibly the Waikato's cheapest holiday park – equipped with grass tennis court, gym and hot pool, 2km southwest of town. The owners also speak German and Japanese.

Eating

Behr Burger BURGERS $
(176 Whitaker St; burgers $9-13; 4-9pm Mon-Wed, 11am-9pm Thu-Sun) Awesome gourmet hamburgers are the go at this buzzy main-street nook. 'The Chief' (NZ rump steak, honey-smoked bacon, a free-range egg, cheddar cheese, salad and aioli) plugs the hungry hollows.

Berlusconi on Whitaker ITALIAN, TAPAS $$
(☎07-884 9307; www.tearoha-info.co.nz/berlusconi; 149 Whitaker St; lunch $14-19, dinner $27-33; lunch Tue-Sun, dinner Wed-Sun) We know the defunct Italian PM has his fingers in a lot of pies, but surely they don't extend to this upmarket wine, tapas and pizza bar in Te Aroha. Mind you, it is suave enough.

Information

Te Aroha i-SITE (☎07-884 8052; www.tearohanz.co.nz; 102 Whitaker St; 9.30am-5pm Mon-Fri, 9.30am-4pm Sat & Sun)

Getting There & Away

Te Aroha is on SH26, 21km south of Paeroa and 55km northeast of Hamilton. Waikato Regional Council's **Busit!** (☎0800 4287 5463; www.busit.co.nz) runs to/from Hamilton (adult/child $8/4, one hour, two daily Monday to Friday). Naked Bus (p210) runs to Hamilton ($20, one hour, one daily) and Cambridge ($20, 1½ hours, one daily).

THE KING COUNTRY

Holding good claim to the title of NZ's rural heartland, this is the kind of no-nonsense place that raises cattle and All Blacks. A bastion of independent Maoridom, it was never conquered in the war against the King Movement. The story goes that King Tawhiao placed his hat on a large map of NZ and declared that all the land it covered would remain under his *mana* (authority), and the region was effectively off limits to Europeans until 1883.

The Waitomo Caves are the area's major drawcard. An incredible natural phenomenon in themselves, they've been jazzed up even more with a smorgasbord of adrenaline-inducing activities.

Kawhia

POP 670

Along with resisting cultural annihilation, Kawhia (think mafia with a K) has avoided large-scale development, retaining its sleepy fishing-village vibe. There's not much here except for the general store, a couple of takeaways and a petrol station. Even Captain Cook blinked and missed the narrow entrance to the large harbour when he sailed past in 1770. But if low-key is what you're craving, look no further.

Sights & Activities

Kayaks can be hired from Kawhia Beachside S-Cape and Kawhia Motel.

Ocean Beach BEACH, SPRING
(Te Puia Rd) Four kilometres west of Kawhia is Ocean Beach and its high, black-sand dunes. Swimming can be dangerous, but one to two hours either side of low tide you can find the Te Puia Hot Springs in the sand – dig a hole for your own natural hot pool.

KAWHIA'S CANOE

The *Tainui waka* – a 14th-century ancestral canoe – made its final landing at Kawhia. The expedition leaders – Hoturoa, the chief/captain, and Rakataura, the *tohunga* (priest) – searched the west coast until they recognised their prophesised landing place. Pulling into shore, they tied the *waka* to a pohutukawa tree, naming it Tangi te Korowhiti. This unlabelled tree still stands on the shoreline between the wharf and Maketu Marae. The *waka* was then dragged up onto a hill and buried: sacred stones were placed at either end to mark its resting place, now part of the *marae*.

Kawhia Regional Museum & Gallery MUSEUM, GALLERY
(www.kawhiaharbour.co.nz; Omimiti Reserve, Kawhia Wharf; admission by gold coin donation; noon-3pm Wed-Sun) Kawhia's cute waterside museum is a modest but engaging affair, with lots of local history, nautical and Maori artefacts, and regular art exhibitions. It doubles as the visitor information centre.

Kawhia Harbour Cruises CRUISE
(021 966 754; www.kawhiaharbourcruises.co.nz; cruises per adult $35) There are some gorgeous beaches and kooky rock formations to check out around isolated Kawhia Harbour: bring your swimming gear! Minimum six adults.

Maketu Marae MARAE
(www.kawhia.maori.nz; Kaora St) From the wharf, a track extends along the coast to Maketu Marae, which has an impressively carved meeting house, Auaukiterangi. Two stones here – Hani and Puna – mark the burial place of the Tainui *waka*. You can't see a lot from the road, but the *marae* is private property – don't enter without permission from the Maketu Marae Committee (info@kawhia.maori.nz).

Dove Charters FISHING
(07-871 5854; www.westcoastfishing.co.nz; full day $105) Offers full-day fishing trips.

Festivals & Events

Kawhia Traditional Maori Kai Festival FOOD
(www.kawhiaharbour.co.nz/maori-kai-festival.html) During the annual Kai Festival in early February, over 10,000 people descend to enjoy traditional Maori *kai* (food) and catch up with *whanau* (relations). Once you've filled up on seafood, *rewana* bread and rotten corn, settle in to watch the bands and rousing *kapa haka* (traditional Maori group singing and dancing) performances.

Sleeping & Eating

Kawhia Motel MOTEL, RENTAL HOUSE $$
(07-871 0865; kawhiamotel@xtra.co.nz; cnr Jervois & Tainui Sts; s $99-155, extra person $20, house $250-300;) These six perkily painted, well-kept, old-school motel units are right next to the shops. There's also a four-bedroom house available. Kayak/bike hire costs $20/15 per hour.

Kawhia Beachside S-Cape HOLIDAY PARK $
(07-871 0727; www.kawhiabeachsidescape.co.nz; 225 Pouewe St; sites from $30, cabins dm/s/d from $30/40/58, cottages $165-185) Perfectly positioned on the water's edge, this camping ground looks shabby from the road but has comfy cottages. There's a smart laundry and ablutions block, but the backpackers' area is rudimentary at best – camping is a better bet. Two-hour kayak hire is $12 per person.

Annie's Cafe & Restaurant CAFE, RESTAURANT $
(146 Jervois St; meals $7-22; breakfast & lunch Wed-Sun winter, breakfast, lunch & dinner daily summer; @) An old-fashioned licensed eatery in the main street, serving espresso, sandwiches and local specialities such as flounder and whitebait with kumara chips. There's also an internet terminal.

Getting There & Away

Kawhia doesn't have a bus service. Take SH31 from Otorohanga (58km) or explore the scenic but rough unsealed road to Raglan (50km, 22km unsealed).

Otorohanga

POP 2700

One of several nondescript North Island towns to adopt a gimmick, Otorohanga's main street is festooned with images of cherished Kiwiana icons: sheep, gumboots, jandals, No 8 wire, All Blacks, pavlova, the beloved Buzzy Bee children's toy... But gimmicks aside, the Kiwi House is well worth a visit.

Sights

Otorohanga Kiwi House & Native Bird Park ZOO
(www.kiwihouse.org.nz; 20 Alex Telfer Dr; adult/child $20/6; ⏲9am-5pm Sep-May, 9am-4.30pm Jun-Aug) This bird barn has a nocturnal enclosure where you can see active kiwi energetically digging with their long beaks, searching for food. This is the only place in NZ where you can see a Great Spotted Kiwi, the biggest of the three kiwi species. Other native birds, such as kaka, kea, morepork and weka, are also on show.

FREE **Ed Hillary Walkway** MEMORIAL
(⏲24hr) As well as the Kiwiana decorating the main street, the Ed Hillary Walkway (running off Maniapoto St) has information panels on the All Blacks, Marmite, NZ competing in the America's Cup, and of course, Sir Ed.

Sleeping

Otorohanga Holiday Park HOLIDAY PARK $
(☎07-873 7253; www.kiwiholidaypark.co.nz; 20 Huiputea Dr; sites from $30, units $65-125; @📶) It's not the most attractive locale, backing onto train tracks and encircled by tractor sales yards, but the owners are quick with a smile and the park's tidy facilities include a fitness centre and sauna. And if you can't find a bed in Waitomo (it happens), Otorohanga is only 16km away.

Eating & Drinking

Thirsty Weta PUB
(www.theweta.co.nz; 57 Maniapoto St; meals $10-37; ⏲10am-1am) The top pick in town, with hearty snacks (of the pizza, pasta, surf 'n' turf and quesadilla variety) and the promise of things kicking off after dinner when the wine-bar vibe takes over and the musos plug in.

Origin Coffee Station CAFE
(www.origincoffee.co.nz; 7 Wahanui Cres; coffee $3-5; ⏲8.30am-4.30pm Mon-Fri) It's a long way from Malawi to the old Otorohanga railway station, but the beans don't seem to mind. The folks at Origin are dead serious about coffee, sourcing, importing and roasting it themselves and then delivering it to your table, strong and perfectly formed, and possibly with a slice of cake.

Countdown SUPERMARKET
(www.countdown.co.nz; 123 Maniapoto St; ⏲7am-10pm) As there's no supermarket at Waitomo Caves, stock up at Oto's Countdown on the Waitomo side of town.

Information

Otorohanga i-SITE (☎07-873 8951; www.otorohanga.co.nz; 27 Turongo St; ⏲9am-5pm Mon-Fri, 10am-2pm Sat & Sun; 📶) Free wi-fi and local information.

Getting There & Away

Bus

InterCity (☎09-583 5780; www.intercity.co.nz) buses run from Otorohanga to Auckland ($50, 3¼ hours, four daily), Te Awamutu ($21, 30 minutes, three daily), Te Kuiti ($20, one hour, three daily) and Rotorua ($53, 2½ hours, two daily).

Naked Bus (☎0900 625 33; www.nakedbus.com) runs one bus daily to Waitomo Caves ($20, 30 minutes), Hamilton ($25, one hour) and New Plymouth ($30, 3¼ hours).

The **Dalroy Express** (☎0508 465 622; www.dalroytours.co.nz) bus runs daily between Auckland ($37, three hours) and New Plymouth ($35, 3¼ hours) via Otorohanga. Other stops include Hamilton ($17, 50 minutes) and Te Awamutu ($12, 25 minutes).

The **Waitomo Shuttle** (☎07-873 8279, 0800 808 279; one-way adult/child $12/7) heads to

KINGITANGA

The concept of a Maori people is relatively new. Until the mid-1800s, NZ effectively comprised many independent tribal nations, operating in tandem with the British from 1840.

In 1856, faced with a flood of Brits, the Kingitanga movement formed to unite the tribes to better resist further loss of land and culture. A gathering of leaders elected Waikato chief Potatau Te Wherowhero as the first Maori king, hoping that his increased *mana* (prestige) could achieve the cohesion that the British had under their queen.

Despite the huge losses of the Waikato War and the eventual opening up of the King Country, the Kingitanga survived – although it has no formal constitutional role. A measure of the strength of the movement was the huge outpouring of grief when Te Arikinui Dame Atairangikaahu, Potatau's great-great-great-granddaughter, died in 2006 after 40 years at the helm. Although it's not a hereditary monarchy (leaders of various tribes vote on a successor), Potatau's line continues to the present day with King Tuheitia Paki.

the Waitomo Caves five times daily, coordinating with bus and train arrivals.

Train

Otorohanga is on the **Overlander** (☎0800 872 467; www.tranzscenic.co.nz; ⊙daily Oct-Apr, Fri-Sun May-Sep) train route between Auckland ($98, 3¼ hours) and Wellington ($129, nine hours) via Hamilton ($68, 50 minutes) and Te Kuiti ($68, 15 minutes).

Waitomo Caves

Even if damp, dark tunnels sound like your idea of hell, take a chill pill and head to Waitomo anyway. The limestone caves and glowing bugs here are one of the North Island's premier attractions.

The name Waitomo comes from *wai* (water) and *tomo* (hole or shaft): dotted across this region are numerous shafts dropping into underground cave systems and streams. There are 300-plus mapped caves in the area: the three main caves – Glowworm, Ruakuri and Aranui – have been bewitching visitors for over 100 years.

Your Waitomo experience needn't be claustrophobic: the electrically lit, cathedral-like Glowworm Cave is far from squeezy. But if it's tight, gut-wrenching, soaking-wet, pitch-black excitement you're after, Waitomo can oblige.

⊙ Sights

Caves

The big-three Waitomo Caves are all operated by the same company, based at the snazzy new **Waitomo Caves Visitor Centre** (☎0800 456 922; www.waitomo.com; Waitomo Caves Rd) behind the Glowworm Cave, which incorporates a cafe and theatre. Various combo deals are available, including a Triple Cave Combo (adult/child $80/39). Try to avoid the large tour groups, most of which arrive between 10.30am and 2.30pm.

Waitomo Caves

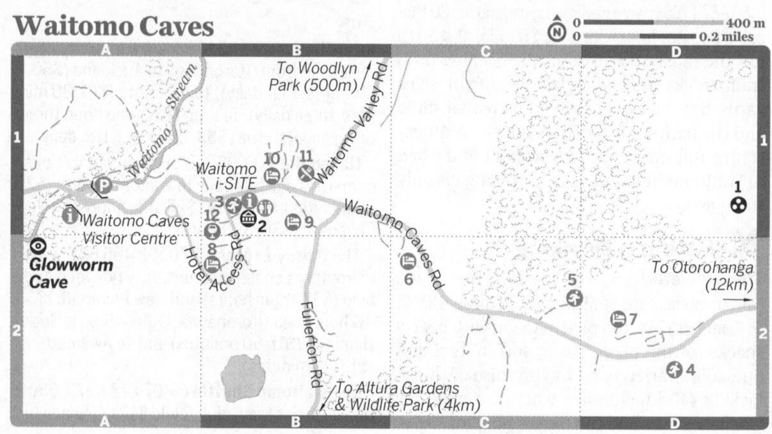

Waitomo Caves

⊙ Top Sights
- Glowworm Cave A2

⊙ Sights
- 1 Opapake Pa D1
- 2 Waitomo Caves Discovery Centre B1

Activities, Courses & Tours
- 3 CaveWorld B1
- 4 Legendary Black Water Rafting Company D2
- Spellbound .... (see 11)
- 5 Waitomo Adventures C2

Sleeping
- 6 Abseil Inn C2
- 7 Juno Hall Backpackers D2
- 8 Kiwi Paka B2
- 9 Waitomo Caves Guest Lodge B1
- 10 Waitomo Top 10 Holiday Park B1

Eating
- 11 Huhu B1
- Morepork Cafe .... (see 8)

Drinking
- 12 Curly's Bar B1

LOCAL KNOWLEDGE

WAITOMO CAVES *DR FARAH RANGIKOEPA PALMER*

The best way to experience the Waitomo glowworm caves is via black-water rafting. It's an exhilarating experience and involves getting dressed up in a wet suit (laughing at how funny everyone looks is half the fun), choosing an inflatable inner tube to sit in (another hilarious experience) and travelling through the limestone caves with two guides, your wits, and the glowworms. It is a real hands-on experience and requires some agility and the guts to jump backwards down some small waterfalls as you make your way through the tunnels. You finish off the trip quietly drifting through the caves in your tube, looking at the glowworms with your head lamp turned off.

Dr Farah Rangikoepa Palmer, former captain of the Black Ferns (NZ's women's rugby team)

Glowworm Cave CAVE
(adult/child $48/21; ⏲45min tours every 30min 9am-5pm) The guided tour of the Glowworm Cave, which is behind the visitor centre, leads past impressive stalactites and stalagmites into a large cavern known as the Cathedral. The acoustics are so good that Dame Kiri Te Kanawa and the Vienna Boys Choir have given concerts here. The highlight comes at the tour's end when you board a boat and swing off onto the river. As your eyes grow accustomed to the dark you'll see a Milky Way of little lights surrounding you – these are the glowworms. Conditions for their growth are just about perfect here so there are a remarkable number of them. Book your tour at the visitor centre.

Aranui Cave CAVE
(adult/child $46/21; ⏲45min tours 10am, 11am, 1pm, 2pm, 3pm) Three kilometres west from the Glowworm Cave is Aranui Cave. This cave is dry (hence no glowworms) but compensates with an incredible array of limestone formations. Thousands of tiny 'straw' stalactites hang from the ceiling. Book tours at the visitor centre. It's an hour's walk to the caves, otherwise the visitors centre can arrange transport.

Ruakuri Cave CAVE
(☎07-878 6219, 0800 782 587; adult/child $67/26; ⏲2hr tours 9am, 10am, 11.30am, 12.30pm, 1.30pm, 2.30pm & 3pm) Culturally significant Ruakuri Cave has an impressive 15m-high spiral staircase, removing the need to trample through the Maori burial site at the cave entrance (as tourists did for 84 years). Tours lead through 1.6km of the 7.5km system, taking in vast caverns with glowworms, subterranean streams and waterfalls, and intricate limestone structures. For as long as this cave has been open to the public, people have described it as spiritual – some claim it's haunted. It's customary to wash your hands when leaving to remove the *tapu* (sacred). Book your tour at the Legendary Black Water Rafting Company (p215) (tours also depart from there).

Other Sights

Waitomo Caves Discovery Centre MUSEUM
(☎07-878 7640, 0800 474 839; www.waitomodiscovery.org; 21 Waitomo Caves Rd; adult/child $5/free; ⏲8.15am-7pm Jan & Feb, 8.45am-5.30pm Nov, Dec & Mar, 8.45am-5pm Apr-Oct) Adjoining the i-SITE, the Waitomo Caves Discovery Centre has excellent exhibits explaining how caves are formed, the flora and fauna that thrive in them and the history of Waitomo's caves and cave exploration.

Altura Gardens & Wildlife Park ZOO, HORSE RIDING
(☎07-878 5278; www.alturapark.co.nz; 477 Fullerton Rd; adult/child $12/5; ⏲9.30am-5pm) At this 2-hectare park you can chat with a cockatoo, outstare a morepork or pat a blue-tongue lizard. There are dozens of bird and animal species here, but it's not a regular zoo – expect llamas and sheep rather than lions and giraffes. It also runs leisurely horse treks (60/90 minutes $65/80) and has B&B accommodation (a self-contained unit sleeping four; double/quad $145/185).

Activities

Underground

Legendary Black Water Rafting Company CAVING, ADVENTURE TOUR
(☎0800 782 5874; www.waitomo.com; 585 Waitomo Caves Rd; ⏲Black Labyrinth tour 9am, 10.30am, noon, 1.30pm & 3pm; Black Abyss tour 9am & 2pm) These guys run a Black Labyrinth tour ($119, three hours), which involves floating in a wet suit on an inner tube down a river that flows through Ruakuri Cave. The highlight

is leaping off a small waterfall and then floating through a long, glowworm-covered passage. The trip ends with showers, soup and bagels in the cafe. The Black Abyss tour ($220, five hours) is more adventurous and includes a 35m abseil into Ruakuri Cave, a flying fox and more glowworms and tubing. Minimum ages apply.

Spellbound CAVING, GUIDED TOUR
(07-878 7622, 0800 773 552; www.glowworm.co.nz; 10 Waitomo Caves Rd; adult/child $70/25; 3hr tours 10am, 11am, 2pm & 3pm) Spellbound is a good option if you don't want to get wet, are more interested in glowworms than an 'action' experience, and want to avoid the big groups in the main caves. Small-group tours access parts of the heavily glowworm-dappled Mangawhitiakau cave system, 12km south of Waitomo (...and you still get to ride in a raft!).

Waitomo Adventures CAVING, ADVENTURE TOUR
(07-878 7788, 0800 924 866; www.waitomo.co.nz; 654 Waitomo Caves Rd) Waitomo Adventures offers five different cave adventures, with discounts for various combos and for advance bookings. The Lost World ($310/445 four/seven hours) trip starts with a 100m abseil down into the cave, then – by a combination of walking, rock climbing, wading and swimming – you journey through a 30m-high cave to get back out, passing glowworms, amazing rock formations, waterfalls and more. The price includes lunch (underground) and dinner. The shorter version skips the wet stuff and the meals.

Haggas Honking Holes ($240, four hours) includes professional abseiling instruction followed by three waterfall abseils, rock climbing and travelling along a subterranean river, traversing narrow passageways and huge caverns. Along the way you see glowworms, cave formations and cave coral.

TumuTumu Toobing ($165, four hours) is a walking, climbing, swimming and tubing trip. St Benedict's Cavern ($165, three hours) includes abseiling and a subterranean flying fox in a cave with amazing straw stalagmites.

Green Glow Eco-Adventures CAVING, ADVENTURE TOUR
(0800 476 459; www.greenglow.co.nz; 1117 Oparure Rd, Te Kuiti; 6hr tours per person $180) Green Glow Eco-Adventures runs customised, small-group Waitomo tours, putting a caving, rock-climbing, abseiling, photographic or glowworm spin on your day (or all of the above!). It's based in Te Kuiti, 20 minutes from Waitomo.

CaveWorld CAVING, ADVENTURE TOURS
(07-878 6577, 0800 228 338; www.caveworld.co.nz; cnr Waitomo Caves Rd & Hotel Access Rd) CaveWorld runs the Tube It ($124, two hours) black-water rafting trip through glowworm-filled Te Anaroa. Also available are a glowworm-illuminated night abseil down a 45m crevice called the Glowworm Canyon (two hours, $199), or the daytime Footwhistle Glowworm Cave Tour ($49, one hour).

Rap, Raft 'n' Rock CAVING, ADVENTURE TOUR
(0800 228 372, 07-873 9149; www.caveraft.com; 95 Waitomo Caves Rd) These small-group expeditions ($160, five hours) start with abseil training, followed by a 27m descent into a natural cave, and then floating along a subterranean river on an inner tube with plenty of glowworms. After some caving, a belayed rock climb up a 20m cliff brings you to the surface.

Tramping

The Waitomo i-SITE has free pamphlets on walks in the area. The walk from **Aranui Cave** to **Ruakuri Cave** is an excellent short path. From the Waitomo Caves Visitor Centre, the 5km, three-hour-return **Waitomo Walkway** takes off through farmland, following Waitomo Stream to the **Ruakuri Scenic Reserve**, where a 30-minute return walk passes by a natural limestone tunnel. There are glowworms here at night – drive to the car park and bring a torch to find your way. Near Waitomo Adventures a steep 20-minute walk leads through bush then along farmland to the abandoned **Opapake Pa**, where terraces and kumara pits are visible.

Dundle Hill Walk TRAMPING
(07-878 7788, 0800 924 866; www.waitomowalk.com; adult/child $75/35) The self-guided privately run Dundle Hill Walk is a 27km, two-day/one-night loop walk through Waitomo's bush and farmland, including overnight bunk-house accommodation high up in the bush.

Sleeping

Abseil Inn B&B $$
(07-878 7815; www.abseilinn.co.nz; 709 Waitomo Caves Rd; d from $150;) A *veeery* steep driveway (abseiling in from a helicopter might be an easier approach) takes you to this de-

GLOWWORM MAGIC

Glowworms are the larvae of the fungus gnat. The larva glowworm has luminescent organs that produce a soft, greenish light. Living in a sort of hammock suspended from an overhang, it weaves sticky threads that trail down and catch unwary insects attracted by its light. When an insect flies towards the light it gets stuck in the threads – the glowworm just has to reel it in for a feed.

The larval stage lasts from six to nine months, depending on how much food the glowworm gets. When it has grown to about the size of a matchstick, it goes into a pupa stage, much like a cocoon. The adult fungus gnat emerges about two weeks later.

The adult insect doesn't live very long because it doesn't have a mouth. It emerges, mates, lays eggs and dies, all within about two or three days. The sticky eggs, laid in groups of 40 or 50, hatch in about three weeks to become larval glowworms.

Glowworms thrive in moist, dark caves but they can survive anywhere if they have the requisites of moisture, an overhang to suspend from and insects to eat. Waitomo is famous for its glowworms but you can see them in many other places around NZ, both in caves and outdoors.

When you come upon glowworms, don't touch their hammocks or hanging threads, try not to make loud noises and don't shine a light right on them. All of these things will cause them to dim their lights. It takes them a few hours to become bright again, during which time the grub will go hungry. The glowworms that shine most brightly are the hungriest.

lightful B&B with four themed rooms, great breakfasts and witty hosts. The biggest room has a double bath and valley views.

Waitomo Caves Guest Lodge B&B $$

(07-878 7641, 0800 465 762; www.waitomocavesguestlodge.co.nz; 7 Te Anga Rd; s $80, d $105-130, extra person $25, all incl breakfast;) Bag your own cosy little hillside en-suite cabin at this central operation with a sweet garden setting. The top cabins have valley views. Large continental breakfast and resident dog included. Simple and unfussy.

Waitomo Top 10 Holiday Park HOLIDAY PARK $

(07-878 7639, 0508 498 666; www.waitomopark.co.nz; 12 Waitomo Caves Rd; sites from $22, units $70-190;) This lovely holiday park in the heart of the village has spotless facilities, some beaut new cabins (the older ones are OK too) and plenty of outdoor distractions to keep the kids busy (pool, spa, playground and neighbouring rugby pitch).

Juno Hall Backpackers HOSTEL $

(07-878 7649; www.junowaitomo.co.nz; 600 Waitomo Caves Rd; sites from $16, dm $28, d with/without bathroom $78/68, tr $98/88, q with bathroom $124;) A slick purpose-built hostel 1km from the village with a warm welcome, a warmer wood fire in the woody lounge area, and an outdoor pool and tennis court. Comfy couches; lots of wood panelling.

Kiwi Paka HOSTEL $

(07-878 3395; www.waitomokiwipaka.co.nz; Hotel Access Rd; dm/s/d $30/65/70, chalets tw/d/q $95/110/150;) It's too big to be social but this classy, purpose-built, Alpine-style hostel has four-bed dorms in the main lodge, plus separate peak-roofed chalets, Morepork Cafe on-site and super-tidy facilities. Popular with big groups.

Woodlyn Park MOTEL $$$

(07-878 6666; www.woodlynpark.co.nz; 1177 Waitomo Valley Rd; d $170-245, extra person $15) Boasting the world's only hobbit motel (set into the ground with round windows and doors), Woodlyn Park's other sleeping options include the cockpit of a combat plane, train carriages and the *Waitanic* – a converted WWII patrol boat fitted with chandeliers, moulded ceilings and shiny brass portholes. It's extremely well done and the kids will love you for it.

Eating & Drinking

The general store in Waitomo sells the basics, but a better bet is to buy provisions in Otorohanga or Te Kuiti before you visit.

TOP CHOICE **Huhu** CAFE, MODERN NZ $$

(07-878 6674; www.huhustore.co.nz/cafe; 10 Waitomo Caves Rd; lunch $11-19, dinner $25-30; 10.30am-9pm;) Come to Huhu twice a day –

you won't be disappointed. Slick and modern with charming service, it has great views from the terrace and sublime contemporary NZ food. Sip a strong coffee, or graze through a seasonal tapas-style menu (large or small plates) of Kiwi delights like rabbit hotpot or organic braised beef, all locally sourced (right down to the specific cow). Wonderful!

Morepork Cafe CAFE, PIZZERIA **$$**
(Kiwi Paka, Hotel Access Rd; breakfast & lunch $7-15, dinner $14-27; ⏲8am-8pm) At the Kiwi Paka backpackers is this cheery joint, a jack-of-all-trades eatery serving breakfast, lunch and dinner either inside or out on the deck. The 'Caveman' pizza is a winner (the first person to ask for more pork will be shown the door).

Curly's Bar PUB
(www.curlysbar.co.nz; Hotel Access Rd; lunch & dinner $10-25; ⏲11am-2am) An easygoing tavern with lots of beers on tap, good-value pub grub (steaks, lamb shanks, nachos...), chunky wooden tables, occasional quiz nights and live music.

Information

Note that there's no petrol in town. Curly's Bar has an ATM.

Waitomo i-SITE (☎07-878 7640, 0800 474 839; www.waitomodiscovery.org; 21 Waitomo Caves Rd; ⏲8.15am-7pm Jan & Feb, 8.45am-5.30pm Nov, Dec & Mar, 8.45am-5pm Apr-Oct; @) Internet access, post office and booking agent.

Getting There & Away

Naked Bus (☎0900 625 33; www.nakedbus.com) runs once daily to Otorohanga ($20, 20 minutes), Hamilton ($20, 1¼ hours) and New Plymouth ($30, three hours).

Waitomo Shuttle (☎07-873 8279, 0800 808 279; waikiwi@ihug.co.nz; one way adult/child $12/7) heads to the caves five times daily from Otorohanga (15 minutes away), coordinating with bus and train arrivals.

Waitomo Wanderer (☎03-477 9083, 0800 000 4321; www.travelheadfirst.com) operates a daily return services from Rotorua or Taupo, with optional caving, glowworm and tubing add-ons (packages from $133). Shuttle-only services are $99 return.

Waitomo to Awakino

This obscure route, heading west of Waitomo on Te Anga Rd, is the definition of off-the-beaten-track. It's a slow but fascinating alternative to SH3 if Taranaki's your goal. Only 12km of the 111km route remains unsealed, but it's nearly all winding and narrow. Allow around two hours (not including stops) and fill up with petrol.

Walks in the **Tawarau Forest**, 20km west of the Waitomo Caves, are outlined in DOC's *Waitomo & King Country Tracks* booklet ($1, available from DOC in Hamilton or Te Kuitifrom), including a one-hour track to the Tawarau Falls from the end of Appletree Rd.

The Mangapohue Natural Bridge Scenic Reserve, 26km west of Waitomo, is a 5.5-hectare reserve with a giant natural limestone arch. It's a five-minute walk to the arch on a wheelchair-accessible pathway. On the far side, big rocks full of 35-million-year-old oyster fossils jut up from the grass, and at night you'll see glowworms.

About 4km further west is **Piripiri Caves Scenic Reserve**, where a five-minute walk leads to a large cave containing fossils of giant oysters. Bring a torch and be prepared to get muddy after heavy rain. Steps wind down into the gloom...

The impressively tiered, 30m **Marokopa Falls** are 32km west of Waitomo. A short track (15 minutes return) from the road leads to the bottom of the falls.

Just past Te Anga you can turn north to Kawhia, 59km away, or continue southwest to Marokopa (population 1560), a small black-sand village on the coast with some scarily big new mansions starting to appear. The whole Te Anga/Marokopa area is riddled with caves.

Marokopa Campground (☎07-876 7444; marokopacampground@xtra.co.nz; Rauparaha St; sites from $24, dm $18) ain't flash but it's in a nice spot, close to the coast. There's a small shop that will cover the catering basics (bread, milk, cheese), as well as a tennis court and tiny library.

The road heads south to Kiritehere, following a bubbling stream through idyllic farmland to Moeatoa then turning right (south) into Mangatoa Rd. Now you're in serious backcountry, heading into the dense **Whareorino Forest**. It would pay not to watch the movie *Deliverance* before tramping in this spectacularly remote tract of native bush. The 16-bunk DOC-run **Leitch's Hut** (☎07-878 1050; www.doc.govt.nz; per adult $5) has a toilet, water and a wood stove.

At Waikawau it's worth taking the 5km detour along the unsealed road to the coast near **Ngarupupu Point**, where a 100m walk through a dank tunnel opens out on an exquisitely isolated stretch of black-sand beach. Visit early and the only footprints in the sand will be yours, but think twice about swimming here; if you get caught in a rip you'll be halfway to Melbourne before your friends can reach help.

The road then continues through another twisty 28km, passing lush forest and the occasional farm before joining SH3 east of Awakino.

Te Kuiti

POP 4380

Cute Te Kuiti sits in a valley between picturesque hills. Welcome to the shearing capital of the world! You won't have any doubt as to the veracity of that statement if you're here for the very sheepish Great New Zealand Muster.

Sights

Big Shearer LANDMARK
(Rora St) The most prominent landmark in town is the 7m, 7½-tonne Big Shearer statue at the south end of the Rora St shopping strip.

Te Kuititanga-O-Nga-Whakaaro MONUMENT
(Rora St) Te Kuititanga-O-Nga-Whakaaro (the Gathering of Thoughts and Ideas) is a beautiful pavilion of etched-glass, *tukutuku* (woven flax panels) and wooden carvings that celebrates the town's history.

Festivals & Events

Great New Zealand Muster CULTURAL, FOOD
(www.waitomo.govt.nz/events/the-great-nz-muster; late Mar/early Apr) The highlight of the Great New Zealand Muster is the legendary Running of the Sheep: Pamplona's got nothing on the sight of 2000 woolly demons stampeding down Te Kuiti's main street. The festival includes sheep-shearing championships, a parade, Maori cultural performances, live music, barbecues, *hangi* and market stalls.

Sleeping

TOP CHOICE **Waitomo Lodge Motel** MOTEL $$
(07-878 0003; www.waitomo-lodge.co.nz; 62 Te Kumi Rd; d/f from $125/195;) Can't find a bed in Waitomo? This snappily designed motel at the Waitomo end of Te Kuiti is a brilliant alternative. Twenty spacious, modern rooms clad in plywood feature contemporary art, moody low-voltage lighting, flat-screen TVs and little decks overlooking Mangaokewa Stream in the units at the back. Bosco Cafe is across the street. Hipness in an un-hip town!

Simply the Best B&B B&B $$
(07-878 8191; www.simplythebestbnb.co.nz; 129 Gadsby Rd; s/d incl breakfast $60/110) It's hard to argue with the immodest name when the prices are this reasonable, the breakfast this generous and the hosts this charming. Warning: the spectacular views may illicit involuntary choruses of Tina Turner anthems.

Eating & Drinking

Bosco Cafe CAFE $
(theteam@boscocafe.co.nz; 57 Te Kumi Rd; mains $10-20; breakfast & lunch;) It's not damning it with faint praise to say that Bosco is the coolest place in Te Kuiti. This excellent industrial-chic cafe offers great coffee, tempting food (try the bacon-wrapped meatloaf with greens) and sweet service. It comes into its own on a sunny afternoon when the doors swing open onto Brook Park.

New World SUPERMARKET
(www.newworld.co.nz; Te Kumi Rd; 8am-8pm) Self-caterers bound for Waitomo should stock up at New World.

Information

Department of Conservation (DOC; 07-878 1050; www.doc.govt.nz; 78 Taupiri St; 8am-4.30pm Mon-Fri)
Te Kuiti i-SITE (07-878 8077; www.waitomo.govt.nz; Rora St; 9am-5pm Mon-Fri, 10am-2pm Sat, noon-4pm Sun; @) Internet access and visitor information.

Getting There & Away

Bus

InterCity (www.intercity.co.nz) uses run daily to the following destinations (among others):

DESTINATION	PRICE	DURATION	FREQUENCY
Auckland	$47	3½hr	3 daily
Mokau	$30	1hr	2 daily
New Pllymouth	$30	2½hr	2 daily
Otorohanga	$20	45min	3 daily
Taumarunui	$28	1¼	1 daily

Naked Bus (www.nakedbus.com) runs once daily to Auckland ($44, four hours), Hamilton ($20, 1½ hours), New Plymouth ($30, 2¼ hours) and Otorohanga ($20, 30 minutes).

The Dalroy Express bus runs daily between Auckland ($39, 3½ hours) and New Plymouth ($29, 2¼ hours), stopping at Te Kuiti. Other stops include Hamilton ($19, 1½ hours), Mokau ($17, one hour) and Otorohanga ($12, 15 minutes).

Train

Te Kuiti is on the Overlander train route between Auckland ($98, 3½ hours) and Wellington ($129, 8¾ hours) via Hamilton ($68, one hour) and Taumarunui ($68, 50 minutes).

Te Kuiti to Mokau

From Te Kuiti, SH3 runs southwest to the coast before following the rugged shoreline to New Plymouth. Along this scenic route the sheep stations sprout peculiar limestone formations before giving way to lush native bush as the highway winds along the course of the Awakino River.

The river spills into the Tasman at **Awakino** (population 60), a small settlement where boats shelter in the estuary while locals find refuge at the down-to-earth (or down-to-sea?) **Awakino Hotel** (☎06-752 9815; www.awakinohotel.co.nz; SH3; meals $9-20; ⏲breakfast & lunch daily, dinner Mon-Sat).

A little further south the impressive **Maniaroa Marae** dominates the cliff above the highway. This important complex houses the anchor stone of the *Tainui waka* (p212) which brought this region's original people from their Polynesian homeland. You can get a good view of the intimidatingly carved meeting house, Te Kohaarua, from outside the fence – don't cross into the *marae* unless someone invites you.

Five kilometres further south, as the perfect cone of Mt Taranaki starts to take shape on the horizon, is the village of **Mokau** (population 400). It offers a fine stretch of black-sand beach and good surfing and fishing. From August to November the Mokau River (the second-longest on the North Island) spawns a whole lot of whitebait, and subsequent swarms of fiercely territorial whitebaiters.

The town's **Tainui Historical Society Museum** (☎06-752 9072; mokaumuseum@vodafone.co.nz; SH3; admission by donation; ⏲10am-4pm; @) has an interesting collection of old photographs and artefacts (pianolas, whale bones, dusty photos of the Queen) from the time when this once-isolated outpost was a coal and lumber shipping port for settlements along the river.

Mokau River Cruises (☎0800 665 2874; www.mokaurivercruises.co.nz; cruises adult/child $50/15) operates a three-hour river cruise with commentary on-board the historic *MV Cygnet*. Twilight cruises are also available.

Just north of Mokau, **Seaview Holiday Park** (☎06-752 9708; seaviewhp@xtra.co.nz; SH3; sites from $10, cabins/units d from $50/85) is basic (dinky pastel-painted cabins with rickety furniture) but it's right on a broad span of big brown beach.

On the hill above the village the austere-looking but actually very friendly **Mokau Motel** (☎06-752 9725; www.mokaumotels.co.nz; SH3; s/d/ste from $90/105/120; 📶) offers fishing advice, no-nonsense self-contained units and three city-standard luxury suites (what a surprise!).

PHONE ZONE

If you've been rabidly punching the 07 area code into your phone for weeks across Waikato and the King Country, note that the code changes to 06 from around Awakino heading south into Taranaki.

Taumarunui

POP 5140

Taumarunui on a cold day can feel a bit miserable, but this town in the heart of the King Country has potential. The main reason to stay here is to kayak on the Whanganui River or as a cheaper base for skiing in Tongariro National Park, and there are some beaut walks and cycling tracks around town.

For details on the Forgotten World Highway between Taumarunui and Stratford, see Taranaki. For details on canoeing and kayaking on the Whanganui River, see Whanganui National Park.

Sights & Activities

The 3km **Riverbank Walk** along the Whanganui River runs from Cherry Grove Domain, 1km south of town, to Taumarunui Holiday Park. **Te Peka Lookout**, across the Ongarue River on the western edge of town, is a good vantage point from which to survey proceedings.

Hakiaha Street STREET

At the eastern end of Hakiaha St is **Hauaroa Whare**, a beautifully carved house. At the western end **Te Rohe Potae** memorialises King Tawhiao's assertion of his *mana* (authority) over the King Country in a sculpture of a top hat on a large rock.

Raurimu Spiral RAILWAY

The Raurimu Spiral, 30km south of town, is a unique feat of railway engineering that was completed in 1908 after 10 years' work. Rail buffs can experience the spiral by taking the *Overlander* train to National Park township (return $136).

Taumarunui Jet Tours JETBOATING

(☎07-896 6055, 0800 853 886; www.taumarunuijettours.co.nz; Cherry Grove Domain; 30min/1hr tour from $60/100) Taumarunui Jet Tours runs high-octane jetboat trips on the Whanganui River.

Sleeping & Eating

Taumarunui Holiday Park HOLIDAY PARK $

(☎07-895 9345; www.taumarunuiholidaypark.co.nz; SH4; sites from $17, cabins & cottage d $50-115; @) On the banks of the Whanganui River, 4km east of town, this shady camping ground offers safe river swimming and clean facilities. The new owners are fierce advocates for the town, and can give you the low-down on what to see and do.

Twin Rivers Motel MOTEL $$

(☎07-895 8063; www.twinrivers.co.nz; 23 Marae St; units $90-215;) The 12 units at Twin Rivers are spick and span and are constantly being upgraded (new bathrooms, new faux-stone wall facing, shiny new oversized door numbers...). The bigger units sleep up to seven.

L'attitude CAFE, TAPAS $$

(☎07-895 6611; 1 Hakiaha St; brunch $13-19, dinner tapas plates $6-12; brunch Wed-Sun, dinner Fri & Sat) This black-painted box on the Te Kuiti side of town is surely the only place in Taumarunui where you can get grilled marinated sesame-seed chicken wings. There are art-hung walls, outdoor tables and plenty of NZ wines to ply yourself with.

Information

Department of Conservation (DOC; ☎07-895 8201; www.doc.govt.nz; Cherry Grove Domain; 8am-5pm Mon-Fri) A field office not always open (call in advance).

Taumarunui i-SITE (☎07-895 7494; www.visitruapehu.co.nz; 116 Hakiaha St; 9am-5pm; @) Visitor information and internet access. Pick up the *Ruapehu Chosen Pathways* brochure for regional information.

Getting There & Away

Taumarunui is on SH4, 81km south of Te Kuiti and 41km north of National Park township.

InterCity (☎0508 353 947; www.intercity.co.nz) buses head to Auckland ($59, 4½ hours, one daily) via Te Kuiti ($28, one hour), and to Palmerston North ($53, 4¾ hours, one daily) via National Park ($22, 30 minutes).

Taumarunui is on the **Overlander** (☎0800 872 467; www.tranzscenic.co.nz; daily Oct-Apr, Fri-Sun May-Sep) train route between Auckland ($98, 4¾ hours) and Wellington ($129, 7½ hours), via Te Kuiti ($68, 1¼ hours) and National Park ($68, 50 minutes).

Owhango

POP 210

A pint-sized village where all the street names start with 'O', Owhango makes a cosy base for walkers, mountain bikers (the 42 Traverse ends here) and skiers who can't afford to stay closer to the slopes in Tongariro National Park. Take Omaki Rd for a two-hour loop walk through virgin forest in **Ohinetonga Scenic Reserve**.

Sleeping

Forest Lodge LODGE

(☎07-895 4854; www.forest-lodge.co.nz; 12 Omaki Rd; dm/s/d $25/45/65, units $95-120; @) A snug backpackers lodge with comfortable, clean rooms, neatly folded towels with bars of soap on top, and good communal spaces. For privacy junkies there are separate self-contained motel and cottage units next door. Breakfast/dinner from $9/22; bike hire from $20 and guided fishing from $250.

Blue Duck Lodge LODGE, HOSTEL $

(☎07-895 6276; www.blueducklodge.co.nz; RD2, Whakahoro; dm from $35, d $80-185, extra adult/child $37/20) Overlooking the Retaruke River 36km southwest of Owhango (take the Kaitieke turn-off 1km south of town), this ecosavvy place is actually three lodges, offering accommodation from dorms in an old shearers' quarters to a self-contained family cottage sleeping eight. The owners are mad-keen conservationists, restoring native bird habitats and historic buildings (you can volunteer and lend a hand).

Fernleaf B&B B&B, FARMSTAY **$$**
(☎07-895 4847; www.fernleaffarmstay.co.nz; 58 Tunanui Rd; s/d incl breakfast $85/120) This characterful villa on a third-generation cattle-and-sheep farm has two en-suite rooms with garden outlooks, plus a twin and a separate cottage double that share a bathroom. Generous breakfast and dinners ($30 per person by arrangement) are labours of love. It's just off SH4, 7km north of Owhango.

Eating & Drinking

Cafe 39 South CAFE **$**
(☎07-895 4800; www.facebook.com/cafe39south; SH4; meals $9-17; ⏲7am-3pm Wed-Sun) Transport this stylishly angular roadside cafe into any major city and it would get by just fine. The food is delicious and reasonably priced, the coffee is excellent and the electric fire will make you want to linger on cold days. The 39° South lattitude marker is just across the road.

Getting There & Away

Owhango is 14km south of Taumarunui on SH4. All the **InterCity** (☎0508 353 947; www.intercity.co.nz) buses that stop in Taumarunui also stop here.

Taranaki & Whanganui

Includes »

New Plymouth 226
Around New Plymouth 234
Mt Taranaki (Egmont National Park) 234
Around Mt Taranaki 237
Surf Highway 45 238
Whanganui 240
Whanganui National Park 246
Palmerston North 252
Around Palmerston North 256
Manawatu Gorge & Around 257

Best Outdoors

» New Plymouth Coastal Walkway (p228)

» Surf Highway 45 (p238)

» A Mt Taranaki walk (p235)

» Whanganui River canoeing (p248)

Best Places to Stay

» Fitzroy Beach Motel (p230)

» Ahu Ahu Beach Villas (p238)

» Anndion Lodge (p243)

» Flying Fox (p251)

Why Go?

Halfway between Auckland and Wellington, Taranaki (aka 'the 'naki') is the Texas of New Zealand: oil and gas stream in from offshore rigs, plumping the region with enviable affluence. New Plymouth is the regional hub, home to an excellent art gallery and provincial museum, and enough decent espresso joints to keep you humming.

Behind the city, the moody volcanic cone of Mt Taranaki demands to be visited. Taranaki also has a glut of black-sand beaches: surfers and holidaymakers swell summer numbers.

Further east the history-rich Whanganui River curls its way through Whanganui National Park down to Whanganui city, a 19th-century river port that's aging with artistic grace.

Palmerston North, the Manawatu's main city, is a town of two peoples: tough-talkin' country fast-foodies in hotted-up cars and caffeinated Massey University literati. Beyond the city the region blends rural grace with yesterday's pace: you might even find time for a little laziness!

When to Go

Mt Taranaki is one of NZ's wettest spots, and frequently cops snowfalls, even in summer: weather on the mountain can be extremely changeable. Ironically, New Plymouth frequently tops the North Island's most-sunshine-hours list. Expect warm summers and cool winters.

Over in Whanganui the winters are milder, but they're chillier on the Palmerston North plains. Sunshine is abundant hereabouts too – around 2000 hours per year!

Taranaki & Whanganui Highlights

1. Walking up or around the massive cone of **Mt Taranaki** (p234)
2. Riding the big breaks along **Surf Highway 45** (p238)
3. Getting experimental at New Plymouth's **Govett-Brewster Art Gallery** (p227)
4. Bouncing from bean to bean in **New Plymouth's cafes** (p231)
5. Watching a glass-blowing demonstration at one of **Whanganui's glass studios** (p241)
6. Redefining serenity on a canoe or kayak trip on the **Whanganui River** (p248)
7. Traversing the rainy **Whanganui River Road** (p247) by car or bike – it's all about the journey, not how fast you get there
8. Flexing your All Blacks–spirit at Palmerston North's **New Zealand Rugby Museum** (p252)

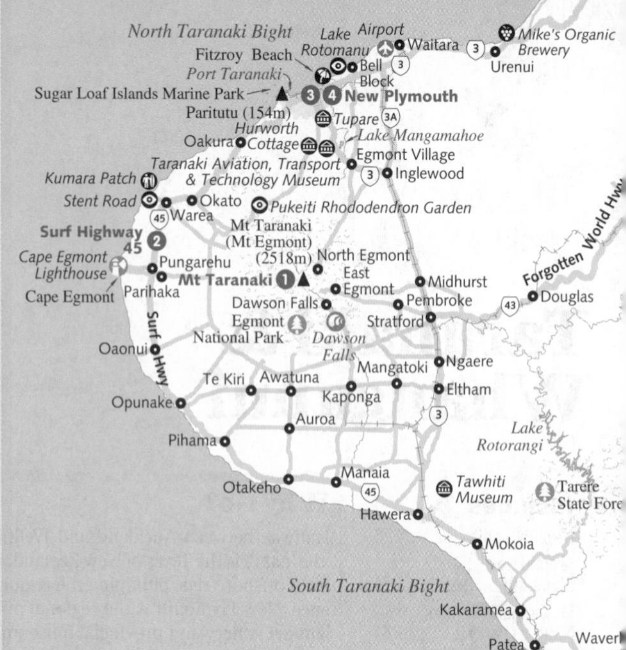

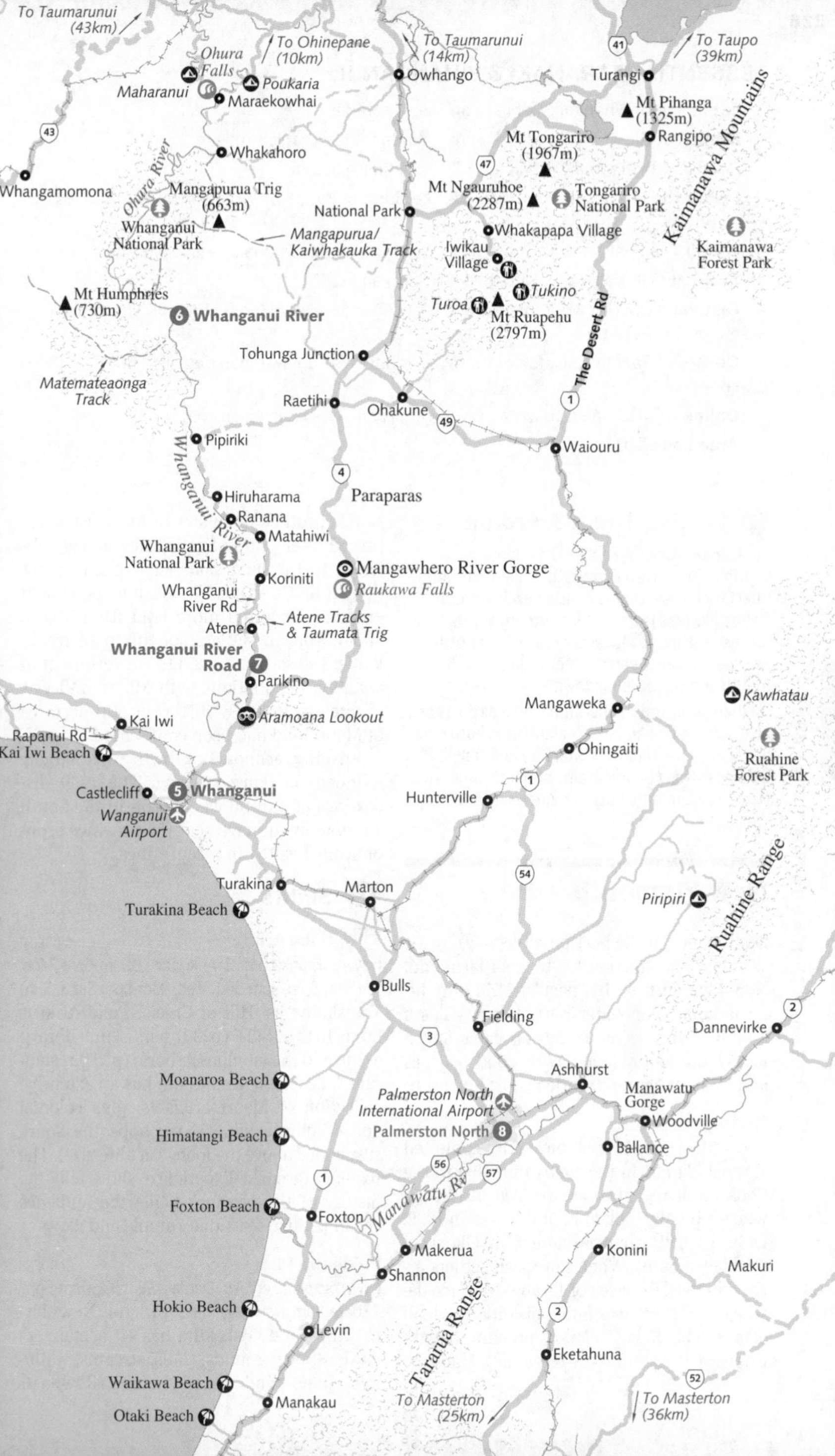

To Taumarunui (43km)
To Ohinepane (10km)
To Taumarunui (14km)
To Taupo (39km)
Ohura Falls
Maharanui
Poukaria
Maraekowhai
Owhango
Turangi
Mt Pihanga (1325m)
Rangipo
Kaimanawa Mountains
Whakahoro
Mt Tongariro (1967m)
Whangamomona
Ohura River
Mangapurua Trig (663m)
Mt Ngauruhoe (2287m)
Tongariro National Park
National Park
Whanganui National Park
Mangapurua/ Kaiwhakauka Track
Whakapapa Village
Iwikau Village
Kaimanawa Forest Park
Tukino
Turoa
Mt Ruapehu (2797m)
Mt Humphries (730m)
6 Whanganui River
The Desert Rd
Tohunga Junction
Matemateaonga Track
Raetihi
Ohakune
Pipiriki
Waiouru
Whanganui River
Paraparas
Hiruharama
Ranana
Matahiwi
Whanganui National Park
Mangawhero River Gorge
Koriniti
Raukawa Falls
Whanganui River Rd
Atene Tracks & Taumata Trig
Atene
Whanganui River Road 7
Parikino
Kawhatau
Mangaweka
Aramoana Lookout
Kai Iwi
Rapanui Rd
Kai Iwi Beach
Ohingaiti
Ruahine Forest Park
Castlecliff
5 Whanganui
Hunterville
Wanganui Airport
Ruahine Range
Turakina
Marton
Piripiri
Turakina Beach
Bulls
Fielding
Dannevirke
Ashhurst
Moanaroa Beach
Palmerston North International Airport
Manawatu Gorge
Woodville
Palmerston North 8
Himatangi Beach
Ballance
Manawatu Rv
Foxton Beach
Foxton
Makerua
Konini
Makuri
Shannon
Hokio Beach
Tararua Range
Levin
Eketahuna
Waikawa Beach
To Masterton (25km)
To Masterton (36km)
Manakau
Otaki Beach
43
41
47
1
49
4
54
3
2
56
57
52

ESSENTIAL TARANAKI & WHANGANUI

» **Eat** In one of Whanganui's hip main-street eateries

» **Drink** A bottle of Mike's Mild Ale from White Cliffs Organic Brewery

» **Read** The *Wanganui Chronicle*, NZ's oldest newspaper

» **Listen to** The rockin' album *Back to the Burning Wreck* by Whanganui riff-monsters The Have

» **Watch** *The Last Samurai*, co-starring Tom Cruise (Mt Taranaki gets top billing)

» **Swim at** Oakura Beach, with its black sand and surf

» **Festival** WOMAD (World of Music Arts and Dance) every March at New Plymouth's Bowl of Brooklands

» **Go Green** Paddle a stretch of the Whanganui River, an awe-inspiring slice of NZ wilderness

» **Online** www.taranaki.co.nz, www.wanganui.com, www.ourregion.co.nz

» **Area code** ☎06

Getting There & Around

In Taranaki, Air New Zealand has domestic flights to/from New Plymouth. Naked Bus and InterCity bus services service New Plymouth; Dalroy Express is a smaller company plying local routes. Getting to Mt Taranaki is easy: shuttle services run between the mountain, New Plymouth and surrounding towns.

Whanganui and Palmerston North airports are also serviced by Air New Zealand, and both cities are also on the radar for InterCity and Naked Bus services. Tranz Scenic trains stop in Palmerston North too, en route between Auckland and Wellington.

New Plymouth

POP 52,500

Dominated (in the best possible way) by Mt Taranaki and surrounded by lush farmland, New Plymouth is this part of NZ's only international deep-water port. The city has a bubbling arts scene, some fab cafes and a rootsy, outdoorsy focus, with good beaches and Egmont National Park a short hop away.

History

Local Maori *iwi* (tribes) have long contested Taranaki lands. In the 1820s they fled to the Cook Strait region to escape Waikato tribes, who eventually took hold of the area in 1832. Only a small group remained, at Okoki Pa (New Plymouth). When European settlers arrived in 1841, the coast of Taranaki seemed deserted and there was little opposition to land claims. The New Zealand Company bought extensive tracts from the remaining Maori.

When other members of local tribes returned after years of exile, they fiercely objected to the land sale. Their claims were upheld by Governor Fitzroy, but the Crown gradually acquired more land from Maori, and European settlers sought these fertile lands. The settlers forced the government to abandon negotiations with Maori, and war erupted in 1860. By 1870 over 500 hectares of Maori land had been confiscated.

Ensuing economic growth was largely founded on dairy farming. The 1959 discoveries of natural gas and oil in the South Taranaki Bight have kept the province economically healthy in recent times.

Sights

FREE **Puke Ariki** MUSEUM

(www.pukeariki.com; 1 Ariki St; ⌚9am-6pm Mon, Tue, Thu & Fri, 9am-9pm Wed, 9am-5pm Sat & Sun) Translating as 'Hill of Chiefs', Puke Ariki is home to the i-SITE (p233), a museum, library, a cafe and the fabulous Arborio (p231) restaurant. The excellent museum has an extensive collection of Maori artefacts, plus colonial and wildlife exhibits (...we hope the shark suspended above the lobby isn't life-size). The regular 'Taranaki Experience' show tells the history of the province while the audience sits in podlike seats that rumble and glow.

Pukekura Park GARDENS

(www.pukekura.org.nz; Liardet St; ⌚7.30am-6pm, 7.30am-8pm Nov-Mar) The pick of New Plymouth's parks, Pukekura has 49 hectares of gardens, playgrounds, trails, streams, waterfalls, ponds and display houses. Rowboats (per half-hour $10, December and January only) meander across the main lake (full of arm-sized eels), next to which the **Tea House** (Liardet St; snacks $4-9; ⏲10am-5pm) serves light meals. The technicoloured Festival of Lights (p229) here draws the summer crowds, as does the classically English cricket oval.

FREE **Govett-Brewster Art Gallery** GALLERY
(www.govettbrewster.com; 42 Queen St; ⏲10am-5pm) The Govett-Brewster Art Gallery is arguably the country's best regional art gallery. Presenting contemporary – often experimental – local and international shows, it's most famous for its connection with NZ sculptor, filmmaker and artist Len Lye (1901–80). His work is well represented here, with showings of his 1930s animation as well as sculpture and super-clever kinetic works. The glass-fronted Café Govett-Brewster is also here.

Puke Ariki Landing SCULPTURE PARK
(St Aubyn St) Along the city waterfront is Puke Ariki Landing, a historic area studded with sculptures, including the wonderfully eccentric Wind Wand (www.windwand.co.nz). Designed by Len Lye – the artist who has put this town on the map in modern times – this 45m-high kooky kinetic sculpture is a beloved icon of bendy poleness.

Paritutu HILL
(Centennial Dr) Just west of town is Paritutu, a steep-sided, craggy hill (154m); its name translates appropriately as 'Rising Precipice'. From the summit you can see for miles around: out to the Sugar Loaves, down to the town and to the mountain beyond. It's a 20-minute scramble to the top.

Sugar Loaf Islands Marine Park ISLAND
(www.doc.govt.nz) A refuge for sea birds and over 400 NZ fur seals 1km offshore, these rugged islets (Nga Motu in Maori) are eroded volcanic remnants. Most seals come here from June to October but some stay all year round. Learn more about the marine park at the tiny interpretation centre on the Lee Breakwater waterfront, or take a tour.

FREE **Real Tart Gallery** GALLERY
(www.tact.org.nz; 19 Egmont St; ⏲10am-5pm Mon-Fri, 10am-4pm Sat & Sun) To see what local artists have to offer, visit the 100-year-old reconstructed warehouse Real Tart Gallery. Exhibitions change regularly and most works are for sale. Don't miss the old graffiti preserved under perspex!

Brooklands Park PARK
(www.newplymouthnz.com; Brooklands Park Dr; ⏲daylight hr) Adjoining Pukekura, Brooklands Park is home to the **Bowl of Brooklands** (www.bowl.co.nz; Brooklands Park Dr), a world-class outdoor sound-shell, hosting festivals such as WOMAD (p229) and old-school rockers like Fleetwood Mac. Park highlights include a 2000-year-old puriri tree, a 300-variety rhododendron dell and the farmy **Brooklands Zoo** (Brooklands Park Dr; ⏲9am-5pm).

Taranaki Cathedral CHURCH
(www.taranakicathedral.org.nz; 37 Vivian St; ⏲services daily) The austere Church of St Mary, built in 1846, is NZ's oldest stone church and its newest cathedral! Its graveyard has the headstones of early settlers and soldiers who died during the Taranaki Land Wars, as well as those of several Maori chiefs. Check out the fabulous vaulted timber ceiling inside.

MAORI NZ: TARANAKI & WHANGANUI

Ever since Taranaki fled here to escape romantic difficulties, the Taranaki region has had a turbulent history. Conflicts between local *iwi* and invaders from the Waikato were followed by two wars with the government – first in 1860–61, and then again in 1865–69. Following the wars there were massive land confiscations and an extraordinary passive-resistance campaign at Parihaka.

Further east, a drive up the Whanganui River Rd takes you deep into traditional Maori territory, passing the Maori villages of Atene, Koriniti, Ranana and Hiruharama along the way. In Whanganui itself, run your eyes over amazing indigenous exhibits at the Whanganui Regional Museum (p241), and check out the superb Maori carvings in Putiki Church (p242).

Over in Palmerston North, Te Manawa museum (p252) has a strong Maori focus, while the New Zealand Rugby Museum (p252) pays homage to Maori All Blacks, without whom the team would never have become a world force.

New Plymouth

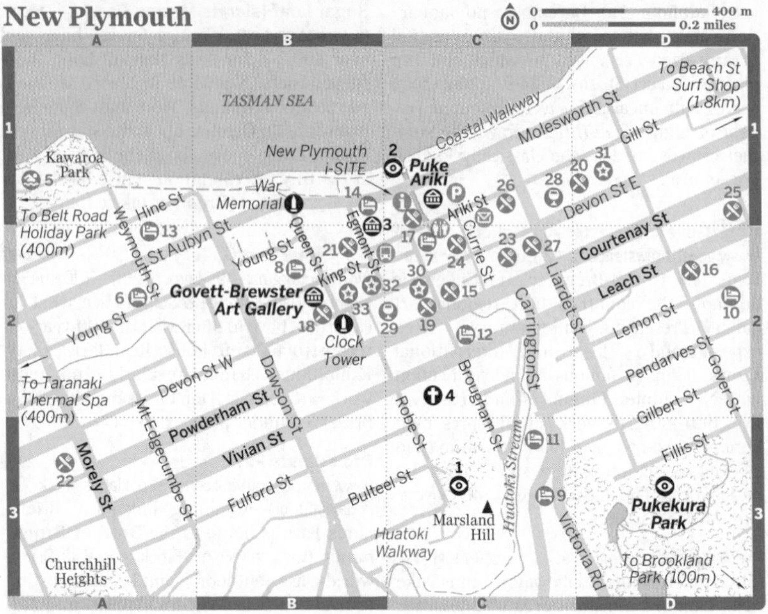

New Plymouth Observatory OBSERVATORY
(www.sites.google.com/site/astronomynp; Marsland Hill, off Robe St; adult/child/family $5/3/10; ⌚7.30-9.30pm Tue Mar-Oct, 8.30-10pm Tue Nov-Feb) Atop Marsland Hill (great views!) is this wee observatory. Public nights include a planetarium program and telescope viewings if the weather is clear. Also on the hill is the cacophonous 37-bell **Kibby Carillon**, a huge automated glockenspiel-like device that tolls out across the New Plymouth rooftops.

Activities

Surfing

The black, volcanic-sand beaches of Taranaki are world renowned for surfing. Close to the eastern edge of town are **Fitzroy Beach** and **East End Beach** (allegedly the cleanest beach in Oceania). There's also decent surf at **Back Beach**, near Paritutu, at the western end of the city.

Beach Street Surf Shop SURFING
(☎06-758 0400; www.taranakisurf.com; 39 Beach St; 2hr lesson $75; ⌚9am-6pm) Close to Fitzroy Beach, this surf shop offers lessons, gear hire and surf tours.

Tarawave Surf School SURFING
(☎06-752 7474, 021 119 6218; www.tarawavesurfschool.com; 1½hr lesson $70) Tarawave is based 15km south of town at Oakura, on Surf Hwy 45.

Tramping

The i-SITE stocks the *Taranaki: A Walker's Guide* booklet, including coastal, local reserve and park walks. The excellent **Coastal Walkway** (13km) from Bell Block to Port Taranaki, gives you a surf-side perspective on New Plymouth and crosses the great new **Te Rewa Rewa Bridge**. The **Te Henui Walkway** (6km), from the coastal East End Reserve to the city's southern boundary, is an interesting streamside amble. **Huatoki Walkway** (5km), following Huatoki Stream, is a rambling walk into the city centre. Alternatively, the *New Plymouth Heritage Trail* brochure, taking in historic hot spots, is a real blast from the past.

Other Activities

Taranaki Thermal Spa SPA, MASSAGE
(☎06-7591666; www.windwand.co.nz/mineralpools; 8 Bonithon Ave; treatments $5-245; ⌚10am-5pm Mon & Tue, 10am-9pm Wed-Fri, 3pm-9pm Sat & Sun) The warm mineral water filling the tanks at Taranaki Thermal Spa was discovered during the search for oil around 1910. The pri-

New Plymouth

Top Sights

- Govett-Brewster Art Gallery ... B2
- Puke Ariki ... C1
- Pukekura Park ... D3

Sights

1 New Plymouth Observatory ... C3
2 Puke Ariki Landing ... C1
3 Real Tart Gallery ... B2
4 Taranaki Cathedral ... C2

Activities, Courses & Tours

5 Todd Energy Aquatic Centre ... A1

Sleeping

6 Arcadia Lodge ... A2
7 Ariki Backpackers ... C2
8 Bella Vista ... B2
9 Carrington Motel ... C3
10 Cottage Mews Motel ... D2
11 Issey Manor ... C3
12 Nice Hotel ... C2
13 Seaspray House ... A2
Shoestring Backpackers ... (see 10)
14 Waterfront ... B1

Eating

15 André L'Escargot ... C2
16 Andre's Pies & Patisserie ... D2
17 Arborio ... C1
18 Café Govett-Brewster ... B2
19 Chaos ... C2
20 Elixir ... D1
Empire Tea & Coffee ... (see 33)
21 Frederic's ... B2
22 Fresha ... A3
23 IndiaToday ... C2
24 Laughing Buddha ... C2
25 Pak 'n Save ... D1
Petit Paris ... (see 24)
26 Portofino ... C1
27 Sandwich Extreme ... C2

Drinking

28 Crowded House ... C1
29 Matinee ... C2

Entertainment

30 Arthouse Cinema ... C2
31 Event Cinemas ... D1
32 The Basement ... B2
33 TSB Showplace ... B2

vate baths are filled on arrival, and there's a suite of massage and beauty therapies available. An absolute tonic.

Todd Energy Aquatic Centre SWIMMING
(☎06-759 6060; www.newplymouthnz.com; Tisch Ave, Kawaroa Park; adult/child $4.50/3.50, waterslide $3.50; ⏱6am-8.30pm Mon-Fri, 8.30am-7pm Sat & Sun) Just west of town in grassy Kawaroa Park is the Todd Energy Aquatic Centre, which has a waterslide, outdoor pool and indoor pool.

Tours

Happy Chaddy's Charters BOAT
(☎06-758 9133; www.windwand.co.nz/chaddies charters; Ocean View Pde; trips adult/child $35/10) Take a trip out to visit the Sugar Loaf Islands with Chaddy: expect at least four laughs a minute on a one-hour bob around on the chop. Departs daily from Lee Breakwater, tide and weather permitting. You can also hire kayaks (single/double per hour $15/30) and bikes ($10 per 30 minutes) here.

Wind Wanderers CYCLING
(☎027 358 1182; www.windwanderers.co.nz; Nobs Line car park, East End Reserve; tours per person $90) Wind Wanderers offers bike hire (single/tandem per hour $20/30) and three-hour guided tours along New Plymouth's excellent Coastal Walkway (cycling, not walking, obviously). Miniumum two people.

Canoe & Kayak Taranaki KAYAKING
(☎06-769 5506; www.canoeandkayak.co.nz; half-day trips incl hire $70) Paddle out to the Sugar Loaf Islands or over the gentle Waitara River rapids.

Festivals & Events

Festival of Lights CULTURAL
(www.festivaloflights.co.nz) Complete with live music and costumed characters roaming the undergrowth, this colourful display lights up Pukekura Park from late December to mid-February.

WOMAD MUSIC, CULTURAL
(World of Music Arts & Dance; ☎06-759 8412; www.womad.co.nz) A diverse array of local and international artists perform at the Bowl of Brooklands each March. Hugely popular, with music fans travelling from across NZ.

Taranaki International Arts Festival ARTS
(www.taft.co.nz/artsfest) The regional big-ticket arts fest happens in August ('It's warm inside' was the 2011 tagline): theatre, dance, music, visual arts, parades and plenty of food and wine.

Taranaki Garden Spectacuclar HORTICULTURAL
(www.taft.co.nz/gardenfestnz) A long-running NZ flower fest, held late October/early November each year. More rhododendrons than you'll ever see in one place again.

Sleeping

TOP CHOICE **Fitzroy Beach Motel** MOTEL $$
(☎06-757 2925; www.fitzroybeachmotel.co.nz; 25 Beach St; s/d $130/150, unit $190;) This quiet, old-time motel (just 160m from Fitzroy Beach) has been thoroughly redeemed with a major overhaul and extension. Highlights include quality carpets, double glazing, lovely bathrooms, LCD TVs, and an absence of poky studio-style units (all one- or two-bedroom). Free bikes too. Winner!

Seaspray House HOSTEL $
(☎06-759 8934; www.seasprayhouse.co.nz; 13 Weymouth St; dm/s/d $30/50/74; @) A big old house with gloriously high ceilings, Seaspray has had a recent makeover inside but remains relaxed and affordable, with well-chosen retro and antique furniture. Fresh and arty, it's a rare bunk-free backpackers with no TV (conversation encouraged). Closed June and July.

Arcadia Lodge B&B, HOSTEL $
(☎06-769 9100; www.arcadialodge.net; 52 Young St; dm/d/f incl breakfast $35/90/150;) A former rest home tacked onto a big old lemon-coloured villa (built in 1904 for the local newspaper editor), Arcadia is a homey B&B with a lovely breakfast room, genteel lounge, spa, barbecue, and a superb timber-ceilinged family room upstairs with sea views.

Ariki Backpackers HOSTEL $
(☎06-769 5020; www.arikibackpackers.com; cnr Ariki & Brougham Sts; dm $25-30, d $60-90; @) Upstairs in the old Royal Hotel (Queen Liz stayed here once!), Ariki offers downtown hostelling with funky carpets, a roomy lounge area with retro couches, and fantastic roof terrace looking across the park to Puke Ariki. Most rooms have their own shower and toilet.

Belt Road Holiday Park HOLIDAY PARK $
(☎06-758 0228, 0800 804 204; www.beltroad.co.nz; 2 Belt Rd; sites from $18, cabins $65-125; @) This environmentally attuned, pohutukawa-covered holiday park sits atop a bluff overlooking the increasingly interesting Lee Breakwater area, about a 10-minute walk from town. The half-dozen best cabins have million-dollar views!

Issey Manor BOUTIQUE HOTEL $$
(☎06-758 2375; www.isseymanor.co.nz; 32 Carrington St; d $150-210) Friendly Issey is hard to miss(ey): two conjoined Victorian timber houses (1875 and 1910) painted with startling panels of white, orange and black. Inside are four stylish units (two with spa), a guest kitchen, and far more designer touches than you'd expect at these prices. Fab!

Cottage Mews Motel MOTEL $$
(☎06-758 0403; www.cottagemews.net.nz; 50 Lemon St; s/d from $115/125;) A small, modest motel where you'll feel like family, rather than a guest. The well-kept rooms have interesting layouts, there's a lawn out the front instead of a car park, and you can pop next door to the co-owned Shoestring Backpackers and remember how travelling was before your career took off.

Shoestring Backpackers HOSTEL $
(☎06-758 0404; www.shoestring.co.nz; 48 Lemon St; dm/s/d/tr $30/58/78/93; @) Inside a labyrinthine 1920s heritage building with stripy wallpaper and fancy timberwork, this isn't the fanciest option but it's well maintained and brimming with character. The upstairs rooms are the pick: secluded, quiet and catching the morning sun. Out the back is a deck and barbecue.

Bella Vista MOTEL $$
(☎0800 235 528, 06-769 5932; www.staybellavista.co.nz; 32 Queen St; d $125-165;) A dependable, vaguely Spanish-looking option right in the centre of town. Basic rooms have toast-making facilities only; fancier rooms have full kitchenettes. Bonuses such as fair-trade plunger coffee and free bicycles abound.

Egmont Eco Lodge HOSTEL $
(☎06-753 5720; www.yha.co.nz; 12 Clawton St; dm/d from $29/74; @) An immaculate YHA in a glade with chirping birds and a chuckling creek (with eels!). Mixed dorms in the main lodge; smaller pinewood cabins down below

(sleeping four). It's a hike uphill from town, but the prospect of free nightly Egmont cake will put a spring in your step. A Mt Taranaki shuttle is available.

Nice Hotel BOUTIQUE HOTEL $$$
(06-758 6423; www.nicehotel.co.nz; 71 Brougham St; d/ste from $250/300;) This hotel is high class from top to tail; 'nice' is the understatement of the decade. The seven rooms feature luxury furnishings, designer bathrooms, imported wallpapers and select *objets d'art*. There's also a classy in-house restaurant, free bikes, and four self-contained suites next door.

New Plymouth Top 10 Holiday Park HOLIDAY PARK $
(06-758 2566, 0800 758 256; www.nptop10.co.nz; 29 Princes St; sites/cabins from $19/75, units $85-180; @) Sequestered in Fitzroy, 3.5km east of town and a seven-minute walk to the beach, this quaint, family-run Top 10 feels a bit like a school camp, with a dinky little row of units, a life-sized chess set, trampoline, laundry and spacious kitchen.

Carrington Motel MOTEL $$
(06-757 9431; www.carringtonmotel.co.nz; 61 Carrington St; s/d/f $95/110/165) Sixteen old but tidy units close to Pukekura Park and a 10-minute walk to town. It's very family friendly and great value (especially in winter), but noisy when the hoons careen up Carrington St. Wildly eclectic furnishings and tsunami-like showers.

BK's Egmont Motor Lodge MOTEL $$
(0800 115 033, 06-758 5216; www.egmontmotorlodge.co.nz; 115 Coronation Ave; d $125-190;) Opposite the racecourse, corporate BK's has ground-floor units and oceans of parking. Rooms are smart, comfortable and clean, and the managers (travellers too) readily share a laugh with the cleaners (a good sign). Free wi-fi and DVDs.

Waterfront HOTEL $$$
(06-769 5301; www.waterfront.co.nz; 1 Egmont St; r $190-550; @) Sleek and snazzy, the Waterfront is *the* place to stay, particularly if the boss is paying. The minimalist studios are pretty flash, while the penthouses steal the show with big TVs and little balconies. It's got terrific views from some – but not all – rooms, but certainly from the curvy-fronted bar and restaurant.

Sunflower Lodge HOSTEL $
(0800 422 257, 06-759 0050; www.sunflowerlodge.co.nz; 33 Timandra St; dm/s/d/tr $28/50/70/85; @) Down a steep driveway a few minutes' drive south of town, Sunflower does its best to transcend its mid-'80s rest-home origins, and (with the exception of some relentless timber panelling) succeeds. Bonuses such as quality mattresses, free local calls and a heavy-duty kitchen help the cause. Weekly rates available.

Eating

TOP CHOICE **Arborio** MEDITERRANEAN $$
(www.arborio.co.nz; Puke Ariki, 1 Ariki St; mains $13-34; breakfast, lunch & dinner) Despite looking like a cheese grater, Arborio, in the Puke Ariki building, is the star of New Plymouth's local food show. It's airy, arty and modern, with sea views and faultless service. The Med-influenced menu ranges from an awesome Moroccan lamb pizza to pastas, risottos and barbecued chilli squid with lychee-and-cucumber noodle salad. Cocktails and NZ wines also available.

Frederic's TAPAS $$
(www.frederics.co.nz; 34 Egmont St; plates $10-19, mains $20-25; 2pm-late Mon-Thu, 11am-late Fri-Sun) Freddy's is a fab gastro-bar with quirky interior design (rusty medieval chandeliers, peacock-feather wallpaper, religious icon paintings), serving generous share plates. Order some meatballs with bell-pepper sauce, or some green-lipped mussels with coconut cream, chilli and coriander to go with your beer.

Elixir CAFE $$
(www.elixircafe.co.nz; 117 Devon St E; brunch $7-18, dinner $18-31; 7am-4.30pm Mon, 7am-late Tue-Sat, 8am-4pm Sun) Behind a weird louvered wall facing onto Devon St, Elixir fosters an American-diner vibe, serving up everything from coffee, cake, bagels and eggs on toast, through to more innovative evening fare. Below a wall of rock posters, sexy staff give the coffee machine a serious work-out.

Bach on Breakwater CAFE, RESTAURANT $$
(06-769 6967; www.bachonbreakwater.co.nz; Ocean View Pde; brunch $10-22, dinner $27-38; 9.30am-10pm Wed-Sun;) Constructed from weighty recycled timbers, this cool cafe-bistro in the emerging Lee Breakwater precinct looks like an old sea chest washed up after a storm. Expect plenty of seafood and

steak, plus Asian- and Middle Eastern–influenced delights (curries, wontons, felafels) and killer coffee. The seafood chowder is a real winter warmer.

Chaos CAFE $

(chaoscafe@xtra.co.nz; 36 Brougham St; meals $6-14; breakfast & lunch;) Not so much chaotic as endearingly boho, Chaos is a dependable spot for a coffee and a zingy breakfast. Beans with bacon, avocado and sour cream, background jazz, smiley staff and arty interior design – hard to beat! Plenty of vegetarian and gluten-free options, too.

IndiaToday INDIAN $$

(06-758 4634; 40 Devon St E; mains $17-19; lunch & dinner;) A sumptuous gold-walled room draped with bolts of silk, IndiaToday wafts with spicy aromas and snaky tabla tunes enticing you in off the street. Dapper waiters, subcontinentally perfect in gold tunics and black pants, serve up classic and creative curries. Takeaway lunch specials from $10.

Laughing Buddha CHINESE $$

(06-759 2065; laughingbuddha@xtra.co.nz; cnr Devon St E & Currie St; mains $16-29; dinner Tue-Sat) Red-glowing windows and a rather menacing-looking Buddha sign suggest 'nightclub'...but a wander upstairs delivers you instead to New Plymouth's best Chinese restaurant. Load up on entree plates ($4 to $8; try the steamed pork buns), or order a steaming main course (the Cantonese roast duck with plum sauce is magic). Great for groups.

Andre's Pies & Patisserie BAKERY $

(44 Leach St; pies $4-8; 6am-3.30pm Mon-Fri) Expanding waistlines since 1972, this is an easy pull-over off the main road through town. Hefty pies, buns, doughnuts and sandwiches and calorific slabs of cake.

Portofino ITALIAN $$

(06-757 8686; www.portofino.co.nz; 14 Gill St; mains $19-60; 5pm-late) This discreet little family-run eatery has been here for years, serving old-fashioned Italian pasta and pizza just like nonna used to make. The rigatoni Portofino is a knock out (spinach, fetta, garlic and sun-dried tomatoes).

Petit Paris FRENCH $

(www.petitparis.co.nz; 34 Currie St; lunch $8-15; 7.30am-4pm) Ooh-la-la: lashings of buttery treats! Flying the tricolore with pride, Petit Paris is a boulangerie and patisserie turning out crispy baguettes and *tart au citron* (lemon tart), or an omelette or croque monsieur for lunch.

Empire Tea & Coffee CAFE $

(112 Devon St W; lunch $7-12; 7.30am-4pm Mon-Fri, 9am-2pm Sat) A perfectly evolved Kiwi tearoom with china plates nailed to the walls and a sunny courtyard. Tasty sandwiches, salads, lasagne and filos, plus delectable cakes and quivering slices of lime-topped custard to finish.

André L'Escargot FRENCH $$$

(06-758 4812; www.andres.co.nz; 37 Brougham St; mains $35-37; dinner Mon-Sat, lunch by appointment) Audaciously serving snails in the 'naki since 1976, we doff our beret to the man who has no doubt raised the bar and kept it there. All classic French fare, indulgent and largely gout-inducing, plus killer cocktails. 'Casual elegance' is the catch-cry here.

Sandwich Extreme SANDWICHES $

(06-759 6999; 52 Devon St E; meals $8-14; 8am-4pm Mon-Fri, 9am-3pm Sat) A buzzy spot for a toastie, sandwich, baked spud, coffee, salad, bagel or slice of cake, served fresh and fast by friendly staff.

Fresha SELF-CATERING $

(www.fresha.net.nz; cnr Devon & Morley Sts; snacks $3-15; 9am-6pm Mon-Fri, 9am-5pm Sat;) A drool-worthy emporium for picnic-basket essentials: meats, wines, olive oil, relish, fruit and veg, cheeses, jams and prepackaged meals (try the fish pie). There's an excellent cafe here too.

Pak 'n Save SUPERMARKET $

(www.paknsave.co.nz; 53 Leach St; 8am-11pm) Just east of downtown NP.

Drinking & Entertainment

Arthouse Cinema CINEMA

(www.arthousecinema.co.nz; 73a Devon St W; adult/child from $12/9; 11.30am-11pm) Run by a nonprofit private trust, this groovy cinema, found up a mirror-clad stairwell (this has to be an old nightclub, doesn't it?), screens the arty and the interesting. Beanbags, food platters and beer complete the picture.

Crowded House BAR

(www.crowdedhouse.co.nz; 93 Devon St E; 10am-late) A sporty hive of boozy activity with pool tables (in good nick), restaurant (fries with everything) and big-screen TVs. No sign of Neil Finn...

The Basement LIVE MUSIC
(www.myspace.com/thebasementnp; cnr Devon St W & Egmont St; admission free-$10; ⊙varies with gigs) Underneath a regulation Irish pub, the grungy Basement is the best place in town for up-and-coming live acts, broadly sheltering under a rock, metal and punk umbrella.

Matinee BAR
(matinee@xtra.co.nz; 69 Devon St W; ⊙9.30am-late Mon-Sat) A good option (one of the only ones, actually) for those who prefer top shelf to Tui, and electronica to '80s rock. Inside a former theatre, the design is all mirrors, silk drapes and art-nouveau wallpaper; the tables outside afford puffing and people-watching. Jazz Fridays; DJs Saturdays.

TSB Showplace PERFORMING ARTS
(☎06-759 0021; 92 Devon St W; ⊙box office 9am-5pm Mon-Fri, 10am-1pm Sat) Housed in an old opera house, the three-venue Showplace stages a variety of big performances (Russian Ballet, Pam Ayers). For online bookings go to Ticketek (www.ticketek.co.nz) or Ticket Direct (www.ticketdirect.co.nz).

Event Cinemas CINEMA
(www.eventcinemas.co.nz; 119 Devon St E; tickets adult/child $13.50/8.50; ⊙10am-11pm) Mainstream main street megaplex, the carpet a sea of popcorn.

Information

Department of Conservation (DOC; ☎06-759 0350; www.doc.govt.nz; 55a Rimu St; ⊙8am-4.30pm Mon-Fri)

New Plymouth i-SITE (☎06-759 6060, 0800 639 759; www.visitnewplymouthnz.co.nz; Puke Ariki, 1 Ariki St; ⊙9am-6pm Mon, Tue, Thu & Fri, 9am-9pm Wed, 9am-5pm Sat & Sun) In the Puke Ariki building, with a fantastic interactive tourist-info database.

Phoenix Urgent Doctors (☎06-759 4295; npdocs@clear.net.nz; 95 Vivian St; ⊙8.30am-8pm) Doctors available for urgent stuff (not blisters).

Post Office (21 Currie St) Foreign exchange available.

Taranaki Base Hospital (☎06-753 6139; www.tdhb.org.nz; David St; ⊙24hr) Accident and emergency.

Getting There & Away

Air

New Plymouth Airport (☎06-755 2250; www.newplymouthairport.com; Airport Dr) is 11km east of the centre off SH3. **Scott's Airport Shuttle** (☎06-769 5974, 0800 373 001; www.npairportshuttle.co.nz; adult from $25) operates a door-to-door shuttle to/from the airport.

Air New Zealand (☎0800 737 000, 06-757 3300; www.airnewzealand.co.nz; 12 Devon St E; ⊙9am-5pm Mon-Wed & Fri, 9.30am-5pm Thu) has daily direct flights to/from Auckland, Wellington and Christchurch, with onward connections.

Bus

The bus centre (p233) is on the corner of Egmont and Ariki Sts.

InterCity (☎09-583 5780; www.intercity.co.nz) services numerous destinations:

DESTINATION	PRICE	DURATION	FREQUENCY
Auckland	$70	6¼hr	4 daily
Hamilton	$58	4hr	4 daily
Palmerston North	$30	4hr	2 daily
Wellington	$41	7hr	2 daily
Whanganui	$38	3hr	2 daily

Naked Bus (☎0900 625 33; www.nakedbus.com) services run to the following destinations (among many others). Book in advance for big savings.

DESTINATION	PRICE	DURATION	FREQUENCY
Auckland	$30	6½hr	1 daily
Hamilton	$27	4hr	1 daily
Palmerston North	$20	3½hr	1 daily
Wellington	$26	6¼hr	1 daily
Whanganui	$18	2½hr	1 daily

The **Dalroy Express** (☎06-759 0197; www.dalroytours.co.nz) bus runs daily to/from Auckland ($60, six hours) via Hamilton ($41, four hours), and extending south to Hawera ($20, 45 minutes).

Getting Around

Citylink (☎0800 872 287; www.taranakibus.info; adult/child $3.50/2) services run Monday to Friday around town, as well as north to Waitara and south to Oakura. Buses depart the bus centre.

Cycle Inn Bike Hire (☎06-758 7418; www.cycleinn.co.nz; 133 Devon St E; per half-/full day $10/15; ⊙8.30am-5pm Mon-Fri, 9am-4pm Sat, 10.30am-2pm Sun) rents out bicycles, as does **Happy Chaddy's Charters** (☎06-758 9133; www.windwand.co.nz/chaddiescharters; Ocean View Pde; per 30min $10).

For cheap car hire, try **Rent-a-Dent** (☎06-757 5362, 0800 736 823; www.newplymouthcarrentals.co.nz; 592 Devon St E); for a cab call **Energy City Cabs** (☎06-757 5580).

Around New Plymouth

SOUTH OF TOWN

FREE **Pukeiti Rhododendron Garden** GARDENS
(www.pukeiti.org.nz; 2290 Carrington Rd; ⏲9am-5pm) This 4-sq-km garden, 20km south of New Plymouth, is home to a masses of rhododendrons and azaleas. The flowers bloom between September and November, but it's worth a visit any time. The drive here passes between the Pouakai and Kaitake Ranges, both part of Egmont National Park. The **Gatehouse Café** (2290 Carrington Rd; meals $7-18; ⏲10am-4pm) is here too.

FREE **Tupare** HISTORIC BUILDING, GARDENS
(www.tupare.info; 487 Mangorei Rd; ⏲9am-5pm, tours 11am Fri-Mon Oct-Mar) Tupare is a Tudor-style house designed by the renowned architect James Chapman-Taylor. It's as pretty as a picture, but the highlight of this 7km trip south of town will likely be the rambling 3.6 hectare garden surrounding it. Bluebells and birdsong under the boughs... picnic paradise.

Hurworth Cottage HISTORIC BUILDING
(www.historic.org.nz; 906 Carrington Rd; adult/child/family $5/2/10; ⏲11am-3pm Sat & Sun) This 1856 cottage, 8km south of New Plymouth, was built by four-time NZ prime minister Harry Atkinson. The cottage is the sole survivor of a settlement abandoned at the start of the Taranaki Land Wars: a rare window into the lives of early settlers.

Taranaki Aviation, Transport & Technology Museum MUSEUM
(http://tatatm.tripod.com/museum; cnr SH3 & Kent Rd; adult/child/family $7/2/16; ⏲10am-4.30pm Sat & Sun) Around 9.5km south of New Plymouth is this roadside museum, with ramshackle displays of old planes, trains, automobiles and general household miscellany. Ask to see the stuff made by the amazing bee guy (hexagons ahoy!).

NORTH VIA SH3

Heading north from New Plymouth along SH3 are various seaward turn-offs to high sand dunes and surf beaches. **Urenui**, 16km past Waitara, is a summer hot spot.

About 5km past Urenui you'll find arguably the highlight of North Taranaki – **Mike's Organic Brewery** (☎06-752 3676; www.organicbeer.co.nz; 487 Mokau Rd; tastings/tours $5/10; ⏲10am-6pm) – which offers tours (book ahead), takeaways, tastings of the legendary Mike's Pale Ale (the pilsener and lager are ace, too), and an Oktoberfest party every (you guessed it) October. A little further on is the turn-off to Pukearuhe and White Cliffs, huge precipices resembling their Dover namesakes. From Pukearuhe boat ramp you can tackle the **White Cliffs Walkway**, a seven-hour walk (one-way) with mesmerising views of the coast and mountains (Taranaki and Ruapehu).

Continuing north towards Mokau, stop at the **Three Sisters** rock formation signposted just south of the Tongaporutu Bridge – you can traverse the shore at low tide. Two sisters stand somewhat forlornly off the coast; their other sister collapsed in a heap 10 years ago, but check the progress of a new sis emerging from the eroding cliffs.

Mt Taranaki (Egmont National Park)

A classic 2518m volcanic cone dominating the landscape, Mt Taranaki is a magnet to all who catch his eye. Geologically, Taranaki is the youngest of three large volcanoes – Kaitake and Pouakai are the others – which stand along the same fault line. With the last eruption over 350 years ago, experts say that the mountain is overdue for another go. But don't let that put you off – this mountain is an absolute beauty and the highlight of any visit to the region.

History

According to Maori legend, Taranaki belonged to a tribe of volcanoes in the middle of the North Island. However, he was forced to depart rather hurriedly when he was caught with Pihanga, the beautiful volcano near Lake Taupo and the lover of Mt Tongariro. As he fled south (some say in disgrace; others say to keep the peace), Taranaki gouged out a wide scar in the earth (now the Whanganui River) and finally settled in the west in his current position. He remains here in majestic isolation, hiding his face behind a cloud of tears.

It was Captain Cook who named the mountain Egmont, after the Earl he sought to flatter at that particular moment. Egmont National Park was created in 1900, making it NZ's second oldest. Mt Taranaki eventually reclaimed its name, although the name Egmont has stuck like, well, egg. The mountain starred as Mt Fuji in *The Last Samurai* (2003), the production of which caused near-hysteria in the locals, especially when Tom Cruise came to town.

Activities

Tramping

Due to its accessibility, Mt Taranaki ranks as the 'most climbed' mountain in NZ. Nevertheless, tramping on this mountain is dangerous and should not be undertaken lightly. It's *crucial* to get advice before departing and to leave your intentions with a DOC visitor centre or i-SITE.

Most walks are accessible from North Egmont, Dawson Falls or East Egmont. Check out DOC's pamphlet *Short Walks in Egmont National Park* ($1.50), and the free *Taranaki: A Walker's Guide* booklet for more info.

From North Egmont, the main walk is the scenic **Pouakai Circuit**, a two- to three-day, 25km loop through alpine, swamp and tussock areas with awesome mountain views. Short, easy walks from here include the **Ngatoro Loop Track** (one hour), **Veronica Loop** (two hours) and **Connett Loop** (40 minutes return). The **Summit Track** also starts from North Egmont. It's a 14km poled route taking eight to 10 hours return, and should not be attempted by inexperienced people, especially in icy conditions and snow.

East Egmont has **Potaema Track** (30 minutes return) and **East Egmont Lookout** (30 minutes return); a longer walk is the steep **Enchanted Track** (two to three hours return).

At Dawson Falls you can do several short walks including **Wilkies Pools Loop** (one hour return) or the excellent but challenging **Fanthams Peak Return** (five hours return), which is snowed-in during winter. The **Kapuni Loop Track** (one-hour loop) runs to the impressive 18m **Dawson Falls** themselves. You can also see the falls on a 20-minute return walk to a viewpoint, starting 400m down the road from the visitor centre.

The difficult 55km **Around-the-Mountain Circuit** takes three to five days and is for experienced trampers only. There are a number of huts en route, tickets for which should be purchased in advance.

The **York Loop Track** (three hours), accessible from York Rd north of Stratford, is a fascinating walk following part of a disused railway line.

DECEPTIVE MOUNTAIN

Mt Taranaki might look like an easy peak to bag, but this cute cone has claimed more than 60 lives. The mountain microclimate changes fast: from summery to white-out conditions almost in an instant. There are also precipitous bluffs and steep icy slopes.

There are plenty of short walks here, safe for much of the year, but for adventurous trampers January to March is the best time to go. Take a detailed topographic map (the Topo50 1:50,000 *Mt Taranaki or Mt Egmont* map is good) and consult a DOC officer for current conditions. You *must* also register your tramping intentions with the DOC visitor centre or i-SITE.

You can tramp without a guide from February to March when snowfalls are low, but at other times inexperienced climbers can check with DOC for details of local clubs and guides. It costs around $300 per day to hire a guide.

Reliable operators include **Adventure Dynamics** (06-751 3589; www.adventuredynamics.co.nz) and **Top Guides** (0800 448 433, 021 838 513; www.topguides.co.nz).

Scenic Flights

Heliview SCENIC FLIGHTS
(06-753 0123, 0800 435 426; www.heliview.co.nz; flights from $110) A 20-minute summit flight costs $200 per passenger.

New Plymouth Aero Club SCENIC FLIGHTS
(06-755 0500; www.airnewplymouth.co.nz; flights from $69) A 50-minute, fixed-wing Mt Taranaki summit buzz costs $159 per person (minimum three people).

Precision Helicopters Limited SCENIC FLIGHTS
(PHL; 06-752 3291, 0800 246 359; www.precisionhelicopters.com; flights from $120) A 50-minute, scenic mountain fly-around costs $300 per person (minimum four people).

Skiing

From Stratford take Pembroke Rd up to Stratford Plateau, from where it's a 1.5km walk to the small **Manganui Ski Area** (snow phone 06-759 1119; www.skitaranaki.co.nz). The Stratford i-SITE (p237) has daily weather and snow reports; otherwise ring the snow phone or check the webcam online.

Sleeping

Several DOC huts are scattered about the mountain, accessible by tramping tracks. Most cost $15 per night (Syme and Kahui cost $5); purchase hut tickets in advance from DOC. BYO cooking, eating and sleeping gear, and bookings are not accepted – it's first come, first served. Remember to carry out *all* your rubbish.

Alpine Lodge B&B **$$**
(06-765 6620; www.andersonsalpinelodge.co.nz; 922 Pembroke Rd; s/tw/d incl breakfast from $50/100/140; P) With picture-postcard mountain views, this lovely Swiss-style lodge is on the Stratford side of the mountain. Inside are four rooms (three with en suite) and lots of nifty timberwork; outside are billions of birds, a hot tub and some wandering black-faced sheep.

Camphouse HOSTEL **$**
(06-756 9093; www.mttaranaki.co.nz; Egmont Rd; dm/d/f $30/70/160) Bunkhouse-style accommodation behind the North Egmont visitor centre in a historic 1850 corrugated-iron building, complete with bullet holes in the walls (from shots fired at settlers by local Maori during the Taranaki Land Wars). Endless horizon views from the porch.

Mountain House LODGE **$$**
(06-765 6100; www.stratfordmountainhouse.co.nz; Pembroke Rd; r $155) This upbeat lodge, on the Stratford side of the mountain (15km from the SH3 turn-off and 3km to the Manganui ski area), has recently renovated, motel-style rooms and a European-style **restaurant/cafe** (Pembroke Rd; mains $30-35; breakfast, lunch & dinner). Dinner, bed and breakfast packages available.

Eco Inn HOSTEL **$**
(06-752 2765; www.ecoinn.co.nz; 671 Kent Rd; s/d $30/60; @) About 6.5km up the road from the turn-off at the Aviation, Transport & Technology Museum, this ecofriendly place is made from recycled timber and runs on solar, wind and hydropower. There's a spa and pool table, too. Good for groups.

Rahiri Cottage B&B **$$**
(06-756-9093; www.mttaranaki.co.nz; Egmont Rd; d with/without breakfast $195/145, whole cottage $225, extra person $45) Right on the edge of Egmont National Park on the way to North Egmont, this 1929 clinker-brick cottage was once the park tollgate (it once cost two shillings and six pence to drive past), and today offers rustic B&B rooms in a bush setting. Sleeps five.

Konini Lodge HOSTEL **$**
(06-756 0990; www.doc.govt.nz; Upper Manaia Rd; dm adult/child $25/10) Basic bunkhouse accommodation 100m downhill from the Dawson Falls visitor centre. The six dorm rooms feed off a huge communal space and kitchen.

Missing Leg Lodge HOSTEL **$**
(06-752 2570; www.missinglegbackpackers.co.nz; 1082 Junction Rd; sites/dm/s/d from $15/27/35/64; @) This eccentric, bicycle-strewn backpackers has a strange lack of natural light – OK for sleeping! Dorm accommodation is up in the loft, plus there's a handful of shabby-chic baches outside.

Information

Dawson Falls Visitor Centre (027 443 0248; www.doc.govt.nz; Manaia Rd; daily Dec-Feb, 9am-4pm Thu-Sun Mar-Nov) On the southeastern side of the mountain, fronted by an awesome totem pole.

MetPhone (0900 999 06) Mountain weather updates.

North Egmont Visitor Centre (06-756 0990; www.doc.govt.nz; Upper Manaia Rd; 8am-4.30pm) Current and comprehensive national park info, plus a greasy-spoon cafe (meals $10 to $18).

Getting There & Away

There are three main entrance roads to Egmont National Park, all of which are well signposted and either pass by or end at a DOC visitor centre. Closest to New Plymouth is North Egmont: turn off SH3 at Egmont Village, 12km south of New Plymouth, and follow the road for 14km. From Stratford, turn off at Pembroke Rd and continue for 15km to East Egmont and the Manganui Ski Area. From the southeast, Upper Manaia Rd leads up to Dawson Falls, 23km from Stratford.

There are no public buses to the national park but numerous shuttle-bus/tour operators will gladly take you there for around $40/55 one-way/return:

Cruise NZ Tours (0800 688 687, 027 497 3908; kirkstall@xtra.co.nz) Mountain shuttle bus departing New Plymouth 7.30am for North Egmont; returns 4.30pm. Other pick-ups/drop-offs by arrangement. Tours also available.

WORTH A TRIP

FORGOTTEN WORLD HIGHWAY

The 150km road between Stratford and Taumarunui (SH43) has become known as the Forgotten World Hwy. The drive winds through hilly bush country with 11km of unsealed road, passing Maori *pa* (fortified villages), abandoned coal mines and memorials to those long gone en route. Allow four hours and plenty of stops, and fill up with petrol at either end (there's no petrol along the route itself). Pick up a pamphlet from i-SITEs or DOC visitor centres in the area.

The town of **Whangamomona** (population 170) is a highlight. This quirky village declared itself an independent republic in 1988 after disagreements with local councils. The town celebrates Republic Day in January every two years, with a military-themed extravaganza. In the middle of town is the unmissable grand old **Whangamomona Hotel** (☎06-762 5823; www.whangamomonahotel.co.nz; 6018 Forgotten World Hwy; accommodation per person incl breakfast $65, meals $10-20; ⏰11am-late), a pub offering simple accommodation and big country meals.

If you're not driving, **Eastern Taranaki Experience** (☎06-765 7482, 027 471 7136; www.eastern-taranaki.co.nz; day trips per person from $45) runs tours through the area.

Eastern Taranaki Experience (☎06-765 7482, 027 471 7136; www.eastern-taranaki.co.nz) Departs from Stratford; extra charge from New Plymouth. Tours also available.

Outdoor Gurus (☎06-758 4152, 027 270 2932; www.outdoorgurus.co.nz) Pick-up points (New Plymouth) and times to suit; gear hire available.

Taranaki Tours (☎06-757 9888, 0800 886 877; www.taranakitours.com) New Plymouth to North Egmont return. Tours also available.

Around Mt Taranaki

INGLEWOOD

POP 3090

Handy to the mountain on SH3, the little main-street town of Inglewood (www.inglewood.co.nz) is an adequate stop for supermarket supplies and a noteworthy stop for a steak-and-egg pie at **Nelsons Bakery** (☎06-756 7123; 45 Rata St; pies $3-4; ⏰ 6am-4.30pm Mon-Fri, 7am-4pm Sat). Inglewood's other shining light is the cute **Fun Ho! National Toy Museum** (☎06-756 7030; www.funhotoys.co.nz; 25 Rata St; adult/child $6/3; ⏰10am-4pm), exhibiting (and selling) old-fashioned sand-cast toys. It doubles as the local visitor information centre.

On the road into town from New Plymouth, **White Eagle Motel** (☎06-756 8252; www.whiteeaglemotel.co.nz; 87b Rata St; s/d from $90/98, extra person $20) is basic but tidy and quiet. The two-bedroom units feel bigger than they are.

Inside a fire-engine-red heritage building, jazzy **Macfarlane's Caffe** (☎06-756 6665; 1 Kelly St; brunch $9-18, dinner $23-30; ⏰9am-5pm Sun-Wed, 9am-late Thu-Sat) sells super-sized custard squares and coffee during the day and wild-boar sausages at night (among other things). The venison Taranaki Burger rules. Nearby, **Funkfish Grill** (☎06-756 7287; www.funkfishgrill.co.nz; 32 Matai St; takeaways $8-10, mains $22-38; ⏰4pm-late Tue-Thu, Sat & Sun, 3pm-late Fri) is a hip pizzeria and fish-and-chippery doing eat-in and takeaway meals, and doubles as a bar at night. Try the tempura scallops.

STRATFORD

POP 5330

Forty kilometres southeast of New Plymouth on SH3, Stratford plays up its namesake of Stratford-upon-Avon, Shakespeare's birthplace, by naming its streets after bardic characters. Stratford also claims NZ's first **glockenspiel**. Four times daily (10am, 1pm, 3pm and 7pm) this clock doth chime out Shakespeare's greatest hits with some fairly wooden performances.

Stratford i-SITE (☎06-765 6708, 0800 765 6708; www.stratfordnz.co.nz; Prospero Pl; ⏰8.30am-5pm Mon-Fri, 10am-3pm Sat & Sun) also houses the **Percy Thomson Gallery** (☎06-765 0917; www.percythomsongallery.org.nz; ⏰10.30am-4pm Mon-Fri, 10.30am-3pm Sat & Sun), a community gallery (named after the former mayor) displaying eclectic local and touring art shows.

One kilometre south of Stratford on SH3, the **Taranaki Pioneer Village** (☎06-765 5399; www.pioneervillage.co.nz; SH3; adult/child/family $10/5/20; ⏰10am-4pm) is a 4-hectare outdoor museum that houses 40 historic buildings. It's very bygone-era and more than a little spooky.

Seemingly embalmed in calamine lotion, the pretty-in-pink **Stratford Top Town Holiday Park** (☎06-765 6440; www.stratfordtoptownholidaypark.co.nz; 10 Page St; sites/dm/cabins/units from $14/22/40/90; @📶) is a trim caravan park offering one-room cabins, motel-style units and backpackers' bunks.

All stone-clad columns, jaunty roof angles, timber louvres and muted cave colours, flashy **Amity Court Motel** (☎06-765 4496; www.amitycourtmotel.co.nz; 35 Broadway N; d $120, apt $140-160; @📶) is the new kid on the Stratford block, upping the town's accommodation standings 100%.

Across the street from Stratford i-SITE is the disarmingly retro, trapped-in-a-time-warp tearoom, **Casa Pequena** (☎06-765 6680; casa@xtra.co.nz; 280 Broadway; snacks $3-5, meals $12-28; ⏲6am-4pm Mon-Fri, 7am-1.30pm Sat), serving classics such as bangers-and-mash and hot beef-and-gravy sandwiches.

Surf Highway 45

Sweeping south from New Plymouth to Hawera, the 105km-long SH45 is known as Surf Hwy 45. There are plenty of black-sand beaches dotted along the route, but don't expect to see waves crashing ashore the whole way. The drive generally just undulates through farmland – be ready to swerve for random tractors and cows. Pick up the *Surf Highway 45* brochure at visitor centres.

OAKURA

POP 1220

From New Plymouth, the first cab off the rank is laid-back Oakura, 15km southwest on SH45. Its broad sweep of beach is hailed by waxheads for its right-hander breaks, but it's also great for families (take sandals – that black sand scorches feet). A surf shop on the main road, **Vertigo** (☎06-752 7363; www.vertigosurf.com; 2hr lessons $75; ⏲9am-5pm Mon-Fri, 10am-4pm Sat), runs surf lessons. See also Tarawave Surf School (p228).

Sleeping & Eating

TOP CHOICE **Ahu Ahu Beach Villas** BOUTIQUE HOTEL $$$

(☎06-752 7370; www.ahu.co.nz; 341 Lower Ahu Ahu Rd; d from $210; 📶) Pricey, but pretty amazing. Set on a knoll overlooking the wide ocean, these luxury, architect-designed villas are superbly eccentric, with huge recycled timbers, bottles cast into walls, lichen-covered French tile roofs and polished-concrete floors with inlaid paua. A new lodge addition sleeps four. Even rock stars stay here!

PARIHAKA

From the mid-1860s Parihaka, a small Maori settlement east of SH45 near Pungarehu, became the centre of a peaceful resistance movement, one that involved not only other Taranaki tribes, but Maori from around the country. Its leaders, Te Whiti-o-Rongomai and Tohu Kakahi, were of both Taranaki and Te Ati Awa descent.

After the Land Wars, confiscation of tribal lands was the central problem faced by Taranaki Maori, and under Te Whiti's leadership a new approach to this issue was developed: resisting European settlement through nonviolent methods.

When the government started surveying confiscated land on the Waimate plain in 1879, unarmed followers of Te Whiti, wearing the movement's iconic white feather in their hair and in good humour, obstructed development by ploughing troughs across roads, erecting random fences and pulling survey pegs. Many were arrested and held without trial on the South Island, but the protests continued and intensified. Finally, in November 1881 the government sent a force of over 1500 troops to Parihaka. Its inhabitants were arrested or driven away, and the village was later demolished. Te Whiti and Tohu were arrested and imprisoned until 1883. In their absence Parihaka was rebuilt and the ploughing campaigns continued into the 1890s.

In 2006 the NZ government issued a formal apology and financial compensation to the tribes affected by the invasion and confiscation of Parihaka lands.

Te Whiti's spirit lives on at Parihaka, with annual meetings of his descendants and a public music-and-arts Parihaka International Peace Festival held early each year. Parihaka is open to the public on the 18th and 19th of each month. For more info see www.parihaka.com.

Wave Haven HOSTEL $
(☎06-752 7800; www.thewavehaven.co.nz; cnr Lower Ahu Ahu Rd & SH45; dm/s/d $25/50/60; @) A surfy backpackers close to the big breaks, this colonial charmer has a coffee machine, a large deck to chill out on, and surfboards and empty wine bottles strewn about the place.

Oakura Beach Holiday Park HOLIDAY PARK $
(☎06-752 7861; www.oakurabeach.com; 2 Jans Tce; sites from $18, cabins $70-140; @) Squeezed between the cliffs and the sea, this classic beachside park caters best to caravans but has simple cabins and well-placed spots to pitch a tent (absolute beachfront!).

Oakura Beach Motel MOTEL $$
(☎06-752 7680; www.oakurabeachmotel.co.nz; 53 Wairau Rd; d from $115;) A very quiet, seven-unit motel set back from the main road, just three minutes' walk to the beach. It's a '70s number, but the Scottish owners keep things shipshape, and there are 300 DVDs to choose from!

Carriage Café CAFE $
(1145 SH45; meals $4-14; 8am-4pm) Housed in a very slow-moving 1914 railway carriage set back from the main street, this is an unusual stop for good-value breakfast stacks, bacon-and-egg pies and cheese scones. Good coffee, too.

Snickerdoodle BAKERY $
(1151 SH45; snacks $4-7; 7am-4pm Mon-Fri, 8.30am-4pm Sat & Sun) On the main road this tiny bakery bakes daily. Swing in for a chunky cheese scone, a chicken-and-apricot quiche, some delectable pumpkin bread or a coffee.

OAKURA TO OPUNAKE

From Oakura, SH45 veers inland, with detours to sundry beaches along the way. On the highway near Okato the buttermilk-coloured, 130-year-old **Stony River Hotel** (☎06-752 4253; www.stonyriverhotel.co.nz; 2502 SH45; s/d/tr incl breakfast $80/120/180, mains $10-28.; dinner Wed-Sat) has simple country-style en suite rooms and a straight-up public bar.

Just after Warea is **Stent Rd**, a legendary shallow reef break suitable for experienced surfers (look for the painted-boulder sign: the street sign kept being stolen). Another famous spot is **Kumara Patch**, down Komene Rd west of Okato, which is a fast 150m left-hander.

Another coastward turn-off at **Pungarehu** leads 4km to **Cape Egmont Lighthouse**, a photogenic cast-iron lighthouse moved here from Mana Island near Wellington in 1881. Abel Tasman sighted this cape in 1642 and called it 'Nieuw Zeeland'. The road to Parihaka leads inland from this stretch of SH45.

OPUNAKE

POP 1500

A summer town and the surfie epicentre of the 'naki, Opunake has a sheltered family beach and plenty of challenging waves further out.

Activities

Dreamtime Surf Shop SURFING
(☎06-761 7570; cnr Tasman & Havelock Sts; surfboards/bodyboards/wetsuits per half-day $30/20/10; 9am-5pm; @) Dreamtime Surf Shop has internet access and surf-gear hire; hours can be patchy – call in advance.

Sleeping & Eating

Headlands HOTEL $$
(☎06-761 8358; www.headlands.co.nz; 4 Havelock St; d $120-250) Just 100m back from the beach, Headlands is a new(ish) operation encompassing a mod, airy **bistro** (mains $10-35; breakfast, lunch & dinner) and an upmarket, three-storey accommodation tower. The best rooms snare brilliant sunsets. B&B and DB&B packages available.

Opunake Motel & Backpackers MOTEL, HOSTEL $
(☎06-761 8330; www.opunakemotel.co.nz; 36 Heaphy Rd; dm $30, d $100-120) Opunake Motel & Backpackers is much more low-key, with old-style motels and a funky dorm lodge (a triumph in genuine retro) on the edge of some sleepy fields.

Opunake Beach Holiday Park HOLIDAY PARK $
(☎0800 758 009, 06-761 7525; www.opunakebeachnz.co.nz; Beach Rd; sites/cabins/cottages $18/68/98; @) Opunake Beach Holiday Park is a mellow spot right on the surf beach. The laugh-a-minute host will direct you to your grassy site, the big camp kitchen and the cavernous amenities block.

TOP CHOICE **Sugar Juice Café** CAFE $$
(42 Tasman St; snacks $4-10, mains $25-29; 8.30am-4pm Tue, 8.30am-late Wed-Sun) Sugar Juice Café has the best food on SH45. It's buzzy and brimming with delicious, filling things

SNELLY!

Opunake isn't just about the surf – it's also the birthplace of iconic middle-distance runner Peter Snell (b 1938), who showed his rivals a clean set of heels at the 1960 Rome and 1964 Tokyo Olympics. Old Snelly won the 800m gold in Italy, then followed up with 800m and 1500m golds in Japan. Legend! Check out his funky running statue outside the library.

(try the basil-crusted snapper or cranberry lamb shanks). Terrific coffee, salads, wraps, tarts, cakes and big brekkies too – don't pass it by. Open Mondays too in summer.

Information

Opunake Library (☎0800 111 323, 06-761 8663; opunakel@stdc.govt.nz; Tasman St; ⏰8.30am-5pm Mon-Fri, 9.30am-1pm Sat; @) The Opunake Library doubles as the local visitor information centre and has internet access.

HAWERA

POP 11,000

Don't expect much urban virtue from agricultural Hawera, the largest town in South Taranaki. Still, it's a good pit stop for supplies, to stretch your legs, or to bed down for a night. And don't miss Elvis!

Sights & Activities

TOP CHOICE KD's Elvis Presley Museum MUSEUM
(www.elvismuseum.co.nz; 51 Argyle St; admission by donation; ⏰by appointment only) Elvis lives! At least he does at Kevin D Wasley's astonishing museum, which houses over 10,000 of the King's records and a mind-blowing collection of Elvis memorabilia collected over 50 years. 'Passion is an understatement', says KD. Just don't ask him about the chubby Vegas-era Elvis: his focus is squarely on the rock 'n' roll King from the '50s and '60s.

Hawera Water Tower TOWER, LOOKOUT
(vistorinfo@stdc.govt.nz; 55 High St; adult/child/family $2.50/1/6; ⏰10am-2pm) The austere Hawera Water Tower beside the i-SITE is one of the coolest things in Hawera. Grab the key from the i-SITE, ascend the 215 steps, then scan the horizon for signs of life (you can see the coast and Mt Taranaki on a clear day).

Tawhiti Museum MUSEUM
(www.tawhitimuseum.co.nz; 401 Ohangai Rd; adult/child $10/3; ⏰10am-4pm Fri-Mon Feb-Apr & Sep-Dec, Sun only Jun-Aug, daily Jan) The excellent Tawhiti Museum houses a collection of exhibits, dioramas and creepily lifelike human figures modelled on people from the region. A large collection of tractors pays homage to rural heritage; there's also a bush railway and 'Traders & Whalers' boat ride here (extra charges for both). It's near the corner of Tawhiti Rd, 4km north of town.

Sleeping & Eating

Hawera Central Motor Lodge MOTEL $$
(☎06-278 8831; www.haweracentralmotorlodge.co.nz; 53 Princes St; d $135-170; 📶) The pick of the town's motels (better than any of those along South Rd), the shiny Hawera Central does things with style: grey-and-eucalypt colour scheme, frameless-glass showers, big flat-screen TVs, good security, DVD players, free movie library... Nice one!

Wheatly Downs Farmstay FARMSTAY $
(☎06-278 6523; www.mttaranaki.co.nz; 484 Ararata Rd; sites from $20, dm/s & tw $30/70, d with/without bathroom $115/70; @) Set in a rural idyll, this heritage building is a classic, with its clunky wooden floors and no-nonsense fittings. Host Gary is an affable bloke, and might show you his special pigs. To get there, head past the turn-off to Tawhiti Museum and continue on Ararata Rd for 5.5km. Pick-ups by arrangement.

Indian Zaika INDIAN $$
(☎06-278 3198; 91 Princes St; mains $16-20; ⏰lunch Tue-Sat, dinner daily; ✎) For a fine lunch or dinner, try this spicy-smelling, black-and-white diner, serving decent curries in upbeat surrounds. The $10 takeaway lunches are a steal.

Information

South Taranaki i-SITE (☎06-278 8599; www.southtaranaki.com; 55 High St; ⏰9.30am-4pm Mon-Fri, 10am-3pm Sat & Sun) The South Taranaki low-down. Reduced winter hours.

Whanganui

POP 39,700

With rafts of casual Huck Finn sensibility, Whanganui is a raggedy historic town on the banks of the wide Whanganui River. The local arts community is thriving: old port buildings are being turned into glass-art studios, and the town centre has been rejuvenated – there are few more appealing

WHANGANUI OR WANGANUI?

Yeah, we know, it's confusing. Is there an 'h' or isn't there? Either way, the pronunciation is identical: 'wan-ga', not (as in the rest of the country) 'fan-ga'.

Everything was originally spelled Wanganui, because in the local dialect *whanga* (harbour) is pronounced 'wan-ga'. However, in 1991 the New Zealand Geographic Board officially adopted the correct Maori spelling (with an 'h') for the Whanganui River and Whanganui National Park. This was a culturally deferential decision: the Pakeha-dominated town and region retained the old spelling, while the river area – Maori territory – adopted the new.

In 2009 the Board assented that the town and region should also adopt the 'h'. This caused much community consternation, opinions on the decision split almost evenly (outspoken Mayor Michael Laws was particularly anti-'h'). Ultimately, NZ Minister for Land Information Maurice Williamson decreed that either spelling was acceptable, and that adopting the querulous 'h' is up to individual businesses or entities. A good old Kiwi compromise! Whanderful...

places to while away a sunny afternoon than beneath Victoria Ave's leafy canopy.

History

Maori settlement at Whanganui dates from around 1100. The first European on the river was Andrew Powers in 1831, but Whanganui's European settlement didn't take off until 1840 when the New Zealand Co could no longer satisfy Wellington's land demands – settlers moved here instead.

When the Maori understood that the gifts the Pakeha settlers had given them were in permanent exchange for their land, they were understandably irate, and seven years of conflict ensued. Thousands of government troops occupied the Rutland Stockade in Queens Park. Ultimately, the struggle was settled by arbitration; during the Taranaki Land Wars the Whanganui Maoris assisted the Pakeha.

Sights & Activities

Whanganui Regional Museum MUSEUM
(www.wrm.org.nz; Watt St, Queens Park; adult/child $8.50/free; ⌚10am-4.30pm) The Whanganui Regional Museum is one of NZ's better natural-history museums. Maori exhibits include the carved Te Mata o Houroa war canoe and some vicious-looking *mere* (greenstone clubs). The colonial and wildlife installations are first rate, and there's plenty of button-pushing and drawer-opening to keep the kids engaged.

FREE **Sarjeant Gallery** GALLERY
(www.sarjeant.org.nz; Queens Park; ⌚10.30am-4.30pm) The elegant neoclassical Sarjeant Gallery covers the bases from historic to contemporary with its extensive permanent art exhibition and frequent special exhibits (including glass from the annual Wanganui Festival of Glass). What a lovely place!

FREE **Whanganui Riverboat Centre** MUSEUM
(www.riverboats.co.nz; 1a Taupo Quay; ⌚10am-4pm) The historical displays are interesting, but everyone's here for the *Waimarie*, the last of the Whanganui River paddle steamers. In 1900 she was shipped from England and paddled the Whanganui until she sank ingloriously at her mooring in 1952. Submerged for 41 years, she was finally raised, restored, then relaunched on the first day of the 21st century. She now offers two-hour tours along the Whanganui.

FREE **Chronicle Glass Studio** GALLERY
(✆06-347 1921; www.chronicleglass.co.nz; 2 Rutland St; ⌚9am-5pm Mon-Fri, 10am-3pm Sat & Sun) The pick of Whanganui's many glass studios is the Chronicle Glass Studio where you can watch glass-blowers working, check out the gallery, take a weekend glass-blowing course ($375) or a one-hour 'Make a Paperweight' lesson ($100), or just hang out and warm up on a chilly afternoon.

Durie Hill Elevator TOWER
(Anzac Pde; adult/child one-way $2/1; ⌚8am-6pm Mon-Fri, 10am-5pm Sat & Sun) Across City Bridge from downtown Whanganui, this elevator was built with grand visions for Durie Hill's residential future. A tunnel burrows 213m into the hillside, from where the

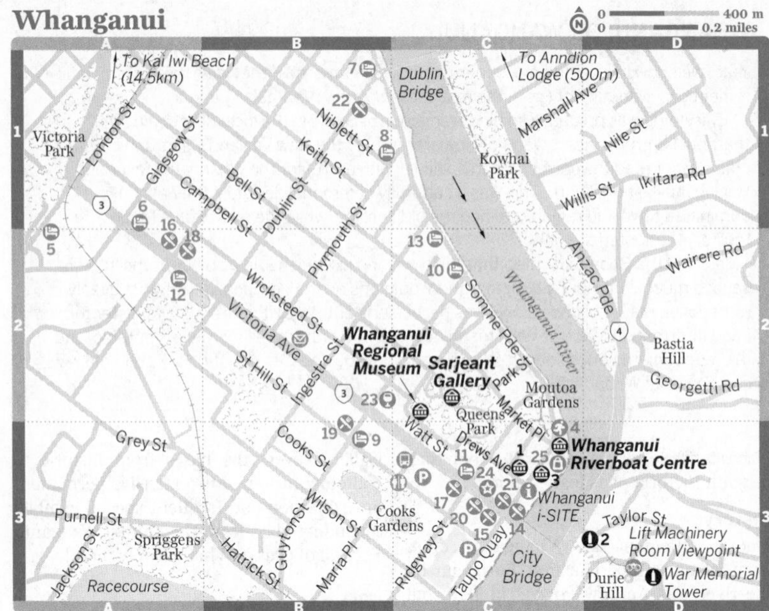

elevator rattles 65.8m to the top. At the summit you can climb the 176 steps of the **War Memorial Tower** and scan the horizon for Mt Taranaki and Mt Ruapehu.

FREE Wanganui Community Arts Centre GALLERY

(www.communityartscentre.org.nz; 19 Taupo Quay; ⏲10am-4pm Mon-Fri, 9am-4pm Sat, 1-4pm Sun) By the river's edge is the Wanganui Community Arts Centre, which exhibits mostly local artists and musters up a decidedly South Pacific vibe with glass, ceramics, jewellery, photography and painting.

Putiki Church CHURCH

(20 Anaua St; per person $2 plus deposit $20; ⏲service 9am Sun) Across the City Bridge from town and 1km towards the sea is the Putiki Church, aka St Paul's Memorial Church. It's unremarkable externally but, just like the faithful pew-fillers, it's what's inside that counts: the interior is magnificent, completely covered in Maori carvings and *tukutuku* (wall panels). Show up for Sunday service, or borrow a key from the i-SITE.

Kai Iwi Beach BEACH

Kai Iwi Beach is a wild ocean frontier, strewn with black sand and masses of broken driftwood. To get here follow Great North Rd 4km north of town, then turn left onto Rapanui Rd and head seawards for 10km.

Splash Centre SWIMMING

(www.splashcentre.co.nz; Springvale Park, London St; adult/child $4.50/3, waterslide $3; ⏲6am-8pm Mon-Fri, 8am-6pm Sat & Sun) If the sea is angry, try the Splash Centre for a safe swim.

Tours

See also Whanghanui National Park for Whanganui River canoe, kayak and jetboat tours.

Waimarie Paddle-Steamer Tours BOAT

(☎06-347 1863, 0800 783 2637; www.riverboats.co.nz; 1a Taupo Quay; adult/child/family $39/15/89; ⏲tours 11.30pm daily) Take a two-hour trip up ol' man Whanganui on the historic *Waimarie,* the last of the river paddle steamers.

Scenic Flights SCENIC FLIGHTS

(☎06-345 0914; www.wanganuiaeroclub.co.nz; Whanganui Airport, Airport Rd; flights from $50) Mile-high fixed-wing panoramas above Whanganui, Mt Ruapehu and Whanganui National Park.

Whanganui

Top Sights

Sarjeant Gallery C2
Whanganui Regional Museum C2
Whanganui Riverboat Centre C3

Sights

1 Chronicle Glass Studio C3
2 Durie Hill Elevator D3
3 Wanganui Community Arts Centre C3

Activities, Courses & Tours

4 Waimarie Paddle-Steamer Tours C3

Sleeping

5 151 on London Motel A2
6 Aotea Motor Lodge A1
7 Astral Motel B1
8 Braemar House YHA B1
9 Grand Hotel B3
10 Riverview Motel C2
11 Rutland Arms Inn C3
12 Siena Motor Lodge A2
13 Tamara Backpackers Lodge C2

Eating

14 Al Ponte C3
Ceramic .... (see 17)
15 Cracked Pepper C3
16 New World A2
17 Orange C3
18 Rapido Espresso House A2
19 Red Eye Café B3
20 Spice Guru C3
21 Stellar C3
22 Yellow House Café B1

Drinking

Grand Irish Pub .... (see 9)
23 Spirit'd B2

Entertainment

24 Embassy 3 Cinemas C3

Shopping

25 River Traders Market C3

Festivals & Events

NZ Masters Games SPORTS
(www.nzmg.com) The country's biggest multisport event (67 sports!), held in early February every odd-numbered year.

Wanganui Festival of Glass ARTS
(www.wanganuiglass.co.nz) Classy glass fest in September. Plenty of open studios, demonstrations and workshops.

Wanganui Literary Festival CULTURAL
(www.writersfest.co.nz) Thoughts, words, and thoughts about words every September.

Cemetery Circuit Motorcycle Race SPORTS
(www.cemeterycircuit.co.nz) Pandemonic Boxing Day motorcycle race around Whanganui's city streets. The southern hemisphere's version of the Isle of Man TT?

Sleeping

TOP CHOICE **Anndion Lodge** HOSTEL $
(☎06-343 3593, 0800 343 056; www.anndionlodge.co.nz; 143 Anzac Pde; s/d/f/ste from $75/88/105/130; @) Hell-bent on constantly improving and expanding their fabulous hyper-hostel, hosts Ann and Dion (Anndion, get it?) go to enormous lengths to make things homey: stereo systems, big TVs, spa, swimming pool, barbecue area, restaurant, bar, courtesy van etc. 'No is not in our vocabulary', says super-helpful Ann.

Aotea Motor Lodge MOTEL $$
(☎06-345 0303; www.aoteamotorlodge.co.nz; 390 Victoria Ave; d/apt from $150/190;) It gladdens the heart to see a job done well, and the owners of one of Whanganui's newest motels have done just that. On the upper reaches of Victoria Ave, this flashy, two-storey contemporary motel features roomy suites, lavish linen, dark-timber furniture and plenty of marble and stone – classy stuff.

Tamara Backpackers Lodge HOSTEL $
(☎06-347 6300; www.tamaralodge.com; 24 Somme Pde; dm $31, s from $54, d & tw with/without bathroom $86/72; @) Tamara is a photogenic, mazelike two-storey heritage house with a wide balcony, lofty ceilings (people weren't taller in 1904 were they?), kitchen, TV lounge, free bikes and a leafy, hammock-hung back garden. Ask for one of the beaut doubles overlooking the river.

Grand Hotel HOTEL $$
(☎0800 843 472, 06-345 0955; www.thegrandhotel.co.nz; cnr St Hill & Guyton Sts; s/d/ste from

$79/99/120;) If you can't face another soulless motel room, rooms at this stately old-school Whanganui survivor (built 1927) have a bit more personality. Singles and doubles are basic but good value; suites are spacious. The Grand Irish Pub and a restaurant are downstairs.

Braemar House YHA HOSTEL $
(06-348 2301; www.braemarhouse.co.nz; 2 Plymouth St; dm/d & tw $29/70, guesthouse incl breakfast s/d $100/130;) Riverside Braemar brings together an 1895 Victorian B&B guesthouse and a reliable YHA backpackers. Centrally heated guesthouse rooms are floral and fancy; airy dorms conjure up a bit more fun out the back.

Kembali B&B B&B $$
(06-347 1727; www.bnb.co.nz/kembali.html; 26 Taranaki St, St Johns Hill; s/d incl breakfast from $80/110) Up on leafy St Johns Hill on the way to Taranaki, this home-spun B&B has two private upstairs guest rooms sleeping four, available on an exclusive-use basis. It's a sedate place overlooking some wetlands, all achirp with tuis, pukekos and native whistling frogs.

151 on London Motel MOTEL $$
(06-345 8668; www.151onlondon.co.nz; 151 London St; d & ste $110-280;) Since opening in 2009, this snappy-looking spaceship of a motel has won plenty of fans with its architectural angles, quality carpets and linen, natty lime, silver and black colour scheme and big TVs. At the top of the price tree are some excellent upstairs/downstairs apartment-style units: about as ritzy as Whanganui accommodation gets.

Siena Motor Lodge MOTEL $$
(06-345 9009, 0800 888 802; www.siena.co.nz; 335 Victoria Ave; d $130-150;) Aiming for Tuscany but hitting Taranaki, the compact rooms here are five star and spotless. Business travellers enjoy double glazing, a DVD library, heated towel rails, coffee plungers and real coffee.

Whanganui River Top 10 Holiday Park HOLIDAY PARK $
(06-343 8402, 0800 272 664; www.wrivertop10.co.nz; 460 Somme Pde; sites/cabins/units from $21/72/135;) This tidy Top 10 park sits on the Whanganui's west bank 6km north of Dublin Bridge. Facilities (including pool and jumping pillow) are prodigious. Kayak hire also available: the owners shuttle you up river then you paddle back to camp. Self-catering or dining in town is your best bet food-wise.

Avro Motel & Caravan Park HOLIDAY PARK $
(0800 367 287, 06-345 5279; www.wanganuiaccommodation.co.nz; 36 Alma Rd; sites/units from $20/85;) Avro's yellow biplane heralds the closest camping to the city centre, 1.5km west. Both powered and unpowered sites have their own freestanding bathrooms, and the camp kitchen is a wee winner. Standard motel units also available.

Riverview Motel MOTEL $$
(06-345 2888, 0800 102 001; www.wanganuimotels.co.nz; 14 Somme Pde; d $98-150;) Take your pick from one of 15 '80s-style kitchenette units in the main block or the five spiffy spa suites out the back. Nothing too flash (and the river views are mostly glimpses), but a decent central option with a charming Irish host.

Astral Motel MOTEL $$
(06-347 9063, 0800 509 063; www.astralmotel.co.nz; 46 Somme Pde; s/d/f from $85/95/110;) Astrally aligned with the very terrestrial Dublin Bridge nearby, rooms here are a bit dated and a tad noisy but are well serviced, roomy and good bang for your buck. There's also 24-hour check-in if you're rolling in off the midnight highway.

Rutland Arms Inn HOTEL $$
(06-347 7677, 0800 788 5263; www.rutlandarms.co.nz; 48 Ridgway St; ste $140-165;) Carving off a slice of the 'upmarket heritage' pie, this restored 1849 building has an old-fashioned pub downstairs with colonial-style accommodation above. Rooms have TV, phone, flowery wall friezes, double glazing and spine-straightening beds. English hunting scenes adorn the bar's beer taps.

Eating

Cracked Pepper CAFE $
(21 Victoria Ave; mains $5-18; 7am-4.30pm;) Hungry? Hungover? Hedonistic? Head straight for Cracked Pepper, the best cafe in Whanganui serving (arguably) the best eggs Benedict in NZ. Staff are spot-on, and the 1890s building is a beauty (formerly a Japanese tearoom, a menswear store and a confectioner). Great coffee and plenty of vegetarian and gluten-free options.

Stellar CAFE, BAR $$
(www.stellarwanganui.co.nz; 2 Victoria Ave; mains $15-35; 3pm-late Mon, 9am-late Tue-Sun;)

Stellar lives up to its name – a cavernous bar-cum-restaurant with a convivial family atmosphere, it's the town's pride and joy. Reclining contentedly on leather couches, locals and tourists alike sip premium lagers and feast on bar morsels, gourmet pizzas and surf 'n' turf fare. Frequent bands, DJs and quiz nights to boot.

Rapido Espresso House CAFE **$**
(rapidoltd@hotmail.com; 71 Liverpool St; snacks $3-6; 7.30am-6pm Mon-Fri, 9am-3pm Sat) If you're hungry, don't expect more than a wedge of cake, a scone or some sushi at this raffish, royal blue cafe – what you're here for is the coffee. Organic and fair-trade all the way, the brew here is the best in town.

Red Eye Café CAFE **$**
(96 Guyton St; meals $6-18; 6.30am-3.30pm Mon-Fri, 7am-10.30pm Sat;) With inexplicable familiarity (maybe it's the friendly staff), this bohemian urban cafe has colourful local art, tasty light snacks (bagels, nachos, salads) as well as more substantial meals (curries, organic chicken sandwiches). Good coffee, too.

Orange CAFE **$**
(51 Victoria Ave; meals $9-22; 7.30am-5pm Mon-Fri, 9am-5pm Sat & Sun;) Inside a gorgeous old Whanganui red-brick building, Orange is a babbling espresso bar serving gourmet burgers, big breakfasts, muffins, cakes and sandwiches (try the BLT). The outdoor tables go berserk during summer.

Ceramic CAFE, LOUNGE **$$**
(51 Victoria Ave; mains $9-22; 3pm-late Tue-Sat;) In a split-business arrangement with adjacent Orange, Ceramic takes over for the dinner shift, serving upmarket cafe food (killer quesadillas) in a low-lit, rust-coloured interior. Occasional DJs ooze tunes across the tables to cocktail-sipping seducers.

Yellow House Café CAFE **$**
(cnr Pitt & Dublin Sts; meals $6-20; 8am-4pm Tue-Sun;) Take a walk away from the main drag for funky tunes, buttermilk pancakes, local art, great omelettes and courtyard tables beneath a chunky-trunk cherry blossom tree. Actually, it's more of a taupe colour...

Spice Guru INDIAN **$$**
(06-348 4851; 23 Victoria Ave; mains $17-23; lunch Mon-Sat, dinner daily;) There are a few Indian joints in the River City (an affinity with the Ganges, perhaps?), but the Guri takes the cake for its charismatic black-and-chocolate coloured interior, attentive service and flavoursome dishes (the chicken tikka masala is great). Plenty of vego options.

Al Ponte ITALIAN **$$**
(06-345 9955; 49 Taupo Quay; mains $18-32; dinner Tue-Sun;) Al Ponte's moody riverside building has been a merchant store and a brothel, but today it's a time-and-space vortex delivering you straight to Roma. There's plenty of seafood for the *poisson*-impassioned, plus zingy pizzas (the Salcicia is a vego delight: tomato, mozzarella, zucchini, artichoke hearts and black olives); or dive into a classic *penne alla putanesca.*

New World SUPERMARKET
(www.newworld.co.nz; 374 Victoria Ave; 7am-9pm) Your best self-catering option.

Drinking

See also Rutland Arms Inn (p244), Stellar (p244) and Ceramic (p245).

Grand Irish Pub IRISH PUB
(www.thegrandhotel.co.nz; cnr St Hill & Guyton Sts; 11am-late) Siphoning into NZ's insatiable (and, it has to be said, annoying) passion for Irish pubs, the Grand Hotel's version is as good a spot as any to elbow down a few pints of Guinness on a misty river afternoon. Good pub meals too.

Spirit'd BAR
(75 Guyton St; 10am-late) Pool tables, Jack Daniels, Metallica on the jukebox and local young bucks trying to out-strut each other – just like 1989 minus the cigarettes.

Entertainment

Embassy 3 Cinemas CINEMA
(www.embassy3.co.nz; 34 Victoria Ave; tickets adult/child $12.50/8.50, Tue tickets $8; 11am-midnight) Nightly new-release blockbusters selling out faster than you can say 'bored Whanganui teenagers'.

Shopping

River Traders Market FARMERS MARKET
(www.therivertraders.co.nz; Taupo Quay; 9am-1pm Sat) The Saturday-morning River Traders Market, next to the Riverboat Centre, is crammed with local crafts and organic produce.

Information

Post Office (119 Victoria Ave)

Whanganui Hospital (☎06-348 1234; www.wdhb.org.nz; 100 Heads Rd; ⏲24hr) Accident and emergency.

Whanganui i-SITE (☎0800 926 426, 06-349 0508; www.wanganui.com; 31 Taupo Quay; ⏲8.30am-5pm Mon-Fri, 9am-3pm Sat & Sun; @📶) Tourist and DOC information in an impressive renovated riverside building (check out the old floorboards!). Internet access available.

Getting There & Away

Air

Whanganui Airport (WAG; ☎06-348 0536; www.wanganuiairport.co.nz) is 4km south of town, across the river towards the sea.

Air New Zealand (☎06-348 3500, 0800 737 000; www.airnewzealand.co.nz; 133 Victoria Ave; ⏲9am-5pm Mon-Fri) has daily direct flights to/from Auckland and Wellington, with onward connections.

Bus

InterCity (☎09-583 5780; www.intercity.co.nz) buses operate from the **Whanganui Travel Centre** (☎06-345 7100; www.tranzit.co.nz; 160 Ridgway St; ⏲8.15am-5.15pm Mon-Fri). Some destinations:

DESTINATION	PRICE	DURATION	FREQUENCY
Auckland	$83	8hr	5 daily
New Plymouth	$32	2½hr	2 daily
Palmerston North	$22	1½hr	3 daily
Taumarunui	$48	2¾hr	1 daily
Wellington	$42	4hr	3 daily

Naked Bus (☎0900 625 33; www.nakedbus.co.nz) departs from Whanganui i-SITE to most North Island centres, including the following:

DESTINATION	PRICE	DURATION	FREQUENCY
Auckland	$40	9¼hr	1 daily
Hamilton	$32	7hr	1 daily
New Plymouth	$18	2½hr	1 daily
Palmerston North	$12	1hr	1 daily
Wellington	$23	4hr	1 daily

Getting Around

Bicycle

Bike Shed (☎06-345 5500; www.bikeshed.co.nz; cnr Ridgway & St Hill Sts; ⏲8am-5.30pm Mon-Fri, 9am-2pm Sat) Hires out bikes from $35 per day, including helmet and lock.

Bus

Tranzit City Link (☎0508 800 800; www.horizons.govt.nz; tickets adult/child $2.50/1.50; ⏲7am-6pm Mon-Fri, 10.30am-5.30pm Sat) Operates four looped local bus routes departing from the Maria Pl bus stop, including routes 5 and 6 past the Whanganui River Top 10 Holiday Park in Aramoho.

Taxi

Rivercity Cabs
(☎06-345 3333, 0800 345 3333)

Wanganui Taxis
(☎06-343 5555, 0800 343 5555)

Whanganui National Park

The Whanganui River – the lifeblood of Whanganui National Park – curls 329km from its source on Mt Tongariro to the Tasman Sea. It's the longest navigable river in NZ, a fact that's been shaping its destiny for centuries. The river today conveys canoes, kayaks and jetboats, its waters shifting from deep mirror greens in summer to turbulent winter browns.

The native bush here is thick podocarp broad-leaved forest interspersed with ferns. Occasionally you'll see poplar and other introduced trees along the river, remnants of long-vanished settlements. Traces of Maori settlements also crop up here, with old *pa* (fortified village) and *kainga* (village) sites, and Hauhau *niu* (war and peace) poles at the convergence of the Whanganui and Ohura Rivers at Maraekowhai.

The impossibly scenic Whanganui River Rd, a partially unsealed river-hugging road from Whanganui to Pipiriki, makes a fabulous alternative to the faster but less magical SH4.

History

In Maori legend the Whanganui River was formed when Mt Taranaki, after brawling with Mt Tongariro over the lovely Mt Pihanga, fled the central North Island for the sea, leaving a long gouge behind him. He turned west at the coast, finally stopping at his current address. Mt Tongariro sent cool water to heal the gouge – thus the Whanganui River was born.

Kupe, the great Polynesian explorer, is believed to have travelled 20km up the Whanganui around AD 800; Maori lived here by 1100. By the time Europeans put down roots in the late 1830s, Maori settlements lined the river valley. Missionaries sailed upstream and their settlements – at Hiruharama, Ranana, Koriniti and Atene – have survived to this day.

Steamers first tackled the river in the mid-1860s, a dangerous time for Pakeha. Aligned with Taranaki Maoris, some river tribes joined the Hauhau Rebellion – a Maori movement seeking to expel settlers.

In 1886 a Whanganui company established the first commercial steamer transport service. Others soon followed, utilising the river between Whanganui and Taumarunui. Supplying river communities and linking the sea with the interior, the steamers' importance grew, particularly after 1903 when the Auckland railway reached Taumarunui from the north.

New Zealand's contemporary tourism leviathan was seeded here. Internationally advertised trips on the 'Rhine of Maoriland' became so popular that by 1905, 12,000 tourists a year were making the trip upriver from Whanganui to Pipiriki or downriver from Taumarunui. The engineering feats and skippering ability required on the river became legendary.

From 1918 land upstream of Pipiriki was granted to returning WWI soldiers. Farming here was a major challenge, with many families struggling for years to make the rugged land productive. Only a few endured into the early 1940s.

The completion of the railway from Auckland to Wellington and the improving roads ultimately signed river transport's death warrant; 1959 saw the last commercial riverboat voyage. Today, just one old-fleet vessel cruises the river – the *Waimarie*.

Whanganui National Park Area

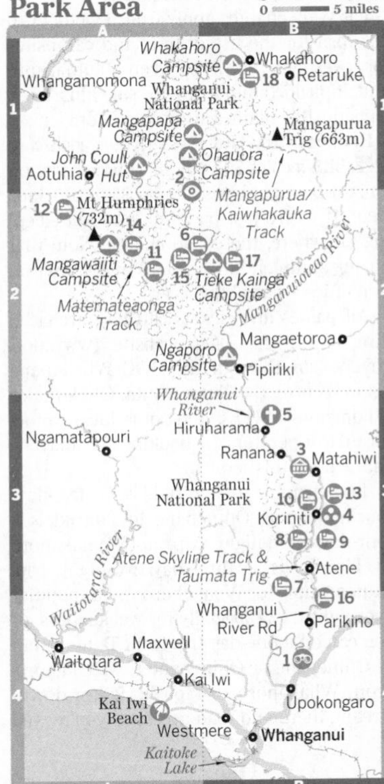

Sights

Whanagnui River Road

The scenery along the Whanganui River Rd en route to Pipiriki is camera conducive – stark, wet mountain slopes plunge into lazy jade stretches of the Whanganui River. A French Catholic mission led by Suzanne Aubert established the Daughters of Our Lady of Compassion in Jerusalem in 1892. Around a corner in the road, the picture-perfect, red-and-mustard spire of **St Joseph's Church** stands tall on a spur of land above a deep river bend.

Whanganui National Park Area

Sights

1 Aramoana Hill B4
2 Bridge to Nowhere A1
3 Kawana Flour Mill B3
4 Operiki Pa B3
5 St Joseph's Church B3

Sleeping

6 Bridge to Nowhere Lodge A2
7 Downes Hut B3
8 Flying Fox B3
9 Kohu Cottage B3
10 Koriniti Marae B3
11 Ngapurua Hut A2
12 Omaru Hut A2
13 Operiki Farmstay B3
14 Pouri Hut A2
15 Puketotara Hut A2
16 Rivertime Lodge B4
St Joseph's Church .... (see 5)
17 Tieke Kainga B2
18 Whakahoro Hut B1

LOCAL KNOWLEDGE

WHANGANUI RIVER *PETER GORDON*

Whanganui has a good black-sand surfing beach out at Castlecliff where I'm from, and a famous 'upside-down' river (as Dad calls it) where all the silt floats on the top – muddy coloured, but still gorgeous. The river is truly breathtaking and also happens to be the longest navigable river in the country. Join a guided canoe or boat trip down the river, over rapids that are challenging but not deathly, through spectacular broody lush bush and visit historical places like Jerusalem – where one of our more famous poets James K Baxter lived for a while.

Peter Gordon, chef, food writer & restaurateur

Other sights along the road include the restored 1854 **Kawana Flour Mill** near Matahiwi, **Operiki Pa** and other *pa* sites, and **Aramoana Hill**, near the southern end of the road, from where there's a panoramic view. The Maori villages of **Atene**, **Koriniti**, **Ranana** and **Hiruharama** crop up along the way – ask a local before you go sniffing around. You can wander around Koriniti Marae (p251; between the road and the river: look for the signs) unless there's a *marae* function happening. The *marae* also offers accommodation for groups. Note that the River Rd is unsealed between Ranana and 4km south of Pipiriki, although road crews are making steady progress in sealing the entire route.

Pipiriki is beside the river at the north end of Whanganui River Rd. It's a rainy river town without much going on (no shops or petrol), but was once a humming holiday hot spot serviced by river steamers and paddleboats. Seemingly cursed, the old Pipiriki Hotel, formerly a glamorous resort full of international tourists, burned to the ground twice. Recent attempts to rebuild it have stalled due to funding issues; it's been vandalised and stripped of anything of value, leaving a hollow brick husk riddled with potential. Pipiriki is the end point for canoe trips coming down the river and the launching pad for jetboat rides.

Standing in mute testimony to the optimism of the early settlers is the **Bridge to Nowhere**, built in 1936. The walking track from Mangapurua Landing (upstream from Pipiriki, accessible by jetboat) to the lonesome bridge was part of a long-lost 4.5m-wide roadway from Raetihi to the river.

Activities

Canoeing & Kayaking

The most popular stretch of river for canoeing and kayaking is downstream from Taumarunui to Pipiriki. This has been added to the NZ Great Walks system and is called the 'Whanganui Journey' (despite the fact that there's more sitting down than walking involved). It's a Grade II river – easy enough for the inexperienced, with enough moiling rapids to keep things interesting.

Great Walk charges apply from 1 October to 30 April for the use of huts and campsites for overnight stays between Taumarunui and Pipiriki (adults $10 to $31, kids free). Outside the main season you'll only need a **Backcountry Hut Pass** (1yr per adult/child $122/61, 6 months $92/46), or you can pay on a night-by-night basis (adults $5 to $15, kids free). If you're just paddling and not sleeping anywhere, there's no charge. Note that during summer, hut wardens and conservation officers patrol the river.

All passes and tickets can be purchased directly on the DOC website (www.doc.govt.nz), or through the DOC Whakapapa visitor centre, the Taumarunui, Ohakune or Whanganui i-SITEs, and some local canoe-hire/trip operators (a booking fee may be charged for this service).

Taumarunui to Pipiriki is a five-day/four-night trip, Ohinepane to Pipiriki is a four-day/three-night trip, and Whakahoro to Pipiriki is a three-day/two-night trip. Taumarunui to Whakahoro is a popular overnight trip, especially for weekenders, or you can do a one-day trip from Taumarunui to Ohinepane or Ohinepane to Whakahoro. From Whakahoro to Pipiriki, 88km downstream, there's no road access so you're wed to the river for a few days; this is the trip everyone clamours to do. Most canoeists stop at Pipiriki.

The season for canoe trips is usually from September to Easter. Up to 5000 people make the river trip each year, mostly between Christmas and the end of January. During winter the river is almost deserted – the winter currents run swift and deep, as cold weather and short days deter potential paddlers.

To hire a two-person Canadian canoe for one/three/five days costs around $80/220/300 per person not including transport (around $50 per person). A single-person kayak costs about $60 per day. Operators provide you with everything you need, including life jackets, waterproof drums (essential if you go bottom-up), and sometimes cover the mandatory DOC camping/hut fees.

GUIDED TRIPS

You can also take guided canoe or kayak trips – prices start at around $300/800 per person for a two-/five-day guided trip.

Operators from include the following; see also Jetboating for operators who also run canoe trips:

Blazing Paddles CANOEING
(☎07-895 5261, 0800 252 946; www.blazingpaddles.co.nz)

Whanganui River Canoes CANOEING
(☎06-385 4176, 0800 408 888; www.whanganuirivercanoes.co.nz)

Wades Landing Outdoors CANOEING
(☎07-895 5995, 0800 226 631; www.whanganui.co.nz)

Canoe Safaris CANOEING
(☎0800 272 335, 06-385.9237; www.canoesafaris.co.nz)

Taumarunui Canoe Hire CANOEING
(☎07-895 7483, 0800 226 6348; www.taumarunuicanoehire.co.nz)

Awa Tours CANOEING
(☎06-385 8012; www.awatours.co.nz)

Whanganui Kayak Hire KAYAKING
(☎021 133 6938; www.kayakhire.co.nz)

Yeti Tours CANOEING
(☎06-385 8197, 0800 322 388; www.canoe.co.nz)

Jetboating

Hold onto your hats – jetboat trips give you the chance to see parts of the river that would otherwise take you days to paddle through. Jetboats depart from Pipiriki and Whanganui; four-hour tours start at around $110 per person. The following operators can also provide transport to the river ends of the Matemateaonga and Mangapurua Tracks:

Spirit of the River Jet JETBOATING
(☎06-342 5572, 0800 538 8687; www.spiritoftheriverjet.co.nz)

Bridge to Nowhere Tours JETBOATING, CANOEING
(☎0800 480 308; www.bridgetonowhere.co.nz) Canoe trips also available.

Whanganui River Adventures JETBOATING, CANOEING
(☎0800 862 743; www.whanganuiriveradventures.co.nz) Canoe trips also available.

Whanganui Scenic Experience Jet JETBOATING, CANOEING
(☎06-342 5599, 0800 945 335; www.whanganuiscenicjet.com) Canoe trips also available.

Tramping

BRIDGE TO NOWHERE TRACK

The most popular track in Whanganui National Park is the 40-minute walk from Mangapurua Landing to the Bridge to Nowhere, 30km upstream from Pipiriki by jetboat. Contact jetboat operators for transport (around $100 per person one way).

TRACKS FROM ATENE

At Atene, on the Whanganui River Rd about 22km north of the SH4 junction, you can tackle the short **Atene Viewpoint Walk**, about a one-hour ascent (quicker on the way down). The track travels through native bush and farmland along a 1959 roadway built by the former Ministry of Works and Development during investigations for a Whanganui River hydro-electric scheme (a dam was proposed at Atene that would have flooded the river valley almost as far as Taumarunui). From the ridge-top there are great views across the national park.

From the Viewpoint Walk you can continue along the circular 18km **Atene Skyline Track**. The track takes six to eight hours, showcasing native forest, sandstone bluffs and the **Taumata Trig** (523m), with its broad views as far as Mt Ruapehu, Mt Taranaki and the Tasman Sea. The track

REMOTE TRACK ACCESS

The Matemateaonga and Mangapurua/Kaiwhakauka Tracks are brilliant longer tramps (DOC booklets $1, or see www.doc.govt.nz for up-to-date track info). Both are one-way tracks beginning (or ending) at remote spots on the river, so you have to organise jetboat transport to or from the river trailheads – ask any jetboat operator. Between Pipiriki and the Matemateaonga Track is around $50 per person; for the Mangapurua Track it's around $100.

ends back on the Whanganui River Rd, 2km downstream from the starting point.

MATEMATEAONGA TRACK

Three to four days from end to end, the 42km Matemateaonga Track gets kudos as one of NZ's best walks. Probably due to its remoteness, it doesn't attract the hordes of trampers that amass on NZ's more famous tracks. Penetrating deep into wild bush and hill country, it traces an old Maori track and a disused settlers' dray road between the Whanganui and Taranaki regions. It follows the crest of the Matemateaonga Range along the route of the Whakaihuwaka Rd, started in 1911 to create a more direct link from Stratford to the railway at Raetihi. WWI interrupted planning and the road was never finished.

On a clear day, a 1½-hour side trip to the top of **Mt Humphries** (730m) rewards you with sigh-inducing views all the way to Mt Taranaki and the volcanoes of Tongariro. There's a steep section between the Whanganui River (75m above sea level) and the Puketotara Hut (427m above sea level) but mostly it's easy walking. There are four DOC backcountry huts along the way: Omaru, Pouri, Ngapurua and Puketotara; hut tickets cost $15 per person per night. There's road access at the track's western end.

MANGAPURUA/KAIWHAKAUKA TRACK

The Mangapurua/Kaiwhakauka Track is a 40km trail between Whakahoro and the Mangapurua Landing, both on the Whanganui River. The track runs along the Mangapurua and Kaiwhakauka Streams (both Whanganui River tributaries). Between these valleys a side track leads to the 663m **Mangapurua Trig**, the area's highest point, from which cloudless views extend to the Tongariro and Egmont National Park volcanoes. The route also passes the Bridge to Nowhere (p248) and abandoned farming land cleared by settlers in the 20th century. Unless you're an insane tramping dynamo, walking the track takes 20 hours (three to four days). The Whakahoro Hut (p251) at the Whakahoro end of the track is the only hut, but there's plenty of good camping. There's road access to the track both at the Whakahoro end and from a side track from the end of the Ruatiti Valley–Ohura Rd (from Raetihi).

Mountain Biking

Aside from cycling down the Whanganui River Rd, the Mangapurua/Kaiwhakauka Track has recently been upgraded to form part of the Mountains to Sea Ohakune-to-Whanganui bike track, part of the **Nga Haerenga, New Zealand Cycle Trail** (www.nzcycletrail.com) project. It takes about six hours to ride along the Mangapurua Track from the Ruatiti Rd end through to the Whanganui River (where you'll need to pre-arrange a jetboat to take you downriver to Pipiriki). After rain, some sections get slippery and muddy: dismount and walk your bike across. For bike hire/track info try Bike Shed (p246) in Whanganui; for info on the track from the Ohakune end see p285.

Tours

See also Activities for info on canoe and jetboat tours on the Whanganui River.

Whanganui Tours VAN

(☎06-345 3475; www.whanganuitours.co.nz) Join the mailman on the Whanganui River Rd to Pipiriki ($63, departs 7am) with lots of social and historical commentary. Returns mid-afternoon. Ask about the option of taking the mail van to Pipiriki then cycling back down the road to Whanganui.

Whanganui River Road Tours BUS

(☎0800 201 234; www.whanganuiriverroad.com; tours per person $80) Take a five-hour minibus ride up the River Rd with lots of stops and commentary. Or, you can take an abbreviated tour up to Pipiriki then cycle back to Whanganui ($100 per person). Minimum four people on both tours.

Sleeping

WHANGANUI NATIONAL PARK

The park has a sprinkling of huts, a lodge and numerous camping grounds. Along the Taumarunui–Pipiriki section are three huts classified as Great Walks Huts during summer and Backcountry Huts in the off-season ($10 to $31 per person per night in summer; $10 to $15 off-season): **Whakahoro Hut** (free), John Coull Hut and Tieke Kainga, which has been revived as a marae (you can stay here, but full marae protocol must be observed). On the lower part of the river, Downes Hut is on the west bank, opposite Atene.

Bridge to Nowhere Lodge LODGE, HOSTEL
(☎06-385 4622, 0800 480 308; www.bridgetonowhere.co.nz; sites from $20, per adult/child self-catering $45/20, incl meals $245/75) Across the river from the Tieke Kainga *marae*, this remote lodge lies deep in the national park, 21km upriver from Pipiriki near the Matemateaonga Track. The only way to get here is by jetboat from Pipiriki or on foot. It has a licensed bar, and meals are quality home-cooked affairs. The lodge also runs jetboat, canoe and mountain-bike trips.

WHANGANUI RIVER RD

There's an informal campsite with toilets and cold water at Pipiriki, and another one (even less formal) just north of Atene.

Book the following places in advance – no one's going to turn you away, but they appreciate a bit of warning! From south to north, accommodation includes the following:

Rivertime Lodge LODGE $$
(☎06-342 5595; www.rivertimelodge.co.nz; 1569 Whanganui River Rd; d $130, extra adult/child $45/35) A rural idyll: grassy hills folding down towards the river and the intermittent bleating of sheep. Rivertime is a moss green farmhouse with three bedrooms, a barbecue, a lovely deck overlooking the river and no TV! Sleeps six.

Flying Fox LODGE, HOSTEL $$
(☎06-342 8160; www.theflyingfox.co.nz; Whanganui River Rd; sites $20, d $100-200) This eco-attuned getaway is on the riverbank across from Koriniti. You can self-cater in the Brewhouse, James K or Glory Cart (self-contained cottages), opt for B&B ($120 per person), or pitch a tent in a bush clearing. Access is by jetboat; otherwise you can park across the river from the accommodation then soar over the river on the flying fox.

Kohu Cottage RENTAL HOUSE $
(☎06-342 8178; kohu.cottage@xtra.co.nz; Whanganui River Rd; d $70) A snug little cream-coloured weatherboard cottage (100 years old!) above the road in Koriniti, sleeping three beds. There's a basic kitchen and a wood fire for chilly riverside nights.

Koriniti Marae LODGE $
(☎06-342 8198; www.koriniti.com; Koriniti Pa Rd; dm $30) This *marae* on the east bank offers dorm-style beds for pre-booked groups; offer *koha* (a donation) plus the fee. It also runs a 24-hour 'cultural experience' for groups, including a *haka* (war dance), weaving, storytelling and three meals ($190 per person).

Operiki Farmstay FARMSTAY $
(☎06-342 8159; operiki@farmside.co.nz; Whanganui River Rd; incl breakfast & dinner s/d $55/110) On a steep hillside 1.5km north of Koriniti, this is a cheery in-with-the-family farmhouse. There are scenic walks around the property, and macadamia-nut muffins come hot from the oven. The friendliest place this side of Disneyland.

St Joseph's Church HOSTEL $
(☎06-342 8190; www.compassion.org.nz; Whanganui River Rd; dm adult/child $25/15, linen $10) Taking in bedraggled travellers and offering 20 dorm-style beds and a simple kitchen, the sisters at St Joe's await to issue your deliverance – book ahead for the privilege. Moutoa Island, site of a historic 1864 battle, is just downriver.

Information

For national park information, try the affable Whanganui (p246) or Taumarunui i-SITEs, or check out www.doc.govt.nz or www.whanganuiriver.co.nz online. Otherwise, a more tangible resource is the NZ Recreational Canoeing Association's *Guide to the Whanganui River* ($10). The **Wanganui Tramping Club** (☎06-346 5597; www.wanganuitrampingclub.org.nz) puts out the quarterly *Wanganui Tramper* magazine.

There's no mobile-phone coverage along the River Rd, and no petrol or shops. There are a couple of takeaway food vans in Pipiriki open during summer, plus the casual **Matahiwi Gallery cafe** (☎06-342 8112; www.matahiwigallery.com; 3926 Whanganui River Rd; snacks $3-5; ⏲9am-3.30pm Thu-Sun) in Matahiwi (call ahead to ensure they're open).

Getting There & Away

From the north, there's road access to the Whanganui River at Taumarunui, Ohinepane and Whakahoro, though the latter is a long, remote drive on mostly unsealed roads. Roads to Whakahoro lead off from Owhango and Raurimu, both on SH4. There isn't any further road access to the river until Pipiriki.

From the south, the Whanganui River Rd veers off SH4, 14km north of Whanganui, rejoining it at Raetihi, 91km north of Whanganui. It takes about two hours to drive the 79km between Whanganui and Pipiriki. The full circle from Whanganui through Pipiriki and Raetihi and back along SH4 takes about four hours. Alternatively, take a River Rd tour from Whanganui.

Palmerston North

POP 82,400

The rich sheep- and dairy-farming Manawatu region embraces the districts of Rangitikei to the north and Horowhenua to the south. The hub of it all, on the banks of the Manawatu River, is Palmerston North, with its moderate high-rise attempts reaching up from the plains. Massey University, NZ's largest, informs the town's cultural and social structures. As a result 'Palmy' has an open-minded, rurally bookish vibe.

None of this impressed a visiting John Cleese who scoffed, 'If you ever do want to kill yourself, but lack the courage, I think a visit to Palmerston North will do the trick.' The city exacted revenge by naming a rubbish dump after him.

Sights & Activities

TOP CHOICE New Zealand Rugby Museum MUSEUM
(www.rugbymuseum.co.nz; 326 Main St; adult/child/family $12.50/5/30; ⏲10am-5pm) Fans of the oval ball holler about the New Zealand Rugby Museum, an amazing new space overflowing with rugby paraphernalia, from a 1905 All Blacks jumper to a scrum machine and the actual whistle used to start the first game of every Rugby World Cup. Of course, NZ hosted the 2011 Rugby World Cup and beat France 7-8 in the final: don't expect anyone here to stop talking about it until 2015...

FREE Te Manawa MUSEUM
(www.temanawa.co.nz; 326 Main St; ⏲10am-5pm) Te Manawa merges a museum, art gallery and science centre into one experience. Vast collections join the dots between 'life, art and mind'. The museum has a strong Maori focus, while the gallery's exhibits change frequently. Kids will get a kick out of the hands-on exhibits at the science centre. The New Zealand Rugby Museum is in the same complex.

The Square LANDMARK
(The Square) Taking the English village-green concept to a whole new level, The Square is Palmy's heart and soul. Seventeen spacey acres, with a clock tower, duck pond, Maori carvings, statues and trees of all seasonal dispositions. Locals eat lunch on the manicured lawns in the sunshine.

Lido Aquatic Centre SWIMMING
(www.lidoaquaticcentre.co.nz; 50 Park Rd; adult/child $4/3, hydroslide $5; ⏲6am-8pm Mon-Thu, 6am-9pm Fri, 8am-8pm Sat & Sun) When the summer plains bake, dive into the Lido Aquatic Centre. It's a long way from Lido Beach in Venice, but it has a 50m pool, waterslides, cafe and gym.

Tours

Feilding Saleyard Tours CULTURAL
(☎06-323 3318; www.feilding.co.nz; 10 Manchester Sq; tours $5; ⏲tours 11am Fri) Local farmers instruct you in the gentle art of selling livestock at this small town north of the city centre. Farmers market from 9am to 2pm every Friday.

Manawatu Gorge Experience Jet JETBOATING
(☎06-342 5599, 0800 945 335; www.manawatugorgejet.com; 25min tours per person $65) Jetboat tours through gorgeous Manawatu Gorge, departing Woodville Ferry Domain on SH3, 25 minutes from Palmy.

Tui Brewery Tours BREWERY
(☎06-370 6600, 0800 471 227; www.tuibrewery.co.nz; 5hr tour per person $50; ⏲noon-5pm Fri) Even if you're more of a craft-beer fan than a drinker of ubiquitous Tui, this boozy tour is a worthwhile outing. Check out the interesting brewery and museum and taste a Tui or two. Minimum numbers apply.

Festivals & Events

Festival of Cultures CULTURAL, FOOD & WINE
(www.foc.co.nz) Massive arts/culture/lifestyle festival in late March, with a food-and-craft market in the Square.

Palmerston North

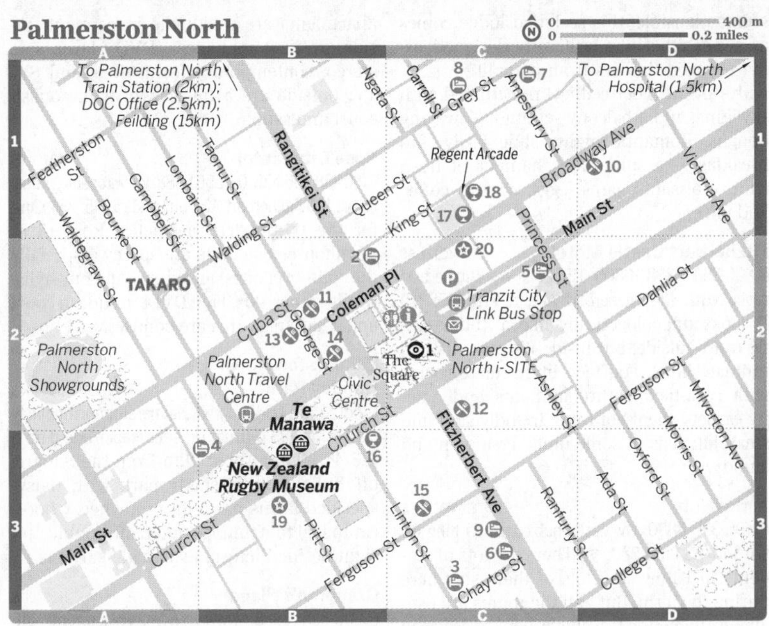

Palmerston North

Top Sights
New Zealand Rugby Museum B3
Te Manawa B3

Sights
1 The Square C2

Sleeping
2 @ the Hub B2
3 Bentleys Motor Inn C3
4 Café de Paris B3
5 Empire Hotel C2
6 Fitzherbert Castle Motel C3
7 Grandma's Place C1
8 Pepper Tree Hostel C1
9 Rose City Motel C3

Eating
10 Aqaba D1
11 Café Cuba B2
12 Halikarnas Café C2
13 Indian2nite B2
14 Moxies B2
15 Pak 'n Save C3

Drinking
16 Brewer's Apprentice B3
17 Celtic Inn C1
18 Fish C1

Entertainment
19 Centrepoint Theatre B3
CinemaGold .... (see 20)
20 Downtown Cinemas C2

Reel Earth Environmental Film Festival FILM
(www.reelearth.org.nz) Nature and environment films from across Oceania flicker onto Palmy's screens in May.

International Jazz & Blues Festival MUSIC
(www.jazzandblues.co.nz) All things jazzy, bluesy and swingin' in late May/early June, including plenty of workshops.

Manawatu Wine & Food Festival FOOD & WINE
(www.mwff.co.nz) Mid-June weekend fiesta of culinary creations and the best local drops.

Sleeping

TOP CHOICE **Plum Trees Lodge** LODGE, B&B $$
(☎06-358 7813; www.plumtreeslodge.co.nz; 97 Russell St; s/d incl breakfast from $135/150;) In a flat-grid town with more motels than

seems plausible, this secluded lodge comes as sweet relief. It's brilliantly designed using recycled timbers from demolition sites, with raked timber ceilings punctuated with skylights, and a balcony set among swaying boughs. Romantic nights slide lazily into breakfast – a sumptuous hamper of fresh fruit, croissants, jams, eggs, cheese, coffee and juice.

Fitzherbert Castle Motel MOTEL **$$**
(☎06-358 3888, 0800 115 262; www.fitzherbertcastle.co.nz; 124 Fitzherbert Ave; d $110-195; 📶) It looks unapologetically like a Tudor castle from outside, but inside it's more like an intimate hotel. Fourteen immaculate rooms with cork-tiled bathroom floors and quality carpets, plenty of trees, friendly staff and small kitchens in some units. Free wi-fi and laundry.

@ the Hub HOTEL, HOSTEL **$**
(☎06-356 8880; www.atthehub.co.nz; 10 King St; s/d $40/55, units $80; 📶) There are lots of students in Palmy, and lots of them stay here during the term. But half the rooms are usually available for travellers: book a serviced en-suite double unit with kitchenette, or a simple student shoebox (also with en suite). Great location, great value!

Pepper Tree Hostel HOSTEL **$**
(☎06-355 4054; www.peppertreehostel.co.nz; 121 Grey St; dm/s/d $28/53/70; @) Inexplicably strewn with green-painted boots, this endearing 100-year-old house is the best budget option in town. Mattresses are thick, the kitchen will never run out of spatulas, and the piano and wood fire make things feel downright homey. Doubles off the kitchen are a bit noisy – angle for one at the back.

Empire Hotel HOTEL **$**
(☎06-357 8002; www.empirehotel.co.nz; cnr Princess & Main Sts; s/d/f $80/80/140; 📶) With slicker-than-average, colonial-style pub rooms upstairs, the Empire is a solid central option. Beyond a tandem bike poised bizarrely in the stairwell, rooms have TV, bathroom and fridge. The pub downstairs gets raucous – steer for a room far from the beer cheer.

Bentleys Motor Inn MOTEL, APARTMENT **$$**
(☎06-358 7074, 0800 2368 5397; www.bentleysmotorinn.co.nz; cnr Linton & Chaytor Sts; ste $155-320) The highest peak on Palmerston North's motel range, Bentleys' five-star apartments are worth the investment. Inside are new appliances, DVD player, spa, stereo, contemporary furnishings and Sky TV; outside are a full-blown gym, squash court and sauna.

Rose City Motel MOTEL **$$**
(☎0508 356 538, 06-356 5388; www.rosecitymotel.co.nz; 120 Fitzherbert Ave; units $125-145; 📶) One for the postmodern aesthetes, Rose City's townhouse-style units are spacey (especially the split-level ones) and shipshape but stylistically rather '90s. Free DVDs, a squash court and a kids' play area are bonuses.

Palmerston North Holiday Park HOLIDAY PARK **$**
(☎06-358 0349; www.palmerstonnorthholidaypark.co.nz; 133 Dittmer Dr; sites/cabin/unit d from $16/45/80; 📶) About 2km from the Square, off Ruha St, this shady park with daisy-speckled lawns has a bit of a wheezy boot-camp feel to it, but it's quiet, affordable and right beside Victoria Esplanade gardens.

Grandma's Place HOSTEL **$**
(☎06-358 6928; www.grandmas-place.com; 146 Grey St; dm/s/d $28/52/70; 📶) Ignore the terrifying spectre of Grandma on the sign out the front – inside are tidy, old-fashioned rooms with floral wallpaper and macramé rugs. There are plenty of beds and a functional kitchen.

Café de Paris HOTEL **$**
(☎06-355 2130; www.cafedeparisinn.co.nz; 267 Main St; s/d $60/80) It ain't Montmartre, but this friendly, 1893 boozer three minutes' walk from the Square has a warren of surprisingly decent pub accommodation upstairs, all rooms with TV, en suite and eclectic furnishings. Off-street parking out the back is limited.

Eating

Moxies CAFE **$$**
(moxies@hotmail.com; 67 George St; meals $6-20; ⏰7am-5pm Mon-Sat, 7.30am-5pm Sun; 🌿) This chipper corner cafe is a real George St fixture, decked out in primary colours with big windows. Staff members are equally upbeat, the all-day menu is top value (stellar omelettes) and if you've got gluten issues, this is the place for you.

Halikarnas Café TURKISH **$$**
(15 Fitzherbert Ave; mains $16-20; ⏰lunch Tue-Fri, dinner daily) Angling for an Ali-Baba-and-the-Forty-Thieves vibe, with magic carpets, brass hookahs and funky trans-Bosphorus

beats, Halikarnas plates up generous Turkish delights, from lamb shish kebabs to felafels and kick-arse Turkish coffee. Takeaway kebabs next door.

Café Cuba CAFE **$$**
(cnr George & Cuba Sts; meals $10-30; ⏰7am-midnight; ✎) Need a sugar shot? Proceed to day-turns-to-night Café Cuba – the cakes here are for professional chocoholics only. Supreme coffees and traditional cafe fare (risottos, salads, corn fritters) also draw the crowds. Live music Friday nights.

Izakaya Yatai JAPANESE **$$**
(☎06-356 1316; www.yatai.co.nz; 316 Featherstone St; dishes $9-24; ⏰dinner Tue-Sat) Simple, fresh, authentic Japanese food cooked by Atsushi Taniyama in an unpretentious suburban house with empty sake bottles lining the window sills. Front-of-house host Barbara comes with a big personality. Set menus available.

Indian2nite INDIAN **$$**
(☎06-353 7400; www.indian2nite.com; 22 George St; mains $10-20; ⏰lunch Wed-Sat, dinner daily; ✎) A million miles from Bollywood schmaltz, this upmarket place won't break the bank. Behind George St picture windows and tucked under a curved wall-cum-ceiling, northern Indian curries are served by super-polite waiting staff. Try the *dahl makhani*.

Aqaba INTERNATIONAL **$$**
(186 Broadway Ave; meals $12-32; ⏰7.30am-late Mon-Fri, 9am-late Sat & Sun) Family-friendly cafe classics (pasta, fish and chips, soups, nachos, steaks, salads and curries) served inside a cavernous, colourful former Masonic Hall (no secret handshake required). R&B beats; Egyptian interiors.

Pak 'n Save SUPERMARKET
(www.paknsave.co.nz; 335 Ferguson St; ⏰7am-11pm) Cheap and cheerful.

Drinking

Fish COCKTAIL BAR
(Regent Arcade; ⏰4-11pm Wed, 4pm-1am Thu, 4pm-3am Fri & Sat) A progressive, stylish, Pacifically-hewn cocktail bar, the Fish has got its finger firmly on the Palmy pulse. DJs smooth over the week's problems on Friday and Saturday nights as a sexy, urbane crew sips Manhattans and Tamarillo Mules (yes, they kick).

Brewer's Apprentice PUB
(www.brewersapprentice.co.nz; 334 Church St; ⏰11am-late Mon-Fri, 10am-late Sat & Sun) What was once a grungy student pub is now a slick Monteiths-sponsored bar. Business crowds flock for lunch ($10 to $17, dinner $27 to $29), and 20-somethings fill the beer terrace after dark. Live music Friday nights.

Celtic Inn IRISH PUB
(www.celticinn.co.nz; Regent Arcade; ⏰11am-3am Mon-Sat, 4pm-11am Sun) The Celtic expertly offsets the Fish nearby with its good old-fashioned pub stuff, labourers, travellers and students bending elbows with a few tasty pints of the black stuff. Friendly staff, live music, red velvet chairs, kids darting around parents' legs – it's all here.

☆ Entertainment

CinemaGold CINEMA
(www.cinemagold.co.nz; Downtown Shopping Arcade, Broadway Ave; adult/child $16/11; ⏰10am-midnight) In the same complex as the Downtown Cinemas, CinemaGold ups the ante with plush seats and a booze licence to enhance art-house classics and limited-release screenings.

Centrepoint Theatre THEATRE
(www.centrepoint.co.nz; 280 Church St) A mainstay of the simmering Palmerston North theatre scene, Centrepoint serves up big-name professional shows, theatre sports and seasonal plays.

Downtown Cinemas CINEMA
(www.dtcinemas.co.nz; Downtown Shopping Arcade, Broadway Ave; adult/child $15.40/9.40; ⏰10am-midnight) The capacious Downtown Cinemas megaplex shows mainstream new-release flicks. All Tuesday tickets $9.40.

Information

Palmerston North i-SITE (☎0800 626 292, 06-350 1922; www.manawatunz.co.nz; The Square; ⏰9am-5pm Mon-Fri, 10am-2pm Sat & Sun; 📶) A super-helpful source of tourist information; free wi-fi throughout the Square.

Department of Conservation (DOC; ☎06-350 9700; www.doc.govt.nz; 717 Tremaine Ave; ⏰8am-4.30pm Mon-Fri) DOC information 3km north of the Square.

Palmerston North Hospital (☎06-356 9169; www.midcentraldhb.govt.nz; 50 Ruahine St; ⏰24hr) Accident and emergency assistance.

Post Office (cnr Main St & the Square)

Radius Medical, The Palms (☎06-354 7737; www.radiusmedical.co.nz; 445 Ferguson St; ⊙8am-7pm Mon-Fri, 9am-6pm Sat & Sun) Accident and emergency, plus doctors by appointment and a pharmacy.

ℹ Getting There & Away

Air

Palmerston North International Airport (PMR; ☎06-351 4415; www.pnairport.co.nz; Airport Dr) is 4km north of the town centre. Air New Zealand runs daily direct flights to Auckland, Christchurch and Wellington.

Bus

InterCity (☎09-583 5780; www.intercity.co.nz) buses operate from the **Palmerston North Travel Centre** (☎06-355 4955; cnr Main & Pitt Sts; ⊙8.45am-5pm Mon-Thu, 8.45am-7.45pm Fri, 9am-2.45pm Sat, 9am-2.45pm & 4-7.15pm Sun). Destinations include the following:

DESTINATION	PRICE	DURATION	FREQUENCY
Auckland	$70	9hr	2 daily
Napier	$34	3hr	2 daily
Taupo	$35	4hr	2 daily
Wellington	$30	2¼hr	7 daily
Whanganui	$24	1½hr	3 daily

Naked Bus (p246) services also depart the Travel Centre, servicing North Island centres including these:

DESTINATION	PRICE	DURATION	FREQUENCY
Auckland	$25	9¼hr	1 daily
Napier	$16	2½hr	2 daily
Taupo	$20	4¼hr	2 daily
Wellington	$14	2¼hr	4 daily
Whanganui	$12	1¼hr	1 daily

Train

Tranz Scenic (☎04-495 0775, 0800 872 467; www.tranzscenic.co.nz) runs long-distance trains between Wellington and Auckland, stopping at the retro-derelict **Palmerston North Train Station** (Mathews Ave), off Tremaine Ave about 2.5km north of the Square. From Palmy to Wellington, take the *Overlander* ($68, 2½ hours, one daily) departing at 5pm (Friday to Sunday, May to November); or the *Capital Connection* ($24, two hours, one daily Monday to Friday) departing Palmy at 6.15am. To Auckland, the *Overlander* ($129, 9½ hours, one daily) departs at 9.45am. Buy tickets from Tranz Scenic directly, or on the train for the *Capital Connection* (no ticket sales at the station).

ℹ Getting Around

To & From the Airport

There's no public transport between the city and airport, but taxis abound or **Super Shuttle** (☎09-522 5100, 0800 748 885; www.supershuttle.co.nz; $18) can whiz you into town in a minivan (pre-booking required).

Bicycle

Crank It Cycles (☎06-358 9810; www.crankitcycles.co.nz; 203 Cuba St; ⊙8am-5.30pm Mon-Fri, 9am-3pm Sat) Hires out mountain bikes from $20/40 per half-/full day, including helmet and lock.

Bus

Tranzit City Link (☎06-952 2800, 0508 800 800; www.horizons.govt.nz; adult/child $2.50/1.50) Runs daytime buses departing from the Main St bus stop on the east side of the Square. Bus 12 goes to Massey University; none go to the airport.

Taxi

A city-to-airport taxi costs around $15. **Gold & Black Taxis** (☎06-351 2345) is a family-run local outfit.

Around Palmerston North

Just south of 'Student City' in the underrated Horowhenua district, **Shannon** (population 1510) and **Foxton** (population 2000) are sedentary country towns en route to Wellington.

Our fine feathered friends at **Owlcatraz** (☎06-362 7872; www.owlcatraz.co.nz; SH57; adult/child incl tour $17.50/8; ⊙9am-5pm) have obligingly adopted oh-so-droll names like Owlvis Presley and Owl Capone. It's a 30-minute drive south from Palmerston North.

Foxton Beach is one of a string of broad, shallow Tasman Sea beaches along this stretch of coast – brown sand, driftwood and holiday houses proliferate. Other worthy beaches include **Himatangi**, **Hokio** and **Waikawa**.

The town of **Levin** (population 19,550) is more sizeable, but suffers from being too close to both Wellington and Palmerston North to warrant the through-traffic making a stop.

Manawatu Gorge & Around

About 15km northeast of Palmerston North, SH2 dips into **Manawatu Gorge**. Maori named the gorge Te Apiti (the Narrow Passage), believing the big reddish rock near the centre of the gorge was its guardian spirit. The rock's colour is said to change intensity when a prominent Rangitane tribe member dies or sheds blood. It takes around four hours to walk through the gorge from either end, or you can see it via jetboat.

On the southwestern edge of the gorge, about 40 minutes drive from Palmerston North, is the **Tararua Wind Farm** (☎07-574 4754, 0800 878 787; www.trustpower.co.nz; Hall Block Rd), allegedly the largest wind farm in the southern hemisphere. From Hall Block Rd there are awesome views of the turbines. Spinning similarly, north of the gorge is **Te Apiti Wind Farm** (☎03-357 9700, 0800 496 496; www.meridianenergy.co.nz; Saddle Rd, Ashhurst). There are great views from Saddle Rd – ask the i-SITE for directions.

Alternatively, flee the city with a visit to **Timeless Horse Treks** (☎06-376 6157; www.timelesshorsetreks.co.nz; Gorge Rd, Ballance; 1/2hr rides from $40/60). Gentle trail rides take in the Manawatu River and surrounding hills, or you can saddle up for an overnight all-inclusive trek ($175). Palmerston North pick-up/drop-off available.

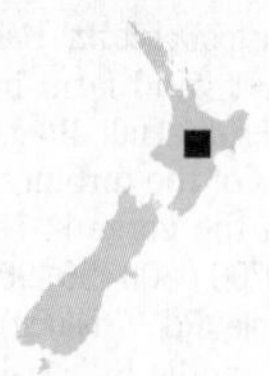

Taupo & the Central Plateau

Includes »

Lake Taupo Region 260
Taupo 260
Around Taupo 272
Turangi & Around 273
The Central Plateau 275
Tongariro National Park 275
National Park Village 282
Ohakune 283
Waiouru 286
Taihape & Around 287

Best Places to Eat

» Bistro Lago (p270)
» Vine Eatery (p270)
» Cyprus Tree (p285)
» Brantry (p270)
» Tongariro Lodge (p275)

Best Places to Stay

» Riverstone Backpackers (p274)
» Creel Lodge (p274)
» Lake (p269)
» Powderhorn Chateau (p285)
» Station Lodge (p285)

Why Go?

From river deep to mountain high, New Zealand's geology takes centre stage in this diverse region – and my-oh-my does it get its shimmy on. Much of the pizzazz comes from the Taupo Volcanic Zone – a line of geothermal activity that stretches, via Rotorua, to Whakaari/White Island in the Bay of Plenty. It's the commotion below the surface that has gifted the region with some of the North Island's star attractions, including the country's largest lake and the three hot-headed peaks of Tongariro National Park.

And the thrills don't stop there, for this area now rivals Rotorua for daredevil escapades. Perhaps you fancy fly-fishing in the trout-filled Tongariro River, hooning up to Huka Falls in a jetboat, or bouncing on a bungy over the Waikato River? Or skydiving, skiing or just soaking in a thermal pool? If so, mark Taupo as a must-do on your North Island itinerary.

When to Go

Equally popular in winter as in summer, there's not really a bad time to visit. The ski season runs roughly from July to October, but storms and freezing temperatures can occur at any time on the mountains, and above 2500m there is a small permanent cap of snow. Due to its altitude, the Central Plateau has a generally cool climate, with average high temperatures ranging from around 3°C in winter up to around 24°C in summer. In summer, the lake becomes the epicentre of a whirl of outdoor activity.

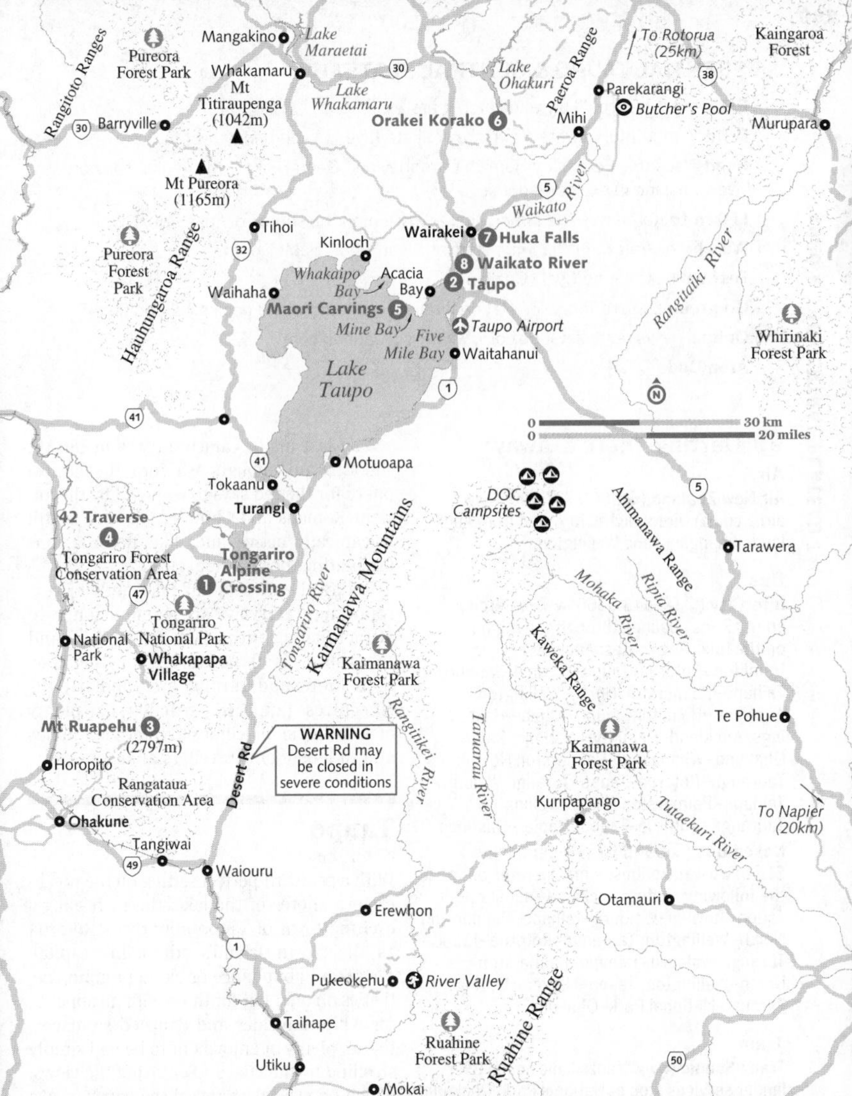

Taupo & Central Plateau Highlights

1. Exploring fascinating volcanic terrain while tramping the **Tongariro Alpine Crossing** (p278)
2. Hurtling to earth strapped to a complete stranger in the world's skydiving capital, **Taupo** (p266)
3. Carving fresh powder on **Mt Ruapehu** (p276)
4. Biking till your bum burns on the **42 Traverse** (p278)
5. Paddling Lake Taupo to check out the modern **Maori carvings** (p261)
6. Rediscovering the 'lost valley' of **Orakei Korako** (p272)
7. Rocketing up the Waikato River to the base of **Huka Falls** (p261) in a jetboat
8. Plunging 47m over the **Waikato River** (p267) on the end of a rubber band

ESSENTIAL TAUPO & CENTRAL PLATEAU

» **Eat** Trout – but you'll have to catch it first!

» **Drink** A mouthful of water from the Waikato River as you bungy over it

» **Read** *Awesome Forces* by Hamish Campbell and Geoff Hicks – the geological story of New Zealand in explosive detail

» **Listen to** *Ka mate* – the famous haka, written on the shores of Lake Rotoaira

» **Watch** *The Return of the King*, starring Ngauruhoe as Mt Doom

» **Festival** Lake Taupo Cycle Challenge

» **Go green** Explore Tongariro National Park's alpine flora and geological oddities

» **Online** www.greatlaketaupo.com; www.visitruapehu.com

» **Area Code** ☎07

Getting There & Away

Air

Air New Zealand (☎0800 737 000; www.airnz.co.nz) Direct flights to Taupo from Auckland, Whanganui and Wellington.

Bus

InterCity (☎07-348 0366; www.intercity.co.nz) Runs coaches through the region on the following routes: Auckland–Hamilton–Rotorua–Taupo–Turangi–Waiouru–Taihape–Palmerston North–Wellington; Auckland–Hamilton–Taupo–Napier–Hastings; Auckland–Hamilton–National Park–Ohakune–Whanganui–Palmerston North Tauranga–Rotorua–Taupo–Turangi–Waiouru–Taihape–Palmerston North–Wellington; Tauranga–Rotorua–Taupo–Napier–Hastings.

Naked Bus (☎0900 62533, per minute $1.99; www.nakedbus.com) Operates on the following routes: Auckland–Hamilton–Taupo–Turangi–Waiouru–Taihape–Palmerston North–Wellington; Tauranga–Rotorua–Taupo–Turangi–Waiouru–Taihape–Palmerston North–Wellington; Taupo–Napier–Hastings; Turangi–National Park–Ohakune.

Train

Tranz Scenic (www.tranzscenic.co.nz) Overlander services stop at National Park, Ohakune and Taihape on the Auckland–Hamilton–Palmerston North–Wellington route.

LAKE TAUPO REGION

NZ's largest lake, Lake Taupo, sits in the caldera of a volcano that began erupting about 300,000 years ago. The caldera was formed by a collapse during the Oruanui eruption about 26,500 years ago, which threw out 750 cu km of ash and pumice, making Krakatoa (8 cu km) look like a pimple.

The last major cataclysm was in 180AD, shooting up enough ash into the atmosphere for the red skys to be noted by the ancient Romans and Chinese. The area is still volcanically active and, like Rotorua, has fascinating thermal hot spots.

Today the 606-sq-km lake and its surrounding waterways are serene enough to attract fishing enthusiasts from all around the world. Well positioned by the lake, both Taupo and Turangi are popular tourist centres. Taupo, in particular, has plenty of activities and facilities to cater for families and independent travellers alike.

Taupo

POP 22,600

With a postcard-perfect setting on the northeastern shores of the lake, the increasingly exciting town of Taupo now rivals Rotorua as the North Island's adrenaline capital. There's an abundance of blood-pumping activities on offer but for those with no appetite for white knuckles and churned stomachs, there's plenty of enjoyment to be had simply strolling by the lake and enjoying the views, which on clear days reveal the snowy peaks of Tongariro National Park. Stop at the lookout on the way into town and you'll see exactly what we mean.

NZ's longest river, the Waikato, originates from Lake Taupo at the township, before crashing its way through the Huka Falls and Aratiatia Rapids and then settling down for a sedate ramble to the west coast, just south of Auckland.

History

When Maori chief Tamatea-arikinui first visited this area, his footsteps reverberated, making him think the ground was hollow; he therefore dubbed the area Tapuaeharuru (Resounding Footsteps). The modern name, however, originates from the story of Tia. After Tia discovered the lake and slept beside it draped in his cloak, the area became known as Taupo Nui a Tia (The Great Cloak of Tia).

Europeans settled here in force during the East Coast Land War (1868–72), when it was a strategic military base. A redoubt was built in 1869 and a garrison of mounted police remained until the defeat of Te Kooti later that year.

In the 20th century the mass ownership of the motorcar saw Taupo grow from a lakeside village of about 750 people to a large resort town, easily accessible from most points of the North Island. Today the population still grows considerably at peak holiday times, when New Zealanders and international visitors alike flock to the lakeshore.

Sights

LAKESIDE

Taupo's main attraction is the lake and all the things you can do in, on and around it. The water is famously chilly, but in several places (such as **Hot Water Beach** (Map p264), immediately south of the centre) there are thermal springs just below the surface. You can swim right in front of the township, but **Acacia Bay**, 5km west, is a particularly pleasant spot. Even better and quieter is **Whakaipo Bay**, another 7km further on.

Maori Carvings CARVINGS

Accessible only by boat, these 10m-high carvings were etched into the cliffs near Mine Bay by master carver Matahi Whakataka-Brightwell in the late 1970s. They depict Ngatoro-i-rangi, the visionary Maori navigator who guided the Tuwharetoa and Te Arawa tribes to the Taupo area a thousand years ago. There are also two smaller Matahi figures here, both of Celtic design, which depict the south wind and a mermaid.

Taupo Museum MUSEUM

(Map p262; www.taupomuseum.co.nz; Story Pl; adult/child $5/free; ⏲10am-4.30pm) With an excellent Maori gallery and quirky displays, which include a 1960s caravan set up as if the occupants have just popped down to the lake, this little museum makes an interesting rainy-day diversion. The centrepiece is an elaborately carved Maori meeting house, *Te Aroha o Rongoheikume*. Set up in a courtyard, the *Ora Garden of Wellbeing* is a re-creation of NZ's gold-medal-winning entry into the 2004 Chelsea Flower Show. Historical displays cover local industries, a mock-up of a 19th-century shop and a moa skeleton, and there's also a gallery devoted to visiting exhibitions.

WAIRAKEI PARK

Huka Falls WATERFALL

(Map p264; Huka Falls Rd) Clearly signposted and with a car park and kiosk alongside, these falls mark the spot where NZ's longest river, the Waikato, is slammed into a narrow chasm, making a dramatic 10m drop into a surging pool. As you cross the footbridge, you can see the full force of this torrent that the Maori called Hukanui (Great Body of Spray). On sunny days the water is crystal clear and you'll be able to

MAORI NZ: CENTRAL PLATEAU

The North Island's central region is home to a group of mountains that feature in several Maori legends of lust and betrayal, which end with a few mountains fleeing to other parts of the island (see Mt Taranaki's sad tale).

Long after all that action was over, the *tohunga* (priest) Ngatoro-i-rangi, fresh off the boat from Hawaiki, explored this region and named the mountains that remained. The most sacred was Tongariro, consisting of at least 12 volcanic cones, seen as the leader of all the other mountains.

The major *iwi* (tribe) of the region is **Ngati Tuwharetoa** (www.tuwharetoa.co.nz), one of the few *iwi* in NZ that has retained an undisputed *ariki* (high chief). The current *ariki* is Sir Tumu Te Heuheu Tukino VIII, whose great-great-grandfather, Te Heuheu Tukino IV (a descendent of Ngatoro-i-rangi), gifted the mountains of Tongariro to NZ in 1887.

To discover the stories of local Maori and their ancestors, visit Taupo Museum, the carved cliff faces at Mine Bay, Wairakei Terraces, or take a tour with pureORAwalks, Rafting NZ, Wai Maori, Awhina Wilderness Experience or Kai Waho.

Central Taupo

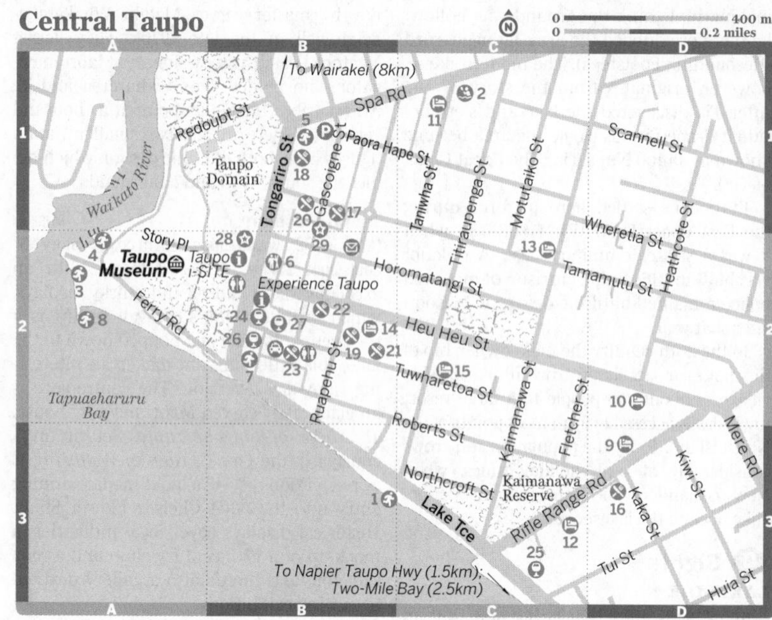

take great photographs from the lookout on the other side of the footbridge. You can also take a few short walks around the area or pick up the Huka Falls Walkway back to town, or the Aratiatia Rapids Walking Track to the rapids.

Wairakei Terraces & Thermal Health Spa THERMAL AREA
(Map p264; ☎07-378 0913; www.wairakeiterraces.co.nz; Wairakei Rd; thermal walk adult/child $18/9, pools $25; ⊙8.30am-5pm) Known to Maori as Waiora and latterly as Geyser Valley, this was one of the most active thermal areas in the world (with 22 geysers and 240 mud pools and springs) until 1958, when it was significantly affected by the opening of the geothermal power station. Today it's the site of a re-created Maori village, a small meeting house, a carving centre, massage rooms and a set of healing thermal pools. These sit alongside artificially made geysers and silica terraces, re-creating, on a smaller scale, the famous Pink and White Terraces, which were destroyed by the Tarawera eruption in 1886.

The nighttime Maori Cultural Experience – which includes a traditional challenge, welcome and concert, as well as a *hangi* meal – gives an insight into Maori life in the geothermal areas of the county (adult/child $95/48).

Craters of the Moon THERMAL AREA
(Map p264; www.cratersofthemoon.co.nz; Karapiti Rd; adult/child $6/2.50; ⊙8.30am-5.30pm) This lesser-known geothermal area sprang to life as a result of the hydroelectric tinkering that created the power station. When underground water levels fell and pressure shifted, new steam vents and bubbling mud pools sprang up. The perimeter loop walk takes about 45 minutes and affords great views down to the lake and mountains beyond. There's a kiosk at the entrance, staffed by volunteers who kindly keep an eye on the car park. It's signposted from SH1, about 5km north of Taupo.

Aratiatia Rapids WATERFALL
(Map p264) Two kilometres off SH5, this was a spectacular part of the Waikato River until the government plonked a hydroelectric dam across the waterway, shutting off the flow. But the spectacle hasn't disappeared completely, with the floodgates opened from October to March at 10am, noon, 2pm and 4pm and from April to September at 10am, noon and 2pm. You can see the water crash through the dam from two good vantage points.

Central Taupo

Top Sights
Taupo Museum A2

Activities, Courses & Tours
1 Big Sky Parasail B3
2 Canoe & Kayak C1
3 Chris Jolly Outdoors A2
4 Fish Cruise Taupo A2
5 Greenstone Fishing B1
6 Pointons Ski Shop B2
7 Taupo Rod & Tackle B2
8 Taupo's Floatplane A2

Sleeping
9 Beechtree D3
10 Bella Vista D2
11 Blackcurrant Backpackers C1
12 Catelli's of Taupo C3
13 Silver Fern Lodge C2
14 Taupo Urban Retreat B2
15 Tiki Lodge C2

Eating
16 Brantry D3
17 Eruption B1
18 Lotus B1
19 Piccolo B2
20 Pimentos B1
21 Plateau B2
22 Replete B2
23 Vine Eatery B2

Drinking
24 Finn MacCuhal's B2
25 Jolly Good Fellows C3
26 Mulligans B2
27 Shed B2

Entertainment
28 Great Lake Centre B2
29 Starlight Cinema Centre B1

Volcanic Activity Centre MUSEUM
(Map p264; www.volcanoes.co.nz; Karetoto Rd; adult/child $10/6; ⌚9am-5pm Mon-Fri, 10am-4pm Sat & Sun) What's with all the geothermal activity around Taupo? This centre has the answers, with excellent, if text-heavy, displays on the region's geothermal and volcanic activity, including a live seismograph keeping a watch on what's currently going on. A favourite exhibit with kids is the Earthquake Simulator, which is a little booth you can sit in to experience an earthquake, complete with teeth-chattering shudders and sudden shakes. You can also configure your own tornado and then watch it wreak havoc, or see a simulated geyser above and below ground. There is a small theatre that screens footage of the 1995 Ruapehu eruption and the 2007 breach of the crater lake.

Huka Prawn Park FARM
(Map p264; www.hukaprawnpark.co.nz; Karetoto Rd; adult/child $24/14; ⌚9.30am-4pm) One of the world's only geothermally heated freshwater prawn farms, this place offers a surprising array of activities, including prawn 'fishing' and Killer Prawn Golf, shooting for rings floating in the prawn ponds. And, of course, there's a restaurant.

FREE **Honey Hive** STORE
(Map p264; www.honeyhivetaupo.com; 65 Karetoto Rd; ⌚10am-5pm) Has a glass-enclosed viewing hive, honey tastings, a cafe and sells all manner of bee products – edible, medicinal and cosmetic – as well as mead.

Activities

Adrenaline addicts should look out for special deals that combine several activities for a reduced price. Some operators offer backpacker discounts.

Water-based

FREE **Spa Park Hot Spring** SWIMMING
(Map p264; Spa Park) The hot thermal waters of the Otumuheke Stream meet the bracing Waikato River at this pleasant and well-worn spot under a bridge, creating a free natural spa bath. Take care: people have been known to drown while trying to cool off in the fast moving river. It's near the beginning of the Huka Falls Walkway, about 20 minutes from the centre of town.

Hukafalls Jet JETBOATING
(Map p264; ☎07-374 8572; www.hukafallsjet.com; 200 Karetoto Rd; trips adult/child $105/59) This 30-minute thrill ride takes you up the river to the spray-filled foot of the Huka Falls and down to the Aratiatia Dam, all the while doing acrobatic 360-degree turns. Trips run all day (prices include transport from Taupo) and you can bundle it in with a helicopter ride.

Rapids Jet JETBOATING
(Map p264; ☎07-374 8066; www.rapidsjet.com; Nga Awa Purua Rd; adult/child $105/60) This sensational 35-minute ride shoots along the

Taupo & Wairakei

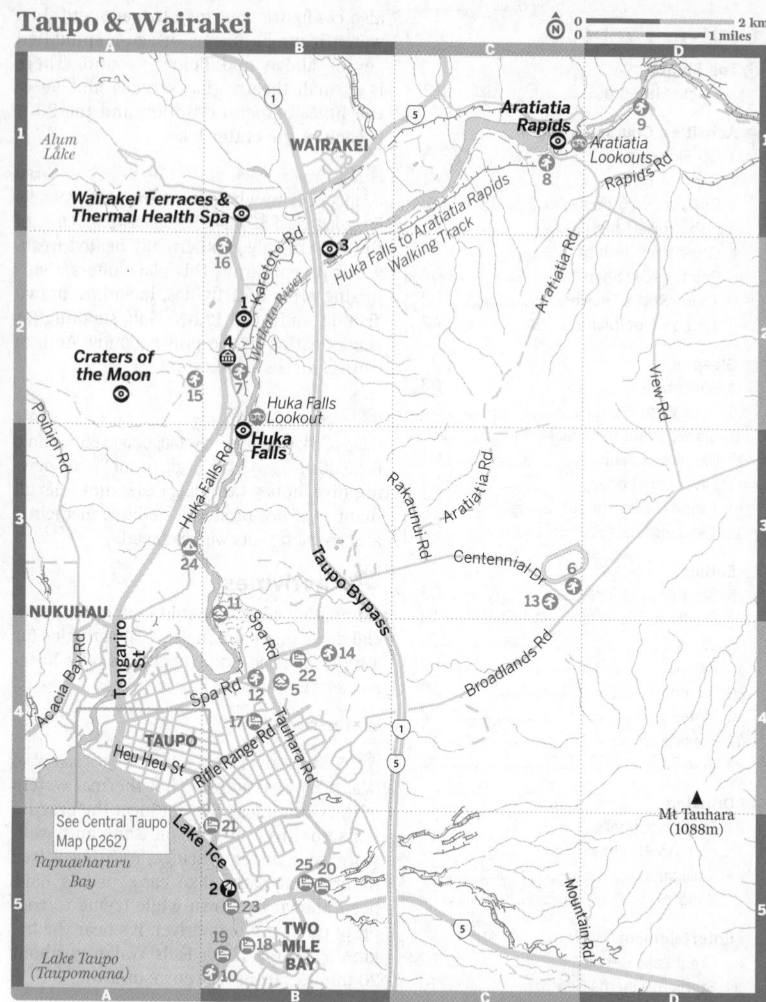

lower part of the Aratiatia Rapids – rivalling the Huka Falls trip for thrills. The boat departs from the end of the access road to the Aratiatia lookouts. Go down Rapids Rd and look for the signpost to the National Equestrian Centre.

Huka Falls River Cruise CRUISE
(Map p264; ☎0800 278 336; www.hukafallscruise.co.nz; Aratiatia Dam; adult/child $35/15; ⏱10.30am, 12.30pm & 2.30pm) For a photo-friendly ride, this boat offers a relaxed jaunt (80 minutes) from Aratiatia Dam to Huka Falls.

Taupo DeBretts Spa Resort SWIMMING
(Map p264; ☎07-377 6502; www.taupodebretts.co.nz; 76 Napier Taupo Hwy; adult/child $20/12; ⏱7.30am-9.30pm) A variety of mineral-rich indoor and outdoor thermal pools are on offer. The kids will love the giant dragon waterslide, while the adults can enjoy a wide choice of treatments, such as massage and body scrubs.

AC Baths SWIMMING, CLIMBING
(Map p264; ☎07-376 0350; www.taupovenues.co.nz; AC Baths Ave; adult/child $7/3, slides $5, climbing wall adult/child $10/6; ⏱6am-9pm,

Taupo & Wairakei

Top Sights

Aratiatia Rapids C1
Craters of the Moon A2
Huka Falls B3
Wairakei Terraces & Thermal Health Spa B1

Sights

1 Honey Hive B2
2 Hot Water Beach B5
3 Huka Prawn Park B2
4 Volcanic Activity Centre B2

Activities, Courses & Tours

5 AC Baths B4
6 Formula Challenge C3
7 Helistar Helicopters B2
8 Huka Falls River Cruise C1
Hukafalls Jet .... (see 3)
Rapid Sensations & Kayaking Kiwi .... (see 7)
9 Rapids Jet D1
Rock'n Ropes .... (see 1)
10 Sailing & Watersports Centre Two Mile Bay B5
11 Spa Park Hot Spring B3
12 Taupo Bungy B4
Taupo DeBretts Spa Resort .... (see 25)
13 Taupo Gliding Club C3
14 Taupo Golf Club B4
15 Taupo Horse Treks A2
16 Wairakei Golf & Sanctuary B2

Sleeping

17 All Seasons B4
18 Chelmswood B5
19 Cottage Mews B5
20 Hilton Lake Taupo B5
21 Lake B5
22 Lake Taupo Top 10 Holiday Resort B4
23 Reef Resort B5
24 Reid's Farm Recreation Reserve A3
Sacred Waters .... (see 23)
25 Taupo DeBretts Spa Resort B5

Eating

Bistro Lago .... (see 20)

climbing wall hours vary) At the Taupo Events Centre, about 2km east of town, this large complex has a big, heated pool with a waterslide, as well as an indoor kids' pool, private mineral pools and a sauna. There are also a climbing wall and gym.

Wilderness Escapes KAYAKING
(☎07-376 8981; www.wildernessescapes.co.nz; half-day $90) Well-regarded, long-standing operator offering half- or full-day kayaking trips to the Maori carvings, as well as sunset paddles on the lake.

Chris Jolly Outdoors CRUISE, KAYAKING
(Map p262; ☎07-378 0623; www.chrisjolly.co.nz; Marina; ⏰9am-5.30pm) Operates the Cruise Cat, a large, modern launch that offers fishing trips and daily cruises to the Maori carvings (adult/child $44/16, 10.30am and 1.30pm). Sunday brunch trips (adult/child $62/34) are especially worthwhile. It also hires kayaks (single/double per hour $20/30) and self-drive boats ($70 to $85 per hour), and offers guided mountain-biking trips.

Barbary SAILING
(☎07-378 3444; www.sailbarbary.com; adult/child $40/10; ⏰10.30am & 2pm year-long plus 5pm summer) A classic 1926 yacht offering 2½-hour cruises to the Maori rock carvings every day, as well as a three-hour movie and barbecue cruise in summer ($65, 8pm, December to April).

Rapid Sensations & Kayaking Kiwi KAYAKING, RAFTING
(Map p264; ☎0800 35 34 35; www.rapids.co.nz; 413 Huka Falls Rd) This operator offers kayak trips to the Maori carvings (four hours, $98), a gentle paddle along the Waikato (two hours, $48), white-water rafting on the Tongariro River ($88 to $145) and guided mountain-bike rides ($75).

Canoe & Kayak CANOEING, KAYAKING
(Map p262; ☎07-378 1003; www.canoeandkayak.co.nz; 77 Spa Rd; ⏰9am-5pm Mon-Sat) Instruction and boat hire, as well as guided tours, including a two-hour trip on the Waikato River ($45) or a half-day to the Maori carvings ($90).

Sailing & Watersports Centre Two Mile Bay SAILING, KAYAKING
(Map p264; ☎0274 967 350; www.sailingcentre.co.nz; Lake Tce; ⏰9am-10pm) Has a lakeside cafe/bar and hires out kayaks (from $25), canoes (from $25), windsurfers (from $30),

ABOUT TROUT

Ever since trout were introduced into Lake Taupo in 1898 there have been yarns of fish weighing more than a sack of spuds and measuring the length of a surfboard. The truth is that more than 28,000 brown and rainbow trout of legal size are bagged annually and fishing enthusiasts head here from all over the world to try their luck.

February and March are the best months for brown trout but rainbow fishing is good year-round on the Tongariro River (near Turangi). Fly-fishing is the only fishing permitted on all rivers flowing into the lake and within a 300m radius of the river mouths. Spin fishing is allowed only on the Waikato River (flowing *out* of the lake) and on the Tokaanu tailrace, flowing into the lake from the Tokaanu Power Station.

This unique fishery is protected by special conditions, including a bag limit of three fish, no use of bait (except flies) and a minimum size of 40cm, depending on where you fish – this is detailed on your licence, which you must carry at all times while fishing. Licences are available from DOC, i-SITEs and fishing stores (per day/week/season $17/38/90).

There are numerous fishing guides operating out of Taupo and Turangi, offering transport, gear, licences and, most importantly, local knowledge. Many are happy to negotiate a price depending on the trip; $250 for a half-day is a rough ballpark. Likewise there are shops in each town that hire and sell gear, and handle bookings for guides and charters. Refer to the activities section of each town for recommended operators.

sailboats ($65) and catamarans (from $70); rates are per hour.

Fish Cruise Taupo BOATING
(Launch Office; Map p262; ☎07-378 3444; www.fishcruisetaupo.co.nz; Marina; ⏰9am-5pm Dec-Mar, 9.30am-3pm Apr-Nov) Representing 18 different boats belonging to the Taupo Launchmen's Association, this is the best place to book a private charter – whether for fishing or for a cruise.

Greenstone Fishing FISHING
(Map p262; ☎07-378 3714; 147 Tongariro St; gear hire from $15; ⏰8am-5pm Mon-Sat, 9am-3pm Sun) Central fishing shop that sells licences, hires gear and arranges guided trips.

Taupo Rod & Tackle FISHING
(Map p262; ☎07-378 5337; www.tauporodandtackle.co.nz; 7 Tongariro St; gear hire $20-35; ⏰8am-6pm Sat & Sun, 8am-8pm Fri) Rental gear, fishing guides and boat charters.

Skydiving

More than 30,000 jumps a year are made from Taupo, which makes it the skydiving capital of the world. It's certainly a terrific spot to do it: all those beautiful places you see from ground level are patchworked together in a brilliant blanket of natural colour, the highlights of which are the deep blue lake and the brilliant white of the snow-capped peaks.

Skydive Taupo SKYDIVING
(☎0800 586 766; www.skydivetaupo.co.nz; 12,000ft/15,000ft $250/340) Packages are available (from $439) that include town pick-ups in a white limousine, DVDs, photos and T-shirts.

Taupo Tandem Skydiving SKYDIVING
(☎0800 826 336; www.taupotandemskydiving.com; 12,000ft/15,000ft $249/339) Various packages that include DVDs, photos, T-shirts etc ($388 to $679) are available.

Freefall! SKYDIVING
(☎0800 373 335; www.freefall.net.nz; 12,000/15,000ft $249/339) DVDs and photos are extra.

Other Activities

There are good mountain-bike tracks just out of town in the Wairakei and Pureora Forests, and along the Waikato River. You can download maps for these from www.biketaupo.org.nz or pick them up at the i-SITE. While you're there, check on the status of the **Great Lake Trail**, a purpose-built 97km track from Whakaipo Bay to Waihaha in the remote western reaches of the lake. At the time of research only the **W2K** section had been completed, from Whakaipo to Kinloch.

There are some great walks in and around Taupo, ranging from sedate ambles to more gnarly all-dayers; collect a booklet from the i-SITE.

Great Lake Walkway WALKING

This pleasant path follows the Taupo lakefront south to Five Mile Bay (8km). It's a flat, easy walk along public-access beaches.

Huka Falls Walkway WALKING

Starting from the Spa Park car park at the end of County Ave (off Spa Rd), this scenic, easy walk takes just over an hour to reach the falls, following the east bank of the Waikato River. Continuing on from the falls is the 7km Huka Falls to Aratiatia Rapids walking track (another two-plus hours).

Taupo Bungy BUNGY

(Map p264; ☎07-377 1135; www.taupobungy.co.nz; 202 Spa Rd; solo/tandem $149/298; ⏰8.30am-5pm, extended in summer) Sitting on a cliff edge over the mighty Waikato River, this picturesque bungy site is the most popular on the North Island, with plenty of vantage points if you're too chicken to jump. Nonchickens will be led onto a platform jutting 20m out over the cliff (the world's first cantilever jump, for engineering boffins) and convinced, with masterly skill, to throw themselves off the edge. A heart-stopping 47m hurtle and a few bounces back and it's safely into the boat. You can opt for a slight dunk in the river, or strap yourself to a friend and leap off together. Alternatively, try the giant swing (solo/tandem $99/180).

If you want all of the glory and none of the terror, the wonders of Photoshop and a blue screen now allow you to 'Fake It' ($25).

Taupo Horse Treks HORSE RIDING

(Map p264; ☎07-378 0356; www.taupohorsetreks.co.nz; Karapiti Rd; per hr $70, pony ride $30) Conducts treks through some fine forest with good views over the Craters of the Moon.

Big Sky Parasail PARASAILING

(Map p262; ☎0800 724 4759; www.bigskyparasail.co.nz; Lake Tce; 400ft/800ft $79/89; ⏰9am-5pm Dec-Apr) Parasailing flights from the lakefront, taking off hourly; bookings essential.

Rock'n Ropes ROPES COURSE

(Map p264; ☎07-374 8111; www.rocknropes.co.nz; 65 Karetoto Rd; giant swing $20, adrenaline combo $40, half-day $65) A vertiginous and challenging high-ropes course that includes balancing in teetering 'tree-tops', negotiating a tricky two-wire bridge and scaling ropes. The combo includes the swing, high beam and trapeze.

Kaimanawa Heli-Biking MOUNTAIN BIKING

(☎07-384 2816; www.kaimanawahelibiking.co.nz; 4hr ride $395) For luxury rough riding, Heli-Biking will pick you up in a helicopter and drop you on top of the highest point in the Kaimanawa range, allowing you to ride all the way down.

Formula Challenge MOTOR RACING

(Map p264; ☎07-377 0338; www.fcr.co.nz; Broadlands Rd; driving experience $340-740) Thrill seekers with petrol-head tendencies should head to the Taupo Motorsport Park, a state-of-the-art 3.5km racetrack and drag circuit that has staged the A1 Grand Prix. There's often something to watch here, from sidecar races to 'drifters' and, on occasion, the police testing their skills. Best of all, this outfit allows you to get behind the wheel in a V8 or Formula Challenge racer.

Taupo Gliding Club GLIDING

(Map p264; ☎07-378 5627; www.taupoglidingclub.co.nz; Centennial Dr; flights $120-195) Flights daily by appointment (weather permitting).

Pointons Ski Shop SKIING

(Map p262; ☎07-377 0087; www.pointons.co.nz; 57 Tongariro St; ski/snowboard hire $30/40) Taupo is tantalisingly close to the ski fields, being 1¼ hours drive from Whakapapa and two hours from Turoa. This shop hires gear and stays open from 7am to 7pm throughout the season.

Wairakei Golf & Sanctuary GOLF

(Map p264; ☎07-374 8152; www.wairakeigolfcourse.co.nz; SH1; 18 holes $155-225) In late 2009 a 2m-high, 5km-long pest-proof fence was erected, turning the whole course into a native bird sanctuary. It's a challenging 18 holes set in 150 hectares of beautiful countryside.

Taupo Golf Club GOLF

(Map p264; ☎07-378 6933; www.taupogolf.co.nz; 32 Centennial Dr; 18 holes $52-60, club hire $25-50) Has two good 18-hole courses; one is a park course and the other an inland links.

Tours

pureORAwalks CULTURAL TOUR

(☎021-042 2722; www.pureorawalks.com; adult/child $105/97) Nature-Culture walks in Pureora Forest Park, Lake Rotopounamu and Whirinaki Forest Park, offering insight into *Maoritanga* (things Maori) – including local history, legends and traditional uses for flora and fauna.

Kai Waho Experience CULTURAL TOUR
(www.kaiwaho.co.nz; price on application) Whisks you to a remote *pa* in wilderness east of the lake for a day of Maori culture and a *hangi*-cooked feast.

Taupo Quad Adventures QUAD BIKES
(07-377 6404; www.taupoquads.co.nz; SH1, Maroa; 1hr to full day $85-299) Offers fully guided off-road quad-bike trips, 24km north of town opposite the turn-off to Orakei Korako.

Helipro SCENIC FLIGHTS
(07-377 8805; www.helipro.co.nz; flights $99-1150) Specialises in heli-tours, which include alpine and White Island landings, as well as shorter scenic flights over the town, lake and volcanoes.

Helistar Helicopters SCENIC FLIGHTS
(Map p264; 07-374 8405; www.helistar.co.nz; 415 Huka Falls Rd; flights $99-995) Offers a variety of scenic helicopter flights, from 10 minutes to two hours. Combine a Helistar trip with the Huka Falls Jet in the Huka Star combo (from $193).

Izardair SCENIC FLIGHTS
(07-378 7835; www.izardair.com; flights $100-310) Luxury light aircraft flights over Taupo, Orakei Korako or the volcanoes.

Taupo Air Services SCENIC FLIGHTS
(07-378 5325; www.taupoair.com; flights $100-550) Runs light aircraft flights, from the 15-minute Local Look to a two-hour trip to White Island.

Taupo's Floatplane SCENIC FLIGHTS
(Map p262; 07-378 7500; www.tauposfloatplane.co.nz; flights $85-625) Located at the entrance to the marina, the floatplane offers a variety of trips, including quick flights over the lake and longer ones over Mt Ruapehu or White Island. Packages include the Taupo Trifecta (floatplane trip, followed by a jet-boat trip and a walk through Orakei Korako; $440).

Paradise Tours BUS TOUR
(07-378 9955; www.paradisetours.co.nz; adult/child $99/45) Three-hour tours to the Aratiatia Rapids, Craters of the Moon and Huka Falls. Also offers day tours to Tongariro National Park, Orakei Korako, Rotorua, Hawke's Bay and Waitomo Caves.

Festivals & Events

Heralding itself as the events capital of NZ, Taupo plays host to numerous big shindigs throughout the year, many of them of a sporting nature – and many of which you can enter and participate in. See www.greatlaketaupo.com for more details.

Epic Swim SPORTS
(www.epicswim.co.nz) Brave the lake waters in mid-January alongside some of the best swimmers in NZ. Courses range from 1km to 10km.

NZ Body Painting Festival ARTS
(www.bodyartawards.co.nz) Three days of decorated flesh brightens up the lakeside in late January.

Great Lake Relay SPORTS
(www.relay.co.nz) Hustle together 10 to 18 mates (or badger some backpackers) for a tag-team circumnavigation of the lake. It takes place mid-February and it doesn't matter whether you walk or run, as long as you finish your allotted leg.

Ironman New Zealand SPORTS
(www.ironman.co.nz) Bring a magnet, as buns of steel are plentiful during this pimped-up triathlon. Held in early March, it's the country's biggest annual one-day event. A half-ironman (half fluffy bunny?) is held in December.

100K Flyer SPORTS
(www.100kflyer.co.nz) A 100km road-cycling race from Rotorua to Taupo; late March.

Erupt Festival ARTS
(www.erupt.co.nz/Erupt-Festival) Biennial arts festival, held over 11 days in May on even numbered years.

Winterfest FAMILY
Billed as a festival of old-fashioned family fun, this July celebration includes a trolley derby and temporary snowpark.

Day-Night Thriller SPORTS
(www.daynightthriller.co.nz; Spa Park) Held in September, this 12-hour event attracts more than 3000 mountain bikers, competing in teams or as individuals.

BikeFest & Lake Taupo Cycle Challenge SPORTS
(www.bikefest.co.nz) One of NZ's biggest annual cycling events, the 160km Lake Taupo Cycle Challenge, sees around 10,000 people pedalling around the lake on the last Saturday in November. It's preceded by a week-long festival.

Sleeping

Taupo is motel central, with many spread out along the lake, especially southeast of the town centre at Waipahihi and Two Mile Bay. Acacia Bay, 5km to the west, has some good B&Bs. Areas have been designated for Freedom Campers between the hours of 5pm and 10am at the Ferry Rd parking bay and at the marina. Best of all is the **Reid's Farm Recreation Reserve** (Map p264; Huka Falls Rd), a beautiful spot beside the Waikato River.

Lake MOTEL **$$**
(Map p264; ☎07-378 4222; www.thelakeonline.co.nz; 63 Mere Rd; apt $155-220) A reminder that 1960s and '70s design wasn't all Austin Powers–style groovaliciousness, this unusual boutique motel is crammed with furniture from the era's signature designers. The studio is a tight fit, but the four one-bedroom units all have kitchenettes and dining/living areas.

Beechtree MOTEL **$$**
(Map p262; ☎07-377 0181; www.beechtreemotel.co.nz; 56 Rifle Range Rd; apt $140-390; @) The Beechtree, and its sister motel Miro next door, offer classy rooms at reasonable rates. The design is fresh and modern, with neutral-toned decor, large windows, ground-floor patios and upstairs balconies.

Cottage Mews MOTEL **$$**
(Map p264; ☎07-378 3004; www.cottagemews.co.nz; 311 Lake Tce, Two Mile Bay; apt $115-210;) Few motels muster much charm, but this cute gable-roofed block, festooned with hanging flowers, manages to seem almost rustic. Some units have lake views, most have spa baths and all have a small private garden.

Blackcurrant Backpackers HOSTEL **$**
(Map p262; ☎07-378 9292; www.blackcurrentbp.co.nz; 20 Taniwha St; dm $27-28, s/d $60/78; @) Fashioned from an ageing motel, our favourite Taupo hostel has private rooms with en suites and supercomfy beds. The staff rival the cartoon blackcurrants in the Ribena ads for chirpiness.

Sacred Waters APARTMENTS **$$$**
(Map p264; ☎07-376 1400; www.sacredwaters.co.nz; 221-225 Lake Tce, Waipahihi; apt $360-670;) Apart from some awful mass-produced 'art', these large apartments are stylish and well-designed. Each has a contemporary kitchen and its own private thermal plunge pool, and most have wonderful lake views.

Acacia Cliffs Lodge B&B **$$$**
(☎07-378 1551; www.acaciacliffslodge.co.nz; 133 Mapara Rd, Acacia Bay; r $700; @) Pushing the romance switch way past 'rekindle', this luxurious B&B, high in the hills above Acacia Bay, offers four modern suites – three with sumptuous lake views and one that compensates for the lack of them with a curvy bath and a private garden.

Taupo Urban Retreat HOSTEL **$**
(Map p262; ☎07-378 6124; www.tur.co.nz; 65 Heu Heu St; dm $25-29, r $70; @) A younger crowd gravitates to this purpose-built hostel, attracted by its publike hub and carefree style. It's refreshingly modern in design with a beach-house feel, despite being on a busy road.

Catelli's of Taupo MOTEL **$$**
(Map p262; ☎07-378 4477; www.catellis.co.nz; 23-27 Rifle Range Rd; apt $135-230;) The exterior is all hobbitish '80s curves, sloping roofs and nipple-pink trim, but these orderly motel units have a fresh feel inside. In summer it's worth paying the extra $5 for a garden studio.

Hilton Lake Taupo HOTEL **$$$**
(Map p264; ☎07-378 7080; www.hilton.com/laketaupo; 80-100 Napier Taupo Hwy; from $230; @) Occupying the historic Terraces Hotel (1889) and a recent extension, this large complex offers the expected Hilton standard of luxury in non-threatening shades of grey. It's a little out of town but is handy for the DeBretts thermal complex.

Taupo DeBretts Spa Resort HOLIDAY PARK **$**
(Map p264; ☎07-378 8559; www.taupodebretts.com; 76 Napier Taupo Hwy; sites from $20, units $90-275; @) More of a holiday park than a flashy resort, DeBretts offers everything from tent sites to motel-style units. It's a five-minute drive from downtown, but it's well worth the hop for the indulgent thermal pools that share its home.

Reef Resort APARTMENTS **$$**
(Map p264; ☎07-378 5115; www.accommodationtaupo.com; 219 Lake Tce; apt $145-480;) Like the ducks that congregate here in winter, warming their butts in the hot springs, so too do Taupo's apartment complexes jostle

for the free thermal waters on this stretch of the lake. Reef offers attractive, well-priced units of varying sizes, including a luxurious three-bedroom apartment that is right by the shore.

Bella Vista MOTEL $$
(Map p262; ☎07-378 9043; www.bellavistamotels.co.nz; 145 Heu Heu St; apt $120-190;) The canine-adverse may find the owners' big docile dog a little offputting, but the units here are clean and comfortable, if a little bland. There's a communal barbecue at the rear of the complex.

Silver Fern Lodge HOSTEL $
(Map p262; ☎07-377 4929; www.silverfernlodge.co.nz; cnr Tamamutu & Kaimanawa Sts; dm $25, r $60-110; @) Rooms range from 10-bed dorms to studio en suite units in this large, custom-built complex, trimmed in shiny corrugated aluminium yet still strangely lifeless, decor-wise. There's a large communal kitchen and lounge.

Tiki Lodge HOSTEL $
(Map p262; ☎07-377 4545; www.tikilodge.co.nz; 104 Tuwharetoa St; dm $27, r $80-90; @) This hostel has lake and mountain views from the balcony, a spacious kitchen, comfy lounges, lots of Maori artwork and a spa pool out the back.

All Seasons HOLIDAY PARK $
(Map p264; ☎07-378 4272; www.taupoallseasons.co.nz; 16 Rangatira St; sites from $20, dm $47, units $75-240;) A pleasant holiday park, located five minutes' walk from town, with well-established trees and hedgerows between sites, a playground, games room, thermal pool, bike hire and good kitchen facilities.

Lake Taupo Top 10 Holiday Resort HOLIDAY PARK $
(Map p264; ☎07-378 6860; www.taupotop10.co.nz; 41 Centennial Dr; sites from $50, units $123-365; @) The slickest of the local camping grounds, this 20-acre park has all the mod cons, including heated swimming pool, tennis courts and an on-site shop. It's about 2.5km from the i-SITE.

Chelmswood MOTEL $$
(Map p264; ☎07-378 2715; www.chelmswood.co.nz; 250 Lake Tce, Waipahihi; r $115-295; @) It's starting to look a little tired, but this Tudor-style motel has simple studios and larger family rooms, most with their own mineral pool. There's a heated outdoor pool, a sauna, and a sandpit for the littlies.

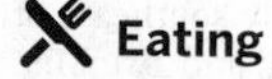

Eating

Bistro Lago ITALIAN $$$
(Map p264; ☎07-377 1400; www.bistrolago.co.nz; 80-100 Napier Taupo Hwy; breakfast $25-35, pizza $22-23, mains $37-42; breakfast, lunch & dinner) Under the long-distance tutelage of Auckland-based celebrity chef Simon Gault, the Hilton's inhouse restaurant delivers inventive Italian-influenced dishes using quality regional ingredients. The view, stretching over the lake to the distant mountains, only adds to the magic.

Vine Eatery TAPAS $$
(Map p262; www.sceniccellars.co.nz; 37 Tuwharetoa St; tapas $9-20; 9am-late) Sharing the Scenic Cellars wine store, this chic eatery continues the communal ethos with a 'shared plates' menu – offering traditional tapas alongside heftier divisible dishes. Of course, the wine list is excellent.

Brantry MODERN NZ $$$
(Map p262; ☎07-378 0484; www.thebrantry.co.nz; 45 Rifle Range Rd; mains $38-42, 2-/3-course set menu $45/60; dinner) It's an unusual set-up, operating out of an unobtrusive 1950s house, but the Campbell sisters have turned Brantry into one of the most well-regarded restaurants in the region. The menu makes use of top-quality cuts of beef and lamb.

Pimentos INTERNATIONAL $$
(Map p262; ☎07-377 4549; 17 Tamamutu St; mains $28-30; dinner Wed-Mon) Pimentos is such a local favourite that you'd be wise to book ahead. The lamb shanks and mash are legendary, but the relatively short menu offers plenty of well-considered experimentation.

Plateau PUB $$
(Map p262; www.plateautaupo.co.nz; 64 Tuwharetoa St; mains $20-35; lunch & dinner) Plateau is a great place for a drink (Monteith's beer being the main poison), but it's as a gastro-pub that it shines. The menu offers rustic pub classics with fancy fusion tweaks.

L'Arté CAFE $
(www.larte.co.nz; 255 Mapara Rd, Acacia Bay; mains $10-19; 9am-4pm Wed-Sun, daily Jan) Lots of mouth-watering treats are made from scratch at this fantastically artful cafe on the hill that backs Acacia Bay. After your arty latte, check out the sculpture garden and gallery.

Eruption CAFE $
(Map p262; www.eruptioncoffee.co.nz; Suncourt Centre, Tamamutu St; mains $7-17; ⏲7.30am-3.30pm) Shelter behind one of the free newspapers while Eruption's espresso machine steams and spurts out black rivers topped with creamy foam. The food selection is limited but good.

Replete CAFE $
(Map p262; www.replete.co.nz; 45 Heu Heu St; mains $7-18; ⏲8.30am-4pm) The counter at Replete is packed full of delicatessen delights – running the gamut from sandwiches and salads to sweets. Its pastry selection is particularly commendable. A blackboard menu offers inexpensive and interesting light meals.

Lotus THAI $$
(Map p262; www.lotusthai.co.nz; 137 Tongariro St; mains $16-21; ⏲lunch Wed-Fri, dinner Wed-Mon; 🌿) A warm and inviting restaurant with Siamese trimmings throughout, offering standard Thai fare in plentiful portions.

Piccolo CAFE $
(Map p262; 41 Ruapehu St; mains $11-19; ⏲7am-4pm; 📶) Good coffee, tasty food and free wifi – that's something to toot your flute about.

Drinking

Things get lively in the height of summer when the town fills up with travellers. The rest of the year it might pay to take a newspaper to read over your pint.

Shed PUB
(Map p262; www.theshedbar.co.nz; 18 Tuwharetoa St; ⏲3pm-late Mon & Tue, noon-late Wed-Sun) A lively place to sup a beer and catch the big game, sit outside and watch the world go by, or strut your stuff to DJs on the weekends. Food is punter-pleasing pub fare in man-sized portions.

Finn MacCuhal's IRISH PUB
(Map p262; www.finns.co.nz; cnr Tongariro & Tuwharetoa Sts; ⏲11am-late) With Irish ephemera nailed to the walls and a backpackers' next door, you can be sure that there will be plenty of craic here. DJs and bands play on the weekends.

Jolly Good Fellows PUB
(Map p262; 76 Lake Tce; ⏲11am-late) Corr, Guvnor! You ain't seen a pub like this since old Blighty, with lashings of cultural cliches and Old Speckled Hen, Tetleys and Bulmers cider on tap.

Mulligans IRISH PUB
(Map p262; 15 Tongariro St; ⏲11am-late) A good spot for a quiet Guinness among the locals.

☆ Entertainment

Great Lake Centre CONCERT VENUE
(Map p262; www.taupovenues.co.nz; Tongariro St) Hosts performances, exhibitions and conventions. Ask at the i-SITE for the current program.

Starlight Cinema Centre CINEMA
(Map p262; www.starlightcinema.co.nz; Starlight Arcade, off Horomatangi St; adult/child $13/8.50) Screens the latest Hollywood blockbusters.

Information

Experience Taupo (☎07-377 0704; www.experiencetaupo.co.nz; 29 Tongariro St; ⏲9am-6pm; @) A private agency booking activities, tours and transport. It also offers internet access.

Taupo i-SITE (☎07-376 0027; www.greatlaketaupo.com; Tongariro St; ⏲8.30am-5pm) Handles bookings for accommodation, transport and activities; dispenses cheerful advice; and stocks Department of Conservation (DOC) maps and town maps.

Getting There & Away

Taupo Airport (☎07-378 7771; www.taupoairport.co.nz; 33 Anzac Memorial Dr) is 8km south of town. InterCity buses stop at the **Taupo Travel Centre** (☎07-378 9005; 16 Gascoigne St), which operates as a booking office. Naked Bus services (p260) stop outside the i-SITE.

Shuttle services (p281) operate year-round between Taupo, Turangi and Tongariro National Park. In winter, services run to Whakapapa Ski Area (1½ hours) and can include package deals for lift tickets and ski hire.

Getting Around

Shuttle 2U (☎07-376 7638; www.shuttle2u.co.nz; per stop $4-10, day pass $15) operates an on-demand shuttle service, picking up from local accommodation and stopping at all major attractions in and around Taupo.

Hotbus (☎0508 468 287; www.alpinehotbus.co.nz; 1st stop $15, then per stop $5) is a hop-on, hop-off minibus that covers similar sights, departing from the i-SITE.

Taxi companies include **Taupo Taxi** (☎07-378 5100; www.taupotaxi.co.nz) and **Top Cabs** (☎07-378 9250; 23 Tuwharetoa St). Expect to pay about $25 for a cab from the airport to the centre of town.

Around Taupo

ORAKEI KORAKO

A bit off the beaten track, **Orakei Korako** (07-378 3131; www.orakeikorako.co.nz; adult/child $34/14; 8am-5pm) gets fewer visitors than other thermal areas. Yet, since the destruction of the Pink and White Terraces, it is arguably the best thermal area left in NZ, even though three-quarters of the original site now lies beneath the dam waters of Lake Ohakuri.

A walking track that's steep in parts largely follows a boardwalk around the colourful silica terraces for which the park is famous, and passes geysers and **Ruatapu Cave** (allow 1½ hours). This impressive natural cave has a jade-green pool, thought to have been used as a mirror by Maori women preparing for rituals (Orakei Korako means 'the place of adorning'). Entry includes a boat ride across Lake Ohakuri.

It's about 35 minutes to Orakei Korako from Taupo. Take SH1 towards Hamilton for 23km, and then travel for 14km from the signposted turn-off. From Rotorua the turn-off is on SH5, via Mihi.

Alternatively, **NZ River Jet** (07-333 7111; www.riverjet.co.nz; SH5, Mihi; 2½hr ride incl entry to Orakei Korako adult/child $159/79) will zip you there in thrilling fashion from Mihi, 20km upstream on the Waikato River. The operator also offers The Squeeze – a highly recommended jetboat ride through Tutukau Gorge to a spot where you can disembark in warm water and edge your way through a crevice to a concealed natural thermal waterfall surrounded by native bush ($139).

If it was difficult to resist all that enticing but scalding water at Orakei Korako, but you don't fancy a squeeze, a 30km detour will take you to **Butcher's Pool** (admission free), a bedecked but otherwise purely natural thermal spring in the middle of a farmer's paddock. Alongside is a small parking area and changing sheds. To get there, turn left onto SH5 at Mihi (follow the signs to Rotorua). After 4km look out for Homestead Rd on your right. Follow it to the end, turn left and look for a row of trees lining a gravel driveway off to your right about 300m away (the signpost can be difficult to spot as it's pointing from the other side of the road).

MANGAKINO & WHAKAMARU

These neighbouring towns, like their respective lakes (Maraetai and Whakamaru), are by-products of hydroelectric schemes on the Waikato River. The power stations are still in operation, but the main drawcards today are activities on or around the lakes.

Activities

Paddleboat Company CRUISE
(07-882 8826; www.paddleboat.co.nz; 1/2hr cruise $25/35) Splash along the lake in a paddleboat, which over the course of a century has transported everything from cattle to the Queen.

M-I-A Wakeboarding WAKEBOARDING
(021 864 254; www.m-i-a.co.nz; wakeboard/wakeskate/wakesurf $100/100/75) M-I-A tears up the water on Mangakino's Lake Maraetai, offering wakeboarding, wakeskating and wakesurfing as well as basic backpacker accommodation (dorm/double $23/54).

Waikato River Trails TRAMPING, CYCLING
(www.waikatorivertrails.com) Mangakino and Whakamaru are stops on this 100km walking and cycling route, which follows the river from near the southern end of Lake Karapiro to Atiamuri, 38km north of Taupo.

Sleeping & Eating

Freedom camping is permitted near the **Bus Stop Café** (mains $6-9; Tue-Sun), which dishes out burgers and toasties from the back of an old Bedford bus on the Maraetai lakefront.

PUREORA FOREST PARK

Fringing the western edge of Lake Taupo, the 78,000-hectare Pureora Forest is home to NZ's tallest totara tree. Logging was stopped in this forest in the 1980s after a long campaign by conservationists, and the subsequent regeneration is impressive. There are mountain-bike tracks and hiking routes through the park, including tracks to the summits of **Mt Pureora** (1165m) and the rock pinnacle of **Mt Titiraupenga** (1042m). A 12m-high tower, a short walk from the Bismarck Rd car park, provides a canopy-level view of the forest for birdwatchers.

To stay overnight in one of three standard DOC huts (adult/child $5.10/2.50) you'll need to buy hut tickets in advance, unless you have a backcountry hut pass. The three campsites (adult/child $8/2) have self-registration boxes. Hut tickets, maps and information on the park are available from DOC.

Awhina Wilderness Experience (www.awhinatours.co.nz; per person $175) offers five-hour walking tours with local Maori guides through virgin bush to the summit of Titiraupenga, their sacred mountain. Farmstay accommodation is also available.

Turangi & Around

POP 3500

Once a service town for the nearby hydro-electric power station, sleepy Turangi's claim to fame nowadays is as the 'Trout Fishing Capital of the World' and as one of the country's premier white water–rafting destinations. Set on the Tongariro River, the town is a shortish hop for snow-bunnies from the ski fields and walking tracks of Tongariro National Park.

Sights & Activities

There are several short walks around town. A favourite is the **Tongariro River Lookout Track** (one-hour loop), a riverside amble affording views of Mt Pihanga. This track joins the **Tongariro River Walkway** (three hours return), which follows the river to the Red Hut suspension bridge, and will eventually hook up with the **Tongariro River Trail** (www.tongarirorivertrail.co.nz), a multiday walking and mountain-biking route, which was being finalised at the time of research.

Other good leg-stretchers include **Hinemihi's Track**, near the top of Te Ponanga Saddle, 8km west of Turangi on SH47 (15 minutes return); **Maunganamu Track**, 4km west of Turangi on SH41 (40 minutes return); and **Tauranga-Taupo River Walk** (30 minutes), which starts at Te Rangiita, 12km north of Turangi on SH1.

The Tongariro River has some superb Grade III rapids for river rafting, as well as Grade I stretches suitable for beginners in the lower reaches during summer.

It's also a likely spot for trout fishing (p266).

Tongariro National Trout Centre AQUARIUM
(Map p277; www.troutcentre.com; SH1; adult/child $10/free; ⌚10am-3pm) The DOC-managed trout hatchery has polished educational displays, a collection of rods and reels dating back to the 1880s and freshwater aquariums displaying river life, both nasty and nice. A gentle stroll along the landscaped walkway leads to the hatchery, keeping ponds, an underwater viewing chamber and a picnic area.

Tokaanu Thermal Pools SWIMMING
(Map p277; Mangaroa St, Tokaanu; adult/child $6/4, private pools per 20min $10/6; ⌚10am-9pm) Soak in thermally heated water at this unpretentious, family-orientated facility, 5km northwest of Turangi. A 20-minute stroll along the boardwalk (wheelchair accessible) showcases boiling mud pools, thermal springs and a trout-filled stream.

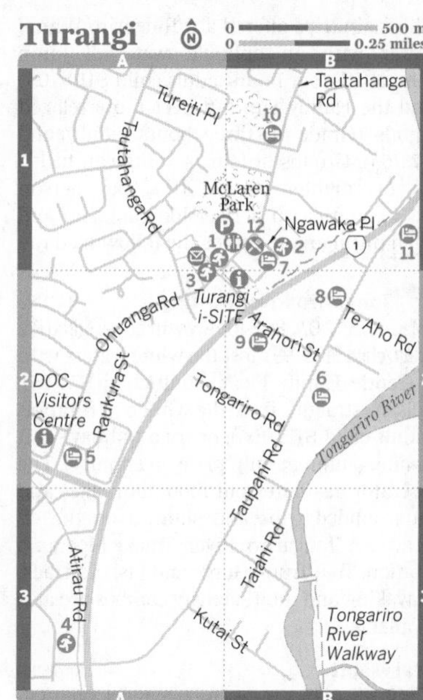

Turangi

Activities, Courses & Tours

1 Barry Greig's Sporting World ... A1
Creel Tackle House ... (see 6)
2 Rafting NZ ... B1
3 Sporting Life ... A2
4 Tongariro River Rafting ... A3
Vertical Assault ... (see 7)

Sleeping

5 Anglers Paradise Motel ... A2
6 Creel Lodge ... B2
7 Extreme Backpackers ... B1
8 Judges Pool Motel ... B2
9 Parklands Motor Lodge ... B2
10 Riverstone Backpackers ... B1
11 Sportmans Lodge ... B1

Eating

12 Grand Central Fry ... B1

Rafting NZ RAFTING
(Map p273; ☎0800 865 226; www.raftingnewzealand.com; 41 Ngawaka Pl) Offering a warm welcome, hot showers and a taste of Maori culture, this operator is a popular choice.

The main trips offered are Tongariro Whitewater with an optional waterfall jump (Grade III, four hours, adult/child $119/109) and the Family Fun raft over more relaxed rapids (Grade II, three hours, adult/child $75/65). Groups of four or more can tackle an overnighter (Grade III+, per person $350), rafting to a riverside campsite and then hitting more rapids the following day.

Tongariro River Rafting RAFTING
(Map p273; ☎07-386 6409; www.trr.co.nz; Atirau Rd; adult/child $109/99) Test the white waters with a Gentle Family Float (adult/child $75/65), splash straight into the Grade III rapids (adult/child $115/105), or try a full day's raft fishing (summer only, price on enquiry). The operator also hires out mountain bikes and runs guided trips and shuttles on the 42 Traverse, Tongariro River Track, Moerangi Station, Tree Trunk Gorge and Fishers Track. Kayaking and multi-activity combos are also available.

Wai Maori KAYAKING
(☎07-386 0315; www.waimaori.com; Tokaanu) Offers guided white-water kayaking (November to April, per person $159) or trips accompanied only by trout down the gentle Tokaanu Stream to Lake Taupo, passing boiling mud, hot pools and wetlands on the way (90 minutes/half-day/full day $30/40/65).

Flyfishtaupo.com FISHING
(☎07-377 8054; www.flyfishtaupo.com; prices on application) Guide Brett Pirie offers a range of fishing excursions, including seniors-focussed 'Old Farts & Tarts' trips.

Central Plateau Fishing FISHING
(☎027 285 6593; www.cpf.net.nz; half-/full day from $300/550) Guided fly-fishing, boat charters (per hour $100) and quad-bike adventure fishing in Tongariro National Park (from $750). Licences extra.

Ian & Andrew Jenkins FISHING
(☎07-386 0840; www.tui-lodge.co.nz; half-/full day $350/600) Father and son fly-fishing guides.

John Somervell FISHING
(☎07-386 5931; www.nymphfish.com; half-/full day from $225/450) Well-priced guided fly-fishing.

AJ Charters FISHING, CRUISE
(☎07-386 7992; www.ajtaupocharters.com; per hr from $120) Fishing trips and scenic lake cruises on a two-storey catamaran.

Barry Greig's Sporting World FISHING
(Map p273; ☎07-386 6911; www.greigsports.co.nz; 59 Town Centre) Hires and sells gear and handles bookings for guides and charters.

Creel Tackle House FISHING
(Map p273; ☎07-386 7929; 183 Taupahi Rd) Fishing equipment and tips.

Sporting Life FISHING
(Map p273; www.sportinglife-turangi.co.nz; Town Centre) This sports store is laden with fishing paraphenalia. Its website details the latest fishing conditions.

Motuoapa Hire Boats BOATING
(☎07-386 7000; Motuoapa Esplanade; per hr $39) Hires aluminium dinghies for lake fishing, 10km northeast of Turangi.

Vertical Assault CLIMBING
(Map p273; www.extremebackpackers.co.nz; 22 Ngawaka Pl; adult/child $20/15; ⌚9am-5pm Thu-Tue, 9am-8pm Wed) For wet-weather thrills, head here to scale walls built to challenge all skill levels.

Sleeping

TOP CHOICE **Riverstone Backpackers** HOSTEL $
(Map p273; ☎07-386 7004; www.riverstonebackpackers.com; 222 Tautahanga Rd; dm $25-30, r $62-84; @) Reborn as a bijou backpackers, this cleverly refitted old house has an enviable kitchen, comfortable lounge and a stylish landscaped yard (with pizza oven). It's a true home away from home.

Creel Lodge LODGE $$
(Map p273; ☎07-386 8081; www.creel.co.nz; 183 Taupahi Rd; s $110-130, d $125-145; 📶) Set in green and peaceful grounds, this heavenly hideaway backs onto a fine stretch of the Tongariro River. It's worth upgrading to an executive garden suite for a smarter unit in an attractive punga-fenced garden.

Oreti Village APARTMENTS $$$
(Map p277; ☎07-386 7070; www.oretivillage.com; Mission House Dr, Pukawa; apt $220-280; 📶) This enclave of luxury self-contained apartments might give you a hankering for 'village' life – which in Oreti's case entails gazing at blissful lake views from the comfort of a rolled-arm leather couch. Take SH41 for 15km, heading northwest of Turangi, and turn right into Pukawa Rd.

Sportmans Lodge GUESTHOUSE $$
(Map p273; ☎07-386 8150; www.sportsmanslodge.co.nz; 15 Taupahi Rd; r $72, cottage $105-130; 📶) Backing on to the river, this lodge is a hidden bargain for trout-fishing folk unbothered by punctuation. All the rooms share the lounge and well-equipped kitchen. The self-contained cottage sleeps four.

Extreme Backpackers HOSTEL $
(Map p273; ☎07-386 8949; www.extremebackpackers.co.nz; 22 Ngawaka Pl; dm $25-27, s $46-56, d $62-72; @📶) Crafted from pine and corrugated iron, this modern backpackers has the bonus of a climbing wall, a cafe, a lounge with an open fire and a sunny courtyard with hammocks. Dorms range from four to eight beds and the pricier private rooms have en suites. The operators also run shuttles to Tongariro National Park.

Parklands Motor Lodge MOTEL $
(Map p273; ☎07-386 7515; www.parklandsmotorlodge.co.nz; 25 Arahori St; sites from $17, units $110-140; 📶🏊) On SH1 but set back beyond an epic front lawn, Parklands offers a small but functional area for campervans and splay of well-presented units. There's a swimming pool and play area for the kids.

Anglers Paradise Motel MOTEL $$
(Map p273; ☎07-386 8980; www.anglersparadise.co.nz; cnr Ohuanga Rd & Raukura St; units $119-160; @🏊) Looking like something out of Twin Peaks, this very old-fashioned motel sits in a 1-hectare leafy pocket where privacy prevails. It's geared up for anglers, with guides happily arranged and a smokehouse on-site.

Judges Pool Motel MOTEL $$
(Map p273; ☎07-386 7892; www.judgespoolmotel.co.nz; 92 Taupahi Rd; units $105-145; 📶) This older motel has tidy, spacious rooms with kitchenettes. All one-bedroom units have outdoor decks for relaxing beers, although the barbecue area is the best place to talk about the one that got away.

Eating

Tongariro Lodge MODERN NZ $$
(Map p277; ☎07-386 7946; www.tongarirolodge.co.nz; 83 Grace Rd; mains $30-42; ⊙dinner) Some of the world's most famous blokes (Robert Mitchum, Liam Neeson, Larry Hagman, Jimmy Carter, Timothy Dalton) have come to this luxury riverside fishing lodge, set in 9 hectares of parkland north of the town, to relax in wood-panelled anonymity. Not surprisingly, the menu is orientated around man-sized slabs of meat but the real squeals of delight come when lucky lodgers are presented with their day's catch, smoked and served to perfection.

Oreti Village FRENCH $$
(Map p277; ☎07-386 7070; Mission House Dr, Pukawa; mains $30-38; ⊙lunch Sat & Sun, dinner Tue-Sun) It's hard to imagine a more romantic spot to while away a balmy summer's evening than looking over the lake from Oreti's terrace. It's an added bonus that the French-influenced food matches up.

Grand Central Fry FAST FOOD $
(Map p273; 8 Ohuanga Rd; meals $3-8; ⊙11am-8.30pm) This local legend serves top fish and chips, plus burgers and anything else fryable.

Licorice CAFE $
(57 SH1, Motuoapa; mains $9-17; ⊙7am-4pm Wed-Sat, 9am-4pm Sun) Look for the giant licorice allsort on the roof of this roadside cafe, 8km north of Turangi. It's better than any of the cafes in the town itself.

Information

Turangi i-SITE (☎07-386 8999; www.greatlaketauponz.com; Ngawaka Pl; ⊙8.30am-5pm; @📶) A good stop for information on Tongariro National Park, Kaimanawa Forest Park, trout fishing, and snow and road conditions. It issues DOC hut tickets, ski passes and fishing licences, and makes bookings for transport, accommodation and activities.

Getting There & Away

Both InterCity (p260) and Naked Bus (p260) coaches stop outside the i-SITE.

THE CENTRAL PLATEAU

Tongariro National Park

Established in 1887, Tongariro was NZ's first, and the world's fourth, national park, and is one of NZ's three World Heritage Sites. Its three towering, active volcanoes – Ruapehu, Ngauruhoe and Tongariro – rise from a vast, scrub-covered alpine plateau, making this one of the nation's most spectacular locations. In summer it offers excellent short walks and longer tramps, most notably the Tongariro Northern Circuit and the Tongariro Alpine Crossing. In winter it's a busy ski area.

The three peaks were a gift to NZ from Ngati Tuwharetoa, the local *iwi* (tribe), who saw the act as the only way to preserve an area of spiritual significance.

Sights

Mt Ruapehu VOLCANO

(www.mtruapehu.com) The multipeaked summit of Ruapehu (2797m) is the highest and most active of the park's volcanoes, and the centrepiece of the national park, with Whakapapa Village (pronounced 'fa-ka-pa-pa'), numerous walking tracks and three ski fields on its slopes.

The name means 'pit of sound', a reference to its regular eruptions. It began erupting over 250,000 years ago and remains active today, with major eruptions roughly every 50 years. During the spectacular 1995 eruptions, Ruapehu spurted volcanic rock and cloaked the area in clouds of ash and steam. From June to September the following year the mountain rumbled, groaned and thrust ash clouds high into the sky, writing off the 1996 ski season. The latest eruption, accompanied by a small earthquake, came out of the blue in September 2007, seriously injuring a climber sleeping in a hut on the mountain.

The mountain was the cause of one of NZ's deadliest natural disasters. Eruptions in 1945 blocked the overflow of the crater lake, causing the water levels to rise dramatically. On Christmas Eve 1953 the dam burst and the flood of volcanic mud (known as a lahar) swept down the mountain and took out a railway bridge at Tangiwai (between Ohakune and Waiouru), just moments before a crowded express train arrived. The train was derailed and 153 people lost their lives.

The crater lake was blocked again by the 1995–96 eruption. As the levels rose, it was foreseen that a major lahar could lead to another catastrophe. Alarm systems were set up at the crater lake's edge and in March 2007 they were triggered when a moderate lahar swept down the Whangaehu Valley. No one was injured and there was little damage to infrastructure.

Mt Ngauruhoe VOLCANO

Much younger than the other two volcanoes, it is estimated that Ngauruhoe (2287m) formed in the last 2500 years. In contrast to the others, which have multiple vents, Ngauruhoe is a conical, single-vent volcano with perfectly symmetrical slopes – which is the reason that it was chosen to star as Mt Doom in Peter Jackson's *Lord of the Rings*. It can be climbed in summer, but in winter (under snow) this steep climb is only for experienced mountaineers.

Mt Tongariro VOLCANO

The Red Crater of Mt Tongariro (1968m) last erupted in 1926. This ancient, but still active, volcano has coloured lakes dotting its uneven summit. The Tongariro Alpine Crossing, a magnificent walk, passes beside the lakes, right through several craters, and down through lush native forest.

Activities

The DOC and i-SITE visitor centres at Whakapapa, Ohakune and Turangi have maps and information on walks in the park, as well as track and weather conditions. Each January, DOC offers an excellent guided-walks program in and around the park; ask at DOC centres for information or book online. The national park is a popular skiing destination (p44).

Whakapapa & Turoa Ski Areas SKIING, SNOWBOARDING

(☎Turoa 06-385 8456, Whakapapa 07-892 4000; www.mtruapehu.com; daily lift pass adult/child $95/57, valid at both resorts) These linked resorts straddle either side of Mt Ruapehu and are NZ's two largest ski areas. Each offers similar skiing at an analogous altitude (around 2300m), with areas to suit each level of experience – from beginners' slopes to

Tongariro National Park & Around

Sights

1 Tongariro National Trout Centre D2

Activities, Courses & Tours

2 Mountain Air B3
3 Ruapehu Homestead A6
4 Tokaanu Thermal Pools D1
5 Tukino Ski Area C4

Sleeping

6 Discovery Lodge B3
7 Oreti Village D1

Eating

Oreti Village .... (see 7)
8 Tongariro Lodge D1

black diamond runs for the pros. The same lift passes cover both ski areas. At the time of research a new lift was being planned for Turoa, providing access to a glacial area further up the mountain.

The only accommodation at the ski fields is in private lodges (mainly owned by ski clubs), so most Whakapaka visitors stay at Whakapaka or National Park Village. Turoa is only 16km from Ohakune, which has the best après-ski scene.

Tongariro National Park & Around

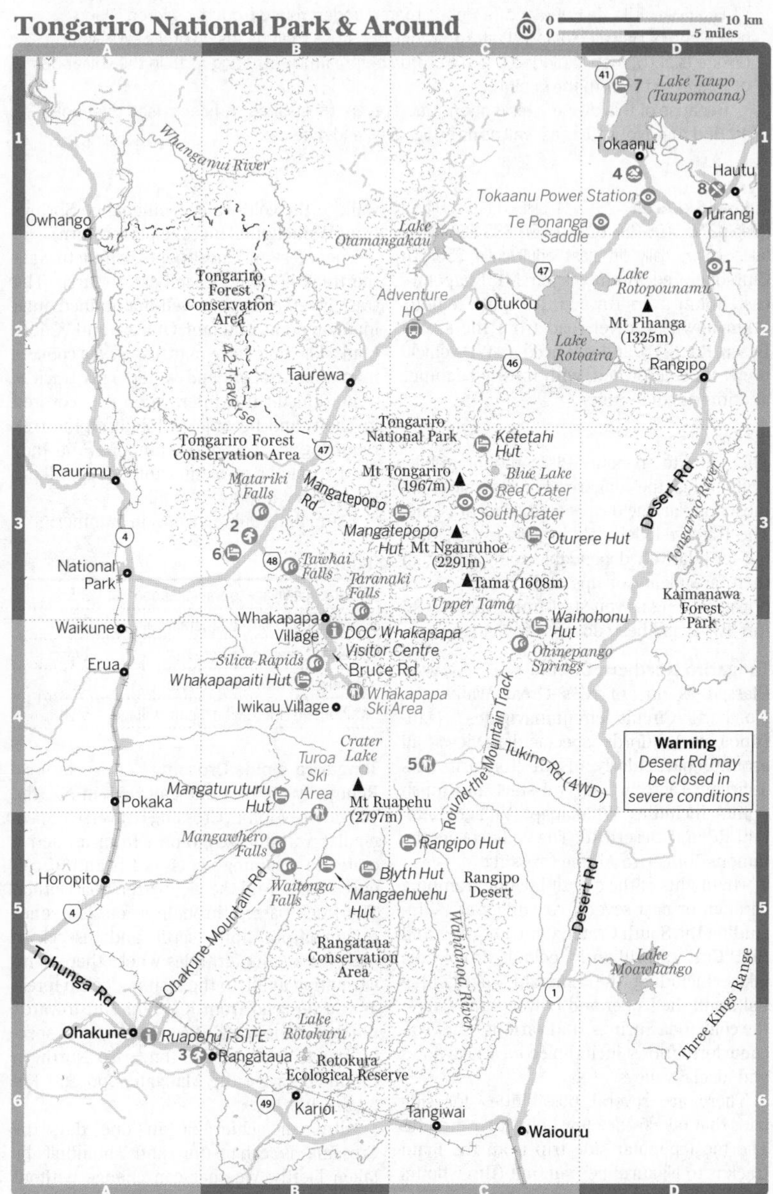

HOTHEADS TO THE RESCUE

Maori legend tells of the great *tohunga* (priest) and explorer Ngatoro-i-rangi, who first climbed Mt Tongariro. At the summit, realising he was close to freezing to death, he called out for assistance: '*ka riro au i te tonga*' ('I am carried away by the cold south wind') – and from these words the name Tongariro is derived.

The fire spirits, Te Pupu and Te Hoata, roared underground from the sacred island homeland of Hawaiki to find Ngatoro-i-rangi, but stuck their heads up first at Whakaari (White Island), then exploded out at Rotorua before finally bursting forth in the volcanoes of Tongariro to warm the explorer.

Because of this divine intervention, Maori revere these sites and once used the pools around them for rituals as well as cooking, dyes and medicine.

Tukino Ski Area SKIING, SNOWBOARDING
(Map p277; ☎06-387 6294, 0800 885 466; www.tukino.co.nz; daily lift pass adult/child $50/30) Club-operated Tukino is on Mt Ruapehu's east, 46km from Turangi. It's quite remote, 14km down a gravel road from the sealed Desert Rd (SH1), and you need a 4WD vehicle to get in. Uncrowded, with mostly beginner and intermediate runs.

42 Traverse MOUNTAIN BIKING
This four- to six-hour, 46km mountain-bike trail through the Tongariro Forest is one of the most popular one-dayers on the North Island. The Traverse follows old logging tracks, making for relatively dependable going, although there are plenty of ups and downs – more downs as long as you start from Kapoors Rd (off SH47) and head down to Owhango.

Tongariro Northern Circuit TRAMPING
Classed as one of NZ's Great Walks, the Northern Circuit circumnavigates Ngauruhoe and affords spectacular views all around, particularly of Mt Tongariro. As a circuit, there are several start and finish points, including Whakapapa Village, Ketetahi Rd and Desert Rd. The walk covers the famous Tongariro Alpine Crossing.

Highlights of the circuit include tramping through or past several volcanic craters, including the South Crater, Central Crater and Red Crater; brilliantly colourful volcanic lakes, including the Emerald Lakes, Blue Lake and the Upper and Lower Tama Lakes; the cold Soda Springs; and various other volcanic formations, including cones, lava flows and glacial valleys.

There are several possibilities for side trips that take from a few hours to overnight. The most popular side trip from the main track is to Ngauruhoe's summit (three hours return), but it is also possible to climb Tongariro from Red Crater (two hours return) or walk to the cold-water Ohinepango Springs from Waihohonu Hut (one hour return).

The safest and most popular time to walk the track is from December to March. The track is served by four well-maintained huts: Mangatepopo, Ketetahi, Oturere and Waihohonu. The huts have mattresses, gas cookers in summer, toilets and water. This track is quite difficult in winter, when it is covered in snow, and becomes a tough alpine trek requiring ice axes and crampons. You may need to factor in significant extra walking time, or not attempt it at all.

Estimated walking times in summer:

ROUTE	TIME
Whakapapa Village to Mangatepopo Hut	3-5hr
Mangatepopo Hut to Emerald Lakes	3½hr
Emerald Lakes to Oturere Hut	1½hr
Oturere Hut to Waihohonu Hut	3hr
Waihohonu Hut to Whakapapa Village	5½hr

Tongariro Alpine Crossing TRAMPING
Reputedly the best one-day walk in NZ, the Tongariro Alpine Crossing traverses spectacular volcanic geography, from an active crater to steaming vents and beautiful coloured lakes. And the views aren't bad either. The track passes through vegetation zones ranging from alpine scrub and tussock to places at higher altitudes where there is no vegetation at all, to the lush podocarp forest as you descend from Ketetahi Hut towards the end of the track. It covers the most spectacular features of the Tongariro Northern Circuit between the Mangatepopo and Ketetahi Huts.

Although achievable in one day, the Crossing is exhausting and shouldn't be taken lightly. Weather can change without warning, so make sure you are adequately equipped. If you're not in top walking condition you may prefer to take two days, spending a night at Ketatahi Hut

Worthwhile side trips from the main track include ascents to the summits of Mts Ngauruhoe and Tongariro. Ngauruhoe can be ascended most easily from the Mangatepopo Saddle, reached near the beginning of the track after the first steep climb. It's a challenging unmarked ascent on a scree surface where rocks are easily dislodged – look out for those falling from above and take care if people are walking below you. The summit of Tongariro is reached by a poled route from Red Crater.

The Tongariro Alpine Crossing can be reached from Mangatepopo Rd, off SH47, and from Ketetahi Rd, off SH46. The Mangatepopo Hut, reached via Mangatepopo Rd, is near the start of the track, and the Ketetahi Hut is a couple of hours before the end. Theft from parked vehicles is a problem at both ends: don't leave valuables in the car and keep everything out of sight.

Because of its popularity, there are plenty of shuttle services to both ends of the track. The shuttles need to be booked and you'll be expected to complete the track in a reasonable time.

Note: this may be one of the world's great walks, but it's not an experience you'll enjoy if you're badly prepared or the weather is awful. In winter, the colourful lakes are hidden under a blanket of snow and the effect is quite different. If it's blowing a gale, pelting with rain or if you're wearing unsuitable clothing (jeans and flip-flops aren't alpine-appropriate), you're all but guaranteed to have a miserable, not to mention potentially dangerous, time.

Estimated summer walking times:

ROUTE	TIME
Mangatepopo Rd end to Mangatepopo Hut	15min
Mangatepopo Hut to South Crater	1½-2hr
South Crater to Mt Ngauruhoe summit (side trip)	2-3hr (return)
Red Crater to Tongariro summit (side trip)	1½hr (return)
South Crater to Emerald Lakes	1-1½hr
Emerald Lakes to Ketetahi Hut	1½hr
Ketetahi Hut to road end	1½hr

Round the Mountain Track TRAMPING

This off-the-beaten-track hike is a quieter alternative to the busy Northern Circuit, but it's particularly tough, has some potentially tricky river crossings, and is not recommended for beginners or the unprepared. Looping around Mt Ruapehu, the trail takes in a diversity of country, from glacial rivers to tussocky moors to majestic mountain views. You should allow at least four days to complete the hike, with six days a realistic estimate if you're including side trips to the Blyth Hut or Tama Lakes.

You can get to the Round the Mountain trail from Whakapapa Village, the junction near Waihohonu Hut, Ohakune Mountain Rd, or Whakapapaiti Hut. Most trampers start at Whakapapa Village and return there to finish the loop.

The track is safest from December to March when there is little or no snow, and less chance of avalanche. At other times of year, navigation and walking is made difficult by snow, and full alpine gear (ice axe, crampons and specialised clothing) is a requirement. To attempt the track you should prepare thoroughly. Take sufficiently detailed maps, check on the latest conditions, and carry clothing for all climes and more-than-adequate food supplies. Be sure to leave your plans and intended return date with a responsible person and check in when you get back.

This track is served by Waihohonu, Rangipo, Mangaehuehu, Mangaturuturu and Whakapapaiti Huts, and a side trip can be made to Blyth Hut. Estimated summer walking times:

ROUTE	TIME
Whakapapa Village to Waihohonu Hut	5-6hr
Waihohonu Hut to Rangipo Hut	5hr
Rangipo Hut to Mangaehuehu Hut	5-6hr
Mangaehuehu Hut to Mangaturuturu Hut	5hr
Mangaturuturu Hut to Whakapapaiti Hut	6hr
Whakapapaiti Hut to Whakapapa Village	2-3hr
Tama Lakes (side trip)	1½hr
Blyth Hut (side trip)	1hr

MOUNTAIN SAFETY

Many visitors to NZ come unstuck in the mountains. The weather can change quicker than you expect, and rescues (and fatalities) are not uncommon. When heading out on remote tracks, you must be properly equipped and take safety precautions, including leaving your itinerary with a responsible person.

Crater Lake TRAMPING

The unmarked rugged route up to Ruapehu's Crater Lake (seven hours return) is a good one, allowing you to see the acidic lake up close, but this walk is strictly off limits when there's volcanic activity. This moderate-to-difficult walk begins at Iwikau Village at the top of the Bruce Rd. You can cut three hours off it by catching the **chairlift** (adult/child $26/16; 9am-3.30pm mid-Dec–April) from Whakapapa Ski Area. **Guided walks** (0508 782 734; www.mtruapehu.com; adult/child incl lift pass $145/95) to Crater Lake run from mid-December to mid-April, weather dependent. Like most of the walks in Tongariro, you'll need to check conditions before heading out and don't attempt it in winter unless you're a mountaineer.

Tama Lakes Track TRAMPING

Starting at Whakapapa Village, this 17km track leads to the Tama Lakes, on the Tama Saddle between Ruapehu and Ngauruhoe (five to six hours return). The upper lake affords fine views of Ngauruhoe and Tongariro (beware of winds on the saddle).

Ridge Track TRAMPING

A 30-minute return walk from Whakapapa that climbs through beech forest to alpine-shrub areas for views of all three peaks.

Silica Rapids Track TRAMPING

From Whakapapa Village this 2½-hour, 7km loop track leads to the Silica Rapids, named for the silica mineral deposits formed there by rapids on the Waikare Stream.

Taranaki Falls Track TRAMPING

A two-hour, 6km loop track heads from Whakapapa to the 20m Taranaki Falls on the Wairere Stream.

Whakapapa Nature Walk WALKING

Suitable for wheelchairs, this 15-minute loop track begins about 200m above the visitor centre, passing through beech forest and gardens typical of the park's vegetation zones.

Tongariro Quads QUAD BIKES

(07-378 2662; www.tongariroquads.com; half-/full day $199/299) Takes guided trips through the Tongariro Forest Park along the 42 Traverse.

Mountain Air SCENIC FLIGHTS

(Map p277; 0800 922 812; www.mountainair.co.nz; junction SH47 & SH48; flights $115-220) Offers scenic flights ranging from 15 to 35 minutes covering the volcanoes and lakes. They also depart from Turangi ($275, 45 minutes) and Taupo ($299, 65 minutes).

Edge to Edge SNOW SPORTS

(0800 800 754; www.edgetoedge.co.nz; Skotel Alpine Resort; 1-day full ski gear $35-65, 1-day snowboard gear $43-71) Stocks a full range of skiing, climbing and alpine gear for hire.

Sleeping & Eating

Whakapapa Village has limited accommodation and prices quoted here are for summer; rates are generally much higher during the ski season. National Park village and Ohakune offer a greater range of options. National Park has the best selection of budget accommodation while Ohakune is a proper town, with a better array of eateries and shops.

Whakapapa Holiday Park HOLIDAY PARK $

(07-892 3897; www.whakapapa.net.nz; Whakapapa Village; sites from $19, dm $25, units $69-149) This popular DOC-associated park has a wide range of accommodation options, including campsites perched on the edge of beautiful bushland, a 32-bed backpackers lodge (linen required), cabins (linen required) and a self-contained unit. The camp store stocks basic groceries.

Skotel Alpine Resort HOSTEL $

(07-892 3719; www.skotel.co.nz; Whakapapa Village; s/tw/tr without bathroom $40/55/75, r with bathroom $110-185, cabin $185) If you think of it more as a hostel than a hotel, you'll excuse the odd bit of stained carpet or cheap lino, and enjoy the timber-lined alpine ambience and decidedly non-hostel-like facilties: sauna, spa pool, gym, ski hire, restaurant and bar.

Bayview Chateau Tongariro HOTEL **$$**
(☎07-892 3809; www.chateau.co.nz; Whakapapa Village; r from $155; @) NZ's great missed tourism opportunity promises much, with its sublime setting and manor house grandeur, but the old-world charm is fading fast. Which is a shame, as a cashed-up interior designer could swiftly transform the Chateau back into the iconic hotel it was when it first opened its doors in 1929. Still, you may just run into one-armed big-game hunters in the bar here, or cane-wielding silver-medal skiers from the seventies, or ex-colonels twisting their fine little moustaches as they eye you through their greasy monocles – it has that kind of vibe. Within the hulking complex are a cinema, the elegant **Ruapehu Room** (mains $36-38; ⏲dinner), **Pihanga Cafe** (mains $20-27; ⏲lunch & dinner) and the T-bar, a cosy spot for a warming winter tipple. The operators also manage the neighbouring nine-hole public golf course, **Fergusson's Cafe** (mains $5-10; ⏲breakfast & lunch; @) and Fergusson Motel, which has self-contained family chalets (from $155).

DOC campsites CAMPSITES **$**
(www.doc.govt.nz; sites per adult/child $6/3) Apart from the huts and associated campsites, there are two basic DOC camping grounds in this area: Mangahuia, between National Park village and the SH48 turn-off heading to Whakapapa; and Mangawhero, near Ohakune. Both have cold water and pit toilets.

Information

Further national park information is available from the i-SITEs in Ohakune (p286) as well as Turangi (p275).

DOC Whakapapa Visitor Centre (☎07-892 3729; www.doc.govt.nz; Whakapapa Village; ⏲8am-5pm) Has maps and info on all corners of the park, including walks, huts and current skiing, track and weather conditions. It also has interesting exhibits on the geological and human history of the area, including an audiovisual display and a small shop – making it the perfect place for rainy days. The detailed *Tongariro National Park* map ($19) is worth buying before tramping.

Getting There & Around

Bus

There are numerous shuttle services to Whakapapa Village, the Tongariro Alpine Crossing and other key destinations from Taupo, Turangi, National Park and Ohakune. In summer tramping trips are their focus, but in winter most offer ski-field shuttles. Book your bus in advance to avoid unexpected strandings. As well as those listed below, most of the Turangi and National Park hostels offer their own shuttles at similar rates.

Adventure HQ (☎07-386 0969; www.adventurehq.co.nz) Runs scheduled Tongariro Alpine Crossing services ($35) from its base on SH47. They also sell and hire gear.

Alpine Hotbus (☎0508 468 287; www.alpinehotbus.co.nz) Provides shuttles to the Crossing from Rotorua ($99), Taupo ($55) and Turangi ($40), and from Taupo to Whakapapa and National Park village ($60).

Matai Shuttles (☎06-385 8724; www.mataishuttles.co.nz) Runs ski shuttles from Ohakune to Turoa (return $25) and Whakapapa (return $30), a winter-only nighttime loop around Ohakune ($4), and shuttles to various walking and cycling trails.

Snow Express (☎06-385 4022; www.dempseybuses.co.nz; return $25) Offers transport from Ohakune to the Turoa ski field.

Tongariro Expeditions (☎0800 828 763; www.tongariroexpeditions.com) Runs shuttles from Taupo ($59, 1½ hours), Turangi ($40, 45 minutes) and Whakapapa ($35, 15 minutes) to the Crossing and the Northern Circuit.

Turangi Alpine Shuttles (☎07-386 8226; www.turangirentals.co.nz) Plys the Turangi–Whakapapa route (one-way/return $35/45) and has Crossing shuttles ($40).

HUT PASSES

Scattered around the park's tramping tracks are 10 huts that can be used for accommodation. Prices vary according to hut and season, but range from $15 to $31 per person. You can camp beside the huts for $5 to $21 per person. The DOC centres and i-SITEs in Turangi, Whakapaka and Ohakune sell hut tickets and Backcountry Hut Passes.

In the Great Walk season – from late October to April – advance reservations are required for the four Tongariro Northern Circuit huts (Mangatepopo, Ketetahi, Oturere and Waihohonu). You're best to book online at www.doc.govt.nz, but bookings may also be made at DOC visitor centres and some i-SITES, where a booking fee may apply.

Car & Motorcycle

Tongariro National Park is bounded by roads: SH1 (called the Desert Rd) to the east, SH4 to the west, SH46 and SH47 to the north and SH49 to the south. The main road up into the park is SH48, which leads to Whakapapa Village and continues further up the mountain as Bruce Rd leading to the Whakapapa Ski Area. Ohakune Mountain Rd leads up to the Turoa Ski Area from Ohakune. The Desert Rd is regularly closed when the weather is bad – large signs will direct you to other routes. Likewise, Ohakune Mountain Rd and Bruce Rd are subject to closures, and access beyond certain points may be restricted to 4WDs or cars with snow chains.

National Park Village

POP 460

Named for nearby Tongariro National Park, this tiny outpost lies at the junction of SH4 and SH47, 15km from the hub of Whakapapa Village. In ski season the township is packed, but in summer it's sleepy – despite being a handy base for activities in and around the park.

There's little to do in the village itself, its major enticement being its proximity to the ski fields, national-park tramps, the 42 Traverse mountain-bike trail and canoe trips on the Whanganui River. Daily shuttles leave from here to the Tongariro Alpine Crossing and Whakapapa Village in summer, and the ski area in winter.

As you'll discover, it's railway country around here. About 20km south on SH4 at Horopito is a monument to the Last Spike, the spike that marked the completion of the Main Trunk Railway Line between Auckland and Wellington in 1908. Five kilometres north from National Park, at Raurimu, is evidence of the engineering masterpiece that is the 'spiral'. Trainspotters will marvel, while non-trainspotters will probably wonder what the hell they're looking at it (there's not much to see).

Activities

Most accommodation in town offers packages for lift passes and ski hire, sparing you the steeper prices further up the mountain. Ski gear can be hired from **Eivins** (07-892 2843; www.nationalpark.co.nz/eivins; Carroll St), **Snow Zone** (07-892 2757; www.snowzone.co.nz; 25-27 Buddo St) and **Ski Biz** (07-892 2717; www.skibiz.co.nz; 10 Carroll St).

Fishers Track MOUNTAIN BIKING

Starting from National Park village, this track is a 17km downhill blast, and now forms part of the Ruapehu Whanganui Trails (p285).

Adrift Guided Outdoor Adventures CANOEING, TRAMPING

(07-892 2751; www.adriftnz.co.nz) Runs guided canoe trips on the Whanganui River (one to six days, $245 to $999), as well as freedom canoe hire and all necessary transfers. It also offers guided tramps in Tongariro National Park (two hours to three days, $95 to $850).

Wade's Landing Outdoors CANOEING, KAYAKING

(07-895 5995; www.whanganui.co.nz; 29 Kaitieke Rd, Raurimu) Offers freedom kayak and canoe hire for Whanganui River expeditions, including jetboat/road transfers to trail heads (one to five days, $80 to $180). There are also mountain-biking shuttles, *Lord of the Rings* tours and a 'prehistoric driftwood sculpture park'.

Climbing Wall CLIMBING

(07-892 2870; www.npbp.co.nz; 4 Findlay St; adult/child $15/10; 9am-8pm) For rainy days there's an 8m-high indoor climbing wall at National Park Backpackers. Outdoor climbers with their own gear can find spots near Manataupo Valley and Whakapapa Gorge.

Sleeping

National Park is a town of budget and midrange accommodation. This makes sense, as you'll probably spend most of your time in the great outdoors. We list summer prices here; be warned that they increase in the ski season, when accommodation is tight and bookings are essential.

Tongariro Crossing Lodge LODGE $$

(07-892 2688; www.tongarirocrossinglodge.com; 27 Carroll St; s $115-125, d $140-185; @) As pretty as a picture, this white weatherboard cottage is decorated with a baby-blue trim and rambling blooms in summer. Accommodation ranges from standard doubles to larger self-contained apartments.

Discovery Lodge LODGE $

(Map p277; 07-892 2744; www.discovery.net.nz; SH47; sites from $16, units $60-300; @) Handy for skiers, this lodge is midway between the village and the Whakapapa turn-off. The restaurant has excellent views of Ruapehu, plus there's a bar and comfy lounge. Cabins are basic, but large chalets provide upmarket getaways for up to four people.

Plateau HOSTEL $
(☎07-892 2993; www.plateaulodge.co.nz; 17 Carroll St; dm $28, d $65-85, apt $155-195; @📶) Plateau has cosy rooms, some with en suite and TV, and an attractive communal lounge, a kitchen and a hot tub. The dorms don't get bigger than two sets of bunks and there are nice two-bedroom apartments (sleeping up to six) available as well. This place also offers Crossing, Northern Circuit and 42 Traverse shuttles.

Park HOSTEL $
(☎07-892 2748; www.the-park.co.nz; 2/6 Millar St; dm $35-40, r $120-140, apt $160-200; @📶) There's no way you can miss this big flashpackers on the highway. Inside it's smart and comfortable, with a garden courtyard surrounded by 200 beds' worth of dorms, doubles and self-contained micro-apartments, as well as an in-house cafe and a railway-inspired bar. Bikes are available for hire (per hour/day $15/60).

Adventure Lodge & Motel HOSTEL, MOTEL
(☎07-892 2991; www.adventurenationalpark.co.nz; 21 Carroll St; lodge dm/r $30/70, units $120-210; @📶) This place caters particularly to Tongariro Alpine crossers, offering accommodation and transfers, with all-inclusive packages available (two nights' accommodation, breakfasts, lunch, dinner, T-shirt and transport for $170 to $240). Chill out post-walk in the relaxing lounge or one of the spa pools. The motel units are clean but unspectacular.

Eating & Drinking

Station CAFE $$
(www.stationcafe.co.nz; Findlay St; lunch $9-16, dinner $29-36; ⊙lunch daily, dinner Wed-Mon) Count your blessings ye who find this little railway station along the line, a lovely old dear, carefully restored and now serving eggy brunch, pies, coffee and cakes, plus an impressive à la carte evening menu.

Schnapps PUB
(www.schnappsbarruapehu.com; Findlay St; mains $19-28; ⊙noon-late) This popular pub serves better-than-average grub and has a handy ATM. Bands pack the place out on wintry Saturday nights.

Mill Bar & Grill PUB
(www.nationalparkhoteltongariro.co.nz; 61 Carroll St; mains $19-25; ⊙10am-11pm) A good old-fashioned Kiwi boozer with real live locals having a few quiet ones, a selection of local microbrewed beers and a menu of stomach-warming favourites.

Information

There's no i-SITE in the village, so visit www.nationalpark.co.nz for info.

Getting There & Away

InterCity (☎09-583 5780; www.intercity.co.nz), Naked Bus and **Tranz Scenic** (☎04-495 0775; www.tranzscenic.co.nz; tickets $49-81) all offer services.

Ohakune

POP 1100

Expect to see carrots crop up all over Ohakune, for this is undisputedly the country's carrot capital. They not only creep into burgers and sneak onto pizzas, but also litter the roadside in season. To learn more (and you know you want to), visit during October's annual **Carrot Carnival** (www.carrotcarnival.org.nz).

But locals needn't mention liver cleansing and eyesight improvement to win us over to the charms of this little town. A pretty retreat in the summer offering outdoor adventure galore, Ohakune springs to life in winter when the snow drifts down on Turoa Ski Area and the snow bunnies invade (they no doubt love carrots themselves).

There are two distinct parts to the town: the commercial hub strings along the highway, but in winter the northern end around the train station, known as the Junction, is the epicentre of action.

Activities

There are several scenic walks near the town, many starting from the Ohakune Mountain Rd, which stretches 17km from Ohakune to the Turoa Ski Area on Mt Ruapehu. The handy DOC brochure *Walks in and around Tongariro National Park* ($3) is a good starting point, available from the i-SITE.

Tramps in Tongariro National Park, including the Tongariro Alpine Crossing, are easily accessible from Ohakune, and shuttle services are provided by Matai Shuttles (p281). The Round the Mountain (p279) track can be accessed by continuing on the Waitonga Falls track.

Old Coach Road WALKING, MOUNTAIN BIKING
(www.ohakunecoachroad.co.nz) The original 16km coach track from Ohakune to Horopito dates from 1886, when it was built largely by hand by workers living in canvas tents and operating in harsh winter conditions. It was gradually upgraded to carry passengers and goods, and used until 1909, when SH49 opened. A recent restoration has rescued it from obscurity, creating this excellent walking and cycling route.

The gently graded route contains a number of unique engineering features, including the historic Hapuawhenua and Toanui viaducts – these are the only two remaining curved viaducts in the southern hemisphere. It passes through ancient forest of giant rimu and totara that survived the Taupo blast, being in the lea of Ruapehu.

If you're cycling, you're best to start at Horopito for a slightly downhill ride finishing at Ohakune Railway Station (allow four hours). Mountain Bike Station offers transfers to Horopito or you can undertake a full-day's return ride.

Mangawhero Forest Walk WALKING
An easy stroll starting near the beginning of Ohakune Mountain Rd (one hour return, 3km), taking in native forest and the Mangawhero River. It is well graded and suitable for wheelchairs and pushchairs.

Waitonga Falls & Lake Surprise Tracks TRAMPING
The path to Waitonga Falls (1½ hours return, 4km), Tongariro's highest waterfall (39m), offers magnificent views of Mt Ruapehu. A more challenging walk climbs to shallow Lake Surprise (five hours return, 9km). Both tracks start from Ohakune Mountain Rd.

Ruapehu Homestead HORSE RIDING
(Map p277; ☎027-267 7057; cnr Piwara St & SH49, Rangataua; 30min-3hr adult $30-120, child $15-90) Located four kilometres east of Ohakune (near Rangataua), Ruapehu Homestead offers guided treks around its paddocks, as well as longer rides along the river and on backcountry trails that have views of the mountain.

Canoe Safaris CANOEING, RAFTING
(☎0800 272 3353; www.canoesafaris.co.nz; 6 Tay St) Offers guided canoeing trips on the Whanganui River (one to five days, $165 to $950) and Rangitikei River (one to four days, $145 to $825), canoe and kayak hire (two to five days, $150 to $195), and guided rafting trips on the Mohaka (two to four days, $425 to $950).

Yeti Tours CANOEING, KAYAKING
(☎06-385 8197; www.yetitours.co.nz; 61 Clyde St; guided tours 2-10 days $420-1500, 2-6 day hire $160-210) Leads guided canoeing safaris on the Whanganui and Mokau Rivers, and hires canoes and kayaks.

Heliview SCENIC FLIGHTS
(☎06-753 0123; www.heliview.co.nz; flights $110-420) Offers scenic helicopter flights ranging from 12 minutes over Ohakune to 45-minute flights over the peaks or Whanganui National Park.

Mountain Bike Station & SLR MOUNTAIN BIKING
(☎06-385 8797; www.mountainbikestation.co.nz; 60 Thames St) Rents mountain bikes (half-/full-day from $35/50) and provides transfers to local mountain-biking routes, including the Old Coach Road ($20); bike and transport packages are available. SLR, the winter sports part of the business, rents ski and snowboard gear (from $25).

TCB EQUIPMENT HIRE
(☎06-385 8433; www.tcbskiandboard.co.nz; 29 Ayr St) A good source of information about local mountain-biking routes, TCB publishes a free bike trail map and rents mountain bikes (from $40) and skiing and snowboarding gear (from $20).

Ski Shed EQUIPMENT HIRE
(☎06-385 9173; www.skished.com; 71 Clyde St) Hires skiing (from $35) and snowboard-

DON'T MISS

THE BIG CARROT

Maybe not so much 'Don't Miss' as 'Impossible to Miss', this roadside tribute to Ohakune's biggest crop, the **Big Carrot** (Rangataua Rd) was erected in 1984 and quickly became one of NZ's most hugged 'Big Things'. Carrots were first grown in the area during the 1920s by Chinese settlers, who cleared the land by hand and explosives. Ohakune now grows two-thirds of the North Island's total crop.

MOUNTAIN BIKING FROM MOUNTAIN TO SEA

Traversing two national parks, the Ruapehu Whanganui Trails (Nga Ara Tuhono) is a 317km route linking up various established tracks and stretches of rural road to provide a mountain-biking route from Mt Ruapehu to the sea at Whanganui.

Starting at Turoa with a descent down the sealed Ohakune Mountain Rd (check those brakes first!), it follows the Old Coach Road (p284) to Horopito. Here it takes rural roads to the Fishers Track (p282), connects to the Mangapurua Track across the Bridge to Nowhere and continues on the Kaiwhakauka Track (p250).

ing (from $43) gear, and snow-appropriate clothing.

Powderhorn Snow Centre EQUIPMENT HIRE
(☎06-385 9100; www.snowcentre.co.nz; 194 Mangawhero Tce) Sells and hires snow gear and mountain bikes (half-/full-day $35/50).

Sleeping

The prices listed here are for summer; expect to pay up to 50% more in winter and book ahead. Savings can be made on winter rates by booking midweek.

TOP CHOICE **Station Lodge** HOSTEL $
(☎06-385 8797; www.stationlodge.co.nz; 60 Thames St; dm $27, r $54, unit $100-200; @ wi-fi) Housed in a lovely old villa with wooden floors and high ceilings, this excellent backpackers has a well-equipped kitchen, comfortable lounge and a spa pool. In winter the demand is so high that it only rent beds, not whole rooms; if you're after privacy, separate chalets and apartments are available. The clued-up young owners also run Mountain Bike Station and SLR.

Powderhorn Chateau HOTEL $$$
(☎06-385 8888; www.powderhorn.co.nz; cnr Thames St & Mangawhero Tce; r from $199; @ wi-fi pool) Enjoying a long-standing reputation as the hub of activity during the ski season, the Powderhorn has a Swiss-chalet feel with woody interiors, slate floors and exposed rafters. The grotto-like indoor pool is a relaxing way to recover from the slopes before enjoying revelry in the popular in-house establishments.

Snowhaven APARTMENTS, B&B $$
(☎06-385 9498; www.snowhaven.co.nz; 92 Clyde St; apt $95-110, r $195, townhouse $245; wi-fi) A tasty trio is on offer at Snowhaven: modern studio apartments in a slate-fronted block on the main drag; three self-contained, three-bedroom townhouses by the Junction; or luxury B&B rooms somewhere between the other two. All are top options.

Peaks MOTEL $$
(☎06-385 9144; www.thepeaks.co.nz; cnr Mangawhero Tce & Shannon St; units $110-124; @ wi-fi) This well-kept motel offers spacious rooms with good bathrooms but dubious decor. Communal facilities include a basic gym, a large outdoor spa and a sauna.

Tussock Grove HOTEL $$
(☎06-385 8771; www.tussockgrove.co.nz; 3 Karo St; r $145-165; wi-fi) Cooking on holiday? No way, mister. In a town full of motels this small hotel fills a gap for those who just want a decent midrange room, perhaps with a mountain view.

Ohakune Top 10 HOLIDAY PARK $
(☎0800 825 825; www.ohakune.net.nz; 5 Moore St; sites from $20, units $32-203; @ wi-fi) A bubbling stream borders this holiday park, and while it's not as flash as some of the Top 10 chain, neither is it as expensive. Extras include a playground, barbecue area and spa pool.

Mountain View MOTEL $
(☎06-385 8675; www.mountain-viewmotel.co.nz; 2 Moore St; units $70-100; wi-fi) In this old, vaguely Tudor-styled motel, the no-nonsense rooms are clean, quiet and good value, with all necessary facilities, including a spa pool.

Eating & Drinking

The Junction is the après-ski place to be, but in summer the action (such that it is) drifts to the other end of town. Many hotels sprout restaurants during the ski season.

Cyprus Tree ITALIAN $$
(☎06-385 8857; www.thecyprustree.co.nz; 19a Goldfinch St; mains $22-31; ⏲4pm-late Mon-Fri, 9am-late Sat & Sun) Open all year round, this restaurant and bar serves up a tasty menu of Italian-influenced dishes – pizza, pasta and

WORTH A TRIP

LAKE ROTOKURA

Rotokura Ecological Reserve is 14km southeast of Ohakune, at Karioi, just off SH49 (*karioi* means 'places to linger'). There are two lakes here: the first is Dry Lake, actually quite wet and perfect for picnicking; the furthest is Rotokura, *tapu* (sacred) to Maori, so eating, fishing and swimming are prohibited. The round-trip walk will take you 45 minutes; longer if you linger to admire the ancient beech trees and waterfowl such as dabchicks and paradise ducks.

antipasto – in a large yet relaxed space. Or you can just drop in for a cocktail.

Bearing Point INTERNATIONAL **$$**
(☎06-385 9006; Clyde St; mains $25-35; ⊙dinner Tue-Sat) Hearty après-ski fare is offered at this upmarket establishment run by local identities. Warm your cockles with aged eye fillet, maple-glazed salmon, lamb rump or a seafood curry.

Mountain Kebabs KEBABS **$**
(29 Clyde St; kebabs $10-13) Any old kebabery can come up with the basic lamb, chicken or felafel varieties – but here camembert, hummus, sprouts and olives are rolled into the mix, too.

Powderkeg & Matterhorn PUB
(www.powderhorn.co.nz; cnr Thames St & Mangawhero Tce; bar menu $12-18, à la carte $31-35; ⊙lunch & dinner) The Powderkeg is the party bar of the Powderhorn Chateau, with bands in winter and regular dancing on the tables – once the detritus of the burgers and nachos have been cleared. Upstairs is the swankier Matterhorn, serving cocktails and relaxed but chic à la carte dining. In summer the Matterhorn closes and its menu moves to the Powderkeg.

Utopia CAFE **$**
(47 Clyde St; mains $10-17; ⊙8am-2.30pm; 📶) A funky, upbeat and perennially popular destination for cooked breakfasts and fresh homemade counter food. If it's pumping downstairs, there are usually quieter tables upstairs.

ℹ Information

Ohakune Public Library (☎06-385 8364; 15 Miro St; ⊙9am-5pm Mon-Fri; @) Offers free internet access.

Ruapehu i-SITE (☎06-385 8427; www.visitruapehu.com; 54 Clyde St; ⊙9am-5pm) Can make bookings for activities, transport and accommodation; DOC officer on hand from 9am to 3.30pm, Wednesday to Sunday.

ℹ Getting There & Around

InterCity (p260) buses and Tranz Scenic (p260) trains service Ohakune, and Matai Shuttles (p281) and Snow Express (p281) run up to Turoa. Matai runs a handy night shuttle around Ohakune's pubs during the ski season.

Waiouru

POP 1400

At the junction of SH1 and SH49, 27km east of Ohakune, Waiouru is primarily an army base and a refuelling stop for the 56km-long Desert Rd leading to Turangi. **Rangipo Desert** isn't a true desert, as it receives plenty of rainfall; its stunted scrubby vegetation is due to its high altitude, windswept nature and the Taupo eruption that obliterated the ancient forests, affected the soil quality and caused a mass sterilisation of seeds. The road often closes in winter due to snow.

Housed in a large, concrete castle at the south end of the township, the **National Army Museum** (www.armymuseum.co.nz; adult/child $15/5; ⊙9am-4.30pm) preserves the history of the NZ army and its various campaigns, from colonial times to the present. Moving stories are told through displays of arms, uniforms, medals and memorabilia.

Once you're done with playing soldier, head 11km south to **Lazy H Horseback Riding & Adventures** (☎06-388 1144; www.lazyh.co.nz; 159 Maukuku Rd; 1hr-overnight $50-295), where you can channel your inner cowboy. Sadly, this is where the Village People–themed pursuits end.

Taihape & Around

POP 1800

If you have an ill-defined interest in rubber boots, a visit to Taihape, 20km south of Waiouru, is a must. The town has the dubious distinction of being the Gumboot Capital of the World, celebrated with – you guessed it – a giant corrugated gumboot on the main street. It is also the access point for **Gravity Canyon** (☎06-388 9109; www.gravitycanyon.co.nz; Mokai; ⏲9am-5pm), 20km southeast, where adrenaline-junkies can take a 1km, 170m-high flying-fox ride at speeds of up to 160km/h ($155); dive from the North Island's highest bridge bungy (80m, $179); or freefall for 50m on a tandem swing ($159). Multi-thrill packages are available.

If you didn't give horseback riding a go in Ohakune or Waiouru, giddy-up to **River Valley** (☎06-388 1444; www.rivervalley.co.nz), 28km northeast of Taihape (follow the signs from Taihape's Gretna Hotel). Enjoy views of Mt Ruapehu, the Ruahine Range and the Rangitikei River on two-hour ($109), half-day ($175) or day-long ($235) excursions. On summer evenings the three-hour Sundowner ride ends with a glass of bubbles ($139). White-water rafting trips are also offered.

Rotorua & the Bay of Plenty

Includes »

Rotorua....290
Around Rotorua....304
Bay of Plenty....308
Tauranga....308
Mt Maunganui....315
Katikati....319
Te Puke....321
Whakatane....322
Whakaari (White Island)....326
Ohope....327
Opotiki....328

Best Outdoors

» Surfing at Mt Maunganui (p315)

» Waimangu Volcanic Valley (p307)

» KG Kayaks (p327)

» Agroventures (p294)

» Redwoods Whakarewarewa Forest (p305)

Best Places to Stay

» Regent of Rotorua (p299)

» Warm Earth Cottage (p320)

» Captain's Cabin (p324)

» Opotiki Beach House Backpackers (p329)

Why Go?

Captain Cook christened the Bay of Plenty when he cruised past in 1769, and plentiful it remains. Blessed with sunshine and sand, the bay stretches from Waihi Beach in the west to Opotiki in the east, with the holiday hubs of Tauranga, Mt Maunganui and Whakatane in between.

Offshore from Whakatane is New Zealand's most active volcano, Whakaari (White Island). Volcanic activity defines this region, and nowhere is this subterranean sexiness more obvious than in Rotorua. Here the daily business of life goes on among steaming hot springs, explosive geysers, bubbling mud pools and the billows of sulphurous gas responsible for the town's 'unique' eggy smell.

Rotorua and the Bay of Plenty are also strongholds of Maori tradition. There are plenty of opportunities to engage with NZ's rich indigenous culture: check out a power-packed concert performance, chow down at a *hangi* (Maori feast) or learn the techniques behind Maori arts and crafts.

When to Go

The Bay of Plenty is a beachy haven: it's one of NZ's sunniest regions, with Whakatane recording a brilliant 2350 average hours of sunshine per year. Summers here are gorgeous, with maximum temperatures hovering between 20°C and 27°C. Of course, everyone else is here too, but the holiday vibe is heady. Winter can see the mercury fall as low as 5°C overnight, although it's usually warmer on the coast. Visit Rotorua any time: geothermal activity is a year-round wonder, and there are enough beds in any season.

Rotorua & the Bay of Plenty Highlights

1. Watching Rotorua's famous geyser Pohutu blow its top at **Te Puia** (p291), then tucking into a steaming-hot Maori *hangi*
2. Ogling kaleidoscopic colours and bubbling mud pools at **Wai-O-Tapu Thermal Wonderland** (p307)
3. Mountain biking on tracks (both humble and hardcore) in the **Redwoods Whakarewarewa Forest** (p305)
4. Carving up the surf over NZ's first artificial reef at **Mt Maunganui** (p315)
5. Flying or boating to NZ's only active marine volcano, **Whakaari (White Island)** (p326)
6. Kicking back in **Whakatane** (p322) – NZ's most underrated seaside town?
7. Swimming with dolphins at **Tauranga** (p308)
8. Drinking in **Mt Maunganui** (p315) after a day at the beach
9. Climbing the pohutukawa-studded flanks of **Mauao** (p315)

ESSENTIAL ROTORUA & THE BAY OF PLENTY

» **Eat** A buttery corn cob, cooked in Rotorua's only genuine thermal *hangi* at Whakarewarewa Thermal Village (p291)

» **Drink** Croucher Brewing Co's microbrewed pale ale in Rotorua

» **Read** *How to Watch a Bird*, an exposition on the joys of avian observation, written by Mt Maunganui schoolboy Steve Braunias

» **Listen to** *Kora*, the eponymous rootsy album from Whakatane's soulful sons

» **Watch** Maori TV and Te Reo, NZ's two Maori TV stations

» **Go green** See www.sustainablenz.com for tips on how to make your Rotorua visit more ecofriendly

» **Online** www.rotoruanz.com, www.bayofplenty.co.nz; www.lonelyplanet.com/new-zealand/rotorua

» **Area code** ☎07

Getting There & Away

Air New Zealand (www.airnewzealand.co.nz) has direct flights from Tauranga and Rotorua to Auckland, Wellington and Christchurch, plus Rotorua to Sydney (every Tuesday and Saturday) and Whakatane to Auckland and Wellington. Qantas (p303) also links Auckland with Tauranga, Whakatane and Rotorua.

InterCity (www.intercity.co.nz) and **Naked Bus** (www.nakedbus.com) services connect Tauranga, Rotorua and Whakatane with most other main cities in NZ. **Bay Hopper** (☎0800 422 928; www.baybus.co.nz) bus services run between Tauranga, Whakatane and Opotiki. **Twin City Express** (☎0800 422 928; www.baybus.co.nz) buses link Tauranga and Rotorua.

ROTORUA

POP 70,400

Catch a whiff of Rotorua's sulphur-rich, asthmatic airs and you've already got a taste of NZ's most dynamic thermal area, home to spurting geysers, steaming hot springs and exploding mud pools. The Maori revered this place, naming one of the most spectacular springs Wai-O-Tapu (Sacred Waters). Today 35% of the population is Maori, with their cultural performances and traditional *hangi* as big an attraction as the landscape itself.

Despite the pervasive eggy odour, 'Sulphur City' is one of the most touristed spots on the North Island, with nearly three million visitors annually. Some locals say this steady trade has seduced the town into resting on its laurels, and that socially Rotorua lags behind more progressive towns like Tauranga and Taupo. And with more motels than nights in November, the urban fabric of 'RotoVegas' isn't particularly appealing... but still, where else can you see a 30m geothermal geyser!

History

The Rotorua area was first settled in the 14th century when the canoe *Te Arawa*, captained by Tamatekapua, arrived from Hawaiki at Maketu in the central Bay of Plenty. Settlers took the tribal name Te Arawa to commemorate the vessel that had brought them here. Tamatekapua's grandson, Ihenga, explored much of the inland forest, naming geographical features as he discovered them. Ihenga unimaginatively dubbed the lake Rotorua (Second Lake) as it was the second lake he came across.

In the next few hundred years, subtribes spread and divided through the area, with conflicts breaking out over limited territory. A flashpoint occurred in 1823 when the Arawa lands were invaded by tribes from the Northland in the so-called Musket Wars. After heavy losses on both sides, the Northlanders eventually withdrew.

During the Waikato Land War (1863–64) Te Arawa threw in its lot with the government against its traditional Waikato enemies, gaining troop support and preventing East Coast reinforcements getting through to support the Kingitanga movement.

With peace in the early 1870s, word spread of scenic wonders, miraculous landscapes and watery cures for all manner of diseases. Rotorua boomed. Its main attraction was the fabulous Pink and White Terraces, formed by volcanic silica deposits. Touted at the time as the eighth natural wonder of the world, they were destroyed in the 1886 Mt Tarawera eruption.

Sights

Te Whakarewarewa THERMAL RESERVE

Rotorua's main drawcard is Te Whakarewarewa (pronounced fa-ka-re-wa-re-wa), a thermal reserve 3km south of the city centre. This area's full name is Te Whakarewarewatanga o te Ope Taua a Wahiao, meaning 'The Gathering Together of the War Party of Wahiao', although many people just call it 'Whaka'. Either way, the reserve is as famous for its Maori cultural significance as its steam and bubbling mud. There are more than 500 springs here, including a couple of famed geysers. The two main tourist operations are Te Puia and Whakarewarewa Thermal Village.

Te Puia GEYSER, CULTURAL TOUR

(Map p306; ☎0800 837 842, 07-348 9047; www.tepuia.com; Hemo Rd; adult/child tour & daytime cultural performance $57.50/29, tour, evening concert & hangi $110/55, combination $145/72.50; ⏱8am-6pm Nov-Apr, to 5pm May-Oct) The most famous Te Whakarewarewa spring is **Pohutu** ('Big Splash' or 'Explosion'), a geyser which erupts up to 20 times a day, spurting hot water up to 30m skyward. You'll know when it's about to blow because the **Prince of Wales' Feathers** geyser will start up shortly before. Both these geysers form part of Te Puia, the most polished of NZ's Maori cultural attractions. Also here is the National Carving School and the National Weaving School, where you can discover the work and methods of traditional Maori woodcarvers and weavers, plus a carved meeting house, a cafe, galleries, a kiwi reserve and a gift shop.

Tours take 1½ hours and depart hourly from 9am (the last tour an hour before closing). Daytime 45-minute cultural performances start at 10.15am, 12.15pm and 3.15pm; nightly three-hour Te Po indigenous concerts and *hangi* feasts start at 6pm.

Whakarewarewa Thermal Village SPRING, CULTURAL TOUR

(Map p306; ☎07-349 3463; www.whakarewarewa.com; 17 Tyron St; tour & cultural performance adult/child $30/13; ⏱8.30am-5pm) Whakarewarewa Thermal Village, on the eastern side of Te Whakarewarewa, is a living village, where *tangata whenua* (the locals) still reside, as they and their ancestors have for centuries. It's these local villagers who show you around and tell you the stories of their way of life and the significance of the steamy bubbling pools, silica terraces and the geysers that, although inaccessible from the village, are easily viewed from vantage points (the view of Pohutu is just as good from here as it is from Te Puia, and considerably cheaper).

The village shops sell authentic arts and crafts, and you can learn more about Maori traditions such as flax weaving, carving, and *ta moko* (tattooing). Nearby you can eat tasty, buttery sweetcorn ($2) pulled straight out of the hot mineral pool – the only genuine geothermal *hangi* in town. There are cultural performances at 11.15am and 2pm, and guided tours at 9am, 10am, 11am, noon, 1pm, 3pm and 4pm.

ROTORUA IN...

Two Days

Order breakfast at **Third Place Cafe**, after which stroll the lakeside at **Ohinemutu**, continuing back into town via steamy **Kuirau Park**. Next stop is the fabulous **Rotorua Museum**, followed by a soak at the **Blue Baths**. In the evening, catch a *hangi* and concert at **Tamaki Maori Village** or **Mitai Maori Village**.

Start the second day with a tour of **Whakarewarewa Thermal Village** and watch **Pohutu** geyser blow its top. From here, it's a quick hop to the **Redwoods Whakarewarewa Forest** for a couple of hours' mountain biking. Head across town to dangle in a gondola at **Skyline Rotorua** or see the swooping falcons at **Wingspan Birds of Prey Trust**.

Four Days

Too much geothermal excitement is barely enough! Explore the hot spots to the south: **Waimangu Volcanic Valley** and **Wai-O-Tapu Thermal Wonderland**. The nearby **Waikite Valley Thermal Pools** are perfect for an end-of-day plunge.

On your last day, head southeast and visit the **Buried Village**, swim in **Lake Tarawera**, or take a long walk on one of the tracks at nearby **Lake Okataina**. Back in town, cruise the restaurants and bars on **Tutanekai St** and toast your efforts with a few cold beers.

Rotorua

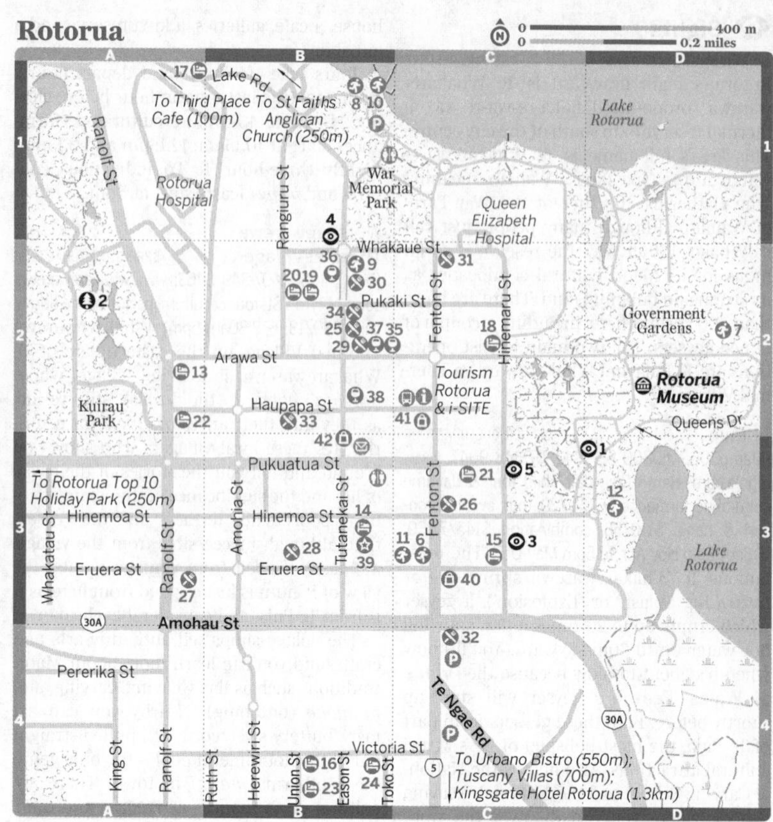

TOP CHOICE **Rotorua Museum** MUSEUM, GALLERY

(Map p292; www.rotoruamuseum.co.nz; Queens Dr, Government Gardens; adult/child $18/7; ⌚9am-5pm Apr-Sep, to 8pm Oct-Mar, tours hourly 10am-4pm plus 5pm Dec-Feb) This outstanding museum occupies a grand Tudor-style edifice. It was originally an elegant spa retreat called the Bath House (1908); displays in the former shower rooms give a fascinating insight into some of the eccentric therapies once practised here, including 'electric baths' and the Bergonie Chair.

A gripping 20-minute film on the history of Rotorua, including the Tarawera eruption, runs every 20 minutes from 9am (not for small kids – the seats vibrate and the eruption noises are authentic). The fabulous new **Don Stafford Wing** houses eight object-rich galleries dedicated to Rotorua's Te Arawa people, featuring woodcarving, flax weaving, jade, interactive audiovisual displays and the stories of the revered WWII 28 Maori Battalion (a movie on the battalion runs every 30 minutes from 9.30am). Also here are two **art galleries** (with air swabbed clean of hydrogen sulphide), and a cool cafe with garden views (although the best view in town can be had from the viewing platform on the roof).

Lake Rotorua LAKE

Lake Rotorua is the largest of the district's 16 lakes and is – underneath all that water – a spent volcano. Sitting in the lake is Mokoia Island, which has for centuries been occupied by various subtribes of the area. The lake can be explored by boat, with several operators situated at the lakefront.

Government Gardens GARDENS

The manicured English-style Government Gardens surrounding the Rotorua Museum are pretty as a picture, with roses aplenty, steaming thermal pools dotted about and civilised amenities such as croquet lawns

Rotorua

Top Sights

Rotorua Museum D2

Sights

1 Blue Baths D3
2 Kuirau Park A2
3 Millennium Hotel Rotorua C3
4 Novotel Rotorua B1
5 Tamaki Maori Village C3

Activities, Courses & Tours

6 Bike Barn C3
7 Government Gardens Golf D2
8 Kawarau Jet B1
9 Lady Jane's Ice Cream Parlour B2
Lakeland Queen .... (see 10)
10 Mana Adventures B1
Mokoia Island Wai Ora Experiences .... (see 8)
11 O'Keefe's Fishing Specialists C3
12 Polynesian Spa D3
The Wall .... (see 14)
Volcanic Air Safaris .... (see 10)

Sleeping

13 Base Rotorua A2
14 Crank Backpackers B3
15 Crash Palace C3
16 Funky Green Voyager B4
17 Jack & Di's Lake View Lodge A1
Millennium Hotel Rotorua .... (see 3)
18 Princes Gate Hotel C2
19 Regent Flashpackers B2
20 Regent of Rotorua B2
21 Rotorua Central Backpackers C3
22 Rotorua YHA A2
23 Six on Union B4
24 Victoria Lodge B4

Eating

25 Ali Baba's Tunisian Takeaway B2
26 Amazing Thai C3
27 Bistro 1284 .... A3
28 Capers Epicurean B3
29 Fat Dog Cafe & Bar B2
30 Indian Star B2
31 Lime Caffeteria C2
32 Pak 'n Save C4
33 Sabroso B2
34 Weilin's Noodle House B2

Drinking

35 Belgian Bar B2
36 Brew B2
37 Pheasant Plucker B2
38 Pig & Whistle B2

Entertainment

39 Basement Cinema B3

Shopping

40 Mountain Jade C3
41 Out of New Zealand C2
42 Rotorua Night Market B3

and bowling greens. Also here is the upmarket Polynesian Spa and Government Gardens Golf.

Blue Baths BATHHOUSE
(Map p292; ☎07-350 2119; www.bluebaths.co.nz; Government Gardens; adult/child/family $11/6/30; ⊙noon-6pm Apr-Nov, 10am-6pm Dec-Mar) The gorgeous Spanish Mission–style Blue Baths opened in 1933 (and, amazingly, were closed from 1982 to 1999). Today you can visit a small museum recalling the building's heyday, with recorded anecdotes and displays in the old changing rooms. If it all makes you feel like taking a dip yourself, the heated pool (adult/child/family $11/6/30) awaits. Ask about occasional dinner-and-cabaret shows (from $125 per person).

Kuirau Park PARK
(Map p292; cnr Ranolf & Pukuatua Sts) Want some affordable geothermal thrills? Just west of central Rotorua is Kuirau Park, a volcanic area you can explore for free. In 2003 an eruption covered much of the park (including the trees) in mud, drawing crowds of spectators. It has a crater lake, pools of boiling mud and plenty of huffing steam. Take care – the pools here really are boiling, and accidents have happened.

Ohinemutu MAORI VILLAGE
Ohinemutu is a charmingly ramshackle lakeside Maori village (access via Kiharoa, Haukotuku or Korokai Sts off Lake St, north of Rotorua Hospital) that traces the fusing of European and Maori cultures. A highlight is the 1905 Tama-te-kapua Meeting House (corner of Kiharoa St and Mataiawhea St),

DON'T MISS

MAORI CONCERTS & HANGI

Maori culture is a big-ticket item in Rotorua and, although it is commercialised, it's a great opportunity to learn about the indigenous culture of New Zealand. The two big activities are concerts and *hangi* feasts, often packaged together in an evening's entertainment featuring the famous *hongi* (Maori greeting; the pressing of foreheads and noses, and sharing of life breath) and *haka* and *poi* dances.

An established favourite, **Tamaki Maori Village** (☎07-349 2999; www.maoriculture.co.nz; booking office 1220 Hinemaru St; adult/child/family $105/60/250; ⊙tours depart 5pm, 6pm & 7.30pm Nov-Apr, 6.30pm May-Oct) does an excellent twilight tour to a *marae* (meeting house) and Maori village 15km south of Rotorua. Buses collect from the Hinemaru St booking office and local accommodation. The experience is very hands-on, taking you on an interactive journey through Maori history, arts, traditions and customs from pre-European times to the present day. The concert is followed by an impressive *hangi*.

The family-run **Mitai Maori Village** (Map p306; ☎07-343 9132; www.mitai.co.nz; 196 Fairy Springs Rd; adult/child 5-9yr/child 10-15yr/family $107/21/53/279; ⊙6.30pm) offers a popular three-hour evening event with a concert, *hangi* and glowworm bushwalk. The experience can be combined with a tour of Rainbow Springs Kiwi Wildlife Park (p304) next door, with coloured nightlights and a walk through the kiwi enclosure (four hours total, adult/child 5-9yr/child 10-15yr $125/35/65). Pick-ups available.

Te Puia (p291) and Whakarewarewa Thermal Village (p291) also put on shows, and many of the big hotels offer Maori concerts and *hangi*, making up for what they lack in ambience with convenience. Some of the main venues:

» **Kingsgate Hotel Rotorua** (Map p306; ☎07-348 0199; www.millenniumhotels.co.nz; 328 Fenton St; concert adult/child $30/15, incl hangi $45/22.50)

» **Millennium Hotel Rotorua** (Map p292; ☎07-347 1234; www.millenniumrotorua.co.nz; cnr Eruera & Hinemaru Sts; concert adult/child $30/15, incl hangi $70/35)

» **Novotel Rotorua** (Map p292; ☎07-346 3888; www.novotelrotorua.co.nz; 11 Tutanekai St; concerts adult/child $39/18, incl hangi $59/28)

» **Pohutu Cultural Theatre** (Map p306; ☎07-348 1189, 0800 476 488; www.pohututheatre.co.nz; cnr Froude & Tryon Sts; concerts & hangi adult/child $69/34.50)

named for the captain of Te Arawa canoe. This sacred meeting house for Te Arawa people isn't open to visitors, but you can check out the exterior.

St Faith's Anglican Church CHURCH
(☎07-348 2393; cnr Mataiawhea & Korokai Sts; admission by donation; ⊙8am-6pm, services 9am Sun & 10am Wed) Ohinemutu's historic timber St Faith's Anglican Church is intricately decorated with Maori carvings, *tukutuku* (woven panels), painted scrollwork and stained-glass windows. One window features an etched image of Christ wearing a Maori cloak as he appears to walk on the waters of Lake Rotorua.

Activities

Note that several of the following operators have teamed up under the banners of **Rotorua Adventure Combos** (☎0800 338 786, 07-357 2236; www.rotoruacombos.com), **Rotorua Hot Deals** (☎0800 768 678; www.rotoruahotdeals.com) and **Rotorua CitySights** (☎0800 744 487; www.citysights.co.nz), delivering a slew of good-value skydiving, white-water rafting, river sledging, jetboating and helicopter experiences (plus zorbing, gondola rides, mountain biking...).

Extreme Sports

Agroventures EXTREME SPORTS
(Map p306; ☎07-357 4747, 0800 949 888; www.agroventures.co.nz; Western Rd; ⊙9am-5pm) Agroventures is a hive of action, 9km north of Rotorua on SH5 (shuttles available). Prices following are for single activities but combo deals abound.

Start off with the 43m bungy (adult/child $95/80) and the Swoop (adult/child $49/35), a 130km/h swing that can be enjoyed alone or with friends. If that's not enough for you, try Freefall Xtreme (3min per adult/child $49/35), which simulates skydiving by blasting you 5m into the air on a column of wind.

Also here is the Shweeb (adult/child $39/29), a monorail velodrome from which you hang in a clear capsule and pedal yourself along recumbently at speeds of up to 60km/h. Alongside is the Agrojet (adult/child $49/35), allegedly NZ's fastest jetboat, splashing around a 1km course.

Zorb EXTREME SPORTS

(Map p306; ☎07-357 5100, 0800 227 474; www.zorb.com; cnr Western Rd & SH5; rides from $30; ⏲9am-5pm, to 7pm Dec-Mar) The Zorb is 9km north of Rotorua on SH5 – look for the grassy hillside with large, clear, people-filled spheres rolling down it. Your eyes do not deceive you! There are three courses: 150m straight, 180m zigzag or 250m 'Drop'. Do your zorb strapped in and dry, or freestyle with water thrown in.

Ogo EXTREME SPORTS

(Map p306; ☎0800 646 768; www.ogo.co.nz; 525 Ngongotaha Rd; rides from $35; ⏲9am-5pm, to 6.30pm Dec-Feb) The Ogo (about 5km north of town) involves careening down a grassy hillside in a big bubble, with water or without. Silly? Fun? Terrifying? All of the above...

Skyline Rotorua EXTREME SPORTS

(Map p306; ☎07-347 0027; www.skyline.co.nz; Fairy Springs Rd; adult/child gondola $25/12.50, luge 3 rides $41/31, sky swing $52/41; ⏲9am-11pm) This gondola cruises up Mt Ngongotaha, about 3km northwest of town, from where you can take in panoramic lake views or ride a speedy luge back down on three different tracks. For even speedier antics, try the Sky Swing, a screaming swoosh through the air at speeds of up to 160km/h. Also at the top are a restaurant, cafe and walking tracks.

The Wall ROCK CLIMBING

(Map p292; ☎07-350 1400; www.thewall.co.nz; 1140 Hinemoa St; adult/child incl harness $16/12, shoe hire $5; ⏲noon-10pm Mon-Fri, 10am-10pm Sat & Sun) Get limbered up at the Wall, which has a three-storey indoor climbing wall with overhangs aplenty.

NZONE SKYDIVING

(Map p306; ☎07-345 7520, 0800 376 796; www.nzone.biz; Rotorua Airport; dives from $269) NZONE offers tandem skydives from 9000ft, 12,000ft or 15,000ft, giving you a bird's-eye view of the lakes and volcanoes. Town pick-ups available.

Kawarau Jet JETBOATING

(Map p292; ☎07-343 7600, 0800 538 7746; www.kjetrotorua.co.nz; Lakefront; 30min adult/child $74/54) Speed things up by jetboating with Kawarau Jet, which tears around the lake. Parasailing also available.

Mountain Biking

On the edge of town is the Redwoods Whakarewarewa Forest (p305), home to some of the best mountain-bike trails in the country. There are close to 100km of tracks to keep bikers of all skill levels happy for days on end. Note that not all tracks in the forest are designated for bikers, so adhere to the signposts. Pick up a trail map at the forest visitor centre.

For more information, the Rotorua i-SITE stocks the *Get on Your Bike* Rotorua cycle

MAORI NZ: ROTORUA & THE BAY OF PLENTY

The Bay of Plenty's traditional name, Te Rohe o Mataatua, recalls the ancestral *Mataatua* canoe, which arrived here from Hawaiki to make an eventful landfall at Whakatane. The region's history stretches back further than that, though, with the Polynesian settler Toi setting up what's claimed to be Aotearoa's first settlement in about AD 800.

Major tribal groups in the region are the Ngati Awa (www.ngatiawa.iwi.nz) of the Whakatane area, Whakatohea (www.whakatohea.co.nz) of Opotiki, Ngai Te Rangi (www.ngaiterangi.org.nz) of Tauranga, and Te Arawa (www.tearawa.iwi.nz) of Rotorua. Tribes in this region were involved on both sides of the Land Wars of the late 19th century, with those fighting against the government suffering considerable land confiscations that have caused legal problems right up to the present day.

There's a significant Maori population in the bay, and there are many ways for travellers to learn about the Maori culture. Opotiki has Hiona St Stephen's Church (p328) – the death here of government spy Reverend Carl Volkner in 1865 inspired the charming eyeball-eating scene in *Utu*. Whakatane has a new main-street marae (p322) (meeting house complex) and Toi's Pa (p297), perhaps NZ's oldest *pa* (fortified village) site. Rotorua has traditional villages at Te Whakarewarewa (p291) and Ohinemutu (p293), cultural performances and *hangi* (p294), and much, much more.

HINEMOA & TUTANEKI

Hinemoa was a young woman of a *hapu* (subtribe) that lived on the western shore of Lake Rotorua, while Tutanekai was a young man of a Mokoia Island *hapu*. The pair met and fell in love during a regular tribal meeting. While both were of high birth, Tutanekai was illegitimate, and so while Hinemoa's family thought he was a fine young man, marriage between the two was forbidden.

Home on Mokoia, the lovesick Tutanekai played his flute for his love, the wind carrying the melody across the water. Hinemoa heard his declaration, but her people took to tying up the canoes at night to ensure she wouldn't go to him.

Finally, Tutanekai's music won her over. Hinemoa undressed and swam the long distance from the shore to the island. When she arrived on Mokoia, Hinemoa found herself in a quandary. Shedding her clothing in order to swim, she could hardly walk into the island's settlement naked. She hopped into a hot pool to think about her next move.

Eventually a man came to fetch water from a cold spring beside the hot pool. In a deep man's voice, Hinemoa called out, 'Who is it?' The man replied that he was Tutanekai's slave on a water run. Hinemoa grabbed the slave's calabash and smashed it to pieces. More slaves came, but she smashed their calabashes too, until finally Tutanekai came to the pool and demanded that the interloper identify himself – imagine his surprise when it turned out to be Hinemoa. He secreted her into his hut.

Next morning, after a suspiciously long lie-in, a slave reported that someone was in Tutanekai's bed. The two lovers were rumbled, and when Hinemoa's superhuman efforts to reach Tutanekai had been revealed, their union was celebrated.

Descendants of Hinemoa and Tutanekai still live around Rotorua today.

map (downloadable from www.rdc.govt.nz) and the *Rotorua Mountain Biking* brochure (www.rotoruanz.com).

Mountain Bike Rotorua BICYCLE RENTAL
(Map p306; ☎0800 682 768; www.mtbrotorua.co.nz; Waipa State Mill Rd; mountain bikes per 2hr/day from $30/45, guided half-/full-day rides $120/185; ⏰9am-5pm) This outfit hires out bikes at the Waipa Mill car park entrance to the Redwoods Whakarewarewa Forest, the starting point for the bike trails. There's also a satellite bike depot across the forest at the visitor centre, so you can ride through the trees one-way then catch a shuttle back.

Bike Barn BICYCLE RENTAL
(Map p292; ☎07-347 1151; www.bikebarn.co.nz; 1275 Fenton St; mountain bikes per half/full day from $45/60; ⏰8.30am-5.30pm Mon-Fri, 9am-5pm Sat, 10am-5pm Sun) Bike hire and repairs in downtown Rotorua.

Lady Jane's Ice Cream Parlour BICYCLE RENTAL
(Map p292; ☎07-347 9340; ladyjanes@xtra.co.nz; 1092 Tutanekai St; bikes per 3hr/day $25/35; ⏰10am-late) Bike hire down near Lake Rotorua.

White-Water Rafting & Sledging

There's plenty of white-water action around Rotorua with the chance to take on the Grade V **Kaituna River**, complete with a startling 7m drop at Okere Falls. Most of these trips take a day. Some companies head further out to the **Rangitaiki River** (Grade III–VI) and **Wairoa River** (Grade V), raftable only when the dam is opened every second Sunday. Sledging (in case you didn't know) is zooming downriver on a body board. Most operators can arrange transport.

River Rats RAFTING
(☎07-345 6543, 0800 333 900; www.riverrats.co.nz) Takes on the Wairoa ($119), Kaituna ($99) and Rangitaiki ($129), and runs a scenic trip on the lower Rangitaiki (Grade II) that is good for youngsters (adult/child $129/100).

Kaituna Cascades RAFTING
(☎07-345 4199, 0800 524 8862; www.kaitunacascades.co.nz) Does rafting on the Kaituna ($82), Rangitaiki ($118) and Wairoa ($98), plus kayaking options.

Wet 'n' Wild RAFTING
(☎07-348 3191, 0800 462 7238; www.wetnwildrafting.co.nz) Runs trips on the Kaituna ($99), Wairoa ($110) and Mokau ($160), as well as easy-going Rangitaiki trips (adult/child $125/90) and longer trips to remote parts of the Motu and Mohaka (two to five days, $595 to $975).

Raftabout RAFTING, RIVER SLEDGING
(☎07-343 9500, 0800 723 822; www.raftabout.co.nz) Does rafting on the Kaituna ($99), Rangitaiki ($129) and Wairoa ($129), plus sledging on the Kaituna ($115).

Kaitiaki Adventures RAFTING, RIVER SLEDGING
(☎07-357 2236, 0800 338 736; www.kaitiaki.co.nz) Offers white-water rafting trips on the Kaituna ($95), Wairoa ($99) and Rangitaki ($125), plus sledging on the Wairoa ($299) and a Grade III section of the Kaituna ($109).

Kayaking

River Rats KAYAKING
(☎07-345 6543, 0800 333 900; www.riverrats.co.nz) Kayaking options include freedom hire (from $30/40 per half/full day) and guided four-hour Lake Rotoiti trips ($95).

Go Wild Adventures KAYAKING
(☎07-533 2926; www.adventurekayaking.co.nz) Takes trips on Lakes Rotorua, Rotoiti, Tarawera and Okataina (from $80/95/140 for two hours/half-day/full day); also offers freedom hire (from $50 per day).

Kaituna Kayaks KAYAKING
(☎07-362 4486; www.kaitunakayaks.com; half-day trip $199, lessons half/full day $199/299) Guided tandem trips and kayaking lessons (cheaper for groups) on the Kaituna River.

Thermal Pools & Massage

Geothermal complexes in the area include Hell's Gate & Wai Ora Spa (p304), 16km northeast of Rotorua, and Waikite Valley Thermal Pools (p307), 30km south.

Polynesian Spa SPA, MASSAGE
(Map p292; ☎07-348 1328; www.polynesianspa.co.nz; Government Gardens, off Hinemoa St; adults-only pools $21.50, private pools per half-hour adult/child from $18.50/6.50, family pool adult/child/family $14.50/6.50/36, spa therapies from $85; ⏲8am-11pm, spa therapies 9am-8pm) A bathhouse opened at these Government Gardens springs in 1882, and people have been swearing by the waters ever since. There is mineral bathing (36°C to 42°C) in several picturesque pools at the lake's edge, marble-lined terraced pools and a larger, main pool. Also here are luxury therapies (massage, mud and beauty treatments) and a cafe.

Tramping

There are plenty of opportunities to stretch your legs around Rotorua, with day walks a speciality. The booklet *Walks in the Rotorua Lakes Area* ($2.50), available from the i-SITE, showcases town walks, including the popular lakefront stroll (20 minutes). See also www.doc.govt.nz.

The **Eastern Okataina Walkway** (three hours one way) goes along the eastern shoreline of Lake Okataina to Lake Tarawera and passes the Soundshell, a natural amphitheatre that has *pa* (fortified village) remains and several swimming spots. The Western Okataina Walkway (five hours one way) mimics this route on the western side of the lake.

The **Northern Tarawera Track** (three hours one way) connects to the Eastern Okataina Walkway, creating a two-day walk from either Ruato or Lake Okataina to Lake Tarawera with an overnight camp at either Humphries Bay (sites free) or Tarawera Outlet (sites per adult/child $6/3). From Tarawera Outlet you can walk on to the 65m **Tarawera Falls** (four hours return). There's a forestry road into Tarawera Outlet from Kawerau, a grim timber town in the shadow of Putauaki (Mt Edgecumbe), off the road to Whakatane; access costs $5, with permits available from the **Kawerau visitor centre** (☎07-323 6300; www.kawerauonline.com; Plunkett St bus terminal; ⏲8am-6pm Nov-Apr, 9am-4pm May-Oct).

The **Okere Falls** are about 21km northeast of Rotorua on SH33, with an easy track (30 minutes return) past the 7m falls (popular for rafting), through native podocarp (conifer) forest and along the Kaituna River. Along the way is a lookout over the river at Hinemoa's Steps.

Just north of Wai-O-Tapu on SH5, the **Rainbow Mountain Track** (1½ hours one way) is a strenuous walk up the peak known to Maori as Maungakakaramea (Mountain of coloured earth). There are spectacular views from the top towards Lake Taupo and Tongariro National Park.

There are also a couple of good walks at Mt Ngongotaha, 10km northwest of Rotorua: the easy 3.2km **Nature Walk** loop through native forest, and the steep 5km return **Jubilee Track** to the (viewless) summit. See www.ngongotaha.org.

Horse Riding

Paradise Valley Ventures HORSE RIDING
(☎07-348 3300; www.paradisetreks.co.nz; 679 Paradise Valley Rd; 60/90min $65/90) The very safe and professional Paradise Valley Ventures takes treks for novices and experienced riders through a 280-hectare farm northwest of Rotorua. Pony rides for the kids, too.

Farmhouse HORSE RIDING
(Map p306; ☎07-332 3771; www.thefarmhouse.co.nz; 55 Sunnex Rd, off Central Rd; 30/60/120min $26/42/74) North of Lake Rotorua at the Farmhouse you can saddle-up for a short horse-riding trip for beginners, or a longer trek for experienced riders.

Fishing

There's always good trout fishing to be had somewhere around Rotorua. Hire a guide or go solo: either way a licence (per day/season $23/116) is essential, available from **O'Keefe's Fishing Specialists** (Map p292; ☎07-346 0178; www.okeefesfishing.co.nz; 1113 Eruera St; ⏲8.30am-5pm Mon-Fri, 9am-2pm Sat, 9am-1pm Sun). You can fish Rotorua's lakefront with a licence, though not all lakes can be fished year-round; check with O'Keefe's or the i-SITE.

Recommended guides include Mana Adventures (p299) and the following operators.

Trout Man FISHING
(☎0800 876 881, 07-357 5255; www.waiteti.com; 2hr/day trip from $35/120) Learn to fish with experienced angler Harvey Clark, from a couple of hours to multiday trips.

Clark Gregor FISHING
(☎07-347 1123; www.troutnz.co.nz; per hr $105) Fly- and boat fishing.

Gordon Randle FISHING
(☎07-349 2555; www.rotoruatrout.co.nz; half-/full-day charters $370/750) Reasonable hourly rates also available.

Golf

Government Gardens Golf GOLF
(Map p292; ☎07-348 9126; www.governmentgardensgolf.co.nz; Queens Dr, Government Gardens; ⏲7.30am-8pm) Government Gardens Golf has a nine-hole course (adult/child $20/14), minigolf ($11/8) and driving range (80 balls $11). A $40 golf package incudes clubs, green fees, balls and tees. There's also a baseball batting cage (bucket of balls $9).

☞ Tours

Geyser Link Shuttle TOUR
(☎07-343 6764; www.geyserlink.co.nz) Tours of some of the major sights, including Wai-O-Tapu (adult/child $65/32.50, half-day) and Waimangu Volcanic Valley ($60/30, half-day), or both ($115/57.50, full day). Transport-only options available too.

Affordable Adventures TOUR
(☎0508 278 946; www.affordableadventures.co.nz) Runs a shuttle to Wai-O-Tapu ($25 return), plus a full-day geothermal tour (adult/child $120/60).

Indigenous Trails TOUR
(☎07-542 1074; www.itrails.co.nz; tours adult/child $338/250) Full-day Maori-guided tours around Rotorua, with a bungy jump, river cruise, kiwi-meeting, cultural show and *hangi*.

Elite Adventures TOUR
(☎07-347 8282; www.eliteadventures.co.nz; tours adult/child half-day from $85/55, full-day from $220/130) Small-group tours covering a selection of Rotorua's major cultural and natural highlights.

Rotorua Duck Tours TOUR
(☎07-345 6522; www.rotoruaducktours.co.nz; adult/child/family $68/38/155; ⏲tours 11am, 1pm & 3.30pm Oct-Apr, 11am & 2.15pm May-Sep) Ninety-minute trips in an amphibious bio-fuelled vehicle taking in the major sites around town and heading out onto three lakes (Rotorua, Okareka and Tikitapu/Blue). Longer Lake Tarawera trips also available.

Tim's Wai-O-Tapu Thermal Cultural Shuttle TOUR
(☎027 494 5508) Goes to Wai-O-Tapu (return including entry $50) and the Buried Village and Waimangu Volcanic Valley on request.

Volcanic Air Safaris SCENIC FLIGHTS
(Map p292; ☎07-348 9984, 0800 800 848; www.volcanicair.co.nz; Lakefront; trips $70-862) A variety of floatplane and helicopter flights taking in Mt Tarawera and surrounding geothermal sites including Hell's Gate, the Buried Village and Waimangu Volcanic Valley. A 3¼-hour Whakaari (White Island)/Mt Tarawera trip is also available.

Helipro SCENIC FLIGHTS
(Map p306; ☎07-357 2515, 0800 435 477; www.helipro.co.nz; Hemo Rd; flights $95-895) Helipro plies the skies over Rotorua in nippy little red choppers (eight-minute city sightseeing flights $95), also extending to Mt Tarawera and as far as Whakaari (White Island). Landings in various places cost extra.

Pure Cruise New Zealand SAILING
(☎0800 272 456, 027 272 4561; www.purecruise.co.nz; cruises adult/child morning or sunset $110/70, half-day $135/75) Slow-boat catamaran

cruises on Lake Rotoiti; take a morning sail with a hot-spring soak, a sunset cruise or half-day exploration.

Mokoia Island Wai Ora Experiences CRUISE, CULTURAL TOUR
(Map p292; ☎07-349 0976; www.mokoiaisland.co.nz; Lakefront; tours adult/child $75/38; ⏰9.30am & 2pm) This operator takes visitors out to Mokoia Island on a 2½-hour Ultimate Island Experience tour. The tour includes wildlife-spotting, hearing tales of the island, and letting you dip your toes in the legendary hot pool of Hinemoa.

Lakeland Queen CRUISE
(Map p292; ☎07-348 0265, 0800 572 784; www.lakelandqueen.com; Lakefront) The *Lakeland Queen* paddlesteamer offers one-hour breakfast cruises (adult/child $45/22.50) and longer cruises (lunch $54/27.50; Saturday-night summer dinner $70/35) on Lake Rotorua.

Mana Adventures CRUISE, KAYAKING
(Map p292; ☎07-348 4186, 0800 333 660; www.manaadventures.co.nz; Lakefront) To explore the lake under your own steam, head for Mana Adventures, which offers (weather permitting) rental pedal boats ($9/6 per adult/child per 20 minutes) and kayaks ($25/50 per hour/half-day). It also runs one-hour lake cruises ($55/39 per adult/child), trout-fishing charters and three-hour tours to Mokoia Island ($75/30 per adult/child).

Sleeping

Rotorua has plenty of holiday parks and an ever-changing backpacker scene. Generic motels crowd Fenton St: better and more interesting rooms are away from the main drag.

TOP CHOICE **Regent of Rotorua** BOUTIQUE HOTEL $$$
(Map p292; ☎07-348 4079, 0508 734 368; www.regentrotorua.co.nz; 1191 Pukaki St; d/ste from $169/239; 📶🏊) Wow! It's about time Rotorua showed some slumbering style, and the Regent (a renovated 1960s motel) delivers. 'The '60s was a glamorous time to travel,' say the owners: the decor follows suit, with hip black-and-white tones, funky mirrors, retro wallpaper and colourful splashes. There's a pool and restaurant too, and the Tutanekai St eateries are an amble away.

🍃 **Funky Green Voyager** HOSTEL $
(Map p292; ☎07-346 1754; www.funkygreenvoyager.co.nz; 4 Union St; dm from $25, d with/without bathroom $68/59; @📶) Green on the outside and the inside – due to several cans of paint and a dedicated environmental policy – the shoe-free Funky GV features laid-back tunes and plenty of sociable chat among a spunky bunch of guests and worldly-wise owners, who know what you want when you travel. The best doubles have bathroom; dorms are roomy with quality mattresses.

Waiteti Trout Stream Holiday Park HOLIDAY PARK $
(Map p306; ☎07-357 5255, 0800 876 881; www.waiteti.com; 14 Okona Cres; sites $36, dm from $22, d cabin/motel from $55/105; @📶) This well-maintained park is a great option if you don't mind the 8km drive into town. Set in 2 acres of garden on the banks of a trout-filled stream, it's a cute classic with character-filled motel units, compact cabins, a tidy backpackers lodge and beaut campsites by the stream. Free kayaks and dinghies; fly-fishing lessons $30.

Tuscany Villas MOTEL $$
(Map p306; ☎07-348 3500, 0800 802 050; www.tuscanyvillasrotorua.co.nz; 280 Fenton St; d from $145; 📶) With its Italian-inspired architecture and pointy conifers, this family-owned eye-catcher is the pick of the Fenton St motels. It pitches itself perfectly at both the corporate and leisure traveller, who will appreciate the lavish furnishings, multiple TVs, DVD players and huge, deep spa baths.

Crank Backpackers HOSTEL $
(Map p292; ☎0508 224 466, 07-348 0852; www.crankbackpackers.co.nz; 1140 Hinemoa St; dm $22-25, d & tw with/without bathroom $62/56; @📶) A cavernous hostel determined to compete with the old stagers, Crank occupies a former shopping mall (you might be sleeping in a florist or delicatessen). Dorms over the street are sunny, and there are sexy co-ed bathrooms, a free gym and the Wall rock-climbing facility, as well as the art-house Basement Cinema downstairs.

Regent Flashpackers HOSTEL $
(Map p292; ☎07-348 5111; www.regentflashpackers.co.nz; 1181 Pukaki St; dm/d from $25/79; @📶) Angling for a mature, upscale backpacker market (is there such a thing?), the very decent Regent does it with style: sturdy bunks, cosy kitchen, quality linen, underfloor heating and fill-your-own mineral pools out the back. There's also a bar, which helps lower the tone a little.

Jack & Di's Troutbeck Lodge LODGE, MOTEL **$$**
(Map p306; ☎07-357 4294, 0800 522 526; www.jackanddis.co.nz; 5 Arnold St; d/lodge from $99/399; 📶) A lakeside position in quiet, secluded Ngongotaha makes this large lodge a good retreat from central Rotorua (no sulphur smell!). The lodge (with full kitchen) caters for families or groups of up to 11, or there are motel-style doubles. Good winter rates; free kayaks.

Rotorua YHA HOSTEL **$**
(Map p292; ☎07-349 4088, 0800 278 299; www.yha.co.nz; 1278 Haupapa St; dm $28-35 d with/without bathroom $87/77; @📶) Bright and sparkling-clean, this classy, purpose-built hostel is great for those wanting to get outdoors, with staff eager to assist with trip bookings, and storage for bikes and kayaks. Pricier rooms come with bathroom, and there's a barbecue area and deck for hanging out on (though this ain't a party pad). Off-street parking a bonus.

Rotorua Top 10 Holiday Park HOLIDAY PARK **$**
(☎07-348 1886, 0800 223 267; www.rotoruatop10.co.nz; 1495 Pukuatua St; sites from $20, d cabin/motel from $65/95; @📶🏊) A small but perfectly formed holiday park with a continual improvement policy that has seen a new playground, shower/toilet blocks and mineral hot pools installed. Cabins are in good nick and have small fridges and microwaves. Plenty of shrubberies and picnic tables.

Sandi's Bed & Breakfast B&B **$$**
(Map p306; ☎0800 726 3422, 07-348 0884; www.sandisbedandbreakfast.co.nz; 103 Fairy Springs Rd; d/f incl breakfast $130/160; 📶🏊) A friendly, family B&B run by the well-humoured Sandi who offers tourist advice with a ready smile. The best bets are the two bohemian chalets with TV and plenty of room to move. It's on a busy road a couple of kilometres north of town, but thoughtful extras include fresh fruit with breakfast and a sun deck.

Rotorua Central Backpackers HOSTEL **$**
(Map p292; ☎07-349 3285; www.rotoruacentralbackpackers.co.nz; 1076 Pukuatua St; dm $25, d $60; @📶) This heritage hostel was built in 1936 and retains historic features including dark-wood skirting boards and door frames, deep bathtubs and radiators that are geothermally powered. Dorms have no more than six beds (and no bunks), plus there's a spa pool and barbecue, all within strolling distance of the museum.

Jack & Di's Lake View Lodge LODGE **$$**
(Map p292; ☎07-357 4294, 0800 522 526; www.jackanddis.co.nz; 21 Lake Rd; r/apt from $99/199 ; 📶) Lake views and a central but secluded location make this unique lodge a persuasive option. The upstairs penthouse is ideal for couples, while downstairs is better for families or groups (three bedrooms, three bathrooms). A spa pool, lazy lounge areas and full kitchens add to the appeal.

Crash Palace HOSTEL **$**
(Map p292; ☎07-348 8842, 0800 892 727; www.crashpalace.co.nz; 1271 Hinemaru St; dm/s/d from $22/35/60; @📶) This newcomer occupies a big, mustard-coloured 1930s hotel near Government Gardens. The atmosphere strikes a balance between party and pristine, without too much of either. The nicest rooms have floorboards, and there's lots of art on the walls. Crash (aka Chris) and Nero the black cat man the reception desk. Limited off-steet parking.

Rotorua Thermal Holiday Park HOLIDAY PARK **$**
(Map p306; ☎07-346 3140; www.rotoruathermal.co.nz; 463 Old Taupo Rd; sites from $16, d cabins/units from $51/98; @📶🏊) This super-friendly holiday park on the edge of town is deep in the leisure groove, with barbecues, a playground, rows of cabins and tourist flats, campsites galore and a shop and seasonal cafe. There's plenty of room to move, with lots of open grassy areas, plus hot mineral pools to soak the day away.

Millennium Hotel Rotorua HOTEL **$$$**
(Map p292; ☎07-347 1234; www.millenniumrotorua.co.nz; cnr Eruera & Hinemaru Sts; d from $250; @📶🏊) The slick Maori-inspired lobby sets the scene for this elegant five-storey motel. Lakefront rooms afford excellent views as does the club lounge, popular with the suits and internationalists swanning about. The poolside *hangi* (p294) is fab, as is the in-house restaurant Nikau.

Six on Union MOTEL **$$**
(Map p292; ☎07-347 8062, 0800 100 062; www.sixonunion.co.nz; 6 Union St; d/f from $105/145; 📶🏊) Hanging baskets ahoy! This modest place is an affordable bonanza with pool, spa and small kitchenettes in all units. Rooms are functional, and the new owners (from Yorkshire) keep the swimming-pool area in good nick. It's away from traffic noise, but still an easy walk into town.

Victoria Lodge MOTEL $$
(Map p292; ☎0800 100 039, 07-348 4039; www.victorialodge.co.nz; 10 Victoria St; d/apt from $115/160;) The friendly Vic has seen a lot of competitors come and go, maintaining its foothold in the market with individual-feeling rooms: the studios are particularly attractive with their thermally heated plunge pools. Fully equipped, freshly painted apartments can squeeze in seven, though four would be very comfortable.

Ann's Volcanic Rotorua Motel MOTEL $$
(Map p306; ☎07-347 1007, 0800 768 683; www.rotoruamotel.co.nz; 107 Malfroy Rd; d/ste from $99/115;) Ann's is an affordable motel that has family charm and an ever-friendly host with loads of advice on things to see and do around Rotorua. Larger rooms feature courtyard spas and facilities for travellers with disabilities, with a house next door available for big groups. Rooms close to the street can be a tad noisy.

Princes Gate Hotel LUXURY HOTEL $$$
(Map p292; ☎07-348 1179, 0800 500 705; www.princesgate.co.nz; 1057 Arawa St; d/ste from $165/220; @) The Princes Gate is a well-loved and warmly welcoming 19th-century dame with 54 different rooms, such as the opulent Marvelly suite – perhaps too pink for all but Barbara Cartland. Sink into the bottomless bath, however, and all is forgiven. Other amenities include cascading mineral baths, sauna and restaurant. Cabaret nights, too.

Base Rotorua HOSTEL $
(Map p292; ☎07-348 8636, 0800 227 369; www.stayatbase.co.nz; 1286 Arawa St; dm/s/d from $28/70/70; @) A link in the Base chain, this huge hostel is ever-popular with partying backpackers who love the Lava Bar (cheap meals, toga parties, disco nights etc). Dorms can be tight (up to 12 beds), but extras such as girls-only rooms, en suites in all doubles, a large outdoor heated pool and off-street parking compensate.

Kiwi Paka HOSTEL $
(☎07-347 0931; www.kiwipaka.co.nz; 60 Tarewa Rd; sites from $15, dm/s/d $29/55/64, chalets with bathroom d/tr/q $87/107/147; @) This rambling complex is a short walk through Kuirau Park to town. The vibe is a bit like a school camp, with acceptable amenities and a range of accommodation from campsites to plain dorms, lodge rooms and two-storey pine-clad chalets. There's a cafe and bar on-site.

Eating

The lake end of Tutanekai St has a strip of good eating places, but there are plenty of other options all over town.

TOP CHOICE **Third Place Cafe** CAFE $$
(☎07-349 4852; www.thirdplacecafe.co.nz; 36 Lake Rd; mains $15-18; 8am-4pm Mon-Fri, 8am-3pm Sat) A really interesting cafe away from the hubbub, Third Place has leapfrogged into first by our reckoning. All-day breakfast/brunch sidesteps neatly between chicken jambalaya, fish and chips, and an awesome 'mumble jumble' of crushed kumara (sweet potato), green tomatoes and spicy chorizo topped with bacon, poached egg and hollandaise sauce. Hangover? What hangover? Slide into a red-leather couch or score a window seat overlooking Ohinemutu.

Lime Caffeteria CAFE $$
(Map p292; ☎07-350 2033; cnr Fenton & Whakaue Sts; mains $13-24; 7.30am-4.30pm;) Occupying a quiet corner near the lake, this refreshing cafe is especially good for alfresco breakfasts and dishes with a welcome twist: try the chicken-and-chorizo salad or prawn-and-salmon risotto in lime sauce. It also offers classy counter snacks, excellent coffee and outdoor tables. 'This is the best lunch I've had in ages,' says one happy punter.

Indian Star INDIAN $$
(Map p292; ☎07-343 6222; www.indianstar.co.nz; 1118 Tutanekai St; mains $14-22; lunch & dinner;) This is one of several Indian eateries around town, elevating itself above the competition with immaculate service and marvellous renditions of subcontinental classics. It has sizeable portions and good vegetarian selections (try the chickpea masala). Book for dinner.

Fat Dog Cafe & Bar CAFE $$
(Map p292; ☎07-347 7586; 1161 Arawa St; mains breakfast & lunch $12-20, dinner $27-32; breakfast, lunch & dinner;) With paw prints and silly poems painted on the walls, this is the town's friskiest and most child-friendly cafe. During the day it dishes up burgers (try the Dogs Bollox version), nachos, salads and sandwiches; in the evening it's candlelit lamb and venison. The only cafe in NZ brave enough to play *Unskinny Bop* by Poison.

Capers Epicurean CAFE, DELICATESSEN
(Map p292; ☎07-348 8818; www.capers.co.nz; 1181 Eruera St; mains breakfast & lunch $6-20, dinner

$13-28; ⏲7.30am-9pm; ✎) This slick, barnlike deli is always busy with diners showing up for cabinets crammed full of delicious gourmet sandwiches, pastries, salads and cakes, and an excellent blackboard menu of breakfasts and other tasty hot foods (try the carrot, leek and feta lasagne). There's also a deli section stocked with olive oils, marinades, relishes, jams and chocolates.

Weilin's Noodle House NOODLES, CHINESE $
(Map p292; ☎07-343 9998; 1148 Tutanekai St; mains $8-17; ⏲lunch & dinner Wed-Mon) A neat and tidy shop serving trad (and refreshingly un-fatty/salty/stodgy) Chinese dumplings and oodles of noodles in soups and stir-fries. Eat in or take away.

Urbano Bistro MODERN NZ, CAFE $$
(Map p306; ☎07-349 3770; www.urbanobistro.co.nz; cnr Fenton & Grey Sts; mains breakfast & lunch $14-21, dinner $24-43; ⏲9am-11pm Mon-Sat, to 3pm Sun) This suburban cafe, with its mega-checkerboard floor and striking wallpaper, is a bold move by reputable local restaurateurs. It serves some of the most delicious fare in town (try the beef, pineapple and kumara curry), rich in flavour and well executed. Fine wines and five-star service.

Sabroso LATIN AMERICAN $$
(Map p292; ☎07-349 0591; www.sabroso.co.nz; 1184 Haupapa St; mains $18-45; ⏲5-10pm Thu-Tue) What a surprise! This modest Latin American cantina – adorned with sombreros, guitars, hessian tablecloths and salt-and-pepper shakers made from Corona bottles – serves adventurous south-of-the-border fare to spice up bland Kiwi palates. The black-bean chilli is a knock-out (as are the margaritas).

Bistro 1284 MODERN NZ $$$
(Map p292; ☎07-346 1284; www.bistro1284.co.nz; 1284 Eruera St; mains $34-39; ⏲6pm-late) Definitely one of RotoVegas' fine-dining hot spots, this intimate place (all chocolate and mushroom colours) serves stylish NZ cuisine with an Asian influence. It's an excellent place to sample local ingredients (the lamb is always good); be sure to leave room for some delectable desserts.

Amazing Thai THAI $$
(Map p292; ☎07-343 9494; 1246 Fenton St; mains $19-28; ⏲lunch & dinner) This large, glass-fronted restaurant dishes up better-than-average, spicy-as-you-like Thai food in generous servings. There are obligatory portraits of Thai royals and sundry elephants, and takeaways available.

Ali Baba's Tunisian Takeaway MIDDLE EASTERN, TUNISIAN $
(Map p292; ☎07-348 2983; 1146 Tutanekai St; meals $9-15; ⏲11.30am-late; ✎) Follow the belly-dancing music (and your nose) into this neat little eatery serving kebabs and Tunisian-inspired pizzas, salads, pastas and rice meals. Eat in or take away.

Pak 'n Save SUPERMARKET
(Map p292; www.paknsave.co.nz; cnr Fenton & Amohau Sts; ⏲8am-10pm) Centrally located.

Drinking & Entertainment

Brew BAR, CRAFT BEER
(Map p292; www.brewpub.co.nz; 1103 Tutanekai St) Run by the lads from Croucher Brewing Co, Rotorua's best microbrewers, Brew sits in a sunny spot on Rotorua's main eat-street. Sip down a pint of fruity pale ale, aromatic drunken hop bitter or malty pilsener and wonder how you'll manage a sleep-in tomorrow morning. Good coffee, too.

Pig & Whistle PUB, BREWERY
(Map p292; www.pigandwhistle.co.nz; cnr Haupapa & Tutanekai Sts) Inside a former police station, this busy microbrewery-pub serves up Swine lager, big-screen TVs, a beer garden and live music Thursday to Saturday, plus simple grub (mains $15 to $30). The menu runs the gamut from crispy pork-belly salad to burgers and vegetarian nachos.

Belgian Bar BAR, LIVE MUSIC
(Map p292; www.facebook.com/pages/belgian-bar/137762819598058; 1151 Arawa St; ⏲Tue-Sun) The best bar in town for lovers of gigs and good beer. Half a dozen Euro-beers on tap and 42 in the bottle accompany regular blues and acoustic acts ('Clapton is God' is spraypainted behind the stage).

Pheasant Plucker PUB, LIVE MUSIC
(Map p292; www.thepheasantplucker.co.nz; 1153 Arawa St) A place for a proper pint, the pleasant Pheasant proffers locally brewed and Brit beers, along with pub food and open-mic, blues, rock, roots and singer-songwriter acts.

Basement Cinema CINEMA
(Map p292; www.basementcinema.co.nz; 1140 Hinemoa St) Part of the same complex as the Wall rock-climbing gym, the Basement offers up offbeat, foreign-language and art-house flicks.

Shopping

Rotorua and souvenirs go hand-in-hand: look for genuine Maori and NZ-made arts and crafts. South of town, Te Puia and Whakarewarewa Thermal Village have excellent selections of genuine Maori-made arts.

Rotorua Night Market MARKET
(Map p292; www.rotoruanightmarket.co.nz; Tutanekai St; ⌚4.30pm-late Thu) Tutanekai St is closed off on Thursday nights between Haupapa and Pukuatua Sts to allow the Rotorua Night Market to spread its wings. Expect local arts and crafts, souvenirs, cheesy buskers, coffee, wine and plenty of deli-style food stalls for dinner.

Mountain Jade ARTS & CRAFTS, JEWELLERY
(Map p292; www.mountainjade.com; 1288 Fenton St; ⌚9am-6pm) High-end hand-crafted greenstone jewellery and carvings. You can watch the carvers at work through the streetside window.

Out of New Zealand ARTS & CRAFTS, JEWELLERY
(Map p292; 1189 Fenton St; ⌚10am-6pm, to 9pm Dec-Mar) Stocks NZ-made craft and gifts including carvings, ceramics and jewellery: affordable, packable souvenirs.

Information

There are plenty of ATMs around town, and a Travelex at the i-SITE. Most banks offer currency exchange.

Lakes Prime Care (☎07-348 1000; 1165 Tutanekai St; ⌚8am-10pm) Urgent medical care.

Police (☎111, non-emergency 07-348 0099; www.police.govt.nz; 1190-1214 Fenton St)

Post office (cnr Tutanekai & Pukuatua Sts)

Rotorua Hospital (☎07-348 1199; www.lakesdhb.govt.nz; Arawa St; ⌚24hr) Round-the-clock medical care.

Rotorua Sustainable Tourism (www.sustainablenz.com) Make your Rotorua visit more ecofriendly.

Tourism Rotorua & i-SITE (☎07-348 5179, 0800 768 678; www.rotoruanz.com; 1167 Fenton St; ⌚8am-6pm Sep-May, to 5.30pm Jun-Aug) The hub for travel information and bookings, including Department of Conservation (DOC) walks. Also has an exchange bureau, a cafe, showers and lockers.

Getting There & Away

Air

Air New Zealand (☎07-343 1100; www.airnewzealand.co.nz; 1267 Tutanekai St; ⌚9am-5pm Mon-Fri) Has direct flights between Rotorua and Auckland, Wellington and Christchurch, plus Sydney (every Tuesday and Saturday).

Qantas (www.qantas.com.au) Links Rotorua with Auckland.

Bus

All the major bus companies stop outside the Rotorua i-SITE, from where you can arrange bookings.

InterCity (www.intercity.co.nz) destinations include the following:

DESTINATION	PRICE	DURATION	FREQUENCY
Auckland	$50	3½hr	7 daily
Gisborne	$82	9hr	1 daily
Hamilton	$32	1½hr	5 daily
Napier	$53	3hr	3 daily
Taupo	$32	1hr	4 daily
Tauranga	$30	1½hr	3 daily
Wellington	$65	8hr	5 daily
Whakatane	$34	1½hr	1 daily

Naked Bus (www.nakedbus.com) services the following destinations. Substantial fare savings can be made by booking in advance.

DESTINATION	PRICE	DURATION	FREQUENCY
Auckland	$19	4hr	6 daily
Gisborne	$27	4¾hr	1 daily
Hamilton	$16	1½hr	5 daily
Napier	$29	3hr	3 daily
Taupo	$15	1hr	2 daily
Tauranga	$12	1½hr	5 daily
Wellington	$36	8hr	2 daily
Whakatane	$18	1½hr	1 daily

Twin City Express (☎0800 422 928; www.baybus.co.nz) buses run twice daily Monday to Friday between Rotorua and Tauranga/Mt Maunganui via Te Puke ($11.60, 1½ hours).

White Island Shuttle (☎07-308 9588, 0800 733 529; www.whiteisland.co.nz; one-way/return $35/60), run by White Island Tours in Whakatane, operates return shuttles to Whakatane from Rotorua. It's ostensibly for tour customers, but you can use the service without taking the tour.

Getting Around

To/From the Airport

Rotorua Airport (☎07-345 8800; www.rotorua-airport.co.nz; SH30) is 10km northeast of town.

Super Shuttle (☎09-522 5100, 0800 748 885; www.supershuttle.co.nz) offers a door-to-door airport service for $22 for the first person then

$6 per additional passenger. Cityride (p304) runs a daily airport bus service ($2.30). A taxi to/from the city centre costs about $25.

Bus

Many local attractions offer free pick-up/drop-off shuttle services. Shuttle services (p298) are also available to/from outlying attractions.

Cityride (☎0800 422 928; www.baybus.co.nz) operates local bus services around town, and also to Ngongotaha (route 1, $2.30) and the airport (route 10, $2.30).

Car

The big-name car-hire companies vie for your attention at Rotorua Airport. The following smaller companies share a premises located on Fenton St.

A2B Car Rentals (☎0800 666 703; www.a2b-carrentals.co.nz; 1234 Fenton St)

Ezi-Rent Car Hire (☎07-349 1629, 0800 652 565; www.ezirentcarhire.co.nz; 1234 Fenton St)

Nationwide Rental Cars (☎0800 803 003; www.nationwiderentalcars.co.nz; 1234 Fenton St)

Taxi

Fast Taxis (☎07-348 2444)

Rotorua Taxis (☎07-348 1111)

AROUND ROTORUA

North of Rotorua

Sights & Activities

Rainbow Springs Kiwi Wildlife Park WILDLIFE RESERVE

(Map p306; ☎0800 724 626; www.rainbowsprings.co.nz; Fairy Springs Rd; 24hr pass adult/child/family $35/22.50/103; ⏰8am-late) About 3km north of central Rotorua, Rainbow Springs is a family-friendly winner. The natural springs here are home to wild trout and eels, which you can peer at through an underwater viewer. There are interpretive walkways, a new 'Big Splash' water ride, and plenty of animals, including tuatara (a native reptile), introduced species (wallabies, rainbow lorikeets) and native birds (kea, kaka and pukeko).

A highlight is the Kiwi Encounter, offering a rare peek into the lives of these endangered birds: excellent 30-minute tours have you tiptoeing through incubator and hatchery areas. Also available are joint four-hour evening tours (adult/child $125/65) with neighbouring Mitai Maori Village (p294).

Wingspan Birds of Prey Trust WILDLIFE CENTRE

(☎07-357 4469; www.wingspan.co.nz; 1164 Paradise Valley Rd; adult/child $25/8; ⏰9am-3pm) Wingspan Birds of Prey Trust is dedicated to conserving three threatened NZ birds: the falcon, hawk and owl. Learn about the birds in the museum display, then take a sneaky peek into the incubation area before walking through the all-weather aviary. Don't miss the 2pm flying display.

aMAZEme MAZE

(Map p306; ☎07-357 5759; www.amazeme.co.nz; 1335 Paradise Valley Rd; adult/child/family $16/9/45; ⏰9am-5pm Dec-Feb, 10am-4pm Mar-Nov) This amazing 1.4km maze is constructed from immaculately pruned, head-high escallonia hedge. Lose yourself (or the kids) in the endless spirals.

Paradise Valley Springs WILDLIFE RESERVE

(☎07-348 9667; www.paradisevalleysprings.co.nz; 467 Paradise Valley Rd; adult/child $29/14.50; ⏰8am-dusk) In Paradise Valley at the foot of Mt Ngongotaha, 8km from Rotorua, is Paradise Valley Springs, a 6-hectare park with trout springs, big slippery eels and various land-dwelling animals such as deer, alpacas, possums and a pride of lions (fed at 2.30pm; see the two new cubs before they grow up). There's also a coffee shop and an elevated treetop walkway.

Agrodome AGRICULTURAL

(Map p306; ☎07-357 1050; www.agrodome.co.nz; Western Rd; 1hr tour adult/child/family $38.50/19.50/82, 1hr show $29/14.50/77, tour & show $56/28/115; ⏰8.30am-5pm, shows 9.30am, 11am & 2.30pm, tours 10.40am, 12.10pm, 1.30pm & 3.40pm) Learn everything you need to know about sheep at the educational Agrodome. Shows include a parade of champion rams, a livestock auction, and shearing and doggy displays. The tour lets you check out farm animals including, among others, sheep. Other agro-attractions include a shearing-shed museum and cafe.

Northeast of Rotorua

Sights & Activities

Hells Gate & Wai Ora Spa VOLCANIC AREA, SPA

(Map p306; ☎07-345 3151; www.hellsgate.co.nz; SH30, Tikitere; admission adult/child/family $30/15/75, mud bath & spa $105, massage per 30/60min $85/135; ⏰8.30am-8.30pm) Known as Tikitere to the Maori, Hells Gate is an impressive geothermal reserve 16km northeast of Rotorua on the Whakatane road (SH30). Tikitere is an abbreviation of *Taku tiki i tere nei* (My youngest daughter has floated away), remembering the tragedy of a young girl jumping into a thermal pool. The English name originates from a 1934 visit by George Bernard Shaw. The reserve covers 10 hectares, with a 2.5km walking track to the various attractions, including a hot thermal waterfall. You can also see a master woodcarver at work, and learn about flax weaving and other Maori traditions.

Long regarded by Maori as a place of healing, Tikitere also houses the Wai Ora Spa, where you can get muddy with a variety of treatments. A courtesy shuttle to/from Rotorua is available.

3D Maze MAZE
(Map p306; ☎07-345 5275; www.3dmaze.co.nz; 1135 Te Ngae Rd; adult/child $9/6; ⏲9am-5pm) Three kilometres beyond Rotorua Airport is this 1.7km-long wooden maze that will entertain kids for an hour or so.

Southeast of Rotorua

Sights & Activities

Redwoods Whakarewarewa Forest FOREST
(www.redwoods.co.nz; ⏲5.30am-8.30pm) This magical forest park is 3km southeast of town on Tarawera Rd. It was originally home to over 170 tree species (a few less now), planted from 1899 to see which could be grown successfully for timber. Radiata pine proved a hit (as evident throughout New Zealand), but it's the mighty Californian redwoods that give the park its grandeur today.

Clearly signposted walking tracks range from a half-hour wander through the Redwood Grove to an enjoyable whole-day route to the Blue and Green Lakes. Most walks start from the **Redwoods Gift Shop & Visitor Centre** (Map p306; ☎07-350 0110; Long Mile Rd; ⏲8.30am-5.30pm Mon-Fri, 10am-5pm Sat & Sun Oct-Mar, 8.30am-4.30pm Mon-Fri, 10am-4pm Sat & Sun Apr-Sep), where you can get maps and view displays about the forest. Aside from walking, the park is great for picnics, and is acclaimed for its accessible mountain biking. Mountain Bike Rotorua (p296) offers bike hire, across the park off Waipa State Mill Rd.

Buried Village ARCHAEOLOGICAL SITE, MUSEUM
(Map p306; ☎07-362 8287; www.buriedvillage.co.nz; 1180 Tarawera Rd; adult/child/family $31/8/62; ⏲9am-5pm Nov-Mar, to 4.30pm Apr-Oct) Fifteen kilometres from Rotorua on Tarawera Rd, beyond the pretty Blue and Green Lakes, is the buried village of Te Wairoa, interred by the eruption of Mt Tarawera in 1886. Te Wairoa was the staging post for travellers coming to see the Pink and White Terraces. Today a museum houses objects dug from the ruins, and guides in period costume escort groups through the excavated sites. There's also a walk to the 30m **Te Wairoa Falls** (not suitable for kids or oldies), and a teahouse if you're feeling more sedate.

Lake Tarawera LAKE
(www.doc.govt.nz) Tarawera means 'Burnt Spear', named by a visiting hunter who left his bird spears in a hut and, on returning the following season, found both the spears and hut had been burnt. The lake is picturesque and good for swimming, fishing, cruises and walks.

A good place to access the lake is at the Landing, about 2km past the buried village. Here you'll find **Clearwater Cruises** (Map p306; ☎07-345 6688, 0508 253 279; www.clearwater.co.nz; per hr cruise vessel/self-drive runabout $550/140), which runs scenic cruises for groups and trout-fishing trips aboard a variety of vessels. Also here is the **Landing Café** (www.thelandinglaketarawera.co.nz; mains $26-30; ⏲breakfast & lunch daily, closed Mon & Tue Jun-Aug), serving hearty mains like spiced lamb rump, salmon pasta and seafood chowder. Around 2km beyond the Landing is **Lake Tarawera Water Taxi** (☎07-362 8080; www.laketaraweraescape.co.nz; 93 Spencer Rd; from $60), which can take you anywhere on the lake, at any time.

There are campsites managed by **DOC** (www.doc.govt.nz) at **Hot Water Beach** (Map p306; adult/child $10/5) (boat access only), **Tarawera Outlet** (Map p306; adult/child $6/3) and **Humphries Bay** (Map p306) (free, but rudimentary). The **Blue Lake Top 10 Holiday Park** (Map p306; ☎07-362 8120, 0800 808 292; www.bluelaketop10.co.nz; 723 Tarawera Rd; sites from $18.50, cabins $56-139, units $99-229; @☜) offers camping next to the Blue Lake (good for swimming and kayaking), 6km before you get to Lake Tarawera; well run, it has spotless facilities and a handy range of cabins.

Around Rotorua

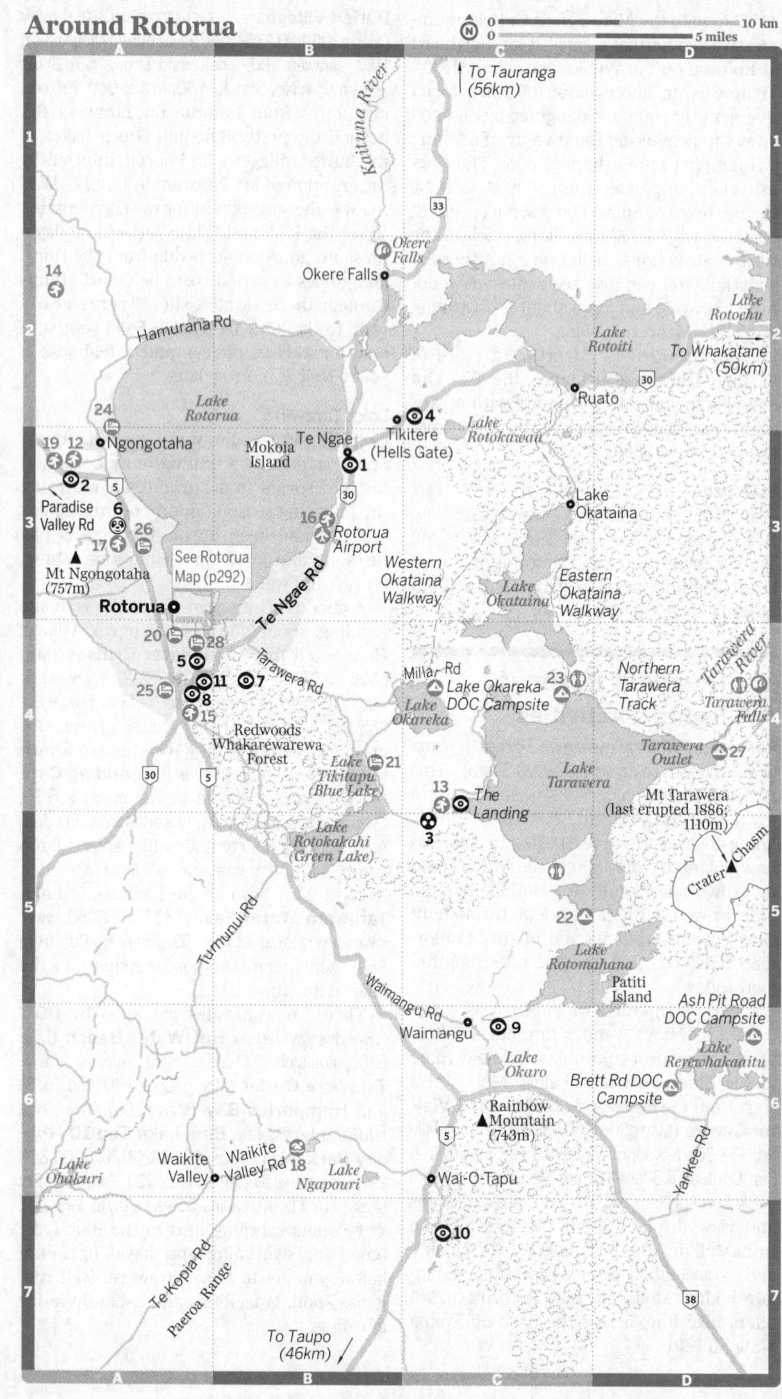

Around Rotorua

Sights

1	3D Maze	B3
2	aMAZEme	A3
3	Buried Village	C5
4	Hells Gate & Wai Ora Spa	C2
5	Kingsgate Hotel Rotorua	A4
	Mitai Maori Village	(see 17)
	Pohutu Cultural Theatre	(see 5)
6	Rainbow Springs Kiwi Wildlife Park	A3
7	Redwoods Gift Shop & Visitor Centre	B4
8	Te Puia	A4
9	Waimangu Volcanic Valley	C6
10	Wai-O-Tapu Thermal Wonderland	C7
11	Whakarewarewa Thermal Village	A4

Activities, Courses & Tours

12	Agrodome	A3
	Agroventures	(see 2)
13	Clearwater Cruises	C4
14	Farmhouse	A2
	Helipro	(see 8)
15	Mountain Bike Rotorua	A4
16	NZONE	B3
	Ogo	(see 17)
17	Skyline Rotorua	A3
18	Waikite Valley Thermal Pools	B6
19	Zorb	A3

Sleeping

20	Ann's Volcanic Rotorua Motel	A4
21	Blue Lake Top 10 Holiday Park	B4
22	Hot Water Beach Campsite	C5
23	Humphries Bay Campsite	C4
24	Jack & Di's Troutbeck Lodge	A2
25	Rotorua Thermal Holiday Park	A4
26	Sandi's Bed & Breakfast	A3
27	Tarawera Outlet Campsite	D4
28	Tuscany Villas	A4
	Waiteti Trout Stream Holiday Park	(see 24)

Eating

	Urbano Bistro	(see 28)

South of Rotorua

Sights & Activities

Waimangu Volcanic Valley VOLCANIC AREA, SPRING
(Map p306; ☎07-366 6137; www.waimangu.com; 587 Waimangu Rd; adult/child walking tour $34.50/11, boat cruise $42.50/11; ⏰8.30am-5pm daily, to 6pm Jan, last admission 3.45pm, 4.45pm Jan) This interesting thermal area was created during the eruption of Mt Tarawera in 1886, making it young in geological terms. Waimangu (Black Water) refers to the dark, muddy colour of much of the water here.

Taking the easy downhill stroll through the valley you'll pass many spectacular thermal and volcanic features, including Inferno Crater Lake, where overflowing water can reach 80°C, and **Frying Pan Lake**, the largest hot spring in the world. The walk continues down to Lake Rotomahana (meaning 'Warm Lake'), from where you can either get a lift back up to where you started or take a 45-minute boat trip on the lake, past steaming cliffs and the former site of the Pink and White Terraces.

Waimangu is 20 minutes south of Rotorua, 14km along SH5 (towards Taupo) and then 6km from the marked turn-off.

Wai-O-Tapu Thermal Wonderland VOLCANIC AREA, GEYSER
(Map p306; ☎07-366 6333; www.waiotapu.co.nz; 201 Waiotapu Loop Rd, off SH5; adult/child/family $32.50/11/80; ⏰8.30am-5pm, last admission 3.45pm) Wai-O-Tapu (Sacred Waters) is a fairly commercial operation with a lot of interesting geothermal features packed into a small area, including the boiling, multi-hued Champagne Pool, bubbling mud pool, stunning mineral terraces and Lady Knox Geyser, which spouts off (with a little prompting from an organic soap) punctually at 10.15am and gushes up to 20m for about an hour (be here by 9.45am to see it).

Wai-O-Tapu is 27km south of Rotorua along SH5 (towards Taupo), and a further 2km from the marked turn-off.

Waikite Valley Thermal Pools SWIMMING
(Map p306; ☎07-333 1861; www.hotpools.co.nz; 648 Waikite Valley Rd; public pools adult/child/family $14/7/35, private pools 40min $18; ⏰10am-9pm) Approximately 30km south of Rotorua are these excellent open-air pools, formalised in the 1970s but utilised for centuries before then. There are four main pools, two more relaxing, smaller pools, and four private spas, all ranging from 35°C to 40°C. There's also a cafe and camping (sites from $18; pools free for campers).

To get here, turn right off SH5 opposite the Wai-O-Tapu turn-off, and continue 6km (worth the drive if only for the gorgeous valley view as you come over the hill).

BAY OF PLENTY

The Bay of Plenty stretches along the pohutukawa-studded coast from Waihi Beach to Opotiki and inland as far as the Kaimai Range. This is where New Zealanders have come on holiday for generations, lapping up salt-licked activities and lashings of sunshine.

Tauranga

POP 121,500

Tauranga (pronounced Tao-wronger) has been booming since the 1990s and remains one of NZ's fastest-growing cities. It's also NZ's busiest port – with petrol refineries and mountains of coal and lumber – but it's beach-seeking holidaymakers who have seen the old workhorse reborn as a show pony. Restaurants and bars line the revamped waterfront, fancy hotels rise high, and the once-sleepy burbs of Mt Maunganui and Papamoa have woken up to new prosperity. This is about as Riviera as NZ gets. Online, www.downtowntauranga.co.nz is a commercial but useful resource.

Sights

FREE Tauranga Art Gallery GALLERY
(www.artgallery.org.nz; cnr Wharf & Willow Sts; ⏲10am-4.30pm) The Tauranga Art Gallery presents historic and contemporary art, and houses a permanent collection along with frequently changing local and visiting exhibitions. The building itself is a former bank, although you'd hardly know it – it's an altogether excellent space with no obvious compromise (cue: applause). Touring the ground and mezzanine galleries, with a stop to poke your nose into the video cube, will take an hour or so.

Elms Mission House HISTORIC BUILDING
(www.theelms.org.nz; 15 Mission St; house adult/child $5/50c, gardens free; ⏲house 2-4pm Wed, Sat & Sun, gardens 9am-5pm daily) Built in 1847, Elms Mission House is the oldest building in the Bay of Plenty. Furnished in period style, it sits among other well-preserved mission buildings in leafy gardens. The spooky **Mission Cemetery** (cnr Marsh St & Dive Cres; ⏲24hr) lies not far away – a shady tangle of trees and headstones, it's good for a little epitaph-reading.

Classic Flyers NZ MUSEUM
(www.classicflyersnz.com; 8 Jean Batten Dr; adult/child/family $10/5/25; ⏲10am-4pm) Out near the airport, Classic Flyers NZ is an interesting aviation museum (biplanes, retired US Airforce jets, helicopters etc) with a buzzy on-site cafe.

FREE Monmouth Redoubt ARCHAEOLOGICAL SITE, PARK
(Monmouth St; ⏲24hr) Shaded by huge pohutukawa trees, spooky Monmouth Redoubt was a fortified site during the Maori Wars. Next door is **Robbins Park** (Cliff Rd), a verdant pocket of roses with sweeping views across to Mt Maunganui. At the foot of the

WORTH A TRIP

WHIRINAKI FOREST PARK

This lush podocarp (conifer) forest park is 90km southeast of Rotorua off SH38, en route to Te Urewera National Park (take the turn-off at Te Whaiti to Minginui). Also here are canyons, waterfalls, lookouts and streams, plus the **Oriuwaka Ecological Area** and **Arahaki Lagoon**.

Walking tracks here vary in length and difficulty: the Department of Conservation (DOC) booklet *Walks in Whirinaki Forest* ($2.50) details walking and camping options. Pick one up at DOC's **Murupara visitor centre** (☎07-366 1080; www.doc.govt.nz; SH38, Murupara).

A good short walk is the **Whirinaki Waterfalls Track** (four hours return), which follows the Whirinaki River. Longer walks include the **Whirinaki Track** (two days), which can be combined with **Te Hoe Track** (four days). There's also a rampaging 16km **mountain-bike track** here.

There are several accessible camping areas and 10 backcountry huts (free to $15) in the park; pay at the DOC office.

Redoubt on the end of the Strand is Te Awa nui Waka, a replica Maori canoe, on display in an open-sided building.

Brain Watkins House HISTORIC BUILDING
(www.nzhistoricalsocieties.org.nz; cnr Elizabeth St & Cameron Rd; adult/child/family $4/2/10; ⏲2-4pm Sun) A demure Victorian villa and one of Tauranga's best-preserved colonial homes, Brain Watkins House was built in 1881 from kauri (wood). It was bequeathed to the Historical Society in 1979 following the death of Elva Brain Watkins.

Minden Lookout LOOKOUT
(Minden Rd) From Minden Lookout, about 10km west of Tauranga towards Katikati, there's a superb view back over the Bay of Plenty. To get there, take SH2 to Te Puna and turn off south on Minden Rd; the lookout is about 4km up the road.

Mills Reef Winery WINERY
(☎07-576 8800; www.millsreef.co.nz; 143 Moffat Rd; ⏲10am-5pm) Stately Mills Reef, 7km from the town centre at Bethlehem, has tastings of its award-winning wines (dig the cab sav) and a refined restaurant (read: great food but not much fun) that's open for lunch daily and dinner by reservation (mains $23 to $39).

Tauranga

Top Sights
Tauranga Art Gallery B2

Sights
1 Brain Watkins House A3
2 Monmouth Redoubt B1

Activities, Courses & Tours
3 Dive Zone A3

Sleeping
4 City Suites A1
5 Harbour City Motor Inn A2
6 Harbourside City Backpackers B2
7 Hotel on Devonport B3
8 Loft 109 Backpackers B3

Eating
9 Cafe Bravo B2
10 City Markets B2
11 Collar & Thai B3
12 Fresh Fish Market B1
13 Mediterraneo Café B3
14 Naked Grape B2
15 Shima B2
16 Zeytin on the Strand B2

Drinking
17 CornerStone B2
18 Crown & Badger B2
19 De Bier Haus B2

Entertainment
20 Bay City Cinemas A3
21 Buddha Lounge B2
Rialto Cinemas .... (see 11)

FREE **Huria Marae** MARAE
(☎07-578 7838; www.ngaitamarawaho.maori.nz; Te Kaponga St) Huria Marae is on a nondescript suburban street, but has sensational carvings both inside and out. Call to organise permission to visit.

Activities

White-water rafting on the Wairoa River (accessible from Tauranga) is definitely for thrill-seekers. The Wairoa's levels are controlled by a dam, so it can only be rafted 26 days of the year: advance bookings are essential. Contact local operators (p296) for more information.

The free *Tauranga City Walkways* pamphlet details walks around Tauranga and Mt Maunganui, including the **Waikareao Estuary Walkway** and the popular **Mauao**

Base Track in Mt Maunganui. History buffs should pick up the free *Historic Tauranga* brochure and stroll around the town's cache of historic sites. Pick up pamphlets at the Tauranga and Mt Maunganui i-SITEs.

FREE **Kaimai Mamaku Forest Park** TRAMPING
(www.doc.govt.nz; SH29) The backdrop to the Western Bay of Plenty is the rugged 70km-long Kaimai Mamaku Forest Park, 35km southwest of Tauranga, with tramps for the intrepid and huts (per person per night $5 to $15) and campsites ($6). For more info see DOC's pamphlet *Kaimai to Coast* ($2.50), or contact **Kaimai New Zealand Tours** (07-552 6338; www.kaimai-new-zealand-tours.com) to arrange a guided tramp.

FREE **McLaren Falls Park** TRAMPING
(07-577 7000; www.tauranga.govt.nz; McLaren Falls Rd; sites adult/child $6/free; 8am-5.30pm May-Oct, to 7.30pm Nov-Apr) In the Wairoa River valley, 15km southwest of Tauranga just off SH29, McLaren Falls Park is a 190-hectare lakeland park with wonderful trees, short walks and picnic areas. There's a basic modern hostel here ($110 per night for exclusive use, or $20 per person) and campsites. Also accessible from McLaren Falls is **Marshalls Animal Park** (07-543 1099; www.marshallsanimalpark.co.nz; McLaren Falls Rd; adult/child/family $12/6/32; 10am-2pm Wed & Thu, to 4.30pm Sat & Sun), which has animal petting, a flying fox, a playground and pony rides.

Butler's Swim with Dolphins WILDLIFE TOUR
(07-578 3197, 0508 288 537; www.swimwithdolphins.co.nz; full-day trips adult/child $135/110; departs Tauranga 9am, Mt Maunganui 9.30am) Even without dolphins (and you're guaranteed of seeing them), these trips are always entertaining, particularly with Cap'n Butler, a real old salt who protested against nuclear testing at Mururoa Atoll.

Dolphin Blue WILDLIFE TOUR
(07-576 4303; www.dolphinblue.co.nz; day trips from $135; departs 8.30am) Small-group, unhurried day trips (15 people maximum) across Tauranga harbour and out onto the Bay of Plenty in pursuit of pods of dolphins.

Dolphin Seafaris WILDLIFE TOUR
(07-577 0105, 0800 326 8747; www.nzdolphin.com; half-day trip adult/child $110/95; departs Tauranga 8am, Mt Maunganui 8.15am) Offers eco-attuned dolphin-spotting trips.

Waimarino Adventure Park KAYAKING, WATER SPORTS
(07-576 4233, 0800 456 996; www.waimarino.com; 36 Taniwha Pl; kayak tours from $65, kayak hire per hr/day $26/55, park day-pass adult/child $40/32; 10am-6pm Aug-Apr, reduced hours May-Jul) On the banks of the Wairoa River 8km west of town, Waimarino offers freedom kayak hire for leisurely paddles along 12km of flat water, and runs self-guided tours further up the river and sea kayaking trips. Its Glowworm Tour ($120 per person) is a magical after-dark journey at McLaren Falls Park where you slip into a secret glowworm-filled wonderland. Waimarino also has an adventure park with all kinds of watery distractions: a kayak slide, a diving board, a ropes course, water-walking zorbs, warm pools, and a terrifying human catapult called 'The Blob' – intense!

Bay Fishing Charters FISHING
(0800 229 347; www.bayfishingcharters.co.nz; adult/child trips from $80/50, game fishing from $1800) Small-group fishing charters (half- and full-day) and longer game-fishing epics.

Blue Ocean Charters FISHING
(07-544 3072, 0800 224 278; www.blueocean.co.nz; day trips from $100) Fishing, diving and sightseeing trips (including one to Tuhua Island) on the TS *Ohorere*, MV *Te Kuia* and MV *Ratahi*.

Dive Zone DIVING
(07-578 4050; www.divezone.co.nz; 213 Cameron Rd; trips/courses from $95/600) PADI-qualifying courses or trips to local wrecks and reefs, plus gear rental.

Earth2Ocean DIVING
(07-571 5286; www.earth2ocean.co.nz; trips/courses from $100/500) Runs an extensive range of diving courses and trips.

Elements Watersports WATER SPORTS
(0800 486 729; www.elementsonline.co.nz; lessons from $80) If you're new to the sea and want to splash safely into the big blue, Elements Watersports runs sailing, windsurfing and jetskiing lessons, and has gear for hire.

Tauranga Tandem Skydiving SKYDIVING
(07-576 7990, 0274 968 408; www.tandemskydive.co.nz; 2 Kittyhawk Way; jumps 8000/10,000/12,000ft $269/299/349) Landlubbers might consider jumping out of a plane...or maybe not.

Tauranga Tandem Skydiving offers jumps from three different heights, with views of Whakaari (White Island), Mt Ruapehu and the East Cape on the way down.

Tours

Adventure Bay of Plenty KAYAKING, MOUNTAIN BIKING
(0800 238 267; www.adventurebop.co.nz; 2hr/half-day/full-day tours from $85/125/175) Offers an enticing array of adventure tours by kayak, mountain bike and horse. Half-day paddles around Mt Maunganui with a stop on Matakana Island cost $125/70 per adult/child. A two-to-three hour cycle around Tauranga costs $85.

No.8 Farm Tours GUIDED TOUR
(07-579 3981; www.no8farmtours.co.nz; tours adult/child from $95/69) Half-day Tauranga tours, plus 4WD tours of a working NZ farm, featuring shearing, milking, sheep dogs, deer and morning tea.

Touring Company GUIDED TOUR
(07-577 0057; www.newzealandadventure.co.nz; tours from $79) Half- and full-day local scenic tours and trips further afield to Waitomo, Rotorua and Whakaari (White Island).

Tauranga Tasting Tours GUIDED TOUR
(07-544 1383; www.tastingtours.co.nz; tours $130) Whips around a local brewery, Mills Reef and Morton Estate wineries, and back to town for cocktails.

Aerius Helicopters SCENIC FLIGHTS
(0800 864 354; www.aerius.co.nz; flights from $59) Local flights and aerial excursions as far away as Waitomo, Rotorua and Whakaari (White Island), departing Mt Maunganui or Te Puke.

Gyrate SCENIC FLIGHTS
(07-575 6583; www.gyrate.co.nz; flights from $95) Flights in a gyroplane (the jetski of the sky), from local, scenic flights to learn-to-fly packages.

Vulcan Helicopters SCENIC FLIGHTS
(07-308 4188, 0800 804 354; www.vulcanheli.co.nz; flights from $870) If you feel like (and can afford) a rotor-propelled spin out to explore Whakaari (White Island), Vulcan Helicopters is for you.

Mount Classics Tours BUS TOUR
(07-574 1779; www.shoretrips.co.nz; half-day tours from $65) Short-hop trips around Tauranga and to Te Puke, aimed at cruise-boat passengers finding their land legs. Longer tours to Rotorua from Tauranga also available.

Festivals & Events

National Jazz Festival MUSIC, FOOD & WINE
(www.jazz.org.nz) An Easter extravaganza of big blowers and scoobee-doobee-doobop, with concerts and food and wine galore.

Tauranga Arts Festival ARTS
(www.taurangafestival.co.nz) Kicking off on Labour weekend in October (in odd-numbered years), showcasing dance, comedy, plays and other things arty.

Sleeping

Ambassador Motor Inn MOTEL $$
(07-578 5665, 0800 735 294; www.ambassador-motorinn.co.nz; 9 Fifteenth Ave; d/f from $110/175;) This tidy motel has noise-reducing glass for peaceful sleeps, a swimming pool, and a long list of 'new' things: TVs, kitchens, bedspreads, towels, sheets... Some rooms have spa baths; all have kitchen facilities. It's not overtly ambassadorial, but spotlessly clean, and the owner calls you 'Honey' and might pick you up from the pub if it's not too late.

Roselands Motel MOTEL $$
(0800 363 093, 07-578 2294; www.roselands.co.nz; 21 Brown St; d/ste from $110/135;) Tarted up with splashes of orange paint and new linen, this sweet, old-style motel is in a quiet but central location. Expect roomy units (all with kitchens), friendly first-name-basis hosts and new TVs. Nice one.

Harbourside City Backpackers HOSTEL $
(07-579 4066; www.backpacktauranga.co.nz; 105 The Strand; dm/d from $28/72; @) Enjoy sea views from this sociable hostel (a renovated former hotel), which is all too handy to the Strand's bars. Rooms are smallish but clean, and you'll spend more time on the awesome roof terrace anyway. There's no car park, but down the road is a public car park that's empty at the right time.

Harbour City Motor Inn MOTEL $$
(0800 253 525, 07-571 1435; www.taurangaharbourcity.co.nz; 50 Wharf St; d from $150;) With a winning location right in the middle of town (and with plenty of parking), this newish, lemon-yellow motor inn has all the mod cons. There are spa baths in each room, and friendly staff who can offer sound advice on your itinerary.

Tauranga YHA HOSTEL $
(07-0800 278 299, 07-578 5064; www.yha.co.nz; 171 Elizabeth St; dm from $29, d with/without bathroom $106/89;) A well-kept, deceptively big YHA with a large grassy backyard and a nearby mangrove swamp boardwalk to explore. Inviting dorms have individual lockers, and there's also info available on local walking trails and a noticeboard for all things green.

Loft 109 Backpackers HOSTEL $
(07-579 5638; www.loft109.co.nz; 109 Devonport Rd, upstairs; dm/d/tr from $28/62/82;) This central spot feels like somebody's flat, with an intimate kitchen and lounge, rooftop balconies in upper rooms, and (oddly) two halves of a boat built into the ceiling. It's bright, with plenty of skylights and a gas fire for colder days. Super-relaxed without being lax about things like security or boozy bad behaviour.

Just the Ducks Nuts Backpackers HOSTEL $
(07-576 1366; www.justtheducksnuts.co.nz; 6 Vale St; dm from $29, d with/without bathroom $78/66;) Just out of the town centre, this is a friendly place with colourful rooms, a fulsome library, TVs strewn about and quirky touches like flowers planted in a bathtub and duck-themed toilets – like a university share-house minus the parties. Free shuttles to/from the bus stop; self-contained flats also available.

Hotel on Devonport HOTEL $$$
(07-578 2668; www.hotelondevonport.net.nz; 72 Devonport Rd; d/ste $165/195;) City-centre Devonport is top of the town, with bay-view rooms, noise-reducing glass, slick interiors and sassy staff, all of which appeal to business travellers and upmarket weekenders. No in-room wi-fi is a surprising downer.

City Suites HOTEL $$
(07-577 1480, 0800 4787 474; www.puriri.co.nz; 32 Cameron Rd; ste $130-225;) A 2011 refurb of this hotel has sent the mood upmarket, the large rooms (all with either terrace or balcony) taking on a decidedly regal feel, with Louis XIV bedspreads, king-sized beds and full kitchens. A swimming pool and secure parking complete the list of essentials for wandering business bods.

Sebel Trinity Wharf Tauranga HOTEL $$$
(0800 937 373, 07-577 8700; www.mirvachotels.com; 51 Dive Cres; d from $180;) This blocky high-rise near the harbour bridge has a slick, contemporary lobby – all retro white vinyl and trendy plush greys – leading to the upmarket in-house restaurant **Halo** (mains lunch $14 to $32, dinner $30 to $39). Rooms are supersized and luxurious in tones au naturel. Amenities include an underutilised gym, an infinity-edge swimming pool and a baby grand piano in the lobby. Very flashy.

Tauranga Tourist Park HOLIDAY PARK $
(07-578 3323; www.taurangatouristpark.co.nz; 9 Mayfair St; sites/cabins from $20/50;) On the harbour's edge, this is a good option for tenters and campervans with decent grassed sites and a new TV lounge. The layout feels a bit tight (don't expect rolling acres), but it's well maintained, clean and tidy.

Eating

Devonport Rd is the place to grab lunch, but places on the Strand excel at dinner with drinks to follow. Tauranga's pubs also do solid meals.

Grindz Café CAFE $
(07-579 0017; grindzcafe@xtra.co.nz; 50 First Ave; meals $5-15; 7am-4pm Mon-Fri, 8am-3pm Sat & Sun;) The undisputed highlight of wide-open First Ave is Grindz, a hip cafe with scattered footpath tables. Inside it's a roomy, split-level affair, with funky wallpaper, antiques and retro relics. Bagels, veggie stacks, muffins, cakes and salads are the order of the day, plus creative coffee (try 'The Trough' if you're sleepy: a four-shot soup bowl of caffeine heaven). Free wi-fi too.

Naked Grape MODERN NZ, WINE BAR $$
(07-579 5555; www.nakedgrape.co.nz; 97 The Strand; breakfast & lunch $9-19, dinner mains $21-32; breakfast & lunch daily, dinner Mon-Sat) With cheery staff, wine-coloured rugs and lilting jazz, this hip Strand wine bar draws the daytime crowds with pastas, pizzas, salads, good coffee and beaut breakfasts. At night it's moodier, with mains like spice-rubbed salmon with citrus salsa and eggplant parmesan with toasted pine nuts.

Mediterraneo Café CAFE, MEDITERRANEAN $$
(The Med; 07-577 0487; www.mediterraneocafe.co.nz; 62 Devonport Rd; mains $12-19; 7am-4pm Mon-Fri, 7.30am-4pm Sat, 8am-4pm Sun;) A hot spot reeling with regulars enjoying terrific coffee and scrumptious all-day breakfasts. Order from the blackboard or from the

cabinet that is crammed with sandwiches, salads, flans and cakes. Lunchtime crowds can be frantic (but the chicken salad is worth it). Plenty of gluten-free and vegetarian options.

Zeytin on the Strand TURKISH **$$**
(☎07-579 0099; 83 The Strand; mains $16-29; ⊙lunch & dinner Tue-Sun) Ask the locals to name their favourite restaurant, and odds-on they'll name Zeytin – a Turkish delight indeed. Real food, real cheap, with something for everyone along the lines of kebabs, delicious homemade breads, dips and healthy salads, wood-fired pizza and a few exotic surprises.

Fresh Fish Market FISH & CHIPS **$**
(☎07-578 1789; 1 Dive Cres; meals from $5; ⊙lunch & dinner) A local legend serving up fresh fish and chips, with hexagonal outdoor tables right on the water's edge and plenty of seagulls to keep you company.

Collar & Thai THAI **$$**
(☎07-577 6655; www.collarandthai.co.nz; Goddards Centre, 21 Devonport Rd; mains lunch $15-17, dinner $21-31; ⊙lunch Mon-Sat, dinner daily) No tie required at this upstairs eatery that artfully elaborates on Thai standards and uses plenty of fresh seafood. Perfect for a pre-movie meal (the Rialto Cinemas are right next door). Good-value lunch specials, too.

Cafe Bravo CAFE, MEDITERRANEAN **$$**
(☎07-578 4700; www.cafebravo.co.nz; Red Sq; mains $22-32; ⊙breakfast & lunch daily, dinner Tue-Sat; ✎) Set back from the Strand fray, this refined restaurant-bar is a quiet spot for breakfast or a substantial lunch (try the cider-braised pork belly), or lighter stuff like sandwiches, salads, wood-fired pizzas and freshly squeezed juices. There's outside seating on the pedestrianised street, and a couple of good vegetarian options.

Shima JAPANESE **$$**
(☎07-571 1382; 15 Wharf St; mains $12-30; ⊙lunch & dinner Mon-Sat) Shima is a simple, unpretentious sushi and sashimi bar, hung with Japanese fans, umbrellas and lanterns. Bento boxes and set-price menus are great bang for your buck.

Somerset Cottage MODERN NZ **$$$**
(☎07-576 6889; www.somersetcottage.co.nz; 30 Bethlehem Rd; mains $38-40; ⊙lunch Wed-Fri, dinner Tue-Sun) The most awarded restaurant in the bay, Somerset Cottage is a simple-but-elegant venue for that special treat. The food is highly seasonal, made from the best NZ ingredients, impressively executed without being too fussy. Standout dishes include blue cheese soufflé, duck with coconut kumara and the famous liquorice ice cream.

City Markets MARKET
(cnr Willow & Hamilton Sts; ⊙9am-5pm Mon-Fri, to noon Sat) Self caterers should swing by the fruit-and-veg City Markets, in a warehouse a block back from the Srand. Freshly baked bread, too.

Pak 'n Save SUPERMARKET
(www.paknsave.co.nz; 476 Cameron Rd; ⊙8am-10pm) This place is a short drive south of central Tauranga.

Drinking

De Bier Haus BAR
(www.debierhaus.com; 109 The Strand) With a pavement packed with happy punters, this hot *haus* features Belgian beers, big-screen TVs and manly hunting-lodge interiors with an antler or two in the midst. Kitchen-work is swift and savvy, turning out cajun chicken sandwiches, roast-duck spring rolls and seafood chowder (mains $15 to $36).

Crown & Badger PUB
(www.crownandbadger.co.nz; cnr The Strand & Wharf St) A particularly convincing black-painted Brit boozer that does pukka pints of Tennent's and Guinness, and food along the lines of bangers and mash and BLTs (mains $15 to $23). Things get happening at the weekends with live bands.

CornerStone PUB
(www.cornerstonepub.net.nz; 55 The Strand) This cheerful watering hole features on-the-ball staff and a mature crowd (let's say over-25s... folks who wouldn't mind Gordon Lightfoot on the sound system). A no-surprises menu offers whopping meals (mains $15 to $31), while sports fans can watch the game on the big TV and groovers can swing a hip (live music Thursday to Sunday).

Entertainment

Rialto Cinemas CINEMA
(www.rialtotauranga.co.nz; Goddards Centre, 21 Devonport Rd) Home to the Tauranga Film Society, the Rialto is the best spot in town to

catch a flick: classic, offbeat, art-house and international. And you can sip a coffee or a glass of wine in the darkness.

Buddha Lounge CLUB, COCKTAIL BAR
(www.thebuddhalounge.co.nz; 61b The Strand; ⏲Thu-Sat) Up a staircase beyond a big set of varnished plywood doors (and some heavy-duty bouncers), this clubby cocktail lounge hosts local and visiting DJs. There's a beaut outdoor terrace up above the street. Don't dress down.

Bay City Cinemas CINEMA
(www.baycitycinemas.co.nz; 45 Elizabeth St) A mainstream Megaplex a few blocks back from the action.

ℹ Information

Paper Plus (17 Grey St; ⏲8.30am-5.30pm Mon-Fri, 9am-4pm Sat, 10am-3pm Sun) The local NZ Post branch.

Tauranga Hospital (☎07-579 8000; www.bopdhb.govt.nz; 375 Cameron Rd; ⏲24hr) A couple of kilometres south of town.

Tauranga i-SITE (☎07-578 8103; www.bayofplentynz.com; 95 Willow St; ⏲8.30am-5.30pm Mon-Fri, 9am-5pm Sat & Sun, reduced winter hours; 📶) Local tourist information, bookings, InterCity bus tickets and DOC maps.

ℹ Getting There & Away

Air

Air New Zealand (☎07-577 7300; www.airnewzealand.co.nz; cnr Devonport Rd & Elizabeth St; ⏲9am-5pm Mon-Fri) Has daily direct flights to Auckland, Wellington and Christchurch, with connections to other centres.

Bus

Twin City Express (☎0800 422 928; www.baybus.co.nz) buses run twice daily Monday to Friday between Tauranga/Mt Maunganui and Rotorua via Te Puke ($11.60, 1½ hours).

InterCity (www.intercity.co.nz) tickets and timetables are available at the i-SITE. Destinations including the following:

DESTINATION	PRICE	DURATION	FREQUENCY
Auckland	$46	4hr	7 daily
Hamilton	$33	2hr	2 daily
Rotorua	$30	1½hr	2 daily
Taupo	$50	3hr	3 daily
Wellington	$59	9hr	4 daily

Naked Bus (www.nakedbus.com) offers substantial fare savings when you book in advance. Destinations include the following:

DESTINATION	PRICE	DURATION	FREQUENCY
Auckland	$15	4¼hr	3 daily
Hamilton	$20	2hr	3 daily
Napier	$50	4½hr	2 daily
Rotorua	$9	1½hr	3-5 daily
Taupo	$25	2½hr	2 daily
Wellington	$27	9hr	1 daily
Whakatane	$19	6¼hr	1 daily

SHUTTLE BUS

White Island Shuttle (☎07-308 9588, 0800 733 529; www.whiteisland.co.nz; shuttle-only one way/return $35/60), run by White Island Tours in Whakatane, runs return shuttles to Whakatane from Tauranga. It's ostensibly for tour customers, but you can use the service without taking the tour.

A couple of companies can pick you up at Auckland or Rotorua airports and bus you to Tauranga (though you'll pay upwards of $100 for the privilege):

Luxury Airport Shuttles (☎07-547 4444, 0800 454 678; www.luxuryairportshuttles.co.nz)

Apollo Connect Shuttles (☎07-218 0791; www.taurangashuttles.co.nz)

Car

If you're heading to Hamilton on route K, don't forget the toll road costs $1.

ℹ Getting Around

Bicycle

Cycle Tauranga (☎07-571 1435, 0800 253 525; www.cycletauranga.co.nz; 50 Wharf St; per half-/full-day $29/49) Cycle Tauranga, at Harbour City Motor Inn, has road-trail hybrid bikes for hire, including helmets, locks, saddle bags and maps. Tours also available.

Bus

Tauranga's bright yellow **Bay Hopper** (☎0800 422 928; www.baybus.co.nz) buses run to most locations around the area, including Mt Maunganui ($2.60, 15 minutes) and Papamoa ($3.20, 30 minutes). There's a central stop on Wharf St; timetables available from the i-SITE.

Car

Numerous car-rental agencies have offices in Tauranga, including **Rent-a-Dent** (☎07-578 1772, 0800 736 823; www.rentadent.co.nz; 19 Fifteenth Ave).

Taxi

A taxi from the centre of Tauranga to the airport costs around $20.

Citicabs (☎07-577 0999)

Tauranga Mount Taxis (☎07-578 6086; www.taurangataxis.co.nz)

Mt Maunganui

POP 18,600

Named after the hulking 232m hill that punctuates the sandy peninsula occupied by the township, up-tempo Mt Maunganui is often just called 'the Mount', or Mauao, which translates as 'caught by the light of day'. It's considered part of greater Tauranga, but really it's an enclave unto itself, with great cafes and restaurants, hip bars and fab beaches. Sun-seekers flock to the Mount in summer, supplied by an increasing number of 10-storey apartment towers studding the spit. Online, see www.mountmaunganui.org.nz for information.

Sights & Activities

The Mount lays claim to being NZ's premier surfing city (they teach surfing at high school!). You can carve up the waves at **Mount Beach**, which has lovely beach breaks and a 100m artificial surf reef not far offshore. Learn-to-surf operators include the following:

Hibiscus (☎07-575 3792, 027 279 9687; www.surfschool.co.nz; 2hr/2-day lesson $80/150)

Discovery Surf School (☎027 632 7873; www.discoverysurf.co.nz; lessons 1hr $60, 2hr group/private $90/150)

Mount Surf Shop (☎07-575 9133; www.mountsurfshop.co.nz; 96 Maunganui Rd; rental per day wetsuit/bodyboard/surfboard $15/20/30, 2hr lesson $80)

East Coast Paddler (☎07-574 2674, 021 0230 0746; www.eastcoastpaddler.co.nz; lessons 1hr group/private $50/75)

TOP CHOICE **Mauao** MOUNTAIN, LOOKOUT

Mauao (Mt Maunganui) itself can be explored via walking trails, winding around it and leading up to the summit. The summit walk takes about 40 minutes and gets steep near the top. You can also climb around the rocks on Moturiki Island, which adjoins the peninsula. The island and the base of Mauao also make up the Mauao base track (3½km, 45 minutes), wandering through magical groves of pohutukawa trees that bloom between November and January. Pick up a map at the i-SITE.

THE WRECK OF THE RENA

On 5 October 2011, the 47,000 tonne cargo ship MV *Rena*, loaded with 1368 containers and 1900 tonnes of fuel oil, ran aground on Astrolabe Reef 22km off the coast of Mt Maunganui. The ship had been attempting to enter Tauranga Harbour, NZ's busiest port, but inexplicably hit one of the most consistently charted obstacles in the way. Pitched acutely on the reef with a rupturing hull, the *Rena* started spilling oil into the sea and shedding containers from its deck. Over subsequent days, disbelieving locals watched as oil slicks, containers and dead fish and seabirds washed up on their glorious beaches.

The blame game began: the captain? The owners? The company that chartered the vessel? Thousands of volunteers pitched in to help with the clean-up as bad weather delayed attempts to pump oil from the vessel and remove the containers still on deck. Salvors eventually managed to remove most of the oil, but on 8 January 2012 the *Rena* finally broke in two, spilling remnant oil and dozens more containers into the sea.

By 10 January, the stern section was almost completely submerged. With the initial focus on preventing an oil spill, the elephant in the corner of the room – the *Rena* herself – seemed a problem too large. With refloating the ship no longer an option, will the bow section of the boat be dragged off the rocks and scuttled, and the stern section sunk in entirety? A future dive site for the Bay of Plenty? Whatever happens, the grounding has been an environmental and economic disaster, with beaches soiled, fisheries ravaged and countless local businesses suffering. Time will tell how far reparations – both environmental and fiscal – will go towards improving the situation.

Mt Maunganui

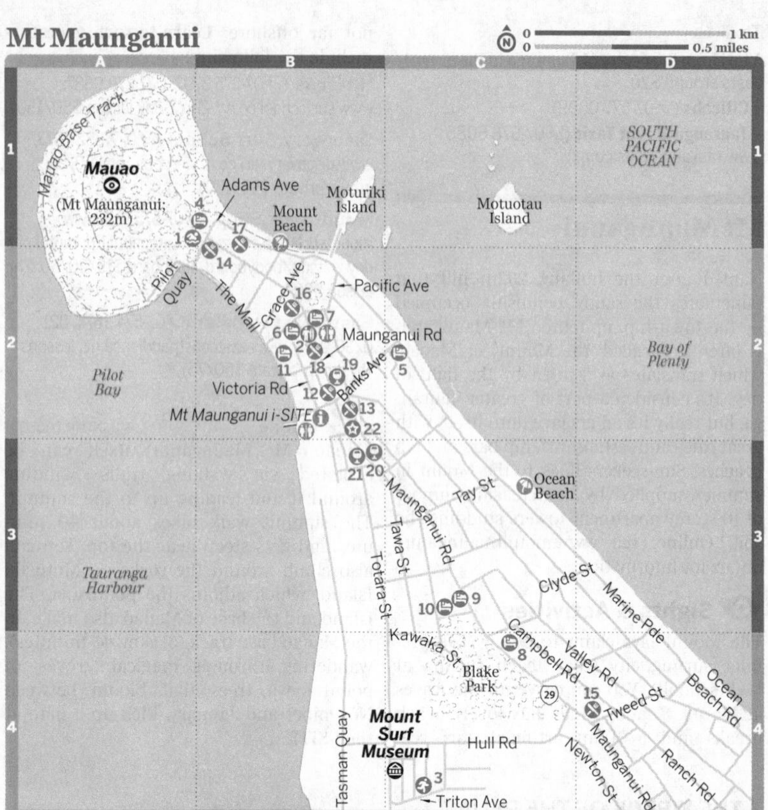

FREE **Mount Surf Museum** MUSEUM
(www.mountsurfshop.co.nz; 139 Totara St; ⊙9am-5pm Mon-Sat, 9.30am-5pm Sun) To learn about surfing in the area (and beyond) visit the amazing Mount Surf Museum, inside the Totara St branch of the Mount Surf Shop.

Mount Maunganui Hot Saltwater Pools SWIMMING
(www.tcal.co.nz; 9 Adams Ave; adult/child/family $11/8/30; ⊙6am-10pm Mon-Sat, 8am-10pm Sun) If you've worked up a sweat walking up and down Mauao, take a long relaxing soak at these hotwater pools at the foot of the hill.

Canoe & Kayak KAYAKING
(☎07-574 7415; www.canoeandkayak.co.nz; tours adult/child from $89/69) Canoe & Kayak run 2½-hour kayaking trips around Mauao checking out seals, rock formations and hearing local legends, plus 1½-hour nocturnal glowworm paddles in nearby McLarens Falls Park.

Rock House ROCK CLIMBING
(www.therockhouse.co.nz; 9 Triton Ave; adult/child $16.50/12.50, gear hire extra; ⊙noon-9pm Tue-Fri, 10am-6pm Sat & Sun) Try rock climbing at the Rock House, a huge blue steel shed with huge blue climbing walls inside it.

Baywave SWIMMING
(☎07-575 0276; www.tcal.co.nz; cnr Girven & Gloucester Rds; adult/child $7.50/5, hydroslide $4.50; ⊙6am-9pm Mon-Fri, 7am-7pm Sat & Sun) Don't like salt in your hair? For traditional swimming-pool action plus NZ's biggest wave pool, a hydroslide and aqua aerobics, visit Baywave.

Sleeping

Seagulls Guesthouse B&B B&B, HOSTEL $
(☎07-574 2099; www.seagullsguesthouse.co.nz; 12 Hinau St; dm/s/d/f from $30/60/70/100; @ 📶) Can't face another crowded, alcohol-soaked hostel? On a quiet street not far from town,

Mt Maunganui

Top Sights
Mauao....A1
Mount Surf Museum....C4

Activities, Courses & Tours
1 Mount Maunganui Hot Saltwater Pools....A1
2 Mount Surf Shop....B2
3 Rock House....C4

Sleeping
4 Beachside Holiday Park....B1
5 Belle Mer....C2
6 Mission Belle Motel....B2
7 Mount Backpackers....B2
8 Mount Maunganui B&B....C4
9 Pacific Coast Lodge & Backpackers....C3
10 Seagulls Guesthouse B&B....C3
11 Westhaven Motel....B2

Eating
12 Gusto....B2
13 Kwang Chow....B2
14 Mount Bistro....B2
15 New World....D4
16 Providores Urban Food Store....B2
17 Slowfish....B1
18 Zeytin at the Mount....B2

Drinking
19 Latitude 37....B2
20 Major Tom's....B3
21 Rosie O'Grady's....B3

Entertainment
22 Bay City Cinemas....B2

Seagulls is a gem: an immaculate, upmarket backpackers where the emphasis is on peaceful enjoyment of one's surrounds rather than wallowing in the excesses of youth (...not that there's anything wrong with that). The best rooms have bathrooms and TVs. Breakfast costs $8; bike hire is $25.

Pacific Coast Lodge & Backpackers HOSTEL $
(☎07-574 9601, 0800 666 622; www.pacificcoastlodge.co.nz; 432 Maunganui Rd; dm/d from $26/72; @📶) Not far from the action, this efficiently run, clean hostel is sociable but not party-focused, with drinkers gently encouraged to migrate into town after 10pm. Purpose-built bunkrooms are roomy and adorned with jungle murals.

Beachside Holiday Park HOLIDAY PARK $
(☎07-575 4471; www.mountbeachside.co.nz; 1 Adams Ave; sites from $35, on-site vans $60-80, cabins $80-130; 📶) With three different camping areas nooked into the foot of Mt Maunganui itself, this community-run park has spectacular camping with all the requisite facilities, plus it's handy to the Mount Maunganui Hot Saltwater Pools (who offer a discount for campers) and a strip of good eateries.

Mission Belle Motel MOTEL $$
(☎07-575 2578, 0800 202 434; www.missionbellemotel.co.nz; cnr Victoria Rd & Pacific Ave; d/f from $125/185; 📶) With a distinctly Tex-Mex exterior (like something out of an old Clint Eastwood movie), this family-run motel goes all modern inside, with especially good two-storey family rooms with large bathtubs, plus sheltered barbecue and courtyard areas.

Westhaven Motel MOTEL $$
(☎07-575 4753; www.westhavenmotel.co.nz; 27a The Mall; units $100-250; 📶) The 1970s architecture here is soooo *Brady Bunch*, with wooden shelving between kitchen and lounge, and funky mirrors to retune your afro. Full kitchens are perfect for self-caterers, plus there are new TVs and DVDs, and free fishing rods and kayaks. The cheapest motel in miles.

Mount Backpackers HOSTEL $
(☎07-575 0860; www.mountbackpackers.co.nz; 87 Maunganui Rd; dm/tw/tr from $28/72/84; @📶) A tight but tidy hostel, bolstered by location – close to the beach and a mere stagger from the Mount's best restaurants and bars – plus extras like a travel desk, cheap weekly rates and deals on activities including surf lessons.

Belle Mer HOTEL, APARTMENTS $$$
(☎0800 100 235, 07-575 0011; www.bellemer.co.nz; 53 Marine Pde; apt $190-450; 📶🏊) A classy beachside complex of one-, two- and three-bedroom apartments, some with sea-view balconies and others opening onto private courtyards (though you'll more likely head for the resort-style pool terrace). Rooms are tastefully decorated in warm tones with soft edges, and have everything you need for

longer stays, with proper working kitchens and laundries.

Cosy Corner Holiday Park HOLIDAY PARK $
(☎0800 684 654, 07-575 5899; www.cosycorner.co.nz; 40 Ocean Beach Rd; sites from $40, cabins & flats $70-120; @🛜🏊) This spartan camping ground has a sociable feel, with barbecues, trampolines and a games room. And it's possibly the only accommodation in NZ where prices have actually come down since the last edition of this book. Handy for the beach, too.

Mount Maunganui B&B B&B $$
(☎07-575 4013; www.mountbednbreakfast.co.nz; 463 Maunganui Rd; s/d incl cooked breakfast from $65/100; @🛜) This good-value five-room B&B on the main road into town offers a cosy guest lounge, basic shared kitchen, pool table, BBQ and cable TV. The two rooms at the front cop a bit of traffic noise, but the rest are fine. Good for groups.

Eating

TOP CHOICE Slowfish CAFE $
(☎07-574 2949; www.slowfish.co.nz; Shop 5, Twin Towers, Marine Pde; meals $7-20; ⏰6.30am-4.30pm; 🌱) There's no slacking-off in the kitchen of this award-winning, eco-aware cafe, which promotes the art of savouring fine, locally sourced food. It's a hit with the crowds: you'll have to crowbar yourself in the door or pounce on any available alfresco seat, but it's worth it for its free-range eggs and ham, Greek salads and divine counter selection, all made on-site.

Providores Urban Food Store CAFE, DELICATESSEN $
(☎07-572 1300; 19a Pacific Ave; meals $5-18; ⏰7.30am-5pm; 🌱) Surf videos set the mood as your eyes peruse fresh-baked breads, buttery croissants, home-smoked meats and cheeses, organic jams and free-range eggs – perfect ingredients for a bang-up breakfast or a hamper-filling picnic on the beach. Superb.

Mount Bistro MODERN NZ $$$
(☎07-575 3872; www.mountbistro.co.nz; 6 Adams Ave; ⏰dinner Tue-Sun) The buttermilk-coloured Mount Bistro, an unpretentious fine-dining experience at the foot of Mauao, is onto a good thing: quality local meats (fish, lamb, beef, crayfish, chicken, duck) creatively worked into classic dishes (lamb shanks, seafood chowder) and served with élan. Makes for a classy night out.

Gusto CAFE $$
(☎07-575 5675; 200 Maunganui Rd; breakfast $7-16, lunch $15-17; ⏰7am-3.30pm, from 8am Sat & Sun; 🌱) This friendly spot keeps its menu affordable but interesting, with pancakes, fritters, bagels, omelettes, BLATs and Kiwi standards like lamb and kumara, given a fresh spin. Cool tunes, sassy staff, no weird culinary surprises... As reliable as a cafe can get.

Zeytin at the Mount TURKISH, MEDITERRANEAN $$
(☎07-574 3040; 118 Maunganui Rd; mains $19-21; ⏰lunch & dinner Tue-Sun; 🌱) Sister establishment to Tauranga's Zeytin on the Strand, this version has earned a following for its slow-cooked tagines, spanakopita and moussaka, plus live jazz every second Wednesday. Stripy cushions and Arabic lanterns adorn the cavelike interior. Magic felafels (you can buy the mixture and whip up some more back at the hotel).

Kwang Chow CHINESE $$
(☎07-575 5063; 241 Maunganui Rd; lunch/dinner $13/20; ⏰lunch & dinner Tue-Sun) This all-you-can-eat Chinese place is a local favourite for a bargain bite that maintains tasty flavours rather than resorting to a bland melange. And great puddings. Cavernous interior with floorboards and refreshingly little gold/crimson/mirror festoonery.

New World SUPERMARKET
(www.newworld.co.nz; cnr Tweed St & Maunganui Rd; ⏰7am-9pm) A haven for self-caterers.

Drinking & Entertainment

TOP CHOICE Major Tom's BAR, LIVE MUSIC
(www.majortomsbar.com; 297 Maunganui Rd; ⏰Tue-Sat) A funky little bar set back from the main drag in what looks like Major Tom's spaceship. Inside it's all kooky antiques, vintage couches, dangling inverted desk lamps and prints of Elvis, the *Mona Lisa* and (of course) David Bowie. Fabulous streetside terrace, cool tunes, free wi-fi and occasional live acts. Everybody sing: 'Planet Earth is blue, and there's nothing I can do...'

Latitude 37 BAR
(www.37.co.nz; 181 Maunganui Rd; 🛜) A slick, upmarket bar with stone-faced walls, fold-back windows and flaming torches out the front. A lot of folk come here to eat (lunch $15 to $22, dinner $22 to $34...oh, the pork-belly

sandwich!), but it's also a beaut spot for a cold Heineken after a day in the surf.

Rosie O'Grady's IRISH PUB
(www.rosiesnz.com; 2 Rata St) Rosie's is usually not too blokey, with NZ boutique beers, jam nights, pool tables, big screens and good-value pub grub (mains $11 to $28). The beer garden has *actual grass* – ideal for a pint or two of the black stuff.

Bay City Cinemas CINEMA
(www.baycitycinemas.co.nz; 249 Maunganui Rd) Mainstream cinematic offerings, run in parallel with Bay City Cinemas in Tauranga.

Information

Mt Maunganui i-SITE (07-575 5099; www.bayofplentynz.com; Salisbury Ave; 9am-5pm) The friendly Mt Maunganui i-SITE can assist with information and bookings (transport, accommodation and activities).

Getting There & Away

Bus

InterCity (www.intercity.co.nz) and **Naked Bus** (www.nakedbus.com) services visiting Tauranga also stop at Mt Maunganui, with fares similar to those to/from Tauranga (p314). All buses depart from the i-SITE.

Car

Mt Maunganui is across the harbour bridge from Tauranga, or accessible from the south via Te Maunga on SH2. For car hire, try **Rite Price Rentals** (0800 250 251; www.ritepricerentals.co.nz; 25 Totara St).

Papamoa

POP 20,100

Papamoa is a burgeoning 'burb next to Mt Maunganui, separated now by just an empty paddock or two, destined for subdivision. With big new houses on pristine streets, parts of Papamoa have the air of a gated community, but the beach beyond the sheltering dunes is awesome – you can't blame folks for moving in.

Back a few kilometres from the beach, **Blo-kart Heaven** (07-572 4256; www.blokartheaven.co.nz; 176 Parton Rd; blokarting 30min $30; 10am-4.30pm) is the place to attempt land-sailing around a custom-built speedway (blokarts are like seated windsurfers on wheels).

The sprawling **Papamoa Beach Top 10 Holiday Resort** (0800 232 243, 07-572 0816; www.papamoabeach.co.nz; 535 Papamoa Beach Rd; sites from $40, villas & units $88-250;) is a spotless, modern park, primed and priced beyond its caravan-park origins, with an array of accommodation including self-contained villas. If you're quiet you'll hear the surf breaking just over the dunes.

With its angular corrugated-iron exterior and tasteful caneware furnishings, **Beach House Motel** (0800 429 999, 07-572 1424; www.beachhousemotel.co.nz; 224 Papamoa Beach Rd; d from $120;) offers an immaculate, upmarket version of the Kiwi bach holiday, relaxed and close to the beach. There's a pool if the beach is too windy, and orange daisies poking up through rock gardens.

Bluebiyou (07-572 2099; www.bluebiyou.co.nz; 559 Papamoa Beach Rd; mains $15-38; breakfast Sat & Sun, lunch & dinner Wed-Sun) is a casual, breezy restaurant riding high on the dunes, serving big brunches and seafood specialities. The orange-scented French toast with maple syprup and bacon is a surefire Saturday start-me-up.

Tuhua (Mayor Island)

Commonly known as Mayor Island, this dormant volcano is 35km north of Tauranga. It's a privately owned island noted for its black, glasslike obsidian rock and birdlife, including a clutch of kiwi, introduced to the predator-free isle in 2006. Walking tracks cut through the overgrown crater valley, and the northwest corner is a marine reserve.

You need permission to visit from the island's *kaitiaki* (guardians), via the **Tuhua Trust Board** (07-577 0942). There's a $5 landing fee, and visitors must observe strict quarantine regulations. Accommodation is limited to basic camping/cabins ($10/30); bring your own food and water (no fridges). The landing fee is included in accommodation costs. Several boat-charter companies will take you to Tuhua, including Blue Ocean Charters (p310). Contact **DOC** (07-578 7677; taurangainfo@doc.govt.nz) in Tauranga for more info.

Matakana Island

About 24km long and forming the seaward side of Tauranga Harbour, Matakana is laced with secluded white-sand surf beaches on its eastern shore (for the experienced only) and enjoys a laid-back island lifestyle. The only way to visit it is on a kayak tour with Adventure Bay of Plenty (p311).

HOT FUZZ: KIWIFRUIT

The humble kiwifruit earns New Zealand more than a billion dollars every year, and with the Bay of Plenty in the thick of the action, it's no wonder the locals are fond of them.

The fruit's origins are in China, where it was called the monkey peach (they were considered ripe when the monkeys munched them). As they migrated to NZ, they were renamed the Chinese gooseberry – they were a lot smaller then, but canny Kiwis engineered them to more generous sizes and began exporting them in the 1950s. The fruit was then sexily rebranded as the Zespri. Today the Zesprians grow two types of kiwifruit: the common fuzzy-covered green fruit, and the gold fruit with its smooth complexion. To learn more about the kiwifruit, visit **Kiwi360** (07-573 6340, 0800 549 4360; www.kiwi360.com; 35 Young Rd, off SH2; admission free, tour adult/child $20/6; 9am-5pm).

For visitors after a dollar or two, there's always kiwifruit-picking work around the area – most of it during harvest (May and June), and odd jobs at other times. Enquire at Mural Town Backpackers (p321) in Katikati and regional i-SITEs, or check online at www.picknz.co.nz.

Katikati

POP 3580

'Katikat' to the locals, this small town was the only planned Ulster settlement in the world, and celebrates this history with colourful murals adorning the town's buildings. The **Mural Town Information Centre** (07-549 1658; www.katikati.co.nz; 36 Main Rd; 8am-5pm Mon-Fri, 9am-2pm Sat, 10am-2pm Sun; @) sells a guide to the various murals for $2.50, but you can also take a small-group guided tour (07-549 2977; per person $5).

Sights & Activities

Katikati Heritage Museum MUSEUM
(katikati.heritage.museum@xtra.co.nz; 3 Wharawhara Rd; adult/child $7.50/5; 8.30am-4.30pm) This rusty old museum traces local history with an engaging mix of Maori artefacts and Ulster history, some moa bones and reputedly the largest bottle collection in the southern hemisphere.

FREE **Haiku Pathway** WALKWAY
(www.katikati.co.nz/kk_text/haiku.html; 24hrs) From the information centre you can also explore the Haiku Pathway, rambling along the Uretara River past boulders inscribed with haiku verses.

Katikati Bird Gardens WILDLIFE RESERVE
(07-549 0912; www.birdgardens.co.nz; 263 Walker Rd E; adult/child/family $9/5/24; 10am-4.30pm) Located about 7km south of town, the 4-hectare Katikati Bird Gardens is all aflap with native birdlife (ever seen a kawaupaka?). There's a cafe and gallery here too, plus boutique cottage accommodation (double rooms $160).

Morton Estate WINERY
(www.mortonestatewines.co.nz; 2389 SH2; 9.30am-5pm) The monastic-looking Morton Estate, one of NZ's bigger wineries, is located on SH2, 8km south of Katikati, and open for tastings and stock-ups. Try the smooth-as-cream chardonnay.

Sleeping

TOP CHOICE **Warm Earth Cottage** CABIN, B&B $$$
(07-549 0962; www.warmearthcottage.co.nz; 202 Thompsons Track; d $220) Re-ignite your romance or simmer in simple pleasures at this rural idyll, 5km south of town then 2km west of SH2. Two pretty, electricity-less cottages sit by the swimmable Waitekohe River. Fire up the barbecue (generous BBQ packs $85), or melt into a wood-fired outdoor bath. Big DIY breakfasts are included in the price, and there's a lovely new guest lounge/library.

Panorama Country Lodge B&B $$$
(07-549 1882; www.panoramalodge.co.nz; 901 Katikati North Rd; d from $185;) Run by jocular Brits, this neat little B&B is set in diverse orchards 9km north of town, and lives up to its name with sweeping views of the bay. It's a real farm experience, with quail and alpacas wandering around. Plush rooms have extras beyond brass beds and DVDs, including slippers and fresh coffee.

Kaimai View Motel MOTEL $$
(07-549 0398; www.kaimaiview.co.nz; 78 Main Rd; d from $120;) Beyond a funky mural on

the streetside wall, this jaunty, mod motel offers neat rooms (all named after NZ native trees) with CD player, kitchenette and, in larger rooms, spa. Breakfast available on request.

Mural Town Backpackers HOSTEL $
(☎07-549 5150, 021 184 1403; 5 Main Rd; dm $25; @) Inside a converted 1935 barbershop, this basic two-storey hostel is *really* casual, and is usually full of backpackers here to work in the local orchards (kiwifruit, citrus, flowers, avocados etc). The owners can help find you farm work and offer good weekly rates.

Eating

Talisman PUB $$
(7 Main Rd; mains $18-36; ⏲lunch & dinner) The Talisman is the local boozer, with occasional live music, and the Landing restaurant serving all-day grub including pizza, steak and chips, lamb Wellington, pan-fried salmon and surf 'n' turf.

Katz Pyjamas CAFE $
(cnr SH2 & Beach Rd; meals $5-15; ⏲8am-4pm Mon-Fri) Royal blue outside, rude orange inside, this informal main-street cafe serves homemade soups, salads, pies and cakes and a reasonable jolt of java.

Twickenham Restaurant & Cafe CAFE, RESTAURANT $$
(www.twickenham.co.nz; cnr SH2 & Mulgan St; mains lunch $17-23, dinner $24-30; ⏲brunch Tue-Sun, dinner Thu-Sun) In a century-old villa surrounded by manicured gardens, this place is a bit twee but makes amends with admirable Devonshire teas. During the day it's Thai beef salad, omelettes and ploughman's platters; at night it's roast duck, pork fillets and steaks.

Te Puke

POP 7150

Welcome to the 'Kiwifruit Capital of the World', a busy town during the picking season when there's plenty of work around. The **Te Puke visitor information centre** (☎07-573 9172; www.tepuke.co.nz; 130 Jellicoe St; ⏲8am-5pm Mon-Fri, 9am-noon Sat) is in the same building as the public library (staff will confirm that 'Puke' rhymes with cookie, not fluke).

For the low-down on all things kiwifruit, swing into Kiwi360 (p320) at the turn-off for Maketu. Sitting among orchards of nashi pears, citrus, avocados and (you guessed it) kiwifruit, this visitor centre peels off a range of attractions, including a 35-minute kiwicart orchard tour, kiwifruit viewing tower and a cafe serving up a variety of kiwifruit delights.

After something sweeter? About 10km south of Te Puke in Paengaroa, **Comvita** (☎07-533 1987, 0800 493 782; www.comvita.com; 23 Wilson Rd S; ⏲8.30am-5pm Mon-Fri, 9.30am-4pm Sat & Sun) is home to NZ's most famous honey- and bee-derived health-care products. There's a gallery, shop, cafe and educational talks available. Grab a pot of vitamin E cream with bee pollen and manuka honey on your way out.

Not far from Comvita, **Spring Loaded** (☎07-533 1515, 0800 867 386; www.springloaded adventures.co.nz; 316 SH33; adult/child jetboat $95/45, 4WD $60/35, helicopter 12min $105; ⏲8.30am-4.30pm Nov-Apr, 9am-4pm May-Oct) offers various adventures from jetboat rides on a lovely stretch of the Kaituna River and Tauranga Harbour, to 'mud bug' 4WD trips, helicopter flights and rafting and sledging trips. There's a cafe on-site.

Homestays and farmstays dapple the Te Puke area: ask the visitor centre for a list. A cute, private self-contained cottage, **Lazy Daze B&B** (☎07-573 8188; www.lazydaze cottage.co.nz; 144 Boucher Ave; d cottage/house incl breakfast $130/110) sits out the back of Mel and Sharron's property and has a deck overlooking its own garden. Breakfast

WORTH A TRIP

PADDLES & PIES: MAKETU

Take SH2 through Te Puke then turn left onto Maketu Rd, and you'll find yourself deposited at this historic seaside town that has seen better days.

Maketu (population 1240) played a significant role in New Zealand's history as the landing site of *Te Arawa* canoe in 1340, commemorated with a somewhat underwhelming 1940 monument on the foreshore. Arguably, though, the town is more famous for **Maketu Pies** (☎07-533 2358; www.maketupies.co.nz; 6 Little Waihi Rd), baked fresh daily here and employing a good proportion of the population. The factory shopfront was being renovated when we visited, but you can buy a pie at the store next door (go for a lamb-and-mint or smoked fish).

provisions are included and there's also a tidy two-bedroom, self-contained house available next door, sleeping six. Call for directions. For fruit-pickers and doyens of dorm-life there's rudimentary hostel accommodation at **Hairy Berry** (☎07-573 8015; www.hairyberrynz.com; 2 No 1 Rd; sites $15, dm/tw/d from $22/56/60), a barn-like affair on the Whakatane side of town with a roomy communal space and small, tidy bedrooms.

Whakatane

POP 18,750

A true pohutukawa paradise, Whakatane (pronounced Fokka-*tar*-nay) sits on a natural harbour at the mouth of the river of the same name. It's the hub of the Rangitaiki agricultural district, but there's much more to Whakatane than farming – blissful beaches, a sunny main-street vibe and volcanic Whakaari (White Island) for starters. And (despite Nelson's protestations) it's officially NZ's sunniest city.

Sights

FREE Te Manuka Tutahi Marae MARAE
(www.mataatua.com; Muriwai Dr) The centrepiece of this brand-new Ngati Awa *marae* isn't new: Mataatua Wharenui (The House That Came Home) is a fantastically carved 1875 meeting house. In 1879 it was dismantled and shipped to Sydney, before spending 71 years in the Otago Museum from 1925. It was returned to the Ngati Awa in 1996. Still a work in progress when we visited, a cultural experience for visitors is planned: until its completion you can enter the *marae* and check out Mataatua Wharenui from the outside (behave respectfully).

Wairere Falls WATERFALL
(Toroa St) Tumbling down the cliffs behind the town, picture-perfect Te Wairere (Wairere Falls) occupies a deliciously damp nook, and once powered flax and flour mills and supplied Whakatane's drinking water. It's a gorgeous spot, and goes almost completely unheralded: in any other county there's be a ticket booth, interpretive audiovisual displays and a hotdog van!

FREE Whakatane Museum & Gallery MUSEUM, GALLERY
(☎07-306 0505; www.whakatanemuseum.org.nz; 51-55 Boon St; ⏰10am-4.30pm Mon-Fri, 11am-3pm Sat & Sun) This impressive regional museum has artfully presented displays on early Maori and European settlerment in the area: *taonga* (treasures) of local Maori trace their lineage back to the *Mataatua* canoe. The art gallery presents a varied program of NZ and international exhibitions. It's rumoured to be relocating: call the number if it's not where it's supposed to be.

Pohaturoa LANDMARK, MONUMENT
(cnr The Strand & Commerce St) Beside a roundabout on the Strand is Pohaturoa, a large *tapu* (sacred) rock outcrop, where baptism, death, war and *moko* (tattoo) rites were performed. The Treaty of Waitangi was signed here by Ngati Awa chiefs in 1840; there's a monument to the Ngati Awa chief Te Hurinui Apanui here too.

Muriwai's Cave CAVE
(Muriwai Dr) The partially collapsed Te Ana o Muriwa (Muriwai's Cave) once extended 122m into the hillside and sheltered 60 people, including Muriwai, a famous seer and aunt of Wairaka (p324). Along with Wairere Falls and a rock in the harbour-mouth, the cave was one of three landmarks Toroa was told to look for by his father Irakewa, when he arrived in the *Mataatua waka*.

Te Papaka & Puketapu ARCHAEOLOGICAL SITES, LOOKOUTS
On the clifftops behind the town are two ancient Ngati Awa *pa* sites – Te Papaka and Puketapu – both of which offer sensational (and very defendable) outlooks over Whakatane.

Whakatane Observatory ASTRONOMY
(www.skyofplenty.com; Hurinui Ave; adult/child/family $15/5/35; ⏰dusk Tue & Fri) Up on a hilltop behind the town, Whakatane Observatory offers a great chance to star-spot when the sky is clear.

Activities

The i-SITE sells Discover the Walks Around Whakatane ($2), a booklet detailing walks ranging from 30 minutes to half a day. Most walks are part of the Nga Tapuewae o Toi Track (Footsteps of Toi; 13 hours, 18km), large loop which actually comprises three separate walks: the Kohi Point Walkway, the walk along Ohope Beach up into Ohope Reserve at the base of Ohope Hill, and the walk back down into Whakatane through Mokoroa Reserve.

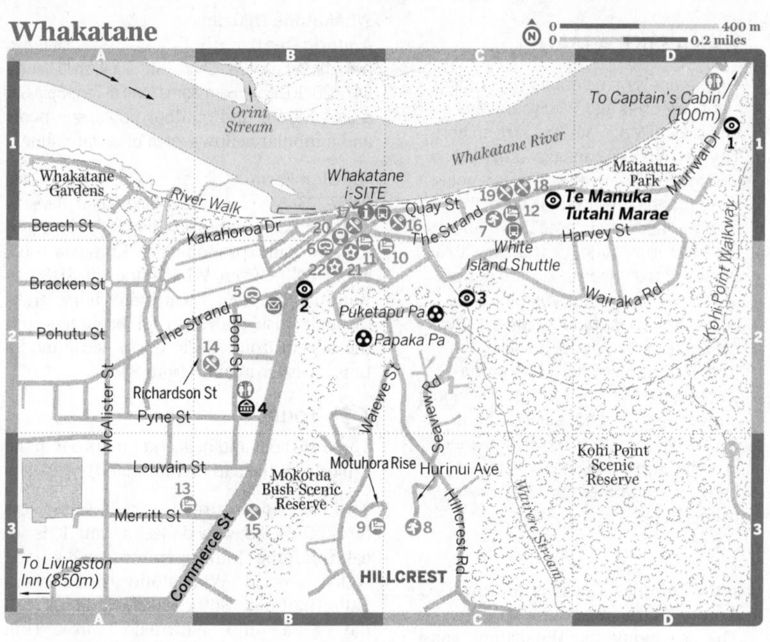

Whakatane

Top Sights

Te Manuka Tutahi Marae C1

Sights

1 Muriwai's Cave D1
2 Pohaturoa B2
3 Wairere Falls C2
4 Whakatane Museum & Gallery B2

Activities, Courses & Tours

5 Dive White Island B2
6 Diveworks Dolphin & Seal Encounters B2
7 Dolphin & Whale Nature Rush C1
8 Whakatane Observatory C3
White Island Tours .... (see 12)

Sleeping

9 Motuhora Rise B&B B3
10 Tuscany Villas C2
11 Whakatane Hotel B2
12 White Island Rendezvous C1
13 Windsor Backpackers A3

Eating

14 Cafe Coco B2
15 Countdown B3
16 Roquette C1
17 The Bean B1
18 Wally's on the Wharf C1
19 Wharf Shed C1

Drinking

Craic .... (see 11)
20 Office B1

Entertainment

21 Boiler Room B2
22 Cinema 5 .... B2

The Kohi Point Walkway is highly recommended: a bushy four-hour, 5.5km track with panoramic clifftop views and a genuine 'gasp' moment when you set eyes on Otarawairere Bay. A short detour rewards you with amazing views from Toi's Pa (Kapua te rangi), reputedly the oldest's pa site in NZ. You can also get to Toi's Pa by a party unsealed access road off the Whakatane-Ohope road. From Ohope, you can catch the bus back to Whakatane if there aren't any more kilometres left in your legs.

A flatter option is the River Walk (two to three hours), following the Whakatane River

WAKA LIKE A MAN

Whakatane's name originated some eight centuries ago, 200 years after the original Maori settlers arrived here. The warrior Toroa and his family sailed into the estuary in a huge ocean-going *waka* (canoe), the *Mataatua*. As the men went ashore to greet local leaders, the tide turned, and the *waka* – with all the women on board – drifted out to sea. Toroa's daughter, Wairaka, cried out *'E! Kia whakatane au i ahau!'* (Let me act as a man!) and, breaking the traditional *tapu* (taboo) on women steering a *waka*, she took up the paddle and brought the boat safely ashore. A whimsical **statue of Wairaka** stands proudly atop a rock in Whakatane's harbour in commemoration of her brave deed.

past the Botanical Gardens, Muruwai's Cave and on to Wairaka's statue.

The sea along the Whakatane coast is alive with marine mammals including dolphins (25,000 of them!), fur seals, orca, pilot and minke whales; plus birdlife including gannets and little blue penguins. The area is also renowned for diving and big-game fishing.

See also Dive White Island (p327).

Dolphin & Whale Nature Rush ECOTOUR, WILDLIFE TOUR
(☎07-308 9588, 0800 733 529; www.dolphinandwhale.co.nz; 15 The Strand; trips adult/child $80/50; ⊙10am daily Jan-Mar) Run by White Island Tours, Dolphin & Whale Nature Rush offers a two-hour trip out to Motuhora (Whale Island), with plenty of critter-spotting in the sea and sky.

Diveworks Dolphin & Seal Encounters DIVING, WILDLIFE TOUR
(☎07-308 2001, 0800 354 7737; www.whaleislandtours.com; 96 The Strand; dolphin & seal swimming adult/child $160/130, diving incl gear from $215) This dive/ecotour company runs dolphin- and seal-swimming trips from Whakatane (cheaper if you're just watching from the boat), plus dive trips to Motuhora (Whale Island) and Whakaari (White Island). Fishing tours and dive lessons also available (two Whale Island dives with instructor and gear $475).

Whakatane District Aquatic Centre SWIMMING
(www.tlc.net.nz; 28 Short St; adult/child/family $4/2.20/10.50; ⊙6am-8pm Mon-Fri, 7am-6pm Sat & Sun) Indoor and outdoor pools, spa pools and a tubular yellow worm of a waterslide.

Tui Glen Farm HORSE RIDING
(☎07-323 6457; www.tuiglenfarm.com; Kawerau Loop Rd; rides adult/child from $40/30) Close to Kawerau (pronounced 'Kuh-*way*-roo'), about 35km from Whakatane off SH30 to Rotorua, Tui Glen Farm offers horse treks through bush and farm for beginners and the adventurous. Basic dorm accommodation, is also available (from $35).

Tours

There are boat and helicopter tours out to the explosive Whakaari (White Island) (p327).

Kiwi Feet Adventures TRAMPING, OUTDOORS
(☎021 077 7789; www.kiwifeetnz.com) This local tramping tour operator runs guided walks around Whakatane to Tarawera Falls (half-day, $60), Lake Okataina (full day, $125) and Whirinaki Forest (full day, $150). All tours include lunch. Horse riding, kayaking and fishing options also available.

Sleeping

Captain's Cabin APARTMENT **$$**
(☎07-308 5719; www.captainscabin.co.nz; 23 Muriwai Dr; r $125) In a serene part of town with sparkling harbour views, this homely self-contained unit is the perfect spot if you're hanging round for a few days (rates drop for stays of two nights or more). A cosy living area cleverly combines bedroom, lounge, kitchen and dining, with a second smaller room and bijou bathroom – all sweetly decorated along nautical lines. Sleeps three (extra person $25).

Whakatane Hotel HOTEL **$**
(☎07-307 1670; www.whakatanehotel.co.nz; 79 The Strand; dm/s $25/40, d with/without bathroom from $75/50; 📶) This lovely old art-deco classic has 27 basic (but very decent) rooms upstairs in two wings. Clean shared bathroons, high celings, communal kitchen... Great value for money. Some rooms do cop a bit of noise from the pub downstairs, but the owners try to shuffle people around to dodge the din.

White Island Rendezvous HOTEL, B&B $$
(☎07-308 9588, 0800 242 299; www.whiteisland.co.nz; The Strand; d from $140, apt $260, B&B $190; 📶) An immaculate 26-room complex run by the on-the-ball White Island Tour people. Lots of balcony and deck space for inhaling the sea air, while interiors are decked out with timber floors for a nautical vibe. Deluxe rooms come with spas; disabled-access facilities available. The B&B next door includes cooked breakfast.

Windsor Backpackers HOSTEL $
(☎07-308 8040; www.windsorlodge-backpackers.co.nz; 10 Merritt St; dm/s/d from $25/48/66; @📶) Whakatane's best backpackers occupies a converted funeral parlour, so expect a restful sleep. Excellent rooms range from serviceable dorms to a couple of motel-standard doubles out the front. The communal kitchen, lounge and barbecue courtyard are spacious and tidy.

Tuscany Villas MOTEL $$
(☎07-308 2244, 0800 801 040; www.tuscanyvillas.co.nz; 57 The Strand; d $155-200; @📶) This mod motel may be a long way from Florence, but still offers a few rays of Italian sunshine with interesting architecture, wrap-around balconies and floral plantings wherever there's room. Rooms are luxurious and comfy, with super-king beds and spa pools.

Motuhora Rise B&B B&B $$$
(☎07-307 0224; www.motuhorarise.com; 2 Motuhora Rise; s/d incl breakfast $205/220; @📶) At the top of the town in both senses (the driveway is steep!), this jaunty hilltop spot feels vaguely Rocky Mountains, and affords a distant glimpse of Motuhora (Whale Island). You can expect a gourmet cheeseboard on arrival, along with other extras such as a DVD home-theatre suite, outdoor spa-pool deck, and fishing rods and golf clubs. Kid-free zone.

Livingston Inn MOTEL $$
(☎07-308 6400, 0800 770 777; www.livingston.co.nz; 42 Landing Rd; d/f $130/220; 📶) This spotless, ranch-style motel is the pick of the half-dozen dotted along the Landing, with spacious, well-kept units and comfy beds. Large spas in executive suites are a great fringe benefit.

Awakeri Hot Springs HOLIDAY PARK $
(☎07-304 9117; www.awakerisprings.co.nz; SH30; sites $32, d cabins/flats/units $70/85/95) Sixteen kilometres from Whakatane on the road to Rotorua (SH30) you'll come to the immaculate Awakeri Hot Springs, an old-fashioned holiday park complete with (as the name suggests) hot springs (adult/child $6/4), picnic areas and a bed for every budget.

Eating

Wally's on the Wharf FISH & CHIPS $
(☎07-307 1100; www.whakatane.info; The Wharf, The Strand; meals $6-19; ⏰11am-7pm) Wally knows a thing or two about fish and chips: hoki, snapper, flounder, john dory and tarakihi – done in the deep fry, on the grill or in a burger. Whitebait fritters in season, and chips that score well on the crispometer. The reconstituted squid rings are a tad disappointing (but the seagulls don't seem to mind).

Cafe Coco CAFE $
(☎07-308 8337; 10 Richardson St; mains $5-17; ⏰7.30am-6.30pm, to 4.30pm winter) Just 10 months old when we visited, Coco is a hip, L-shaped corner spot serving bright, fresh cafe fare: bagels, paninis, corn fritters, juices, French toast, cakes, organic fair-trade coffee, eggs any-which-way...and the 'Crepe of the Week'. Very kid-friendly, too.

Wharf Shed INTERNATIONAL $$
(☎07-308 5698, 0800 863 463; www.wharfshed.com; The Wharf, The Strand; mains $18-32; ⏰lunch & dinner) An award winner for beef and lamb but famous for fish (this is Whakatane, after all), which includes locally bagged crayfish, corpulent mussels and fresh Pacific oysters. Right on the waterside with alfresco dining on balmy evenings.

Roquette MODERN NZ, MEDITERRANEAN $$$
(☎07-307 0722; www.roquette-restaurant.co.nz; 23 Quay St; mains $20-35; ⏰10am-late Mon-Sat) A modern waterside restaurant on the ground floor of one of the town's big new apartment building, sunny Roquette serves up refreshing Mediterranean-influenced fare with lots of summery salads, risotto and fish dishes. Laid-back tunes, lots of glass and mosaics, good coffee and sexy staff to boot. Try the haloumi salad nicoise.

The Bean CAFE $
(☎07-307 0494; www.thebeancafe.co.nz; 72 The Strand; snacks $5-12; ⏰8am-4pm Mon-Sat , 9am-3pm Sun) The loungiest spot in town to get good coffee (roasted on the premises). Pull up a chair, and get yourself going with a quick fix and a freshly baked biscuit, roll or

bagel. Local art on the walls; retro furniture on the floor.

Countdown SUPERMARKET
(www.countdown.co.nz; 105 Commerce St; ⏰7am-10pm) Stock up on supplies.

Drinking & Entertainment

Craic IRISH PUB
(www.whakatanehotel.co.nz; Whakatane Hotel, 79 The Strand) The Craic is a busy locals' boozer of the Irish ilk, good for a pint or two, or a mug of hot chocolate if you're feeling sub-par. Fantastic streetside terrace for sunny afternoons, and solid pub-grub (mains $13 to $22).

Office BAR
(82 The Strand) The upmarket Office does what it does well: beer, big meals with chips and salad all over (mains $17 to $27), and live bands and/or DJs on Friday and Saturday nights.

Boiler Room CLUB, LIVE MUSIC
(www.whakatanehotel.co.nz; Whakatane Hotel, 79 The Strand) Next door to the Craic at the Whakatane Hotel, the Boiler Room is a cavernous, hedonistic space dotted with pool tables. In fact, it's Whakatane's only club. DJs and live bands engage your ears for Friday and Saturday nights respectively.

Cinema 5 CINEMA
(www.cinema5.co.nz; 101 The Strand) Right in the middle of the Strand, Cinema 5 screens new-release movies. Cheap tickets before 4.30pm.

Information

Post office (4 Commerce St) Also has foreign exchange.

Whakatane Hospital (☎07-306 0999; www.bopdhb.govt.nz; cnr Stewart & Garaway Sts; ⏰24hr) For emergency medical treatment.

Whakatane i-SITE (☎07-306 2030, 0800 924 528; www.whakatane.com; cnr Quay St & Kakahoroa Dr; ⏰8am-5pm Mon-Fri, 10am-4pm Sat & Sun; @📶) Free internet access (including 24-hour wi-fi on the terrace outside the building), tour bookings, accommodation and general enquiries for DOC.

Getting There & Around

Air

Air New Zealand (☎07-308 8397, 0800 737 000; www.airnewzealand.com) has daily flights linking Whakatane to Auckland, with connections to other centres.

Bus

InterCity (www.intercity.co.nz) buses stop outside the i-SITE and connect Whakatane with Rotorua ($34, 1½ hours, one daily), Tauranga ($27, three hours, one daily; via Rotorua) and Gisborne ($45, three hours, one daily; via Opotiki), with onward connections.

Naked Bus (www.nakedbus.com) services run to the following destinations. Book in advance for big savings.

DESTINATION	PRICE	DURATION	FREQUENCY
Auckland	$33	5½hr	1 daily
Gisborne	$20	3¼hr	1 daily
Hamilton	$20	1½hr	1 daily
Rotorua	$15	1½hr	1 daily
Tauranga	$18	5½hr	1 daily
Wellington	$70	10½hr	1 daily

Local **Bay Hopper and Beach Runner** (☎0800 422 928; www.baybus.co.nz) buses run to Ohope ($2.60, 45 minutes, seven daily), Opotiki ($8, 1¼ hour, two daily Monday and Wednesday) and Tauranga ($12.60, five hours, one daily Monday to Saturday).

SHUTTLE BUS

White Island Shuttle (☎0800 733 529; www.whiteisland.co.nz) runs Rotorua–Whakatane and Tauranga–Whakatane return shuttles that can be used by nontour travellers (adult/child return $60/35 from either town).

GKM Shuttles (☎0800 007 005, 07-308 9906; www.whakatane.info) to/from the airport cost $20 per adult for the first adult, with discounted prices per additional passenger.

Taxi

Dial a Cab (☎07-308 0222, 0800 342 522)

Whakaari (White Island)

NZ's most active volcano (it last erupted in 2000) lies 49km off the Whakatane coast. The small island was originally formed by three separate volcanic cones of different ages. The two oldest have been eroded, while the younger cone has risen up between them. Mt Gisborne is the highest point on the island at 321m. Geologically, Whakaari is related to Motuhora (Whale Island) and Putauaki (Mt Edgecumbe), as all lie along Taupo Volcanic Zone.

The island is dramatic, with hot water hissing and steaming from vents over most of the crater floor. Temperatures of 600°C to 800°C have been recorded.

WORTH A TRIP

MOTUHORA (WHALE ISLAND)

Nine kilometres off Whakatane is Motuhora (Whale Island) – so-called because of its leviathan shape. This island is yet another volcano along the Taupo Volcanic Zone but is much less active, although there are hot springs along its shore. The summit is 353m high and the island has several historic sites, including an ancient *pa* (fortified village) site, a quarry and a camp.

Whale Island was originally home to a Maori settlement. In 1829, Maori massacred sailors from the trading vessel *Haweis* while it was anchored at Sulphur Bay. In 1867 the island passed into European ownership and remains privately owned, although since 1965 it has been a Department of Conservation–protected wildlife refuge for seabirds and shorebirds.

The island's protected status means landing is restricted, with tours running only from January to March. Operators include Dolphin & Whale Nature Rush (p324), Diveworks Dolphin & Seal Encounters (p324) and KG Kayaks (p327).

The island is privately owned so you can only visit it with a licensed tour operator. Fixed-wing air operators run flyover tours only, while boat and helicopter tours will usually include a walking tour around the island including a visit to the ruins of the sulphur-mining factory – an interesting story in itself.

Numerous helicopter and fixed-wing operators run trips out of Rotorua and Tauranga; there are also a number of local operators.

Tours

White Island Tours BOAT TOUR
(07-308 9588, 0800 733 529; www.whiteisland.co.nz; 15 The Strand, Whakatane; 6hr tours adult/child $185/120; departures btwn 7am-12.30pm) The only official boat trip to Whakaari (on board the good ship *Pee Jay*), with dolphin-spotting en route and a two-hour tour of the island.

Dive White Island DIVING
(07-307 0714, 0800 348 394; www.divewhite.co.nz; 186 The Strand, Whakatane; snorkelling/diving trips per person $190/345) Full-day snorkelling and diving trips with lunch and gear provided; underwater volcanic terrain and lots of fish to look at.

Vulcan Helicopters SCENIC FLIGHTS
(07-308 4188, 0800 804 354; www.vulcanheli.co.nz; flights per person from $550) A two-hour trip to Whakaari (departing from Whakatane) that includes a one-hour guided walk on the volcano.

White Island Flights SCENIC FLIGHTS
(0800 944 834; www.whiteislandflights.co.nz; flights per person $220) Fixed-wing scenic flights over Whakaari, with lots of photo opportunities. A Whakaari/Mt Tarawera combo flight costs $299.

Ohope

POP 2760

Just 7km over the hill from Whakatane, Ohope has great beaches, perfect for lazing or surfing, and is backed by sleepy Ohiwa Harbour. Just beyond the harbour is the small Sandspit Wildlife Refuge.

Activities

KG Kayaks KAYAKING
(027 272 4073; www.kgkayaks.co.nz; tours $75-145, 2hr hire s/d $50/70) Explore the harbour with KG Kayaks, which offers freedom hire and 2½-hour guided tours, plus four-hour kayak trips around Motuhora (Whale Island), which involves a boat trip initially.

By Salt Surf School SURFING
(07-312 4909, 0211 491 972; beaver@e3.net.nz; 2hr lesson $90) If you want to splash around in the Ohope Beach surf, get some lessons from Beaver at By Salt Surf School, which provides all gear and offers discounts for groups.

Sleeping

Ohope Beach Top 10 Holiday Park HOLIDAY PARK $
(0800 264 673, 07-312 4460; www.ohopebeach.co.nz; 367 Harbour Rd; sites/cabins/units/apts from $23/90/136/190;) The Ohope Beach Top 10 Holiday Park is the very model of a modern holiday park, with a raft of family-friendly facilities: sports courts, minigolf,

pool... Plus some great apartments peeking over the dunes at the Bay of Plenty. Busy as a woodpecker in summer.

Aquarius Motor Lodge MOTEL $
(☎07-312 4550; www.aquariusmotorlodge.co.nz; 103 Harbour Rd; d $85-150;) For a quiet, affordable motel-style option, roll into Aquarius Motor Lodge, a basic complex with various room configurations, all with kitchens and just 100m from the beach (you don't need a swimming pool).

Eating

Ohiwa Oyster Farm SEAFOOD, FAST FOOD $
(Wainui Rd; meals $6-17; ⏲9am-8pm, to 7pm winter) Poised over a swampy back-reach of Ohiwa Harbour (serious oyster territory), this classic roadside fish shack is perfect for a fish-and-chip (and oyster) picnic.

Toi Toi Bar & Brasserie MODERN NZ $$
(☎07-312 5623; www.toitoi-ohope.co.nz; 19 Pohutukawa Ave; mains lunch $13-18, dinner $25-35; ⏲breakfast & lunch Sat & Sun, dinner Tue-Sun) With polished wooden floorboards, white vinyl chairs and a fold-back window wall, Toi Toi is a ritzy new bistro making a splash in little Ohope's shopping strip. Try some sautéed paua (shellfish) with chilli, lime and mussel fritters, or some peppered duck breast with orange, ginger and honey glaze. There are occasional jazz-and-dinner nights, too. Classy stuff indeed.

Opotiki

POP 4180

The Opotiki area was settled from at least 1150, some 200 years before the larger 14th-century Maori migration. Maori traditions are well preserved here, with the work of master carvers lining the main street and the occasional facial *moko* passing by. The town acts as a gateway to the East Coast, and has excellent beaches – Ohiwa and Waiotahi – and an engaging museum.

Sights & Activities

Pick up the *Historic Opotiki* brochure from the i-SITE (or download from www.opotikinz.com) for the low-down on the town's heritage buildings.

Opotiki Heritage & Agriculture Museum MUSEUM
(ohas@xtra.co.nz; 123 Church St; adult/child $10/5; ⏲10am-4pm Mon-Fri, to 2pm Sat) Opotiki's excellent museum offers a chance to learn much about the rich history of the area. Run by volunteers, the museum has interesting heritage displays including Maori *taonga,* militaria, recreated shop-fronts (a barber, carpenter, printer...), and agricultural items including tractors and a horse-drawn wagon. Admission to the Shalfoon & Francis Museum is included in the ticket price.

Shalfoon & Francis Museum MUSEUM
(ohas@xtra.co.nz; 129 Church St; adult/child $10/5) Opotiki's original general store has been born again, with shelves piled high with old grocery and hardware products. Handbags, sticky-tape dispensers, sets of scales, books – you name it, they had it. An amazing collection. Admission is included in your ticket to the Opotiki Heritage & Agriculture Museum.

Hiona St Stephen's Church CHURCH
(hiona-st.stephens@xtra.co.nz; 128 Church St; ⏲services 8am & 9.30am Sun, 10am Thu) White-weatherboard St Stephen's (1862) is an Anglican church with a perfectly proportioned timber-lined interior. Reverend Carl Volkner, known by the local Whakatohea tribe to have acted as a government spy, was murdered here in 1865. In 1992 the Governor-General granted Mokomoko, the man who hanged for the crime, a full pardon, which hangs in the lobby.

FREE **Hukutaia Domain** FOREST, ARCHAEOLOGICAL SITE
(☎07-315 6167; Woodlands Rd; ⏲daily) Around 8km south of the town centre is Hukutaia Domain, home to one of the finest collections of native plants in NZ. In the centre is Taketakerau, a 23m puriri tree estimated to be more than 2000 years old and a burial place for the distinguished dead of the Upokorehe *hapu* (subtribe) of Whakatohea. The remains have since been reinterred elsewhere.

Waioeka River Kayaks KAYAKING, WATER SPORTS
(☎07-315 5553; www.newzealandsbestspot.co.nz; 3666 Waioeka Rd; adult/child $20/10; ⏲Dec-Apr) Have a paddle on the scenic and easy Waioeka River, or try a rope swing, an 8m cliff jump or just bobbing around in an innertube. About 16km south of Opotiki on SH2 on the way to Gisborne.

Motu River Jet Boat Tours JETBOATING
(www.motujet.co.nz; trips from $90) Runs as many as three 1½-hour trips on the Motu River (which runs through the Raukumara Ranges near Opotiki) every day through summer. Winter trips by arrangement.

Wet 'n' Wild RAFTING
(☎0800 462 7238, 07-348 3191; www.wetnwildrafting.co.nz; trips from $875) Offers two- to five-day rafting and camping adventures on the Motu (Grade III–IV rapids).

Festivals & Events

Opotiki Rodeo RODEO
(www.opotikirodeo.co.nz) Dust off your spurs and cowboy hat for the annual Opotiki Rodeo in December. Giddyup.

Sleeping

Opotiki Beach House Backpackers HOSTEL $
(☎07-315 5117; www.opotikibeachhouse.co.nz; 7 Appleton Rd; sites/dm/d $20/28/66; wi-fi) A cruisy, shoe-free beachside pad with a sunny, hammock-hung deck, sea views and plenty of opportunities to get in the water (kayaks/body boards cost $5/3 per hour). Beyond the dorms and breezy lounge are decent doubles and a quirky caravan for those who want a real taste of the Kiwi summer holiday. About 5km west of town; sleeps 12.

Capeview Cottage COTTAGE
(☎07-315 7877, 0800 227 384; www.capeview.co.nz; 167 Tablelands Rd; d $145; wi-fi) Set amid chirruping birds and kiwifruit orchards, this serene, self-contained cottage has two bedrooms, a barbecue and a brilliant outdoor spa from which you can soak up some rather astonishing coastal views. Weekly rates available.

Central Oasis Backpackers HOSTEL $
(☎07-315 5165; www.centraloasisbackpackers.co.nz; 30 King St; dm/d $24/54; ✻ wi-fi) Inside a late-1800s kauri (timber) house, this central backpackers is run by a super-laid-back German a long way from home. It's a snug spot with spacious rooms, a crackling fire and a big front yard to hang out in. The pet rabbit keeps the grass down.

Kukumoa Lodge LODGE, GUESTHOUSE
(☎07-315 8545; www.kukumoalodge.co.nz; 19a Bairds Rd; d $90-110, f $300; wi-fi, pool) This imposing farmhouse is five minutes from town on the way to Ohope, and sports a spacious double and a family area sleeping up to six. There's a games room for the kids, a pool and spa, and a large balcony and patio for swanning around in the sunshine.

Eastland Pacific Motor Lodge MOTEL $$
(☎0800 103 003, 07-315 5524; www.eastlandpacific.co.nz; cnr Bridge & St John Sts; d/units from $105/145; wi-fi) Bright, clean Eastland is a well-kept motel with new carpets, spa baths as standard, and a tidy rose garden in the car park. The two-bedroom units are top value.

Eating

TOP CHOICE **Two Fish** CAFE $
(mudslide@xtra.co.nz; 102 Church St; snacks $4-8, mains $9-19; ⏲8am-4pm Mon-Fri, 8.30am-2pm Sat) Decent eating options are thin on the ground in Opotiki, so what a surprise to discover the best cafe this side of Tauranga! Serving up hefty burgers, chowder, toasties, fab muffins and salads plus a jumbo selection in the cabinet, Two Fish has happy staff, Cuban tunes and a retro-groovy interior and courtyard. Nice one.

Nikau CAFE, RESTAURANT $$
(☎07-315 5760; 95 Church St; mains lunch $9-16, dinner $16-28; ⏲breakfast & lunch daily, dinner Tue-Sun) Seemingly the only real restaurant within miles, Nikau does a steady cafe trade during the day (good coffee, toasted sandwiches, BLATs, eggs florentine), and more sophisticated dinners at night ('The warm beef salad is di-VINE!' says one happy customer). Hip, minimal, informal.

New World SUPERMARKET
(www.newworld.co.nz; 19 Bridge St; ⏲8am-8pm) Self-catering supplies.

Entertainment

De Luxe Cinema CINEMA
(127 Church St) The beguiling old De Luxe Cinema shows the occasional movie and brass-band concert. Check the window for upcoming events, including the annual Silent Film Festival in September.

Information

DOC (☎07-315 1001; www.doc.govt.nz; 70 Bridge St; ⏲8am-2.30pm Mon-Fri) In the same building as the i-SITE.

Opotiki i-SITE (☎07-315 3031; www.opotikinz.com; 70 Bridge St; ⏲9am-4.30pm Mon-Fri, 9am-1pm Sat & Sun) The i-SITE takes bookings for activities and transport and stocks the indispensable free East Coast booklet *Pacific Coast Highway*.

 Getting There & Away

Travelling east from Opotiki there are two routes: SH2, crossing the spectacular Waioeka Gorge, or SH35 around East Cape. The SH2 route offers some day walks in the Waioeka Gorge Scenic Reserve, with the gorge getting steeper and narrower as you travel inland, before the route crosses typically green, rolling hills, dotted with sheep, on the descent to Gisborne.

Bus

Buses pick up/drop off at the Hot Bread Shop on the corner of Bridge and St John Sts, though tickets and bookings are made through the i-SITE or **Travel Shop** (☎07-315 8881; travelshop@xtra.co.nz; 104 Church St; ⊙8am-5pm Mon-Fri, to noon Sat). The Travel Shop also rents out bikes (per half-/full day $30/45).

InterCity (www.intercity.co.nz) has daily buses connecting Opotiki with Whakatane ($22, 45 minutes), Rotorua ($34, 2½ hours) and Auckland ($69, seven hours). Heading south, daily buses connect Opotiki with Gisborne ($34, two hours).

Naked Bus (www.nakedbus.com) runs daily services to destinations including the following. Book in advance for big savings.

DESTINATION	PRICE	DURATION
Auckland	$35	6¼hr
Gisborne	$18	2¼hr
Rotorua	$23	2¼hr
Tauranga	$36	6¼hr
Wellington	$50	11¼hr

The local **Bay Hopper** (☎0800 422 928; www.baybus.co.nz) bus runs to Whakatane ($8, 1¼ hour, two daily Monday and Wednesday).

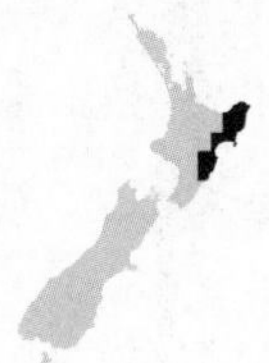

The East Coast

Includes »

East Cape 334
Pacific Coast Hwy 334
Gisborne 338
Te Urewera National Park 344
Hawke's Bay 347
Napier 348
Hastings & Around 356
Cape Kidnappers 361
Central Hawke's Bay 362
Kaweka & Ruahine Ranges 363

Best Outdoors

» Cape Kidnappers (p361)

» Cooks Cove Walkway (p338)

» Hawke's Bay Cycle Trails (p352)

» Surf Gisborne (p340)

» Lake Waikaremoana Track (p345)

Best Places to Stay

» Kennedy Park Top 10 Resort (p353)

» Waikawa B&B (p336)

» Clive Colonial Cottages (p358)

» Knapdale Eco Lodge (p341)

Why Go?

New Zealand is known for its mix of wildly divergent landscapes, but in this region it's the sociological contours that are most pronounced. From the earthy settlements of the East Cape to Havelock North's wine-soaked streets, there's a full spectrum of NZ life.

Maori culture is never more visible than on the East Coast. Exquisitely carved *marae* (meeting house complexes) dot the landscape, and while the locals may not be wearing flax skirts and swinging *poi* (flax balls on strings) like they do for the tourists in Rotorua, you can be assured that *te reo* and *tikanga* (the language and customs) are alive and well.

Intrepid types will have no trouble losing the tourist hordes – along the Pacific Coast Hwy, through rural back roads, on remote beaches, or in the mystical wilderness of Te Urewera National Park.

When the call of the wild gives way to caffeine withdrawal, a fix will quickly be found in the urban centres of Gisborne and Napier. You'll also find plenty of wine, as the region strains under the weight of grapes. From *kaimoana* (seafood) to berry fruit and beyond, there are riches here for everyone.

When to Go

The East Coast basks in a warm, mainly dry climate. Summer temperatures around Napier and Gisborne nudge 25°C, rarely dipping below 8°C in winter. The Hawke's Bay region also suns itself in mild, dry, grape-growing conditions, with an average annual rainfall of 800mm. Heavy downpours sometimes wash out sections of the Pacific Coast Hwy (State Hwy 35, SH35).

East Coast Highlights

1. Time-warping to the 1930s amid the art-deco delights of **Napier** (p348)
2. Sniffing and sipping your way around the wineries of **Hawke's Bay** (p360) or **Gisborne** (p339)
3. Losing yourself in the mighty forests and Maori culture of **Te Urewera National Park** (p344)
4. Cruising the coast, taking in landmarks such as **Cape Kidnappers** (p361), **Tolaga Bay** (p337), **Tokomaru Bay** (p337) and the **East Cape Lighthouse** (p336)
5. Searching for wood nymphs among the magical forest paths of **Eastwoodhill Arboretum** (p9)

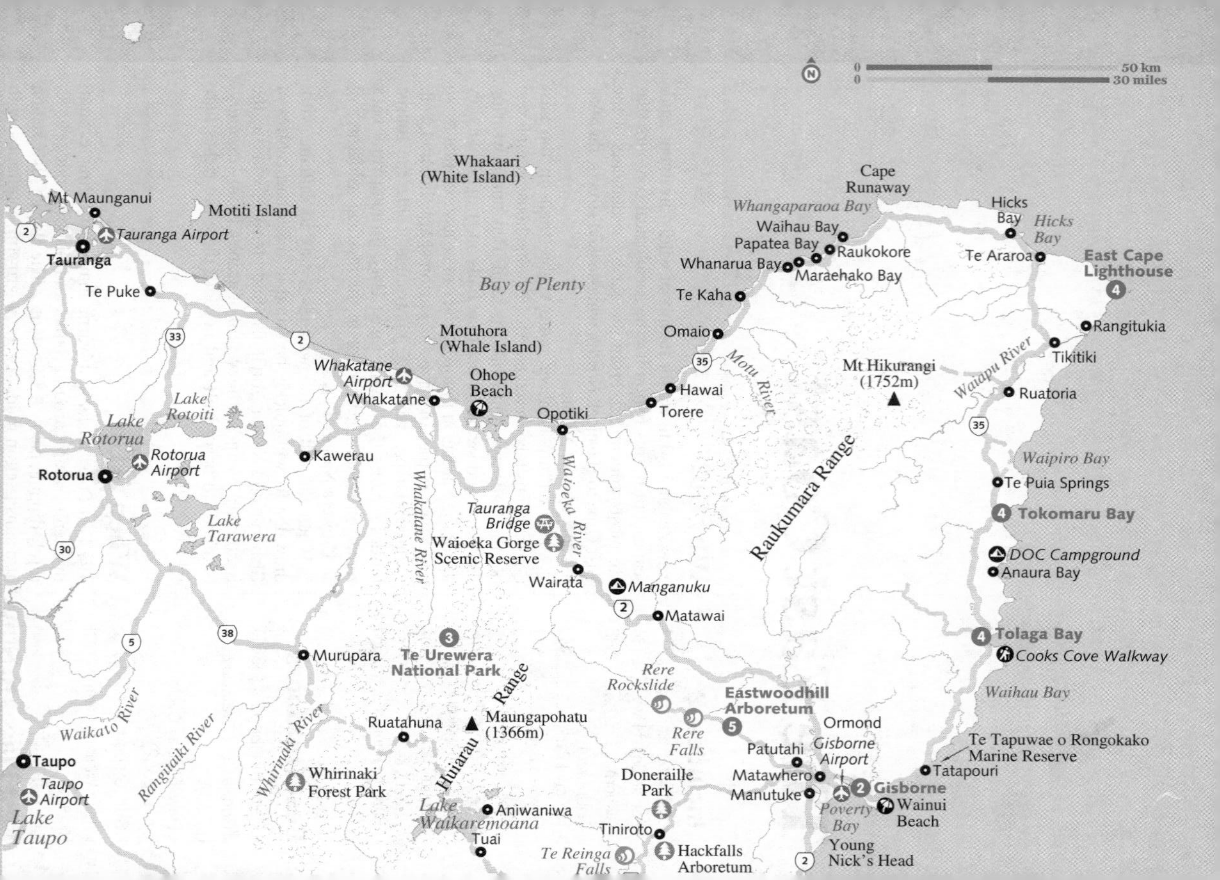

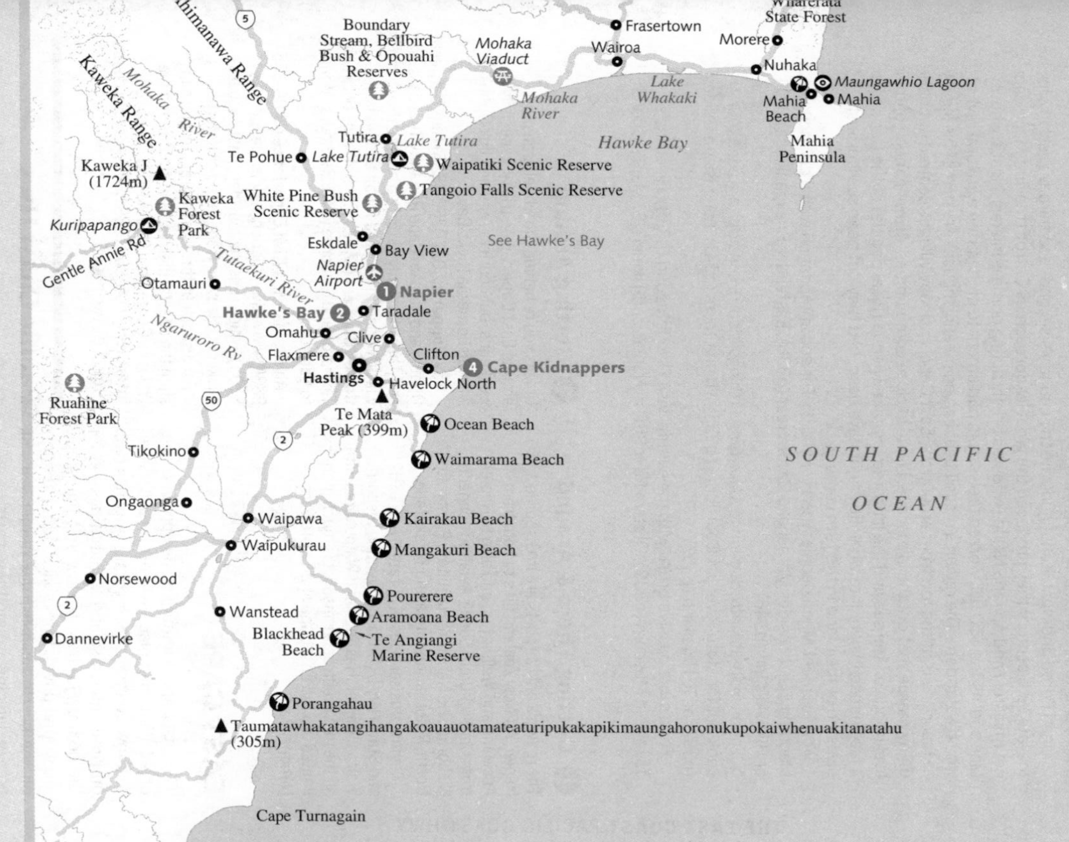

Whareata State Forest
Frasertown
Morere
Wairoa
Nuhaka
Maungawhio Lagoon
Mahia
Mahia Beach
Mahia Peninsula
Lake Whakaki
Mohaka Viaduct
Mohaka River
Boundary Stream, Bellbird Bush & Opouahi Reserves
Hawke Bay
Kaweka Range
Mohaka River
Tutira
Lake Tutira
Te Pohue
Lake Tutira
Waipatiki Scenic Reserve
Tangoio Falls Scenic Reserve
Kaweka J (1724m)
Kaweka Forest Park
White Pine Bush Scenic Reserve
Kuripapango
Gentle Annie Rd
Eskdale
Bay View
See Hawke's Bay
Napier Airport
Tutaekuri River
1 Napier
Otamauri
Hawke's Bay 2
Taradale
Ngaruroro Rv
Omahu
Clive
Flaxmere
Clifton
4 Cape Kidnappers
Hastings
Havelock North
Ruahine Forest Park
50
Te Mata Peak (399m)
Ocean Beach
2
Tikokino
Waimarama Beach
SOUTH PACIFIC OCEAN
Ongaonga
Waipawa
Kairakau Beach
Waipukurau
Mangakuri Beach
Norsewood
2
Pourerere
Wanstead
Aramoana Beach
Dannevirke
Blackhead Beach
Te Angiangi Marine Reserve
Porangahau
Taumatawhakatangihangakoauauotamateaturipukakapikimaungahoronukupokaiwhenuakitanatahu (305m)
Cape Turnagain

MAORI NZ: THE EAST COAST

The main *iwi* (tribes) in the region are Te Whanau-a-Apanui (west side of East Cape), Ngati Porou (east side of East Cape), Ngati Kahungunu (the coast from Hawke's Bay down) and Tuhoe (inland in Te Urewera).

Ngati Porou and Ngati Kahungunu are the country's second- and third-biggest *iwi*. In the late 19th century they produced the great leaders James Carroll (the first Maori cabinet minister) and Apirana Ngata (who was briefly acting prime minister). Ngata, whose face adorns the $50 bill, worked tirelessly in parliament to orchestrate a cultural revival within Maoridom. The region's magnificent carved meeting houses are part of his legacy.

Maori life is at the forefront around the East Cape, in sleepy villages centred upon the many *marae* that dot the landscape. Living in close communities, drawing much of their livelihoods off the sea and the land, the *tangata whenua* (local people) of the Cape offer a fascinating insight into what life might have been, had they not been so vigorously divested of their land in the 19th century.

You will meet Maori people wherever you go. For accommodation with a distinctly Maori flavour, consider Maraehako Bay Retreat (p336), Eastender Backpackers (p337) or Hikihiki's Inn (p346).

For an intimate introduction to *Maoritanga* (things Maori), consider a guided tour. Look out for Motu River Jet Boat Tours (p335), Tipuna Tours (p341), Long Island Guides (p357) or Te Hakakino (p357).

For a more passive brush with the culture, visit Dive Tatapouri (p338), Gisborne's Tairawhiti Museum (p338), Otatara Pa (p351) in Napier, and Tikitiki's St Mary's Church.

Getting There & Around

The region's only airports are in Gisborne and Napier. Air New Zealand flies to both from Auckland and Wellington, and also to Napier from Christchurch. Sunair Aviation connects Gisborne and Napier to Hamilton, Palmerston North, Rotorua, Tauranga and Whakatane.

Regular bus services ply State Hwy 2 (SH2) and State Hwy 5 (SH5), connecting Gisborne, Wairoa, Napier, Hastings and Waipukurau with all the main centres. Transport is much more limited around East Cape and Te Urewera National Park.

EAST CAPE

The East Cape is a unique and special corner of NZ. It's a quiet place, where everyone seems to know everyone, their community ties built on rural enterprise and a shared passion for the ocean. The pace is slow and the people are wound down. Horse-back riding, tractors on the beach, fresh fish for dinner – it's all part of daily life around these parts.

Inland, the wild Raukumara Range forms the Cape's jagged spine. Near the edge of the sea, the 323km Pacific Coast Hwy (SH35) runs from Opotiki to Gisborne. Lonely shores lie strewn with driftwood, while picture-postcard sandy bays lure in a handful of visitors.

Getting Around

Unless you're behind the wheel, transport around East Cape can be tricky, especially on weekends, but couriers regularly link Opotiki with Gisborne via Hicks Bay.

Bay Hopper (☎021 0260 4885) runs between Opotiki and Potaka/Cape Runaway Tuesdays and Thursdays only ($15, two hours); they will drive on to Te Araroa for an additional fee. **Cook's Couriers** (☎021 371 364) runs between Te Araroa and Gisborne ($40, 3½ hours) Monday to Saturday.

An alternative is **Kiwi Experience** (☎09-366 9830; www.kiwiexperience.com; per person $395), which runs the four-day 'East As' backpacker bus leaving from Taupo or Rotorua.

For a shortcut through this region, you can shun the coastal highway and zip through the Waioeka Gorge from Opotiki to Gisborne on **InterCity** (☎06-868 6139; www.intercity.co.nz) (from $15, two hours).

Pacific Coast Hwy

The long and often winding road around the North Island's easternmost point has long been somewhat of a rite of road-trip passage for New Zealanders, but overseas visitors could be forgiven for wondering what all the fuss is about. It has its highlights, for sure, but for much of the journey between Opotiki and Gisborne, the Pacific Coast is far away beyond the hills, and the road snakes through farmland that missed its makeover by the quaintillator.

That said, if you like cruisy drives or are skilled in cadging lifts, and don't mind attractions that are few, far between and largely centred upon people, horses, and piles of driftwood, you will likely find this journey surprisingly intrepid and captivating.

If you're short on time or not up for hit-and-miss, you can head for Gisborne via the **Waioeka Gorge**. This 144km alternative route takes 2½ hours to drive, although you could easily make a day of it by the time you stop at various picnic spots including the historic **Tauranga Bridge**. The loop walk here (three hours) is well worth the effort if you like bushy valleys or haven't yet had a glimpse into the pioneer past that was 'farm fails: terrain too tough'.

For a taste of the Pacific Coast Hwy, drive from Opotiki to the macadamia farm (p336). It's a picturesque section that captures the essence of this scenic route: shimmering turquoise ocean seen betwixt the crimson blooms of gnarled pohutukawa trees.

Both routes, along with several more in the region, are covered in the excellent *Pacific Coast Highway Guide*, available at Gisborne and Opotiki i-SITEs and outlets along the way.

Set off with a full petrol tank, and stock up on snacks and groceries – shops and petrol stations are in short supply. Sleeping and eating options are pretty spread out, so we've listed them in the order you'll find them.

OPOTIKI TO TE KAHA

The first leg offers hazy views across to Whakaari (White Island), a chain-smoking active volcano. The desolate beaches at **Torere**, **Hawai** and **Omaio** are steeply shelved and littered with flotsam. Check out the magnificent *whakairo* (carving) on the Torere school gateway. Hawai marks the boundary of the Whanau-a-Apanui tribe whose *rohe* (traditional land) extends to Cape Runaway.

About 42km east of Opotiki the road crosses the broad pebbly expanse of the **Motu River**, the first river in NZ to be designated as a protected wilderness area. Departing from the Motu bridge on the highway, **Motu River Jet Boat Tours** (☎07-325 2735; www.motujet.co.nz; 45min ride $85, min 2 people) blats up the river all year round, weather permitting. **Wet 'n' Wild Rafting** (☎0800 462 7238; www.wetnwildrafting.co.nz; 2-5 days $825-975) offers multiday excursions, with the longest taking you 100km down the river. The two-day tour requires you to be helicoptered in, therefore costing almost as much as the five-day trip.

Twenty-five kilometres further along, the fishing town of **Te Kaha** once sounded the death knell for passing whales. There's a shop here, a modern waterside hotel with a bar and restaurant, and several accommodation options including **Tui Lodge** (☎07-325 2922; www.tuilodge.co.nz; Copenhagen Rd, Te Kaha; s/d incl breakfast $125/150; @). This capacious guesthouse sits on groomed three-acre gardens, irresistible to tui and many other birds. Meals are available by arrangement, as are horse-trekking, fishing and diving trips.

TE KAHA TO CAPE RUNAWAY

A succession of sleepy bays extends from Te Kaha. At **Papatea Bay** stop to admire the gateway of **Hinemahuru marae**, intricately carved with images of WWI Maori Battalion soldiers. Nearby **Christ Church Raukokore** (1894) is a sweet beacon of belief on a lonely promontory (look out for the mouse on high). **Waihau Bay** has an all-in-one petrol station–post office–store-takeaway at its western end, alongside the pub. **Cape Runaway**, where

ESSENTIAL EAST COAST

» **Eat** Delicious fresh produce from the Hastings Farmers Market (p359)

» **Read** Witi Ihimaera's novel *Whale Rider*, then watch the powerful movie adaptation

» **Listen to** Uawa FM (88.5, 88.8, 99.3 FM) in Tolaga Bay

» **Watch** *Boy* (2010), Taika Waititi's record-breaking and hilarious film, shot at Waihau Bay

» **Festival** Art Deco Weekend (p353) in Napier and Hastings

» **Go Green** Millton vineyard (p339)–organic, biodynamic, and delicious to boot

» **Online** www.hawkesbaynz.com; www.gisbornenz.com

» **Area code** Opotiki east to Hicks Bay ☎07; rest of the region ☎06.

FREEDOM TO CAMP

Gisborne District Council (GDC) is one of the few authorities to permit freedom camping (extremely cheap informal camping), but only at a handful of designated sites from the end of September to April. You can apply for a permit online (www.gdc.govt.nz/freedom-camping/) for two, 10 or 28 consecutive nights at a cost of $10, $25 and $60 respectively. Freedom camping is a privilege, so please follow the requirements in the GDC *Freedom Camping* leaflet, available online or at visitor centres. Your own gas cooker, chemical toilet and water supply are obligatory.

kumara was first introduced to NZ, can only be reached on foot.

There are few accommodation options in these parts, and what you will find will be small and personal. Nestled among ancient pohutukawa trees, the waterfront **Maraehako Bay Retreat** (07-325 2648; www.maraehako.co.nz; SH35; dm/s/d $28/43/66; @) is a hostel that looks like it was cobbled together from flotsam and jetsam washed up in the craggy cove. It's rustic, but unique, for what it lacks in crossed t's and dotted i's it more than makes up for in *manaakitanga* (hospitality). Enjoy a spa under the stars ($5), free kayaks, as well as fishing charters, *marae* tours, guided walks, horse treks and more, at reasonable prices. Run by the same *hapu* (subtribe) as the retreat next door is **Maraehako Camping Ground** (07-325 2901; SH35; sites per adult/child $12/8). Little more is offered than clean toilets, showers and beachfront nirvana.

Towards **Whanarua Bay**, the magical **Waikawa B&B** (07-325 2070; www.waikawa.net; 7541 SH35; d $120-135; @) sits in a private rocky cove with views of the sunset and White Island. The artful buildings blend weathered timber, corrugated iron and paua inlay to great effect. There are two double B&B rooms, and a two-bedroom self-contained bach ($150 to $220), perfect for two to four people.

There are plenty of beds at **Oceanside Apartments** (07-325 3699; www.waihaubay.co.nz; 10932 SH35; d $110-130; @), between two nicely-kept apartments and a next-door bach. Meals and picnic lunches are available by arrangement. Bookings can be made for kayak hire and local activities.

Heaven is a tub of homemade macadamia and honey ice cream at **Pacific Coast Macadamias** (07-325 2960; www.macanuts.co.nz; SH35, Whanarua Bay; snacks $2-9; 9am-4pm), accompanied by views along one of the most spectacular parts of the coast. Toasted sandwiches and nutty sweet treats make this a great lunch stop.

CAPE RUNAWAY TO EAST CAPE

The road heads inland from Whangaparaoa, crossing into Ngati Porou territory before hitting the coast at **Hicks Bay**, a real middle-of-nowhere settlement with a grand beach. Brilliant views distract from the barrack ambience at the sprawling **Hicks Bay Motel Lodge** (06-864 4880; www.hicksbaymotel.co.nz; 5198 SH35; dm $23, d $75-145;), perched high above the bay. The old-fashioned rooms are nothing flash, although the restaurant, shop, pool and glowworm grotto offer some compensation.

Nearly 10km further is **Te Araroa**, a lone-dog village with two shops, petrol station, takeaway and beautifully carved *marae*. The geology changes here from igneous outcrops to sandstone cliffs, but it is the dense regenerating bush backdrop that gives this place its flavour. More than 350 years old, 20m high and 40m wide, Te-Waha-O-Rerekohu, allegedly NZ's largest pohutukawa tree, stands in Te Araroa schoolyard. The progressive **East Cape Manuka Company** (www.eastcapemanuka.co.nz; 4464 Te Araroa Rd; 9am-4pm daily Nov-Mar, Mon-Fri Apr-Oct) is also here, selling soaps, oils, creams and honey made from potent East Cape manuka. It's a good stop for coffee.

From Te Araroa, drive out to see the **East Cape Lighthouse**, the easterly tip of mainland NZ. It's 21km (30 minutes) east of town along a mainly unsealed road, with a 25-minute climb to the lighthouse. Set your alarm and get up there for sunrise.

EAST CAPE TO TOKOMARU BAY

Heading through farmland south of Te Araroa, the first town you come to is **Tikitiki**. If you haven't yet made it onto a *marae*, you'll get a fair idea of what you're missing out on by visiting the extraordinary **St Mary's Church** (1924). It's nothing special from the outside, but step inside for a sensory overload. There are woven *tukutuku* (flax panels) on the walls, geometrically patterned stained-glass windows, painted beams and amazing carvings – check out the little guys holding up the pulpit. A stained-glass crucifixion scene behind the pulpit depicts WWI Maori Battalion soldiers in attendance.

The farming sprawl of **Rangitukia**, 8km down towards the coast from Tikitiki, would be unremarkable were it not for a couple of welcoming visitor experiences. **Eastender Backpackers** (06-864 3820; eastenderbackpackers@xtra.co.nz; 836 Rangitukia Rd; campsites per person $10, dm $25, d $50) is a down-to-earth farmstay with a choice of dorms or cabins. Conveniently, **Eastender Horse Treks** (06-864 3033; www.eastenderhorsetreks.co.nz; 836 Rangitukia Rd; 2hr treks $85) can be found next door, and either operator can hook you up with bone-carving lessons (from $55), and you might even get to try a *hangi* (Maori feast; $14). The nearby beach is dicey for swimming but there's a safe waterhole if you're keen.

Mt Hikurangi (1752m), jutting out of the Raukumara Range, is the highest non-volcanic peak on the North Island and the first spot on Earth to see the sun each day. According to local tradition it was the first piece of land dragged up when Maui snagged the North Island. The Ngati Porou version of the Maui story has his canoe and earthly remains resting here on their sacred mountain.

Continuing south, the road passes **Ruatoria** and **Te Puia Springs**. Along this stretch a 14km loop road offers a rewarding detour to **Waipiro Bay**.

Eleven kilometres south of Te Puia is **Tokomaru Bay**, perhaps the most interesting spot on the entire route, with its broad beach framed by sweeping cliffs. The town has weathered hard times since the freezing works closed in the 1950s, but it still sports several attractions including good beginner surfing, swimming, and **Te Puka Tavern** (06-864 5465; www.tepukatavern.co.nz; Beach Rd; meals $10-25; 11am-10pm; @). The well-run pub with cracker ocean views is a cornerstone of the community, keeping everyone fed and watered, and now offering visitors a place to stay. Four units sleep up to five and there's room for a couple of campervans. You'll also find a small supermarket, takeaway and post office, and some crumbling surprises at the far end of the bay. Up on the hill, **Brian's Place** (06-864 5870; www.briansplace.co.nz; 21 Potae St; campsites per person $15, dm/s/d $28/45/66) scores the awards for views and eco-loos. There are two tricky loft rooms for sharing, a double downstairs and three sweet cabins. Tenters have a panoramic knoll on which to pitch.

LOCAL KNOWLEDGE

THE BALLAD OF FOOTROOT FLATS *MURRAY BALL*

Where the black Raukumara Ranges
Lie out east of everywhere,
The land's been stripped by sun and rain,
Until its bones are bare.
In this land of snarl-lipped razor backs
Of possums, deer and rats,
They talk a lot of working dogs
And the man from Footrot Flats.

TOKOMARU BAY TO GISBORNE

After a bucolic 22km of highway is the turn-off to **Anaura Bay**, 7km away. It's a definite 'wow' moment when it springs into view far below. Captain Cook arrived here in 1769 and commented on the 'profound peace' in which the people were living and their 'truly astonishing' cultivations. **Anaura Bay Walkway** is a two-hour ramble through steep bush and grassland, starting at the northern end of the bay. There's a standard Department of Conservation (DOC) campsite here (adult/child $6/3); fully self-contained campers only).

Campers are catered for best around these parts, although a few B&Bs come and go in the midst. **Anaura Bay Motor Camp** (06-862 6380; anaurabay@farmside.co.nz; Anaura Bay Rd; sites per adult/child from $16/6) is all about the location – right on the beachfront by the little stream where James Cook once stocked up with water. There's a decent kitchen, showers and toilets.

Back on the highway it's 14km south to **Tolaga Bay**, East Cape's largest community. There's an **information centre** (06-862 6862; 55 Cook St; 6am-6pm Mon-Fri) in the foyer of the local radio station (Uawa FM; 88.5, 88.8, 99.3FM). Just off the main street, **Tolaga Bay Cashmere Company** (www.cashmere.co.nz; 31 Solander St; 10am-4pm Mon-Fri) inhabits the art-deco former council building. Watch the knitters at work, then perhaps purchase one of their delicate handiworks; the seconds are sold at a discount.

Tolaga is defined by the remarkable **historic wharf** (1929) – the longest in the southern hemisphere at 660m – which is slowly surrendering to the sea (although work is under way to preserve it). Take the time to walk its length. Nearby is **Cooks Cove Walkway** (5.8km, 2½ hours; closed August to October), an easy loop through farmland and native bush to another cove where the captain landed. At the northern end of the beach is the **Tatarahake Cliffs Lookout**, a sharp 10-minute walk to an excellent vantage point.

Tolaga Bay Holiday Park (☎06-862 6716; www.tolagabayholidaypark.co.nz; 167 Wharf Rd; sites from $14, units $55-90) is right next to the wharf. The stiff ocean breeze tousles Norfolk Island pines as open lawns bask in the sunshine. It's a pretty special spot. Back in town, the 1930s faux-Tudor **Tolaga Inn** (☎06-862 6856; 12 Cook St; dm/s/d $25/50/75) is an up-and-comer with basic but clean rooms. Downstairs is a pub and cafe (meals $9 to $30) with home-baking.

Around 16km north of Gisborne, **Te Tapuwae o Rongokako Marine Reserve** is a 2450-hectare haven for many species of marine life including fur seals, dolphins and whales. Get out amongst it with **Dive Tatapouri** (☎06-868 5153; www.divetatapouri.com; SH35, Tatapouri Beach, Tatapouri Beach), which offers an array of watery activities including dive trips, snorkel hire, a reef ecology tour, shark-cage diving and even stingray feeding.

Gisborne

POP 34,300

Gizzy to her friends, Gisborne's a pretty thing, squeezed between surf beaches and a sea of chardonnay. It proudly claims to be the first city on Earth to see the sun, and once it does it hogs it and heads to the seaside. Poverty Bay starts here, hooking south to Young Nick's Head.

Perhaps it's the isolated location that's helped Gisborne maintain its small-town charm and interesting main street. Grand Edwardian buildings sit alongside modernist 1950s, five-storey 'skyscrapers' and the odd slice of audacious art deco.

It's a good place to put your feet up for a few days, hit the beaches and sip heavenly wine.

History

The Gisborne region has been settled for over 700 years. A pact between two migratory *waka* (canoe) skippers, Paoa of the *Horouta* and Kiwa of the *Takitimu*, led to the founding of Turanganui a Kiwa (now Gisborne). Kumara flourished in the fertile soil and the settlement blossomed.

In 1769 this was the first part of NZ sighted by Cook's expedition. Eager to replenish supplies and explore, they set ashore, much to the amazement of the locals. Setting an unfortunate benchmark for intercultural relations, the crew opened fire when the Maori men performed their traditional bloodcurdling challenge, killing six of them.

The *Endeavour* set sail without provisions. Cook, perhaps in a fit of petulance, named the area Poverty Bay as 'it did not afford a single item we wanted'.

European settlement began in 1831 with whaling and farming, with missionaries following. In the 1860s battles between settlers and Maori erupted. Beginning in Taranaki, the Hauhau insurrection spread to the East Coast, culminating in the battle of Waerenga a Hika in 1865.

To discover Gisborne's historical spots, pick up the *Historic Walk* pamphlet from the i-SITE.

Sights

Tairawhiti Museum MUSEUM

(www.tairawhitimuseum.org.nz; 18 Stout St; adult/child $5/free, Mon free; ⏲10am-4pm Mon-Sat, 1.30-4pm Sun) The Tairawhiti Museum focuses on East Coast Maori and colonial history. Its gallery is Gisborne's arts hub, with rotating exhibits, and excellent historic photographic displays. There's also a maritime wing, with displays on *waka*, whaling and Cook's Poverty Bay, although these pale in comparison to the vintage surfboard collection.

There's a shop and tearoom-style cafe overlooking Kelvin Park, while outside is the reconstructed **Wyllie Cottage** (1872), Gisborne's oldest house.

Titirangi Park PARK

High on Kaiti Hill overlooking the city, Titirangi was once a *pa* (fortified village). You can reach it by driving or walking up Queens Dr, or pick up the walking track at the Cook Monument. Near the summit is **Titirangi Lookout** and yet another Cook edifice, **Cook's Plaza**. Due to a cock-up of historic proportions, the Cook statue here looks nothing like Cap'n Jim. A plaque proclaims, 'Who was he? We have no idea!' Further on is the **Cook Observatory** (public viewing $5; ⏲viewing 8.30pm Tue Oct-Mar, 7.30pm Tue Apr-Sep), the world's easternmost stargazing facility.

Cook Monument MONUMENT
At the foot of Titirangi Park is the spot where Cook first got NZ dirt on his boots. This important site is little more than a patch of lawn with a grim obelisk facing the end of the wharves. The scrappy site is made even more significant by being the landing point of the *Horouta waka*. Look out for the remnants of terracing and kumara pits on the steep track to the top of Kaiti Hill, which starts near the monument.

Statue of Young Nick MONUMENT
There's no let-up in the *Endeavour* endeavours, because in the riverside park is a statue of Nicholas Young, Cook's cabin boy, whose eagle eyes were the first to spot NZ (the white cliffs at Young Nick's Head). There's a **Captain Cook statue** nearby, erected on a globe etched with his roaming routes.

Te Tauihu Turanga Whakamana MONUMENT
(The Canoe Prow; cnr Gladstone Rd & Customhouse St) Te Tauihu Turanga Whakamana is a large modern sculpture in the shape of a *tauihu* (canoe prow) that celebrates early Maori explorers.

Gisborne Botanic Gardens GARDENS
(Aberdeen Rd) The town gardens sit prettily beside the Taruheru River and are a pleasant place for a picnic.

TOP CHOICE **Eastwoodhill Arboretum** GARDENS
(☎06-863 9003; www.eastwoodhill.org.nz; 2392 Wharekopae Rd, Ngatapa; adult/child $15/free; ⏲9am-5pm) Arboreal nirvana, Eastwoodhill Arboretum is the country's largest collection of imported trees and shrubs. It's staggeringly beautiful, and you could easily lose a day wandering around the 25km of themed tracks in this pine-scented paradise. It's well signposted, 35km northwest of Gisborne.

East Coast Museum of Technology & Transport MUSEUM
(www.ecmot.org.nz; SH2, Makaraka; adult/child $5/2; ⏲10am-4.30pm) Think analogue, rather than digital; old-age rather than space-age. Located 5km west of the town centre, this improbable medley of farm equipment, fire engines, domestic appliances and an electron microscope has found an appropriate home in a motley old milking barn and surrounding outhouses. Oh, the irony of the welcome sign...

GISBORNE WINERIES

With hot summers and fertile loam soils, the land to the northwest of Gisborne is of New Zealand's foremost grape-growing areas. Centred upon the Waipaoa River valley, geographically and climatically diverse terroir – river plains, gently sloping hills, sheltered valleys and plateau – produce a wide variety of distinct wines. It is traditionally famous for its chardonnay but increasingly being noticed for other white varietals, particularly gewürztraminer and pinot gris.

Some vineyards charge a nominal fee, deducted from subsequent purchases. Pick up the winery guide from the i-SITE, or visit www.gisbornewine.co.nz for a map of all cellar doors. The following are open daily from around 11am to 4pm, but scale back opening hours out of peak season.

» **Bushmere Estate** (www.bushmere.com; 166 Main Rd, Matawhero) Great chardonnay, gewürztraminer, cafe lunches, and live music on summer Sundays.

» **Kirkpatrick Estate** (www.kew.co.nz; 569 Wharekopae Rd, Patutahi) Sustainable winery with lovely wines across the board, including a delicious malbec. Enjoy a guided tour and antipasto platter in the sun.

» **Matawhero** (www.matawhero.co.nz; Riverpoint Rd, Matawhero) Home of a particularly buttery chardy. Enjoy your picnic in a bucolic setting, accompanied by a flight of fine wines.

» **Millton** (www.millton.co.nz; 119 Papatu Rd, Manutuke) Sustainable, organic and biodynamic to boot. Bring a picnic and linger in the beautiful gardens.

» **Gisborne Wine Centre** (www.gisbornewine.co.nz; Shed 3, 50 The Esplanade; ⏲10am-5pm Sun-Wed, 10am-7pm Thu-Sat) Harbourside spot with a wide selection of the region's vino to sample, plus local winery information.

Gisborne

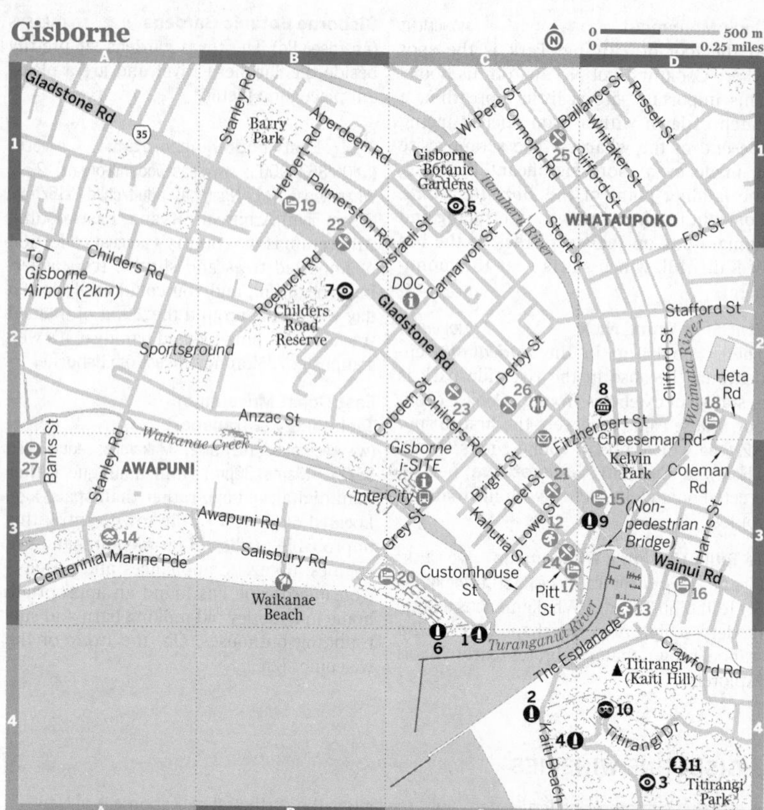

Presbyterian Church CHURCH
(Church Ln, Matawhero) Some 7km west of the centre in the suburb of Matawhero, this historic Presbyterian church is the only building in the village to have survived Te Kooti's 1868 raid. It's a sweetly simple affair with lovingly tended gardens.

FREE **Sunshine Brewing Company** BREWERY
(☎06-867 7777; www.gisbornegold.co.nz; 109 Disraeli St; ⊙9am-6pm Mon-Sat) Sunshine Brewing Company, Gisborne's own natural brewery, offers four quality beers including the famous Gisborne Gold and its big brother Green. Free tours and tastings by arrangement.

Activities

Water Sports

Surfing is mainstream in Gisborne, with the teenage population looking appropriately shaggy. **Waikanae Beach** and **Roberts Road** are good for learners and young ones; experienced surfers get tubed south of town at the **Pipe**, or east at **Sponge Bay** and **Tuamotu Island**. Further east along SH35, **Wainui** and **Makorori** also have quality breaks.

Wainui is home to **Surfing with Frank** (☎021 119 0971; www.surfingwithfrank.com; 58 Murphy Rd, Wainui Beach, Wainui Beach; lessons $50-75), which offers lessons as well as tours of the best East Coast and Taranaki breaks. Don't miss the Wainui Store if you're in the vicinity and are looking for something to fill your belly.

There's plenty of good swimming in the area. In town, swim safely between the flags at **Waikanae** and **Midway** beaches, or if you prefer the parameters of a swimming pool, the **Olympic Pool** (Centennial Marine Pde, Midway Beach; adult/child $3.60/2.60; ⊙6am-8pm) has 50m lane-swimming, and a wormlike waterslide.

Gisborne

Sights

1 Captain Cook Statue C4
2 Cook Monument C4
3 Cook Observatory D4
4 Cook's Plaza C4
5 Gisborne Botanic Gardens C1
6 Statue of Young Nick C4
7 Sunshine Brewing Company B2
8 Tairawhiti Museum D2
9 Te Tauihu Turanga Whakamana D3
10 Titirangi Lookout D4
11 Titirangi Park D4

Activities, Courses & Tours

12 Gisborne Cycle Tours C3
13 Gisborne Wine Centre D3
14 Olympic Pool A3

Sleeping

15 Emerald Hotel D3
16 Gisborne YHA D3
17 Pacific Harbour Motor Inn C3
18 Te Kura B&B D2
19 Teal Motor Lodge B1
20 Waikanae Beach Top 10 Holiday Park C3

Eating

21 Bookshop Café C3
Café 1874 .... (see 12)
22 Morrell's B1
23 Pak N Save C2
24 USSCO Bar & Bistro C3
25 Villaggio C1
26 Yoko Sushi C2

Drinking

27 Smash Palace A3
The Rivers .... (see 15)

Entertainment

Poverty Bay Club .... (see 12)

Awaken your sense of mortality with a shark-cage dive from **Surfit Charters** (☎06-867 2970; www.surfit.co.nz; per person $310). Tamer fishing and snorkelling trips can also be arranged.

The extreme in local watery sports has to be **Rere Rockslide** (Wharekopae Rd). This natural phenomenon occurs in a section of the Rere River 50km northwest of Gisborne along Wharekopae Rd. Grab a tyre tube or boogie board to cushion the worst of the bumps and slide down the 60m-long rocky run into the pool at the bottom. Three kilometres downriver, the **Rere Falls** send a 30m-wide curtain of water over a 10m drop; you can walk behind it if you don't mind getting wet.

Walking

There are stacks of walks to tackle in the area, starting with a gentle stroll along the river. The i-SITE can provide you with brochures for the **Historic Walk** and the **Arts & Crafts Trail**. The *Walking Trails of Gisborne City* brochure details a further five walks around the city cenre.

Winding its way through farmland and forest with commanding views, the **Te Kuri Walkway** (two hours, 5.6km, closed August to October) starts 4km north of town at the end of Shelley Rd.

Tours

Tipuna Tours CULTURAL TOUR
(☎027 240 4493, 06-862 6118; www.tipunatours.com; half-day tour $60-120) Anne offers meaningful insights into Maori culture on her small-group tours, including the half-day trip to Tolaga Bay. Visit the sites and hear the stories, including the *Whale Rider* legend.

Gisborne Cycle Tours CYCLING
(☎06-927 7021; www.gisbornecycletours.co.nz; Poverty Bay Club, 38 Childers Rd; half-day tour $100, freedom hire from $50 per day) Half-day to multiday guided cycle tours around local sights and further afield including wineries and Eastwoodhill Aboretum. Take the half-day cultural tour and you can keep the bike all day. Cheaper rates for multiday freedom bike hire (maps and advice on tap).

Festivals & Events

Gisborne Food & Wine Festival FOOD & WINE
(www.gisbornewine.co.nz; tickets $75) On October's Labour Day weekend, local wine makers and foodies pool talents for the Gisborne Food & Wine Festival held at a local vineyard. Top NZ musical talent usually makes an appearance.

Sleeping

Gisborne's speciality is midrange motor lodges and the ubiquitous beachside motel. Budget travellers will find their options limited.

Knapdale Eco Lodge LODGE $$$
(☎06-862 5444; www.knapdale.co.nz; 114 Snowsill Rd, Waihirere; d incl breakfast $398-472; @☎)

Indulge and relax at this tranquil idyll complete with lake, farm animals and home-grown produce. The stunning modern lodge is filled with international artwork, its glassy frontage flowing out to an expansive patio area, with brazier, barbecue and pizza oven. Five-course dinner by arrangement ($85). The lodge is 10km northwest of Gisborne, via Back Ormond Rd.

Te Kura B&B B&B $$
(06-863 3497; www.tekura.co.nz; 14 Cheeseman Rd; d $120-140;) Play lord of the manor at this lovely 1920s Arts and Crafts-style riverside home. Two guest rooms (one with clawfoot-bath en suite) share a stately lounge and a bright breakfast room opening on to the swimming pool and Waimata River.

Teal Motor Lodge MOTEL $$
(0800 838 325, 06-868 4019; www.teal.co.nz; 479 Gladstone Rd; d $125-135, tr/q $175/215; @) With super street appeal on the high street (500m to town), the mildly aeronautical Teal boasts a solid offering of tidy, family-friendly units with the bonus of a pleasant swimming-pool area and lots of lawn to run around on.

Gisborne YHA HOSTEL $
(06-867 3269; www.yha.co.nz; 32 Harris St; dm/s/d $26/48/64; @) A short stroll across the river from town, this rambling mansion houses a well-kept hostel. The rooms are large and comfortable, while outside there's a pleasant deck and lawns for communing. Family ensuite unit available.

Eastwoodhill Arboretum LODGE $
(06-863 9003; www.eastwoodhill.org.nz; 2392 Wharekopae Rd, Ngatapa; dm/tw $40/70) The bunks and private rooms are basic and you'll still need to pay the garden admission on the first day (adult/child $15/free), but once you're here, endless woody delights can fill your days and nights. Meals can be provided by arrangement, or you can use the fully-equipped kitchen. Remember to bring food though as there's nothing for miles around.

Waikanae Beach Top 10 Holiday Park HOLIDAY PARK $
(0800 867 563, 06-867 5634; www.waikanaebeachtop10.co.nz; Grey St; sites from $18, units $60-145; @) Right by the beach and a pleasant 10-minute walk to town, this grassy holiday park offers good-value built accommodation and grassy lanes for pitching tents and parking vans.

Emerald Hotel HOTEL $$
(06-868 8055; www.emeraldhotel.co.nz; cnr Reads Quay & Gladstone Rd; r $140-280; @) The modern Emerald is all about the swimming pool and patio area, which makes a reasonable fist of looking like a foxy international. Surrounding it are 48 luxury suites running along epic corridors connecting the various wings. There's a gym, day spa, and the Grill Room restaurant (mains $28 to $35).

Pacific Harbour Motor Inn MOTEL $$
(06-867 8847; www.pacific-harbour.co.nz; 24 Reads Quay; r $130-190, ste $130-195; @) Overlooking the harbour, this apartment-style inn offers well-kept units with no-frills decor and the bonus of good balconies.

Eating

TOP CHOICE **USSCO Bar & Bistro** MODERN NZ $$
(06-868 3246; 16 Childers Rd; mains $30; dinner) Housed in the restored Union Steam Ship Company building (hence the name), this place is all class. Silky kitchen skills shine in a highly seasonal menu featuring the likes of pan-fried fish with ratatouille and creamed mussel sauce. Devilishly good desserts, plus plenty of local wines and NZ craft beers. Generous portions, multi-course deals and live piano on some nights.

Villaggio CAFE $$
(06-863 3895; 57 Ballance St; lunch mains $18-28, dinner mains $28-32; 8am-4pm Sun-Wed, til late Thu-Sat) On the north side of the river, not far from the Botanic Gardens, this dear old art-deco home has been respectfully stripped back, its new scheme of red, white and wood making this cafe super-smart and edgy. The food's on the modern side too, offering fresh takes on the classics (seafood chowder, fish and chips), as well as a colourful array of Med-style dishes such as spaghetti with tomato, goat cheese and herbs, and Moroccan vegetable tagine. Pleasant garden invites loitering over lunchtime wines.

Café 1874 CAFE $
(38 Childers Rd; meals $10-22;) The creaky old grandeur of the Poverty Bay gentleman's club (1874) is reason enough to visit. This cafe within it certainly adds impetus: appealing counter food, all-day brunch, pizza, blackboard specials, reasonable prices and

a pleasant garden. Bike hire and boutique shopping share the building.

Bookshop Café CAFE $

(62 Gladstone Rd; meals $7-12;) Situated above Muirs Bookshop, a beloved, age-old independent in a lovely heritage building, this simple cafe offers a small but sweet selection of counter food and excellent salads. Fans of fine espresso coffee and literature may need to be forcibly removed. Atmospheric balcony for those balmy days.

Morrell's BAKERY $

(437 Gladstone Rd; 7am-2pm Tue-Sat;) Artisan bakers with killer pies, wholesome bread and delicious patisserie.

Yoko Sushi SUSHI $

(87 Grey St; sushi $5-12) Looks like the Gisbonites have well and truly taken to sushi, if the lunchtime trade at this sparky sushi bar is anything to go by. Commendable sushi, along with the usual miso-lany of extras including the bento box and octopus dumplings. Ample seating for eating in, plus pavement tables.

Pak N Save SUPERMARKET

(274 Gladstone Rd; 7am-9pm) Fill up the trolley, and don't forget your Gisborne oranges.

Drinking & Entertainment

The Rivers PUB

(cnr Gladstone Rd & Reads Quay) This well-run, British-style pub does the business, offering steak-and-ale pie, proper pudding, big-screen telly and pool. It's also family-friendly and cosy, with some stonework and choice artefacts adding a veneer of history in what could otherwise be a plain, corner pub in the bottom of a big new hotel.

Smash Palace PUB

(24 Banks St) Get juiced at the junkyard. Iconic drinking den full to the gunwales with ephemera and its very own DC3 crash-landed in the garden bar. Occasional live music.

Poverty Bay Club LIVE MUSIC, CINEMA

(www.thepovertybayclub.co.nz; 38 Childers Rd) Sharing this lovely old historic building with a cafe and art shop is Winston's Bar where occasional music events are held, as well as the bean-bagged **Dome Cinema** (08-324 3005; www.domecinema.co.nz), which shows arthouse films on Wednesday, Thursday and Sunday evenings.

Information

The major banks are located along Gladstone Rd.

DOC (06-869 0460; www.doc.govt.nz; 63 Carnarvon St; 8am-4.30pm Mon-Fri) Tourist information.

Gisborne Hospital (06-869 0500; Ormond Rd)

Gisborne i-SITE (06-868 6139; www.gisbornenz.com; 209 Grey St; 8.30am-5.30pm Mon-Fri, 9am-5pm Sat, 10am-4pm Sun; @) Beside a doozy of a Canadian totem pole, this information centre has all and sundry, as well as a travel booking office, internet access, toilets and a minigolf course ($4).

Police Station (06-869 0200; cnr Gladstone Rd & Customhouse St)

Post Office (cnr Gladstone Rd & Bright St)

Getting There & Around

The **Travel Centre** (06-868 6139; 209 Grey St) at the i-SITE handles bookings for many local and national transport services.

Air

Gisborne Airport (www.eastland.co.nz/airport; Aerodrome Rd) is 3km west of the city. **Air New Zealand** (0800 737 000; www.airnewzealand.co.nz) flies to/from Auckland and Wellington, with onward connections. Check the website for fares and special offers.

Sunair Aviation (0800 786 247; www.sunair.co.nz) offers flights on weekdays to Hamilton, Napier, Paparaumu, Rotorua and Tauranga (from $280).

Bus

InterCity (p334) buses depart daily from the i-SITE for Napier (from $30) via Wairoa (from $15), and Auckland (from $38) via Opotiki (from $18) and Rotorua (from $23).

Organised penny-pinchers can take advantage of limited $1 advance fares on **Naked Bus** (www.nakedbus.com) to Auckland via Opotiki and Rotorua.

For courier services from Gisborne to Opotiki travelling via East Cape's scenic SH35, see East Cape (p334).

Car

Conveniently, **Gisborne Airport Car Rental** (0800 556 606; www.gisborneairportcarhire.co.nz) is an agent for 10 car-hire companies including the big brands and local outfits.

Taxi

A city-to-airport taxi fare costs about $20.

Eastland Taxis
(0800 282 947, 06-867 6667)

Gisborne Taxis
(0800 505 55523, 06-867 2222)

Gisborne to Hawke's Bay

From Gisborne, heading south towards Napier you're confronted with a choice: follow SH2, which runs closer to the coast, or take SH36 inland via Tiniroto. Either way you'll end up in Wairoa.

The coastal route is a marginally better choice, being quicker and offering occasional views out to sea. However, SH36 (Tiniroto Road) is also a pleasant drive with several good stopping points en route. **Doneraille Park**, 49km from Gisborne, is a peaceful bush reserve with a frigid river to jump into and freedom camping for self-contained vehicles. Avid tree-lovers might like to check out **Hackfalls Arboretum** (entry $10), a 4km detour from the turn-off at the tidy Tiniroto Tavern. The snow-white cascades of **Te Reinga Falls**, 12km further south, are well worth a stop.

The busier SH2 route heads inland and soon enters the **Wharerata State Forest** (so beware of logging trucks around these parts). Just out of the woods, 55km from Gisborne, **Morere Hot Springs** (www.morerehotsprings.co.nz; SH2; adult/child $6/3; ⏲10am-5pm, to 9pm summer) burble up from a fault line in the **Morere Springs Scenic Reserve**. You might want to tackle the bushwalks (20 minutes to two hours) before taking the plunge. The main swimming pool is near the entrance, but a five-minute walk through virgin rainforest leads to the Nikau Baths. The reserve is quite lovely, much favoured by locals who visit for a family day out. Long may it continue, although with the spring outlet threatened by landslips upriver, the day may soon come when the hot tap is turned off.

There's accommodation at Morere. You won't miss the **Morere Tearooms & Camping Ground** (☎06-837 8792; SH2; campsites from $30, d $60-90) where you can get a respectable toasted sandwich and avail yourself of campsites and basic cabins alongside the babbling Tunanui Stream. Just over the stream is **Morere Hot Springs Lodge** (☎06-837 8824; www.morerehotsprings.co.nz; SH2; s/d/tr/q $80/95/115/135), a farmy enclave where the lambs gambol and the dog wags her tail at you nonstop. Sleeping options are a classic 1917 farmhouse with sweet sleep-out, or two adorable cabins.

From Gisborne on SH2, keep an eye out for the unusually brightly painted **Taane-nui-a-Rangi Marae**. You can get a decent view from the road; don't enter unless invited.

SH2 continues south to Nuhaka at the northern end of Hawke Bay. From here it's west to Wairoa or east to the salty **Mahia Peninsula**. Not far from the Nuhaka roundabout is **Kahungunu Marae**. From the street you can see the carving at the house's apex of a standing warrior holding a *taiaha* (spear). It's less stylised than most traditional carving, opting for simple realism.

Te Urewera National Park

Shrouded in mist and mysticism, Te Urewera National Park is the North Island's largest, encompassing 212,673 hectares of virgin forest cut with lakes and rivers. The highlight is **Lake Waikaremoana** (Sea of Rippling Waters), a deep crucible of water encircled by the Lake Waikaremoana Track, one of NZ's Great Walks. Rugged bluffs drop away to reedy inlets, the lake's mirror surface disturbed only by mountain zephyrs and the occasional waterbird taking to the skies.

The name Te Urewera still has the capacity to make Pakeha New Zealanders feel slightly uneasy – and not just because

WORTH A TRIP

MAHIA PENINSULA

The Mahia Peninsula's eroded hills, sandy beaches and vivid blue sea make it a mini-ringer of the Coromandel, without the tourist hordes and fancy subdivisions, and with the bonus of dramatic Dover-ish cliffs. It's an enduring holiday spot for East Coasters, who come largely for boaty, beachy stuff, and you can easily get in on the action if you have your own transport. A day or two could easily be spent visiting the scenic reserve and the bird-filled Maungawhio Lagoon, hanging out at the beach (Mahia Beach at sunset can be spectacular), or even playing a round of golf at the friendly golf course.

Mahia has several small settlements offering between them a couple of guesthouses, a grotty campsite, a decent pub and a dairy. See www.voyagemahia.co.nz for more information.

Lake Waikaremoana Track

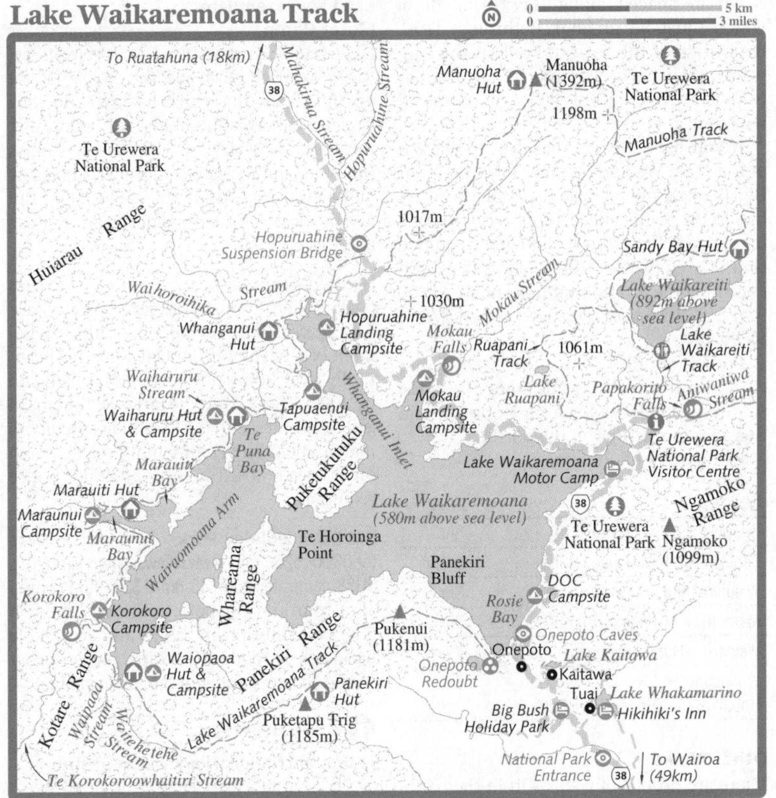

it translates as 'The Burnt Penis'. There's something primal and untamed about this wild woodland, with its rich history of Maori resistance.

The local Tuhoe people – prosaically known as the 'Children of the Mist' – never signed the Treaty of Waitangi and fought with Rewi Maniapoto at Orakau during the Waikato Wars. The army of Te Kooti (p347) took refuge here during running battles with government troops. The claimant of Te Kooti's spiritual mantle, Rua Kenana, led a thriving community beneath the sacred mountain Maungapohatu (1366m) from 1905 until his politically motivated 1916 arrest. This effectively erased the last bastion of Maori independence in the country. Maungapohatu never recovered, and only a small settlement remains. Nearby, Ruatahuna's extraordinary Mataatua Marae celebrates Te Kooti's exploits.

Tuhoe remain proud of their identity and traditions, with around 40% still speaking *te reo* (the language) on a regular basis.

Activities

Lake Waikaremoana Track

The 46km, three- to four-day tramp scales the spectacular Panekiri Bluff, with open panoramas interspersed with fern groves and forest. The walk is rated as moderate with the only difficult section being the Panekiri ascent, and during summer it can get busy.

Although it's a year-round track, winter rain deters many people and makes conditions much more challenging. At this altitude (580m above sea level), temperatures can drop quickly, even in summer. Walkers should take portable stoves and fuel as there are no cooking facilities en route.

There are five huts (adult/child $32/free) and campsites (per night adult/child

$14/free) spaced along the track, all of which must be prebooked through DOC, regardless of the season. Book at the Aniwaniwa, Gisborne, Wairoa, Whakatane or Napier DOC offices, i-SITEs or online at www.doc.govt.nz.

If you have a car, it is safest to leave it at the Lake Waikaremoana Motor Camp or Big Bush Holiday Park then take a water taxi to the trailheads. Alternatively, you can take the fully catered, four-night guided tour offered by the enthusiastic and experienced people at **Walking Legends** (☎0800 925 569; www.walkinglegends.com; adult/child $1290/1000).

Propel yourself onto the trail either clockwise from just outside **Onepoto** in the south or anticlockwise from **Hopuruahine Suspension Bridge** in the north.

Estimated walking times:

ROUTE	TIME
Onepoto to Panekiri Hut	5hr
Panekiri Hut to Waiopaoa Hut	3-4hr
Waiopaoa Hut to Marauiti Hut	5hr
Marauiti Hut to Waiharuru Hut	2hr
Waiharuru Hut to Whanganui Hut	2½hr
Whanganui Hut to Hopuruahine Suspension Bridge	2hr

Other Walks

There are dozens of walks within the park's vast boundaries, most of which are outlined in DOC's *Lake Waikaremoana Walks* and *Recreation in Northern Te Urewera* pamphlets ($2.50).

With its untouched islands, **Lake Waikareiti** (892m) is an enchanting place. Starting nearby the DOC visitor centre, it's an hour's walk to its shore. Once you're there, a fitting way to explore it is in a rowboat (unlock one with a key collected from the visitor centre for $20 for four hours). You may also be lured in for a skinny dip.

The **Ruapani Track** (six hours), starting at the same place, is a circuit that passes seven wetlands as it wends through dense, virgin forest.

Numerous shorter walks (less than an hour) are easily accessible from the visitor centre and Waikaremoana Motor Camp.

Sleeping & Eating

DOC has more than 30 huts and campsites within the park, most of which are very basic.

Lake Waikaremoana Motor Camp HOLIDAY PARK **$**
(☎06-837 3826; www.lake.co.nz; campsites per adult/child $15/5, cabins $55, units $90-160) Right on the shore, this place has Swiss-looking chalets, fisherman's cabins and campsites, most with watery views. The on-site shop is full of essentials such as hot pies, chocolate and a swarm of fishing flies. The camp can also hook you up with water taxis, shuttles and petrol.

Hikihiki's Inn B&B **$$**
(☎06-837 3701; www.hikihiki.co.nz; 9 Rotten Row, Tuai; s/d $80/160) In the sweet little settlement of Tuai, 6km from Onepoto, this beautifully kept home now serves as a B&B run by '100% Kiwi' hosts. The little weatherboard gem is quintessential NZ, with hospitality to match, including continental breakfast and other meals at extra cost (24 hours notice required).

Big Bush Holiday Park HOLIDAY PARK **$**
(☎0800 525 392; www.lakewaikaremoana.co.nz; SH38; campsites from $15, dm/d $30/95) Located 4km from the Onepoto trailhead, Big Bush offers tent sites, trim cabins and acceptable backpacker rooms. Pick-ups, water taxis/scenic charters and storage are available.

Information

Te Urewera National Park Visitor Centre (☎06-837 3803; www.doc.govt.nz; SH38, Aniwaniwa; ⏲8am-4.45pm) has weather forecasts, accommodation information and hut or campsite passes for the Lake Waikaremoana Track.

See also www.teurewera.co.nz.

Getting There & Around

Approximately 95km of SH 38 between Wairoa and Rotorua remains unsealed and it'll take around four bone-rattling hours to do the entire journey (Wairoa to Aniwaniwa 61km, Aniwaniwa to Rotorua 139km).

Big Bush Water Taxi (☎0800 525 392; www.lakewaikaremoana.co.nz) will ship you to either Onepoto or Hopuruahine trailhead ($35 return), with hut-to-hut pack transfers for the less gung-ho. It also runs shuttles to and from Wairoa ($40 one way). More shuttle action is offered by **Route 38 Shuttles** (☎021 042 9972).

Home Bay Water Taxi & Shuttles (☎06-837 3826; www.waikaremoana.com) does boat runs from Lake Waikaremoana Motor Camp to stops all around the lake (trailhead $40 return), offers lake cruises ($40) and runs a shuttle to Wairoa ($80 for four people).

TE KOOTI

Maori history is littered with mystics, prophets and warriors, one of whom is the legendary Te Kooti (rhymes with naughty, not booty).

In 1865 he fought with the government against the Hauhau (adherents of the Pai Marire faith, founded by another warrior-prophet) but was accused of being a spy and imprisoned on the Chatham Islands without trial.

While there, Te Kooti studied the Bible and claimed to receive visions from the archangel Michael. His charismatic preaching and 'miracles' – including producing flames from his hands (his captors claimed he used phosphorus from the head of matches) – helped win over the Pai Marire to his distinctly Maori take on Christianity.

In 1867 Te Kooti led an astounding escape from the Chathams, hijacking a supply ship and sailing to Poverty Bay with 200 followers. En route he threw a doubter overboard as a sacrifice. Upon their safe arrival, Te Kooti's disciples raised their right hands in homage to God rather than bowing submissively; *ringa tu* (upraised hand) became the name of his church.

Te Kooti requested a dialogue with the colonial government but was once again rebuffed, with magistrate Reginald Biggs demanding his immediate surrender. Unimpressed by Pakeha justice, Te Kooti commenced a particularly effective guerrilla campaign – starting by killing Biggs and around 50 others (including women and children, Maori and Pakeha) at Matawhero near Gisborne.

A four-year chase ensued. Eventually Te Kooti took refuge in the King Country, the Maori king's vast dominion where government troops feared to tread.

Proving the pointlessness of the government's approach to the whole affair, Te Kooti was officially pardoned in 1883. By this time his reputation as a prophet and healer had spread and his Ringatu Church was firmly established – at the most recent census it boasted over 16,000 adherents.

HAWKE'S BAY

Hawke Bay, the name given to the body of water that stretches from the Mahia Peninsula to Cape Kidnappers, looks like it's been bitten out of the North Island's eastern flank. Add an apostrophe and an 's' and you've got a region that stretches south and inland to include fertile farmland, surf beaches, mountainous ranges and forests.

The southern edge of the bay is a travel-channel come to life – food, wine and architecture are the shared obsessions. It's smugly comfortable but thoroughly appealing, and is best viewed through a rosé-tinted wineglass. If the weather's putting a dampener on your beach-holiday plans, it's a great place to head.

Wairoa to Napier

The small town of **Wairoa** is trying hard to shirk its rough-edged reputation, and a walk along its riverside promenade on a sunny day will leave you wondering whether those edges are smoothing off. Not scintillating enough to warrant an extended stay, the town has a couple of points of interest, including an exceptional pie shop called **Oslers**. Non-consumable attractions include the **Wairoa Museum** and the nearby **Whakaki Lake** wetland. The town has a couple of motels and a cracker little campsite.

The stretch of highway between Wairoa and Napier traipses through unphotogenic farmland and forestry blocks for much of its 117km. Most of it follows a railway line that is currently only used for freight – you'll see what a travesty that is when you pass under the **Mohaka viaduct** (1937), the highest rail viaduct in Australasia (97m). The litter-strewn roadside rest area here does little to honour this grand construction.

Occupied by early Maori, **Lake Tutira** has walkways and a bird sanctuary. At Tutira village, just north of the lake, Pohokura Rd leads to the wonderful **Boundary Stream Reserve**, a major conservation area. Three loop tracks start from the road, ranging in length from 40 minutes to three hours. Also along this road you'll find the **Opouahi** and **Bellbird Bush Scenic Reserves**, which both offer rewarding walks.

Hawke's Bay

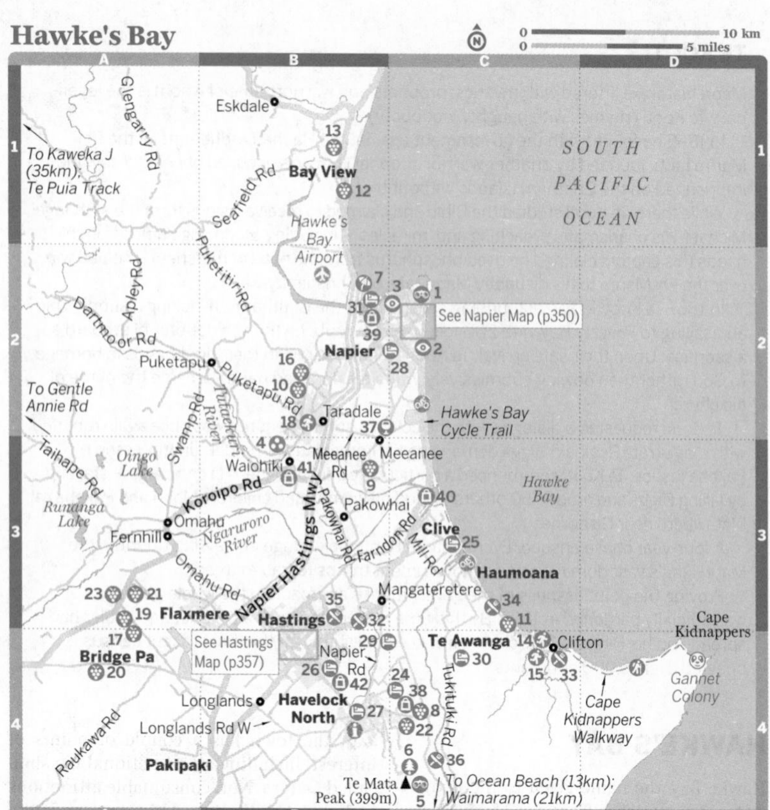

Off Waipatiki Rd, 34km outside Napier, Waipatiki Beach is a beaut spot boasting a low-key campsite and the 64-hectare **Waipatiki Scenic Reserve**. Further down the line, **White Pine Bush Scenic Reserve**, 29km from Napier on SH2, bristles with kahikatea and nikau palms. **Tangoio Falls Scenic Reserve**, 27km north of Napier, has Te Ana Falls, stands of wheki-ponga (tree ferns) and native orchids. Between White Pine and Tangoio reserves the **Tangoio Walkway** (three hours return) follows Kareaara Stream.

The highway surfs the coast for the last 25km, with impressive views towards Napier. Hawke's Bay wine country starts in earnest at the mouth of the Esk River. Even the driver should safely be able to stop for a restrained tasting at one of the excellent vineyards just off SH2 (or both if you're spitting).

Esk Valley Estate is a lovely spot to bring your picnic and enjoy some great reds. With its relaxed, rustic feel, **Crab Farm Winery** (Map p348; www.crabfarmwinery.co.nz; 511 Main Rd, Bay View; tastings free; ⏲10am-5pm Fri-Sun, cafe 12-3pm Fri-Sun, dinner Fri) is a good stop for lunch and a glass of rosé (among others).

Napier

POP 58,800

The Napier of today is the silver lining of the dark cloud that was one of NZ's worst natural disasters. Rebuilt after the deadly 1931 earthquake in the popular styles of the time, the city retains a unique concentration of art-deco buildings to which architecture obsessives flock from all over the world. Don't expect the Chrysler Building – Napier's art deco is resolutely low-rise – but you will find intact 1930s streetscapes, which can

Hawke's Bay

Sights

1 Bluff Hill Lookout C2
2 National Aquarium of New Zealand C2
3 National Tobacco Company Building C2
4 Otatara Pa B3
5 Te Mata Peak Lookout C4
6 Te Mata Trust Park C4
7 Westshore Beach B2

Activities, Courses & Tours

8 Black Barn Vineyards C4
9 Brookfields B3
10 Church Road B2
11 Clearview Estate C3
12 Crab Farm Winery B1
13 Esk Valley Estate B1
14 Gannet Beach Adventures C4
15 Gannet Safaris C4
Hawke's Bay Wine Country Cat .... (see 3)
16 Mission Estate B2
17 Ngatarawa A4
Pandora Kayaks .... (see 39)
18 Pedal Power B2
19 Salvare Estate A3
20 Sileni Estates A4
Splash Planet .... (see 26)
21 Te Awa A3
22 Te Mata Estate C4
23 Trinity Hill A3

Sleeping

24 Arataki Holiday Park C4
25 Clive Colonial Cottages C3
Crown Hotel .... (see 3)
26 Hastings Top 10 Holiday Park B4
27 Havelock North Motor Lodge B4
28 Kennedy Park Top 10 Resort C2
29 Mangapapa Petit Hotel B4
30 Millar Road C4
31 Rocks Motorlodge B2

Eating

32 Bay Espresso B3
BJs Bakery .... (see 27)
33 Clifton Bay Café C4
Deliciosa .... (see 27)
Diva .... (see 27)
34 Elephant Hill C3
35 Hastings Farmers Market B3
Pipi .... (see 27)
36 Terrôir at Craggy Range C4
Vidal .... (see 26)
Westshore Fish Café .... (see 31)

Drinking

37 Filter Room B2
Loading Ramp .... (see 27)
Rose & Shamrock .... (see 27)

Entertainment

Gintrap .... (see 3)
Globe Theatrette .... (see 3)
Shed 2 .... (see 3)
Thirsty Whale .... (see 3)

Shopping

38 Arataki Honey C4
39 Classic Sheepskins B2
40 Hohepa Organic Cheeses C3
41 Silky Oak Chocolate Company B3
Strawberry Patch .... (see 27)
42 Telegraph Hill B4

provoke a *Great Gatsby* swagger in the least romantic soul.

For the layperson it's a charismatic, sunny, composed city with the air of an affluent English seaside resort about it.

History

The area has been settled since around the 12th century and was known to Maori as Ahuriri. By the time James Cook eyeballed it in October 1769, Ngati Kahungunu was the dominant tribe, controlling the coast to Wellington.

In the 1830s whalers malingered around Ahuriri, establishing a trading base in 1839. By the 1850s the Crown had purchased – by often dubious means – 1.4 million acres of Hawke's Bay land, leaving Ngati Kahungunu with less than 4000 acres. The town of Napier was planned in 1854 and obsequiously named after the British general and colonial administrator Charles Napier.

At 10.46am on 3 February 1931, the city was levelled by a catastrophic earthquake (7.9 on the Richter scale). Fatalities in Napier and nearby Hastings numbered 258. Napier suddenly found itself 40 sq km larger, as the earthquake heaved sections of what was once a lagoon 2m above sea level (Napier airport was once more 'port', less 'air'). A fevered rebuilding program ensued, constructing one of the world's most uniformly art-deco cities.

Napier

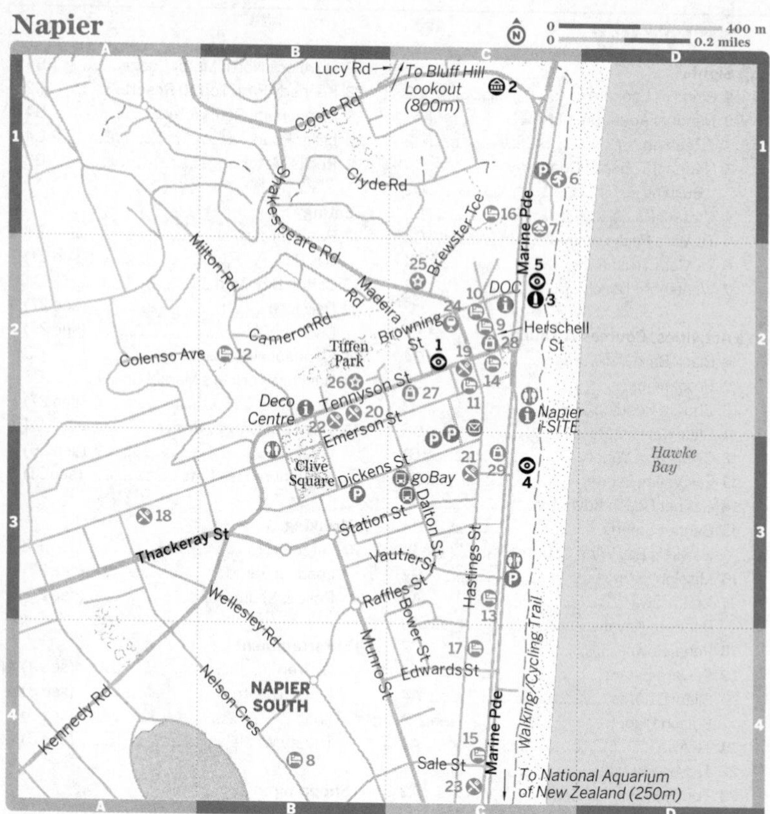

Sights

Napier's claim to fame is undoubtedly its architecture, and a close study of these treasures could take several days (especially if you stop often to shop and eat). There are, however, many other interesting diversions, not least of all the area's many wineries (p360).

Architecture

The 1931 quake demolished most of Napier's brick buildings. Frantic reconstruction between 1931 and 1933 caught architects in the throes of global art-deco mania. Art deco, along with Spanish Mission and Stripped Classical, was cheap (debts were high), safe (falling stone columns and balconies had killed many during the earthquake) and contemporary (residents wanted to make a fresh start).

The place to start your art-deco exploration is the home of the Art Deco Trust, the **Deco Centre** (www.artdeconapier.com; 163 Tennyson St; ⊙9am-5pm) opposite colourful Clive Sq. Its one-hour guided deco walk ($16) departs the i-SITE daily at 10am; the two-hour version ($21) leaves the Centre at 2pm daily and includes an introductory spiel. These excellent walks include an introductory spiel, DVD screening and refreshments. The Deco Centre has a lovely little shop, and stocks brochures for the excellent self-guided *Art Deco Walk* ($5), *Art Deco Scenic Drive* ($5) and *Marewa Meander* ($3). You can also hire art-deco–style bikes from here, and set off on a self-guided tour of up to four hours ($50).

If you haven't got time for guided or self-guided art-deco walking tours of Napier, just take to the streets – particularly Tennyson and Emerson. Remember to look up! The **Daily Telegraph Building** (Map p350; 49 Tennyson St) is one of the stars of the show, with superb zigzags, fountain shapes and ziggurat aesthetic. If the building is open, nip inside and ogle at the painstakingly restored foyer.

Napier

Sights
1 Daily Telegraph Building C2
2 Napier Prison C1
3 Pania of the Reef C2
4 Sunken Gardens C3
5 Tom Parker Fountain C2

Activities, Courses & Tours
6 Fishbike C1
7 Ocean Spa C1

Sleeping
8 Aqua Lodge B4
9 Archie's Bunker C2
10 County Hotel C2
11 Criterion Art Deco Backpackers C2
12 Green House on the Hill B2
13 Manor on Parade C3
14 Masonic Hotel C2
Napier YHA ..... (see 13)
15 Nautilus C4
Sea Breeze ..... (see 13)
16 Seaview Lodge B&B C1
17 Stables Lodge Backpackers C4

Eating
18 Burger Fuel A3
19 Café Ujazi C2
Farmers Market ..... (see 1)
20 Groove Kitchen Espresso B2
21 Kilim Café C3
22 Kitchen Table B2
23 Restaurant Indonesia C4

Drinking
24 Brazen Head C2
Med Bar ..... (see 14)

Entertainment
25 Cabana Bar C2
26 Napier Municipal Theatre B2

Shopping
27 Beattie & Forbes C2
28 Decorum C2
29 Opossum World C3

Around the shore at Ahuriri, the **National Tobacco Company Building** (Map p348; cnr Bridge & Ossian Sts) is arguably the region's deco masterpiece. Built in 1933, it combines art-deco forms with the natural motifs of art nouveau. Roses, *raupo* (bulrushes) and grapevines frame the elegantly curved entrance. During business hours it's possible to pull on the leaf-shaped brass door handles and enter the first two rooms.

Other Sights

Marine Parade STREET

Napier's elegant avenue is lined with huge Norfolk Island pines, and dotted with motels and charming timber villas. Along its length are parks, **sunken gardens** (Map p350), a minigolf course, a swimming complex and aquarium. Near the north end of the parade is the **Tom Parker Fountain** (Map p350), which is best viewed at night when it is lavishly lit. Next to it is **Pania of the Reef** (Map p350) (1954), with her dubious boobs.

National Aquarium of New Zealand AQUARIUM

(Map p348; www.nationalaquarium.co.nz; 546 Marine Pde; adult/child/family $17.40/8.70/41.90; 9am-5pm, feedings 10am & 2pm) Inside this modern complex with its stingray-inspired roof are piranhas, terrapins, eels, kiwi, tuatara and a whole lotta fish. 'Behind the Scenes' tours (adult/child $34.80/17.40) leave at 9am and 1pm and snorkellers can swim with sharks ($60).

Napier Prison HISTORIC BUILDING

(Map p350; www.napierprison.com; 55 Coote Rd; tours $20) If you fancy going to jail, Napier Prison Tours offers fascinating self-guided audio tours in 16 languages (9am to 9pm) and hosted tours (9.30am and 3pm).

Bluff Hill Lookout LOOKOUT

(Map p348) The circuitous route to the top (102m) makes a pleasant wander and rewards with expansive views. The well-loved lookout itself is a nice spot for a picnic, which might just give you the excuse you need to drive up in your car.

Otatara Pa ARCHAEOLOGICAL SITE

(Map p348) Wooden palisades, carved *pou* (memorial posts) and a carved gate help bring this *pa* site to life. An hour-long loop walk across grassy hills passes barely-discernible archaeological remains but affords terrific views of the surrounding countryside. From the city head southwest on Taradale Rd and Gloucester St. Turn right into Springfield Rd just before the river.

Activities

Most of the city's activities require energy to burn and moderate risk of personal injury. Speaking of which, Napier's pebbly beach isn't safe for swimming; locals head north

CYCLE THE BAY

The expanding network of **Hawke's Bay Cycle Trails** offers cycling opportunities from short, city scoots to hilly, single-track shenanagins.

Napier is cycle-friendly, particularly along Marine Parade where you'll find **Fishbike** (Map p350; www.fishbike.co.nz; 26 Marine Pde; bike hire from $15; ⏲9am-5pm) renting comfortable bikes – including tandems for those willing to risk divorce.

Dedicated cycle trails stretch from Napier, north to Westshore and Bay View, inland to Taradale and the wineries around Flaxmere, and south along the coast all the way to Clifton. The *Hawke's Bay Cycle Map* can be picked up from the i-SITE or www.hawkesbaynz.com/visit/cyclinghawkesbay. Fit mountain bikers should head to **Eskdale Mountain Bike Park** (www.hawkesbaymtb.co.nz; 3-week permit $7) for a whole lot of fun in the forest. Hire mountain bikes from **Pedal Power** (Map p348; ☎06-844 9771; www.pedalpower.co.nz; 340 Gloucester St; half-/full day from $30/60), just out of the city centre in Taradale.

Given the condusive climate, terrain and multitudinous tracks, it's no surprise that numerous cycle companies pedal their fully geared-up tours around the Bay. These include:

» **Bike About Tours** (☎06-845 4836; www.bikeabouttours.co.nz; half- to full day $35-60)
» **Bike D'Vine** (☎06-833 6697; www.bikedevine.com; adult/child from $45/25)
» **On Yer Bike** (☎06-879 8735; www.onyerbikehb.co.nz; full day without/with lunch $50/60)
» **Takaro Trails** (☎06-836 5385; www.takarotrails.co.nz; half- to full day $55-85)
» **Village Cycle Tours & Hire** (☎06-650 7722; www.villagecycletours.co.nz; half-/full day $40/60)

of the city to **Westshore** (Map p348) or to the surf beaches south of Cape Kidnappers.

Ocean Spa SWIMMING
(Map p350; www.oceanspa.co.nz; 42 Marine Pde; adult/child $9/7, private pools 30min adult/child $12/9; ⏲6am-10pm Mon-Sat, 8am-10pm Sun) A spiffy waterfront pool complex that features a lane pool, hot pools, a beauty spa and gym.

Pandora Kayaks KAYAKING
(Map p348; www.pandorakayaks.co.nz; 53 Pandora Rd; kayaks per hr from $14, bikes per day from $30) Situated on the shore of Pandora Pond, these folks hire out kayaks, surfboards, windsurfers, stand-up paddle boards, small yachts and bikes. Windsurfing and sailing lessons available.

Mountain Valley ADVENTURE SPORTS
(☎06-834 9756; www.mountainvalley.co.nz; 408 McVicar Rd, Te Pohue; horse treks from $30, rafting from $60) Sixty kilometres north of Napier on SH5, Mountain Valley is a hub of outdoorsy activities including horse trekking, whitewater rafting, kayaking and fly fishing. There's also accommodation on-site.

Tours

Numerous operators offer tours of the art-deco delights and excursions around the local area.

Absolute de Tours GUIDED TOUR
(☎06-844 8699; www.absolutedetours.co.nz) Runs the 'Deco Tour' of the city, Marewa and Bluff Hill ($38, 75 minutes) in conjunction with the Deco Centre, as well as half-day tours of Napier and Hastings ($60).

Ferg's Fantastic Tours GUIDED TOUR
(☎0800 428 687; www.fergstours.co.nz; tours $40-120) Tours from two to seven hours, exploring Napier and surrounding areas.

Hawke's Bay Scenic Tours GUIDED TOUR
(☎06-844 5693; www.hbscenictours.co.nz; tours $50-90) Five tour options including the 'Napier Whirlwind' and wineries.

Hawke's Bay Wine Country Cat BOAT TOUR
(Map p348; ☎0800 946 322; www.experiencehawkesbay.co.nz; West Quay; cruises $30-70) Schmooze out on a lunch or dinner cruise, or shorter trips morning and afternoon. Also operates the fun, family-friendly Duck tours (one hour adult/child/family $45/30/130), jet boat rides (adult/child $55/30), and winery tours (from $55).

Packard Promenade GUIDED TOUR
(☎06-835 0022; www.packardpromenades.co.nz; tours up to 4 people $140-600) Offers deco and wine tours, in a 1939 Packard Six vintage car.

Festivals & Events

Art Deco Weekend CULTURAL
(www.artdeconapier.com) In the third week of February, Napier and Hastings co-host the sensational Art Deco Weekend. Dinners, picnics, dances, balls, bands and Gatsby-esque fancy dress fill the week with shenanigans, many of which are free. Bertie, Napier's art-deco ambassador, is omnipresent. (See if he'll flex his biceps for you.)

Sleeping

TOP CHOICE Kennedy Park Top 10 Resort HOLIDAY PARK $
(Map p348; ☎0800 457 275, 06-843 9126; www.kennedypark.co.nz; Storkey St; sites $48, units $89-227; @🛜🏊) Less a campsite and more an entire suburb of holidaymakers, this complex is top dog on the Napier camping scene and winner of many awards. It's the closest campsite to town (2.5km out, south-west of the centre) and has every facility imaginable, although a larger kitchen would be nice.

Criterion Art Deco Backpackers HOSTEL $
(Map p350; ☎06-835 2059; www.criterionartdeco.co.nz; 48 Emerson St; dm $26, s $49-85, d $65-85, tr/q $90/120 all incl continental breakfast; @🛜) If it's interesting architecture and a central location you're after, here you have it. The vast communal area showcases the impressive internal features of what is Napier's best Spanish Mission specimen. Deals for guests in the bar-restaurant downstairs.

Masonic Hotel HOTEL $$
(Map p350; ☎06-835 8689; www.masonic.co.nz; cnr Herschell & Tennyson Sts; s $85-95, d $95-130, tr $120-140; 🛜) The art-deco Masonic is arguably the heart of town, its accommodation, restaurants and bars taking up most of a city block. It's undergoing a gradual but much-needed refurb, and is shaping up nicely around its charming old bones. Lovers of heritage hotels will likely fall in love with it, especially once they've experienced the 1st-floor balcony.

Archie's Bunker HOSTEL $
(Map p350; ☎06-833 7990; www.archiesbunker.co.nz; 14 Herschell St; dm/s $24/35, d $60-64; @🛜) One street back from the foreshore, Archie's is a shipshape modern hostel in an old office building. A few of the rooms are windowless, but on the whole this is a well-ventilated, quiet and secure arrangement with friendly owners and bike hire.

Napier YHA HOSTEL $
(Map p350; ☎06-835 7039; www.yha.co.nz; 277 Marine Pde; dm $29-32, s/d $40/70; @🛜) Napier's friendly YHA is housed in a beachfront earthquake survivor with a seemingly endless ramble of rooms. There's a fabulous overhanging reading nook and a sunny rear courtyard. Bob will help with bookings and local info.

Stables Lodge Backpackers HOSTEL $
(Map p350; ☎06-835 6242; www.stableslodge.co.nz; 370 Hastings St; dm $22-28, d $64; @🛜) Formerly an actual stables, this is a friendly place to get off your horse with pot-luck dinners, a barbecue courtyard, murals, resident cats and free internet.

Aqua Lodge HOSTEL $
(Map p350; ☎06-835 4523; aquaback@inhb.co.nz; 53 Nelson Cres; campsites per person $18, dm $26, d $62-76; @🛜🏊) Aqua Lodge sprawls between neighbouring houses on a quiet suburban street, with campsites on the back lawn. It's a fun place, with a wee pool and gardens.

Seaview Lodge B&B B&B $$
(Map p350; ☎06-835 0202; www.aseaviewlodge.co.nz; 5 Seaview Tce; s $130-140, d $170-180; 🛜) This grand Victorian villa (1890) is queen of all she surveys – which is most of the town and a fair bit of ocean. The elegant rooms have tasteful period elements and either bathroom or en suite. It's hard to resist a sunset tipple on the veranda, which opens off the relaxing guest lounge.

Rocks Motorlodge MOTEL $$
(Map p348; ☎06-835 9626; www.therocksmotel.co.nz; 27 Meeanee Quay, Westshore; units $110-180; @🛜) Located just 80m from the beach, the Rocks has corrugated stylings and wood-carving that have raised the bar on Westshore's motel row. Interiors are plush with a colour-splash, and some have a spa bath, others a clawfoot. Free internet, free gym, and laundry.

Sea Breeze B&B $$
(Map p350; ☎06-835 8067; seabreeze.napier@xtra.co.nz; 281 Marine Pde; s $95, d $110-130; 🛜) Inside this Victorian seafront villa are three richly coloured themed rooms (Chinese, Indian and Turkish), decorated with a cornucopia of artefacts and exotic flair.

Manor on Parade B&B $$
(Map p350; ☎06-834 3885; www.manoronparadenapier.co.nz; 283 Marine Pde; d $155-195; 🛜) Comfortable and friendly, this two-storey wooden villa on the waterfront has proved itself a

solid option, having survived the earthquake and in its latter-day incarnation as a B&B. The back room has a sunny deck while at the front are views out to sea.

Green House on the Hill B&B **$$**
(Map p350; ☎06-835 4475; www.the-green-house.co.nz; 18b Milton Rd; s/d $110/135; 📶) This meat-free B&B is up a steep hill and rewards with leafy surrounds and city 'n' sea views. The guest floor has one en suite room and one with its own bathroom. Home-baked goodies and fine herbal teas are likely to make an appearance. Free wi-fi most definitely on.

County Hotel HOTEL **$$$**
(Map p350; ☎06-835 7800; www.countyhotel.co.nz; 12 Browning St; r/ste $350/488; @📶) There's luxury infused between the masonry at this elegantly restored Edwardian building (a rare brick earthquake survivor). Chambers restaurant breathes refined formality at dinner (mains $30 to $40) while Winston's portrait gazes victoriously over Churchill's Champagne and Snug Bar.

Nautilus MOTEL **$$$**
(Map p350; ☎0508 628 845, 06-974 6550; www.nautilusnapier.co.nz; 387 Marine Pde; d $175-225; @📶) A newish hotel and a relatively good bit of architecture, too. Views from every room, kitchenettes, decor with spunk, spa baths, private balconies and an in-house restaurant. Apartments can sleep up to six ($300).

Crown Hotel HOTEL **$$$**
(Map p348; ☎06-833 8300; www.thecrownnapier.co.nz; cnr Bridge St & Hardinge Rd, Ahuriri; apt from $200; @📶) The conversion of this 1932 pub into a ritzy apartment-style hotel must have broken a few fishermen's hearts. The new wing may be generically modern but it offers superb ocean views. There's also a gym.

Eating

Napier is strong on cafes, but sketchy when it comes to evening dining. Some of the best food can be found at the Bay's wineries (p360).

Groove Kitchen Espresso CAFE **$**
(Map p350; www.groovekitchen.co.nz; 112 Tennyson St; meals $9-19; ⏰breakfast & lunch ; ✎) A sophisticated cafe squeezed into small, groovy space where the turntable spins and the kitchen cranks out A1 brunch along with trendsetting wraps, baps and salads, plus ginger gems your granny would be proud of. Killer coffee. With luck you'll be around for one of the intermittent Thursday night gigs.

Kitchen Table CAFE **$**
(Map p350; 138 Tennyson St; brunch $8-19; ⏰breakfast & lunch; ✎) Sharing an airy gallery space with a local photography studio, this colourful and crafty cafe produces classic modern fare from scones to goat cheese salad. Plenty to inspire, both on the walls and on the menu.

Restaurant Indonesia INDONESIAN **$$**
(Map p350; ☎06-835 8303; 409 Marine Pde; mains $20-27; ⏰dinner Tue-Sun; ✎) Crammed with Indonesian curios, this intimate space oozes authenticity. Lip-smacking Indo-Dutch *rijsttafel* smorgasbords are the house speciality (14 dishes, $30 to $36). A romantic option for those inclined. Bookings advisable.

Café Ujazi CAFE **$**
(Map p350; 28 Tennyson St; snacks $4-10, meals $9-19; ✎) The most bohemian of the city's cafes, Ujazi folds back its windows and lets the alternative vibe spill out onto the pavement where coffee and conversation carry on all day long. This is a long-established, consistent performer offering blackboard meals and hearty counter food. Try the classic *rewana* special – a big breakfast on traditional Maori bread.

Burger Fuel BURGERS **$**
(Map p350; 70 Carlyle St; burgers $9-15; ✎) Big, beautiful burgers that feel like a good square meal, especially if you add a side of fries with aioli and a malted milkshake. Pleasant dine-in experience – a little bit Fonzie, a little bit Prince in *Purple Rain*.

Westshore Fish Café FISH & CHIPS **$**
(Map p348; 112a Charles St, Westshore; takeaway $5-8, meals $14-28; ⏰lunch Thu-Sun, dinner Tue-Sun) If you're the type who needs cutlery, sit-down meals are served in the dining room. Otherwise grab some of the acclaimed fish and chips and contend with the gulls on the beach.

Kilim Café TURKISH **$**
(Map p350; ☎06-835 9100; 193 Hastings St; meals $9-17; ⏰11am-late; ✎) Authentic Turkish cuisine in a smart cafe environment, adorned with suitably Ottoman cushions and wall hangings. The kebabby, felafelly, salady meals are fresh and tasty, which is just as well as the service can be a bit on the sluggish side.

Farmers Market FARMERS MARKET
(Map p350; Lower Emerson St; ⏰8.30am-12.30pm Sat) This is your chance to score super-fresh local produce including fruit, veggies, bread and dairy products.

Drinking & Entertainment

When it comes to nightlife, Napier hedges its bets between the more traditional options downtown, and the strip of brassy restaurant-cum-bars around the shore at Ahuriri. Here you'll find a numer of fairly average establishments tailored to the weekend fun-lovers who flock here, particularly in high summer. Expect barnlike interiors, big screens, nautical themes, open fires, outdoor seating (a highlight) and limited beer options. A definite upside is the possibility of live music, as is the spectacle of excitable people breaking out their best dance moves – there's nothing like a bit of '70s twang-rock to bring folk out of their shell. Ahuriri's best is arguably **Shed 2** (Map p348), followed closely the **Thirsty Whale** (Map p348) and the **Gintrap** (Map p348). Oh, hang on a minute: that's just about all of them.

Napier town's options for an evening out have a bit more character, and are pretty much centred around Hastings St.

Med Bar BAR
(Map p350; Masonic Hotel, cnr Herschell & Tennyson Sts) Napier's s most civilised bar by a long shot, the Med's warm terracotta tones, tiling and mosaic make for atmosphere plus. Brisk staff, cocktails, good coffee, bistro fare ($24 to $30) and location in the waterfront Masonic Hotel complete the package.

Brazen Head BAR
(Map p350; 21 Hastings St) Poker machines compromise the vibe at this Irish bar, but the beer's cold and the outdoor deck is a brazen spot to get through a few.

Cabana Bar LIVE MUSIC
(Map p350; www.cabana.net.nz; 11 Shakespeare Rd) This legendary music venue of the '70s, '80s and '90s died in 1997, but thanks to some forward-thinking, toe-tapping folk, it's risen from the grave to save the day for Napier's gig lovers.

Napier Municipal Theatre THEATRE
(Map p350; www.napiermunicipaltheatre.co.nz; 119 Tennyson St) Not only the city's largest venue for the likes of concerts, dance and drama, but also one of the world's few working art-deco theatres. Worth going for the foyer lighting alone. Box office on-site.

Globe Theatrette CINEMA
(Map p348; www.globenapier.co.nz; 15 Hardinge Rd, Ahuriri) A vision in purple, this boutique cinema screens art-house flicks in a sumptuous cinema lounge with ready access to upmarket snacks.

Shopping

Although a relatively small town centre, Napier has plenty of interesting, independent retailers stocking a surprisingly diverse range of goods. Antiques, unsurprisingly, are in reasonable supply, although for a thorough trawl pick up the free *Hawke's Bay Antique Trail* brochure from the i-SITE. Instant gratification can be found at **Decorum** (Map p350; www.decorum-napier.com; cnr Tennyson & Herschell Sts), especially if you like crazy clothing from a bygone era.

Art and craft galleries are listed in another free brochure, the *Hawke's Bay Art Guide*, published annually.

For all-natural snugly gear, head straight to **Opossum World** (Map p350; 157 Marine Pde), or to **Classic Sheepskins** (Map p348; 22 Thames St) on the edge of the city centre.

Bookworms should wriggle into **Beattie & Forbes** (Map p350; www.beattieandforbes.co.nz; 70 Tennyson St), a long-standing independent, strong on NZ titles.

Information

Banks cluster around the corner of Hastings and Emerson Sts, with ATMs scattered throughout the centre. Internet access is available at the i-SITE and several cafes in the city.

DOC (☎06-834 3111; www.doc.govt.co.nz; 59 Marine Pde; ⏰9am-4.15pm Mon-Fri) Maps, advice and passes.

Napier Health Centre (☎06-878 8109; 76 Wellesley Rd; ⏰24hr)

Napier i-SITE (☎06-834 1911; www.napiercity.co.nz; 100 Marine Pde; ⏰9am-5pm; @) Handy and helpful.

Napier Police Station (☎06-831 0700; Station St; ⏰24hr)

Napier Post Office (151 Hastings St)

Getting There & Away

Air

Hawke's Bay Airport (☎06-835 3427; www.hawkesbay-airport.co.nz) is 8km north of the city.

Air New Zealand (☎06-833 5400; www.airnewzealand.co.nz; cnr Hastings & Station Sts) Daily direct flights to Auckland (from $89), Wellington (from $79) and Christchurch (from $129).

Sunair Aviation (☎0800 786 247; www.sunair.co.nz) Offers direct flights on weekdays between Napier and Gisborne ($280) with connections to other select North Island towns.

Bus

InterCity (www.intercity.co.nz) buses can be booked online or at the i-SITE, and depart from the **Dalton St Bus Stop**. Services run daily to Auckland (from $51, seven hours) via Taupo (from $18, two hours), Gisborne ($30, four hours) via Wairoa (from $13, 2½ hours), and Wellington (from $22, 5½ hours) via Waipukurau (from $13, one hour), plus four daily services to Hastings (from $18, 30 minutes).

If you're super-organised you can take advantage of $1 advance fares on **Naked Bus** (www.nakedbus.com) on the Auckland–Wellington route via Hastings and Taupo.

Getting Around

Most key sights in the city are reachable on foot, or you can speed things up by hiring a bicycle from Fishbike (p352).

Bus

goBay (06-878 9250; www.hbrc.govt.nz) runs the local bus service, covering Napier, Hastings, Havelock North and thereabouts. There are ample services between the main centres Monday to Friday, including three different routes between Napier and Hastings (adult/child $4.50/2.50) taking between 30 minutes (express) and 55 minutes (all stops). Buses depart from the Dalton St Bus Stop.

Car

Conveniently, **Napier Airport Car Rental** (0800 556 606; www.napierairportcarehire.co.nz) acts as agent for 10 car-hire companies including the big brands and local outfits. **Rent-a-Dent** (06-834 0688; www.napiercarrentals.co.nz) is locally owned and based at the airport.

Taxi

A city-to-airport taxi ride will cost you around $22.

Napier Taxis (06-835 7777)

Super Shuttle (0800 748 885; www.supershuttle.co.nz)

Hastings & Around

POP 66,100

Positioned at the centre of the Hawke's Bay fruit bowl, bustling Hastings is the commercial hub of the region, 20km south of Napier. A few kilometres of orchards still separate it from Havelock North, with its prosperous village atmosphere and the towering backdrop of Te Mata Peak.

Sights & Activities

As with Napier, Hastings was similarly devastated by the 1931 earthquake and also boasts some fine art-deco and Spanish Mission buildings, built in the aftermath. Main street highlights include the **Westerman's Building** (Map p357; cnr Russell & Heretaunga St E, Hastings), arguably the Bay's best example of the Spanish Mission style, although there are many other architectural gems if you cast your eye around. The i-SITE stocks the *Art Deco Hastings* brochure ($2), detailing two self-guided walks of the CBD.

FREE Hastings City Art Gallery GALLERY

(Map p357; www.hastingscityartgallery.co.nz; 201 Eastbourne St E, Hastings; 10am-4.30pm) The city's gallery presents contemporary NZ and international art in a pleasant, purpose-built space.

Te Mata Peak PARK

Rising melodramatically from the Heretaunga Plains, Te Mata Peak, 16km south of Havelock North, is part of the 98-hectare **Te Mata Trust Park** (Map p348). The road to the 399m summit passes sheep trails, rickety fences and vertigo-inducing stone escarpments cowled in a bleak, lunar-meets-Scottish-Highland atmosphere. The **lookout** (Map p348) still awaits its makeover, but it's really all about the views which – on a clear day – fall away to Hawke Bay, Mahia Peninsula and distant Mt Ruapehu.

The view *of* Te Mata is also extraordinary. To local Maori this is the sleeping giant Te Mata O Rongokako. From the fields around Havelock North, a little imagination will conjure up the giant, lying on his back with his head to the right. The park's network of trails offers walks from 30 minutes to two hours. Our pick is the Peak Trail for views, but all are detailed in the *Te Mata Trust Park* brochure available from local visitor centres.

Splash Planet SWIMMING

(Map p348; www.splashplanet.co.nz; Grove Rd, Hastings; adult/child $26/18; 10am-5.30pm Nov-Feb) This massive complex has plenty of pools, slides and aquatic excitement.

Airplay Paragliding PARAGLIDING

(06-845 1977; www.airplay.co.nz) Te Mata Peak is a paragliding hotspot, with voluminous updraughts offering exhilarating whooshes through the air. Airplay Paragliding has tandem paragliding ($140) and full-day beginners' courses (from $180).

Hastings

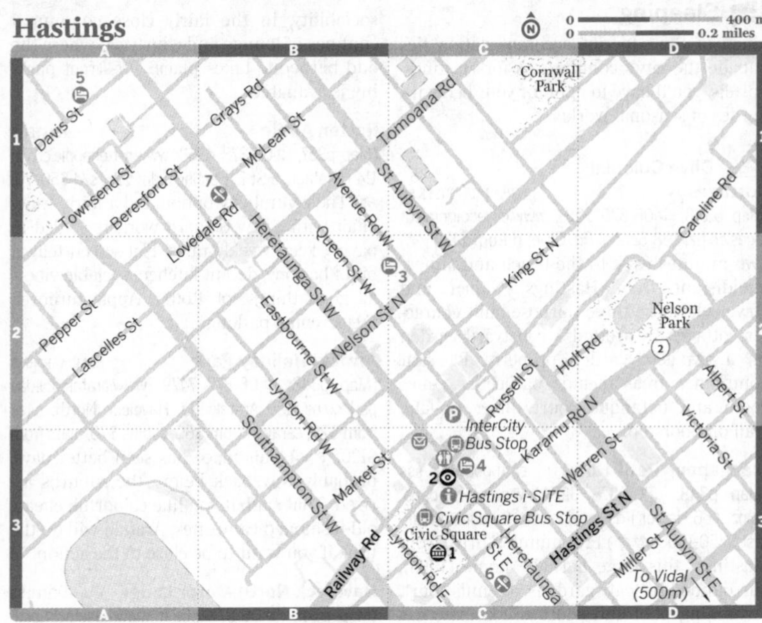

Hastings

Sights

1 Hastings City Art Gallery C3
2 Westerman's Building C3

Sleeping

3 Gloucester House Motel C2
4 Rotten Apple C3
5 Sleeping Giant A1

Eating

6 Opera Kitchen C3
7 Rush Munro's B1

Tours

Long Island Guides GUIDED TOURS

(☎06-874 7877; www.longislandtoursnz.com; half-day from $180) Customised and personalised tours across a wide range of interests including Maori culture, bushwalks, kayaking, horse riding and, inevitably, food and wine.

Te Hakakino CULTURAL TOUR

(☎021 057 0935; www.waimaramaori.com; 2-3hr tours $60-120) Guided tours of a historic hill fortress revealing archaeological remains and cultural insights en route.

Early Morning Balloons BALLOONING

(☎06-879 4229; www.hotair.co.nz; per person $345) Provides inflated views over grapey Hawke's Bay.

Wine Tours

The majority of tours in this part of the world are focused on wine. Plenty of operators offer self-guided cycle tours (p352) of the vines, but there are also plenty of motorised options, usually by minibus, lasting three to seven hours and starting at $60 per person.

» **Bay Tours & Charters**
(☎06-845 2736; www.baytours.co.nz)

» **Grape Escape**
(☎0800 100 489; www.grapeescape.net.nz)

» **Odyssey NZ**
(☎0508 639 773; www.odysseynz.com)

» **Prinsy's**
(☎06-845 3703; www.prinsyexperience.co.nz)

» **Vince's World of Wine**
(☎06-836 6705; www.vincestours.co.nz)

Festivals & Events

Hastings Blossom Festival CULTURAL

(☎06-878 9447; www.blossomfestival.co.nz) The Hastings Blossom Festival, a petalled spring fling, happens in the second half of September, with parades, arts, crafts and visiting artists.

Sleeping

Much of the superior accommodation lies outside the city's confines. As for Hastings' hostels, you'll have to fight for your bed with hordes of seasonal workers.

TOP CHOICE Clive Colonial Cottages RENTAL HOUSES $$
(Map p348; 06-870 1018; www.clivecolonialcottages.co.nz; 198 School Rd, Clive; d from $135;) Two minutes walk to the beach and almost equidistant from Hastings, Napier and Havelock, these three purpose-built character cottages sit around a courtyard garden on a two-acre garden property. Pleasant communal areas include barbecue, games room and pétanque court. Bikes on-site; trail on doorstep.

Mangapapa Petit Hotel BOUTIQUE HOTEL $$$
(Map p348; 06-878 3234; www.mangapapa.co.nz; 466 Napier Rd, Havelock North; d incl breakfast $450-1500; @) Five minutes' drive from Hastings, this large heritage home (1885), surrounded by leafy gardens, a tennis court, swimming pool and short golf course, has been sympathetically adapted into a boutique hotel. Twelve suites offer period-style luxury; a restaurant and day spa up the indulgence factor.

Hastings Top 10 Holiday Park HOLIDAY PARK $
(Map p348; 06-878 6692; www.hastingstop10.co.nz; 610 Windsor Ave, Hastings; sites $42, units $78-145; @) Putting the 'park' back into holiday park, within its leafy confines are sycamore hedges, a topiary 'welcome' sign, stream, ducks and plenty of serenity. New pool and spa complex will satisfy young and old.

Gloucester House Motel MOTEL $$
(Map p357; 06-876 3741; www.gloucesterhousemotel.co.nz; 404 Avenue Rd W, Hastings; units $99-125;) Picket fences and colourful roses welcome you to this spick-and-span motel, five minutes' walk from the centre of town. The 11 units are spotlessly clean and spacious, with kitchen facilities and separate lounge-dining areas. Cool off with a dip in the pool.

Sleeping Giant HOSTEL $
(Map p357; 06-878 5393; sleepinggiant@xtra.co.nz; 109 Davis St, Hastings; dm/tw/d $20/50/60;) A comfy backpackers in a suburban street, 10 minutes walk to town. A posse of tanned, wiry agricultural workers ensures an atmosphere of laid-back sociability, in the fairly close communal confines of lounge and courtyard where the odd barbeque takes place. Off-street parking is available.

Rotten Apple HOSTEL $
(Map p357; 06-878 4363; www.rottenapple.co.nz; 114 Heretaunga St E, Hastings; dm $26, s/d $50/70;) The central city option and a fairly fruity affair with a few orchard workers settled in paying keen weekly rates. Flat-screen telly, a bit of balcony, decent kitchen, sociable vibe – all good things for Rotten Apple turnover. Free evening parking.

Arataki Holiday Park HOLIDAY PARK $
(Map p348; 06-877 7479; www.aratakiholidaypark.co.nz; 139 Arataki Rd, Havelock North; sites from $20, caravan from $60, cabins $70, units from $130;) This place has seen better days, probably way back before the suburbs arrived. That said, if you like colourful, cheap, old-fashioned campsites, Arataki will do the trick if you want to be close to the action.

Havelock North Motor Lodge MOTEL $$
(Map p348; 06-877 8627; www.havelocknorthmotorlodge.co.nz; 7 Havelock Rd, Havelock North; units $135-195; @) Smack-bang in the middle of Havelock North, this modern motel is a cut above the rest. Tidy one- and two-bedroom units feature spa baths, Sky TV and kitchenettes.

Millar Road RENTAL HOUSES $$$
(Map p348; 06-875 1977; www.millarroad.co.nz; 83 Millar Rd; villa $600, house $950;) Set in the Tuki Tuki Hills with vineyard and bay views, Millar Road is architecturally heaven-sent. Two plush villas (each sleep four) and a super-stylish house (sleeps up to eight) are filled with NZ-made furniture and local artworks. Explore the 20-hectare grounds or look cool by the communal pool.

Eating

It is the wineries and artisan food producers we have to thank for this area's culinary highlights, which include some particularly fine vineyard lunches (p360), ice cream, and a perplexing amount of pickle.

Opera Kitchen CAFE $$
(Map p357; 312 Eastbourne St E, Hastings; snacks $5-7, meals $9-22; breakfast & lunch;) This modern and stylish cafe has an interesting menu including healthy brekkie options, such as granola and fruit compote. For the less calorie-conscious, the farmer's breakfast is a real

winner, too. Heavenly baked goods, great coffee and snappy staff round things out nicely. Eat in or outside in the suntrap courtyard.

Deliciosa TAPAS $$

(Map p348; ☎06-877 6031; 21 Napier Rd, Havelock North; tapas $8-17; ⊙4pm-late Mon-Wed, 11am-late Thu-Sat) Great things come in small packages at this intimate tapas bar with a rosy glow. The menu has almost as many influences as the United Nations, as duck rillette battles Lebanese seven-spice beef and Waldorf salad. Luckily for diners, flare in the kitchen and great local ingredients keep the peace.

BJs Bakery BAKERY $

(Map p348; 12 Havelock Road, Havelock North; pies $3-5; ✎) This outpost of one of the Bay's biggest bakeries is stacked with handsome cakes and sandwiches as well as arguably the region's best pies. It also offers hot meals, good espresso, wine if you fancy it, a pleasant environment, and whip-cracking service.

Diva MODERN NZ $$

(Map p348; ☎06-877 5149; 1/10 Napier Rd, Havelock North; meals $12-32; ⊙lunch Tue-Fri, dinner Tue-Sat) The most happening place in Havelock, Diva offers good-value lunch (from fish and chips to Caesar salad) and a bistro-style menu featuring fresh seafood and seasonal specialities. Eating is divided between flash dining room and groovy bar (snacks from $6), plus lively pavement tables.

Pipi PIZZERIA $$

(Map p348; ☎06-877 8993; 16 Joll Rd, Havelock North; mains $16-24; ⊙4-10pm Tue-Sun; ✎) Shockingly pink with candy stripes and mismatched furniture, Pipi cheekily thumbs its nose at small-town conventionality. The food focus is on simple pasta dishes and Roman-style thin-crusted pizza.

Bay Espresso CAFE $

(Map p348; 141 Karamu Rd, Hastings; snacks & lunchees $6-19; ⊙7am-4pm; ✎) An easy pit stop on the main road, this enduringly popular cafe serves up house-roasted organic coffee as well as handsome counter food and reasonable brunch, best enjoyed in the sunny courtyard out back.

Rush Munro's ICE CREAM $

(Map p357; 704 Heretaunga St W, Hastings; ice cream $3-8) Rush Munro's is a Hastings icon, serving up locally made ice cream since 1926.

Hastings Farmers Market FARMERS MARKET

(Map p348; Showgrounds, Kenilworth Rd; ⊙8.30am-12.30pm Sun) If you're around on Sunday, the Hastings market is not to be missed. Bring an empty stomach, cash and a roomy shopping bag.

Drinking

Few standout options exist beyond the winery gates.

Rose & Shamrock PUB

(Map p348; cnr Napier Rd & Porter Dr, Havelock North) A carpeted, dark-wood, British-style boozer complete with a few British brews on tap and hearty pub grub (mains $14 to $26). Occasional live music on Saturday nights.

Loading Ramp PUB

(Map p348; 6 Treachers Lane, Havelock North; ⊙3pm-late) This lofty timber space pulls a mixed crowd of young 'uns up to high jinks, especially on the weekends when the queue can stretch well down the road. Also offers pub-style meals.

Filter Room BREWERY

(Map p348; www.hbib.co.nz; Awatoto Rd, Meeanee; ⊙10am-5pm Sun-Thu, 10am-7pm Fri & Sat) Surrounded by orchards, these folk offer a large range of craft beers and ciders, all brewed on-site, plus a great-value $15 tasting tray and tummy-filling food.

Shopping

The Hastings area appears to exist largely for the satisfaction of our appetites. Beyond a great big bunch of wineries (p360), there is a plethora of boutique food producers, of which the following are just a few:

Arataki Honey FOOD

(Map p348; www.aratakihoney.co.nz; 66 Arataki Rd, Havelock North; ⊙9am-5pm) Stock up on buzzy by-products for your toast or your skin. There are family-fun, hands-on displays outlining the whole sticky cycle from flower to jar.

Hohepa Organic Cheeses FOOD

(Map p348; www.hohepa.com; 363 Main Rd, Clive; ⊙9am-5pm Mon-Fri, 9.30am-2.30pm Sat) Part of a Steiner-based community of people with intellectual disabilities, this shop sells local produce, including cheese (made on-site), biodynamic fruit and vegetables, candles and clothing.

HAWKE'S BAY WINERIES

Once upon a time, this district was most famous for its orchards. Today it's vines that have top billing, with Hawke's Bay now NZ's second-largest wine-producing region. A bunch of grapes are grown around Havelock North and the Tuki Tuki River, by the coast at Te Awanga, and in the stony Gimblett Gravels west of Flaxmere. Between them they produce some excellent Bordeaux-style reds, syrah and chardonnay.

Best Wining & Dining

» **Vidal** (Map p348; ☎06-872 7440; www.vidal.co.nz; 913 St Aubyn St, Hastings; lunch mains $20-30, dinner mains $28-39; ⊙11.30am-late) There's nothing pedestrian about this winery restaurant despite being tucked into the backstreets of suburban Hastings. The warm, wood-lined dining room is a worthy setting for the elegant food. The pancetta and tarragon roasted baby chicken was a summer highlight.

» **Elephant Hill** (Map p348; ☎06-872 6060; www.elephanthill.co.nz; 86 Clifton Rd, Te Awanga; mains $32-38; ⊙11am-10pm) Ubermodern winery with edgy architecture, and food, wine and service to rival the stunning sea views; we went quackers over the duck tasting plate. At night, enjoy an aperitif or dessert in the slinky sunken bar.

» **Terrôir at Craggy Range** (Map p348; ☎06-873 0143; www.craggyrange.com; 253 Waimarama Rd, Havelock North; mains $37-40; ⊙lunch Mon-Sun, dinner Mon-Sat) Housed in a cathedral-like 'wine barrel', Terrôir is one of the region's most consistent fine-dining experiences. Impressive views of Te Mata peak from the terrace.

A Taste of the Tastings

Cellar doors are open for tastings throughout the summer, with shorter hours in winter. Tastings are generally free, but there's a small charge at some (refundable on purchase). Pick up the *Hawke's Bay Winery Guide*, or download it from www.winehawkesbay.co.nz.

» **Black Barn Vineyards** (Map p348; ☎06-877 7985; www.blackbarn.com; Black Barn Rd, Havelock North) Bistro, gallery, popular Saturday growers market and an amphitheatre.

» **Brookfields** (Map p348; www.brookfieldsvineyards.co.nz; 376 Brookfields Rd, Meeanee) Excellent reds. The 'sun-dried' malbec is a delicious rendition of Italy's amarone.

» **Church Road** (Map p348; www.churchroad.co.nz; 150 Church Rd, Taradale) Winery and museum tours (11am and 2pm).

» **Clearview Estate Winery** (Map p348; ☎06-875 0150; www.clearviewestate.co.nz; 194 Clifton Rd, Te Awanga) Award-winning wines, quality restaurant, relaxed and family-friendly.

» **Crab Farm Winery** (☎06-836 6678; www.crabfarmwinery.co.nz; 511 Main North Rd, Bay View; ⊙10am-5pm Fri-Sun, 6pm-late Fri) Decent, reasonably priced wines and a great cafe.

» **Esk Valley Estate** (Map p348; www.eskvalley.co.nz; 745 Main North Rd, Bay View) Excellent Bordeaux-style reds, chardonnay and riesling.

» **Mission Estate** (Map p348; ☎06-845 9354; www.missionestate.co.nz; 198 Church Rd, Napier) NZ's oldest winery; beautiful grounds and restaurant housed within a restored seminary.

» **Ngatarawa** (Map p348; www.ngatarawa.co.nz; 305 Ngatarawa Rd, Bridge Pa) Historic stables with rustic cellar door and picnicking opportunities.

» **Salvare** (Map p348; www.salvare.co.nz; 403 Ngatarawa Rd, Bridge Pa) Small winery punching well above its weight in terms of wine and cellar-door experience.

» **Sileni Estates** (Map p348; www.sileni.co.nz; 2016 Maraekakaho Rd, Bridge Pa) Wine, cheese, chocolate and charming cellar-door experience.

» **Te Awa** (Map p348; ☎06-879 7602; www.teawa.com; 2375 SH50) Casually stylish winery and a good lunch option, where the kids can come too.

» **Te Mata Estate** (Map p348; www.temata.co.nz; 349 Te Mata Rd, Havelock North) Legendary Coleraine red and Elston chardonnay.

» **Trinity Hill** (Map p348; www.trinityhill.com; 2396 SH50) Sip serious reds and top-ranking chardonnay at this baroque-industrial cellar door.

Silky Oak Chocolate Company FOOD
(Map p348; www.silkyoakchocs.co.nz; 1131 Links Rd, Waiohiki; ⏲9am-5pm Mon-Thu, to 4pm Fri, 10am-4pm Sat & Sun) Watch the chocolatiers at work while deliberating over mouth-watering truffles and chocolate rugby balls. The museum (adult/child $8/5) offers a chocolate-drenched history and the odd ancient Mayan artefact. There's a cafe next door.

Strawberry Patch FOOD
(Map p348; www.strawberrypatch.co.nz; 76 Havelock Rd, Havelock North; ⏲9am-5.30pm) Pick your own berries in season, and call in all year round for fresh produce, picnic supplies and real fruit ice cream.

Telegraph Hill FOOD
(Map p348; www.telegraphhill.co.nz; 1279 Howard St, Hastings; ⏲9am-5pm Mon-Fri, 10am-3pm Sat) A small producer of olives, oils and all sorts of Mediterranean-influenced gourmet treats. Four-person picnic baskets ($30) available for on-site indulgence.

Information

Hastings i-SITE (☎06-873 0080; www.hastings.co.nz; cnr Russell St & Heretaunga St E; ⏲8.30am-5pm Mon-Fri, 9am-4pm Sat, to 3pm Sun; @) Internet access, free maps, trail brochures and bookings.

Havelock North Information Centre (☎06-877 9600; www.havelocknorthnz.com; cnr Te Aute & Middle Rds, Havelock North; ⏲10am-4pm Mon-Fri, to 2pm Sat & Sun) Information, bike hire and more.

Hawke's Bay Hospital (☎06-878 8109; Omahu Rd)

Police Station (☎06-873 0500; Railway Rd)

Post Office (cnr Market St & Heretaunga St W)

Getting There & Away

Napier's Hawke's Bay Airport (p355) is a 20-minute drive away. **Air New Zealand** (☎06-873 2200; www.airnewzealand.co.nz; 117 Heretaunga St W) has an office in central Hastings.

The **InterCity Bus Stop** is on Russell St. Book **InterCity** (☎06-835 4326; www.intercity.co.nz) and **Naked Bus** (www.nakedbus.com) buses online or at the i-SITE.

Getting Around

goBay (p356) runs the local bus service, covering Napier, Hastings, Havelock North and thereabouts. There are ample daily services between the main centres including three different routes between Napier and Hastings taking between 30 minutes (express) and 55 minutes (all stops). Buses depart from the **Civic Square Bus Stop**. Fares are up to adult/child $4.50/2.50. Services between Hastings and Havelock North run from Monday to Saturday (adult/child $3/2, 35 minutes). Signal the driver and pay on the bus.

Hastings Taxis (☎06-878 5055) is the local cab service.

Cape Kidnappers

From mid-September to late April, Cape Kidnappers (named when local Maori tried to kidnap Cook's Tahitian servant boy) erupts with squawking gannets. These big birds usually nest on remote islands but here they settle for the mainland, completely unfazed by human spectators.

The birds nest as soon as they arrive, and eggs take about six weeks to hatch, with chicks arriving in early November. In March the gannets start their migration; by May they're gone.

Early November to late February is the best time to visit. Take a tour or the walkway to the colony: it's about five hours return from the Clifton Reserve car park (parking $3), located at the Clifton Motor Camp. You'll find interesting cliff formations, rock pools, a sheltered picnic spot, and the birds themselves. The walk is tide dependent. Leave no earlier than three hours after high tide; start back no later than 1½ hours after low tide.

No regular buses go to Clifton, but the tour operators below will transport you for an additional fee, or you could bike (p352).

Refreshments out this way can be had at the pleasant **Clifton Bay Café** (Map p348; 468 Clifton Rd; meals $12-25; ⏲10am-4pm), a breezy place for a meal before or after you run the gannet gauntlet.

Tours

All trips depart according to tide times; the region's i-SITEs and individual operators have schedules.

TOP CHOICE **Gannet Beach Adventures** ECOTOUR
(Map p348; ☎0800 426 638; www.gannets.com; adult/child/family $39/24/95) Ride along the beach on a tractor-pulled trailer before wandering out on the Cape for 90 minutes. A great, guided return trip of four hours, departing from Clifton Reserve.

Gannet Safaris ECOTOUR
(Map p348; ☎0800 427 232; www.gannetsafaris.co.nz; Summerlee Station; adult/child $60/30)

Overland 4WD trips across farmland into the gannet colony. Three-hour tours depart at 9.30am and 1.30pm. Also operate small-group Wilderness Safaris (www.kidnapperssafaris.co.nz) heading behind the vermin-proof fence into the conservation zone.

Central Hawke's Bay

Grassy farmland stretches south from Hastings, dotted with the grand homesteads of Victorian pastoralists. It's an untouristed area, rich in history and deserted beaches. Waipukurau (aka 'Wai-puk'), the main town, isn't exactly thrilling but it's worth calling in to the extremely helpful **Central Hawke's Bay Information Centre** (06-858 6488; www.centralhawkesbay.co.nz; Railway Esp; 9am-5pm Mon-Fri, to 1pm Sat) in the old railway station. It can sort you out with the comprehensive *Experience Central Hawke's Bay* brochure and pamphlets outlining heritage trails and DOC reserves and walkways.

Sights

There are no fewer than six windswept and interesting beaches along the coast here: **Kairakau**, **Mangakuri**, **Pourerere**, **Aramoana**, **Blackhead** and **Porangahau**. The first five are good for swimming, and between the lot they offer a range of sandy, salty activities including surfing, fishing, and driftwoody, rock-pooly adventures. Between Aramoana and Blackhead Beach lies the **Te Angiangi Marine Reserve** – bring your snorkel.

It's a nondescript hill in the middle of nowhere, but the place with the world's second-longest name is good for a photo op. **Taumatawhakatangihangakoauauotamateaturipukakapikimaungahoronukupokaiwhenuakitanatahu** is actually the abbreviated form of 'The Brow of a Hill Where Tamatea, the Man with the Big Knees, Who Slid, Climbed, and Swallowed Mountains, Known as Land Eater, Played his Flute to his Brother'. To get there, fuel-up in Waipukurau and drive 40km to the Mangaorapa junction on route 52. Turn left and go 4km towards Porangahau. At the intersection with the signposts, turn right and continue 4.3km to the sign.

Ongaonga, an historic village 16km west of Waipawa, has interesting Victorian and Edwardian buildings. Pick up a pamphlet for a self-guided walking tour from the information centre in Waipukurau.

The **Central Hawke's Bay Settlers Museum** (www.chbsettlersmuseum.co.nz; 23 High St; $2; 10am-4pm) in **Waipawa** has pioneer artefacts, informative 'homestead' displays and a good specimen of a river *waka* (canoe).

Sleeping & Eating

Lochlea Backpacker Farmstay FARMSTAY $
(06-855 4816; 344 Lake Rd, Wanstead; campsites from $23, dm/d/q $26/60/106;) As far removed from urban stress as possible, this idyllic farm has breezy stands of trees on grazing slopes. Rooms are simple but the communal lounge is cosy. There's a pool, tennis court and endless paddocks to wander.

Gwavas Garden Homestead B&B $$$
(06-856 5810; www.gwavasgarden.co.nz; 5740 SH50, Tikokino; d incl breakfast $245-285;) Six kilometres from Tikokino, this grand old 1890 homestead has enjoyed a faithful room-by-room renovation with pretty floral wallpaper, period furnishings and divine linens. Enjoy breakfast on the veranda before a spot of lawn tennis or a wander through the internationally renowned 9-hectare 'Cornish' garden.

Misty River Café CAFE $$
(12 High Street, Waipawa; mains $14-20; 9am-4pm Wed-Sun) A little bit of continental chic on the functional high street, this darling cafe makes lip-smacking salads as well as fresh ham, pasta, nachos and other global favourites. Drop-dead-gorgeous baking.

Paper Mulberry Café CAFE $
(SH2, Pukehou; meals $8-17; 7am-4pm Thu-Mon) Halfway between Waipukurau and Hastings, this rustic cafe and art gallery serves excellent coffee and home-style food (and yummy fudge). Well worth a stop for a chomp and a shop.

Oruawharo CAFE $$
(06-855 8274; www.oruawharo.com; 379 Oruawharo Rd, Takapau; morning and afternoon tea $15, lunch $20-25) One of the area's rural mansions, Oruawharo (1879) is a grand setting for high tea or lunch served on fine bone china. Call ahead for sittings.

Getting There & Away

InterCity (www.intercity.co.nz) and **Naked Bus** (www.nakedbus.com) pass through Waipawa and Waipukurau on their Wellington–Napier routes.

Kaweka & Ruahine Ranges

The remote Kaweka and Ruahine ranges separate Hawke's Bay from the Central Plateau. These forested wildernesses offer some of the North Island's best tramping. See the DOC pamphlets *Kaweka Forest Park & Puketitiri Reserves* and *Eastern Ruahine Forest Park* for details of tracks and huts.

An ancient Maori track, now know as the **Gentle Annie Road**, runs inland from Omahu near Hastings to Taihape, via Otamauri and Kuripapango (where there is a basic but charming DOC campsite, $5). The route is scenic and will take around three hours.

Kaweka J, the highest point of the range (1724m), can be reached by a three-to-five-hour tramp from the end of Kaweka Rd; from Napier take Puketitiri Rd then Whittle Rd. The drive is worthwhile in itself; it's partly unsealed and takes three hours return.

Enjoy a soak in natural hot pools before or after the three-hour walk on **Te Puia Track**, which follows the picturesque **Mohaka River**. From Napier, take Puketitiri Rd, then Pakaututu Rd, then Makahu Rd to the road-end **Mangatutu Hot Pools**.

The Mokaha can be rafted with **Mohaka Rafting** (☎027 825 8539, 06-839 1808; www.mohakarafting.com; from $75).

Wellington Region

Includes »

Wellington 366
Sights 367
Activities 373
Tours 374
Festivals & Events 374
Sleeping 375
Eating 379
Drinking 383
Entertainment 384
Shopping 386
Kapiti Coast 389
The Wairarapa 391

Best Places to Eat

- » Ortega Fish Shack (p380)
- » Trio Café at Coney Winery (p393)
- » Moore Wilson Fresh (p383)
- » Logan Brown (p381)
- » Scopa (p381)
- » Schoc Chocolates (p395)

Best Places to Stay

- » YHA Wellington City (p376)
- » Ohtel (p376)
- » Martinborough Top 10 Holiday Park (p393)
- » Moana Lodge (p376)

Why Go?

If your New Zealand travels thus far have been all about the great outdoors and sleepy rural towns, Wellington will blow the cobwebs away. Art-house cinemas, funky boutiques, hip bars, live-music venues and lashings of restaurants – all can be found in the 'cultural capital'.

As the crossing point between the North and South Islands, travellers have long been passing through these parts. Te Papa and Zealandia now stop visitors in their tracks, and even a couple of days' pause will reveal myriad other attractions, including a beautiful harbour and walkable waterfront, hillsides clad in pretty weatherboard houses, ample inner-city surprises, and some of the freshest city air on the planet.

Less than an hour away to the north, the Kapiti Coast offers more settled weather and a beachy vibe, with Kapiti Island nature reserve a highlight. An hour away over the Rimutaka Range, the Wairarapa farm plains are dotted with sweet towns and famed wineries, hemmed in by a windswept coastline.

When to Go?

'You can't beat Wellington on a good day', they say, and such days are a lot more frequent than you might think. For while the nickname 'Windy Welly' is justly deserved, Wellington's climate is largely pleasant, and the Kapiti Coast and Wairarapa are even better.

November to April are the warmer months, with average maximums hovering around 20°C. From May to August it's colder and wetter – daily temperatures lurk around 12°C. No matter: there's plenty to do indoors.

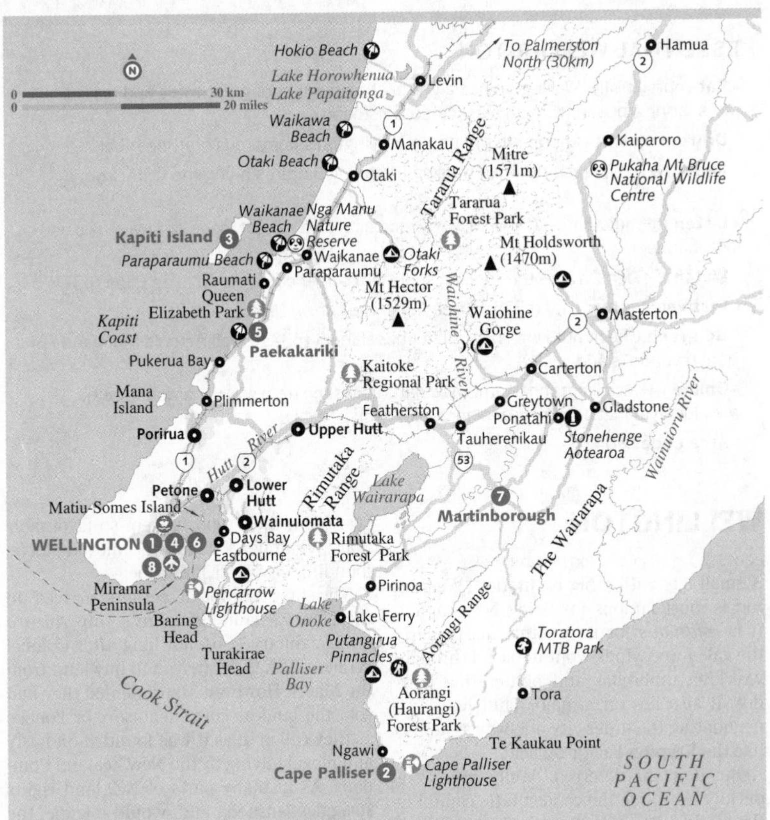

Wellington Region Highlights

1. Getting interactive at NZ's finest museum, Wellington's **Te Papa** (p374)
2. Scaling the lighthouse steps on wild and remote **Cape Palliser** (p394)
3. Meeting real live kiwi on a **Kapiti Island** night-time walk (p391)
4. Exploring the capital's creative side on **Cuba Street**
5. Rambling the dunes of **Queen Elizabeth Park** (p389) near beachy **Paekakariki**
6. Riding the ratchety **cable car** (p371) from Lambton Quay to the leafy **Wellington Botanic Gardens** (p371)
7. Maintaining a straight line on your bicycle as you tour the picturesque **Martinborough wineries** (p394)
8. Discovering the joys of NZ single-track on the trails of **Makara Peak Mountain Bike Park** (p373)

Getting There & Around

Wellington is the North Island port for the inter-island ferries. Long-distance **Tranz Scenic** (☎0800 872 467, 04-495 0775; www.tranzscenic.co.nz) trains run from Wellington to Auckland via Palmerston North. Wellington Airport is serviced by international and domestic airlines.

InterCity (☎04-385 0520; www.intercity.co.nz) is the main North Island bus company, travelling just about everywhere. Approaching Wellington city from the north, you'll pass through either the Kapiti Coast to the west via State Hwy1 (SH1), or the Wairarapa and heavily populated Hutt Valley to the east via State Hwy2 (SH2).

Getting into and out of Wellington on regional trains and buses is a breeze. Metlink (p388) is the one-stop-shop for regional transport services, from Wellington to the Kapiti Coast and the Wairarapa.

ESSENTIAL WELLINGTON

» **Eat** yourself silly: Wellington has a gut-busting number of great cafes and restaurants; bring trousers with an elasticated waistband

» **Drink** in pursuit of hoppiness at one of Wellington's numerous craft beer bars

» **Read** the moving, sometimes rousing literary sculptures along the waterfront's Writers Walk

» **Listen** to Radio Active (88.6FM, www.radioactive.co.nz), for loads of Kiwi music and local banter

» **Watch** 'Golden Days' – the frenetic short film screened non-stop at Te Papa (p374)

» **Festival** Summer City (p375) – free fun in the sun, *in theory*

» **Go green** Check out rare NZ wildlife at Zealandia (p373), Wellington's mainland 'conservation island'

» **Online** www.wellingtonnz.com, www.naturecoast.co.nz, www.wairarapanz.com; www.lonelyplanet.com/new-zealand/wellington

» **Area code** ☎04

WELLINGTON

POP 199,200 (CITY), 393,400 (REGION)

A small city with a big reputation, Wellington is most famous for being NZ's capital. It is *infamous* for its weather, particularly the gale-force winds wont to barrel through, wrecking umbrellas and obliterating hair-dos. It also lies on a major fault line. And negotiating the inner-city one-way system is like the Krypton Factor on acid.

But don't be deterred. 'Welly' is a wonderful city, voted 'the coolest little capital in the world' in Lonely Planet's *Best in Travel* (2011). For a starter it's lovely to look at, draped around bushy hillsides encircling a magnificent harbour. There are super lookouts on hilltops, golden sand on the prom, and spectacular craggy shores along the south coast. Downtown, the city is compact and vibrant, buoyed by a surprising number of museums, theatres, galleries and boutiques. A cocktail- and caffeine-fuelled hospitality scene fizzes and pops among the throng.

History

Maori legend has it that the explorer Kupe was first to discover Wellington harbour. Wellington's original Maori name was Te Whanganui-a-Tara (great harbour of Tara), named after the son of a chief named Whatonga who had settled on the Hawke's Bay coast. Whatonga sent Tara and his half-brother to explore the southern part of the North Island. When they returned over a year later, their reports were so favourable that Whatonga's followers moved there, founding the Ngati Tara tribe.

The first European settlers arrived in the New Zealand Company's ship *Aurora* on 22 January 1840, not long after Colonel William Wakefield arrived to buy land from the Maori. However, Maori denied they had sold the land at Port Nicholson, or Poneke as they called it, as it was founded on hasty and illegal buying by the New Zealand Company. As in many parts of NZ, land rights struggles ensued, and would plague the country for years to come.

By 1850 Wellington was a thriving settlement of around 5500 people, despite a lack of flat land. Originally the waterfront was along Lambton Quay, but reclamation of parts of the harbour began in 1852. In 1855 a significant earthquake razed many parts of Wellington, including the lower Hutt Valley and the land on which the modern Hutt Rd now runs.

In 1865 the seat of government was moved from Auckland to Wellington, due to its central location in the country.

One blustery day back in 1968 the wind blew so hard it pushed the almost-new Wellington–Christchurch ferry *Wahine* onto Barrett Reef at the harbour entrance. The disabled ship dragged its anchors, drifted into the harbour and slowly sank – 51 people perished. The Museum of Wellington City & Sea has a moving exhibit commemorating this tragedy.

Sights

Museums & Galleries

FREE Museum of Wellington City & Sea MUSEUM
(Map p368; www.museumofwellington.co.nz; Queens Wharf; ⏲10am-5pm) For an imaginative, interactive experience of Wellington's social and salty maritime history, swing into the Museum of Wellington. Highlights include a moving documentary about the tragedy of the *Wahine*, and ancient Maori legends dramatically told using tiny hologram actors and special effects. The building itself is an old Bond Store dating from 1892.

FREE City Gallery GALLERY
(Map p378; www.citygallery.org.nz; Civic Sq, Wakefield St; charges may apply for major exhibits; ⏲10am-5pm) Housed in the monumental old library in Civic Sq, Wellington's much-loved City Gallery does a cracking job of securing acclaimed contemporary international exhibitions, as well as unearthing and supporting those at the forefront of the NZ scene. A jam-packed events calendar and excellent Nikau Gallery Cafe enhance endearment.

FREE New Zealand Film Archive CINEMA
(Map p378; ☎film info line 04-499 3456; www.filmarchive.org.nz; cnr Taranaki & Ghuznee Sts; movies $8; ⏲9am-5pm Mon-Fri, evening cinema screenings Wed-Sat) The Film Archive is a veritable vortex of NZ moving images, into which you could well get sucked for days on end. Its library holds more than 150,000 titles spanning feature films, documentaries, short films, home movies, newsreels, TV programs and advertisements. There are regular screenings in the cinema ($8), as well as a viewing library (free) where you can ferret out and watch films until you're square-eyed. Groovy on-site cafe.

Carter Observatory ASTRONOMY
(Map p368; ☎04-910 3140; www.carterobservatory.org; 40 Salamanca Rd; adult/child $18.50/8; ⏲10am-5pm, to 9.30pm Tue & Sat) At the top of the Botanic Gardens (p371), the Carter Observatory features a full-dome planetarium offering regular shows with virtual tours of the local skies; a multimedia display of Polynesian navigation, Maori cosmology and European explorers; and some of NZ's finest telescopes and astronomical artefacts. Check the website for evening star-gazing times.

FREE Academy Galleries GALLERY
(Map p368; www.nzafa.com; 1 Queens Wharf; ⏲10am-5pm) The showcase of the New Zealand Academy of Fine Arts, Academy Galleries presents frequently changing exhibitions by NZ artists.

FREE New Zealand Portrait Gallery GALLERY
(Map p368; www.portraitgallery.nzl.org; Shed 11, Queens Wharf; ⏲10.30am-4.30pm) Housed in historic waterfront Shed 11, this gallery presents

WELLINGTON IN ...

Two Days

To get a feel for the lie of the land, walk (or drive) up to the **Mt Victoria Lookout**, or ride the **cable car** up to the **Wellington Botanic Gardens**. After lunch on cool **Cuba Street,** immerse yourself in all things Kiwi at **Te Papa** or the **Museum of Wellington City & Sea**. Drink beer by the jug and meet fun-loving locals at **Mighty Mighty**.

The next day, fuel-up with coffee and eggs at **Nikau** in the City Gallery, then head to **Zealandia** to meet the birds and learn about NZ conservation, or encounter some other bird-brains in a tour of **Parliament House**. For dinner, try **Chow** or **Phoenician Falafel**, then spend your evening **bar-hopping** along Courtenay Pl. Nocturnal entertainment could involve live music, a movie at the gloriously restored **Embassy Theatre**, or a midnight snack at a late-closing cafe – or all three.

Four Days

Shake and bake the two-day itinerary, then decorate with the following: hightail it out of Wellington for some wine-tasting around **Martinborough**, followed by a seal-spotting safari along the wild **Cape Palliser.** The next day, have a picnic in **Paekakariki**, plunge in for a swim, and take a wander around **Queen Elizabeth Park** next door.

Greater Wellington

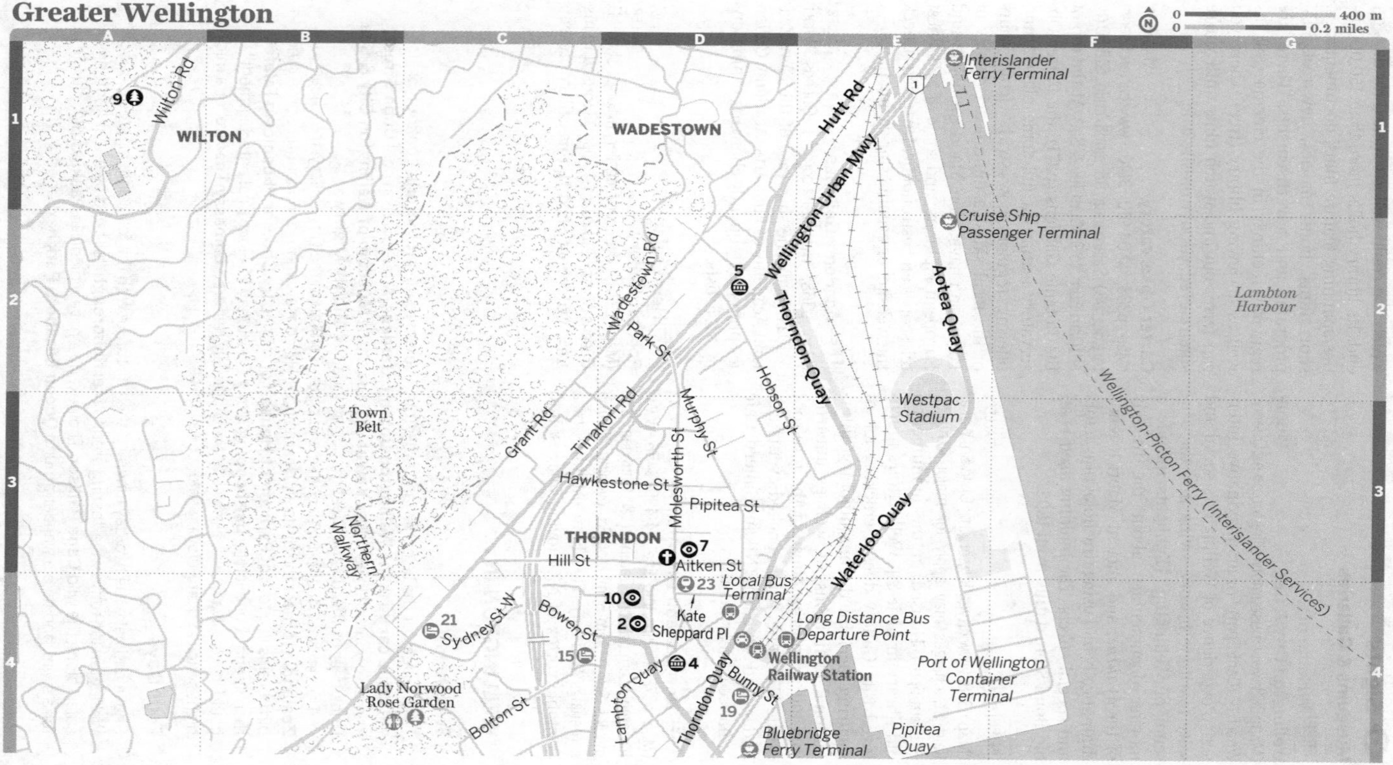

0 400 m
0 0.2 miles

A B C D E F G
1 2 3 4

9
Wilton Rd
WILTON
WADESTOWN
Hutt Rd
Wellington Urban Mwy
Interislander Ferry Terminal
1
Cruise Ship Passenger Terminal
5
Wadestown Rd
Park St
Thorndon Quay
Aotea Quay
Lambton Harbour
Hobson St
Westpac Stadium
Town Belt
Grant Rd
Tinakori Rd
Murphy St
Molesworth St
Hawkestone St
Pipitea St
Wellington-Picton Ferry (Interislander Services)
Waterloo Quay
THORNDON
7
Northern Walkway
Hill St
Aitken St
23
Local Bus Terminal
10
Kate Sheppard Pl
2
Sydney St W
21
Bowen St
Long Distance Bus Departure Point
15
Wellington Railway Station
4
Lambton Quay
Thorndon Quay
Bunny St
19
Port of Wellington Container Terminal
Lady Norwood Rose Garden
Bolton St
Bluebridge Ferry Terminal
Pipitea Quay

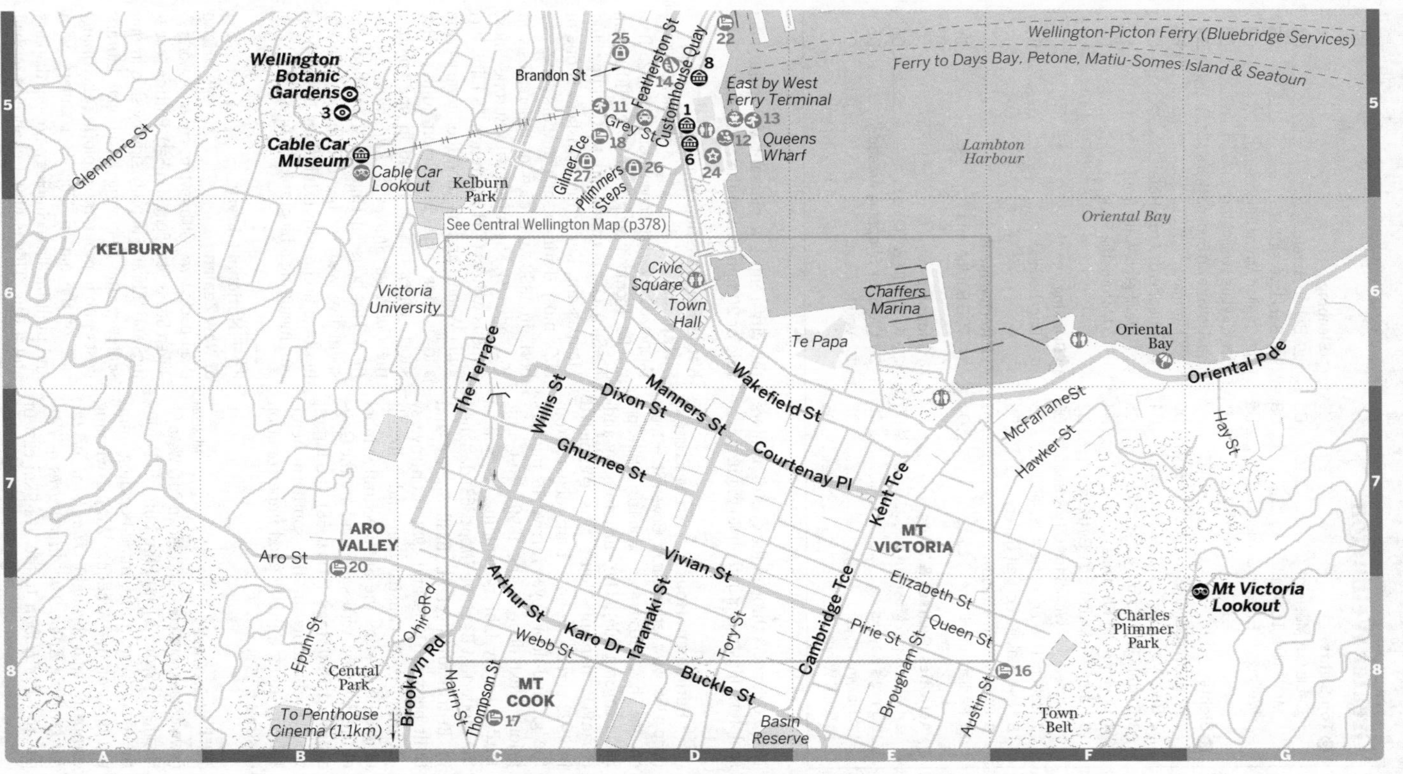
Wellington-Picton Ferry (Bluebridge Services)
Ferry to Days Bay, Petone, Matiu-Somes Island & Seatoun
Wellington Botanic Gardens
3
Cable Car Museum
Cable Car Lookout
Kelburn Park
Glenmore St
KELBURN
Brandon St
25
Featherston St
14
Customhouse Quay
8
22
East by West Ferry Terminal
13
11
Grey St
18
1
6
12
Queens Wharf
24
Gilmer Tce
27
Plimmers Steps
26
Lambton Harbour
Oriental Bay
See Central Wellington Map (p378)
Civic Square
Town Hall
Te Papa
Chaffers Marina
Oriental Bay
Oriental Pde
Victoria University
The Terrace
Willis St
Dixon St
Manners St
Wakefield St
Courtenay Pl
Ghuznee St
Kent Tce
McFarlane St
Hawker St
Hay St
MT VICTORIA
ARO VALLEY
Aro St
20
Vivian St
Cambridge Tce
Elizabeth St
Mt Victoria Lookout
Charles Plimmer Park
Ohiro Rd
Arthur St
Taranaki St
Tory St
Pirie St
Queen St
Epuni St
Central Park
Brooklyn Rd
Webb St
Karo Dr
Buckle St
Brougham St
16
Austin St
Town Belt
To Penthouse Cinema (1.1km)
Nairn St
Thompson St
17
MT COOK
Basin Reserve
5
6
7
8
A
B
C
D
E
F
G

Greater Wellington

Top Sights

	Cable Car Museum	B5
	Mt Victoria Lookout	G8
	Wellington Botanic Gardens	B5

Sights

1	Academy Galleries	D5
2	Beehive	D4
3	Carter Observatory	B5
4	Government Buildings	D4
5	Katherine Mansfield's Birthplace	D2
6	Museum of Wellington City & Sea	D5
7	National Library of New Zealand	D3
8	New Zealand Portrait Gallery	D5
9	Otari-Wilton's Bush	A1
10	Parliament House	D4

Activities, Courses & Tours

11	Cable Car & Museum	D5
12	Ferg's Kayaks	D5
13	Helipro	D5
14	Wild Winds	D5

Sleeping

15	Bolton Hotel	C4
16	Booklovers B&B	F8
17	Carillon Motor Inn	C8
18	CityLife Wellington	D5
19	Downtown Backpackers	D4
20	Mermaid	B7
21	Shepherds Arms Hotel	C4
22	Wellington Waterfront Motorhome Park	D5

Drinking

23	Backbencher	D4

Entertainment

24	TSB Bank Arena	D5

Shopping

25	Kirkcaldie & Stains	D5
26	Old Bank Shopping Arcade	D5
27	Vault	C5

New Zealanders through the eyes of painters, sculptors, illustrators and photographers.

FREE **Parliament House** CULTURAL BUILDING
(Map p368; www.parliament.nz; Bowen St; tours on the hour 10am-4pm Mon-Fri, 10am-3pm Sat, 11am-3pm Sun) The austere grey-and-cream Parliament House was completed in 1922. Free one-hour tours depart from the ground-floor foyer (arrive 15 minutes prior). Next door is the 1899 neo-Gothic Parliamentary Library building, as well as the modernist **Beehive** (Map p368) designed by British architect Sir Basil Spence and built between 1969 and 1980. Controversy surrounded its construction and – love it or loathe it – it's the architectural symbol of the country. Across the road are the **Government Buildings** (Map p368), the largest wooden building in the southern hemisphere, doing a pretty good impersonation of stone.

FREE **Weta Cave** MUSEUM
(www.wetanz.com; cnr Camperdown Rd & Weka St, Miramar; 9am-5.30pm) Film buffs will enjoy the Weta Cave, a fun, mind-boggling mini-museum of the Academy Award–winning company that brought *The Lord of the Rings, King Kong, The Adventures of Tintin* and *The Hobbit* to life. It's 9km east of the city centre, a pleasant waterside bike ride or 20 minutes on the No 2 bus.

Katherine Mansfield's Birthplace HISTORIC BUILDING
(Map p368; www.katherinemansfield.com; 25 Tinakori Rd, Thorndon; adult/child $8/2; 10am-4pm Tue-Sun) Often compared to Chekhov and Maupassant, Katherine Mansfield is one of NZ's most distinguished authors. She was born in 1888, and died of tuberculosis in 1923 aged 34. She mixed with Europe's most famous writers (DH Lawrence, TS Eliot, Virginia Woolf), and married the literary critic and author John Middleton Murry. Her short stories can be found in one volume, the *Collected Stories of Katherine Mansfield*. This house in Tinakori Rd is where she spent five years of her childhood, a lovely heritage home with exhibitions in her honour, including a biographical film.

FREE **National Library of New Zealand** CULTURAL BUILDING
(Map p368; www.natlib.govt.nz; cnr Molesworth & Aitken Sts; 9am-5pm Mon-Sat) Putting 'exciting' and 'library' happily side by side in one sentence, the re-emerged National Library hosts public programs exploring the brainy side of the nation. There's a gallery, wi-fi and multimedia technology, pop-up displays and a cafe. This is also a chance to eyeball

nationally significant documents such as the Treaty of Waitangi and the women's suffrage petition.

FREE **The Dowse** GALLERY
(www.dowse.org.nz; 45 Laings Rd, Lower Hutt; ⏲10am-4.30pm Mon-Fri, 10am-5pm Sat & Sun) Fifteen minutes' drive or via regular buses from downtown Wellington, the Dowse is worth visiting for its architecture alone (the pink is positively audacious). It's also a friendly, accessible art museum showcasing NZ art, craft and design. Nice cafe.

FREE **Petone Settlers Museum** MUSEUM
(www.newdowse.org.nz; The Esplanade, Petone; ⏲10am-4pm Wed-Sun) On the shell-strewn Petone foreshore, 10 to 15 minutes' drive from downtown Wellington or reachable by regular bus services, the art-deco Petone Settlers Museum recalls local migration and settlement, in its charming *Tatou Tatou* exhibition.

Gardens & Lookouts

FREE **Wellington Botanic Gardens** GARDENS
(Map p368) The hilly, 25-hectare botanic gardens can be *almost* effortlessly visited via a cable-car ride (nice bit of planning, eh?). They boast a tract of original native forest along with varied collections including a beaut rose garden and international plant collections. Add in fountains, a cheerful playground, sculptures, duck pond, cafe, magical city views and much more, and you've got a grand day out. The gardens are also accessible from the Centennial Entrance on Glenmore St (Karori bus 3).

Cable Car & Museum CABLE CAR
(Map p368; www.wellingtoncablecar.co.nz; one-way adult/child $3.50/1, return $6/2; ⏲departs every 10min, 7am-10pm Mon-Fri, 8.30am-10pm Sat, 9am-9pm Sun) One of Wellington's most famous attractions is the little red cable car that clanks up the steep slope from Lambton Quay to Kelburn. At the top are the Wellington Botanic Gardens, the Carter Observatory (p367) and the small-but-nifty **Cable Car Museum** (Map p368; www.cablecarmuseum.co.nz; admission free), which tells the cable car's story since it was built in 1902 to open up hilly Kelburn for settlement. Take the cable car back down the hill, or ramble down through the gardens (a 30- to 60-minute walk, depending on your wend).

Mt Victoria Lookout LOOKOUT
(Map p368) For a readily accessible viewpoint of the city, harbour and surrounds, venture up to the lookout atop the 196m Mt Victoria, east of the city centre. You can take bus 2 some of the way up, but the rite of passage is to sweat it out on the walk (ask a local for directions or just follow your nose). If you've got your own wheels, take Oriental Pde along the waterfront and then scoot up Carlton Gore Rd. If this whets your appetite, ask a local how to get to the wind turbine or Mt Kaukau – these are even higher viewpoints that'll blow your socks off.

FREE **Otari-Wilton's Bush** PARK
(Map p368; 160 Wilton Rd; ⏲dawn-dusk) About 3km west of the city is Otari-Wilton's Bush, the only botanic gardens in NZ specialising in native flora. There are more than 1200 plant species here, including some of the

MAORI NZ: WELLINGTON

In legend the mouth of Maui's Fish, and traditionally known as Te Whanganui-a-Tara, the Wellington area became known to Maori in the mid-19th century as 'Poneke' (a transliteration of Port Nicholas, its European name at the time).

The major *iwi* (tribes) of the region were Te Ati Awa and Ngati Toa. Ngati Toa was the *iwi* of Te Rauparaha, who composed the now famous *Ka Mate haka*. Like most urban areas the city is now home to Maori from many *iwi*, sometimes collectively known as Ngati Poneke.

New Zealand's national museum, Te Papa (p374), presents excellent displays on Maori culture, traditional and modern, as well as a colourful *marae* (meeting house). In its gift store you can see excellent carving and other crafts, as you can in both Kura (p386) and Ora (p386) galleries nearby.

Kapiti Island Nature Tours (p391) offers an intimate insight into the Maori culture of Wellington.

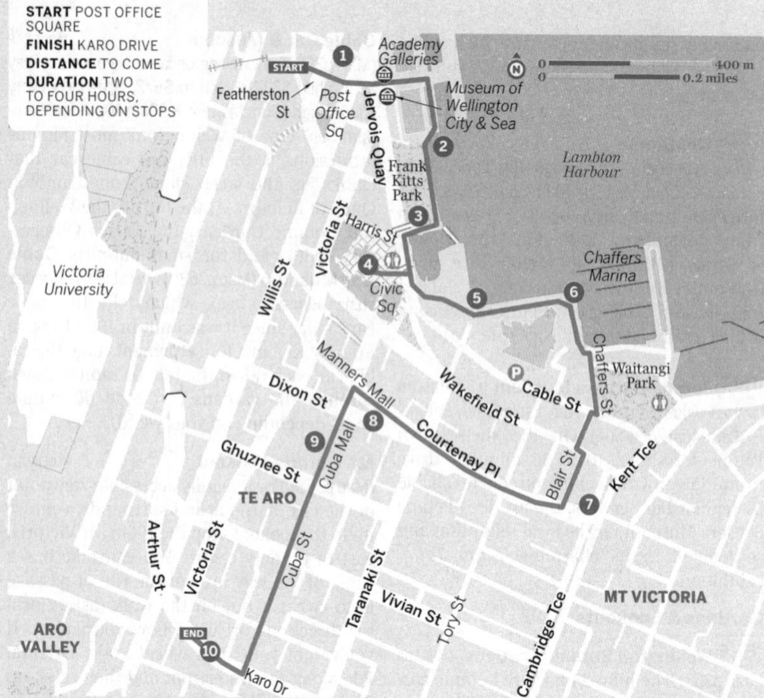

Walking Tour
City Sculpture

To begin, send yourself to Post Office Sq, where Bill Culbert's 1 **SkyBlues** spaghetti's into the air, then cross Jervois Quay to pass between the New Zealand Academy of Fine Arts and Museum of Wellington City & Sea. At the Queens Wharf waterfront, turn south, past the big shed to the 2 **Water Whirler**, the largely lifeless needle of experimental kineticist Len Lye that whirrs crazily into life on the hour several times a day.

Continue along the promenade or deviate through Frank Kitts Park, under which lies Kaffe Eis on the edge of the lagoon and next to the 3 **Albatross Fountain**. A short detour over the flotsam City to Sea Bridge, Civic Sq is surrounded by the i-SITE, library, and City Gallery. Neil Dawson's 4 **Ferns** hangs in the air, attendant by a stand of nikau palms.

Back on the waterfront, continue past Te Raukura *whare waka* (canoe house), and 5 **Hikitia**, the world's oldest working crane ship. Keep to the wharf, past the bronze form of 6 **Solace in the Wind** leaning over the edge, alongside Katherine Mansfield's breezy contribution to the Wellington Writers Walk.

Cross the footbridge to Waitangi Park to eyeball the graffiti wall and some roller action, before heading south to Courtenay Pl via Chaffers St, and Blair St with its century-old warehouses.

On Courtenay Pl, check out the leggy form of the industrial 7 **Tripod**, before heading west. Cross Taranaki St to 8 **Te Aro Park** with its canoe prow and other ceramic elements.

Both Dixon and Manners St will see you intersect with Cuba St, where you should turn south and head up the pedestrian mall, home of the ridiculous, malicious 9 **Bucket Fountain**. It's out to get you. See the sly, schadenfreude smile on the face of the tuatara slide?

Change down to granny gear and wander through doorways, all the way to the top of Cuba, into the remnant heritage precinct cut through by the controversial inner-city bypass. The Lady McLeods at Arthur's & Martha's cafes could well tell the tale, poignantly illustrated by Regan Gentry's brilliant but ghostly 10 **Subject to Change**, and the Tonk's Well alongside.

WORTH A TRIP

DAYS BAY & MATIU-SOMES ISLAND

The small **East By West Ferry** (☎04-499 1282; www.eastbywest.co.nz; Queens Wharf) plies Wellington harbour between Queens Wharf and Days Bay in Eastbourne, via Matiu-Somes Island, and on fine weekends Petone and Seatoun as well.

Locals have been jumping on a boat to **Days Bay** for decades, where there's a beach, park and cafe, and a boatshed with kayaks, rowboats and bikes for hire. A 10-minute walk from Days Bay leads to Eastbourne, a beachy township with more cafes, a cute pub, and numerous other diversions.

The ferry also stops at at **Matiu-Somes Island** in the middle of the harbour, a DOC-managed reserve where you might see weta, tuatara, kakariki and little blue penguins, among other critters. The island is rich in history, having once been a prisoner-of-war camp and quarantine station. Take a picnic lunch, or even stay overnight in the campsite (adult/child $10/5) or in the DOC house – book online at www.doc.govt.nz or at Wellington's DOC visitor centre (p387).

It's a 20- to 30-minute chug across the harbour. There are 16 sailings on weekdays, eight on Saturday and Sunday (return fare adult/child $22/11.50).

city's oldest trees, as well as 11km of walking trails and delightful picnic areas. Bus 14 from the city passes the gates.

Wildlife

Zealandia WILDLIFE RESERVE
(☎04-920 9200; www.visitzealandia.com; Waiapu Rd; adult/child/family exhibition only $18.50/9/46, exhibition & valley $28.80/14.50/71.50; ⏰10am-5pm, last entry 4pm) This groundbreaking eco-sanctuary is tucked in the hills about 2km west of town (bus 3 passes nearby, or see the Zealandia website for the free shuttle). Living wild within the fenced valley are more than 30 native bird species, including rare takahe, saddleback, hihi and kaka, as well as NZ's most accessible wild population of tuatara and little spotted kiwi. An excellent exhibition relays NZ's natural history and world-renowned conservation story. More than 30km of tracks can be explored and there's a daily tour (11.15am). The night tour provides an opportunity to spot nocturnal creatures including kiwi, frogs and glow-worms (adult/child $76.50/36). Cafe and shop on-site.

Wellington Zoo ZOO
(www.wellingtonzoo.com; 200 Daniell St; adult/child $20/10; ⏰9.30am-5pm, last entry 4.15pm) Committed to conservation, research and rescuing wayward Antarctic penguins, Wellington Zoo is also home to a plethora of native and non-native wildlife, including lions and chimpanzees. The nocturnal house has kiwi and tuatara. Check the website for info on 'close encounters', which allow you to meet the big cats, red pandas and giraffes (for a fee). The zoo is 4km south of the city; catch bus 10 or 23.

Staglands Wildlife Reserve WILDLIFE RESERVE
(www.staglands.co.nz; Akatarawa Rd, Upper Hutt; adult/child $19/8; ⏰10am-5pm) The drive from Upper Hutt to Waikanae (on the Kapiti Coast) along the windy, scenic Akatarawa Rd passes the 10-hectare Staglands Wildlife Reserve, which helps to conserve native NZ birds and animals, such as the blue duck (whio). It's 16km from SH2, 20km from SH1.

Activities

Ferg's Kayaks KAYAKING
(Map p368; www.fergskayaks.co.nz; Shed 6, Queens Wharf; ⏰10am-8pm Mon-Fri, 10am-6pm Sat & Sun) Punish your tendons with indoor rock climbing (adult/child $15/10), cruise the waterfront on a pair of in-line skates ($15 for two hours) or paddle around the harbour in a kayak or on a stand-up paddleboard (from $15 for one hour). There's also bike hire (one hour from $15) and guided kayaking trips.

Makara Peak Mountain Bike Park MOUNTAIN BIKING
(www.makarapeak.org; South Karori Rd, Karori; admission by donation) In the hills of Karori, 4km west of the city centre (bus 3, 17 or 18), this excellent 200-hectare park is laced with 24km of single-track ranging from beginner to expert. The nearby **Mud Cycles** (☎04-476 4961; www.mudcycles.co.nz; 421 Karori Rd, Karori; half-/full-day/weekend bike hire from $30/45/75; ⏰8.30am-6.30pm Mon-Fri, 9am-5pm Sat, 10am-5pm Sun) has mountain bikes for hire, and

runs guided tours for riders of all abilities. Wellington is fast becoming a MTB mecca – visit tracks.org.nz for details of the dozens of other rides around the capital.

Wild Winds WINDSURFING
(Map p368; ☎04-384 1010; www.wildwinds.co.nz; 36 Customhouse Quay) With all this wind and water, Wellington was made for windsurfing, kiteboading, and stand-up paddleboarding. Take on one or all three with Wild Winds, with lessons starting from $110 for two hours.

Tours

Walk Wellington GUIDED TOUR
(☎04-802 4860; www.walkwellington.org.nz; adult/child $20/10; ⊙tours 10am daily, plus 5.30pm Mon, Wed & Fri Nov-Mar) Informative and great-value two-hour walking tours focusing on the city and waterfront, departing the i-SITE. Book online, phone or just turn up.

Flat Earth GUIDED TOUR
(☎0800 775 805, 04-472 9635; www.flatearth.co.nz; half- & full-day tours $159-385) An array of themed small-group tours (city highlights, Maori treasures, arts and Middle-earth filming locations).

Hammonds Scenic Tours GUIDED TOUR
(☎04-472 0869; www.wellingtonsightseeingtours.com; city tour adult/child $55/27.50, Kapiti Coast $100/50, Wairarapa $195/97.50) Runs a 2½-hour city highlights tour, four-hour tour of the Kapiti Coast, and a full-day Wairarapa experience including Cape Palliser.

Zest Food Tours GUIDED TOUR
(☎04-801 9198; www.zestfoodtours.co.nz; tours from $128) Runs 2½- to 5½-hour small-group city sightseeing tours; longer tours include lunch with matched wines at Logan Brown (p381).

Wild About Wellington GUIDED TOUR
(☎027 441 9010; www.wildaboutwellington.co.nz; tours from $95) Small-group walking and public-transport tours including City of Style, Sights & Bites, Wild About Chocolate or Boutique Beer Tasting. From a few hours to a full day.

Movie Tours GUIDED TOUR
(☎027 419 3077; www.adventuresafari.co.nz; tours from adult/child $45/30) Half- and full-day tours for real movie fiends – more props, clips, film locations and Middle-earth than you can shake a staff at.

Wellington Rover GUIDED TOUR
(☎0800 426 211, 04-471 0044; www.wellingtonrover.co.nz; tours from adult/child $50/25) Half- to full-day tours of the city and plenty of Hobbit action.

Helipro SCENIC FLIGHTS
(Map p368; ☎04-472 1550; www.helipro.co.nz; Shed 1, Queens Wharf; 10/15/25/35min flights per person $95/190/240/375) Buzz around Welly in a chopper. Heli-lunch trips to the Wairarapa and Marlborough Sounds also available.

Festivals & Events

Check at the Wellington i-SITE or visit www.wellingtonnz.com/event for comprehensive festival listings; most tickets can be booked through Ticketek (p385).

DON'T MISS

TREASURES OF TE PAPA

Te Papa (Map p378; www.tepapa.govt.nz; 55 Cable St; admission free; ⊙10am-6pm Fri-Wed, to 9pm Thu) is the city's 'must-see' attraction, and for reasons well beyond the fact that it's NZ's national museum. It's highly interactive, fun and full of surprises.

Aptly, 'Te Papa Tongarewa' loosely translates as 'treasure box'. The riches inside include an amazing collection of Maori artefacts and the museum's own colourful *marae*; natural history and environment exhibitions; Pacific and NZ history galleries; national art collection, and themed hands-on 'discovery centres' for children. Exhibitions occupy impressive gallery spaces with a high-tech twist (eg motion-simulator rides and a house shaking through an earthquake). Big-name, temporary exhibitions incur an admission fee.

You could spend a day exploring Te Papa's six floors but still not see it all. To cut to the chase, head to the information desk on level two. For exhibition highlights and to get your bearings, the one-hour 'Introducing Te Papa' tour ($14) is a good idea; tours leave from the info desk at 10.15am, noon and 2pm daily in winter, more frequently in summer. Two cafes and two gift shops complete the Te Papa experience, one which could well take a couple of visits.

LOCAL KNOWLEDGE

TANA UMAGA, FORMER ALL BLACK CAPTAIN

Wellington is a beautiful city, with a striking waterfront surrounded by bush-clad hills, and sightseeing and photo opportunities are plentiful. Downtown, it's easy to get around on foot and there are plenty of cafes and restaurants to stop at for a break. It's also a very family-friendly city: Wellington Zoo (p373) is a special place to take the family to check out the brave one-legged kiwi, while just a short bus ride away, Te Papa (p374), the national museum, mixes history and modern technology under the one roof. Wellingtonians are always really friendly and welcoming and ready to help visitors to their city.

Summer City CULTURAL
(www.wellingtonnz.com) A two-month celebration commencing mid-January that includes countless free outdoor events.

New Zealand International Sevens SPORTS
(www.sevens.co.nz) The world's top seven-a-side rugby teams compete, but it's the crowd that plays up. Held in February.

Fringe NZ CULTURAL
(www.fringe.org.nz) Three weeks across February and March of way-out-there experimental visual arts, music, dance and theatre.

New Zealand International Arts Festival CULTURAL
(www.festival.co.nz) A month-long biennial (even years) spectacular of theatre, dance, music, visual arts and literature. International acts aplenty. Usually held late February to March.

ASB Gardens Magic CULTURAL
(www.wellingtonnz.com) Free evening concerts in the Botanic Gardens. Get there early with blanket and picnic. In March.

New Zealand Comedy Festival COMEDY
(www.comedyfestival.co.nz) Three weeks of hysterics across April/May. World-famous-in-NZ comedians, and some truly world-famous ones, too.

Matariki CULTURAL
(www.tepapa.govt.nz) Celebrating the Maori New Year (in June) with a free festival of dance, music and other events at Te Papa.

International Film Festival FILM
(www.nzff.co.nz) Two-week indie film fest screening the best of NZ and international cinema. Held over July/August.

Beervana BEER
(www.beervana.co.nz) A barrel-load of craft-beer aficionados roll into town for a weekend of supping and beard-stroking. In August.

Wellington on a Plate FOOD
(www.wellingtononaplate.com) Lip-smacking program of gastronomic events, and bargains aplenty at restaurants around the city. Held in August.

World of WearableArt FASHION
(www.worldofwearableart.com) A two-week run in September of the spectacular nightly extravaganza of amazing garments. Tickets are hot property.

Toast Martinborough FOOD & DRINK
(www.toastmartinborough.co.nz) A day of hedonism around the Martinborough vineyards. Tickets = hot cakes. Held in November.

Sleeping

Wellington accommodation is generally more expensive than in regional areas. Standards are reasonably high, and there are plenty of options right in or within easy walking distance of the city centre. One hassle is the lack of parking; if you have your own wheels, ask about car parking when you book (and be aware you'll probably have to pay for it).

Wellington's budget accommodation largely takes the form of multistorey hostel megaliths. There's no 'motel alley' in Wellington, but motels are scattered around the city fringe. Being the hub of government and business, self-contained apartments are popular, and bargains can often be found at weekends.

During the peak season (December to February), or during major festivals, book your bed well in advance.

Campsites are as rare as bad coffee in Wellington. Tenters should head to the Harcourt Holiday Park (p379) in the Hutt Valley, the Wellington Top 10 Holiday Park (p379) in Seaview, or Paekakariki Holiday Park (p390). Motorhomers, however, can enjoy

WELLINGTON FOR CHILDREN

With ankle-biters in tow, your best bet is a visit to colourful **Capital E** (Map p378; ☎04-913 3740; www.capitale.org.nz; Civic Sq; events free-$15; ⊙9am-5pm Mon-Fri, 10am-4pm Sat), an educational entertainment complex designed especially for kids. Expect interactive rotating exhibitions, children's theatre and TV, readings, workshops and courses. Call or check the website for the events calendar and prices.

Te Papa (p374) is fantastic for children. The Discovery Centres are loaded with interactive activities, and StoryPlace is designed for children aged five and under. See the dedicated Kids page on the website for more details. Along the waterfront on either side of Te Papa are **Frank Kitts Park** and **Waitangi Park**, both with playgrounds perfect for expending pent-up energy.

A ride up the cable car (p371) and a lap around the Wellington Botanic Gardens (p371) will pump plenty of fresh air into young lungs, and when darkness descends head to the Carter Observatory (p367) where kids can gaze at galaxies far, far away. On a more terrestrial bent, check out some living dinosaurs (aka tuatara) at the Wellington Zoo (p373) or Zealandia (p373).

For online ideas, search the Sights & Activities section of www.wellingtonnz.cm.

the unbelievably convenient Wellington Waterfront Motorhome Park (p379).

TOP CHOICE YHA Wellington City HOSTEL $
(Map p378; ☎04-801 7280; www.yha.co.nz; cnr Cambridge Tce & Wakefield St; dm $29-36, d with/without bathroom $120/88; @☜) Wellington's best hostel wins points for fantastic communal areas including two big kitchens and dining areas, games room, reading room and dedicated movie room with high-tech projector. Sustainable initiatives (recycling, composting and energy-efficient hot water) impress, and there's a comprehensive booking service at reception, along with espresso.

Ohtel BOUTIQUE HOTEL $$$
(Map p378; ☎04-803 0600; www.ohtel.com; 66 Oriental Parade; d $265-395; ☜) Aesthetes check in and don't want to check out at this bijou hotel on Oriental Parade. Individually decorated rooms are beautified with stylish furniture and contemporary artwork and ceramics, avidly collected by the architect-owner. The bathrooms in the deluxe rooms and suites, with their vista walls and deep tubs, are a designer's wet dream.

Nomads Capital HOSTEL $
(Map p378; ☎0508 666 237, 04-978 7800; www.nomadscapital.com; 118 Wakefield St; dm $28-36, d with bathroom $95-105; @☜) Smack-bang in the middle of town, Nomads has good security, spick-and-span rooms, an on-site cafe-bar (free modest nightly meals) and discounts for longer stays. Kitchen and lounge spaces are short on elbow room, but heritage features (such as the amazing stairwell) stop you dwelling on the negatives.

Moana Lodge HOSTEL $
(☎04-233 2010; www.moanalodge.co.nz; 49 Moana Rd, Plimmerton; dm $33, d with shared bathroom $76-94; @☜) Just off SH1 and only a short train ride or drive from Wellington (25km), this exceptional backpackers right on the beach is immaculate and inviting, with friendly owners super-keen to infuse you with their local knowledge. Kayaks and bikes available. From Wellington catch the Tranz Metro Kapiti train to Plimmerton.

Cambridge Hotel HOSTEL $
(Map p378; ☎04-385 8829; www.cambridgehotel.co.nz; 28 Cambridge Tce; dm $23-25, s with/without bathroom $95/65, d $105/85; @☜) Comfortable, affordable accommodation in a heritage hotel. En suite rooms have Sky TV, phone and fridge (try for a room at the back if you're a light sleeper). The backpacker wing has a snug kitchen/lounge, flash bathrooms and dorms with little natural light but sky-high ceilings. The $2 breakfast is a plus.

Capital View Motor Inn MOTEL $$
(Map p378; ☎0800 438 505, 04-385 0515; www.capitalview.co.nz; 12 Thompson St; d $125-160; ☜) Many of the rooms in this well-maintained, multistorey buiilding close to Cuba St do indeed enjoy capital views – especially the large, good-value penthouse (sleeps five, $220). All are self-contained, and recent renovations have freshened things up.

Booklovers B&B B&B $$
(Map p368; ☎04-384 2714; www.booklovers.co.nz; 123 Pirie St; s/d from $150/180; @📶) This gracious, book-filled B&B run by award-winning author Jane Tolerton has four guest rooms with TV, CDs and CD/DVD player. Three have en suites, one has a private bathroom. Bus 2 runs from the front gate to Courtenay Pl and the train station, and the city's 'green belt' begins right next door. Free wi-fi and parking.

Comfort & Quality Hotels HOTEL $$
(Map p378; ☎04-385 2156, 0800 873 553; www.hotelwellington.co.nz; 223 Cuba St; d $104-200; @📶🏊) Two hotels in one: the sympathetically renovated historic Trekkers building with its smaller, cheaper rooms (Comfort); and the snazzier high-rise Quality with modern styling and a swimming pool. Both share the in-house bar and dining room (mains $22 to $30). Two solid options in the heart of Cuba.

City Cottages RENTAL HOUSES $$
(Map p378; ☎021 073 9232; www.citybedandbreakfast.co.nz; Tonks Grove; d/q $170/200; 📶) Saved only after protracted public protest when the new bypass went through, these two tiny 1880 cottages sit amongst a precious precinct of historic Cuba St buildings. Clever conversion has transformed them into all-mod-con, self-contained one-bedroom pads, comfortable for two but sleeping up to four thanks to a sofa bed. Stylish, convenient, and veerrrry Cuba. Ask about road noise.

Museum Hotel HOTEL $$$
(Map p378; ☎0800 994 335, 04-802 8900; www.museumhotel.co.nz; 90 Cable St; r & apt Mon-Thu $205-399, Fri-Sun $199-349; @📶🏊) Formerly known as 'Museum Hotel de Wheels' (to make way for Te Papa, it was rolled here from its original location 120m away), this art-filled hotel keeps the quirk-factor high. Bright-eyed staff, a very good restaurant with outrageous decor, and groovy tunes piped into the lobby make a refreshing change from homogenised business hotels. Tasty weekend/weekly rates.

Mermaid GUESTHOUSE $$
(Map p368; ☎04-384 4511; www.mermaid.co.nz; 1 Epuni St; s $95-130, d $105-145; 📶) In the uber-cool Aro Valley 'hood, Mermaid is a small women-only guesthouse in a colourfully restored villa. Each room is individually themed with artistic flair (one with private bathroom, three with shared facilities). The lounge, kitchen and deck are homely and laid-back. Great cafe, bakery and deli on the doorstep.

Victoria Court MOTEL $$
(Map p378; ☎04-385 7102; www.victoriacourt.co.nz; 201 Victoria St; r $149-205; 📶) Our top motel choice in the city centre, with plenty of parking. The affable owners offer modern, spacious studios and apartments with spa baths, kitchenettes, slick blond-wood joinery and TVs. Two disabled-access units; larger units sleep six.

Trek Global HOSTEL $
(Map p378; ☎04-471 3480, 0800 868 735; www.trekglobal.net; 9 O'Reilly Ave; s $59, tw with/without bathroom $89/69, d with/without bathroom $99/79; 📶) Wellington's groovy new hostel is slightly squeezed into its back-lane location, hence some tight but funky communal areas (the lounge is a highlight). Multistorey, colour-coded accommodation wings are a little bit rabbit-warren, but what counts is that it's relatively quiet, the rooms are fresh, the service is good, and there are laudable extras such as bike hire, bookings, and a fab women-only dorm with a suntrap terrace.

Downtown Backpackers HOSTEL $
(Map p368; ☎0800 225 725, 04-473 8482; www.downtownbackpackers.co.nz; 1 Bunny St; dm $25-29, s $65, d $82-95; @📶) An old charmer at the railway end of town, housed in a grand art-deco building. Downtown has clean, bright rooms and plenty of character-filled communal areas (be sure to check out the carved fireplace in the bar). Budget meals available in the cafe morning and night.

🍃 **Bolton Hotel** HOTEL $$$
(Map p368; ☎0800 996 622, 04-472 9966; www.boltonhotel.co.nz; cnr Bolton & Mowbray Sts; d $174-334; @📶🏊) Slick and well serviced, the lofty Bolton deserves its five stars. Room options are varied but share a common theme of muted tones, fine linens and colourful artwork. Most are spacious with full kitchen facilities and some enjoy park or city views. Warm your cockles in the heated pool, spa and sauna.

CityLife Wellington APARTMENTS $$$
(Map p368; ☎04-922 2800, 0800 368 888; www.heritagehotels.co.nz; 300 Lambton Quay; d Mon-Thu $229-249, Fri-Sun $179-199; @📶) Luxurious serviced apartments in the city centre,

Central Wellington

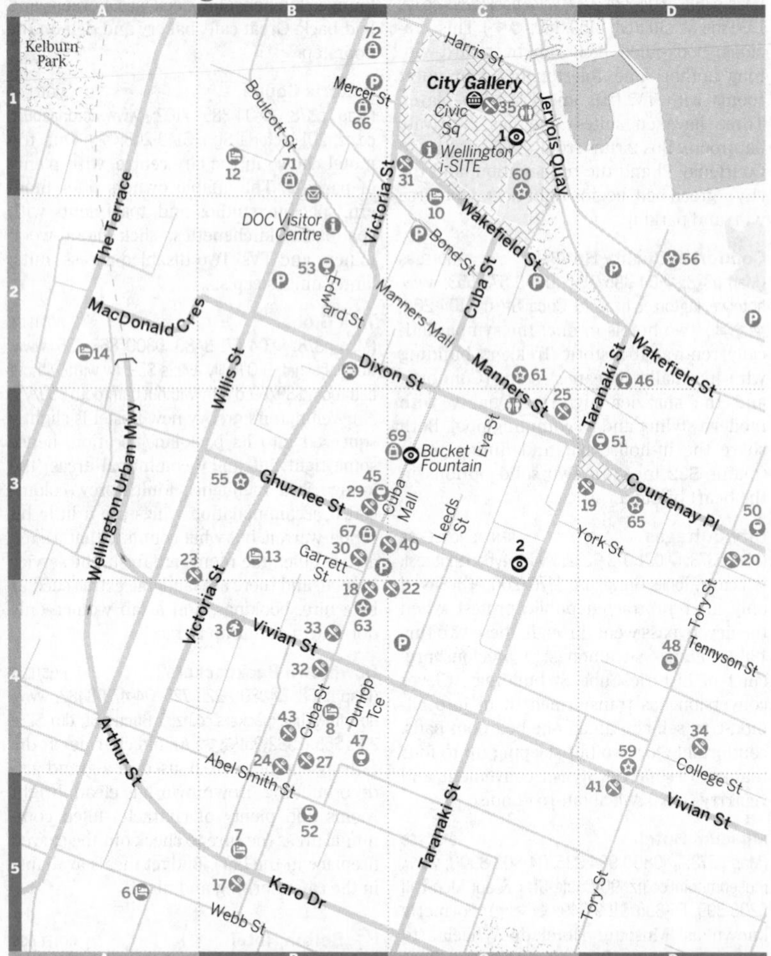

ranging from studios to three-bedroom arrangements, some with a harbour glimpse. Features include full kitchen, CD/DVD player, and in-room laundry facilities. Weekend rates are great bang for your buck. The vehicle entrance is from Gilmer Tce, off Boulcott St (parking $15.50 per day).

Shepherds Arms Hotel HISTORIC HOTEL **$$**
(Map p368; ☎0800 393 782, 04-472 1320; www.shepherds.co.nz; 285 Tinakori Rd; s without bathroom $65-75, d with bathroom $100-140; 📶) With wall-to-wall heritage buildings and proximity to the Botanic Gardens, Thorndon makes an atmospheric home base. This well-preserved hotel serves its patrons in fitting style, with a restaurant and bar, and good-value rooms upstairs. The ovine artwork isn't baaaad.

Apollo Lodge MOTELS **$$**
(Map p378; ☎0800 361 645, 04-385 1849; www.apollolodge.co.nz; 49 Majoribanks St; d $135-160, q $190-260; 📶) Within staggering distance of Courtenay Pl, Apollo Lodge is a loose collation of 35 varied units (one and two bedrooms), ranging from studios to family-friendly units with full kitchen. Nearby apartments available for longer-term stays.

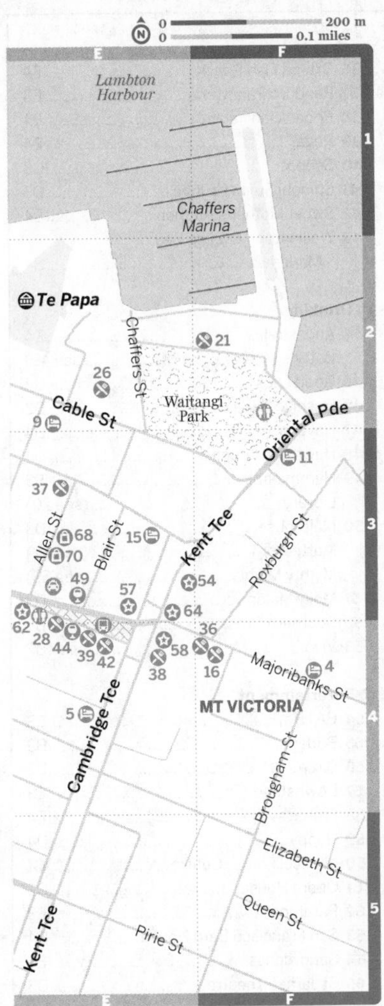

Carillon Motor Inn GUESTHOUSE $
(Map p368; ☎04-384 8795; www.carillon.co.nz; 33 Thompson St; s/d $85/95; 📶; 🚌7) Wow, what a relic! Carillon is a rickety old Victorian mansion that's somehow evaded the wrecking ball, developers' ambitions and renovators' brushstrokes. With its air of *Fawlty Towers* and cheap price, its en suite rooms are a character-filled alternative to the city hostels.

Worldwide Backpackers HOSTEL $
(Map p378; ☎04-802 5590, 0508 888 555; www.worldwidenz.co.nz; 291 The Terrace; dm/d with shared bathroom incl breakfast $29/75; @📶) In a 110-year-old house, Worldwide is a small hostel that's reasonably tidy, with winning features such as free wi-fi, breakfast, and regular barbecues. It's youthful, down-to-earth and chilled out.

Wellington Waterfront Motorhome Park MOTORHOME PARK $
(Map p368; ☎04-472 3838; www.wwmp.co.nz; 12 Waterloo Quay; powered sites $50; 📶) In reality it's simply a waterfront car park, but it's nonetheless unbelievably convenient, offering overnight stays, and modest hourly rates for day-parking. Facilities comprise a sharp ablution block and power supply. Book online.

Wellington Top 10 Holiday Park HOLIDAY PARK $
(☎04-568 5913, 0800 948 686; www.wellingtontop10.co.nz; 95 Hutt Park Rd, Seaview; sites $45, cabins $58-105, motels $111-168; @📶) Holiday park, 13km northeast of Wellington, that's convenient for the ferry. Family-friendly facilities include communal kitchens, games room, jumping pillow and a playground, but its industrial location detracts. Follow the signs off SH2 for Petone and Seaview, or take regular public transport.

Harcourt Holiday Park HOLIDAY PARK $
(☎04-526 7400; www.harcourtholidaypark.co.nz; 45 Akatarawa Rd, Upper Hutt; unpowered/powered sites $32/44, cabins & tourist flats $45-100, motels $120; @📶) Veritably verdant park 35km northeast of Wellington (a 35-minute drive), just off SH2, set in parkland by the trout-filled Hutt River.

✕ Eating

Wellington is an exciting place in which to eat. There's a bewildering array of options in a very small area, and keen competition keeps standards high and prices reasonable. Varied, contemporary NZ dining is nicely complemented by legions of budget fare including oodles of noodles. The recent opening of Le Cordon Bleu cookery school puts some icing on Wellington's culinary cake, bolstering its status as a bona fide gastronomic destination.

Three excellent food markets run from dawn till around 2pm on Sundays – the seriously fruit-and-veggie **Farmers Market** (Map p378; cnr Victoria & Vivian Sts), and the more varied **Harbourside Market** (Wakefield St) next to Te Papa where you'll also find artisan producers seducing foodies with their wares in the **City Market** (Map p378; Chaffers Dock Bldg, 1 Herd St; ⏰8.30am-12.30pm Sun).

Central Wellington

Top Sights
City Gallery ... C1
Te Papa ... E2

Sights
1 Capital E ... C1
2 New Zealand Film Archive ... C3

Activities, Courses & Tours
3 On Yer Bike ... B4

Sleeping
4 Apollo Lodge ... F4
5 Cambridge Hotel ... E4
6 Capital View Motor Inn ... A5
7 City Cottages ... B5
8 Comfort & Quality Hotels ... B4
9 Museum Hotel ... E2
10 Nomads Capital ... C2
11 Ohtel ... F3
12 Trek Global ... B1
13 Victoria Court ... B3
14 Worldwide Backpackers ... A2
15 YHA Wellington City ... E3

Eating
16 Ambeli ... F4
17 Arthur's & Martha's ... B5
18 Aunty Mena's ... B4
19 Burger Fuel ... D3
Capitol ... (see 58)
20 Chow ... D3
21 City Market ... F2
Deluxe ... (see 58)
22 Duke Carvell's ... C4
23 Farmers Market ... A3
24 Fidel's ... B4
25 Great India ... C3
26 Harbourside Market ... E2
27 Heaven ... B4
28 Kaffe Eis ... E4
29 KK Malaysian Cafe ... B3
30 Le Métropolitain ... B3
31 Lido ... C1
32 Logan Brown ... B4
33 Midnight Espresso ... B4
34 Moore Wilson Fresh ... D4
35 Nikau Gallery Cafe ... C1
36 Ortega Fish Shack ... F4
37 Pandoro Panetteria ... E3
38 Phoenician Falafel ... E4
39 Regal ... E4
40 Scopa ... C3
41 Shinobi Sushi Lounge ... D5
42 Sweet Mother's Kitchen ... E4
43 Wellington Trawling Sea Market ... B4

Drinking
44 Ancestral ... E4
Betty's ... (see 49)
45 Good Luck ... B3
46 Hashigo Zake ... D2
47 Havana ... B4
48 Hawthorn Lounge ... D4
49 Hummingbird ... E3
Library ... (see 20)
50 Malthouse ... D3
Matterhorn ... (see 69)
Mighty Mighty ... (see 69)
51 Molly Malone's ... D3
52 Southern Cross ... B5
53 Vivo ... B2

Entertainment
54 BATS ... E3
55 Bodega ... B3
56 Circa ... D2
57 Downstage ... E3
58 Embassy Theatre ... E4
59 Happy ... D4
60 Michael Fowler Centre ... C1
61 Opera House ... C2
62 Paramount ... E3
63 San Francisco Bath House ... B4
64 Sandwiches ... E3
65 St James Theatre ... D3

Shopping
66 Bivouac Outdoor ... B1
67 Hunters & Collectors ... B3
68 Kura ... E3
69 Mandatory ... C3
70 Ora Design Gallery ... E3
71 Starfish ... B1
72 Unity Books ... B1

TOP CHOICE **Ortega Fish Shack** SEAFOOD **$$$**
(Map p378; ☎04-382 9559; www.ortega.co.nz; 16 Marjoribanks St; mains $32-34; ⊙dinner Tue-Sat) Fishing floats, salty portraits and Egyptian floor tiles set a colourful Mediterranean scene, a good hook on which to hang a seafood dinner. Fish comes many ways (with ratatouille and crayfish butter; on pork-and-prawn kedgeree with *nam prik* spicy relish) while the afters head straight for France

courtesy of orange crêpes and one of Welly's best cheeseboards. Excellent food in a relaxed yet upbeat environment.

Scopa ITALIAN **$$**
(Map p378; cnr Cuba & Ghuznee Sts; mains $15-26; 9am-late Mon-Sun;) Perfect pizza, proper pasta and other authentic Italian treats make dining at this modern *cucina* a pleasure. The *bianche* (white) pizzas make a refreshing change as do the *pizzaiolo* – pizzas of the week. Watch the groovy 'Cubans' from a seat in the window. Lunchtime specials; sexy evenings complete with cocktails.

Fidel's CAFE **$**
(Map p378; 234 Cuba St; meals $9-20; 7.30am-late;) A Cuba St institution for caffeine-craving, alternative types. Eggs any-which-way, pizza and splendid salads are cranked out of the itsy kitchen, along with Welly's best milkshakes. Revolutionary memorabilia adorns the walls of the funky interior; decent outdoor areas too. A superbusy crew copes with the chaos admirably.

Capitol MODERN NZ **$$**
(Map p378; www.capitolrestaurant.co.nz; cnr Kent Tce & Majoribanks St; mains $23-33; lunch & dinner daily, brunch from 9.30am Sat & Sun) Simple, seasonal food using premium local ingredients, lovingly prepared with a nod to the classic Italian style. The rabbit pappardelle is to die for (for the rabbit, at least). The dining room is a bit cramped and noisy, but elegant nonetheless. And who's going to gripe when presented with food of this quality for the price? No dinner bookings are taken, but it's well worth waiting with an aperitif at the tiny bar.

Phoenician Falafel LEBANESE **$**
(Map p378; 10 Kent Tce; meals $8-16; 11.30am-9.30pm;) Authentic falafel, shish and *shawarma* (kebab) served up by cheery Lebanese owners. The best kebabs in town, although its sistership, Phoenician Cuisine at 245 Cuba St, comes a very close second.

Nikau Gallery Cafe CAFE **$$**
(Map p378; City Gallery, Civic Sq; lunch $14-25; 7am-4pm Mon-Fri, 8am-4pm Sat;) An airy affair at the sophisticated end of the cafe scene, Nikau consistently dishes up some of the simplest but most delightful fare in town. Refreshing aperitifs, legendary kedgeree and sage eggs, divine sweets, and sunny courtyard.

Logan Brown MODERN NZ **$$$**
(Map p378; 04-801 5114; www.loganbrown.co.nz; 192 Cuba St; mains $39-48; noon-2pm Mon-Sat, 5.30pm-late Mon-Sun) Located in a 1920s banking chamber, Logan-Brown oozes class without being pretentious or overly formal. Believe the hype, sample the lamb two ways, snapper and paua, and peruse the epic wine list. The pre-theatre menu ($39.50) is a fine way of indulging without cleaning out your account. Bookings recommended.

KK Malaysian Cafe MALAYSIAN **$**
(Map p378; 54 Ghuznee St; mains $9-14; lunch Mon-Sat, dinner Mon-Sun;) Decked out like a dirty protest, tiny KK is one of Wellington's most popular cheap Malaysian joints in a city obsessed with Southeast Asian cuisine. Scrumptious satay and rendang to put a smile on your face, accompanied by the ubiquitous roti, of course.

Chow FUSION **$$**
(Map p378; 45 Tory St; small plates $7-17, mains $15-24; noon-midnight;) Home of the legendary blue-cheese-and-peanut wonton, Chow is a stylish pan-Asian restaurant-cum-bar: a must-visit for people who love exciting food in sociable surroundings, accompanied by the odd cocktail. Daily deals, free wi-fi, and the fun Library bar through the back door.

Midnight Espresso CAFE **$**
(Map p378; 178 Cuba St; meals $8-17; 7.30am-late Mon-Fri, 8am-late Sat & Sun;) The city's original hip cafe, with food that's hearty, tasty and inexpensive – heavy on the wholesome and vegetarian. Sitting in the window with Havana coffee and cake is the quintessential Wellington cafe experience.

Aunty Mena's VEGETARIAN **$**
(Map p378; 167 Cuba St; meals $10-18; 11.30am-9.30pm;) One of many Cuba St noodle houses, cheap-and-cheerful Aunty Mena's cranks out yummy veggie/vegan Malaysian and Chinese dishes to a diverse clientele. Easy-clean, over-lit interior.

Sweet Mother's Kitchen AMERICAN **$**
(Map p378; 5 Courtenay Pl; mains $10-27; 8am-late;) Perpetually full, predominantly with young cool cats, Sweet Mother's serves dubious takes on the Deep South, such as burritos, nachos, po' boys and jambalaya. Key lime pie is about as authentic as it gets. It's cheap, cute, has craft beer and good sun.

Ambeli MODERN NZ $$$
(Map p378; ☎04-385 7577; www.theambeli.co.nz; 18 Marjoribanks St; ⏰lunch Tue-Fri, dinner daily) Seriously good, super-fine fare served in the refined surroundings of an inner-city colonial cottage. Exciting dishes flavoured with seasonal, top-end ingredients (confit pork cheek with hand-pounded broad beans; citrus-cured salmon) are complemented by a wine list much-lauded maître d' Shae Moleta claims to know better than he knows his mother. Exquisite desserts. Bookings recommended.

Le Métropolitain FRENCH $$
(Map p378; www.lemetropolitain.co.nz; cnr Garrett & Cuba Sts; mains $19-34; ⏰lunch & dinner Tue-Sat) Prepare to be transported to the heart of France via unpretentious bistro fare in a suitably Gallic environment. Classics are well covered and include *moules* (mussels), onion soup, *steak frites,* coq au vin and escargot. Scrumptious cheese for afters, although you'll probably want the tart that you saw in the window.

Great India INDIAN $$
(Map p378; 141 Manners St; mains $15-29; ⏰lunch & dinner; ✎) This is not your average curry house. While a tad more expensive than its competitors, this place consistently earns its moniker. With any luck you'll be served by Rakesh, one of the capital's smoothest maître d's.

Regal CHINESE $$
(Map p378; ☎04-384 6656; 7 Courtenay Pl; yum cha around $20) Yum cha is popular in Wellington, with Regal just one of many Chinese restaurants clustered around Courtenay Pl that pack in the punters for their weekend ritual. Despite having arguably the least charm of the lot, Regal nevertheless pleases with excellent delivery speed, volume and quality, and excellence in the departments of prawn steamed dumplings, barbecue pork buns, Peking duck and coconut buns. Booking advised.

Shinobi Sushi Lounge SUSHI $$
(Map p378; 43 Vivian St; sushi plates $19-35, California rolls $7-19; ⏰noon-2pm Tue-Fri, 5.30pm-10pm Tue-Sun) Super-fresh fish, Japanese training and Kiwi flair combine to create the most exciting sushi joint in town, while seriously good cocktails and a quality drinks list keeps things lubricated. Non-fishy dishes include killer *karaage* (fried) chicken, *kounomono* (pickled vegetables) and seaweed salad.

Burger Fuel BURGERS $
(Map p378; 101 Courtenay Pl; burgers $5-15; ⏰11am-late; ✎) Fast food how it should be. Tasty burgers of all description made with fresh, natural ingredients, beating the pants off Ronald and the Colonel.

Deluxe CAFE $
(Map p378; 10 Kent Tce; snacks $4-10; ⏰7am-late Mon-Fri, 8am-late Sat & Sun; ✎) A stalwart of the late-night cafe scene, with off-beat, oft-changing local art adorning the walls. Cranking, teeny wee space next to the Embassy Cinema that serves hundreds of coffees a day and mainly vegetarian/vegan counter food and pizza slices to loyal customers.

Duke Carvell's TAPAS $$
(Map p378; 6 Swan Ln; lunch $12-20, small plates $15-19, large plates $30-42; ⏰noon-late Mon-Fri, 9am-late Sat & Sun) Join the Duke for a culinary tour of the Mediterranean, and choose from small plates and large plates, or get piggy with a charcuterie platter. A mish-mash of classic artwork adorns the walls while thrift-shop chandeliers cast a low, sexy light on proceedings. Snappy staff brighten the atmosphere as do dishes of flaming ouzo cheese.

Lido CAFE $$
(Map p378; cnr Victoria & Wakefield Sts; brunch & lunch $9-21, dinner $19-26; ⏰7.30am-3pm Mon, to late Tue-Sat, 9am-9pm Sun) Swing into Lido, at the bottom of a racy old office block, for a wide selection of consistent and reasonably priced Med-inspired food. Pancakes and pasta sit happily alongside fish, burgers, antipasto and salad. Great coffee and sweet treats, too. Live jazz Saturday and Sunday evenings.

Wellington Trawling Sea Market FISH & CHIPS $
(Map p378; 220 Cuba St; meals $7-15; ⏰11.30am-9.30pm) Locals' favourite fresh-off-the-boat fish and chips, plus other salty delicacies in season. Burgers, too.

Arthur's & Martha's CAFE $
(Map p378; 272 & 276 Cuba St; snacks $3-8, meals $12-22) Run by the McLeods, whose roots in this neighbourhood descend several generations, this pair of Ladies & Gentlemen tearooms commemorate their heritage in delicious style. Martha proffers finger sand-

wiches, delicate tarts, and tea in fine bone china, while Arthur wears plaid and dishes up a manly fry-up and pork crackling snacks.

Heaven PIZZERIA $

(Map p378; 247 Cuba St; pizzas $8-22; ⏲noon-late;) Divine pizzas emerge from the flames of a woodfired oven, straddled by a monolithic sculpture of St George and the Dragon. Eat inside this groovy space with its rustic and recycled decor, or take away. Pizzas also available by the slice.

Kaffe Eis ICE CREAM $

(Map p378; 29 Courtenay Pl; ice cream $3-7) Ice cream made the Italian way, but with NZ ingredients (think extraordinarily good cream, luscious fruit including the inimitable feijoa) – Kaffe Eis brings you heaven by way of waffle or spoon. Go for the double scoop: vanilla on the bottom, gingernut on top. Look out for satellite branches along the waterfront.

Pandoro Panetteria BAKERY $

(Map p378; 2 Allen St; items $3-6; ⏲7am-5pm Mon-Fri, to 4pm Sat & Sun;) An excellent Italian bakery with smooth coffee, cakes, pastries and a range of yummy savoury, bready, scrolly, rolly things.

Moore Wilson Fresh SUPERMARKET

(Map p378; cnr College & Tory Sts; ⏲7.30am-7pm Mon-Fri, to 6pm Sat, 9am-5pm Sun) An unsurpassed array of (predominantly NZ) produce, baked treats, smallgoods, mountains of cheese...just endless goodies. Positively swoon-inducing.

Drinking

Wellingtonians love a late night, and it's common to see the masses heading into town at a time when normal folk would be boiling the kettle for cocoa. A lively music scene keeps things cranking, along with some famously good bar food, competitive cocktail concocting, fine wines and microbrews.

In fact it's the craft-beer scene that has most recently gone through the roof, with updraught encouraged by a burgeoning local brewing scene and more beer bars than you can lob a hop at. See www.craftbeercapital.com for more propaganda.

Most of the action in Wellington's clusters around two hubs: Courtenay Pl – bustling, brassy and positively let-your-hair-down; and Cuba St – edgy, groovy and sometimes too cool for school.

TOP CHOICE **Mighty Mighty** BAR

(Map p378; 104 Cuba St; ⏲4pm-late Wed-Sat) This is the hippest of the capital's drinking and music venues. Inside-a-pinball-machine decor, pink velvet curtains, kitsch gewgaws and Wellington's best barmaid make this an essential port of call for those wanting to tilt or bang a bumper. A colourful slice of NZ bar life.

Hashigo Zake CRAFT BEER

(Map p378; www.hashigozake.co.nz; 25 Taranaki St) The headquarters of the capital's underground beer movement, this brick-walled basement bar pours only quality craft brews to a wide range of hopheads. An oft-changing selection of a dozen beers on tap is reinforced by a United Nations of around 140 beers by the bottle.

Havana BAR

(Map p378; www.havanabar.co.nz; 32 Wigan St; ⏲11am-late Mon-Fri, 3pm-late Sat) Much like the proverbial light under a bushel, one of Welly's most seductive bars is hidden away down a side-street you'll never stumble across. (This is your cue to turn to our map.) You'll find it in two adjacent heritage cottages, where you can eat tapas, drink your way along the top shelf, then chinwag, smoke, flirt and dance until very near dawn.

Malthouse CRAFT BEER

(Map p378; www.themalthouse.co.nz; 48 Courtenay Pl; ⏲3pm-late Sun-Thu, noon-3am Fri & Sat) At last count there were 150 reasons to drink at this, the capital's original craft-beer bar. Savvy staff will recommend brews from an epic list that showcases beers from NZ and around the globe. Enquire about new arrivals, and the aged selection of brews if you're a well-heeled beer geek.

Southern Cross PUB

(Map p378; www.thecross.co.nz; 35 Abel Smith St; ⏲9am-late) Welly's most stylish crowd-pleasing pub combines a laid-back restaurant, lively bar, regular music, dance floor, pool table, the best garden bar in town and a welcoming attitude to children. Independent beer on tap and a good bowl of chips. Choice!

Ancestral BAR

(Map p378; www.ancestral.co.nz; 31 Courtenay Pl; ⏲11am-late Tue-Fri, 3pm-late Mon & Sat) Asian-infused Ancestral has broken new ground in the Wellington bar scene. It's designed by the architects responsible for the legendary Matterhorn, and no effort has been spared to get every line and level right – lighting, music, shirt collars and cocktails. Whisky and cigars in the stripped and pimped garden bar are a highlight, but there's heaps to please here, including sake and the smoke, spark and crackle of the yakitori grill ($4 to $17).

Matterhorn BAR
(Map p378; www.matterhorn.co.nz; 106 Cuba St; ⏲3pm-late Mon-Fri, 10am-late Sat & Sun) We're still gettin' the Horn, despite a change of ownership and some stiff competition. A perennially popular joint with three distinct but equally pleasing areas (long bar, dining room and garden bar), the Matterhorn still honours its patrons with reputable food (tapas from mid-arvo, dinner daily, brunch weekends), solid service and regular live music.

Vivo WINE BAR
(Map p378; www.vivowinebar.co.nz; 19 Edward St; ⏲3pm-late Mon-Fri, 5pm-late Sat) A tomelike list of approximately 600 wines from around the world, with more than 60 available by the glass. Exposed bricks and timber beams give Vivo an earthy cellarlike feel, while the fairy lights look like stars set against the dark ceiling. Excellent, inexpensive tapa-esque food (small plates $6 to $14).

Good Luck BAR
(Map p378; basement, 126 Cuba St; ⏲5pm-late Tue-Sun) Cuba St's Chinese opium den, without the opium. This is a slickly run, sultry basement bar playing multiflavoured upbeat tunes. It also mixes the best mint juleps in town, and sports a middle-of-the-mall al fresco lounge – great for watching the Cubacade.

Hawthorn Lounge BAR
(Map p378; 82 Tory St; ⏲6pm-late Tue-Sat) Akin to a 1920s speakeasy, complete with waistcoats and wide-brimmed fedoras. Sip cocktails and play poker, or simply enjoy the behind-the-bar theatrics.

Library BAR
(Map p378; 53 Courtenay Pl; ⏲5pm-late Mon-Thu, 4pm-late Fri-Sun) Velveteen booths, books, booze and board games. A real page-turner, with cocktails you won't want to put down.

Betty's BAR
(Map p378; 32 Blair St; ⏲5pm-3am Wed-Sat) Brassy joint with on-to-it staff, apothecary theme and wraparound digital screen covering three walls. DJs and VJs drop quality beats.

Hummingbird WINE BAR
(Map p378; www.hummingbird.net.nz; 22 Courtenay Pl; ⏲3pm-late Mon-Fri, 10am-late Sat & Sun) Popular with the sophisticated set, Hummingbird is usually packed – both inside in the intimate, stylish dining room and bar, and outside on street-side tables. Croony music (with regular live jazz), exciting brunch-to-supper menus, and impressive drinks including fine wines and cocktails.

Molly Malone's PUB
(Map p378; cnr Courtenay Pl & Taranaki St) A highly polished Irish bar, complete with daily live music, well-priced pub grub (bar menu $6 to $19, meals $23 to $30) and a suntrap balcony. If the craic downstairs is too much for you, head up to the piano bar for a calming dram.

Backbencher PUB
(Map p368; 34 Molesworth St; ⏲11am-late) You might spot the odd parliamentarian on the turps at this pub opposite the Beehive, where rubbery puppets of NZ pollies are mounted trophy-style on the walls (Aunty Helen is much more beautiful in real life). Quiz nights and other events keep things lively.

☆ Entertainment

Wellington's entertainment scene is a bit like the Tardis: it looks small from the outside, but inside it holds big surprises. Not only does it boast an inordinate number of local performers, plenty of high-quality acts visit from around NZ and abroad, too. Hungry, appreciative crowds help things along.

Listings can be found in the *Capital Times* – the free weekly rag found all over town. Look out, also, for the *Groove Guide* (www.grooveguide.co.nz), which has a gig guide and pertinent articles.

Entry to most gigs and club nights can be gained via a door sale. Popular gigs, however, may well sell out, so it pays to buy advance tickets from advertised outlets – often Ticketek (p385), www.undertheradar.co.nz or **Cosmic** (www.cosmiccorner.co.nz; 97-99 Cuba Mall).

Live Music & Clubs

Listed below are Wellington's main players, although live music is also a staple of many of the capital's bars, including Mighty

Mighty (p383), Havana (p383), Molly Malone's (p384), the Matterhorn (p384) and the Southern Cross (p383).

San Francisco Bath House LIVE MUSIC
(Map p378; www.sfbh.co.nz; 171 Cuba St; ⌚4pm-late Tue-Sat) Wellington's best midsized live-music venue, playing host to the cream of NZ artists, as well as quality acts from abroad. Somewhat debauched balcony action, five deep at the bar, but otherwise well run and lots of fun when the floor starts bouncing.

Bodega LIVE MUSIC
(Map p378; www.bodega.co.nz; 101 Ghuznee St; ⌚4pm-late) A trailblazer of the city's modern live-music scene, and still considered an institution despite its move from a derelict heritage building to a concrete cavern. 'The Bodge' offers a full and varied program of gigs in a pleasant space with a respectable dance floor.

Happy LIVE MUSIC
(Map p378; www.happybar.co.nz; cnr Tory & Vivian Sts; ⌚Wed-Sun 5pm-late) A loungey basement bar championing performance-focused acts from virtually all genres – expect indie folk right through to hardcore. Craft beers, sushi from Shinobi (p382) across the road and free jazz on Sundays.

Sandwiches CLUB
(Map p378; www.sandwiches.co.nz; 8 Kent Tce; ⌚4pm-late Wed-Sat) Get yourself a slice of NZ's electronic artists and DJs, regular multiflavoured international acts and a great sound system. Gritty club run by a dedicated team that isn't just in it for the bread.

Theatres

Wellington's accessible performing-arts scene sustains a laudable number of professional and amateur companies. Tickets for many events can be purchased from the **Ticketek box offices** (www.ticketek.co.nz) at two of the major venues: **St James Theatre** (Map p378; ☎04-802 4060; www.stjames.co.nz; 77 Courtenay Pl) and the **Michael Fowler Centre** (Map p378; ☎04-801 4231; www.wellingtonconventioncentre.com; 111 Wakefield St). Discount same-day tickets for some productions are often available at the i-SITE. The two other key show venues are the **Opera House** (Map p378; www.stjames.co.nz; 111 Manners St) and **TSB Bank Arena** (Map p368; 4 Queens Wharf).

The capital has three noteworthy theatre companies presenting regular performances:

BATS THEATRE
(Map p378; ☎04-802 4175; www.bats.co.nz; 1 Kent Tce) Wildly alternative BATS presents cutting-edge and experimental NZ theatre – varied, cheap and intimate.

Circa THEATRE
(Map p378; ☎04-801 7992; www.circa.co.nz; 1 Taranaki St) Circa's main auditorium seats 240 people, its studio 100. Cheap tickets are available for preview shows, and there are standby tickets available an hour before the show (anything from pantomime to international comedy).

Downstage THEATRE
(Map p378; ☎04-801 6946; www.downstage.co.nz; 12 Cambridge Tce) Original NZ plays, dance, comedy and musicals in a 250-seat auditorium.

Cinemas

Movie times are listed in the local newspapers and at www.film.wellington.net.nz, and most cinemas have discounts early in the week or during the day. We can't list all the many excellent indy cinemas in Wellywood – we just ain't got the room! Here are our inner-city picks.

Embassy Theatre CINEMA
(Map p378; ☎04-384 7657; www.deluxe.co.nz; 10 Kent Tce; from adult/child $15.50/12.50) Wellywood's cinema mothership, built in the 1920s. Screens mainstream films; bars and cafe on-site.

WELCOME TO WELLYWOOD

In recent years Wellington has stamped its place firmly on the world map as the home of NZ's dynamic film industry, earning itself the nickname 'Wellywood'. Acclaimed director Peter Jackson still calls Wellington home; the success of his *The Lord of the Rings (LOTR)* films and subsequent productions such as *King Kong*, *The Adventures of Tintin* and *The Hobbit* have made him a powerful Hollywood player, and have bolstered Wellington's reputation.

LOTR fans and movie buffs can experience some local movie magic by visiting minimuseum, the Weta Cave (p370), or one of many film locations around the region – a speciality of local guided-tour companies (p374).

Paramount CINEMA

(Map p378; ☎04-384 4080; www.paramount.co.nz; 25 Courtenay Pl; from adult/child $13/9; ⌚noon-midnight) A lovely old complex screening largely art-house, documentary and foreign flicks.

Penthouse Cinema CINEMA

(☎04-384 3157; www.penthousecinema.co.nz; 205 Ohiro Rd, Brooklyn; from adult/child $11.50/9.50) Art-deco charmer screening a smart range of films. Nice cafe too. Well worth the bus ride – take number 7 or 8 south from town.

Shopping

Wellington supports a high number of independent shops including scores of designer boutiques. To 'Buy Kiwi Made', head straight to Cuba St to score a good hit rate, or try the gift shop at Te Papa.

A short drive or train ride away, Petone's Jackson Street is well worth a wander for lunching and shopping.

Starfish CLOTHING

(Map p378; 128 Willis St) Wellingtonian fashionista favourite treat. Beautiful clothing, sustainably made.

Hunters & Collectors VINTAGE

(Map p378; 134 Cuba St) Off-the-rack and vintage clothing (punk, skate and mod), plus shoes and accessories. Best-dressed window in NZ.

Mandatory CLOTHING

(Map p378; 108 Cuba Mall) Great service and sharp men's tailoring for the capital's cool cats.

Kura ARTS & CRAFTS

(Map p378; 19 Allen St) Contemporary indigenous art: painting, ceramics, jewellery and sculpture.

Ora Design Gallery ARTS & CRAFTS

(Map p378; 23 Allen St) The latest in Pacific and Maori art: beautiful sculpture, weaving and jewellery.

Vault ARTS & CRAFTS

(Map p368; 2 Plimmer Steps) Jewellery, clothing, bags, ceramics, cosmetics – a bonny store with beautiful things.

Unity Books BOOKS

(Map p378; 57 Willis St) Setting the standard for every bookshop in the land.

Bivouac Outdoor OUTDOOR EQUIPMENT

(Map p378; 39 Mercer St) The best of several outdoor shops clustered around Mercer St.

Old Bank Shopping Arcade SHOPPING CENTRE

(Map p368; www.oldbank.co.nz; cnr Lambton Quay & Willis St) This is a dear old building home to some satisfying and self-indulgent boutiques.

Kirkcaldie & Stains DEPARTMENT STORE

(Map p368; 165-177 Lambton Quay) NZ's answer to Bloomingdale's or Harrods, established in 1863. Bring your travels documents with you for tax-free bargains.

Information

Emergency

Ambulance, fire service & police (☎111)

Wellington Police Station (☎04-381 2000; www.police.govt.nz; cnr Victoria & Harris Sts)

Internet Access

Free wi-fi is available in most of the CBD (www.cbdfree.co.nz); the i-SITE (p387) also has internet access.

Media

Best of Wellington (www.bestofwellington.co.nz) 'Insiders', independent guidebook aimed at longer-staying visitors.

Capital Times (www.capitaltimes.co.nz) Free weekly newspaper with local news, gossip and gig listings.

Stuff (www.stuff.co.nz) Online news service incorporating Wellington's newspaper, the *Dominion Post*.

Medical Services

Wellington Accident & Urgent Medical Centre (☎04-384 4944; 17 Adelaide Rd, Newtown; ⌚8am-11pm) No appointment necessary; also home to the after-hours pharmacy. It's close to the Basin Reserve around the northern end of Adelaide Rd.

Wellington Hospital (☎04-385 5999; www.ccdhb.org.nz; Riddiford St, Newtown; ⌚24hr) One kilometre south of the city centre.

Money

Major banks have branches on Courtenay Pl, Willis St and Lambton Quay. Moneychangers include the following:

City Stop (107 Manners St; ⌚24hr) Convenience store that exchanges travellers cheques.

Travelex (www.travelex.co.nz; 120 Lambton Quay; ⌚8.30am-5.30pm Mon-Fri) Foreign-exchange office. Also has branches at the airport.

Post

Post Office (2 Manners St)

Tourist Information

DOC Visitor Centre (Department of Conservation; ☎04-384 7770; www.doc.govt.nz; 18 Manners St; ⊙9am-5pm Mon-Fri, 10am-3.30pm Sat) Bookings, passes and information for national and local walks, parks, huts and camping, plus permits for Kapiti Island.

Hutt City i-SITE (☎04-560 4715; www.huttvalleynz.com; 25 Laings Rd; ⊙9am-5pm Mon-Fri, to 4pm Sat & Sun) Information centre covering Upper Hutt, Lower Hutt and Petone.

Wellington i-SITE (☎04-802 4860; www.wellingtonnz.com; Civic Sq, cnr Wakefield & Victoria Sts; ⊙8.30am-5pm) Staff book almost everything, and cheerfully distribute Wellington's *Official Visitor Guide*, other maps and walking guides. Internet access and cafe.

Websites

Positively Wellington Tourism (www.wellingtonnz.com) Official tourism website for the city.

Word on the Street (www.wordonthestreet.co.nz) Magazine-style site dedicated to news, previews and reviews.

Wotzon.com (www.wotzon.com) Arts and events listings for Wellington and surrounds.

Getting There & Away

Air

Wellington is an international gateway to NZ.

Wellington Airport (WLG; ☎04-385 5100; www.wellington-airport.co.nz; Stewart Duff Dr, Rongotai; ⊙4am-1.30am) has touch-screen information kiosks in the luggage hall. There's also currency exchange, ATMs, car-rental desks, cafes, shops etc. If you're in transit or have an early flight, you can't linger overnight inside the terminal. Departure tax on international flights is adult/child $25/10.

Air New Zealand (☎0800 737 000, 04-474 8950; www.airnewzealand.co.nz; cnr Lambton Quay & Grey St; ⊙9am-5pm Mon-Fri, 10am-1pm Sat) offers flights between Wellington and most domestic centres, including Auckland (from $69), Christchurch (from $59), Queenstown (from $89) and Nelson (from $79).

Jetstar (☎0800 800 995; www.jetstar.com) flies between Wellington and Auckland (from $49), Christchurch (from $49) and Queenstown (from $59).

Soundsair (☎0800 505 005, 03-520 3080; www.soundsair.com) flies between Wellington and Picton up to eight times daily (from $90), Nelson (from $107) and Blenheim (from $90).

Air2there (☎0800 777 000, 04-904 5130; www.air2there.com) flies between Wellington and Blenheim ($99), and from Kapiti Coast Airport (p389) to Blenheim ($125) and Nelson ($135).

Travel agents include Air New Zealand and **Flight Centre** (www.flightcentre.co.nz; cnr Cuba & Manners Sts; ⊙9am-5.30pm Mon-Wed & Fri, 9am-7pm Thu, 10am-4pm Sat).

Boat

On a clear day, sailing into Wellington Harbour or through the Marlborough Sounds is magical. Cook Strait is notoriously rough, but the big ferries handle it well, and sport lounges, cafes, bars, information desks and cinemas but no pool tables. There are two options for crossing the strait between Wellington and Picton: Bluebridge and the Interislander.

Book ferries at hotels, by phone, online, at travel agents and with operators directly (online is the cheapest option). Bluebridge is based at Waterloo Quay, opposite the Wellington train station. The Interislander terminal is about 2km northeast of the city centre; a shuttle bus ($2) runs to the Interislander from platform 9 at Wellington train station (where long-distance buses also depart). It also meets arriving ferries, returning passengers to platform 9. There's also a taxi stand at the terminal.

Car-hire companies allow you to pick-up/drop-off vehicles at ferry terminals. If you arrive outside business hours, arrangements can be made to collect your vehicle from the terminal car park.

Bluebridge Ferries (☎04-471 6188, 0800 844 844; www.bluebridge.co.nz; 50 Waterloo Quay; adult/child from $51/26) Crossing takes three hours 20 minutes; up to four sailings in each direction daily. Cars and campervans up to 5.5m from $118; motorbikes $51; bicycles $10.

Interislander (☎04-498 3302, 0800 802 802; www.interislander.co.nz; Aotea Quay; adult/child from $55/28) Crossing takes three hours 10 minutes; up to five sailings in each direction daily. Cars are priced from $118; campervans (up to 5.5m) from $133; motorbikes from $56; bicycles $15.

Bus

Wellington is a bus-travel hub, with connections north to Auckland and all major towns in between. **InterCity** (☎04-385 0520; www.intercity.co.nz) and **Newmans** (☎04-385 0521; www.newmanscoach.co.nz) buses depart from platform 9 at the train station. Tickets are sold at the Intercity/Newmans ticket window in the train station. Typical fares include Auckland (from $29, 11 hours), Palmerston North (from $14, 2¼ hours) and Rotorua (from $26, 7½ hours). There are good savings when booked online.

Naked Bus (☎0900 625 33; www.nakedbus.com) runs north from Wellington to all major North Island destinations, including Palmerston North (from $11, 2½ hours), Napier (from $19, five hours), Taupo (from $25, 6½ hours) and

Auckland (from $28, 11½ hours), with myriad stops en route. Buses depart from opposite the Amora Hotel in Wakefield St, and collect more passengers at Bunny St opposite the railway station. Book online or at Wellington i-SITE; get in early for the cheapest fares.

Train

Wellington train station has six **ticket windows** (☎0800 801 700; ⏰6.30am-8pm Mon-Thu, to 1pm Fri & Sat, to 3pm Sun), two selling tickets for Tranz Scenic trains, Interislander ferries and InterCity and Newmans coaches; the other four ticketing local/regional **Tranz Metro** (☎0800 801 700; www.tranzmetro.co.nz) trains (Johnsonville, Melling, Hutt Valley, Kapiti and Wairarapa lines).

Long-haul **Tranz Scenic** (☎0800 872 467; www.tranzscenic.co.nz) routes include the daily *Overlander* between Wellington and Auckland (from $79, 12 hours, Thursday to Sunday May to September); and the *Capital Connection* between Wellington and Palmerston North (from $26, two hours, one daily Monday to Friday).

Getting Around

Metlink (☎0800 801 700; www.metlink.org.nz) is the one-stop shop for Wellington's regional bus, train and harbour ferry networks all detailed below.

To & From Airport

Super Shuttle (☎0800 748 885; www.super shuttle.co.nz; 1/2 passengers $16/21; ⏰24hr) provides a door-to-door minibus service between the city and airport, 8km southeast of the city. It's cheaper if two or more passengers are travelling to the same destination. Shuttles meet all arriving flights.

The **Airport Flyer** (☎0800 801 700; www.metlink.co.nz; airport–city per adult/child $8.50/5) bus runs between the airport, Wellington and the Hutt Valley. Buses run from around 6am to 9.30pm.

A taxi between the city centre and airport costs around $30.

Bicycle

If you're fit or keep to the flat, bicycle hire is a viable option. City hirers include **On Yer Bike** (Map p378; ☎04-384 8480; www.onyerbikeavanti plus.co.nz; 181 Vivian St; half-day $20-30, full day $30-40, week $150) and **Penny Farthing** (☎04-385 2279; www.pennyfarthing.co.nz; 65 Dixon St; half-/full day from $40/60).

Bus

Frequent and efficient bus services cover the whole Wellington region and run between approximately 6am and 11.30pm. Major bus terminals are at the Wellington train station, and on Courtenay Pl near the Cambridge Tce intersection. Pick up route maps and timetables from the i-SITE and convenience stores, or online from Metlink (p388). Fares are determined by zones: a trip across the city centre (Zone 1) costs $2, and all the way up the coast to Otaki (Zone 13) costs $16.50.

Metlink also runs the **After Midnight** bus service, departing from two convenient city stops (Courtenay Pl and Cuba St) between midnight and 4.30am Saturday and Sunday. on a number of routes to the outer suburbs. Fares range from $6 to $12, depending on how far away your bed is.

Car

There are a lot of one-way streets in Wellington, the traffic is surprisingly snarly and parking can be a royal (and expensive) pain in the rump. If you've got a car or a caravan, park on the outskirts and walk or take public transport into the city centre. Campervans can also park during the day at the Wellington Waterfront Motorhome Park (p379) and the car park outside Te Papa (p374).

Aside from the major international rental companies, Wellington has several operators that will negotiate cheap deals, especially for longer-term rental of two weeks or more, but rates generally aren't as competitive as in Auckland. Rack rates range from around $40 to $80 per day; cars are usually a few years old and in pretty good condition. Operators include the following:

Ace Rental Cars (☎0800 535 500, 04-471 1176; www.acerentalcars.co.nz; 126 Hutt Rd, Kaiwharawhara)

Apex Car Rental (☎04-385 2163, 0800 300 110; www.apexrentals.co.nz; 186 Victoria St)

Omega Rental Cars (☎04-472 8465, 0800 667 722; www.omegarentalcars.com; 96 Hutt Rd)

If you plan on exploring both North and South Islands, most companies suggest you leave your car in Wellington and pick up another one in Picton after crossing Cook Strait. This is a common (and more affordable) practice, and car-hire companies make it a painless exercise.

There are often cheap deals on car relocation from Wellington to Auckland (most renters travel in the opposite direction). A few companies offer heavy discounts on this route, with the catch being that you may only have 24 or 48 hours to make the journey.

Taxi

Packed ranks can be found on Courtenay Pl, at the corner of Dixon and Victoria Sts, on Featherston St, and outside the railway station. Two of many operators:

Green Cabs (☎0508 447 336)

Wellington Combined Taxis (☎04-384 444)

Train

Tranz Metro (p388) operates four train routes running through Wellington's suburbs to regional destinations. Trains run frequently from around 6am to 11pm, departing Wellington train station. The routes: Johnsonville, via Ngaio and Khandallah; Kapiti, via Porirua, Plimmerton, Paekakariki and Paraparaumu; Melling, via Petone; the Hutt Valley via Waterloo to Upper Hutt. A train service also connects with the Wairarapa, calling at Featherston, Carterton and Masterton. Timetables are available from convenience stores, the train station, Wellington i-SITE and online. Standard fares from Wellington to the ends of the five lines range from $4.50 to $17.50. A Day Rover ticket ($13) allows unlimited off-peak and weekend travel on all lines except Wairarapa.

KAPITI COAST

With wide, crowd-free beaches, the Kapiti Coast acts as a summer playground and suburban extension for Wellingtonians. The region takes its moniker from Kapiti Island, a bird and marine sanctuary 5km offshore from Paraparaumu.

In the Tararua Range, Tararua Forest Park forms a dramatic backdrop along the length of the coastline and has some accessible day walks and longer tramps.

The Kapiti Coast makes an easy day trip from Wellington, but if you're after a few restful days there's enough of interest to keep you happy.

Information

Comprehensive visitor information can be found at **Paraparaumu visitor information centre** (04-298 8195; www.naturecoast.co.nz; Coastlands, Rimu Rd; 9am-5pm Mon-Fri, 10am-3pm Sat & Sun). Pick up the *Nature Coast* brochure while you're there.

Getting There & Around

Getting here from Wellington is a breeze: just track north on SH1. By car, it's about a 30-minute drive to Paekakariki, and around 45 minutes to Paraparaumui, much of it by motorway.

Air

Kapiti Coast Airport (PPQ; www.kapitiairport.co.nz; Toru Rd, Paraparaumu Beach) in Paraparumu was expanded in 2011, and is a regular destination for **Air2there** (0800 777 000; www.air2there.com), with daily flights to Blenheim and Nelson, and Air New Zealand (p387), which flies direct to Auckland.

Bus

InterCity (p387) stops at major Kapiti Coast towns on its services between Wellington and the north. At the outside, you're looking at $34 from Wellington, and $68 from Taupo; cheaper if you book in advance and online.

The daily services into/out of Wellington run by **White Star Express** (04-478 4734, 0800 465 622; www.whitestarbus.co.nz) and Naked Bus (p387) also stop at major Kapiti Coast towns.

Metlink (p388) runs good local bus services around Paraparaumu, and up to Waikanae and Otaki, calling at highway and beach settlements.

Train

Tranz Metro (p388) commuter trains between Wellington and the coast are easier and more frequent than buses. Services run from Wellington to Paraparaumu ($12, generally half-hourly off-peak between 6am and 11pm, with more services at peak times), stopping en route in Paekakariki ($9.50). Weekday off-peak fares (9am to 3pm) are up to $3 cheaper.

Tranz Scenic (p388) has long-distance *Overlander* trains connecting Wellington and Auckland stopping at Paraparaumu, while the weekday-only, peak-hour *Capital Connection*, travelling to Wellington in the morning and back to Palmerston North in the evening, stops at Paraparaumu, Waikanae and Otaki.

Paekakariki

POP 1730

Paekakariki is a little seaside village stretched along a black-sand beach, serviced by a train station and passed by the highway to Wellington, 41km to the south.

Sights & Activities

FREE **Queen Elizabeth Park** PARK

(SH1; gates open 8am-8pm) This rambling but rather beautiful 650-hectare beachside park offers plenty of opportunities for swimming, walking, cycling and picnicking, as well as being the location of the Stables on the Park and Tramway Museum. There are three entrances: off Wellington Rd in Paekakariki, at MacKay's Crossing on SH1, and off the Esplanade in Raumati to the north.

Tramway Museum MUSEUM

(www.wellingtontrams.org.nz; MacKay's Crossing entrance, Queen Elizabeth Park; admission by donation, all-day tram rides adult/child/family $8/4/20; museum 10am-4.30pm daily, trams 11am-4.30pm Sat & Sun, daily 26 Dec–late Jan) A glimpse into historic Wellington by way of restored wooden trams and museum displays inside their big garage. A 2km track curls through Queen Elizabeth Park down to the beach. On-site ice-cream kiosk.

Stables on the Park HORSE RIDING
(☎027 448 6764, 06-364 3336; www.stablesonthe park.co.nz; MacKay's Crossing entrance, Queen Elizabeth Park; 30-90min ride $35-90; ⊙open most days in summer) Mandy and friends run guided rides on well-mannered horses. The 1½-hour ride will see you trot along the beach with views of Kapiti Island before heading inland on park tracks. Beginners are welcome.

Sleeping & Eating

Paekakariki Holiday Park HOLIDAY PARK $
(☎04-292 8292; www.paekakarikiholidaypark.co.nz; 180 Wellington Rd; sites per adult $15, cabins & flats from $65; @🛜) A pleasant, large, leafy park approximately 1.5km north of the township at the southern entrance to Queen Elizabeth Park. Just a hop, skip and a jump from the beach.

Hilltop Hideaway GUESTHOUSE $
(☎04-902 5967; www.wellingtonbeachbackpackers.co.nz; 11 Wellington Rd; d $80; @🛜) Formerly Paekakariki Backpackers, Peter and Denise now offer two double en suite rooms in their hilltop home, one with sea and sunset views. The great-value rooms are homely but elegant, much like the hosts themselves.

Finn's HOTEL $$
(☎04-292 8081; www.finnshotel.co.nz; 2 Beach Rd; d $125-135; 🛜) Finn's is the flashy beige suit of the cutesy railway village, but redeems itself with spacious rooms, good-value meals (mains $17 to $27), and independent beer on tap. The hush glass keeps the highway at bay.

Beach Road Deli CAFE $
(5 Beach Rd; snacks $3-8, pizza $13-22; ⊙7am-8pm Wed-Sun) Bijou deli and pizzeria, packed with home-baked bread and patisserie, cheese, charcuterie and assorted imported goodies. Heaven-sent for the highway traveller, picnic provisioner, or those looking for a sausage to fry and a bun to put it in. Ace coffee.

Paraparaumu

POP 6840

Low-key Paraparaumu is the principal town on the Kapiti Coast, and a suburban satellite of Wellington. The rough-and-tumble beach is the coast's most developed, sustaining cafes, motels and takeaway joints. Boat trips to Kapiti Island set sail from here.

The correct pronunciation is 'Pah-ra-pah-ra-oo-moo', meaning 'scraps from an oven', which is said to have originated when a Maori war party attacked the settlement and found only scraps of food remaining. It's a bit of a mouthful to pronounce; locals usually just corrupt it into 'Para-par-am'.

Sights & Activities

There are two hubs to Paraparaumu: the main town on the highway, with shopping galore, and Paraparaumu Beach with its waterside park and walkway, decent swimming and other beachy attractions, including the stunning view out to Kapiti Island.

Southward Car Museum MUSEUM
(www.southwardcarmuseum.co.nz; Otaihanga Rd; adult/child $12/3; ⊙9am-4.30pm) This museum has one of Australasia's largest collections of antique and unusual cars. Check out the DeLorean and the 1950 gangster Cadillac.

Paraparaumu Beach Golf Club GOLF
(☎04-902 8200; www.paraparaumubeachgolfclub.co.nz; 376 Kapiti Rd; green fees $150; ⊙7.30am-dusk) This challenging and beautiful links course is ranked among NZ's best. It has hosted the New Zealand Open 12 times and tamed Tiger in 2002. Visitors are welcome: call for tee times, or book online. Clubs, carts and shoes can be hired.

Sleeping

Barnacles Seaside Inn HOSTEL $
(☎04-902 5856; www.seasideyha.co.nz; 3 Marine Pde; dm/s/f $29/50/93, d $72-82; @🛜) Opposite Paraparaumu Beach, this homely YHA hostel resides in a 1920s heritage building. Snug rooms are individually decorated with antique dressers and have sinks and heaters; some have electric blankets and sea views. Note that all rooms share a bathroom.

Wrights by the Sea MOTEL $$
(☎0508 902 760, 04-902 7600; www.wrightsmotel.co.nz; 387 Kapiti Rd; units $120-160; @🛜) In fact about a minute's walk to the sea, this modern motel complex in the conservative style has light, airy rooms, Sky TV and off-road parking. Some rooms have full kitchen.

Eating

If you're around on a Saturday, head for the **farmers market** (9am to 1pm) held in a carpark on Marine Parade at Paraparaumu Beach. Picnic heaven!

Fed Up Fast Foods FISH & CHIPS $
(40 Marine Pde; meals $6-15; ⏲10am-9pm Mon-Thu, 9.30am-9.30pm Fri-Sun) A beachside chippy with the usual battery of fries as well as good-value dinner deals, eggy brekkies, espresso and Kapiti ice cream. Alfresco tables with views to the blue yonder.

Ambience Café CAFE $
(10 Seaview Rd; lunch $12-20; ⏲8am-4pm Sun-Thu;) A very 'Wellington' cafe, with both light and substantial meals made with relish, such as fish cakes, the BLT, and colourful veggie options. Cake cabinet at full capacity, and great coffee (of course).

Soprano Ristorante ITALIAN $$
(☎04-298 8892; 7 Seaview Rd; mains $25-30; ⏲6pm-late Mon-Sat) A welcoming family-run joint with the liveliest evening atmosphere at the beach township. Pasta and other Italian-influenced fare, *carne e pesce*. Sweet treats include the ubiquitous tiramisu and delicious homemade *limoncello* (lemon liqueur). No-nonsense, affordable food and wine in a homely environment – *bella*!

Mediterranean Food Warehouse PIZZA $
(Coastlands car park, SH1; meals $11-20; ⏲9am-9pm) A handy highway pit stop in Paraparaumu town, with excellent wood-fired pizza, luscious cakes and gelato – food so good you'll forget you're in the middle of a car park.

Information

Coastlands shopping centre has all the services you'll need: banks, ATMs, post office, supermarkets and cinema, as well as the Paraparaumu visitor information centre (p389).

Kapiti Island

Kapiti Island is the coatline's dominant feature, a 10km by 2km slice that since 1897 has been a protected reserve. It's largely predator-free, allowing a remarkable range and number of birds – including many species that are now rare or extinct on the mainland – to thrive on the island.

The island is open to visitors, limited to 86 people per day (or you can stay overnight with Kapiti Island Nature Tours), and it's essential that you book and obtain a permit (adult/child $11/5) online (www.doc.govt.nz), in person at Wellington's DOC visitor centre (p387), or via email (wellingtonvc@doc.govt.nz).

Transport is booked separately from the permit (arrange your permit before your boat trip). Two commercial operators are licensed to take visitors to the island, both running to/from Paraparaumu Beach (which can be reached by train). Departures are between 9am and 9.30am daily, returning between 3pm and 4pm; call in the morning to confirm departure (sailings are weather dependent). And don't forget to bring your lunch.

Make all your bookings in advance; more information can be found in DOC's *Kapiti Island Nature Reserve* brochure.

Tours

TOP CHOICE **Kapiti Island Nature Tours & Lodge** LODGE
(☎06-362 6606; www.kapitiislandnaturetours.co.nz; per person incl 3 meals $250-330) The Barrett and Clark *whanau* (family), which have a long-standing connection to the island, run very special nature tours that touch on the birds (in incredible range and number), seal colony, history and Maori traditions. Lodge accommodation is in four-bunk cabins or two-bedroom house and, importantly, offers the after-dark chance to spot the cutest-ever bird, the rare little spotted kiwi.

Getting There & Away

The following operators provide boat transport to and from Kapiti Island, a couple of times a day:

Kapiti Marine Charter (☎04-297 2585, 0800 433 779; www.kapitimarinecharter.co.nz; adult/child $60/35)

Kapiti Tours (☎04-237 7965, 0800 527 484; www.kapititours.co.nz; adult/child $60/35)

THE WAIRARAPA

The Wairarapa is the large slab of land east and northeast of Wellington, beyond the craggy Tararua and Rimutaka Ranges. Named after Lake Wairarapa (Shimmering Waters), a shallow. 8000-hectare lake, the region has traditionally been a frenzied hotbed of sheep farming. More recently, wineries have sprung up, accompanied by a vigorous foodie culture – around Martinborough, most famously – which has turned the region into a decadent weekend retreat.

See www.wairarapanz.com for regional info, but also check out the **Classic New Zealand Wine Trail** (www.classicwinetrail.co.nz) – a useful tool for joining the dots

WORTH A TRIP

WAIKANAE

With a particularly nice stretch of beach, NZ's 2008 'Top Town' (and retirees' favourite) is a viable option as your Kapiti Coast rest stop.

As well as the beach and a couple of good cafes right next to it, the main attraction here is **Nga Manu Nature Reserve** (www.ngamanu.co.nz; 281 Ngarara Rd; adult/child/family $15/6/35; ⏲10am-5pm), a 15-hectare bird sanctuary dotted with picnic areas, bushwalks, aviaries and a nocturnal house with kiwi, owls and tuatara. The eels are fed at 2pm daily, and guided tours run at weekends at 2pm (Sunday only in winter). To get here, turn seawards from SH1 onto Te Moana Rd and then right down Ngarara Rd and follow the signs.

The Waikanae Estuary is a hotspot for birds, with around 60 species visiting during the year. **Waikanae Estuary Bird Tours** (☎04-905 1001; www.kapitibirdtours.co.nz; 2hr tours $35) offer highly personalised, passionate tours, so if you're looking to make feathered friends (and like a cup of tea and a freshly baked scone), this is a great opportunity.

A couple of breezy cafes sit side by side on the road that runs behind the dunes. The crowd-pleasing **Long Beach** (40 Tutere St; meals $16-22) offers an extensive menu from Cloudy Bay clams and beef cheek, though to pizza and fish and chips. With a large conservatory, it's bright, airy and suitably beachy.

Next door, the **Front Room** (42 Tutere St; meals $10-31) has a stylish, pared-back interior and is home to some simple and seasonal yet rather sophisticated fare such as watermelon and feta salad, and Waikanae crab, a regional speciality. The pleasant garden out back sports a fireplace, welcome on cool evenings.

throughout the Wairarapa and its neighbouring wine regions of Hawke's Bay and Marlborough.

Note that the telephone area code over here is 06, not 04 like most of the rest of the Wellington region.

Getting There & Around

From Wellington, **Tranz Metro** (☎0800 801 700; www.tranzmetro.co.nz) commuter trains run to Masterton ($17.50, five or six daily on weekdays, two daily on weekends), calling at seven Wairarapa stations including Featherston and Carterton. For towns off the railway line, catch a local bus.

Tranzit Coachlines (☎0800 471 227, 06-370 6600; www.tranzit.co.nz) runs services between all major Wairarapa towns (maximum fare $7.50) as well as north to Palmerston North ($21).

Martinborough

POP 1360

The sweetest visitor spot in the Wairarapa, Martinborough is a pretty town with a leafy town square and some charming old buildings, surrounded by a patchwork of pasture and a pinstripe of grapevines. It is famed for its wineries, which draw in visitors to nose the pinot, avail themselves of excellent eateries, and snooze it off at boutique accommodation.

Sights & Activities

With so many wineries scattered around town (p394), there are no points for guessing what is the town's main attraction. That said, there's plenty more to do and see, mostly in the surrounding countryside.

Patuna Farm Adventures HORSE RIDING, WALKING

(☎06-306 9966; www.patunafarm.co.nz; Ruakokoputuna Rd) This operator offers horse treks (from $50), a challenging pole-to-pole rope course (from $25), and a four-hour self-guided walk through native bush and a limestone chasm (adult/child $15/10). The chasm is open late October until Easter; other activities operate year-round (bookings essential). It's a pleasant 18km drive to get there.

Toratora Mountain Bike Park MOUNTAIN BIKING

(☎06-307 8151; www.toratora.co.nz; 460 Tora Rd; day pass adult/child $25/15, bike hire $45; ⏲open daily, call in advance) Half an hour's drive from Martinborough, this new, purpose-built mountain-bike track offers bike-fit visitors a classic NZ offroad experience. More than 25km of track loops through a native bush reserve, with accommodating climbs, huge views, and frightening but fun downhills. Farmstay accommodation is offered in a 100-year-old villa and a couple of small cabins (double $200 including track day pass), with the bonuses of a pool, tennis court and games room.

Sleeping

TOP CHOICE Martinborough Top 10 Holiday Park HOLIDAY PARK $
(☎0800 780 909, 06-306 8946; www.martinboroughholidaypark.com; cnr Princess & Dublin Sts; unpowered sites from $20, cabins $65-120; @📶) An appealing campsite with grapevine views, just five minutes' walk to town. It has shady trees and the town pool over the back fence, making it a cooling oasis on sticky days. Cabins are basic but great value, freeing up your dollars for the cellar door. Bike hire available for $35 per day.

Aylstone Retreat BOUTIQUE HOTEL $$$
(☎06-306 9505; www.aylstone.co.nz; 19 Huangarua Rd; d incl breakfast $230-260; 📶) Set among the vines on the edge of the village, this elegant retreat is a winning spot for the romantically inclined. Six en suite rooms exude a lightly floral, French-provincial charm, and share a pretty posh reading room. The on-site bistro does a magnificent croissant, and the whole shebang is surrounded by micro-mansion garden sporting lawns, boxed hedges and chichi furniture.

Claremont MOTEL $$
(☎06-306 9162, 0800 809 162; www.theclaremont.co.nz; 38 Regent St; d $130-158, 4-person apt $280; @) A classy accommodation enclave off Jellicoe St, the Claremont has two-storey, self-contained units in great nick, modern studios with spa baths, and sparkling two-bedroom apartments, all at reasonable rates (even cheaper in winter and/or midweek). Attractive gardens, barbecue areas and bike hire.

Eating & Drinking

TOP CHOICE Trio Café at Coney Winery MODERN NZ $$
(☎06-306 8345; www.coneywines.co.nz; Dry River Rd; snacks $12, mains $22-24; ⊙noon-3pm Sat & Sun; 🖉) Wine and dine in a courtyard of gorgeous white roses or in the light and airy dining room. The great-value food is sophisticated, fresh and delicious, and all made from scratch. The atmosphere is relaxed and fun, a testament to your host Tim Coney, an affable character who makes a mighty syrah and may sing at random. Booking advisable.

Tirohana Estate MODERN NZ $$
(☎06-306 9933; www.tirohanaestate.com; 42 Puruatanga Rd; lunch mains $25-33, 3-course prix fixe dinner $59; ⊙lunch noon-3pm, dinner 6pm-late Tue-Sun) On sunny days, casual brunches and lunches are served on the terrace at this pretty vineyard, while evenings are set aside for finer dining in the elegant dining room with global decor and artwork. There's something for everyone on the good-value prix fixe menu; we'll vouch for the olive-crusted lamb with mint and tomato salad. Impeccable service; dinner booking essential.

Village Cafe CAFE $
(6 Kitchener St; mains $9-22; ⊙8am-4.30pm, dinner Fri; 🖉) In the barnlike back-end of the Wine Centre and opening out onto a sunny courtyard, this on-song cafe cranks out fine works: from a properly composed feijoa and ginger muffin, through a pallete of eggy brekkiness and smoothies, towards serious stuff like mince on toast and pizza.

Martinborough Hotel PUB
(Memorial Sq; mains $12-22) The Settlers Bar in the historic Martinborough Hotel is deservedly and perenially popular, welcoming to all and setting them up with some craft beers, local wines and honest grub. Best enjoyed outside on pavement tables on sunny days, or gathered inside with all the other out-of-towners and a clutch of down-to-earth locals.

Entertainment

Circus CINEMA, CAFE
(☎06-306 9442; www.circus.net.nz; 34 Jellicoe St; adult/child $15/10; ⊙4pm-late Wed-Mon) The town's cultural hub is arguably Circus, a stylish art-house cinema (movieline 056-306 9434) where you can watch the cream of contemporary movies in a a modern, micro-size complex. There are two comfy studio theatres, as well as a stylish foyer and cafe that open out on to a rather Zen garden. Reasonably priced food (mains $20 to $28) includes bar snacks, pizza, mains with plenty of seasonal veg, and gelato.

Information

The **Martinborough i-SITE** (☎06-306 5010; www.wairarapanz.com; 18 Kitchener St; ⊙9am-5pm Mon-Fri, 10am-4pm Sat & Sun) is small, helpful and cheery. It stocks the *Martinborough Wine Village Map*, produced by the people behind the useful site www.martinboroughnz.com.

WAIRARAPA WINE COUNTRY

Wairarapa's world-renowned wine industry was nearly crushed in infancy. The region's first vines were planted in 1883, but the prohibition movement in 1908 soon put a cap on that corker idea. It wasn't until the 1980s that winemaking was revived, after Martinborough's *terroir* was discovered to be similar to Burgundy in France. A few vineyards soon sprang up, but the number has now ballooned to nearly 50 regionwide. Martinborough is the undisputed hub of the action, but vineyards around Gladstone and Masterton are also on the up.

Martinborough plays host to **Toast Martinborough** (☎06-306 9183; www.toastmartinborough.co.nz; tickets $70), held annually on the third Sunday in November. Enjoyable on many levels (standing up and quite possibly lying on the grass), this is a hugely popular wine, food and music event, and you'll have to be quick on the draw to get a ticket.

The **Wairarapa Wines Harvest Festival** (www.wairarapawines.co.nz; tickets $40) celebrates the beginning of the harvest with an extravaganza of wine, food and family fun. It's held at a remote riverbank setting 10 minutes from Carterton on a Saturday in mid-March.

Wairarapa's wineries thrive on visitors; Martinborough's 20-odd are particularly welcoming with well-oiled cellar doors and noteworthy food served in some gorgeous gardens and courtyards. The *Wairarapa Wine Trail Map* (available from the i-SITE and many other locations) will aid your navigations. Read all about it at www.winesfrommartinborough.com.

An excellent place to sample and purchase many wines, and for advice on local cellar doors, is the **Martinborough Wine Centre** (www.martinboroughwinecentre.co.nz; 6 Kitchener St; ⏲10am-5pm), which also sells olive oils, books, clothing and art.

Recommended Wineries

Ata Rangi (www.atarangi.co.nz; 14 Puruatanga Rd; ⏲1pm-3pm Mon-Fri, noon-4pm Sat & Sun) One of the region's pioneering winemakers. Great drops across the board and cute cellar door.

Coney (www.coneywines.co.nz; Dry River Rd; ⏲11am-4pm Fri-Sun) Friendly, operatic tastings and lovely restaurant.

Margrain (www.margrainvineyard.co.nz; cnr Ponatahi & Huangarua Rds; ⏲11am-5pm Fri-Sun) Pretty winery and site of the Taste Vin Café, a good pit stop overlooking the vines.

Palliser (www.palliser.co.nz; Kitchener St; ⏲10.30am-4pm Mon-Fri, 10.30am-5pm Sat & Sun) Wines so good, even the Queen has some stashed away in her cellar. Slick outfit.

Cape Palliser

The Wairarapa coast south of Martinborough around Palliser Bay and Cape Palliser is remote and sparsely populated. The bendy road to the Cape is stupendously scenic: a big ocean and black-sand beaches on one side; barren hills and sheer cliffs on the other. Look for hints of the South Island, visible on a clear day.

Standing like giant organ pipes in the Putangirua Scenic Reserve are the **Putangirua Pinnacles**, formed by rain washing silt and sand away and exposing the underlying bedrock. Accessible by a track near the car park on Cape Palliser Rd, it's an easy three-hour return walk along a streambed to the pinnacles, or take the 3½-hour loop track past hills and coastal viewpoints. For some rugged tramping nearby, head to **Aorangi (Haurangi) Forest Park**. Maps and more information (including details on camping and a DOC cottage for rent) can be obtained from DOC in Masterton and Wellington.

Further south is the wind-worn fishing village **Ngawi**. The first things you'll notice here are the rusty bulldozers on the beach, used to drag fishing boats ashore. Next stop is the malodorous **seal colony**, the North Island's largest breeding area. Whatever you do in your quest for a photo, don't get between the seals and the sea. If you block their escape route they're likely to have a go at you!

Get your thighs thumping on the steep, 250-step (or is it 249?) climb to **Cape Palliser Lighthouse**, from where there are yet more amazing coastal views.

On the way there or back, take the short detour to the wind-blown settlement of **Lake Ferry**, overlooking Lake Onoke, where there's birdwatching to be enjoyed. This area is also good for exploration – discover the lake edge, the wild and woolly coastline

Vynfields (www.vynfields.com; 22 Omarere Rd; ⏱11am-4pm) Five-star, savoury pinot noir and a lush lawn on which to enjoy a platter. Organic/biodynamic wines.

Bicycle Tours

The best and most eco-friendly way to explore the Wairarapa's wines is by bicycle, as the flat landscape makes for puff-free cruising. Martinborough has four options:

Christina Estate Vineyard (☎06-306 8920; christinaestate@xtra.co.nz; 28 Puruatanga Rd; half-day $25-40, full day $35-50; ⏱8.30am-6pm) Bikes, plus tandems for the coordinated.

March Hare (☎021 668 970; www.march-hare.co.nz; 18 Kitchener St; $65) Two wheels and a picnic.

Martinborough Top 10 Holiday Park (☎0800 780 909, 06-306 8946; www.martinboroughholidaypark.com; cnr Princess & Dublin St; full day $40) Super-convenient if you're staying on-site.

Martinborough Wine Centre (☎06-306 9040; www.martinboroughwinecentre.co.nz; 6 Kitchener St; half-day $25, full day $35) Morning, afternoon or all-day rentals.

Guided Tours

The following companies will guide you round the vines:

Dynamic Tours (☎04-478 8533; www.dynamictours.co.nz; from $250) Customised wine tours, run from Wellington.

Hammond's Scenic Tours (☎04-472 0869; www.wellingtonsightseeingtours.com; full-day tour adult/child $200/100) Full-day winery tours including gourmet lunch.

Tour Wairarapa (☎06-372 7554; www.tourwairarapa.co.nz; $190) Wine tastings, chocolate and lunch at the historic Gladstone Inn.

Tranzit Tours (☎0800 471 227, 06-370 6600; www.tranzittours.co.nz; from $142) Four vineyards and a platter lunch at Martinborough's Village Café.

Zest Food Tours (☎04-801 9198; www.zestfoodtours.co.nz; $369) Small-group food and wine tours in Greytown and Martinborough.

(prime for surfing), and the cliffs behind. You'll also find the **Lake Ferry Hotel** (mains $12-28; ⏱from 11am) with its retro fitout (check out the formica), which has great views and fish and chips.

Martinborough i-SITE can help with accommodation options in the Lake Ferry and Cape Palliser area, which include campsites and holiday homes for rent.

Greytown

POP 2000

The most seductive of several small towns along SH2, Greytown has tarted itself up over recent years and is now full of Wellingtonians on the weekend. It has plenty of accommodation, some decent food, three high-street pubs and some swanky shopping. Check out www.greytown.co.nz for more information.

Sights

Cobblestones Village Museum MUSEUM
(www.cobblestonesmuseum.org.nz; 169 Main St; adult/child/family $5/2/10; ⏱10am-4.30pm) Greytown was the country's first planned inland town: intact Victorian architectural specimens line the main street. The quaint Cobblestones Village Museum is an enclave of period buildings and various historic objects, dotted around pretty grounds inviting a lie-down on a picnic blanket.

TOP CHOICE **Schoc Chocolates** FOOD
(www.chocolatetherapy.com; 177 Main St) No picnic? No worries. Visit Schoc in its 1920s cottage beside Cobblestones Village Museumvillage. Sublime flavours, worth every single penny of 10 bucks a tablet. Truffles, rocky road and peanut brittle, too. Free tastings.

Stonehenge Aotearoa MONUMENT
(06-377 1600; www.stonehenge-aotearoa.com; tours adult/child $16/8; 10am-4pm, tours 11am Sat & Sun & by appointment) About 10km southeast of Carterton, this full-scale adaptation of the UK's Stonehenge is orientated for its location on a grassy knoll overlooking the Wairarapa Plain. Its mission: to bring the night sky to life, even in daylight. The pre-tour talk and audiovisual presentation are excellent, and the henge itself a pretty surreal sight – especially when interpreted by one of its tour guides, who are consummate storytellers. Self-guided 'Stone Trek' tours are also available for adult/child $6/3.

Sleeping & Eating

Greytown Campground CAMPSITE $
(06-304 9837; Kuratawhiti St; unpowered/powered sites $18/22) A basic camping option (with equally basic facilities) scenically spread through Greytown Park, 500m from town.

Greytown Hotel HOTEL $
(06-304 9138; www.greytownhotel.co.nz; 33 Main St; s/d with shared bathroom $50/80) A serious contender for 'oldest hotel in New Zealand', the Top Pub (as it's known) is looking great for her age. Upstairs rooms are small and basic but comfortable, with no-frills furnishings and shared bathrooms. Downstairs is a chic dining room, alongside an ol' faithful lounge-bar (meals $12 to $20) and popular garden-courtyard.

Oak Estate Motor Lodge MOTEL $$
(06-304 8188, 0800 843 625; www.oakestate.co.nz; cnr Main St & Hospital Rd; r $125-185) A stand of gracious roadside oaks and pretty gardens shield a smart complex of self-contained units: studios, one- and two-bedroom options.

Salute TAPAS $$
(83 Main St; tapas $8-15, pizza $19; noon-late Wed-Sat, 12.30-3.30pm Sun;) Heavy on the Med vibe but with a delicate touch on the food front, Salute will suit you down to the ground if you like saucy, succulent, crisp, charred and fried, along with lashings of olive oil and wedges of lemon. Food so colourful you'll forget you're in grey-town.

Cuckoo Cafe ITALIAN $$
(06-304 8992; 128 Main St; meals $15-25; 10am-late Wed-Sun;) Refreshingly unruly joint littered with mismatched retro furniture in a shocking-pink villa on the main street. Substantial pizzas are the mainstay, along with pasta and blackboard specials, with house-churned ice cream and cheesecake for pud. Inexpensive local wines.

French Baker BAKERY $
(81 Main St; snacks $4-7, mains $13-19) Buttery croissants, tempting tarts and authentic breads; artisan baker Moïse Cerson is le real McCoy. Great coffee too and a compact menu of suitably Gallic offerings, such as Roquefort salad and French toast.

Masterton & Around

POP 19,500

Masterton is the Wairarapa's utilitarian hub, an unselfconscious town getting on with its business. Its main claim to immortality is the 50-year-old sheep-shearing competition, the international **Golden Shears** (www.goldenshears.co.nz), held annually in the first week of March.

Masterton spins the wool out a bit longer at the **Wool Shed** (www.thewoolshednz.com; Dixon St; adult/child/family $8/2/15; 10am-4pm), a baaaa-loody marvellous little museum dedicated to NZ's sheep-shearing and wool-production industries.

Next door is the region's foremost cultural institution, the small but rather splendid **Aratoi Wairarapa Museum of Art & History** (www.aratoi.co.nz; cnr Bruce & Dixon Sts; admission by donation; 10am-4.30pm), which hosts an impressive program of exhibitions and events (and has a very nice shop!)

Opposite the Wool Shed and Aratoi is **Queen Elizabeth Park** (Dixon St), perfect for stretching your legs. Feed the ducks, dump someone on the see-saw, have a round of minigolf or practise your high catches on the cricket oval. You could also eat a magnificent meat pie, purchased from Masterton's notable bakery, the **Ten O'Clock Cookie** (180 Queen St).

There are a few interesting sights further afield, one of which is , on the coast 68km east of Masterton. It's a truly awesome, end-of-the-world place, with a reef, the lofty 162m-high Castle Rock, largely safe swimming and walking tracks. There's an easy (but sometimes ludicrously windy) 30-minute return walk across the reef to the lighthouse, where 70-plus shell species are fossilised in the cliffs. Another one-hour return walk runs to a huge limestone cave (take a torch), or take the 1½-hour return track from Deliverance Cove to Castle Rock.

Keep well away from the lower reef when there are heavy seas. Ask the staff at Masterton i-SITE about accommodation here.

Thirty kilometres north of Masterton on SH2, **Pukaha Mt Bruce National Wildlife Centre** (www.pukaha.org.nz; adult/child/family $20/6/50; ⌚9am-4.30pm) is not only one of NZ's most successful wildlife and captive breeding centres, it's also the most readily accessible bush experience off the highway. The visitor centre has various exhibits including an interactive gallery, while outside there's a new kiwi house with a nursery, aviaries, virgin forest and a scenic one-hour loop track taking in some great views. Huge eels, tuatara and other creatures also reside here. The daily visitor program allows you to see tuatara being fed (11.30am), attend the eel-feeding (1.30pm) and watch the kaka circus (3pm). There are also guided tours on weekends (adult/child $35/15). There's a cafe on-site.

The turn-off to the main eastern entrance of the **Tararua Forest Park** (www.doc.govt.nz) is just south of Masterton on SH2; follow Norfolk Rd about 15km to the gates. Mountain streams dart through virgin forest in this reserve, known as 'Holdsworth'. At the park entrance are swimming holes, picnic areas, campsites and a lodge. Walks include short, easy family tramps, excellent one- or two-day tramps, and longer, challenging tramps for experienced bush-bods (west through to Otaki Forks). The resident caretaker has maps and hut accommodation info. Check weather and track updates before setting off, and be prepared to be baked, battered and buffeted by fickle conditions.

As you've had the stamina to read this far, it's only fair that we share with you one final tip. If you've got your own wheels, and you like a good garden bar, head to the **Gladstone Inn** (51 Gladstone Rd, Gladstone). Cheers!

ℹ Information

The **Masterton i-SITE** (☎06-370 0900; www.wairarapanz.com; cnr Dixon & Bruce Sts; ⌚9am-5pm Mon-Fri, 10am-4pm Sat & Sun) can sort you out with oodles of information including a copy of the *Wairarapa Visitor Guide*, advice on accommodation, and directions to the Gladstone Inn.

Marlborough & Nelson

Includes »

Marlborough Region.... 400
Picton.......................... 400
Marlborough Sounds ...404
Queen Charlotte Track...407
Kenepuru & Pelorus Sounds.............409
Blenheim........................411
Kaikoura........................ 416
Nelson........................... 423
Nelson Lakes National Park................430
Motueka........................ 432
Motueka to Abel Tasman.........................435
Golden Bay....................440
Kahurangi National Park...............................444

Best Places to Eat

» Green Dolphin (p422)
» Wither Hills (p414)
» Hopgood's (p428)
» Sans Souci Inn (p442)
» Wakamarinian Cafe (p411)

Best Places to Stay

» Hopewell (p410)
» Ratanui (p442)
» Kerr Bay (p430)
» Dylan's Country Cottages (p422)

Why Go?

For many travellers, Marlborough and Nelson will be their introduction to what South Islanders refer to as the 'Mainland'. Having left windy Wellington, and made a white-knuckled crossing of Cook Strait, folk are often surprised to find the sun shining and the temperature up to 10 degrees warmer.

Good pals, these two neighbouring regions have much in common beyond an amenable climate: both boast renowned coastal holiday spots, particularly the Marlborough Sounds and Abel Tasman National Park. There are two other national parks (Kahurangi and Nelson Lakes) and more mountain ranges than you can poke a stick at.

And so it follows that these two regions have an abundance of luscious produce: summer cherries for a starter, but most famously the grapes that work their way into the wineglasses of the world's finest restaurants. Keep your penknife and picnic set at the ready.

When to Go?

The forecast is good: Marlborough and Nelson soak up some of New Zealand's sunniest weather. January and February are the warmest months, with daytime temperatures averaging 22°C; July is the coldest, averaging 12°C. It's wetter and more windswept the closer you get to Farewell Spit and the West Coast.

From around Christmas to mid February, the top of the South teems with Kiwi holidaymakers, so plan ahead during this time and be prepared to jostle for position with a load of jandal-wearing families.

Marlborough & Nelson Highlights

1. Getting up close to wildlife, including whales, seals, dolphins and albatross, in **Kaikoura** (p416)
2. Nosing your way through the **Marlborough Wine Region** (p414)
3. Tramping or biking the **Queen Charlotte Track** (p407) in the Marlborough Sounds
4. Embracing the craft-beer scene around **Nelson** (p429)
5. Sea kayaking in postcard-perfect **Abel Tasman National Park** (p437)
6. Getting blown away at Blenheim's **Omaka Aviation Heritage Centre** (p411), one of New Zealand's best museums
7. Reaching the end of the road around **Farewell Spit** (p444), where there'll be gannets and godwits for company

ESSENTIAL MARLBOROUGH & NELSON

» **Eat** Doris' bratwurst at the weekend markets in Nelson and Motueka

» **Drink** A pint of Captain Cooker at Golden Bay's Mussel Inn (p444)

» **Read** The *Nelson Mail* and the *Marlborough Express*

» **Listen to** the dawn chorus in Nelson Lakes National Park

» **Watch** The tide roll in, and then watch it roll away again...

» **Festival** Marlborough Wine Festival

» **Go Green** on the Heaphy Track, a hotbed of ecological wonderment

» **Online** www.destinationmarlborough.com; www.nelsonnz.com; www.kaikoura.co.nz

» **Area code** ☎03

Getting There & Around

Cook Strait can be crossed slowly and scenically on the ferries between Wellington and Picton, and swiftly on flights servicing key destinations.

InterCity is the major bus operator, but there are also local shuttles. Tranz Scenic's *Coastal Pacific* train takes the scenic route from Picton to Christchurch, via Blenheim and Kaikoura.

Renting a car is easy, with a slew of car-hire offices in Picton and depots throughout the region.

Popular coastal areas such as the Marlborough Sounds and Abel Tasman National Park are best navigated on foot or by kayak, with water-taxi services readily available to join the dots.

MARLBOROUGH REGION

Picton is the gateway to the South Island and the launching point for Marlborough Sounds exploration. A cork's pop south of Picton is agrarian Blenheim and its world-famous wineries, and further south still is Kaikoura, the whale-watching town.

History

Long before Abel Tasman sheltered on the east coast of D'Urville Island in 1642 (more than 100 years before James Cook blew through in 1770), Maori knew the Marlborough area as Te Tau Ihu o Te Waka a Maui ('the prow of Maui's canoe'). When Cook named Queen Charlotte Sound, his detailed reports made the area the best-known sheltered anchorage in the southern hemisphere. In 1827 French navigator Jules Dumont d'Urville discovered the narrow strait now known as French Pass. His officers named the island just to the north in his honour. In the same year a whaling station was established at Te Awaiti in Tory Channel, which brought about the first permanent European settlement in the district.

Picton

POP 4000

Half asleep in winter, but hyperactive in summer (with up to eight fully laden ferry arrivals per day), boaty Picton clusters around a deep gulch at the head of Queen Charlotte Sound. It's the main traveller port for the South Island, and the best place from which to explore the Marlborough Sounds and tackle the Queen Charlotte Track. Over the last few years this little town has really bloomed, and offers visitors plenty of reason to linger even after the obvious attractions are knocked off the list.

Sights & Activities

The majority of activity happens around the Marlborough Sounds (p404), but landlubbers will still find plenty to occupy themselves.

The town has some very pleasant **walks**. A free i-SITE map details many of these, including an easy 1km track to Bob's Bay. The Snout Track (three hours return) continues along the ridge offering superb water views. Climbing a hill behind the town, the Tirohanga Track is a two-hour leg-stretching loop offering the best view in the house.

Edwin Fox Maritime Museum MUSEUM
(www.edwinfoxsociety.co.nz; Dunbar Wharf; adult/child $10/4; ⌚9am-5pm) Purportedly the world's third-oldest wooden ship, the *Edwin Fox* was built of teak in Calcutta and launched in 1853. During its chequered career it carried troops to the Crimean War, convicts to Australia and immigrants to NZ. This museum has maritime exhibits, including the venerable old dear, preserved under cover.

Eco World Aquarium WILDLIFE CENTRE
(www.ecoworldnz.co.nz; Dunbar Wharf; adult/child/family $20/10/55; ⌚10am-8pm Dec-Feb, 10am-5.30pm Mar-Nov) The primary purpose

of this centre is animal rehab, but we're not talking in the Amy Winehouse sense here. All sorts of critters come here for fix-ups and rest-ups, and the odd bit of how's-your-father goes on, too. Very special specimens include NZ's 'living dinosaur' – the tuatara – as well as blue penguins, gecko and giant weta. Fish-feeding time (11am and 2pm) is a splashy spectacle. Sharing the building is the **Picton Cinema** (03-573 6030; www.pictoncinemas.co.nz; Dunbar Wharf; adult/child $15/9; 10am-8pm), bringing the likes of Werner Herzog to town. The manager deserves a medal

Picton Museum MUSEUM
(London Quay; adult/child $5/1; 10am-4pm) If you dig local history – whaling, sailing and the 1964 Roller Skating Champs – this will float your boat. The photo displays are well worth a look, especially for five bucks (funds go towards much-needed development).

Sleeping

Villa Backpackers HOSTEL $
(03-573 6598; www.thevilla.co.nz; 34 Auckland St; dm $26-30, d with/without bathroom $76/67;) This bright backpackers has a blooming garden and sociable outdoor areas (with spa pool), cheery kitchen and free bikes. In-demand en-suite rooms, switched-on staff, fresh flowers and free apple crumble (fruit supply permitting) make this a real home away from home. Queen Charlotte Track bookings and camping gear for hire.

Tombstone Backpackers HOSTEL $
(03-573 7116, 0800 573 7116; www.tombstonebp.co.nz; 16 Gravesend Pl; dm $28, d with/without bathroom $75/81;) Rest in peace in hotel-worthy dorms, double rooms and a self-contained apartment. Also on offer are a spa overlooking the harbour, free breakfast, sunny reading room, pool table, DVD library, free ferry pick-up and drop-off… The list goes on.

Jugglers Rest HOSTEL $
(03-573 5570; www.jugglersrest.com; 8 Canterbury St; sites from $19, dm $31, d $66-70; closed from Jun-Sept;) The jocular host keeps all her balls up in the air at this well-run and homely bunk-free backpackers. Peacefully located 10 minutes' walk from town or even less on a free bike. Cheery, private gardens are a good place to socialise with fellow travellers, especially during the evening fire shows.

Sequoia Lodge Backpackers HOSTEL $
(0800 222 257, 03-573 8399; www.sequoialodge.co.nz; 3a Nelson Sq; dm $25-28, d with/without bathroom $78/66;) A well-managed backpackers in a colourful, high-ceilinged Victorian house. It's a little out of the centre, but has bonuses including free internet, DVDs, hammocks, barbecues, spa and nightly chocolate pudding! Free breakfast May to November.

Buccaneer Lodge LODGE $
(03-573 5002; www.buccaneerlodge.co.nz; 314 Waikawa Rd; s/d/tr/q $72/80/93/124;) Enthusiastic owners have spruced up this Waikawa Bay lodge to offer good en-suite rooms, many with expansive views from the 1st-floor balcony. Courtesy town transfers, free bike hire and the pretty foreshore just five minutes' walk away.

Parklands Marina Holiday Park HOLIDAY PARK $
(0800 111 104, 03-573 6343; www.parktostay.co.nz; 10 Beach Rd, Waikawa; sites from $30, units $50-90;) Large, leafy campground with roomy sites, satisfactory cabins, plus ready access to boat-ilicious Waikawa Bay and Victoria Domain (pleasant 3km walk/cycle from town). Courtesy transfers available.

Picton Top 10 Holiday Park HOLIDAY PARK $
(03-573 7212, 0800 277 444; www.pictontop10.co.nz; 70-78 Waikawa Rd; sites from $20, units

MAORI NZ: MARLBOROUGH & NELSON

While Maori culture on the South Island is much less evident than in the north, it can still be found in pockets, and particularly around coastal Marlborough.

Kaikoura is rich in Maori history, into which Maori Tours Kaikoura (p420) can offer an insight. The Marlborough Sounds, too, has some stories to tell. Plug into them on eco-oriented tours and wildlife cruises with Myths & Legends Eco-Tours (p404).

Maori history is no more powerfully relayed than through oral traditions and carving. Encounter both of these *tikanga* (customs) at Shark Nett Gallery (p410) in Havelock, with its impressive collection of contemporary carvings.

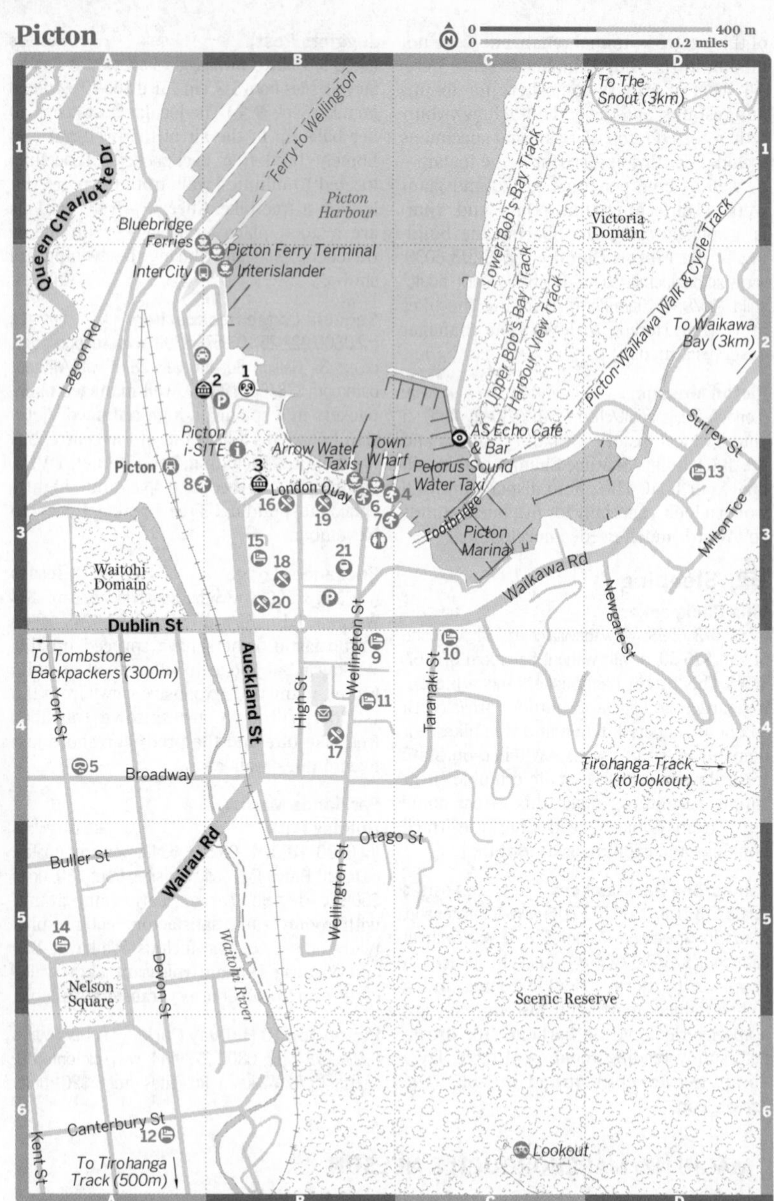

$70–110; @🛜≋) About 500m from town, this compact, well-kept place has modern, crowd-pleasing facilities including playground, barbecue area, heated swimming pool and a super recreation room.

Harbour View Motel MOTEL **$$**
(☎03-573 6259, 0800 101 133; www.harbourviewpicton.co.nz; 30 Waikawa Rd; d $125-200; 🛜) The elevated position of this motel commands good views of Picton's mast-filled harbour from its tastefully decorated, self-contained studios with timber decks.

Picton

Sights

1 Eco World Aquarium ... B2
2 Edwin Fox Maritime Museum ... B2
3 Picton Museum ... B3

Activities, Courses & Tours

4 Beachcomber Fun Cruises ... B3
Cougar Line ... (see 4)
5 Dive Picton ... A4
Dolphin Watch Ecotours ... (see 6)
6 Endeavour Express ... B3
7 Marlborough Sounds Adventure Company ... B3
8 Wilderness Guides ... A3

Sleeping

9 Gables B&B ... B4
10 Harbour View Motel ... C4
11 Jasmine Court ... B4
12 Jugglers Rest ... A6
13 Picton Top 10 Holiday Park ... D3
14 Sequoia Lodge Backpackers ... A5
15 Villa Backpackers ... B3

Eating

16 Café Cortado ... B3
17 Fresh Choice Supermarket ... B4
18 Gusto ... B3
19 Le Café ... B3
20 Picton Village Bakkerij ... B3

Drinking

21 Seamus's ... B3

Entertainment

Picton Cinema ... (see 1)

Jasmine Court MOTEL $$
(☎0800 421 999, 03-573 7110; www.jasminecourt.co.nz; 78 Wellington St; d $145-235, f $185-245; @📶) Top-notch, spacious motel with plush interiors, kitchenette, DVD player, plunger coffee and locally milled soap. Some rooms have a spa, and the odd one has a decent harbour view. Flash new studio units exhibit further excellence.

Bay Vista Waterfront Motel MOTEL
(☎03-573 6733; www.bayvistapicton.co.nz; 303 Waikawa Rd, Waikawa; d $130-165; 📶) Recently revamped and neat as a new pin, this motel enjoys an enviable position at the water's edge, with lush lawn and views down Queen Charlotte Sound. All units have kitchen facilities. Located 4km from Picton (courtesy transfer available by request).

Gables B&B B&B $$
(☎03-573 6772; www.thegables.co.nz; 20 Waikawa Rd; s $100, d $140-170, units $155-200, all incl breakfast; @📶) This historic B&B (once home to Picton's mayor) has three spacious, themed en-suite rooms in the main house and two homely self-contained units out the back. Prices drop if you organise your own breakfast. Lovely hosts show good humour (ask about the Muffin Club).

Whatamonga Home Stay HOMESTAY $$
(☎03-573 7192; www.whsl.co.nz; 425 Port Underwood Rd; d incl breakfast $140-165; @📶) Follow Waikawa Rd, which becomes Port Underwood Rd, for 8km and you'll bump into this classy waterside accommodation with two detached, self-contained units with king-sized beds and balconies with magic views. Two other rooms under the main house (also with views) share a bathroom. Free kayaks, dinghies and fishing gear are available.

Eating & Drinking

Picton Village Bakkerij BAKERY $
(cnr Auckland & Dublin Sts; items $2-8; ⏰6am-4pm; ✎) Dutch owners bake trays of European goodies here, including interesting breads, decent pies and filled rolls, cakes and custardy, tarty treats. Be prepared to queue.

Le Café CAFE $$
(London Quay; lunch $10-23, dinner $19-33; ⏰7.30am-10.30pm; ✎) A perennially popular spot both for its quayside location, dependable food and Havana coffee. The likes of salami sandwiches and sweets are in the cabinet, while a good antipasto platter, generous pasta, local mussels, lamb loin and expertly cooked fresh fish feature a la carte. Laid-back atmosphere, craft beer and occasional live gigs make this a good evening hang-out.

Gusto CAFE $
(33 High St; meals $14-20; ⏰7.30am-2.30pm; ✎) This workaday joint, with friendly staff and outdoor tables, does beaut breakfasts including first-class salmon-scrambled egg and a 'Morning Glory' fry-up worth the calories. Lunch options may include local mussels and a steak sandwich.

EXPLORING THE MARLBOROUGH SOUNDS

The Marlborough Sounds are a geographic maze of inlets, headlands, peaks, beaches and watery reaches, formed when the sea flooded into deep valleys after the last ice age. To get an idea of how convoluted the sounds are, Pelorus Sound is 42km long but has 379km of shoreline.

You can reach many spectacular locations by car. The wiggly 35km drive along **Queen Charlotte Drive** from Picton to Havelock is a great Sounds snapshot (even on a rainy day), but if you've got time to burn, take a pilgrimage to **French Pass** (or even **D'Urville Island**) for some big picture framing of the Outer Sounds. Roads are predominantly narrow and occasionally unsealed, so allow plenty of driving time and keep your wits about you.

Sounds travel is invariably quicker by boat (for example, Punga Cove from Picton by car takes two to three hours, but just 45 minutes by boat). Fortunately, a multitude of vessels await to ferry you around, either to schedule or on-demand, with the bulk operating out of Picton for the Queen Charlotte Sound, and some from Havelock for Kenepuru and Pelorus Sounds.

There are loads of walking, kayaking and biking opportunities, but there's **diving** as well – notably the wreck of the *Mikhail Lermontov*, a Russian cruise ship that sank in Port Gore in 1986.

From Picton

Numerous operators ply the Picton waters, most of which can be found at the new Town Wharf. They offer everything from a quick zip across to a lodge and back, to cruises taking in sites such as Ship Cove and Motuara Island bird sanctuary, to round-trip Queen Charlotte Track transport and pack transfers that allow trampers to walk with a small daypack. Bikes and kayaks can also be transported.

Cougar Line (Map p402; ☎0800 504 090, 03-573 7925; www.cougarlinecruises.co.nz; Town Wharf; track round trip $103, full day tour from $75) QC Track transport, plus various half- and full-day cruise/walk trips, including the rather special (and flexible) ecocruise to Motuara Island (p404) and a Ship Cove picnic.

Beachcomber Fun Cruises (Map p402; ☎03-573 6175, 0800 624 526; www.beachcombercruises.co.nz; Town Wharf; mail run $89, cruises $61-99, track round trip $99) Two- to four-hour cruises, some with resort lunches. Cruise/walk, cruise/bike and QC Track options also available.

Endeavour Express (Map p402; ☎03-573 5456; www.boatrides.co.nz; Town Wharf; track round trip $97) Backpacker-friendly company offering QC Track transfers and day adventures. Mountain bikes and camping gear for hire. QCT Pass vendor.

Marlborough Sounds Adventure Company (Map p402; ☎0800 283 283, 03-573 6078; www.marlboroughsounds.co.nz; Town Wharf; half- to 3-day packages $85-545) Bike-walk-kayak trips, with options to suit every inclination. The kayak trip ($105) to Lochmara Lodge includes a fish and chips lunch as reward. Gear rental (bikes, kayaks and camping equipment) also available.

Wilderness Guides (Map p402; ☎0800 266 266, 03-573 5432; www.wildernessguidesnz.com; Picton Railway Station; 1 day trip from $125, kayak or bike hire per day $60) Host of the popular and flexible 'multisport' day trip (kayak/walk/cycle) plus many other guided and independent biking, hiking and kayaking tours around the Queen Charlotte Sound.

Dolphin Watch Ecotours (Map p402; ☎0800 9453 5433, 03-573 8040; www.naturetours.co.nz; Town Wharf; dolphin swimming/viewing $165/100, other tours from $75) Half-day 'swim with dolphins' and wildlife tours including trips to Motuara Island (p404).

Café Cortado CAFE **$$**
(cnr High St & London Quay; mains $17-36; ⏲8am-late) A pleasant corner cafe and bar with sneaky views of the harbour through the foreshore's pohutukawa and palms, this fairly consistent performer turns out fish and chips, meaty mains, good pizza and respectable salads.

Myths & Legends Eco-Tours (☎03-573 6901; www.eco-tours.co.nz; half-/full-day cruises $200/250) A chance to get out on the water with a local Maori family – longtime locals, storytellers and environmentalists. There are six different trips to choose from, including birdwatching and visiting Ship Cove.

GoDive Marlborough (☎03-573 9181, 0800 463 483; www.godive.co.nz; 1-day wreck dive incl lodge accommodation from $255) PADI training and dive trips to the Sounds' most famous wreck, the *Mikhail Lermontov*.

Dive Picton (Map p402; ☎0800 423 483, 03-573 7323; www.divepicton.co.nz; cnr York St & Broadway; half-/full-day $190/290) Dive trips around the Sounds and to the *Mikhail Lermontov*, plus PADi and SSI training.

Active Eco Tours (☎03-573 7199; www.sealswimming.com; half-day dive trip/snorkel/seal swim $185/90/135) See the seals, plus wreck dives and jaunts to other Sounds sights, under and over the water.

Arrow Water Taxis (Map p402; ☎03-573 8229, 027 444 4689; www.arrowwatertaxis.co.nz; Town Wharf) Pretty much anywhere, on demand, for groups of four or more.

Picton Water Taxis (☎027 227 0284, 03-573 7853; www.pictonwatertaxis.co.nz) Water taxi and sightseeing trips around Queen Charlotte, on demand.

Float Plane (☎021-704 248; www.nz-scenic-flights.co.nz; Ferry Terminal; flights from $75) Offers Queen Charlotte Track and Sounds accommodation transfers, scenic flights, and flights and trips to Nelson, the Abel Tasman National Park and across to the lower North Island.

From Anakiwa

Sea Kayak Adventure Tours (Map p406; ☎03-574 2765, 0800 262 5492; www.nzseakayaking.com; cnr Queen Charlotte Dr & Anakiwa Rd; half-/full-day kayak rental $40/60, bike $40/50) Freedom kayak and mountain-bike rental, plus guided and 'guided then go' kayaking trips around Queen Charlotte, Kenepuru and Pelorus Sounds (from $75).

From Havelock

Pelorus Mail Boat (Map p406; ☎03-574 1088; www.mail-boat.co.nz; Jetty 1; adult/child $128/free; ⏲departs 9.30am Tue, Thu & Fri) Popular full-day boat cruise through the far reaches of Pelorus Sound on a genuine NZ Post delivery run. Bookings essential; BYO lunch. Picton and Blenheim pick-up and drop-off available.

Greenshell Mussel Cruise (☎03-577 9997, 0800 990 800; www.greenshellmusselcruise.co.nz; adult/child $115/39; ⏲departs 1.30pm) Three-hour cruise on a catamaran to mussel in on Kenepuru's aquaculture. Includes a tasting of steamed mussels and a glass of wine. Bookings essential.

Waterways Boating Safaris (Map p406; ☎03-574 1372; www.waterways.co.nz; 745 Keneperu Rd; half-day adult/child $110/55, full day $150/75) Be guided around the majestic Marlborough Sounds while piloting your own zippy boat. A unique and fun way to get out on the water, see the scenery and learn about the area's ecology and history. BYO lunch. Local pick-up/drop-offs.

Pelorus Sound Water Taxi (Map p402; ☎027 444 2852, 03-574 2151; www.pelorussoundwatertaxis.co.nz; Jetty 1a) Taxi and sightseeing trips from Havelock, around Pelorus, on demand.

Kenepuru Water Taxi (☎021 455 593, 03-573 4344; www.kenepuru.co.nz; 7170 Kenepuru Rd) Taxi and sightseeing trips around Kenepuru Sound, on demand.

Seamus's PUB

(25 Wellington St; meals $12-27; ⏲noon-1am) Seamus's is a snug little drinking den, pouring a reliable Guinness as well as a good selection of whiskies. Mix it all up with hearty bar food and regular live music, and you've got the recipe for the liveliest joint in town.

Marlborough Sounds

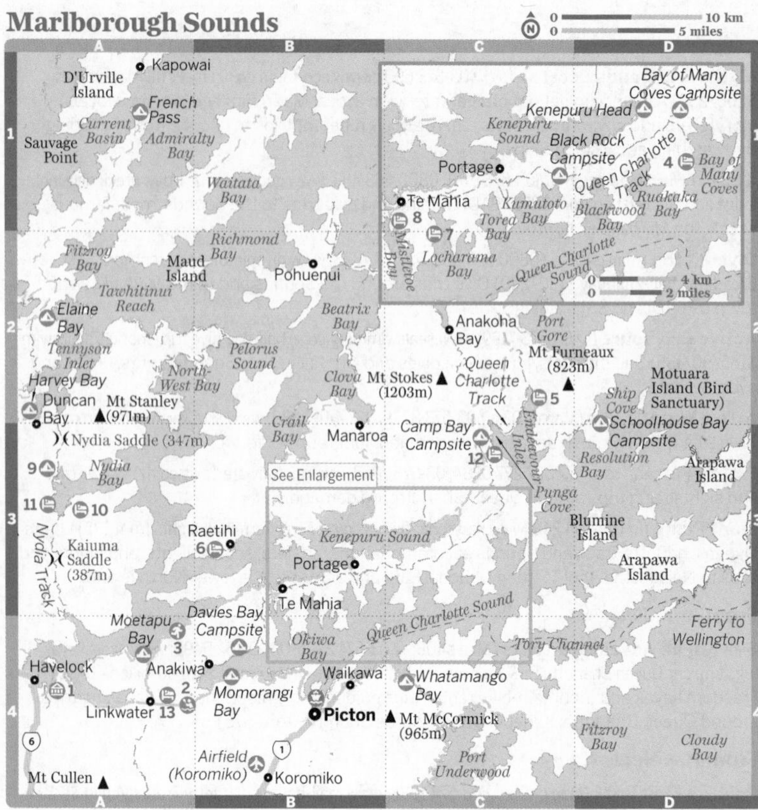

Marlborough Sounds

Sights

1 Shark Nett Gallery A4

Activities, Courses & Tours

Pelorus Mail Boat .... (see 1)
2 Sea Kayak Adventure Tours A4
3 Waterways Boating Safaris A4

Sleeping

4 Bay of Many Coves Resort D1
5 Furneaux Lodge C2
6 Hopewell B3
7 Lochmara Lodge C2
Mahana Lodge .... (see 12)
8 Mistletoe Bay C1
Noeline's Homestay .... (see 12)
9 Nydia Bay DOC Campsite A3
10 Nydia Lodge A3
11 On the Track Lodge A3
12 Punga Cove Resort C3
13 Smiths Farm Holiday Park A4

Fresh Choice Supermarket SUPERMARKET (Mariners Mall, 100 High St; 7am-9pm) Pretty much the only choice, and actually pretty good.

Information

Picton i-SITE (03-520 3113; www.destinationmarlborough.com; Foreshore; 9am-5pm Mon-Fri, to 4pm Sat & Sun) All vital tourist guff including maps, Queen Charlotte Track information, lockers and transport bookings. Department of Conservation (DOC) counter staffed during summer.

Picton Library (03-520 7493; 67 High St; 8am-5pm Mon-Fri, 10am-1pm Sat;) Free wi-fi internet access.

Police Station (03-520 3120; 36 Broadway)

Post Office (03-573 6900; Mariners Mall, 72 High St)

Getting There & Away

Make bookings for ferries, buses and trains at Picton i-SITE.

Air

Soundsair (☎03-520 3080, 0800 505 005; www.soundsair.com) flies daily between Picton and Wellington (adult/child $100/88). There are discounts for online bookings, and a shuttle bus ($7) to/from the airstrip at Koromiko, 8km south.

Boat

There are two operators crossing Cook Strait between Picton and Wellington, and although all ferries leave from more or less the same place, each has its own terminal. The main transport hub (with car-rental depots) is at the Interislander Terminal, which also has public showers, a cafe and internet facilities.

Bluebridge Ferries (☎0800 844 844, in Wellington 04-471 6188; www.bluebridge.co.nz; adult/child from $51/26) crossings takes three hours 20 minutes; there are up to four sailings in each direction daily. Cars and campervans up to 5.5m from $118, motorbikes $51, bicycles $10. Passenger fares are from $51/26 per adult/child.

Interislander (☎0800 802 802, in Wellington 04-498 3302; www.interislander.co.nz; adult/child from $46/23) crossings takes three hours 10 minutes; up to five sailings in each direction daily. Cars are priced from $118, campervans (up to 5.5m) from $133, motorbikes $56, bicycles $15. Passenger fares from adult/child $55/28.

Bus

Buses serving Picton depart from the Interislander terminal or nearby i-SITE.

InterCity (☎03-365 1113; www.intercitycoach.co.nz; Picton Ferry Terminal) runs services south to Christchurch (from $26, 5½ hours) via Kaikoura (from $17, 2½ hours), with connections to Dunedin, Queenstown and Invercargill. Services also run to/from Nelson (from $26, 2¼ hours), with connections to Motueka and the West Coast; and to/from Blenheim (from $10, 30 minutes). At least one bus daily on each of these routes connects with a Wellington ferry service.

Smaller shuttle buses running from Picton to Christchurch include **Atomic Shuttles** (☎03-349 0697; www.atomictravel.co.nz) and **Naked Bus** (☎0900 625 33; www.nakedbus.com).

Ritchies Transport (☎03-578 5467; www.ritchies.co.nz) buses traverse the Picton–Blenheim line daily (from $12), departing from the Interislander ferry terminal.

Train

Tranz Scenic (☎0800 872 467, 04-495 0775; www.tranzscenic.co.nz) runs the *Coastal Pacific* service daily each way between Picton and Christchurch via Blenheim and Kaikoura (and 22 tunnels and 175 bridges!), departing Christchurch at 7am, Picton at 1pm. Adult one-way Picton–Christchurch fares range from $59 to $99. The service connects with the Interislander ferry.

Getting Around

Shuttles (and tours) around Picton and wider Marlborough are offered by **Marlborough Sounds Shuttles** (☎03-573 7122; www.marlboroughsoundsshuttles.co.nz). Between Picton and Havelock (via Anakiwa), you can hitch a van ride with **Coleman Post** (☎027 255 8882; $15). It departs Picton at 8.15am and Havelock at 10.45am, with other services on request.

Renting a car in Picton is easy-peasy – as low as $35 per day if you shop around. Most agencies allow drop-offs in Christchurch; if you're planning to drive to the North Island, most companies suggest you leave your car at Picton and pick up another one in Wellington after crossing Cook Strait. The i-SITE can help you with recommendations and bookings, or try one of the following direct:

Ace (☎03-573 8939; www.acerentalcars.co.nz; Ferry Terminal)

NZ Rent A Car (☎03-573 7282; www.nzrentacar.co.nz; Ferry Terminal)

Omega (☎03-573 5580; www.omegarentalcars.com; 1 Lagoon Rd)

Pegasus (☎03-573 7733; www.carrentalspicton.co.nz; 1 Auckland St)

Queen Charlotte Track

The hugely popular, meandering 71km Queen Charlotte Track offers gorgeous coastal scenery on its way from historic Ship Cove to Anakiwa, passing through a mixture of privately owned land and DOC reserves. Access depends on the cooperation of local landowners; respect their property by utilising designated campsites and toilets, and carrying out your rubbish. Your purchase of the Track Pass ($12), available from operators in town and on the track, provides the co-op the means to maintain and enhance the experience for all.

Queen Charlotte is a well-defined track, suitable for people of average fitness. You can do the walk in sections using local water-taxi transport, walk the whole three- to five-day journey, or embark on a combo of walking, kayaking or biking. We're talking mountain biking here, and a whole lot of fun for fit, competent off-roaders: it's possible to ride the track in two or three days, guided or self-guided. Note that the section between Ship Cove and Camp Bay is off-limits to cyclists from 1 December to the end of February. During these months you can still be dropped by boat at the Saddle and ride to Anakiwa.

Numerous boat and tour operators service the track (p404), allowing you to start and finish where you like, on foot or bike or by kayak.

Sleeping options are no more than a few hours' walk apart; boat operators will transport your pack along the track for you. Ship Cove is the usual (and recommended) starting point – mainly because it's easier to arrange a boat from Picton to Ship Cove than vice versa – but the track can be started from Anakiwa. There's a public phone at Anakiwa but not at Ship Cove.

Estimated walk times:

TRACK SECTION	DISTANCE	DURATION
Ship Cove to Resolution Bay	4.5km	1½-2hr
Resolution Bay to head of Endeavour Inlet	10.5km	2½-3hr
Endeavour Inlet to Camp Bay/Punga Cove	12km	3-4hr
Camp Bay/Punga Cove to Torea Saddle/Portage	24km	6-8hr
Torea Saddle/Portage to Te Mahia Saddle	7.5km	3-4hr
Te Mahia Saddle to Anakiwa	12.5km	3-4hr

Sleeping & Eating

Unless you're camping, it pays to book your Queen Charlotte Track accommodation *waaay* in advance, especially in summer. There are six **DOC campsites** (adult/child $6/3) along the track, each with toilets and a water supply but no cooking facilities. There's also a variety of resorts, lodges, backpackers and guesthouses.

The following select listings are arranged in order heading south from Ship Cove. Your overnight stops will depend on how far you can/want to walk on any given day – do your research and book ahead. Not every accommodation option is covered here; see the map for campsites, and www.qctrack.co.nz for all possibilities.

Furneaux Lodge LODGE $$
(☎03-579 8259; www.furneauxlodge.co.nz; Endeavour Inlet; dm $38, cabins from $45, units $199-269, meals $20-36; @) One of the Sounds' stalwart resorts, Furneaux's highlights are the historic lodge building and a big flat lawn right down to the water's edge. This place welcomes pit-stoppers (coffee, beer, lunch, etc), but there's also adequate accommodation here, the most pleasant of which are the swish but pricey waterfront studios.

Punga Cove Resort RESORT $$$
(☎03-579 8561; www.pungacove.co.nz; Endeavour Inlet; dm $45, lodge $150-180, chalets $180-450, restaurant mains $29-40; @≋) A rustic but charming resort offering self-contained studios and family and luxury A-frame chalets, most with sweeping sea views. The backpackers is basic but Punga's location easily atones. Ample activities (pool, spa, games, kayak and bike hire), plus a restaurant and boatshed bar/cafe (decent local beers and $25 pizza).

Mahana Lodge LODGE $$
(☎03-579 8373; www.mahanalodge.co.nz; Endeavour Inlet; d $180; ⊙closed May-Aug) This beautiful property features a pretty waterside lawn and purpose-built lodge with four en-suite doubles. Eco-friendly initiatives include bush regeneration, pest trapping and organic veggie patch; in fact, feel-good factors abound: free kayaks, robes, home-baking and a blooming conservatory where the evening meal is served (three courses $55).

Noeline's Homestay HOMESTAY $
(☎03-579 8375; Endeavour Inlet; dm without/with linen $30/35) Follow the pink arrows from Camp Bay to this relaxed homestay and be greeted by 70-something Noeline, 'the Universal Grandma', and her home-baked treats. It's a friendly arrangement with beds for five people, cooking facilities and great views.

Bay of Many Coves Resort RESORT $$$
(☎0800 579 9771, 03-579 9771; www.bayofmanycoves.co.nz; Bay of Many Coves; 1-/2-/3-bedroom apt $620/830/995; @🛜≋) Honeymooning? These plush and secluded apartments are appropriately romantic, with all mod cons and private balconies overlooking the water. The upmarket cafes and restaurant are staffed by a crew of iron chefs. Additional indulgences include room service, massage, spa and a hot tub.

Portage Resort Hotel RESORT $$
(☎03-573 4309; www.portage.co.nz; The Portage; dm $40, d $165-365; @🛜≋) This fancy resort is centred upon a smart lodge building housing Te Weka restaurant and Retro Bar (meals $14 to $35), with a sundeck overlooking the pool patio and grounds. The 22-bed backpacker wing has a small lounge and cooking facilities. Moderately stylish rooms climb the price ladder from there. The on-site Kenepuru Store sells limited snacks and groceries, while underneath is an outpost of Marlborough Sounds Adventure Company (p404), offering trips and freedom hire of bikes and boats.

DeBretts & Treetops GUESTHOUSE $
(☎03-573 4522; www.stayportage.co.nz; Portage Bay; s without/with linen $40/45) The family-run enclave of DeBretts and **Treetops** (☎03-573 4404) offers a combined total of six bedrooms in two homely backpackers high on the hill above Portage Resort. Torea Bay bag transfers included.

Lochmara Lodge RESORT $$
(☎0800 562 462, 03-573 4554; www.lochmaralodge.co.nz; Lochmara Bay; units $90-280; @🛜) A superb retreat on Lochmara Bay, reached from the Queen Charlotte Track or from Picton aboard the lodge's water taxi ($55 return). Relaxation-inducing facilities include massage and the indulgent bath house overlooking the bay. There are en-suite doubles, units and chalets, all set in lush surroundings, and a fully licensed cafe and restaurant offering fine food and decent coffee.

TOP CHOICE **Mistletoe Bay** HOLIDAY PARK $
(☎03-573 4048; www.mistletoebay.co.nz; unpowered sites adult/child $16/10, dm $20, cabins $140, linen $7.50) Surrounded by bushy hills, sweet Mistletoe Bay offers attractive camping with a brand new communal facilities block, eight irresistible cabins sleeping up to six, and a cottage with bunks for overflow. Environmental sustainability abounds, as does the opportunity to jump off the jetty, kayak in the bay, or walk the Queen Charlotte Track.

Te Mahia Bay Resort RESORT $$
(☎03-573 4089; www.temahia.co.nz; d $140-248; 🛜) This lovely low-key resort is within cooee of the Queen Charlotte Track in a picturesque bay on Kenepuru Sound. It has a range of delightful rooms-with-a-view, our pick of which is the great-value heritage units. The on-site store has pre-cooked meals, pizza, coffee and camping supplies (wine!), and there are kayaks for hire and massage.

Anakiwa Backpackers HOSTEL $
(☎03-574 1388; www.anakiwabackpackers.co.nz; 401 Anakiwa Rd, Anakiwa; dm $33, d $85-105, q $155; @🛜) This former schoolhouse (1926) greets you at the southern end of the track – a soothing spot to rest and reflect. There are two doubles (one with en-suite), a four-bed dorm and a beachy self-contained unit. Jocular owners will have you jumping off the jetty for joy and imbibing espresso and ice cream (hallelujah) from their little green caravan (open summer afternoons). Provisions available by arrangement and free kayak hire.

ℹ Information

The Picton i-SITE (p406) books and stocks everything Queen Charlotte Track, and loads more besides. Picton's Villa Backpackers (p401) is also a hotbed of info, and handles bookings. Check online details at www.qctrack.co.nz.

Kenepuru & Pelorus Sounds

Kenepuru and Pelorus Sounds, to the west of Queen Charlotte Sound, are less populous and therefore offer fewer traveller services, including transport. There's some cracking scenery, however, and those with time to spare will be well rewarded by their explorations.

Havelock is the hub of this area, the western bookend of the 35km Queen Charlotte Drive (Picton being the eastern) and the self-proclaimed 'Greenshell Mussel Capital of the World'. While hardly the most rock-and-roll of NZ towns, Havelock makes a practical base from which to set off, as you'll readily locate most necessaries, including fuel and food. As you get out into the Sounds be prepared to encounter only the odd service station and the occasional shop, which *may* have frozen bread and and out-of-date Popsicles.

For finer detail, including a complete list of visitor services, visit www.pelorus.co.nz, which covers Havelock, Kenepuru and Pelorus Sounds, and the extreme extremeties of French Pass and D'Urville Island.

DON'T MISS

PELORUS BRIDGE

A pocket of deep, green forest tucked away among paddocks of bog-standard pasture, 18km west of Havelock, this scenic reserve contains one of the last stands of river-flat forest in Marlborough. It survived only because a town planned in 1865 didn't get off the ground by 1912, by which time obliterative logging made this little remnant look precious. The reserve was born, and hats off to that, because now visitors can explore its many tracks, admire the historic bridge, take a dip in the limpid Pelorus River (beautiful enough to star in Peter Jackson's *Hobbit*), and even indulge in some home-baking at the cafe. The fortunate few can stay overnight in the DOC's small but perfectly formed **Pelorus Bridge Campsite** (☎03-571 6019; www.doc.govt.nz; unpowered/powered sites from $10/11), with its snazzy new facilities building.

Sights & Activities

If a stroll through the streets of Havelock leaves you thinking that there *must* be more to this area, you're right – and to get a taste of it you need go no further than the **Cullen Point Lookout**, 10 minutes from Havelock along the Queen Charlotte Drive. A short walk leads up and around a headland overlooking Havelock, the surrounding valleys and Pelorus Sound. The *Havelock Map & Walkway Guide*, available around town, details more walks in the area.

Nydia Track

The Nydia Track (27km, 10 hours) starts at Kaiuma Bay and ends at Duncan Bay (or vice versa). Around halfway is beautiful Nydia Bay, where there's a **DOC campsite** (adult/child $6/3) and **Nydia Lodge** (☎03-520 3002; www.doc.govt.nz; dm $15.30), an unhosted 50-bed lodge (four-person minimum). You'll need water and road transport to complete the journey; Havelock's Blue Moon lodge runs a shuttle to Duncan Bay. **On the Track Lodge** (☎03-579 8411; www.nydiatrack.org.nz; Nydia Bay; dm $40, d/tw $110, d cabins $130) provides alternative accommodation at Nydia Bay in a tranquil, ecofocused lodge offering everything from packed lunches to evening meals and a hot tub.

Shark Nett Gallery GALLERY

(☎03-574 2877; www.sharknett.co.nz; 129 Queen Charlotte Dr, Havelock; adult/child $12/6.50; ⏲10am-4pm) Overlooking the tidal Pelorus estuary, Shark Nett showcases contemporary Maori carving relating to the local Rangitane *iwi* (tribes). Guided tours provide an educational and evocative insight into how carving is used to record tribal *tikanga* (customs) and *whakapapa* (ancestry).

Sleeping & Eating

There's plenty of accommodation along the Kenepuru Road, most of which is readily accessible off the Queen Charlotte Track (p411). Other options in this area include some picturesque DOC campgrounds (most full to bursting in mid-summer), a few remote lodges and a handy holiday park at Linkwater, the cross-roads for Queen Charlotte and Kenepuru, where you'll find a petrol station with snacks. Havelock has a couple of dependable offerings and a smattering that are less so.

Smiths Farm Holiday Park HOLIDAY PARK $

(☎0800 727 578, 03-574 2806; www.smithsfarm.co.nz; 1419 Queen Charlotte Dr, Linkwater; sites from $16, cabins $60-130, units $130; @ wi-fi) Located on the apty named Linkwater flat between Queen Charlotte and Pelorus, friendly Smiths makes a handy basecamp. Well-kept cabins and motel units face out onto the bushy hillside, while livestock nibble around the lush camping lawns. Walks extend to a nearby waterfall and glowworm dell.

Hopewell LODGE $

(☎03-573 4341; www.hopewell.co.nz; 7204 Kenepuru Rd, Double Bay; dm from $40, d with/without bathroom from $130/100, 4-person cottage $200; @ wi-fi) Beloved of travellers from near and far, remote Hopewell sits waterside surrounded by native bush. Savour the long, winding drive to get there, or take a water taxi from Te Mahia. Stay at least a couple of days, so you can chill out or enjoy the roll-call of activities: mountain biking, kayaking, sailing, fishing, eating gourmet pizza, soaking in the outdoor spa, and more.

Havelock Garden Motel MOTEL $$

(☎03-574 2387; www.gardenmotels.com; 71 Main Rd, Havelock; d 105-160; wi-fi) Set in a large, graceful garden complete with dear old trees and a duck-filled creek, these 1960s units have been tastefully revamped to offer homely comforts. Local activities are happily booked for you.

Blue Moon GUESTHOUSE $
(☎03-574 2212; www.bluemoonhavelock.co.nz; 48 Main Rd, Havelock; dm $25, d $66-86; @☎) This largely unremarkable lodge has homely rooms in the main house (one with en suite), as well as cabins and a bunkhouse in the yard (along with a spa pool). The lounge and kitchen are pleasant and relaxed, as is the sunny barbecue deck. Hosts run shuttle transport servicing the Nydia Track, Queen Charlotte, and surrounds.

Wakamarinian Café CAFE $
(☎03-574 1180; 70 Main Rd, Havelock; snacks $2-9; ⊙9.30am-5pm) Heavenly home baking in a sweet cottage. Get in early to grab one of the popular pies, or console yourself with proper quiche and a sweet slice – the raspberry and white-chocolate shortcake defies description. Great coffee and excellent value, too, from Beth and Laurie: Havelock's culinary saviours.

Getting There & Away

InterCity (☎03-365 1113; www.intercitycoach.co.nz) runs daily from Picton to Havelock via Blenheim ($22, one hour), and from Havelock to Nelson ($23, 1¼ hours). **Atomic Shuttles** (☎03-349 0697; www.atomictravel.co.nz) plies the same run. You can travel between Havelock and Picton for $15 via the scenic Queen Charlotte Drive with Coleman Post (p407). Buses depart from the high street in the middle of town – look for the restaurant with the mussels on the roof.

Blenheim

POP 26,500

Blenheim (pronounced 'Blenum') is an agricultural town 29km south of Picton on the Wairau Plain between the Wither Hills and the Richmond Ranges. The town has yet to demonstrate any real power as a visitor magnet; it is the neighbours over the back fence that pull in the punters.

Sights & Activities

Omaka Aviation Heritage Centre MUSEUM
(Map p412; www.omaka.org.nz; 79 Aerodrome Rd; adult/child/family $25/10/55; ⊙10am-4pm) Blenheim's 'big attraction' has always been its wineries, but the Omaka Aviation Heritage Centre has blown the wine out of the water. Aided by Peter Jackson and his team of creative types, this captivating collection of original and replica Great War aircraft is brought to life with a series of dioramas depicting dramatic wartime scenes such as the death of Manfred von Richthofen, the Red Baron. Memorabilia and photographic displays deepen the experience. The guided tour is an extra $5 extremely well spent. A cafe and shop are on-site, and next door is **Omaka Classic Cars**, with over 100 vehicles from the '50s to the '80s (adult/child $12.50/5).

Marlborough Museum MUSEUM
(Map p412; www.marlboroughmuseum.org.nz; 26 Arthur Baker Pl off New Renwick Rd; adult/child $10/5; ⊙10am-4pm) Besides a replica township, vintage mechanicals, train rides (every first and third Sunday) and well-presented artefact displays, there's the *Wine Exhibition* for those looking to cap off their vineyard experiences.

Wither Hills Farm Park WALKING
In a town as flat as a pancake, this 1100-hectare park provides welcome relief, offering a range of walks and mountain-bike trails with grand views across the Wairau Valley and out to Cloudy Bay. Pick up a map from the i-SITE or check the information panels at the gates.

High Country Horse Treks HORSE RIDING
(☎03-577 9424; www.high-horse.co.nz; 961 Taylor Pass Rd; 1-3hr treks $70-120) Runs equine exploration from its base 11km southwest of town (call for directions).

Molesworth Tours GUIDED TOUR
(☎03-577 9897; www.molesworthtours.co.nz) New Zealand's largest high-country station – which is complete with cob cottages and vistas galore – can be discovered in depth with Molesworth Tours. It offers one- to four-day all-inclusive heritage and 4WD trips ($190 to $1655), as well as four-day fully supported (and catered) mountain-bike adventures ($1295).

Festivals & Events

Marlborough Wine Festival FOOD & WINE
(www.wine-marlborough-festival.co.nz; tickets $48) Held on the second weekend of February at Montana's Brancott Estate, this is an extravaganza of local wine, fine food and entertainment. Book accommodation well in advance.

Marlborough Wine Region

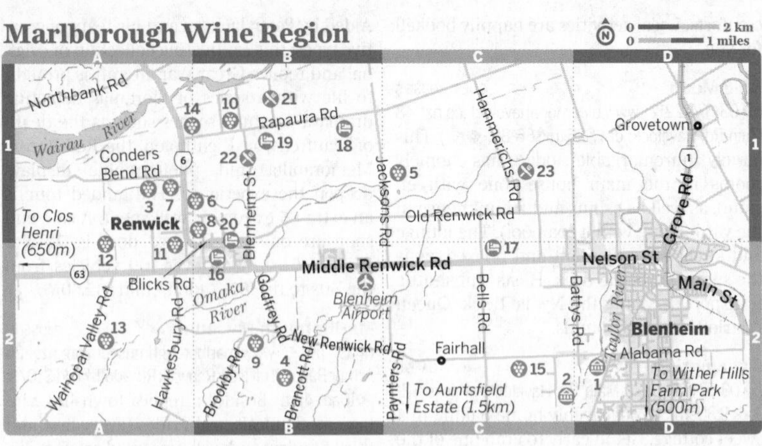

Marlborough Wine Region

Sights
1 Marlborough Museum D2
2 Omaka Aviation Heritage Centre C2

Activities, Courses & Tours
3 Bladen Estate A1
4 Brancott Estate Heritage Centre B2
5 Cloudy Bay C1
6 Forrest B1
7 Framingham A1
8 Gibson Bridge B1
9 Highfield Estate B2
10 Huia B1
11 Mahi Wines A2
12 Seresin Estate A2
13 Spy Valley Wines A2
14 Wairau River A1
15 Wither Hills C2

Sleeping
16 Olde Mill House B2
17 St Leonards C2
18 Stonehaven B1
19 Vintners Hotel B1
20 Watson's Way Lodge B1

Eating
21 Herzog Winery B1
22 La Veranda B1
23 Rock Ferry C1
Wairau River .... (see 14)
Wither Hills .... (see 15)

Sleeping

IN TOWN

Blenheim's budget beds fill with long-stay guests doing seasonal work; hostels will help find work and offer reasonable weekly rates. There are masses of midrange motels, with rich pickings on Middle Renwick Rd west of the town centre, and a handful on SH1 towards Christchurch.

Koanui Lodge & Backpackers HOSTEL $
(☎03-578 7487; www.koanui.co.nz; 33 Main St; dm $25, d with/without bathroom $82/58; @☜) This pink palace on the main street caters to both workers and casual visitors. Both the old villa and newer lodge wing are clean and tidy, but otherwise unremarkable.

Grapevine Backpackers HOSTEL $
(☎03-578 6062; www.thegrapevine.co.nz; 29 Park Tce; tent sites $18, dm $24, d $58-68, tr $81; @☜) Located inside an old maternity home just out of the town centre, Grapevine is a worker-focused hostel with a peaceful sunset deck by Opawa River. There are free canoes, and bike hire is $20 per day. Avoid the three-tier bunks if vertigo is an issue.

Blenheim Top 10 Holiday Park HOLIDAY PARK $
(☎03-578 3667, 0800 268 666; www.blenheimtop10.co.nz; 78 Grove Rd; sites from $35, cabins $78-90, units & motels $110-145; @☜) About five minutes north of town, this holiday park has campervan pads and campsites spread out along Opawa River, as well as a spa, a playground and the usual cabin/unit sus-

pects. Bike hire costs $20 per half-day. Park up right at the far end of the camp to mute some of the road and railway noise.

171 on High MOTEL $$
(0800 587 856, 03-579 5098; www.171onhighmotel.co.nz; 171 High St; d $140-180; @) A welcoming option close to town, these tasteful, splash-o-purple studios and apartments are bright and breezy in the daytime, warm and shimmery in the evening. Expect a wide complement of facilities and 'extra mile' service.

WINE REGION ACCOMMODATION

TOP CHOICE **Watson's Way Lodge** LODGE $
(Map p412; 03-572 8228; www.watsonswaybackpackers.co.nz; 56 High St, Renwick; dm $30, d $70-90; closed Aug-Sep; @) This traveller-focused, purpose-built hostel has spick-and-span rooms, mainly twins and doubles, some with en suite. There are spacious leafy gardens dotted with fruit trees and hammocks, an outdoor claw-foot bath, bikes for hire (guest/public rate $15/25 per day) and local information aplenty.

Olde Mill House B&B $$
(Map p412; 03-572 8458; www.oldemillhouse.co.nz; 9 Wilson St, Renwick; s/d $120/145; @) On an elevated section in otherwise flat Renwick, this charming old house is a treat. Dyed-in-the-wool local hosts run a welcoming B&B, with stately decor and home-grown fruit and homemade goodies for breakfast. Free bikes, outdoor spa and gardens make this a tip-top choice in the heart of the wine country.

St Leonards COTTAGES $$
(Map p412; 03-577 8328; www.stleonards.co.nz; 18 St Leonards Rd; d $115-310, extra adult $35;) Tucked into the grounds of an 1886 homestead, these four rustic cottages offer privacy and a reason to stay put. (Anyone for tennis?) Each has its own history, layout and individual outlook to the gardens and vines. Our pick is the Stables, with its lemon-grove view.

Stonehaven B&B $$$
(Map p412; 03-572 9730; www.stonehavenhomestay.co.nz; 414 Rapaura Rd; d incl breakfast $262-288; @) A stellar stone-and-timber B&B nestled among the picturesque vines with two ensuite guest rooms. Beds are piled high with pillows, breakfast is served in the summer house, dinner is provided by request with rare wines from the cellar.

Vintners Hotel HOTEL $$$
(Map p412; 0800 684 190, 03-572 5094; www.mvh.co.nz; 190 Rapaura Rd; d $150-295;) Sixteen architecturally designed suites make the most of wine-valley views, while inside classy suites boast wet-room bathrooms and abstract art. The stylish reception building has a bar and restaurant opening out on to a cherry orchard and organic vegie garden. Staff are keen to connect you with the best experiences the region has to offer.

Eating & Drinking

Hospitality can be pretty hit and miss in Blenny, with some of the best food found yonder at the wineries. While you're at it, keep an eye out for the scrumptious craft beers made by local brewers, **Renaissance** (www.renaissancebrewing.co.nz), and their associate **8-Wired** (www.8wired.co.nz), 2011 Brewer's Guild champion. Josh Scott, a winemaker's son, also brews the good range of bottle-fermented beers and thirst-quenching ciders known as **Moa** (www.moabeer.co.nz).

Café le Cupp CAFE $
(30 Market St; snacks $2-5, meals $5-16) The best tearoom in town by a country mile. Ogle your way along the counter (egg sandwiches, mince savouries, luscious lamingtons, carrot cake) or get yourself a brekkie such as the full fry-up, French toast or muesli. Heaven descends on Thursdays in the form of the ginger gem.

Raupo MODERN NZ $$
(6 Symons St; breakfast $13-19, lunch & dinner $18-33; 7.30am-late) Blenheim's best restaurant since the day it opened. It boasts stylish timber-and-stone architecture and a pleasant riverside location. This promise is backed up by consistent, modern cafe fare along the lines of macadamia muesli, aged feta and chorizo salad, local mussels and salmon, and super-fine Euro-sweets: truffles, sorbet and pastries.

CPR CAFE
(18 Wynen St) Get a fix of Blenheim's own-roast coffee. There are muffins if you're lucky, but it's really all about the beans.

Information

Blenheim i-SITE (0800 777 181, 03-577 8080; www.destinationmarlborough.com; 8 Sinclair St; 8.30am-5.30pm Mon-Fri, 9am-5pm Sat, 9am-4pm Sun) Information on

MARLBOROUGH WINERIES

Marlborough is NZ's vinous colossus, producing around three quarters of the country's wine. At last count, there were 23,900 hectares of vines planted – that's approximately 28,000 rugby pitches! Sunny days and cool nights create the perfect microclimate for cool-climate grapes: world-famous sauvignon blanc, top-notch pinot noir, and notable chardonnay, riesling, gewürztraminer, pinot gris and bubbly. Spending a day or two drifting between tasting rooms and dining among the vines is a quintessential South Island experience.

The majority of Marlborough's nearly 140 wineries lie within the Wairau Valley, mainly around Blenheim and Renwick, with others blanketing the cooler Awatere Valley or creeping up the southern-side valleys of the Wairau. Of the 40 or so that are open to the public, those listed below are well worth a look, and provide a range of quality cellar-door experiences.

A Taste of the Tastings

Most cellar doors are open from around 10.30am till 4.30pm, with some scaling back operations in winter. Wineries may charge a small fee for tasting, normally refunded if you purchase a bottle. Pick up a copy of *The Marlborough Wine Trail* map from Blenheim i-SITE (p413), available online at www.wine-marlborough.co.nz.

Auntsfield Estate (☎03-578 0622; www.auntsfield.co.nz; 270 Paynters Rd) Quality handcrafted wines from this historic and picturesque vineyard at the foot of the hills. Tours by arrangement ($15).

Bladen Estate (Map p412; www.bladen.co.nz; 83 Conders Bend Rd) Bijou family winery that's big on charm.

Brancott Estate (Map p412; ☎03-520 6975; www.brancottestate.com; 180 Brancott Rd) Ubermodern cellar door and restaurant complex atop a hillock overlooking one of the original sauvignon blanc vineyards.

Clos Henri (www.closhenri.com; 639 SH63) French winemaking meets Marlborough terroir with *très bien* results. Beautifully restored local country church houses the cellar door.

Cloudy Bay (Map p412; www.cloudybay.co.nz; Jacksons Rd) Understated exterior belies the classy interior of this blue-ribbon winery and cellar door. Globally coveted sauvignon blanc, bubbly and pinot noir.

Forrest (Map p412; www.forrest.co.nz; 19 Blicks Rd) Doctor-owners produce and prescribe a range of fine vinous medicines, including some mood-altering riesling.

Framingham (Map p412; www.framingham.co.nz; 19 Conders Bend Rd) Consistent, quality wines including exceptional rieslings and stellar stickies.

Gibson Bridge (Map p412; www.gibsonbridge.co.nz; cnr Gee St & SH6) Peachy pinot gris, and a grandiose cellar door in a miniscule space.

Highfield Estate (Map p412; www.highfield.co.nz; 27 Brookby Rd) Impressive views over the Wairau Valley from the tower atop this rosy Tuscan-style winery. The fizz is the biz.

Huia (Map p412; www.huia.net.nz; 22 Boyces Rd) Sustainable, small-scale winegrowing and the cutest yellow tasting room in town. Delectable dry-style gewürztraminer.

Mahi Wines (Map p412; www.mahiwine.co.nz; 9 Terrace Rd) Knowledgeable and friendly staff who are rightly proud of Mahi's stable of fine wines, with a strong focus on single-vineyard varieties.

Seresin Estate (Map p412; www.seresin.co.nz; 85 Bedford Rd) Organic and biodynamic wines and olive oils from cinematographer Michael Seresin. Shedlike cellar door and groovy sculptures dotted about.

Spy Valley Wines (Map p412; www.spyvalleywine.co.nz; 37 Lake Timara Rd, Waihopai Valley) Stylish, edgy architecture at this espionage-themed winery with great wines across the board. Memorable merchandise.

Wairau River (Map p412; www.wairauriverwines.com; 11 Rapaura Rd) Carbon-neutral family estate with some of Marlborough's oldest vines. Relaxing gardens and a fancy new cellar door.

Wither Hills (Map p412; www.witherhills.co.nz; 211 New Renwick Rd) One of the region's flagship wineries and an architectural gem. Premium wines and enthralling winemaker-for-a-day tours ($35).

Best Wining & Dining

With wine there must be food. This is our pick of the bunch for dining among the vines. Opening hours are for summer, when bookings are recommended.

La Veranda (Map p412; ☎03-572 7230; www.georgesmichel.com; 56 Vintage Ln; platters $19-22; ⏲11am-4pm Tue-Sun) Keenly priced platters of quality charcuterie, fromages and French desserts – the sort of lunch you should be eating at a vineyard. Eat outside or in Domaine George Michel's elegant restaurant.

Wairau River (Map p412; ☎03-572 9800; www.wairauriverwines.com; 11 Rapaura Rd; mains $19-24; ⏲noon-3pm) Modishly modified mudbrick bistro with wide veranda, and beautiful gardens with plenty of shade. Order the mussel chowder or the rare beef salad with noodles. Relaxing and thoroughly enjoyable.

Wither Hills (Map p412; ☎03-520 8284; www.witherhills.co.nz; 211 New Renwick Rd; mains $18-35, platters $25-38; ⏲11am-4pm Tue, 11am-4pm & 6pm-late Wed-Sun) Simple, well executed food in a stylish space. Pull up a beanbag on the Hockneyesque lawns and enjoy a french onion tart, bouillabaisse or platter (after 3pm), before climbing the ziggurat for impressive views across the Wairau.

Rock Ferry (Map p412; ☎03-579 6431; www.rockferry.co.nz; 80 Hammerichs Rd; mains $18-24; ⏲noon-3pm) Pleasant environment inside and out, with a slightly groovy edge. The compact summery menu – think salmon and lime leaves or fish cakes on noodle salad – is accompanied by wines from Marlborough and Otago.

Herzog Winery (Map p412; ☎03-572 8770; www.herzog.co.nz; 81 Jefferies Rd; mains $46-82, 5-course degustation menu with/without wine $197/125; ⏲restaurant 6.30pm-9.30pm, bistro 11am-10pm (closed mid-May to mid-Oct)) Refined dining in Herzog's opulent dining room. Beautifully prepared food and a remarkable wine list. Less extravagant bistro meals (mains $26 to $28) also available.

Wine Tours

Wine tours are generally conducted in a minibus, last between four and seven hours, take in four to seven wineries and range in price from $55 to $90 (with a few grand tours up to around $200 for the day, including a winery lunch). The following are grand crus:

Bubbly Grape (☎0800 228 2253, 027 672 2195; www.bubblygrape.co.nz) Three different tours including a gourmet lunch option.

Highlight Wine Tours (☎03-577-9046, 027 434 6451; www.highlightwinetours.co.nz) Visit a chocolate factory, too. Custom tours available.

Sounds Connection (☎03-573 8843, 0800 742 866; www.soundsconnection.co.nz) This operator partners up with Herzog for a wine and food matched lunch.

Bike2Wine (☎0800 653 262, 03-572 8458; www.bike2wine.co.nz; 9 Wilson St, Renwick; standard/tandem $30/60 per day, delivery/pick-up $5-10 per bike) Your other option is to get around the grapes on two wheels. This operator offers a self-guided, fully geared and supported tours.

Marlborough and beyond. Wine-trail maps and bookings for everything under the sun.

Blenheim Police Station (☎03-578 5279; 8 Main St)

Post Office (cnr Scott & Main Sts)

Wairau Hospital (☎03-520 9999; www.nmdhb.govt.nz; Hospital Rd)

Getting There & Around

Air

Blenheim Airport is 6km west of town on Middle Renwick Rd. **Air New Zealand** (☎03-577 2200, 0800 747 000; www.airnewzealand.co.nz; 29 Queen St; ⏲9am-5pm Mon-Fri) has direct flights to/from Wellington (from $99), Auckland (from $139) and Christchurch (from $99) with onward connections. Soundsair (p407) and **Air2There** (☎0800 777 000; www.air2there.com) connect Blenheim with Wellington and Paraparaumu.

Bicycle

Avantiplus (☎03-578 0433; www.bikemarlborough.co.nz; 61 Queen St; hire per half-/full day touring bike $25/40, mountain bike $40/60) rents bikes; longer hire and delivery by arrangement.

Bus

InterCity (☎03-365 1113; www.intercitycoach.co.nz) buses run daily from the Blenheim i-SITE to Picton (from $11, 30 minutes) continuing through to Nelson (from $18, 1¾ hours). Buses also head down south to Christchurch (from $25, three daily) via Kaikoura (from $16).

Naked Bus (☎0900 625 33; www.nakedbus.com) runs from Blenheim to many South Island destinations, including Kaikoura ($18, two hours), Nelson ($23, 1¾ hours) and Motueka ($36, 3¾ hours). Buses depart the i-SITE. Book online or at the i-SITE; cheaper fares for advance bookings.

Ritchies Transport (p407) buses traverse the Blenheim–Picton line daily (from $12), departing from Blenheim Railway Station.

Shuttles (and tours) around Picton and wider Marlborough are offered by Marlborough Sounds Shuttles (p407).

Taxi

Call for bookings or for a post-wine-tour ride back to your hotel with **Marlborough Taxis** (☎03-577 5511).

Train

Tranz Scenic (☎0800 872 467, 04-495 0775; www.tranzscenic.co.nz) runs the daily *Coastal Pacific* service, stopping at Blenheim en route to Picton (from $29) heading north, and Christchurch (from $59) via Kaikoura (from $59) heading south.

Kaikoura

POP 3850

Take SH1 132km southeast from Blenheim (or 183km north from Christchurch) and you'll wind around the panoramic coast to Kaikoura, a pretty peninsula town backed by the snowcapped peaks of the Seaward Kaikoura Range. There are few places in the world with so much wildlife around: whales, dolphins, NZ fur seals, penguins, shearwaters, petrels and wandering albatross all stop by or make this area home.

Marine animals are abundant here due to ocean-current and continental-shelf conditions: the seabed gradually slopes away from the land before plunging to more than 800m where the southerly current hits the continental shelf. This creates an upwelling, bringing nutrients up from the ocean floor into the feeding zone.

Until the 1980s Kaikoura was a sleepy crayfishing town ('Kai' meaning food, 'koura' meaning crayfish) with grim prospects. These days it's a tourist mecca, with quality accommodation and many other enticements including eye-popping wildlife tours.

History

In Maori legend, Kaikoura Peninsula (Taumanu o Te Waka a Maui) was the seat where the demigod Maui placed his feet when he fished the North Island up from the depths of the sea. The area was heavily settled before Europeans arrived – at least 14 Maori *pa* (fortified village) sites have been identified, and excavations show that the area was a moa-hunter settlement about 800 to 1000 years ago.

James Cook sailed past the peninsula in 1770, but didn't land. His journal states that 57 Maori in four double-hulled canoes came towards the *Endeavour*, but 'would not be prevail'd upon to put along side'.

In 1828 Kaikoura's beachfront was the scene of a tremendous battle. A Ngati Toa war party, led by chief Te Rauparaha, bore down on Kaikoura, killing or capturing several hundred of the Ngai Tahu tribe.

Europeans established a whaling station here in 1842, and the town remained a whaling centre until 1922. Sheep farming and agriculture also flourished. After whaling ended, the sea and fertile farmland continued to sustain the community.

Sights

Point Kean Seal Colony WILDLIFE RESERVE
At the end of the peninsula seals laze around in the grass and on the rocks, lapping up all the attention. Give them a wide berth (10m), and never get between them and the sea – they will attack if they feel cornered and can move surprisingly fast.

Fyffe House HISTORIC BUILDING
(www.fyffehouse.co.nz; 62 Avoca St; adult/child/family $9/2/18; ⏲10am-6pm daily Nov-Apr, to 4pm Thu-Mon May-Oct) Kaikoura's oldest surviving building is Fyffe House, built upon foundations of whale vertabrae. Built by Scotsman George Fyffe, cousin of Kaikoura's first European settler, Robert Fyffe, it started life as a small cottage in 1842. There's plenty to see inside and out, including the original brick oven, historical displays and gardens.

Kaikoura District Museum MUSEUM
(14 Ludstone Rd; adult/child $5/1; ⏲10am-4.30pm Mon-Fri, 2-4pm Sat & Sun) This provincial museum houses the old town jail, historical photos, Maori and colonial artefacts, a huge sperm-whale jaw and the fossilised remains of a plesiosaur.

Point Sheep Shearing Show FARM
(☎03-319 5422; www.pointsheepshearing.co.nz; Fyffe Quay; adult/child $10/5; ⏲shows 1.30pm & 4pm) The 30-minute Point Sheep Shearing Show at the Point B&B is fun and educationally ovine. You can also feed a ram, and lambs between September and February. Classic NZ!

Activities

There's a safe swimming beach in front of the Esplanade, and a pool (adult/child $3/1.50; 10am to 5pm November to March) if you have a salt aversion.

Decent surfing can be found in the area, too, particularly at Mangamaunu Beach (15km north of town), where there's a 500m point break, fun in good conditions. Get the low-down, transport, learn to surf or hire gear from **Board Silly Surf Adventures** (☎0800 787 352, 027 418 8900; 76 West End; 3hr lesson $80, board & suit from $30) based at South Bay. Gear hire and advice is also available from **R&R Sports** (☎03-319 5028; 14 West End; bike hire half-day $20, full day $30-40) and **Surf Kaikoura** (☎03-319 7173; www.surfkaikoura.co.nz; 4 Beach Rd).

Kaikoura Peninsula Walkway WALKING
A foray along this walkway is a must-do if humanly possible. Starting from the town, this three- to four-hour loop heads out to Point Kean, along the cliffs to South Bay, then back to town over the isthmus (or in reverse, of course). En route you'll see fur seals and red-billed seagull and shearwater (aka mutton bird) colonies. Lookouts and interesting interpretive panels abound. Collect a map at the i-SITE or follow your nose.

Dive Kaikoura DIVING
(☎0800 348 352, 03-319 6622; www.divekaikoura.co.nz; Yarmouth St; half-day $250) The whole coastline, with its rocky formations and abundant marine life, offers interesting snorkelling and diving. Dive Kaikoura runs small-group trips and diver training.

Skydive Kaikoura SKYDIVING
(☎0800 843 759; www.skydivekaikoura.co.nz; Kaikoura Airport; 9000-13,000ft $260-380; ⏲ closes for winter) Come down to earth with Henk and Sarah, who offer personal service and jumps with stupendous mountain-to-sea views. Handicam and photo packages available. The airport is 7km south of town.

Fyffe View Ranch Adventure Park FARM
(☎03-319 5069; www.kaikourahorsetrekking.co.nz; 82 Chapmans Rd off Postmans Rd; 30min/90min treks $30/120; ⏲10.30am-late) Fun, down-to-earth farmy folk offer horse treks. Hilarious gravity-fuelled mountain kart luge, woolshed archery and farm-animal feeding are also available. The ranch is 9km west of town at the foot of Mt Fyffe.

Clarence River Rafting RAFTING
(☎03-319 6993; www.clarenceriverrafting.co.nz; 3802 SH1, at Clarence Bridge; 5hr trip adult/child $120/80) The bouncy Grade II rapids of the scenic Clarence River can be rafted on a popular half-day trip, or on longer journeys including a five-day journey with wilderness camping ($1300). The operator's base is on SH1, 40 km north of Kaikoura near Clarence Bridge.

Tours

Tours are big business in Kaikoura. It's all about marine mammals: whales (sperm, pilot, killer, humpback and southern right), dolphins (Hector's, bottlenose and dusky) and NZ fur seals up close. During summer, book your tour a few weeks ahead, and give yourself some leeway to allow for lousy weather.

Whale-Watching

Your choices are boat, plane or helicopter. Aerial options are shorter and pricier, but allow you to see the whole whale, as opposed to just a tail, flipper or spout from a boat.

Kaikoura

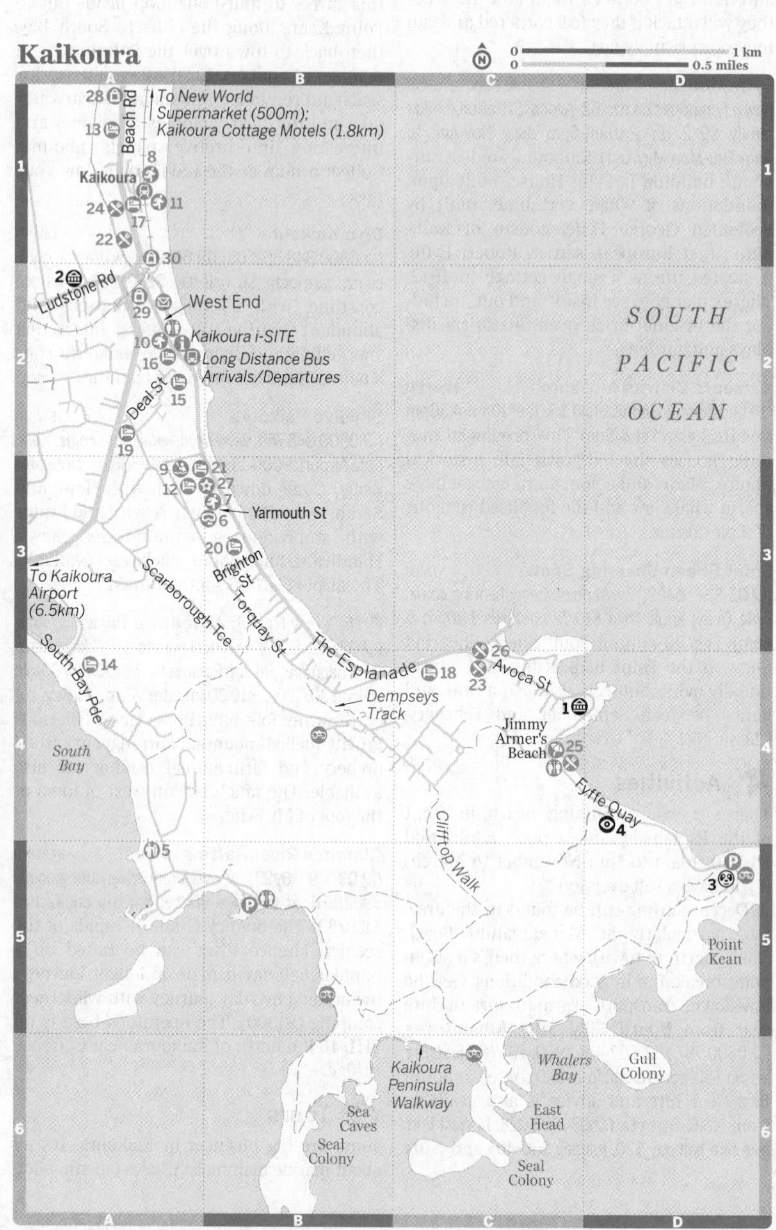

Whale Watch Kaikoura ECOTOUR
(☎03-319 6767, 0800 655 121; www.whalewatch.co.nz; Railway Station; 3hr tour adult/child $145/60) With knowledgeable guides and fascinating 'world of whales' onboard animation, Kaikoura's biggest operator heads out on boat trips (with admirable frequency) to introduce you to some of the big fellers. It'll refund 80% of your fare if no whales are sighted (success rate: 98%). If this trip is a must for you, allow a few days flexibility in case the weather turns to custard.

Kaikoura Helicopters SCENIC FLIGHTS
(☎03-319 6609; www.worldofwhales.co.nz; Railway Station; 15-60min flight from $100-490) Reliable whale-spotting flights (standard tour 30 minutes $220 each for three or more people), plus jaunts around the peninsula, Mt Fyffe and peaks beyond.

Wings Over Whales ECOTOUR
(☎03-319 6580, 0800 226 629; www.whales.co.nz; 30min flight adult/child $165/75) Light-plane flights departing from Kaikoura Airport, 7km south of town. Spotting success rate: 95%.

Dolphin & Seal Spotting

Dolphin Encounter ECOTOUR
(☎03-319 6777, 0800 733 365; www.dolphin.co.nz; 96 Esplanade; swim adult/child $175/160, observation $90/45; ⏲tours 8.30am & 12.30pm year-round, plus 5.30am Nov-Apr) Here's your chance to rub shoulders with pods of dusky dolphins on three-hour tours. Limited numbers, so book in advance.

Seal Swim Kaikoura ECOTOUR
(☎0800 732 579, 03-319 6182; www.sealswimkaikoura.co.nz; 58 West End; tours $70-110; ⏲Oct-May) Two-hour guided snorkelling tours, from shore or boat.

TOP CHOICE **Kaikoura Kayaks** KAYAKING
(☎0800 452 456, 03-319 7118; www.kaikourakayaks.co.nz; 19 Killarney St; seal tours adult/child $95/70; ⏲tours 8.30am, 12.30pm & 4.30pm Nov-Apr, 9am & 1pm May-Oct) Guided sea-kayak tours to view fur seals and explore the peninsula's coastline. Kayaking lessons, freedom hire, family-friendly options and kayak fishing also available.

Birdwatching

Albatross Encounter BIRDWATCHING
(☎03-319 6777, 0800 733 365; www.albatrossencounter.co.nz; 96 Esplanade; adult/child $120/60; ⏲tours 9am & 1pm year-round, plus 6am Nov-Apr) Kaikoura is heaven for bird-nerds, who fly at the opportunity for a close encounter with pelagic species such as shearwaters,

Kaikoura

Sights
1 Fyffe House ... C4
2 Kaikoura District Museum ... A2
3 Point Kean Seal Colony ... D5
4 Point Sheep Shearing Show ... D4

Activities, Courses & Tours
Albatross Encounter ... (see 7)
5 Board Silly Surf Adventures ... A5
6 Dive Kaikoura ... B3
7 Dolphin Encounter ... B3
8 Kaikoura Helicopters ... A1
9 Kaikoura Kayaks ... A3
10 Seal Swim Kaikoura ... A2
11 Whale Watch Kaikoura ... A1

Sleeping
12 Albatross Backpacker Inn ... A3
13 Alpine Pacific Holiday Park ... A1
14 Bay Cottages ... A4
15 Dolphin Lodge ... A2
16 Fish Tank Lodge ... A2
17 Kaikoura Top 10 Holiday Park ... A1
18 Maui YHA ... C4
19 Nikau Lodge ... A2
20 Sails Motel ... B3
21 Waves on the Esplanade ... A3

Eating
Café Encounter ... (see 7)
22 Corianders ... A1
23 Green Dolphin ... C4
24 Hislops ... A1
25 Original Kaikoura Seafood BBQ ... C4
26 Pier Hotel ... C4
Reserve Hutt ... (see 10)

Entertainment
27 Mayfair Theatre ... B3

Shopping
28 Cods & Crayfish ... A1
29 R&R Sport ... A2
30 Surf Kaikoura ... A1

CRAY CRAZY

Among all of Kaikoura's munificent marine life, the one species you just can't avoid is the crayfish, whose delicate flesh dominates local menus. Unfortunately (some say unnecessarily), it's pricey – at a restaurant, you'll shell out (pardon the pun) around $55 for half a cray or over $100 for the whole beast. You can also buy fresh, cooked or uncooked crays from **Cods & Crayfish** (81 Beach Rd; ⏲8am-6pm) and iconic **Nins Bin** (SH1; ⏲8am-6pm), a surf-side caravan 23km north of town. Upwards of $50 should get you a decent specimen.

A good alfresco option is the **Original Kaikoura Seafood BBQ** (Fyffe Quay; ⏲10.30am-early evening), a roadside stall near the peninsula seal colony – the fish or scallop sandwiches (white bread of course) are worthy, affordable substitutes if crayfish doesn't float your boat. Alternatively, take a fishing tour, or buddy-up with a local who might take you crayfishing and share the spoils.

shags, mollymawks, petrels and the inimitable albatross.

Fishing Trips

Fishing is a common obsession in Kaikoura, with local boaties angling for any excuse to go out for a little look-sea. It's a good opportunity to *kai koura* (eat crayfish). Trips start from around $60; the i-SITE has a full list of operators.

Fishing at Kaikoura FISHING
(☎03-319 3003; gerard.diedrichs@xtra.co.nz) Fishing, crayfishing, scenic tours and waterskiing, on the 6m *Sophie-Rose*.

Kaikoura Fishing Charters FISHING
(☎03-319 6888, 0800 225 297; www.kaikourafishing.co.nz) Dangle a line from the good ship *Takapu*, then take your filleted, bagged catch home to eat.

Kaikoura Fishing Tours FISHING
(☎0800 246 6597; www.kaikoura-fishing-tours.co.nz) Serious about scenery and seafood. Your catch is filleted ready for dinner.

Walking Tours

Walks Kaikoura WALKING
(☎03-319 6617; www.walkskaikoura.com; half-/full day from $95/145) Experienced local guides offering tailored walks around the area, from mountains to coast. Helihikes to mountaintops also possible.

Kaikoura Coast Track WALKING
(☎03-319 2715; www.kaikouratrack.co.nz; package $215) A three-day, 40km, self-guided walk through private farmland and along the Kaikoura Coast, 43km south of town. The price includes three nights' farm-cottage accommodation and pack transport; BYO sleeping bag and food. A two-day mountain-bike option (BYO bike) costs $85.

Kaikoura Wilderness Walks WALKING
(☎03-319 6966, 0800 945 337; www.kaikourawilderness.co.nz; 1-/2-night package $1195/1595) Two- or three-day guided walks through the privately owned Puhi Peaks Nature Reserve high in the Seaward Kaikoura range. Package includes accommodation and meals at the luxurious Shearwater Lodge.

Other Tours

Maori Tours Kaikoura CULTURAL TOUR
(☎0800 866 267, 03-319 5567; www.maoritours.co.nz; 3½hr tour adult/child $125/65; ⏲tours 9am & 1.30pm) Fascinating half-day, small-group tours laced with Maori hospitality and local lore. Visit historic sites, hear legends and learn indigenous use of trees and plants. Advance bookings required.

Kaikoura Mountain Safaris DRIVING TOUR
(☎021 869 643; www.kaikouramountainsafaris.co.nz; half-day tour adult/child $100/55, 1-day tour adult/child $165/100) Journey into the backcountry in a 4WD or Unimog – three different tours (departing from the i-SITE) taking in alpine vistas, remote farms and the Clarence River valley.

Festivals & Events

Seafest FOOD & WINE
(www.seafest.co.nz; tickets $35; ⏲early Oct) A one-day showcase of piscatorial prowess, plus live bands, family entertainment and a big Friday-night bash to kick things off.

Sleeping

Summer sees accommodation fill up, so book in advance or save your visit for the off-season when reduced rates are in the offing.

Fish Tank Lodge HOSTEL $
(03-319 7408; www.fishtanklodge.co.nz; 86 West End; dm/d $25/65; @) Nemo meets Michaelangelo at this newly muraled and freshly upgraded hostel in the middle of town. Expect clean, bright and breezy all-round, especially out on the 1st-floor balcony, which enjoys expansive views. Smart management are keen to keep you happy: bike hire and snorkel gear make a good start.

Albatross Backpacker Inn HOSTEL $
(0800 222 247, 03-319 6090; www.albatross-kaikoura.co.nz; 1 Torquay St; dm $25-29, s/d $49/69; @) This arty backpackers resides in two sweet heritage buildings, one a former post office. It's colourful and close to the beach but sheltered from the breeze. As well as a laid-back lounge, and a separate one for tele-viewers, there are decks and verandas to chill out on.

Dolphin Lodge HOSTEL $
(03-319 5842; www.dolphinlodge.co.nz; 15 Deal St; dm $27, d with/without bathroom $67/60; @) This small home-away-from-home hostel has onsite managers showing the love and owners visiting often to fuss over their lovely scented garden (hammocks ahoy). Inside is a bit squeezed, but on dry days most of the action will be out on the fantastic deck, or around the barbecue, or in the spa pool...

Maui YHA HOSTEL $
(0800 278 299, 03-319 5931; www.yha.co.nz; 270 Esplanade; dm $33, d $89-110, tr $102; @) This excellent YHA boasts unimpeded views across the bay to the pine-lined esplanade and mighty peaks beyond. Many rooms enjoy similar views, as does the big-windowed dining room, which you'll find in the same state as the rest of this purpose-built (1962) hostel: tidy, functional and conservatively dressed. Half-/full-day bike hire $20/30.

Alpine Pacific Holiday Park HOLIDAY PARK $
(0800 692 322, 03-319 6275; www.alpine-pacific.co.nz; 69 Beach Rd; sites from $40, cabins $75, units & motels $140-180; @) This compact and proudly trimmed park copes well with its many visitors, and offers excellent facilities, including a shiny kitchen, resorty pool area and barbecue pavilion. Rows of cabins and units are slightly more stylish than average. Mountain views can be had from many angles.

Kaikoura Top 10 Holiday Park HOLIDAY PARK $
(0800 363 638, 03-319 5362; www.kaikoura top10.co.nz; 34 Beach Rd; sites from $44, cabins $80-95, units & motels $150-210; @) Hiding from the highway behind a massive hedge, this busy, well-maintained campground offers family-friendly facilities (heated pool, spa, trampoline) and cabins and units to the usual Top 10 standard.

Nikau Lodge B&B
(03-319 6973; www.nikaulodge.com; 53 Deal St; d $190-250; @) A waggly-tailed welcome awaits at this beautiful B&B high on the hill with grand-scale vistas. Four ensuite rooms are plush and comfy, with additional satisfaction arriving in the form of cafe-quality breakfasts accompanied by fresh local coffee. Good-humour, home-baking, free wi-fi, hot-tub and blooming gardens: you may want to move in.

Bay Cottages MOTEL $$
(03-319 5506; www.baycottages.co.nz; 29 South Bay Pde; cottages/motels $100/130) Here's a great value option on South Bay, a few kilometres south of town: five tourist cottages with kitchenette and bathroom sleeping up to four, and two slick motel rooms with stainless-steel benches, low-voltage lighting and flat-screen TVs. The friendly owner may even take you crayfishing in good weather.

Sails Motel MOTEL $$
(03-319 6145; www.sailsmotel.co.nz; 134 Esplanade; d $115, q $140) There are no sea (or sails) views at this motel, so the cherubic owners have to impress with quality. Their four secluded, tastefully appointed self-contained units are down a driveway in a garden setting (private outdoor areas abound).

Kaikoura Cottage Motels MOTEL $$
(0800 526 882, 03-319 5599; www.kaikoura cottagemotels.co.nz; cnr Old Beach & Mill Rds; d $120-140) This enclave of eight modern tourist flats is looking mighty fine, surrounded by attractive native plantings now in full flourish. Oriented for mountain views, the self-contained units sleep four between an open plan studio-style living room and one private bedroom. Soothing sand-and-sky colour scheme and quality chattels.

TOP CHOICE **Dylan's Country Cottages** COTTAGES $$

(☎03-319 5473; www.lavenderfarm.co.nz; 268 Postmans Rd; d $175; ⊙closed May-Aug; 📶) On the grounds of the delightful Kaikoura Lavender Farm, northwest of town, these two self-contained cottages make for an aromatic escape from the seaside fray. One has a private outdoor bath and a shower emerging from a tree; the other an indoor spa and handkerchief lawn. Homemade scones, preserves and free-range eggs for breakfast. Sweet, stylish and romantic.

Waves on the Esplanade APARTMENT $$$

(☎0800 319 589, 03-319 5890; www.kaikouraapartments.co.nz; 78 Esplanade; apt $240-350; 📶) Can't do without the comforts of home? Here you go: spacious, luxury two-bedroom apartments with Sky TV, DVD player, two bathrooms, laundry facilities and full kitchen. Oh, and superb ocean views from the balcony. Rates are for up to four people.

The Factory B&B $$$

(☎03-319 3034; www.hapukufactory.com; 5 Old Beach Rd, Hapuku; d incl breakfast $480; 📶) About 10 minutes' drive north of Kaikoura in the cute beach settlement of Hapuku is this 100-year-old dairy factory, divinely converted and bejewelled with designer furniture. The guest wing is fully self-contained and sleeps up to six, although it looks like honeymoon heaven. One night will never be enough.

Eating & Drinking

Kaikoura has some very good cafes and restaurants, and some that are well-past their use-by date.

Green Dolphin SEAFOOD $$$

(☎03-319 6666; www.greendolphinkaikoura.com; 12 Avoca St; mains $25-46; ⊙5pm-late) Quality Kaikoura fish multiple ways, and the omnipresent bovine, porcine and lobstery treats, all made with care and a fondness for good local produce. On busy nights, book ahead or nurse a cocktail or aperitif in the pleasant bar or garden. Those with foresight should plump for a table with a view by the floor-to-ceiling windows.

Hislops CAFE $$

(33 Beach Rd; lunch $9-24, dinner $22-37; ⊙9am-late, closed Tue & Wed May-Sep; 🌿) This snappy, feel-good cafe maintains its reputation for fresh, wholesome food. Start the morning with a guilt-free fry-up, then come back at night for organic meats plus local seafood, veg and vegan choices. Notable salads, such as goats feta and avocado.

Pier Hotel MODERN NZ $$

(www.thepierhotel.co.nz; 1 Avoca St; snacks $7-18, mains $24-34; ⊙11am-late) Wide views of bay and the mountains beyond make this the grandest dining room in town. A cheerful crew serves up generous portions of honest food, such as fresh local fish, baby back spare ribs and bbq crayfish for those with fat wallets. The enticing public bar has reasonably priced beer and bar snacks, historical photos and a garden bar. Upstairs lodgings are worn and creaky, but good value (double room, including breakfast, from $115).

Café Encounter CAFE $

(96 Esplanade; meals $8-19; ⊙7.30am-5pm; 🌿) Housed in the Dolphin Encounter complex, this cafe is more than just somewhere to wait for your trip. Great counter food and coffee, plus cakes, pastries, bagels, toasties and daily specials, such as braised pork belly and fennel slaw. Ocean and esplanade views from the sunny patio.

Reserve Hutt CAFE $

(72 West End; meals $10-18) The best coffee in the town centre, roasted on site and espressed by dedicated baristas in Kaikoura's grooviest cafe. Puttin' out that rootsy retro-Kiwiana vibe we love so much, this is a neat place to linger over a couple of flatties and down a muffin, delicious ham croissant or the full eggy brunch.

Corianders INDIAN $$

(17 Beach Rd; mains $14-20; 🌿) Spicing up Kaikoura life, this branch of the Corianders chain keeps the bar raised with dependable Indian food in a pleasant environment. The epic menu has all your favourites and some you've never heard of. Excellent *pakora*, good breads and extensive vegie options.

New World Supermarket SUPERMARKET

(124-128 Beach Rd; ⊙7.30am-9pm) Ten minutes' walk from the town centre.

Entertainment

Mayfair Theatre CINEMA

(☎03-319 5859; 80 Esplanade; adult/child $10/6) Resembling a pink liquorice allsort, this seafront picture house screens almost-recent releases.

Information

Kaikoura i-SITE (☎03-319 5641; www.kaikoura.co.nz; West End; ⏲ 9am-5pm Mon-Fri, to 4pm Sat & Sun, extended hours Dec-Mar) Helpful staff make tour, accommodation and transport bookings, and help with DOC-related matters.

Coffee Hit (22 Beach Rd; wi-fi) Free wi-fi when you buy a cup or two of top-notch espresso served to you by Mr Good Guy from his coffee caravan right on SH1. Choice.

Paperplus/Post Office (☎03-319 6808; 41 West End) Postal agent.

Getting There & Away

Bus

InterCity (☎03-365 1113; www.intercity.co.nz) buses run between Kaikoura and Nelson (from $49, 3½ hours), Picton (from $17, 2¼ hours) and Christchurch (from $15, 2¾ hours). The bus stop is at the car park next to the i-SITE (tickets and info inside).

Naked Bus (☎0900 625 33; www.nakedbus.com) also runs to/from Kaikoura to most South Island destinations, departing from the i-SITE. Book online or at the i-SITE; cheaper fares for advance bookings.

Train

Tranz Scenic (☎0800 872 467, 04-495 0775; www.tranzscenic.co.nz) runs the *Coastal Pacific* service, stopping at Kaikoura on its daily run between Picton (from $59, 2¼ hours) and Christchurch (from $59, three hours). The northbound train departs Kaikoura at 9.54am; the southbound at 3.28pm.

Getting Around

Hire bicycles from R&R Sport (p417). Surf Kaikoura and Maui YHA also hire bikes.

Kaikoura Shuttles (☎03-319 6166; www.kaikourashuttles.co.nz) will run you around the local sights as well as to and from the airport.

NELSON REGION

The Nelson region, centred upon Tasman Bay but stretching north to Golden Bay and Farewell Spit, and south to Nelson Lakes, is a popular travel destination for both international visitors and locals. It's not hard to see why. Not only does it boast three national parks (Kahurangi, Nelson Lakes and Abel Tasman), but it can also satisfy nearly every other whim, from food, wine and beer to art, craft and festivals, to that most precious of pastimes for which the region is well known: lazing about in the sunshine.

Nelson

POP 60,800

Dishing up a winning combination of great weather and beautiful surroundings, Nelson is hailed as one of New Zealand's most 'liveable' cities. In summer it fills up with local and international visitors, who lap up its offerings, including proximity to diverse natural attractions.

Sights

Nelson has an inordinate number of galleries, most of which are listed in the *Art & Crafts Nelson City* brochure (with walking-trail map) available from the i-SITE. A fruitful wander can be had by starting at the **Fibre Spectrum** (www.fibrespectrum.co.nz; 280 Trafalgar St), where you can pick up handwoven woollens, before moving on to 'Lord of the Ring' jeweller **Jens Hansen** (www.jenshansen.com; 320 Trafalgar Sq), glassblower **Flamedaisy** (www.flamedaisy.com; 324 Trafalgar Sq), then around the corner to the home of Nelson pottery, **South Street Gallery** (www.nelsonpottery.co.nz; 10 Nile St W). More interesting local creations can be found at the **Nelson Market** (Montgomery Sq; ⏲8am-1pm Sat) on Saturday.

Christ Church Cathedral CHURCH
(www.nelsoncathedral.org; Trafalgar Sq; admission free; ⏲8am-7pm Nov-Mar, to 5pm Apr-Oct) The enduring symbol of Nelson, the art-deco Christ Church Cathedral lords it over the city from the top of Trafalgar St. Work began in 1925, but this architectural hybrid wasn't completed until 1965.

Nelson Provincial Museum MUSEUM
(www.nelsonmuseum.co.nz; cnr Hardy & Trafalgar Sts; admission from adult/child $5/3; ⏲10am-5pm Mon-Fri, 10am-4.30pm Sat & Sun) This modern museum space is filled with cultural heritage and natural history exhibits with a regional bias, as well as regular touring exhibitions (admission price varies). It also features a great rooftop garden.

Suter GALLERY
(www.thesuter.org.nz; 208 Bridge St; adult/child $3/50c, free on Sat; ⏲10.30am-4.30pm) Adjacent to Queen's Gardens, Nelson's public art gallery presents changing exhibitions, floor talks, musical and theatrical performances, and films. It also houses a small but good art store and a popular cafe.

Central Nelson

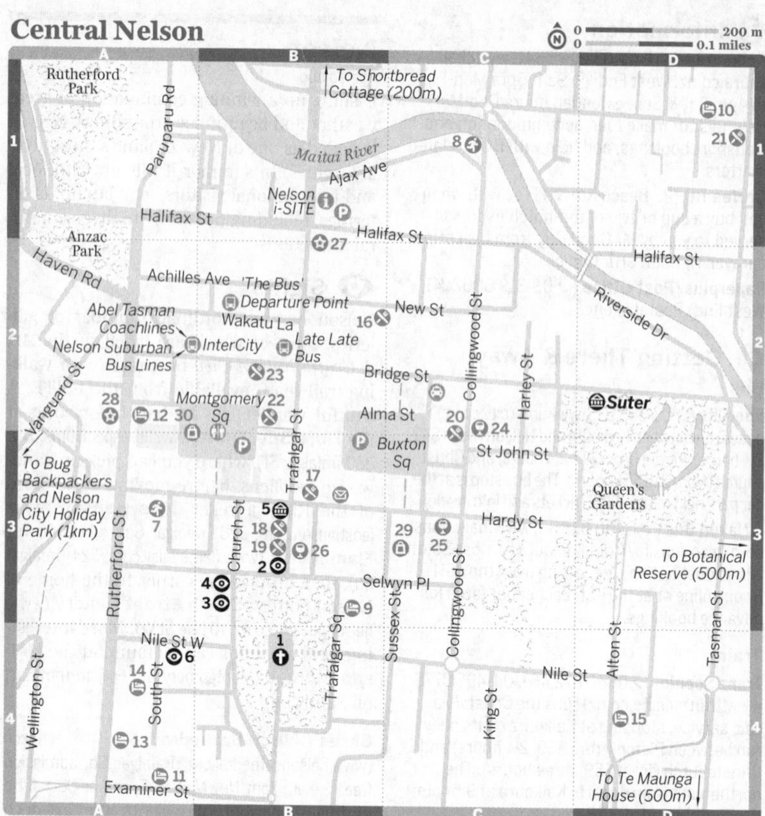

Founders Heritage Park MUSEUM
(www.founderspark.co.nz; 87 Atawhai Dr; adult/child/family $7/5/15; ⏲10am-4.30pm) Two kilometres from the city centre, this park comprises a replica historic village with a bakery, chocolatier and museums. It makes for a fascinating wander, which you can augment with a visit to the onsite **Founders Brewery & Café** (www.foundersbrewery.co.nz; meals $11-15), NZ's first certified organic brewery, where you can get brunch and wood-fired pizza. Tastings are $10; a 'backpacker special' grants park entry plus a tasting of three beers for $12.

Miyazu Japanese Garden GARDENS
(Atawhai Dr) This serene garden is full of sculptures, lanterns and ducks on placid ponds. Sit for a while and ponder something profound.

Botanical Reserve PARK
(Milton St) Walking tracks ascend Botanical Hill, where a spire proclaims it the 'Centre of New Zealand'. NZ's first-ever rugby match was played at the foot of the hill on 14 May 1870. Nelson Rugby Football Club trounced the lily-livered players from Nelson College 2-0.

Activities

Nelson offers boundless opportunities to embrace the great outdoors.

Walking & Cycling

There's plenty of walking and cycling to be enjoyed in and around the town, for which the i-SITE has maps. The classic walk from town is to the top of the Botanical Reserve, while the new **Dun Mountain Trail** network ranging over the hills to the south of the city centre has lots of interesting options and supberb riding for fit, keen mountain bikers.

Central Nelson

Top Sights
Suter ... D2

Sights
1 Christ Church Cathedral ... B4
2 Fibre Spectrum ... B3
3 Flamedaisy Glass Design ... B3
4 Jens Hansen ... B3
5 Nelson Provincial Museum ... B3
6 South Street Gallery ... A4

Activities, Courses & Tours
7 Stewarts Avanti Plus Nelson ... A3
8 UBike ... C1

Sleeping
9 Accents on the Park ... B3
10 Almond House ... D1
11 Lynton Lodge ... A4
12 Nelson YHA ... A2
13 Palazzo Motor Lodge ... A4
14 South Street Cottages ... A4
15 Trampers Rest ... D4

Eating
16 DeVille ... B2
17 Falafel Gourmet ... B3
18 Ford's ... B3
19 Hopgood's ... B3
20 Indian Café ... C2
21 Organic Greengrocer ... D1
22 Penguino Ice Cream Café ... B2
Stefano's ... (see 27)
23 Swedish Bakery & Café ... B2

Drinking
24 Free House ... C2
25 Sprig & Fern ... C3
26 Vic ... B3

Entertainment
27 State Cinema 6 ... B2
28 Theatre Royal ... A2

Shopping
29 Nelson Farmers' Market ... C3
30 Nelson Market ... A2

UBike CYCLING
(0800 282 453; www.ubike.co.nz; Collingwood St Bridge; half-/full day from $40/60) A short walk from the i-SITE, UBike hires city and mountain bikes from its caravan. Trail maps and tips, plus espresso to get you going.

Biking Nelson MOUNTAIN BIKING
(0800 224 532, 021 861 725; www.bikingnelson.co.nz; 3hr guided ride $115, bike hire half-/full day $45/65) Hit the hillside mountain-bike trails with Dave and company, who run guided rides (all gear provided) and offer freedom rental and advice.

Paragliding, Hang Gliding & Kiteboarding

Nelson is a great place to get airborne. Most operators are some way out of town, but will pick-up or drop-off in Nelson.

Tandem paragliding costs around $180, while introductory courses are around $250. Tandem hang gliding is around $185, and introductory kiteboarding starts at $150.

Nelson Paragliding PARAGLIDING
(03-544 1182, 0508 359 669; www.nelsonparagliding.co.nz)

Adventure Paragliding & Kiteboarding PARAGLIDING, KITEBOARDING
(03-540 2183, 0800 212 359; www.skyout.co.nz)

Cumulus Paragliding PARAGLIDING
(03-929 5515; www.tandem-paragliding.co.nz)

Kitescool KITEBOARDING
(021 354 837; www.kitescool.co.nz)

Kite Surf Nelson KITEBOARDING
(0800 548 363; www.kitesurfnelson.co.nz)

Nelson Hang Gliding Adventures HANG GLIDING
(03-548 9151; www.flynelson.co.nz)

Hang Gliding New Zealand HANG GLIDING
(03-540 2183, 0800 212 359; www.hanggliding.co.nz; flight $180)

Other Activities

TOP CHOICE **Nelson Bonecarving** CARVING
(03-546 4275; www.carvingbone.co.nz; 87 Green St, Tahunanui; full-day course $79) Admirers of Maori design will love Stephan's acclaimed bonecarving course. He'll supply all materials, tools, instruction, encouragement and cups of tea (plus free pick-up/drop-off in town if needed); you supply inspiration and talent and you'll emerge with your very own bone carving.

Happy Valley Adventures ADVENTURE SPORTS
(03-545 0304, 0800 157 300; www.happyvalleyadventures.co.nz; 194 Cable Bay Rd; Skywire adult/

child $85/55, quad bike tours from $80, horse trek $95) Dangle 150m above the forest in the 'Skywire' (a chairlift/flying-fox hybrid), then soar through the air for its 1.65km length. If that ain't enough, take a quad-bike tour, or if it's too much, try a 2½-hour horse trek. Or just have coffee and cake in the cafe – a 15-minute drive northeast of Nelson along SH6.

Cable Bay Kayaks KAYAKING
(☎0508 222 532, 03-545 0332; www.cablebaykayaks.co.nz; Cable Bay Rd; half-/full day guided trip $85/145) Fifteen minutes' drive from Nelson city, Nick and Jenny offer guided sea-kayaking trips exploring the local coastline where you'll likely meet local marine life (snorkelling gear on board) and may even enter a cave.

Tours

Bay Tours GUIDED TOUR
(☎0800 229 868, 03-548 6486; www.baytoursnelson.co.nz; half-/full-day tours from $89/144) Nelson city, region, wine, beer, food and art tours. The full-day scenic tour includes a visit to Kaiteriteri and a cruise in Abel Tasman National Park.

JJ's Quality Tours GUIDED TOUR
(☎0800 229 868, 03-548 6486; www.jjstours.co.nz; tours from $89) Scenic, wine-focused and craft tours, plus a half-day brewery trail.

Wine, Art & Wilderness GUIDED TOUR
(☎03-539 4477, 0800 326 868; www.wineartandwildernesstours.co.nz; tours from $214) Upmarket wine, scenic and nature tours around Nelson, Marlborough, Golden Bay and the West Coast.

Simply Wild GUIDED TOUR
(☎03-548 8500; www.simplywild.co.nz) A swathe of half- to five-day active wilderness adventures: walking, mountain biking, sailing, caving, rafting and canoeing around Nelson's national parks. Prices on application.

Festivals & Events

For current info on Nelson's active events program, visit www.itson.co.nz.

Nelson Jazz & Blues Festival MUSIC
(www.nelsonjazzfest.co.nz) More than 50 scoobedoobop events over a week in January. Local and international acts in halls and on street corners, regionwide.

Nelson Arts Festival
(www.nelsonfestivals.co.nz) Over two weeks in October; events include a street carnival, exhibitions, cabaret, writers, theatre and music.

Sleeping

Accents on the Park HOSTEL $
(☎03-548 4335, 0800 888 335; www.accentsonthepark.com; 335 Trafalgar Sq; sites $30, dm $20-28, d with/without bathroom from $92/60; @) This perfectly positioned hostel has a hotel feel with its professional staff, balconies, groovy cafe-bar (meals around $15), movie nights with free popcorn, free daily bread and wi-fi, soundproofed rooms, quality linen, fresh bathrooms and bikes for hire. Bravo! (Book early.)

Bug Backpackers HOSTEL $
(☎03-539 4227; www.thebug.co.nz; 226 Vanguard St; dm $25-28, d $66-80; @) A fresh, excellent hostel about 15 minutes' walk from town, occupying a converted villa and a modern building next door. The Bug emits joie de vivre, with an unashamedly bold colour scheme and a swarm of cutesy VW Beetle paraphernalia. Quality beds, nice kitchens, girls' dorm and a homely backyard. Free bikes and pick-up/drop-offs.

Tasman Bay Backpackers HOSTEL $
(☎03-548 7950, 0800 222 572; www.tasmanbaybackpackers.co.nz; 10 Weka St; sites from $18, dm $25-27, d $66-85; @) Typical of Nelson's breed of quality backpackers, this well-designed hostel has airy communal spaces, hyper-coloured rooms, a sunny outdoor deck and a well-used hammock. Good freebies: bikes, breakfast during winter, and chocolate pudding and ice cream year-round.

Trampers Rest HOSTEL $
(☎03-545 7477; 31 Alton St; dm/s/d $29/46/66; @) With just a few beds (no bunks), the tiny but much-loved Trampers is hard to beat for a homely environment. The enthusiastic owner is a keen tramper and cyclist, and provides comprehensive local information and free bikes. It has a small kitchen, a book exchange, and a piano for evening singalongs.

Almond House HOSTEL $
(☎03-545 6455; www.almondbackpackers.co.nz; 63 Grove St; dm/s/d $29/46/68; @) Stylish and homely addition to Nelson's collection of quality backpackers. Four-bed dorms and

THE WONDROUS WORLD OF WEARABLE ART

Nelson exudes creativity, so it's hardly surprising that NZ's most inspiring fashion show was born here. It began humbly in 1987 when creator Suzie Moncrieff held a local off-beat fashion show. The concept was to create a piece of art that could be worn and modelled. The idea caught on, and the World of WearableArt Awards Show became an annual event. Wood, papier mâché, paua shell, earplugs, soft-drink cans, ping-pong balls and more have been used to create garments; 'Bizarre Bra' entries are showstoppers.

The awards show has been transplanted to Wellington, but you can ogle entries at Nelson's **World of WearableArt & Classic Cars Museum** (WOW; ☎03-547 4573; www.wowcars.co.nz; 1 Cadillac Way; adult/child $22/8; ⊙10am-5pm). High-tech galleries include a carousel mimicking a catwalk, and a glow-in-the-dark room.

More car than bra? Under the same roof are 50 mint-condition classic cars and motorbikes. Exhibits change, but may include a 1959 pink Cadillac, a yellow 1950 Bullet Nose Studebaker convertible and a BMW bubble car. You can view another 70 vehicles in *The Classic Collection* next door ($8 extra). Cafe and art gallery on-site.

double rooms are decked out with colourful local art and quality linen, while the friendly vibe makes you feel like part of the family. Free internet and bikes.

Shortbread Cottage HOSTEL $
(☎03-546 6681; www.shortbreadcottage.co.nz; 33 Trafalgar St; dm/s/d $26/60/60; @📶) This renovated 100-year-old villa has room for only a dozen or so beds but it's packed with charm and hospitality. It offers free internet, fresh-baked bread, and shortbread on arrival. It's also only a stone's throw from the town centre.

Nelson YHA HOSTEL $
(☎03-545 9988; www.yha.co.nz; 59 Rutherford St; dm/s/d from $28/60/86, d with bathroom $100; @📶) A tidy, purpose-built, central hostel with high-quality facilities including a soundproof TV room (free DVDs), two well-organised kitchens and a sunny outdoor terrace. Solid service on tour and activity bookings.

Paradiso Backpackers HOSTEL $
(☎0800 269 667, 03-546 6703; www.backpackernelson.co.nz; 42 Weka St; sites from $18, dm $25-29, d $66; @📶🏊) Club Med for the impoverished, Paradiso is a sprawling place that lures a backpacker-body-beautiful crowd to its poolside terrace. There are two kitchens, hammocks, volleyball court, spa and sauna. Bikes for hire ($15 per day).

Tahuna Beach Accommodation Park HOLIDAY PARK $
(☎03-548 5159, 0800 500 501; www.tahunabeach.co.nz; 70 Beach Rd; sites/cabins/units from $17/50/110; @📶) A few minutes' walk from the beach, 5km from the city, this huge park is home to thousands in high summer, which you'll find hellish or bloody brilliant, depending on your mood. During the shoulder season, you'll have the minigolf mostly to yourself.

Palazzo Motor Lodge MOTELS $$
(☎03-545 8171, 0800 472 5293; www.palazzomotorlodge.co.nz; 159 Rutherford St; studios $130-225, apt $225-390; @📶) Hosts with the most offer a cheerful welcome at this popular, modern, Italian-tinged motor lodge. The stylish studios and one- and two-room apartments feature enviable kitchens with decent cooking equipment, classy wineglasses and a dishwasher. The odd bit of dubious art is easily forgiven, particularly as Doris' sausage is available for breakfast.

Te Maunga House B&B $$
(☎03-548 8605; www.nelsoncityaccommodation.co.nz; 15 Dorothy Annie Way; s $90, d $100-135; @📶) Aptly named ('the mountain'), this is a grand old family home on a knoll with exceptional views. Two doubles and a single, with their own bathrooms, are filled with characterful furniture and made up with good linens. Your hearty breakfast can be walked off up and down *that* hill. It's only a 10-minute climb (15 minutes in all, from town), but only the leggy ones will revel in it. Closed from May to September.

Nelson City Holiday Park HOLIDAY PARK $
(☎03-548 1445, 0800 778 898; www.nelsonholidaypark.co.nz; 230 Vanguard St; sites $40, cabins & units $60-120; @📶) The closest option to town: convenient, well-maintained, clean, but cramped

(although the motel units are pretty good). Limited campsites by the creek out back.

Lynton Lodge LODGE $$
(☎03-548 7112; www.lyntonlodge.co.nz; 25 Examiner St; apt $95-130;) On the hill near the cathedral and with city views, unashamedly dated Lynton Lodge offers self-contained apartments and a guesthouse vibe – try for one of the balcony units. Affable hosts, grassy garden and super-close to town.

South Street Cottages RENTAL HOUSE $$$
(☎03-540 2769; www.cottageaccommodation.co.nz; South St; d from $225) Stay on NZ's oldest preserved street in one of several endearing, two-bedroom self-contained cottages built in the 1860s. Each has all the comforts of home, including kitchen, laundry and courtyard garden; breakfast provisions supplied. There is a two-night minimum stay.

Eating

Nelson has a lively cafe scene as well as a varied array of restaurants. Self-caterers should steer resolutely towards the fruitful Nelson Market (p423) on Saturday and the **Farmers Market** (Fashion Island, cnr Morrison & Hardy Sts ; 12pm–4.30pm Wed) on Wednesday.

DeVille CAFE $$
(22 New St; meals $13-20; 9am-4pm Mon-Sat;) Most of DeVille's tables lie in its sweet walled courtyard, a hidden boho oasis in the inner city and the perfect place for a meal or morning tea. The food's good – from fresh baked goods to the eggy brunch, caesar salad and sticky pork sandwich. Open late for live music Friday and Saturday in summer.

Stefano's PIZZERIA $
(☎03-546 7530; 91 Trafalgar St; pizzas $6-29; lunch & dinner;) Located upstairs in the State Cinema complex, this Italian-run joint turns out some of NZ's best pizza. Thin, crispy and delicious, and some variations really very cheap. Wash it down with a beer or wine in the ambience-free interior or out on the tiny balcony.

Swedish Bakery & Café BAKERY $
(54 Bridge St; snacks $2-7; 8.30am-3.30pm Mon-Fri, 9am-1.30pm Sat) Delicious breads, pastries, cakes and small chocolate treats from the resident Scandinavian baker. Lovely fresh filled rolls such as meatball and beetroot salad. Take your goodies away or eat in the bijou cafe.

Indian Café INDIAN $$
(94 Collingwood St; mains $16-21; lunch Mon-Fri, dinner daily;) This saffron-coloured Edwardian villa houses an Indian restaurant that keeps the *bhaji* raised with impressive interpretations of Anglo-Indian standards, such as chicken tandoori, rogan josh and beef madras. Share the mixed platter to start, then mop up your mains with one of 10 different breads.

Hopgood's MODERN NZ $$$
(☎03-545 7191; 284 Trafalgar St; mains $34-37; 5.30pm-late Mon-Sat) Tongue-and-groove-lined Hopgood's is perfect for a romantic dinner or holiday treat. The food is decadent and skilfully prepared but unfussy, allowing quality local ingredients to shine. The Asian crispy duck followed by twice-cooked pork belly with butter beans, spinach and bacon are knockouts. Desirable, predominantly Kiwi wine list. Bookings advisable.

Penguino Ice Cream Café ICE CREAM $
(Montgomery Sq; ice creams $4-7; noon-5pm) Indulge yourself with superb gelato and sorbet, from traditional vanilla and boysenberry to apple pie and beyond. Next day, visit for a shake, fruit smoothie, sundae, mango lassi...

Ford's MODERN NZ $$
(www.fordsnelson.co.nz; 276 Trafalgar St; lunch $16-22; from 8am) Sunny pavement tables at the top of Trafalgar Street make this a popular lunchtime spot, as does the chef-owner's menu of modern classics such as the excellent seafood chowder, steak sandwich on sourdough, and tuna niçoise. Make a short stop for coffee and a scone, or linger over dinner which leaps up a tenner.

Falafel Gourmet MIDDLE EASTERN $
(195 Hardy St; meals $9-23;) A cranking joint dishing out the best kebabs in town, full of salad.

Haven Fish & Chips FISH & CHIPS $
(268 Wakefield Quay; fish & chips $8-10; 11.30am-1.30pm & 4.30-8pm) Pick your own fillet, then eat your meal by the waterfront. What could be better?

Organic Greengrocer FOOD, DRINK $
(cnr Tasman & Grove Sts; 9am-6pm Mon-Fri, to 3pm Sat;) Stocks foods for the sensitive, plus produce, organic tipples and natural bodycare. Food to go and coffee also on offer.

IN PURSUIT OF HOPPINESS

The Nelson region lays claim to the title of craft-brewing capital of New Zealand. With world-class hops grown here since the 1840s, and a dozen breweries spread between Nelson and Golden Bay, it's got a pretty good case.

Pick up a copy of the *Nelson Craft Beer Trail* map (available from the i-SITE and other outlets, and online at www.craftbrewingcapital.co.nz) and wind your way between brewers and pubs. Top picks for a tipple include the Free House (p429), the Moutere Inn (p432), Golden Bear (p432), and the Mussel Inn (p444).

Drinking

Nelson's got a bad (read: good) case of craft-beer fever, so if your budget allows it, hoppiness awaits. Cheaper thrills can be found at numerous establishments clustered on Bridge St towards the intersection with Collingwood. If you're out late, walk home with a friend.

Free House CRAFT BEER
(www.freehouse.co.nz; 95 Collingwood St) Come rejoice at this church of ales. Tastefully converted from its original, more reverent purpose, it's now home to an excellent, oft-changing selection of NZ craft beers. You can imbibe inside or out. Hallelujah.

Sprig & Fern CRAFT BEER
(www.sprigandfern.co.nz; 280 Hardy St) The Sprig & Fern brewery in Richmond supplies an extensive range of beers to S&F pubs springing up around the region. Around 20 brews on tap, from lager through to doppelbock and berry cider. No pokies, no TV, just decent beer, occasional live music and a pleasant outdoor area. Pizzas can be ordered in.

Vic PUB
(www.vicbrewbar.co.nz; 281 Trafalgar St) A commendable example of a Mac's Brewbar, with trademark, quirky Kiwiana fit-out, including a striped, knitted stag's head. Quaff a few handles of ale, maybe grab a bite to eat (mains $10 to $30) and tap a toe to regular live music, including Tuesday night jazz. Good afternoon sun and people-watching from streetside seating.

Entertainment

Theatre Royal THEATRE
(☎03-548 3840; www.theatreroyalnelson.co.nz; 78 Rutherford St) Joan Rivers, eat your heart out, because the 'grand old lady of Nelson' (aged 134) has just had the face lift to end all face lifts. If you love heritage buildings and the performing arts, visit **Everyman Records** (249 Hardy St), find out what she's showing and book a ticket.

State Cinema 6 CINEMA
(☎03-548 3885; www.statecinema6.co.nz; 91 Trafalgar St) This is the place to see mainstream, new-release flicks.

Information

Banks and ATMs pepper Trafalgar St.

After Hours & Duty Doctors (☎03-546 8881; 96 Waimea Rd; ⏲8am-10pm)

Nelson i-SITE (☎03-548 2304; www.nelsonnz.com; cnr Trafalgar & Halifax Sts; ⏲8.30am-5pm Mon-Fri, 9am-5pm Sat & Sun; @) A slick centre complete with DOC information desk for the low-down on national parks and walks (including Abel Tasman and Heaphy tracks). Pick up a copy of the *Nelson Tasman Visitor Guide*.

Police Station (☎03-546 3840; cnr St John & Harley Sts)

Post Office (www.nzpost.co.nz; 209 Hardy St)

Nelson Hospital (☎03-546 1800; www.nmdhb.govt.nz; Waimea Rd)

Getting There & Away

Air

Air New Zealand (☎03-546 3100, 0800 737 000; www.airnewzealand.co.nz; cnr Trafalgar & Bridge Sts; ⏲9am-5pm Mon-Fri) has direct flights to/from Wellington (from $79), Auckland (from $99) and Christchurch (from $79).

Soundsair (☎03-520 3080, 0800 505 005; www.soundsair.com) flies daily between Nelson and Wellington (from $107).

Air2there (p416) flies between Nelson and Paraparaumu on the Kapiti Coast ($135).

Bus

Book Abel Tasman Coachlines, InterCity, Tranz Scenic and Interisland ferries at the **Nelson SBL Travel Centre** (☎03-548 1539; www.nelsoncoaches.co.nz; 27 Bridge St).

Also based here are **Abel Tasman Coachlines** (☎03-548 0285; www.abeltasmantravel.co.nz; 27

Bridge St, departs SLB Travel Centre), operating services to Motueka ($12, one hour), Takaka ($35, two hours), Kaiteriteri and Marahau (both $20, two hours). These services also connect with Golden Bay Coachlines (p442) services for Takaka and around. Transport to/from the three national parks is provided by **Trek Express** (☎0800 128 735; www.trekexpress.co.nz).

Atomic Shuttles (☎03-349 0697; www.atomictravel.co.nz) runs from Nelson to Picton ($25, 2¼ hours), and daily to West Coast centres like Greymouth ($54, 5¾ hours) and Fox Glacier ($78, 9½ hours). Services can be booked at (and depart from) Nelson i-SITE.

InterCity (☎03-548 1538; www.intercity.co.nz; Bridge St, departs SLB Travel Centre) runs from Nelson to most key South Island destinations including Picton (from $18, two hours), Kaikoura (from $49, 3½ hours), Christchurch (from $54, seven hours) and Greymouth (from $40, six hours).

Getting Around

To/From the Airport

Nelson Airport is 6km southwest of town, near Tahunanui Beach. A taxi from there to town will cost around about $25, or **Super Shuttle** (☎03-522 5100, 0800 748 885; www.supershuttle.co.nz) offers door-to-door service for $21 (additional passengers $17).

Bicycle

Hire a bike from **Stewarts Avanti Plus Nelson** (☎03-548 1666; www.avantiplusnelson.co.nz; 114 Hardy St; hire per day $30-95, per week from $140) or UBike (p425).

Bus

Nelson Suburban Bus Lines (SBL; ☎03-548 3290; www.nelsoncoaches.co.nz; 27 Bridge St, departs SLB Travel Centre, Bridge St) operates NBUS, the local service between Nelson, Richmond via Tahunanui and Stoke until about 7pm weekdays, 4.30pm on weekends. It also runs the **Late Late Bus** (hourly 10pm-3am Fri & Sat) from Nelson to Richmond via Tahunanui, departing from the Westpac Bank on Trafalgar St. Maximum fare for these services is $4.

Taxi

Nelson City Taxis (☎03-548 8225, 0800 108 855)

Sun City Taxis (☎03-548 2666, 0800 422 666)

Nelson Lakes National Park

Pristine Nelson Lakes National Park surrounds two lakes – Rotoiti and Rotoroa – fringed by sweet-smelling beech forest with a backdrop of greywacke mountains. Located at the northern end of the Southern Alps, and with a dramatic glacier-carved landscape, it's an awe-inspiring place to get up on high.

Part of the park, east of Lake Rotoiti, is classed as a 'mainland island' where a conservation scheme aims to eradicate introduced pests (possums, stoats), and regenerate native flora and fauna. It offers excellent tramping, including short walks, lake scenery and one or two sandflies... The park is flush with bird life, and is famous for brown-trout fishing.

Activities

Many spectacular walks allow you to appreciate this rugged landscape, but before you tackle them, stop by the DOC Visitor Centre for maps and track/weather updates, to leave intentions and to pay your hut or camping fees.

The five-hour **Mt Robert Circuit Track** starts south of St Arnaud and circumnavigates the mountain, with options for a side trip along Robert Ridge. Alternatively, the **St Arnaud Range Track** (five hours return), on the east side of the lake, climbs steadily to the ridgeline via Parachute Rocks. Both tracks are strenuous, but reward with jaw-dropping views of glaciated valleys, arête peaks and Lake Rotoiti. Only attempt these walks in fine weather. At other times they are both pointless (no views) and dangerous.

There are also plenty of shorter (and flatter) walks starting from Lake Rotoiti's Kerr Bay and the road end at Lake Rotoroa. These and the longer day tramps in the park are described in DOC's *Walks in Nelson Lakes National Park* pamphlet ($2).

The fit and well-equipped can enjoy the **Lake Angelus Routes**, including a magnificent overnight (or three-day) tramp along Robert Ridge to Lake Angelus. Stay at the fine Angelus Hut (adult/child $20/10) before returning to St Arnaud via one of three routes. Pick up or download DOC's *Angelus Hut Tracks & Routes* pamphlet ($2) for more details.

Sleeping & Eating

DOC Campsites CAMPSITE $

(☎03-521 1806; www.doc.govt.nz; Kerr Bay sites from $10, West Bay $6) Located on the shores of Lake Rotoiti at Kerr Bay, this inviting and hugely popular site has toilets, hot showers, a laundry and a kitchen. Three kilometres from St Arnaud, West Bay campsite has the bare necessities and is open in summer only.

Bookings are essential over the Christmas and Easter holidays.

Travers-Sabine Lodge LODGE $
(☎03-521 1887; www.nelsonlakes.co.nz; Main Rd; dm/d $26/62; @📶) This modern lodge is a great base for outdoor adventure, being a short walk to Lake Rotoiti, inexpensive, clean and comfortable. It also has particularly cheerful technicolour linen in the dorms, doubles and a family room. The owners are experienced adventurers themselves, so tips come as standard; tramping equipment and snowshoes available for hire.

Nelson Lakes Motels MOTEL $$
(☎03-521 1887; www.nelsonlakes.co.nz; Main Rd; d $115-135; @📶) These log cabins and newer board-and-batten units offer all the creature comforts, including kitchenettes and Sky TV. Bigger units sleep up to six.

Alpine Lodge LODGE $$
(☎03-521 1869; www.alpinelodge.co.nz; Main Rd; d $150-205; @📶) Trying its darnedest to create an alpine mood, this lodge has a a range of accommodation, the pick of which are the split-level doubles with mezzanine bedroom, spa and pine timberwork aplenty. The adjacent backpacker lodge (dorm/double $27/69) is spartan but clean and warm. The in-house restaurant is snug, with mountain views, and serves very good food (meals $10 to $29). Long may the Sunday night barbecue continue.

Tophouse Historic Hotel HISTORIC HOTEL $$
(☎0800 544 545, 03-521 1848; www.tophouse.co.nz; Tophouse Rd; s/d $110/135, lunch $10-18) Nine kilometres from St Arnaud, this 1887 hotel retells fireside tales, tall and true. A good stop for refreshments (cake and coffee, wild game pies, and a $49 four-course dinner, for which bookings are essential), Tophouse also boasts New Zealand's smallest bar and a garden with mountain views. There are old-fashioned rooms within the hotel, and four chalets sleeping up to five.

St Arnaud Alpine Village Store SUPERMARKET $
(Main Rd; ⏲8am-6pm, takeaways 4.30-8pm Fri & Sat, daily Dec-Feb) The settlement's only general store sells groceries, petrol, beer and possum-wool socks. Mountain-bike hire per half-/full day is $20/40. It has tramping food, sandwiches, pies and milkshakes, with the fish and chips cranking up on weekends and daily in peak season ($6 to $10).

ℹ Information

The **DOC Visitor Centre** (☎03-521 1806; www.doc.govt.nz; View Rd; ⏲8am-4.30pm) proffers park information (weather, activities), hut passes, plus displays on park ecology and history. See also www.starnaud.co.nz.

ℹ Getting There & Around

Nelson Lakes Shuttles (☎021 490 095, 03-521 1900; www.nelsonlakesshuttles.co.nz) provides on-demand transport from St Arnaud to (all prices per person) Mt Robert car park ($15), Lake Rotoroa ($30), Nelson ($35), Picton ($45) and tramping trailheads as far away as Canterbury. Minimum numbers apply; check the website for budget fares and up-to-the-minute movements.

Rotoiti Water Taxis (☎021 702 278; www.rotoitiwatertaxis.co.nz) runs to/from Kerr Bay and West Bay to Lakehead Jetty ($90, up to four people) and Coldwater Jetty ($105, up to four people). Kayaks, canoes and rowboats can also be hired from $40 per half-day; fishing trips and scenic lake cruises by arrangement.

Nelson to Motueka

From Richmond, south of Nelson, there are two routes to Motueka: the busier, more populated coastal highway (SH60) and the inland Moutere Hwy, a pleasant alternative, particularly if you want to make a loop. Either way, this area is densely packed with attractions, so you should allow enough time to pull off the road.

There are numerous wineries in this area; the *Nelson Wine Guide* pamphlet (www.wineart.co.nz) will help you find them.

Art and craft galleries are also in the vicinity. Find these in the *Nelson Art Guide* or *Nelson's Creative Pathways* pamphlets, both available from local i-SITEs, where you can also get information on accommodation around these parts.

SH60 via Mapua

Skirting around Waimea Inlet and along the Ruby Coast, this is the quickest route from Nelson to Motueka (around 45 minutes), although there are various distractions to slow you down. Here are just a few highlights.

Just 10 from Richmond you'll hit **Waimea** (www.waimeaestates.co.nz; SH60; ⏲11am-5pm) winery with its jazzy cafe and tables by the vines. Located a little further away, masterpiece glass is blown at **Höglund Glass Art** (www.hoglundartglass.com; 52 Lansdowne Rd, Appleby; ⏲10am-5pm), where you can watch Ola and his trainees working the furnace.

Just up the road is the turn-off to **Rabbit Island**, a recreation reserve offering estuary views from many angles, sandy beaches and plenty of quiet pine forest. The bridge to the island closes at sunset; overnight stays are not allowed.

Seifried (www.seifried.co.nz; cnr SH60 & Redwood Rd; ⏲10am-5pm) winery sits at the Rabbit Island turn off. It's one of the region's biggest, and is home to a pleasant garden restaurant and the delicious Sweet Agnes riesling.

As you reach the end of the inlet, you can either continue along SH60, or detour along the original coast road, now named the Ruby Bay Scenic Route. Along it lies the settlement of Mapua at the mouth of the Waimea River. It features numerous pleasant establishments including the **Smokehouse** (www.smokehouse.co.nz; Mapua Wharf; fish & chips $7-12; ⏲11am-8pm). Order up fish and chips, and eat them on the wharf while the gulls eye up your crispy bits. Delicious wood-smoked fish and pâté to go.

In the same wharfside cluster you will undoubtedly sniff out the **Golden Bear Brewing Company** (www.goldenbearbrewing.com; Mapua Wharf; meals $8-19), a micro-brewery with tons of stainless steel out back and a dozen or so brews out front. Authentic Mexican food (burritos, quesadillas and *huevos rancheros*) will stop you from getting a sore head. Occasional live music, takeaway beers and tours.

Art browers will enjoy Mapua's **Cool Store Gallery** (www.coolstoregallery.co.nz; 7 Aranui Rd; ⏲11am-4.30pm), packed with high-quality work.

A few kilometres before the scenic route rejoins SH60 is **Jester House** (320 Aporo Rd, Tasman; meals $13-23; ⏲9am-5pm). It alone is a good reason to take this detour, as much for its tame eels as for the peaceful sculpture gardens that encourage you to linger over lunch. A short, simple menu puts a few twists into the staples (wild pork burger, lavender shortbread), and there are local beer and wines. It's 8km to Mapua or Motueka.

Moutere Hwy

This drive traverses gently rolling countryside, dotted with farms, orchards and lifestyle blocks. Visitor attractions are fewer and farther between along here, but it's a nice drive nonetheless, and will prove particularly fruitful in high summer when the berry farms are on song.

The turn-off to the Moutere is sign-posted at Appleby on SH60. Not far along is the turn off to Old Coach Rd, from where you can follow the signposts to **Woollaston** (www.woollaston.co.nz; School Rd; ⏲11am-5pm), a flash hilltop winery complete with tasting room and contemporary art gallery. The patio is a spectacular place to enjoy a platter for lunch.

Upper Moutere is the main settlement along this route. First settled by German immigrants and originally named Sarau, today it's a sleepy hamlet with a shop, a cafe and allegedly New Zealand's oldest pub, the **Moutere Inn** (www.moutereinn.co.nz; 1046 Moutere Hwy; meals $5-27). This welcoming establishment serves honest meals (toasties, pizza, mussels and hot-pot) and very good beer, including its own house brews. Pull up a pew with a beer-tasting platter, play pool, sit outside on the sunny patio, or come along at night to hear regular live music.

Continuing along the Moutere Highway, Neudorf Rd is well signposted, leading as it does to berries and other delectables. Call into **Neudorf Dairy** (www.neudorfdairy.co.nz; 226 Neudorf Rd) for award-winning hand-crafted sheeps'-milk cheeses, or **Neudorf** (www.neudorf.co.nz; 138 Neudorf Rd) winery for gorgeous pinot noir and some of the country's finest chardonnay.

Motueka

POP 6900

Motueka (pronounced Mott-oo-ecka, meaning 'Island of Wekas') is a bustling town, one which visitors will find handy for stocking up en route to Golden Bay and the Abel Tasman and Kahurangi National Parks. It has all the vital amenities, ample accommodation, cafes, roadside fruit stalls, and a clean and beautiful river offering swimming and fishing.

Sights & Activities

While most of Mot's drawcards are out of town, there are a few attractions worth checking out, the best of which is the active aerodrome, home to several air-raising activities. With a coffee cart on site, it's a good place to soak up some sun and views, and watch a few folks drop in.

To get a handle on the town, visit the i-SITE and collect the *Motueka Art Walk* pamphlet, detailing sculpture, murals and occasional peculiarities around town.

Motueka District Museum MUSEUM
(140 High St; admission by donation; ⊙10am-4pm Mon-Fri Dec-Mar, 10am-3pm Tue-Fri Apr-Nov) An interesting collection of regional artefacts, housed in a dear old school building; cafe on site.

Skydive Abel Tasman EXTREME SPORTS
(☎0800 422 899, 03-528 4091; www.skydive.co.nz; Motueka Aerodrome, College St; jumps 13,000ft/16,500ft $299/399) Move over Taupo tandems: we've jumped both and think Mot takes the cake (presumably so do the many sports jumpers who favour this drop zone, some of whom you may see rocketing in). DVDs and photos cost extra, but pick-up/drop-off from Motueka and Nelson are free.

Tasman Sky Adventures SCENIC FLIGHTS
(☎027 229 9693, 0800 114 386; www.skyadventures.co.nz; Motueka Aerodrome, College St; 30min flight $185) A rare opportunity to fly in a microlight. Keep your eyes open and blow your mind on a scenic flight above Abel Tasman National Park. Wow. And there's tandem hang gliding for the eager (15/30 minutes, 2500ft/5280ft $185/275).

U-fly Extreme SCENIC FLIGHTS
(☎0800 360 180, 03-528 8290; www.uflyextreme.co.nz; Motueka Aerodrome, College St; 15min $299) Here's one for the courageous: you handle the controls doing aerobatics in an open cockpit Pitts Special plane. No experience necessary, just a stomach for stunts.

Sleeping

Numerous midrange B&Bs and holiday homes are secreted in the surrounds – ask the i-SITE for suggestions.

TOP CHOICE **Motueka TOP 10 Holiday Park** HOLIDAY PARK $
(☎03-528 7189, 0800 668 835; www.motuekatop10.co.nz; 10 Fearon St; sites from $40, cabins $50-125, units/motels $95-140; @☎☒) Busy it may

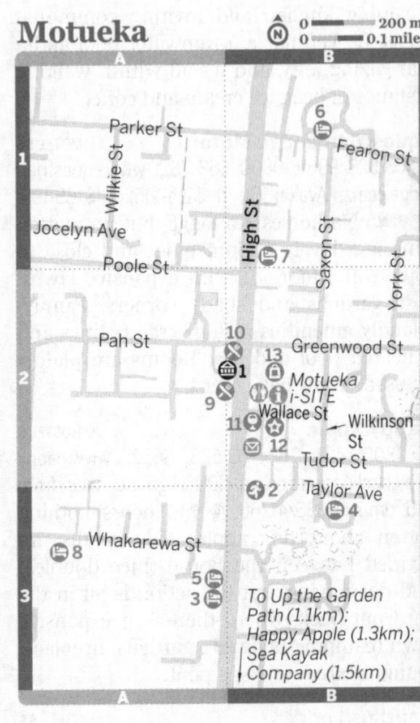

Motueka

Sights
1 Motueka District Museum B2

Activities, Courses & Tours
2 Wilsons Abel Tasman B3

Sleeping
3 Avalon Manor Motel A3
4 Equestrian Lodge Motel B3
5 Laughing Kiwi A3
6 Motueka TOP 10 Holiday Park B1
7 Nautilus Lodge B1
8 White Elephant A3

Eating
9 Patisserie Royale A2
10 Simply Indian B2

Drinking
11 Sprig and Fern B2

Entertainment
12 Gecko Theatre B2

Shopping
13 Motueka Sunday Market B2

be, but this park retains plenty of grassy, green charm. Love those lofty kahikatea trees! All the bells and whistles are in evidence, including several amenities blocks and family-friendly facilities such as swimming pool and jumping pillow. Local wine tours by arrangement.

Eden's Edge Backpacker Lodge HOSTEL $
(☎03-528 4242; www.edensedge.co.nz; 137 Lodder Ln, Riwaka; sites from $17, dm $28, d with/without bathroom $80/70; @🛜🏊) Surrounded by orchards, 4km from Motueka, this purpose-built lodge comes pretty close to backpacker heaven. Well-designed facilities include a gleaming kitchen and inviting communal areas. It even has a a rainwater pool and a star-gazing jetty, and it's all within walking distance of beer, ice cream and coffee.

Equestrian Lodge Motel MOTEL $$
(☎03-528 9369, 0800 668 782; www.equestrianlodge.co.nz; Avalon Ct; d $115-145, q $165-195; @🛜🏊) No horses, no lodge, but no matter. This is a lovely option: quiet and close to town (off Tudor St), with expansive lawns, rose gardens and shady corners. Family-friendly amenities include trampolines and a heated pool and spa. Rooms are plainly dressed; many have ovens.

Happy Apple HOSTEL $
(☎0800 427 792, 03-528 8652; www.happyapplebackpackers.co.nz; 500 High St; sites from $15, dm/s/d $26/41/60; @🛜) There's nothing rotten about this apple. Tidy rooms are divided between the house (nice doubles) and dorm wing, but the action is all in the yard out back, where there's an expansive lawn (camping allowed), gardens, fireplace, lounging areas and spa pool.

Nautilus Lodge MOTELS $$
(☎0800 628 845, 03-528 4658; www.nautiluslodge.co.nz; 67 High St; d $160-220; @🛜) A top-notch motel complex with 12 units decorated in neutral tones with low-profile furniture including European slatted beds. There are kitchenettes in larger units, spa baths in some, full Sky TV and classy bathrooms in all, and balconies and patios collecting afternoon sun.

Avalon Manor Motel MOTEL $$
(☎0800 282 566, 03-528 8320; www.avalonmotels.co.nz; 314 High St; d $150-215; 🛜) Prominent L-shaped motel five minutes' walk from the centre of town. Spacious four-star rooms have a contemporary vibe, with cooking facilities, Sky TV and free DVDs. Sumptuous studios have king-size beds and large flat-screen TVs. It also has a guest barbecue, a laundry and views of Mt Arthur.

Resurgence LODGE, CHALETS $$$
(☎03-528 4664; www.resurgence.co.nz; Riwaka Valley Rd; lodge from $625, chalets from $525; @🛜🏊) Choose a luxurious en-suite lodge room or self-contained chalet at this magical 50-acre bushland retreat 15 minutes' drive north of Motueka, and half an hour's walk from the picturesque source of the Riwaka River. Lodge rates include cocktails and a four-course dinner as well as breakfast, or you can fire up the barbecue if you're staying in one of the chalets. Chalet rates are for B&B; lodge dinner extra ($90).

Laughing Kiwi HOSTEL $
(☎03-528 9229; www.laughingkiwi.co.nz; 310 High St; dm $27, d with/without bathroom $68/62; @🛜) Constant upgrades and improvements at this smart hostel keep the punters smiling. Rooms are spread between an old villa and a purpose-built backpacker lodge with an excellent kitchen/lounge, while the self-contained bach is ideal for groups (double $120).

White Elephant HOSTEL $
(☎03-528 6208; www.whiteelephant.co.nz; 55 Whakarewa St; dm $27, d with/without bathroom $76/72; @🛜) Dorms in a high-ceilinged colonial villa have a creaky charm, but your best bets are the en-suite cabins in the garden. Free wi-fi.

Eating & Drinking

TOP CHOICE **Patisserie Royale** BAKERY $
(152 High St; baked goods $2-8; ⏰6am-4pm Mon-Sat, 6am-2pm Sat & Sun) The best of several Mot bakeries and worth every delectable calorie. Lots of French fancies and a darn good pie.

Up the Garden Path CAFE $$
(473 High St; meals $15-27; ⏰9am-5pm Mon-Sun; 🌿) Perfect for lunch or a peppy coffee, this licensed cafe-gallery kicks back in an 1890s house amid idyllic gardens. Unleash the kids in the playroom and linger over your panini, cheese platter, mushroom burger, seafood chowder, pasta or lemon tart. Vegetarian, gluten- and dairy-free options, too.

Simply Indian INDIAN $$
(130 High St; mains $16-23; ⏰lunch & dinner Mon-Sat, dinner Sun; 🌿) As the name suggests:

no-nonsense curry in a no-frills setting. The food, however, is consistently good and relatively cheap. Expect the usual suspects such as tikka, tandoori, madras and vindaloo, and the ubiquitous naan prepared eight different ways. Takeaways are available.

Sprig and Fern PUB
(www.sprigandfern.co.nz; Wallace St; meals $14-19; ⏲2pm-late) Recently born of the expanding Sprig and Fern family, this branch has upped the ante among Motueka's drinking holes. Small but pleasant, with two courtyards, it offers 20 hand-pulled beers, simple food (burgers, pizza, platters) and occasional live music.

☆ Entertainment

Gecko Theatre CINEMA
(☎03-528 9996; www.geckotheatre.co.nz; 23b Wallace St; Tue & Wed $9, Thu-Sun $13; ⏲5pm-midnight) When the weather closes in, pull up an easy chair at this wee, independent theatre for interesting art-house flicks.

Shopping

Motueka Sunday Market MARKET
(Wallace St; ⏲8am-1pm) On Sunday the car park behind the i-SITE fills up with trestle tables for the Motueka Sunday Market: produce, jewellery, buskers, arts, crafts and Doris's divine bratwurst.

Information

Motueka i-SITE (☎03-528 6543; www.abeltasmanisite.co.nz; 20 Wallace St; ⏲8.30am-5pm Mon-Fri, 9am-4pm Sat & Sun) An excellent centre with helpful staff who will make bookings from Kaitaia to Bluff and provide local national-park expertise and necessaries.

Motueka Police Station (☎03-528 1220; 68 High St)

Take Note/Post Office (207 High St) Bookshop moonlighting as a post office.

Getting There & Away

All services depart from Motueka i-SITE.

Abel Tasman Coachlines (☎03-528 8850; www.abeltasmantravel.co.nz) runs two to four times daily from Motueka to Nelson ($12, one hour), Marahau ($10, 30 minutes), Kaiteriteri ($10, 25 minutes) and Takaka ($26, one hour). In summer these services connect with Golden Bay Coachline services to the Heaphy Track, Abel Tasman National Park and other Golden Bay destinations; from May to September all buses run less frequently.

Golden Bay Coachlines (☎03-525 8352; www.goldenbaycoachlines.co.nz) runs from Motueka to Takaka ($26, one hour) and Collingwood ($39, 1½ hours), as well as other Golden Bay destinations in summer, including the Heaphy Track and Totaranui.

Naked Bus (☎0900 625 33; www.nakedbus.com) runs from Motueka to Nelson ($11, one hour). Book online or at the i-SITE; cheaper fares for advance bookings.

Motueka to Abel Tasman

KAITERITERI

Known simply as 'Kaiteri', this seaside hamlet 13km from Motueka is the most popular resort town in the area. On a sunny summer's day, its gorgeous, golden, safe-swimming beach feels more like Noumea than NZ, with more towels than sand. Compounding this is the fact that it's a major gateway to Abel Tasman National Park (various trips depart Kaiteriteri beach, though Marahau is the main base). Kaiteri now also boasts an all-comers mountain-bike park; see www.kaiteriterimtbpark.org.nz for more info.

Sleeping & Eating

Kaiteri Lodge LODGE $
(☎03-527 8281; www.kaiterilodge.co.nz; Inlet Rd; dm $20-35, d $80-160; @📶) Modern, purpose-built lodge with small, simple rooms – dorms and en-suite doubles. A nautical navy-and-white colour scheme has been splashed throughout, and there are tidy communal facilities including a barbecue area, as well as bike hire. The on-site **Beached Whale** (dinner $13-28; ⏲4pm-late) bar is a sociable affair serving wood-fired pizza, burgers, fish dinners and the like. Drink and dine while the host busts out a few tunes on his guitar. The Whale will be open when the big bus pulls in.

Kaiteriteri Beach Motor Camp HOLIDAY PARK $
(☎03-527 8010; www.kaiteriteribeach.co.nz; Sandy Bay Rd; sites from $18, cabins $43-75; @📶) A gargantuan park in pole position across from the beach. It's hugely popular, so book in advance. The on-site general store is very well stocked, as is the ice-cream hatch were a queue often forms.

Bellbird Lodge B&B $$$
(☎03-527 8555; www.bellbirdlodge.co.nz; Sandy Bay Rd; d $275-325; @📶) An upmarket B&B located 1.5km up the hill from Kaiteri Beach, offering two ensuite rooms, bush and sea views, extensive gardens, spectacular breakfasts (featuring homemade muesli and fruit compote), and gracious hosts. Dinner

by arrangement in winter, when local restaurant hours are irregular.

Torlesse Coastal Motels MOTELS $$
(☎03-527 8063; www.torlessemotels.co.nz; Kotare Pl, Little Kaiteriteri Beach; d $120-170, q & f $180-280;) Just 200m from Little Kaiteriteri Beach (around the corner from the main beach) is this congregation of roomy hillside units with pitched ceilings, full kitchens and laundries. Most have water views.

Shoreline RESTAURANT $$
(cnr Inlet & Sandy Bay Rds; meals $15-28; 8am-9pm, reduced hours Apr-Nov) A modern, beige cafe-bar-restaurant right on the beach. Punters chill out on the sunny deck, lingering over sandwiches, pizzas, burgers and other predictable fare, or pop in for coffee and cake. Erratic winter hours; takeaway booth out the back.

Getting There & Away

Kaiteriteri is serviced by **Abel Tasman Coachlines** (☎03-528 8850; www.abeltasmantravel.co.nz).

MARAHAU

POP 200

Further along the coast from Kaiteriteri and 18km north of Motueka, Marahau is the main gateway to the Abel Tasman National Park. It's less of a town, more like a procession of holiday homes and tourist businesses.

If you're in an equine state of mind, **Pegasus Park** (☎0800 200 888; www.pegasuspark.co.nz) and **Marahau Horse Treks** (☎03 527-8425), both along Sandy Bay Rd, offer the chance to belt along the beach on a horse, your hair streaming out behind you (children's pony rides $35, two-hour rides $85 to $90).

Sleeping & Eating

Kanuka Ridge HOSTEL $
(☎03-527 8435; www.abeltasmanbackpackers.co.nz; Moss Rd, off Marahau-Sandy Bay Rd; dm $28, d & tw with/without bathroom $82/62) Five minutes' drive from Marahau and the start of the Abel Tasman track, this purpose-built cottage arrangement is ringed by forest, offering birdy, bushy surroundings for a bit of peace and quiet. Hosts are willing and able to hook you up to the nature buzz, with mountain bikes, activity bookings and car storage.

Ocean View Chalets CHALET $$
(☎03-527 8232; www.accommodationabeltasman.co.nz; 305 Sandy Bay-Marahau Rd; d $118-180, q $235-280;) Positioned on a leafy hillside for maximum privacy, these well-priced cypress-lined chalets are 300m from the Abel Tasman Track and have views across Tasman Bay to Fisherman Island. All are self-contained; breakfast and packed lunches available.

Barn HOSTEL $
(☎03-527 8043; www.barn.co.nz; 14 Harvey Rd; sites from $12, dm $26-30, d $64-76; @) Architecturally chaotic, this rustic place surrounded by eucalypts offers no-frills micro-cabins, and bunks and attic doubles in the main house. The centrepiece of the outfit is a deck with shade sails, bean bags and a fireplace, but there are also the necessaries, including tour bookings, secure parking and a separate kitchen for the cabins and campers.

Abel Tasman Marahau Lodge MOTELS $$
(☎03-527 8250; www.abeltasmanmarahaulodge.co.nz; Marahau Beach Rd; d $130-255; @) Enjoy halcyon days in this arc of 12 lovely studios and self-contained units with cathedral ceilings, fan, TV, phone and microwave. There's also a fully equipped communal kitchen for self-caterers, plus spa and sauna. Cuckoos, tui and bellbirds squawk and warble in the bushy surrounds.

Fat Tui BURGERS $
(Franklin St, next to Kahu Kayaks; burgers $11-14; noon-8.30pm Wed-Sun;) Everyone's heard about this bird, based in a caravan that ain't rollin' anywhere fast. Thank goodness. Superlative burgers, such as the Cowpat (beef), the Ewe Beaut (lamb) and the Sparrow's Fart breakfast burger. Fish and chips, and coffee, too.

Hooked on Marahau CAFE $$
(☎03-527 8576; Marahau-Sandy Bay Rd; lunch $10-28, dinner $26-34; 8am-late Dec-Apr, 6pm-late Oct-May) This place has the natives hooked – dinner reservations are prudent. The art-bedecked interior opens onto an outdoor terrace with distracting views. Lunch centres on sandwiches and salads, while the dinner menu boasts fresh fish of the day, green-lipped mussels and NZ lamb.

Park Café CAFE $
(Harvey Rd; lunch $7-18, dinner $15-28; 8am-late mid-Sep–May;) Sitting at the start (or the end) of the Abel Tasman Track, this breezy, licensed cafe is perfectly placed for fuelling up or restoring the waistline. High-calorie options include the big breakfast, burgers, seafood pasta and homemade cakes. Enjoy

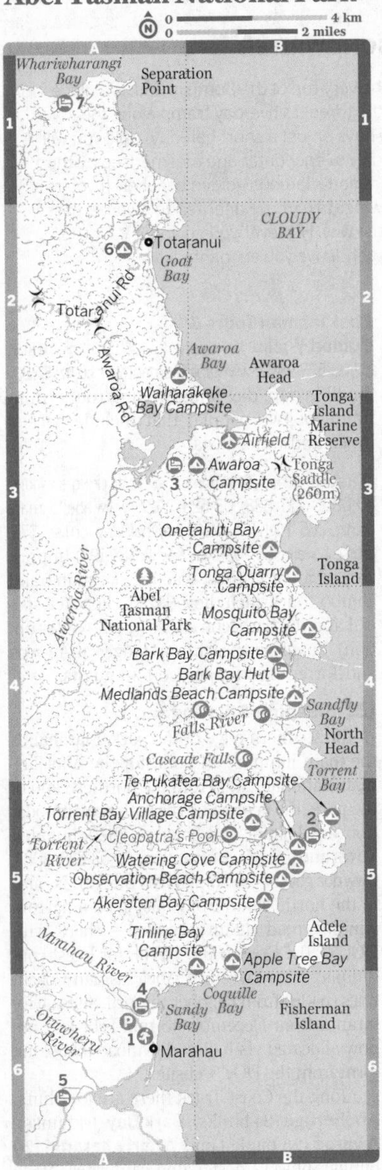

in the the room with a view or in the sunny courtyard garden.

Getting There & Away

Marahau is serviced by **Abel Tasman Coachlines** (☎03-528 8850; www.abeltasmantravel.co.nz).

Abel Tasman National Park

Activities, Courses & Tours
1 Abel Tasman Seal Swim A6

Sleeping
2 Anchorage Hut B5
Aquapackers .... (see 2)
3 Awaroa Hut A3
4 Barn A6
5 Kanuka Ridge A6
Ocean View Chalets .... (see 1)
6 Totaranui DOC Campsite A2
7 Whariwharangi Hut A1

Eating
Park Café .... (see 4)

ABEL TASMAN NATIONAL PARK

The accessible, coastal Abel Tasman National Park blankets the northern end of a range of marble and limestone hills extending from Kahurangi National Park. Various tracks in the park include an inland route, although the coast track is what everyone is here for – it sees more foot traffic than any other Great Walk in New Zealand.

ABEL TASMAN COAST TRACK

This 51km, three- to five-day track is one of the most scenic in the country, passing through native bush overlooking golden beaches lapped by gleaming azure water. Numerous bays, small and large, are like a travel brochure come to life. Visitors can walk into the park, catch water taxis to beaches and resorts along the track, or kayak along the coast.

In summer hundreds of trampers tackle the track at the same time. Track accommodation works on a booking system: huts and campsites must be prebooked year-round. There's no charge for day walks – if you're after a taster, the two- to three-hour stretch from Tonga Bay to Bark Bay is as photogenic as any, or get dropped at a beach and just hang out.

Between Bark Bay and Awaroa Head is an area classified as the **Tonga Island Marine Reserve** – home to a seal colony and visiting dolphins. Tonga Island itself is a small island offshore from Onetahuti Beach.

For a full description of the route, see DOC's *Abel Tasman Coast Track* brochure.

WALKING THE TRACK

The Abel Tasman area has crazy tides (up to a 6m difference between low and high tide),

LOCAL KNOWLEDGE

HAYLEY WESTENRA, SINGER & SONGWRITER

The Abel Tasman National Park, situated at the very top of the South Island, is a place of breathtaking beauty. Whether you opt for the three- to five-day tramp along the coastal track, some sea-kayaking around the bays or just a short half-day walk, you will be left spellbound by the native flora and fauna you encounter and mesmerised by the spectacular ocean views, not to mention the region's famous golden beaches. If you're feeling a little lazy, you could perhaps take a water taxi from Kaiteriteri to Awaroa, passing by Split Apple Rock and a seal colony on the way. However you go about your trip, though, the Abel Tasman National Park will surely leave you enchanted.

which has an impact on walking. Two sections of the main track are tidal, with no high-tide track around them: Awaroa Estuary and the narrow channel at Onetahuti Beach. Tide tables are posted along the track and on the DOC website; regional i-SITES also have them.

Take additional food so that you can stay longer should you have the inclination. Bays around all the huts are beautiful, but definitely bring plenty of sandfly repellent and sunscreen.

Estimated walking times from south to north:

ROUTE	TIME
Marahau to Anchorage Hut	4hr
Anchorage Hut to Bark Bay Hut	4hr
Bark Bay Hut to Awaroa Hut	4hr
Awaroa Hut to Totaranui	1½hr

Many walkers finish at Totaranui, the final stop for the boat services and bus pick-up point, but it is possible to keep walking around the headland to Whariwharangi Hut (p438) (three hours) and then on to Wainui (1½ hours), where buses service the car park.

Tours

Tour companies usually offer free Motueka pick-up/drop-off, with Nelson pick-up available at extra cost.

Abel Tasman Sailing Adventures SAILING
(☎03-527 8375, 0800 467 245; www.sailingadventures.co.nz; Kaiteriteri; half-/full day $85/169) A catamaran that offers the only scheduled sailing trips into the park. Sail/walk/kayak combos available; day-trip includes lunch.

Abel Tasman Seal Swim WILDLIFE TOUR
(☎0800 252 925, 03-527 8383; www.sealswim.com; Aqua Taxi Base, Sandy Bay-Marahau Rd, Marahau; 5hr seal swim adult/child $179/130, seal watch $90/70) Tide-scheduled trips to the seal colony.

Abel Tasman Tours & Guided Walks WALKING
(☎03-528 9602; www.abeltasmantours.co.nz; $220) Small-group, day-long walking tours (minimum of two people) that include packed lunch and water taxis.

Wilsons Abel Tasman WALKING, KAYAKING
(☎0800 221 888, 03-528 2027; www.abeltasman.co.nz; 265 High St, Motueka; half-day cruise $70, cruise & walk $55-70, kayak & walk $89-195) Impressive array of cruises, walking, kayaking and combo tours, including $32 backpacker special and the barbecue cruise (great winter option). Luxurious beachfront lodges at Awaroa and Torrent Bay for guided-tour guests.

Sleeping & Eating

At the southern edge of the park, Marahau is the main jumping-off point for the Abel Tasman National Park. From the northern end of the park, the nearest towns with accommodation are Pohara and Takaka. The whopping **Totaranui DOC Campsite** (☎03-528 8083; www.doc.govt.nz; summer/winter $15/10) is also in the north, 32km from Takaka on a narrow, winding road (12km unsealed – check with DOC or the Golden Bay i-SITE for latest conditions). It's serviced by Abel Tasman Coachlines (p436) from October to April. Sites at Totaranui from December to mid-February are now allocated via ballot; download a booking form from the DOC website.

Along the Coast Track there are four huts: **Anchorage** (24 bunks), **Bark Bay** (34 bunks), **Awaroa** (26 bunks) and **Whariwharangi** (20 bunks), plus 19 designated campsites. None have cooking facilities – BYO stove. Some of the campsites have fireplaces but, again, you must carry cooking equipment. Hut and camp passes should be purchased before you enter the park. From Christmas Day to February, huts and campsites fill to the rafters (book with DOC).

Moored permanently in Anchorage Bay, the **Aquapackers** (☎0800 430 744; www.aquapackers.co.nz; Anchorage; dm/d incl breakfast $70/195) is a rockin' option. This specially converted 13m *Catarac* catamaran provides unusual but buoyant backpacker accommodation for 22. Facilities are basic but decent; prices include bedding, dinner and breakfast. Bookings essential.

Further sleeping options in the park (accessible on foot, by kayak or water taxi, but not by road) are largely confined to holiday homes. Ask about these at the Nelson (p429) or Motueka (p435) i-SITEs or browse online.

ℹ Information

The track operates on DOC's **Great Walks Pass** (sites/huts per person $12.20/35.70). Children are free but booking is still required. Book online (www.doc.govt.nz), contact the **Nelson Marlborough Bookings Helpdesk** (☎03-546 8210; nmbookings@doc.govt.nz), or book in person at the Nelson (p429), Motueka (p435) and Takaka i-SITES or DOC offices, where staff can offer suggestions to tailor the track to your needs and organise transport at each end. Book your trip well ahead of time, especially the huts between December and March.

ℹ Getting Around

Common setting-out points for the Abel Tasman are Kaiteriteri and Marahau in the south, and Takaka in the north. All are serviced by Abel Tasman Coachlines (p436), with connections to Nelson and Motueka. Totaranui is serviced by **Golden Bay Coachlines** (☎03-525 8352; www.gbcoachlines.co.nz) from November to April ($22 from Takaka).

Once you hit the park, it is easy to get to/from any point on the track by water taxi, either from

PADDLING THE ABEL TASMAN

The Abel Tasman Coast Track has long been trampers' territory, but its coastal beauty makes it an equally seductive spot for sea kayaking, which can be combined with walking and camping. A variety of professional outfits are able to float you out on the water, and the possibilities and permutations for guided or freedom trips are vast. You can kayak from half a day up to three days, camping ($14 per night) or staying in DOC huts ($32 per night), baches, even a floating backpackers, either fully catered for or self-catering. You can kayak one day, camp overnight then walk back, or walk further into the park and catch a water taxi back.

Most operators offer similar trips at similar prices. Marahau is the main base, but trips also depart from Kaiteriteri. A popular choice if time is tight is to spend a few hours kayaking in the Tonga Island Marine Reserve, followed by a walk from Tonga Quarry to Bark Bay. This will cost around $160 including water taxis. Three-day trips usually drop you at the northern end of the park, then you paddle back (or vice versa) and cost around $600 including food. One-day guided trips are around $200.

Freedom rentals (double-kayak and equipment hire) are around $100 per person for two days; none allow solo hires, and all depart from Marahau with the exception of Golden Bay Kayaks (p442), which is based at Tata Beach in Golden Bay.

Instruction is given to everyone, and most tour companies have a minimum age of either eight or 14, depending on the trip. Camping gear is usually provided on overnight trips; if you're disappearing into the park for a few days, most operators provide free car parking.

November to Easter is the busiest time, with December to February the absolute peak. You can, however, paddle all year round, with winter offering its own rewards. The weather is surprisingly amenable, the seals are more playful, there's more bird life and less haze.

The following are the main players in this competitive market; shop around.

Abel Tasman Kayaks (☎03-527 8022, 0800 732 529; www.abeltasmankayaks.co.nz; Main Rd, Marahau)

Kahu Kayaks (☎03-527 8300, 0800 300 101; www.kahukayaks.co.nz; cnr Marahau Valley Rd)

Kaiteriteri Kayaks (☎03-527 8383, 0800 252 925; www.seakayak.co.nz; Kaiteriteri Beach)

Marahau Sea Kayaks (☎03-527 8176, 0800 529 257; www.msk.co.nz; Abel Tasman Centre, Franklin St, Marahau)

Sea Kayak Company (☎03-528 7251, 0508 252 925; www.seakayaknz.co.nz; 506 High St, Motueka)

Wilsons Abel Tasman (☎0800 221 888, 03-528 2027; www.abeltasman.co.nz; 265 High St, Motueka)

Kaiteriteri or Marahau. Typical one-way prices from either Marahau or Kaiteriteri: Anchorage and Torrent Bay ($33), Bark Bay ($38), Tonga ($40), Awaroa ($43) and Totaranui ($45). The following are key operators:

Abel Tasman Aqua Taxi (☎03-527 8083, 0800 278 282; www.aquataxi.co.nz; Kaiteriteri & Marahau) Scheduled and on-demand services as well as boat/walk options.

Abel Tasman Sea Shuttle (☎03-527 8688, 0800 732 748; www.abeltasmanseashuttles.co.nz; Kaiteriteri) Scheduled services plus cruise/walk options. Also runs between Nelson and Kaiteriteri during peak season (adult/child $30/15).

Wilsons Abel Tasman (☎03-528 2027, 0800 223 582; www.abeltasman.co.nz; 265 High St, Motueka; pass adult/child $145/72.50) Offers an explorer pass for unlimited taxi travel on three days over a five-day period, plus backpacker specials and an array of tours.

Marahau Water Taxis (☎03-527 8176, 0800 808 018; www.abeltasmancentre.co.nz; Abel Tasman Centre, Franklin St, Marahau) Scheduled services plus boat/walk options.

Golden Bay

MOTUEKA TO TAKAKA

From Motueka, SH60 takes a stomach-churning meander over Takaka Hill. On the way it passes dramatic lookouts over Tasman Bay and Abel Tasman National Park before swooping down towards Takaka and Collingwood. The best way to tackle this region is with your own wheels.

Takaka Hill (791m) butts-in between Tasman Bay and Golden Bay. Just below the summit (literally) are the **Ngarua Caves** (SH60; adult/child $15/7; ⏲45min tours hourly 10am-4pm Sep-May, open Sat & Sun only Jun-Aug), a rock-solid attraction karst in stone, where you can see myriad subterranean delights including moa bones. Access is restricted to tours – you can't go solo spelunking.

Also just before the summit is the turn-off to **Canaan Downs Scenic Reserve**, reached at the end of an 11km gravel road. This area stars in both the *Lord of the Rings* and *Hobbit* movies, but **Harwood's Hole** is the most famous feature here. It's one of the largest *tomo* (caves) in the country at 357m deep and 70m wide, with a 176m vertical drop. It's a 30-minute walk from the car park, and allow us to state the obvious: the cave is off-limits to all but the most experienced cavers.

Canaan is mountain-bikers' heaven. Riders with reasonable off-road skills can venture along a couple of new loop tracks, while those of intermediate skill can head off on the famous **Rameka Track** (bikes and drop-offs can be negotiated from Takaka). There's a basic **DOC Campsite** (per person $6) here, too.

Close to the zenith also lies the **Takaka Hill Walkway**, a three-hour loop walk through marble karst rock formations, native forest and private farmland (owned by the Harwoods, of Hole fame), and **Harwood Lookout**, affording fine views down the Takaka River Valley to Takaka and Golden Bay.

TAKAKA

POP 1230

Boasting NZ's highest concentration of yoga pants, dreadlocks and various types of drop-outs, Takaka is nevertheless a largely a down-to-earth town and the last 'big' centre before the road west ends at Farewell Spit. You'll find most things you need here, and a few things you don't, but we all have an unworn tie-dye tanktop in our wardrobe, don't we?

Sights & Activities

Te Waikoropupu Springs SPRING

'Pupu Springs' are the largest freshwater springs in Australasia and reputedly the clearest in the world. About 14,000 litres of water per second surges from underground vents dotted around the reserve, including one with 'dancing sands' propelled upwards by gushing water. The water looks enticing, but swimming or even touching the water is a no-no. From Takaka, head 4km northwest on SH60, turn inland at Waitapu Bridge and keep going for 3km.

Grove Scenic Reserve LOOKOUT

(signposted down Clifton Rd) Around 10 minutes' drive from Takaka, a signpost at Clifton Rd points you to this worthwhile stop, where a 10-minute walk leads through a crazy limestone maze punctuated by gnarled old Rata trees. The lookout point is quite something. If you dig this, look out for the signpost to **Labyrinth Rocks Park** (Scotts Rd; admission free) closer to Takaka.

Rawhiti Cave CAVE

(www.doc.govt.nz) The ultimate in geological eye-candy around these parts are the phytokarst features of Rawhiti Cave. Get there from Motupipi, by driving along Packard Rd for 2.5km. Walk from the farm gates, then clamber along the river bed and up a zigzag track to the right. The rugged two-hour-return walk (steep in places; dangerous in the wet) may well leave you speechless (although we managed 'monster', 'fangs', and even 'Sarlacc').

Golden Bay Museum & Gallery MUSEUM
(Commercial St; admission by donation; ⏲10am-4pm) This small museum's stand-out exhibits include a diorama depicting Abel Tasman's 1642 landing and some dubious human taxidermy. Ask about the albatross. The adjoining gallery offers satisfying browsing of local and national knickknackery and quite possibly the purchase of a quality souvenir. For additional arty ambling, look for the free *Artists in Golden Bay* pamphlet.

Pupu Hydro Walkway WALKING
Not far from Pupu Springs, this enjoyable two-hour circuit passes through beech forest, past engineering and gold-mining relics to the restored (and operational) Pupu Hydro Powerhouse, built in 1929. To get here, take the 4km gravel road (signed 'Pupu Walkway') off Pupu Springs Rd.

Escape Adventures CYCLING
(☎03-525 8783; www.escapeadventures.co.nz; behind the Post Shop; bike hire per day $75, 1-day guided ride from $150) The Bay offers a range of fantastic cycling opportunities, on- and off-road, for riders of every ability. The flinty folk at Escape can get you out there (including Canaan and Rameka tracks) with guided trips, bike hire and transport.

Remote Adventures SCENIC FLIGHTS
(☎0800 150 338, 03-525 6167; www.remoteadventures.co.nz; Takaka Airfield) Scenic flights around Golden Bay and over Kahurangi National Park for as little as $40.

Golden Bay Air SCENIC FLIGHTS
(☎0800 588 885; www.goldenbayair.co.nz) Scenic and charter flights around the Golden Bay, and Farewell Spit, Abel Tasman and Kahurangi; from $49.

Sleeping & Eating

Kiwiana HOSTEL $
(☎03-525 7676, 0800 805 494; www.kiwianabackpackers.co.nz; 73 Motupipi St; tent sites per person $18, dm/s/d $28/44/68; @📶) Beyond the welcoming garden is a cute cottage where rooms are named after classic Kiwiana (the jandal, Buzzy Bee...). The garage has been converted into a fun games room, with wood-fired stove, pool table, CD player, books and games, and free bikes for guest use.

Annie's Nirvana Lodge HOSTEL $
(☎03-525 8766; www.nirvanalodge.co.nz; 25 Motupipi St; dm/d $28/66; @📶) It's clean, it's tidy, and it smells good: dorms in the main house, four doubles at the bottom of the secluded courtyard garden. This YHA hostel is lovely and has friendly owners. Fluffy the cat seals the deal – what a charmer. Free bikes for guests.

Golden Bay Motel MOTEL $$
(☎0800 401 212, 03-525 9428; www.goldenbaymotel.co.nz; 132 Commercial St; d $95-140, extra person $20; 📶) It's golden, all right: check out the paint job. Clean, spacious, self-contained units with decent older-style fixtures and decent older-style hosts. The rear patios overlook a lush green lawn with a playground.

Dangerous Kitchen CAFE $
(46a Commercial St; meals $12-28; ⏲10am-10pm Mon-Sat) Dedicated to Frank Zappa ('In the kitchen of danger, you can feel like a stranger'), DK serves largely healthy, good-value fare such as falafel, pizza, burritos, mega-cake and fresh juice. Mellow and laid-back, with a sun-trap courtyard out back and a people-watching patio on the main drag.

Top Shop DAIRY
(9 Willow St; items $2-9) One of your best bets for a quick eat. A dairy, tearoom and takeaway at the entrance to town; high-rating pies.

Fresh Choice SUPERMARKET
(☎03-525 9383; 13 Willow St; ⏲8am-7pm) Stock up while you can.

Drinking

Brigand CAFE, BAR
(www.brigand.co.nz; 90 Commercial St; meals $16-35; ⏲11am-late Mon-Sat) Beyond the gates you'll find good food such as sandwiches, chowder and meaty mains served in a relaxed atmosphere. A garden bar and great baking feature, too. Equally important, the Brigand is the mainstay of the local entertainment scene; go for Thursday open mic and look out for other gigs.

Roots Bar BAR
(www.rootsbar.co.nz; 1 Commercial St) Popular with the young 'uns and those who can still tap a toe, this music-focused joint has decent beer on tap, a garden bar, lively evenings and the odd tree root lending a little rusticity.

Paul's Coffee Caravan CAFE
The dude with the tunes does the best brew in town from his van tucked into the Library carpark.

Entertainment

Village Theatre CINEMA
(03-525 8453; www.villagetheatre.org.nz; 32 Commercial St; adult/child $12.50/7) Demonstrating, yet again, provincial New Zealand's appetite for quality movies.

Information

DOC Office (03-525 8026; www.doc.govt.nz; 62 Commercial St; 8.30am-4pm Mon-Fri) Information on Abel Tasman and Kahurangi National Parks, the Heaphy Track, Farewell Spit and Cobb Valley. Sells hut passes.

Golden Bay i-SITE (03-525 9136; www.goldenbaynz.co.nz; Willow St; 9am-5pm Nov-Apr, 10am-4.30pm Mon-Fri, to 4pm Sat & Sun May-Oct; @) A friendly little information centre with all the necessary information, including the indispensible yellow map. Bookings and DOC passes.

Getting There & Around

Abel Tasman Coachlines (03-528 8850; www.abeltasmantravel.co.nz) runs between Takaka and Nelson ($35, 2½ hours).

Golden Bay Air (03-525 8725, 0800 588 885; www.goldenbayair.co.nz) flies daily between Wellington and Takaka ($139 to $189) and between Takaka and Karamea for Heaphy Track trampers (minimum two people, per person $175).

Golden Bay Coachlines (03-525 8352; www.gbcoachlines.co.nz) works in conjunction with Abel Tasman Coachlines. Connects Takaka with Collingwood ($19, 25 minutes), the Heaphy Track ($33, one hour), Totaranui ($22, one hour) and other stops en route.

Remote Adventures (03-525 6167, 0800 150 338; www.remoteadventures.co.nz) offers daily flights between Takaka and Nelson (from $150).

A sustainable, butt-enhancing method of transport is available from the **Quiet Revolution Cycle Shop** (03-525 9555; www.quietrevolution.co.nz; 11 Commercial St; bike hire per day $25-45). Local ride maps and a car-relocation service for the Heaphy Track in winter, too.

POHARA

POP 350

About 10km northeast of Takaka is pint-sized Pohara, a beachside resort with a population that quadruples over summer. It's more 'yuppified' than other parts of Golden Bay, with large modern houses cashing in on sea views, but an agreeable air persists and there's some good accommodation.

The beach is on the way to the northern end of the Abel Tasman Coastal Track; the largely unsealed road into the park passes Tarakohe Harbour (Pohara's working port) where **Golden Bay Kayaks** (03-525 9095; www.goldenbaykayaks.co.nz; Tata Beach; half-day guided tours adult $75-80, child $35, freedom hire half-/full day $90/110) rents kayaks for hour-long paddles, or can launch you on a three-day exploration of Abel Tasman National Park.

Further along, **Ligar Bay** has a lookout and a memorial to Abel Tasman, who anchored here in December 1642.

Signposted from the Totaranui Rd at Wainui Bay is a leafy walk to the best cascade in the bay: **Wainui Falls**. It's a 1½-hour return trip, but you could easily take longer by dipping a toe or two in the river.

Sleeping & Eating

Pohara Beach Top 10 Holiday Park HOLIDAY PARK $
(0800 764 272, 03-525 9500; www.poharabeach.com; 809 Abel Tasman Dr; sites from $20, cabins & units $72-164; @) Wow, what a big 'un! On a long grassy strip between the dunes and the main road, this place has a primo location – love that beach! – but in summer it can feel more like a suburb than the seaside. General store and takeaway on site.

Nook GUESTHOUSE $
(03-525 8501, 0800 806 665; www.thenookguesthouse.co.nz; 678 Abel Tasman Dr; sites from $15, dm/tw/d $32/65/75, cottage $180-200;) Low-key, nook-sized guesthouse with timber floors, and rooms opening out onto gardens. A self-contained straw-bale cottage sleeps six, while the back paddock has space for tents. Bikes available.

Sans Souci Inn LODGE $$
(03-525 8663; www.sanssouciinn.co.nz; 11 Richmond Rd; s/d/f $90/115/135, self-contained unit from $180, dinner mains $32 to $35; closed Jul–mid-Sep;) Sans Souci means 'no worries' in French, and this will be your mantra too after staying in one of the seven mudbrick, Mediterranean-flavoured rooms. Guests share a plant-filled, mosaic bathroom that has composting toilets, and an airy lounge and kitchen opening out onto the semi-tropical courtyard. Dinner in the on-site restaurant (bookings essential) is highly recommended; breakfast is by request.

Ratanui LODGE $$
(03-525 7998; www.ratanuilodge.com; 818 Abel Tasman Dr; d $155-269; @) This beautiful new boutique lodge is a contender for NZ's most romantic, with plush and elegant rooms, and sensual stimulators such as swimming pool, massage room, mean mar-

LOCAL KNOWLEDGE

RHYS DARBY, ACTOR & STAND-UP COMIC

Golden Bay has all the elements of wonder for me: beautiful, rugged terrain, an amazing array of artists and world-class food. It's my annual trip there, however, that really gets the wildlife excited. You haven't lived until you've been chased by a wild seal. That's what happened to me the last time I visited Wharariki Beach with its wild windswept dunes and giant rock formations. It really is the land of the lost. You must traverse farmland, hills and bush to get there, but it's well worth it for the stunning ocean views. Then, to complete the day, you should aim for the Mussel Inn (p444) for its wonderful Captain Cooker Manuka Honey Beer, but be sure to stop on the way for a cold dip in any one of the refreshing rivers.

garitas and a candleabra-lit restaurant (open to the public; bookings required). Victorian grandeur inside; colourful cottage garden out the front. Affordable luxury that delivers.

Penguin Café & Bar PUB **$$**
(818 Abel Tasman Dr; lunch $13-22, dinner $20-33; ⌚10am-late Nov-Apr; 4pm-late Mon-Wed & 11am-late Thu-Sun May-Oct) A buzzy spot with a large outdoor area suited to sundowners and thirst-quenchers on sunny days. There's an open fire inside for the odd inclement day. Brunch treats include chowder, mussels and steak sandwiches. Come dinner time, keep an eye out for the local seafood specials.

Getting There & Away

Golden Bay Coachlines (☎03-525 8352; www.gbcoachlines.co.nz) runs daily from Takaka to Pohara ($15, 15 minutes) on the way to Totaranui.

COLLINGWOOD & AROUND

Far-flung Collingwood (population 250) is the last town in this part of the country, and has a real end-of-the-line vibe. It's busy in summer, though for most people it's simply a launch pad for the Heaphy Track or trips to Farewell Spit.

The **Collingwood Museum** (Tasman St; admission by donation; ⌚10am-4pm) fills a tiny, unstaffed corridor with a quirky collection of saddlery, Maori artefacts, moa bones, shells and old typewriters, while the **Aorere Centre** next-door houses multimedia presentations, including the works of the wonderful pioneer photographer, Fred Tyree.

No Collingwood visit would be complete without visiting **Rosy Glow** (54 Beach Rd; chocolates $3-5; ⌚10am-5pm Sat-Thu). Chocoholics: this is your cue. Don't miss it!

A foray to Farewell Spit is essential. From there, follow the sign to **Wharariki Beach** (☎03-524 8507; www.whararikibeachholidaypark.co.nz; sitres from $16, dm $25) (6km unsealed road, then a 20-minute walk through Puponga Farm Park). It's a wild introduction to the West Coast, with mighty dune formations, looming rock islets just offshore and a seal colony at its eastern end (keep an eye out for seals in the stream on the walk here). As inviting as a swim here may seem, there are strong undertows – what the sea wants, the sea shall have...

Befitting a frontier, this is the place to saddle up: **Cape Farewell Horse Treks** (☎03-524 8031; www.horsetreksnz.com; McGowan St, Puponga; ⌚treks from $75). Treks in this wind-blown country range from 1½ hours (to Pillar Point) to three hours (to Wharariki Beach), with longer (including overnight) trips by arrangement.

On the road to Wharariki Beach you'll pass **Wharariki Beach Holiday Park** (☎03-524 8507; www.whararikibeachholidaypark.co.nz; sitres from $16, dm $25), a pretty, young campground with a pleasant communal building.

Sleeping & Eating

There's little in the way of refreshment round these parts, so keep some cheese and crackers up your sleeve.

Innlet Backpackers & Cottages HOSTEL **$**
(☎03-524 8040; www.goldenbayindex.co.nz; Main Rd; sites from $24, dm/d $31/73, cabins from $83; @) A great option 10km from Collingwood on the way to Farewell Spit. The main house has elegant backpacker rooms, and there are various campsites and self-contained options, including a cottage sleeping six. Bush walks and bike hire raise the environmental-consciousness quotient.

Somerset House HOSTEL **$**
(☎03-524 8624; www.backpackerscollingwood.co.nz; 10 Gibbs Rd, Collingwood; dm/s/d incl breakfast $30/46/72; @) A small, low-key hostel

DON'T MISS

FAREWELL SPIT

Bleak, exposed and slighly sci-fi, **Farewell Spit** is a wetland of international importance and a renowned bird sanctuary – the summer home of thousands of migratory waders, notably the godwit (which flies all the way from the Arctic tundra), Caspian terns and Australasian gannets. The 35km beach features colossal, crescent-shaped dunes, from where panoramic views extend across Golden Bay and a vast low-tide salt marsh. Walkers can explore the first 4km of the spit via a network of tracks, but beyond that point access is via tour only.

At the time of writing, the visitor centre and cafe at the spit was between managers; this we take as a positive because the only way is up.

Farewell Spit Eco Tours (☎0800 808 257, 03-524 8257; www.farewellspit.com; Tasman St, Collingwood; tours $120-145) Operating for more than 65 years, this outfit runs tours that range from three to 6½ hours, taking in the spit, lighthouse, gannets and godwits. Tours depart from Collingwood.

Farewell Spit Nature Experience (☎0800 250 500, 03-524 8992; www.farewellspittours.com; tours $120-135) Four-hour spit tours depart Farewell Spit Visitor Centre; six-hour tours depart the Old School Café, Pakawau.

in a bright, historic building on a hill with views from the deck. Get tramping advice from the knowledgeable owners, who offer track transport, free bikes and kayaks, and freshly baked bread for breakfast.

Collingwood Park Motel MOTEL **$$**
(☎03-524 8499, 0800 270 520; www.collingwoodpark.co.nz; 1 Tasman St; d $100-140; @) Clean, spacious self-contained units in excellent nick, wedged between the road and Aorere estuary. Good-value family-sized units have nifty mezzanine floors, plus compact campervan sites ($35) and a backpacker double ($85 to $95).

TOP CHOICE **Mussel Inn** PUB **$$**
(www.musselinn.co.nz; 1259 SH60, Onekaka; all-day menu $5-18, dinner $23-29; ⏰11am-late, closed Jul-Aug) Halfway between Takaka and Collingwood, this earthy tavern-cafe-brewery is a Golden Bay institution. A totem pole with crucified mobile phones heralds the mood: this is no place for urban trappings, just excellent beer, wholesome food (mussels, seasonal scallops, fresh fish and steak), open fires and live music. Try a handle (beer glass) or two of 'Captain Cooker', a brown beer brewed naturally with manuka, or the delicious 'Bitter Ass'.

Old School Cafe CAFE **$$**
(1115 Collingwood Puponga Rd; mains $14-30; ⏰4pm-late Thu-Fri, 11am-late Sat & Sun) These folks get an A for effort by providing honest food to an unpredictable flow of passing trade. What it lacks in imagination (steak, pizza and even a shrimp cocktail), it more than makes up for with arty ambience, a garden bar and a welcoming disposition.

ℹ Getting There & Away

Golden Bay Coachlines (☎03-525 8352; www.goldenbaycoachlines.co.nz) runs from Takaka to Collingwood ($19, 25 minutes, two daily).

Kahurangi National Park

Kahurangi, meaning 'Treasured Possession', is the second largest of NZ's national parks and undoubtedly one of the greatest. Its 452,000 hectares are a hotbed of ecological wonderment: 18 native bird species, over 50% of all NZ's plant species, including over 80% of its alpine plant species, a karst landscape and the largest known cave system in the southern hemisphere (explored by local caving groups, but only for the experienced).

HEAPHY TRACK

One of the best-known tracks in NZ, the four- to six-day 78.5km Heaphy Track doesn't have the spectacular scenery of the Routeburn or Milford Tracks, but revels in its own distinct beauty. The track is almost entirely within Kahurangi National Park, and its highlights include the mystical Gouland Downs, and the nikau-palm-dotted coast, especially around Heaphy Hut, where you could easily spend spend a day or two.

There are seven huts en route, the smallest accommodating only eight people, the largest 28; all have gas stoves, except Brown and Gouland Downs, which need wood. There are nine campsites along the route, with limited capacity (eight campers maximum at James Mackay Hut, as many as 40 at Heaphy Hut). Huts/campsites cost $32/14; all must be prebooked through DOC and the Nelson and Golden Bay i-SITEs.

WALKING THE TRACK

Most people tramp southwest from the Collingwood end to Karamea. From Brown Hut the track passes through beech forest to Perry Saddle. The country opens up to the swampy Gouland Downs, then closes in with sparse bush all the way to Mackay Hut. The bush becomes more dense towards Heaphy Hut, with beautiful nikau palms growing at lower levels.

The final section is along the coast through nikau forest and partly along the beach. Unfortunately, sandflies love this beautiful stretch too. The climate here is surprisingly mild, but don't swim in the sea, as the undertows and currents are vicious. The lagoon at Heaphy Hut is good for swimming, and the Heaphy River is full of fish.

Kilometre markers crop up along the track – the zero marker is at the track's southern end at Kohaihai River near Karamea. Estimated walking times:

ROUTE	TIME
Brown Hut to Perry Saddle Hut	5hr
Perry Saddle Hut to Gouland Downs Hut	2hr
Gouland Downs Hut to Saxon Hut	1½hr
Saxon Hut to James Mackay Hut	3hr
James Mackay Hut to Lewis Hut	3½hr
Lewis Hut to Heaphy Hut	2½hr
Heaphy Hut to Kohaihai River	5hr

CYCLING THE TRACK

For a trial period ending in September 2013, the Heaphy Track can be cycled by experienced mountain bikers from May to September each year. The ride takes two to three days. Two local companies can help you with gear and advice: Escape Adventures (p441) and Quiet Revolution Cycle Shop (p442).

Information

The best spot for detailed Heaphy Track information and bookings is the DOC counter at the Nelson i-SITE (p429). You can also book at the Golden Bay i-SITE (p442) or DOC (p442) in Takaka, online at www.doc.got.nz, by email (nmbookings@doc.govt.nz) or phone (03-546 8210). See also www.heaphytrack.com. For a detailed track description, see DOC's *Heaphy Track* brochure.

OTHER KAHURANGI TRACKS

After tackling the Heaphy north to south, you can return to Golden Bay via the more scenic (though harder) **Wangapeka Track**. It's not as well known as the Heaphy, but many consider the Wangapeka a more enjoyable walk. Taking about five days, the track starts 25km south of Karamea at Little Wanganui, running 52km east to Rolling River near Tapawera. There's a chain of huts along the track.

See www.doc.govt.nz for detailed information on both tracks, and for some excellent full-day and overnight walks around the Cobb Valley, Mt Arthur and the Tableland.

Tours

Bush & Beyond TRAMPING
(☎03-528 9054; www.bushandbeyond.co.nz) Offers various tramping trips, ranging from Mt Arthur or Cobb Valley day walks ($220) through to a guided six-day Heaphy Track package ($1795).

Southern Wilderness TRAMPING
(☎03-545 7544, 0800 666 044; www.southernwilderness.com) Guided four- to five-day tramps on the Heaphy Track ($1495 to $1595) and day walks in Nelson Lakes National Park ($220).

Kahurangi Guided Walks TRAMPING
(☎03-525 7177; www.kahurangiwalks.co.nz) Small-group adventures such as five-day Heaphy tramps ($1500) and various one-day trips, including Abel Tasman and the Cobb (from $170).

Getting There & Away

Golden Bay Coachlines (☎03-525 8352; www.gbcoachlines.co.nz) will get you to the Heaphy Track from Takaka via Collingwood ($33, one hour).

Heaphy Bus (☎0800 128 735, 03-540 2042; www.theheaphybus.co.nz) offers a round-trip shuttle service: drop off and pick up from Kohaihai ($110), and other on-demand local track transport.

Heaphy Track Help (☎03-525 9576; www.heaphytrackhelp.co.nz) offers car relocations ($200 to $300, depending on the direction and time), food drops, shuttles and advice.

Remote Adventures (p441) flies Takaka to Karamea from $170 per person (up to four people and bicycles). Golden Bay Air (p441) flies the same route from $155 per person, as does Helicopter Charter Karamea (p455), who will take up to three people for $675 ($750 with three mountain bikes).

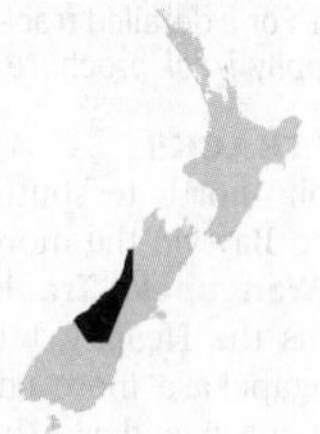

The West Coast

Includes »

Murchison & Buller Gorge 448
Karamea & Around 452
Punakaiki & Paparoa National Park 455
The Coast Road 457
Reefton 457
Lake Brunner 459
Greymouth 459
Hokitika 463
Westland Tai Poutini National Park 469
Franz Josef Glacier 469
Fox Glacier 474
Haast Region 477

Best Outdoors

- » Heaphy Track (p453)
- » Hokitika Gorge (p465)
- » Charming Creek Walkway (p453)
- » Denniston Plateau (p452)

Best Places to Stay

- » Fox Glacier Holiday Park (p476)
- » Lantern Court Motels (p458)
- » Okarito Campground (p469)
- » Beaconstone Eco Lodge (p455)

Why Go?

What a difference a mountain range makes. Hemmed in by the wild Tasman Sea and the Southern Alps, the West Coast (aka Westland) is like nowhere else in New Zealand.

Both ends of the coast have a remote end-of-the-road feel. In the north the surf-battered highway leads to sleepy Karamea, surrounded by farms and home to alternative lifestylers drawn by its isolation and surprisingly mild climate. The southern end of spectacular State Hwy 6 continues to Haast, gateway to a magnificent pass and Central Otago beyond.

Built on the wavering fortunes of gold, coal and timber, the stories of Coast settlers are hair-raising. Today just 32,000 reside here, typically a hardy and individual breed: they make up less than 1% of NZ's population, scattered amid almost 9% of the country's area.

During summer a phalanx of campervans and tourist buses tick off the 'must see' Punakaiki Rocks and Franz Josef and Fox Glaciers. Deviate from the trail even a short way, however, and be awed by the spectacles that await you alone.

When to Go

During summer the coast road gets relatively busy. May to September can be warm and clear, with fewer crowds and cheaper accommodation. The West Coast has serious rainfall (around 5m annually) but Westland sees as much sunshine as Christchurch. When it's pouring in the east it's just as likely to be fine here.

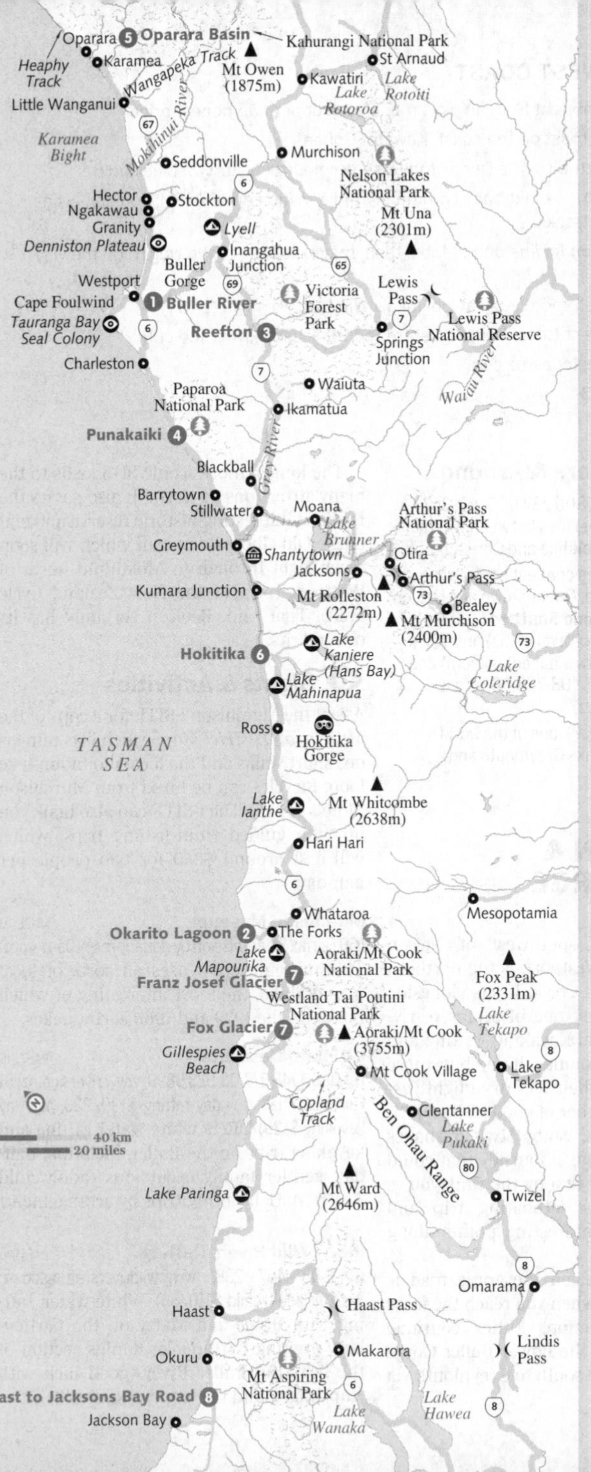

The West Coast Highlights

1. Getting wet 'n' wild on the mighty **Buller River** (p448)
2. Kayaking through the bird-filled channels of **Okarito Lagoon** (p468)
3. Delving into the golden past around **Reefton** (p457)
4. Marvelling at nature's beautiful fury at the Pancake Rocks at **Punakaiki** (p455)
5. Exploring the limestone landscape of the **Oparara Basin** (p453)
6. Hunting out authentic local greenstone in the galleries of **Hokitika** (p463)
7. Flying high into the Southern Alps via **Franz Josef** (p469) and **Fox Glaciers** (p474)
8. Reaching the end of the line on the scenic and historical highway from **Haast** to **Jackson Bay** (p478)

ESSENTIAL WEST COAST

» **Eat** Whitebait, bought from an old-timer's back door at an honest price

» **Drink** The only roast on the coast, Kawatiri Coffee

» **Read** Jenny Pattrick's *The Denniston Rose*, a colourful history of black gold

» **Listen to** Karamea's laid-back community radio station on 107.5FM; you can even choose your own tracks

» **Watch** *Denniston Incline* on YouTube, then imagine sitting in the wagon on the way down

» **Festival** Go bush-food crazy at Hokitika's Wildfoods Festival (p465)

» **Go Green** At West Coast Wildlife Centre (p469) – baby kiwis! Too cute!

» **Online** www.westcoastnz.com

» **Area code** ☎03

Getting There & Around

Air New Zealand (☎0800 737 000, 09-357 3000; www.airnz.co.nz) flies between Westport and Wellington, and Hokitika and Christchurch.

Coaches and shuttles connect centres like Christchurch, Dunedin, Queenstown and Nelson; major players are **Atomic Shuttles** (☎03-349 0697; www.atomictravel.co.nz), InterCity (p694), **Naked Bus** (www.nakedbus.com) and **West Coast Shuttle** (☎03-768 0028; www.westcoastshuttle.co.nz).

The TranzAlpine (p462), one of the world's great train journeys, links Greymouth and Christchurch.

MURCHISON & BULLER GORGE

POP 800

Murchison, 125km southwest of Nelson and 95km east of Westport, is the northern gateway to the West Coast. It sits alongside the Buller River, just one of scores of rivers around this area. Kayaking, rafting and trout-fishing are popular here, but those who want to keep their feet dry might *just* manage it on a number of good walks.

From Murchison, State Hwy 6 snakes through Buller Gorge, a journey that could easily take a day or two by the time you've taken a rafting or jetboating trip and stopped at other interesting points along the way.

Your big decision on the gorge road is which way to head when you reach the forks at Inangahua Junction. Either continue along SH6 through the Lower Buller Gorge to Westport, or head south to Greymouth via Reefton on SH69.

The longer, more scenic SH6 leads to the many attractions up north. It also passes the Lyell, an interesting historic reserve and end of the Old Ghost Road trail which will soon reach right through to Mokihinui north of Westport (part of the New Zealand Cycle Trail). That said, Reefton certainly has its own merits.

Sights & Activities

Ask at the Murchison i-SITE for a copy of the *Murchison District Map*, which lists numerous short walks and the local mountain-bike loop. Bicycles can be hired from Murchison Motels (p449). The i-SITE can also hook you up with guided trout-fishing trips, which will cost around $350 for two people per half-day.

Murchison Museum MUSEUM
(60 Fairfax St; admission by donation; ⏲10am-4pm) This museum showcases all sorts of local memorabilia, the most interesting of which relates to the 1929 and 1968 earthquakes.

Ultimate Descents RAFTING
(☎0800 748 377, 03-523 9899; www.rivers.co.nz; 51 Fairfax St; half-/full day rafting $130/220, half-day kayaking $125) Offers white-water rafting and kayaking trips on the Buller, including half-day, gentler family excursions (adult/child $105/85). Heli-rafting trips by arrangement.

TOP CHOICE **Wild Rivers Rafting** RAFTING
(☎0508 467 238; www.wildriversrafting.co.nz; 3hr trip adult/child $110/85) White-water rafting with Bruce and Marty on the particularly exciting Earthquake Rapids section of the beautiful Buller River (good luck with 'gunslinger' and the 'pop-up toaster'!).

Buller Gorge Swingbridge BRIDGE
(www.bullergorge.co.nz; SH6; bridge crossing adult/child $5/2; ⏲8am-7pm Oct-Apr, 9am-5pm May-Sep) About 14km west of Murchison is NZ's longest swingbridge (110m). Across it are some short walks, one to the White Creek Faultline, epicentre of the 1929 earthquake. Coming back, ride the 160m Cometline Flying Fox, either seated (adult/child $30/15) or 'Supaman' ($45, or tandem adult/child $30/15).

Buller Canyon Jet JETBOATING
(☎03 523 9883; www.bullercanyonjet.co.nz; SH6; adult/child $95/50; ⏲Sept-Apr) Claiming 'NZ's best jet boating', and it might just be right: 40 minutes of ripping through the Buller. Whoo hoo! It's located at the Buller Gorge Swingbridge.

Festivals & Events

Buller Festival SPORTS
(www.bullerfestival.co.nz) A kayaking and rafting extravaganza held over the first weekend in March.

Sleeping & Eating

Murchison is decent place for stocking up on supplies, with a dairy, mini-supermarket and a butchery curing notable bacon.

Lazy Cow HOSTEL $
(☎03-523 9451; www.lazycow.co.nz; 37 Waller St; dm $28, d $74-84; @) It's easy to be a lazy cow here, with all the comforts of home including free muffins or cake and freshly cooked evening meals ($12). The great hosts take pride in their pad, and it shows throughout the house and gardens.

Commercial Hotel HOTEL $
(☎03-523 9696; www.commercialhotel.co.nz; cnr Waller & Fairfax Sts; s/d/tr $40/75/100; ⏲8am-8.30pm; @) Super street-appeal and brightly coloured bar walls are just the starters. The guest wing offers the best possible shock with its checkerboard and crimson hallway clashing with the heritage-charm bedrooms. Great value; all share bathrooms and a cupboard-sized kitchen. The popular pub offers bar snacks and meals ($13 to $29).

Murchison Motorhome Park HOLIDAY PARK $
(☎03-523 9666; www.murchisonmotorhomepark.co.nz; SH6; sites from $26; ⏲closed Jul & Aug;) The landscaping at this new park has yet to reach maturity, but warm and well-designed facilities more than make up for it, as does the lovely stretch of Buller River (with swimming holes) that runs alongside. It's 8km north of Murchison.

Murchison Lodge B&B $$
(☎03-523 9196; www.murchisonlodge.co.nz; 15 Grey St; s incl breakfast $130-190, d incl breakfast $155-215; ⏲closed May-Aug; @) Surrounded by native trees, this B&B has access to the Buller River and some decent swimming holes. Nice interior design touches and friendly hosts add to the comfortable feel. Evening meals by arrangement, if you can't be bothered with the short walk to town.

Murchison Motels MOTEL $$
(☎0800 166 500, 03-523 9026; www.murchisonmotels.co.nz; 53 Fairfax St; d $140-180;) Tucked behind Rivers Cafe, with snazzy one- and two-bedroom units complete with kitchenettes. There's also a swimming pool, and mountain bikes for hire (half-day $15).

Hu-Ha Bikepackers FARMSTAY $
(☎03-548 2707; huhabikepackers@farmside.co.nz; 2937 Kohatu-Kawatiri Hwy, Glenhope; unpowered sites from $14, dm $28, d with/without bathroom $72/62;) Friendly hosts give their ground floor over to guests who can enjoy a charming open-plan communal area with wooden floors, log-burner, and a dining table with a rural view. There's a piano, an enviable collection of vinyl records, and farm animals including a very fat pig. It's 45km to Murchison from here. Cash only.

Rivers Cafe CAFE $$
(51 Fairfax St; meals $12-30; ⏲8.30am-9pm Oct-Mar, 9am-3pm Apr-Sep) The town's old garage is now home to a questionable craft gallery,

MAORI NZ: THE WEST COAST

For Maori, the river valleys and mountains of the West Coast were the traditional source of highly prized *pounamu* (greenstone), carved into tools, weapons and adornments. View the Pounamu exhibit at Holitika Museum (p463) to polish your knowledge of the precious rock before admiring the classy carving done by the town's artists. Kotuku Gallery (p468), further south in Whataroa, is also a good spot for the genuine article.

but myriad quality pastries. Sample the delicious lamb shank pie with decent coffee or a pint of craft beer.

Information

There is no ATM in town; the postal agency is on Fairfax St.

The **Murchison i-SITE** (03-523 9350; www.nelsonnz.com; 47 Waller St; 10am-6pm Oct-May, reduced hours Apr-Sept) has info on local activities and transport.

Getting There & Away

Buses passing through Murchison between the West Coast and Picton are **InterCity** (03-365 1113; www.intercity.co.nz) and **Naked Bus** (www.nakedbus.com), both of which stop at Beechwoods Café on Waller St.

WESTPORT & AROUND

POP 4850

The port of Westport made its fortune in coal mining, though today the main mine is at Stockton, 38km north. The proposed expansion of West Coast coal mining is the subject of heated debates which pit traditional adversaries – the greens versus the go-aheads – against each other. There's no doubt that this industry keeps the town stoked up: it's looking purposeful, pretty, and even slighly 'go ahead'. Beyond some respectable hospitality, the town contains little of prolonged interest, but makes a good base for exploring the fascinating coast north to Karamea, Oparara and the Heaphy Track.

Sights & Activities

Westport is good for a stroll – the i-SITE can direct you to the **Millenium Walkway** and the freshly revamped **Kawatiri Beach Reserve**. The most thrilling adventure in the area is cave rafting with Norwest Adventures (p450).

Tauranga Bay Seal Colony WILDLIFE

Depending on the season, anything from 20 to 200 NZ fur seals dot the rocks at this seal colony, 16km from Westport. Pups are born from late November to early December.

The Cape Foulwind Walkway (1½ hours return) extends from the seal colony near its southern end, 4km along the coast to Cape Foulwind, passing a replica of Abel Tasman's astrolabe (a navigational aid) and a lighthouse. The walk's northern end is car-accessible from Lighthouse Rd.

The Maori called the cape Tauranga, meaning 'Sheltered Anchorage'. The first European here was Abel Tasman in December 1642; he named it Clyppygen Hoek (Rocky Point). When James Cook moored the *Endeavour* here in March 1770, a furious storm made it anything but a 'sheltered anchorage', hence Cape Foulwind's modern name.

West Coast Brewing Co BREWERY

(www.westcoastbrewing.com; 10 Lyndhurst St; tastings $10; 8.30am-5pm Mon-Fri, 10am-4pm Sat & Sun) Taste up to a dozen craft beers, including the organic Green Fern lager and a notable India pale ale. Pop in for a tasting, or get a rigger to go (or, quite possibly, pull up a stool and struggle to leave).

Coaltown Museum MUSEUM

(165 Queen St; adult/child $12.50/5; 9am-4.30pm) This earnest but decidedly old-fashioned museum will appeal to those with an interest in local history. Expect plenty of musty mining artefacts, maritime displays, and a huge engine from a steam dredge. The Denniston film is worth watching.

Norwest Adventures CAVING, RAILWAY

(0800 116 686, 03-788 8168; www.caverafting.com; SH6, Charleston) At Charleston, 26km south of Westport, this friendly bunch run 'Underworld' cave-rafting trips ($165, four hours) into the glowworm-filled Nile River Caves. If you want the glow without the flow (no rafting), it's $105 per person. Both options start with a fun rainforest railway ride, available separately (adult/child $20/15, 1½ hours). The Adventure Caving trip ($330, five hours) includes a 40m abseil into Te Tahi *tomo* (hole) with rock squeezes, waterfalls, prehistoric fossils and trippy cave formations.

Sleeping

Archer House B&B **$$**

(03-789 8778, 0800 789 877; www.archerhouse.co.nz; 75 Queen St; d incl breakfast $185; @) This big and beautiful 1890 heritage home sleeps up to eight in three rooms with their own bathrooms, all sharing no less than three lounges and peaceful gardens. Lovely hosts, complimentary sherry, generous continental breakfast and free wi-fi make this Westport's most refined accommodation option.

Buller Court Motel MOTEL **$$**

(03-789 7979; www.bullercourtmotel.co.nz; 253 Palmerston St; d $120-170, q $195-215;) One of many main road options, this older-style complex has had a tasteful make-over and impresses with an away-from-the-road aspect and small but private grassy gardens.

Trip Inn HOSTEL $
(☎0800 737 773, 03-789 7367; www.tripinn.co.nz; 72 Queen Street; dm/s/d $27/55/66; @) Feel like lord of the manor at this grand 150-year old villa with beautiful gardens. There's a variety of tidy rooms in and out of the house to choose from, and voluminous communal areas.

Seal Colony TOP 10 Holiday Park HOLIDAY PARK $
(☎0508 937 876, 03-789 8002; www.top10westport.co.nz; 57 Marine Pde, Carters Beach; sites from $36, units $70-140; @) Right on Carters Beach and conveniently located between Westport (4km) and the Tauranga Bay seal colony (12km), this no-frills outfit offers a full range of facilities of a more than acceptable standard. A good option for tourers seeking a clean and peaceful stop-off, and perhaps even a swim.

Omau Settlers Lodge LODGE $
(☎03-789 5200; www.omausettlerslodge.co.nz; 1054 Cape Rd; r incl breakfast $135-155;) Close to Cape Foulwind and across the road from the excellent Star Tavern, these contemporary and stylish units offer rest, relaxation and huge buffet breakfasts. Rooms have kitchenette, but you can also share a kitchen and dining room. A hot tub surrounded by bush maximises the take-it-easy quotient.

Westport Holiday Park HOLIDAY PARK $
(☎03-789 7043; www.westportholidaypark.co.nz; 31 Domett St; sites from $32, d $95-145; @) A-frame 'chalets' stud this back-street park with adequate amenities and a mini-golf course.

Eating & Drinking

A small town it may be, but Westport has more than its fair share of pubs, along with plenty of places to eat and a couple of supermarkets for stocking up.

TOP CHOICE **Town House** MODERN NZ $$
(☎03-789 7133; www.thetownhouse.co.nz; cnr Cobden & Palmerston Sts; mains $15-32; ⌚10am-4pm Sun & Mon, 10am-late Tue-Sat) The most upmarket option in town, fit for the finest of cities. Shift between the sunny terrace, groovy bar and dining room with art deco styling while you enjoy excellent contemporary fare from morning til night. Too many highlights to mention, but the home-cured confit duck leg and gingernut ice-cream did it for us.

Jay's Cafe CAFE $
(260 Palmerston St; mains $9-17; ⌚8am-5pm Mon-Sat) Mimicking the cafe's native bird theme, locals flock here for the best coffee in town and consistent cafe food, ranging from eggy brekkies through to grilled turbot and steak sammies.

Porto Bello BAR $$
(www.westportrestaurant.co.nz; 62 Palmerston St; meals $12-29; ⌚4pm-late Mon-Thur, 11am-late Fri-Sun) Roman columns and renaissance artwork give this place a Coliseum feel, but the food has its roots firmly in the US of A. Six local craft beers on tap, $15 steak specials and occasional live music keep the locals happy.

Information

The major banks are along Palmerston St. There's free wi-fi at the **Westport Library** (87 Palmerston St).

Buller Hospital (☎03-788 9030; Cobden St)

Department of Conservation Office (DOC; ☎03-788 8008; www.doc.govt.nz; 72 Russell St; ⌚8am-noon & 1-4.30pm Mon-Fri) Tickets for the Heaphy and Wangapeka Tracks plus general tramping info.

Police Station (☎03-788 8310; 13 Wakefield St)

Post Office (cnr Brougham & Palmerston Sts)

Westport i-SITE (☎03-789 6658; www.westport.org.nz; 1 Brougham St; ⌚9am-5pm Nov-Mar, to 4.30pm Apr-Oct) Information on local tracks, walkways, tours, accommodation and transport.

Getting There & Around

Air

Air New Zealand (☎0800 737 000; www.airnewzealand.co.nz) has one or two flights per day to/from Wellington (from $89).

Bus

InterCity (☎03-365 1113; www.intercity.co.nz) buses depart daily from outside the i-SITE and **Caltex Petrol Station** (197 Palmerston St) to Nelson (from $30, 3½ hours), Greymouth (from $17, 2¼ hours) and Franz Josef (from $38, six hours).

Naked Bus (www.nakedbus.com) goes three times a week to Nelson (from $10, four hours), Greymouth (from $10, two hours) and Franz Josef (from $10, 5¼ hours), departing from the i-SITE.

East West Coach (p458) operates a Christchurch service ($63, Sunday to Friday, 4¾ hours) departing from the Caltex Petrol Station.

Karamea Express (☎03-782 6757; info@karamea-express.co.nz) links Westport and Karamea ($30, two hours, 11.30am Monday to Friday May to September, plus Saturday from October to April), departing from the i-SITE.

Car

Hire some wheels at **Wesport Hire** (☎0508 974 473, 03-789 5038; wesporthire@xtra.co.nz; 294 Palmerston St).

Taxi

Buller Taxis (☎03-789 6900) can take you to/from the airport (around $20).

WESTPORT TO KARAMEA

North along SH67, the road is pressed against the rocky shoreline by verdant hills. If you're heading all the way up to Karamea, fill your tank in Westport as it's 98km to the next petrol station.

The first town beyond Westport is **Waimangaroa**, with a shop worth a stop for a home-made pie and ice cream. Here you'll also find the turn-off to the **Denniston Plateau**, 9km inland and 600m above sea level.

Denniston was once NZ's largest coal producer, with 1500 residents in 1911. By 1981 there were eight. Its claim to fame was the fantastically steep **Denniston Incline**, an engineering spectacular. Empty coal trucks were hauled back up the 45-degree slope by the weight of descending loaded trucks.

Today this historic site is a fascinating place to visit, recently improved and enhanced with information panels. The *Denniston Rose Walking Tour* brochure ($2 from DOC and Westport Llibrary) may lead keen readers to the local bookshop to buy Jenny Pattrick's evocative novels set in the area. The **Denniston Mine Experience** (☎0800 881 880; www.dennistonminexperience.co.nz; Denniston; 2hr tour adult/child $85/55) guided tours ride the 'gorge express' train into the historic Banbury mine for what is a slightly spooky but fascinating exploration of the tunnels. Other features of the plateau include the **Denniston Bridle Track**, which follows sections of the Incline, excellent mountain biking (maps and bikes from Habitat Sports (p454)) and some picnic sports with awesome views.

At sleepy **Granity**, 30km north of Westport, head 5km uphill to the semi-ghost town of **Millerton**, and a further 3km to **Stockton**, home of NZ's largest operational coal mine. (Orange fluro vests ahoy!) The **Millerton Incline Walk** (20 minutes return) takes in parts of the old Incline, a bridge and dam. Just north at **Hector** you can see a monument to Hector's dolphins, NZ's smallest, although you'll be lucky to see them unless your timing is impeccable.

In these parts you'll find the Charming Creek Walkway (p453). Further north, the Seddonville road leads to the **Rough and Tumble Bush Lodge** (☎03-782 1337; www.roughandtumble.co.nz; Mokihinui Rd; r $200; wi-fi). In a gentle bend of the Mohikinui River, this upmarket self-catering option is surrounded by forest and walking trails. The rooms and shared main lodge house exude rustic chic, while the kitchen is equipped to feed a small army. Advance bookings are essential.

At the Mohikinui River mouth, 3km off the highway, is the not-so-gentle **Gentle Annie Beach** and the **Gentle Annie Coastal Enclave** (☎03-782 1826, 0274 188 587; www.gentleannie.co.nz; De Malmanche Rd, Mohikinui; sites from $12, s/d $25/50, cabins $120-200), perfect for quiet contemplation. There are campsites, a lodge, a range of self-contained accommodation and a seasonal cafe. There's also a maze on top of a lookout point, and glow worms if you know who to ask.

Between Mohikinui and Little Wanganui the road meanders over **Karamea Bluff**, with rata and matai forests, and expansive views of the Tasman Sea below. It's worth stopping to do the **Lake Hanlon** walk (30 minutes return) on the Karamea side of the hill.

KARAMEA & AROUND

The relaxed town of Karamea (population 650) considers itself the West Coast's 'best kept secret', but those who've visited tend to boast about its merits far and wide. An end-of-the-road town it may well be, but it still has a bit of the 'hub' about it, servicing the end (or start) of the Heaphy and Wangapeka Tracks, and the unmissable Oparara Basin. With a friendly climate, and a take-it-easy mix of locals and chilled-out imports, the Karamea area is a great place to jump off the well-trodden tourist trail for a few lazy days.

Sights & Activities

Hats off to the Karamea community who have established the very pleasant **Karamea Estuary Walkway**, a short stroll (one

DON'T MISS

A CHARMING CREEK INDEED

One of the best day-walks on the Coast, the **Charming Creek Walkway** (six hours return) is an all-weather trail following an old coal line through the Ngakawau River Gorge. Along its length are rusty relics galore, tunnels, a suspension bridge and waterfall, and lots of interesting plants and geological formations.

You can start the track at **Ngakawau**, where you'll find the **Charming Creek B&B** (☎0800 867 3529, 03-782 8007; www.bullerbeachstay.co.nz; Ngakawau; d incl breakfast $139-169; 📶) – a good base for the track. The rooms are clean and, well, charming, and there's a driftwood-fired hot tub right by the sea. A two-night walking package ($420) includes dinners and a picnic lunch while on the track.

You can also start the track at the northern trailhead 10km beyond **Seddonville**, a small bush town on the Mohikinui River where **Seddonville Holiday Park** (☎03-782 1314) offers respectable camping in the grounds of the old school. A local may fix you up with transport if you don't want to walk it both ways.

Experienced mountain bikers can make a loop of it: park your car at the Seddonville pub and ride in a clockwise direction. The coastal highway is a fab way to finish, as is a pint at the pub when you're done.

hour) bordering the estuary and Karemea River. You can ask a local where it is, follow your nose, or pick up a leaflet from the Karamea Information & Resource Centre. While you're there, pick up the free *Karamea* brochure, which details other walks, including **Big Rimu** (45 minutes return), **Flagstaff** (one hour return) and the **Zig Zag** (one hour return).

Longer walks around Karamea include the **Fenian Track** (four hours return) leading to **Cavern Creek Caves** and **Adams Flat**, where there's a replica gold-miner's hut; and the first leg of the **Wangapeka Track** to Belltown Hut. The Wangapeka Track is a day traverse of Kahurangi National Park, generally started at Tapawera in the Motueka Valley.

Other activities include swimming, fishing, whitebaiting, kayaking and mountain biking. Your best bet for advice on these is to ask a local and always use common sense – especially when it comes to the watery stuff. **Karamea Outdoor Adventures** (☎03-782 6181, 03-782 6646; www.karameaadventures.co.nz; Bridge St; guided kayak trips from $45, kayak hire 2hrs $25, bike hire 2hrs $25) offers guided kayaking trips on the Oparara and Karamea Rivers, plus kayak and mountain-bike hire, and advice on local excursions.

OPARARA VALLEY

North of Karamea, the **Oparara Basin** contains justifiably famous natural wonders. Spectacular limestone arches and unique caves are surrounded by a karst landscape blanketed by primitive rainforest. To get here from Karamea, drive 10km along the main north road north and turn off at McCallum's Mill Rd. Continue 15km past the sawmill along a winding gravel (sometimes rough) road.

It's an easy walk (45 minutes return) through old-growth forest to the 200m-long, 37m-high **Oparara Arch**, spanning its namesake river. Its rival is the **Moria Gate Arch** (43m long, 19m high), accessed via a similar track (one hour return). Other highlights are **Mirror Tarn** (an easy 20 minutes return), and the **Crazy Paving & Box Canyon Caves** (10 minutes return, BYO torch).

Beyond these, in a protected area of Kahurangi National Park, are the superb **Honeycomb Hill Caves & Arch**, accessible only by prebooked guided tours (five hours, $150) run by the people at the Karamea Information and Resource Centre (p454). Ask about their other guided tours of the area.

For a full-day freedom walk, the rewarding **Oparara Valley Track** takes you through ancient forest, along the river, and will take five hours and pop you out at the **Fenian Walk** carpark. Ask at the Information & Resource Centre about track transport, and also about gentle river kayaking trips on offer from mid-December to April (two hours, $95).

HEAPHY TRACK

The West Coast road runs out at **Kohaihai**, the western trailhead (and most commonly, the finish point) of the Heaphy Track, where there's also a **DOC campsite** (per person $6). A day walk or overnight stay can readily be had from here. Walk to **Scotts Beach** (1½ hours return), or go as far as **Heaphy Hut** (huts/campsites $32/14) (five hours) and stay a night or two before returning.

This section can also be mountain-biked, as can the whole track (two to three days) from May to September under a trial period ending in September 2013; ask at Westport's **Habitat Sports** (☎03-788 8002; www.habitatsports.co.nz; 204 Palmerston St) for bike hire and details.

Helicopter Charter Karamea (p455) will fly up to three people through to the northern trailhead in Golden Bay for $675 ($750 with three bikes); ask about other possible drop-off/pick-up points.

For detailed information on negotiating the Heaphy Track, see www.heaphytrack.com.

Sleeping & Eating

Cafes and restaurants are thin on the ground around these parts, so stock up at Karamea's 4 Square and keep an eye out for 'open' signs.

Last Resort RESORT $
(☎0800 505 042, 03-782 6617; www.lastresort.co.nz; 71 Waverley St, Karamea; dm $37, d $78-155; @☎) When we visited, renovations were well underway at this iconic, rambling and rustic resort. Rooms and facilities are simple but hallmarked by the extensive use of local timbers and artwork. The communal areas are warm and welcoming, including the cafe (lunch $9 to $15, dinner $18 to $29) serving simple all-day food like burgers, fish and chips and Caesar salad.

Rongo Backpackers HOSTEL $
(☎03-782 6667; www.rongobackpackers.com; 130 Waverley St, Karamea; sites from $20, dm $30-32, d & tw $75; @☎) Part neo-hippie artists' haven and part organic vegie garden, this uber-relaxed hostel even has its own community radio station (107.5 FM, www.karamearadio.com). Popular with long-term guests who often end up working within – either tending the garden or as de facto DJs. Every fourth night free.

Karamea Farm Baches CABINS $
(☎03-782 6838; www.karameamotels.com; 17 Wharf Rd, Karamea; d/tr/q $90/115/140; @☎) Pushing reuse/recycle to the limit, these 1960s fully self-contained baches are the real McCoy, right down to cobwebby corners and frayed bedspreads. If you dig organic gardening, friendly dogs and colourful hosts, this will win you over.

Karamea River Motels MOTEL $$
(☎03-782 6955; www.karameamotels.co.nz; 31 Bridge St, Karamea; r $125-165; ☎) The smart rooms at this modern, rural motel range from studios to two-bedroom units. Features include long-range views, barbecues and lush gardens complete with lily pond.

Karamea Holiday Park HOLIDAY PARK $
(☎03-782 6758; www.karamea.com; Maori Point Rd, Karamea; sites from $28, cabins $40-50, d $86; @☎) A simple, old-fashioned camp alongside the estuary in bush surrounds, 3km south of Market Cross. The classic weatherboard cabins are clean and well maintained.

Wangapeka Backpackers Retreat & Farmstay HOSTEL $
(☎03-782 6663; www.wangapeka.co.nz; Atawhai Farm, Wangapeka Valley; campsites from $10, dm $20, s/d $45/75; ☎) This laid-back and friendly farmstay close to the Wangapeka Track has crusty dorms with clean linen, and meals by arrangement. Turn down Wangapeka Rd just north of Little Wanganui and follow the signs. It's a 20km drive south of Karamea.

Karamea Village Hotel PUB $$
(karameahotel@xtra.co.nz; cnr Waverley St & Wharf Rd, Karamea; mains $18-29; ⏲11am-11pm) Treat yourself to life's simple pleasures: a game of pool with the locals, a pint of Monteith's Original Ale, and a whitebait-fritter sandwich. Sorted.

Information

Karamea Information & Resource Centre (☎03-782 6652; www.karameainfo.co.nz; Market Cross; ⏲9am-5pm daily Jan-May, 9am-1pm Sat & Sun only Jun-Dec; @) This excellent, community-owned centre has the local low-down, internet access, maps and DOC hut tickets. It also doubles as the petrol station.

Getting There & Away

Karamea Express (p452) links Karamea and Westport ($30, two hours, 7.50am Monday to Friday May to September, plus Saturday from October to April). It also services Kohaihai twice daily during peak summer, and other times on demand. Wangapeka transport is also available.

Heaphy Bus (☎0800 128 735, 03-540 2042; www.theheaphybus.co.nz), based in Nelson, also runs between both ends of the Heaphy, as well as the Wangapeka.

Fly from Karamea to Takaka with **Helicopter Charter Karamea** (☎03-782 6111; www.adventuresnz.co.nz; 79 Waverley St, Karamea) or Golden Bay Air (p442), for around $175 per person, then walk back on the Heaphy Track; contact the Information & Resource Centre for details.

Rongo Backpackers run on-demand track and town transport around the place including to Heaphy, Wangapeka, Oparara Basin and Westport.

WESTPORT TO GREYMOUTH

SH6 along the surf-pounded coastline here proffers fine ocean views. Fill up in Westport if you're low on petrol and cash – there's no fuel until Runanga, 92km away, and the next ATM is in Greymouth. The main attractions along this stretch are the geologically fascinating Pancake Rocks at Punakaiki. To break the journey, consider the following.

Set on 52 serene hectares 17km south of Westport, solar-powered, energy-efficient **Beaconstone Eco Lodge** (☎027 431 0491; www.beaconstoneecolodge.co.nz; Birds Ferry Rd; dm $28-31, d $66-74; ⏲Oct-Jun) is both earth- and guest-friendly. The style is a little bit Americana cool, while the comforts are many, including cosy beds and a laid-back communal area. Bush walks on the doorstep. There's only room for 12, so booking is recommended.

Jack's Gasthof (☎03-789 6501; www.jacksgasthof.co.nz; SH6; sites from $5, d $50; ⏲Oct-May) is 21km south of Westport on the Little Totara River. Laconic Jack swapped Berlin for this gentle spot more than 22 years ago, and he and Petra still run this eternally popular pizzeria (mains $10 to $25; open from 11am) with adjacent bar improbably bejewelled with a disco ball. Rooms and camping for horizonal dancing.

For a true taste of the region's gold mining past, swing into **Mitchell's Gully Gold Mine** (☎03-789 6553; www.mitchellsgullygoldmine.co.nz; SH6; adult/child $10/free; ⏲9am-5pm), 22km south of Westport, where you'll meet a pioneer's descendants and explore the family mine. There are interesting tales, relics, tunnels and railtracks, plus a giant waterwheel and the odd trap-door spider.

The next stop is **Charleston**, 26km south of Westport. It's hard to believe it now, but this place boomed during the 1860s gold rush, with 80 hotels, three breweries and hundreds of thirsty gold-diggers staking claims along the Nile River. There's not much left now except a motel, campground, a clutch of local houses and the brilliant Norwest Adventures (p450) with whom you can explore some utterly amazing hidden treasures.

From here to Punakaiki is an attractive mixture of lowland pakihi scrub and lush green forest alongside a series of bays dramatically sculpted by relentless ocean fury. Drive as slowly as the traffic behind you will allow.

Punakaiki & Paparoa National Park

Located midway between Westport and Greymouth is Punakaiki, a small settlement beside the rugged 38,000-hectare Paparoa National Park. For most travellers, it's a quick stop for an ice cream and a squiz at the Pancake Rocks; a shame because there's excellent tramping on offer and some tragically underused accommodation.

Sights

Paparoa National Park is blessed with sea cliffs, a dramatic mountain range, gorgeous limestone river valleys, diverse flora and a Westland petrel colony, the world's only nesting site of this rare sea bird.

Pancake Rocks NATURAL FEATURE

Punakaiki is famous for its fantastic Pancake Rocks and blowholes. Through a layering-weathering process called stylobedding, the Dolomite Point limestone has formed into what looks like piles of thick pancakes. When the tide is high (tide times are posted at the visitor information centre), the sea surges into caverns and booms menacingly through blowholes. See it on a wild day and be reminded that Mother Nature really is the boss. An easy 15-minute walk loops from the highway out to the rocks and blowholes.

Activities

Tramps around Punakaiki include the **Truman Track** (30 minutes return) and the **Porari River Track** (3½ hours), which goes up the spectacular limestone Pororari River gorge before popping over a hill to come down the bouldery Punakaiki River to rejoin the highway.

Surefooted types can visit the **Fox River Tourist Cave** (three hours return), 12km north of Punakaiki and open to amateur explorers. BYO torch and sturdy shoes.

Other tramps in the national park are detailed in the DOC *Paparoa National Park* pamphlet ($1), and include the **Inland Pack Track** (two to three days), a route established by miners in 1867 to dodge difficult coastal terrain.

Many of Paparoa's inland walks are susceptible to river flooding; check in with the DOC Visitor Centre in Punakaiki before you depart. Better still, go with a guide.

Nature's Tours ECOTOUR
(☎03-731 1442; www.naturestours.co.nz; 4hr tour $125) Fresh-faced Zane of Nature's Tours brims with passion for the wilderness and successfully translates this into insightful hiking tours packed with stories with a dash of fun. Four-hour trips take in the Pancake Rocks, the Truman Track and Pororari River, with customised trips (two hours to two days) by arrangement.

Punakaiki Canoes KAYAKING
(☎03-731 1870; www.riverkayaking.co.nz; SH6; canoe hire 2hr/full day $35/55, family rates avail) The Pororari River offers gentle, family-friendly paddling. This outfit rents canoes near the Pororari River bridge.

Punakaiki Horse Treks HORSE RIDING
(☎03-731 1839; www.pancake-rocks.co.nz; SH6; 2½hr ride $145; ⊙Oct-June) Punakaiki Horse Treks, based at Hydrangea Cottages, conducts four-legged outings in the Punakaiki Valley, with river crossings, finishing at the beach.

Sleeping & Eating

There's good news and bad news. The good news is that there's heaps of good accommodation in Punakaiki. The bad news is that there's no grocery shop or petrol, and that the two cafes next to the main visitor car park may well fail to please. The tavern down the road, however, has proven a consistently good performer. Keep it up, Team Pub!

TOP CHOICE **Punakaiki Beach Hostel** HOSTEL $
(☎03-731 1852; www.punakaikibeachhostel.co.nz; 4 Webb St; sites per person $20, dm/s/d $27/53/71; @☰) A canary-yellow, beach-bumming hostel with a sea-view verandah, just a short way from Pancake Rocks. Co-operative owners have been-there-done-that and know exactly what you want: a clean hostel with good beds, great communal facilities, and staff who smile because they mean it.

Punakaiki Beach Camp HOLIDAY PARK $
(☎03-731 1894; beachcamp@xtra.co.nz; 5 Owen St; sites $31, d $46) With a back-drop of sheer cliffs, this salty park with good grass is studded with clean, old-style cabins and shipshape amenities.

Te Nikau Retreat LODGE $
(☎03-731 1111; www.tenikauretreat.co.nz; Hartmount Pl; sites from $18, dm $27, d $71-86, cabins from $96; @☰) This unconventional property consists of numerous buildings nestled into their own rainforest nooks, just a short walk to the beach. There are dorms in the main building, several cute cabins, and the larger Nikau Lodge sleeping up to 10. The clear-roofed stargazer hut is tiny, but fun for those who want to sleep under the night sky.

Hydrangea Cottages COTTAGES $$
(☎03-731 1839; www.pancake-rocks.co.nz; SH6; d $140-220; ☰) On a hillside overlooking the Tasman, these five stand-alone and mostly self-contained cottages (largest sleeping up to seven) are built from salvaged river timber and river stones. It's a classy but relaxed enclave, with splashes of colourful mosaic and pretty cottage gardens. The owners also run the horse-trekking stables.

Punakaiki Tavern PUB $$
(www.punakaikitavern.co.nz; SH6; mains $19-32; ⊙8am-late) Whether it's breakfast, lunch or dinner, this pub does decent portions of honest food served in comfortable surrounds. Most nights the punters are a mix of local and international, so there's ample opportunity for conversation and friendly debate over the rules of pool.

Information

The **Paparoa National Park visitor information centre and i-SITE** (☎03-731 1895; www.doc.govt.nz; SH6; ⊙9am-5pm Oct-Nov, to 6pm Dec-Mar, to 4.30pm Apr-Sep) has information on the park and track conditions, and handles bookings for local attractions and accommodation, including hut tickets.

See also www.punakaiki.co.nz.

Getting There & Away

InterCity (☎03-365 1113; www.intercity.co.nz) links to Westport daily (from $13, three hours), Greymouth (from $10, 45 minutes) and Franz Josef (from $33, four hours). **Naked Bus** (www.nakedbus.com) has a similar service along SH6 operating three days a week. Both companies allow enough time to check out Pancake Rocks.

The Coast Road

The highway from Punakaiki to Greymouth is flanked by white-capped waves and rocky bays on one side, and the steep, bushy Paparoa Ranges on the other.

At **Barrytown**, 16km south of Punakaiki, Steve and Robyn run **Barrytown Knifemaking** (☎0800 256 433, 03-731 1053; www.barrytownknifemaking.com; 2662 SH6, Barrytown; classes $130; ⊙closed Mon), where you can make your own knife – from hand-forging the blade to crafting a handle from native rimu timber. The day-long course features lunch, archery, axe-throwing and a stream of entertainingly bad jokes from Steve. Bookings essential, and transport from Punakaiki can be arranged.

With a backdrop of subtropical rainforest, **Ti Kouka House** (☎03-731 1460; www.tikoukahouse.co.nz; 2522 SH6, Barrytown; d incl breakfast $295; 📶) is all rugged sea views, global antiques and lots of recycled wood including history-laden doors and windows. It's an excellent B&B, with three luxury rooms.

Breakers (☎03-762 7743; www.breakers.co.nz; 1367 SH6, Nine Mile Creek; d incl breakfast $215-355; @📶), 14km north of Greymouth, is one of the best-kept secrets on the coast. Beautifully appointed en suite rooms overlook the sea, with fine surfing opportunities at hand for the intrepid. The hosts are both friendly and mountain-biking mad.

REEFTON & GREY VALLEY

From Murchison, an alternative to the SH6 coast route is to turn off at Inangahua Junction and travel inland across winding valley roads via Reefton, and over the mountains into the Grey Valley.

Amid the regenerating forests, small towns are reminders of futile farming attempts, and of the gold rush of the 1860s.

Reefton

POP 1000

For generations, Reefton's claims to fame have been mining and its early adoption of the electricity grid and street lighting. Hence the tagline, 'the city of light'. Today, however, it's a different story, one that starts – improbably – with the building of the world-class Roller Park, which attracts stunt-lovers from all corners of NZ. To quote a local, 'It's more than we deserve.' We disagree. If so many volunteers and sponsors are prepared to build such an edgy civic amenity in a town that still looks like the set of *Bonanza*, we suggest there's something a little bit special about this crazy little town.

Sights & Activities

With loads of crusty old buildings within a 200m radius, Reefton is a fascinating town for a stroll. To find out who lived where and why, undertake the short **Heritage Tour** outlined in the woefully photocopied Historic Reefton leaflet ($1), available from the i-SITE.

The i-SITE also stocks the free Reefton leaftlet, detailing historic sites and more short walks including the **Reefton Walkway** (40 minutes), and **Powerhouse Walk** (40 minutes). Rewarding walks can be had at the old goldfields around Blacks Point and Murray Creek, with the enjoyable **Murray Creek loop** taking five hours (round trip). It's mountain-biking heaven around here, with bikes available to hire from the **Picture Framers** (☎03-732 8293; 45 Broadway; bikes from $10).

Reefton lies on the edge of the 206,000-hectare **Victoria Forest Park** (NZ's largest forest park), sporting five different species of beech tree. Tramps here include the three-day **Kirwans**, **Lake Christabel** and **Robinson River Tracks**, and the two-day **Big River Track**, which is fast becoming a must-do for mountain bikers. It ends at historic Waiuta, 21km south of Reefton, once a burgeoning gold town but abandoned in 1951 after the mine collapsed. Ask at the i-SITE for information and maps.

Blacks Point Museum MUSEUM
(Blacks Point, SH7; adult/child/family $5/3/15; ⊙9am-noon & 1-4pm Wed-Fri & Sun year-round, plus 1-4pm Sat Oct-Apr) This community-run museum, 2km east of Reefton on the Christchurch road, is inside an old church and crammed with prospecting paraphernalia. Just up the driveway is the still functional **Golden Fleece Battery** (adult/child $1/free; ⊙1-4pm Wed & Sun Oct-Apr), used for crushing gold-flecked quartz. The Blacks Point walks also start from here.

Bearded Mining Company ODDBALL ENCLAVE
(Broadway; admission by donation; ⊙9am-2pm) Looking like a ZZ Top tribute band, the fellers hangin' at this high-street mining hut

are champing at the bit to rollick your socks off with tales tall and true. If you're lucky you'll get a cuppa from the billy.

Tours

Globe Gold Mine Tours CULTURAL TOUR
(☎027 442 4777; www.reeftongold.co.nz) If you want to dig deeper into Reefton, book into Paul and Ronnie's tours at the i-SITE or pop into their Broadway Tearooms. The Heritage Tour (two hours, $25) takes in town highlights. The Gold Mine Tour (adult/child/family $55/30/120) visits the local mine. You'll get views over the pit-edge and see plenty of huge machiney in action. Tours run at noon and 2pm, with evening tours in summer.

Festivals & Events

Reefton Summer Festival CULTURAL
(www.reefton.co.nz) Go-ahead Reefton has cobbled together a month of fun from mid-December onwards, kicking off with carols and a visit from Santa, and pressing on with quiz nights, go-kart races and the Reefton Gallops.

Sleeping & Eating

Lantern Court Motels MOTEL **$$**
(☎03-732 8574, 0800 526 837; www.lanterncourtmotel.co.nz; 63 Broadway; old units d $95-120, new units d $140-165; 📶) The original accommodation in this heritage hotel has had a right old spruce-up, and offers great-value self-catering for everyone from singles to family groups. The verandah is the best chilling-out spot in town. Meanwhile, the well-assimilated motel block next door offers all mod cons with a nod to classical styling.

Reefton Motor Camp HOLIDAY PARK **$**
(☎03-732 8477; roa.reuben@xtra.co.nz; 1 Ross St; sites from $25, d $45) On the Inangahua River and a minute's walk to Broadway, this older style camp ticks the right boxes and offers the bonuses of a big green sportsfield and shady fir trees.

Old Nurses Home GUESTHOUSE **$**
(☎03-732 8881; reeftonretreat@hotmail.com; 104 Shiel St; s/d $40/80; @📶) Your best bet for a cheap sleep, this stately old building is warm and comfortable, with noteworthy communal areas including pretty gardens and patios. Bedrooms are clean and airy with comfy beds.

Broadway Tearooms BAKERY **$**
(31 Broadway; snacks $3-8, meals $10-20; ⏰5am-3pm) This rustic old joint gets by far the most day-time traffic, and for good reason. The bakers out back turn out everything from cream-filled donuts to decent meat pies to meticulous golden shortbread. Hot meals range from the egg breakfast to a whitebait lunch. Good alfresco, or eat in and survey the cute cruet set collection.

Wilson's PUB
(32 Broadway; mains $15-29; ⏰11am-11pm) A solid town pub pleasing all, from smokin' youth through to soup-slurping pensioners. Meat and two veg dominate the menu, but it's all hearty and homemade. Occasional bands and DJs raise the excitement level to somewhere under fever pitch.

Information

The **Reefton i-Site** (☎03-732 8391; www.reefton.co.nz; 67 Broadway; ⏰9am-5pm Nov-Mar, to 4.30pm Apr-Oct; @) has helpful staff, and a compact re-creation of the Quartzopolis Mine (gold coin entry). There's internet at the library, which doubles as the postal agency.

Getting There & Away

East West Coach (☎03-789 6251, 0800 142 622; eastwestco@xtra.co.nz) runs daily to Westport ($29, 1¼ hours) and Christchurch ($54, 3¾ hours).

Blackball

In the Grey Valley northeast of the river, about 25km north of Greymouth, is Blackball – established in 1866 to service gold diggers; coal mining kicked in between 1890 and 1964. The National Federation of Labour (a trade union) was conceived here, born from influential strikes in 1908 and 1931.

The hub of Blackball is **Formerly the Blackball Hilton** (☎03-732 4705, 0800 425 225; www.blackballhilton.co.nz; 26 Hart St; s without/with breakfast $40/55), famous because a certain global hotel chain got antsy when it was renamed a few years back. Hence the 'formerly'. This official Historic Place has memorabilia galore, hot meals, cold beer, heaps of afternoon sun, and a host of clean rooms oozing the charm of yesteryear.

Competing with the Hilton in the fame stakes are smallgoods made by the **Blackball Salami Co** (www.blackballsalami.co.nz; 11 Hilton St; ⏰8am-4pm Mon-Fri, 9am-2pm Sat). The venison and beef salami are super tasty, as are the snarlers (as they say in Kiwi-speak) – that's sausages for the uninitiated.

Lake Brunner

Lying inland from Greymouth, Lake Brunner can be reached via the SH7 turn-off at Stillwater (or from the south via Kumara Junction). Locals reckon Lake Brunner and the Arnold River have the world's best trout fishing – not an uncommon boast in NZ. The Greymouth i-SITE can hook you up with a guide.

Moana is the main settlement, and where several short walks start including the **Velenski Walk** (20 minutes one way) and the **Rakaitane** (45 minutes return), between them taking in lake, river and forest views.

The **Station House Cafe** (40 Koe St; lunch $12-19, dinner $28-30; ⌚9.30am-10pm Dec-Feb, 10.30am-10pm Mar-Nov) is a reliable stop for refreshment, sitting on a hillside opposite the station where the *TranzAlpine* train pulls in. With a view that grand a glass of wine might be in order.

Lake Brunner Country Motel (☎03-738 0144; www.lakebrunnermotel.co.nz; 2014 Arnold Valley Rd; sites from $30, cabins $54-145) is a wonderful place for a night or two, even if the lake wasn't on your itinerary. Cabins, cottages and campervan sites are tucked into native plantings, while tenters can enjoy the lush grassy camping field down the back. This is proper peace and quiet, unless you count birdsong and the bubbling of the spa pool. It's 37km from Greymouth, 2km north of Moana.

GREYMOUTH

POP 10,000

Welcome to the 'Big Smoke' of Westland. Crouched at the mouth of the imaginatively named Grey River, the West Coast's largest town has a proud gold-mining history, and a legacy of occasional river floods, now somewhat alleviated by a flood wall.

On the main road and rail route through Arthur's Pass and across the Southern Alps from Christchurch, Greymouth sees its fair share of travellers. The town is well geared to looking after them, with all the necessary services and the odd tourist attraction, the most famous of which is Shantytown.

Sights & Activities

Shantytown MUSEUM

(www.shantytown.co.nz; Rutherglen Rd, Paroa; adult/child/family $31.50/15.50/74; ⌚8.30am-5pm) Eight kilometres south of Greymouth and 2km inland from SH6, Shantytown recreates an 1860s gold-mining town, complete with steam-train rides, post office, pub and Rosie's House of Ill Repute. There's also gold panning, a flying fox, sawmill, a gory hospital and 10-minute holographic movies in the new Princess Theatre.

TOP CHOICE **Left Bank Art Gallery** GALLERY

(www.leftbankarts.org.nz; 1 Tainui St; admission by donation; ⌚10am-4pm daily) This 90-year-old former bank houses contemporary NZ jade carvings, prints, paintings, photographs and ceramics. The gallery also fosters and supports a wide society of West Coast artists.

History House Museum MUSEUM

(www.history-house.co.nz; 27-29 Gresson St; adult/child $6/2; ⌚10am-4pm Mon-Fri) This museum documents Greymouth's pre-1920 history with an impressive collection of photographs.

Floodwall Walk WALKING

Take a 10-minute stroll along Mawhera Quay from Cobden Bridge, or keep going for an hour or so taking in the fishing harbour, breakwater and Blaketown Beach.

Point Elizabeth Walkway WALKING

Starting 6km north of Greymouth at Dommett Esplanade, this impressive walkway (three hours return) heads up the coast to the Rapahoe Range Scenic Reserve and a fine tract of mixed podocarp forest with flashes of bright-red rata blooming in the summer.

Tours

Kea Heritage Tours GUIDED TOURS

(☎0800 532 868; www.keatours.co.nz) Top-quality tours with well-informed guides, visiting coast sites and those beyond. Short tours include the half-day Punakaiki Tour ($105), and the day-long Twin Glaciers ($287). Myriad other options include a multi-day exploration of the Maori greenstone trails.

Monteith's Brewing Co GUIDED TOUR

(www.monteiths.co.nz; cnr Turumaha & Herbert Sts) When we visited, Monteith's brand-new brewery was getting ready to open: testatment to the power of a loyal public. Tours and tastings are available: ask for details at the i-SITE or just turn up at the front door.

Greymouth

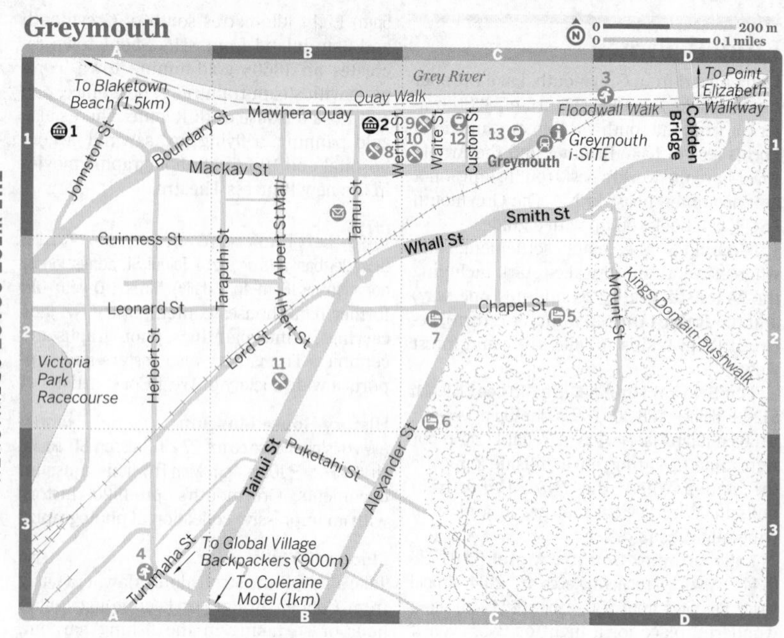

Greymouth

Sights

1 History House Museum A1
2 Left Bank Art Gallery B1

Activities, Courses & Tours

3 Floodwall Walk D1
4 Monteith's Brewing Co A3

Sleeping

5 Ardwyn House C2
6 Kaianga-ra YHA C2
7 Noah's Ark Backpackers C2

Eating

8 Ali's Eating & Drinking B1
9 DP:One Cafe C1
10 Frank's Late Night Lounge C1
11 Priya B2

Drinking

12 Royal Hotel C1
13 Speight's Ale House C1

Sleeping

Global Village Backpackers HOSTEL $
(03-768 7272; www.globalvillagebackpackers.co.nz; 42 Cowper St; sites from $17, dm/d/tr/q $28/68/96/120; @) A collage of African and Asian art is infused with a passionate travellers' vibe here. Free kayaks – the Lake Karoro wetlands reserve is just metres away – and mountain bikes are on tap, and relaxation comes easy with a spa, sauna, barbecue and fire pit.

Noah's Ark Backpackers HOSTEL $
(0800 662 472, 03-768 4868; www.noahsarkbackpackers.co.nz; 16 Chapel St; sites $32, dm/s/d $27/52/66; @) Originally a monastery, Noah's now has eccentric animal-themed rooms and a sunset-worthy balcony. In true Ark style, the camping price is for two people. Mountain bikes and fishing rods are provided free of charge.

Kaianga-ra YHA HOSTEL $
(03-768 4951; www.yha.co.nz; 15 Alexander St; dm $31, s/d $68/80; @) Built in 1937 as a Marist Brothers' residence, this hostel is big, clean, functional and well behaved – everything you'd expect from YHA. A good night's sleep in the chapel dorm is sacrosanct.

Ardwyn House B&B $
(03-768 6107; ardwynhouse@hotmail.com; 48 Chapel St; s/d incl breakfast from $55/85;)

This old-fashioned B&B nestles amid steep gardens on a quiet dead-end street. Mary, the well-travelled host, cooks a splendid breakfast.

Greymouth Seaside Top 10 Holiday Park HOLIDAY PARK $
(☎03-768 6618, 0800 867 104; www.top10greymouth.co.nz; 2 Chesterfield St; sites $44, d $64-193; @📶) This well-appointed beachside park is 2.5km south of town. The facilities are a little worn, but there are plenty of accommodation options, and a jumping pillow and go-karts to keep the kids amused.

Coleraine Motel MOTEL $$
(☎03-768 077, 0800 270 0027; www.colerainemotel.co.nz; 61 High St; d $152-225; @📶) Rattan furniture, spa baths and king-sized beds add up to the smartest luxury rooms in town. Cheaper one- and two-bedroom studios are not far behind. Extra-mile courtesy is shown in the provision of a communal guest lounge.

South Beach Motel & Motorpark MOTEL, HOLIDAY PARK $
(☎0800 101 222, 03-762 6768; www.southbeach.co.nz; 318 Main South Rd; sites $30, d $50-110, tr $125; @📶) Run by good-humoured hosts, this low-rise accommodation complex offers a range of simple but cosy accommodation, unless you count the campsites on a rainy day. Decent communal facilities will help on that score, and as it's only 6km to town this is a pleasant alternative to the big town camp.

Paroa Hotel HOTEL $$
(☎03-762 6860, 0800 762 6860; www.paroa.co.nz; 508 Main South Rd, Paroa; d $125-140; 📶) This family-owned hotel (60 years and counting) is located opposite the Shantytown turn-off and has spacious, garden-fronted units. The onsite restaurant plates up notable schnitzel and huge roasts ($17 to $31) amid a display of rugby jerseys.

New River Bluegums B&B $$
(☎03-762 6678; www.bluegumsnz.com; 985 Main South Rd, Camerons; d incl breakfast $180; @📶) Stay in the cosy upstairs room in the rustic family home, or settle into one of two self-contained units with a rural outlook. Take a bush bath or a farm walk, or work off that extra rasher of bacon or Sharon's gooey brownies on the tennis court. Look for the signpost, 11km south of Greymouth.

Jacksons Retreat HOLIDAY PARK $
(☎03-738 0474; www.jacksonscampervanretreat.co.nz; Jacksons, SH73; sites from $35; @📶) Heading east across Arthur's Pass on SH73, 63km from Greymouth, the tiny settlement of Jackons can be found nestled beside the Taramakau River. Campervan travellers and tenters can stay at Jacksons Retreat, a superb holiday park set upon 15 sloping acres with exceptional views and stacks of excellent amenities. Up the road, the historic Jackson's Tavern can fix you up with a pie and a pint.

Eating & Drinking

Just in case you've missed the gist, big supermarkets are few and far between on the Coast. In Greymouth there are several, so stock up while the going is good.

DP:One Cafe CAFE $
(104 Mawhera Quay; meals $6-15; ⏲9am-9pm; @📶) A stalwart of the Greymouth cafe scene, this hip cafe cups up the best espresso in town, along with good-value grub. Groovy NZ tunes, wi-fi, a relaxed vibe and quayside tables make this a great place for a meet-up to while away a grey day.

THE COAST TO COAST

Kiwis really are a mad bunch. Take, for instance, the annual **Coast to Coast** (www.coasttocoast.co.nz), the most coveted one-day multisport race in the country. Held in mid-February, the race starts in Kumara on the West Coast. Intrepid racers start in the wee hours of the morning with a gentle 3km run, followed by a 55km cycle. Next it's a 33km mountain run over Goat Pass – you know any pass named after a goat isn't going to be flat. From there all there is to do is ride your bike another 15km, paddle your kayak 67km and get back on the bike for the final 70km to Christchurch.

The strong, the brave and the totally knackered will cross the finish line to much fanfare. The course is 243km long and the top competitors will dust it off in just under 11 hours – with slowpokes taking almost twice that.

THE TRANZALPINE

The **TranzAlpine** (☎0800 872 467, 03-768 7080; www.tranzscenic.co.nz; adult/child one way from $89/62), one of the world's great train journeys, traverses the Southern Alps between Christchurch and Greymouth, from the Pacific Ocean to the Tasman Sea – a sequence of unbelievable landscapes. Leaving Christchurch at 8.15am, it speeds across the flat, alluvial Canterbury Plains to the Alps' foothills. Here it enters a labyrinth of gorges and hills called the Staircase, a climb made possible by three large viaducts and a plethora of tunnels.

The train emerges into the broad Waimakariri and Bealey Valleys and (on a good day) the vistas from the new carriages with their panoramic windows are stupendous. The beech-forested river valley gives way to the snowcapped peaks of Arthur's Pass National Park. At Arthur's Pass itself (a small alpine village), the train enters the longest tunnel, the 8.5km 'Otira', burrowing under the mountains to the West Coast.

The western side is just as stunning, with the Otira, Taramakau and Grey River valleys, patches of podocarp forest, and the trout-filled Lake Brunner, fringed with cabbage trees. The train rolls into Greymouth at 12.45pm, heading back to Christchurch an hour later, arriving at 6.05pm.

This awesome journey is diminished only when the weather's bad, but if it's raining on one coast, it's probably fine on the other.

Ali's Eating & Drinking CAFE **$$**
(9 Tainui St; mains $15-27; ⌚10am-late Mon-Sat, to 3pm Sun) Offering little in the way of ambience other than a splash of deep purple, Ali's atones with all-day food made from scratch. Salads, soup and homemade cheesecake make an appearance, although our pick is the chicken parmigiana and the $15 pasta, which filled us to the brim.

Frank's Late Night Lounge INTERNATIONAL **$$**
(☎03-768 9075; 115 Mackay St; mains $19-28; ⌚5pm-late Thu-Sat; ⓥ) This effortlessly cool, retro late-night lounge-bar-cafe is your best bet for getting a groove on. Art deco architecture, eclectic decoration and excellent fresh food (including stellar fish dishes and salads) are just a few reasons for visit. Regular gigs, and it's family friendly. Nice one, Frank.

Priya INDIAN **$$**
(☎03-768 7377; 84 Tainui St; mains $16-22; ⌚lunch & dinner) With an explosion of subcontinental Indian spices on temperate West Coast taste buds, this seasoned performer is heavily patronised.

Speight's Ale House PUB
(130 Mawhera Quay; lunch $12-29, dinner $19-35; ⌚11am-late) Housed in the imposing 1909 'Brick House' building, one of the big brands of NZ beer stands its ground with a well-stocked bar, manly meals and several epic dining and drinking rooms of such warmth and style that you could probably bring your granny here.

Royal Hotel PUB
(128 Mawhera Quay; ⌚11am-late) The old-fashioned Royal welcomes all comers with gusto, and flies a little flag for independent NZ brewing while it's at it. Get yourself a pint of something fine, get chatting or watch the soccer on Sky TV.

ℹ Information

Free town and regional maps are available at the i-SITE. Major banks huddle around Mackay and Tainui Sts. There's internet access at the i-SITE and at the **library** (18 Albert St; @📶).

Greymouth i-SITE (☎03-768 5101; www.greydistrict.co.nz; Railway Station, 164 Mackay St; ⌚8.30am-7pm Mon-Fri, 9am-6pm Sat, 10am-5pm Sun Nov-Apr, reduced hours May-Oct; @📶) Inside the railway station you'll find a very helpful crew, and an abundance of local and DOC information.

Grey Base Hospital (☎03-769 7400; High St)

Police Station (☎03-768 1600; 45-47 Guinness St)

Post Office (36 Tainui St)

ℹ Getting There & Around

Sharing the old railway station with the i-SITE, the **West Coast Travel Centre** (☎03-768 7080; www.westcoasttravel.co.nz; Railway Station, 164 Mackay St; ⌚9am-5pm Mon-Fri, 10am-4pm Sat & Sun; @📶) books all forms of transport, including buses, trains and inter-island ferries, and has luggage-storage facilities. It also serves as the bus depot.

Bus

All buses stop at the railway station.

InterCity (☎03-365 1113; www.intercity.co.nz) has daily buses north to Westport (from \$17, two hours) and Nelson (from \$40, six hours), and south to Franz Josef Glacier (from \$29, 3½ hours) and Fox Glacier (from \$31, 4¼ hours).

Naked Bus (p448) runs north to Nelson and south to Queenstown stopping at Hokitika, Franz Josef and Fox Glaciers, Haast and Wanaka.

Atomic Shuttles (p448) runs daily to Queenstown (\$70, 10½ hours) stopping at Hokitika (from \$13, one hour), Franz Josef (from \$30, 3½ hours) and Fox Glaciers (from \$35, 4¼ hours), Haast (\$65, 5¾ hours) and Wanaka (\$65, nine hours). It also heads north daily to Nelson (\$54, 6¼ hours) on the InterCity service, via Westport (\$24, 2¾ hours).

Car

The West Coast Travel Centre will hook you up with hire cars.

Local companies include **Alpine West** (☎0800 257 736, 03-736 4002; www.alpinerentals.co.nz; 11 Shelley St) and **NZ Rent-a-Car** (☎0800 800 956, 03-768 0379; www.nzrentacar.co.nz; 170 Tainui St).

Taxi

Try **Greymouth Taxis** (☎03-768 7078).

HOKITIKA

POP 3100

Visit Hokitika's wide and quiet streets in the off-season, and you might be excused for thinking you've stumbled into a true Wild West town. Throughout summer, though, there's no room for rogue tumbleweeds in the expansive thoroughfares, and 'Hoki' gets as busy with visitors as when the town was a thriving port during the 1860s gold rush, only now, green (stone), and not gold, is the colour of choice.

Sights & Activities

An extensive network of moutain-biking trails lurks near Hokitika. Hire bikes and get maps and advice from **Sports World & Hokitika Cycles** (☎03-755 8662; 33 Tancred St; per day \$30-65).

Sunset Point LOOKOUT

(Gibson Quay) A spectacular vantage point at any time of day, this is – as the name suggests – the primo place to watch the light fade away. Surfers, seagulls, and fish and chips: *this* is New Zealand.

Hokitika Museum MUSEUM

(☎03-755 6898; www.hokitikamuseum.co.nz; 17 Hamilton St; adult/child \$5/2.50; ⊙9.30am-5pm) Housed in the imposing Carnegie Building (1908), this is an exemplary provincial museum, with intelligently curated exhibitions presented in a clear, modern style. Highlights include the fascinating *Whitebait!* exhibition, and the *Pounamu* room – the ideal primer before you hit the galleries looking for greenstone treasures.

Glowworm Dell NATURAL FEATURE

Just north of town, a short stroll from SH6 leads to a Glowworm Dell, an easy opportunity to enter the other-wordly home of NZ's native fungus gnat lavae (so not even a worm at all). An information panel at the entrance will further illuminate your way.

Hokitika Heritage Walk WALK

Pick up the free leaflet from the i-SITE and wander the waterfront, imagining when the wharves were choked with old-time sailing ships.

Galleries

Art and craft galleries are a strong spoke in Hoki's wheel, and you could easily spend a day spinning around the lot. There are plenty of opportunities to meet the artists, and in some studios you can watch them at work. Be aware that some galleries sell jade imported from Europe and Asia, as precious local *pounamu* (greenstone) is not given up lightly by the wilds.

Hokitika Craft Gallery GALLERY

(www.hokitikacraftgallery.co.nz; 25 Tancred St) The town's best one-stop shop, this co-op showcases a wide range of stunning local work including greenstone, jewellery, textiles, ceramics and some feel-good woodwork.

Tectonic Jade GALLERY

(www.tectonicjade.com; 67 Revell St) The work by local carver Rex Scott is arguably the best in town.

Te Waipounamu Maori Heritage Centre GALLERY

(www.maoriheritage.co.nz; 39 Weld St) Scrupulously authentic, selling only NZ *pounamu* handcrafted into both traditional and contemporary designs.

Jagosi Jade GALLERY

(246 Sewell St) Carver Aden Hoglund produces traditional and modern Maori designs

Hokitika

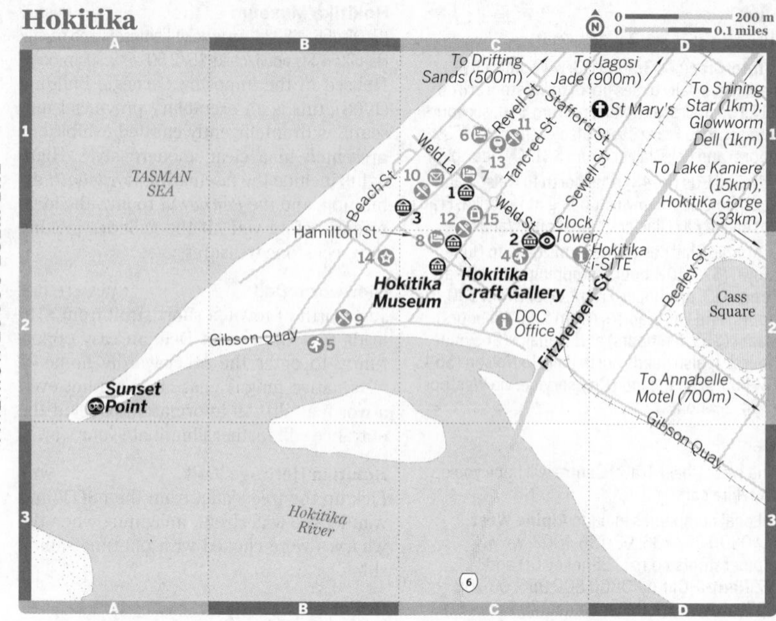

Hokitika

Top Sights
Hokitika Craft Gallery.......C2
Hokitika Museum.......C2
Sunset Point.......A2

Sights
1 Hokitika Glass Studio.......C1
2 Te Waipounamu Maori Heritage Centre.......C2
3 Tectonic Jade.......C1

Activities, Courses & Tours
4 Bonz 'N' Stonz.......C2
5 Hokitika Heritage Walk.......B2

Sleeping
6 Beachfront Hotel.......C1
7 Stumpers.......C1
8 Teichelmann's B&B.......C2

Eating
9 Dulcie's on the Quay.......B2
10 Fat Pipi Pizza.......C1
11 New World.......C1
Stumpers Cafe & Bar.......(see 7)
12 Sweet Alice's Fudge Kitchen.......C1

Drinking
13 West Coast Wine Bar.......C1

Entertainment
14 Crooked Mile Talking Movies.......B2

Shopping
15 Sports World & Hokitika Cycles.......C1

from jade sourced from around the South Island.

Hokitika Glass Studio GALLERY
(www.hokitikaglass.co.nz; 9 Weld St) Glass art and covering a continuum from garish to glorious; watch the blowers at the furnace on weekdays.

Bonz 'N' Stonz CARVING
(www.bonz-n-stonz.co.nz; 27 Sewell St; full-day workshop $75-150) Design, carve and polish your own jade, bone or paua masterpiece, with tutelage from Steve. Prices vary with materials and design complexity. Bookings are recommended.

Tours

Wilderness Wings SCENIC FLIGHTS
(☎0800 755 8118; www.wildernesswings.co.nz; Hokitika Airport; flights $375) Offers 75-minute flights over Hokitika, Aoraki (Mt Cook) and the glaciers.

Festivals & Events

Wildfoods Festival FOOD
(www.wildfoods.co.nz) Held in early March, this festival attracts 20,000 curious and brave gourmands. It's your chance to eat a whole lot of things you would usually either run away from or flick out of your hair. Legendary fun; book early.

Sleeping

Shining Star Beachfront Accommodation HOLIDAY PARK $
(☎0800 744 646, 03-755 8921; www.shiningstar.co.nz; 11 Richards Dr; sites from $30, d $90-169; @) Attractive and versatile beachside spot with everything from camping to classy self-contained seafront units. Kids will love the menagerie, including ducks and alpacas straight from Dr Doolittle's appointment book. Mum and dad might prefer the spa and sauna ($15 for two).

Drifting Sands HOSTEL $
(☎03-755 7654; www.driftingsands.co.nz; 197 Revell St; sites from $15, dm/s/d $29/58/74; @) Access to the beach from the back garden and this hostel's family-home feel make it our pick of Hoki's budget accommodation. The cheery manager and crisp new linen don't hurt either.

Birdsong HOSTEL $
(☎03-755 7179; www.birdsong.co.nz; SH6; dm/s $29/58, d $74-89; @) Located 2.5km north of town, this bird-themed hostel has sea views and a homely atmosphere. Free bikes, handy beach access and hidden extras will entice you into extending your stay.

Stumpers HOTEL $
(☎03-755 6154, 0800 788 673; www.stumpers.co.nz; 2 Weld St; d $70-120; @) Stumpers has a range of rooms above its bustling cafe-bar, including freshly renovated en-suite doubles and simple doubles with shared facilities. Winner of the award for continuous improvement.

Teichelmann's B&B B&B $$$
(☎03-755 8232; www.teichelmanns.co.nz; 20 Hamilton St; d $195-240;) Once home to surgeon, mountaineer and professional beard cultivator Ebenezer Teichelmann, now a charming B&B with amicable hosts. All rooms have en suites, including the more private Teichy's Cottage, situated in the garden oasis out back.

Beachfront Hotel HOTEL $$
(☎0800 400 344, 03-755 8344; www.beachfronthotel.co.nz; 111 Revell St; d $125-330;) This split-personality hotel offers budget rooms in the original wing (where noise from the adjacent pub can be an issue at times), and fancy rooms in the modern Ocean View building with fabulous views from the balconies. The in-house bar is a good spot for a sundowner.

WORTH A TRIP

THE GORGEOUS HOKITIKA GORGE

A picturesque 33km drive leads to **Hokitika Gorge**, a ravishing ravine with turquoise waters. Glacial flour (suspended rock particles) imbues the milky hues. Cross the swing bridge for a couple of short forest walks. To get here, head up Stafford St past the dairy factory and follow the signs.

Kowhitirangi, en route to the gorge, was the scene of a massive 12-day manhunt involving the NZ army in 1941. Unhinged farmer Stanley Graham shot dead four Hokitika policemen, disappeared into the bush then returned to murder three others, before eventually being killed. A grim roadside monument lines up the farmstead site through a stone gun shaft. The 1982 film *Bad Blood* re-enacts the awful incident.

To loop back to Hokitika, take the narrow and winding 10km gravel forest road that skirts **Lake Kaniere**, passing **Dorothy Falls**, **Kahikatea Forest** and **Canoe Cove**. The Hokitika i-SITE has details on these and other local walks, including the **Lake Kaniere Walkway** (3½ hours one way), along the lake's western shore, the historic **Kaniere Water Race Walkway** (3½ hours one way),

Annabelle Motel MOTEL $$
(☎0508 549 494, 03-755 8160; www.annabellemotel.co.nz; 214 Weld St; s $130, d $140-180; 📶) Less than 1km from the Hoki clock tower, pretty Annabelle is away from beach and town action but well located for peace and convenience. Tip-top units, decorated in green garden hues with plush furnishings, meet middle-of-the-road modern standards.

Stations Inn MOTEL $$
(☎0508 782 846, 03-755 5499; www.stations.co.nz; Blue Spur Rd; d $170-250) King-sized beds and spa baths feature in these new units amid rolling hills and rocking alpacas. Next door an ambient restaurant shows off its award-winning relationship with venison, beef and lamb. Follow Hampden St and Hau Hau Rd to Blue Spur Rd.

Awatuna Homestead B&B $$$
(☎0800 006 888, 03-755 6834; www.awatunahomestead.co.nz; 9 Stafford Rd; d incl breakfast $290-370; 📶) Set down on a quiet road 11km north of Hokitika, Awatuna Homestead has three lovely guest rooms and a self-contained apartment. Dinner is available by prior arrangement, and in the evening owners Hemi and Pauline may share fascinating stories of Maori culture and Pacific exploration.

Eating & Drinking

TOP CHOICE **Fat Pipi Pizza** PIZZERIA $$
(89 Revell St; pizzas $19-24; ⏲noon-9pm; 🖉) Vegetarians, carnivores and everyone in between will be salivating for the pizza (including a whitebait version) made with love right before your eyes. Lovely cakes, honey buns and Bengers juices. The beachfront garden bar is shaping up to be the best dining spot in town.

Dulcie's on the Quay FISH & CHIPS $
(cnr Gibson Quay & Revell St; fish & chips $5-10; ⏲lunch & dinner) Net yourself some excellent fush 'n' chups (try the turbot or blue cod), then scoff them straight from the paper at Sunset Point – a Hokitika highlight.

Sweet Alice's Fudge Kitchen SWEETS $
(27 Tancred St) Treat yourself with a slice of Alice's handmade all-natural fudge ($6), or a real fruit ice cream, or a bag of boiled lollies, or maybe all three.

Stumpers Cafe & Bar CAFE, BAR $$
(2 Weld St; lunch $11-21, dinner $18-34; ⏲7am-late) There's something for everyone here, at any time of the day. In the evening you'll find meaty mains, along with a whole host of locals meeting up for a pint and a powwow.

West Coast Wine Bar WINE BAR
(108 Revell St; ⏲11am-4pm Tue-Thu & Sat, 11am-late Fri) Upping Hoki's sophistication factor, this weeny joint with a cute garden bar pours all sorts of deliciousness, and plates up some cheese. Cigars for puffers; fine wines to go.

New World SUPERMARKET
(116 Revell St; ⏲8am-8pm Mon-Fri, 8am-7pm Sat, 9am-7pm Sun) If you're heading south, this is your last proper supermarket before Wanaka, 426 km away!

Entertainment

Crooked Mile Talking Movies CINEMA
(www.crookedmile.co.nz; 36 Revell St; tickets adult/child $12/10) Vintage building, plus old couches, plus organic chocolate and house bar, plus art-house films, equals a perfect night out.

Information

Banks can be found on Weld and Revell Sts.

DOC Office (☎03-756 9100; 10 Sewell St; ⏲8am-4.45pm Mon-Fri) Get basic information from the i-SITE; intrepid adventurers should come to the source.

Hokitika i-SITE (☎03-755 6166; www.hokitika.org; Weld St; ⏲8.30am-6pm Mon-Fri, 9am-5pm Sat & Sun) Extensive bookings including all bus services, car rental agent, DOC information and passes, plus local maps and guides.

Police Station (☎03-756 8310; 50 Sewell St)

Post Office (Revell St)

Westland Medical Centre (☎03-755 8180; 54a Sewell St; ⏲8.30am-10pm)

Getting There & Around

Air

Hokitika Airport (Airport Dr, off Tudor St) is 1.5km east of the centre of town. Air New Zealand (p448) has four flights daily (from $65 one way) to/from Christchurch.

Bus

InterCity (☎03-365 1113; www.intercity.co.nz) buses depart from Tancred St daily for Greymouth (from $14, 45 minutes), Nelson (from $44, seven hours) and Franz Josef Glacier (from $30, two hours).

Atomic Shuttles (☎03-349 0697; www.atomictravel.co.nz) departs i-SITE to Fox Glacier ($36, 3½ hours), Greymouth ($15, one hour) and Queenstown ($70, 10 hours).

WHITEBAIT FEVER

On even the swiftest of visits to the Coast, you are sure to come across a little whitebait or two, whether being sold from the back door of Womble's house, in sandwiches, in museums or in tales tall and true.

These tiny, transparent fish are the young of some of NZ's precious native fish, including inanga, kokopu, smelt and and even eels. Strangely enough, they all look and taste the same, especially once transformed into a fritter.

Commanding up to $80 a kilo round these parts (and much elsewhere), competition is tough to net the elusive fish. The season runs from August to November, when riverbanks and fishing stands are busy from Karamea to Haast.

The classic fritter recipe involves little more than an egg, and is accompanied by a wedge of lemon, although some would say that mint sauce is the best embellishment. The *Whitebait!* exhibition at Hokitika Museum (p463) will give you some idea as to what all the fuss is about.

Naked Bus (www.nakedbus.com) heads north to Greymouth, and south to Queenstown stopping at Franz Josef and Fox Glaciers, Haast and Wanaka.

Car

There are several car-hire branches at Hokitika Airport. **Hokitika Airport Car Rental** (☎0800 556 606; www.hokitikaairportcarhire.co.nz) offers on-line price comparisons, or you could enquire and book at the i-SITE.

Taxi

Try **Hokitika Taxis** (☎03-755 5075).

HOKITIKA TO WESTLAND TAI POUTINI NATIONAL PARK

From Hokitika it's 140km south to Franz Josef Glacier. Most travellers fast forward without stopping, but there are some satisfying stopping points for the inclined. Intercity and Atomic Shuttles stop along this stretch of SH6.

Lake Mahinapua to Okarito

LAKE MAHINAPUA

Eight kilometres south of Hokitika there's a signpost and car park for the **Mahinapua Walkway** (two hours one way), a wonderful walk along an old logging tramway with relics and a diverse range of forest. It's an even better bike ride. Two kilometres further on is the entrance to **Lake Mahinapua Scenic Reserve**, with a picnic area, DOC campsite and several short walks.

ROSS

Ross, 30km south of Hokitika, is where the unearthing of NZ's largest gold nugget, the 2.772kg 'Honourable Roddy', caused a kerfuffle in 1907. The **Ross Goldfields Information Centre** (☎03-755 4077; www.ross.org.nz; 4 Aylmer St; ⏲9am-4pm Dec-Mar, to 3pm Apr-Nov) displays a replica Roddy, along with a scale model ($2) of the town in its shiny years.

The **Water Race Walk** (one hour return) starts near the museum, passing old gold-diggings, caves, tunnels and a cemetery. Try **gold panning** by hiring a pan from the information centre ($10) and head to Jones Creek to look for Roddy's great, great grandnuggets.

The bar at the **Empire Hotel** (19 Aylmer St; meals $15-20) is one of the West Coast's hidden gems – imported directly from a bygone era. It reeks of authenticity, especially when propped up by a few locals. Look out for jam night.

HARI HARI

About 22km south of Lake Ianthe, Hari Hari made headlines in 1931 when swashbuckling Australian aviator Guy Menzies completed the first solo trans-Tasman flight from Sydney. Menzies crash-landed his plane into La Fontaine swamp. Menzies' flight took 11¾ hours, 2½ hours faster than fellow Australian Charles Kingsford Smith's flight in 1928. At the southern end of town is a replica of Menzies' trusty biplane, and there are good photo displays at the Motor Inn.

The **Hari Hari Coastal Walk** (2¾ hours return) is a well-trodden low-tide loop passing the Poerua and Wanganui Rivers. The walk starts 20km from SH6, the last 8km unsealed; follow the signs from Wanganui

Flats Rd. Tide times are posted at the Pukeko Tearooms, which also has decent food and coffee.

Flaxbush Motels (☎03-753 3116; www.flaxbushmotel.co.nz; SH6; d $65-120; wi-fi) has characterful cabins and units covering a wide range of budgets. The owners are certainly animal lovers, with peacocks wandering the grounds and a pet possum that has its own room – in the house. Prices negotiable for extra nights.

The **Hari Hari Motor Inn** (☎0800 833 026, 03-753 3026; hhmi@xtra.co.nz; 42 Main Road; unpowered/powered sites from $12.50/17.50, dm $22.50, d $65-110) has serviceable doubles but doesn't have a shared kitchen for campers or backpackers. The bistro (mains $12 to $28; open noon till late) is Hari Hari's only evening eatery, with pizzas, whitebait sammies, steak, roasts and cold pints of beer.

WHATAROA

Near Whataroa, 35km south of Hari Hari, is the **Kotuku Sanctuary**, NZ's only nesting site for the kotuku (white heron), which roost here between November and February. The herons then fly off individually to reconsider the single life over winter.

White Heron Sanctuary Tours (☎03-753 4120, 0800 523 456; www.whiteherontours.co.nz; SH6; adult/child $120/55; ⏲4 tours daily late Oct-Mar) has the only DOC concession to see the herons. An enjoyable 2½-hour tour involves a gentle jetboat ride and short boardwalk to a viewing hide. Seeing the scores of birds perched in the bushes is a magical experience. A scenic rainforest tour without the herons is available year-round for the same price.

The tour people also run the **Sanctuary Tours Motel** (☎0800 523 456, 03-753 4120; www.whiteherontours.co.nz; SH6; cabins $55-65, d $95-125), with basic cabins with shared facilities ($8 extra for bedlinen), and enthusiastically painted motel units.

Kotuku Gallery (☎03-753 4249; SH6, Whataroa) is chock-full of beautiful Maori bone and pounamu carving. This is a great place to pick up an authentic memento of your visit to Aotearoa.

Glacier Country Scenic Flights (☎0800 423 463, 03-753 4096; www.glacieradventures.co.nz; SH6, Whataroa; flights $175-415) offers a range of scenic flights and heli-hikes, lifting off from Whataroa Valley. These guys give you more mountain-gawping for your buck than many of the operators flying from the glacier townships.

OKARITO

Fifteen kilometres south of Whataroa is the Forks, the turn-off to the tiny seaside hamlet of Okarito, 13km further away on the coast. It sits alongside **Okarito Lagoon**, the largest unmodified wetland in NZ. Okarito has no shops and limited visitor facilities, so stock up and book up before you arrive.

Sights & Activities

From a carpark on the Strand you can begin the easy **Wetland Walk** (25 minutes), or two spectacular longer walks to **Three Mile Lagoon** (three hours return; beach section passable low tide only) and to **Okarito Trig** (1½ hours return). Expect Southern Alps and Okarito Lagoon views.

Andris Apse Wilderness Gallery GALLERY
(☎03-753 4241; www.andrisapse.com; 109 The Strand) Okarito is home to world-class landscape photographer Andris Apse. His precisely composed gallery showcases his beautiful works, printed on site and available to purchase, as are infinitely more affordable books. Ring ahead to check it's open, or look for the sandwich board at the end of the driveway.

Okarito Nature Tours TOURS
(☎0508 652 748, 03-753 4014; www.okarito.co.nz; kayak half-/full day $55/65; wi-fi) Hires out kayaks for paddles into the lagoon and up into the stunning rainforest channels where all sorts of birds hang out. Guided tours are available (from $75), while overnight rentals ($80) allow experienced paddlers to check out deserted North Beach or Lake Windemere. There's excellent espresso and wi-fi in the welcoming office and lounge.

Okarito Boat Tours TOURS
(☎03-753 4223; www.okaritoboattours.co.nz) The lagoon can be explored with Okarito Boat Tours, on morning and afternoon sightseeing tours starting at $45. Bookings are recommended for the nature tour, which departs in the mornings for better wildlife-viewing potential (two hours, $85). Paula and Swade can also fix you up with accommodation in the town

Okarito Kiwi Tours TOURS
(☎03-753 4330; www.okaritokiwitours.co.nz; 2-3hr tours $75) Runs nightly expeditions to spot the rare bird (95% success rate) with a interesting education along the way. Numbers are limited to eight, so booking is recommended

Sleeping

Okarito Campground CAMPSITE
(off Russell St; sites adult/child $10/free) Okarito Campground is a breezy patch of community-managed greenery complete with kitchen and hot showers ($1). Drop your cash in the honesty box and you're sweet as. Gather driftwood from the beach for the fire-pit, or build your bonfire on the beach while the sun goes down.

Old School House GUESTHOUSE
(☎03-752 0796; www.doc.govt.nz; The Strand; house $100) An old 1892 school building is now the DOC-run Old School House, a charming heritage building available for rent (sleeps up to 12).

Okarito Beach House HOSTEL
(☎03-753 4080; www.okaritohostel.com; The Strand; dm $25, d $60-100; wi-fi) The Okarito Beach House has a variety of accommodation. The weathered, self-contained 'Hutel' ($100) is worth every cent. The Summit Lodge has commanding views and the best dining-room table you've ever seen.

WESTLAND TAI POUTINI NATIONAL PARK

Literally the biggest highlights of the Westland Tai Poutini National Park are the Franz Josef and Fox Glaciers. Nowhere else at this latitude do glaciers come so close to the ocean. The glaciers' staggering development is largely due to the West Coast's ample rain. Snow falling in the glaciers' broad accumulation zones fuses into clear ice at 20m depth then surges down the steep valleys.

The rate of descent is mind-blowing: wreckage of a plane that crashed into Franz Josef in 1943, 3.5km from the terminal face, made it down to the bottom 6½ years later – a rate of 1.5m per day. Franz usually advances about 1m per day, but sometimes ramps it up to 5m per day, over 10 times faster than the Swiss Alps' glaciers.

Some say Franz Josef is the superior ice experience, and while it's visually more impressive, the walk to Fox is shorter, more interesting and often gets you closer to the ice. Both glacier faces are roped off to prevent people being caught in icefalls and river surges. The danger is very real – in 2009 two tourists were killed after being hit by falling ice when they ventured too close. Take a guided tour to get close without being too close.

Beyond the glaciers, the park's lower reaches harbour deserted Tasman Sea beaches, rising up through colour-splashed podocarp forests to NZ's highest peaks. Diverse and often unique ecosystems huddle next to each other in interdependent ecological sequence. Seals frolic in the surf as deer sneak through the forests. The resident endangered bird species include kowhiowhio, kakariki (a parrot), kaka and rowi (Okarito brown kiwi), as well as kea, the South Island's native parrot. Kea are inquisitive and endearing, but feeding them threatens their health.

Heavy tourist traffic often swamps the twin towns of Franz and Fox, 23km apart. Franz is the more action-packed of the two, while Fox has a more subdued alpine charm. From December to February, visitor numbers can get a little crazy in both, so consider travelling in the off-season (May to September) for cheaper accommodation.

Franz Josef Glacier

The early Maori knew Franz Josef as Ka Roimata o Hine Hukatere (Tears of the Avalanche Girl). Legend tells of a girl losing her lover who fell from the local peaks, and her flood of tears freezing into the glacier. The glacier was first explored by Europeans in 1865, with Austrian Julius Haast naming it after the Austrian emperor. The glacier is 5km from Franz Josef village; the terminal face is a 40-minute walk from the car park.

Sights & Activities

West Coast Wildlife Centre WILDLIFE
(www.wildkiwi.co.nz; cnr Cron & Cowan Sts; day pass adult/child/family $25/15/75, backstage pass $20/15/60; wi-fi) This feel-good attraction ticks all the right boxes (exhibition, cafe and retail, wi-fi), then goes a whole lot further by actually breeding the rowi – the rarest kiwi in the world. The day-pass is well worthwhile by the time you've viewed the conservation, glacier and heritage displays, and hung out with real, live kiwi in their ferny enclosure. The additional backstage pass into the incubating and chick-rearing area is a rare opportunity to learn how a species can be brought back from the brink of extinction, and a chance to go ga-ga over what may be the cutest babies on the planet.

Franz Josef Glacier & Village

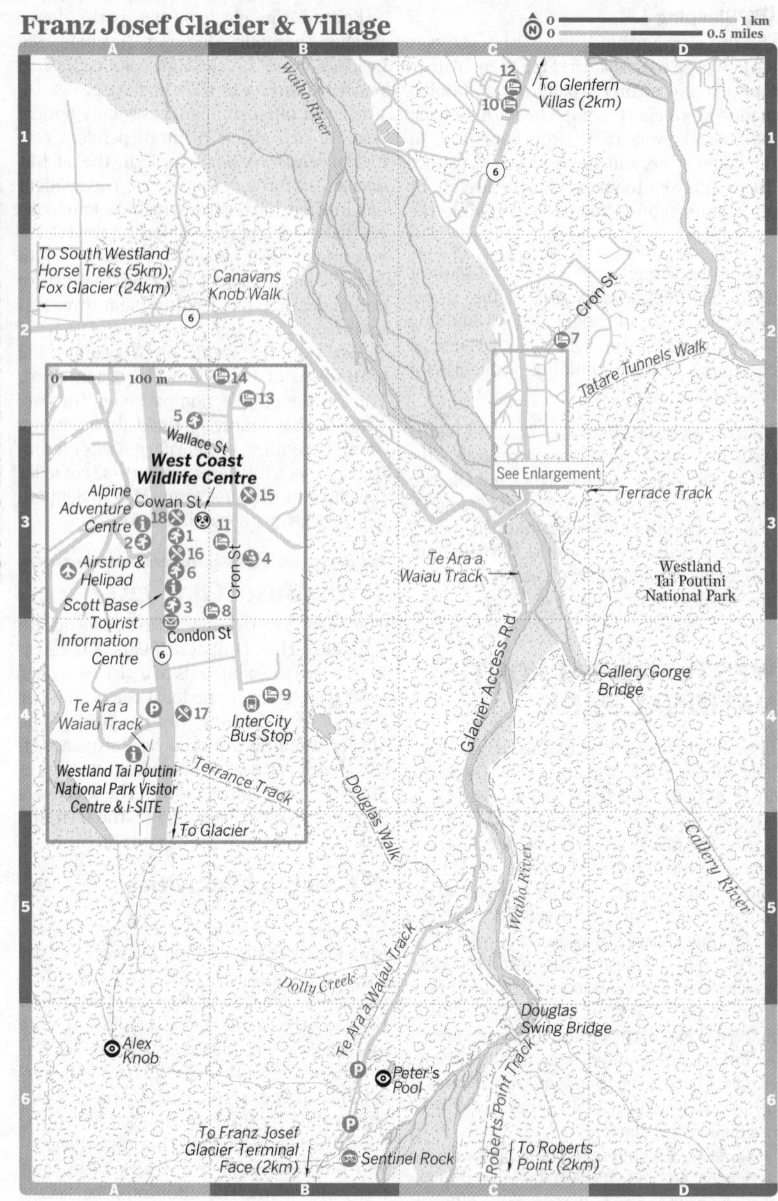

Independent Walks

Courtesy of DOC, the new **Te Ara a Waiau Walkway/Cycleway** provides pleasant rainforest trail access to the glacier car park. Pick up the track at the DOC Visitor Centre. It's an hour each way to walk, 30 minutes maximum to cycle (leave your bikes at the car park – you can't cycle on the glacier walkways). Hire bikes from Across Country Quad Bikes (p472).

Several glacier viewpoints are accessed from the car park, including **Sentinel Rock**

Franz Josef Glacier & Village

Top Sights

West Coast Wildlife Centre........A3

Activities, Courses & Tours

Across Country Quad Bikes.........(see 1)
1 Air Safaris........A3
2 Fox & Franz Josef Heliservices........A3
3 Franz Josef Glacier Guides........A3
4 Glacier Country Tours & Kayaks........B3
5 Glacier Hot Pools........A2
Mountain Helicopters........(see 1)
6 Skydive Franz........A3

Sleeping

7 58 on Cron........C2
8 Alpine Glacier Motel........B3
9 Franz Josef Glacier YHA........B4
10 Franz Josef Top 10 Holiday Park........C1
11 Glow Worm Cottages........B3
12 Holly Homestead........C1
13 Rainforest Retreat........B2
14 Te Waonui Forest Retreat........B2

Eating

15 Alice May........B3
16 Four Square Supermarket........A3
17 Picnics........A4
18 Speights Landing Bar & Restaurant........A3

(20 minutes return) and the **Ka Roimata o Hine Hukatere Walk** (1½ hours return), leading you to the terminal face (read the signs; respect the barriers).

Other longer walks include the **Douglas Walk** (one hour return), off the Glacier Access Rd, which passes moraine from the 1750 advance and Peter's Pool, a small kettle lake. The **Terrace Track** (30 minutes return) is an easy amble over bushy terraces behind the village, with Waiho River views. Two good rainforest walks, **Tatare Tunnels** and **Callery Gorge Walk** (both around 1½ hours return), start from Cowan St.

The rougher **Roberts Point Track** (approximately five hours return) heads off from the Douglas swing bridge (access via the Douglas Walk). The **Alex Knob Track** (eight hours return) runs from the Glacier Access Rd to the 1303m peak of Alex Knob. Look forward to three glacier lookouts and views to the coast (cloud cover permitting). Both **Roberts Point** and Alex Knob are suitable only for well-equipped and experienced trampers.

Check out the glacier in the morning or evening, before the cloud cover sets in or after it lifts. Expect fewer tour buses as well.

Guided Walks & Helihikes

Small group walks with experienced guides (boots, jackets and equipment supplied) are offered by **Franz Josef Glacier Guides** (☎0800 484 337, 03-752 0763; www.franzjosefglacier.com). Half-/full-day walks are $123/180 per adult (slightly cheaper for children). Full-day trips have around six hours on the ice, half-day trips up to two hours. Full-day ice-climbing trips ($256 including training), and three-hour helihikes ($399), which take you further up the glaciers to see more interesting formations and include two hours on the ice, are also available.

Aerial Sightseeing

Forget sandflies and mozzies. The buzzing you're hearing is more likely to be helicopters and planes cruising past the glaciers and Aoraki/Mt Cook. Many flights also include a snow landing. A 20-minute flight to the head of Franz Josef (or Fox Glacier) costs around $200. Flights past both of the glaciers and to Aoraki/Mt Cook cost from $300 to $380. These are adult prices; fares for children under 15 are between 60% and 70% of the adult price. Shop around: most operators are situated on the main road in Franz Josef.

Air Safaris SCENIC FLIGHTS
(☎03-752 0716, 0800 723 274; www.airsafaris.co.nz) Fixed wing.

Fox & Franz Josef Heliservices SCENIC FLIGHTS
(☎03-752 0793, 0800 800 793; www.scenic-flights.co.nz)

Helicopter Line SCENIC FLIGHTS
(☎0800 807 767, 03-752 0767; www.helicopter.co.nz)

Mountain Helicopters SCENIC FLIGHTS
(☎0800 369 432, 03-752 0046; www.mountainhelicopters.co.nz)

Other Activities

TOP CHOICE **Glacier Hot Pools** BATHHOUSE
(www.glacierhotpools.co.nz; 63 Cron St; adult/child $23/16.50; ⏰noon-10pm) Setting a new standard for outdoor hot pools, this complex has been skillfully built within dense rainforest.

GLACIERS FOR DUMMIES

During the last ice age (15,000 to 20,000 years ago) the Franz Josef and Fox Glaciers reached the sea; in the ensuing thaw they may have crawled back further than their current positions. In the 14th century a mini ice age descended and for centuries the glaciers advanced, reaching their greatest extent around 1750. The terminal moraines from this time are still visible. Since then the West Coast's twin glaciers have both ebbed and advanced on a cyclic basis.

If you get rained in during your time in glacier country, here are a few glacier-geek conversation starters for the pub.

Ablation zone – where the glacier melts.

Accumulation zone – where the snow collects.

Bergschrund – a large *crevasse* in the ice near the glacier's starting point.

Blue ice – as the accumulation zone *(névé)* snow is compressed by subsequent snowfalls, it becomes *firn* and then *blue ice.*

Crevasse – a crack in the glacial ice formed as it crosses obstacles while descending.

Dead ice – isolated chunks of ice left behind when a glacier retreats.

Firn – partly compressed snow en route to becoming *blue ice.*

Glacial flour – finely ground rock particles in the milky rivers flowing off glaciers.

Icefall – when a glacier descends so steeply that the upper ice breaks into ice blocks.

Kettle lake – a lake formed by the melt of an area of isolated *dead ice.*

Moraine – walls of debris formed at the glacier's sides (lateral moraine) or end (terminal moraine).

Névé – snowfield area where *firn* is formed.

Seracs – ice pinnacles formed, like *crevasses,* by the glacier rolling over obstacles.

Terminal – the final ice face at the bottom of the glacier.

Perfect après-hike or on a rainy day. Enjoy the communal pools, or private ones ($42 per 45 minutes) and massages ($85 per half-hour) if you want to really indulge.

Skydive Franz SKYDIVING
(☎0800 458 677, 03-752 0714; www.skydivefranz.co.nz; Main Rd) Claiming NZ's highest jump (18,000ft, 75 seconds freefall, $549), this company also offers 15,000 for $399, and 12,000 for $299. With Aoraki/Mt Cook in your sights, this could be the most scenic jump you ever do.

Glacier Country Tours & Kayaks KAYAKING
(☎03-752 0230, 0800 423 262; www.glacierkayaks.com; 20 Cron St; 3hr tours $95) Take a guided kayak trip on Lake Mapourika (7km north of Franz), and get ecological commentary, mountain views and a serene channel detour. The family deal (from $210) is suitable for the whole crew, with mornings generally offering better conditions. You can also hire kayaks ($60 for 2½ hours).

Eco-Rafting RAFTING
(☎0508 669 675, 03-755 4254; www.ecorafting.co.nz; 6hr trip $450) Rafting adventures throughout the coast, including the six-hour 'Grand Canyon' trip on the Whataroa River with its towering granite walls. Includes a 15-minute helicopter ride.

South Westland Horse Treks HORSE RIDING
(☎0800 187 357, 03-752 0223; www.horsetreknz.com; Waiho Flats Rd; 2h trek $99) Located 5km south of town, this trekking company runs one- to six-hour equine excursions across farmland and remote beaches.

Glacier Valley Eco Tours GUIDED TOUR
(☎0800 999 739; www.glaciervalley.co.nz) Offers leisurely three- to eight-hour walks around local sights ($70 to $160), packed with local knowledge.

Across Country Quad Bikes QUAD BIKING
(☎0800 234 288, 03-752 0123; www.acrosscountryquadbikes.co.nz; Air Safaris Bldg, SH6) Four-wheeled outings, rockin' and rollin' through

the rainforest (two hours, rider/passenger $160/70). A heliquad option ($435, 2½ hours) traverses the mountains and coastline by air before taking on a remote West Coast beach. Mountain bike hire available (half-/full day $25/40).

Sleeping

Franz Josef Top 10 Holiday Park HOLIDAY PARK $
(☎03-752 0735, 0800 467 897; www.franzjoseftop10.co.nz; 2902 Franz Josef Hwy; sites from $40, d $65-165; @📶) This spacious holiday park, 1.5km from the township, has tip-top facilities and more sleeping options than you can shake a stick at. Tenters are well catered for with their own attractive, free-draining grassy area at the back of the park.

Glow Worm Cottages HOSTEL $
(☎03-752 0172, 0800 151 027; www.glowwormcottages.co.nz; 27 Cron St; dm $24-26, d $65-100; @📶) Relax at this quiet haven with homely communal areas and a nice nod to local history in the bedrooms. If you are back by 6pm, there's free vegie soup on offer. If the rain settles in, chill out in the spa or with a good DVD.

Te Waonui Forest Retreat HOTEL $$$
(☎0800 696 963, 03-752 0555; www.tewaonui.co.nz; 3 Wallace St; s/d $620/795; @📶) The damp, earthy surrounds and unflashy exterior of Franz's fancy new hotel hide the fact that inside is porter service, degustation dinners (included, along with breakfast, in the price) and a snazzy bar. The interior is dark – there's definitely a rainforest feel to the place – but you'll sleep like a log in the luxurious beds, and appreciate the modern styled rooms, all natural tones textured in wood and stone.

58 on Cron MOTEL $$
(☎0800 662 766, 03-752 0627; www.58oncron.co.nz; 58 Cron St; d $175-245; 📶) No prizes for the name, but these newish units impress with refreshed furnishings and all mod cons. A smart, clean, consistent performer.

Rainforest Retreat LODGE $
(☎0800 873 346, 03-752 0220; www.rainforestretreat.co.nz; 46 Cron St; sites from $19.50, dm $27-29, d $85-215; @📶) This large complex has something for everyone, from slightly unruly dorms to quieter double units, a handful of cottages and tree houses sleeping up to seven. Campervans can park up in leafy nooks. The on-site Monsoon Bar (motto: 'It rains, we pour') may be enjoyed by the young 'uns.

Franz Josef Glacier YHA HOSTEL $
(☎03-752 0754; www.yha.co.nz; 2-4 Cron St; dm $27-32, s $57, d $83-120; @📶) A large, tidy and colourful place with over 100 beds, and warm, spacious communal areas. There are family rooms available, a free sauna (keep your bathers on, please) and the rainforest at the back door.

Alpine Glacier Motel MOTEL $$
(☎03-752 0226, 0800 757 111; www.alpineglaciermotel.com; 14 Cron St; d $135-230; 📶) Standard motel offerings in the middle of the township. Two units have spas, and most have cooking facilities. Opt for the newer, more stylish units.

Glenfern Villas APARTMENT $$$
(☎03-752 0054, 0800 453 633; www.glenfern.co.nz; SH6; d $210-266; 📶) A handy 3km out of the tourist hubbub, these delightful one- and two-bedroom villas sit amid nikau palms and have top-notch beds, full kitchens, and private decks with views. This is the sort of place that says 'holiday', not 'stop-off'.

Holly Homestead B&B $$$
(☎03-752 0299; www.hollyhomestead.co.nz; SH6; d $265-430; @📶) Guests are welcomed with fresh home baking at this wisteria-draped 1926 B&B. Choose from three character ensuite rooms and a suite, all of which share a deck perfect for that sun-downer. Children over 12 welcome.

Eating & Drinking

Alice May MODERN NZ $$
(cnr Cowan & Cron Sts; mains $18-33; ⏲4pm-late) Resembling an old staging post, this sweet dining room serves up meaty, home-style meals like pork ribs and venison casserole. Park yourself outside and enjoy mountain views and bar snacks during happy hour (4pm to 7pm).

Picnics BAKERY $
(SH6; snacks $2-10; ⏲7am-5pm) Follow your nose (and the stream of foot traffic) to this fantastic little bakery. Heaps of good-value ready-to-scoff baked goods, including epic pasties suitable for bagging for a picnic lunch, or heating up later at dinner time.

Speights Landing Bar & Restaurant PUB $$
(SH6; mains $19-39; ⌚7.30am-late) A slighty frenzied but well-run pub serving up mega-portions of crowd-pleasing food; think big burgers, steaks and pizzas. The patio – complete with heaters and umbrellas – is a good place to unwind after a day on the ice.

Four Square Supermarket SUPERMARKET $
(SH6; ⌚7.45am-9.30pm) Mr Four Square comes to the party, big time.

Information

There's internet at Glacier Country Tours & Kayaks (p472) and Scott Base Tourist Information Centre (p474), and an ATM on the main street – if travelling south this is the last one you will see until Wanaka. The postal agency is located at the Mobil service station.

Alpine Adventure Centre (☎03-752 0793, 0800 800 793; www.scenic-flights.co.nz; SH6) Books activities and screens the 20-minute *Flowing West* movie (adult/child $12/6) on a giant screen. Shame about the '80s soundtrack.

Franz Josef Health Centre (☎03-752 0700, after hours 027 464 1192; 97 Cron St; ⌚8.30am-4pm Mon-Fri) South Westland's main medical centre.

Scott Base Tourist Information Centre (☎03-752 0288; SH6; 9am-9pm; @📶) Internet, Atomic agent, and bookings.

Westland Tai Poutini National Park Visitor Centre & i-SITE (☎03-752 0796; www.glaciercountry.co.nz; SH6; ⌚8.30am-6pm Oct-Apr, to 5pm May-Sept) Regional DOC office with good exhibits, weather information and track updates.

Getting There & Around

Buses leave from outside the Four Square supermarket.

InterCity (☎03-365 1113; www.intercity.co.nz) has daily buses south to Fox Glacier (from $10, 35 minutes) and Queenstown (from $62, eight hours); and north to Nelson (from $56, 10 hours). Book at the DOC Visitor Centre or YHA.

Atomic Shuttles (☎03-349 0697; www.atomictravel.co.nz) has services Sunday to Thursday south to Queenstown ($50, 6½ hours) via Fox Glacier ($15, 35 minutes), and north to Greymouth ($30, four hours). Book at the Scott Base Tourist Information Centre.

Glacier Valley Eco Tours (☎03-752 0699, 0800 999 739; www.glaciervalley.co.nz) runs scheduled shuttle services to the glacier car park (return trip $12.50).

Naked Bus (www.nakedbus.com) runs north to Hokitika, Greymouth and Nelson, and south to Fox Glacier.

Fox Glacier

Fox is smaller and quieter than Franz Josef, with a farmy feel and more open aspect. Lake Matheson is a highlight, as is the beach and historic walk down at Gillespies Beach.

Sights & Activities

Glacier Valley Walks

It's 1.5km from Fox Village to the glacier turn-off, and a further 2km to the car park. Thanks to DOC you can now reach the car park under your own steam via the new **Te Weheka Walkway/Cycleway**, a pleasant rainforest trail starting just south of the Bella Vista motel. It's just over an hour each way to walk, or 30 minutes to cycle (leave your bikes at the car park – you can't cycle on the glacier walkways). Hire bikes from Westhaven (p476).

From the car park, the terminal face is 30 to 40 minutes' walk. How close you can get to it depends on conditions. Obey all signs: this place is dangerously dynamic.

Short walks near the glacier include the **Moraine Walk** (over a major 18th-century advance) and **Minnehaha Walk**. The **River Walk** extends to the **Chalet Lookout Track** (1½ hours return) leading to a glacier lookout. The fully accessible **River Walk Lookout Track** (20 minutes return) starts from the Glacier View Road car park and allows people of all abilities the chance to view the glacier.

Fox Glacier Guiding WALKS
(☎03-751 0825, 0800 111 600; www.foxguides.co.nz; 44 Main Rd) Guided walks (equipment provided) are organised by Fox Glacier Guiding. Half-day walks cost $115/95 per adult/child; full-day walks are $165 (over-13s only). Helihikes cost $399 per person, while a day-long introductory ice-climbing course costs $275 per adult. There are also easy-going two-hour interpretive walks to the glacier (adult/child $49/35). Longer guided heli-hike adventures are also available.

Skydiving & Aerial Sightseeing

With Fox Glacier's backdrop of Southern Alps, rainforest and ocean, it's hard to imagine a better place to jump out of a plane. Aerial sightseeing costs at Fox

Fox Glacier & Village

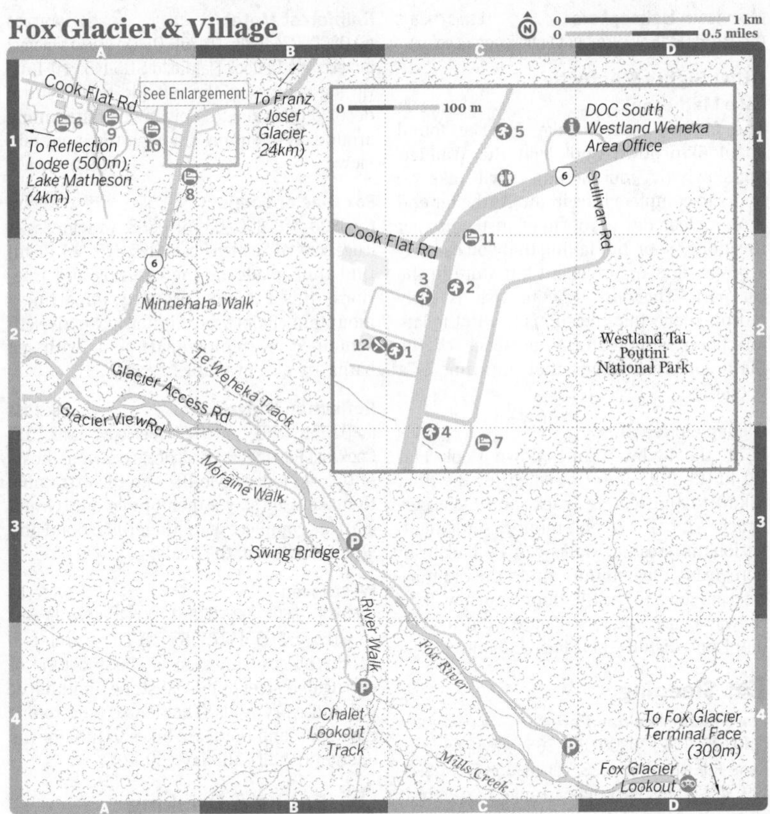

parallel those at Franz Josef. All four operators can be found on SH6 in Fox Glacier Village.

Skydive Glacier Country SKYDIVING
(☎03-751 0080, 0800 751 0080; www.skydivingnz.co.nz; Fox Glacier Airfield, SH6) This professional outfit challenges Isaac Newton, with thrilling leaps from 16,000ft ($399) or 12,000ft ($299).

Fox & Franz Josef Heliservices SCENIC FLIGHTS
(☎03-751 0866, 0800 800 793; www.scenic-flights.co.nz)

Glacier Helicopters SCENIC FLIGHTS
(☎0800 800 732, 03-751 0803; www.glacierhelicopters.co.nz)
See p471.

Helicopter Line SCENIC FLIGHTS
(☎0800 807 767, 03-752 0767; www.helicopter.co.nz)

Fox Glacier & Village

Activities, Courses & Tours

Fox & Franz Josef Heliservices....(see 1)
1 Fox Glacier Guiding....C2
2 Glacier Helicopters....C2
3 Helicopter Line....C2
4 Mountain Helicopters....C3
5 Skydive Glacier Country....C1

Sleeping

6 Fox Glacier Holiday Park....A1
7 Fox Glacier Inn....C3
8 Fox Glacier Lodge....A1
9 Lake Matheson Motels....A1
10 Rainforest Motel....A1
11 Westhaven....C2

Eating

12 Hobnail Café....B2
Plateau Café & Bar....(see 4)

Mountain Helicopters SCENIC FLIGHTS
(☎03-751 0045; www.mountainhelicopters.co.nz)

Other Sights & Activities

Lake Matheson LAKE
The famous 'mirror lake' can be found about 6km down Cook Flat Rd. Wandering slowly (as you should), it will take 1½ hours to complete the circuit. At the far end – on a clear day – you may, just *may*, get the money shot, but failing that you can buy a postcard at the excellent gift store in the car park. The best time to visit is early morning, or when the sun is low in the late afternoon, although the presence of the Matheson Café means that any time is a good time.

Gillespies Beach BEACH
From the highway, turn down Cook Flat Rd for its full 21km (unsealed for the final 12km) to the remote black-sand Gillespies Beach, site of an old mining settlement. Various interesting walks can be had from here, from a five-minute zip to the old miners' cemetery, to the 3½ hour return walk to Galway Beach where seals are wont to haul out. Don't disturb their lazing about.

Sleeping

Fox Glacier Holiday Park HOLIDAY PARK $
(☎03-751 0821, 0800 154 366; www.fghp.co.nz; Kerrs Rd; sites from $38, cabins $58-60, d $94-199; @📶) This park has a range of different sleeping options to suit all budgets. Renovations, including a swanky facilities block, playground and barbecues, have improved what was already a good choice.

Fox Glacier Inn HOSTEL $
(☎03-751 0022; www.foxglacierinn.co.nz; 39 Sullivan Rd; dm $23-27, d $60-90; @📶) Hard-working managers have transformed this backpackers from hellhole to haven. Improvements include female-only 'sanctuary rooms' and bright new linen. Bar/restaurant and information centre on-site.

Lake Matheson Motels MOTEL $$
(☎0800 452 2437, 03-751 0830; www.lakematheson.co.nz; cnr Cook Flat Rd & Pekanga Dr; d $135-145, q $190; 📶) From the outside this place looks pretty ordinary, but inside the rooms come into their own. The owners have continued to pour profits back into the property, where you'll find ultra-tidy rooms with up-market amenities that contradict the mid-range price.

Rainforest Motel MOTEL $$
(☎0800 724 636, 03-751 0140; www.rainforestmotel.co.nz; 15 Cook Flat Rd; d $115-145; 📶) Rustic log cabins on the outside with neutral decor on the inside. Epic lawns for running around on or simply enjoying the mountain views.

Fox Glacier Lodge B&B $$$
(☎0800 369 800, 03-751 0888; www.foxglacierlodge.com; 41 Sullivan Rd; d $195-225; 📶) Beautiful timber adorns the exterior and interior of this attractive property, imparting a mountain chalet vibe. Similarly woody self-contained mezzanine apartments with spa baths are also available.

Reflection Lodge B&B $$$
(☎03-751 0707; www.reflectionlodge.co.nz; 137 Cook Flat Rd; d $210; 📶) The gregarious hosts of this ski-lodge style B&B go the extra mile to make your stay a memorable one. Grand gardens complete with Monet-like pond and alpine views seal the deal.

Westhaven MOTEL $$
(☎0800 369 452, 03-751 0084; www.thewesthaven.co.nz; SH6; d $125-185; 📶) These architecturally precise suites are a classy combo of corrugated steel and local stone amid burnt red and ivory walls. The deluxe king rooms have spas, and there are bikes to hire for the energetic (half-/full day $20/40).

Eating & Drinking

TOP CHOICE **Matheson Café** MODERN NZ $$
(www.lakematheson.com; Lake Matheson Rd; breakfast & lunch $9-19, dinner $24-36; ⏲7.30am-late Nov-Mar, 8am-4pm Apr-Oct) Near the shores of Lake Matheson, this cafe does everything right: slick interior design, inspiring mountain views, strong coffee and upmarket Kiwi fare. Get your sketchpad out and while away the afternoon. Next door is the ReflectioNZ Gallery stocking quality, primarily NZ-made art and souvenirs.

Plateau Café & Bar CAFE $$
(cnr Sullivan Rd & SH6; lunch $10-23, dinner $22-33; ⏲noon-late) Buzzy and sophisticated (for the West Coast anyway), Plateau combines snappy service with rustic faves like lamb burgers, Akaroa salmon and decent veggie creations. If the sun is shining, you can chill out on the wisteria-covered deck with a Kiwi craft beer or glass of wine.

Hobnail Café CAFE $

(44 Main Rd; meals $11-19; ⏲7.30am-3pm) Cabinets full of high-quality stodge including mightily stuffed jacket potatoes, pastries, panini, biscuits and cake. Hearty breakfasts such as bubble and squeak fuel folk headed for the ice. Located in the same building as Fox Glacier Guiding.

ℹ Information

At the time of research there were plans afoot to build a Four Square supermarket on the corner of SH6 and Frames Road; here you should find an ATM. The BP petrol station is the last fuel stop until Haast, 120km south. Get online at the Internet Outpost, beside the Helicopter Line office.

DOC South Westland Weheka Area Office (☎03-751 0807; SH6; ⏲9am-noon & 1-4.30pm Mon-Fri) This is no longer a general visitor information centre, but has the usual DOC information, hut tickets and weather and track updates.

Fox Glacier Guiding (☎0800 111 600, 03-751 0825; www.foxguides.co.nz; 44 Main Rd) Books Atomic Shuttles, and provides postal and currency exchange services.

Fox Glacier Health Centre (☎03-751 0836, after hours 027 464 1193; SH6) Staffed most mornings from 9am to noon; doctor available on Tuesdays. Call the clinic for the latest hours.

ℹ Getting There & Around

Most buses stop outside the Fox Glacier Guiding building.

InterCity (☎03-365 1113; www.intercity.co.nz) runs two buses a day north to Franz Josef (from $10, 40 minutes), the morning bus continuing to Nelson (from $57, 11 hours). Daily southbound services run to Queenstown (from $58, 7½ hours).

Atomic Shuttles (☎03-349 0697; www.atomictravel.co.nz) runs daily to Franz Josef ($15, 30 minutes), continuing to Greymouth (from $35, 3¼ hours). Southbound buses run daily to Queenstown ($45, 6½ hours).

Fox Glacier Shuttles & Tours (☎0800 369 287) will drive you around the immediate surrounds such as Lake Matheson, Gillespies Beach, the glaciers or beyond (from $10 return).

Naked Bus (www.nakedbus.com) runs north to Franz Josef Glacier, Hokitika, Greymouth, Westport and Nelson, and south to Queenstown, stopping at Haast and Wanaka.

SOUTH TO HAAST

About 26km south of Fox Glacier, along SH6, is the **Copland Valley** trailhead, the western end of the **Copland Track**. Earn one of the best pay-offs of any walk in Aotearoa by tramping six to seven hours to the **Welcome Flat DOC Hut** (adult/child $15/7.50) where thermal springs bubble just metres from the hut door. Backcountry Hut Passes don't apply here, but you can buy tickets online or at any West Coast DOC office or visitor information centres.

Popular with Haast–Fox cyclists and Copland Track trampers, the **Pine Grove Motel** (☎03-751 0898; SH6; sites $25, d $50-90) is 8km south of the trailhead. Units are affordable and in reasonable shape, and the owners offer secure parking.

Lake Moeraki, 31km north of Haast, is a rippling fishing lake. An easy 40-minute walk from here brings you to **Monro Beach**, a gravel beach copping the full Tasman Sea force. There's a breeding colony of Fiordland crested penguins here (July to December) and fur seals. **Wilderness Lodge Lake Moeraki** (☎03-750 0881; www.wildernesslodge.co.nz; SH6; d incl breakfast & dinner $640-1000) is ecofriendly accommodation in a vibrant wilderness setting. The comfortable rooms and four-course dinners are lovely, but the real treats here are the outdoor activities, including nature tours guided by people with conservation in their blood.

About 5km south of Lake Moeraki is the much-photographed **Knights Point** (named after a surveyor's dog) where the Haast road was eventually opened in 1965. Stop here if humanly possible.

Ship Creek, 15km north of Haast, has a lookout platform and two interesting interpretive walks: the **Dune Lake Walk** (30 minutes return) and the **Kahikatea Swamp Forest Walk** (20 minutes return).

If you haven't had your fill of whitebait yet, call into the **Curly Tree Whitebait Company** (☎03-750 0097), 5km north of Haast at the Waita River bridge. Exemplary whitebait patties for $7, plus bait to go at the market price.

HAAST REGION

The Haast region is a major wilderness area. The area's kahikatea and rata forests, wetlands, sand dunes, seal and penguin

WORTH A TRIP

JACKSON BAY ROAD

From Haast Junction, the road most travelled is SH6, upwards or across. But there is another option, and that is south... to the end of the line.

The road to Jackson Bay is quiet and intensely scenic. Towered over by Southern Alps, the farms on the flat and the settlements dotted between them stand testament to some of the hardiest souls who ever attempted settlement in NZ. Until the 1950s, the only way to reach Haast overland was via bush tracks from Hokitika and Wanaka. Supplies came in by a coastal shipping service that called in every couple of months or so.

Besides the ghosts and former glories, which make an appearance here and there, there's plenty to warrant a foray down to Jackson Bay.

Near Okuru is the **Hapuka Estuary Walk** (20 minutes return), a winding boardwalk that loops through a sleepy wildlife sanctuary with good interpretation panels en route.

The road continues west to **Arawhata Bridge**, where a turn-off leads to the **Ellery Creek Walkway**, 3.5km away. This pleasant amble through mossy beech forest (1½ hours return) leads to **Ellery Lake**, where a picnic bench encourages lunch with perhaps a skinny dip for afters.

It's less than an hour's drive from Haast town to the fishing hamlet of **Jackson Bay**, the only natural harbour on the West Coast. Migrants arrived here in 1875 under a doomed settlement scheme, their farming and timber-milling aspirations mercilessly shattered by never-ending rain and the lack of a wharf, not built until 1938. Those families who stayed turned their hands to largely subsistence living.

With good timing you will arrive when the **Cray Pot** (☎03-750 0035; fish & chips $17-29; ⊙11am-8pm Nov-Mar) is open. This place is just as much about the dining room (a caravan) and location (looking out over the bay) as it is about the honest seafood, including a good feed of fish and chips, crayfish, chowder and whitebait.

Walk off your fries on the **Wharekai Te Kou Walk** (40 minutes return) to Ocean Beach, a tiny bay that hosts pounding waves and some interesting rock formations.

colonies, bird life and sweeping beaches ensued its inclusion in the Southwest New Zealand (Te Wahipounamu) World Heritage Area.

Haast & Jackson Bay

Some 120km south of Fox Glacier, Haast crouches around the mouth of the wide Haast River in three distinct pockets: Haast Junction, Haast Village and Haast Beach. While certainly a handy stop for filling the tank and tummy, it's also the gateway to some spectacular scenery, and the end of the line at Jackson Bay.

Activities

Haast River Safari JETBOATING

(☎0800 865 382, 03-750 0101; www.haastriver.co.nz; Haast Village; adult/child $132/55; ⊙trips 9am, 11am & 2pm) Based in the Red Barn between Haast Village and the visitor information centre, these folks runs leisurely 90-minute covered-jetboat cruises on the Haast River.

Waiatoto River Safaris JETBOATING

(☎03-750 0780; www.riversafaris.co.nz; Jackson Bay Rd; adult/child $139/59; ⊙trips 10am, 1pm & 4pm) Take a hair-tousling 2½-hour 'sea to mountain' jetboat trip on the wild Waiatoto River, 30km south of Haast.

Sleeping

Haast Beach Holiday Park HOLIDAY PARK $

(☎03-750 0860, 0800 843 226; www.haastbeachholidaypark.co.nz; 1348 Jackson Bay Rd, Haast Beach; sites from $28, dm $25, d $45-110) New managers are working hard to improve this old but pleasant holiday park with a variety of accommodation options. It's a 20-minute walk from an epic West Coast beach and about 14km south of the Haast Junction. The Hapuka Estuary Walk is across the road.

Haast River Top 10 HOLIDAY PARK $

(☎0800 624 847, 03-750 0020; www.haasttop10.co.nz; SH6, Haast Village; sites from $25, dm $30, s $60, d $90-130, q $130-170; @☎) New holiday park with top-notch amenities including a bright-red, open-plan shed housing facilities for campers and great communal areas in the converted lodge. Motel units are light, spacious and enjoy great views when the weather's kind.

Haast Lodge LODGE **$**
(☎0800 500 703, 03-750 0703; www.haastlodge.com; Marks Rd, Haast Village; sites from $16, dm/d $25/65, units d $95-120; @) Covering all bases, Haast Lodge offers well-maintained, clean lodgings from dorms and doubles complete with an excellent communal area, to motel units at the Aspring Court next door. Powered bays for campervans.

Collyer House B&B **$$$**
(☎03-750 0022; www.collyerhouse.co.nz; Cuttance Rd, Haast Village; r from $220; @) This gem of a B&B has thick bathrobes, quality linen, beach views and a sparkling host who cooks a terrific breakfast. This all adds up to make Collyer House an indulgent and comfortable choice. Follow the signs off SH6 for 12km down Jackson Bay Rd.

Eating & Drinking

Hard Antler PUB **$$**
(Marks Rd, Haast Village; dinner $20-30; ⏲dining 11am-9pm) This expanding array of deer antlers is enough to give you the horn. So is the fine home cooking (meat all ways) and welcoming attitude of this big, bold pub.

Okoto Espresso CAFE **$**
(Haast Village; snacks $2-10) Look out for the rusty hut being towed by the orange Landrover. Where you find it you'll encounter Robyn and her excellent coffee, whitebait fritters, smoothies, biscotti and pancakes.

Information

The **DOC Haast Visitor Information Centre** (☎03-750 0809; www.haastnz.com; cnr SH6 & Jackson Bay Rd; ⏲9am-6pm Nov-Mar, to 4.30pm Apr-Oct) has wall-to-wall regional information and screens the all-too-brief Haast landscape film *Edge of Wilderness* (adult/child $3/free).

Getting There & Away

InterCity (☎03-365 1113; www.intercity.co.nz) and **Atomic Shuttles** (☎03-349 0697; www.atomictravel.co.nz) buses stop at the visitor information centre on their Fox to Wanaka runs.

Naked Bus (www.nakedbus.com) runs north to the glaciers, Hokitika, Greymouth and Nelson, and south to Queenstown, stopping at Wanaka.

Haast Pass Highway

Turning inland from Haast towards Wanaka (145km, 2½ hours), SH6 snakes alongside the Haast River, climbing up to Haast Pass and Mt Aspiring National Park. As you move inland the vegetation thins away until you reach the 563m pass – snow country covered in tussock and scrub. There are some stunning waterfalls en route (especially if it's been raining), tumbling down just minutes from the highway: **Fantail** and **Thunder Creek** falls are worth a look. There's also the **Bridle Track** (1½ hours one-way) between the pass and Davis Flat. See the DOC booklet *Walks along the Haast Highway* ($2).

The Haast Pass road (Tioripatea, meaning 'Clear Path' in Maori) opened in 1965; before then Maori walked this route bringing West Coast greenstone to the Makarora River in Otago. The pass (and river and township) take their European name from geologist Julius Haast, who passed through in 1863.

There are food and fuel stops at Makarora and Lake Hawea. If you're driving north, check your fuel gauge: Haast petrol station is the last one before Fox Glacier, 120km north.

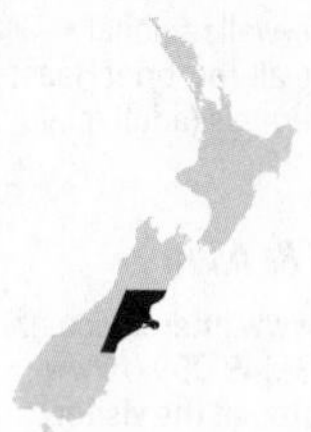

Christchurch & Canterbury

Includes »

Christchurch 482
Lyttelton 502
Akaroa & Banks Peninsula 503
Hanmer Springs 510
Lewis Pass Hwy 513
Craigieburn Forest Park 514
Arthur's Pass 515
Methven 516
Mt Somers 518
Timaru 518
Inland & Mackenzie Country 521
Aoraki/Mt Cook National Park 528

Best Places to Eat

» Bodhi Tree (p495)
» Simo's Deli (p497)
» Christchurch Farmers Market (p498)
» Almeidas Tapas Bar (p496)
» The Little Bistro (p509)

Best Places to Stay

» Orari B&B (p492)
» Le Petit Hotel (p496)
» Coombe Farm (p508)
» Okuti Garden (p508)

Why Go?

Nowhere in New Zealand is changing and developing as fast as post-earthquake Christchurch, and visiting the country's second largest city as it's being rebuilt and reborn is both interesting and inspiring.

A short drive from Christchurch's dynamic re-emergence, Banks Peninsula conceals hidden bays and beaches – a backdrop for kayaking and wildlife cruises with a sunset return to the attractions of Akaroa. To the north are the vineyards of the Waipara Valley and the family-holiday ambience of Hanmer Springs. Westwards, the well-ordered farms of the Canterbury Plains morph quickly into the rough-and-tumble wilderness of the Southern Alps.

Canterbury summertime attractions include tramping along the braided rivers and alpine valleys around Arthur's Pass and mountain biking around the turquoise lakes of the Mackenzie Country. During winter, the attention switches to the mountains, with skiing at Mt Hutt. Throughout the seasons, Aoraki/Mt Cook, the country's tallest peak, stands sentinel over this diverse region.

When to Go

Overall Canterbury is one of NZ's driest regions because moisture-laden westerlies from the Tasman Sea dump their rainfall on the West Coast before hitting the eastern South Island. Head to Christchurch and Canterbury from January to March for settled summer weather and plenty of opportunities to get active amid the region's spectacular landscapes. It's also festival time in Christchurch with January's World Buskers Festival and the Ellerslie International Flower Show in March. Hit the winter slopes from July to October at Mt Hutt or on Canterbury's smaller club ski fields.

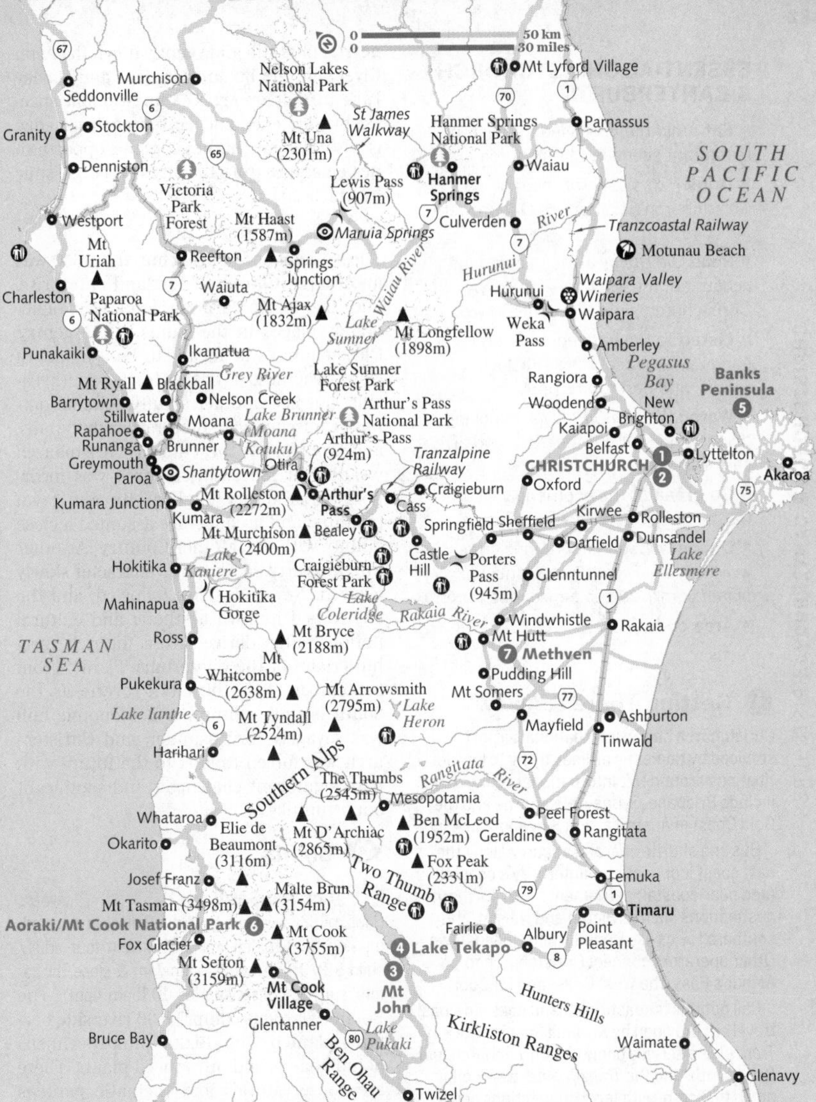

Christchurch & Canterbury Highlights

1. Supporting the exciting rebuilding and re-emergence of **Christchurch** (p482)
2. Meandering along Christchurch's **Avon River** (p487) by punt or bicycle
3. Marvelling at the views of the Mackenzie Country from atop **Mt John** (p524)
4. Taking a soothing soak at Lake Tekapo's **Alpine Springs & Spa** (p524)
5. Negotiating the outer reaches of **Banks Peninsula** (p503) by bike, kayak or boat
6. Tramping in the shadow of NZ's highest peak in **Aoraki/ Mt Cook National Park** (p528)
7. Being surprised by the size of the Canterbury Plains on a balloon flight from **Methven** (p516)

ESSENTIAL CHRISTCHURCH & CANTERBURY

» **Eat** Amid the emerging Addington restaurant scene in Christchurch

» **Drink** NZ's best craft beer at Christchurch's Pomeroy's Old Brewery Inn (p498)

» **Read** *Old Bucky & Me*, a poignant account of the 2011 earthquake by Christchurch journalist Jane Bowron

» **Listen** To the best up-and-coming bands at Christchurch's Dux Live (p499) and darkroom (p499)

» **Watch** *When a City Falls*, a moving documentary about the 2010 and 2011 earthquakes

» **Go green** At the ecofriendly Okuti Garden (p508) on Banks Peninsula

» **Online** www.christchurchnz.com, www.mtcooknz.com; www.lonelyplanet.com/new-zealand/christchurch

» **Area code** ☎03

ℹ Getting There & Away

Christchurch has an international airport serviced by domestic airlines flying to key destinations around NZ. International connections include Brisbane, Sydney, Melbourne and the Gold Coast in Australia, and Singapore in Asia.

Bus and shuttle operators scurry along the east coast, connecting Canterbury's coastal (and near-coastal) settlements with northern destinations such as Picton and Nelson, and southern towns like Dunedin and Queenstown. Other operators connect Christchurch to Arthur's Pass, the West Coast and Mt Cook.

Rail options for east-coast and coast-to-coast travel are provided by KiwiRail Scenic. The *TranzAlpine* service connects Christchurch and Greymouth, and the *TranzCoastal* trains chug north to Picton, with ferry connections across Cook Strait to the North Island.

CHRISTCHURCH

POP 380,900

Welcome to a vibrant city in transition, coping resiliently and creatively with the aftermath of NZ's second-biggest natural disaster (especially as tremors can still be felt regularly). Traditionally the most English of NZ cities, Christchurch is now adding a modern and innovative layer to its damaged heritage heart. Punts still glide gently down the Avon River, and the Botanic Gardens and Hagley Park are still among NZ's finest public spaces, but an energetic entrepreneurial edge is also evident, harnessing the opportunities emerging from the city's recent seismic heartache.

History

The settlement of Christchurch in 1850 was an ordered Church of England enterprise, and the fertile farming land was deliberately placed in the hands of the gentry. Christchurch was meant to be a model of class-structured England in the South Pacific, not just another scruffy colonial outpost. Churches were built rather than pubs, and wool made the elite of Christchurch wealthy. In 1862, Christchurch was incorporated as a very English city, and town planning and architecture assumed a close affinity with the 'Mother Country'. As other migrants arrived, the city's character slowly evolved. New industries followed, and the city forged its own aesthetic and cultural notions, often derived from the rich rural hinterland of the Canterbury Plains. From September 2010, the city's reverie as the South Island's cultural and economic hub was savagely torn asunder, and Christchurch was forced to look to the future with both significant challenges and significant opportunities.

Sights

Botanic Gardens GARDENS

(Map p488; www.ccc.govt.nz; Rolleston Ave; admission free, guided walks $10, train tour adult/child $18/9; ⏲grounds open 7am & close 1hr before sunset, conservatories 10.15am-4pm) The Botanic Gardens comprise 30 riverside hectares planted with 10,000-plus specimens of indigenous and introduced plants. There are conservatories and thematic gardens to explore, lawns to sprawl on, and a cafe at the **Botanic Gardens visitors centre** (Map p488; ⏲pam-4pm Mon-Fri, 10.15-4pm Sat & Sun). Get the kids active in the playground adjacent to the cafe. Guided walks ($10) depart daily at 1.30pm (September to April) from the Canterbury Museum, or you can ride around the gardens in the electric **Caterpillar train** (www.gardentour.co.nz; hop on/hop-off tickets adult/child $18/9; ⏲10am-4pm). Tickets are valid for two days and include a commentary.

Canterbury Museum MUSEUM

(Map p488; ☎03-366 5000; www.canterburymuseum.com; Rolleston Ave; admission by donation; ⏰9am-5pm Apr-Sep, to 5.30pm Oct-Mar) The absorbing Canterbury Museum has a wonderful collection of items of significance to NZ. Highlights include the Maori gallery, with some stunning *pounamu* (greenstone) pieces on display; the coracle in the Antarctic Hall that was used by a group shipwrecked on Disappointment Island in 1907; and a wide array of stuffed birds from the Pacific and beyond: don't miss the statuesque Emperor penguin. Guided tours (donations appreciated) run from 3.30pm to 4.30pm on Tuesday and Thursday. Kids will enjoy the interactive displays in the Discovery Centre (admission $2). Don't miss the gloriously kitsch Kiwiana of Fred & Myrtle's Paua Shell House.

Arts Centre HISTORIC SITE

(Map p488; www.artscentre.org.nz; 2 Worcester St; admission free) This precinct is currently closed, pending strengthening and repairs estimated to cost $240 million. An enclave of Gothic Revival buildings (built from 1877), it was the original site of Canterbury College, which later became Canterbury University. One graduate of the college was Sir Ernest Rutherford, the NZ-born physicist who first split the atom in 1917. Before the earthquakes, the Arts Centre was a popular cultural precinct comprising artists' studios and galleries, weekend craft markets, restaurants and cinemas. One business still operating from a modern building within the Arts Centre is the excellent Canterbury Cheesemongers (p498).

Cathedral Square SQUARE

(Map p488; ☎03-366 0046; www.christchurchcathedral.co.nz; admission free; ⏰8.30am-7pm Oct-Mar, 9am-5pm Apr-Sep) Christchurch's historic hub is Cathedral Square. At the time of research the square was in the heart of the city's cordoned-off CBD (Central Business District), but was planned to be reopened sometime from mid-2012. See the CBD Red Zone Cordon Map (www.cera.govt.nz) for the latest information.

At the centre of the square is (or was) ChristChurch Cathedral, originally constructed in 1881, and a much-loved icon of the city. The February 2011 earthquake caused devastating damage, bringing down the Gothic church's 63m-high spire and leaving only the bottom half of the tower remaining. It was feared up to 20 people had been in the spire when it collapsed, but it was later found that no one had died at the site. Subsequent earthquakes in June 2011 and December 2011 destroyed the cathedral's prized stained-glass rose window, and the cathedral was deconsecrated in October 2011.

The deconstruction and demolition of the cathedral was announced in March 2012 by the Anglican Diocese of Christchurch,

MAORI NZ: CHRISTCHURCH & CANTERBURY

Only 5% of NZ's Maori live on the South Island. The south was settled a few hundred years later than the north, with significant numbers coming south only after land became scarcer on the North Island. Before that, Maori mostly travelled to the south in search of moa, fish and West Coast *pounamu* (greenstone).

The major *iwi* (tribe) of the South Island is **Ngai Tahu** (www.ngaitahu.iwi.nz), ironically now one of the country's wealthiest as it's much richer in land and natural resources (per person) than the North Island tribes. In Christchurch, as in other cities, there are urban Maori of many other *iwi* as well.

Ko Tane at the Willowbank Wildlife Reserve (p486) features traditional dancing, including the *haka* and the *poi* dance. Future plans at Willowbank include the establishment of a replica Maori village.

If you're feeling creative, the Bone Dude (p490), John Fraser, teaches visitors to do their own bone carving at his studio in Christchurch.

You'll unearth Maori artefacts at Christchurch's Canterbury Museum (p483), and at Akaroa Museum (p504) and Maori & Colonial Museum (p504) in Okains Bay on the Banks Peninsula.

Further south in Timaru, the Te Ana Maori Rock Art Centre (p518) presents the fascinating story of NZ's indigenous rock art, and also arranges tours to see the centuries-old work in situ.

Greater Christchurch

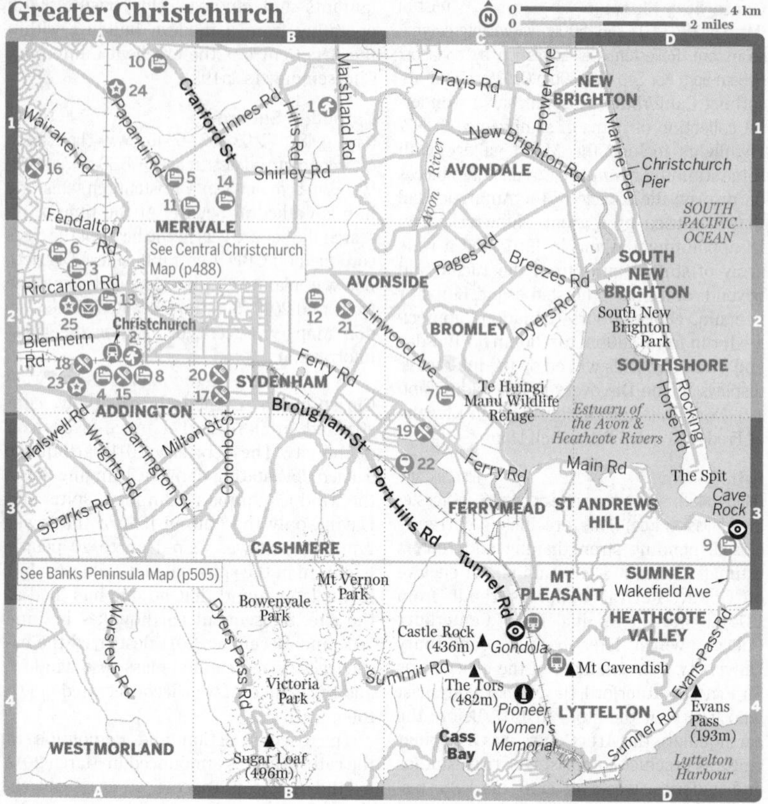

but at the time of research there remained significant public opposition to this decision. See www.christchurchcathedral.co.nz for the latest information. The draft plan to rebuild Christchurch recommends that Cathedral Square be transformed into a park. In April 2012, plans were announced to build a 'cardboard cathedral' designed by Japanese architect Shigeru Ban. Located on the corner of Madras and Hereford Sts near Latimer Square, the $5 million construction would seat 700 worshippers and is planned to open in December 2012. The cathedral will become the temporary centre for Christchurch's Anglican St John's parish, and will also be used for concerts and art exhibitions.

Other heritage buildings around Cathedral Square were also badly damaged, but one modern landmark left unscathed is the 18m-high metal sculpture *Chalice*, designed by Neil Dawson. It was erected in 2001 to commemorate the new millennium.

International Antarctic Centre WILDLIFE
(☎03-353 7798, 0508 736 4846; www.iceberg.co.nz; 38 Orchard Rd, Christchurch Airport; adult/child/family from $35/20/95; ⏰9am-5.30pm)
The International Antarctic Centre is part of a huge complex built for the administration of the NZ, US and Italian Antarctic programs. See penguins and learn about the icy continent via historical, geological and zoological exhibits. There's also an aquarium of creatures gathered under the ice in McMurdo Sound. Other attractions include a '4D' theatrette – a 3D film plus moving seats and a watery spray – and the Antarctic Storm chamber, where you can get a first-hand taste of -18°C wind chill. An Extreme Pass (adult/child/family $65/35/165) includes unlimited rides on the Hägglund outdoor adventure course. An optional extra is the Penguin Backstage Pass (adult/child/family $25/15/80), which takes visitors behind the scenes of the Penguin Encounter. Transport

Greater Christchurch

Activities, Courses & Tours
1 Bone Dude B1
2 Turners Auctions A2

Sleeping
3 Anslem House A2
4 Arena Motel A2
5 Elm Tree House A1
6 Fendalton House A2
7 Haka Lodge C2
8 Jailhouse A2
9 Le Petit Hotel D3
10 Meadow Park Top 10 Holiday Park A1
11 Merivale Manor A1
12 Old Countryhouse B2
13 Roma on Riccarton A2
Sumner Bay Motel and Apartments ..... (see 9)
14 Wish B1

Eating
15 Addington Coffee Co-op A2
Almeidas Tapas Bar ..... (see 9)
Bamboozle ..... (see 9)
16 Bodhi Tree A1
17 Burgers & Beers Inc B2
Christchurch Farmers Market ..... (see 3)
Cornershop Bistro ..... (see 9)
18 Edesia A2
19 Holy Smoke C3
20 Honey Pot Cafe B2
Serious Sandwich ..... (see 17)
Simo's Deli ..... (see 15)
21 Under the Red Verandah B2

Drinking
22 The Brewery C3
Volstead Trading Company ..... (see 13)
Wood's Mill ..... (see 15)

Entertainment
23 Christchurch Stadium A2
24 Club 22 ..... A1
Court Theatre ..... (see 15)
Hollywood 3 ..... (see 9)
25 Hoyts Riccarton A2

Shopping
Backpackers Car Market ..... (see 20)
Sunday Artisan Market ..... (see 3)
Westfield Riccarton Mall ..... (see 25)

options include the City Flyer (p502) airport bus (it's just a short walk from the main terminal) or the free Penguin Express shuttle that departs from outside the Canterbury Museum.

FREE Christchurch Art Gallery GALLERY
(Map p488; www.christchurchartgallery.org.nz; cnr Worcester & Montreal Sts; 10am-5pm Thu-Tue, to 9pm Wed) Set in an eye-catching metal-and-glass construction built in 2003, the city's art gallery – closed at the time of writing, with a definite reopening being planned – has an engrossing permanent collection divided into historical, 20th-century and contemporary galleries, plus temporary exhibitions featuring NZ artists. Before the gallery closed following the earthquakes, free guided tours were offered at 11am Monday to Sunday, plus 2pm Saturday and Sunday and 7.15pm Wednesday. Check the website for the latest information about gallery reopenings. The gallery's shop is currently open.

Tramway TRAM
(03-366 7830; www.tram.co.nz) Prior to the February 2011 earthquake, historic trams operated on a 2.5km inner-city loop, taking in local attractions and shopping areas. At the time of writing the tramway was not operating because the city's CBD was closed. Check the website for an update.

Orana Wildlife Park WILDLIFE RESERVE
(www.oranawildlifepark.co.nz; McLeans Island Rd, Papanui; adult/child $25/8; 10am-5pm) Orana has an excellent, walk-through native-bird aviary, a nocturnal kiwi house and a reptile exhibit featuring the wrinkly tuatara. Most of the grounds are devoted to Africana, including lions, rhinos, giraffes, zebras, lemurs, oryx and cheetahs. Guided walks start at 10.40am daily, taking in feeding time for the Sumatra tigers; the 2.30pm departure visits the lion enclosure. Check the website for feeding times and other optional Orana experiences for more personal interactions with some of the animals. Phone 03-379 1699 for shuttle transport to Orana.

THE CHRISTCHURCH EARTHQUAKES

Christchurch's seismic nightmare began at 4.35am on 4 September 2010. Centered 40km west of the city, a 40-second, 7.1-magnitude earthquake jolted Cantabrians from their sleep, and caused widespread damage to older buildings in the central city. Close to the quake's epicentre in rural Darfield, huge gashes erupted amid grassy pastures, and the South Island's main railway line was bent and buckled. Because the tremor struck in the early hours of the morning, when most people were home in bed, there were no fatalities, and many Christchurch residents felt the city had dodged a bullet.

Fast forward to 12.51pm on 22 February 2011, when central Christchurch was busy with shoppers and office and retail workers enjoying their lunch break. This time the 6.3-magnitude quake was much closer, centred just 10km southeast of the city and only 5km deep. The tremor was significantly more extreme, and many locals report being flung violently and almost vertically into the air. The peak ground acceleration (PGA) exceeded 1.8, almost twice the acceleration of gravity.

When the dust settled after 24 traumatic seconds, NZ's second-largest city had changed forever. The towering spire of the iconic ChristChurch Cathedral lay in ruins; walls and verandahs had cascaded down on the city's central retail hub; and two multi-storey buildings had pancaked, causing scores of deaths. Around half of the 185 deaths (including 20 nationalities) occurred in the Canterbury TV building, where many international students at a language school were killed. Elsewhere in the city, the historic port town of Lyttelton was badly damaged; roads and bridges were crumpled; and residential suburbs in the east were inundated as a process of rapid liquefaction saw tonnes of oozy silt rise from the ground

After 22 February, the resilience and bravery of Cantabrians quickly became evident. From the region's rural heartland, the 'Farmy Army' descended on the city, armed with shovels and food hampers. Social media mobilised 10,000 students, and the Student Volunteer Army became a vital force for residential clean-ups in the city's beleaguered eastern suburbs. Heartfelt aid and support arrived from among NZ's close-knit population of just 4.4 million, and seven other nations sent specialised urban-search-and-rescue teams.

At the time of writing, the city's population was still bravely getting on with their lives, besieged by thousands of aftershocks, including significant jolts in June 2011 and December 2011. Most tremors, however, have been small and there have been no fatalities or injuries since February 2011. The earthquake activity is reported to be moving further east into the Pacific Ocean, and peak ground acceleration is decreasing.

The impact of a warm summer's day in early 2011 will take longer than a generation to resolve. Around a quarter of the buildings within the city's famed four avenues need to be demolished. Entire streets and family neighbourhoods in the eastern suburbs will be abandoned, and Christchurch's heritage architecture is irrevocably damaged. The cost to repair and rebuild the city could exceed NZ$30 billion, making it history's third most costly natural disaster.

In December 2011, the influential United States magazine *Foreign Policy* nominated Christchurch one of the urban centres of the 21st century, opining that the 'massive rebuilding effort is a unique opportunity to rethink urban form'. Draft plans for the city's rebuilding over 20 years include a compact, low-rise city centre, neighbourhood green spaces, and parks and cycleways along the Avon River. Coupled with the endurance and energy of the people of Christchurch, the city's future promises to be both interesting and innovative.

Willowbank Wildlife Reserve WILDLIFE RESERVE
(www.willowbank.co.nz; 60 Hussey Rd, Northwood; adult/child/family $25/10/65; ⌚9.30am-dusk) About 6km north of the city, Willowbank focuses on native NZ animals and hands-on enclosures with alpacas, wallabies and deer. Tours are held several times a day, and the after-dark tours are a good opportunity to see a kiwi. Phone ☎*03-359 6226* or ask at the Christchurch i-SITE about free shuttle transport to Willowbank.

Gondola CABLE CAR
(www.gondola.co.nz; 10 Bridle Path Rd; return adult/child/family $24/10/59; ⌚10am-9pm) At the time

of writing, this attraction was closed but was planned to reopen by September 2012. Check the website for the latest information.

Activities

Christchurch's most popular activities are gentler than the adrenaline-fuelled pursuits of Queenstown and Wanaka: the city is better suited to punting down the Avon River, cycling through the easy terrain of Hagley Park or negotiating the walking trails at Lyttelton Harbour. The closest **beaches** to the city are Waimairi, North Beach, New Brighton and South Brighton; buses 5, 49 and 60 head here. Sumner, to the city's southeast, is another popular beach, with good restaurants (take bus 3), while further east at Taylors Mistake are some good **surfing** breaks. Several **skiing** areas lie within a two-hour drive of Christchurch. Other active options accessible from Christchurch include cruising on Akaroa Harbour, rafting on the Rangitata River, tandem skydiving, hot-air ballooning, jetboating the Waimakariri River and horse trekking. Inquire at the Christchuch i-SITE (p501).

Walking

The i-SITE has information on walks around Christchurch and in the Port Hills. Some popular walks were closed at the time of writing due to rock falls and instability following the earthquakes, so it's vital to check the current situation at the i-SITE before setting off. Also search www.ccc.govt.nz with the keywords 'Port Hills' for the current status of the following tracks.

For great views of the city, take the walkway from the Sign of the Takahe on Dyers Pass Rd. The various 'Sign of the...' places in this area were originally roadhouses built during the Depression as rest stops. This walk leads up to the Sign of the Kiwi through Victoria Park and then along Summit Rd to Scotts Reserve, with several lookout points along the way.

You can walk to Lyttelton on the Bridle Path (1½ hours), which starts at Heathcote Valley (take bus 28). The Godley Head Walkway (two hours return) begins at Taylors Mistake, crossing and recrossing Summit Rd, and offers beautiful views on a clear day.

The Crater Rim Walkway (nine hours) around Lyttelton Harbour goes some 20km from Evans Pass to the Ahuriri Scenic Reserve. From the gondola terminal on Mt Cavendish, walk to Cavendish Bluff Lookout (30 minutes return) or the Pioneer Women's Memorial (one hour return).

Cycling

City Cycle Hire BICYCLE RENTAL

(☎0800 424 534; www.cyclehire-tours.co.nz; bike half/full day $25/35, mountain bike half/full day $30/45) Mountain bikes will get you nicely off-road: before the earthquakes, a mountain-bike ride from the top of the gondola was on offer (check the website for the latest updates). Bikes can be delivered to where you're staying.

Natural High BICYCLE RENTAL

(☎03-982 2966, 0800 444 144; www.naturalhigh.co.nz; 690a Harewood Rd, Harewood; per day/week from $40/154) Rents touring and mountain bikes, and can advise on guided and

CHRISTCHURCH IN...

Two Days

After breakfast at the Addington Coffee Co-op (p496), amble back to the city through leafy South Hagley Park. Stop at the Antigua Boatsheds (p490) for punting on the Avon, and put together your own informal lunch at Canterbury Cheesemongers (p498) in the Arts Centre. After lunch, explore the excellent Canterbury Museum (p483) before heading to meet the locals over NZ craft beers and great pub food at Pomeroy's Old Brewery Inn (p498).

On day two, explore Hagley Park on a vintage bike courtesy of Vintage Peddler Bike Hire Co (p490), or walk through the lovely Botanic Gardens (p482), perhaps picking up some goodies from Vic's Cafe & Bakery (p497) or Simo's Deli (p497) for a riverside picnic. In the evening, jump on a bus to hit the excellent restaurants at Lyttelton or Sumner.

Four Days

Follow the two-day itinerary, then head to Akaroa to explore its wildlife-rich harbour and the peninsula's beautiful outer bays. On day four it's time for shopping in the funky Re:START (p500) precinct before chilling at the International Antarctic Centre (p484) or enjoying a traditional Maori feast at Willowbank Wildlife Reserve (p486).

Central Christchurch

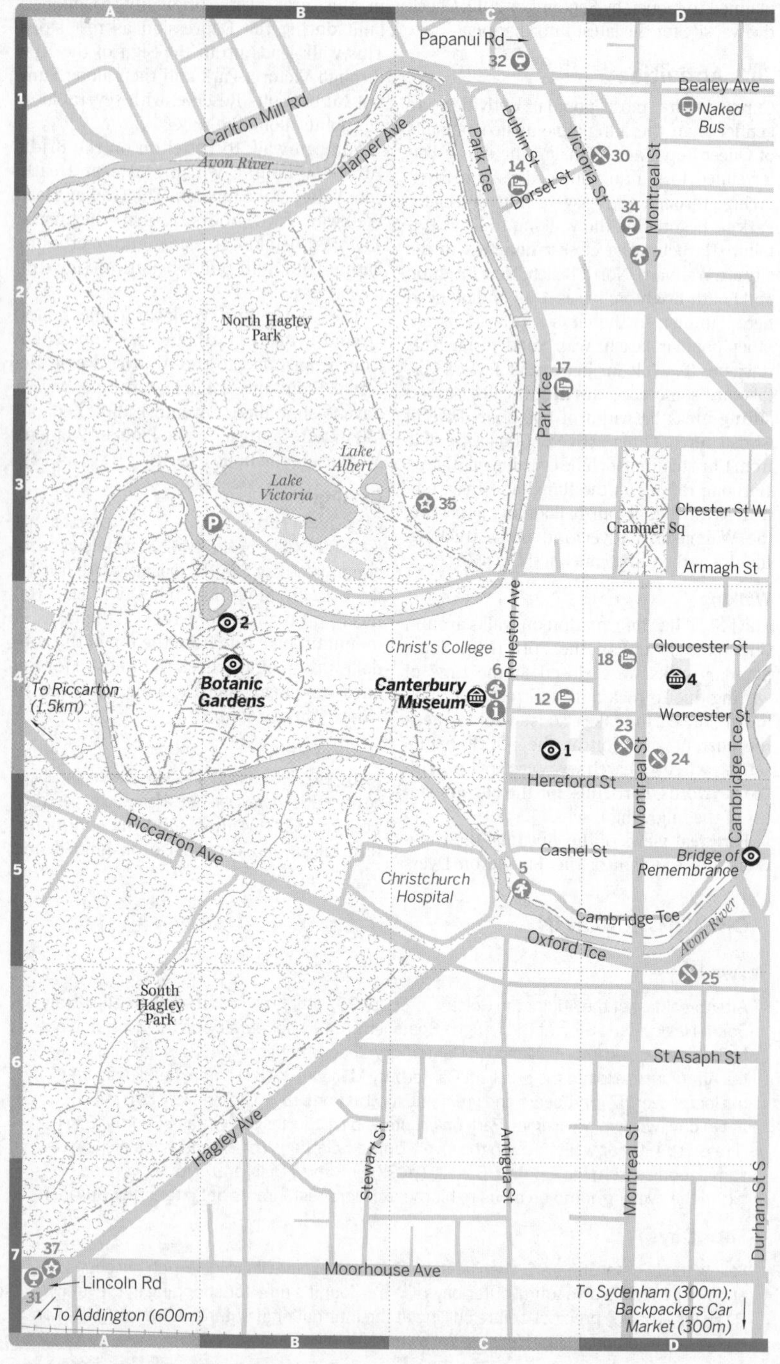

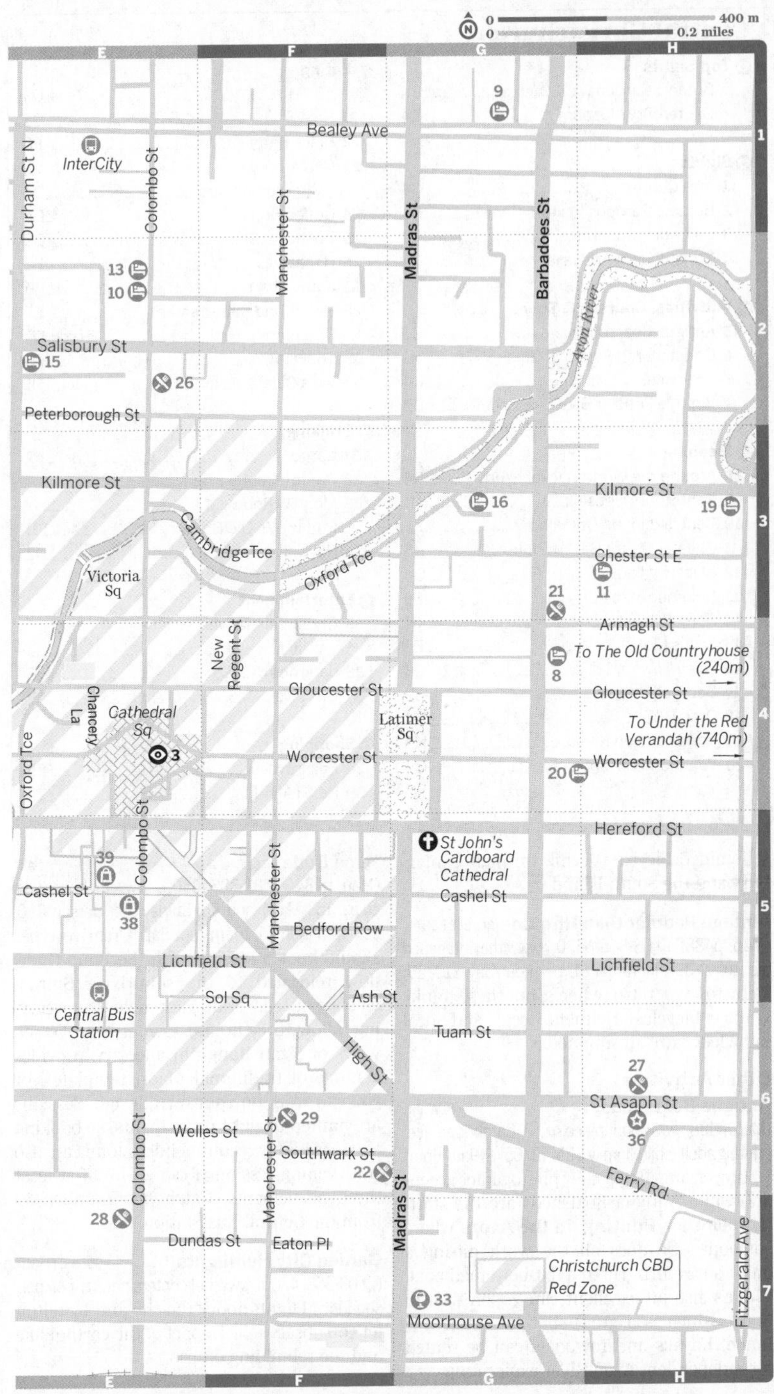
0 400 m
0 0.2 miles
E
F
G
H
1
2
3
4
5
6
7
Bealey Ave
InterCity
Durham St N
Colombo St
Manchester St
Madras St
Barbadoes St
Avon River
9
13
10
Salisbury St
15
26
Peterborough St
Kilmore St
16
Kilmore St
19
Cambridge Tce
Oxford Tce
Chester St E
11
Victoria Sq
21
Armagh St
New Regent St
8
To The Old Countryhouse (240m)
Gloucester St
Gloucester St
Chancery La
Cathedral Sq
Latimer Sq
To Under the Red Verandah (740m)
3
Worcester St
Worcester St
20
Oxford Tce
Hereford St
St John's Cardboard Cathedral
39
Colombo St
Manchester St
Cashel St
Cashel St
38
Bedford Row
Lichfield St
Lichfield St
Sol Sq
Ash St
Central Bus Station
Tuam St
High St
27
St Asaph St
36
29
Welles St
Southwark St
22
Colombo St
Manchester St
Madras St
Ferry Rd
28
Dundas St
Eaton Pl
Fitzgerald Ave
Christchurch CBD Red Zone
33
Moorhouse Ave
E
F
G
H

Central Christchurch

Top Sights
- Botanic Gardens B4
- Canterbury Museum C4

Sights
- 1 Arts Centre C4
- 2 Botanic Gardens Visitors Centre B4
- 3 Cathedral Square E4
- 4 Christchurch Art Gallery D4

Activities, Courses & Tours
- 5 Antigua Boatsheds C5
- 6 Christchurch Personal Guiding Service C4
- 7 Vintage Peddler Bike Hire Co D2

Sleeping
- 8 Around the World Backpackers G4
- 9 Canterbury House G1
- 10 CentrePoint on Colombo E2
- 11 Chester Street Backpackers H3
- 12 Classic Villa C4
- 13 Colombo in the City E2
- 14 Dorset House C1
- 15 Focus Motel E2
- 16 Foley Towers G3
- 17 George C2
- 18 Orari B&B D4
- 19 Pomeroy's on Kilmore H3
- 20 Vagabond Backpackers G4

Eating
- 50 Bistro .... (see 17)
- 21 Beat St G3
- 22 Black Betty F6
- 23 Canterbury Cheesemongers D4
- 24 Coffee House D4
- 25 Dose D6
- 26 Himalayas E2
- 27 Lotus Heart H6
- 28 New World Supermarket E7
- Pescatore .... (see 17)
- 29 Topkapi F6
- 30 Vic's Cafe & Bakery D1

Drinking
- 31 Cargo A7
- 32 Carlton Country Club C1
- 33 Monday Room G7
- Pomeroy's Old Brewery Inn .... (see 19)
- 34 Revival D2

Entertainment
- 35 Christchurch Events Village C3
- 36 darkroom H6
- 37 Dux Live A7

Shopping
- 38 Ballantynes E5
- 39 Re:START Mall E5

self-guided bicycle touring through Canterbury and the South Island.

Vintage Peddler Bike Hire Co BICYCLE RENTAL
(Map p488; ☎03-365-6530; www.thevintagepeddler.co.nz; 399 Montreal St; per hour/day $10/25) Take to two retro wheels on these funky vintage bicycles. Helmets, locks and local knowledge are all supplied.

Other Activities

Antigua Boatsheds BOATING
(Map p488; www.punting.co.nz; 2 Cambridge Tce; punting adult/child/family $25/12/65; 9am-6pm) Dating from 1882, the photogenic green-and-white Antigua Boatsheds are the starting point for **Punting on the Avon**, where someone else does all the work during a half-hour return trip in a flat-bottomed boat. There's also an excellent cafe (open 7am to 5pm), which is a great spot for brunch or lunch. Kayaks and rowboats can be rented for independent Avon River exploration.

Bone Dude ART
(Map p484; ☎03-385 4509; www.thebonedude.co.nz; 153 Marshland Rd, Shirley; per person $60; 1-4pm Mon-Fri, 10am-1pm Sat) Creative types should book a session with the Bone Dude, now relocated to the suburb of Shirley, where you can craft your own bone carving (allow three hours). Owner John Fraser, who's of Ngati Rangitihi ancestry, provides a range of traditional Maori templates, or you can work on your own design. Sessions are limited to eight participants, so booking ahead is highly recommended. John can also run evening sessions for a group of at least three participants. Catch bus number 60 from the Central Bus Station.

Garden City Heliflights SCENIC FLIGHT
(☎03-358 4360; www.helicopters.net.nz; per person $145) Flights above the city and Lyttelton let you observe the impact of the earthquake and the rebuilding efforts.

Tours

Ask at the i-SITE about city tours and excursions to Lyttelton, Akaroa, Arthur's Pass, Hanmer Springs and the Waipara Valley.

Canterbury Leisure Tours GUIDED TOUR
(☎03-384 0999, 0800 484 485; www.leisuretours.co.nz; tours from $60) Touring options in and around Christchurch, with everything from three-hour city tours to full-day outings to Akaroa, Mt Cook, Arthur's Pass and Kaikoura.

Canterbury Wine Tours WINE TASTING
(☎0800 081 155; www.waiparavalley.co.nz; tours from $90) Experience three Waipara vineyards on the half-day trip, or make a day of it and sample four different wineries with lunch ($125).

Christchurch Bike Tours GUIDED TOUR
(☎0800 733 257; www.chchbiketours.co.nz; tours from $40; ⊙departs 2pm) Informative, two-hour tours loop around the city along quiet cycleways and leafy park tracks. Also available is a gourmet food tour and a Saturday morning foodie spin that takes in the Christchurch Farmers Market. Prior booking is essential. Tours leave from the Antigua Boatsheds (p490).

Christchurch Personal Guiding Service WALKING TOUR
(Map p488; ☎03-379 9629; tours $15; ⊙11am & 1pm Oct-Apr, 1pm May-Sep) Nonprofit organisation offering informative two-hour city walks. Buy tickets and join tours at the i-SITE departure point.

Christchurch Sightseeing Tours GUIDED TOUR
(☎03-366 9660, 0508 669 660; www.christchurchtours.co.nz; tours from $75) City tours, plus further-afield detours to Akaroa, Hanmer Springs and the Waipara wine region.

Discovery Tours GUIDED TOUR
(☎0800 372 879; www.discoverytravel.co.nz; tours from $130) Excursions to Akaroa, Hanmer Springs, Kakoura and the Waipara Valley wine region. The Alpine Safari option (adult/child $375/276) packs the *TranzAlpine*, jetboating and a spin in a 4WD into one action-packed day.

Hassle Free Tours GUIDED TOUR
(☎0800 141 146; www.hasslefree.co.nz; tours from $29) Explore Christchurch on an open-top, bright-red double-decker bus. Regional options include a 4WD alpine safari, jetboating on the Waimakariri River, and visiting the location of Edoras from the *Lord of the Rings* trilogy. Combo deals with the International Antarctic Centre (p484) are also available.

Hiking Guys TRAMPING
(☎09-281 4481; www.hikingguys.co.nz; adult/child $395/198) Day trips incorporating the *Tranz Alpine* train and tramping around Arthur's Pass.

Welcome Aboard GUIDED TOUR
(☎0800 242 486; www.welcomeaboard.co.nz; adult/child $79/49) The operators of the gondola and tramway operate this comprehensive tour taking in punting on the Avon River, the Botanic Gardens, Sumner and the Re:START container mall.

Festivals & Events

Check www.bethere.co.nz for a comprehensive listing of festivals and events.

CHRISTCHURCH FOR CHILDREN

There's no shortage of kid-friendly sights and activities in Christchurch. If family fun is a priority, consider planning your travels around NZ's biggest children's festival, **KidsFest** (www.kidsfest.org.nz). It's held every July and is chock-full of shows, workshops and parties. The annual World Buskers Festival (p492) is also bound to be a hit.

For picnics and open-air frolicking, visit the Botanic Gardens (p482); there's a playground beside the cafe, and the kids will love riding on the Caterpillar train. Extend your nature-based experience with a wildlife encounter at the Orana Wildlife Park (p485) or the Willowbank Wildlife Reserve (p486), or get them burning off excess energy in a rowboat or paddleboat from the Antigua Boatsheds (p490). At the engrossing International Antarctic Centre (p484), kids will love the Antarctic Storm chamber, the Hägglund Ride and (of course) the penguins. Educational and attention-getting factors also run high at the Discovery Centre at Canterbury Museum (p483).

If the weather's good, hit the beaches at Sumner or New Brighton.

WORTH A TRIP

THE SLOW ROAD TO LITTLE RIVER

The **Little River Rail Trail** (www.littleriverrailtrail.co.nz) will eventually traverse 45km, from the Christchurch suburb of Hornby to the Banks Peninsula hamlet of Little River. At the time of writing, all sections excluding a 14km stretch were open: see the website for the latest information. Join the trail 20km from Little River at Motukarara for the best of the ride. Ask at the Christchurch i-SITE about bike rental and public transport options. Rail trail day trips including transport can be booked with Natural High (p487). Natural High also rents out bikes and offers advice for multiday, self-guided cycling trips incorporating the Little River Rail Trail. Two funky accommodation options at Little River are Okuti Garden (p508) and the Little River Campground (p509); both are also well placed for exploring Akaroa and Banks Peninsula.

World Buskers Festival ARTS
(www.worldbuskersfestival.com) National and international talent entertain passers-by for 10 days in mid- to late January. Check the website for locations – and don't forget to put money in the hat.

Garden City SummerTimes MUSIC
(www.summertimes.co.nz) Say g'day to summer at a huge array of outdoor events between December and March. Sweet as.

Festival of Flowers CULTURAL
(www.festivalofflowers.co.nz) A blooming spectacle around Christchurch's heritage gardens in February and March.

Ellerslie Flower Show CULTURAL
(www.ellersileflowershow.co.nz) Hagley Park comes alive in early March with NZ's biggest flower show.

Christchurch Arts Festival ARTS
(www.artsfestival.co.nz) Midwinter arts extravaganza in August and September celebrating music, theatre and dance.

NZ Cup and Show Week CULTURAL
(www.nzcupandshow.co.nz) Includes the NZ Cup horse race, fashion shows, fireworks and the centrepiece A&P Show, where the country comes to town. Held in November.

Sleeping

At the time of writing, Christchurch's CBD was closed following earthquake damage, and accommodation was focused in and around the city's inner suburbs. Several international hotels within the CBD were demolished after the earthquake, but the Novotel (www.novotel.com), Ibis (www.ibishotel.com) and Rendezvous (www.rendezvoushotels.com) hotels were preparing to reopen once the CBD cordon was lifted. Check the hotel websites and www.cera.govt.nz for the status of Christchurch's CBD.

Motels are clustered around Bealey Ave and Papanui Rd, north of the centre, and Riccarton Rd, west of town beyond Hagley Park. Many inner-city hostels closed after the earthquake. Most of the hostels still operating are located to the east of the CBD or in Addington.

Booking ahead for accommodation is recommended as motels and hostels in the city are in high demand for tradespeople working on the city's rebuilding.

Orari B&B B&B $$$
(Map p488; ☎03-365 6569; www.orari.net.nz; 42 Gloucester St; d $195-255; P ☎) Orari is a late-19th-century home that has been stylishly updated with light-filled, pastel-toned rooms and inviting guest areas, as well as a lovely front garden. Art connoisseurs take note: it's right across the road from Christchurch Art Gallery. Wine connoisseurs can look forward to complimentary wine after a busy day.

Pomeroy's on Kilmore B&B $$
(Map p488; ☎03-365 1523; www.pomeroysonkilmore.co.nz; 292 Kilmore St; d $145-245; P) What could be better than staying in an elegantly furnished five-room boutique guesthouse? How about knowing it's just a short, thirsty stroll to Pomeroy's Old Brewery Inn (p498), Christchurch's best craft beer pub? Rates include breakfast, and you're also welcome to have a private beer tasting with the friendly owners. Several of the rooms open onto a sunny garden.

Wish B&B $$
(Map p484; ☎03-356 2455; www.wishnz.com; 38 Edgeware Rd, St Albans; s/d incl breakfast from $125/150; P @ ☎) The rooms and beds at the

stylish Wish are supercomfy, but it could be the locally sourced, sustainable and organic breakfasts that you recommend to other travellers. Contemporary NZ art dots the walls, and the huge native-timber kitchen table is just made for catching up with other guests over an end-of-day glass of wine. Wish is very popular and booking ahead is necessary. It's located slightly north of the CBD, in St Albans.

Jailhouse HOSTEL $

(Map p484; ☎03-982 7777, 0800 524 546; www.jail.co.nz; 338 Lincoln Rd, Addington; dm/s/d $30/79/85; P@) Housed in an old prison that was built in 1874 (and only decommissioned in 1999), the Jailhouse is one of NZ's most unique hostels. Twins and doubles are a bit on the small side – remember, it *was* a prison – but it's still an exceptionally well run and friendly spot. The surrounding Addington area has good cafes, restaurants and entertainment venues.

CentrePoint on Colombo MOTEL $$

(Map p488; ☎0800 859 000, 03-377 0859; www.centrepointoncolombo.co.nz; 859 Colombo St; d $155-165, apt $180-260; P@) CentrePoint on Colombo has super-comfortable facilities and the bonus of a friendly Kiwi-Japanese management. The owners are a mine of information on how Christchurch is bouncing back after the earthquakes, and happily provide guests with up-to-date information on the best places to eat around town.

George BOUTIQUE HOTEL $$$

(Map p488; ☎0800 100 220, 03-379 4560; www.thegeorge.com; 50 Park Tce; d $506-886; P@) The George has 53 handsomely decorated rooms and suites on the fringe of Christchurch's sweeping Hagley Park. Discreet staff attend to every whim; there are two excellent restaurants; and ritzy features include huge TVs, luxury toiletries and glossy magazines. Check online for good-value packages and discounts.

Classic Villa B&B $$$

(Map p488; ☎03-377 7905; www.theclassicvilla.co.nz; 17 Worcester Ave; d incl breakfast $269-489; P) Ideally located near the Botanic Gardens and Canterbury Museum, the Classic Villa is one of Christchurch's most elegant accommodation options. Rooms are trimmed with antiques and Turkish rugs for a classy ambience, and the expansive, Mediterranean-style breakfast is a shared social occasion around the dining room's big wooden table. No children under 12 years old allowed.

Elm Tree House B&B $$$

(Map p484; ☎03-355 9731; www.elmtreehouse.co.nz; 236 Papanui Rd, Merivale; d $365-445; P@) Originally built in the 1920s, the elegant Elm Tree House has six stylish rooms, a dining area leading to sunny rose gardens, and a spacious, wood-lined guests' lounge. Top-end shopping and Merivale's good restaurants are a short walk away, and yes, the classic Wurlitzer jukebox downstairs is still in working order.

Anslem House B&B $$$

(Map p484; ☎03-343 4260; www.anselmhouse.co.nz; 34 Kahu Rd, Fendalton; s/d $190/230; P) Designed by renowned NZ architect Heathcote Helmore and constructed partially of unique Oamaru pink marble, Anselm House in Fendalton is one of the city's iconic heritage residences. The decor is elegant and restrained, and the property features a beautiful riverside garden, just perfect for an end-of-the-day glass of wine and conversation with the friendly, well-travelled owners.

Merivale Manor MOTEL $$

(Map p484; ☎03-355 7731; www.merivalemanor.com; 122 Papanui Rd, Merivale; d $145-185; P) A gracious 19th-century Victorian residence is now the hub of an elegant motel. Accommodation ranges from studios (some with spa baths) to one- and two-bedroom apartments. In keeping with the property's history, decor is understated, and the classy shopping and good bars and restaurants of Merivale are just a few hundred metres away.

Roma on Riccarton MOTEL $$

(Map p484; ☎03-341 2100; www.romaonriccarton.com; 38 Riccarton Rd, Riccarton; d $150-205; P) Handily located near Hagley Park and the city end of Riccarton Rd, the Mediterranean-style Roma on Riccarton is also a short stroll from cinemas, bars and restaurants, and Christchurch's best shopping mall. Studio units – some with spa baths – and larger, two-bedroom apartments are all spotless and thoroughly modern.

Chester Street Backpackers HOSTEL $

(Map p488; ☎03-377 1897; www.chesterst.co.nz; 148 Chester St E; dm/tw/d $30/64/66; P@) This relaxed wooden villa is painted in bright colours and has a huge library in the sunny front room. The friendly house cat is a regular guest at hostel barbecues. It's popular, so try to book ahead. The equally charming Entwhistle Cottage across the road is often used as an overflow facility, offering twin and double rooms.

Fendalton House B&B $$
(Map p484; ☎03-343 1661, 0800 374 298; www.fendaltonhouse.co.nz; 28a Kotare St, Fenadlton; d $145; P) A friendly, homestay-style B&B amid the pleasant streets of leafy Fendalton. Rates include a cooked breakfast, and on Wednesday nights and Saturday mornings, the foodie attractions of the Christchurch Farmers Market (p498) are just around the corner.

Foley Towers HOSTEL $
(Map p488; ☎03-366 9720; www.backpack.co.nz/foley.html; 208 Kilmore St; dm $24-26, d with/without bathroom $68/62; P@) Sheltered by well-established trees, Foley Towers provides well-maintained rooms encircling quiet inner courtyards and a friendly welcome in dorms warmed by underfloor heating. Check-in after 9pm is available only by arrangement.

Dorset House HOSTEL $
(Map p488; ☎03-366 8268; www.dorsethouse.co.nz; 1 Dorset St; dm/s/d $32/69/84; P@) This 145-year-old wooden villa has a large regal lounge with log fire, pool table, DVDs and beds instead of bunks. It's a short stroll to Hagley Park and the bars and restaurants of Victoria St and Papanui Rd.

Old Countryhouse HOSTEL $
(Map p484; ☎03-381 5504; www.oldcountryhousenz.com; 437 Gloucester St; dm $31-35, d $90-110; P@) The Old Countryhouse features two separate villas with handmade wooden furniture, a reading lounge and a lovely garden filled with native ferns. It's slightly further out than other hostels, but still only 1km east of Latimer Sq. Bus 21 stops opposite.

Around the World Backpackers HOSTEL $
(Map p488; ☎03-365 4363; www.aroundtheworld.co.nz; 314 Barbadoes St; dm/d/tw $30/68/68; P@) Around the World gets rave recommendations for its 'Kiwiana' decor and sunny back garden (complete with a private outdoor bath). Ask about the hostel's 'Love Shack' if you're visiting with the closest of travelling companions.

Haka Lodge HOSTEL $
(Map p484; ☎03-980 4252; www.hakalodge.com; 518 Linwood Ave, Woolston ; dm $28, d&tw $70, self-contained apt $160; P) Sprawled across three floors of a modern suburban house, Haka Lodge is one of Christchurch's newest hostels. Shared dorms and rooms are spotless and colourful, and end-of-day treats include a comfy lounge with big-screen TV and a bird-friendly garden. The lodge is around 10 minutes' drive from the city, and there's a bus stop nearby.

Arena Motel MOTEL $$
(Map p484; ☎03-338 4579, 0800 232 565; www.arenamotel.co.nz; 30 Whiteleigh Ave, Addington; d $130-180;) Handily located in up-and-coming Addington, the Arena Motel is also the closest accommodation to the Christchurch Railway Station – convenient if you're planning a morning departure on the *Tranz Alpine* (p462) through the Southern Alps.

Colombo in the City MOTEL $$
(Map p488; ☎0800 265 662, 03-366 8775; www.motelcolombo.co.nz; 863 Colombo St; d $160-185, apt $185-270; P@) Colombo in the City has attractive units that are luxuriously equipped with Sky TV, CD players, double-glazed windows and spa baths.

Focus Motel MOTEL $$
(Map p488; ☎03-943 0800, 0800 943 0800; www.focusmotel.com; 344 Durham St N; d $150-200; P@) Sleek and centrally located, with big-screen TVs, self-contained studios and super-modern decor.

Airport Gateway Motor Lodge MOTEL $$
(☎0800 242 8392, 03-358 7093; www.airportgateway.co.nz; 45 Roydvale Ave, Burnside; d $155-195; P@) Handy for those early flights, this motel has a variety of rooms with good facilities. A 24-hour airport pick-up is available at no extra charge. The newly opened Premier Suites are very comfortable and good value.

Vagabond Backpackers HOSTEL $
(Map p488; ☎03-379 9677; vagabondbackpackers@hotmail.com; 232 Worcester St; dm/s/d $26/42/60; P@) This small, friendly place is reminiscent of a big shared house. There's an appealing garden, rustic but comfy facilities, and frisbees and barbecues that remind you that you're definitely in NZ. Take the airport shuttle to Cathedral Sq.

Canterbury House HOSTEL $
(Map p488; ☎03-377 8108; http://canterburyhousebp.web.fc2.com; 257 Bealey Ave; dm/s $30/45, d&tw $70; P) More of a homestay than a hostel, Canterbury House is run by a friendly Kiwi-Japanese couple, and enjoys a quiet right-of-

way location off busy Bealey Ave. The decor is slightly chintzy and old-fashioned, but the spacious and well-kept garden is a real asset during summer.

Meadow Park Top 10 Holiday Park HOLIDAY PARK $
(Map p484; ☎0800 396 323, 03-352 9176; www.christchurchtop10.co.nz; 39 Meadow St, Papanui; sites from $40, units $75-169; P@) Wall-to-wall campervans here, while other accommodation ranges from cabins to motel units. It's also well equipped for leisure activities, with an indoor pool, games rooms and a playground for the kids.

North South Holiday Park HOLIDAY PARK $
(☎03-359 5993, 0800 567 765; www.northsouth.co.nz; cnr John's & Sawyers Arms Rds, SH1, Harewood; sites from $35, units $58-125; P@) This place is just five minutes from the airport, and a good place to spend the night after you've picked up your campervan. Facilities include a pool, sauna, playground and newer motel units. Airport transfers are available.

Eating

Following the February 2011 earthquake, many cafes and restaurants were damaged, or left shuttered behind the cordon around the city's CBD. The CBD was scheduled to reopen sometime from mid-2012, and the area will again become a focus for dining out. However, for this edition we have only included restaurants and cafes that were open at the time of research; check www.christchurchnz.com for the latest updates. Bookings are recommended for dinner.

Key dining precincts are along Victoria St to the immediate northwest of the CBD. South of Moorhouse Ave, Addington and Sydenham have become hubs for new post-earthquake eateries.

To the west and north respectively of the CBD, Riccarton and Merivale are dotted with cafes and restaurants, and the beachside suburb of Sumner also features great eating. To the southeast, Lyttelton is again emerging as one Christchurch's best areas for eating and drinking.

Restaurants

Bodhi Tree BURMESE $$
(Map p484; ☎03-377 6808; www.bodhitree.co.nz; 39 Ilam Rd, Bryndwr; dishes $13-24; ⊙6-10pm Tue-Sun;) Christchurch's only Burmese restaurant is also one of the city's best eateries. Don't come expecting spicy flavours from neighbouring Thailand, but look forward to subtle food crafted from exceptionally fresh ingredients. Standout dishes include the *le pet thoke* (pickled tea-leaf salad) and the *ciandi thoke* (grilled eggplant). Meat and seafood also feature. Dishes are starter-sized, so drum up a group and sample lots of different flavours. Bookings are essential.

50 Bistro RESTAURANT $$
(Map p488; ☎03-371 0250; www.thegeorge.com; 50 Park Tce, The George; dinner from $35; ⊙6.30am-late) The more casual restaurant at the George is a bustling affair, doing savvy local twists on classic bistro flavours. Try the Nifty 50 lunch menu – $29 for soup and a main dish – or sample more robust evening meals like lamb shoulder ragu with kumara (sweet potato) gnocchi.

Pescatore RESTAURANT $$$
(Map p488; ☎03-371 0250; www.thegeorge.com; 50 Park Tce; mains $42-50; ⊙6pm-late Tue-Sat) Travelling gourmands should book for Pescatore, the George's more formal restaurant. Dishes like citrus-cured salmon or Canterbury lamb help make Pescatore a regular finalist in *Cuisine* magazine's NZ Restaurant of the Year awards.

Edesia MODERN NZ $$
(Map p484; ☎03-943 2144; www.edesia.co.nz; 12 Show Pl, Addington ; lunch $21-29, dinner $28-39; ⊙11.30am-3pm Mon-Fri & 5.30pm-late Mon-Sat) Ignore the office-park location; Edesia's version of fine dining is worth seeking out. The dinner menu includes innovative spins on local venison, salmon and quail, while lunch is a more informal affair, with prime Canterbury steaks and gossamer-light pasta. The wine list is one of Christchurch's best, and after work Edesia morphs into a cosy bar for local desk jockeys.

Himalayas INDIAN $$
(Map p488; ☎03-377 8935; www.himalayas.co.nz; 830a Colombo St; mains $18-22; ⊙11.30am-2pm Tue-Fri & 5pm-late Tue-Sun;) Every city needs a great Indian eatery, and Himalayas ticks the box in Christchurch. A stylish dining room showcases lots of subcontinental favourites, including vegetarian options like the creamy *dal makhani* (black lentils cooked with aromatic spices). The *kadhai* chicken is studded with chilli, ginger and coriander – perfect with a cold beer. Takeaways are also available.

WORTH A TRIP

SEASIDE AT SUMNER

Just 12km southeast of Christchurch by bus 3, the beachy suburb of Sumner is a relaxing place to stay. Commute to central Christchurch for sightseeing and return to Sumner for good restaurants and an arthouse cinema at night.

Le Petit Hotel (Map p484; ☎03-326 6675; www.lepetithotel.co.nz; 16 Marriner St; d $135; P@) Relaxed coffee, croissant breakfasts and Kara the friendly Scottish terrier are among the highlights at this intimate, French-themed boutique hotel. Factor in the friendly owners, the close proximity to Sumner beach and some of Christchurch's best restaurants, and it's a definite *oui* from us.

Sumner Bay Motel and Apartments (Map p484; ☎0800 496 949, 03-326 5969; www.sumnermotel.co.nz; 26 Marriner St; d $159-185) Studios and one- and two-bedroom units all have a balcony and courtyard, quality furniture, and Sky TV and DVD players. Bikes and surfboards can be rented.

Almeidas Tapas Bar (Map p484; ☎03-326 5220; 41a Nayland St; tapas $8-12; ⊙5pm-late Wed-Sat) Beachy Sumner meets the back streets of Barcelona at this rustic, Spanish-themed tapas bar. More than 20 different small-plate offerings include haloumi and roasted garlic in prosciutto, artichoke hearts wrapped in lemon and mint, and prawns sautéed in garlic, lime and coriander. Try and resist the urge for 'just one more plate' before settling on *churros* (Spanish donuts) for dessert.

Bamboozle (Map p484; ☎03-326 7878; 6 Wakefield St; mains $25-30) Asian fusion is the name of the game at the stylish Bamboozle, where talented chefs conjure up innovative spins on traditional flavours. Dishes include Burmese-style fish with chilli, and wasabi, salmon and cream-cheese dumplings. Leave room for dessert with one of Christchurch's best crème brûlées, or ginger steamed-pudding topped with a lime sauce and coffee ice cream.

Cornershop Bistro (Map p484; ☎03-326 6720; www.cornershopbistro.co.nz; 32 Nayland St; brunch & lunch $12-17, dinner $23-34; ⊙5pm-late Wed-Fri & 10am-late Sat-Sun) This is a superior, French-style bistro that never forgets it's in a relaxed beachside suburb. Spend longer than you planned to lingering over brunch.

Holy Smoke STEAKHOUSE $$

(Map p484; www.holysmoke.co.nz; 650 Ferry Rd, Woolston; brunch & lunch $18-25, dinner $26-36; ⊙9am-late Mon-Sat, to 4pm Sun) Here's your chance to get acquainted with the unique smoky character of *manuka* (NZ tea tree). At Holy Smoke, the native wood is used to smoke everything from pork ribs and chicken wings to bacon and salmon. Other menu items include robust slabs of venison, lamb and beef, all teamed with Kiwi craft beers and Central Otago wines.

Lotus Heart VEGETARIAN $$

(Map p488; www.thelotusheart.co.nz; 363 St Asaph St; mains $14-25; ⊙8am-4pm daily & 6-10pm Thu-Sat;) Relocated to the edge of the CBD, this organic and vegetarian eatery does curries, freshly squeezed organic juices and filled pita pockets. Try the chilli, coriander and garlic-studded eggs Akoori for breakfast, or drop by for a healthy pizza, wrap or shared platter for lunch or dinner. Organic, vegan and gluten-free options abound, and there's an interesting gift shop onsite.

Topkapi TURKISH $$

(Map p488; www.topkapi.co.nz; 64 Manchester St; mains $14-22; ⊙closed Mon) Grab yourself a cushioned, low-slung bench in the tapestry-draped interior and enjoy some great Turkish food, including a wide range of meat or veg kebabs and the all-important baklava finisher. The takeaway counter also does brisk business.

Cafes

TOP CHOICE **Addington Coffee Co-op** CAFE $

(Map p484; www.addingtoncoffee.org.nz; 297 Lincoln Rd, Addington; snacks & mains $6-20;) One of Christchurch's biggest and most bustling cafes is also one of its best. Fair-trade coffee and a compact stall selling organic cotton T-shirts jostle for attention with delicious cakes and slices, while a cross-section of the city comes for the free wi-fi, gourmet pies and wraps, and the legendary big breakfasts. An onsite laundromat completes the deal for busy travellers.

Black Betty CAFE $

(Map p488; www.blackbetty.co.nz; 163a Madras St; mains $10-20;) Infused with glorious caffeine-enriched aromas from Switch Espresso's roasting operation, Black Betty's chic industrial warehouse is a popular destination for students from nearby CPIT. Essential culinary attractions include all-day breakfasts – try the ciabatta toast with creamy mushrooms – and excellent counter food including wraps and bagels, as well as the best of NZ wine and craft beers.

Under the Red Verandah CAFE $$

(Map p484; www.utrv.co.nz; cnr Tancred & Worcester Sts, Linwood ; mains $15-25;) After losing their original premises in the 2011 earthquake, Under the Red Verandah reopened in a spacious villa at the same location. Christchurch foodie types quickly returned, and now fill the shady garden for leisurely combinations of coffee, oaty pancakes and the city's best corn fritters. Look forward also to lots of organic and gluten-free baking.

Beat St CAFE $

(Map p488; 324 Barbadoes St; snacks & mains $8-16;) Welcome to the grungy hub of Christchurch cafe-cool. Free range this and organic that combine with terrific eggy breakfasts, gourmet pies (try the feta and vegie one) and robust Havana coffee. Beat Street hosts a bohemian open mic night featuring music and poetry on the third Thursday of every month from 6pm.

Honey Pot Cafe CAFE $$

(Map p484; www.honeypotcafe.co.nz; 458 Colombo St, Sydenham ; mains $20-30) One of the first CBD cafes to relocate after the earthquakes, the Honey Pot Cafe set the scene for the emergence of Sydenham as a dining destination. Great eggs Benedict for breakfast give way to spiced lamb and feta salad for lunch, and sirloin steak and chunky, hand-cut chips for dinner. Christchurch's very own 3 Boys beer is on tap.

Coffee House CAFE $$

(Map p488; 290 Montreal St; breakfast & lunch $11-22 & dinner $27-32) Housed in a heritage villa complete with sunny patio, the Coffee House has a great location near the Arts Centre and the Botanic Gardens. Highlights include feta-studded Mediterranean scrambled eggs for breakfast and herb-marinated lamb for dinner. Emerson's beer on tap and a concise wine list will probably see you lingering over something stronger than coffee.

Dose CAFE $

(Map p488; 77 Tuam St; snacks & mains $8-18; closed Sun) Excellent coffee from the Lyttelton Coffee Company and superior counter food combine here with toasted bagels and what may just be Christchurch's best eggs Benedict. Downstairs is almost unbearably cosy, so head upstairs for bigger tables and a quirky ambience with graffiti-style art. From Wednesday to Saturday from 4pm, Dose morphs into a *yakitori* bar with tasty grilled skewers and ice-cold Japanese beer.

Vic's Cafe & Bakery CAFE $

(Map p488; www.vics.co.nz; 132 Victoria St; snacks & mains $8-20) Always busy, Vic's attracts a wide cross-section of Christchurch folk – we even saw the city's mayor there on our Sunday-morning visit. Pop in for a robust breakfast on the big shared tables, or grab baked goodies and still-warm artisan bread for an affordable DIY riverside picnic. Get there early (before 10am) for Vic's world-famous-in-Christchurch nutty porridge ($10.50).

Quick Eats

TOP CHOICE **Simo's Deli** MOROCCAN $

(Map p484; www.simos.co.nz; 3/300 Lincoln Rd, Addington; wraps $6.50-$9.50, tapas & mains $7-17) Part cafe and part deli, Simo's in Addington is popular for its takeaway *bocadillos* (grilled wraps filled with a huge selection of Middle Eastern and African-inspired fillings, sauces and toppings). Other tasty offerings include small plates of grilled calamari or spicy *merguez* sausages, or more robust *tagines* (Moroccan casseroles) and beef kofta with pomegranate sauce.

Serious Sandwich SANDWICHES $

(Map p484; www.theserioussandwich.com; 363 Colombo St, Sydenham; sandwiches $7-10) Serious in name and serious in flavour. Concealed in Sydenham's new Colombo shopping mall, this compact kitchen dishes up tasty gourmet sammies, including the breakfast BLAT (available from 9am) and a meatballs-on-toasted-ciabatta variant (available from around 11am). Look forward to a serious attitude to good coffee, too.

Burgers & Beers Inc BURGERS $

(Map p484; www.burgersandbeersinc.co.nz; 355 Colombo St, Sydenham; burgers $12-16) Quirkily named gourmet burgers – try the Moroccan-spiced Woolly Sahara Sand Hopper (lamb with lemon yoghurt) or the Shagged Stag (venison with tamarillo and plum chutney) – give this place a funky, laid-back air. An ever-changing selection of Kiwi craft beers give you further reasons to tarry longer. Definitely worth the short hop south to Sydenham.

Self-Catering

Canterbury Cheesemongers SANDWICHES $
(Map p488; www.cheesemongers.co.nz; Arts Centre Old Registry Building, 301 Montreal St; sandwiches from $7; ⌚Tue-Sat) Pop in to buy artisan cheeses, or craft your own sandwich by combining freshly baked *ficelles* and ciabatta with a whole cheese shop of dairy goodies. Coffee and juices are also available to complete a good-value lunch. No Monty Python jokes, please.

TOP CHOICE **Christchurch Farmers Market** FARMERS MARKET $
(Map p484; www.christchurchfarmersmarket.co.nz; Riccarton House, 16 Kahu Rd, Riccarton ; ⌚9am-noon Sat year-round & 4-7pm Wed Nov-Sat) Welcome to one of New Zealand's best farmers markets, a tasty labyrinth of organic fruit and vegies, South Island cheeses and salmon, local craft beer and ethnic treats including Colombian *empanadas* and Moroccan *briouats* (filo parcels). Other tasty stalls to track down are Posh Porridge and She Chocolat. Check out the website before you go to create your own foodie hit list.

New World Supermarket SUPERMARKET
(Map p488; South City Centre, Colombo St) Centrally located.

Drinking

Before the earthquakes, Christchurch's after-dark scene was focused around Oxford Tce ('the Strip') and the inner-city laneways around SOL ('South of Lichfield') Sq and Poplar St. Both precincts were closed at the time of research, and areas like Riccarton, Addington, Victoria St and Merivale were becoming popular.

TOP CHOICE **Pomeroy's Old Brewery Inn** CRAFT BEER
(Map p488; www.pomeroysonkilmore.co.nz; 292 Kilmore St) The welcoming Pomeroy's is the city's hoppy hub for fans of NZ's rapidly expanding craft beer scene. A wide range of guest taps showcase brews from around the country, often including seasonal beers and limited releases. Check the website for what's coming up. There's occasional live music, and the attached Victoria's Kitchen does great pub food (mains $20 to $30).

Volstead Trading Company BAR
(Map p484; www.volstead.co.nz; 55 Riccarton Rd, Riccarton) Volstead is a great example of what Christchurch has always done better than the rest of NZ: shabbily chic bars with a real sense of individuality. Comfy old sofas from your last student flat combine with quirky artwork, interesting beers from the Moa Brewery, and funky cocktails. If you're peckish, dig into unpretentious popcorn, nachos and toasted sandwiches.

The Brewery CRAFT BEER
(Map p484; www.casselsbrewery.co.nz; 3 Garlands Rd, Woolston) Out in Woolston, it's a fair schlep from the city, but the Brewery is an essential destination for beer-loving travellers. Cassels & Sons craft all their beer using a wood-fired brew kettle, resulting in big, bold beers like their 1PA and Best Bitter. Tasting trays are available for the curious and the indecisive, and the food – including wood-fired pizzas – is top-notch, too.

Monday Room WINE BAR
(Map p488; www.themondayroom.co.nz; 367 Moorhouse Ave; ⌚8am-late) Part cafe, part restaurant and part wine bar, the versatile Monday Room is the kind of place to hang out at any time of any day of the week. Occupying a restored heritage building, the funky interior is a background for interesting brunch and lunch options; later in the day, tapas, craft beers and cocktails take centre stage.

Cargo BAR
(Map p488; 379 Lincoln Rd, Addington) Welcome to the city of shipping containers, a popular option for business owners re-establishing after the earthquake. In the case of Addington's Cargo, there's even an astroturf putting green in the corner. The utilitarian decor won't score points for a romantic night out, but on Friday and Saturday nights it's crammed with locals celebrating the end of the working week.

Carlton Country Club PUB
(Map p488; 1 Papanui Rd) Only in innovative, post-earthquake Christchurch would a bunch of shipping containers and a truck-and-trailer come together as one of the city's most popular pubs. Perched on a busy urban corner, the Carlton is a thoroughly unpretentious spot, with lots of thirsty locals tucked away in its nooks and crannies. Don't miss the rooftop deck on a sunny afternoon.

Revival BAR
(Map p488; www.revivalbar.co.nz; 94 Victoria St) More shipping-container bar tomfoolery, this time with the added attraction of its own onsite Lebanese food caravan, Revival is the hippest of Christchurch's container bars, with regular DJs and a funky lounge area dotted with a quirky collection of automotive rear ends and vintage steamer trunks. Yet another classic example of post-earthquake Christchurch drinking chic.

Wood's Mill BAR, CAFE
(Map p484; Addington) Before the earthquakes, Christchurch had a thriving eating and drinking scene in the bricklined thoroughfares around SOL Sq and Lichfield Lane. At the time of research these areas were still cordoned off, but the Wood's Mill precinct in Addington was being repurposed as a similar precinct. The area is scheduled to open in mid-2012.

✩ Entertainment

Like the city's pub and bar scene, many of Christchurch's traditional entertainment venues were damaged by the earthquakes, and newer, more suburban areas have emerged. For live music and club listings, see www.christchurchmusic.org.nz or www.mukuna.co.nz. Also look out for the *Groove Guide* magazine in cafes.

Pomery's Old Brewery Inn (p498) and the Brewery (p498) are good live-music venues. Check their websites for listings.

Christchurch Events Village CONCERT VENUE
(Map p488; www.eventsvillage.co.nz; Hagley Park) This Hagley Park collection of temporary venues is being used for everything from concerts to live theatre.

Dux Live LIVE MUSIC
(Map p488; www.duxlive.co.nz; 363 Lincoln Rd; ⌚hours vary) Dux de Lux was an excellent restaurant, microbrewery and live-music venue in Christchurch's Arts Centre, but it was forced to close after the February 2011 earthquake. The beer is still being brewed (try it here and at Dux de Lux in Queenstown) and in late 2011 this Addington venue opened for live music.

Darkroom LIVE MUSIC
(Map p488; www.facebook.com/darkroom.nz; At the Archive, 336 St Asaphs St; ⌚5pm-late Thu-Sun) A hip combination of live-music venue and bar, darkroom has lots of Kiwi beers, great cocktails and the moreish delights of mini-pizzas and the 'Pie of the Week'. There's lots of live gigs, often free – it's a cool introduction to the renaissance of Christchurch's music scene. Check its Facebook page for gig info.

Court Theatre THEATRE
(Map p484; www.courttheatre.org.nz; off Bernard St, Addington) Christchurch's original Court Theatre was an iconic part of the city's Arts Centre, but it was forced to relocate after the earthquakes. Its new premises in up-and-coming Addington are more modern and spacious, and it's a great venue to see popular international plays and works by NZ playwrights. Check the website for what's playing.

Club 22 CLUB
(Map p484; 22 Harewood Rd, Papanui; ⌚8pm-2am Thu-Sat) Energetic DJ-driven dance club for the younger traveller – some nights the good people of suburban Papanui don't know what's hit them. Search Facebook for Club 22 to see what's planned and who's playing.

The Venue CLUB
(6 Tower St, Hornby; ⌚Wed-Sat 4pm-2am) Another suburban nightclub worth the trek to Hornby for occasional hip hop, dubstep and gloriously noisy rock and roll from Kiwi acts. Check www.christchurchmusic.org.nz for what's on or search Facebook for the Venue.

Christchurch Stadium STADIUM
(Map p484; www.crfu.co.nz; 95 Jack Hinton Drive, Addington) Along with much of Christchurch's sporting infrastructure, the earthquakes forced the closure of AMI Stadium, the traditional home of rugby and cricket in the city. After a 2011 season playing all their games away from home – and still coming in as runners-up – the Canterbury Crusaders Super 15 rugby team moved to a new ground in Addington for the 2012 season. Super-15 games are played from late February to July; from July to September, Canterbury plays in NZ's domestic championship.

Hoyts Riccarton CINEMA
(Map p484; www.hoyts.co.nz; Riccarton Rd, Westfield Riccarton; adult/child $16.50/11.50) Hollywood blockbusters and the occasional art-house gem feature at Christchurch's most central multiplex. Catch a bus to Riccarton Mall from platform C at the Central Bus Station. Check listings in the *Press* newspaper or at www.flicks.co.nz.

Hollywood 3 CINEMA
(Map p484; www.hollywoodcinema.co.nz; 28 Marriner St; adult/child $16/10) Mainly arthouse and foreign language flicks in the seaside suburb of Sumner. Catch bus 3 from platform A at the Central Bus Station.

Shopping

Since the earthquakes, shopping in Christchurch has largely been focused on the city's suburban malls. The most convenient for visitors is the Westfield Riccarton Mall. At the time of writing, the CBD was closed, but green shoots of retail commerce were evident nearby in the new RE:Start shopping precinct. The gift shops at the Canterbury Museum (p483) and the Christchurch Art Gallery (p485) are also worth browsing.

Re:START Mall MALL
(Map p488; www.restart.org.nz; Cashel Mall) Opened in late October 2011, this colourful labyrinth of shops based in shipping containers was the first retail activity in the Christchurch CBD after the February 2011 earthquake. With a couple of decent cafes, and including two iconic Christchurch stores – Scorpio Books and Johnson's Grocers – it's a pleasant place to stroll. Visit Hapa for a good selection of design and crafts from local artists.

Ballantynes DEPARTMENT STORE
(Map p488; cnr Colombo & Cashel Sts) A venerable Christchurch department store selling men's and women's fashions, cosmetics, travel goods and speciality NZ gifts. Ballantynes was one of the first stores to reopen in the CBD following the earthquakes.

Sunday Artisan Market MARKET
(Map p484; www.sundayartisanmarket.co.nz; Riccarton House, 16 Kahu Rd, Riccarton; ⌚11am-3pm Sun) This Sunday morning market in the leafy grounds of Riccarton House combines local arts and crafts vendors with gourmet food stalls and live music and entertainment.

Westfield Riccarton Mall MALL
(Map p484; www.westfield.co.nz; Riccarton Rd, Riccarton) To the west of central Christchurch, this mega mall has a huge selection of fashion, homeware and entertainment outlets. There's a cinema multiplex and the surrounding area around Riccarton Rd also has many shops. Catch a bus from platform C at Christchurch's Central Bus Station

Information

Emergency

Ambulance, fire service & police (☎111)

Police station (☎03-348 6640; www.police.govt.nz; Church Corner, Riccarton Rd, Riccarton) The police kiosk in Cathedral Sq was inaccessible at the time of research, so the station in Riccarton is the most central police station.

Internet Resources

Christchurch & Canterbury (www.christchurchnz.com) Official tourism website for the city and region. Also see www.popupcity.co.nz for its blog of new eating and drinking opportunities around town.

Christchurch.org.nz (www.christchurch.org.nz) The Christchurch City Council's website.

CERA (www.cera.govt.nz) Check the website of the Canterbury Earthquake Recovery Authority for up-to-date maps of the cordon around the city's CBD. Also available is a download of the draft plan to rebuild the city.

Neat Places (www.neatplaces.co.nz) A local blogger's authoritative view of the best of Christchurch's shopping, eating and drinking.

Media

Cityscape (www.cityscape-christchurch.co.nz) Entertainment and events magazine available in inner-city cafes and retailers. Check its website for updates on new openings around town.

Press (www.stuff.co.nz) Christchurch's newspaper, published Monday to Saturday. Check out Friday's edition for the best entertainment listings.

Medical Services

24-Hour Surgery (☎03-365 7777; www.pegasus.org.nz; Bealey Ave Medical Centre, cnr Bealey Ave & Colombo St; ⌚24hr) Located north of town, with no appointment necessary.

After-Hours Pharmacy (☎03-366 4439; 931 Colombo St; ⌚6-11pm Mon-Fri, 9am-11pm Sat & Sun, plus public holidays) Located beside the 24-Hour Surgery.

Christchurch Hospital (☎03-364 0640, emergency dept 03-364 0270; www.cdhb.govt.nz; 2 Riccarton Ave) Centrally located.

Post

Post Office (103 Riccarton Rd) At the time of research, Christchurch's main post office was closed. The most central location is in Riccarton.

Tourist Information

Airport Information Desks (☎03-353 7774; www.christchurchairport.co.nz; ⌚7.30am-8pm) Transport and accommodation bookings, and a handy post office (open 8am to 4.30pm)

Christchurch i-SITE (☎03-379 9629; www.christchurchnz.com; Rolleston Ave, beside the Canterbury Museum; ⌚8.30am-5pm, later in summer) Transport, activities and accommodation. Note that this location may change during the life of this book. Check online for the current location when you visit.

Department of Conservation (DOC; ☎03-371 3700; www.doc.govt.nz; 38 Orchard Rd, International Antarctic Centre; ⌚8.30am-5pm Mon-Fri) Has information on South Island national parks and walkways. At the time of writing DOC had relocated to the International Antarctic Centre near the airport, but check online for the current location.

Getting There & Away

Air

Christchurch Airport (CHC; ☎03-358 5029; www.christchurchairport.co.nz) is the South Island's main international gateway. The newly modernised and expanded airport has excellent facilities, including baggage storage and visitor information desks in both the domestic and international terminals.

INTERNATIONAL

Air New Zealand (☎0800 737 000; www.airnewzealand.co.nz) Direct flights (one-way prices) to/from Melbourne (from $139), Sydney ($159) and Brisbane ($159).

Jetstar (☎800 800 995; www.jetstar.com) Direct flights (one-way prices) to/from Melbourne (from $139), Sydney (from $139), Brisbane (from ($169) and the Gold Coast (from $139). Corporate cousin Qantas also flies the same routes at higher fares.

Singapore Airlines (www.singaporeair.com) Direct flights to/from Singapore from around $1100 one way.

Virgin Australia (www.virginaustralia.com) Direct flights (prices one-way) to/from Sydney (from $149), Melbourne (from $149) and Brisbane (from $149).

DOMESTIC

Air New Zealand (☎0800 737 000; www.airnewzealand.co.nz) Direct flights (prices one-way) to/from Auckland (from $79), Blenheim (from $99), Dunedin (from $79), Hamilton (from $109), Hokitika (from $109), Invercargill (from $109), Napier (from $109), Nelson (from $79), New Plymouth (from $109), Palmerston North (from $119), Queenstown (from $59), Rotorua (from $119), Tauranga (from $109), Wanaka (from $99) and Wellington (from $59).

Jetstar (☎0800 800 995; www.jetstar.com) Direct flights (prices one-way) to/from Auckland ($79),Queenstown ($59) and Wellington ($59).

Bus

Shuttles run to Akaroa, Arthur's Pass, Dunedin, Greymouth, Hanmer Springs, Picton, Queenstown, Twizel, Wanaka, Westport and points in between; see the Christchurch i-SITE. Departure points vary, so check when you book.

InterCity (☎03-365 1113; www.intercity.co.nz; 118 Bealey Ave) Buses depart from 118 Bealey Ave, but that may change during the life of this book – check the website. North bound buses go to Kaikoura (2¾ hours), Blenheim (five hours) and Picton (5½ hours), with connections to Nelson (eight hours). One daily bus also goes southwest to Queenstown direct (eight hours). There are services to Wanaka (seven hours) involving a change in Tarras. Heading south, two buses run daily along the coast via the towns along SH1 to Dunedin (six hours), with connections via Gore to Invercargill (9¾ hours) and Te Anau (10½ hours). Book online or at the i-SITE.

Naked Bus (www.nakedbus.com; 70 Bealey Ave, cnr Montreal & Bealey Ave) Heads north to Picton and Nelson, south to Dunedin and southwest to Queenstown. Most buses depart from 70 Bealey Ave, but buses to Kaikoura, Picton and Nelson depart from outside the Canterbury Museum (p483). Check the website or when you book.

Train

Christchurch railway station (☎0800 872 467, 03-341 2588; www.tranzscenic.co.nz; Troup Dr; ⌚ticket office 6.30am-3.30pm Mon-Fri, to 3pm Sat & Sun) is serviced by a free shuttle that picks up from various accommodation; ring the i-SITE to request pick-up. An alternative is Steve's Airport Shuttle (p501) for $5.

The *Coastal Pacific* runs daily each way between Christchurch and Picton via Kaikoura and Blenheim, departing from Christchurch at 7am and arriving at Picton at 12.13pm. The standard adult one-way fare to Picton is $99, but fares can be discounted to $59.

The *TranzAlpine* has a daily route between Christchurch and Greymouth via Arthur's Pass. The standard adult one-way fare is $129, but fares can be discounted to $89.

Contact **Kiwi Rail Scenic** (☎0800 872 467; www.tranzscenic.co.nz) for timetables and tickets.

Getting Around

To/From the Airport

The airport is 12km from the city centre.

Super Shuttle (☎0800 748 885; www.supershuttle.co.nz) operates 24 hours and charges $24 for one person between the city and the airport, plus $5 for each additional person. A cheaper alternative is **Steve's Airport Shuttle**

(☎0800 101 021; 1 person $15, 2&3 people $20) offering a door-to-door service from 3am.

The airport is serviced by the **City Flyer bus** (☎0800 733 287; www.redbus.co.nz; adult/child $7.50/4.50), which runs to/from the Central Bus Station between 7.15am and 10.15pm Monday to Friday and 7.15am to 9.15pm Saturday and Sunday. Pick up the red City Flyer timetable at the i-SITE.

A taxi between the city centre and airport costs around $45 to $55.

Car & Motorcycle

HIRE Most major car- and campervan-rental companies have offices in Christchurch, as do numerous smaller local companies. Operators with national networks often want cars to be returned from Christchurch to Auckland because most renters travel in the opposite direction, so special rates may apply on this northbound route.

Ace Rental Cars (☎03-360 3270, 0800 202 029; www.acerentalcars.co.nz; 20 Abros Pl) Located near the airport.

First Choice (☎03-357 3243, 0800 736 822; www.firstchoice.co.nz; 577 Wairekei Rd) Located near the airport.

Omega Rental Cars (☎03-377 4558, 0800 112 121; www.omegarentalcars.com; 20 Lichfield St) Centrally located.

Pegasus Rental Cars (☎0800 354 504; www.rentalcars.co.nz; 578 Wairakei Rd) Located near the airport.

New Zealand Motorcycle Rentals & Tours (☎03-348 1106; www.nzbike.com; 22 Lowther St) Also does guided motorbike tours.

PURCHASE Many vehicles are offered for sale on noticeboards at hostels, cafes and internet places. Check out **Backpackers Car Market** (Map p484; ☎03-377 3177; www.backpackerscarmarket.co.nz; 33 Battersea St; ⏲9.30am-5pm), or the weekly **Canterbury Car Fair** (☎03-338 5525; Wrights Rd entrance; ⏲9am-noon Sun) held at Addington Raceway. Turners Auctions (p697) buys and sells used cars by auction; vehicles priced under $7000 are auctioned at 6pm on Tuesday and Thursday.

Online see www.trademe.co.nz and www.autotrader.co.nz.

Public Transport

The Christchurch **bus network** (Metro; ☎03-366 8855; www.metroinfo.org.nz; ⏲7am-9pm Mon-Sat, 9am-7pm Sun) is inexpensive and efficient. Most buses run from the **Central Bus Station** (46-50 Lichfield St) between Tuam and Lichfield Sts. Get timetables from the i-SITE or the station's information kiosk. Tickets (adult/child $3.20/1.60) include one free transfer within two hours. Metrocards allow unlimited two-hour/full-day travel for $2.30/4.60, but the cards must be loaded up with a minimum of $10.

Taxi

Blue Star (☎0800 379 979; www.bluestartaxis)

First Direct (☎0800 505 555; www.firstdirect.nz.nz)

Gold Band (☎0800 379 5795; www.goldbandtaxis.co.nz)

AROUND CHRISTCHURCH

Lyttelton

POP 3100

Southeast of Christchurch are the prominent Port Hills, which slope down to the city's port at Lyttelton Harbour. Christchurch's first European settlers landed here in 1850 to embark on their historic trek over the hills.

Lyttelton was badly damaged during the 2010 and 2011 earthquakes, and many of the town's heritage buildings along London St were subsequently demolished. Also fatally damaged was the neogothic **Timeball Station** (www.timeball.co.nz), built in 1876, and where for 58 years a huge time-ball was hoisted on a mast and then dropped at exactly 1pm Greenwich Mean Time. This allowed ships in Lyttelton Harbour to set their clocks and thereby accurately calculate longitude.

Following the earthquakes, Lyttelton has re-emerged as one of Christchurch's most interesting and resilient communities. The town's artsy, independent and bohemian vibe is stronger than ever, and it's again becoming a hub for good bars, cafes and restaurants. It's well worth catching the bus from Christchurch and getting immersed in the local scene.

From Lyttelton, ferries and boat cruises provide access to sheltered Quail Island, as well as to sleepy Diamond Harbour. See www.blackcat.co.nz for details.

If you've got your own transport, the harbour road wends a scenic 15-minute route to pretty Governors Bay, with a couple of good spots for lunch.

The **Lyttelton visitor information centre** (☎03-328 9093; www.lytteltonharbour.info; London St; ⏲9am-5pm Sep-May, to 4pm Jun-Aug) has accommodation and transport information.

Sights

Lyttelton is linked to Christchurch via a road tunnel, but there's a more scenic (and 10km longer) route along the narrow Summit Rd, which has breathtaking city, hill and harbour views, as well as vistas of the Southern Alps.

Eating & Drinking

Freeman's Dining Room RESTAURANT $$
(www.freemansdiningroom.co.nz; 47 London St; pizza $20, mains $25-35; ⏲3pm-late Mon-Thu, from 11.30am Fri, from 9am Sat & Sun) Freeman's does fresh pasta, top-notch pizzas and regular wine and beer specials featuring brews from Christchurch's Cassels & Son Brewery. Grab a spot on the deck for great town and harbour views, and take in Sunday afternoon jazz concerts from 3pm. Definitely the kind of neighbourhood local you'd like in your town.

Lyttelton Coffee Company CAFE $
(www.lytteltoncoffee.co.nz; 29 London St; mains $10-20) This iconic Lyttelton cafe was destroyed in the February 2011 earthquake, but at the time of writing was planning to reopen in late 2012. Check the website: hopefully you can drop by to sample some of Canterbury's best coffee and tasty and robust brunches. Live music on Saturday afternoons was also a pre-earthquake staple.

Fisherman's Wharf SEAFOOD $$
(www.lytteltonwharf.co.nz; 39 Norwich Quay; snacks $7-12, mains $26-34; ⏲11am-8pm) Part alfresco bar and part gourmet fish-and-chippie, Fisherman's Wharf is a top spot for a cold beer and tasty seafood bar snacks and mains. Try the fish of the day – prepared any of three ways – or smaller plates like salmon with lemongrass, chilli and lime, and look forward to views of the harbour and the rugged working port.

Porthole BAR
(cnr Canterbury & London Sts) On the former site of the much-loved Volcano Cafe and Lava Bar, Porthole is another funky reinvention of the humble shipping container. Local wines and Kiwi craft beers are served in the buzzy interior, while laid-back Lyttelton folk chill on the alfresco deck. The Volcano Cafe is still involved too, serving up tasty bar snacks.

Wunderbar BAR
(www.wunderbar.co.nz; 19 London St; ⏲5pm-late Mon-Fri, 1pm-late Sat & Sun) Wunderbar is a top spot to see NZ's more interesting acts, from raucous rock to late-night/early-morning dub. The funky decor alone is worth a trip to Lyttelton. Following the earthquakes, Wunderbar reopened in March 2012. Check the website or www.christchurchmusic.org.nz for what's on.

Governor's Bay Hotel PUB $$
(☎03-329 9433; www.governorsbayhotel.co.nz; Main Rd; mains $14-33) Serves tasty burgers, steaks and fish and chips, and more international meals like slow-cooked lamb shanks with Moroccan cous cous. Enjoy a beer on the cool verandah that's dotted with mementos of the hotel's 145 years of history. Upstairs is accommodation in chic and recently refurbished rooms with shared bathrooms (doubles $100 to $150).

She Chocolat CAFE $$
(☎03-329 9825; www.shechocolat.com; 79 Main Rd; mains $15-34) She Chocolat serves excellent brunches and lunches with an organic and New Age tinge. After ricotta-and-raisin crepes, make room for locally made Belgian chocolates and take in the harbour views. The cafe is also open for dinner on Friday and Saturday nights; the menu includes a unique chocolate-imbued degustation menu with Pegasus Bay wine matches (per person $125). Bookings recommended.

Farmers Market
(www.lyttelton.net.nz; ⏲10am-1pm Sat) Lyttelton's foodie credentials are enhanced by the farmers market held in the local primary school on Saturdays.

Getting There & Away

Buses 28 and 35 run from Christchurch to Lyttelton (25 minutes). From Lyttelton by car, you can continue around Lyttelton Harbour on to Akaroa. This winding route is longer and more scenic than the route via SH75 between Christchurch and Akaroa.

Akaroa & Banks Peninsula

Banks Peninsula and its hills were formed by two giant volcanic eruptions about 8 million years ago. Small harbours such as Le Bons, Pigeon and Little Akaloa Bays radiate out from the peninsula's centre, giving it a cogwheel shape. The historic town of Akaroa, 83km from Christchurch, is a highlight, as is the absurdly beautiful drive along Summit Rd around the edge of the original crater.

Akaroa ('Long Harbour' in Maori) was the site of the country's first French settlement; descendants of the original French settlers still reside here. It's a charming town that strives to re-create the feel of a French provincial village, down to the names of its streets (Rues Lavaud, Balguerie and Jolie) and houses (Langlois-Eteveneaux). There are also a few choice eateries.

If you're not in a hurry, it's definitely worth spending a few leisurely days in the excellent budget accommodations that dot the outer bays of Banks Peninsula. Most accommodation will arrange pick-up in Akaroa.

History

James Cook sighted the peninsula in 1770. Thinking it was an island, he named it after the naturalist Sir Joseph Banks. The Ngai Tahu tribe, who occupied the peninsula at the time, was attacked at the fortified Onawe *pa* (Maori village) by the Ngati Toa chief Te Rauparaha in 1831 and its population was dramatically reduced.

In 1838, whaling captain Jean Langlois negotiated the purchase of Banks Peninsula from local Maori and returned to France to form a trading company. With French government backing, 63 settlers headed for the peninsula in 1840, but only days before they arrived, panicked British officials sent their own warship to raise the flag at Akaroa, claiming British sovereignty under the Treaty of Waitangi. Had the settlers arrived two years earlier, the entire South Island could have become a French colony, and NZ's future might have been quite different.

The French did settle at Akaroa, but in 1849 their land claim was sold to the New Zealand Company, and in 1850 a large group of British settlers arrived. The heavily forested land was cleared and soon farming became the peninsula's main industry.

Sights

The Giant's House GARDEN

(Map p507; www.thegiantshouse.co.nz; 68 Rue Balguerie; adult/child/family $20/10/45; ⏲noon-5pm Dec 26-April 22, 2-4pm in May-late Dec) An ongoing labour of love from local artist Josie Martin, this playful and whimsical combination of sculpture and mosaics cascades down a hillside garden above Akaroa. Echoes of Gaudí and Miró can be found in the intricate collages of mirrors, tiles and broken china, and there are many surprising nooks and crannies to discover and explore. Martin also exhibits her paintings and sculpture in the lovely 1880 house, the former residence of Akaroa's first bank manager.

Akaroa Museum MUSEUM

(Map p507; cnr Rues Lavaud & Balguerie; adult/child/family $4/1/8; ⏲10.30am-4.30pm Oct-Apr, to 4pm May-Sep) This interesting museum is spread over several historic buildings, including the old courthouse; the tiny Custom House by Daly's Wharf; and one of NZ's oldest houses, Langlois-Eteveneaux. It has modest displays on the peninsula's once-significant Maori population, a courtroom diorama, a 20-minute audiovisual on peninsular history, and Akaroa community archives.

Tree Crop Farm WALKING

(☎03-304 7158; www.treecropfarm.com; admission $10; ⏲10am-5pm in good weather only; 📶) The quirky Tree Crop Farm is 1.8km off the main road through Akaroa (take Rue Grehan). This private wilderness garden has rambling, overgrown tracks, sheepskin-covered couches on a ramshackle verandah, and a cafe and travel library with loads of old *National Geographic* magazines. Rustic, romantic accommodation ($200 to $250) is also available.

Maori & Colonial Museum MUSEUM

(Map p505; www.okainsbaymuseum.co.nz; adult/child $10/2; ⏲10am-5pm) At Okains Bay, northeast of Akaroa, this collection of indigenous and pioneer artefacts includes a reproduction Maori meeting house, a sacred 15th-century god stick and a war canoe.

Barrys Bay Cheese

(Map p505; ☎03-304 5809; www.barrysbaycheese.co.nz; ⏲9am-5pm) At Barrys Bay, on the western side of Akaroa Harbour (12km from Akaroa), is the enticing Barrys Bay Cheese, where you can taste and purchase fine cheddar, havarti and gouda. Crackers and chutney are available for a spontaneous seaside snack.

Activities

See the visitor information centre if you like the sound of jetboating, kayaking or sailing on Akaroa Harbour, touring a working sheep farm or visiting a seal colony.

The *Akaroa – An Historic Walk* booklet ($9.50) details a walking tour starting at the 1876 **Waeckerle Cottage** (Map p507; Rue Lavaud) and finishing at the old Taylor's Emporium premises near the main wharf. The route takes in the old wooden buildings

Banks Peninsula

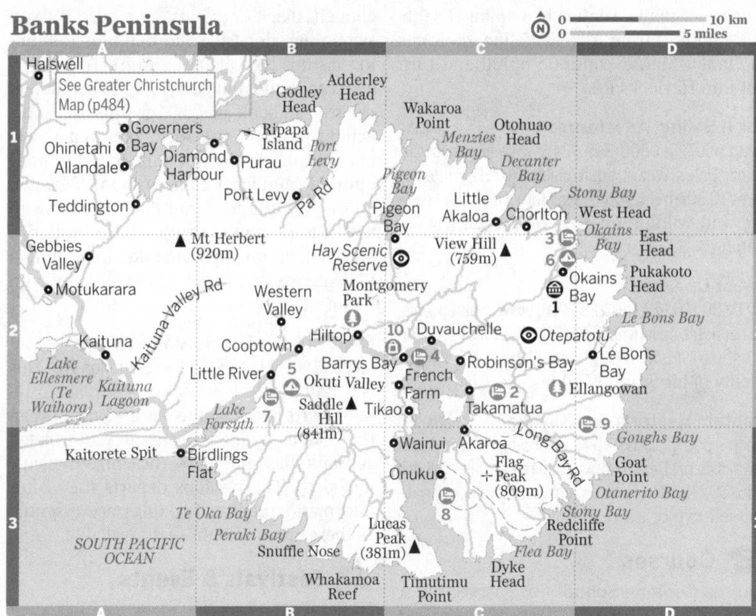

and churches that give Akaroa its character. Audio guides for self-guided walking tours ($10 per 90 minutes) are also available at the visitor information centre.

Banks Peninsula Track WALKING
(☎03-304 7612; www.bankstrack.co.nz; per person $220) This 35km four-day walk traverses private farmland around the dramatic coastline of Banks Peninsula. Costs includes transport from Akaroa and hut accommodation. A two-day option ($145) covers the same ground at twice the speed.

Akaroa Walk WALKING
(☎0800 377 378, 03-962 3280; www.tuataratours.co.nz; per person $1575; ⌚Nov-Apr) A leisurely upmarket 46km stroll, across three days, from Christchurch to Akaroa. Includes good accommodation and lots of gourmet food. You'll only need to carry your daypack.

Akaroa Adventure Centre ADVENTURE SPORTS
(Map p507; ☎03-304 8709; Rue Lavaud; ⌚8.30am-5.30pm) The Akaroa Adventure Centre rents out sea kayaks, bikes, golf clubs, fishing rods and windsurfing gear. Ask here about staying at Purple Peak Backpackers (p509).

Pohatu Plunge WILDLIFE
(☎03-304 8552; www.pohatu.co.nz) Runs evening penguin-viewing tours (adult/child $70/55); spying the white-flippered penguin is best between August and January. Sea kayaking (adult/child $80/60) and 4WD nature tours (adult/child $90/50) are also available, with the option of staying overnight in a secluded cottage (additional $20 per person) in the Pohatu Nature Reserve.

Banks Peninsula

Sights

1 Maori & Colonial Museum C2

Sleeping

2 Coombe Farm C2
3 Double Dutch C2
4 Halfmoon Cottage C2
5 Little River Campground B2
6 Okains Bay Camping Ground C2
7 Okuti Garden B2
8 Onuku Farm Hostel C3
9 Purple Peak Backpackers D2

Shopping

10 Barrys Bay Cheese C2

Onuku Heights Horse Treks HORSE RIDING
(☎03-304 7112; www.onuku-heights.co.nz; 166 Haylocks Rd; from $110; ⌚Nov-May) Surround yourself with the best of the spectacular

scenery of Banks Peninsula. Onuku Heights is 15 minutes from Akaroa: follow the signs to Onuku Marae, continue uphill and turn left into Haylocks Rd.

Fox II Sailing Adventures SAILING
(Map p507; ☎0800 369 7245; www.akaroafoxsail.co.nz; Daly's Wharf; adult/child $70/30; ⊙departures 10.30am & 1.30pm Dec-May) History, scenery and wildlife on NZ's oldest gaff-rigged ketch.

Coast Up Close BOAT TOUR
(☎0800 126 278, 021 228 8091; www.coastupclose.co.nz; adult/child from $65/25; ⊙departs 10.15am & 1.45pm) Fishing and scenic boat trips with plenty of birds and wildlife.

Captain Hector's Sea Kayaks KAYAKING
(Map p507; ☎03-304 7866; www.akaroaseakayaks.co.nz; Beach Rd; kayak hire per half-/full day $35/60) Rental kayaks, canoes and rowboats for self-exploration.

Courses

Akaroa Cooking School COOKING COURSE
(Map p507; ☎021 166 3737; www.akaroacooking.co.nz; 81 Beach Rd; per person $195) Options include popular 'Gourmet in a Day' sessions (10am to 4pm) on Saturdays, and occasional specialised seafood and barbecue classes. All sessions end with tucking into your self-prepared feast, all accompanied by local wines. Check the website for the school's occasional forays into specific ethnic cuisines, including Thai and Italian. Booking ahead is highly recommended.

Tours

Akaroa Dolphins WILDLIFE
(Map p507; ☎0800 990 102, 03-304 7866; www.akaroadolphins.co.nz; 65 Beach Rd; adult/child $70/35; ⊙departures 10.15am, 12.45pm & 3.15pm Oct-Apr, 10.15am only May-Sep) Two-hour wildlife cruises, plus evening cruises and birdwatching trips by arrangement. Say hi to Murphy – wildlife-spotting dog extraordinaire – for us. He even stars in his own children's picture book, available at the Akaroa Dolphins office.

Black Cat Cruises WILDLIFE
(Map p507; ☎03-304 7641; www.blackcat.co.nz; Main Wharf; cruise & swim adult/child $139/115, cruise only $72/35; ⊙5 tours daily 6am-3.30pm Oct-April, 1 tour daily 11.30am May-Sep) The waters around Akaroa are home to the world's smallest and rarest dolphin, the Hector's dolphin, found only in NZ waters. If viewing the dolphins on a harbour cruise isn't enough, Black Cat Cruises can also get you swimming alongside the dolphins (assuming it's not the calving season). Trips operate year-round and carry only 10 swimmers per trip, so book ahead. Wet suits and snorkelling gear are provided, plus hot showers back on dry land. Count on a 2½-hour outing including time in and on the water, and a $59 refund if you don't get to swim with the dolphins. Cruises have around a 98% success rate in seeing dolphins, and an 81% success rate in actually swimming with them.

Eastern Bays Scenic Mail Run TOUR
(☎03-304 8600; tour $60; ⊙9am Mon-Fri) This is a 120km, 4½-hour delivery service to remote parts of the peninsula, and visitors can travel along with the posties to visit isolated communities and bays (beachfront picnic included). The minibus departs the visitor information centre; bookings are essential as there are only eight seats available.

Festivals & Events

French Fest Akaroa FOOD & WINE
(www.frenchfest.co.nz) French Fest Akaroa is a Gallic-inspired get-together, with an emphasis on food, wine, music and art. Don't miss (or stand on) *Le Race D'Escargots,* where sleek, highly trained snails negotiate a compact course. There's also a French Waiter's Race. It's held in late October on a biannual basis in odd-numbered years.

Sleeping

Most Banks Peninsula accommodation is around Akaroa, but the outer bays are also blessed with excellent and interesting budget lodgings. Akaroa has some splurge-worthy, romantic B&B accommodation.

AKAROA

Garthowen B&B $$$
(Map p507; ☎03-304 7419; www.garthowen.co.nz; 7 Beach Rd; s & d incl breakfast $280-345; @ 📶) With two vintage Citroën cars, two friendly Jack Russell terriers and four super-comfy en suite rooms, (almost) everything comes in twos at this upscale B&B rebuilt in heritage style using recycled cedar. Breakfast on the deck comes with a side order of the best view in town.

Oinako Lodge B&B $$$
(☎03-304 8787; www.oinako.co.nz; 99 Beach Rd; d incl breakfast $245-285; @ 📶) This glorious timber mansion was built in 1865 for the

Akaroa

Akaroa

Top Sights
Akaroa Museum ... B2
The Giant's House ... D3

Sights
1 Waeckerle Cottage ... B1

Activities, Courses & Tours
2 Akaroa Adventure Centre ... B2
3 Akaroa Cooking School ... B4
4 Akaroa Dolphins ... B4
5 Black Cat Cruises ... A4
6 Captain Hector's Sea Kayaks ... B4
7 Fox II Sailing Adventures ... B2

Sleeping
8 Bon Accord ... B2
9 Chez la Mer ... B2
10 Garthowen ... B3
11 La Rive Motel ... B1
12 Old Shipping Office ... B4
13 Tresori Motor Lodge ... B4

Eating
14 Akaroa Fish & Chips ... B4
Bully Hayes ... (see 14)
15 Four Square Supermarket ... B2
16 L'Escargot Rouge ... B4
17 The Little Bistro ... B2
18 Vangionis ... B2

Drinking
19 Truby's Bar on the Beach ... B3

Entertainment
20 Cine Café ... B4

British magistrate. It's now an upmarket bed and breakfast with five themed rooms and expansive bay windows with sea and garden views. The lodge was damaged during the 2010 and 2011 Canterbury earthquakes, but at the time of writing was scheduled to reopen in September 2012. Check the website for the latest news.

Chez la Mer HOSTEL $
(Map p507; ☎03-304 7024; www.chezlamer.co.nz; 50 Rue Lavaud; dm $25-28, d with/without bathroom $80/70; @📶) A friendly backpackers with well-kept rooms and a shaded garden, complete with fish ponds, hammocks, barbecue and outdoor seating; it's also a TV-free zone. Free bikes and fishing rods are available.

Bon Accord HOSTEL $
(Map p507; ☎03-304 7782; www.bon-accord.co.nz; 57 Rue Lavaud; dm $27-30, d $59-89; @📶) This colourful and quirky backpackers fills a compact 155-year-old house. Relax on the deck or in the two cosy lounges, or dive into the herb-filled garden to release your inner French chef. There are free bikes to get you exploring.

Old Shipping Office APARTMENT $$$
(Map p507; ☎0800 695 2000; www.akaroavillageinn.co.nz; Church St; d $230) A self-contained apartment in a restored heritage building with an interesting past. (No prizes for guessing the building's former incarnation.) Two bedrooms, a spacious shared lounge and an outdoor spa pool make the Old Shipping Office a good option for families or for two couples. Check-in is at the adjacent Akaroa Village Inn.

Tresori Motor Lodge MOTEL $$
(Map p507; ☎03-304 7500, 0800 273 747; www.tresori.co.nz; cnr Rue Jolie & Church St; d $155-205; @📶) For designer-conscious lodgings treat yourself to the Tresori; its rich, colourful decor is anything but bland. It's a short walk to Akaroa's waterfront cafe and restaurant strip.

La Rive Motel MOTEL $$
(Map p507; ☎03-304 7651, 0800 247 651; www.larive.co.nz; 1 Rue Lavaud; d $125-135; 📶) Old-style motel with big rooms and good facilities; well priced considering each unit (studio, two- and three-bedroom options) is fully self-contained. The decor is slightly dated compared to other, more modern motels, but La Rive represents good value in a sometimes pricey destination. Most downstairs units open out onto compact courtyards.

Akaroa Top 10 Holiday Park HOLIDAY PARK $
(☎03-304 7471, 0800 727 525; www.akaroa-holidaypark.co.nz; 96 Morgans Rd; sites from $35, units $70-118; @📶) On a terraced hillside above town and connected by a pathway to Woodhills Rd, this pleasant park has good harbour views and versatile options for every budget.

AROUND BANKS PENINSULA

TOP CHOICE **Coombe Farm** B&B
(☎03-304 7239; www.coombefarm.co.nz; 18 Old Le Bons Track; d incl breakfast $145-165) Choose between staying in the private and romantic Shepherd's Hut – complete with an outdoor bath – or in the historic farm house, now lovingly restored and dotted with interesting contemporary art and Asian antiques. Hosts Hugh and Kathrine are a friendly Kiwi-English couple. After breakfast (including homemade jam and organic yoghurt), you can negotiate Coombe Farm's private forest and stream walkway.

Okuti Garden ECO-STAY $
(☎03-325 1913; www.okuti.co.nz; 216 Okuti Valley Rd; per person $40; ⊙closed May-Oct; @📶) Part eco-aware homestay, part WWOOFer's haven and an all-round funky and friendly place to stay. Options include sleeping in a teepee, a Mongolian yurt, house truck, earth-brick cottage or farmhouse. Vegetarian breakfasts ($15) are available, with many ingredients sourced from Okuti's own gardens. There are plenty of natural nooks and crannies for reading or relaxing, and there's a generous supply of fresh herbs to kickstart your creativity in the shared kitchen.

Halfmoon Cottage HOSTEL $
(Map p505; ☎03-304 5050; www.halfmoon.co.nz; dm/s/d $30/52/75; ⊙often closed Jun-Sep; 📶) This marvellous cottage at Barrys Bay (12km from Akaroa) is a blissful place to spend a few days lazing on the big verandahs or in the hammocks dotting the lush gardens. The rooms – mostly doubles – are warmly decorated, and the local landscapes and seascapes can be explored by bicycle or kayak.

Double Dutch HOSTEL $
(Map p505; ☎03-304 7229; www.doubledutch.co.nz; 32 Chorlton Rd; dm/s $30/55, d with/without bathroom $76/70; @) Posh enough to be a B&B but budget-friendly, this relaxed hostel is perched on a secluded river estuary

in farmland. There's a general store (and a beach) just a short walk away, but it's best to bring your own ingredients for the flash kitchen.

Onuku Farm Hostel HOSTEL $
(Map p505; 03-304 7066; www.onuku.co.nz; Onuku Rd; sites per person from $12.50, dm/d from $28/66; closed Jun-Aug;) An eco-minded backpackers with basic huts, tent sites and a comfy house on a sheep farm near Onuku, 6km south of Akaroa. From November to March the owners organise swimming-with-dolphins tours ($100) and kayaking trips ($50) for both guests and non-guests, and will pick up from Akaroa. The same family has owned the farm since the 1860s, so you should trust them when they say there's some great walks on the 340-hectare spread. A newly-developed campsite area makes it a great option for travellers with tents or campervans.

Purple Peak Backpackers HOSTEL $
(Map p505; 03-420 0199; www.purplepeak.co.nz; camping by donation, dm/d $25/60;) This rustic surf lodge and backpackers has glorious sea views and a rugged, out-of-the-way location. Accommodation is simple but clean, and during summer there's the occasional tasty seafood barbecue, and pizzas served up from the outdoor wood-fired pizza oven. Surfboards and gear are available for hire. Free shuttles are provided from Akaroa. See Darin at the Akaroa Adventure Centre (p505) for accommodation.

Little River Campground HOLIDAY PARK $
(03-325 1014; www.littlerivercampground.co.nz; 287 Okuti Valley Rd; sites from $25, cabins $40-110) This sprawling campground near the hamlet of Little River is arrayed around a forest and riverside setting. Accommodation ranges from grassy tent sites through to rustic Kiwiana cabins. There's a really cruisy family atmosphere: added benefits for the kids include campfires, trampolines and a natural swimming hole in the river.

Okains Bay Camping Ground CAMPSITE $
(Map p505; 03-304 8789; www.okainsbaycamp.co.nz; 1162 Okains Bay Rd; sites adult/child $12/6) On pine tree–peppered ground right by a beach, with spick-and-span kitchen facilities and coin-operated hot showers. Pay your fees at the house at the camping ground's entrance. There's a small general store around 1km down the road, and a terrific adventure playground for the kids.

Eating & Drinking

TOP CHOICE **The Little Bistro** FRENCH $$
(Map p507; 03-304 7314; 33 Rue Lavaud; mains $27-35; 6pm-late Tue-Sun;) *Très petite, très chic* and very tasty. Look forward to classic bistro style given a proud Kiwi spin with local seafood, South Island wines and Canterbury craft beers. The menu changes seasonally, but usually includes favourites like pistachio-encrusted lamb or Akaroa salmon terrine; vegetarians are not ignored. Booking ahead is definitely necessary. Sometimes open for lunch in summer – check the blackboard out the front.

Vangionis ITALIAN
(Map p507; www.vangionis.co.nz; Rue Brittan; tapas $8-18, pizza $18-28) Thin-crust pizzas, tapas, pasta and Canterbury beers and wines all feature at this Tuscan-style trattoria. Secure an outside table and while away lunchtime, afternoon or evening. Takeaway pizzas are also available.

L'Escargot Rouge CAFE $
(Map p507; www.lescargotrouge.co.nz; 67 Beach Rd; meals $8-14) Tasty gourmet pies ($7), picnic fixings and French-accented breakfasts are the main attractions at the 'Red Snail'. Try the homemade toasted muesli with fruit, yoghurt and honey ($12) before exploring Akaroa harbour by kayak.

Bully Hayes RESTAURANT $$
(Map p507; www.bullyhayes.co.nz; 57 Beach Rd; lunch $15-25, dinner mains $22-35) Named after a well-travelled American buccaneer, the menu at this sunny spot kicks off with Akaroa salmon before touching down for gourmet burgers, pasta and tapas. Try the seafood platter ($31) for lots of briny bounty from local waters. Monteith's beers and a good local wine list make it a worthwhile place to linger. It's a good spot for breakfast, too.

Akaroa Fish & Chips FISH & CHIPS $
(Map p507; 59 Beach Rd; snacks & meals $6-15) Order takeaways and sit beside the ocean, or grab a table and tuck into blue cod, scallops, oysters and other assorted deep-fried goodness. Either way, keep a close eye on the local posse of eager cats and seagulls.

Truby's Bar on the Beach BAR
(Map p507; Rue Jolie) A perfect waterfront location combines with rustic outdoor seating to produce Akaroa's best place for a sundowner

drink. Truby's blue cod and chips for dinner are world-famous in Akaroa, and baked cheesecake and good coffee are other distractions earlier in the day.

Four Square Supermarket SUPERMARKET $
(Map p507; Rue Lavaud; ⏲8am-8pm) Good deli and wine selection.

☆ Entertainment

Cine Café CINEMA
(Map p507; ☎03-304 7678; www.cinecafe.co.nz; cnr Rue Jolie & Selwyn Ave; adult/child $15/13; ⏲2-10pm; wi-fi) Part cafe with excellent pastries, soups and wi-fi, and part cinema showing art-house flicks.

ℹ Information

Akaroa Information Centre (☎03-304 8600; www.akaroa.com; 80 Rue Lavaud; ⏲9am-5pm) Tours, activities and accommodation.

ℹ Getting There & Away

From November to April the **Akaroa Shuttle** (☎0800 500 929; www.akaroashuttle.co.nz; return $45) departs Christchurch daily at 8.30am and 2pm, returning from Akaroa at 10.30am, 3.35pm and 4.30pm. Bookings are recommended. From May to September, there's only a 10am departure from Christchurch. Check the website for Christchurch pick-up options. Scenic tours from Christchurch exploring Banks Peninsula are also available.

French Connection (☎0800 800 575; www.akaroabus.co.nz; return $45) has a year-round daily departure from Christchurch at 9.15am, returning from Akaroa at 4pm.

NORTH CANTERBURY

From Christchurch, SH1 heads north for 57km through Woodend and Amberley to Waipara. From here it continues northeast to Kaikoura, while SH7 branches due north to Hurunui, through flat farming country, to reach Culverden. About 27km from Culverden is the turn-off from SH7 to Hanmer Springs, a thermal resort. The *Alpine Pacific Triangle Touring Guide* (available from Hanmer Springs and Christchurch i-SITES) outlines things to see and do in this region. See also www.visithurunui.co.nz.

If you're a wine buff or foodie, look for the *North Canterbury Food & Wine Trail* touring map at the i-SITE in Christchurch. Online, see www.foodandwinetrail.co.nz.

The **Brew Moon Garden Café & Brewery** (www.brewmooncafe.co.nz; 150 Ashworths Rd; mains $15-26; @ family) on SH75 in Amberley crafts four different beers; sample them all for $12. Our favourite is the gloriously hoppy Hophead IPA. Gourmet pizzas ($20 to $25) and meals including Akaroa salmon and steak sandwiches are also available. Coffee and New York–style baked cheesecake ($10) are other tasty options.

A few kilometres up SH1, the scenic **Waipara Valley** is home to around 20 wineries; see www.waiparawines.co.nz. Sample a pinot noir or riesling and stop for lunch at one of the spectacular vineyard restaurants. **Waipara Springs** (www.waiparasprings.co.nz; SH1, north of Waipara), **Pegasus Bay** (www.pegasusbay.com; Stockgrove Rd, south of Waipara; mains $27-39; ⏲noon-4pm) and the **Mud House** (www.themudhousewinery.co.nz; SH1, south of Waipara) are open daily for wine tasting and sales, and all have restaurant-cafes for a leisurely lunch. During summer, the Mud House also hosts occasional local and international concerts; see www.adayonthegreen.com.au. The annual **Waipara Wine and Food Festival** (www.waiparawineandfood.co.nz) is held in early March. Wine tours are available from several Christchurch-based companies.

The **Pegasus Bay Restaurant** (☎03-314 6869; www.pegasusbay.com; Stockgrove Rd, south of Waipara; mains $27-39; ⏲noon-4pm) has an old-world ambience set amid a lovely European-style garden. The menu takes advantage of superb local produce and recommends appropriate wine matches – Pegasus Bay is a regular contender for NZ's Best Winery Restaurant award. Booking ahead is recommended.

Near the intersection with SH7 is **Waipara Sleepers** (☎03-314 6003; www.waiparasleepers.co.nz; 12 Glenmark Dr; sites from $20, dm $25, s $35-45, d $55-65; @ wi-fi), where you can camp, bunk down in converted train carriages and cook your own meals in the 'station house'. The local pub and general store are located close by.

Hanmer Springs

POP 750

Hanmer Springs, the main thermal resort on the South Island, is 10km off SH7. It's a pleasantly low-key spot to indulge in bathing in hot pools and being pampered in the spa complex. There are good restaurants and lots of family-friendly activities.

Hanmer Springs

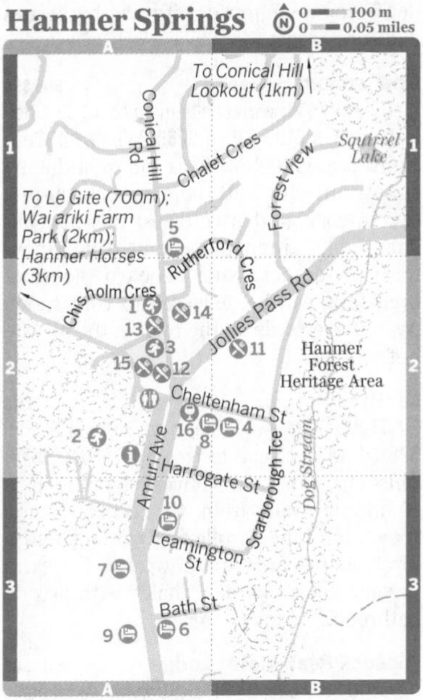

Hanmer Springs

Activities, Courses & Tours

1 Hanmer Springs Adventure Centre ... A2
2 Hanmer Springs Thermal Pools ... A2
3 Thrillseekers Canyon Booking Office ... A2

Sleeping

4 Cheltenham House ... B2
5 Hanmer Backpackers ... A1
6 Hanmer Springs Top 10 Holiday Park ... A3
7 Kakapo Lodge ... A3
8 Rosie's ... A2
9 Scenic View Motels ... A3
10 Tussock Peak Motor Lodge ... A3

Eating

11 Chantellini's ... B2
12 Four Square Supermarket ... A2
13 Hanmer Springs Bakery ... A2
14 Malabar Restaurant & Bar ... A2
15 Powerhouse Café ... A2
Thai Chilli ... (see 15)

Drinking

16 Monteith's Brewery Bar ... A2

Sights & Activities

Hanmer Springs Thermal Pools BATHHOUSE
(☎03-315 0000; www.hanmersprings.co.nz; entry on Amuri Ave; adult/child $18/9; ⏲10am-9pm) Visitors have been soaking in the waters of Hanmer Springs Thermal Pools for over 100 years. Local legend has it that the thermal springs are the fires of Tamatea, which fell from the sky after an eruption of Mt Ngauruhoe on the North Island; Maori call the springs Waitapu (Sacred Waters).

The hot-spring water mixes with freshwater to produce pools of varying temperatures. In addition to mineral pools, there are landscaped rock pools, a freshwater 25m lap pool, private thermal pools ($25 per 30 minutes) and a restaurant. There are loads of fun for kids of all ages, including a waterslide and the exciting Superbowl ($10). The adjacent **Hanmer Springs Spa** (☎03-315 0029, 0800 873 529; www.hanmerspa.co.nz; ⏲10am-7pm) has massage and beauty treatments from $70. A recent refurbishment has lifted the spa to international standards, and entry to the pools is discounted to $12 if you also partake of the spa's facilities.

Molesworth Station WORKING FARM
At 180,500 hectares, Molesworth Station, northeast of Hanmer Springs, is NZ's largest farm, with the country's largest cattle herd (up to 10,000). Inquire at the i-SITE about independent visits to Molesworth, which is under DOC control. Visits are usually possible only when the Acheron Rd through the station is open from late December to early April (weather permitting). The drive from Hanmer Springs north to Blenheim on this narrow, unsealed backcountry road takes around six hours; note that the gates are open only from 7am to 7pm, and overnight camping (adult/child $6/1.50) is permitted in certain areas (no open fires allowed). Pick up the Department of Conservation's *Molesworth Station* brochure from the Hanmer Springs i-SITE or download it from www.doc.govt.nz. **Molesworth Heritage Tours** (☎03-315 7401; www.molesworth.co.nz; tours $198-695; ⏲Oct-May) offer 4WD tours of the station and the remote private land stretching north to St Arnaud. Day tours include a picnic lunch, but there's also a five-hour 'no frills' option.

Other Activities

Other Hanmer Springs activities include kayaking, scenic flights, fishing trips and claybird shooting. Family-friendly activities include mini-golf and tandem bicycles.

There are two skiing areas nearby. **Hanmer Springs Ski Field** is the closest, 17km (unsealed road) from town, and **Mt Lyford Ski Field** is 60km away. They're cheaper than larger resorts. The Hanmer Springs Adventure Centre operates transport.

Thrillseekers Adventures ADVENTURE SPORTS
(03-315 7046; www.thrillseekers.co.nz; SH7) Bungy off a 35m-high bridge ($169), jetboat the Waiau Gorge (adult/child $115/60) or go white-water rafting (Grade II to III) down the Waiau River (adult/child $149/79). Other activities include quad-biking (adult/child $129/99). Book at the Thrillseekers Adventure centre, next to the bridge where the Hanmer Springs turn-off meets SH7. There's another **booking office** (03-315 7346; www.thrillseekerscanyon.co.nz; Conical Hill Rd; 10am-6pm) in town.

Hanmer Springs Adventure Centre ADVENTURE SPORTS
(03-315 7233, 0800 368 7386; www.hanmeradventure.co.nz; 20 Conical Hill Rd; 9am-5pm) Books activities, and rents quad bikes (from $129), mountain bikes (per hour/day from $19/45), fishing rods (per day $25) and ski and snowboard gear. Mountain biking maps are available at the i-SITE.

Wai Ariki Farm Park FARM
(03-315 7772; www.waiariki-farmpark.co.nz; 108 Rippingale Rd; adult/child/family $12/6/35; 10am-4pm Tue-Sat, open daily during school holidays) With more animals than Dr Dolittle's Facebook page, Wai Ariki is a great spot for kids. Llamas, Tibetan yaks, rabbits, guinea pigs and goats all feature, and many of the critters can be hand-fed; horse treks for the young ones are also available. For mum and dad there's a cafe and craft gallery.

Hanmer Horses HORSE RIDING
(0800 873 546; www.hanmerhorses.co.nz; 1hr rides adult/child $59/49, 2½hr treks $99) Rides depart from a forested setting 10 minutes from town on Rogerson Rd. Younger children can be led on a pony for 30 minutes ($25).

Sleeping

Woodbank Park Cottages COTTAGES $$
(03-315 5075; www.woodbankcottages.co.nz; 381 Woodbank Rd; d $180-200) These two matching cottages in a woodland setting are around 10 minutes' drive from Hanmer, but feel a million miles away. Decor is crisp and modern, bathrooms and kitchens are well appointed and expansive wooden decks come equipped with gas barbecues and rural views.

Cheltenham House B&B $$$
(03-315 7545; www.cheltenham.co.nz; 13 Cheltenham St; s $195-235, d $235-265; @) Centrally located B&B with six snooze-inducing suites, all with bathroom, and including two in cosy garden cottages; there's a billiard table, grand piano and complimentary pre-dinner wine. Cooked gourmet breakfasts can be delivered to your room. Avoid the crowds up the road in the private hot tub.

Le Gîte HOSTEL $$
(03-315 5111; www.legite.co.nz; 3 Devon St; dm $28, d with/without bathroom $76/64; @) This charming old converted home is a 10-minute walk from the centre. Large rooms (no bunks), relaxing gardens and a lovely lounge area are drawcards. For extra privacy, book a garden 'chalet' with private bathroom.

Tussock Peak Motor Lodge MOTEL $$
(0800 8877 625, 03-315 5191; www.tussockpeak.co.nz; cnr Amuri Ave & Leamington St; d $145-225;) Modern, spotless and central, Tussock Peak has colourful decor and friendly service that's an eclectic cut above other motels on Hanmer's main drag. The hardest part is choosing what kind of room to get: studio, one- or two-bedroom unit, spa, courtyard or balcony.

Scenic View Motels MOTEL $$
(03-315 7419; www.hanmerscenicviews.co.nz; 10 Amuri Ave; d $135-200; @) An attractive timber-and-stone complex with modern, colourful studios and two- and three-bedroom apartments. Mountain views come as standard.

Hanmer Backpackers HOSTEL $
(03-315 7196; www.hanmerbackpackers.co.nz; 41 Conical Hill Rd; dm $27, s $55, d $58-70; @) Centrally located, the township's original backpackers is a cosy, woodlined haven with a friendly and well-travelled host. Well-maintained shared social areas, cheap wi-fi access and free fruit and coffee all add further big ticks. There's even another edible surprise that we can't talk about.

Rosie's B&B $
(03-315 7095; roxyrosie@clearnet.nz; 9 Cheltenham St; s incl breakfast $55-90, d incl breakfast $85-130) Rosie is originally from Australia, but she's now offering great Kiwi hospitality at

this welcoming and reader-recommended spot. Rooms offer either en suite or shared facilities. Look forward to recently decorated bathrooms and a friendly cat called Kiri. The garden cottage ($130) is a nicely private option. Rates include breakfast.

Hanmer Springs Top 10 Holiday Park HOLIDAY PARK **$**
(☎03-315 7113, 0800 904 545; www.mountainviewtop10.co.nz; Bath St; sites from $32, units $80-160; @📶) Family-friendly park a few minutes' walk from the Hanmer thermal reserve. Kids will love the playground and the trampoline. Take your pick from basic cabins (BYO everything) to two-bedroom motel units with everything supplied. There are two more camping grounds in town if it's full.

Kakapo Lodge HOSTEL **$**
(☎03-315 7472; www.kakapolodge.co.nz; 14 Amuri Ave; dm $28, d $66-90; @📶) The spartan, YHA-affiliated Kakapo has a roomy kitchen and lounge, chill-busting underfloor heating and an outdoor deck. Bunk-free dorms (some with bathroom) are joined by a motel-style unit ($100) with TV and cooking facilities.

Eating & Drinking

Chantellini's FRENCH **$$**
(☎03-315 7667; www.chantellinis.com; 11 Jollies Pass Rd; mains $30-36; ⏲10am-10:30ampm) Tucked away behind the main street, this quiet oasis is a relaxed cafe with outdoor garden seating by day, and an intimate French bar and restaurant by night. Chandeliers and black drapes create an elegant ambience. Portions are generous, and the daily two/three-course lunch for $25/30 is great value – try the leek tart or onion soup. Bookings are recommended for dinner.

Powerhouse Café CAFE **$$**
(☎03-315 5252; www.powerhousecafe.co.nz; 6 Jacks Pass Rd; mains $12-20; 📶🌿) Recharge your batteries with a huge High Country breakfast, or linger for a more sophisticated lunch of a creamy goats-cheese salad. During summer, return for dinner of Akaroa salmon in the Powerhouse's spacious courtyard. An organic fair-trade coffee is a good trade for wi-fi access, and there are plenty of gluten-free and vegetarian options.

Thai Chilli THAI **$$**
(The Mall; mains $14-20) Run by a friendly Thai family, the cosy Thai Chilli respects requests for 'spicy, please', and also offers good-value lunch specials ($14). Service – usually by the family's kids – can be hit and miss, but that's part of the low-key charm. Takeaways are also available.

Malabar Restaurant & Bar ASIAN **$$**
(☎03-315 7745; www.malabar.co.nz; 5 Conical Hill Rd; lunch & breakfast $10-22 dinner $28-36) This elegant eatery presents Asian cuisine from Beijing to Bangalore. Try the Malabar *thali* showcasing four different curries, or the moreish five-spice crackling pork belly. Breakfast and lunch options are less Asian influenced – think bagels, omelettes or burgers – but equally tasty. A limited takeaway menu of Indian, Chinese and Thai favourites is also available (around $13).

Monteith's Brewery Bar PUB
(wwww.mbbh.co.nz; 47 Amuri Ave) The best pub in town features lots of different Monteiths beers and tasty tucker from bar snacks ($10 to $17) to full meals ($17 to $32). Platters ($27 to $54) are good value if you've just met some new friends in the hot pools across the road.

Hanmer Springs Bakery BAKERY **$**
(16 Conical Hill Rd; pies $5; ⏲6am-4pm) Grab a takeaway coffee or gourmet pie.

Four Square Supermarket SUPERMARKET **$**
(Conical Hill Rd) In Hanmer's shopping mall.

Information

Hanmer Springs i-SITE (☎0800 733 426, 03-315 7128; www.visithanmersprings.co.nz; 42 Amuri Ave; ⏲10am-5pm) Books transport, accommodation and activities.

Getting There & Away

Hanmer Backpackers run daily shuttles between Hanmer and Christchurch (90 minutes) and also operates a convenient service to and from Kaikoura (two hours; Monday, Wednesday and Friday). **Hanmer Connection** (☎0800 242 663; www.atsnz.com) also links Hanmer Springs to Christchurch. Shuttles depart from the Hanmer i-SITE.

Check the websites of both companies for current departure points from Christchurch.

Lewis Pass Hwy

At the northern end of the Southern Alps, the beautiful Lewis Pass Hwy (SH7) wiggles west from the Hanmer Springs turn-off to Lewis Pass, Maruia Springs and Springs Junction. The 907m-high **Lewis Pass** is not as steep or the forest as dense as Arthur's and Haast Passes, with mainly red and silver beech and kowhai trees growing along river terraces.

The area has some interesting tramps; see the DOC pamphlet *Lake Sumner & Lewis Pass* ($2). Most tracks pass through beech forest with a backdrop of snow-capped mountains, lakes, and alpine tarns and rivers. The most popular tramps are around Lake Sumner in the Lake Sumner Forest Park and the **St James Walkway** (66km; three to five days) in the Lewis Pass National Reserve. Subalpine conditions apply, so make sure you sign the intentions books at the huts.

Maruia Springs (☎03-523 8840; www.maruiasprings.co.nz; SH7; d $179-199, f $259; @📶) is a small, Japanese-style hot-spring resort on the banks of the Maruia River, 69km from the Hanmer turn-off, with fairly spartan accommodation, a cafe-bar and a Japanese restaurant (breakfast & dinner only). Despite the name, the cheaper Garden View rooms actually offer the best mountain views. In the **thermal pools** (adult/child $19/9, free for guests), water with black mineral flakes of 'hot spring flowers' is pumped into a gender-segregated traditional Japanese bathhouse and outdoor rock pools. It's a magical setting during a winter snowfall, but mind the sandflies in summer. Massages (30/50 minutes $45/65) and private spa houses (per person 45 minutes for $25) are available.

SH7 continues to **Springs Junction**, where the Shenandoah Hwy (SH65) branches north to meet SH6 near Murchison, while SH7 continues west to Reefton and down to Greymouth. Springs Junction has a petrol station and cafe.

CENTRAL CANTERBURY

Two hours west from Christchurch on SH73 is Arthur's Pass National Park. The trans-island crossing from Christchurch to Greymouth over Arthur's Pass is covered by buses and the *TranzAlpine* train.

From Christchurch the road traverses the Canterbury Plains and then escalates rapidly into the Porters and Craigieburn skiing areas before following the Waimakariri and Bealey Rivers and Lakes Pearson and Grasmere to Arthur's Pass. Southwest of Christchurch (reached by SH73 and SH77) is the Mt Hutt ski resort and Methven.

Craigieburn Forest Park

Accessed from SH73, this forest park is 110km northwest of Christchurch and 42km south of Arthur's Pass. The park has many walking tracks, with longer tramps possible in the valleys west of the Craigieburn Range; see the DOC pamphlet *Craigieburn Forest Park: Day Walks* ($1). The surrounding country is also suitable for skiing and rock climbing. Dominating the vegetation is beech, tussock and turpentine scrub, and even a few patches of South Island edelweiss (*Leucogenes grandiceps*).

Craigieburn has a rise of 503m so is one of NZ's best skiing areas, with wild-country slopes that suit advanced skiers.

Near Broken River Bridge is the **Cave Stream Scenic Reserve**, with a 594m-long cave with a small waterfall at one end. Take all the necessary precautions (two light sources per person etc) if you're doing the one-hour walk in waist-deep cold water through the pitch-black cave. For details, get the DOC brochure *Cave Stream Scenic Reserve* (50c). The reserve is in the **Castle Hill** area, with prominent limestone outcrops loved by rock climbers and boulderers. Scenes from *The Chronicles of Narnia: The Lion, the Witch and the Wardrobe* were filmed in the area.

Sleeping & Eating

Smylie's Accommodation HOSTEL $
(☎03-318 4740; www.smylies.co.nz; Main Rd; dm/s/d $28/45/60; @📶) This welcoming YHA-associated hostel and ski lodge is in the town of Springfield, around 30km southeast of Craigieburn. A handful of self-contained motel units ($85 to $120) and a three-bedroom cottage ($180) are also available. In winter, packages including ski-equipment rental and ski-field transport are on offer. Nearby year-round activities include jetboating, rock climbing, mountain biking and horse trekking.

Flock Hill Lodge LODGE $$
(☎03-318 8196; www.flockhill.co.nz; SH73; sites from $30, dm/d $31/155; @📶) This is a high-country sheep station 44km east of Arthur's Pass, adjacent to Lake Pearson and the Craigieburn Forest Park. Backpackers can stay in rustic shearers' quarters, while large groups can opt for two-bedroom motel units or large cottages with kitchenettes. After fishing, exploring, horse riding or mountain

biking, recharge in the cosy bar-restaurant. Unpowered camping sites are also available.

Wilderness Lodge LODGE $$$
(☎03-318 9246; www.wildernesslodge.co.nz; SH73; s incl breakfast $499-649 d incl breakfast $798-998; @) Luxurious lodge on a mountain-beech-speckled sheep station (2400 hectares in size), 16km east of Arthur's Pass. Alpine views and the world's longest driveway produce an absolute middle-of-nowhere atmosphere, and standalone studios with private spa baths feel even more remote. Walking, birdwatching and canoeing are all on tap.

Bealey Hotel HOTEL $$
(☎03-318 9277; www.bealeyhotel.co.nz; s/d without bathroom $60/80, units $150-180; @) Just 12km east of Arthur's Pass, tiny Bealey is famous for a hoax by the local pub owner in 1993. He reckoned he'd seen a real live moa, hence the bogus Big Bird statue standing on a rocky outcrop. There are self-contained motel units and the budget and basic Moa Lodge. Enjoy expansive alpine views from the Mad Moa restaurant.

Famous Sheffield Pie Shop BAKERY $
(Main Rd; pies $4-6) This roadside bakery in the quiet Canterbury Plains hamlet of Sheffield turns out some of NZ's best pies. There are more than 20 different varieties on offer.

Arthur's Pass

POP 62

Arthur's Pass village is 4km from the pass of the same name and is NZ's highest-altitude settlement. The 924m pass was used by Maori to reach Westland, but its European discovery was made by Arthur Dobson in 1864, when the Westland gold rush created the need for a crossing over the Southern Alps from Christchurch. A coach road was completed within a year, but later on the coal and timber trade demanded a railway, duly completed in 1923.

The town is a handy base for tramps, climbs, views and wintertime skiing in Arthur's Pass National Park. Online see www.arthurspass.com. For specific information on weather conditions see www.softrock.co.nz.

Sights & Activities

Near DOC is a small interfaith chapel, with wonderful views.

Day tramps offer 360-degree views of snowcapped peaks, many of them over 2000m; the highest is Mt Murchison (2400m). There are huts on the tramping tracks and several areas suitable for camping. Tramping is best in the drier months (January to April). The leaflet *Walks in Arthur's Pass National Park* ($2) details walks to scenic places including **Devils Punchbowl Waterfall** (one hour return), **Temple Basin** (three hours return) and the **Bealey Spur** track (four to six hours return) with expansive views of the Waimakariri River valley and surrounding mountains. The pleasant **Dobson Nature Walk** (30 minutes return) is best from November to February when the alpine flowers are blooming. Recommended for fit trampers is the **Avalanche Peak** track (six to eight hours return). Longer tramps with superb alpine backdrops include the **Goat Pass Track** (two days) and the longer and more difficult **Harman Pass** and **Harpers Pass Tracks**. These tracks require previous tramping experience as flooding can make the rivers dangerous and the weather is extremely changeable; ask DOC first.

Sleeping & Eating

Camp within Arthur's Pass township at the basic **public shelter** (adult/child $6/3), opposite DOC, where there's running water, a sink, tables and toilets. At the time of research, camping was free at **Klondyke Corner**, 8km south of Arthur's Pass, where there is a toilet. Note that the water here must be boiled before drinking.

Arthurs Pass Village B&B B&B $$
(☎021 394 776; www.arthurspass.org.nz; d $100; wi-fi) This former railway cottage is now a cosy B&B, complete with open fire, free-range bacon and eggs and homebaked bread for breakfast, and the company and conversation of the interesting owners. Ask Geoff about his time working for Greenpeace, and tuck into tasty, home-cooked dinners like organic roast chicken ($35). The two guest bedrooms share one bathroom.

Mountain House YHA Backpackers & Cottages HOSTEL $
(☎03-318 9258, 027 419 2354; www.trampers.co.nz; SH73; dm $27-29, s/d/tr/q $79/82/99/124, cottage d $140 plus $15 per person; @ wi-fi) Excellent dorms and private rooms on one side of the highway, and older, but still comfortable, rooms across the road. The owners also provide transport to trailheads. Self-

contained cottages with cosy open fires are also available. Bookings are recommended from November to April. You can sometimes camp ($20 per person) near the cottages. Phone ahead to check availability first.

Arthur's Pass Alpine Motel MOTEL $$
(☎03-318 9233; www.apam.co.nz; SH73; d $115-135; @ wifi) In the southern part of town, with comfortable motel units (some recently refurbished) and with new beds. If you're snowed in there's a good DVD library and Freeview satellite TV.

Arthur's Pass Village Motel MOTEL $$
(☎021 131 0616, 03-318 9233; www.apmotel.co.nz; SH73; d $145) Centrally located, with two luxury units with cosy leather furniture and warm, natural colours. Booking ahead from November to April is highly recommended.

Wobbly Kea CAFÉ $$
(www.wobblykea.co.nz; SH73; meals $15-32) This friendly cafe-bar serves steaks, pasta and pizza. Takeaway pizza ($28) is also available. Breakfast at the Wobbly Kea ($10 to $18) is a local tradition designed to set you up for the most active of days.

Arthur's Pass Store CAFE $
(SH73; @ wifi) Sells sandwiches, burgers, pies and good breakfasts.

Information

There is no ATM in Arthur's Pass. Limited groceries and petrol are very expensive, so fill up in Christchurch or Greymouth.

DOC Arthur's Pass Visitor Centre (☎03-318 9211; www.doc.govt.nz; SH73; ⏱8am-5pm) Information on all park tramps, including route guides for longer hut-lined tramps. It doesn't make onward bookings or reservations, but can help with local accommodation and transport information. The centre screens a 17-minute video on the history of Arthur's Pass. Purchase detailed topographical maps ($9) and hire locator beacons ($30, highly recommended). DOC also advises on the park's often savagely changeable weather. Check conditions here and fill out an intentions card before venturing out. Sign in again after returning to avoid a search party being organised.

Getting There & Around

Arthur's Pass sees buses travelling between Christchurch (two hours) and Greymouth (2½ hours). **Atomic Shuttles** (www.atomictravel.co.nz) and **West Coast Shuttle** (☎027 492 7488, 03-768 0028; www.westcoastshuttle.co.nz) stop here; check their websites for current departure ponts in Christchurch. Bus tickets are sold at the Arthur's Pass Store.

The *TranzAlpine* train runs between Christchurch and Greymouth via Arthur's Pass.

The road over the pass was once winding and very steep, but the spectacular Otira viaduct has removed many of the treacherous hairpin bends.

Mountain House Shuttle (☎03-318 9258, 027 419 2354), based at Mountain House YHA Backpackers, provides transport to various trailheads. See the Trampers Shuttle tab on www.trampers.co.nz for costs.

Methven

POP 1140

Methven is busiest in winter, when it fills up with snow-sports fans heading to nearby Mt Hutt. In summer, Methven town is a laid-back option with quieter (and usually cheaper) accommodation than elsewhere in the country, and a 'what shall I do today?' range of warm-weather activities.

Activities

Ask at the i-SITE about walking trails, horse riding, mountain biking, fishing, scenic helicopter flights and jetboating through the nearby Rakaia Gorge.

Aoraki Balloon Safaris BALLOONING
(☎0800 256 837, 03-302 8172; www.nzballooning.co.nz; flights $385) Early-morning combos of snowcapped peaks and a champagne breakfast.

Methven Heliskiing SKIING
(☎03-302 8108; www.methvenheli.co.nz; Main St; 5-run day trips $950; ⏱May-Oct) Trips include guide service, safety equipment and lunch.

Black Diamond Safaris SKIING
(☎03-302 1884; www.blackdiamondsafaris.co.nz; ⏱May-Oct) Provides access to uncrowded club ski fields by 4WD. Prices start at $150 for 4WD transport only, while $270 gets you transport, a lift pass, guiding and lunch.

Skydiving NZ SKYDIVING
(☎03-302 9143; www.skydivingnz.com; Pudding Hill Airfield) Offers tandem jumps from 3600m ($440).

Sleeping

Some accommodation is closed in summer, but the following are open year-round, with lower prices often available outside the ski season. During the ski season, it pays to book well ahead, especially for budget accommodation.

Alpernhorn Chalet HOSTEL $
(☎03-302 8779; www.alpenhorn.co.nz; 44 Allen St; dm $28, d $60-85; @☎) This small, inviting home has a conservatory housing an indoor garden and a spa pool; a log fire, free internet and complimentary espresso coffee seal the deal. Bedrooms are spacious and brightly coloured, there's lots of warm, natural wood, and an in-house reflexologist and massage therapist are on hand if you've come a-cropper on the slopes.

Beluga Lodge B&B $$
(☎03-302 8290; www.beluga.co.nz; 40 Allen St; d incl breakfast $165-260; @) Highly relaxing B&B with king-sized beds, fluffy bathrobes, luscious bathrooms and private decks. Extreme privacy-seekers should consider the garden suite, with its own patio and barbecue. A four-bedroom cottage is also available ($275 to $375 per night; minimum three-night stay from June to October).

Glenthorne Station LODGE $$
(☎0800 926 868, 03-318 5818; www.glenthorne.co.nz; lodges per person $25-35, holiday house per person $50) This beautifully isolated 25,800-hectare sheep station is 60km northwest of Methven, on the northern shore of Lake Coleridge. The high-country accommodation ranges from budget lodges to a self-contained holiday house. Activities include 4WD tours, fishing, horse riding and walking.

Redwood Lodge LODGE $
(☎03-302 8964; www.snowboardnz.com; 3 Wayne Pl; r $58-130; @☎) Turkish rugs and a bright decor give this family-friendly spot with single, double, triple and quad rooms plenty of charm. En suite rooms with TV provide privacy and there's a huge shared TV lounge and kitchen. Larger rooms can be reconfigured to accommodate families.

Big Tree Lodge LODGE $
(☎03-302 9575; www.bigtreelodge.co.nz; 25 South Belt; dm $30-32, d/tw/tr $69/69/95; @☎) Transformed from a one-time vicarage, this relaxed lodge has lovely, wood-trimmed bathrooms and a comfy, heritage ambience. Long-term discounts are available. Tucked just behind is Little Tree Studio, a self-contained unit sleeping up to four people ($90/110 summer/winter).

Flashpackers Methven YHA HOSTEL $
(☎03-302 8999; www.methvenaccommodation.co.nz; cnr McMillan & Bank Sts; dm/d $25/70, d with bathroom $80; @☎) This YHA-associated lodge has appealing dining and living areas, a large kitchen and indoor and outdoor spa pools. Prices include breakfast and equipment hire (bikes, golf clubs, fishing gear etc).

Eating & Drinking

Café Primo CAFE $$
(38 McMillan St; meals $10-18) A treasure trove of retro Kiwiana, and the coolest part is that everything is for sale. Sandwiched in and around the souvenir teaspoons and Buzzy Bee bookends are tasty cakes, panini and legendary bacon and egg sandwiches. You'll also unearth Methven's best coffee. Grab a sunny table in the recently added courtyard and kick-start your day with super-healthy granola.

Cafe 131 CAFE $
(Main St; meals $10-20; ☎) A warm space with polished timber and leadlight windows. Serves up all-day breakfasts, good-value platters and soup, pasta, and sandwiches. Beer and wine takes over later in the day. There's also paid wi-fi.

Blue Pub PUB $$
(www.thebluepub.co.nz; Main St; mains $15-30) Drink at the bar crafted from a huge slab of native timber, or tuck into robust meals like sausage and mash or blue cod in the quieter restaurant. Challenge the locals to a game of pool or watch rugby on the big screen (most Friday and Saturday nights from March to June). Across the road, the Brown Pub is the rowdier choice of locals.

Supervalue Supermarket SUPERMARKET $
(cnr The Mall & MacMillan St; ⌚7am-9pm) Good wine and beer selection.

Entertainment

Cinema Paradiso CINEMA
(☎03-302 1957; www.cinemaparadiso.co.nz; Main St; adult/child $14/10) Quirky cinema with an arthouse skew.

Information

Methven i-SITE (☎03-302 8955; www.methveninfo.co.nz; 160 Main St; ⌚9am-5pm; @) Books accommodation, skiing packages, transport and activities.
Medical Centre (☎03-302 8105; Main St)

Getting There & Around

Methven Travel (☎03-302 8106, 0800 684 888; www.methventravel.co.nz; 93 Main St) picks up from Christchurch (one hour; once daily Monday, Wednesday, Friday and Saturday Nov-Apr; up to three times daily May-Oct). Christchurch airport departures are also available.

Shuttles operate from Methven to Mt Hutt ski field in winter ($38).

Mt Somers

Mt Somers is a small settlement just off SH72, the main road between Geraldine and Mt Hutt. The **Mt Somers Subalpine Walkway** (17km, 10 hours) traverses the northern face of Mt Somers, linking the popular picnic spots of Sharplin Falls and Woolshed Creek. Trail highlights include volcanic formations, Maori rock drawings, deep river canyons and botanical diversity. There are two huts on the tramp: Pinnacles Hut and Woolshed Creek Hut ($10 each). This route is subject to sudden changes in weather and precautions should be taken. Download the Mt Somers track guide from www.doc.govt.nz. Hut tickets and information are available at the **Mt Somers General Store** (Pattons Rd). There are other shorter walks in the area.

The **Mt Somers Holiday Park** (☎03-303 9719; www.mountsomers.co.nz; Hoods Rd; sites from $22, cabins $54-79) is small and well maintained.

At the highway turn-off to Mt Somers is **Stronechrubie** (☎03-303 9814; www.stronechrubie.co.nz; SH72; d $120-160), with studios and luxury chalets. The intimate restaurant (mains $33 to $38, open 6.30pm to late Wednesday to Saturday, noon to 2pm Sunday) features excellent Canterbury lamb and local venison and duck. Consider a DB&B package (per two people $230 to $280).

SOUTH CANTERBURY

SH1 heading south from Christchurch along the coast passes through the port city of Timaru on its way to Dunedin, and carries a lot of traffic. The inland route along SH8 is also busy, but showcases the stunning landscapes of the Mackenzie Country. Studded with the intense blue lakes of Tekapo and Ohau, SH80 veers off at Twizel in the Mackenzie Country to hug Lake Pukaki all the way to the magnificent heights of Aoraki/Mt Cook National Park.

Timaru

POP 26,750

The port city of Timaru is a handy stopping-off point halfway between Christchurch and Dunedin. Many travellers prefer to kick on 85km further south to the smaller, more charming Oamaru, but a few good restaurants and good-value motels means Timaru is worthy of a spot of travellers' R&R. The recently opened Te Ana Maori Rock Art Centre is also of interest for travellers seeking to understand NZ's indigenous Maori heritage.

The town's name comes from the Maori name Te Maru, meaning the 'Place of Shelter'. No permanent settlement existed here until 1839, when the Weller brothers from Sydney set up a whaling station. The *Caroline,* a sailing ship that picked up whale oil, gave the picturesque bay its name.

Sights

Te Ana Maori Rock Art Centre MUSEUM
(☎0800 468 3262; www.teana.co.nz; 2 George St; adult/child/family $20/10/50; ⏲10am-3pm) Interesting showcase of the significance of Maori rock art to the Ngai Tahu tribe. Passionate Maori guides really bring the innovative exhibition to life. You can also take a three-hour excursion (departing 3pm, adult/child/family $125/50/250) around the surrounding region to see isolated rock art in situ. Prior booking is essential for the tours. Entrance is via the i-SITE.

South Canterbury Museum MUSEUM
(www.timaru.govt.nz; Perth St; admission by donation; ⏲10am-4.30pm Tue-Fri, 1.30-4.30pm Sat & Sun) Historical and natural artefacts of the region, including a replica of the aeroplane designed and flown by local pioneer aviator and inventor Richard Pearse. Many believe his mildly successful attempts at manned flight came before the Wright brothers first flew in 1903.

FREE **Aigantighe Art Gallery** GALLERY
(www.aigantighe.org; 49 Wai-iti Rd; ⏲10am-4pm Tue-Fri, noon-4pm Sat & Sun) One of the South Island's largest public galleries, with a 900-piece collection of NZ and European art from the past four centuries set up in a 1908 mansion, and adorned externally by a sculpture garden (always open). The gallery's Gaelic name means 'at home' and is pronounced 'egg-and-tie'.

Timaru

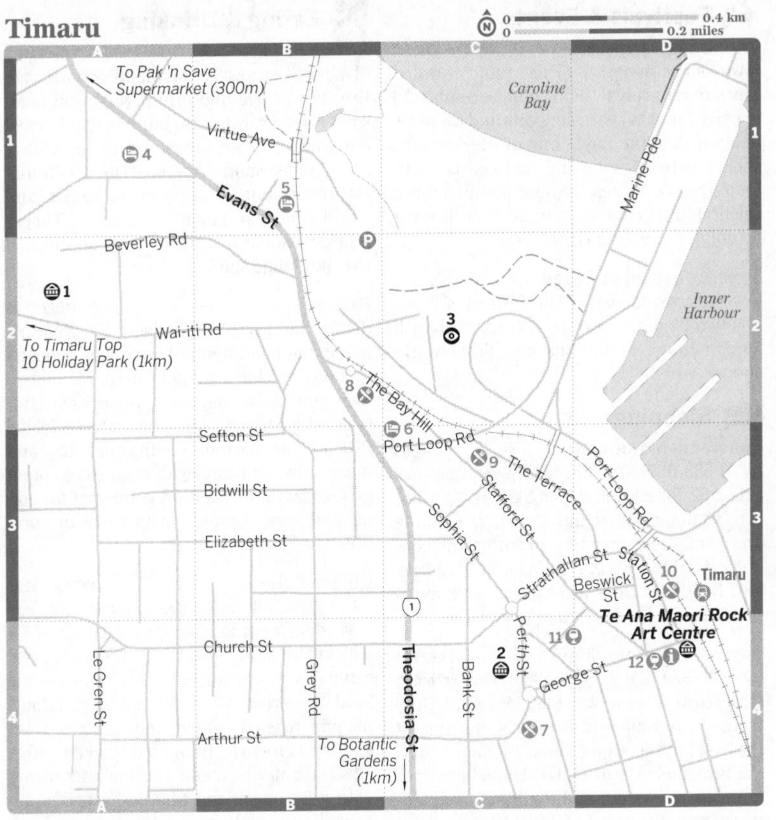

Timaru

Top Sights
Te Ana Maori Rock Art Centre D4

Sights
1 Aigantighe Art Gallery A2
2 South Canterbury Museum C4
3 Trevor Griffiths Rose Garden C2

Sleeping
4 Anchor Motel and Timaru Backpackers A1
5 Baywatch Motor Lodge B1
6 Panorama Motor Lodge C3

Eating
7 Arthur St Café C4
8 Fusion B2
9 Ginger & Garlic C3
10 Off the Rail Café D3

Drinking
11 Petite Wine & Dine C4
12 Speight's Ale House D4

FREE **Botanic Gardens** GARDENS
(cnr King & Queen Sts; 8am-dusk) Established in 1864, Timaru's Botanic Gardens feature ponds, a conservatory and a notable collection of roses and native tree ferns. The gardens are south of town; enter from Queen St.

FREE **Trevor Griffiths Rose Garden** GARDENS
(Caroline Bay; open daylight hours) Rose fans should visit the Trevor Griffiths Rose Garden, with more than 1000 romantic blooms set around arbours and water features. The finest display is from December to February.

Festivals & Events

Christmas Carnival MUSIC
(www.carolinebay.org.nz) This fun, crowded Christmas Carnival (held from December 26 to early January) with concerts and events is held on Caroline Bay – one of the few safe, sheltered beaches on the east coast. South Canterbury's biggest annual summer bash celebrated its centenary in 2012, so it must be doing something right.

Timaru Festival of Roses CULTURAL
(www.festivalofroses.co.nz) The Festival of Roses fills two blooming weeks in November with garden tours, exhibitions and floral workshops.

Sleeping

Panorama Motor Lodge MOTEL $$
(☎03-688 0097, 0800 103 310; www.panorama.net.nz; 52 The Bay Hill; d from $135; @📶) Modern, well-appointed units with spa, sauna and gym. More greenery to soften the concrete would be nice, but Caroline Bay Park and Bay Hill's cafes are a short walk away. Family units are particularly spacious.

Baywatch Motor Lodge MOTEL $$
(☎0800 929 828, 03-688 1886; www.baywatchtimaru.co.nz; 7 Evans St; d $130-145; @📶) Busy Evans St is wall-to-wall motels, but one of the best options along Timaru's main drag is the Baywatch Motor Lodge. Units here offer fantastic bay views, and double-glazed windows mask the worst of the road noise from SH1, though it's worth asking for a room at the back if you're a light sleeper.

Anchor Motel and Timaru Backpackers MOTEL $
(☎03-684 5067; www.anchormotel.co.nz; 42 Evans St; backpackers dm/d $25/60, motels s/d $49/99; @📶) Following a recent refurbishment and with energetic new management, the sprawling Anchor complex is a good-value spot a shortish walk from Caroline Bay. Rooms and dorms are simple, but kept spotless, and just fine if you're transiting north or south.

Timaru Top 10 Holiday Park HOLIDAY PARK $
(☎03-684 7690, 0800 242 121; www.timaruholidaypark.co.nz; 154a Selwyn St; sites from $34, units $65-120; @📶) Parkland site with excellent amenities and a golf course next door that's included in your park tariff.

Eating & Drinking

Arthur St Café CAFE $
(8 Arthur St; snacks & meals $15-18; ⊙closed Sun) Excellent coffee and cruisy Kiwi dub is always a good way to ease into the day. Decked out with retro furniture and tinged with a green and sustainable ethic, Timaru's funkiest eatery offers sandwiches, bagels and world-famous-in-Timaru breakfasts. There's also occasional live music with an alternative and folkie spin.

Fusion RESTAURANT $$
(64 Bay Hill; lunch $17-20, dinner $26-30) Cool and cosmopolitan in red and black, Fusion's modern cuisine channels both Mediterranean and Asian flavours. Pair a Kiwi craft beer with shared plates of kofta or felafel ($12.50), or partner confit duck leg and Asian slaw with a spicy Central Otago pinot gris. Between meals it's a good spot for coffee and cake, complete with views of Caroline Bay.

Ginger & Garlic MODERN NZ $$
(☎03-688 3981; www.gingerandgarlic.co.nz; 335 Stafford St; mains $25-34; ⊙noon-2pm Mon-Fri & 5-10pm Mon-Sat) Timaru's take on sophisticated food is showcased at this long-running local favourite. Asian-influenced standouts include roasted prawn and sesame toast, and tandoori-style marinated chicken with a laksa cream. The menu also includes dishes with a European and Middle Eastern influence. Try the garlic-crusted Canterbury lamb with a walnut and pumpkin salad. Desserts include a mighty mandarin-infused crème brûlée.

Petite Wine & Dine BAR
(18 Royal Arcade; ⊙4pm-late Tue-Sat) The coolest spot in town is concealed in an arcade showcasing Timaru's most funky and interesting shopping. Look forward to cannily mixed cocktails and a stellar array of local and international beers. Tuck into shared antipasto platters ($29) and gourmet pizzas ($12 to 25). A guaranteed bogan-free zone.

Speight's Ale House PUB
(www.timarualehouse.co.nz; 2 George St) Hands down the best of Timaru's pubs, and also worth a visit to see the 19th-century Landing Building. Hearty pub meals – burgers, steak and seafood – and the full range of Speight's beers on tap definitely make a trek downtown worthwhile.

Off the Rail Café CAFE $

(Station St; meals $10-20; @ 📶) This funky licensed cafe is at the train station. Fire up the jukebox crammed with '70s tunes, and sample Kiwi baked goodies and more contemporary globally influenced dishes. It's open late for drinks and occasional live music on Saturday night.

Pak'n Save Supermarket SUPERMARKET $

(cnr Ranui & Evans Sts; ⏲8am-9pm Mon-Fri, to 7pm Sat & Sun) On the main road north.

Information

Timaru i-SITE (☎03-687 9997; www.southisland.org.nz; 2 George St; ⏲8.30am-5pm Mon-Fri, 10am-3pm Sat & Sun; @) Activities, information, and transport and accommodation bookings. Inside is the Te Ana Maori Rock Art Centre.

Getting There & Away

InterCity (www.intercity.co.nz) stops outside the train station, with buses to Christchurch (2½ hours), Oamaru (one hour) and Dunedin (three hours).

Atomic Shuttles (www.atomictravel.co.nz) stop in Timaru en route to Christchurch and Dunedin. Departs Timaru from the i-SITE.

There are no direct buses from Timaru to Lake Tekapo and Mt Cook – you'll need to first get to Geraldine or Fairlie to catch buses to the Mackenzie Country. Ask at the i-SITE.

Inland & Mackenzie Country

Heading to Queenstown and the southern lakes from Christchurch means a turn off SH1 onto SH79, a scenic route towards the high country and the Aoraki/Mt Cook National Park's eastern foothills. The road passes through Geraldine and Fairlie before joining SH8, which heads over Burkes Pass to the blue intensity of Lake Tekapo.

The expansive high ground from which the scenic peaks of Aoraki/Mt Cook National Park escalate is known as Mackenzie Country, after the legendary James 'Jock' Mackenzie, who ran his stolen flocks in this then-uninhabited region in the 1840s. When he was finally caught, other settlers realised the potential of the land and followed in his footsteps. The first people to traverse the Mackenzie were the Maori, trekking from Banks Peninsula to Otago hundreds of years ago.

See www.mtcooknz.com and www.mackenziewinter.co.nz for more information.

GERALDINE

POP 2210

Geraldine has a country-village atmosphere with pretty private gardens and an active arts scene.

The **Geraldine i-SITE** (☎03-693 1006; www.gogeraldine.co.nz; cnr Talbot & Cox Sts; ⏲8.30am-5pm Mon-Fri, 10am-4pm Sat & Sun) has brochures detailing the gardens and galleries in town, and can book rural B&Bs and farmstays.

Sights

Vintage Car & Machinery Museum MUSEUM

(178 Talbot St; adult/child $8/free; ⏲10am-4pm mid-Sep–early Jun) The Vintage Car & Machinery Museum has more than 30 vintage and veteran cars from as far back as 1907. There's also a rare 1929 Spartan biplane.

FREE **Medieval Mosaic** MUSEUM

(www.1066.co.nz; 10 Wilson St; ⏲9am-5pm Mon-Fri, 10am-4pm Sat-Sun, closed Aug) The mind-bending Medieval Mosaic is ideal for fans of medieval history, word games and clever-clogs mathematics. If you're feeling chilly, the world's biggest woollen jersey is also on display.

Sleeping

Scenic Route Motor Lodge MOTEL $$

(☎0800 723 643; www.motelscenicroute.co.nz; 28 Waihi Terrace; d $125-160; @ 📶) This spacious motel is built in early-settler style, but the modern studios include double-glazing, flat-screen TVs and broadband internet. Larger studios have spa baths. You'll find Scenic Route at the northern end of town.

Rawhiti House HOSTEL $

(☎03-693 8252; www.rawhitihouse.co.nz; 27 Hewlings St; dm/s/d/tr $32/50/72/96; @ 📶) This former maternity hospital is now a sunny and spacious budget accommodation with solar electricity and colourfully furnished rooms. Mountain bikes are available, and guests rave about the comfy beds. It's above town off Peel St. If you ask when you book, they'll usually pick you up from the bus stop.

Geraldine Holiday Park HOLIDAY PARK $

(☎03-693 8147; www.geraldineholidaypark.co.nz; 39 Hislop St; sites from $24, cabins & units $45-105; @) This holiday park is set amid well-established trees across the road from a grassy oval. Besides budget cabins and self-contained units, there's a TV room and playground.

WORTH A TRIP

MT COOK SALMON FARM

Some 15km west of Lake Tekapo along SH8 is the signposted turn-off to the **Mt Cook Salmon Farm** (www.mtcookaplinesalmon.com; Canal Rd; adult/child $2/free), the highest salmon farm on the planet. The farm, 12km from the turn-off, operates in a hydroelectric canal system; a scenic drive along the canal has popular fishing spots and enjoys great views of Mt Cook. Stop at the farm to feed the fish, or pick up something smoked or fresh for dinner. The sashimi ($15) is the freshest you'll ever have, guaranteed.

Eating

Four Peaks Plaza (cnr Talbot & Cox Sts; ⊙9am-5pm) has a bakery, cafes and the Talbot Forest cheese shop. Also here is **Barker's** (www.barkers.co.nz), a fruit-products emporium selling (and sampling) kiwifruit wines, juices, sauces, smoothies and jams. Look out also for **Prenzel** (www.prenzelofgeraldine.co.nz), offering regular tastings of luscious fruit schnapps. Every Saturday during summer the town kicks into organic action with a **farmers market** (⊙9.30am-12.30pm).

Cafe Verde CAFE $

(45 Talbot St; mains $10-18; ⊙9am-4pm) Down the lane beside the old post office is this delightful garden cafe. Grown-ups will appreciate the tasty lunch options such as salmon in filo pastry, while the kids can go crazy – with a small, well-behaved 'c', please – in the sweet, postage stamp–sized playground.

Taste RESTAURANT $$

(www.tasterestaurant.co.nz; 7 Talbot St; mains $28-34; ⊙5pm-9pm Tue-Sat) The ritziest place in town features robust meals with a cosmopolitan spin. Try the Canterbury lamb rump dusted with *horopito* (a native NZ pepper). Gourmet pizzas or shared platters and a few local beers are more informal alternatives.

Village Inn PUB $$

(41 Talbot St; mains $15-24) Geraldine's best pub meals are available for alfresco dining in the garden bar at the Village Inn. Indecisive travellers may struggle with the 13 different beers on tap.

Coco SWEETS $

(10 Talbot St) For a quality sugar rush, visit Coco for handmade choccies, plus designer teas, coffee, hot chocolate and cake.

Entertainment

Geraldine Cinema CINEMA

(www.facebook.com/GeraldineCinema; Talbot St; adult/child $12/8) This quirky local cinema has old sofas and features a mix of Hollywood favourites and arthouse surprises. There's also occasional live music, usually with a folk, blues or country spin. Check Facebook for what's on.

PEEL FOREST

Peel Forest, 22km north of Geraldine (signposted off SH72), is among NZ's most important indigenous podocarp (conifer) forests. A road from nearby Mt Peel station leads to **Mesopotamia**, the run of English writer Samuel Butler (author of the satire *Erewhon*) in the 1860s.

Sights & Activities

The magnificent podocarp forest consists of totara, kahikatea and matai. One fine example of totara on the **Big Tree Walk** (30 minutes return) has a circumference of 9m and is over 1000 years old. Local bird life includes the rifleman, kereru (NZ pigeon), bellbird, fantail and grey warbler. There are also trails to **Emily Falls** (1½ hours return), **Rata Falls** (two hours return) and **Acland Falls** (one hour return).

Get the *Peel Forest Park: Track Information* brochure ($1) from Peel Forest Store.

Rangitata Rafts WHITEWATER RAFTING

(☎03-696 3534, 0800 251 251; www.rafts.co.nz; ⊙Oct-Apr) Rangitata goes white-water rafting on the Rangitata River, which contains exhilarating Grade V rapids. The company's base is at Mt Peel, 13km past the camping ground, and includes budget accommodation (sites/dm/d $20/25/48). Rafting trips can be joined from either the Rangitata lodge ($185) or from Christchurch ($195 including return transport), and include hot showers and a barbecue. Count on three hours on the river. A less frantic option for families is a Family Fun trip (adult/child $165/120) on the Grade II Lower Rangitata River. Inflatable kayaks are used, and you'll have around two hours on the river followed by a meal at the lodge.

Hidden Valleys WHITEWATER RAFTING
(☎03-696 3560; www.hiddenvalleys.co.nz; from $200; ⏲Sep-May) If you can't get enough of NZ's rivers, consider a longer three-day rafting expedition with Hidden Valleys. See its website for other rafting journeys exploring the most exciting and remote of the South Island's rivers. One-day rafting trips on the Rangitata River are also available.

Peel Forest Horse Trekking HORSE RIDING
(☎03-696 3703, 027 246 4423; www.peelforesthorsetrekking.co.nz; 1hr/2hr/half-day/full day $55/110/220/380) Horse trekking in the lush forest is on offer at Peel Forest Lodge, even if you're not staying there. Longer multiday treks ($982 to $1623), and accommodation and horse-trekking packages ($550) are available in conjunction with the lodge.

Sleeping & Eating

Peel Forest Lodge LODGE
(☎03-696 3703; www.peelforestlodge.co.nz; d $350) This self-contained log cabin–style lodge is deep in the forest. Bring your own food along for leisurely barbecues; meals are also available (breakfast/dinner per person $25/50) if you don't want cook. The owners don't live on-site so you'll need to book ahead.

DOC Camping Ground CAMPSITE
(☎03-696 3567; www.peelforest.co.nz; sites from $17 per person, cabins per person $22) The pleasant DOC camping ground beside the Rangitata River, about 3km beyond the Peel Forest Store, is equipped with basic two- to four-berth cabins, showers, a kitchen, laundry and card phone. Check in at the Peel Forest Store and ask about renting a mountain bike ($12/35 per hour/day).

Peel Forest Store
(☎03-696 3567; www.peelforest.co.nz; ⏲9am-6pm Mon-Thu, to 7pm Fri & Sat, 10am-5.30pm Sun) Stocks petrol, groceries and takeaway food, and has internet access. The attached Little Mt Peel Cafe & Bar is a cosy spot for steaks, burgers and beers. Also manages the DOC camping ground.

FAIRLIE

POP 725

Fairlie is often described as 'the gateway to the Mackenzie'. To the west the landscape changes as the road ascends Burkes Pass to the open spaces of Mackenzie Country. It's a great place to stop for lunch. Make time to stroll around the **Fairlie Heritage Museum** (www.fairlieheritagemuseum.co.nz; Mt Cook Rd; ⏲9am-5pm), packed full of fascinating mementos of NZ rural life.

The **Fairlie visitor information centre** (☎03-685 8496; www.fairlie.co.nz; Allandale St; ⏲10am-4pm) can provide information on nearby **mountain biking** tracks. There's **skiing** 29km northwest at Fox Peak in the Two Thumb Range. Mt Dobson, 26km northwest of Fairlie, is in a 3km-wide basin.

Sleeping & Eating

Fairlie Gateway Top 10 Holiday Park HOLIDAY PARK $
(☎0800 324 754, 03-685 8375; www.fairlietop10.co.nz; 10 Allandale Rd; sites from $40, units $60-129; @📶) Tranquil, creek-side park that's perfect for families, with mini-golf and a large playground for the kids. Fishing gear is available for hire. Options range from campsites to motel units.

Pinewood Motels MOTEL $$
(☎03-685 8599, 0800 858 599; www.pinewoodmotels.co.nz; 25-27 Mt Cook Rd; d $99-115; 📶) Comfortable, good-value and self-contained units, recently redecorated, and with Sky TV and new flat-screen TVs.

Eat Deli & Bar CAFE $$
(www.eatdeliandbar.co.nz; 76 Main St; mains $10-20; ⏲8am-5pm Tue-Sun; @) Family-friendly, with a kids' play area, Eat also drags in grown-ups with its excellent coffee and counter food, often with a subtle Asian spin. More robust appetites should go for a steak sandwich ($19). There's also beer, wine and complimentary internet access.

Old Library Café CAFE $$
(6 Allandale Rd; dinner $18-35; @) Damaged in a fire in 2011, this cafe-restaurant in a former Andrew Carnegie library opened better than ever in 2012. Look forward to fresh, award-winning local food such as roasted Mackenzie rack of lamb or blue cod with a citrus butter. There's also a more casual all-day menu featuring pasta, salads and soups.

Whisk & Page CAFE $
(49 Mt Cook Rd; coffee & cake $5-7; ⏲closed Sat) Scones, chocolate brownies and damn fine coffee partner with a retro bookshop. You'll probably recognise a few of the iconic tomes from your childhood, and there's also a good selection of NZ-themed books.

LAKE TEKAPO

POP 315

At the southern end of its namesake lake, this town has unobstructed views across turquoise water and a backdrop of rolling hills and mountains.

Lake Tekapo is a popular stop on tours of the Southern Alps, with buses bound for Mt Cook and Queenstown allowing passengers to pop in for a quick ice cream or coffee. Rather than rushing on, it's actually worth staying to experience the region's glorious night sky from atop nearby Mt John.

Sights & Activities

Popular walks include the track to the summit of **Mt John** (three hours return), accessible from just beyond the camping ground. From there, continue on to Alexandrina and McGregor Lakes, making it an all-day walk. Other walks are detailed in the brochure *Lake Tekapo Walkway* ($1). Mountain bikes can be hired (per hour/half day $10/25) from Lakefront Backpackers Lodge and the Lake Tekapo YHA.

In winter, Lake Tekapo is a base for **downhill skiing** at Mt Dobson or Round Hill, and **cross-country skiing** on the Two Thumb Range.

Church of the Good Shepherd CHURCH

(⌚9am-5pm) The lakeside Church of the Good Shepherd was built of stone and oak in 1935, and is a firm favourite for weddings. Nearby is a statue of a collie dog, a tribute to the sheepdogs that helped develop the Mackenzie Country. It's at its scenic best before and after the tour buses, so come early morning or late afternoon.

Earth & Sky ASTRONOMY TOURS

(☎03-680 6960; www.earthandskynz.com; SH1; stargazing adult/child $105/60) Thanks to clear skies and its distance from any main towns, Lake Tekapo has top-notch stargazing, and the area is known as one of the finest spots on the planet to explore the heavens. Departure times vary, so check when you book. On some night tours visitors can use their own cameras to delve into astrophotography with local photographer Fraser Gunn (www.laketekapo.cc). Forty-minute daytime tours (adult/child $50/25) of the University of Canterbury observatory also operate on demand from 10am to 4pm.

Alpine Springs & Spa DAY SPA

(☎0800 353 8283; www.alpinesprings.co.nz; 6 Lakeside Dr; hot pools adult/child $18/10; ⌚10am-9pm) Open all year round, with hot pools scattered amid quickly growing native trees. Private pools and saunas ($26 per hour) are also available, and spa packages start at $120. 'Skate and Soak' combo deals are available at the adjacent Winter Park. There's a good cafe (snacks $5 to $10, open 10am to 7pm) for coffee and cake, or a snack and something stronger.

Lake Tekapo Winter Park SNOW SPORTS

(☎0800 353 8283; www.alpinesprings.co.nz; 6 Lakeside Dr; skating adult/child $16/12, snow tubing adult/child $19/15; ⌚10am-9pm) At the western edge of the lake, the Lake Tekapo Winter Park at the Alpine Springs complex features a year-round skating rink and a winter mini-snow slope for gentle snow-tubing action. Loads-of-fun tubing is even available in summer on a specially constructed artificial slope.

Cruise Tekapo BOAT TOUR

(☎027 479 7675; www.cruisetekapo.co.nz; cruises per person $40-125, fishing per hour $60-80) Fishing and lake cruises from 25 minutes to two hours.

Mackenzie Alpine Horse Trekking HORSE RIDING

(☎0800 628 269; www.maht.co.nz; 1/2hr ride $50/90, half-/full day $140/260) Organises high-country equine explorations. Overnight camping trips ($350) are also available.

Tours

Air Safaris SCENIC FLIGHTS

(☎03-680 6880; www.airsafaris.co.nz; SH8) Does 50-minute 'Grand Traverse' flights over Mt Cook and its glaciers (adult/child $325/215), taking you up the Tasman Glacier, over the upper part of the Fox and Franz Josef Glaciers, and by Mts Cook, Tasman and Elie de Beaumont. A similar flight goes from Glentanner Park, but with higher prices (adult/child $375/265).

Tekapo Helicopters SCENIC FLIGHTS

(☎03-680 6229, 0800 359 835; www.tekapohelicopters.co.nz; SH8) Has five options, from a 25-minute flight ($195) to a 70-minute trip taking in Mt Cook and Fox and Franz Josef Glaciers ($500). All flights include icefield landings and views of Mt Cook.

Sleeping

Hamilton Drive and the surrounding streets in the eastern part of town have other good B&Bs.

Glacier Rock Bed and Breakfast B&B $$
(☎03-680 6669; www.glacierrock.co.nz; 35 Lochinver Ave; d incl breakfast $195-250; @📶) This architecturally designed home doubles as an art gallery. An artist's – or maybe an architect's – eye is evident in the spacious and airy rooms. Breakfast is served in sunny rooms with huge picture windows.

Tailor-Made-Tekapo Backpackers HOSTEL $
(☎03-680 6700; www.tailor-made-backpackers.co.nz; 9-11 Aorangi Cres; dm $29-33, s $60, d with/without bathroom $80/70; @) This hostel favours beds rather than bunks and is spread over a pair of well-tended houses on a peaceful street away from the main road. The interior is spick and span and there's a barbecue-equipped garden complete with well-established trees, lovely birdsong and a children's playground.

Lakefront Backpackers Lodge HOSTEL $
(☎03-680 6227; www.laketekapo-accommodation.co.nz; Lakeside Dr; dm/d $28/80; @📶) An impressive lakeside place owned by the nearby holiday park (about 1km from the township). Relax by the open fire in the comfy lounge area or take in the sensational views from the front deck. Rooms are modern and bathrooms are top-notch. Backpacker buses stop by so it can get a tad social.

Lake Tekapo Motels & Holiday Park HOLIDAY PARK $$
(☎0800 853 853, 03-680 6825; www.laketekapo-accommodation.co.nz; Lakeside Dr; sites from $30, units $60-150; @📶) Has a pretty and peaceful lakeside locale, plus accommocation options from basic cabins to motel units with full kitchens and Sky TV. Newer chalets come with shared picnic tables, barbecues and spectacular lake vistas.

Peppers Bluewater Resort MOTEL $$
(☎0800 275 373; www.peppers.co.nz; SH8; d from $140; 📶) A sprawling resort arrayed around rocky pools and tussocky gardens. Rooms are chic and modern – if sometimes on the small side – but last-minute online discounts make this a place worth considering.

Lake Tekapo YHA HOSTEL $
(☎03-680 6857; www.yha.co.nz; 3 Simpson Lane; dm $37-78, d&tw $96; @📶) Friendly, well-equipped little place with a living room adorned with open fireplaces, a piano and outstanding views across the lake to the mountains beyond.

✕ Eating

The dining scene at Lake Tekapo has traditionally been lacklustre, but a few recent openings have improved culinary choices.

TOP CHOICE **Astro Café** CAFE $
(Mt John Observatory; coffee & cake $4-8, snacks $7-12) This glass-walled pavilion atop Mt John has spectacular 360-degree views across the entire Mackenzie Basin – quite possibly one of the planet's best locations for a cafe. Tuck into bagels with local Aoraki salmon, or fresh ham-off-the-bone sandwiches; the coffee and cake is pretty good, too. After dark, Astro becomes the location for astrophotography with local photographer Fraser Gunn.

Kohan JAPANESE $$
(SH8; lunch $10-16, dinner $22-35) The Japanese food at Kohan is among the South Island's best, and with a salmon farm just up the road, you know the sashimi is ultrafresh. Lunch specials are good value, and you should definitely leave room for their handmade green-tea ice-cream.

Pepe's ITALIAN $$
(SH8; mains $15-30; ⏲6pm-late) With large booths and walls decorated with skiing paraphernalia, the rustic Pepe's is a cosy little place, with good pizza and pasta. Some of the names are a bit naff (Vinnie's Venison or Spag Bol Bada Bing, anyone?), but the dishes are tasty, and later at night it becomes a good spot for a few quiet drinks.

Mackenzie's Bar & Grill PUB $$
(SH8; mains $22-34) Serving up interesting spins on steak, chicken and seafood, everything at Mackenzie's comes with a side order of stellar lake and mountain views. Robust dishes like lamb shanks and beef Wellington are the perfect response to an active day's adventuring. Even if you're dining somewhere else, pop in for a Monteiths Summer Ale or glass of sauvignon blanc.

Run 77 CAFE $
(SH8; mains $10-24) Relax on chunky wooden furniture and enjoy Tekapo's good coffee, or sandwiches, burgers and pies made from local salmon and organic, free-range beef and venison from the owner's high-country spread (the *real* Run 77). Soups, salads and anitipasto platters tick both the healthy and tasty boxes.

Four Square Supermarket SUPERMARKET
(SH8) Located beside a handy bakery.

Information

There are no ATMs at Lake Tekapo (p526).

Lake Tekapo i-SITE (03-680 6579; www.laketekapountouched.co.nz; Godley Hotel, SH8; 9am-6pm) Accommodation, activities and transport information.

Getting There & Away

Southbound services to Queenstown (four hours) and Wanaka (three hours via Tarras), and northbound services to Christchurch (four hours), are offered by **Atomic Shuttles** (www.atomictravel.co.nz), **InterCity** (www.intercity.co.nz) and **Southern Link Coaches** (0508 458 835; www.southernlinkcoaches.co.nz).

Cook Connection (0800 266 526; www.cookconnect.co.nz) operates to Mt Cook (two hours) and Twizel (one hour). Travel can be over more than one day.

LAKE PUKAKI

On the southern shore of Lake Pukaki, 45km southwest of Lake Tekapo and 2km northeast of the turn-off to Mt Cook, is the **Lake Pukaki visitor information centre** (03-435 3280; www.mtcooknz.com; SH8; 9am-6pm Oct-Apr, 10am-4pm May-Sep). The real highlight here is the sterling **lookout**, which on a clear day gives a picture-perfect view of Mt Cook and its surrounding peaks, with the ultrablue lake in the foreground.

TWIZEL

POP 1015

It wasn't long ago that New Zealanders maligned the town of Twizel, just south of Lake Pukaki. The town was built in 1968 to service construction of the nearby hydroelectric power station, and was due to be abandoned in 1984 when the construction project was completed. Now the town's residents are having the last laugh as new lakeside subdivisions have been built to take advantage of the area's relaxed lakes-and-mountains lifestyle. Accommodation and eating options are better value in Twizel than in Mt Cook, but you will be forgoing waking up right in the mountains.

The **Twizel i-SITE** (03-435 0066; www.twizel.info; Twizel Events Centre; 9am-6pm Mon-Fri, noon-3pm Sat-Sun; @) is right in town, and there's an ATM in the main shopping area. Note there's no ATM at Mt Cook or Lake Tekapo. Self-drive travellers should also fill up with petrol in Twizel before heading to Mt Cook.

Sights & Activities

Nearby Lake Ruataniwha is popular for rowing, boating and windsurfing. Fishing in local rivers, canals and lakes is also big business and there are a number of guides in the region. Ask at the i-SITE.

Kaki Visitor Hide WILDLIFE RESERVE
(03-435 3124; adult/child $15/7; 9.30am & 4.30pm late Oct-Apr) The rare *kaki* (black stilt bird) is found only in NZ, and a breeding program is aiming to increase the population at the Ahuriri Conservation Park. Just south of Twizel, the Kaki Visitor Hide gives you a close-up look at these elusive birds. Bookings are essential for the one-hour tour. Book at the Twizel i-SITE (you'll need your own transport).

Tours

Discovery Tours GUIDED TOUR
(03-435 0114, 0800 213 868; www.discoverytours.co.nz) Guided, small-group tours around the Mackenzie Country, including hiking and helibiking, plus a popular two-hour tour (adult/child $75/40) to the site of the Pelennor battlefield in the *Lord of the Rings* movies. You can even charge around like a mad thing wearing *LOTR* replica gear. A shorter one-hour *LOTR* tour (adult/child $55/30) is also available.

Helicopter Line SCENIC FLIGHTS
(03-435 0370, 0800 650 652; www.helicopter.co.nz; SH8, Pukaki Airport) Helicopter Line fly over the Mt Cook region, departing from the Lake Pukaki aiport. Sightseeing flights last from 25 minutes ($230) to 60 minutes ($535) and include a snow landing.

BLUE CRUSH

The blazing turquoise colour of Lake Pukaki, a characteristic it shares with other regional bodies of water such as Lake Tekapo, is due to 'rock flour' (sediment) in the water. This so-called flour was created when the lake's basin was gouged out by a stony-bottomed glacier moving across the land's surface, with the rock-on-rock action grinding out fine particles that ended up being suspended in the glacial melt water. This sediment gives the water a milky quality and refracts the sunlight beaming down, hence the brilliant colour.

Sleeping

Matuka Lodge B&B $$$
(☎03-435 0144; www.matukalodge.co.nz; Old Station Rd; d $465-535; @☜) Surrounded by farmland and mountain scenery, this luxury B&B blends modern design with antiques and Oriental rugs sourced on the owners' travels. A library of well-thumbed Lonely Planet guides is testament to their wanderlust, so look forward to interesting chats over pre-dinner drinks. Breakfast often includes salmon smoked just up the road at the Twizel Aoraki Smokehouse.

Omahau Downs B&B $$
(☎03-435 0199; www.omahau.co.nz; SH8; cottages d $135, B&B d $165; ⊙closed Jun-Aug) This rural homestead 2km north of Twizel has two cosy, self-contained cottages sleeping up to four, and a B&B lodge with sparkling, modern rooms and a deck looking out on the Ben Ohau Range. An essential experience is a moonlit, wood-fired outdoor bath ($20). Don't make the mistake of booking for only one night.

Mountain Chalet Motels MOTEL $$
(☎03-435 0785, 0800 629 999; www.mountainchalets.co.nz; Wairepo Rd; dm $25, d $95-135; ☜) A reader-recommended place with friendly owners and cosy, well-equipped, self-contained A-frame chalets. The cheapest units are studios, but there are a number of two-bedroom set-ups for larger groups or families. There's also a small, laid-back lodge that's perfect for backpackers.

Parklands Alpine Tourist Park HOLIDAY PARK $
(☎03-435 0507; www.parklandstwizel.co.nz; 122 Mackenzie Dr; sites from $36, dm $30, units $90-150; @☜) Offers green, flower-filled grounds and accommodation in a colourfully refurbished maternity hospital. There are a few basic cabins, and room for tents and campervans. The modern, self-contained cottages are particularly good value.

High Country Lodge & Backpackers HOSTEL $
(☎03-435 0671; www.highcountrylodge.co.nz; Mackenzie Dr; dm $29-35, d $50-90, units $125-155; @☜) This sprawling place used to be a basic hostel for construction workers, and is now trimmed with colourful curtains and bright bed linen. Beyond the dorms and the double rooms, a few standalone motel units also see your Kiwi pesos going a long way.

Eating & Drinking

Poppies Cafe CAFE $$
(www.poppiescafe.com; 1 Benmore Pl; breakfast & lunch $9-18, dinner $24-32) Lunch showcases lighter meals like salmon filo parcels, while dinner is a more formal experience with lamb rump or an Asian-style trio of duck; excellent pizzas ($18 to 26) occupy a tasty middle ground. Where possible, organic and locally sourced produce is used. Poppies is on the outskirts of town near the Mackenzie Country Inn.

Shawty's Café CAFE $$
(4 Market Pl; breakfast & lunch $9-19, dinner mains $21-31; ☜) Cool beats and craft beers create a mood that's surprisingly sophisticated for Twizel. Big breakfasts and gourmet pizzas ($12 to $25) are a good way to start and end an active day amid the surrounding alpine vistas. The adjacent Grappa Lounge has occasional DJs and live music from Wednesday to Saturday across summer.

Jasmine Thai Café THAI $$
(1 Market Pl; lunch $12, dinner $17-22; ⊙noon-2pm Tue-Sun & 5-9pm daily) Thailand comes to Twizel, and the zesty and zingy flavours of your favourite Southeast Asian beach holiday have travelled well to get this far inland. Alcohol is BYO, so grab a few cold beers from the Four Square supermarket to ease Jasmine's authentic Thai heat.

Getting There & Away

Onward services to Mt Cook (one hour) and Queenstown (three hours), and northbound services to Christchurch (five hours) are offered by **Atomic Shuttles** (www.atomictravel.co.nz) and **InterCity** (☎03-365 1113; www.intercity.co.nz).

Cook Connection (☎0800 266 526; www.cookconnect.co.nz) operates to Mt Cook (one hour) and Lake Tekapo (one hour). Travel can be over more than one day.

Naked Bus (www.nakedbus.com) travel to Christchurch and Queenstown/Wanaka.

LAKE OHAU & OHAU FORESTS

Six forests in the Lake Ohau area (Dobson, Hopkins, Huxley, Temple, Ohau and Ahuriri) are administered by DOC. The numerous walks in this vast recreation grove are detailed in the DOC pamphlet *Ohau Conservation Area* ($1); huts and camping areas are also scattered throughout for adventurous trampers.

Lake Ohau Lodge LODGE **$$**
(☎03-438 9885; www.ohau.co.nz; Lake Ohau Rd; s $99-175, d $105-200) Lake Ohau Lodge is idyllically sited on the western shore of rower-friendly Lake Ohau, 42km west of Twizel. Prices listed are for accommodation only (everything from backpacker-style to upmarket rooms with deck and mountain views). DB&B packages are good value. The lodge is the wintertime service centre for the Ohau Ski Field. In the summer it's a quieter retreat.

Aoraki/Mt Cook National Park

The spectacular 700-sq-km Aoraki/Mt Cook National Park, along with Fiordland, Aspiring and Westland National Parks, incorporates the Southwest New Zealand (Te Wahipounamu) World Heritage Area, which extends from Westland's Cook River down to Fiordland. Fenced in by the Southern Alps and the Two Thumb, Liebig and Ben Ohau Ranges, more than a third of the park has a blanket of permanent snow and glacial ice.

Of the 27 NZ mountains over 3050m, 22 are in this park. The highest is the mighty Mt Cook – at 3755m it's the tallest peak in Australasia. Known to Maori as Aoraki (Cloud Piercer), after an ancestral deity in Maori mythology, the mountain was named after James Cook by Captain Stokes of the survey ship HMS *Acheron*.

The Mt Cook region has always been the focus of climbing in NZ. On 2 March 1882, William Spotswood Green and two Swiss alpinists failed to reach the summit of Cook after an epic 62-hour ascent. But two years later a trio of local climbers – Tom Fyfe, George Graham and Jack Clarke – were spurred into action by the news that two well-known European alpinists were coming to attempt Cook, and set off to climb it before the visitors. On Christmas Day 1884 they ascended the Hooker Glacier and north ridge, a brilliant climb in those days, and stood on the summit.

In 1913, Australian climber Freda du Faur became the first woman to reach the summit. In 1948, Edmund Hillary's party, along with Tenzing Norgay, climbed the south ridge; Hillary went on to become the first to reach the summit of Mt Everest. Since then, most of the daunting face routes have been climbed. Among the region's many great peaks are Sefton, Tasman, Silberhorn, Malte Brun, La Perouse, Hicks, De la Beche, Douglas and the Minarets. Many can be ascended from Westland National Park, and there are climbers' huts on both sides of the divide.

Mt Cook is a wonderful sight, assuming there's no cloud in the way. Most visitors arrive on tour buses, stop at the Hermitage hotel for photos, and then zoom off back down SH80. Hang around to soak up this awesome peak and the surrounding landscape and to try the excellent short walks. On the trails, look for the thar, a goatlike creature and excellent climber; the chamois, smaller and of lighter build than the thar; and red deer. Summertime brings the large mountain buttercup (the Mt Cook lily), and mountain daisies, gentians and edelweiss.

 Sights

TASMAN GLACIER

The Tasman Glacier is a predictably spectacular sweep of ice, but further down it's downright ugly. Normally as a glacier retreats it melts back up the mountain, but the Tasman is unusual because its last few kilometres are almost horizontal. In recent decades it has melted from the top down, exposing a jumble of stones, rocks and boulders and forming a lake. In other words, in its 'ablation zone' (where it melts), the Tasman is covered in a solid mass of debris, which slows down its melting rate and makes it unsightly.

Despite this considerable melt, the ice by the site of the old Ball Hut is still estimated to be over 600m thick. In its last major advance (17,000 years ago), the glacier crept south far enough to carve out Lake Pukaki. A later advance did not reach out to the valley sides, so the Old Ball Hut Rd runs between the outer valley walls and the lateral moraines of this later advance.

Like the Fox and Franz Josef Glaciers on the other side of the divide, the Mt Cook glaciers move fast. The **Alpine Memorial**, near the old Hermitage site on the Hooker Valley Track, commemorating one of the mountain's first climbing disasters. Three climbers were killed by an avalanche in 1914; only one of the bodies was recovered at the time, but 12 years later a second one melted out of the bottom of the Hochstetter Icefall, 2000m below where the party was buried, illustrating the glaciers' speed.

HERMITAGE

With fantastic views of Mt Cook, this is arguably the most famous hotel in NZ. Originally constructed in 1884, when the trip from

Aoraki/Mt Cook National Park

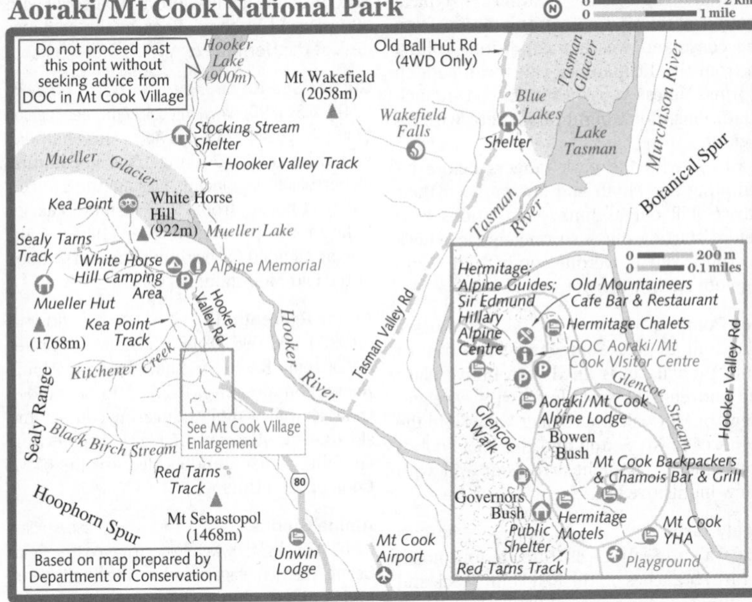

Christchurch took several days, the first hotel was destroyed in a flash flood in 1913. You can still see the foundations in Hooker Valley, 2km from the current Hermitage. Rebuilt, it survived until 1957, when it burnt down. The present Hermitage was built on the same site and a new wing was added for the new millennium.

Sir Edmund Hillary Alpine Centre MUSEUM, PLANETARIUM
(www.hermitage.co.nz; The Hermitage; 1 movie adult/child $18/8, 6 movies adult/child/family $27/14/54; ⏲7.30am-8.30pm) The Sir Edmund Hillary Alpine Centre opened in late 2007 – just three weeks before the January 2008 death of the man often regarded as the greatest New Zealander of all time. His commentary tracks were recorded only a few months before he died. The centre includes a full-dome digital planetarium showing four different digital presentations, and a cinema screen showing the *Mt Cook Magic* 3D movie and a fascinating 75-minute documentary about Sir Ed's conquest of Mt Everest. Another documentary, screened in the museum on a continual basis, reflects the charity and development work that Sir Edmund Hillary achieved in the decades after his conquest of Mt Everest in 1953. Admission to the museum itself is free.

Big Sky ASTRONOMY
(www.hermitage.co.nz; adult/child $50/25; ⏲nightly, weather permitting) NZ's southern sky is introduced by a 30-minute presentation in the Alpine Centre's digital planetarium, before participants venture outside to study the celestial real deal with telescopes, binoculars and an astronomy guide.

Activities

Various easy walks from the Hermitage area are outlined in the brochures available from DOC. Always be prepared for sudden weather changes. Longer walks are recommended only for those with mountaineering experience, as conditions at higher altitudes are severe and the tracks dangerous. Many people have died here, and most walkers shouldn't consider tackling these trails. If you intend on staying at any of the park's huts, it's essential to register your intentions at the DOC visitor centre and pay the hut fee.

For the experienced, there's unlimited scope for climbing, but regardless of your skills, take every precaution – more than 200 people have died in climbing accidents in the park. The bleak In Memoriam book in the visitor information centre begins with the first death on Mt Cook in 1907, and since then more than 70 climbers have died on the peak.

Highly changeable weather is typical around here; Mt Cook is only 44km from the coast and weather conditions rolling in from the Tasman Sea can mean sudden storms. Unless you're experienced in such conditions, don't climb anywhere without a guide.

Check with the park rangers before attempting any climb and always heed their advice. Fill out a climbers-intentions card before starting out – so rangers can check on you if you're overdue coming out – and sign out again when you return.

Kea Point TRAMPING
The trail to Kea Point (two-hours return from the village) is lined with native plant life and ends at a platform with excellent views of Mt Cook, the Hooker Valley and the ice faces of Mt Sefton and the Footstool. If you're lucky, you might share your walk with a few inquisitive kea.

Sealy Tarns TRAMPING
The walk to Sealy Tarns (three to four hours return) branches off the Kea Point Track and continues up the ridge to Mueller Hut (dorm $36), a comfortable 30-bunk hut with gas and cooking facilities.

Hooker Valley TRAMPING
The walk up the Hooker Valley (three hours return) crosses a couple of swing bridges to Stocking Stream and the terminus of the Hooker Glacier. After the second swing bridge, Mt Cook totally dominates the valley.

Tasman Glacier View Track TRAMPING
The Tasman Valley walks are popular for their views of the Tasman Glacier. Walks start at the end of the unsealed Tasman Valley Rd, 8km from the village. The Tasman Glacier View Track (50 minutes return) leads to a viewpoint on the moraine wall, passing the Blue Lakes (more green than blue these days) on the way.

Ultimate Hikes TRAMPING
(☎03-435 1899, 0800 686 800; www.ultimatehikes.co.nz; adult/child $108/67; ⏲Nov-Apr) Offers a day-long 8km walk from the Hermitage through the Hooker Valley to the terminal lake of the Hooker Glacier.

Glacier Explorers BOAT TOUR
(☎0800 686 800, 03-435 1809; www.glacierexplorers.com; per person $145) Heads out on the terminal lake of the Tasman Glacier. It starts with a 20-minute walk to the shore of Lake Tasman, where you board a custom-built MAC boat and get up close and personal with 300-year-old icebergs. Book at the activities desk at the Hermitage.

Glacier Sea-Kayaking KAYAKING
(☎03-435 1890; www.mtcook.com; per person $130-145; ⏲early Oct–mid-Apr) Has half-day and three-hour kayaking trips negotiating icebergs across glacial bays in the Hooker Valley. Choose from the Tasman Glacier Lake or the pristine Mueller Glacier Lake (recommended for beginner kayakers). Book at the Old Mountaineers Cafe.

Alpine Recreation TRAMPING
(☎0800 006 096, 03-680 6736; www.alpinerecreation.com) Based in Lake Tekapo, Alpine Recreation organises high-altitude guided treks, as well as mountaineering courses and ski touring. Also on offer are summertime climbing courses, and guided ascents of Mt Cook or Mt Tasman.

Alpine Guides SNOW SPORTS
(☎03-435 1834; www.alpineguides.co.nz; Retail Centre, The Hermitage) Ski-touring, heliskiing, and guided climbs and mountaineering courses.

Southern Alps Guiding SNOW SPORTS
(☎03-435 1890, 027 342 277; www.mtcook.com) Heliskiing and boarding options including the Tasman Glacier. Ask at the Old Mountaineers Cafe

Glentanner Horse Trekking HORSE RIDING
(☎03-435 1855; www.glentanner.co.nz; 1/2/3hr ride $60/80/150; ⏲Nov-Apr) Leads guided treks on a high-country sheep station. All levels of experience are welcome.

Tours

Mount Cook Ski Planes SCENIC FLIGHTS
(☎0800 800 702, 03-430 8034; www.mtcookskiplanes.com) Based at Mt Cook Airport, offering 40-minute (adult/child $405/295) and 55-minute (adult/child $530/405) flights, both with snow landings. Flightseeing without a landing is a cheaper option; try the 25-minute Mini Tasman trip (adult/child $275/255).

Helicopter Line SCENIC FLIGHTS
(☎03-435 1801, 0800 650 651; www.helicopter.co.nz) From Glentanner Park, the Helicopter Line does 20-minute Alpine Vista flights ($215), an exhilarating 30-minute flight over the Ben Ohau Range ($295) and a 45-minute Mountains High flight over the Tasman Glacier and by Mt Cook ($399). All feature snow landings.

Tasman Valley 4WD Argo Tours 4WD TOUR
(☎0800 686 800, 03-435 1601; www.mountcooktours.co.nz; adult/child $75/38; ⏰year round) Offers a 90-minute Argo (actually an *8WD* all-terrain vehicle) tour checking out the Tasman Glacier and its terminal lake. Expect plenty of alpine flora and an interesting commentary along the way. Pre-book online (recommended) or book at the Hermitage hotel activities desk.

Sleeping

Accommodation is more expensive in Mt Cook Village than in Twizel, but the thrill of waking up so close to the mountains is definitely worth the additional expense.

Campers and walkers can use the **public shelter** (⏰8am-7pm Oct-Apr, to 5pm May-Sep) in the village, which has running water, toilets and coin-operated showers. Note that this shelter cannot be used for overnight stays.

Aoraki/Mt Cook Alpine Lodge LODGE $$
(☎03-435 1860; www.aorakialpinelodge.co.nz; Bowen Dr; d $159-189, tr/q $164/164, f $220-240; @📶) This modern lodge – with twin, double and family rooms – is the best place to stay in the village. With Turkish rugs and underfloor heating, you're guarenteed a warm welcome. Shared facilities include a huge lounge and kitchen area, and the alfresco barbecue with superb mountain views will have you arguing over who's going to grill the steak for dinner.

Mt Cook Backpackers HOSTEL $
(☎03-436 1653, 0800 100 512; www.mountcookbackpackers.co.nz; Bowen Dr; dm $35, d/tw $120, unit $170; @📶) Recently redecorated and refurbished, Mt Cook Backpackers is a sprawling, double-storey spot with four-bed dorms, twins and doubles, and self-contained flats with kitchens. All rooms have en suite facilities and feature private balconies, perfect for taking in the superb alpine views. Attached is the Chamois Bar & Grill.

Hermitage HOTEL $$$
(☎0800 686 800, 03-435 1809; www.hermitage.co.nz; Terrace Rd; r $209-575; @📶) This sprawling complex has long monopolised Mt Cook accommodation in the village. Rooms in well-equipped A-frame chalets (double $269) sleep up to four and include a kitchen. Also available are motel units ($239) and refurbished rooms in various wings of the hotel proper. The higher-end hotel rooms are very smart indeed, and include cinematic views of Mt Cook through huge picture windows.

Mt Cook YHA HOSTEL $
(☎03-435 1820; www.yha.co.nz; cnr Bowen & Kitchener Dr; dm $37, d&tw $118; @📶) This excellent hostel has a free sauna, drying room, warming log fires and DVDs. Rooms are clean and spacious, and family rooms and facilities for travellers with disabilities are also available. Try to book a few days in advance. If you're mountain-bound you can store luggage here.

Glentanner Park Centre HOLIDAY PARK $
(☎0800 453 682, 03-435 1855; www.glentanner.co.nz; SH80; sites from $34, dm $28, units $80-155) On the northern shore of Lake Pukaki, this is the nearest facility-laden camping ground to the national park and has great views of Mt Cook, 25km to the north. It's well set up with various cabins and motel units, a dormitory (open October to April) and a restaurant. Tours and activities can also be booked.

Unwin Lodge HOSTEL $
(☎03-435 1100, 027 817 6860; www.alpineclub.org.nz; SH80; dm $30) About 3.5km before the village, this lodge belongs to the New Zealand Alpine Club (NZAC). Members get preference, but beds are usually available for climbing groupies. There are basic bunks in a recently renovated bunkroom, and a big common room with a fireplace and kitchen.

White Horse Hill Camping Area CAMPSITE $
(☎03-435 1186; Hooker Valley; adult/child $10/5) A basic DOC-run, self-registration camping ground at the starting point for the Hooker Valley Track, 2km from Aoraki/Mt Cook village. There's running water (boil before drinking) and toilets, but no electricity or cooking facilities.

Eating & Drinking

Old Mountaineers Café, Bar & Restaurant CAFE $$
(www.mtcook.com; Bowen Dr; lunch $17-24, dinner $22-35; @📶) This place is cosy in winter, and offers mountain views from outside tables in summer. It delivers top-notch burgers, pizza, pasta and salad, and is a good-value alternative to the eateries at the Hermitage. Linger to study the old black-and-white pics and mountaineering memorabilia. The menu features lots of organic, free-range and GM-free options as well.

TITANIC SCENE ON LAKE TASMAN

When you're only a few kilometres from NZ's highest mountain, the last thing you expect to see is a maze of huge icebergs straight from the planet's polar regions. It's a surreal feeling cruising in an inflatable boat amid 500-year-old islands of ice on Lake Tasman in the Aoraki/Mt Cook National Park. An icing-sugar-like dusting of snow may have fallen overnight, and even that could be enough to rebalance an iceberg and send it spinning and rotating in the frigid water. With a decent wind the location of the floating islands can change by the hour.

The ice may be centuries old, but the lake has been around only a few decades. Lake Tasman was first formed around 30 years ago, when huge swathes of ice sheared off the Tasman Glacier's terminal face. The ice-strewn lake continues to be a dynamic environment and there's always the danger of one of the icebergs breaking up. On 22 February 2011, the Christchurch earthquake caused a 30-million-tonne chunk of ice to shear away from the Tasman Glacier. The huge piece of ice was 1.3km long and 300m high, causing substantial waves to roll into tourist boats on the lake at the time. (Fortunately, no one was injured by the waves.)

The ongoing impact of climate change continues to increase the size of one of NZ's newest and coldest lakes, and it's estimated it will eventually grow to a maximum length of 16km.

Glentanner Restaurant CAFE $
(SH80, Glentanner; meals $10-20) The decor might resemble a school cafeteria, but there's plenty of robust Kiwi tucker on offer. Steak sandwiches and fish and chips will get you through the longest of exploring days.

Hermitage RESTAURANT $$
(☎0800 686 800, 03-435 1809; www.hermitage.co.nz; Terrace Rd) Dining options at the Hermitage include a cafe with light meals and pizzas; fine dining in the Panorama Room (mains $35 to $42); and breakfast, lunch and dinner buffets in the Alpine Room.

Chamois Bar & Grill PUB
(www.mountcookbackpackers.co.nz; Bowen Dr) Chamois Bar & Grill is upstairs in Mt Cook Backpackers, 500m from the YHA, where it entertains with a pool table, big-screen TV and the occasional live gig.

Shopping

Alpine Guides OUTDOOR EQUIPMENT
(www.alpineguides.co.nz; Retail Centre, The Hermitage; ⏲8am-5pm) Sells travel clothing, outdoor and mountaineering gear, and rents ice axes, crampons, daypacks and sleeping bags.

Information

Stock up on groceries and petrol at Twizel or Lake Tekapo. The nearest ATM is in Twizel.

DOC Aoraki/Mt Cook Visitor Centre (☎03-435 1186; www.doc.govt.nz; 1 Larch Grove; ⏲8.30am-5pm Oct-Apr, to 4.30pm May-Sep) Advises on weather conditions, guided tours and tramping routes, and hires out beacons for trampers ($35). The centre includes excellent displays on the flora, fauna and history of the Mt Cook region. Most activities can be booked here. Trampers must complete intentions cards when leaving for walks.

Getting There & Away

The village's small airport only serves aerial sightseeing companies. Some of these may be willing to combine transport to the West Coast (ie Franz Josef) with a scenic flight, but flights are heavily dependent on weather.

InterCity (www.intercity.co.nz) links Mt Cook to Christchurch (five hours), Queenstown (four hours) and Wanaka (with a change in Tarras; 4¼ hours). Buses stop at the YHA and the Hermitage, both of which handle bookings.

The **Cook Connection** (☎0800 266 526; www.cookconnect.co.nz) has services to Twizel (one hour) and Lake Tekapo (two hours). Bus services in these towns link to Christchurch, Queenstown, Wanaka and Dunedin.

If you're driving, fill up at Lake Tekapo or Twizel. There is petrol at Mt Cook, but it's expensive and involves summoning an attendant from the Hermitage (for a fee).

Dunedin & Otago

Includes »

Dunedin....535
Otago Peninsula....546
Cromwell....551
Clyde....553
Alexandra....554
Alexandra to Palmerston....555
Alexandra to Dunedin....558
Clutha District....558
North Otago & Waitaki....558
Oamaru....559
Waitaki Valley....564
Oamaru to Dunedin....566

Best Places to Eat

» Dunedin Farmers Market (p543)

» Plato (p541)

» Riverstone Kitchen (p562)

» Fleur's Place (p566)

» Mt Difficulty Wines (p552)

Best Places to Stay

» Arden Street House (p540)

» Kaimata Retreat (p550)

» Sublime Bed & Breakfast (p565)

» The Church Mouse (p556)

Why Go?

Coastal Otago has attractions both urban and rural, offering a chance to escape Queenstown's crowds, party in the South Island's coolest city, and come face to face with the island's most accessible wildlife.

Otago's historic heart is Dunedin. With excellent bars, restaurants and cafes, it also hosts a vibrant student culture and arts scene. From Dunedin's stately Victorian train station, catch the famous Taieri Gorge Railway inland, and continue further on the craggily scenic Otago Central Rail Trail.

Those seeking backcountry NZ can soak up historic Clyde, atmospheric St Bathans and scenic, rustic Naseby. For wildlife, head to the Otago Peninsula, where penguins, albatross, sea lions and seals are easily sighted. Seaside Oamaru has a wonderful historic precinct, resident penguin colonies and a quirky devotion to Steampunk culture.

Unhurried, and overflowing with picturesque scenery, Otago is undeniably generous to explorers after something a little less intense.

When to Go

February and March have settled, sunny weather (usually...), and the juicy appeal of fresh apricots, peaches and cherries. Take to two wheels on the Otago Central Rail Trail during the quieter months of May and December, or ride graciously into the past on a penny farthing bicycle at Oamaru's Victorian Heritage Celebrations in November.

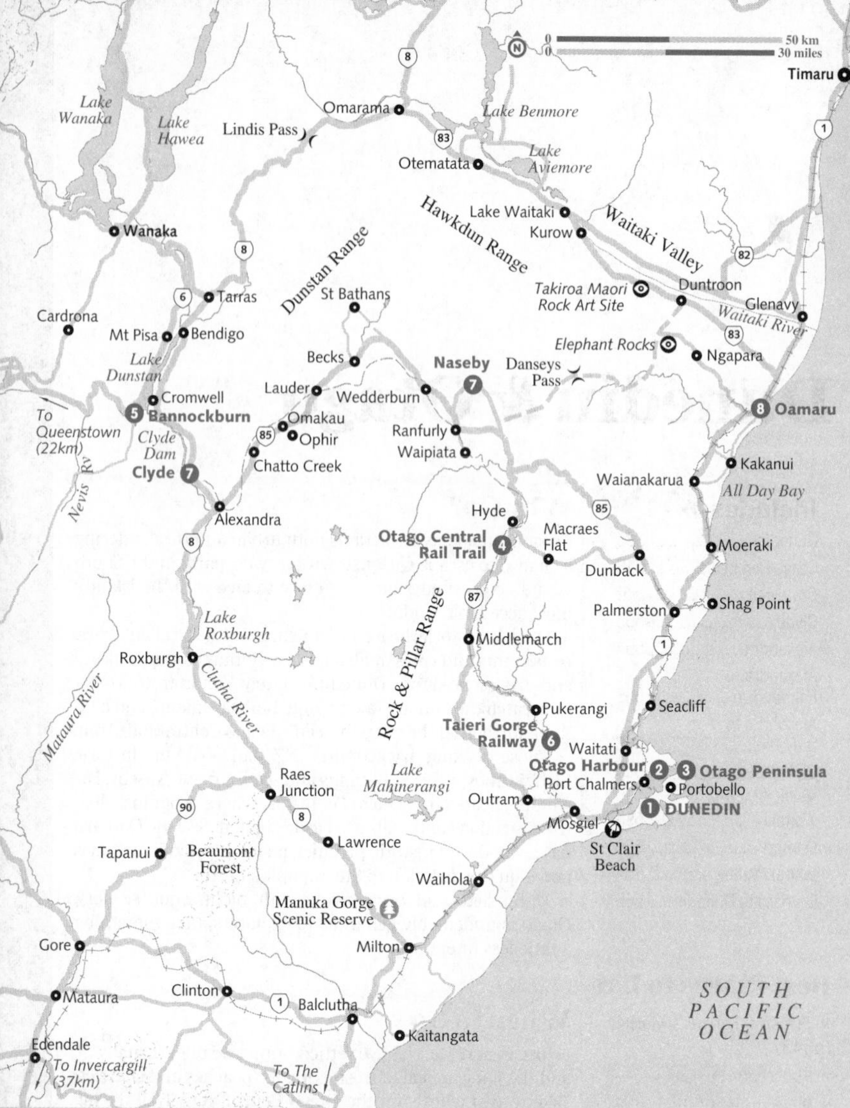

Dunedin & Otago Highlights

1. Sampling local beers and gastronomic excellence in the cafes and restaurants of **Dunedin** (p535)
2. Discovering laid-back charm along the quiet northern shore of **Otago Harbour** (p545)
3. Peering at penguins, admiring albatross and staring at sea lions and fur seals on **Otago Peninsula** (p547)
4. Cycling through lonely vistas of brown and gold along the **Otago Central Rail Trail** (p554)
5. Tasting some of the planet's best pinot noir amid the vineyards of **Bannockburn** (p552)
6. Winding through gorges, alongside canyons and across tall viaducts on the snaking **Taieri Gorge Railway** (p546)
7. Exploring NZ's southern heritage in villages like **Clyde** (p553) and **Naseby** (p556)
8. Experiencing a heritage past and a Steampunk future in historic **Oamaru** (p559)

Getting There & Around

Air New Zealand (☎0800 737 000; www.airnewzealand.co.nz) flies from Dunedin to Christchurch, Wellington and Auckland. Australian destinations are Brisbane, Sydney and Melbourne. **Virgin Australia** (www.virginaustralia.com) links Dunedin to Brisbane, and **Jetstar** (☎0800 800 995; www.jetstar.com) flies to Auckland.

Major bus and shuttle operators include InterCity (p546), Atomic Shuttles (p546), Bottom Bus (p546), **Catch-A-Bus** (☎03-449 2024; www.catchabus.co.nz), Naked Bus (p546) and Wanaka Connexions (p546).

DUNEDIN & THE OTAGO PENINSULA

Nestled at the end of Otago Harbour, Dunedin is a surprisingly artsy town with lots of bars and eateries. If you can unglue yourself from the city's live music and cafe scene, the rugged Otago Peninsula and northern harbour provide easy day trips (or longer), rich with wildlife and outdoor activities.

Dunedin

POP 123,000

Dunedin's compact town centre blends the historic and the contemporary, reflected in its alluring museums and tempting bars, cafes and restaurants. Weatherboard houses ranging from stately to ramshackle pepper its hilly suburbs, and bluestone Victorian buildings punctuate the centre. The country's oldest university provides loads of student energy to sustain thriving theatre, live-music and after-dark scenes.

MAORI NZ: DUNEDIN & OTAGO

In pre-European times, the Otago region was known as Otakou, a name still referenced at the Otakou *marae* (Maori meeting place) on the far reaches of the Otago Peninsula.

Dunedin's Otago Museum (p535) has the finest Maori exhibition in the South Island, including an ornately carved *waka* (war canoe) and finely crafted *pounamu* (green stone). Explore the Maori rock art locations of the Waitaki Valley.

Dunedin is an easy city in which to while away a few days, and many travellers find themselves staying here longer than expected as they recover from the buzz of Queenstown. The wildlife-viewing opportunities of the Otago Peninsula are also nearby.

History

The Otakou area's early history was particularly bloody, involving a three-way feud between peninsular tribes that escalated in the early 19th century. This brutal warfare was followed by devastating diseases and interracial conflict ushered in via coastal sealing and whaling. The first permanent European settlers, two shiploads of pious, hard-working Scots, arrived at Port Chalmers in 1848, and included the nephew of the patron saint of Scottish poetry, Robbie Burns. That the city's founders were Scottish is a source of fierce pride today. A statue of Robbie still frowns down upon the city centre, there are a handful of civic haggis 'n' bagpipe occasions every year, and the city even has its own tartan.

Sights

Some popular things to do in Dunedin involve leaving town, including visiting the Otago Peninsula, the Otago Central Rail Trail and the Taieri Gorge Railway.

Otago Museum MUSEUM
(www.otagomuseum.govt.nz; 419 Great King St; admission by donation; ⏲10am-5pm) Explores Otago's cultural and physical past and present, from geology and dinosaurs to the modern day. The Tangata Whenua Maori gallery houses an impressive *waka taua* (war canoe), wonderfully worn old carvings and some lovely *pounamu* (greenstone) works. If you've already been out on the peninsula admiring penguins and albatrosses, the museum's wildlife collection will also fascinate. Join themed guided tours ($12, see website for times and themes). Children can explore at the hands-on Discovery World (adult/child/family $10/5/25). Check the website for always-excellent temporary exhibitions and special gallery talks.

FREE **Otago Settlers Museum** MUSEUM
(www.otago.settlers.museum; 31 Queens Gardens; ⏲10am-5pm) This eclectic collection gives insights into past residents, whether Maori or Scots, whalers or farmers. Petrol heads and trainspotters will love the old Buick straight eight and 1872-built steam engine, now

showcased in the museum's stunning entrance area. A $38 million upgrade in 2012 introduced many new interactive displays.

Railway Station HISTORIC BUILDING
(Anzac Ave) Featuring mosaic-tile floors and glorious stained-glass windows, Dunedin's striking Edwardian Railway Station claims to be NZ's most-photographed building. The station houses the NZ Sports Hall of Fame (p536), hosts the Dunedin Farmers Market (p543), and is the departing point for the Taieri Gorge Railway (p546). If you get in early enough, grab a tasty haggis pie ($5) at the cafe.

Orokonui Ecosanctuary WILDLIFE RESERVE
(www.orokonui.org.nz; adult/child/family $15.90/7.90/39.90; ⌚9.30am-4.30pm) This ecosanctuary occupies a 300-hectare nature reserve on Otago Harbour's north shore. Its mission is to provide a predator-free refuge to repopulate species previously exiled to smaller offshore islands. Around 20 different species of birds now make the sanctuary their forest home. Options to visit include self-guided tours, or to join a one-guided tour (adult/child/family $29.90/14.90/74.90; departs daily at 11am) or a two-hour guided tour (adult/child/family $44.90/22.50/112.50; departs daily at 1.30pm). Two-hour twilight tours (adult/child/family $69.90/39.90/186) depart one hour before sunset on Tuesday and Sunday afternoons. Check the website for current times. The sanctuary can also visited on the Orokonui Express, a combination rail and road excursion on the Seasider train (p546) departing from the Dunedin Railway Station. Check the website or ask at the i-SITE.

FREE **Public Art Gallery** GALLERY
(www.dunedin.art.museum; 30 The Octagon; ⌚10am-5pm) Explore NZ's art scene at Dunedin's expansive and airy Public Art Gallery. Works on permanent show are mainly contemporary, including a big NZ collection featuring local kids Ralph Hotere and Frances Hodgkins, Cantabrian Colin McCahon and some old CF Goldie oils. Climb the iron staircase for great city views.

New Zealand Sports Hall of Fame MUSEUM
(www.nzhalloffame.co.nz; Dunedin Railway Station; adult/child $5/2; ⌚10am-4pm) At the New Zealand Sports Hall of Fame you can try and match bike-champ Karen Holliday's average speed of 45.629km/h, or check out the high-stepping style of iconic All Black fullback George Nepia.

ESSENTIAL DUNEDIN & OTAGO

» **Eat** Alfresco from the diverse stalls at the Dunedin Farmers Market

» **Drink** The fine brews from Dunedin's Emerson's and Green Man breweries

» **Read** *Owls Do Cry* by Oamaru's Janet Frame

» **Listen to** *Tally Ho! Flying Nun's Greatest Bits, a* 2011 compilation marking the 30th anniversary of the iconic record label

» **Watch** *Scarfies* (1999), about murderous Dunedin university students

» **Festival** Oamaru's Victorian Heritage Celebrations in late November

» **Go green** Tiptoe down to Otago Peninsula beaches in search of yellow-eyed penguins

» **Online** www.dunedinnz.com, www.centralotagonz.com

» **Area code** ☎03

FREE **Temple Gallery** GALLERY
(29 Moray Pl; ⌚10am-6pm Mon-Fri, 10am-2pm Sat) Up the staircase, the Temple Gallery was Dunedin's first synagogue (1864), and then for 30 years a Masonic temple. The building retains marks of both, and is a fabulous art space. Artists represented are predominantly Otago locals and exhibitions change regularly.

FREE **Dunedin Botanic Gardens** GARDENS
(cnr Great King St & Opoho Rd; ⌚dawn-dusk) The Dunedin Botanic Gardens date from the 1860s and spread across 22 peaceful, grassy and shady hectares. There's also a playground and a cafe.

Baldwin St STREET
The world's steepest residential street (or so says the *Guinness Book of World Records*), Baldwin St has a gradient of 1 in 1.286 (19°). From the city centre, head 2km north up Great King St to where the road branches sharp left to Timaru. Get in the right-hand lane and continue straight ahead. This becomes North Rd, and Baldwin St is on the right after 1km. Alternatively, grab a Normanby bus at the Octagon and ask the driver. The annual 'Gutbuster' race in Febru-

ary sees up to 1000 athletes run to the top of Baldwin St and back. The record is just under two minutes.

Activities

There's excellent walking and kayaking out on the Otago Peninsula.

Swimming, Surfing & Diving

St Clair and St Kilda are both popular swimming beaches (though you need to watch for rips at St Clair). Both have consistently good left-hand breaks, and you'll also find good surfing at Blackhead further south, and at Aramoana on Otago Harbour's North Shore.

For St Clair, catch bus 8, 9, 28 or 29 from the Octagon. For St Kilda, catch bus 27, also from the Octagon

St Clair Pool SWIMMING
(Esplanade, St Clair Beach; adult/child $5.70/2.60; 6am-7pm Mon-Fri, 7am-7pm Sat & Sun Nov-Mar) A heated, outdoor saltwater pool.

Esplanade Surf School SURFING
(455 8655; www.espsurfschool.co.nz; lessons from $60) Based at St Clair Beach and provides equipment and lessons.

Moana Pool SWIMMING
(60 Littlebourne Rd; adult/child $5.70/2.60; 6am-10pm Mon-Fri, 7am-7pm Sat & Sun) Waterslides, wave machines and a spa.

Tramping & Walking

The **Otago Tramping and Mountaineering Club** (www.otmc.co.nz) organises weekend day and overnight tramps, often to the Silver Peaks Reserve north of Dunedin. Nonmembers are welcome, but must contact trip leaders beforehand.

TUNNEL BEACH WALKWAY

The Tunnel Beach Walkway (45 minutes return; closed August 20 to October 31 for lambing) crosses farmland before descending the sea cliffs to Tunnel Beach. Sea stacks, arches and unusual rock shapes have been carved out by the wild Pacific, and a few fossils stud the sandstone cliffs. It impressed civic father John Cargill so much that he had a hand-hewn stone tunnel built to give his family access to secluded beachside picnics. The walk is southwest of central Dunedin. Catch a Corstorphine bus from the Octagon to Stenhope Cres and walk 1.4km along Blackhead Rd to Tunnel Beach Rd, then 400m to the start of the walkway. Strong currents make swimming here dangerous.

MT CARGILL-BETHUNES GULLY WALKWAY

Catch a Normanby bus to the start of Norwood St, which leads to Cluny St and the Mt Cargill-Bethunes Gully walkway (3½ hours return). The highlight is the view from Mt Cargill (also accessible by car). From Mt Cargill, a trail continues to the 10-million-year-old, lava-formed Organ Pipes and, after another half-hour, to Mt Cargill Rd on the other side of the mountain.

Climbing

Traditional rock climbing (nonbolted) is popular at Long Beach and the cliffs at Mihiwaka, both accessed via Blueskin Rd north of Port Chalmers, and Lovers Leap (bolted and natural) on the peninsula.

Other Activities

Cycle Surgery BICYCLE RENTAL
(www.cyclesurgery.co.nz; 67 Lower Stuart St; per day $40) Rents out bikes and has mountain-biking information.

Hare Hill HORSE RIDING
(0800 437 837, 03-472 8496; www.horseriding-dunedin.co.nz; 207 Aramoana Rd) Horse treks ($75 to $210) including thrilling beach rides and farm treks.

Tours

See the Dunedin i-SITE for more specialised city tours.

Cadbury World FACTORY TOUR
(www.cadburyworld.co.nz; 280 Cumberland St; from adult/child/family $14/7/37; full tour 9am-3.30pm Mon-Fri, reduced tour 9am-3.30pm Sat & Sun) The full 75-minute tour of the factory includes a spiel on history and production, a liquid-chocolate waterfall, and a taste of the end product. The shorter 45-minute weekend tour omits the factory tour and concentrates the yummy parts. Combination tickets (adult/child $39/20) also visiting Speight's Brewery are available.

Speight's Brewery BREWERY
(www.speights.co.nz; 200 Rattray St; adult/child/family $23/10/48) Speight's has been churning out beer on this site since the late 1800s. The 90-minute tour (noon, 2pm, 4pm, 6pm, plus 10am and 7pm in summer) offers samples of Speight's six different beers.

First City Tours BUS TOUR
(adult/child $20/10; buses depart the Octagon 9am, 10.15am, 1pm, 2.15pm & 3.30pm) Hop-on/hop-off double-decker bus tour that loops around the city. Stops include the Otago

Dunedin

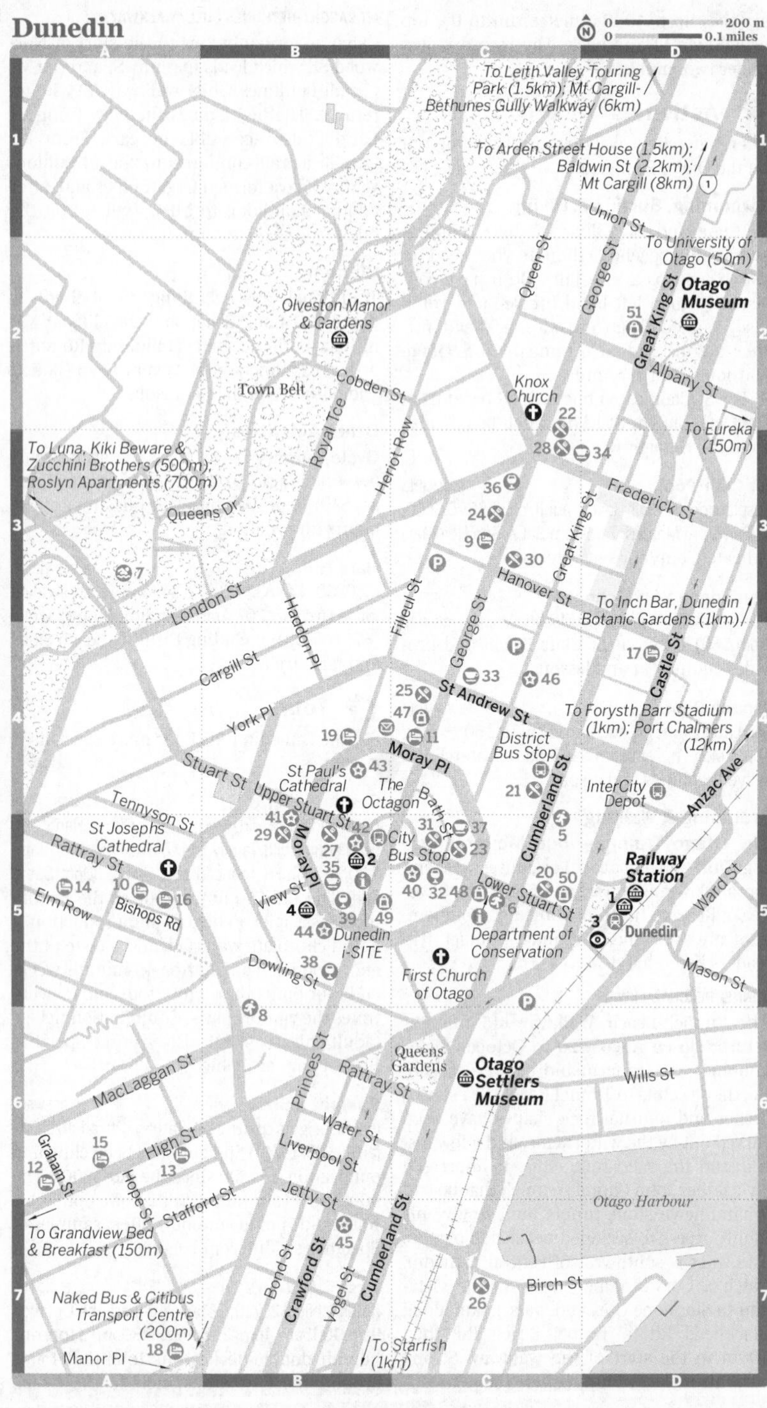

0 200 m
0 0.1 miles
To Leith Valley Touring Park (1.5km); Mt Cargill-Bethunes Gully Walkway (6km)
To Arden Street House (1.5km); Baldwin St (2.2km); Mt Cargill (8km)
Union St
To University of Otago (50m)
Otago Museum
Queen St
George St
Great King St
Albany St
Olveston Manor & Gardens
Town Belt
Cobden St
Royal Tce
Heriot Row
Knox Church
To Eureka (150m)
To Luna, Kiki Beware & Zucchini Brothers (500m); Roslyn Apartments (700m)
Frederick St
Queens Dr
Filleul St
Hanover St
London St
Haddon Pl
To Inch Bar, Dunedin Botanic Gardens (1km)
Cargill St
Castle St
St Andrew St
York Pl
To Forysth Barr Stadium (1km); Port Chalmers (12km)
Moray Pl
District Bus Stop
Stuart St
Upper Stuart St
St Paul's Cathedral
The Octagon
Bath St
Cumberland St
InterCity Depot
Anzac Ave
Tennyson St
St Josephs Cathedral
Rattray St
City Bus Stop
Railway Station
Lower Stuart St
Elm Row
Bishops Rd
View St
Dunedin i-SITE
Department of Conservation
Dunedin
Ward St
Dowling St
First Church of Otago
Mason St
Queens Gardens
Otago Settlers Museum
MacLaggan St
Princes St
Rattray St
Wills St
Water St
Graham St
High St
Liverpool St
Hope St
Stafford St
Jetty St
Otago Harbour
To Grandview Bed & Breakfast (150m)
Bond St
Crawford St
Vogel St
Cumberland St
Birch St
Naked Bus & Citibus Transport Centre (200m)
Manor Pl
To Starfish (1km)

Dunedin

Top Sights

	Otago Museum	D2
	Otago Settlers Museum	C6
	Railway Station	D5

Sights

1	New Zealand Sports Hall of Fame	D5
2	Public Art Gallery	B5
3	Taieri Gorge Railway	D5
4	Temple Gallery	B5

Activities, Courses & Tours

5	Cadbury World	C5
6	Cycle Surgery	C5
7	Moana Pool	A3
8	Speight's Brewery	B6

Sleeping

9	315 Euro	C3
10	Brothers Boutique Hotel	A5
11	Central Backpackers	C4
12	Chalet Backpackers	A6
13	Dunedin Palms Motel	A6
14	Elm Lodge	A5
15	Fletcher Lodge	A6
16	Hogwartz	A5
17	Living Space	D4
18	Manor House Backpackers	A7
19	On Top Backpackers	B4

Eating

20	Best Cafe	C5
21	Countdown Supermarket	C4
	Dunedin Farmers Market	(see 3)
22	Governors	C2
	Guilty by Confection	(see 20)
23	Izakaya Yuki	C5
24	Modaks	C3
	Nova Cafe	(see 2)
25	Paasha	C4
26	Plato	C7
	Saigon Van	(see 33)
27	Scotia	B5
28	Seoul	C3
29	Tangenté	B5
30	The Good Oil	C3
31	The Perc	C5
	Velvet Burger	(see 31)

Drinking

32	Albar	C5
33	Circadian Rhythm Café	C4
34	Fix	D3
35	Mazagran Espresso Bar	B5
36	Mou Very	C3
	Pequeno	(see 39)
	Speight's Ale House	(see 8)
37	Strictly Coffee	C5
38	Tonic	B5
39	XIIB	B5

Entertainment

40	di lusso	C5
41	Fortune Theatre	B5
42	Hoyts Cinema	B5
43	Metro Cinema	B4
	Pop	(see 40)
44	Rialto Cinemas	B5
45	Sammy's	B7
46	Urban Factory	C4

Shopping

47	Bivouac Outdoor	C4
48	De Novo Art Prints and Posters	C5
49	Fern	B5
50	Stuart St Potters Cooperative	C5
51	University Book Shop	D2

Museum, Speight's, Botanic Gardens and Baldwin St.

Tasty Tours FOOD & WINE

(03-453 1455, 021 070 1658; www.tastytours.co.nz; adult/child from $89/59) Tuck into local seafood, cheese, chocolate and beer on specialised foodie tours.

Walk Dunedin WALKING TOUR

(03-477 5052; 2hr walk $20; 10am) History-themed strolls around the city, organised by the Otago Settlers Museum. Book at the i-SITE, or pick up a self-guided tour brochure ($4).

Walk This Way WALKING

(03-473 8338; www.walkthisway.co.nz; per person $65-75) Bush and coastal walks.

Wine Tours Otago WINE TASTING

(021 070 1658, 03-453 1455; www.winetoursotago.co.nz; per person $159) Wine-tasting excursions exploring Central Otago or the Waitaki Valley.

Sleeping

Most accommodation is within easy walking distance of the city centre, though some spots offer a challenging uphill stroll back from town. Most motels are at the northern end of George St.

TOP CHOICE **Arden Street House** B&B $
(☎03-473 8860; www.ardenstreethouse.co.nz; 36 Arden St; s/d/tw/tr $50/60/60/90, s/d incl breakfast from $75/85; P@) North of the city up Northeast Valley, this pair of homes atop a (steep) hill share an organic garden and a very welcoming host. With crazy artworks and a porthole in the bathroom, the main B&B is an amazing space. Readers rave about the shared dinners ($15 to $25) with neighbours, artists, wwoofers and assorted guests. Next door is a comfortable backpacker villa ($30). Head up North Rd from the city, turn right into Glendining St and then left into Arden St.

Grandview Bed & Breakfast B&B $$
(☎03-474 9472, 0800 749 472; www.grandview.co.nz; 360 High St; d incl breakfast $125-200; P@) Bold colours, exposed brick walls and snazzy art deco bathrooms are the highlights at this family-owned B&B. The building dates back to 1861, there are superb harbour views from the barbecue and deck area, and lots of sunny shared spaces. The larger rooms have private spa baths, and there's even a compact gym and sauna.

Roslyn Apartments APARTMENT $$
(☎03-477 6777; www.roslynapartments.co.nz; 23 City Rd; d $150-300; P) Modern decor and brilliant city and harbour views are on tap at these chic apartments just a short walk from the restaurants and cafes of Roslyn Village. Leather furniture and designer kitchens add a touch of class, and it's a quick 10-minute downhill walk to the Octagon. You may need to consider a taxi on the way back up, though.

315 Euro MOTEL $$
(☎0800 387 638, 03-477 9929; www.eurodunedin.co.nz; 315 George St; d $150-250; P) This sleek complex is in the absolute heart of George St's daytime retail strip and after-dark eating and drinking hub. Choose from modern studio apartments or larger one-bedroom apartments with full kitchens. Access via an alleyway is a bit odd, but soundproofing and double-glazed windows keeps George St's irresistible buzz at bay.

Brothers Boutique Hotel BOUTIQUE HOTEL $$$
(☎0800 477 004, 03-477 0043; www.brothershotel.co.nz; 295 Rattray St; d incl breakfast $170-320; P@) Rooms in this distinctive old 1920s Christian Brothers residence have been refurbished beyond any monk's dreams, while still retaining many unique features. The chapel room ($320) includes the original arched stained-glass windows of its past life. There are great views from the rooftop units.

Dunedin Palms Motel MOTEL $$
(☎0800 782 938, 03-477 8293; www.dunedinpalmsmotel.co.nz; 185-195 High St; d $170-210; P@) A short stroll from the Speight's Ale House, the art deco Palms has smartly decorated studios and one- and two-bedroom units arrayed around a central courtyard. You're handily just out of the CBD, but don't have to endure a long walk uphill.

Fletcher Lodge B&B $$$
(☎03-477 5552; www.fletcherlodge.co.nz; 276 High St; d $325-595, apt $650-750; P@) Originally home to one of NZ's wealthy industrialist families, this gorgeous redbrick manor is just minutes from the city, but the secluded gardens feel wonderfully remote. Rooms are elegantly trimmed with antique furniture and ornate plaster ceilings.

Hotel St Clair HOTEL $$
(☎03-456 0555; www.hotelstclair.com; 24 Esplanade; d $175-235;) Southern ocean views and chic and modern rooms provide a surf-side haven in beachy St Clair. Downstairs it's just metres to top cafes and restaurants.

Hogwartz HOSTEL $
(☎03-474 1487; www.hogwartz.co.nz; 277 Rattray St; dm $25-28, s $60, d $62-76; @) The Catholic bishop's residence since the 1870s, this beautiful building is now a fascinating warren of comfortable and sunny rooms, many with harbour views. The five-bed dorm is actually the bishop's old formal dining room. In a renovated heritage building nearby, the recently opened Coach House has a modern kitchen and features cosy ensuite rooms (per person $45).

Chalet Backpackers HOSTEL $
(☎0800 242 538, 03-479 2075; www.chaletbackpackers.co.nz; 296 High St; dm/s/d $26/40/60; @) This rambling old building quickly makes guests feel at home. The kitchen is big, sunny and festooned with flowers, and the dining room has one long table to help you meet your neighbours. There's also a compact garden, pool table, piano and rumours of a ghost.

Elm Lodge HOSTEL $
(☎03-474 1872; www.elmlodge.co.nz; 74 Elm Row; dm/s/d from $26/47/62; @) Elm Lodge is a

popular, laidback choice for travellers looking to relax a while. Rooms are quaint but comfortable, and the back garden – including a spa pool – is just made for barbecues and a few cold beers. Elm Lodge is a fairly steep walk into (or particularly *out from*) town.

Living Space HOTEL **$$**
(☎03-951 5000; www.livingspace.net; 192 Castle St; d $89-119; P@📶) Living Space combines kitchenettes in funky colours, whip-smart ergonomic design and a central location. There's an on-site laundry and huge shared kitchen, conversation-friendly lounges and a private DVD cinema. Some rooms are pretty compact, but they're good value and all you need.

On Top Backpackers HOSTEL **$**
(☎03-477 6121, 0800 668 672; www.ontopbackpackers.co.nz; cnr Filleul St & Moray Pl; dm $26-$27, s $54, d with/without bathroom $88/64; @📶) A modern, well-located hostel sitting atop a pool hall and bar, with a large sundeck, shared barbecue area and free basic breakfast. The three new ensuite doubles are hotel quality.

Central Backpackers HOSTEL **$**
(☎0800 423 6872; www.centralbackpackers.co.nz; 243 Moray Pl; dm/tw/d $27/66/70; @📶) Located in the heart of town, this hostel has inviting common TV lounge and kitchen areas, and a welcoming host in Gizmo the cat. Dorm rooms sleep four to 10 on bunks, and private rooms are spacious.

Manor House Backpackers HOSTEL **$**
(☎03-477 0484, 0800 477 0484; www.manorhousebackpackers.co.nz; 28 Manor Pl; dm $22-26, s $53, d $64-74; @) Two stately old villas surrounded by gardens and trees.

Leith Valley Touring Park HOLIDAY PARK **$**
(☎0800 555 331, 03-467 9936; www.leithvalleytouringpark.co.nz; 103 Malvern St; sites $36, units $56-106; P@📶) This holiday park is surrounded by native bush studded with walks, glowworm caves and a wee creek. Self-contained modern motel units are spacious, and tourist flats are smaller but have a more earthy feel (linen required).

✖ Eating

Inexpensive Asian restaurants are clustered along George St around the intersection with St Andrew St. Most also do takeaways.

Uphill from the Octagon, Roslyn has good restaurants and cafes, and the beachy ambience of St Clair is great for a lazy brunch.

TOP CHOICE **Plato** MODERN NZ **$$**
(☎03-477 4235; www.platocafe.co.nz; 2 Birch St; brunch $15-23, dinner $27-33; ⏲6pm-late Mon-Sat, 11am-late Sun) A regular contender in *Cuisine* magazine's Best of NZ gongs, Plato has a retro-themed location near the harbour and a strong beer and wine list. Try standouts like the Indian seafood curry or grilled salmon on potato gnocchi. Sunday brunch is worth the shortish trek from the CBD. Bookings are recommended.

Scotia RESTAURANT **$$**
(☎03-477 7704; www.scotiadunedin.co.nz; 199 Upper Stuart St; mains $18-32; ⏲lunch Mon-Fri, dinner Mon-Sat) Occupying a cosy heritage townhouse, Scotia toasts all things Scottish with a wall full of single malt whisky, and hearty fare such as smoked salmon and Otago rabbit. The two Scottish Robbies – Burns and Coltrane – look down approvingly on a menu that also includes haggis, and duck and whisky pâté.

Best Cafe FISH & CHIPS **$$**
(30 Stuart St; from $8; ⏲lunch & dinner, takeaway until late) Serving up fish and chips since 1932, this local icon has its winning formula down pat, complete with vinyl tablecloths, hand-cut chips and curls of butter on white bread. If there's two or more of you, try the 'Old School' platter with juicy oysters, whitebait, scallops, squid rings and fish of your choice ($29.50, or $35 with Bluff oysters).

Luna MODERN NZ **$$**
(☎03-477 2227; www.lunaroslyn.co.nz; 314 Highgate; lunch $13-22, dinner $27-36; ⏲11am-late) Make the trek to Roslyn for outstanding harbour views from this hilltop glass-encased pavilion. Ask for a window seat when you book, and tuck in dishes like nori-encased salmon with wasabi mash, or gnocchi with pumpkin, sage and walnuts. A more relaxed option is a drink in the classy bar and shared plates including scallops with chilli, lime and ginger.

Zucchini Bros PIZZA **$$**
(www.zucchinibros.co.nz; 292 Highgate; pizza & pasta $15-21; ⏲from 5pm) Unpretentious, colourful and bustling, Zucchini Bros is the go-to spot for Dunedin folk for great pizza and pasta. Work from local photographers fills the walls, and Central Otago wines and Dunedin's own Emerson's beers are the perfect adjunct to all the wood-fired and hand-rolled goodness. Takeaways are also available.

Paasha TURKISH $$

(www.paasha.co.nz; 32 St Andrew St; kebabs & mains $12-25;) Authentic Turkish kebabs, dips and salads are faithfully created at this long-running Dunedin icon. It's a top place for takeaways, and most nights the spacious and warm interior is filled with groups drinking Efes Turkish beer and sharing heaving platters of tasty Ottoman goodness.

Izakaya Yuki JAPANESE $$

(29 Bath St; dishes $5-12; lunch Mon-Sat, dinner Mon-Sun;) Cute and cosy, with a huge array of small dishes on which to graze, Yuki is a lovely spot for supper or a relaxed, drawn-out Japanese meal. Make a night of it with sake or draught Asahi beer, sushi and sashimi, and multiple plates of *kushiyaki* (grilled skewers) such as asparagus with bacon.

Saigon Van VIETNAMESE $

(66 St Andrew St; mains $10-15; lunch & dinner Tue-Sun;) The elegant decor looks high-end Asian, but the Vietnamese food is definitely budget-friendly. Try the combination spring rolls ($8 for six) and a bottle of Vietnamese beer to recreate lazy nights in Saigon. The bean-sprout-laden *pho* (noodle soup) and salads are also good.

Seoul KOREAN $

(11 Frederick St; lunch $8, mains $15-17; 11am-9pm Mon-Sat) Behind the unprepossessing exterior lurks a warm orange space filled with students merrily tucking into cast-iron pots of authentic Korean fare. Warm up with *dolsot bibimbap* ($15), a sizzling-hot stone bowl of rice and myriad toppings, and cool down with a chunky red-bean ice cream ($3).

The Perc CAFE $

(142 Lower Stuart St; mains $10-18) Always busy, and for good reason – the Perc is a grand place to kick-start your day. The decor's kinda retro and kinda art deco, and there's hearty cafe fare ranging from salmon bagels and panini to warming porridge.

Kiki Beware CAFE $

(302 Highgate; snacks & light meals $8-15; Mon-Fri) This friendly neighbourhood cafe sees a loyal band of Roslyn locals popping in for excellent coffee, lots of design and travel magazines, and classy counter food including top-notch salmon bagels and classy cupcakes.

Governors CAFE $

(438 George St; mains $9-16) Popular with students, Governors does a nice line in early morning pancakes and other light meals. If you're feeling a little off the pace after the previous night, a strong coffee and an eggy omelette are just what the doctor ordered.

The Good Oil CAFE $

(314 George St; mains $10-18) This sleek little cafe is Dunedin's top spot for coffee and cake. Try the lemon and sour cream cake ($4). If you're still waking up, maybe resurrect the day with innovative brunches such as kumara hash with hot smoked salmon ($16).

Nova Cafe CAFE $$

(29 The Octagon; mains $15-30;) Not surprisingly, this extension of the Public Art Gallery has a stylish look about it. Cakes and snacks are famously creative, and Nova is also licensed for beer and wine. Escape into Dunedin's best choice of interesting food, travel and arts magazines.

Tangenté CAFE $

(111 Moray Pl; meals $7.50-17; 8am-3pm Tue-Sat, 9am-3pm Sun, 4.30-9pm Fri;) A cheerful, welcoming space with mismatched tables, toys for the kids, a funky soundtrack and the glorious aroma of freshly baked bread. Tangente's food is generally organic, free-range and locally sourced.

Modaks CAFE $

(337-339 George St; snacks & meals from $9;) This funky little cafe and bar, with brick walls, mismatched Formica tables and couches for slouching, is popular with students and those who appreciate chilled-out reggae while they nurse a pot of tea. Sundaes, smoothies and beer make it a great escape from summer's heat, while plump toasted bagels warm the insides in winter.

Circadian Rhythm Café CAFE

(72 St Andrew St; curry buffet $10; 9am-8pm Mon-Sat) Specialising in organic Indian curries, this all-vegan cafe is also known for its cookies and cakes. Circadian Rhythm is also a music venue, with a variety of interesting acts on Friday nights from 5.30pm. Dunedin's Emerson's and Green Man beers are both available, so you don't have to be *too* healthy.

Starfish CAFE

(www.starfishcafe.co.nz; 7/240 Forbury Rd; mains $18-30) Starfish is part of the growing restaurant scene at St Clair Beach. Pop out on a weekday to score an outside table to enjoy a gourmet pizza ($19.50) and wine. Dinner is more sophisticated with aged beef fillet on smoky bacon and onion mash. Catch bus 8, 9, 28 or 29 from the Octagon.

Dunedin Farmers Market FARMERS MARKET **$**
(www.otagofarmersmarket.org.nz; Dunedin Railway Station; ⏲8am-12.30pm Sat) The thriving Dunedin Farmers Market is all local, all eatable (or drinkable) and mostly organic. Grab felafels or espresso to sustain you while you browse, and stock up on fresh meats, seafood, vegies and cheese for your journey. Also pick up some locally brewed Green Man organic beer. Sorted.

Velvet Burger BURGERS **$**
(150 Lower Stuart St; mains $10-18; ⏲11.30am-late; 🖉) Best consumed after a few beers, but Velvet Burger is also licensed if the night is young. There's another VB at 375 George St (same hours).

Guilty by Confection SWEETS **$**
(www.guiltybyconfection.co.nz; 44-46 Lower Stuart St; ⏲10am-4pm Mon, Wed, Sat, noon-5pm Thu-Fri) Handmade chocolates, fudges and sweets.

Countdown Supermarket SUPERMARKET **$**
(309 Cumberland St; ⏲6am-midnight) Self-catering central.

Drinking

Mou Very BAR
(www.mouvery.co.nz; 357 George St) Welcome to one of the world's smallest bars – it's only 1.8m wide, but is still big enough to host regular funk and soul DJ sessions most Fridays from 5pm. There are just six bar stools, so Mou Very's boho regulars usually spill out into an adjacent laneway. By day, it's a handy refuelling spot for your morning or afternoon espresso.

Eureka BAR
(www.eurekadunedin.co.nz; 116 Albany St) Despite its proximity to occasional student sofa burnings around the corner on Hyde St, Eureka attracts a diverse crowd from first-year university newbies to their more grizzled tutors and other academics. The food's hearty and good value, and it's yet another Dunedin bar showcasing Kiwi microbreweries.

Inch Bar BAR
(8 Bank St) Bigger than Mou Very, but not by much. Make the short trek from town for lots of Kiwi craft beers, tasty tapas including prawns and calamari, and the company of a bohemian team of regulars.

Pequeno BAR
(www.pequeno.co.nz; behind 12 Moray Pl; ⏲Mon-Sat) Down the alleyway opposite the Rialto cinema, Pequeno attracts a more sophisticated crowd with leather couches, a cosy

LOCAL KNOWLEDGE

RICHARD EMERSON, BREWER

Richard Emerson is the head brewer at Dunedin's iconic Emerson's Brewery.

Which of the Emerson's beers is the quintessential Dunedin brew? Our Pilsner is a twist on the classic German Pilsner, and features that distinctive NZ 'sauvignon blanc' hop flavour.

Where are Dunedin's best places to drink Emerson's? The funky Inch Bar (p543) near the Botanic Gardens, Albar (p544) in Stuart St, and Eureka (p543), which is always a favourite with lunching academics. Tonic (p544) is a great craft beer bar, and down Dunedin's laneways is Pequeno (p543), just off Moray Pl. Another must-visit spot is Mou Very (p543), the tiny 'hole in the wall' bar on George St.

What's your favourite Dunedin food and beer match? The Carey's Bay Hotel (p545) near Port Chalmers serves excellent Queen scallops harvested by the local fishermen. They're really good served with Emerson's Pilsner.

Enough about beer – where do you recommend for a coffee? Nova Café (p542).

What are your favourite Dunedin and Otago experiences? The Farmer's Market (p543) held at Dunedin Railway Station on a Saturday morning is hard to beat. Also take the Taieri Gorge Railway (p546) from Dunedin to Middlemarch to start the Otago Central Rail Trail, a brilliant bike ride through to Clyde. Definitely stop at the Waipiata Country Hotel (p557) for a cold beer.

JUST GIVE ME THE COFFEE & NO ONE WILL GET HURT

Dunedin has some excellent coffee bars where you can refuel and recharge.

Fix (15 Frederick St; Mon-Sat) Wage slaves queue at the pavement window every morning, while students and others with time on their hands relax in the courtyard. Fix doesn't serve food, but you can bring along your own food or takeaways.

Mazagran Espresso Bar (36 Moray Pl; Mon-Sat) The godfather of Dunedin's coffee scene, this compact wood-and-brick coffee house is the source of the magic bean for many of the city's restaurants and cafes.

Strictly Coffee (23 Bath St; 8am-4pm Mon-Fri) Stylish retro coffee bar hidden down grungy Bath St. Different rooms provide varying views and artworks to enjoy while you sip and sup.

fireplace and an excellent wine and tapas menu. Music is generally laid-back and never too loud to intrude on conversation.

Albar BAR
(135 Lower Stuart St) This former butchers is now a bohemian little bar attracting just maybe the widest age range in Dunedin. Most punters are drawn by the 50 single-malt whiskies, interesting tap beers and cheap-as-chips bar snacks ($4 to $8).

Tonic BAR
(www.tonicbar.co.nz; 138 Princes St; 4pm-late Tue-Fri, 6pm-late Sat) Limited-release Kiwi craft beers, single-malt whiskies and good cocktails appeal to an older crowd than Dunedin's student pubs. Antipasto plates and cheese boards are good reasons to stay for another drink.

Speight's Ale House PUB
(200 Rattray St) Busy even in non-university months, the Ale House is a favourite of strapping young lads in their cleanest dirty shirts. A good spot to watch the rugby on TV, and to try the full range of Speight's beers.

XIIB BAR
(www.bennu.co.nz/xiib.html; alleyway behind 12 Moray Pl; Tue-Sat) XIIB (aka 12 Below) is an intimate underground bar with comfy seats and couches, and cosy nooks aplenty. There's also floor space for live-music acts (look forward to lots of funk and reggae), or to wriggle along to hip-hop and drum 'n' bass.

☆ Entertainment

di lusso BAR
(www.dilusso.co.nz; 12 The Octagon; Wed-Sat) Cool with crimson walls and a backlit drinks display, di lusso serves seriously good cocktails.

Urban Factory CLUB
(www.urbanfactory.co.nz; 101 Great King St) The hippest of NZ's touring bands, regular DJ sessions and carefully crafted cocktails.

Pop BAR
(downstairs, 14 The Octagon; 9pm-late Wed-Sat) Pop serves Dunedin's best martinis and prides itself on seriously good DJs playing funk and house.

Hoyts Cinema CINEMA
(03-477 3250, info line 03-477 7019; www.hoyts.co.nz; 33 The Octagon; adult/child $16/10) Blockbuster heaven. Rates are often cheaper on Tuesdays.

Metro Cinema CINEMA
(03-471 9635; www.metrocinema.co.nz; Moray Pl; adult/student $13/12) Behind the town hall, Metro shows art-house and foreign flicks.

Rialto Cinemas CINEMA
(03-474 2200; www.rialto.co.nz; 11 Moray Pl; adult/child $15.50/9.50) Blockbusters and art-house flicks. Rates often cheaper on Tuesdays.

Fortune Theatre THEATRE
(03-477 8323; www.fortunetheatre.co.nz; 231 Upper Stuart St; adult/student/child $40/20/15) The world's southernmost professional theatre company has been running dramas, comedies, pantomimes, classics and contemporary NZ productions for almost 40 years. Shows are performed – watched over by the obligatory theatre ghost – in a Gothic-style old Wesleyan church.

Sammy's LIVE MUSIC
(65 Crawford St) Dunedin's premier live-music venue draws an eclectic mix of genres from noisy-as-hell punk to chilled reggae and gritty dubstep. It's also usually venue of choice for visiting Kiwi bands and up-and-coming international acts.

Chicks Hotel LIVE MUSIC
(2 Mount St) Across in Port Chalmers, Chicks is the archetypal rock-and-roll pub, hosting everything from US alt-country bands to local metal noise merchants. Search Facebook for 'Friends of Chicks'. Catch bus 13 or 14 from Cumberland St in Dunedin.

Forsyth Barr Stadium STADIUM
(www.forsythbarrstadium.co.nz; Awatea St) Constructed for the 2011 Rugby World Cup, Dunedin's best sports venue is 1.5km from the centre of town. It's the only major stadium in NZ with a fully covered roof and hosts the Highlanders Super 15 rugby team (www.highlanders-rugby.co.nz) and the Otago NPC rugby team (www.orfu.co.nz).

Shopping

George St is Dunedin's main shopping strip. Moray Pl is also a funky area. Note the following harder-to-find and more interesting spots.

De Novo Art Prints and Posters ARTS & CRAFTS
(www.gallerydenovo.co.nz; 91 Lower Stuart St) Everything from vintage NZ tourism posters and Kiwiana to fine art prints by modern Kiwi artists such as Colin McCahon and Ralph Hotere.

Stuart St Potters Cooperative ARTS & CRAFTS
(14 Lower Stuart St; Mon-Sat) Locally designed and made pottery and ceramic art from 12 Dunedin and Otago region craftspeople.

Fern JEWELLERY
(67 Princes St; Mon-Sat) Unique clothing, design and jewellery, often from up-and-coming Dunedin artists and designers.

Bivouac Outdoor OUTDOOR EQUIPMENT
(www.bivouac.co.nz; 171 George St) Clothing, footwear and rugged gear.

University Book Shop BOOKS
(www.unibooks.co.nz; 378 Great King St) Fiction, poetry, Maori, Pacific and NZ titles.

Information

Call 111 for ambulance, fire service and police. Internet access is available at most hostels and accommodation. Wi-fi can be found at the airport and the Otago Museum.

Urgent Doctors & Accident Centre (03-479 2900; 95 Hanover St; 8am-11.30pm) Also a pharmacy open outside normal business hours.

Dunedin Hospital (03-474 0999, Emergency Department 0800 611 116; www.southerndhb.govt.nz; 201 Great King St)

Post Office (233 Moray Pl)

Department of Conservation (DOC; 03-477 0677; www.doc.govt.nz; 1st fl, 77 Lower Stuart St; 8.30am-5pm Mon-Fri) Information and maps on regional walking tracks and Great Walks bookings.

Dunedin i-SITE (03-474 3300; www.dunedinnz.com; 26 Princes St; 8.30am-5pm Mon-Fri, 8.45am-5pm Sat & Sun) Accommodation, activities, transport and walking tours.

WORTH A TRIP

OTAGO HARBOUR'S NORTH SHORE

The north shore of Otago Harbour provides a worthy detour from the main tourist track.

Little **Port Chalmers** (population 3000) is only 15km out of the city (15 minutes' drive, or bus 13 or 14 from Dunedin's Cumberland St), but it feels a world away. Somewhere between working class and bohemian, Port Chalmers has a history as a port town but has increasingly attracted Dunedin's arty types. Dunedin's best rock-and-roll pub, **Chicks Hotel** is an essential after-dark destination, and daytime attractions include a few raffish cafes, design stores and galleries.

The 150-year-old bluestone **Carey's Bay Hotel** (www.careysbayhotel.co.nz; 17 MacAndrew Rd, Carey's Bay; mains $15-30), 1km past the docks, has a bar with views of fishing boats and the harbour. There is a great collection of art from local painter Ralph Hotere, plus other Otago artworks. Meals tend to be focused on seafood. The salmon fish cakes ($18.50) are good.

On a sheep-and-deer farm 5km down the road from Port Chalmers, **Billy Brown Backpackers** (03-472 8323; www.billybrowns.co.nz; 423 Aramoana Rd, Hamilton Bay; dm/d $28/70) has magnificent views across the harbour to the peninsula. There's a lovely rustic shared lounge with a cosy wood-burner, and plenty of retro vinyl to spin.

WORTH A TRIP

TAIERI GORGE RAILWAY

With narrow tunnels, deep gorges, winding tracks, rugged canyons and more than a dozen stone and wrought-iron viaduct crossings (up to 50m high), the scenic **Taieri Gorge Railway** (☎03-477 4449; www.taieri.co.nz; Dunedin Railway Station, Anzac Ave; ⊙office 8am-5pm Mon-Fri, 8.30am-3pm Sat-Sun) consistently rates highly with visitors.

The four-hour return trip aboard 1920s heritage coaches travels to Pukerangi (one-way/return $56/84), 58km away. Some trips carry on to Middlemarch (one-way/return $65/97) or you can opt for a train–coach trip to Queenstown (one-way $138). From Middlemarch, you can also bring your bike along and hit the Rail Trail. In summer (October to April), trains depart 2.30pm daily for Pukerangi, plus trips to Middlemarch or Pukerangi some mornings. In winter (May to September) trains depart for Pukerangi at 12.30pm daily.

Getting There & Away

Air

Air New Zealand (p535) flies from Dunedin to Christchurch, Wellington and Auckland. Australian destinations are Brisbane, Sydney and Melbourne. Virgin Australia (p535) links Dunedin to Brisbane, and Jetstar (p535) flies to Auckland.

Bus

Buses and shuttles leave from the Dunedin Railway Station, excluding InterCity and Naked Bus. Check when you make your booking.

InterCity (☎03-471 7143; www.intercity.co.nz; 205 St Andrew St; ⊙ticket office 7.30am-5pm Mon-Fri, 11am-3pm Sat, 11am-5.15pm Sun, tickets by phone 7am-9pm daily) has services to Oamaru (one hour 40 minutes), Christchurch (six hours), Queenstown (4½ hours), Te Anau (4½ hours) and Invercargill – via Gore (4 hours). Buses leave from St Andrew St.

Naked Bus (www.nakedbus.com) connects Dunedin with Christchurch (six hours) and Invercargill (four hours). Buses leave from the **Citibus Transport Centre** (630 Princes St).

Southern Link (☎0508 458 835; www.southernlinkcoaches.co.nz) connects Dunedin to Christchurch (six hours), Oamaru (one hour 50 minutes) and Invercargill (three hours 40 minutes). **Coastline Tours** (☎03-434 7744; www.coastline-tours.co.nz) runs between Dunedin and Oamaru (two hours), and will detour to Moeraki or the airport if needed. Coastline departures leave Dunedin from The Octagon.

A couple of services connect Dunedin to the Catlins and Southland. The **Bottom Bus** (☎03-477 9083; www.bottombus.co.nz) does a circuit from Dunedin through the Catlins to Invercargill, Te Anau, Queenstown and back to Dunedin. **Catlins Coaster** (☎03-477 9083; www.catlinscoaster.co.nz) connects Dunedin with Invercargill, returning via the scenic Catlins.

Other services:

Atomic Shuttles (☎03-349 0697; www.atomictravel.co.nz) To/from Christchurch (six hours), Oamaru (two hours), Invercargill (four hours), and Queenstown and Wanaka (both four hours).

Trail Journeys (☎03-449-2024; www.trailjourneys.co.nz) Door-to-door daily between Dunedin and Wanaka stopping at Otago Central Rail Trail towns along the way. Bikes can be transported.

Knightrider (☎03-342 8055; www.knightrider.co.nz) Night-time service to Christchurch (six hours), Oamaru (two hours) and Invercargill (four hours). A handy service if you've got an early morning departure from Christchurch airport.

Wanaka Connexions (☎03-443 9120; www.alpinecoachlines.co.nz) Shuttles between Dunedin and Wanaka (four hours) and Queenstown (four hours). Alternate seven-hour services also include key stops for participants on the Otago Central Rail Trail. See the website for details.

Train

Two interesting train journeys start at Dunedin's railway station (p536): the Taieri Gorge Railway journey, and the **Seasider** (www.seasider.co.nz; one-way/return $54/81; ⊙departs 9.30am, returns 1.30pm), which journeys along the coast to Palmerston and back. Book via the Taieri Gorge Railway (p546).

Getting Around

To & From the Airport

Dunedin Airport (DUD; ☎03-486 2879; www.dnairport.co.nz) is 27km southwest of the city. A door-to-door shuttle is around $15 per person. Try **Kiwi Shuttles** (☎03-487 9790; www.kiwishuttles.co.nz), **Super Shuttle** (☎0800 748 885; www.supershuttle.co.nz) or **Southern Taxis** (☎03-476 6300; www.southerntaxis.co.nz). There is no public bus service.

A standard taxi ride between the city and the airport costs around $80.

Bus

City buses (☎03-474 0287; www.orc.govt.nz) leave from stops in the Octagon, while buses to districts around Dunedin depart a block away from stands along Cumberland St near the Countdown supermarket. Buses run regularly during the week, but services are greatly reduced (or nonexistent) on weekends and holidays. View the Dunedin bus timetable at the Dunedin i-SITE (p545), or see www.orc.govt.nz.

Car

The big rental companies all have offices in Dunedin, and inexpensive local outfits include **Getaway** (☎0800 489 761, 03-489 7614; www.getawaycarhire.co.nz) and **Driven Rentals** (☎03-456 3600; www.drivenrentals.co.nz).

Taxi

Dunedin Taxis (☎03-477 7777, 0800 50 50 10; www.dunedintaxis.co.nz) and **Otago Taxis** (☎03-477 3333).

Otago Peninsula

Otago Peninsula has the South Island's most accessible diversity of wildlife. Albatross, penguins, fur seals and sea lions are some of the highlights of the region, as well as rugged countryside, wild walks and beaches, and interesting historical sites. Despite a host of tours exploring the peninsula, the area maintains its quiet rural air. Get the *Otago Peninsula* brochure and map from the Dunedin i-SITE and visit www.otago-peninsula.co.nz.

Sights

FREE Royal Albatross Centre WILDLIFE RESERVE

(☎03-478 0499; www.albatross.org.nz; Taiaroa Head; 9am-dusk summer, 10am-4pm winter) Taiaroa Head, at the peninsula's eastern tip, has the world's only mainland royal albatross colony. The best time to visit is from December to February, when one parent is constantly guarding the young while the other delivers food throughout the day. Sightings are most common in the afternoon when the winds pick up, and calm days don't see much bird action. The only public access is through the Royal Albatross Centre where 45-minute tours (adult/child/family $40/20/100) include viewing from a glassed-in hut overlooking the nesting sites. There's no viewing from mid-September to late November. From late November to December the birds are nestbound so it's difficult to see their magnificent wingspan. The first tour of each day runs at 10.30am; bookings can be made online. Ask the staff whether the birds are flying before you pay.

Discounted combo deals are available with Nature's Wonders (p548) and Monarch Wildlife Cruises & Tours (p549). Visit www.albatross.org.nz for details.

Fort Taiaroa HISTORIC SITE

(www.albatross.org.nz) Nearby are the remains of Fort Taiaroa and its 1886 Armstrong Disappearing Gun, built when NZ was certain a Russian invasion was imminent. The gun was loaded and aimed underground, then popped up like the world's slowest jack-in-the-box to be fired. The Fort Taiaroa tour (adult/child/family $20/10/50) or the Unique Taiaroa Experience (adult/child/family $50/25/125) include the guns and the birds.

Yellow-Eyed Penguin Conservation Reserve WILDLIFE RESERVE

(☎03-478 0286; www.penguinplace.co.nz; McGrouther's Farm, Harington Point Rd; tours adult/child $49/12) Activities include building nesting sites, caring for sick and injured birds, and trapping predators. Ninety-minute tours focus on penguin conservation and close-up viewing from a system of hides. Between October and March, tours run regularly from 10.15am to 90 minutes before sunset. Between April and September they run from 3.15pm to 4.45pm. Booking ahead is recommended.

Larnach Castle CASTLE

(www.larnachcastle.co.nz; Camp Rd; castle & grounds adult/child $27/10, grounds only $12.50/4; 9am-7pm Oct-Mar, 9am-5pm Apr-Sep) Standing proudly on the peninsula's highest point, Larnach Castle was an extravagance of the Dunedin banker, merchant and politician, William Larnach. Built in 1871 to impress his French-nobility-descended wife, the Gothic mansion is filled with exquisite antique furnishings. The gardens offer fantastic views of the peninsula and harbour. Without your own transport, a tour is the only way to visit.

Glenfalloch Woodland Garden GARDENS

(www.glenfalloch.co.nz; 430 Portobello Rd; admission by donation; gardens 9.30am-dusk, cafe-wine bar 11am-3.30pm Mon-Fri, 11am-4.30pm Sat & Sun Sep-Apr) Glenfalloch Woodland Garden covers 12 hectares with flowers, walking tracks and swaying, mature trees including a 1000-year-old matai. Expect spectacular

Otago Peninsula

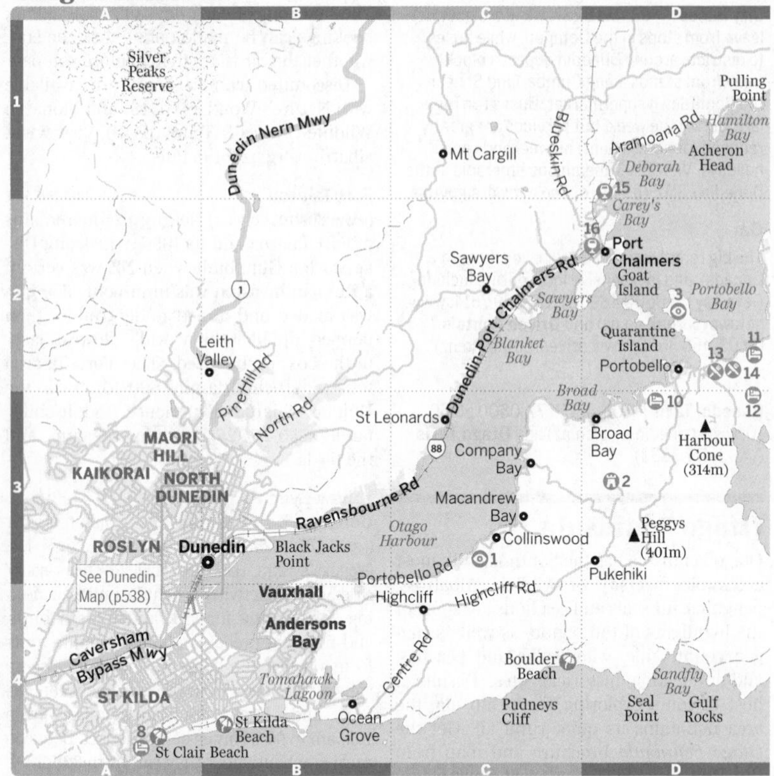

harbour views. The Portobello bus stops out the front.

Marine Studies Centre AQUARIUM
(www.marine.ac.nz; Hatchery Rd; adult/child/family $12.50/6/25; ⏲10am-4.30pm) View octopuses, seahorses, crayfish and sharks, help with fish-feeding (Wednesday and Saturday 2pm to 3pm), or join a guided tour at 10.30am (adult/child/family $21.50/11/49 including entry). The centre showcases the work of the adjacent university-run marine laboratory.

Activities

The peninsula's coastal and farmland walkways offer stunning views and the chance to see wildlife on your own. Pick up a free copy of the detailed *Otago Peninsula Tracks* from the Dunedin i-SITE. A popular walking destination is the beautiful **Sandfly Bay**, reached from Seal Point Rd (moderate; 40 minutes) or Ridge Rd (difficult; 40 minutes). From the end of Sandymount Rd, you can follow a trail to the impressive **chasm** (20 minutes). Note that the Lovers Leap track and the Chasm track at Sandymount are closed from 20 August to 31 October for lambing.

Wild Earth Adventures KAYAKING
(☎03-489 1951; www.wildearth.co.nz; trips from $115) Offers trips in double sea kayaks, with wildlife often being sighted en route. Trips run between four hours and a full day. Some trips start in Dunedin and some on the peninsula.

Tours

Nature's Wonders WILDLIFE
(☎0800 246 446, 03-478 1150; www.natureswondersnaturally.com; Taiaroa Head; tours adult/child/family $55/45/170; ⏲tours from 10.15am) Situated 1km past the albatross colony, and based on a sprawling coastal sheep farm, Nature's Won-

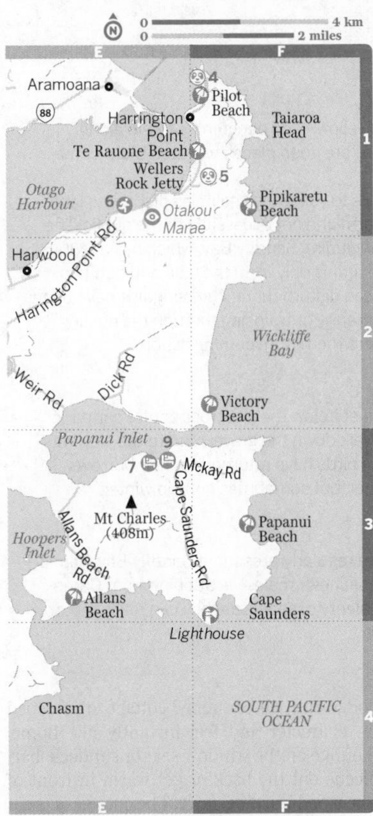

Otago Peninsula

Sights
- Fort Taiaroa .... (see 4)
- 1 Glenfalloch Woodland Garden C3
- 2 Larnach Castle D3
- 3 Marine Studies Centre D2
- 4 Royal Albatross Centre F1
- 5 Yellow-Eyed Penguin Conservation Reserve F1

Activities, Courses & Tours
- 6 Monarch Wildlife Cruises & Tours E1
- Nature's Wonders .... (see 4)

Sleeping
- 7 Betty's Bach E3
- 8 Hotel St Clair A4
- 9 Kaimata Retreat E3
- Larnach Lodge .... (see 2)
- 10 McFarmers Backpackers D3
- Penguin Place Lodge .... (see 5)
- 11 Portobello Motels D2
- 12 Portobello Village Tourist Park D3

Eating
- 1908 Café .... (see 13)
- 13 Portobello Coffee Shop & Café D2
- 14 Portobello Hotel D2
- Starfish .... (see 8)

Drinking
- 15 Carey's Bay Hotel D1
- 16 Chick's Hotel D2

ders runs one-hour tours taking in Stewart Island shags, NZ fur seals and yellow-eyed penguins. The tour is conducted in 'go-anywhere' Argos vehicles and is an exciting combo of improbable scenery and wildlife adventure.

Back to Nature Tours WILDLIFE
(☎03-478 0499, 0800 528 767; www.backtonaturetours.co.nz; adult/child $95/55) Good value peninsula tours getting you up close and personal with yellow-eyed penguins, NZ fur seals and sea lions. From November to March they also offer a tour including a spectacular coastal hike (adult/child $85/45).

Citibus WILDLIFE
(☎03-477 5577; www.citibus.co.nz; adult/child from $95/47.50) Tours combining albatross and penguin viewing.

Elm Wildlife Tours WILDLIFE
(☎03-454 4121, 0800 356 563; www.elmwildlifetours.co.nz; standard tour $99) Small-group tours of up to six hours. Pick-up and drop-off from Dunedin is included.

Monarch Wildlife Cruises & Tours WILDLIFE
(☎03-477 4276; www.wildlife.co.nz) One-hour boat trips from Wellers Rock (adult/child $49/22), and half- ($89/32) and full-day ($235/118) tours from Dunedin. Tours include breeding grounds for sea lions, penguins, albatross and seals often inaccessible by land.

Otago Explorer CULTURAL TOUR, WILDLIFE
(☎03-474 9083; www.otagoexplorer.com) Runs 2½-hour tours of Larnach Castle (adult/child $65/32.50) and summertime wildlife tours.

BEST PLACES TO SPOT...

Yellow-Eyed Penguins

One of the world's rarest penguins, the hoiho (yellow-eyed penguin) is found along the Otago coast, and several peninsula beaches are good places to watch them come ashore (any time after 4pm).

There are two private operators leading tours to yellow-eye colonies on private land, and other tours also visit habitats on private farmland not accessible to the public. The birds also nest at a couple of public beaches, including Sandfly Bay, which has a DOC hide. If you go alone, stay on the trails, view penguins only from the hide and don't approach these shy creatures; even loud voices can disturb them. The penguins have been badly distressed by tourists using flash photography or traipsing through the nesting grounds. Don't loiter on the beach, as this deters them from coming ashore.

Blue Penguins

Blue penguins can be viewed at Pilots Beach, just below the albatross centre car park. The penguins come ashore just before dusk. Walk down the gravel road to the viewing area near the beach, and remain there until the birds have returned to their burrows. There may be as many as 80 or more in summer, but sometimes none in winter.

Sea Lions

Sea lions are most easily seen on a tour, but are regularly present at Sandfly Bay, Allans and Victory Beaches. They are predominantly bachelor males vacationing from Campbell Island or the Auckland Islands. Give them plenty of space, as they can really motor over the first 20 metres.

Sleeping

TOP CHOICE Kaimata Retreat LODGE **$$$**
(03-456 3443; www.kaimatanz.com; 297 Cape Saunders Rd; s/d incl breakfast $390/460) This luxury ecolodge has three rooms overlooking a gloriously isolated inlet on the eastern edge of Otago Peninsula. Watch sea lions and bird life from the spacious decks, or get even closer with an eco-expedition with local farmer Dave. Be sure to include a private three-course dinner ($99 per person), and don't make the mistake of staying just one night.

Betty's Bach RENTAL HOUSE **$$**
(03-456 3443; www.bettysbach.co.nz; 267 Cape Saunders Rd; d $160) This cute retro bach enjoys superb, ever-changing views of Otago Peninsula's isolated Papanui Inlet. Get busy in the funky kitchen, fire up the wood-burning heater and have an old-school Kiwi holiday. Kaimata Retreat (p550) is nearby, and guests at Betty's Bach can join their eco-expeditions exploring the surrounding area.

McFarmers Backpackers LODGE **$**
(03-478 0389; www.otago-peninsula.co.nz; 774 Portobello Rd; s $50, d/tw $60-90) On a working farm with harbour views, this rustic timber lodge and self-contained cottage are steeped in character and feel instantly like home. Lounge on the window seat or sundeck, barbecue out the back or get warm in front of the wood-burning stove. The cottage is great for families, and the Portobello bus goes past the gate.

Larnach Lodge LODGE **$$**
(03-476 1616; www.larnachcastle.co.nz; Camp Rd; incl breakfast stable d $155, lodge d $260-280; @) Larnach Castle's back-garden lodge has 12 individually decorated rooms. The Queen Victoria Room has a giant four-poster bed, while in the Goldrush Room guests sleep in an old horse-drawn carriage. Less frivolous are the atmospheric rooms in the 125-year-old Coach House with sloping Tudor ceilings. Dinner is available by arrangement. A few hundred metres from Larnach Castle, the newly opened Camp Estate country house has luxury suites (doubles $380) worthy of a romantic splurge.

Portobello Village Tourist Park HOLIDAY PARK **$**
(03-478 0359; www.portobellopark.co.nz; 27 Hereweka St; sites from $31, units $55-130;) With lots of trees and grass, this is a pleasant place to stake your tent. There's a kids' play

area, a modern kitchen and wheelchair-accessible facilities. Backpacker rooms are BYO everything – bed linen can be hired – and self-contained units are smartly decorated.

Portobello Motels MOTEL **$$**
(☎03-478 0155; www.portobellomotels.com; 10 Harington Point Rd; d $135-145;) Sunny, modern, self-contained units just off the main road in Portobello. Studio units have small decks overlooking the bay. One- and two-bedroom units are also available, but lack the stunning views.

Penguin Place Lodge LODGE **$**
(☎03-478 0286; McGrouther's Farm, Harington Point Rd; adult/child $25/10) Atop the hill and surrounded by farmland, this lodge has a good shared kitchen, a bright lounge, and basic double and twin rooms. There are views across the farm and harbour, you're close to seals and albatross, and you're next-door neighbours with the penguins. Linen costs $5 extra.

Eating

Other Otago Peninsula dining options include the **Portobello Hotel**, and the **Portobello Coffee Shop & Café** for excellent burgers ($15). There's takeaways at the Portobello Store, and cafes attached to Larnach Castle, Nature's Wonders, Glenfalloch Woodland Garden and the Royal Albatross Centre.

There are also plenty of 'hey-let's-stop-here' places for picnics, so stock up before you leave Dunedin.

1908 Café RESTAURANT **$$**
(www.1908cafe.co.nz; 7 Harington Point Rd; mains $20-34; 11.30am-2pm Wed-Sat, 6-10pm daily) Salmon, venison and steak are joined by fresh fish and blackboard specials, and there's a box of toys for the kids. It's a beautiful old building, cheerfully embellished with local art.

Getting There & Around

Up to 10 buses travel each weekday between Dunedin's Cumberland St and Portobello Village, with one or two a day continuing on to Harington Point. Weekend services are more limited. Once on the peninsula, it's tough to get around without your own transport. Most tours will pick you up from your Dunedin accommodation.

There's a petrol station in Portobello, but opening hours are unpredictable. Fill up in Dunedin before driving out.

CENTRAL OTAGO

Rolling hills, grassy paddocks and a succession of tiny, charming gold-rush towns make this region worth exploring. Naseby and Clyde compete for the title of NZ's cutest towns, and rugged, laconic 'Southern Man' types can be seen propping up the bar in backcountry hotels. There are also fantastic opportunities for those on two wheels, whether mountain biking along old gold-mining trails, or taking it easy on the Otago Rail Trail.

Visit www.centralotagonz.com.

Cromwell

POP 2610

Cromwell has a charming lakeside historic precinct, a great weekly farmers market and, courtesy of local farms and orchards, a few good eateries. If you're travelling east to Dunedin or west to Queenstown, it's a good spot to stop for lunch. The nearby Bannockburn region has fine vineyards crafting excellent pinot noir and also some lovely vineyard restaurants. The **Cromwell i-SITE** (☎03-445 0212; www.centralotagonz.com; 9am-6pm; @) is in the central shopping mall. Its *Walk Cromwell* brochure covers local mountain-bike and walking trails, including the nearby gold-rush ghost-town of Bendigo.

Sights & Activities

Old Cromwell Town HISTORIC BUILDINGS
(www.oldcromwell.co.nz) When the Clyde Dam was completed in 1992, it flooded the original Cromwell village including the town centre, 280 homes, six farms and 17 orchards. Many historic buildings were disassembled before the flooding and have since been restored as Old Cromwell Town. This pedestrianised zone sits beside Lake Dunstan and now showcases good eating and interesting galleries. Ask for the *Old Cromwell Town Historic Precinct* map at the i-SITE. During summer an excellent farmers market kicks off at 8am every Sunday.

Goldfields Jet JETBOATING
(☎03-445 1038, 0800 111 038; www.goldfieldsjet.co.nz; adult/child $90/49) Zip around the Kawarau River on a 40-minute jetboat ride with Goldfields Jet.

Central Otago Motorcycle Hire MOTORBIKE RENTAL
(☎03-445 4487; www.comotorcyclehire.co.nz; 271 Bannockburn Rd; motorcycle hire per day from $275)

WORTH A TRIP

SEARCHING FOR THE PERFECT PINOT NOIR

The Bannockburn Valley near Cromwell is home to NZ's finest pinot noir wines, and accounts for over half of Central Otago's total wine production. Vineyards to visit include **Mt Difficulty Wines** (☎03-445 3445; www.mtdifficulty.co.nz; Felton Rd; platters $17-50, mains $30-33; ⏲cellar door 10.30am-4.30pm, restaurant noon-3pm) and **Carrick Wines** (☎03-445 3480; www.carrick.co.nz; Cairnmuir Rd; platters $12-25, mains $18-25; ⏲cellar door 11am-4pm, restaurant noon-3pm). Both vineyards also have highly regarded restaurants open for lunch; it's worth phoning head to book. Before you head off to Bannockburn, visit the Cromwell i-SITE and check out the handy display showcasing the area's vineyards. Pick up the *Central Otago Wine Map* brochure.

Central Otago vineyard tours can be arranged through **Active Travel** (☎0800 326 228, 03-445 4927; www.activetravelco.com; 8 Pinot Noir Dr; per person $140). Tours include visiting four different vineyards and a high-country sheep station. Other options include exploring Bannockburn's gold-mining heritage with **Bannockburn Historic Goldfields Tours** (☎03-445 1559, 027 221 0799; www.bannockburngold.co.nz; per person $15-29).

See www.otagowine.com and www.cowa.org.nz.

The sinuous and hilly roads of Central Otago are perfect for negotiating on two wheels. Hire a bike – including Harley Davidson – from Central Otago Motorcycle Hire. Much smaller Italian scooters ($90 per day) are perfect for zipping around the area's lakes, orchards and vineyards, and only require a car driver's licence. The company can also advise on improbably scenic routes around Queenstown, Glenorchy and Wanaka.

Sleeping

Most of Cromwell's motels are huddled near the town's central shopping mall.

Burn Cottage Retreat COTTAGE **$$**
(☎03-445 3050; www.burncottageretreat.co.nz; 168 Burn Cottage Rd; d $185) In a rural setting 3km northwest of Cromwell, Burn Cottage has three luxury self-contained cottages set in walnut trees and flower-studded woodland. Decor is classy and chic including king-size beds, spacious self-contained kitchens and modern bathrooms. Ask about the cosy Rascal Cottage, the most secluded of the three. Bed-and-breakfast accommodation (double $165) is available in the main house.

Carrick Lodge MOTEL **$$**
(☎0800 445 495, 03 445 4519; www.carricklodge.co.nz; 10 Barry Ave; d $138-160) One of Cromwell's more stylish motels, with spacious, modern rooms just a short stroll from good restaurants and cafes in the town's mall. Ask the owners about viewing the DVD about when the original Cromwell village was flooded to accommodate the construction of the Clyde Dam and Lake Dunstan.

Cromwell Top 10 Holiday Park HOLIDAY PARK **$**
(☎0800 107 275, 03-445 0164; www.cromwellholidaypark.co.nz; 1 Alpha St; sites from $40, units $75-135; @🛜) The size of a small European nation, packed with cabins, self-contained units and rooms of various descriptions, all set in tree-lined grounds.

Eating & Drinking

Armando's Kitchen ITALIAN **$$**
(71 Melmore Tce, Old Cromwell Town; mains $25-32; ⏲9am-4pm Tue-Sun, 6.30-10pm Thu-Sat) Old Cromwell Town is best enjoyed with an espresso or gourmet ice cream – try the Thai coconut and lime – on the heritage veranda of Armando's Kitchen. Excellent cake, gourmet pies, and open sandwiches are other daytime distractions. Italian-influenced dinner options include wild mushroom risotto with pancetta, and slow-braised lamb shank with polenta and silverbeet.

Feast RESTAURANT **$$**
(The Mall; mains $25-35; ⏲5pm-late Tue-Sat) Ignore the incongruous location in Cromwell's shopping mall, and stop by for tasty gourmet pizzas ($22.50), including woodfired spins on Moroccan lamb and Peking duck. Central Otago lamb and briny South Island blue cod and scallops also make an appearance, all served with local wine.

Grain & Seed Café CAFE **$**
(meals $10-15; ⏲9am-4pm) Set in a beautiful stone building that was once Jolly's Grain Store, this cute cafe serves up big, delicious, inexpensive meals. Grab an outside table beside the lake.

Cider House Cafe & Bar CAFE $$
(SH8; $10-30; ⌚7.30am-4pm Sun-Thu, 7.30am-late Fri-Sat) Sitting beside the state highway at the entry to town, this sunny little cafe dishes up healthy salads, good pizzas ($22.50) and world-famous-in-Cromwell fresh fruit smoothies ($7). Try a glass of their wild apple cider – tart and very tasty.

Getting There & Away

Atomic Shuttles (☎03-349 0697; www.atomictravel.co.nz), **InterCity** (www.intercity.co.nz), **Naked Bus** (www.nakedbus.com) and **Wanaka Connexions** (☎03-443 9122; www.alpinecoachlines.co.nz) all run to/from Queens-town (one hour) and Alexandra (30 minutes). Some services connect to Christchurch and Invercargill. Catch-a-Bus (p535) runs a convenient service linking Dunedin and Wanaka, stopping at Middlemarch, Ranfurly, Alexandra and Cromwell. Other stops near the Otago Central Rail Trail (including Naseby) can also be requested.

Clyde

POP 850

On the banks of the emerald-green Clutha River, the little village of Clyde (www.clyde.co.nz) looks more like a cute 19th-century gold-rush film set than a real town. Despite a recent influx of retirees, Clyde retains a friendly, small-town feel, and even when holidaymakers arrive in numbers over summer, it's a great place to chill out. It's also one end of the Otago Central Rail Trail.

Sights & Activities

Pick up a copy of *Walk Around Historic Clyde* from the Alexandra i-SITE (p555). The **Alexandra–Clyde 150th Anniversary Walk** (three hours one-way) is a riverside trail that's fairly flat with ample resting spots and shade.

Clyde Historical Museum MUSEUM
(Blyth St; adult/child $3/1; ⌚2-4pm Tue-Sun) Showcases Maori and Victorian exhibits and provides information about the Clyde Dam.

Trail Journeys BICYCLE RENTAL
(☎0800 724 587; www.trailjourneys.co.nz; Clyde Railhead; ⌚tours Sep-Apr) Trail Journeys rents bikes (from $35 per day) and offers cycling tours.

Festivals & Events

Clyde Wine & Food Festival WINE & FOOD
(www.promotedunstan.org.nz; ⌚Easter Sunday) Showcasing the region's produce and wines.

Sleeping

In February and March Clyde gets very busy so advance booking of accommodation is recommended.

Oliver's Lodge B&B $$$
(☎03-449 2600; www.oliverscentralotago.co.nz; 34 Sunderland St; d $195-315; wi-fi) Showcasing an outstanding collection of old maps, Oliver's Lodge fills a 19th-century merchant's house and stables with luxurious rooms decked out with Oriental rugs, heritage furniture and claw-foot baths. Most rooms open onto a secluded garden courtyard, and breakfast of freshly baked bread, homemade yoghurt and preserves is included.

Hartley Arms Backpackers HOSTEL $
(☎03-449 2700; hartleyarms@xtra.co.nz; 25 Sunderland St; per person $40) In the old stables behind a beautiful 1869 building that was once the Hartley Arms Hotel, these three cosy rooms look out to a peaceful, private, stone-walled garden and share a small kitchen and lounge. Tables and chairs in the shade of the cherry tree are a fine place to stretch limbs weary from 150km of cycling. The cat's called Radler, German for cyclist.

Dunstan House B&B $$
(☎03-449 2295; www.dunstanhouse.co.nz; 29 Sunderland St; d incl breakfast $120-220; ⌚Sep-May; @) This restored Victorian-age, balconied inn has lovely bar and lounge areas. Rooms with ensuite bathrooms, individually decorated in period style, are a little pricier, but most have claw-foot tubs. Less expensive (but still comfortable) rooms are next door in 'Miners Lane'.

Old Postmaster's House B&B $
(☎03-449 2488; www.postofficecafeclyde.co.nz; Blyth St; d $95-125) Has lovely rooms dotted with antique furnishings.

EATING

Bank Café CAFE $
(31 Sunderland St; $10-18; ⌚9am-4.30pm) Owned by a group of passionate local foodies, everything at the Bank Café is made fresh daily. That includes cakes and slices, corn fritters for breakfast and robust takeaway sandwiches that are perfect for lunch on two wheels.

Post Office Café & Bar CAFE $$
(2 Blyth St; mains $15-30; ⌚10am-9pm) Clyde's 1899 post office houses a popular restaurant famous for its garden tables and favourites such as grilled chicken sandwiches and hot-

WORTH A TRIP

TWO WHEELS GOOD: OTAGO CENTRAL RAIL TRAIL

Stretching from Dunedin to Clyde, the Central Otago rail branch linked small, inland goldfield towns with the big city from the early 20th century through to the 1990s. After the 150km stretch from Middlemarch to Clyde was permanently closed, the rails were ripped up and the trail resurfaced. The result is a year-round trail that takes bikers, walkers and horseback riders along a historic route containing old rail bridges, viaducts and tunnels. With excellent trailside facilities (toilets, shelters and information), no steep hills, gob-smacking scenery and profound remoteness, the trail attracts well over 25,000 visitors annually. March to April is the busiest time, when the trail is packed with urban visitors from Auckland, Wellington, Christchurch and Australia.

The trail can be followed in either direction. One option is to travel from Dunedin on the scenic Taieri Gorge Railway (p546), cycle from Pukerangi to Middlemarch (19km by road) and begin the trail the following day. The entire trail takes approximately four to five days to complete by bike (or a week on foot), but you can obviously choose to do as short or long a stretch as suits your plans. There are also easy detours to towns such as Naseby and St Bathans. Many settlements along the route offer accommodation and dining, including lodgings in restored cottages and rural farmhouses.

Mountain bikes can be rented in Dunedin, Middlemarch, Alexandra and Clyde. Any of the area's major i-SITEs can provide detailed information. See www.otagocentralrailtrail.co.nz and www.otagorailtrail.co.nz for track information, recommended timings, accommodation options and tour companies.

pots. There's loads of nooks and crannies conducive to reading fascinating newspapers featuring momentous days in NZ history.

The Packing Shed CAFE $
(68 Boulton Rd; $10-20) An interesting sculpture garden and a funky rural ambience make the Packing Shed a popular detour for Rail Trailers from Clyde to Alexandra.

Shopping

Central Gourmet Galleria FOOD
(www.centralone.co.nz; 27 Sunderland St) Expect a great collection of award-winning local wines, many of which you won't find anywhere else. There's also plenty of Central Otago foodie treats such as jams and chutneys – all easy-to-transport gifts and souvenirs.

Getting There & Away

Although no company has a dedicated stop here, buses travelling between Cromwell and Alexandra pick up and drop off in Clyde on request (it may incur a small surcharge).

Alexandra

POP 4620

Unless you've come here especially for the Easter Bunny Hunt or September's NZ Merino Shearing Championships, the best reason to visit Alexandra is the nearby mountain biking. Some travellers stay for seasonal fruit-picking work.

Sights & Activities

Mountain bikers will love the old gold trails weaving through the hills. Collect maps from the i-SITE (p555). **Altitude Adventures** (☎03-448 8917; www.altitudeadventures.co.nz; 88 Centennial Ave) and **Trail Journeys** (☎0800 724 587; www.trailjourneys.co.nz; Clyde Railhead) both rent bikes, offer backcountry cycling tours and provide transport to trailheads.

Central Stories MUSEUM
(www.centralstories.co.nz; 21 Centennial Ave; admission by donation; ⏰9am-5pm) Visit this excellent regional museum in the Alexandria i-SITE to understand Central Otago's history of goldmining, winemaking and sheep farming.

Clutha River Adventures KAYAKING
(☎03-449 3155; www.clutharivveradventures.co.nz; from $95) Commandeer inflatable kayaks to explore Lake Roxburgh. A popular self-guided option is from Alexandra to the interesting Doctor's Point gold-mining town.

Clutha River Cruise BOAT TOUR
(☎03-449 3155; www.cluthariver cruises.co.nz; adult/child $90/40; ⏰11am & 2pm Boxing Day-Feb, 1pm Oct-Christmas Eve & Mar-Apr) To experience the scenery and history of the region

by boat, join a 2½-hour Clutha River Cruise. Book at the Alexandra i-SITE.

Sleeping

Motels line Centennial Ave on the way into town.

Quail Rock B&B $$
(☎03-448 7224; www.quailrock.co.nz; 5 Fairway Dr; s/d from $100/150; @☎) Perched high above town, this very comfortable B&B offers equal servings of privacy and mountain views. Homemade preserves give breakfast a unique touch, and dinners are also available. And yes, quail are often seen scratching around the rocks in the garden.

Marj's Place HOSTEL $
(☎03-448 7098; www.marjsplace.co.nz; 5 Theyers St; per person $35; @☎) Two houses have myriad higgledy-piggledy shared rooms and a nice communal vibe, helped by the peaceful rose garden out back. There's a compact Finnish sauna onsite, and friendly owner Marj can also arrange seasonal work. Cash only.

Alexandra Holiday Park HOLIDAY PARK $
(☎03-448 8297; www.alexandraholidaypark.com; 44 Manuherikia Rd; sites from $30, units $50-70; @☎) Sitting beside the road to Ranfurly, with plenty of shade and backing onto the swimmer-friendly Manuherikia River, this holiday park is close to where the Rail Trail enters town. Self-contained units (sleeping up to six) start at $95 for two.

Eating

Tin Goose Cafe CAFE $
(www.thetingoosecafe.com; 22 Centennial Ave; $10-20) Home-style baking and superior counter food – try the chicken, cranberry and cream cheese pizza – combine with interesting salads and Alexandra's best coffee. Local mushrooms on ciabatta or the omelette of the day are healthy ways to start the day, especially if you're en route to the Rail Trail in nearby Clyde.

Red Brick Café CAFE $$
(Centrepoint car park off Limerick St; lunch $15-30, dinner $30-35) This funky cafe–wine bar with a sunny courtyard is positioned beside an Alexandra shoppers' carpark, the last place you'd expect to find blue cod, venison and pork belly so well prepared. Most ingredients and wines are locally sourced. The building was originally Alexandra's first bakery, and a hip utilitarian warehouse ambience lingers.

Shaky Bridge Café CAFE $$
(Graveyard Gully Rd; mains $15-30) Over a 110-year-old footbridge near the Rail Trail, Shaky Bridge is a winery-cafe in a heritage mudbrick building with views of the Manuherikia River. Tuck into locally sourced delicacies such as venison, duck or salmon. Coffee and cake come with a side order of vineyard views.

Foursquare SUPERMARKET $
(91 Tarbert St) Self-catering central.

Information

Alexandra i-SITE (☎03-448 9515; www.centralotagonz.com; 22 Centennial Ave; ⏰9am-6pm; @) The Alexandra i-SITE has internet access and a necessary free map of this very spread-out town.

Getting There & Away

See Cromwell for buses that pass along this route. From Alexandra you can head northwest past Cromwell towards Queenstown, or south past Roxburgh towards the east coast.

Alexandra to Palmerston

Northeast of Alexandra an irrigated strip of land tags alongside the highway, with the Dunstan and North Rough Ranges rising impressively on either side. This is the Manuherikia Valley, which tumbles into the Maniototo Plain as State Hwy 85 (SH85).

Chatto Creek Tavern (☎03-447 3710; www.chattocreektavern.co.nz; SH85; meals $12-23) is a cute 1880s stone hotel beside the Rail Trail and the highway. Pop in for a whitebait fritter (in season) or steak sandwich, or rest your weary calf muscles in a dorm bed ($50) or double room ($120). Rates include breakfast.

Made up of half a handful of historic buildings, and home to just 50 souls, tiny **Ophir** lies across the Manuherikia River and lays claim to the country's largest range of temperatures (from 35°C above to 22°C below). Take the gravel exit south off SH85 to rattle across the cute, 1870s wooden-planked Dan O'Connell Bridge, a bumpy but scenic crossing. **Black's Hotel** (☎03-447 3826; steven.chapman@clear.net.nz; per person incl breakfast $60) has cycle-friendly accommodation.

Back on SH85, **Omakau** and **Lauder** are good stops if you're a hungry rail-trailer with a sore bum and a need for a bed. Good-value rooms, excellent food and local company are all on tap at the **Omakau Commercial Hotel** (☎03-447 3715; www.omakauhotel.co.nz; 1 Harvey

St; dm/s/d from $35/45/80). Accommodation in nearby Lauder includes **Pedal Inn** (☎03-447 3460; benandcatherine@farmside.co.nz; SH85; d $120), which has two modern self-contained units on a working farm, and the cosy **Muddy Creek Cutting** (☎03-447 3682; www.muddycreekcutting.co.nz/; per person $60), a charmingly restored 1930s mudbrick farmhouse. Dinners with a local, organic spin are also available ($50 per person).

In Omakau township, take a break from the Rail Trail at the **Muddy Creek Cafe** (2 Harvey St; pies & mains $10-15), a friendly spot festooned with old radios. Organic ice cream and deservedly famous chicken and mushroom pies are some of the treats your tired legs have earned. Just up the road in Lauder, trailside **Stationside Cafe** (Lauder; snacks & mains $10-20) has healthy salads, sandwiches, soups and pasta. You'll probably hear Rosemary, the pet sheep, before you see her.

Take the turn-off north, into the foothills of the imposing Dunstan Range and on to diminutive **St Bathans**, 17km from SH85. This once-thriving gold-mining town of 2000 people is now home to only half a dozen permanent residents. Blue Lake is an accidental attraction: a large hollow filled with amazingly blue mineral water that has run off abandoned gold workings. Walk around the alien-looking lake's edge to a lookout (one hour return).

The **Vulcan Hotel** (☎03-447 3629; www.stbathansnz.co.nz; Main Rd; r per person $50; meals $20-25) is an atmospheric spot to drink in or stay. Considering it has a population of only six people (plus one Labrador and a ghost or two), you'll find the bar here pretty busy on a Friday night as thirsty shearers from around the valley descend en masse. The Vulcan also rents out some empty houses nearby. Jack (the black Labrador) will escort you down to a handful of cute cottages (doubles from $100 to $220 per night) including the old gaol. He's also very keen on his battered old rugby ball. Try not to lose it like we almost did.

Back on SH85, the road swings around to run southeast and passes the historic **Wedderburn Tavern** (☎03-444 9548; www.wedderburntavern.co.nz; SH85; per person incl breakfast $55). Seven kilometres later is the turn-off for Naseby; otherwise it's straight through to Ranfurly.

NASEBY

Cute as a button, surrounded by forest and dotted with 19th-century stone buildings, Naseby is the kind of small town where life moves slowly. That the town is pleasantly obsessed with the fairly insignificant world of NZ curling indicates there's not much else going on. It's that lazy small-town vibe, along with good mountain-biking and walking trails through the surrounding forest, that make Naseby an interesting place to stay for a couple of days.

Sights & Activities

Naseby Information & Crafts (☎03-444 9961; Derwent St; ⏰11am-2pm Fri-Mon), in the old post office, has information on local walks and bike trails. For more mountain-biking information and to hire a bike, head to **Kila's Bike Shop** (☎03-444 9088; kilasbikeshop@xtra.co.nz; Derwent St; per day $35) near the Black Forest Café. **Naseby Forest Headquarters** (☎03-444 9995; Derwent St) is also good for maps of walks through the Black Forest.

All year round you can shimmy after curling stones at the indoor ice rink in the **Naseby Alpine Park** (☎03-444 9878; www.curling.co.nz; Channel Rd; curling per hr adult/family $20/50; ⏰10am-5pm). Curling tuition is also available. From June to August there's ice skating at an adjacent outdoor rink, and a seasonal ice **luge** (☎03-444 9270; www.lugenz.co.nz; ⏰Jul-Aug) runs for a thrilling 360m down a nearby hillside. The luge is open to the public, but booking ahead is essential.

Sleeping & Eating

Church Mouse RENTAL HOUSE $$
(☎03-444 9440, 027 714 1209; www.holidayhouses.co.nz; d $190) For a romantic stay, consider the Church Mouse, a lovingly restored former Catholic church, now revitalised as luxury rental accommodation. Rich wooden floors are partnered with stylish modern furniture, and the main bedroom fills a private mezzanine floor. Mod cons include a brand-new kitchen, and there's a private sunny courtyard for enjoying those southern summer nights.

Naseby Trail Lodge LODGE $$
(☎03-444 8374, 0508 627 329; www.nasebylodge.co.nz; cnr Derwent & Oughter Sts; d $160) Popular with international luging visitors, the Nasbey Trail Lodge features modern units constructed of environmentally friendly straw-bale walls sheathed in rustic corrugated iron.

Ancient Briton PUB $
(☎03-444 9990; www.ancientbriton.co.nz; 16 Leven St; s $60, d from $105) A mudbrick ho-

tel dating from 1863, Ancient Briton has a rambling range of basic-to-comfortable accommodation. Have some traditional pub grub (mains from $17 to $27), or prop yourself up at the bar to admire the trophies of the pub's 'Blue Hats' curling team and get to know the locals.

Royal Hotel HOTEL $

(☎03-444 9990; www.naseby.co.nz; Earne St; dm $30, d $89-115) Another pub with good food and accommodation is the Royal Hotel, right beside what just may be NZ's most rustic garden bar.

Larchview Holiday Park HOLIDAY PARK $

(☎03-444 9904; www.larchviewholidaypark.co.nz; Swimming Dam Rd; sites from $26, units $45-81; @) Set in 17 acres of woods, Larchview Holiday Park has an alpine feel, a small on-site playground and swimming at a dam nearby. There are also basic timber cabins and cottages.

Black Forest Café CAFE $

(☎03-444 9820; 5 Derwent St; mains $10-15; ⏲9am-4pm) Fresh baking and good coffee features at the Black Forest Café, gorgeous inside with its stone walls, bright colours and warm polished wood. The wide-ranging menu features bagels, panini and creamy smoothies using local Central Otago fruit.

Getting There & Away

The Ancient Briton pub (p556) has a courtesy van and will pick up from Ranfurly or the Rail Trail. If prebooked, **Catch-a-Bus** (☎03-449 2024; www.catchabus.co.nz) stops in Naseby on its Dunedin–Cromwell route. If you're driving, take the exit off SH85, just north of Ranfurly. From Naseby, you can wind your way northeast through spectacular scenery to Danseys Pass and through to Duntroon and the Waitaki Valley.

RANFURLY

Ranfurly is trying hard to cash in on its art deco buildings – much of the town was rebuilt in the architecture of the day after a series of fires in the 1930s – and a few attractive buildings and antique shops line its sleepy main drag. The town holds an annual **Art Deco Festival** (www.ranfurlyartdeco.co.nz) on the last weekend of February.

The **Ranfurly i-SITE** (☎03-444 1005; www.maniototo.co.nz; Charlemont St; ⏲10am-4pm daily Oct-Apr, Mon-Fri May-Sep; @) is in the old train station. Grab a copy of *Rural Art Deco – Ranfurly Walk* for a self-guided tour.

The art deco **Ranfurly Lion Hotel** (☎03-444 9140; www.ranfurlyhotel.co.nz; 10 Charlemont St; s $55-70, d $75-98; @) has 16 comfortable rooms and a couple of bars, and does substantial pub meals (dinner from $20 to $27). All you'll need after a long day on two wheels and a bike seat.

Cheery and warm, with an open fire, local art and the Maniototo sports wall of fame, **E-Central Café** (☎03-444 8300; 14 Charlemont St; mains $7-15; ⏲breakfast & lunch) is definitely the best lunch option in town.

To explore the rugged terrain made famous by local landscape artist Grahame Sydney, contact **Maniototo 4WD Safaris** (☎03-444 9703; www.maniototo4wdsafaris.co.nz; per person half-/full day $80/140).

A daily **Catch-a-Bus** (☎03-449 2024; www.catchabus.co.nz) shuttle passes through Ranfurly on its way between Wanaka and Dunedin.

WAIPIATA

About 10km southeast of Ranfurly and right on the Rail Trail, tiny Waipiata has the **Waipiata Country Hotel** (☎03-444 9470; www.waipiatahotel.co.nz; dinner mains $20-25; @). There's a sunny CYO ('Cook Your Own') barbecue area, and the restaurant menu includes goodies such as Pig Root Spare Ribs and Bike Faster Pasta. It's the only pub on the Rail Trail serving Dunedin's Emerson's beer, and comfortable accommodation is available from $70 per person. Ask about the recently refurbished Mudbrick room.

Set on farmland 4km from Waipiata, **Peter's Farm Lodge** (☎0800 472 458, 027 686 1692; www.petersfarm.co.nz; Tregonning Rd; per person incl breakfast $50) has simple, comfortable rooms in a rustic 19th-century farmhouse. Shared dining tables encourage an end-of-the-day social vibe, and hearty barbecue dinners are $25. Kayaks, fishing rods and gold pans are all available, so it's worth staying a couple of nights. Peter also runs the nearby Tregonnings Cottage, built in 1880, but now with a well-equipped, modern kitchen. He'll also pick you up for nix from the Waipiata stop on the Rail Trail.

RANFURLY TO DUNEDIN

After Ranfurly, SH85 runs 62km to Palmerston, then 55km south to Dunedin or 59km north to Oamaru. Another option is to hop on the southbound SH87 directly to Dunedin, 129km via **Hyde** and Middlemarch. In Hyde, the **Otago Central Hotel** (☎03-444 4800; www.hydehotel.co.nz; s/d with shared bathroom $80-130, s/d with ensuite $100-190) provides boutique accommodation. Linger in the sunny terrace cafe for a second espresso before setting out on two wheels again.

With the Rock and Pillar Range as an impressive backdrop, the small town of **Middlemarch** (www.middlemarch.co.nz) is one end of the Taieri Gorge Railway, and also a start or end-point of the Otago Central Rail Trail. Rent bikes and gear from **Cycle Surgery** (☎03-464 3630; www.cyclesurgery.co.nz; Snow Ave; per day $35). The company has another branch at the other end of the Rail Trail in Clyde.

At the famous **Middlemarch Singles Ball** held across Easter in odd-numbered years, southern men from the region gather to woo city gals.

On a family-owned farm just a few hundred metres from the Rail Trail, **Trail's End** (☎03-464 3474; www.trailsend.co.nz; 91 Mason Rd; d incl breakfast $150) combines secluded cabins with views of the Rock and Pillar Mountain Range, and has the muscle-easing diversion of a spa pool.

Opposite the railway station, **Quench Café & Bar** (☎03-464 3070; 29 Snow Ave; mains $10-30; ⏲8am-late) is versatility plus, with goodies such as the Rail Burger ($15 – recommended if you're beginning the Rail Trail) and ice-cold Speight's on tap (*definitely* recommended if you've just finished the trail).

Alexandra to Dunedin

Heading south from Alexandra, SH8 winds along rugged, rock-strewn hills above Lake Roxburgh, then follows the Clutha River as it passes lush fruit farms and Central Otago's famous orchards. In season, roadside fruit stalls sell just-picked stone fruit, cherries and berries. En route are a number of small towns, many from gold-rush days.

Only 13km south of Alexandra, **Speargrass Inn** (☎03-449 2192; www.speargrassinn.co.nz; SH8; d $155-170) has three units in attractive gardens behind a charming 1860s building with elegant guest areas. An on-site **restaurant** (SH8; mains $15-30; ⏲9am-4pm Mon & Thu,9am-7pm Fri & Sat, 9am-6pm Sun) offers cosmopolitan tastes including beef parmigiana and mushroom-and-blue-cheese tart. At the very least, stop for coffee and cake, and stock up on tasty homemade preserves and chutneys.

From here, the road passes through Roxburgh, Lawrence and the Manuka Gorge Scenic Reserve, a scenic route through wooded hills and gullies. SH8 joins SH1 in Milton.

ROXBURGH

The orchards surrounding Roxburgh provide excellent roadside stalls and equally plentiful seasonal fruit-picking work. **Roxburgh i-SITE** (☎03-446 8920; www.centralotagonz.com; 120 Scotland St; ⏲9.30am-4pm) has information on mountain biking and water sports.

Villa Rose Backpackers (☎03-446 8761; www.villarose.co.nz; 79 Scotland St; dm/unit $30/95) is an old-fashioned villa with spacious dorm rooms and a huge modern kitchen. Adjacent heritage-style, self-contained units are supercomfortable. The manager can help sort out seasonal fruit-picking work, and provide discounted weekly rates.

Stop at Roxburgh's iconic **Jimmy's Pies** (☎03-444-8596; 143 Scotland St; pies $4-6; ⏲7.30am-5pm Mon-Fri). Renowned across the South Island since 1960, Jimmy's pastry delights are at their best just out of the oven. Try the apricot and apple flavour – you're in orchard country after all. Heading south, you'll find Jimmy's on your right just as you're leaving town.

Clutha District

The mighty Clutha River is NZ's highest-volume river, and is dammed in several places to feed hydroelectric power stations. **Balclutha** is South Otago's largest town but is of little interest to travellers other than as a place to stock up on supplies before setting off into the Catlins. The **Balclutha i-SITE** (☎03-418 0388; www.cluthacountry.co.nz; 4 Clyde St) has local info and internet access. For more local information, see www.cluthacountry.co.nz.

NORTH OTAGO & WAITAKI

The broad, braided Waitaki River rushes across the northern boundary of Otago, setting the boundary with Canterbury to the north. South of the river, on the coast, lies Oamaru, a town of penguins and glorious heritage architecture. The Waitaki Valley is an alternative route inland, featuring freaky rock formations, Maori rock paintings and ancient fossils. The area is also one of NZ's newest winemaking regions, and a major component of the new Alps2Ocean Cycle Trail, linking Aoraki/Mt Cook National Park to Oamaru. See www.nzcycletrail.com for more information.

Oamaru

POP 12,700

Nothing moves very fast in Oamaru. Tourists saunter, locals linger and penguins waddle. Even oft-celebrated heritage modes of transport – penny farthings and steam trains – reflect an unhurried pace. For travellers, the focus is mostly on penguins and the historic district, but eccentric gems such as the South Island's yummiest cheese factory, cool galleries and a peculiar live-music venue provide other distractions. Another recent layer to Oamaru's unique appeal is the quirky Steampunk movement, boldly celebrating the past and the future with an ethos of 'tomorrow as it used to be'.

A history of refrigerated-meat shipping made Oamaru prosperous enough in the 19th century to build the imposing limestone buildings that grace the town today. In its 1880s heyday, Oamaru was about the same size as Los Angeles was at the same time. Oamaru also has an affinity with the arts that may well be rooted in its claim to Janet Frame, but extends to a lively arty and crafty community today.

Sights

HARBOUR-TYNE HISTORIC PRECINCT

Oamaru has some of NZ's best-preserved historic commercial buildings, particularly around the harbour and Tyne St, an area designated the **Historic Precinct**. They were built from the 19th century, largely using the local limestone (known as Oamaru stone or whitestone) in fashionable classic forms, from Gothic revival to neoclassical Italianate and Venetian palazzo. Pop into the Oamaru Whitestone Civic Trust (p564) for information and the *Victorian Oamaru* pictorial guide. On Thames St, Oamaru's expansive main drag – laid out to accommodate the minimum turning circle of a bullock cart – don't miss the **National Bank** at No 11 and the **Oamaru Opera House** at No 92.

The fascinating area of narrow streets in the historic precinct is now home to bookshops, antique stores, galleries, vintage clothing shops and craft bookbinders. Guided walking tours ($10) leave from the Oamaru i-SITE at 10am daily from November to April.

The **Woolstore** (1 Tyne St) has a cafe and souvenirs, and the **Auto Museum** (1 Tyne St; adult/child $6/free; ⌚10am-4.30pm) is perfect for *Top Gear* fans. On adjoining Harbour St, the **Grainstore Gallery** (☎027-261 3764; ⌚noon-4pm Mon-Fri, 10am-2pm Sat & Sun) features an ever-changing array of quirky artwork. Another thoroughly Victorian-era thrill is steering a penny farthing bicycle from **Oamaru Cycle Works** (☎03-439 5333, 027 439 5331; Wansbeck St; lesson & afternoon tea $25). Ask David the owner about his intrepid penny farthing trek down the entire length

OAMARU IN FRAME

One of NZ's best-known novelists, Janet Frame, is intimately linked with Oamaru. The town, disguised in her novels as 'Waimaru', was Frame's home throughout most of her early years. Her writing is often described as 'dense', with early books also somewhat grim, a reflection of her own troubled life. But they are also unique in the construction of their stories and the nature in which the story is told. Later books remain intense, with wordplays, mythological clues and illusions, but are less gloomy.

It was in 1951 that Frame, a (misdiagnosed) sufferer of schizophrenia at Seacliff Lunatic Asylum, found sudden recognition as a writer, happily causing her doctors to rethink her planned lobotomy. Released, with frontal lobe intact, she moved on to gain international recognition in 1957 with her first novel *Owls Do Cry*, in which 'Waimaru' features strongly. Her subsequent literary accomplishments include *Faces in the Water* (1961), *The Edge of the Alphabet* (1962), *Scented Gardens for the Blind* (1963), *A State of Siege* (1967) and *Intensive Care* (1970). Jane Campion's film version of *An Angel at My Table* (1990), is based on the second volume of Frame's autobiographical trilogy. Pick up a free copy of *Janet Frame's Oamaru* from the Oamaru i-SITE (p564) and follow the 1½-hour self-guided tour.

Frame received numerous NZ and international awards, and was twice short-listed for the Nobel Prize for literature, most recently in 2003. She died the following year.

Janet Frame's **childhood house** (56 Eden St; $6; ⌚2-4pm Nov-Apr) is also open for viewing.

of New Zealand. He also rents out retro 1940s bikes (half/full day $15/20).

Try to visit this historical precinct at the weekend, especially on a Sunday for the excellent **Oamaru Farmers Market** (www.oamarufarmersmarket.co.nz; Tyne St; ⌚9.30am-1pm Sun). Note that some historic precinct shops and attractions are closed on a Monday.

Also check out the Oamaru limestone being carved at **Ian Andersen's gallery** (www.ianandersensculptor.co.nz; 15 Tyne St) and buy some smaller works to take home. Art buffs should seek out the *Oamaru Arts & Crafts* brochure at the i-SITE.

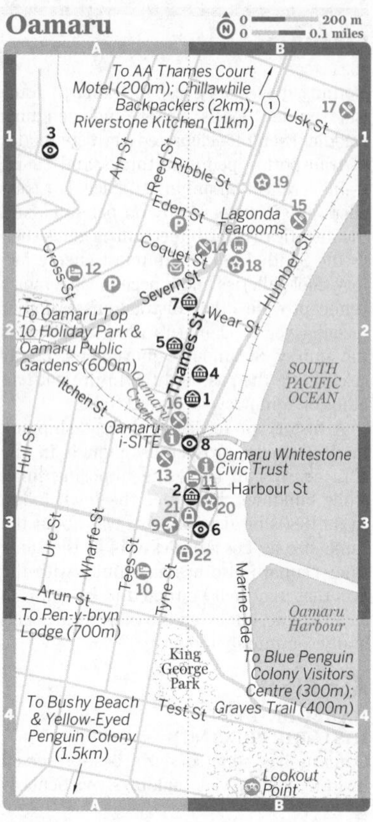

ELSEWHERE IN OAMARU

Blue-Penguin Colony WILDLIFE
(www.penguins.co.nz; adult/child/family $25/10/65; ⌚10am-sunset) In an old limestone quarry near the waterfront, you can see the little tykes from Oamaru's blue-penguin colony surfing in and wading ashore. The penguins arrive just before dark (around 5.30pm in midwinter and 9.30pm midsummer), and it takes them about an hour to all come ashore. You'll see the most penguins (up to 150) in November and December. From March to August there may be only 30 to 50 birds. Nightly viewing times are posted at the i-SITE (p564). Use of camera flashes is prohibited, and you should dress warmly.

To understand the centre's conservation work, take the 30-minute, daytime, behind-the-scenes tour (self-guided adult/child/family $12/5/30 or guided $18/8/50). Forward bookings can be made on www.penguins.co.nz, and packages combining night viewing and the behind-the-scenes tour are also available. Drop some coins in the centre's donation box. Their conservation efforts have helped increase the bird population dramatically.

Do not under any circumstances wander around the rocks beside the sea here at night looking for penguins. It's damaging to their environment as well as stuffing up studies on the effect of humans on the little birds.

FREE **Yellow-Eyed Penguin Colony** WILDLIFE
There are large hides and good trails to the yellow-eyed penguin colony at Bushy Beach, where the penguins come ashore in late afternoon to feed their young. Two hours before dark is the best time to see them. Despite their Maori name, *hoiho* (noisy shouter), they're extremely shy; if they see or hear you they'll head back into the water. Graves Trail, a 2.5km low-tide walk, starts from the end of Waterfront Rd and follows the rugged coastline around to the yellow-eyed colony at Bushy Beach. Watch out for fur seals, and do not use a flash when photographing the penguins.

FREE **Steampunk HQ** GALLERY
(www.steampunkoamaru.co.nz; 1 Itchen St; ⌚10am-4pm) Discover the past – or maybe a quirky version of the future – in this wonderful gallery celebrating Steampunk culture. Ancient machines wheeze and splutter, and the industrial detritus of the last century or so is repurposed and reimagined to funky effect. Don't miss firing up the sparking, space-age locomotive out the front – definitely at its best after dark.

Oamaru

Sights

Auto Museum .... (see 11)
1 Forrester Gallery B2
2 Grainstore Gallery B3
3 Janet Frame's House A1
4 National Bank B2
5 North Otago Museum A2
6 NZ Malt Whisky Company B3
7 Oamaru Opera House B2
8 Steam Train B3
Steampunk HQ .... (see 8)

Activities, Courses & Tours

9 Oamaru Cycle Works A3

Sleeping

10 Anne Mieke Guest House A3
11 Criterion Hotel B3
12 Red Kettle YHA A2

Eating

13 Annie's Victorian Tearooms A3
14 Countdown Supermarket B2
Harbour St Bakery .... (see 11)
Loan & Merc Tavern & Eating House .... (see 6)
15 Midori B1
16 Steam A2
17 Whitestone Cheese Factory & Café B1

Drinking

Birdlands Wine Company .... (see 11)
Criterion Hotel .... (see 11)
Fat Sallys .... (see 5)

Entertainment

18 Globe B2
19 Movie World 3 .... B1
20 Penguin Club B3

Shopping

21 Ian Andersen's Gallery B3
22 Oamaru Farmers Market A3
Woolstore .... (see 11)

FREE **Forrester Gallery** GALLERY
(www.forrestergallery.com; 9 Thames St; ⏲10.30am-4.30pm) Housed in a beautiful, columned 1880s bank building, the Forrester Gallery has an excellent collection of regional and NZ art. This gallery is a good place to see works by Colin McCahon, renowned for his darkly melancholic style. Check the website for regular special exhibitions.

FREE **North Otago Museum** MUSEUM
(www.northotagomuseum.co.nz; 60 Thames St; ⏲10.30am-4.30pm Mon-Fri, 1-4.30pm Sat & Sun) In the grand 19th-century library, the North Otago Museum has exhibits on Maori and Pakeha history, writer Janet Frame, architecture and geology.

Steam Train TRAIN
(www.oamaru-steam.org.nz; adult/child/family one-way $5/2/12, return $8/3/20; ⏲11am-4pm Sun & Public Holidays) On Sundays ride the old Steam Train from the historic district to the waterfront area. The two steam trains date from 1877 and 1924, although in winter they're occasionally replaced by a diesel.

NZ Malt Whisky Company DISTILLERY
(☎03-434 8842; www.nzmaltwhisky.co.nz; 14 Harbour St; gallery free, tastings $10-15; ⏲11am-5pm) The NZ Malt Whisky Company offers whisky tastings amid the heritage bones of a former Victorian warehouse. Don't miss taking the labyrinthine wooden stairs to the art gallery on the upper floors.

FREE **Oamaru Public Gardens**
(main entry on Severn St) The Oamaru public gardens were first opened in 1876 and are a lovely place to chill out on a hot day, with endless lawns, waterways, bridges and a children's playground.

Activities

Vertical Ventures MOUNTAIN BIKING, CLIMBING
(☎021 894 427, 03-434 5010; www.verticalventures.co.nz) Contact Rob to rent mountain bikes ($45 per day), or join guided mountain-biking trips along forest tracks and coastal roads (from $100 per person). To get vertical, join an abseiling or climbing group (from $130). Locations include the Elephant Rocks in the Waitaki Valley.

Festivals & Events

Oamaru Wine & Food Festival FOOD & WINE
(www.oamaruwineandfoodfest.co.nz; ⏲3rd Sun in Feb) Showcasing North Otago's food and wine scene.

Victorian Heritage Celebrations CULTURAL
(www.historicoamaru.co.nz; late November) Five days of locals wearing Victorian garb, with penny-farthing races, singing, dancing and street theatre.

Tours

MP3 players ($15) for self-guided tours are available at the i-SITE (p564). Ask about guided walking tours of Oamaru's historic precinct, often with a ghostly spin.

Penguins Crossing WILDLIFE
(03-477 9083; www.travelheadfirst.com; adult/child/family $50/25/125) Door-to-door, 2½-hour tour taking in the blue and yellow-eyed colonies. Price includes admission to the blue penguin colony. Pick up times vary from 4pm to 7pm throughout the year.

Sleeping

Oamaru's motel mile kicks off at the northern end of town as SH1 morphs into Thames St. There's also good accommodation a short drive from Oamaru at Old Bones Backpackers (p566) and the Olive Grove Lodge and Holiday Park (p566).

Pen-y-bryn Lodge LODGE $$$
(03-434 7939; www.penybryn.co.nz; 41 Towey St; d incl breakfast/breakfast & dinner $625/875; @) Well-travelled foodie owners have thoroughly revitalised this beautiful 125-year-old residence. Rates include a full breakfast, predinner drinks in the antiques-studded drawing room, and a four-course, gourmet dinner in the fabulous dining room. Retire afterwards to the billiard room and show off on the full-sized table. Dinner is also available to outside guests by prior arrangement (three/four courses $85/135).

Chillawhile Backpackers HOSTEL $
(03-437 0168; www.chillawhile.co.nz; 1 Frome St; dm $29-31, s $48, d/tw 58-66; @) Unleash your creative spirit at this funky and colourful hostel in a restored two-storey Victorian residence. Guests are encouraged to draw and paint, or create sweet soul music on the hostel's guitars, pianos, didgeridoo and African drums. With all that creative energy, there's definitely a laidback social vibe, and Chillawhile is one of NZ's best and most unique hostels.

Criterion Hotel HOTEL $$
(03-434 6247; www.criterion.net.nz; 3 Tyne St; d with bathroom $165, s/tw/d without bathroom $85/100/135, all incl breakfast) Period rooms at this 1877 hotel are smallish, but the guest lounge is large, and both are lovingly restored with glowing wooden floors and Turkish rugs. Rates also include home baking and preserves in the cosy dining room. Downstairs there's the distraction of a great corner pub with more than a few good beers on tap.

Anne Mieke Guest House B&B $
(03-434 8051; www.theoamarubnb.com; 47 Tees St; s/d incl $60/90) The decor is a tad chintzy, and the ambience hushed like your Nana's house, but visitors are guaranteed harbour views at this good-value B&B. Look forward to spotless shared bathrooms and a spacious guest lounge.

Red Kettle YHA HOSTEL $
(03-434 5008; www.yha.co.nz; cnr Reed & Cross Sts; dm/d $28/62; @) This red-roofed cottage has colourfully painted inner walls, a well-equipped kitchen and a cosy lounge. A good old-school vinyl collection will keep you and fellow guests entertained. It's on a quiet side street, a short walk from the town centre.

AAA Thames Court Motel MOTEL $$
(0800 223 644, 03-434 6963; www.aaathamescourt.co.nz; 252 Thames St; d $115-140; @) Good option for families with comfortable, recently renovated units and a play area for kids. All bookings include free wi-fi, and the cafes and pubs of Oamaru are a pleasant 500m stroll away.

Oamaru Top 10 Holiday Park HOLIDAY PARK $
(03-434 7666, 0800 280 202; www.oamarutop10.co.nz; Chelmer St; sites from $40, units $65-140; @) Grassy and well maintained, with trees out the back and the public gardens next door. Cabins are basic, but units with kitchen (with varying levels of self-contained comfort) are much nicer.

Eating

TOP CHOICE **Riverstone Kitchen** RESTAURANT $$
(03-431 3505; www.riverstonekitchen.co.nz; 1431 SH1; brunch & lunch mains $15-20, dinner mains $29-32; 9am-5pm Thu-Mon, 6pm-late Thu-Sun;) This award-winning haven 12km north of Oamaru on SH1 blends leather couches and polished concrete for a sophisticated ambience. Much of Riverstone's produce is from their own onsite gardens, with standout options including free-range pork with fennel and apple slaw, or delicious panko-crumbed red cod with chunky hand-cut

chips. Beers and wines showcase smaller vineyards and craft breweries. Booking for dinner is recommended.

Loan & Merc Tavern & Eating House RESTAURANT $$
(www.loanandmerc.co.nz; 14 Harbour St; mains $20-30, dinner carvery $32.50) Attention travelling carnivores. Here's your opportunity to tuck into superbly roasted meats including lamb, beef and pork, all served with overflowing platters of innovatively prepared vegetables. Ask if the honey-roasted fennel bulbs are in season. À la carte offerings include rabbit, venison and pickled walnut pies, and during the day, the high-ceilinged heritage warehouse showcases ploughman's lunches with smoked and cured meats.

Annie's Victorian Tearooms CAFE $
(cnr Itchen & Thames St; afternoon tea $10; ⏲10am-7pm Thu-Mon) Step into a gracious past courtesy of the delightful Annie Baxter. Waitstaff are dressed in Victorian period costume, the heritage ambience is thoroughly authentic and the afternoon tea spread includes delicate sandwiches and freshly baked cakes. Sipping on Earl Grey tea from bone china cups, you won't mind off switching off your flash 21st-century smartphone at all.

Harbour St Bakery BAKERY $
(Harbour St; ⏲Tue-Sun) In the historic precinct the Harbour St Bakery has the South Island's best sourdough bread – just perfect with a slab of local Whitestone cheese. Another tasty option is to buy a freshly baked gourmet pie. Grab an outdoor seat and watch Oamaru's heritage vibe scroll past like an old-time movie.

Midori JAPANESE $$
(cnr Humber & Ribble Sts; sushi $8-11, mains $12-18; ⏲11am-2.30pm & 5-8.30pm Mon-Wed, 11.30am-9pm Thu-Sat) Housed in a heritage whitestone building, this Japanese restaurant makes the most of the South Island's good seafood. Sashimi and sushi are super-fresh, and other carefully prepared dishes include salmon on rice and teriyaki blue cod. Here's your tasty opportunity to (kind of) replicate the diet of a little blue penguin.

Steam CAFE $
(7 Thames St; mains $10-18) Steam specialises in coffees and fruit juices, and is a good spot to stock up on freshly ground java for your own travels. Settle in for breakfast, or partake of a freshly baked Mainland-sized muffin.

Whitestone Cheese Factory & Café CAFE $
(www.whitestonecheese.co.nz; 3 Torridge St) The home of tasty, award-winning organic cheeses. Try the creamy Mature Windsor Blue or the ultrarich Mt Domet Double Cream. Sample the $5 cheese tasting plate or the $18 charcuterie platter. The cheese rolls are an Otago delicacy, and there are also local fruit juices and Central Otago wines. Unsurprisingly, the cheesecake is also very good.

Countdown Supermarket SUPERMARKET $
(cnr Thames & Coquet Sts) Centrally located.

Drinking

Criterion Hotel PUB
(3 Tyne St) This restored property is the ultimate corner pub. The owner maintains an ever-changing selection of draught beers – look for brews from Christchurch's Harrington Breweries and Dunedin's Green Man – and there's also excellent pub food. Don't blame us if you progress to the single-malt heaven also on offer. Weekend evenings sometimes see impromptu gigs from local musos.

Birdlands Wine Company WINE BAR
(3 Harbour St; 4pm-late Thu-Sat, 1pm-late Sun) Oamaru's hippest spot is this cool wine bar in the historic precinct. Local wines and Kiwi craft beers combine with antipasto platters and Whitestone cheese boards, and there's chilled live music or DJs most Saturday nights.

Fat Sallys PUB
(☎03-434 8368; 84 Thames St; ⏲Tue-Sun) Popular with locals, especially early on when they're often tucking into a substantial pub meal. Come along on a Wednesday night for the rollicking pub quiz.

Entertainment

Check out the Criterion Hotel (p563) and Birdlands Wine Company (p563) for occasional live music.

Penguin Club LIVE MUSIC
(☎03-434 1402; www.thepenguinclub.co.nz; Emulsion Lane off Harbour St; admission varies) Tucked down a sleepy alley off a 19th-century street, the Penguin's bizarre location matches its acts: everything from touring Kiwi bands to punky/grungy/rocky/country locals. Fridays are open-stage jam night. It's nominally Members Only, so ask at the Oamaru i-SITE about scoring a guest pass. See the website for listings.

Movie World 3 CINEMA
(03-434 1070; www.movieworld3.co.nz; 239 Thames St; adult/child $13.50/8.50) Cheaper on Tuesdays.

Globe CLUB
(12 Coquet St; Fri & Sat) Oamaru's sole nightclub.

Information

Oamaru i-SITE (03-434 1656; www.visitoamaru.co.nz; 1 Thames St; 9am-5pm Mon-Fri, 10am-4pm Sat-Sun; @) Mountains of information including details on local walking trips and wildlife. There's internet, bike hire and an interesting 10-minute DVD on the history of the town. Daily penguin-viewing times are also posted outside.

Oamaru Whitestone Civic Trust (03-434 5385; www.historicoamaru.co.nz; 2 Harbour St; 10am-4pm) Vintage B&W photos of Oamaru's heritage, maps, information and walking tours of the historic precinct.

Post Office (cnr Coquet & Severn Sts)

Getting There & Around

Bookings can be made through the i-SITE (p564) and at the **Lagonda Tearooms** (191 Thames St; 9am-4.30pm). Buses and shuttles depart from here.

The following companies have shuttles to Dunedin (two hours) and Christchurch (3½ hours).

Atomic Shuttles (03-349 0697; www.atomictravel.co.nz)

Coastline Tours (03-434 7744, 027 256 5651; www.coastline-tours.co.nz) Runs to/from Dunedin and will detour to Dunedin airport

InterCity (www.intercity.co.nz)

Knightrider (www.knightrider.co.nz) Handy for morning flights from Christchurch airport.

Naked Bus
(0900 625 33; www.nakedbus.com)

Southern Link (0508 458 835; www.southernlink.co.nz)

Waitaki Valley

The little-travelled Waitaki Valley includes some unique sights and scenery between the turn-off at SH1 and Omarama. The valley is also an outdoors paradise, and is a good place to catch trout and salmon, or waterski on the strikingly blue hydrolakes. This is a possible route to Wanaka and Queenstown if you're heading south, or to Twizel and Mt Cook if you're heading north.

After following SH83 almost to Duntroon, detour left at the turn-off to Danseys Pass. Nearby on the left, under an impressive limestone overhang, are the Maraewhenua **Maori rock paintings**. The charcoal-and-ochre paintings date back several centuries, tracing everything from pre-European hunting to sailing ships.

Follow the road another 4km then turn left towards Ngapara. Two kilometres further on are **Elephant Rocks**. Sculpted by wind, rain and rivers, the huge limestone boulders of this bizarre landscape were utilised as Aslan's Camp in the NZ-filmed *Narnia* blockbuster (2005). If you're feeling adventurous, continue over Danseys Pass to Naseby from 2km back at the intersection.

Back on SH83 at Duntroon is the **Vanished World Centre** (www.vanishedworld.co.nz; 7 Campbell St; adult/family $5/10; 10am-4pm Oct-Jun, 11am-3pm Sat-Sun only Jul-Sep), with interesting displays of 25-million-year-old fossils, including NZ's shark-toothed dolphins and giant penguins. Pick up a copy of the *Vanished World Fossil Trail* map outlining 20 different locations around North Otago. Just west of Duntroon is the **Takiroa Maori Rock Art Site**, with more drawings dating back many centuries.

Tiny **Kurow** is at the junction of the Waitaki and Hakataramea Rivers. For good coffee, stop at the **Te Kohurau Restaurant & Café** (8am-6pm Thu-Tue). Pop into the **Kurow Heritage & Information Centre** (03-436 0950; museum@kurow.co.nz; SH83), which has an interesting museum, including a mini-shrine to local boy Richie McCaw, captain of the mighty All Blacks when they won the Rugby World Cup in 2011.

Instead of continuing west from Kurow on SH83, take the 21km scenic detour over the Aviemore Dam, around the northern lake shore past walking tracks and scenic campsites ($10), then over the huge Benmore Dam earthworks. Rejoin SH83 just west of Otematata.

OMARAMA

POP 360

At the head of the Waitaki Valley, Omarama is surrounded by mountain ranges and fabulous landscapes. Busy times in town include the Omarama rodeo (28 December) and the Omarama sheepdog trials (March).

Sights & Activities

Clay Cliffs CLIFFS
(admission $5) The bizarre moonscape of the Clay Cliffs is the result of two million years of erosion on layers of silt and gravel that

WAITAKI WINE ON THE WAY UP

The wines of nearby Central Otago already have a robust global reputation, but a few winemaking pioneers in North Otago's Waitaki Valley are also making international wine experts drink up and take notice. Pop into the **Vintner's Drop** (03 436 0545, 021 431 559; www.ostlerwine.co.nz; 45 Bledisloe St; noon-2pm Thu-Sun Dec-Apr, 11am-4pm Thu & noon-2pm Sun Jul-Oct) – housed in Kurow's old post office – to taste a wide range of wines from the emerging vineyards of the Waitaki, including varietals from Ostler Wines.

Just 4km east of Kurow on SH83, the **Kurow Winery** (03 3 436 0443; www.kurowwinery.co.nz; Duntroon Rd; cellar door 11am-5pm, reduced hours in winter) offers well-balanced Riesling, and smoky and spicy pinot noir. Drop in for a wine-tasting session and a winery platter ($38), including smoked Aoraki salmon, Whitestone cheese from nearby Oamaru, and local venison salami.

Pinot gris and pinot noir are the stars at **Sublime Wine** (www.sublimewine.co.nz; 511 Grants Rd, RD7K), a compact, family-owned vineyard around 2km further east on SH83 past the Kurow Winery. The well-travelled owners also operate the funky **Sublime Bed & Breakfast** (03-436 0089, 021 943 969; www.sublimewine.co.nz; d $150;). The rambling old homestead is surrounded by vineyards and mountain valleys, and a twin and double room are decorated with an eclectic combo of old advertising signs and retro furniture. Special Taste of Waitaki three-course dinners ($50 per person including wine) showcasing local produce are available.

were exposed along the active Osler fault line. The cliffs are on private land; the turn-off is 3.5km north of Omarama, then it's another 10km on an unsealed road. Pay $5 for admission at Omarama Hot Tubs.

Wrinkly Rams ANIMAL SHOW

(03-438 9751; www.thewrinklyrams.co.nz; SH8; adult/child/family $25/12.50/60) Wrinkly Rams does 30-minute stage shows of merino sheep being shorn using both modern and traditional methods, along with a sheepdog show. A barbecue lunch is included. Phone ahead to tag along with a tour group, or book your own one-off show. Attached to Wrinkly Rams is one of the town's better restaurants (p566).

Omarama Hot Tubs

(03-438 9703; www.hottubsomarama.co.nz; 25 Omamara Ave; 10am-10pm) If your legs are weary after mountain biking or hiking, or you just want to cosy up with your significant other, pop into the Omarama Hot Tubs. The concept, combining private hot tubs (per person $30 to $40), and private 'wellness pods' ($125 for two people) including intimate, personal saunas, is Japanese, but with the surrounding mountain ranges and a pristine night sky, you could only be on the South Island of New Zealand. Therapeutic massages (30/60 minutes $40/80) are another relaxing option. The chemical-free mountain water is changed daily, and used water is recycled for irrigation.

Omarama Hot Tubs also doubles as the local information office, and can assist with accommodation and transport information. See www.discoveromarama.co.nz for more information.

GLIDING

The area's westerlies and warm summer thermals allow for world-class gliding over the hills and spectacular Southern Alps, and a national gliding meet is held here in December or January. Two companies will get you aloft from around $325:

Glide Omarama

(03-438 9555; www.glideomarama.com)

Southern Soaring

(0800 762 746; www.soaring.co.nz)

Sleeping & Eating

Buscot Station FARMSTAY $

(027 222 1754, 03-438 9646; SH8; dm/s/d $23/43/55; @) A slightly chintzy but very comfortable farmhouse on a huge sheep farm with expansive views. Large doubles in the main house and a large modern dormitory out back are all comfortable. Tony the owner shares his kitchen and lounge, as well as his theories on farming and politics. You'll find the turn-off to Buscot Station 10km north of Omarama.

Omarama Top 10 Holiday Park HOLIDAY PARK $
(☎03-438 9875; www.omaramatop10.co.nz; SH8; sites from $32, units $54-125; @☏) Streamside and duck-ponded, this is a peaceful green space to camp in. Cabins are compact, and larger ensuite and self-contained motel units cost $110 for two.

Ladybird Hill Vineyard Restaurant RESTAURANT $$
(www.ladybirdhill.co.nz; lunch $10-29, dinner $26-32; ⊙10.30am-late Thu-Sun) Drop into this slice of Tuscany for a leisurely lunch of venison open sandwich or wild rabbit pie, or come back at night for pan-fried salmon or prime rib-eye steak with roasted beetroot. Wines include the restaurant's own tipples, and vintages from the nearby Waitaki Valley. Other attractions include a kids' playground and walking tracks through the hillside vineyard.

Wrinkly Rams RESTAURANT $$
(☎03-438 9751; www.thewrinklyrams.co.nz; SH8; breakfast $10-15, lunch & dinner $15-30) Restaurants attached to tourist attractions can be dodgy, but the dinners here (pan-fried cod, tender lamb shanks) are quite delicious. Big glass windows and outside tables give a nice view of the mountains while you eat. Wines from the nearby Waitaki Valley also feature.

ℹ Getting There & Away

From Omarama head north up SH8 past beautiful Lake Ohau to Twizel and Mt Cook, or southwest through the striking Lindis Pass towards Cromwell and Queenstown. Stop before the Lindis Pass to add your own roadside cairn.

Omarama is on the route from Christchurch (five hours) to Lake Tekapo and Mt Cook. Both **Atomic Shuttles** (☎03-349 0697; www.atomictravel.co.nz) and **InterCity** (www.intercity.co.nz) swing by.

Oamaru to Dunedin

It's a 114km blast along SH1 from Oamaru to Dunedin, but the narrow, ocean-hugging road travelling south from Oamaru provides a break from the main highway. Take Wharfe St out of town (following the signs for Kakanui) for gorgeous coastal views.

About 5km south of Oamaru on this coast road, **Old Bones Backpackers** (☎03-434 8115; www.oldbones.co.nz; Beach Rd; per person $45, campervans per person $20; @☏) has spacious rooms off a sunny, central space. Close enough to the sea to hear the surf at night, this is a place to just relax in front of the huge windows looking over farmland to the sea, or get stuck into your favourite book. It's under new ownership, but is still one of NZ's best hostels.

Rejoining SH1 again at Waianakarua, backtrack 300 metres north to the **Olive Grove Lodge and Holiday Park** (☎03-439 5830; www.olivebranch.co.nz; SH1, Waianakarua; sites from $24, dm/s $27/45, d/tw $60-70). Surrounded by farmland and encircled by the Waianakarua River, this is a popular camping ground during summer. The rooms are brightly painted with interesting artworks, and the sunny communal lounge is a treat. Kids will love the adventure playground and highland cattle; parents will love the spa, eco lifestyle, organic vegies and peaceful vibe. En suite rooms (doubles $70) are good options for families.

Further south on SH1, 30km south of Oamaru, stop to check out the **Moeraki Boulders** (*Te Kaihinaki*), a collection of large spherical boulders on a stunning stretch of beach, scattered about like a giant kid's discarded marbles. Try to time your visit for low tide.

Moeraki township is a charming fishing village. It's a nice 1½-hour walk along the beach between the village and the boulders. Head in the other direction towards the Kaiks wildlife trail and a cute old wooden lighthouse – a great spot to see yellow-eyed penguins and fur seals. Moeraki has nurtured the creation of several national treasures, from Frances Hodgkins' paintings to Keri Hulme's *The Bone People*...and Fleur Sullivan's cooking.

Fleur's Place (☎03-439 4480; www.fleursplace.com; Old Jetty; mains $25-38; ⊙10.30am-late Wed-Sat) has a rumble-tumble look about it, but this timber hut serves up some of the South Island's best food. The speciality is seafood, fresh off Moeraki's fishing boats. Head for the upstairs deck and tuck into fresh chowder, tender mutton bird and other briny-fresh ocean bounty. Bookings are strongly recommended, but they'll probably squeeze you in between the busy lunch and dinner times. Fleur is also the energy behind Oamaru's Loan & Merc (p563).

Moeraki Motel (☎03-439 4862; www.moerakibeachmotels.co.nz; cnr Beach & Haven Sts; d $100) has self-contained units with balconies, while the **Moeraki Village Holiday Park** (☎03-439 4759; www.moerakivillageholidaypark.co.nz; 114 Haven St; sites from $29, units $55-130; @☏) has cabins and motel units.

Queenstown & Wanaka

Includes »

Queenstown Region.....568
Queenstown.................568
Arrowtown...................587
Glenorchy.....................591
Lake Wakatipu Region.........................593
Wanaka Region.............595
Wanaka........................595
Makarora......................603
Hawea...........................604
Cardrona......................604

Best Places to Eat

» Bella Cucina (p582)
» Fishbone Bar & Grill (p582)
» Amisfield Winery & Bistro (p585)
» Vudu Cafe & Larder (p582)
» Federal Diner (p601)

Best Places to Stay

» The Dairy (p579)
» Glenorchy Lake House (p592)
» Wanaka Bakpaka (p599)
» Riversong (p599)
» Warbrick Stone Cottage (p579)

Why Go?

With a cinematic background of mountains and lakes you actually have seen in the movies, and a 'what can we think of next?' array of adventure activities, it's little wonder Queenstown tops the itineraries of many travellers.

Slow down (slightly) in Wanaka – Queenstown's junior cousin – which also has good restaurants, bars, and outdoor adventures on tap. Explore nearby Mt Aspiring National Park to reinforce the fact that you're only a short drive from true New Zealand wilderness.

Slow down even more in Glenorchy, an improbably scenic reminder of what Queenstown and Wanaka were like before the adventure groupies moved in. Negotiate the Greenstone and Routeburn Tracks for extended outdoor thrills, or kayak the upper reaches of Lake Wakatipu.

Across in historic Arrowtown, consider the town's goldmining past over a chilled craft beer or dinner in a cosy bistro. The following day there'll be plenty more opportunities to dive into Queenstown's cavalcade of action.

When to Go

The fine and settled summer weather from January to March is the perfect backdrop to Queenstown's active menu of adventure sports and lake and alpine exploration. From June to August, the ski slopes surrounding Queenstown and Wanaka are flush with an international crew of ski and snowboard fans. For the best in local festivals, make a date for June's exciting Queenstown Winter Festival, or experience the region's food and wine scene at March's Gibbston Valley Festival and Wanaka Fest in October.

Getting There & Around

Air New Zealand (☎03-441 1900; www.airnewzealand.co.nz; 8 Church St) links Queenstown to Auckland, Wellington and Christchurch, and Sydney and Melbourne. Virgin Australia has flights between Queenstown and Sydney and Brisbane. Jetstar links Queenstown with Auckland, Christchurch and Wellington, and Sydney, Melbourne and the Gold Coast. From Wanaka, Air New Zealand flies to Christchurch. Bus and shuttle companies criss-cross Otago from Dunedin to Queenstown and Wanaka. Several divert south to Te Anau and Invercargill, and others migrate north to Christchurch or travel through the Haast Pass and up the West Coast. The major operators include InterCity, Atomic Shuttles, Naked Bus, Tracknet, Alpine Coachlines and Wanaka Connexions.

QUEENSTOWN REGION

POP 11,000

Surrounded by the soaring indigo heights of the Remarkables, crowned by Coronet Peak, and framed by the meandering coves of Lake Wakatipu, it's little wonder that Queenstown is a show-off. The town wears its 'Global Adventure Capital' badge proudly, and most visitors take the time to do crazy things they've never done before. But a new Queenstown is also emerging, with a cosmopolitan restaurant and arts scene and excellent vineyards. Go ahead and jump off a bridge or out of a plane, but also slow down and experience Queenstown without the adrenaline. And once you've eased up, look forward to more of the same in historic Arrowtown or beautiful Glenorchy.

Queenstown

No one's ever visited Queenstown and said, 'I'm bored'. Looking like a small town, but displaying the energy of a small city, Queenstown offers a mountain of outdoor activities.

Maximise bragging rights with your souvenir T-shirt in the town's atmospheric restaurants, laid-back cafes and bustling bars. Be sure to also find a lakeside bench at sunrise or dusk and immerse yourself in one of NZ's most beautiful views.

Queenstown is well used to visitors with international accents, so expect great tourist facilities, but also great big crowds, especially in summer and winter. Autumn (March to May) and spring (October to November) are slightly quieter, but Queenstown is a true year-round destination. The town's restau-

Queenstown & Wanaka Highlights

1. Sampling superb wines amid the dramatic scenery of the **Gibbston Valley** (p585)
2. Relaxing and dining in **Arrowtown** (p587) after the last of the day-trippers have left
3. Doing things you've only dreamed about in **Queenstown** (p570), the adrenaline-rush capital of NZ
4. Walking the peaceful **Routeburn Track** (p593)
5. Exploring by horseback, kayak and jetboat the upper reaches of Lake Wakatipu from sleepy and stunning **Glenorchy** (p591)
6. Watching a flick at **Cinema Paradiso** (p602) in Wanaka, with pizza during intermission
7. **Bar-hopping** (p584) and **dining** (p582) in cosmopolitan Queenstown
8. Experiencing Queenstown's **mountain biking** (p575) mecca on two knobbly wheels

ESSENTIAL QUEENSTOWN & WANAKA

» **Eat** A leisurely lunch at a vineyard restaurant

» **Drink** One of Wanaka Beerworks' (p595)' surprising seasonal brews

» **Read** *Walking the Routeburn Track* by Philip Holden for a wander through the history, flora and fauna of this tramp

» **Listen to** The silence as you kayak blissfully around Glenorchy and Kinloch

» **Watch** Art-house movies at Arrowtown's quirky Dorothy Browns (p591) boutique cinema

» **Online** www.queenstownnz.co.nz; www.lakewanaka.co.nz; www.lonelyplanet.com/new-zealand/queenstown

» **Area code** ☎03

rants and bars are regularly packed with a mainly young crowd that really know how to enjoy themselves on holiday. If you're a more private soul, drop in to see what all the fuss is about, but then get out and about by exploring the sublime wilderness further up the lake at Glenorchy.

History

The region was deserted when the first Pakeha (white person) arrived in the mid-1850s, although there is evidence of previous Maori settlement. Sheep farmers came first, but after two shearers discovered gold on the banks of the Shotover River in 1862, a deluge of prospectors followed. Within a year Queenstown was a mining town with streets, permanent buildings and a population of several thousand. It was declared 'fit for a queen' by the NZ government, hence Queenstown was born. Lake Wakatipu was the principal means of transport, and at the height of the boom there were four paddle steamers and 30 other craft plying the waters.

By 1900 the gold had petered out and the population was a mere 190. It wasn't until the 1950s that Queenstown became a popular holiday destination.

Sights

Skyline Gondola CABLE CAR

(Map p572; www.skyline.co.nz; Brecon St; adult/child/family return $25/14/71) Hop on the Skyline Gondola for fantastic views of Queenstown, the lake and the mountains. At the top are a cafe, a restaurant with regular Maori cultural shows (p586), and souvenir shops. Walking trails include the loop track (30 minutes return), or you can try the Luge or new mountain-bike trails. The energetic can forgo the gondola and hike to the top; take the upper, left-hand gravel track from the trailhead on Lomond Cres for an hour's uphill hike.

Kiwi Birdlife Park WILDLIFE

(Map p576; www.kiwibird.co.nz; Brecon St; adult/child $38/19; ⏲9am-5pm, shows 11am & 3pm) Here's your best bet to spy a kiwi. There are also 10,000 native plants and scores of birds, including the rare black stilt, kea, morepork and parakeets. Stroll around the sanctuary, watch the conservation show and tiptoe quietly into the darkened kiwi houses.

The Kingston Flyer TRAIN EXCURSION

(☎03-248 8888, 0800 435 937; www.kingstonflyer.co.nz; Kingston; adult/child/family 1 way $35/17.50/87.50, return $45/22.50/112.50; ⏲departs Kingston 10am & 1.30pm) Based in Kingston, a lakeside village 40 minutes south of Queenstown, this restored 130-year-old steam train runs on a preserved 14km stretch of track linking Kingston and Fairlight. Shuttles ($20 return) are available from Queenstown if you don't have transport.

Williams Cottage HISTORIC BUILDING

(Map p576; cnr Marine Pde & Earl St; ⏲10am-5.30pm) Williams Cottage is Queenstown's oldest home. An annexe of Arrowtown's Lake District Museum and Gallery, it was built in 1864 and retains plenty of character, including 1930s wallpaper. The cottage and its 1920s garden are now home to the very cool Vesta store showcasing local designers and artists. Much of the work is exclusive to Vesta.

Church of St Peter CHURCH

(Map p576; www.stpeters.co.nz; cnr Church & Camp Sts; ⏲services 10am Wed, 10.30am Sun) This pretty wood-beamed building has a beautiful organ and colourful stained glass. Take a look at the cedar lectern, which was

MAORI NZ: QUEENSTOWN & WANAKA

Kiwi Haka (p586) perform nightly atop the Queenstown gondola, Two Queenstown galleries worth checking out for contemporary Maori art and design are Kapa (p586) and toi o tahuna (p586).

Queenstown Region

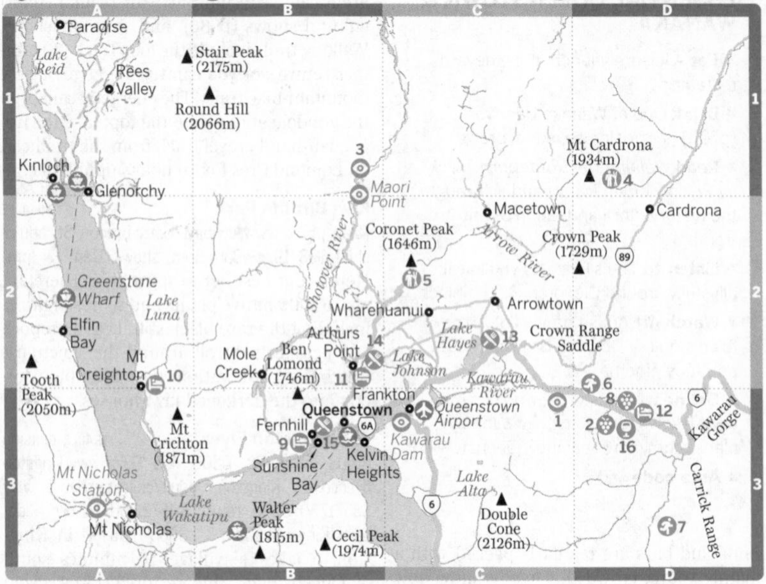

Queenstown Region

Sights

1 Chard Farm C3
2 Gibbston Valley Wines D3
3 Skippers Canyon B1

Activities, Courses & Tours

4 Cardrona D1
5 Coronet Peak C2
6 Kawarau Bridge D2
Kawarau Bungy Centre .... (see 6)
7 Nevis Highwire D3
Onsen Hot Pools .... (see 14)
8 Peregrine D3

Sleeping

9 Evergreen Lodge B3
10 Little Paradise Lodge A2
11 Shotover Top 10 Holiday Park B2
12 Warbrick Stone Cottage D3

Eating

13 Amisfield Winery & Bistro C2
14 Gantley's B2
15 VKnow B3
Winehouse & Kitchen .... (see 6)

Drinking

16 Gibbston Tavern D3

carved by Ah Tong, a Chinese immigrant, in the 1870s. On Saturday mornings in summer, the church grounds host the Queenstown Farmers Market.

Underwater Observatory WILDLIFE
(Map p576; Queenstown Bay Jetty; adult/child/family $5/3/10; ⏲9am-5pm) Underwater Observatory has six giant windows showcasing life under the lake. Brown trout abound, and look out for freshwater eels and scaup (diving ducks), which cruise right past the windows.

Activities

Purchase discounted combination tickets from **Queenstown Combos** (☎03-442 7318, 0800 423 836; www.combos.co.nz). Some activity operators have offices on Shotover St, or you can book at the i-SITE or your accommodation.

Bungy Jumping

Queenstown is famous for bungy jumping. For all the following bungy jumping and bungy variations, contact AJ Hackett Bungy at the Station (p587) or book through your accommodation or the i-SITE. Most bungy trips also include transport to the jump location.

Kawarau Bridge BUNGY
(Map p570; per person $180) The historic 1880 Kawarau Bridge, 23km from Queenstown, became the world's first commercial bungy site in 1988 and allows you to leap 43m.

FREE **Kawarau Bungy Centre** BUNGY
(Map p570; SH6; ⊙8am-5.45pm) Looks through the Secrets of Bungy Tour, explaining the history of bungy; you can try the more gentle Bungy Trampoline (adult/child $20/15). It's loads of fun for children, even two-year-olds.

Ledge Bungy BUNGY
(Map p572; Brecon St; per person $180) From atop the Skyline Gondola, the 47m-high Ledge Bungy also operates after dark.

Nevis Highwire BUNGY
(Map p570; per person $260) Jump from a 134m-high pod above the Nevis River.

Bungy Variations

Shotover Canyon Swing BUNGY
(☎0800 279 464, 03-442 6990; www.canyonswing.co.nz; per person $199, additional swings $39) Be released loads of different ways – backwards, in a chair, upside down. From there it's a 60m free fall and a wild swing across the canyon at 150km/h.

Nevis Arc BUNGY
(☎0800 286 4958; www.nevisarc.co.nz) Fly in tandem ($320) or go it alone ($180) on the planet's highest swing.

Ledge Sky Swing BUNGY
(Map p572; ☎0800 286 4958; www.bungy.co.nz; per person $150) A shorter swing than at the Nevis Arc, but equally stunning views of Queenstown from atop the Skyline Gondola.

Jetboating

The Shotover and Kawarau are Queenstown's most popular rivers to hurtle along. The lengthier and more scenic Dart River is less travelled.

Shotover Jet JETBOATING
(☎0800 746 868; www.shotoverjet.co.nz; adult/child $119/69) Half-hour trips through the rocky Shotover Canyons, with lots of thrilling 360-degree spins.

Kawarau Jet JETBOATING
(Map p576; ☎03-442 6142, 0800 529 272; www.kjet.co.nz; Queenstown Bay Jetty; adult/child $110/65) Does one-hour trips on the Kawarau and Lower Shotover Rivers.

Skippers Canyon Jet JETBOATING
(☎03-442 9434, 0800 226 996; www.skipperscanyon.co.nz; adult/child $129/79) Incorporates a 30-minute blast in the narrow gorges of **Skippers Canyon** (Map p570) in three-hour trips that also cover the area's gold-mining history.

White-Water Rafting

The choppy Shotover and calmer Kawarau Rivers are both great for rafting. Trips take four to five hours with two to three hours on the

QUEENSTOWN IN...

Two Days

Start your day with breakfast at **Vudu Cafe & Larder** before heading to Shotover St to book your adrenaline-charged activities for the next day. Spend the rest of the day visiting **Williams Cottage** and the **Kiwi Birdlife Park**, before boarding the exciting **Shotover Jet** or taking a lake cruise on the **TSS Earnslaw**. Wind up with a walk through **Queenstown Gardens** to capture dramatic views of the **Remarkables** at dusk. Have a sunset drink at **Pub on Wharf** or the **Atlas Beer Cafe** before dinner at **Fishbone Bar & Grill** or **Wai Waterfront Restaurant & Wine Bar**. The evening's still young, so head to **Minibar** or **Bardeaux**. Devote the next morning to bungy jumping, skydiving or white-water rafting, and take to two wheels at the **Queenstown Bike Park** in the afternoon. If you're a wine buff, book a cycle tour through the **Gibbston Valley** with **Cycle de Vine**. Enjoy dinner at **Winnies**, and stay on for the live music or DJs.

Four Days

Follow the two-day itinerary, then head to **Arrowtown** to wander the enigmatic **Chinese settlement**, browse the local shops and sample the beers at the **Arrow Brewing Company**. The following day drive along the shores of Lake Wakatipu to tiny **Glenorchy.** Have lunch at the **Glenorchy Café** and then strap on your hiking boots and head into **Mt Aspiring National Park** to do some wonderful short tramps in the vicinity of the **Routeburn Track.** If you'd rather exercise your arms, go kayaking across the lake at **Kinloch**.

Queenstown

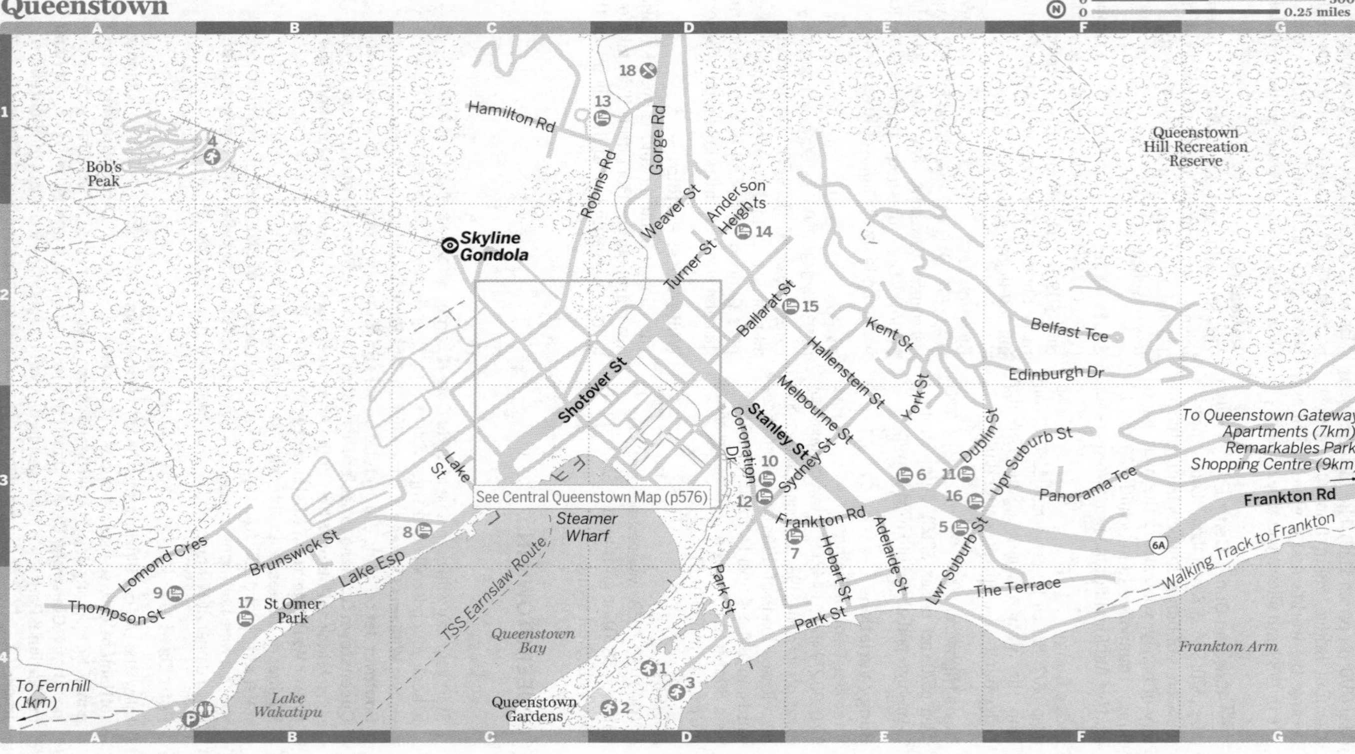
0 500 m
0 0.25 miles
Queenstown Hill Recreation Reserve
Bob's Peak
Skyline Gondola
Hamilton Rd
Robins Rd
Gorge Rd
Weaver St
Anderson Heights
Turner St
Ballarat St
Kent St
Hallenstein St
Melbourne St
York St
Belfast Tce
Edinburgh Dr
Dublin St
Upr Suburb St
Panorama Tce
Shotover St
Stanley St
Coronation Dr
Sydney St
Frankton Rd
Hobart St
Adelaide St
Lwr Suburb St
The Terrace
Park St
Lake St
See Central Queenstown Map (p576)
Steamer Wharf
TSS Earnslaw Route
Queenstown Bay
Queenstown Gardens
Lomond Cres
Brunswick St
Lake Esp
Thompson St
St Omer Park
Lake Wakatipu
To Fernhill (1km)
Frankton Arm
Walking Track to Frankton
To Queenstown Gateway Apartments (7km); Remarkables Park Shopping Centre (9km)
6A

Queenstown

Top Sights
Skyline Gondola C2

Activities, Courses & Tours
1 Frisbee Golf D4
Ledge Bungy .... (see 4)
Ledge Sky Swing .... (see 4)
Luge .... (see 4)
Queenstown Bike Park .... (see 4)
2 Queenstown Gardens D4
3 Queenstown Ice Arena D4
4 Tandem Paragliding B1
Ziptrek Ecotours .... (see 4)

Sleeping
5 Alexis Motor Lodge & Apartments E3
6 Amity Lodge E3
7 Black Sheep Lodge E3
8 Bumbles C3
9 Butterfli Lodge A4
10 Central Ridge Boutique Hotel D3
11 Chalet Queenstown B&B E3
12 Coronation Lodge D3
13 Creeksyde Top 10 Holiday Park D1
14 Hippo Lodge D2
15 Historic Stonehouse E2
16 Queenstown Motel Apartments E3
17 YHA Queenstown Lakefront B4

Eating
18 Freshchoice D1

Entertainment
Kiwi Haka .... (see 4)

river. There's generally a minimum age of 13 years and a minimum weight of around 40kg. An exciting alternative are heli-rafting trips.

Queenstown Rafting RAFTING
(☎03-442 9792, 0800 723 8464; www.rafting.co.nz; rafting/heli-rafting $195/279) One of Queenstown's most established rafting companies.

Extreme Green Rafting RAFTING
(☎03-442 8517; www.nzraft.com; rafting/heli-rafting $195/279) Trips on both the Kawarau and Shotover Rivers.

Challenge Rafting RAFTING
(☎03-442 7318, 0800 423 836; www.raft.co.nz; rafting/heli-rafting $195/279) On the Shotover and Kawarau Rivers.

QUEENSTOWN & WANAKA ON A RAINY DAY

Book in for a Japanese-style spa experience at Onsen Hot Pools (p574), or catch a bus across to Arrowtown for a movie at the quirky cinema Dorothy Browns (p591) . If you're holed up in Wanaka, Cinema Paradiso (p602) or Ruby's (p602) are equally cool. Other all-weather attractions in Wanaka include Puzzling World (p595) and the excellent Wanaka Transport & Toy Museum (p595) or Warbirds & Wheels (p595). If you're visiting from April to October, go ice-skating at the Queenstown Ice Arena (p576).

Family Adventures RAFTING
(☎03-442 8836, 0800 4723 8464; www.familyadventures.co.nz; adult/child $179/120) Gentler (Grade I to II) trips on the Shotover suitable for children three years and older. Operates in summer only.

River Surfing & White-Water Sledging

Serious Fun RIVER SLEDGING
(☎03-442 5262, 0800 737 468; www.riversurfing.co.nz; per person $175) The only company to raft the infamous Chinese Dogleg section of the Kawarau River.

Frogz Have More Fun RIVER SLEDGING
(☎0800 437 649, 03-441 2318; www.frogz.co.nz; per person $175) Steer buoyant sleds on the rapids and whirlpools of the Kawarau River.

Canyoning

Canyoning.co.nz CANYONING
(☎03-441 3003; www.canyoning.co.nz; per person $185) Half-day trips in the nearby 12-Mile Delta Canyons. Canyoning in the remote Routeburn Valley ($210) is also available.

Flying, Gliding & Skydiving

Tandem Paragliding PARAGLIDING
(Map p572; ☎0800 759 688, 03-441 8581; www.nzgforce.com; per person $199) Tandem paragliding from the top of the gondola or from Coronet Peak (9am departures are $20 cheaper).

Skytrek Hang Gliding HANG GLIDING
(☎0800 759 873; www.skytrek.co.nz; flights from $210) Soar on tandem flights from Coronet Peak or the Remarkables.

REMEMBER, YOU'RE ON HOLIDAY...

So much of the Queenstown experience is about active adventure and adrenaline-fuelled shenanigans. Here's our pick of the best experiences to slow down, recharge and remind your body there's more to the travelling life than scaring yourself silly.

» **Onsen Hot Pools** (Map p570; ☎03-442 5707; www.onsen.co.nz; 160 Arthurs Point Rd; adult/child $46/10; ⌚11am-10pm) has private Japanese-style hot tubs with mountain views. Book ahead and one will be warmed up for you.

» To reboot your system after a few days of bungying, biking and jetboating, ease into in-room massage and spa treatments with the **Mobile Massage Co** (☎027 442 6161, 0800 426 161; www.queenstownmassage.co.nz; 1hr from $125; ⌚9am-9pm).

» Slow down even more by checking into **Hush Spa** (Map p576; ☎03-4009 0901; www.hushspa.co.nz; 1st fl, 32 Rees St; 30/60min massage from $70/125; ⌚9am-9pm Tue-Fri, to 7pm Sat) for a massage, aroma stone therapy or a deep bath soak.

» For truly world-class spa treatments, make the short trek to Millbrook near Arrowtown, where the Spa at Millbrook (p588) has been voted one of the world's top 10 spas.

» Queenstown's newest spa escape is **Eforea: Spa at Hilton** (☎03-450 9416; www.queenstownhilton.com; Peninsula Rd, Hilton Queenstown; treatments from $120), enjoying a lakeside location at Kawarau Village, a short water-taxi ride from Steamer Wharf.

Flight Park Tandems PARAGLIDING
(☎0800 467 325; www.tandemparagliding.com; 1140m/1620m $185/205) Offering spectacular takeoffs from Coronet Peak. Rates apply to winter months.

Queenstown Paraflights PARAGLIDING
(Map p576; ☎0800 225 520; www.paraflights.co.nz; adult & child solo $139, adult/child tandem $109/$79) Glide 200m above the lake as you're pulled behind a boat.

Elevation Paragliding School PARAGLIDING
(☎0800 359 444; www.elevation.co.nz; instruction from $240) Learn the paragliding ropes and graduate to four solo flights.

NZONE SKYDIVING
(☎03-442 5867, 0800 376 796; www.nzone.biz; jumps from $269) Jump out of a perfectly good airplane – with a tandem skydiving expert.

Tramping & Climbing

Pick up the *Wakatipu Walks* brochure ($2) from DOC for local tramping tracks ranging from easy one-hour strolls to tough eight-hour slogs.

Bob's Peak WALKING
Walk up Bob's Peak to the gondola terminus. The walk is not particularly scenic, but the views at the top are excellent.

Queenstown Hill WALKING
Another short climb is up 900m Queenstown Hill (two to three hours return). Access is from Belfast Tce.

Ben Lomond WALKING
Climb 1746m Ben Lomond (six to eight hours return), accessed from Lomond Cres. It's a difficult tramp requiring a high level of fitness and shouldn't be underestimated.

Encounter Guided Day Walks TRAMPING
(☎03-442 8200; www.ultimatehikes.co.nz; Routeburn Track adult/child $145/85; Milford Track adult/child $165/95; Mt Cook adult/child $105/65; ⌚Oct-Apr) Day walks on the Routeburn Track, the Milford Track and near Mt Cook, as well as multiday tramps.

Guided Nature Walks WALKING
(☎03-442 7126; www.nzwalks.com; adult/child from $105/65) Excellent walks in the Queenstown area, including a Walk and Wine option and even snow-shoeing in winter.

Climbing Queenstown CLIMBING
(☎03-450 2119; www.climbingqueenstown.com; rock climbing from $139, abseiling adult/child $139/99, Via Ferrata adult/child $139/89 and mountaineering from $499.) Rock climbing, abseiling, Via Ferrata (climbing fixed metal rungs, rails, pegs and cables) and mountaineering. All activities are run by qualified guides.

Horse Treks

Moonlight Stables HORSE RIDING
(☎03-442 1229; www.moonlightcountry.co.nz; adult/child $120/95) Ride through a stunning landscape on a 324-hectare working farm. Horseriding is also on offer around **Cardrona** (☎03-443 8151; www.backcountrysadddles.

co.nz; Crown Range Rd; adult/child from $80/60) and Glenorchy (p592).

Fishing

The rivers and lakes around Queenstown are home to brown and rainbow trout. All companies practise catch-and-release.

Stu Dever Fishing Charters FISHING
(☎03-442 6371; www.fishing-queenstown.co.nz; per hour from $60) Salmon and trout fishing from the 34ft launch *Chinook*. Owner Stu can arrange for your catch to be cooked at a local restaurant.

Other Activities

You can also golf, minigolf, quad bike, sail, dive and much more.

Central Otago Wine Experience WINE TASTING
(Map p576; ☎03-409 2226; www.winetastes.com; 14 Beach St; tasting cards $20; ⏰10am-10pm) A $20 card provides tastes of around eight to 10 different wines from a menu of 80. Cheese and antipasto platters ($28 to $34) accompany the tasty tastings, and all wine can be shipped home.

Ziptrek Ecotours ZIPLINE
(Map p572; ☎0800 947 8735; www.ziptrek.com; Brecon St; adult/child from $129/79) Incorporating a series of zip-lines (flying foxes), this harness-clad thrill-ride takes you from treetop to treetop high above Queenstown. Ingenious design and ecofriendly values are a bonus on this adrenaline-fuelled activity. Choose from the two-hour, four-line 'Moa' tour or the gnarlier three-hour, six-line 'Kea' option (adult/child $179/129).

Luge LUGE
(Map p572; ☎03-441 0101; www.skyline.co.nz; Brecon St; 1/2/3/5 rides incl gondola ride adult $33/38/43/48, child $23/28/33/38; ⏰daylight hours) Hop on a three-wheeled cart to ride the Luge at the top of the gondola. Nail the 'scenic' run once, and then you're allowed on the advanced track with its banked corners and tunnel.

MOUNTAIN-BIKING MECCA

With the opening of the Queenstown Bike Park (p575), the region is now firmly established as an international focus for the sport. See also www.wakatiputrails.co.nz for details on the ongoing development of new mountain-bike trails around the area. Visit in late March for the annual Queenstown Bike Festival (www.queenstownbikefestival.co.nz).

The Queenstown Trail – more than 90km in total – links five scenic smaller trails showcasing Queenstown, Arrowtown, the Gibbston Valley, Lake Wakatipu and Lake Hayes. Overall the trail is technically easy and suitable for cyclists of all levels.

Pop into Outside Sports or Vertigo for more trail information. If you're in town for a while, consider joining the **Queenstown Mountain Bike Club** (www.queenstownmtb.co.nz).

Queenstown Bike Park (Map p572; ☎03-441 0101; www.skyline.co.nz; Brecon St; ⏰half-day pass adult/child/family $45/25/115, day pass adult/child/family $60/30/150) Nine different trails – from easy to extreme – traverse Bob's Peak high above the lake. Once you've descended on two wheels, simply jump on the gondola and do it all over again. The best trail for novice riders is the 6km-long Hammy's Track, which is studded with lake views and picnic spots all the way down.

Vertigo (Map p576; ☎03-442 8378, 0800 837 8446; www.vertigobikes.co.nz; 4 Brecon St; rental from $79 per day) Options include downhill rides into Skippers Canyon ($169) and a Remarkables helibike option ($399). Skills training (from $139) and guided sessions ($159) on the Queenstown Bike Park are also available. If you're serious about getting into mountain biking QT-style, Vertigo is an essential first stop.

Fat Tyre Adventures (☎0800 328 897; www.fat-tyre.co.nz; from $199) Tours cater to different abilities with day tours, multiday tours, helibiking and singletrack riding. Bike hire and trail snacks are included.

Outside Sports (Map p576; www.outsidesports.co.nz; 36-38 Shotover St) One-stop shop for bike rentals and trail information.

Queenstown Bike Hire (Map p576; cnr Marine Pde & Church St) Best for tandems and lakefront rides.

Central Queenstown

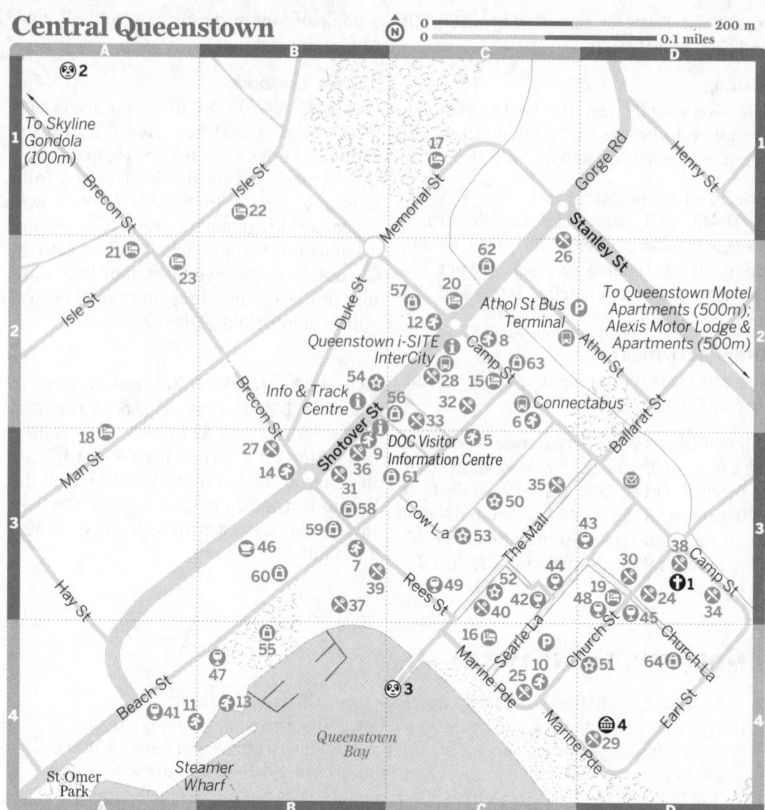

Frisbee Golf
FRISBEE

(Map p572; www.queenstowndiscgolf.co.nz) On a marked course in Queenstown Gardens. Targets are tree-mounted chain baskets. BYO frisbee.

Queenstown Ice Arena
ICE SKATING

(Map p572; ☎03-441 8000; www.queenstownicearena.co.nz; 29 Park St; adult/child incl skate hire $20/15; ⏲10am-6pm, to 9.30pm Fri Apr-Oct) Come for a skate or a game of ice hockey. Closed in summer.

Tours

Scenic Flights

Aerostunts
SCENIC FLIGHT

(☎0800 788 687; www.aerostunts.co.nz; 15/25 minutes $310/400) To see the sights upside down, take a G-force-defying aerobatic flight.

Over the Top Helicopters
SCENIC FLIGHT

(☎03-442 2233, 0800 123 359; www.flynz.co.nz; from $265) Around Queenstown and beyond.

Sunrise Balloons
BALLOONING

(☎03-442 0781, 0800 468 247; www.ballooningnz.com; adult/child $445/295) One-hour rides including a champagne breakfast.

4WD Tours

Nomad Safaris
4WD TOUR

(☎03-442 6699, 0800 688 222; www.nomadsafaris.co.nz; adult/child from $130/65) Trips take in stunning scenery and hard-to-get-to backcountry vistas around Skippers Canyon and Macetown. The operators will even let you drive ($260), or you can quad-bike it ($245).

Off Road Adventures
4WD TOUR

(☎03-442 7858, 0800 633 7623; www.offroad.co.nz; 4WD adult/child from $99/49) Exciting off-road 4WD, quad-bike (from $189) and dirt-bike ($249) tours.

Skippers Canyon Heritage Tours
4WD TOUR

(☎03-442 5949; www.queenstown-heritage.co.nz; adult/child $160/80) Skippers Canyon is

Central Queenstown

Sights

1 Church of St Peter ... D3
2 Kiwi Birdlife Park ... A1
3 Underwater Observatory ... C4
4 Williams Cottage ... D4

Activities, Courses & Tours

5 Central Otago Wine Experience ... C3
6 Double-Decker Bus Tour ... C2
7 Hush Spa ... B3
Kawarau Jet ... (see 3)
8 Kiwi Discovery ... C2
9 Outside Sports ... B3
10 Queenstown Bike Hire ... C4
Queenstown Paraflights ... (see 3)
11 Real Journeys ... A4
12 The Station ... C2
13 TSS Earnslaw ... B4
14 Vertigo ... B3

Sleeping

15 Adventure Queenstown Hostel & Chalet ... C2
16 Eichardt's Private Hotel ... C4
17 Last Resort ... C1
18 Lomond Lodge ... A3
19 Nomads ... D3
20 Queenstown Accommodation Centre ... C2
21 Queenstown Lakeview Holiday Park ... A2
22 Southern Laughter ... B1
23 The Dairy ... A2

Eating

24 @Thai ... D3
25 Aggy's Shack ... C4
26 Alpine Supermarket ... C2
27 Bella Cucina ... B3
28 Bob's Weigh ... C2
29 Botswana Butchery ... D4
30 Devil Burger ... D3
Fergbaker ... (see 31)
31 Fergburger ... B3
32 Fishbone Bar & Grill ... C2
33 Habebes ... C2
34 Halo ... D3
35 Kappa Sushi Cafe ... C3
36 Lick & Slurp Soup ... B3
37 Patagonia ... B3
38 Queenstown Farmers Market ... D3
39 Vudu Cafe & Larder ... B3
Wai Waterfront Restaurant & Wine Bar ... (see 11)
40 Winnies ... C3

Drinking

41 Atlas Beer Cafe ... A4
Ballarat Trading Company ... (see 52)
42 Bardeaux ... C3
43 Barmuda ... D3
44 Minibar ... C3
45 Monty's ... D3
46 Motogrill ... B3
47 Pub on Wharf ... B4
48 Searle Lane & Social ... D3
49 Surreal ... C3

Entertainment

50 Debajo ... C3
51 Dux de Lux ... D4
52 Reading Cinemas ... C3
Subculture ... (see 45)
53 Tardis Bar ... C3
54 The World Bar ... B2

Shopping

55 Arts & Crafts Market ... B4
56 Fetch ... C2
57 Green Toad ... C2
58 Kapa ... B3
59 Kathmandu ... B3
Outside Sports ... (see 9)
60 Rockies ... B3
61 Small Planet Outlet Store ... C3
62 Small Planet Sports Co ... C2
63 Snowrental ... C2
64 toi o tahuna ... D4

reached by a narrow, winding road which was built by gold panners in the 1800s. This scenic but hair-raising 4WD route runs from Arthurs Point towards Coronet Peak and then above the Shotover River, passing along the way some gold-rush sights. Specialist wine and photography tours are also available.

Lake Cruises

TSS Earnslaw BOAT TOUR

(Map p576; ☎0800 656 503; www.realjourneys.co.nz; Steamer Wharf, Beach St) The stately, steam-powered *TSS Earnslaw* celebrated a centenary of continuous service in 2012. Once the lake's major means of transport, it originally carried more than 800 passengers. Climb aboard for the standard

1½-hour Lake Wakatipu tour (adult/child $50/22) or take a 3½-hour excursion to the high-country Walter Peak Farm (adult/child $75/22) for sheep-shearing demonstrations and sheep-dog performances.

Milford Sound

Day trips via Te Anau to Milford Sound take 12 to 13 hours and cost around $225/115 per adult/child, including a two-hour cruise on the sound. Bus–cruise–flight options are also available, as is pick-up from the Routeburn Track finish line. To save on travel time and cost, consider visiting Milford from Te Anau.

Real Journeys GUIDED TOURS
(Map p576; ☎03-249 7416, 0800 656 501; www.realjourneys.co.nz; Beach St, Steamer Wharf) Lake trips and tours.

BBQ Bus TOUR
(☎03-442 1045, 0800 421 045; www.milford.net.nz; adult/child $182/100) Smaller groups (up to 22 people) and a barbecue lunch.

Winery Tours

Most tours include a visit to the wineries around Banockburn (p552).

Appellation Central Wine Tours WINE TASTING
(☎03-442 0246; www.appellationcentral.co.nz; $165-215) Tours include an all-day gourmet excursion that also samples local cheeses.

Cycle de Vine WINE TASTING
(☎0800 328 897; www.queenstown-trails.co.nz; adult/child $155/95; ⊙Sep-Jun) Cruise on a retro bicycle around the Gibbston Valley. Tours include two different wineries and a picnic lunch beside the meandering Kawarau River.

Queenstown Wine Trail WINE TASTING
(☎03-441 3990, 0800 827 8464; www.queenstownwinetrail.co.nz; adult $129, shorter tour with lunch $148) Choose from a five-hour tour with tastings at four wineries or a shorter tour with lunch included.

Other Tours

Double-Decker Bus Tour BUS TOUR
(Map p576; www.doubledecker.co.nz; adult/child $48/25) Visits historic Arrowtown, taking in Gibbston Valley Wines and Lake Hayes. The three-hour tours depart from in front of O'Connell's Shopping Centre at 9.30am.

Segway on Q GUIDED TOUR
(☎03-442 8687, 0800 734 386; www.segwayonq.com) Explore the town and Queenstown Gardens on a two-hour spin (adult/child/family $109/99/375), or cruise for an hour around Queenstown Bay on Lake Wakatipu (adult/child/family $75/65/250).

Art Adventures GUIDED TOUR
(☎0800 582 878; www.artadventures.co.nz; studio & gallery tours half/full day $180/350, tuition from $300) Art Adventures provide studio and gallery tours – including lunch and wine-tasting at local vineyards – or the opportunity to work with professional tutors on your own masterpiece.

Festivals & Events

Gibbston Harvest Festival FOOD & WINE
(www.gibbstonharvestfestival.com; ⊙mid-Mar) Food and wine buffs should time their visit to coincide with this annual festival.

Queenstown Winter Festival SPORTS
(www.winterfestival.co.nz; ⊙late Jun/early Jul) Wacky ski and snowboard activities, live mu-

GETTING ACTIVE ON THE SLOPES

The ski season generally lasts from around June to September. Time your visit for the loads-of-fun Queenstown Winter Festival (p578).

Around Queenstown, the Remarkables and Coronet Peak ski fields are the key snow-sport centres. Across the Crown Range near Wanaka, Treble Cone and Cardrona host the downhill action, and you can try cross-country skiing at **Snow Farm New Zealand** (☎03-443 7542; www.snowfarmnz.com). **Snowpark NZ** (☎03-443 9991; www snowparknz .com) is a winter wonderland of freestyle terrain with half-pipes and rails. For serious skiers, check out **Heli Ski Queenstown** (☎03-442 7733; www.flynz.co.nz; from $895), **Harris Mountains Heli-Ski** (☎03-442 6722; www.heliski.co.nz; from $795) or **Southern Lakes Heliski** (☎03-442 6222; www.southernlakesheliski.co.nz; from $6729).

Tune into 99.2FM from 6.45am to 9am to hear snow reports. Online, visit www.snowreports.co.nz. For equipment hire, including apparel, toboggans and snowboards, see Green Toad (p586) in Queenstown and Outside Sports (p586) in Queenstown and Wanaka.

sic, a Mardi Gras party, fireworks and plenty of frigid frivolity.

Queenstown Bike Festival SPORTS
(www.queenstownbikefestival.co.nz) Ten full days of two-wheeled action and fun; held in late March.

Sleeping

Queenstown has endless places to stay, but many visitors seeking accommodation. Midrange travellers won't find much choice. Consider a top-end place or go for one of the excellent budget options and spend up on activities. Places book out and prices rocket during the peak summer (December to February) and ski (June to September) seasons; book well in advance at these times. Rooms with guaranteed lake views often have a surcharge.

The **Queenstown Accommodation Centre** (Map p576; ☎03-442 7518; www.qac.co.nz; 1st fl, 19 Camp St) has a range of holiday homes and apartments on its website, with prices ranging from around $200 to $500 per week. There is often a minimum-stay period.

Ask at the DOC office for directions to the **12-Mile Delta campsite**, 11km out of town towards Glenorchy, and **Skippers campsite**, near Coronet Peak.

The Dairy B&B $$$
(Map p576; ☎03-442 5164, 0800 333 393; www.thedairy.co.nz; 10 Isle St; s/d incl breakfast from $435/465, Jun-Aug 3-night packages d $900-990; P@) Once a corner store, the Dairy is now a luxury B&B with 13 rooms packed with classy touches like designer bed linen, silk cushions and luxurious mohair rugs. Rates also include freshly baked afternoon tea. From June to August three-night packages are good value for skiers.

Warbrick Stone Cottage COTTAGE $$
(☎03-442 7520, 021 558 321; www.gibbston.co.nz; 2403 Gibbston Hwy; d $150) Relax in this Gibbston Valley (p585) heritage cottage restored by an award-winning architect. A modern kitchen and bathroom partner wooden floors and walls made of local schist (river stone), and there's an outdoor table perfect for lazy breakfasts or a twilight tipple from one of the local vineyards. The cottage is around 30km from Queenstown, en route to Cromwell and Central Otago.

Chalet Queenstown B&B B&B $$$
(Map p572; ☎0800 222 457, 03-442 7117; www.chaletqueenstown.co.nz; 1 Dublin St; d $195-225; P) This chic and friendly B&B is one of the best boutique accommodation options in Queenstown. Perfectly appointed rooms sparkle with flat-screen TVs, interesting original artworks and quality bed linen. Book well ahead to secure one of the rooms with a lake view – easily one of the best vistas in town.

Eichardt's Private Hotel BOUTIQUE HOTEL $$$
(Map p576; ☎03-441 0450; www.eichardtshotel.co.nz; cnr Marine Pde & Searle Lane; d $1639-1892; P) Originally opened in the 1860s, this reopened and restored boutique hotel enjoys an absolute lakefront location. Each of the five giant suites has a fireplace, lake views and a blend of antique and modern decor. King-sized beds, heated floors and lake-sized bath tubs provide the ideal welcome after a day cruising the vineyards of Central Otago. Four newer lakeside apartments (double $1190 to $1449) are equally luxurious.

Evergreen Lodge B&B $$$
(Map p570; ☎03-442 6636; www.evergreenlodge.co.nz; 28 Evergreen Pl; d $895; P@) Handcrafted wooden furniture from a local Queenstown artisan is showcased at this modern lodge. Add in a supremely private location with unfettered views of the Remarkables, complimentary beer and wine, and a sauna and gym, and you've got a very relaxing escape from Queenstown's global hoi polloi.

Central Ridge Boutique Hotel BOUTIQUE HOTEL $$$
(Map p572; ☎03-442 8832; www.centralridge.co.nz; 4 Sydney St; d incl breakfast $270-455; P) Visitors rave about the breakfasts, but there's more to be effusive about, such as pre-dinner canapés with Central Otago wines, underfloor

QUEENSTOWN ON A BUDGET

Play Frisbee golf (p576) in the Queenstown Gardens, or hire a **bike** or **kayak** at the lakefront. For more thrilling two-wheeled action, consider a half-day pass at the Queenstown Bike Park (p575), or getting active on the many bike trials around the town. Foodies should head to the Mediterranean Market (p584) for lakeside picnic supplies, or graze the tasty – and often free – samples at the Queenstown Farmers Market (p584). Market fans should also check out the Saturday morning arts and crafts market (p586).

QUEENSTOWN FOR CHILDREN

While Queenstown is brimming with activities, some of them have age restrictions that may exclude the youngest in your group. Nevertheless, you shouldn't have any trouble keeping the youngsters busy.

For a high that will make sugar rushes seem passé, take wilder kids on the Shotover Jet (p571). For older kids, consider a tamer variation on the classic bungy jump with the Ledge Sky Swing (p571) or go tandem with them on Queenstown Paraflights (p574). At Kawarau Bungy Centre, (p571) kids can watch people plunging off the bridge, and also challenge gravity themselves on the bungy trampoline.

The Skyline Gondola (p569) offers a slow-moving activity from dizzying heights. At the top of the hill lies the wonderfully curvy Luge (p575), suitable for ages three and up. An alternative way of getting down the hill is with Ziptrek Ecotours (p575), suitable for zipline daredevils six years and older. Supervised kids from five to 14 can also zig and zag at the Queenstown Bike Park (p575).

Several places in town hire out tandem bicycles and child-sized mountain bikes. Queenstown Bike Hire (p575) also rents foot scooters and baby buggies, plus toboggans in winter. Rockies (p586) hires out snowsuits for children.

The conservation shows at Kiwi Birdlife Park (p569) are especially geared to a younger crowd. **Queenstown Gardens** (Map p572) has a good beachside playground near the entrance on Marine Pde. Also in the park, Queenstown Ice Arena (p576) is great for a rainy day, and there's Frisbee Golf (p576).

Consider also lake cruises on the TSS *Earnslaw* (p577) and 4WD tours of narrow, snaking Skippers Canyon (p576). Train buffs will love the Kingston Flyer (p569), and family rafting trips are run by Family Adventures (p573).

For more ideas and information – including details of local babysitters – see the i-SITE (p586) or visit online at www.kidzgo.co.nz.

heating, and spacious, modern bathrooms. With only 14 rooms here, you're guaranteed a winning way with personal service.

Adventure Queenstown Hostel & Chalet HOSTEL **$**
(Map p576; ☎03-409 0862; www.aqhostel.co.nz; 36 Camp St; dm $29-35, d/tw/tr $120/110/135; @ 📶) Run by experienced travellers, the Adventure Queenstown Hostel & Chalet has spotless dorms, modern kitchens and bathrooms, and double, twin and triple rooms. Free this and free that includes international calling to 30 countries, bicycles and frisbees. It's got a more subdued ambience than other hostels, but the best of Queenstown's nightlife is nearby.

Amity Lodge MOTEL **$$**
(Map p572; ☎0800 556 000; www.amitylodge.co.nz; 7 Melbourne St; d from $165; P 📶) In a quiet street around five minutes' (uphill) walk from central Queenstown, Amity Lodge combines older but recently renovated units, and more comfortable and modern two-bedroom units. The friendly owners offer a wealth of local information, and in an expensive destination, Amity Lodge is good value.

Historic Stonehouse APARTMENT **$$$**
(Map p572; ☎03-442 9812; www.historicstonehouse.co.nz; 47 Hallenstein St; d $225-395; P) One of Queenstown's loveliest old private residences – built in 1874 – now houses three very comfortable self-contained apartments. Formerly the mayor's digs, the apartments are surrounded by established gardens and trimmed with antique furniture and a heritage vibe. They're not at all stuffy though, and mod cons include modern kitchens and bathrooms and an outdoor spa pool.

Bumbles HOSTEL **$**
(Map p572; ☎03-442 6298, 0800 286 2537; www.bumblesbackpackers.co.nz; cnr Lake Esplanade & Brunswick St; sites/dm/tw/d $20/29/62/62; P @ 📶) This popular hostel is colourfully decorated. Its prime lakeside location near the heart of town ensures excellent views and easy access to the best of Queenstown. It's an easygoing spot, with a quieter and more laidback vibe compared to other larger hostels around town. There's also limited space for tents and campervans.

Last Resort HOSTEL **$**
(Map p576; ☎03-442 4320; www.tlrqtn.com; 6 Memorial St; dm $30; @ 📶) Super-central, this

friendly smaller hostel is reached by a tiny brick-and-timber bridge traversing a bubbling brook in the backyard. It's just a short stroll from where most transport will drop you off, and you can expect an excited canine welcome from Cocco, an Alaskan Malamute.

Coronation Lodge MOTEL $$
(Map p572; ☎0800 420 777, 03-442 0860; www.coronationlodge.co.nz; 10 Coronation Dr; d $150-220; @ 📶) Right beside the Queenstown Gardens, this lodge has plush bed linen, wooden floors and cosy Turkish rugs. In a town that's somewhat lacking in good midrange accommodation, Coronation Lodge is recommended. Larger rooms have kitchenettes, and some of Queenstown's best restaurants and bars are a short stroll downhill.

Little Paradise Lodge LODGE $$
(Map p570; ☎03-442 6196; www.littleparadise.co.nz; Glenorchy-Queenstown Rd; s $45, d $120-160; 🏊) Wonderfully eclectic, this slice of arty paradise is the singular vision of its Swiss owner. Each rustic room features wooden floors, quirky artwork and handmade furniture. Outside the fun continues with a back-to-nature swimming hole and well-crafted walkways along a nearby hillside. Outside visitors are welcome to enjoy afternoon tea and stroll around the gardens for $6.

Queenstown Gateway Apartments MOTEL $$
(☎0800 656 665, 03-442 3599; www.gateway.net.nz; 1066 Frankton Rd; d from $160; P 📶) This modern motel complex near the airport is handy if you're flying in and picking up transport to explore other parts of the South Island. It's also a good base if you're planning on visiting Central Otago, Wanaka and Arrowtown on day trips.

Nomads HOSTEL $
(Map p576; ☎03-441 3922; www.nomadshostels.com; 5 Church St; dm $29-34, tw/d $130-150; @ 📶) With a prime location near Queenstown's nightlife, Nomad's has top-notch facilities including its own mini-cinema, ensuite rooms aplenty, massive kitchens and an on-site travel agency. The only potential downside is its size – Nomads is massive – so it's not the place to stay if you're looking for a quieter, more laidback ambience.

Southern Laughter HOSTEL $
(Map p576; ☎03-441 8828; www.southernlaughter.co.nz; 4 Isle St; dm $26-28, tw $58, d $60-75; @ 📶) This funky hostel has various kitchens scattered throughout the sprawling complex. Check out the retro B&W pics of old Queenstown before strolling into town to see new Queenstown. Free vegie soup and a spa pool are added benefits.

Hippo Lodge HOSTEL $
(Map p572; ☎03-442 5785; www.hippolodge.co.nz; 4 Anderson Heights; dm $28, s/d from $41/68; @ 📶) Well-maintained, relaxed hostel with good views and a correspondingly high number of stairs. Pitch a tent for $19 per person.

Butterfli Lodge HOSTEL $
(Map p572; ☎03-442 6367; www.butterfli.co.nz; 62 Thompson St; dm/d/tr $26/62/78; @) This smaller hostel sits in a quiet hillside suburb. Commandeer the barbecue on the deck and take in beaut views as you turn your steaks and sausages.

Lomond Lodge LODGE $$
(Map p576; ☎03-442 8235; www.lomondlodge.com; 33 Man St; d $138-169; P @ 📶) A recent make-over has modernised Lomond Lodge's cosy decor. Share your on-the-road stories with fellow travellers in the communal kitchen and around the garden barbecue. Larger family apartments ($270 for up to four people) are also available.

Alexis Motor Lodge & Apartments MOTEL $$
(Map p572; ☎03-409 0052; www.alexisqueenstown.co.nz; 69 Frankton Rd; d $170; @ 📶) This modern hillside motel with self-contained units is an easy 10-minute walk from town along the lakefront. Ask for an end unit with snap-happy views of one of the best mountain and lake views on the planet.

Queenstown Motel Apartments MOTEL $$
(Map p572; ☎0800 661 668, 03-442 6095; www.qma.co.nz; 62 Frankton Rd; d $35-195; P) This well-run spot has newer units with spa bathrooms, trendy decor and private mini gardens, and older 1970s-style units that represent good value for budget travellers. There's a handy onsite laundry, and the lake and mountain views are uniformly great – even from the cheaper, budget accommodation.

Black Sheep Lodge HOSTEL $
(Map p572; ☎03-442 7289; www.blacksheepbackpackers.co.nz; 13 Frankton Rd; dm/d from $25/70; @ 📶) This place keeps younger social types happy with a spa, a pool table and a truckload of DVDs. Rooms are recently decorated, and it's a friendly affair that maximises plenty of R&R before your next Queenstown outdoor adventure. Newer rooms are

excellent value, and there are plenty of private nooks and crannies for escaping with your favourite book.

YHA Queenstown Lakefront HOSTEL $
(Map p572; 03-442 8413; www.yha.co.nz; 88-90 Lake Esplanade; dm/d from $36/87;) This friendly alpine lodge has staff well versed in Queenstown's myriad activities. Rooms are basic but clean; some rooms and the dining area have lake and mountain views. Queenstown's nightlife is a 10- to 15-minute lakeside stroll away.

Creeksyde Top 10 Holiday Park HOLIDAY PARK $
(Map p572; 0800 786 222, 03-442 9447; www.camp.co.nz; 54 Robins Rd; sites $47, d $62-164;) In a garden setting, this pretty spot has accommodation ranging from basic tent sites to self-contained motel units. An ecofriendly green tinge is added with a disciplined approach to recycling and a commitment to increase planting of native trees.

Shotover Top 10 Holiday Park HOLIDAY PARK $
(Map p570; 03-442 9306; www.shotoverholidaypark.co.nz; 70 Arthurs Point Rd; sites from $35, units $65-155;) High above the Shotover River, this family-friendly park is 10 minutes' drive from the hustle and bustle of Queenstown. Fall out of your campervan straight onto the famous Shotover Jet.

Queenstown Lakeview Holiday Park HOLIDAY PARK $
(Map p576; 0800 482 735, 03-442 7252; www.holidaypark.net.nz; Brecon St; sites $40, units $140-200;) A short stroll from the gondola, this park has a big open field to camp in and great facilities. A few larger trees would soften the slightly spartan ambience for campers, but there are also flasher motel units and lodges.

Eating

Queenstown's town centre is peppered with busy eateries. Many target the tourist dollar, but dig a little deeper and you'll discover local favourites covering a surprising range of international cuisines. At the more popular places, it's wise to make a reservation for evening dining.

TOP CHOICE **Fishbone Bar & Grill** SEAFOOD $$
(Map p576; 03-442 6768; www.fishbonequeenstown.co.nz; 7 Beach St; mains $26-32) Queenstown's more than a few miles inland, but that doesn't stop Fishbone from sourcing the best of NZ seafood. Everything from scallops to snapper is treated with a light and inventive touch. Try the zingy prawn tacos on handmade tortillas or the robust South Indian-style seafood curry. A recent makeover has reinforced Fishbone's coolly cosmopolitan ambience.

Vudu Cafe & Larder CAFE $
(Map p576; 16 Rees St; mains $10-18) Excellent home-style baking – try the pork and fennel sausage rolls or the delicate mini-pavlovas – feature at this cosmopolitan cafe. Top-notch breakfast and lunch options include buttermilk pancakes and a cheesy quesadilla. Check out the huge photo inside of a much less populated Queenstown, or head through to the rear garden for lake and mountain views.

Bella Cucina ITALIAN $$
(Map p576; 03-442 6762; www.bellacucina.co.nz; 6 Brecon St; pizza & pasta $29, mains $29-34; 5pm-late) Fresh pasta and risotto are highlights at Bella Cucina, while the rustic woodfired pizzas are perfect for sharing. Beautifully simple food done just right and a perfectly concise winelist, all served in one of Queenstown's cosiest and most romantic dining rooms.

VKnow RESTAURANT $$
(Map p570; 03-442 5444; www.vknow.co.nz; 155 Fernhill Rd; mains $26-36) This bistro/wine bar is located in the suburb of Fernhill, but it's definitely worth the short taxi or bus ride (Bus 9 to the Aspen on Queenstown stop). Gourmet pizzas ($19 to $27) feature smoked salmon, Indian and vegetarian spins, and the main menu showcases local venison, blue cod and Canterbury lamb. Look forward to a casual ambience that's like dining at a friend's place.

Wai Waterfront Restaurant & Wine Bar MODERN NZ $$$
(Map p576; 03-442 5969; www.wai.net.nz; Steamer Wharf, Beach St; mains $40-55, 7-course degustation menu without wine $138, with wine $215; 11am-10pm) Small and intimate, Wai (meaning 'water' in Maori) is white-linen classy with lake and mountain views. It's known for lamb and seafood, and the Oyster Bar does the world's favourite bivalve five different ways. The seven-course degustation menu is a splurge-worthy opportunity for a great culinary adventure. Think about it seriously. It's actually about how much you'll spend on another round of outdoor adventure activities, and will last a lot longer.

Botswana Butchery MODERN NZ **$$$**
(Map p576; ☎03-442 6994; Marine Pde; mains $35-45; ⏰noon-late) Botswana Butchery's meals are a divine combination of seasonal vegetables augmenting prime cuts of beef, lamb, poultry and seafood. The winelist is almost as long as a telephone directory. Come along for the $15 Express Lunch menu for a more affordable slice of the Botswana Butchery experience.

@Thai THAI **$$**
(Map p576; www.atthai.co.nz; 3rd fl, 8 Church St; mains $16-24) Head up the semi-hidden set of stairs for pad Thai worth writing home about, and the *hor-mok* seafood red curry will blow your mind. Definitely kick off your meal with the coconut prawns ($12) and an icy Singha beer. Takeaways are also available.

Winnies PIZZA **$$**
(Map p576; www.winnies.co.nz; 1st fl, 7 The Mall; pizza $16-27) Part-bar and part-restaurant, Winnies alway seems busy. Guess why? Pizzas with a Thai, Mexican or Moroccan accent, massive burgers, pasta and steaks, and occasional live music and DJs keep energy levels high. If you need more convincing, happy hour kicks in at 9pm.

Gantley's MODERN NZ **$$$**
(Map p570; ☎03-442 8999; www.gantleys.co.nz; Arthurs Point Rd; mains $35-42; ⏰6.30pm-late) This atmospheric dining experience is showcased in a historic 1863 stone-and-timber house. The contemporary NZ cuisine and highly regarded wine list are worth the journey. Reservations are essential. A courtesy bus is availabe to ferry diners from town. A six-course degustation menu is $90 per person.

Motogrill CAFE
(Map p576; 62 Shotover St; snacks & mains $10-15; wi-fi) Squeeze in beside off-duty adventure guides and other discerning locals for eggy breakfasts, chunky toasted sandwiches and great coffee from hip and savvy baristas. The coffee has actually been judged Central Otago's finest by NZ's *Cuisine* magazine.

Kappa Sushi Cafe JAPANESE **$$**
(Map p576; Level 1, 36a The Mall; sushi $7-13, lunch $9-5, dinner mains $13-29; ⏰noon-2.30pm Mon-Sun, 5.30pm-late Mon-Sat) Queenstown's best Japanese eatery is also its most casual. Fresh tuna and salmon feature in good-value bento boxes for lunch. Later at night linger longer with excellent tempura and Japanese beer and sake. In summer watch the passing parade in the Mall from the upstairs deck.

Halo CAFE **$$**
(Map p576; Camp St; breakfast & lunch $10-20, dinner $24; ⏰7am-9pm) A stylish and sunny place that effortlessly blurs the line between breakfast, lunch and dinner. The breakfast burrito will definitely set you up for a day's adventuring. Come back at night for a Moroccan lamb burger and a glass of local wine. There's plenty of outdoor seating.

Bob's Weigh CAFE **$**
(Map p576; 6 Shotover St; snacks & mains $7-17) Bob's Weigh is the perfect start to any day promising extreme sports and active adventure. Join a steady stream of locals grabbing their first caffeine fix of the day, and boost your own energy levels with muesli or bagels. Lunch options include regular pasta and soup specials.

Patagonia CAFE **$**
(Map p576; wwww.patagoniachocolates.co.nz; 50 Beach St; coffee & chocolate $6-8; wi-fi) Delicious hot chocolate, homemade choccies and Queenstown's best ice cream. What more do you want? How about a lakefront location and free wi-fi? Patagonia is open until 10pm, so it's your best bet for a late-night coffee. The warm *churros* (Spanish doughnuts) will probably have you coming back for a second (or third) night.

Lick & Slurp Soup ICE-CREAM
(Map p576; 40 Shotover St; ice cream from $4.50, soups from $7; ⏰10am-10pm) Winter? Summer? Soup? Ice-cream? Head to this versatile spot for gourmet treats like toffee apple or macadamia-nut ice cream, or hearty cool-weather concoctions including mushroom and thyme soup.

Fergburger BURGERS **$**
(Map p576; www.fergburger.com; 42 Shotover St; burgers $10-17; ⏰8.30am-5am) Queenstown's iconic Fergburger has now become a tourist attraction in itself, forcing a few locals to look elswhere for their regular gourmet burger fix. Ferg's was the innovative original in town, though, and international travellers of all ages still crowd in for their burger fix. Queue nicely, please.

Devil Burger BURGERS **$**
(Map p576; www.devilburger.com; 5-11 Church St; burgers and wraps $10-18) Look out Ferg – you've got competition in the Queenstown burger wars. This diabolical new kid on the block also does tasty wraps. Try the hangover-busting Walk of Shame wrap, stuffed with bacon, egg, hash browns and grilled mushrooms.

Fergbaker BAKERY $

(Map p576; 42 Shotover St; pies $5-7; ⏲7.30am-5am) Hearty pies including lamb and kumara (sweet potato), and assorted baked goodies including ciabatta sandwiches and banoffee pie tart. A perfect early morning treat after an extended bar hop.

Habebes MIDDLE EASTERN $

(Map p576; btwn Beach & Shotover Sts; meals $7-12; 🌿) Middle Eastern–inspired salads and wraps are the go at Habebes. Soups and yummy pies – try the chicken, kumara and mushroom one – are tasty diversions if you're in town for a winter-sports sojourn.

Aggy's Shack FISH & CHIPS $

(Map p576; Church St; $10-20; ⏲11am-10pm) Pull up a chair at this simple lakeside gazebo for fish and chips, including juicy blue cod and the opportunity to try a few local flavours like smoked eel and *titi* (muttonbird).

Queenstown Farmers Market FARMERS MARKET $

(Map p576; cnr Church & Camp Sts; ⏲9am-12.30pm Sat Dec-Mar) Gourmet goodies and ethical foodie choices from all around Central Otago.

Mediterranean Market SELF CATERING $

(cnr Gorge & Robins Rds) Fill up a basket for a lakeside picnic from this fantastic deli and bakery.

New World Wakatipu SUPERMARKET $

(Remarkables Park Shopping Centre) Near the airport and convenient if you've just picked up a campervan.

Freshchoice SUPERMARKET $

(Map p572; 64 Gorge Rd) Queenstown's biggest supermarket.

Alpine Supermarket SUPERMARKET $

(Map p576; cnr Stanley & Shotover Sts) Queenstown's most central supermarket.

Drinking

Drinking is almost a competitive sport in Queenstown, and there's a good range of options for after-dark carousing. Bars shut at 4am.

Atlas Beer Cafe CRAFT BEER

(Map p576; Steamer Wharf, Beach St; ⏲10am-2am) Perched at the end of Steamer Wharf, this pint-sized bar specialises in beers from Dunedin's Emerson's Brewery and regular guest beers from further afield. A concise but tasty food menu includes good-value sandwiches and wraps for lunch (around $10), and shared plates and tapas ($10 to $15) for dinner. If you're a craft beer fan, also head to Dux de Lux (p586).

Searle Lane & Social BAR

(Map p576; www.searlelane.co.nz; 11 Church St) Pool tables, pizza and lunch specials, and shared rotisserie chickens make this a top spot for getting to know any new arrivals at your hostel. Free-flowing beer and well-mixed cocktails definitely enhance the Social part. DJs kick in around 11pm from Wednesday to Saturday.

Ballarat Trading Company PUB

(Map p576; www.ballarat.co.nz; 7-9 The Mall) Stuffed bears, rampant wall-mounted ducks and a recreated colonial general store – there's really no competition for the title of Queenstown's most eclectic decor. Beyond the grab bag of infuences, Ballarat's gastro pub combo is quite a traditional spot, with gleaming beer taps, occasional lapses into 1980s music, and robust meals, including confit duck leg, lamb pie, burgers and steaks.

Pub on Wharf PUB

(Map p576; www.pubonwharf.co.nz; Steamer Wharf) Ubercool interior design meets handsome woodwork and lighting fit for a hipster hideaway. Stuffed animal heads reinforce that you're still in NZ, and Mac's beers on tap, scrummy nibbles and a decent wine list make this a great place to settle in for the evening. Check the website for live-music listings.

Bardeaux WINE BAR

(Map p576; Eureka Arcade, 11 The Mall; ⏲6pm-late) This small, low-key wine bar is all class. Under a low ceiling await plush leather armchairs and a fireplace made from Central Otago's iconic schist rock. Come along for one of Queenstown's best wine selections, many also from Central Otago.

Surreal COCKTAIL BAR

(Map p576; www.surrealbar.co.nz; 7 Rees St) With funky music, low lighting and red-velvet booths, this unpretentious and private spot is good for a quiet drink and nibbling on tasty shared platters. Later in the evening DJ-inspired goings-on kick off and the dance floor comes to life. Happy hour is from 10pm.

Monty's PUB

(Map p576; www.montysbar.co.nz; Church St) On warm summer days the patio at Monty's is prime real estate. Most nights the band cranks up and gets the crowd tapping their feet as they down a few.

EXPLORING THE GIBBSTON VALLEY

Gung-ho visitors to Queenstown might be happiest dangling off a giant rubber band, but as they're plunging towards the Kawarau River, they'll be missing out on some of Central Otago's most interesting winemaking areas just up the road in the stunning Gibbston Valley.

On a spectacular river terrace near the Kawarau Bridge, AJ Hackett's original bungy partner Henry van Asch set up the **Winehouse & Kitchen** (Map p570; ☎03-442 7310; www.winehouse.co.nz; mains $15-30; ⏰10am-5pm). A restored wooden villa includes a garden cafe, and in early 2012, the Winehouse's annual Summer Playgound Series music festival was also launched from January to April. Check the website for listings.

Almost opposite, a winding and scenic road leads to beautiful **Chard Farm** (Map p570; ☎03-442 6110; www.chardfarm.co.nz; ⏰11am-5pm), and a further 700m along is **Gibbston Valley Wines** (Map p570; www.gvwines.co.nz), the area's largest wine producer. Try its pinot noir and take a tour of the impressive wine cave. There are also a 'cheesery' and a restaurant.

A further 4km along SH6, **Peregrine** (Map p570; ☎03-442 4000; www.peregrinewines.co.nz; ⏰10am-5pm) produces excellent sauvignon blanc, pinot noir and pinot gris, and hosts occasional outdoor concerts during summer, sometimes featuring international names.

Further west near the shores of Lake Hayes, the **Amisfield Winery & Bistro** (Map p570; ☎03-442 0556; www.amisfield.co.nz; small plates $16.50; ⏰11.30am-8pm Tue-Sun) is regularly lauded by NZ's authoritative *Cuisine* magazine. The highly regarded eatery serves tapas-sized plates perfect for sharing with a few friends on the sunny deck, and Amisfield's pinot noir has been awarded internationally. Also available is the 'Trust the Chef' menu (per person $55), where Amisfield's canny chefs magic up tasty diversions based on whatever is in season. Bookings recommended.

Ask at the Queenstown i-SITE (p586) for maps and information about touring the Gibbston Valley. Recent developments in the area include mountain biking and walking trails along the spidery Kawarau River. You could also join a guided wine tour. A fun option is by retro bicycle with Cycle de Vine (p578). Visit www.gibbstonvalley.co.nz for more info about this compact wine-growing area with its own unique microclimate.

For accommodation, the cosy Warbrick Stone Cottage (p579) is a convenient option en route from Queenstown to Cromwell. Campervan travellers can park up at the compact well-equipped campsite at the **Gibbston Tavern** (☎03-409 0508; www.gibbstontavern.co.nz; 8 Coal Pit Rd; sites $30). Expect a warm welcome from the locals at the adjacent pub. Ask to try the tavern's own Moonshine Wines, as you won't find them anywhere else.

Barmuda BAR
(Map p576; Searle Lane; ⏰3pm-late) A huge open fire makes Barmuda's atmospheric courtyard the place to be in cooler weather. In summer, live jazz on Friday and Saturday nights is sometimes on the cards.

Minibar CRAFT BEER
(Map p576; Eureka Arcade, 11 The Mall; ⏰4pm-late) Beer, beer and more beer. More than 100 local and international beers are poured in this compact space. A cool name for a cool bar, oozing with style.

☆ Entertainment

Pick up the *Source* (www.thesourceonline.com), a free weekly flyer with a gig guide and events listings. Live music and clubbing are a nightly affair and most Queenstown venues stay open until the wee hours.

Nightclubs

Subculture CLUB
(Map p576; www.subculture.net.nz; downstairs 12-14 Church St) Drum 'n' bass, hip-hop, dub and reggae noises that get the crowds moving.

Debajo CLUB
(Map p576; Cow Lane) The perennial end-of-night boogie spot – house and big-beat gets the dance floor heaving till closing time.

Tardis Bar BAR
(Map p576; www.tardisbar.com; 20 Cow Lane, Skyline Arcade) A good dance bar. Regular DJs play hip-hop, dancehall and dub. Like Dr Who's phone booth, it's surprisingly roomy inside.

Cinema

Reading Cinemas CINEMA
(Map p576; ☎03-442 9990; www.readingcinemas.co.nz; 11 The Mall; adult/child $16.20/10.50) Discounts on Tuesdays.

Live Music

The World Bar BAR

(Map p576; www.theworldbar.co.nz; 27 Shotover St; ⏲4pm to late) Still retaining its raucous backpacker roots, the World Bar is also one of Queenstown's best music clubs with regular DJs and live gigs. Check the website for what's on, or drop by for teapot cocktails and legendary Fat Badgers pizzas.

Dux de Lux PUB

(Map p576; 14 Church St) Lots of live bands and DJs with everything from reggae to drum 'n' bass. Look forward to occasional summer visits from NZ's biggest touring acts. The 'Dux' also brew their own beers.

Haka

Kiwi Haka TRADITIONAL DANCE

(Map p572; ☎03-441 0101; www.skyline.co.nz; Brecon St; adult/child/family incl gondola $59/32/166; ⏲from 5.15pm) For traditional Maori dancing and singing, come watch this group at the top of the gondola. There are four 30-minute shows nightly, but bookings are essential.

Shopping

Queenstown is a good place to shop for souvenirs and gifts. Many shops also specialise in outdoor and adventure gear. Begin your shopping along the Mall, Shotover St and Beach St. Explore Church Lane linking Church St to Earl St for art galleries.

Fetch CLOTHING

(Map p576; www.fetchnz.com; 34 Shotover St) Grab an iconic Kiwi T-shirt - our favourite is 'New Zealand – Damn Better than Old Zealand' or create your own design as a wearable souvenir of the time you bungyed, mountain-biked and ziplined to adventure-sports Nirvana.

Kapa ARTS & CRAFTS

(Map p576; www.kapa.co.nz; 29 Rees St) Quirky and eclectic NZ design infused with a healthy dose of contemporary Maori culture.

Rockies CLOTHING

(Map p576; www.rockies.co.nz; 49 Beach St) Rent or buy kids' clothes from Rockies to keep them cosy on the slopes.

Kathmandu OUTDOOR EQUIPMENT

(Map p576; wwww.kathmandu.co.nz; 88 Beach St) A well-known and good-value chain with regular sales making things even cheaper. Join Kathmandu's 'Summit Club' for extra discounts on its rugged backpacks, active footwear and stylish travel and adventure clothing.

Green Toad OUTDOOR EQUIPMENT

(Map p576; ☎03-442 5311; www.greentoad.co.nz; 48 Camp St) Equipment hire including apparel, snowboards and toboggans.

Snowrental OUTDOOR EQUIPMENT

(Map p576; www.snowrental.co.nz; 39 Camp St) Ski-equipment hire company.

Outside Sports OUTDOOR EQUIPMENT

(Map p576; www.outsidesports.co.nz; 36 Shotover St) Ski-equipment hire, mountain-bike hire and outdoor gear for sale

Small Planet Sports Co OUTDOOR EQUIPMENT

(Map p576; www.smallplanetsports.co.nz; 17 Shotover St) New and used outdoor equipment. It's also got a cheaper **outlet store** (Map p576; www.smallplanetsports.co.nz; 23 Beach St).

toi o tahuna ARTS & CRAFTS

(Map p576; www.toi.co.nz; 11 Church Lane) Exclusively NZ art, with around half the work from contemporary Maori artists. Around toi o tahuna, you can also explore other galleries in chic Church Lane. Ask for the *Fine Arts Galleries Walking Trail* map at the i-SITE.

Arts & Crafts Market ARTS & CRAFTS

(Map p576; www.marketplace.net.nz; ⏲9am 4.30pm Nov-Apr, 10am-3.30pm May-Oct) On Saturdays, visit this creative market at Earnslaw Park on the lakefront beside Steamer Wharf. Here's your chance to get a few truly local gifts or souvenirs.

Information

Emergency

Ambulance, fire service and police (☎111)

Post

Post Office (13 Camp St)

Tourist Information

Queenstown i-SITE (☎03-442 4100, 0800 668 888; www.queenstownnz.co.nz; Clocktower Centre, cnr Shotover & Camp Sts; ⏲8am-6.30pm) Booking service, accommodation and information on Queenstown, Arrowtown and Glenorchy.

DOC Visitor Centre (Department of Conservation; ☎03-442 7935; www.doc.govt.nz; 38 Shotover St; ⏲8.30am-5.30pm) Backcountry Hut Passes and weather and track updates; on the mezzanine floor above Outside Sports. Head here to pick up confirmed bookings for the Milford, Kepler and Routeburn Tracks.

Info & Track Centre (☎03-442 9708; www.infotrack.co.nz; 37 Shotover St; ⏲7am-9pm) Information on transport to trailheads.

Travel Agencies

Kiwi Discovery (Map p576; ☎03-442 7340, 0800 505 504; www.kiwidiscovery.com; 37 Camp St) Ski packages and tramping and trailhead transport.

Real Journeys (☎03-249 7416, 0800 656 501; www.realjourneys.co.nz; Beach St, Steamer Wharf) Lake trips and tours.

The Station (Map p576; ☎03-442 5252; www.thestation.co.nz; cnr Camp & Shotover Sts) Houses AJ Hackett Bungy and Shotover Jet.

Getting There & Away

Air

Air New Zealand (p568) links Queenstown to Auckland, Wellington and Christchurch, and Sydney and Melbourne. Virgin Australia has flights between Queenstown and Sydney and Brisbane.

Jetstar (☎0800 800 995; www.jetstar.com) links Queenstown with Auckland, Christchurch and Wellington, and Sydney, Melbourne and the Gold Coast.

Bus

Most buses and shuttles leave from the **Athol St bus terminal** or the Station (p587). Check when you book. Approximate times from Queenstown are the following: Christchurch (seven hours), Dunedin (4½ hours), Invercargill (three hours), Te Anau (two hours), Milford Sound (six hours), Wanaka (30 minutes), Cromwell (one hour), Haast (four hours), Greymouth (nine hours), West Coast glaciers (six hours).

InterCity (www.intercity.co.nz) Book at the i-SITE. Travels to Christchurch, Te Anau, Milford Sound, Dunedin and Invercargill, plus a daily West Coast service to the glaciers and Haast.

Naked Bus (www.nakedbus.com) To the West Coast, Te Anau, Christchurch, Dunedin, Cromwell, Wanaka and Invercargill.

Atomic Shuttles (www.atomictravel.co.nz) To Wanaka, Christchurch, Dunedin and Greymouth.

Catch-a-Bus (☎03-479 9960; www.catchabus.co.nz) To Dunedin and Central Otago – also links to the Taeri Gorge Railway.

Bottom Bus (☎03-477 9083; www.bottombus.co.nz) Does a loop service around the south of the South Island.

Wanaka Connexions (☎03-443 9120; www.alpinecoachlines.co.nz) Links Queenstown with Wanaka and the Rail Trail towns of Central Otago.

Trampers' & Skiers' Transport

Bus services between Queenstown and Milford Sound via Te Anau can also be used for track transport.

For the ski slopes, catch a shuttle ($15 return) to Coronet Peak or the Remarkables from the Queenstown Snow Centre at the Station (p587).

The Info & Track Centre (p586) and Kiwi Discovery (p587) both provide transport to trailheads.

See **Alpine Coachlines** (☎03-443 9120; www.alpinecoachlines.co.nz) and Kiwi Discovery (p587) for details of transport to Cardrona and Treble Cone.

Trackhopper (☎021-187 7732; www.trackhopper.co.nz; from $230 plus fuel costs) Offers a handy car-relocation service from either end of the Routeburn Track, so you don't have to backtrack over parts of the country you've already seen. Similar services are available for the Greenstone & Caples Track and the Rees-Dart Track.

Getting Around

To/From the Airport

Queenstown Airport (ZQN; ☎03-450 9031; www.queenstownairport.co.nz; Frankton) is 8km east of town. **Super Shuttle** (☎0800 748 885; www.supershuttle.co.nz) picks up and drops off in Queenstown (around $20). **Connectabus** (☎03-441 4471; www.connectabus.com; cnr Beach & Camp Sts) runs to to the airport ($6) every 15 minutes from 6.50am to 10.20pm. **Alpine Taxis** (☎0800 442 6666) or **Queenstown Taxis** (☎03-442 7788) charge around $30.

Public Transport

Connnectabus (☎03-441 4471; www.connectabus.com) has various colour-coded routes. Catch the blue route for accommodation in Fernhill and the red routes for accommodation in Frankton. A day pass (adult/child $17/12) allows travel on the entire network. Pick up a route map and timetable from the i-SITE. Buses leave from the corner of Beach and Camp Sts.

Arrowtown

POP 2400

Beloved by day-trippers from Queenstown, exceedingly quaint Arrowtown sprang up in the 1860s following the discovery of gold in the Arrow River. Today the town retains more than 60 of its original wooden and stone buildings, and has pretty, tree-lined avenues, excellent galleries and an expanding array of fashionable shopping opportunities.

The only gold being flaunted these days is on credit cards, and surrounded by a bonanza of daytime tourists, you might grow wary of the quaint historical ambience. Instead take advantage of improved public transport to stay in the town, and use it as a base for exploring Queenstown and the wider region. That way you can enjoy Arrowtown's history, charm and excellent restaurants when the tour buses have decamped back to Queenstown.

Sights & Activities

Try your luck **gold panning** on the Arrow River. Rent pans from the visitor information centre ($3) and head to the northern edge of town. This is also a good spot for **walking**. Pick up *Arrowtown Area Walks* (free) from the visitor information centre. You'll find routes and history on walks to **Macetown** (14km, seven hours) and on **Tobins Track** (one hour).

Chinese Settlement HISTORIC SITE
(admission by gold coin donation; ⏲24hr) Arrowtown has NZ's best example of a gold-era Chinese settlement. Interpretive signs explain the lives of Chinese 'diggers' during and after the gold rush, while restored huts and shops make the story more tangible. Subjected to significant racism, the Chinese often had little choice but to rework old tailings rather than seek new claims. The Chinese settlement is off Buckingham St.

Lake District Museum & Gallery MUSEUM
(www.museumqueenstown.com; 49 Buckingham St; adult/child $8/2; ⏲8.30am-5pm) Exhibits on the gold-rush era and the early days of Chinese settlement around Arrowtown. Younger travellers will enjoy the Museum Fun Pack ($5), which includes activity sheets, museum treasure hunts, stickers and a few flecks of gold.

Millbrook Golf Course GOLF
(☎03-441 7010; www.millbrook.co.nz; Malaghans Rd; green fees $180, club hire $60) Flasher golfers should head to Millbrook Golf Course.

Arrowtown Bike Hire BICYCLE RENTAL
(☎03-442 1466; www.arrowtownbikehire.co.nz; Ramshaw Lane; half/full day rental $35/49) Get active on two wheels on the many new mountain-biking trails around Arrowtown, or join a Mountain Bike Mania tour ($199, October to April) combining 4WD and mountain-biking action and exploring the former gold-rush village of Macetown. Multiday rentals are also available. Rent bikes on Ramshaw Lane or visit Poplar Lodge (p588) for bookings and track information.

Tours

Southern Explorer 4WD TOUR
(☎03-441 1144; www.southernexplorer.co.nz; 4 Merioneth St; day tours per person $65-140) 4WD day tours exploring the improbably scenic landscapes and old mining history around Arrowtown, Skippers Canyon and Glenorchy. Options include overnight camping in Skippers Canyon or Macetown. Based at Poplar Lodge (p588).

Sleeping

There's accommodation from budget to top end, but during summer rooms fill up fast.

The Arrow BOUTIQUE HOTEL $$$
(☎03-409 8600; www.thearrow.co.nz; 63 Manse Rd; d from $415) Five understated but luxurious suites feature at this modern property set in stunning landscapes on the outskirts of Arrowtown. Accommodation is chic and contemporary with huge picture windows showcasing the countryside. Breakfast is included, and there's an original stone cottage that's the perfect socialising hub for guests. The bright lights of Arrowtown are a picturesque five-minute walk away.

Millbrook RESORT $$$
(☎03-441 7000, 0800 800 604; www.millbrook.co.nz; Malaghans Rd; d from $499; P@≋) Just outside Arrowtown, this enormous resort is a town unto itself. Cosy private villas have recently been refurbished and there's a top-class golf course right at your front door. At the end of the day, take your pick from four restaurants, or relax at the **Spa at Millbrook** (☎03-441 7017; www.millbrook.co.nz; Malaghans Rd; treatments from $230), recently voted one of the world's top 10 hotel spas.

Arrowtown Lodge B&B $$
(☎03-442 1101; www.arrowtownlodge.co.nz; 7 Anglesea St; d incl breakfast $160; @≋) From the outside, the guest rooms look like heritage cottages, but inside they're cosy and modern. The family owners are friendly, the breakfast is hearty and some of the units include compact private gardens,

Poplar Lodge HOSTEL $
(☎03-442 1466; www.poplarlodge.co.nz; 4 Merioneth St; dm/s/d $29/62/70; ≋) Budget accommodation options are limited in A-town, but this is your best bet. A converted house, Poplar Lodge has a cosy feel and is off the bus-bound tourist trail. A couple of self-contained units ($99 to $120) are also available. It's also home base for Arrowtown Bike Hire (p588) and Southern Explorer (p588).

Shades MOTEL $$
(☎03-442 1613; www.shadesofarrowtown.co.nz; cnr Buckingham & Merioneth Sts; d $100-155; ≋) A garden setting gives these bungalow-style cottages a relaxed air. Sleeping up to eight, the two-storey family unit (from $175) is

Arrowtown

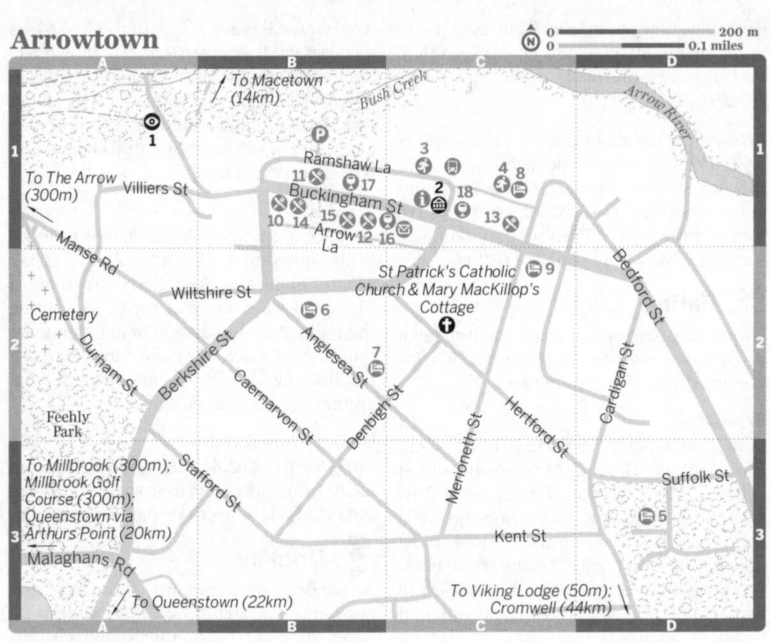

Arrowtown

Sights
1 Chinese Settlement A1
2 Lake District Museum & Gallery C1

Activities, Courses & Tours
3 Arrowtown Bike Hire C1
4 Southern Explorer C1

Sleeping
5 Arrowtown Holiday Park D3
6 Arrowtown Lodge B2
7 Old Villa Homestay B&B B2
8 Poplar Lodge C1
9 Shades C2

Eating
10 Arrowtown Bakery B1
11 Bonjour Cafe B1
12 Cook's Store & Deli B1
Pesto .... (see 14)
13 Provisions C1
14 Saffron B1
15 Stables B1

Drinking
16 Arrow Brewing Company C1
Blue Door .... (see 14)
17 New Orleans Hotel B1
18 The Tap C1

Entertainment
Dorothy Browns .... (see 14)

good value if you're travelling with the whole clan. Savvy budget travellers should book the more compact studio units ($100).

Old Villa Homestay B&B B&B **$$**
(☎03-442 1682; www.arrowtownoldvilla.co.nz; 13 Anglesea St; s/d $120/160) Freshly baked bread and homemade preserves welcome visitors to this heritage-style villa with a garden just made for summer barbecues. Two en-suite double rooms come trimmed with fresh sprigs of lavender. One of the rooms has an additional single bed if you've got an extra travelling companion.

Viking Lodge MOTEL **$$**
(☎03-442 1765; www.vikinglodge.co.nz; 21 Inverness Cres; d $95-150; @🛜🏊) These older A-frame units have a comfortable and family-friendly stamp. If the kids still have energy after a

day's travelling, wear them out even more in the swimming pool or on the playground. Barbecues aplenty make it easy to to dine alfresco.

Arrowtown Holiday Park HOLIDAY PARK **$$**
(03-442 1876; www.arrowtownholidaypark.co.nz; 11 Suffolk St; sites $36, d $65-140;) Mountain views come as standard, even if you're paying more for the flash new studio units. Amenities blocks are equally pristine.

Eating

For its size, Arrowtown has a good range of restaurants. Booking is recommended for evening dining during summer.

Provisions CAFE **$**
(www.provisions.co.nz; 65 Buckingham St; snacks & meals $8-15) One of Arrowtown's oldest cottages is now a cute cafe surrounded by fragrant gardens. Pop in for breakfast or a coffee, and don't leave town without trying one of their deservedly famous sticky buns. Foodie goodies to stock up the campervan with include still-warm bread, and jams and chutneys made from Central Otago fruit.

Saffron INTERNATIONAL **$$$**
(03-442 0131; www.saffronrestaurant.co.nz; 18 Buckingham St; lunch $20-30, dinner mains $38-40; noon-late) Saffron has grown-up food, including lamb rump or Hereford beef with interesting variations on local vegetables. The trio of curries featuring pork, duck and king prawns effortlessly traverses Asia, and you can also purchase the *Saffron* cookbook, showcasing the restaurant's most iconic recipes. The ambience is more formal and sophisticated than the buzz of adjacent Pesto.

Pesto ITALIAN **$$**
(03-442 0885; 18 Buckingham St; mains $18-33; 5pm-late) This candlelit restaurant serves Italian food with a contemporary spin. It's Saffron's slightly rowdier, younger, family-friendly sibling, and the culinary expectations are kept high with good pasta and gourmet pizzas ($20 to $34).

Bonjour Cafe FRENCH **$$**
(03-409 8946; www.bonjour-arrowtown.com; Ramshaw Lane; mains $18-30; 8.30am-3pm Sun & Sat, 5.30-9pm Thu-Sat) Come for breakfast and tuck into one of the 18 different crepe options – you'll definitely struggle to choose. Come back for dinner to treat yourself to cheese fondue or the Kiwi-French combo of herb-crusted rack of lamb.

Arrowtown Bakery BAKERY **$**
(Buckingham St; gourmet pies $5.50) We can recommend the bacon and egg or satay chicken pies. Don't blame us if you order a second. A tasty back-up plan would have to be coffee and a slice of just maybe Central Otago's best boysenberry cheesecake.

Stables CAFE **$$**
(28 Buckingham St; lunch $10-18, dinner $14-30) With courtyard tables adjoining a grassy square, Stables is a good spot to share a pizza and wine. Later at night, step inside the 1860s stone building for a more intimate dining experience. If you're travelling with the kids, they can let off some steam tearing around the adjacent village green.

Cook's Store & Deli DELI **$**
(www.cooksdeli.co.nz; 44 Buckingham St) Pick up picnic fixings including local cheeses and artisan breads at this retro-themed deli and cafe.

Drinking

Arrow Brewing Company CRAFT BEER
(www.arrowbrewing.co.nz; 48-50 Buckingham St) Seven different beers and a sunny courtyard make the Arrow Brewing Company an essential stop. We're especially keen on the honey-infused Gentle Annie lager and the hoppy Arrow Pilz pilsner. Occasional seasonal beers create havoc for the indecisive drinker, and good-value meals and bar snacks include quite possibly the South Island's best lamb burger.

Blue Door BAR
(18 Buckingham St; 3pm-late) Hidden away behind a tricky-to-find blue door. Low ceilings, diffuse light and abundant candles create an intimate quaffing location. Blue Door has a formidable wine list and enough rustic ambience to keep you entertained for the evening.

New Orleans Hotel PUB
(27 Buckingham St) With looks transplanted more from the Wild West than the Deep South, this heritage pub is a good escape from Arrowtown's array of expensive designer shops. The hearty meals are a step back in time, too, and occasional live music infiltrates the town's hushed ambience most weekends.

The Tap PUB
(51 Buckingham St) The Tap dates back to the gold rush. Inside, there are wines, a pool table, pub grub and liquid gold on tap. Sit outside in the sunny garden bar and slow down to Arrowtown's languid pace.

Entertainment

Dorothy Browns CINEMA
(☎03-442 1964; www.dorothybrowns.com; Ballarat Arcade, Buckingham St; adult/child/student $18.50/8/12.50) This is what a cinema should be. Ultra-comfortable seating with the option to cuddle with your neighbour. Fine wine and cheese boards are available to accompany the mostly art-house films on offer. Every screening has an intermission – the perfect opportunity to tuck into a tub of gourmet ice cream.

Information

Arrowtown Visitor Information Centre (☎03-442 1824; www.arrowtown.com; 49 Buckingham St; ⊙8.30am-5pm; @📶) Shares premises with the Lake District Museum & Gallery.

Getting There & Away

From Queenstown, **Connectabus** (☎03-441 4471; www.connectabus.com) runs regular services (7.45am to 11pm) on its No 10 route from Frankton to Arrowtown. You'll need to catch a No 11 bus from Queenstown to the corner of Frankton and Kawarau Rd, and change to a No 10 bus there. The cheapest way is a one-day pass (adult/child $17/12).

The **Double-Decker Bus Tour** (☎03-441 4421; www.doubledeckerbus.co.nz; $48) does a three-hour round-trip tour to Arrowtown (departs Queenstown at 9.30am). **Arrowtown Scenic Bus** (☎03-442 1900; www.arrowtownbus.co.nz) runs a daily four-hour round trip from Queenstown at 10am ($69).

Around Arrowtown

Fourteen kilometres north of Arrowtown lies Macetown, a ghost town reached via a rugged, flood-prone road (the original miners' wagon track), which crosses the Arrow River more than 25 times. Don't even think about taking the rental car here – instead four-hour trips are made from Queenstown and Arrowtown by 4WD vehicle, with gold panning included. Operators include **Nomad Safaris** (☎03-442 6699, 0800 688 222; www.nomadsafaris.co.nz; adult/child from $165/80) and Southern Explorer (p588), and you can also join a mountain-bike trip there with Arrowtown Bike Hire (p588).

Glenorchy

POP 220

Set in achingly beautiful surroundings, postage-stamp-sized Glenorchy is the perfect low-key antidote to Queenstown. An expanding range of adventure operators will get you active on the lake and in nearby mountain valleys by kayak, horse or jetboat, but if you prefer to strike out on two legs, tiny Kinloch, just across the lake, is the starting point for some of the South Island's finest tramps. Glenorchy lies at the head of Lake Wakatipu, a scenic 40-minute (68km) drive northwest from Queenstown.

Activities

Almost all organised activities offer shuttles to and from Queenstown for a small surcharge. Other activities on offer include farm tours – complete with the opportunity to shear sheep – trout fishing, guided photography tours and cookery classes. See www.glenorchyinfocentre.co.nz or ask at the Queenstown i-SITE (p586).

Tramping & Scenic Driving

The DOC brochure *Head of Lake Wakatipu* ($2) details an easy waterside walk around the outskirts of town, and other tramps from two hours to two days, taking in the Routeburn Valley, Lake Sylvan, Dart River and Lake Rere. For track snacks or meals, stock up on groceries in Queenstown. If you're planning on doing short day walks around the region, note that track transport can be at a premium during summer, as it is the Great Walks season. Try to book transport in advance if possible. Those with sturdy wheels can explore the superb valleys north of Glenorchy. **Paradise** lies 15km northwest of town, just before the start of the Dart Track. Keep your expectations low: Paradise is just a paddock, but the gravel road there runs through beautiful farmland fringed by majestic mountains. You can also explore the Rees Valley or take the road to Routeburn, which goes via the Dart River Bridge. Near the start of the Routeburn Track is the Routeburn Nature Walk (one hour) and the Lake Sylvan tramp (one hour 40 minutes).

Glenorchy Base TRAMPING
(☎03-409 0960; www.glenorchybase.co.nz; adult/child from $60) Specialises in guided walks (two hours to one day) in the Glenorchy area. Highlights include birdwatching around Lake Sylvan and a Routeburn Track day walk.

Rural Discovery Tours 4WD
(☎03-442 2299; www.rdtours.co.nz; adult/child $185/92) Half-day tours of a high-country sheep station in a remote valley between Mts Earnslaw and Alfred.

LOCAL KNOWLEDGE

THE REES VALLEY

JANE CAMPION

As many times a year as I can, I travel to a holiday hut up the Rees Valley, at the top end of Lake Wakatipu. I love the lake, the majesty of the surrounding mountains, the good weather in the basin, the walks, the rivers, the end-of-the-world feeling and the laconic people who live nearby. Everyone who has visited me up here is infected by the ready magic of the landscape and the sensation of worldly troubles dissolving. Lake Sylvan is one of many good bush walks in the area – a fairly short walk for this scale of landscape, but the intimacy of being inside the bush immediately gives you a sense of delight. Recently the lake has been high and is phenomenal to swim in.

Jane Campion, film director, writer & producer.

Jetboating & Kayaking

Dart River Safaris JET BOATING
(☎03-442 9992, 0800 327 8538; www.dartriver.co.nz; adult/child $219/119) Journeys into the heart of the spectacular Dart River wilderness, followed by a short nature walk and a 4WD trip. The round trip from Glenorchy takes three hours. You can also combine a jetboat ride with a river descent in an inflatable three-seater 'funyak' (adult/child $289/189).

Kayak Kinloch KAYAKING
(☎03-442 4900; www.kayakkinloch.co.nz; adult $40-80, child $35-50) Excellent guided trips exploring the lake. Trips depart from Queenstown, Glenorchy or Kinloch.

Other Activities

Dart Stables HORSE RIDING
(☎0800 474 3464, 03-442 5688; www.dartstables.com) Offer a two-hour ride ($129), a full-day trot ($279) and a 1½-hour Ride of the Rings trip ($169) for Hobbitty types. If you're really keen, consider the overnight two-day trek with a sleepover in Paradise ($695). All trips can be joined in Queenstown.

Paradise Skydive SKYDIVING
(☎03-442 8333, 0800 475 934; www.skydiveparadise.co.nz; Glenorchy Airport; $325-399) Tandem skydiving above some the planet's most spectacular scenery.

High Country Horses HORSE RIDING
(☎0508 595 959, 03-442 9915; www.high-country-horses.co.nz) Runs two-hour rides ($125) and full-day rides ($295). Trips can be joined in Queenstown.

Sleeping & Eating

At the base of the Kinloch Lodge there's a DOC campsite ($6), which has basic lakeside facilities.

Glenorchy Lake House B&B $$$
(☎03-442 7084; www.glenorchylakehouse.co.nz; Mull St; d incl breakfst $325-400) This luxury lakefront B&B features Egyptian cotton sheets, flat-screen TVs and luxury toiletries. Good luck tearing yourself away to get active out and about in the Wakatipu area. Once you return, recharge in the spa or with a massage. An award-winning chef is in residence (dinner per person $85), and transfers to the Routeburn and Greenstone Tracks are available.

Kinloch Lodge LODGE
(☎03-442 4900; www.kinlochlodge.co.nz; Kinloch Rd; dm $33, d $82-132) Across Lake Wakatipu from Glenorchy, this is a great place to unwind or prepare for a tramp. Rooms in the bunkhouse are comfy and colourful, and there's a hot tub. The 19th-century Heritage Rooms are small but plusher, and come with breakfast and dinner (double $278 to $298). A bar and a good restaurant are on-site. Kinloch is a 26km drive from Glenorchy, or you can organise a five-minute boat ride across the lake. Kinloch Lodge can also arrange track transfers to various trailheads.

Glenorchy Holiday Park HOLIDAY PARK $
(☎03-441 0303; www.glenorchyaccommodation.co.nz; 2 Oban St; sites $28, dm $20, units $32-80; @) Set up camp in a field surrounded by basic cabins and handy barbecues. Out front is a small shop and information centre.

Glenorchy Lodge PUB $$
(☎03-442 9968; www.wakatipu.com; Mull St; d $30-150) Tidy yet tiny rooms live upstairs from this centrally located pub. Some rooms have loft-style ceilings and some have en suites – all have great views.

Glenorchy Hotel HOSTEL $
(☎03-442 9902; www.glenorchy-nz.co.nz; Mull St; dm $30-35) Basic dorms and an adequate base for returning trampers.

Glenorchy Café CAFE $$
(Mull St; breakfast & lunch mains $15-20, pizza $25; ⏲8am-5pm May-Oct, dinner Nov-Apr) Pizza and

breakfast stacks are perennial favourites with locals.

Information

The best place for local information, weather and track information is the **Glenorchy visitor information centre** (☎03-409 2049; www.glenorchy-nz.co.nz; Oban St) in the Glenorchy Hotel. It's website is also an excellent resource. Fishing rods and mountain bikes can be hired. Ask about trail maps for walking or mountain biking in the nearby **Whakaari Conservation Area.**

There is a petrol station in Glenorchy, but fill up with cheaper fuel before you leave Queenstown. There's an ATM at the Glenorchy Hotel.

Getting There & Away

With sweeping vistas and gem-coloured waters, the sealed Glenorchy to Queenstown Rd is wonderfully scenic. Its constant hills are a killer for cyclists. Pick up the *Queenstown to Glenorchy Road* leaflet from the Queenstown i-SITE (p586) for points of interest along the way. The Info & Track Centre (p586) provides transport to Glenorchy from Queenstown. It also services the trailheads of the Routeburn and Greenstone Tracks.

Lake Wakatipu Region

The mountainous region at the northern head of Lake Wakatipu showcases gorgeous, remote scenery, best viewed while tramping along the famous Routeburn and lesser-known Greenstone, Caples and Rees-Dart Tracks. For shorter tracks, see the DOC brochure *Wakatipu Walks* ($5). Glenorchy is a convenient base for all these tramps.

Ultimate Hikes (☎03-450 1940; www.ultimatehikes.co.nz) has a three-day guided tramp on the Routeburn ($1125/1270 low/high season); a six-day Grand Traverse ($1560/1765), combining walks on the Routeburn and Greenstone Tracks; and a one-day Routeburn Encounter ($169), available November to mid-April.

TRACK INFORMATION

For details on accommodation, transport to and from all trailheads, and DOC centres, see coverage of Queenstown and Te Anau. DOC staff advise on maps and sell Backcountry Hut Passes and Great Walks passes. Before setting out, it's essential that you contact them for up-to-date track conditions. Be sure to register your intentions with DOC. For more details on all these tracks, see Lonely Planet's *Tramping in New Zealand*.

ROUTEBURN TRACK

Passing through a huge variety of landscapes with fantastic views, the 32km-long, two- to four-day Routeburn Track is one of the most popular rainforest/subalpine tracks in NZ. Increased pressure on the track has necessitated the introduction of a booking system. Reservations are required throughout the main season (October to April). Book huts or campsites online at www.doc.govt.nz or at a DOC office prior to the trip. Hut fees are $54 per person and camping fees are $18.

For the Routeburn Track, trampers must call in to the DOC visitor centres in either Queenstown (p586) or Te Anau (p612) to collect actual tickets, either the day before or on the day of departure.

Outside the main season, passes are still required; huts cost $15/free per adult/child per night. Camping is $5/free in the off season. The Routeburn track remains open in winter. However, to traverse the alpine section after the snow falls is not recommended for hikers, as winter mountaineering skills required. There are 32 avalanche paths across the section between Routeburn Falls hut and Howden hut, and avalanche risk remains until spring. Always check conditions with DOC.

There are car parks at the Divide and Glenorchy ends of the Routeburn, but they're unattended, so don't leave any valuables in your car. If you do have a car, a relocation service is offered by Trackhopper (p587) in Queenstown from either end of the track.

The track can be started from either end. Many people travelling from Queenstown try to reach the Divide in time to catch the bus to Milford and connect with a cruise on the sound. En route, you'll take in breathtaking views from Harris Saddle and the top of nearby Conical Hill, from where you can see waves breaking at Martins Bay. From Key Summit, there are panoramic views of the Hollyford Valley and the Eglinton and Greenstone River Valleys.

Estimated walking times:

ROUTE	TIME
Routeburn Shelter to Flats Hut	1½-2½hr
Flats Hut to Falls Hut	1-1½hr
Falls Hut to Mackenzie Hut	4½-6hr
Mackenzie Hut to Howden Hut	3-4hr
Howden Hut to the Divide	1-1½hr

Routeburn, Greenstone & Caples Tracks

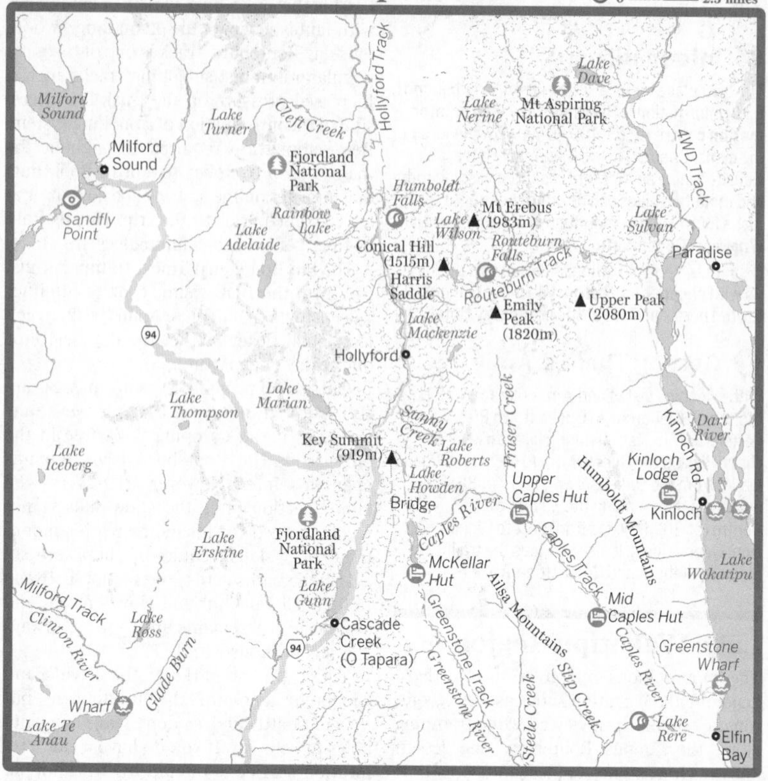

GREENSTONE & CAPLES TRACKS

Following meandering rivers through lush, peaceful valleys, these two tracks form a loop that many trampers stretch out into a moderate four- or five-day tramp. Basic huts en route are **Mid Caples**, **Upper Caples**, **McKellar** and Greenstone. All are $15/5 per adult/child (11 to 17 years) per night, and Backcountry Hut Passes must be pre-purchased.

You can camp for free 50m away from the main track, but not on the private land and around the McKellar Saddle. Check the Environment Care Code on the DOC website. Both tracks meet up with the Routeburn Track; you can either follow its tail end to the Divide or (if you've prebooked) pursue it back to Glenorchy.

From McKellar Hut you can tramp two or three hours to Howden Hut on the Routeburn Track (you'll need to book this hut from October to April), which is an hour from the Divide.

Access to the Greenstone and Caples Tracks is from **Greenstone Wharf**; nearby you'll find unattended parking. Bus transport by Info & Track (p586) runs betwen the Greenstone Car Park and Glenorchy and Queenstown. Another option is the car relocation service offered by Trackhopper (p587).

Estimated walking times:

ROUTE	TIME
Greenstone Wharf to Mid Caples Hut	3hr
Mid Caples Hut to Upper Caples Hut	2-3hr
Upper Caples Hut to McKellar Hut	5-8hr
McKellar Hut to Greenstone Hut	5-7hr
Greenstone Hut to Greenstone Wharf	4-6hr

REES-DART TRACK

This is a difficult, demanding four- to five-day circular route from the head of Lake

Wakatipu, taking you through valleys and over an alpine pass, with the possibility of a side trip to the Dart Glacier if you're suitably equipped and experienced. Access by vehicle is possible as far as Muddy Creek on the Rees side, from where it's six hours to Shelter Rock Hut.

Park your car at Muddy Creek or arrange transport with Queenstown's Info & Track Centre (p586). Another option is the car relocation service offered by Trackhopper (p587). Most people go up the Rees track first and come back down the Dart. The three basic DOC huts (Shelter Rock, Daleys Flat and the Dart) cost $15 per person and Backcountry Hut Passes must be purchased in advance.

Estimated walking times:

ROUTE	TIME
Muddy Creek to Shelter Rock Hut	6hr
Shelter Rock Hut to Dart Hut	5-7hr
Dart Hut to Daleys Flat Hut	6-8hr
Daleys Flat Hut to Paradise	6-8hr

WANAKA REGION

With overgrown valleys, unspoiled rivers and tumbling glaciers, the Wanaka region is crowned with the colossal Mt Aspiring (Tititea; 3035m), the highest peak outside the Mt Cook region. Enter this area from the north via Haast Pass, and you encounter Lakes Wanaka and Hawea, wedged between awesome hills and cliffs. From the south via Cardrona, stunning valley views and mountain vistas are on tap. The Wanaka region, and especially the activity-filled town of Wanaka itself, is seeing more and more travellers, but it's still quieter than Queenstown. It's also very easy to escape the town's growing tourist buzz by exploring Mt Aspiring National Park or the forested wilderness around Makarora.

Wanaka

POP 5000

Beautiful scenery, tramping and skiing opportunities and a huge roster of adrenaline-inducing activities have transformed the lakeside town of Wanaka into a year-round tourist destination. Travellers come here as an alternative to Queenstown, and while some locals worry their home is starting to resemble its hyped-up Central Otago sibling across the Crown Range, Wanaka's lakefront area retains a laid-back, small-town feel. It's definitely not a sleepy hamlet anymore, though, and new restaurants and bars are adding a veneer of sophistication. Note that Wanaka wakes up in a big way for New Year's Eve.

Wanaka is located at the southern end of Lake Wanaka, just over 100km northeast of Queenstown via Cromwell. It's the gateway to Mt Aspiring National Park and to the Treble Cone, Cardrona, Harris Mountains and Pisa Range Ski Areas.

Sights

With its emphasis on the stunning outdoors, Wanaka isn't brimming with conventional sights, but you can keep surprisingly busy on a rainy day.

Warbirds & Wheels MUSEUM
(www.warbirdsandwheels.com; Wanaka Airport, 11 Lloyd Dunn Av; adult/child/family $20/5/45; 9am-5pm) Dedicated to NZ combat pilots, the aircraft they flew, and the sacrifices they made, this excellent museum features Hawker Hurricanes, a de Havilland Vampire and vintage Soviet fighter planes. Classic cars make up the 'wheels' part. Grab a bite to eat and fire up the jukebox in the retro diner.

Wanaka Beerworks BREWERY
(www.wanakabeerworks.co.nz; SH6; tours & tasting $10; 9am-4pm) This small brewery's three main beers, a Vienna lager, a German-style black beer and a hops-laden Bohemian pilsner are complemented by up to 12 different seasonal brews each year. Dave the owner is a real-deal Belgian brewing supremo, and is usually available for tastings and brewery tours.

Wanaka Transport & Toy Museum MUSEUM
(www.wanakatransportandtoymuseum.com; SH6; adult/child/family $12/5/30; 8.30am-5pm) Around 30,000 items include a Cadillac Coupe de Ville, a mysteriously acquired MiG jet fighter, and toys you're guaranteed to remember from rainy childhood afternoons.

Puzzling World AMUSEMENT PARK
(www.puzzlingworld.com; 188 Main Hwy 84; adult/child $15/10; 8.30am-5.30pm) A 3-D Great Maze and lots of 'now-you-see-it, now-you-don't' visual tomfoolery to keep kids of all ages bemused, bothered and bewildered. It's en route to Cromwell, 2km from town.

Wanaka

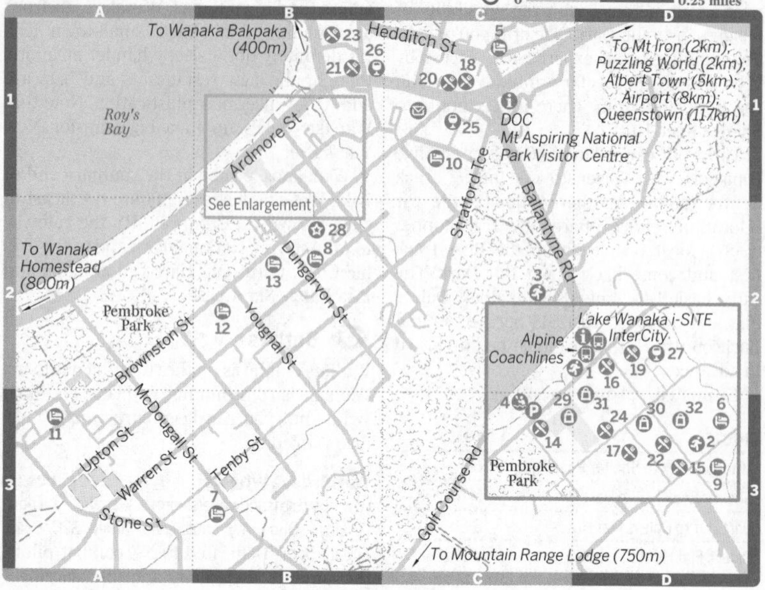

Wanaka

Activities, Courses & Tours

1 Lakeland Adventures D2
2 Thunderbikes D3
3 Wanaka Golf Club C2
4 Wanaka Kayaks C3

Sleeping

5 Archway Motels C1
6 Brook Vale D3
7 Harpers B3
8 Holly's B2
9 Matterhorn South D3
10 Mountain View Backpackers C1
11 Wanaka Lakeview Holiday Park A3
12 Wanaka View Motel B2
13 YHA Wanaka Purple Cow B2

Eating

14 Bistro on Ardmore C3
Botswana Butchery .... (see 25)
Café Gusto .... (see 23)
15 Federal Diner D3
16 Kai Whakapai D2
17 New World Supermarket D3
18 Red Star C1
19 Relishes D2
20 Sasanoki C1
21 Soulfood Store & Cafe B1
22 Spice Room D3
23 The Landing B1
24 Yohei D3

Drinking

25 Barluga C1
26 Opium B1
27 Uno D2
Wanaka Ale House .... (see 14)

Entertainment

28 Cinema Paradiso B2

Shopping

29 Chop Shop C3
30 Gallery Thirty Three D3
31 MT Outdoors D3
32 Picture Lounge D3

Activities

Wide valleys, alpine meadows, more than 100 glaciers and sheer mountains make **Mt Aspiring National Park** an outdoor enthusiast's paradise. Protected as a national park in 1964, and later included in the Southwest New Zealand (Te Wahipounamu) World Heritage Area, the park now blankets more than 3500 sq km along the Southern Alps, from the Haast River in the north to its border with Fiordland National Park in the south.

Tramping

While the southern end of Mt Aspiring National Park is well trafficked by visitors and includes popular tramps such as the Routeburn Track, there are great short walks and more demanding multiday tramps in the Matukituki Valley, close to Wanaka; see the DOC brochure *Matukituki Valley Tracks* ($2). The dramatic **Rob Roy Valley Track** (two to three hours return) takes in glaciers, waterfalls and a swing bridge. It's a moderate walk, but some parts are quite steep. The road to the carpark also crosses many streams. The **West Matukituki Valley** track goes on to Aspiring Hut (four to five hours return), a scenic walk over mostly grassy flats. For overnight or multiday tramps, continue up the valley to **Liverpool Hut** for great views of Mt Aspiring.

Many of these tramps are subject to snow and avalanches and can be treacherous. Register your intentions, and it is also extremely important you consult DOC in Wanaka before heading off. Also purchase hut tickets. Tracks are reached from Raspberry Creek at the end of Mt Aspiring Rd, 54km from Wanaka.

For walks closer to town, pick up the DOC brochure *Wanaka Outdoor Pursuits* ($3.50). This includes the easy lakeside stroll to **Eely Point** (20 minutes) and on to **Beacon Point** (30 minutes), as well as the **Waterfall Creek Walk** (1½ hours return) east along the lakeshore.

The fairly gentle climb to the top of **Mt Iron** (549m, 1½ hours return) reveals panoramic views. After a view, fit folks can undertake the taxing, winding 11km tramp up **Roy's Peak** (1578m, five to six hours return), starting 6km from Wanaka on Mt Aspiring Rd. The high track crosses private land and is closed from October to mid-November for lambing. From Roy's Peak continue along the **Skyline Route** (five to six hours) to Cardrona Rd, 10km south of Wanaka. Don't do this in winter; low cloud eliminates views and makes it treacherous.

To the north of Wanaka, the **Minaret Burn Track** (six to seven hours) in the Mt Alta Conservation Area is suitable for walking and mountain biking. You can pick up a map ($1) at DOC.

Many outfits offer guided walking tours around Wanaka, some into Mt Aspiring National Park.

Alpinism & Ski Wanaka TRAMPING
(☎03-442 6593; www.alpinismski.co.nz; from $200) Day walks and overnight tramps.

Eco Wanaka Adventures TRAMPING
(☎0800 926 326; www.ecowanaka.co.nz; half-/full day from $105/170) Day, half-day and multiday trips.

Wild Walks TRAMPING
(☎03-443 9422; www.wildwalks.co.nz; 3 days from $960) Multiday tramps.

Jetboating & Rafting

Pioneer Rafting RAFTING
(☎03-443 1246; www.ecoraft.co.nz; half-day adult/child $145/85, full day $195/105) Ecorafting on the high-volume Clutha, with Grade II to III rapids, gold panning and birdwatching.

Lakeland Adventures JETBOATING
(☎03-443 7495; www.lakelandadventures.co.nz; i-SITE; adult/child $109/55) One-hour jetboat trips across the lake and including the winding Clutha River.

Wanaka River Journeys JETBOATING
(☎0800 544 555; www.wanakariverjourneys.co.nz; adult/child $240/145) Combination bush walk (50 minutes) and jetboat ride in the stunning Matukituki Valley.

Canyoning & Kayaking

Deep Canyon CANYONING
(☎03-443 7922; www.deepcanyon.co.nz; from $240; ⏲mid-Nov–Apr) Loads of climbing, swimming and waterfall-abseiling through confined, wild gorges.

Alpine Kayak Guides KAYAKING
(☎03-443 9023; www.alpinekayaks.co.nz; half-/full day $149/195; ⏲Nov-May) Paddles down the Hawea, Clutha and Matukituki Rivers. Kids can join a more leisurely half-day Grandview trip (two adult and two kids $450).

Wanaka Kayaks KAYAKING
(☎0800 926 925; www.wanakakayaks.co.nz; from per hour $12; ⏲summer only) Rents kayaks and offers guided lake tours (from $75 per person).

Lakeland Adventures KAYAKING
(☎03-443 7495; www.lakelandadventures.co.nz) Hire kayaks on the waterfront for $15 per hour.

Skydiving & Paragliding

Skydive Lake Wanaka SKY DIVING

(☎03-443 7207; www.skydivewanaka.com; from $329) Jumps from 12,000ft and a scary 15,000ft; the latter lets you fall for 60 seconds.

Wanaka Paragliding PARAGLIDING

(☎0800 359 754; www.wanakaparagliding.co.nz; $189) Count on around 20 minutes soaring on the Central Otago thermals.

Rock Climbing & Mountaineering

Mt Aspiring National Park is a favourite playground of mountaineering and alpine climbing companies. The following all offer beginners' courses and multiday guided ascents of Mts Aspiring, Tasman and Tutoko.

Aspiring Guides MOUNTAINEERING

(☎03-443 9422; www.aspiringguides.com; 3 days from $960) Over 20 years of alpine experience.

Adventure Consultants MOUNTAINEERING

(☎03-443 8711; www.adventureconsultants.com; 5 days from $4100) Also offers two- and three-day excursions on Brewster Glacier and Gillespies Pass in Mt Aspiring National Park ($880 to $990).

Hospital Flat CLIMBING

Excellent rock climbing can be found at Hospital Flat – 25km from Wanaka towards Mt Aspiring National Park.

Wanaka Rock Climbing ROCK CLIMBING

(☎03-443 6411; www.wanakarock.co.nz; from $140) Introductory rock-climbing course (half/full day $140/210), a half-day abseiling intro ($140), and bouldering and multipitch climbs for the experienced.

Basecamp Wanaka ROCK CLIMBING

(www.basecampwanaka.co.nz; 50 Cardrona Valley Rd; adult/child $20/17; ⌚noon-8pm Mon-Fri, from 10am Sat & Sun) Before you hit the mountains, learn the ropes on climbing walls. Climbing gear can also be hired.

Mountain Biking

Many tracks and trails in the region are open to cyclists. Pick up the DOC brochure *Wanaka Outdoor Pursuits* ($3.50), describing mountain-bike rides ranging from 2km to 24km, including the Deans Bank Loop Track (11.5km).

The *Bike Wanaka Cycling Map* ($2) is available at local cycle shops and features forested tracks for more adventurous riders. To hire a bike and get local track information go to **Thunderbikes** (cnr Helwick & Bronwston St).

Freeride NZ MOUNTAIN BIKING

(☎0800 743 369, 021 712 996; www.freeridenz.com; per person from $185) Guided full-day trips including helibiking options, and a three-day ($1370) Central Otago adventure. Self-guided tours and rental is $95.

Fishing

Lakes Wanaka and Hawea (16km away) have excellent trout fishing, and the surrounding rivers are also popular angling spots.

Hatch FISHING

(☎03-443 8446; www.hatchfishing.co.nz; 2 adults half-/full day $490/750) Adventure fishing trips incorporating hiking and including an overnighter (one/two persons $1690/1890) with gourmet food, wine and beer.

Riversong FISHING

(☎03-443 8567, 021 113 6396; www.wanakaflyfishingguides.co.nz; half-/full day $400/600) For $75 per hour, tuition in the dark art of fly-fishing.

Other Activities

Wanaka Golf Club GOLF

(☎03-443 7888; www.wanakagolf.co.nz; Ballantyne Rd; green fees $60, club hire from $20) A spectacular 18-hole course.

 Tours

Book at the i-SITE.

Aerial Sightseeing

Classic Flights SCENIC FLIGHTS

(☎03-443 4043, 0508 435 9464; www.classicflights.co.nz; from $235) Runs sightseeing flights in a vintage Tigermoth. 'Biggles' goggles provided, but BYO flowing silk scarf.

The Silver Demon SCENIC FLIGHT

(☎0508 435 9464; www.silverdemon.co.nz; $185-285) G-force-defying, upside-down, loop-the-loop aerobatic madness.

Wanaka Flightseeing SCENIC FLIGHTS

(☎03-443 8787; www.flightseeing.co.nz; adult/child from $200/120) Spectacular flyovers of Mt Aspiring, Milford Sound and Mt Cook.

Helicopter Rides

The following offer 20-minute flights around Wanaka for about $195, and 60-minute tours of Mt Aspiring and the glaciers for about $495.

Alpine Helicopters SCENIC FLIGHTS

(☎03-443 4000; www.alpineheli.co.nz) Also offer views-a-plenty alpine picnics.

Aspiring Helicopters SCENIC FLIGHTS
(☎03-443 7152; www.aspiringhelicopters.co.nz) Also includes flights to Milford Sound.

Wanaka Helicopters SCENIC FLIGHTS
(☎03-443 1085; www.heliflights.co.nz) Snow landings from $199 per person.

Other Tours

Lakeland Adventures BOAT TOUR
(☎03-443 7495; www.lakelandadventures.co.nz; Wanaka i-SITE) Has 2½-hour trips to Stevensons Island (adult/child $85/55 and a 3½-hour trip with a guided bushwalk on Mou Waho (adult/child $145/55). Kayaks ($15 per hour) and aqua bikes ($15 per 20 minutes) are also available.

Lake Wanaka Cruises BOAT CRUISE
(☎03-443 1230; www.wanakacruises.co.nz; from $70) Lake cruising aboard a catamaran with overnight options.

Ridgeline WINE TASTING
(☎0800 234 000; www.ridgelinenz.com; per person from $165) Tours incorporating wine, spas and 4WD excursions.

Festivals & Events

Warbirds over Wanaka AIRSHOW
(☎0800 496 920, 03-443 8619; www.warbirdsoverwanaka.com; Wanaka Airport; 3-day adult/child from $170/25, 1st day only from $50/10, each of last 2 days from $75/10) Every second Easter (even-numbered years) Wanaka hosts this incredibly popular international airshow attracting 100,000 people. With a backdrop of sun-kissed summertime mountains, it's hard to imagine a more spectacular location to watch heritage and iconic aircraft strut their stuff.

Rippon Festival MUSIC
(www.ripponfestival.co.nz) Music fans should diarise this popular festival held every second year in early February at the lakeside Rippon Vineyard. Big-name Kiwi acts headline with a variety of styles represented – dance, reggae, rock and electronica to name a few. If the music doesn't relax you (highly unlikely), the wine certainly will.

Wanaka Fest ARTS & CULTURAL
(www.wanakafest.co.nz; ⊙mid-Oct) This four-day event has the feel of a small-town fair. Street parades, live music and wacky competitions get the locals saying g'day to the warmth of spring. Look forward to also sampling fine Central Otago produce.

Sleeping

Like Queenstown, Wanaka is bursting with hostels and luxury accommodation, but good midrange options are harder to find. Across summer, and especially around New Year, prices and demand increase considerably. During winter, the town is hit with an influx of international snowboarders.

TOP CHOICE **Riversong** B&B $$
(☎03-443 8567; www.riversongwanaka.co.nz; 5 Wicklow Tce; d $160-180) On the banks of the Clutha River in nearby Albert Town, Riversong has two rooms in a lovely heritage B&B. The well-travelled owners may well have the best nonfiction library in NZ, and if you can tear yourself away from the books, there's excellent trout fishing just metres away. Dinner including wine is $55 per person.

Wanaka Bakpaka HOSTEL $
(☎03-443 7837; www.wanakabakpaka.co.nz; 117 Lakeside Rd; dm $27, s $53, d & tw $64-80; @🛜) An energetic husband-and-wife team run this friendly hostel high above the lake with just about the best views in town. Amenities are top-shelf and the onto-it staff consistently offer a red carpet welcome to weary travellers. The rooms are good value and the outlook from the spacious lounge will inspire you to (finally) get your blog up to date.

Wanaka Homestead LODGE $$$
(☎03-443 5022; www.wanakahomestead.co.nz; 1 Homestead Close; d $265, cottages $410-525; @🛜) Wooden interiors, oriental rugs and local artwork punctuate this boutique lodge, which has won awards for its ecofriendly approach to sustainability. Despite the focus on green good deeds, it's still luxurious, with underfloor heating and an under-the-stars hot tub. Choose from rooms in the main lodge or in self-contained cottages. Say g'day to Douglas, the friendly canine host, for us.

Mountain Range Lodge LODGE $$$
(☎03-443 7400; www.mountainrange.co.nz; Heritage Park, Cardrona Valley Rd; d incl breakfast $320-335; @🛜) Seven rooms named after nearby mountain ranges showcase comfy duvets, fluffy robes and views that'll distract you from the nearby skiing and tramping options. Cool touches like a complimentary glass of Central Otago wine and an on-site hot tub complete an already pretty picture. There's a minimum stay of two nights.

Archway Motels MOTEL $$
(☎0800 427 249, 03-443 7698; www.archwaymotels.co.nz; 64 Hedditch St; $105-150; 📶) This older motel with clean and spacious units and chalets is a short uphill walk from the lakefront. Friendly and helpful owners, new flat screen TVs, and cedar hot tubs with mountain views make Archway great value in a sometimes expensive town. Check online for good offpeak discounts.

Altamont Lodge LODGE $
(☎03-443 8864; www.altamontlodge.co.nz; 121 Mt Aspiring Rd; s/d $49/69; @📶) At the quieter end of town, natural wood gives this place a ski-lodge ambience. Tennis courts, a spa pool and a lounge with a big fire provide plenty of off-piste action. There's also a spacious and well-equipped kitchen. Altamont Lodge is often booked by groups, so it's worthwhile booking ahead. Bathroom facilities are shared.

Aspiring Campervan & Holiday Park HOLIDAY PARK $
(☎03-443 6603, 0800 229 8439; www.campervanpark.co.nz; Studholme Rd; sites fom $37, units $65-160; @📶) Grassy sites for tents and campervans, lots of trees and pretty views add up to a relaxing spot. Superior facilities include a barbecue area with gas heaters, and free wi-fi, spa pool and sauna. Older-style motel units have all been totally renovated, and the newest budget cabins are warm and cosy with wooden floors.

Brook Vale MOTEL $$
(☎0800 438 333, 03-443 8333; www.brookvale.co.nz; 35 Brownston St; d $145-185; 📶🏊) Self-contained studio and family units with a few classy touches; patios open onto a grassy lawn complete with a gently flowing creek. You'll also find a barbecue, a spa and a swimming pool for those sunny Central Otago days.

Wanaka View Motel MOTEL $$
(☎03-443 7480; www.wanakaviewmotel.co.nz; 122 Brownston St; d $110-150) Formerly called Fern Lodge, the relaunched and refurbished Wanaka View Motel has comfortable doubles through to flasher chalet rooms with Sky TV, spa baths and ritzy gas kitchens. The common themes throughout are excellent value for money and mountain views.

YHA Wanaka Purple Cow HOSTEL $
(☎03-443 1880; www.yha.co.nz; 94 Brownston St; dm $28-35, d $86-130) Warmed by a wood stove, the lounge at this ever-popular hostel holds commanding lake and mountain views; that's if you can tear yourself away from the regular movie nights. There are four- and six-bed dorms and a small array of nice doubles with en suites.

Harpers B&B $$
(☎03-443 8894; www.harpers.co.nz; 95 McDougall St; d incl breakfast $140-160; 📶) The garden (with pond and waterfall no less...) is a labour of love at this friendly B&B in a quiet location down a long driveway. Legendary breakfasts are served on a sunny deck with expansive views. You'd be wise to factor a leisurely second cup of breakfast coffee into your day's plans.

Matterhorn South HOSTEL $
(☎03-443 1119; www.matterhornsouth.co.nz; 56 Brownston St; ⏲dm $26-30, s $68, d $68-95, tr $115, q $125; @📶) Right at the edge of central Wanaka, this friendly spot has clean, good-value dorms and studios, and a sunny TV and games room. It has a shared country-style kitchen and a private garden to relax in after a day's outdoor adventuring.

Mountain View Backpackers HOSTEL $
(☎03-443 9010, 0800 112 201; www.wanakabackpackers.co.nz; 7 Russell St; dm $26-28, d $68; @📶) Run by a friendly family, this colourfully renovated and characterful house features an expansive lawn and warm, comfortable rooms. Fire up the alfresco barbecue after a busy day's exploring.

Holly's HOSTEL $
(☎03-443 8187; www.hollys-backpacker.co.nz; 71 Upton St; dm $27-29, d/tw $66; @📶) A family-run, low-key hostel that's a good antidote to busier places around town. Showing a bit of wear and tear, but a friendly spot. Bikes are for hire, and it's a good-value place to stay if you're looking to hit Wanaka for an extended snowboarding sojourn.

Wanaka Lakeview Holiday Park HOLIDAY PARK $
(☎03-443 7883; www.wanakalakeview.co.nz; 212 Brownston St; sites $34, units $55-100) Grassy sites set amid established pine trees with a kids' playground and lots of space to set up camp. Rooms range from basic cabins to en-suite flats.

Eating

Wanaka has a surprising range of places to eat, drink and generally celebrate the fact that you're on holiday. The best coffee in town is at Chop Shop (p602) in Pembroke Mall.

Federal Diner CAFE
(www.federaldiner.co.nz; 47 Helwick St; snacks & mains $10-20; ⏲7.30am-4pm, open later for tapas in summer) Seek out this cosmopolitan cafe tucked away off Wanaka's main shopping street. The all-day menu delivers robust spins on breakfast, excellent coffee and chunky gourmet sandwiches. Try the 'Roaster Coaster' with slow-roasted pork shoulder and apple sauce on ciabatta. Beers and wines are proudly local, and there's occasional live music with a blues or folk flavour on Friday nights.

Spice Room INDIAN **$$**
(www.spiceroom.co.nz; 43 Helwick St; mains $20-25;) The combo of an authentic curry, crispy garlic naan and cold beer is a great way to recharge after a day's snowboarding or tramping. Beyond the spot-on renditions of all your subcontinental favourites, the Spice Room springs a few surprises with starters including a zingy scallops masala salad. Time for one more chilled Kingfisher, maybe?

Kai Whakapai CAFE **$$**
(cnr Helwick & Ardmore Sts; meals $10-30;) An absolute Wanaka institution, Kai (the Maori word for food) is definitely the place to be on a sunny day. Massive sandwiches and pizzas, great coffee and occasionally slow service are all a part of the experience. Locally brewed Wanaka Beerworks beers are on tap – often including the brewery's regular seasonal concoctions – and there are Central Otago wines as well.

Relishes CAFÉ **$$**
(99 Ardmore St; breakfast & lunch $12-20, dinner $27-34) A cafe by day with good breakfast and lunch options, this place whips out the white tablecloths at night and becomes a classy restaurant with a good wine list. Try the free-range pork belly or Aoraki salmon, and toast the lakefront setting with a glass of Central Otago's finest.

Botswana Butchery MODERN NZ **$$$**
(03-443 6745; Post Office Lane; mains $30-45; ⏲5pm-late) In a sophisticated dining room, locally inspired dishes like Central Otago hare and Cardrona Merino lamb shoulder go head to head with Botswana Butchery's signature aged beef steaks. Definitely food for grown-ups, as is the serious Central Otago-skewed wine list. After dinner, pop next door for a night cap at Barluga.

Soulfood Store & Cafe ORGANIC **$**
(74 Ardmore St; mains $8-16;) Park yourself in a rustic wooden booth and stay healthy with organic soups, pizza, pasta and muffins. Not everything's strictly vegetarian, and breakfast with free-range eggs breaks the spell in a tasty way. The attached organic food store, which has freshly baked bread, is a good spot for a pre-picnic stock-up. Juices and smoothies are both tasty and virtuous.

The Landing MODERN NZ **$$$**
(www.missyskitchen.com; Level 1, 80 Ardmore St; mains $25-37; ⏲from 4pm) A dramatic upstairs dining room with equally spectacular lake views serves up local beef, lamb and salmon in innovative and award-winning ways. Try the Asian-style pork belly with black-pepper caramel and mashed aubergine and coriander with a Central Otago pinot gris.

Yohei SUSHI
(Spencer House Mall, 23 Dunmore St; snacks $8-12;) Tucked away in a shopping arcade, this funky Japanese-inspired eatery does interesting local spins on sushi (how about venison or lamb?), and superlative juices and smoothies. Very cool music, a good range of vego options and free wi-fi with any $4 purchase.

Bistro on Ardmore CAFE
(155 Ardmore St; meals $12-20;) This cosmopolitan lakefront cafe has everything from muffins the size of Mt Aspiring to equally robust steak sandwiches and lamb burgers. The food is hearty and honest, the welcome genuine, and it's all washed down with good coffee, free wi-fi and a concise but considered array of local wines and beers.

Café Gusto CAFE **$**
(1 Lakeside Rd; mains $15-20) Gusto provides robust meals like a breakfast burrito with jalapeno peppers, or smoked salmon and scrambled eggs. Both will set you up for the most active of days, and after you've kayaked/mountain biked/rafted/hiked, come back in the afternoon for excellent cakes and good coffee.

Sasanoki JAPANESE **$**
(26 Ardmore St; mains $10-15) Good value, sushi, sashimi, and noodle and rice dishes. Push the boat out with a bento box ($28) and a few Japanese beers if you're feeling flush.

Red Star BURGERS
(26 Ardmore St; burgers $10-15;) Red Star spoils diners with a menu featuring inventive

ingredients and 21 different burgers. Everybody is catered for – even vegetarians, who get a show-stopping three options.

New World Supermarket SELF-CATERING **$**
(Dunmore St) Excellent deli, wine and beer selection.

Drinking

Barluga BAR
(Post Office Lane; ⏲4pm-late) In the funky Post Office Lane area, Barluga's leather armchairs and coolly retro wallpaper at first make you think of a refined gentlemen's club. Wicked cocktails and killer back-to-back beats soon smash that illusion.

Wanaka Ale House PUB
(155 Ardmore St) Celebrating a lakefront location, this place also owns the coveted corner office. The rustic ambience morphs into a Southern Man reverie of exposed beams and mountain views, and an ample supply of Monteith's beer flows like water.

Uno BAR
(99 Ardmore St; ⏲5pm-late) This slick and contemporary wine bar is the perfect place to watch the sun go down. It's a pretty good spot to head back to after dinner as well.

Opium CLUB
(Level 1, 68 Ardmore St; ⏲5pm-late) Asian-themed bar with DJs and occasional live music. It's popular in winter with the snowboarder crowd, but in summer the lakefront bars are busier.

Entertainment

Cinema Paradiso CINEMA
(☎03-443 1505; www.paradiso.net.nz; 72-76 Brownston St; adult/child $16/10; @) Wanaka's original Cinema Paradiso in Ardmore St was a true NZ icon, and it reopened at these more modern and spacious premises in March 2012. Look forward to an entertaining slice of the old Paradiso magic with comfy couches and extra cushions on the floor to stretch out on. At intermission the smell of freshly baked cookies wafts through the theatre, and you can also order light meals to be ready for you at the break. Try the homemade ice cream and don't forget to arrive early to get a good couch. The best of Hollywood and arthouse flicks run across three screens.

Ruby's CINEMA
(www.rubyscinema.co.nz; 50 Cardrona Valley Rd; adult/child $18.50/12.50) Channelling a lush New York or Shanghai vibe, this hip arthouse cinema meets chic cocktail bar is a real surprise in outdoorsy Wanaka. Luxuriate in the huge cinema seats, or chill out in the red velvet lounge with craft beers, classic cocktails and sophisticated bar snacks ($6 to $14). You'll find Ruby's concealed within the Basecamp Wanaka building on the outskirts of town.

Shopping

Picture Lounge PHOTOGRAPHY
(48 Helwick St) Showcase gallery and shop for stunning large-format shots by local and NZ photographers. Central Otago's rugged scenery has never looked so good.

Chop Shop CLOTHING
(www.chop.co.nz; Pembroke Mall) The best coffee in town, funky alfresco seating and a natty range of locally designed beanies and cool T-shirts for the discerning snowboarder

Gallery Thirty Three ARTS & CRAFTS
(www.gallery33.co.nz; 33 Helwick St) Has pottery, glass and jewellery from local artists.

MT Outdoors OUTDOOR EQUIPMENT
(www.mtoutdoors.co.nz; Dunmore St) Camping and tramping gear.

Outside Sports OUTDOOR EQUIPMENT
(www.outsidesports.co.nz; 17-23 Dunmore St) Both winter and summer outdoor equipment for sale or rent.

Information

DOC Mt Aspiring National Park Visitor Centre (☎03-443 7660; www.doc.govt.nz; Ardmore St; ⏲8am-5pm Nov-Apr, 8.30-5pm Mon-Fri, 9.30am-4pm Sat May-Oct) In an A-framed building on the edge of town. Enquire about tramps. There's a small museum (admission free) on Wanaka geology, flora and fauna.

Lake Wanaka i-SITE (☎03-443 1233; www.lakewanaka.co.nz; 100 Ardmore St; ⏲8.30am-5.30pm, to 7pm in summer) In the log cabin on the lakefront.

Wanaka Medical Centre (☎03-443 7811; www.wanakamedical.co.nz; 23 Cardrona Valley Rd; ⏲9am-5pm Mon-Fri, clinics at 9am & 5pm Sat & Sun) Patches up adventure-sports mishaps.

Getting There & Away

Air

Air New Zealand (☎0800 737 000; www.airnewzealand.co.nz) has daily flights between Wanaka and Christchurch (from $99).

Bus

InterCity (www.intercity.co.nz) The bus stop is outside the lakefront i-SITE. Wanaka receives daily buses from Queenstown (two hours), which motor on to Franz Josef (six hours) via Haast Pass (three hours). For Christchurch (6½ hours) you'll need to change at Tarras.

Atomic Shuttles (www.atomictravel.co.nz) Services to Christchurch (seven hours), Dunedin (4½ hours) and the West Coast.

Catch-a-Bus (☎03-479 9960; www.catchabus.co.nz) Links Wanaka with Dunedin and the Rail Trail towns of Central Otago.

Naked Bus (www.nakedbus.com) Services to Queenstown, Christchurch, Cromwell and the West Coast.

connectabus (☎0800 405 066; www.connectabus.com; one-way/return $35/65) Handy twice-daily service linking Wanaka with the Queenstown airport and Queenstown. Free pickup from most accommodation.

Wanaka Connexions (☎03-443-9120; www.alpinecoachlines.co.nz) Links Wanaka with Queenstown and the Rail Trail towns of Central Otago.

ℹ Getting Around

Alpine Coachlines (☎03-443 7966; www.alpinecoachlines.co.nz; Dunmore St) meets and greets flights at Wanaka Airport ($15), and in summer has twice-daily shuttles for trampers ($35) to Mt Aspiring National Park and Raspberry Creek. See it also for winter transport to Treble Cone. **Wanaka Taxis** (☎0800 272 2700) also looks after airport transfers, while **Adventure Rentals** (☎03-443 6050; www.adventurerentals.co.nz; 20 Ardmore St) hires cars and 4WDs, and **Yello** (☎0800 443 5555; www.yello.co.nz) provide charter transport, airport transfers and regional sightseeing.

Makarora

POP 40

At Makarora you've left the West Coast and entered Otago, but the township still has a West Coast frontier feel. Visit the **DOC Visitor Information Centre** (DOC; ☎03-443 8365; www.doc.govt.nz; SH6; ⏲8am-5pm Dec-Mar, Mon-Fri only Nov & Apr) for conditions and routes before undertaking any regional tramps. The **Makarora Tourist Centre** (☎03-443 8372, 0800 800 443; www.makarora.co.nz; ⏲8am-8pm) can help with accommodation and booking tours and activities.

 Activities

Tramping

Short tramps in this secluded area include the **Bridal Track** (1½ hours one-way, 3.5km), from the top of Haast Pass to Davis Flat, and the **Blue Pools Walk** (30 minutes return), where you can see huge rainbow trout.

Longer tramps go through magnificent countryside but shouldn't be undertaken lightly. Changeable alpine and river conditions mean you must be well prepared; consult with DOC before heading off. DOC's brochure *Tramping in the Makarora Region* ($1) is a worthwhile investment.

Gillespie Pass TRAMPING

The three-day Gillespie Pass loop tramp goes via the Young, Siberia and Wilkin Valleys. This is a high pass with avalanche danger in winter and spring. With a jetboat ride down the Wilkin to complete it, this rates alongside the Milford Track as one of NZ's must-do tramps.

Wilkin Valley Track TRAMPING

The Wilkin Valley Track heads off from Kerin Forks Hut – at the top of the Wilkin River – and on to Top Forks Hut and the picturesque Lakes Diana, Lucidus and Castalia (one hour, 1½ hours and three to four hours respectively from Top Forks Hut). Jetboats go to Kerin Forks, and a service goes across the Young River mouth when the Makarora floods. Another option is to use the High River Route from the Blue Pools (7km and two hours). Enquire at Wilkin River Jets or DOC.

Other Activities

Siberia Experience ADVENTURE TOUR

(☎03-443 8666, 0800 345 666; www.siberiaexperience.co.nz; adult/child $355/285) The Siberia Experience is a thrill-seeking extravaganza combining a half-hour scenic small-plane flight, a three-hour bush walk through a remote mountain valley and a half-hour jetboat trip down the Wilkin and Makarora Rivers in Mt Aspiring National Park. To avoid getting lost, keep your eye on the markers as you descend from Siberia Valley. It's possible to join in Wanaka.

Wilkin River Jets JET BOATING

(☎0800 538 945, 03-443 8351; www.wilkinriverjets.co.nz; Kerin Forks transfer $85) A superb 50km, one-hour jetboating trip (adult/child $98/57) into Mt Aspiring National Park, following the Makarora and Wilkin Rivers. It's cheaper than Queenstown options, and also offers trips including helicopter rides or tramping.

Southern Alps Air SCENIC FLIGHTS

(☎03-443 4385, 0800 345 666; www.southernalpsair.co.nz) Trip to Mt Cook and the glaciers (adult/child $410/215) or landings at Milford Sound ($395/245).

Sleeping & Eating

The nearest DOC camping grounds (adult/child $6/3) are on SH6 at Cameron Flat, 10km north of Makarora, and at Boundary Creek Reserve, 18km south of Makarora on the shores of Lake Wanaka.

Makarora Homestead Wilderness Accommodation B&B $$
(03-443 1532; www.makarora.com; Rapid 53 Rata Rd; d $130-150) Country-style studio units and cottages have compact kitchenettes, or you can stay on a B&B basis in the sprawling main homestead. Look forward to a quiet rural location with the occasional company of deer, lambs and native birds. Cottages have wide verandas and tranquil country views.

Makarora Tourist Centre HOLIDAY PARK
(03-443 8372; www.makarora.co.nz; SH6; sites from $24, dm $30, units $70-120; @) In scrubby bush are self-contained chalets, basic cabins, and backpacker doubles and dorms. They've all got a snug, alpine feel, and you'll also find a cafe, an outdoor pool, a grocery store and a petrol station. Campervan travellers are also welcome, and later at night the cafe assumes the role of Makarora's pub.

Getting There & Away

InterCity (www.intercity.co.nz) and **Atomic Shuttles** (www.atomictravel.co.nz) both travel through Makarora en route to Haast and the West Coast.

Hawea

POP 1600

The small town of Hawea, 15km north of Wanaka, has spectacular lake and mountain views. From Lake Hawea look out at the indomitable Corner Peak on the western shore and out to the distant Barrier Range. Separated from Lake Wanaka by a narrow isthmus called the Neck, Lake Hawea is 35km long and 410m deep, and home to trout and landlocked salmon. The lake was raised 20m in 1958 to facilitate the power stations downriver.

Lake Hawea Motor Inn (03-443 1224, www.lakehawea.co.nz; 1 Capell Ave; dm $30, d $150-180) has smart recently refurbished rooms with unbeatable views across the lake. Downstairs is the cosy Stag's Head bar and restaurant with equally stellar vistas.

On the lakeshore is the spacious and relatively peaceful **Lake Hawea Holiday Park** (03-443 1767; www.haweaholidaypark.co.nz; SH6; sites from $30, units $50-120; @), a favourite of fishing and boating enthusiasts.

Cardrona

The sealed **Crown Range Road** from Wanaka to Queenstown via Cardrona is shorter than the route via Cromwell, but it's a narrow, twisting-and-turning mountain road that needs to be tackled with care, especially in poor weather. In winter it is often snow covered, necessitating chaining up the wheels, and is often subject to closure because of snow. You've been warned.

With views of lush valleys, foothills and countless snowy peaks, this is one of the South Island's most scenic drives. The road passes through tall, swaying tussock grass in the **Pisa Conservation Area**, which has a number of short walking trails. There are plenty of rest stops to drink in the view. Particularly good ones are at the Queenstown end of the road, as you switchback down towards Arrowtown.

The unpretentious-looking **Cardrona Hotel** (03-443 8153; www.cardronahotel.co.nz; Crown Range Rd; d $135-185) first opened its doors in 1863. Today you'll find lovingly restored, peaceful rooms with snug, country-style furnishings and patios opening onto a garden. You'll also find a deservedly popular pub with a good **restaurant** (mains $15-20) and a great garden bar.

The hotel is located near the turn-off for Snow Farm New Zealand (p578). In winter this is home to fantastic cross-country skiing. Lessons and ski hire are available ($90 for both). Also nearby is Snowpark NZ (p578), the country's only specialist freestyle and snowboard area.

Also situated nearby is Backcountry Saddle Expeditions (p574), with horse treks through the Cardrona Valley on Appaloosa horses.

Alternatively, the altogether less placid **Cardrona Adventure Park** (www.adventurepark.co.nz; monster trucks from $140, quad-bikes from $75, go-karts from $60; 10am-5pm) is a rambunctious and noisy collection of monster trucks (including a self-drive option), quad-bikes, and off-road go-karts.

Fiordland & Southland

Includes »

Fiordland 607
Te Anau 607
Te Anau–Milford Hwy 612
Milford Sound 615
Manapouri 617
Doubtful Sound 618
Southern Scenic Route 619
Tuatapere 619
Central Southland 621
Invercargill 621
The Catlins 625
Stewart Island 630

Best Outdoors

- » Milford Sound (p615)
- » Doubtful Sound (p618)
- » Nugget Point (p629)
- » Ulva Island (p632)

Best Places to Stay

- » Misty Mountain Eco-Retreat (p617)
- » Milford Sound Lodge (p615)
- » Hilltop (p628)
- » Pounawea Motor Camp (p630)

Why Go?

Welcome to scenery that travellers dream of and cameras fail to capture.

To the west is Fiordland National Park, with jagged misty peaks, glistening lakes and a remote and pristine stillness. Enter this beautiful isolation via the world-famous Milford Track, one of the various trails that meander through dense forest and past spectacular mountains and glacier-sculpted canyons. Fiordland is also home to Milford and Doubtful Sounds, with verdant cliffs soaring almost vertically from deep, indigo waters. Both fiords are relatively easy to access by road, boat or kayak.

In Southland's east, a sharp left turn off the beaten track, the peaceful Catlins showcase bird-rich native forests and rugged, windswept coasts. Abundant southern Pacific waters host penguins, seals, sea lions, dolphins and the occasional whale.

Keep heading south for the rugged isolation of Stewart Island, and the opportunity to spy New Zealand's beloved kiwi in the wild.

When to Go

Visit from February to March for the best opportunity of settled weather amid Fiordland's notoriously fickle climate. Linger until May for the opportunity to sample local beers and NZ's favourite bivalve and at the annual Bluff Oyster and Food Festival. The Milford, Kepler and Routeburn Tracks are three of NZ's iconic tramping routes, and classified as Great Walks by NZ's Department of Conservation. During the Great Walks season from late October to late April you'll need to book your time exploring these three popular tracks in advance.

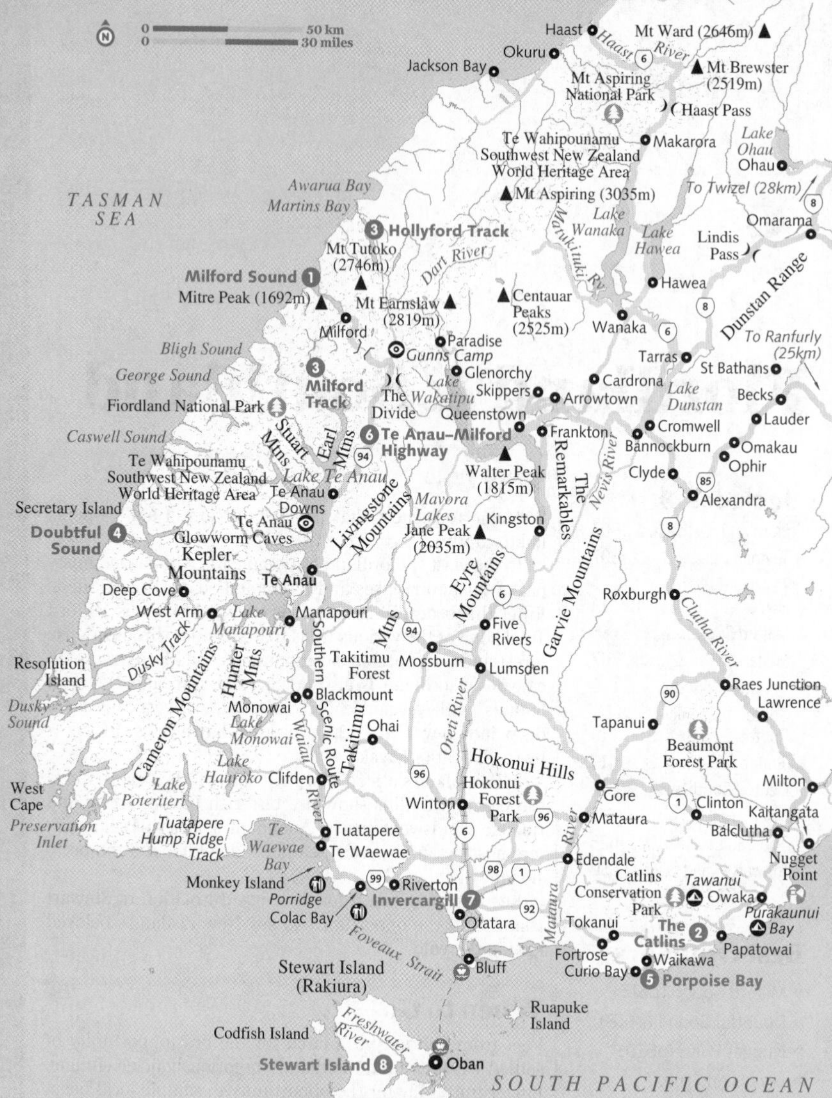

Fiordland & Southland Highlights

1. Sea kayaking, dwarfed by the steep cliffs of **Milford Sound** (p615)
2. Exploring side roads, forest waterfalls and lonely southern beaches in the peaceful, windswept **Catlins** (p625)
3. Walking through forest and mountains on the **Milford** and **Hollyford Tracks** (p613)
4. Overnighting on the vast, remote **Doubtful Sound** (p618)
5. Sharing a beach with dolphins, whales, sea lions and penguins at **Porpoise Bay** (p627) in the Catlins
6. Diverting from **Te Anau–Milford Hwy** (p612) to explore forest walks and still mountain lakes
7. Saying g'day to the tuatara, New Zealand's living dinosaurs, at Invercargill's **Southland Museum & Art Gallery** (p621)
8. Chancing on a snuffling, shuffling band of kiwi on a twilight kiwi-spotting expedition on **Stewart Island** (p630)

Getting There & Around

Air New Zealand (p624) connects Invercargill with Christchurch, while Stewart Island Flights (p624) connects Invercargill with Oban.

Major bus operators shuttle to Te Anau and Invercargill from Queenstown or Dunedin, and some ply the Southern Scenic Route and take in Milford Sound. These include Tracknet, InterCity, Topline Tours, Atomic Shuttles, Bottom Bus and Naked Bus.

FIORDLAND

Fiordland is NZ's rawest wilderness area, a jagged, mountainous, forested zone sliced by numerous deeply recessed sounds (which are technically fiords) reaching inland like crooked fingers from the Tasman Sea. Part of the Te Wahipounamu Southwest New Zealand World Heritage Area, it remains formidable and remote.

Of the region's wonderful bushwalks, Milford Track may be king, but Kepler and Hollyford are worthy knights, and the Routeburn, Greenstone and Caples Tracks all link Fiordland with the Queenstown region.

ESSENTIAL FIORDLAND & SOUTHLAND

» **Eat** Bluff oysters in Bluff or Tuatapere sausages in Tuatapere

» **Drink** The fine beers crafted by the Invercargill Brewery

» **Read** *The Gorse Blooms Pale* by Dan Davin, a collection of Southland short stories

» **Listen to** The sound of silence while kayaking in Doubtful Sound

» **Watch** *South* (2009), a TV series (available on DVD) hosted by quirky local media identity Marcus Lush

» **Go green** Take ecologically focused tours by boat on Doubtful Sound or by foot in the Catlins

» **Online** www.fiordland.org.nz, www.southlandnz.com

» **Area Code** ☎03

Te Anau

POP 3000

Peaceful, lakeside Te Anau township is a good base for trekkers and visitors to Milford Sound, and an ideal place to recharge or get active in the surrounding landscapes.

To the east are the pastoral areas of central Southland, while west across Lake Te Anau lie the rugged forested mountains of Fiordland. The lake, NZ's second largest, was gouged out by a huge glacier and has several arms that penetrate into the mountainous forested western shore. Its deepest point is 417m, about twice the depth of Loch Ness.

Sights

Te Anau Glowworm Caves CAVE

Once present only in Maori legends, these impressive caves were rediscovered in 1948. Accessible only by boat, the 200m-long system of caves is a magical place with sculpted rocks, waterfalls small and large, whirlpools and a glittering glowworm grotto in its inner reaches. **Real Journeys** (☎0800 656 501; www.realjourneys.co.nz) runs 2¼-hour guided tours ($70/22 per adult/child), reaching the heart of the caves by a walkway and a short underground boat ride.

DOC Te Anau Wildlife Centre WILDLIFE CENTRE

(☎03-249 0200; Te Anau-Manapouri Rd; admission by donation; ⏲dawn-dusk) Native bird species – including the rare flightless takahe, NZ pigeons, tui, kaka and weka.

Fiordland Astronomy ASTRONOMY

(☎0508 267 667; www.astronomyfiordland.co.nz; adult/child $45/35) See the Southern Cross and Milky Way in Fiordland's pristine skies; weather permitting.

Stardome ASTRONOMY

(☎0508 267 667; www.astronomyfiordland.co.nz; Events Centre, Luxmore Dr; adult/child $30/20) Book at the i-SITE for this interactive digital planetarium.

Activities

Tramping

Register your intentions at the Department of Conservation Visitor Centre (p612).

KEPLER TRACK

This 60km circular Great Walk starts less than an hour's walk from Te Anau and heads west into the Kepler Mountains, taking in the lake, rivers, gorges, glacier-carved valleys and beech forest. The walk can be done in four days, or three if you exit at Rainbow Reach. On the first day you reach the tree line, giving panoramic views. The alpine stretch between Luxmore and Iris Burn

Te Anau

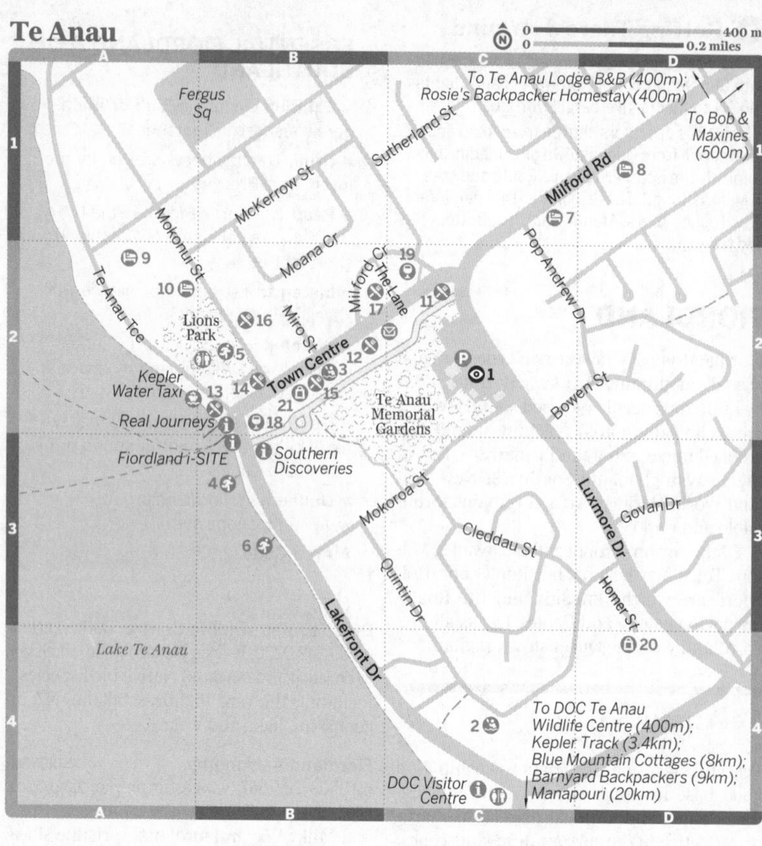

Te Anau

Sights
- 1 Stardome C2

Activities, Courses & Tours
- 2 Fiordland Wilderness Experiences C4
- 3 Rosco's Milford Kayaks B2
- 4 Southern Lakes Helicopters B3
- 5 Te Anau Bike Hire B2
- 6 Wings & Water Te Anau B3

Sleeping
- 7 Cosy Kiwi C1
- 8 Keiko's B&B D1
- 9 Te Anau Top 10 Holiday Park A2
- 10 Te Anau YHA A2

Eating
- 11 Fat Duck C2
- Fresh Choice Supermarket .... (see 17)
- 12 Kebabs 2 Go B2
- 13 Mainly Seafood B2
- 14 Miles Better Pies B2
- 15 Olive Tree Café & Restaurant B2
- 16 Redcliff Bar & Restaurant B2
- 17 Sandfly Café B2

Drinking
- 18 Moose B2
- 19 Ranch Bar & Grill C2

Entertainment
- Fiordland Cinema .... (see 17)

Shopping
- 20 Bev's Tramping Gear D4
- 21 Te Anau Outside Sports B2

Kepler Track

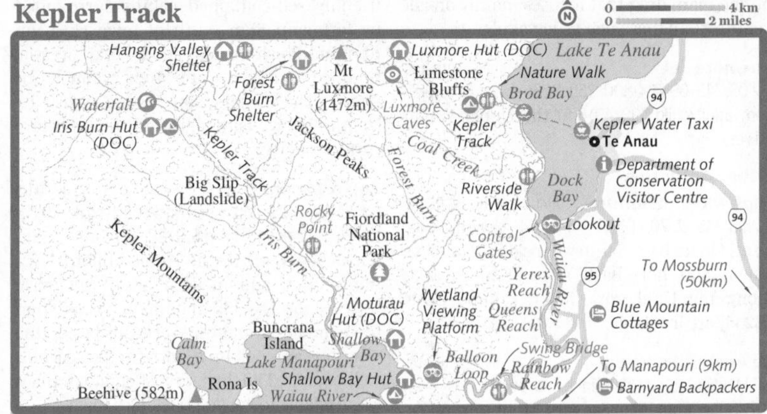

Huts goes along a high ridge, well above the bush, and offers fantastic views when it's clear; in poor weather it can be treacherous. It's recommended that the track be done in the Luxmore–Iris Burn–Moturau direction.

The weather impacts greatly on this walk, and you should expect rain and be prepared for wading. Good rain gear is essential. The alpine sections require a good level of fitness and may be closed in winter. Other sections are considered moderate, with climbs and descents of up to 1000m and unbridged stream crossings.

During the main walking season (October to April), advance bookings must be made by all trampers online at www.doc.govt.nz or at any DOC visitor centre. Pick up tickets at Te Anau's DOC visitor centre before departure.

Accommodation here is in three well-maintained huts. A **camping pass** (per night adult/child $18/free) allows camping at two designated campsites. Outside the main season, a **Backcountry Hut Pass** (per night adult/child $15/free) must be prepurchased, but no heating or cooking is on offer. Off-season camping is free.

Estimated walking times:

DAY	ROUTE	TIME
1	Te Anau DOC visitor centre to control gates	45min
1	Control gates to Brod Bay	1½hr
1	Brod Bay to Luxmore Hut	3½-4½hr
2	Luxmore Hut to Iris Burn Hut	5-6hr
3	Iris Burn Hut to Moturau Hut	5-6hr
4	Moturau Hut to Rainbow Reach	1½-2hr
4	Rainbow Reach to control gates	2½-3½hr

Tracknet (0800 483 262; www.tracknet.net) and **Topline Tours** (03-249 8059; www.toplinetours.co.nz) provide trailhead transport.

SHORT WALKS

Set out along the Kepler Track on free day walks. **Kepler Water Taxi** (03-249 8364; stevsaunders@xtra.co.nz; one-way/return $25/50) will scoot you over to Brod Bay from where you can walk to Mt Luxmore (seven to eight hours) or along the southern lakeshore back to Te Anau (two to three hours). Regular shuttles leave Te Anau lakefront at 8.30am and 9.30am during summer.

During summer, **Trips'n'Tramps** (03-249 7081, 0800 305 807; www.tripsandtramps.com; Oct-Apr) offers small-group, guided hikes on sections of the Routeburn and Kepler and Hollyford Tracks. Some departures incorporate kayaking on Milford Sound. **Real Journeys** (800 656 501; www.realjourneys.co.nz) runs guided day hikes (adult/child $195/127, November to mid-April) along an 11km stretch of the Milford Track.

Grab a copy of *Fiordland National Park Day Walks* ($1 from the Fiordland i-SITE or free at www.doc.govt.nz).

Kayaking & Jetboating

Fiordland Wilderness Experiences KAYAKING
(0800 200 434; www.fiordlandseakayak.co.nz; from $145) One-day and multiday kayaking explorations of Lake Te Anau and Lake Manapouri.

Rosco's Milford Kayaks KAYAKING
(0800 476 726; www.roscosmilfordkayaks.com; 72 Town Centre; 9am-5pm) A good local operator. Has a booking and information kiosk

on the main drag that focuses mainly on adventure activities such as kayaking.

Luxmore Jet JETBOATING
(☎03-249 6951, 0800 253 826; www.luxmorejet.com; adult/child $99/49) On the Upper Waiau River.

Other Activities

High Ride Adventures QUAD BIKES, HORSE RIDING
(☎03-249 7570, 0508 444 474; www.highride.co.nz) Offers backcountry trips on quad bikes ($155) and horseback rides ($80 to $95) along the Upukerora River. Combo deals ($235) are available.

Te Anau Bike Hire BICYCLE RENTAL
(7 Mokonui St; mountain bikes per hr/day from $12/30; ⏲from 10am Sep-Apr) Mountain bikes, kids' bikes and tandems.

Tours

Southern Lakes Helicopters SCENIC FLIGHTS
(☎03-249 7167; www.southernlakeshelicopters.co.nz; Lakefront Dr) Flights over Te Anau for 25 minutes ($195), longer trips over Doubtful, Dusky and Milford Sounds (from $540), and a chopper/walk/boat option on the Kepler Track ($185).

Wings & Water Te Anau SCENIC FLIGHTS
(☎03-249 7405; www.wingsandwater.co.nz; Lakefront Dr) Ten-minute local flights (adult/child $95/55), and longer flights over the Kepler Track and Doubtful and Milford Sounds (from $225).

Sleeping

Accommodation can get booked out in the peak season (late December to February). Book early if possible.

Ask at DOC for directions to **Queens Reach campsite**, 6km south of town towards Manapouri. Basic facilities only (no toilets).

Te Anau Lodge B&B B&B $$$
(☎03-249 7477; www.teanaulodge.com; 52 Howden St; d $240-350; @📶) The former 1930s-built Sisters of Mercy Convent, relocated to a grand location just north of town, is a positively decadent accommodation option. Sip your drink in a chesterfield in front of the fire, retire to your spa before collapsing on a king-size bed, then awaken to a fresh, delicious breakfast in the old chapel.

Blue Mountain Cottages LODGE $$$
(☎03-249 9030; www.bluemountaincottages.co.nz; Hwy 95; cabins $260) These family-friendly self-contained cabins surrounded by farmland 8km south of town sleep up to four. Fresh baked goods and organic produce and vegies are often available for guests. The owners' son Jayden is usually keen to show visitors around the 8-hectare rural property.

Bob & Maxines HOSTEL $
(☎03-249 7429; bob.anderson@woosh.co.nz; 20 Paton Pl, off Oraka St; dm/d $31/82; @) Only 2.5km out of town, off the Te Anau–Milford Hwy, this relaxed and modern hostel gets rave reviews for the big mountain vistas from the communal lounge. Warm up beside the woodburner, cook up a storm in the spacious well-equipped kitchen, or just chill out. Bikes are available to get you back into town.

Keiko's B&B B&B $$
(☎03-249 9248; www.keikos.co.nz; 228 Milford Rd; d $165-195; ⏲closed Jun-Aug; 📶) The private, self-contained cottages here are lovely, and the entirety is surrounded by Japanese-style gardens. A Japanese breakfast in the morning and a bamboo-bordered hot tub in the evening are other essential extras.

Cosy Kiwi MOTEL $$
(☎0800 249 700, 03-249 7475; www.cosykiwi.com; 186 Milford Rd; d $150-210; @📶) This smart motel with modern, well-appointed rooms is just a short stroll from bustling downtown Te Anau. Breakfast is included, and host Eleanor usually offers a couple of cooked options.

Barnyard Backpackers HOSTEL $
(☎03-249 8006; www.barnyardbackpackers.com; 80 Mt York Rd, off SH95; dm $29-33, d $76; @) On a deer farm 9km south of town, this rustic communal building and its collection of log cabins sit on a view-laden hillside. Cabins are comfortable, with en-suite bathrooms, and the main lodge is great for playing pool or sitting around the central fireplace.

Rosie's Backpacker Homestay HOSTEL $
(☎03-249 8431; backpack@paradise.net.nz; 23 Tom Plato Dr; dm/d $31/74; ⏲closed Jun-Jul; @📶) You're immediately made to feel part of the family in this small and intimate homestay. It's a short walk north of the town centre.

Te Anau Top 10 Holiday Park HOLIDAY PARK $
(☎03-249 7462, 0800 249 746; www.teanautop10.co.nz; 128 Te Anau Tce; sites $38, units $72-160; @📶) Near the town and lake with private camping sites, a playground, a sauna, bike hire, a barbecue area and modern kitchen facilities. Cabins and units run from basic to fancy.

Te Anau Lakeview Holiday Park HOLIDAY PARK $
(☎03-249 7457, 0800 483 262; www.teanauholidaypark.co.nz; 77 Te Anau-Manapouri Rd; sites from $20, dm $35, s $40, units $84-270) This sprawling lakeside complex combines the Te Anau Lakeview campsite with West Arm singles accommodation (pretty basic and institutional, but more private than dorms), and Steamers backpackers (characterless rooms but sharing modern communal areas). The new Marakura Apartments are chic and modern.

Te Anau YHA HOSTEL $
(☎03-249 7847; www.yha.co.nz; 29 Mokonui St; dm $33-42, s $70, d $90-120; @📶) This centrally located and modern hostel has great facilities and comfortable, colourful rooms. Lounge in the hammock, barbecue in the grassy backyard, or get cosy by the wood fire.

Eating

Fat Duck RESTAURANT $$
(☎03-249 8480; 124 Town Centre; breakfast $10-17, lunch & dinner mains $22-38; ⏱8.30am-late; 📶) Dishes are tasty and hearty in proportions, with imaginative variations on crispy duck, pork belly and salmon. There's a bar as long as Doubtful Sound if you just want a drink before kicking on somewhere else. Sometimes closed Monday and Tuesday outside the peak season.

Redcliff Bar & Restaurant RESTAURANT $$$
(☎03-249 7431; 12 Mokonui St; mains $29-42; ⏱5pm-late) Housed in a replica old settler's cottage, Redcliff showcases locally sourced produce in a convivial atmosphere. Try the wild Fiordland venison or tender herby hare. Bookings aren't taken, so kick off with a drink in the rustic front bar. There's occasional live music and a permanent friendly vibe with excellent service.

Sandfly Café CAFE $
(9 The Lane; breakfast & lunch $7-17) This is a lovely, chilled-out place to relax. Enjoy excellent coffee and cruisy music, all-day breakfasts, and yummy baking including excellent wraps, muffins and hearty bacon-and-egg pies.

Olive Tree Café & Restaurant CAFE $$
(52 Town Centre; snacks & burgers $10-15, mains $23-34) Olive Tree is warm and funky inside, with excellent outdoor areas to sip coffee in the sun or enjoy a tasty Mediterranean-tinged meal. Build up your pre–Milford Track energy reserves with eggs Benedict or hearty pizzas with organic toppings.

Miles Better Pies PIES $
(cnr Town Centre & Mokonui St; pies $4-6) The selection includes gourmet venison, Thai curry or apricot pies. There are a few pavement tables, but sitting beside the lake is nicer; the pies also make a good snack for the road.

Mainly Seafood FISH & CHIPS $
(Te Anau Tce; snacks & burgers $6-15; ⏱noon-9pm) A lakefront location, mountain views and perfectly executed fish and chips and gourmet burgers. Make this humble food truck your Te Anau snack stop of choice.

Kebabs 2 Go KEBABS $
(Town Centre; kebabs & burgers $10-16) Celebrate your return to civilisation after the Kepler or Milford Tracks with the gulity pleasure of a chilli lamb kebab and a sweet slice of baklava.

Fresh Choice Supermarket SUPERMARKET
(1 The Lane) Good wine and beer selection.

Drinking & Entertainment

Ranch Bar & Grill PUB
(Town Centre) Look forward to happy hour from 8pm to 9pm and good-value Sunday-night roast dinners ($15). It's the locals' choice for the best pub meals in town.

Moose PUB
(84 Lakefront Dr) The cavernous lakefront Moose has big-screen sports and a sunny patio. It also does meals ($20 to $35) and bar snacks.

Fiordland Cinema CINEMA
(☎03-249 8812; www.fiordlandcinema.co.nz; 7 The Lane; 📶) In between back-to-back showings of the excellent *Ata Whenua* (adult/child $10/5), essentially a 32-minute advertisement for stunning Fiordland scenery, Fiordland Cinema also screens Hollywood and art-house titles. The cinema's Black Dog Bar has occasional live gigs.

Shopping

Bev's Tramping Gear OUTDOOR EQUIPMENT
(☎03-249 7389; www.bevs-hire.co.nz; 16 Homer St; ⏱9am-noon & 5.30-7pm Nov-Apr, closed Sun morning) Topographical maps for sale and tramping and camping equipment for hire. From May to October, open by prior arrangement.

Te Anau Outside Sports OUTDOOR EQUIPMENT
(www.outsidesports.co.nz; 38 Town Centre) Tramping and camping equipment for sale or hire.

Information

Department of Conservation Visitor Centre (DOC; ☎03-249 0200; www.doc.govt.nz; cnr Lakefront Dr & Te Anau-Manapouri Rd; ⏰8.30am-4.30pm) Includes the Great Walks counter for bookings and confirmed tickets for the Milford, Routeburn and Kepler Tracks. Computer terminals with NZ-wide DOC information are also available.

Fiordland i-SITE (☎03-249 8900; www.fiordland.org.nz; 85 Lakefront Dr; ⏰8.30am-5.30pm) Activities, accommodation and bus bookings.

Fiordland Medical Centre (☎03-249 7007; Luxmore Dr; ⏰8am-5.30pm Mon-Fri, 9am-noon Sat)

Post office (102 Town Centre) Located in bookshop.

Real Journeys (☎0800 656 501; www.realjourneys.co.nz; Lakefront Dr; ⏰9am-5pm) Fiordland-focused tours and activities.

Southern Discoveries (☎0800 264 536; www.southerndiscoveries.co.nz; Lakefront Dr; ⏰8am-6pm Mon-Fri & 9.30am-6pm Sat-Sun) For information and booking activities. Outside opening hours there's a handy 24-hour information touch screen.

Getting There & Away

InterCity (www.intercity.co.nz) has daily bus services between Te Anau and Queenstown (2½ hours), Invercargill (2½ hours) and Dunedin (4¾ hours). Buses depart outside Kiwi Country on Miro St.

Bottom Bus (☎03-477 9083; www.travelheadfirst.com) is a hop-on, hop-off bus service linking Te Anau to Queenstown, Invercargill and Milford Sound (1½ hours). **Naked Bus** (www.nakedbus.com) links Te Anau with Queenstown, Invercargill and Milford Sound.

From November to April, **Topline Tours** (☎03-249 8059; www.toplinetours.co.nz) run a Te Anau–Queenstown shuttle.

For trampers:

Tracknet (☎0800 483 262; www.tracknet.net) has daily shuttles to the Kepler, Hollyford and Milford Tracks, and to the western end of the Routeburn, Greenstone and Caples Tracks at the Divide. The Kepler Water Taxi (p609) runs regularly across the lake to Brod Bay on the Kepler Track in summer. **Wings & Water** (☎03-249 7405; www.wingsandwater.co.nz) provides transport to Supper Cove ($330 per person, minimum two passengers) for Dusky Sound trampers.

Te Anau–Milford Hwy

If you don't have the opportunity to hike into Fiordland's wilderness, the 119km road from Te Anau to Milford (SH94) is the most easily accessible taste of its vastness and beauty.

Head out from Te Anau early (8am) or later in the morning (11am) to avoid the tour buses heading for midday sound cruises. See the Milford Sound section for important information about chains and avalanches (in winter) and petrol (always).

The trip takes two to 2½ hours if you drive straight through, but take time to stop and experience the majestic landscape. Pull off the road and explore the many viewpoints and nature walks en route. Pick up the *Fiordland National Park Day Walks* brochure ($1 from the DOC or Fiordland i-SITE in Te Anau or free at www.doc.govt.nz).

The first part of the road meanders through rolling farmland atop the lateral moraine of the glacier that once gouged out Lake Te Anau. The road passes **Te Anau Downs** (there's accommodation here at Fiordland National Park Lodge) after 29km and heads towards the entrance of Fiordland National Park, passing patches of beech (red, silver and mountain), alluvial flats and meadows.

Just past the **McKay Creek** campsite (at 51km) are great views over Eglinton Valley with sheer mountains either side and Pyramid Peak (2295m) and Ngatimamoe Peak (2164m) ahead. The boardwalk at Mirror Lakes (at 58km) takes you through beech forest and wetlands, and on a calm day the lakes reflect the mountains across the valley. **Knob's Creek** (at 63km) also has accommodation.

At the 77km mark is the area referred to as O Tapara, or more commonly as **Cascade Creek**. O Tapara is the original name of nearby Lake Gunn, and was a stopover historically for Maori parties heading to Anita Bay in search of *pounamu* (greenstone). A walking track (45 minutes return) passes through tall red beech forest ringing with bird calls. Side trails lead to quiet lakeside beaches.

At 84km the vegetation changes as you pass across the **Divide**, the lowest east–west pass in the Southern Alps. There's a large roadside shelter here for walkers either finishing or starting the Routeburn, Greenstone or Caples Tracks; it's also used as a terminal for trampers' bus services. A walk from the shelter, initially through beech forest along the start of the Routeburn, then climbing up alpine tussockland to **Key Summit** (two hours return), offers spectacular views of the three valleys that radiate from this point.

From the Divide, the road falls into the beech forest of the **Hollyford Valley** (stop at Pop's View for a great outlook) and there's a worthwhile detour to Gunns Camp (p615) 8km along an unsealed road. About 9km further, at the end of that road, is a walk to the high **Humboldt Falls** (30 minutes return) and the start of the Hollyford Track.

Back on the main road to Milford, the road climbs to the **Homer Tunnel**, 101km from Te Anau and framed by a spectacular, high-walled, ice-carved amphitheatre. The tunnel is one-way outside avalanche season, with the world's most alpine set of traffic lights to direct traffic. Kea (alpine parrots) hang around the eastern end of the tunnel looking for food from tourists. Don't feed them as it's bad for their health. Dark, magnificently rough-hewn and dripping with water, the 1207m-long tunnel emerges at the other end at the head of the spectacular **Cleddau Valley**.

About 10km before Milford, the **Chasm Walk** (20 minutes return and even accessible by wheelchair, though you might appreciate assistance on the steeper parts) is well worth a stop. The forest-cloaked Cleddau River plunges through eroded boulders in a narrow chasm, creating deep falls and a natural rock bridge. From here, watch for glimpses of **Mt Tutoko** (2746m), Fiordland's highest peak, above the beech forest just before Milford.

HOLLYFORD TRACK

This dramatic track starts in the midst of lowland forest, crossing mountain streams and passing pretty waterfalls as it follows the broad Hollyford River valley all the way to the sea. The Tasman coast makes a satisfying end point, with dolphins, seals and penguins often greeting hikers on their arrival. However, it does mean backtracking another four days back to your start point unless you take one of the sneaky shortcut options.

The 56km track is graded as a moderate hike, but involves some creek crossings and suffers frequent flash floods that can leave trekkers waiting it out en route for several days until the trail becomes passable. The trickiest part of the route is the ominously named Demon Trail (10km) alongside Lake McKerrow. It's imperative that you check with DOC in Te Anau for the latest track and weather conditions and have detailed maps.

Tracknet (☎0800 483 262; www.tracknet.net) has shuttles between the Hollyford Rd turn-off and Te Anau ($52, one hour) and Queenstown ($90, 3¾ hours).

Options for reducing the length of the there-and-back journey include hitching a jetboat ride south with **Hollyford Track Guided Walks** (☎03-442 3000, 0800 832 226; www.hollyfordtrack.com; $110) for the length of Lake McKerrow; book in advance. A more luxurious, three-day guided walk ($1795) includes fancy accommodation, jetboat trips in both directions along Lake McKerrow and a flight back to Milford Sound from the coastal finish line at Martins Bay.

You can also arrange a flight between Martins Bay and civilisation with **Air Fiordland** (☎03-249 6720; www.airfiordland.com) for up to four people (Te Anau/Milford Sound $620/1240). The price is per flight, so you can share the cost. Hollyford Track Guided Walks sometimes has empty seats when it flies from Milford Sound to pick up its walkers at Martins Bay, and can drop you at Martins Bay by plane ($145) or helicopter ($195).

These services run only on specific dates from October to April, and independent walkers must pre-book with Hollyford Track Guided Walks.

MILFORD TRACK

The 53.5km Milford Track is one of the world's finest walks. The number of walkers is limited in the Great Walks season (late October to late April), and you must follow a one-way, four-day set itinerary. Accommodation is only in huts (camping isn't allowed).

Even in summer, expect *lots* of rain, in the wake of which water will cascade everywhere and small streams will become raging torrents within minutes.

In the off-season, there's limited trail transport, the huts aren't staffed, and some

TE WAHIPOUNAMU SOUTHWEST NEW ZEALAND WORLD HERITAGE AREA

In the southwest corner of New Zealand, the combination of four huge national parks make up Te Wahipounamu Southwest New Zealand World Heritage Area. Te Wahipounamu (the Place of Greenstone) covers 2.6 million hectares and is recognised internationally for its cultural significance to the Ngai Tahu, as well as for the area's unique fauna and wildlife. Te Wahipounamu incorporates the following national parks:

» Fiordland National Park

» Aoraki/Mt Cook National Park

» Westland Tai Poutini National Park

» Mt Aspiring National Park

Milford Track

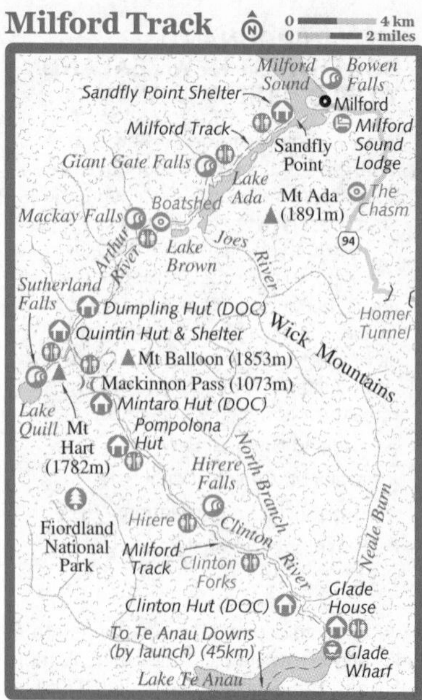

bridges are removed. During winter, snow and avalanches make it unsafe. It's vital to check avalanche risk with DOC.

BOOKINGS

You can walk the track independently or with a guided tour. For independent bookings, contact DOC in Te Anau or book online at www.doc.govt.nz. Pick up track tickets at DOC in Te Anau before departure.

The track must be booked during the Great Walks season (late October to late April). Book as far ahead as possible. Bookings open up 12 months before the start of the following season.

Ultimate Hikes (☎03-450 1940, 0800 659 255; www.ultimatehikes.co.nz; adult/child Dec-Mar from $1995/1790, Apr & Nov $1830/1640) has five-day guided walks staying at private lodges. A one-day 11km sampler is also available (adult/child $195/123).

WALKING THE TRACK

The trail starts at Glade House, at the northern end of Lake Te Anau, accessed by boat from Te Anau Downs or Te Anau. The track follows the flat bottom of the Clinton River Valley up to its head at Lake Mintaro, passing through rainforest and crystal-clear streams. From Mintaro you cross the dramatic **Mackinnon Pass**, which on a clear day gives spectacular views back to yesterday's Clinton Valley and forward to tomorrow's Arthur Valley. (If the pass appears clear when you arrive at Mintaro Hut, make the effort to climb it, as it may not be clear the next day.) From the pass a long, wooden staircase leads you down to Arthur River, following alongside the rapids. The trail then continues down to Quintin and Dumpling Huts and through the valley rainforest to Milford Sound. You can leave your pack at the Quintin public shelter while you make the return walk to the graceful, 630m-high **Sutherland Falls**, NZ's tallest falls.

Estimated walking times:

DAY	ROUTE	TIME
1	Glade Wharf to Glade House	20min
1	Glade House to Clinton Hut	1-1½hr
2	Clinton Hut to Mintaro Hut	6hr
3	Mintaro Hut to Dumpling Hut	6-7hr
3	Side trip to Sutherland Falls	1½hr return
4	Dumpling Hut to Sandfly Point	5½-6hr

TRANSPORT TO GLADE WHARF

During the Great Walks season, **Tracknet** (☎0800 483 262; www.tracknet.net) drives up from Te Anau to Te Anau Downs ($22). Tracknet also offers the option of transport from Queenstown to Te Anau Downs ($65). **Real Journeys** (☎0800 656 501; www.realjourneys.co.nz; adult/child $190/123.50; ⊙Nov-mid-Apr) will then run you by boat from Te Anau Downs to Glade Wharf near the start of the track. Both of these trips can be booked at DOC in Te Anau at the same time as you book your walk. Outside the Great Walks season, talk to Tracknet about transport the whole way to Glade Wharf.

TRANSPORT FROM SANDFLY POINT

There are ferries leaving Sandfly Point at 2pm and 3.15pm for the Milford Sound cruise wharf (adult/child $34/19.50). From there you can bus back to Te Anau with Tracknet ($47, 2½ hours). These can both be booked via DOC at Te Anau.

PACKAGES

Cruise Te Anau (☎03-249 7593; www.cruiseteanau.co.nz) does a bus-boat combination trip for around $180.

Sleeping

Along SH94 are basic DOC campsites ($6 per person), the majority of them situated between 45km and 81km from Te Anau. You'll find them in *Conservation Campsites – South Island* (free from DOC in Te Anau) or at www.doc.govt.nz.

Milford Sound Lodge LODGE $$
(☎03-249 8071; www.milfordlodge.com; just off SH94; sites per person from $18, dm $30-33, d $85) Alongside the Cleddau River, this simple but comfortable lodge has an unhurried, ends-of-the-earth air. There's no TV, and travellers and trampers relax in the large lounges to discuss their experiences. There's a tiny shop/cafe/bar and a free shuttle to Milford Sound, just 1.5km away. Very comfortable chalets ($255) enjoy an absolute riverside location. Booking ahead is strongly recommended.

Gunns Camp CABINS $
(gunnscamp@ruralinzone.net; Hollyford Rd; sites/dm/cabins $12/20/55) Gunns Camp, also known as Hollyford Camp, is on Hollyford Rd about halfway between SH94 (8km) and the start of the Hollyford Track (9km). The old Public Works cabins are very basic (linen hire is $5 per bed), and heating is via a coal or wood-fired stove (fuel provided). A generator supplies limited electricity, turning off at 10pm, and there are hot showers and a spacious new kitchen block. There's also a small shop and an eccentric museum (adult/child $1/30c; guests free) with pioneering memorabilia. Cash and credit cards only – no Eftpos.

Knob's Flat MOTEL $$
(☎03-249 9122; www.knobsflat.co.nz; sites per person $10, studio/motel units $120/150) In the grassy Eglinton Valley, 63km from Te Anau, Knob's Flat has comfortable units catering to walkers and anglers. TV, email and stress have no place here, and mountain bikes can be hired. Recent developments include a campsite (unpowered sites only) and a spacious amenities block.

Fiordland National Park Lodge LODGE $$
(☎0800 500 805, 03-249 7811; www.teanau-milfordsound.co.nz; SH94; dm $28, d hotel $65-75, d motel $130; @📶) At Te Anau Downs (29km from Te Anau) at the head of the lake where boats depart for the Milford Track, Fiordland National Park Lodge has accommodation ranging from dorms and backpacker doubles to self-contained motel units. It's popular with Milford Track walkers, but other travellers are also welcome.

Milford Sound

POP 170

The first sight of Milford Sound is stunning. Sheer rocky cliffs rise out of still, dark waters, and forests clinging to the slopes sometimes relinquish their hold, causing a 'tree avalanche' into the waters. The spectacular, photogenic 1692m-high Mitre Peak rises dead ahead.

A cruise on Milford Sound is Fiordland's most accessible experience, complete with seals, dolphins and an average annual rainfall of 7m – more than enough to fuel cascading waterfalls and add a shimmering moody mist to the scene.

Milford Sound receives about half a million visitors each year, many of them crammed into the peak months (January and February). Some 14,000 arrive by foot, via the Milford Track, which ends at the sound. Many more drive from Te Anau, but most arrive via the multitude of bus tours. But don't worry. Out on the water all this humanity seems tiny compared to nature's vastness.

Sights & Activities

Unique environmental circumstances have allowed the sound to become home to some rarely glimpsed marine life. Heavy rainfall sluicing straight off the rocky slopes washes significant organic matter into the ocean, creating a 5m-deep permanent tannin-stained freshwater layer above the warmer sea water. This dark layer filters out much of the sunlight and, coupled with the sound's calm, protected waters, replicates deep-ocean conditions. The result is that deep-water species thrive not far below the surface. A similar situation exists at Doubtful Sound. One of the best perspectives you can get of Milford Sound is from a kayak at water level, dwarfed by the cliffs.

Rosco's Milford Kayaks KAYAKING
(☎03-249 8500, 0800 476 726; www.roscosmilfordkayaks.com; trips $130-175) Recommended excursions include the 'Morning Glory', a challenging early-morning kayak (around five hours in the boat) the full length of the fiord to Anita Bay, and the 'Stirling Sunriser', which includes kayaking under the 151m-high Stirling Falls. Another option includes a 20-minute paddle around Deepwater Basin to Sandfly Point and a 3½-hour walk on the Milford Track ($89). Rosco's has a booking office in Te Anau's main drag.

Fiordland Wilderness Experiences KAYAKING
(☎0800 200 434, 03-249-7700; www.seakayakfiordland.co.nz; per person $145; ⊙Sep-Apr) Guided six-hour paddles on Milford Sound.

Milford Discovery Centre AQUARIUM
(adult/child $36/18; ⊙9am-3.45pm) Incorporates interactive displays on the natural history, geology and environment of Milford Sound, and the Deep Underwater Observatory, a five-storey mostly submerged building suspended from pontoons. Four storeys underwater are deep-water corals, tube anemones and bottom-dwelling sea perch. The Discovery Centre can be visited on boat trips with Milford Sound Cruises and Mitre Peak Cruises.

Tawaki Adventures DIVING
(☎0800 829 254; www.southernaqua.co.nz) Trips include a three-hour boat cruise and two guided dives of a total of 30 minutes ($159); it's an extra $99 for gear hire. If you don't dive you can join the boat trip anyway ($99 plus $45 to hire snorkelling gear).

Tours

Each Milford Sound cruise company claims to be quieter, smaller, bigger, cheaper or in some way preferable to the rest. What really makes a difference is the timing of the cruise. Most bus tours aim for 1pm sailings so if you avoid that time of day there'll be less people on the boat (and on the road). With some companies you get a better price on cruises outside rush hour too.

If you're particularly keen on wildlife, ask whether there'll be a nature guide on board. It's wise to book ahead regardless. You generally need to arrive 20 minutes before departure. Most companies offer coach transfers from Te Anau for an additional cost. Day trips from Queenstown make for a very long 13-hour day.

All the cruises visit the mouth of the sound, only 15km from the wharf, poking their prow into the choppy waves of the Tasman Sea. The shorter cruises visit less of the en route 'highlights', which include Bowen Falls, Mitre Peak, Anita Bay and Stirling Falls. You'll have a good chance of seeing dolphins, seals and penguins. All cruises leave from the huge **cruise terminal** (⊙8am-5.15pm Oct-Apr, 9am-4.15pm May-Sep), a 10-minute walk from the cafe and car park.

Real Journeys BOAT TOUR
(☎03-249 7416, 0800 656 501; www.realjourneys.co.nz; adult/child from $68/22) Lots of cruises from this big company including 1¾-hour scenic cruises (adult $68 to $90, child $22). The company also does 2½-hour nature cruises (adult $75 to $95, child $22) with a nature guide for commentary and Q&A. Real Journeys does overnight cruises on two of its boats. You can kayak and take nature tours in tender crafts en route. The cost includes all meals but transport from Te Anau is additional. All depart from the Milford terminal around 4.30pm and return around 9.30am the following day. Cheaper prices apply in May and September. The *Milford Wanderer*, modelled on an old trading scow, accommodates 36 passengers in two- and four-bunk cabins (with shared bathrooms) and costs $325/162.50 per adult/child. The *Milford Mariner* sleeps 60 in more upmarket, en-suite, twin-share cabins ($495/247.50 per adult/child).

Jucy Cruize BOAT TOUR
(☎0800 500 121; www.jucycruize.co.nz; adult/child from $65/15) A smaller, less-crowded experience with 1½-hour trips on a comfortable boat with lots of deck space.

Mitre Peak Cruises BOAT TOUR
(☎0800 744 633, 03-249 8110; www.mitrepeak.com; adult/child from $68/16.50) Cruises in smallish boats with a maximum capacity of 75. The 4.30pm cruise is good because many larger boats are heading back at this time.

Milford Sound Cruises BOAT TOUR
(☎03-441 1137, 0800 264 536; www.southerndiscoveries.co.nz; adult/child from $73/15) A range of trips exploring Milford Sound, all lasting around two hours. The 2¼-hour wildlife cruise (adult $73 to $90, child $15) is more intimate, and operates on a smaller boat.

Eating & Drinking

Blue Duck Café & Bar CAFE $$
(snacks $5-15, buffet lunch $17-21; ⊙cafe 8.30am-4pm, bar 4pm-late; @) Serving sandwiches and a lunch buffet, and at night the attached bar sees a mix of travellers and trampers tucking in to the $25 beer and pizza deal. You'll find the Blue Duck on the edge of the main carpark at Milford Sound.

Getting There & Away

Bus

InterCity (www.intercity.co.nz) runs daily bus services from Queenstown (4½ hours) and Te Anau (1½ hours) to Milford Sound. **Naked Bus** (www.nakedbus.com) also runs from Te Anau to the sound. Many bus trips include a boat cruise on the sound; most are around $150 from Te Anau (or around $200 from Queenstown).

Trampers' buses from **Tracknet** (☎0800 483 262; www.tracknet.net) also operate from Te Anau and Queenstown and will pick up at the Milford Sound Lodge. All these buses pass the Divide and the start/end of the Routeburn, Greenstone and Caples Tracks.

Car

Fill up with petrol in Te Anau before setting off. Chains must be carried on avalanche-risk days from May to November (there will be signs on the road), and can be hired from most service stations in Te Anau.

Manapouri

POP 210

Manapouri is largely used as a jumping-off point for cruises to the sublime Doubtful Sound, and as a base for walking expeditions.

In 1969, Manapouri was the site of NZ's first major environmental campaign. The original plan for the West Arm power station, built to provide cheap electricity for the aluminium smelter near Invercargill, included raising the level of the lake by 30m. A petition gathered a staggering 265,000 signatures (17% of voting-age New Zealanders at the time) and the issue contributed to the downfall of the government at the following election. The action was successful: the power station was built but the lake's level remains unchanged. It was a success that spawned increasing national environmental action through the 1970s and '80s. West Arm power station is NZ's largest producer of electricity: a tunnel dug through the mountain from Lake Manapouri to Doubtful Sound drops a hefty 180m from lake to sound, driving the power station's turbines.

Activities

Day Walks TRAMPING

With some form of water transport (kayak, dinghy or water taxi), you can cross the Waiau River for some easy low-altitude day walks, detailed in the DOC brochure *Fiordland National Park Day Walks* (www.doc.govt.nz). A walk along the **Circle Track** (three hours return) can be extended to **Hope Arm** (five to six hours return), crossing the uninvitingly named Stinking Creek. Although Te Anau is the usual access point for the Kepler Track, the trail touches the northern end of Lake Manapouri and part of it can be done as a day walk from Manapouri; access is via the swing bridge at Rainbow Reach, 10km north of town. From Pearl Harbour there's also a walk that doesn't require crossing the river: to **Frasers Beach** (1½ hours return), from where you can gaze across the beautiful lake.

Dusky Track TRAMPING

Manapouri is also a staging point for the remote 84km Dusky Track, a walk that takes eight days if you tramp between Lakes Manapouri and Hauroko, with an extra two-day detour possible from Loch Maree Hut to Supper Cove on Dusky Sound. With regular tree falls, deep mud, river crossings, delaying floods and 21 three-wire bridges, this is an extremely challenging wilderness walk, suitable only for well-equipped, very experienced trampers. Contact DOC, and read Lonely Planet's *Tramping in New Zealand*, for more details. For transport options from either Te Anau or Tuatapere to the Dusky Track, contact **Lake Hauroko Tours** (☎03-226 6681; www.duskytrack.co.nz).

Adventure Kayak & Cruise KAYAKING

(☎0800 324 966; www.fiordlandadventure.co.nz) Rents kayaks from $50 per person per day for paddles on Lake Manapouri from October to April; will rent only to groups of two paddlers or more, and provide VHF radios free of charge for safety. Also offers kayaking trips on Doubtful Sound (from $239 per person).

Adventure Manapouri BOATING

(☎03-249 8070; www.adventuremanapouri.co.nz) Rowboat hire ($20 per day), water taxis and fishing trips.

Manapouri Stores BOATING

Rowboats for rent ($30 per day) and a handy map showing nearby walking trails.

Sleeping

Misty Mountain Eco-Retreat RENTAL HOUSE $$

(☎03-249 6661; www.waitahanui-hideaway.co.nz; 313 Hillside-Manapouri Rd; d $150) Surrounded by native trees and birdsong, this cosy cottage combines timber from seawashed logs retrieved from Doubtful Sound with a modern kitchen and bathroom. Decor is stylish with wooden floors and Oriental rugs, and there's a sunny deck with mountain views.

Freestone Backpackers HOSTEL $

(☎03-249 6893; www.freestone.co.nz; 270 Hillside-Manapouri Rd; dm $22-33, d $66-150) These clean, comfortable and rustic cabins nestle on a hillside about 3km east of town. Each cabin has a small kitchen, potbelly stove and verandah. Bathrooms are communal. Dorms and bedrooms in a shared house are also available. More comfortable options include accommodation ($75) with a kitchen and private bathroom, and a deluxe bed and breakfast ($150) with a spa.

Manapouri Lakeview Chalets & Motor Park HOLIDAY PARK $
(☎03-249 6624; www.manapourimotels.co.nz; SH95; sites from $33, units $58-130; @🛜) This camping ground features eclectic cabins, ranging from mock Swiss Alpine to mock shanty town. There's a fabulous fleet of old Morris Minors in various states of repair and a vintage pinball-machine collection to relive your youth.

Possum Lodge HOLIDAY PARK $
(☎03-249 6623; www.possumlodge.co.nz; 13 Murrell Ave; sites $34, dm $23, units $55-105; ⊙Oct-Easter; @🛜) A charming, shady little campsite near the lakeside, this property has old-school, relatively basic cabins and modern motel-style units. Best bring some sandfly repellent.

Eating & Drinking

Lakeside Café & Bar PUB
(68 Cathedral Dr; pizza $18-20, mains $18-34; @🛜) Serves substantial meals with a generous side order of lake views from the sunny garden bar. The public bar attached is a large, cheery affair, with crazy silver helicopters providing the wacky ventilation.

Getting There & Away

On request, **Topline Tours** (☎03-249 8059; www.toplinetours.co.nz; $20) can divert to Manapouri on their from Queenstown to Te Anau.

Doubtful Sound

Massive, magnificent Doubtful Sound is a wilderness area of rugged peaks, dense forest and thundering post-rain waterfalls. It's one of NZ's largest sounds: three times the length and 10 times the area of Milford Sound. Doubtful is also much, *much* less trafficked. If you have the time and the money, it's an essential experience. Fur seals, dolphins, Fiordland crested penguins and seals are also regular visitors.

Until relatively recently, only the most intrepid tramper or sailor ever explored Doubtful Sound. Even Captain Cook only observed it from off the coast in 1770, because he was 'doubtful' whether the winds in the sound would be sufficient to blow the ship back out to sea. The sound became more accessible when the road over Wilmot Pass opened in 1959 to facilitate construction of the West Arm power station.

Tours

Doubtful Sound is only accessible by tour. You'll cross Lake Manapouri by boat from Manapouri to the West Arm power station, drive by bus the winding 22km through dense rainforest to Deep Cove (permanent population: one), then head out on Doubtful Sound on another boat. Many tours include the power station. The easiest place to base yourself is Manapouri, although many tours pick up in Te Anau and Queenstown.

Real Journeys BOAT TOUR
(☎0800 656 501; www.realjourneys.co.nz) Has a Wilderness Cruise day trip (adult/child $235/65), beginning with a 45-minute boat ride across Lake Manapouri to West Arm power station, followed by a bus ride over Wilmot Pass to the sound, which you explore on a three-hour cruise. Pick up options from Te Anau or Queenstown are also available. To venture underground and admire a power station, take a separate Lake Manapouri cruise (adult/child $70/22, October to April). From September to May, Real Journeys also runs a Doubtful Sound overnight cruise. The *Fiordland Navigator* sleeps 70 and has twin-share, en-suite cabins (per adult/child from $675/337.50) and quad-share bunkrooms ($375/187.50). Transport to and from Te Anau or Queenstown is available. Prices include meals and kayaking or tender-craft trips.

Adventure Kayak & Cruise KAYAKING
(☎0800 324 966; www.fiordlandadventure.co.nz; ⊙late Sep-May) Kayaking day trips ($239) and overnight kayaking and camping trips ($269).

Fiordland Wilderness Experiences KAYAKING
(☎0800 200 434; www.seakayakfiordland.co.nz; per person $399-2250; ⊙Oct-Apr) Two- to five-day kayaking and camping trips around Doubtful Sound, and five-day kayaking trips in remote Dusky Sound. Accommodation is on the expedition vessel *Breaksea Girl* and includes all meals and helicopter transfers.

Deep Cove Charters CRUISE
(☎0800 249 682; www.doubtful-sound.com; bunk beds per person $500, private cabin $1200) Intimate overnight cruises with a maximum of

12 passengers. Includes meals, and you can fish for your own dinner.

Fiordland Cruises CRUISE
(☎0800 483 262; www.fiordlandcruises.co.nz; from $550) Overnight cruise including wildlife viewing and fishing. Maximum 12 passengers. Includes meals and transfers to/from Te Anau.

Fiordland Expeditions CRUISE
(☎0508 888 656; www.fiordlandexpeditions.co.nz; from $495) Overnight cruise. Ten-passenger maximum. Kayaking, diving, fishing, and dinner is whatever is caught from the boat.

Fiordland Explorer Charters CRUISE
(☎0800 434 673; www.doubtfulsoundcruise.com; day cruise adult/child $220/80) Day cruise with maximum of 20 people. Includes power-station tour and three hours on the sound.

Sleeping

Simple accommodation is available on the sound, but most travellers join an overnight cruise or kayak/camping trip to stay on the sound.

Deep Cove Hostel HOSTEL $
(☎03-218 7655; www.deepcovehostel.co.nz; per person $26-41; @) Bunks, cooking facilities and dinghies, all situated right on Doubtful Sound with a number of bush walks radiating from it. It's predominantly used by school groups, but casual guests are welcome. Booking ahead is essential.

SOUTHERN SCENIC ROUTE

The quiet, unhurried Southern Scenic Route begins in Queenstown and heads south via Te Anau to Tuatapere, Riverton and Invercargill. From Invercargill it continues north through the Catlins to Dunedin. See www.southernscenicroute.co.nz or pick up the free *Southern Scenic Route* map. Public transport is limited, but **Bottom Bus** (☎03-477 9083; www.travelheadfirst.com) offers regular shuttles.

From Manapouri the road follows the Waiau River south between the forested Takitimu and Hunter Mountains. Near Clifden is the elegant **Clifden Suspension Bridge**, built in 1899 and one of the longest bridges in the South Island. **Clifden (Waiau) Caves** are signposted on Otautau Rd, 2km from the Clifden Rd corner. These caves offer a scramble through crawl spaces and up ladders. Bring a friend, a spare torch and lots of caution. Visit Tuatapere visitor information centre for conditions and a map beforehand.

Just south of the suspension bridge is a turn-off to a walking track through **Dean Forest**, a reserve of ancient totara trees, 23km off the main road. From Clifden you can drive 30km of mostly unsealed road to Lake Hauroko, the deepest lake in NZ and surrounded by dark, brooding, steeply forested slopes. The area has many ancient *urupa* (burial sites) so be respectful and keep to trails. The Dusky Track also ends (or begins) here. **Lake Hauroko Tours** (☎03-226 6681; www.duskytrack.co.nz; tours incl lunch $120; ⊙Nov-Apr) has day-trip return tours from Tuatapere.

Tuatapere

POP 740

Formerly a timber-milling town, sleepy Tuatapere is now largely a farming centre. Those early woodcutters were very efficient, so only a remnant of a once large tract of native podocarp (conifer) forest remains.

Tuatapere visitor information centre (☎03-226 6739, 0800 486 774; www.humpridgetrack.co.nz; 31 Orawia Rd; ⊙9.30am-5pm, limited hours in winter) assists with visits to the Clifden Caves, Hump Ridge hut passes and transport. Adjacent is the **Bushman's Museum** (admission by donation), featuring an interesting photographic record of the area's timber-milling past

For more information on Tuatapere and the Western Southland area, see www.westernsouthland.co.nz. Don't leave without trying some of the excellent local sausages.

Activities

Tuatapere Hump Ridge Track TRAMPING
(☎03-226 6739; www.humpridgetrack.co.nz) The excellent 53km Tuatapere Hump Ridge Track climbs to craggy subalpine heights with views north to Fiordland and south to Stewart Island, and then descends through lush native forests of rimu and beech to the rugged coast. There's bird life aplenty, and the chance to see Hector's dolphins on the lonely windswept coast back to the start point. En route the path crosses a number of towering historic wooden viaducts, including NZ's highest. Beginning and ending at Bluecliffs Beach on Te Waewae Bay, 20km from Tuatapere, the track takes three fairly long days to complete.

Estimated walking times:

ROUTE	TIME
Bluecliffs Beach Car Park to Okaka Lodge	7-9hr
Okaka Lodge to Port Craig Village	7-9hr
Port Craig Village to Bluecliffs Beach Car Park	5-6hr

It's essential to book for this track, which is administered privately rather than by DOC. No-frills summer bookings cost from $130 for two nights, and there are also guided, jetboating and helihiking options.

Humpridge Jet JETBOATING

(☎0800 270 556; www.wildernessjet.co.nz; from $210) Options include a jetboat/helicopter combo or overnighting at the remote Waitutu Lodge.

W-Jet JETBOATING

(☎0800 376 174; www.wjet.co.nz; from $225) Includes a guided nature walk and barbecue.

Sleeping & Eating

Last Light Lodge HOLIDAY PARK $

(☎03-226 6667; www.lastlightlodge.com; 2 Clifden Hwy; sites from $15, dm $30, units $56-66) A funky spot in Tuatapere with loads of simple overnight options including camping, dorms and cabins. The attached Last Light Cafe does robust breakfasts and yummy snacks amid coolly retro furniture. Most of the food is organic, and lots of ingredients are sourced from their own gardens.

Shooters Backpackers & Tuatapere Motel HOLIDAY PARK $

(☎03-226 6250; www.tuataperaccommodation.co.nz; 73 Main St; sites from $30, dm $28, units $60-110; @📶) Communal spaces include a spacious kitchen with a wood stove, a big deck and barbecue, plus a spa and sauna. Camping is on a grassy lawn; more private are double rooms and self-contained units. Jetboating, diving and fishing trips can also be arranged.

Yesteryears Café CAFE $

(3a Orawia Rd; light meals $10-15) Rip into Aunt Daisy's sugar buns and a quintessentially Kiwi milkshake, and buy homemade jams for on-the-road breakfasts. There's an interesting jumble of quirky household items from local Tuatapere families.

Tuatapere to Riverton

On SH99, around 10km south of Tuatapere, stop at the spectacular lookout at **McCracken's Rest**. Cast your eye down the arcing sweep of **Te Waewae Bay** – where Hector's dolphins and southern right whales are sometimes seen – to the snowy peaks of Fiordland.

Colac Bay is a popular holiday place and a good surfing spot. Southerlies provide the best swells here, but it's pretty consistent year-round and never crowded. **Dustez Bak Paka's & Camping Ground** (☎03-234 8399; www.dustezbakpakas.co.nz; 15 Colac Bay Rd; sites from $29, dm $29, units $55-59) has basic rooms and campsites in a grassy field. Guests can borrow surfboards. Get dinner next door at the Colac Bay Tavern. Down at the beach, the Pavilion is known around Southland for its fish, organic lamb and garden-fresh herbs. It's also a top spot for a coffee and cake break.

Riverton

POP 1850

Quiet little Riverton, only 38km short of Invercargill, is worth a lunch stop and, if near-Antarctic swimming takes your fancy, the **Riverton Rocks** area and **Taramea Bay**

LOCAL KNOWLEDGE

COLAC BAY *KERI HULME*

Where two different strands of my ancestry found themselves: an American whaler captain, rumoured to be part-Tahitian, and a Kai Tahu/Kati Mamoe woman had a son who was my great-grandfather. There's not a lot in Colac Bay except beach and surf and the local *marae*. Oh, and there's Surfer Dude riding his wave at a slant angle. Classic baches and rock-fishing...a bit of fossicking along the low-tide line, and perhaps a trip to Cozy Nook? But the quintessential attraction of Colac Bay is the sound of those seas, that surf homing in: I have spent days, listening, wandering, listening, pondering, going to sleep with sea-song in my ears. It's a really choice place to blob out for a day or three or more. Be warned that the winds can be exceedingly strong, and bear Antarctic coldness with them – but there is also frequent calm and sun...

Keri Hulme, author & poet

(don't venture past the point) are good for a dip. A few **funky galleries** are definitely worth a browse.

Riverton visitor information centre (☎03-234 8260; www.riverton-aparima.co.nz; 127 Palmerston St; ⏰10am-4pm Oct-Apr, 11am-3pm Nov-Mar) has information about exploring the region's interesting geological heritage and can advise on accommodation.

Inside the centre, **Te Hikoi Southern Journey** (☎03-234 8260; www.tehikoi.co.nz; adult/child $5/free; ⏰10am-4pm summer, 11am-3pm winter) tells the story of the area's early Maori and Pakeha history.

Beach House (126 Rocks Hwy; mains $20-34; @) is a stylish, comfortable cafe that is famous for its seafood, especially its creamy chowder. On a sunny day with a warm breeze wafting off Foveaux Strait, the outside tables are a must. The other 90% of the time, retire inside to admire the sea view warm behind the windows. To find the cafe, follow signs along the coast to the lookout.

The chic little **Mrs Clark's Café** (108 Palmerston St; meals $12-123), with lots of reused timbers, chilled-out music and South Island beers and wines, occupies an insanely turquoise building that has been various forms of eatery since 1891. We doubt if its espressos and big breakfasts were quite so delicious back then.

The **South Coast Environment Centre** (www.sces.org.nz; 154 Palmerston St) has a good range of organic fruit, vegies and meats, is the local WWOOF (World Wide Opportunities on Organic Farms) agent, and organises the Riverton farmers market (Friday afternoons).

CENTRAL SOUTHLAND

Central Southland is the gateway to Stewart Island, and also a good jumping-off point for the Catlins and Fiordland.

Invercargill

POP 50,328

Flat and suburban, with endlessly treeless streets, Invercargill won't enthrall you if you came here via the Catlins or Fiordland. Nevertheless, most travellers in Southland will find themselves here at some point – perhaps stocking up on supplies and equipment before setting off to the Catlins or Stewart Island. Discover the town's arty bits, some good restaurants and a great little microbrewery.

Sights & Activities

Southland Museum & Art Gallery GALLERY
(www.southlandmuseum.com; Queens Park, 108 Gala St; admission by donation; ⏰9am-5pm) The art gallery hosts visiting exhibitions from contemporary Maori and local artists and occasional international shows. If you're headed for Stewart Island, visit the museum's 'Beyond the Roaring Forties' exhibition.

The museum's rock stars are undoubtedly the tuatara, NZ's unique lizardlike reptiles, unchanged for 220 million years. If the slow-moving 100-years-old-and-counting patriarch Henry is any example, they're not planning to do much for the next 220 million years either.

You'll find Henry and his reptilian mates in the tuatara enclosure. Feeding time is 4pm on Fridays, and outside opening hours, there are viewing windows at the rear of the pyramid.

Burt Munro MOTORBIKES, FILM LOCATION
If you're a fan of motorcyclist Burt Munro's speedy achievements, captured in *The World's Fastest Indian* (2005), you can see his famous motorbike at **E Hayes & Sons** (www.ehayes.co.nz; 168 Dee St). Other retro two-wheelers are on display and film merchandise is for sale. **Oreti Beach** (site of Burt's race against the troop of insolent young tearaways) is 10km to the southwest and a nice spot for a swim. The **Burt Munro Challenge** (www.burtmunrochallenge.com) is a popular motorbike event held each November. There's also a good display of Munrobilia at the Southland Museum.

Invercargill Brewery BREWERY
(☎03-214 5070; www.invercargillbrewery.co.nz; 8 Wood St; ⏰11am-5.30pm Mon-Thu, to 6.30pm Fri, to 4pm Sat) Tastings are free of charge, and if you're a real beer buff, the staff may be able to show you around the brewery. Phone ahead to check. Our favourites are the crisp Biman Pilsner and the hoppy Stanley Green Pale Ale. Regular seasonal brews include the Smokin' Bishop, a German-style *rauchbier* made with smoked malt.

Anderson Park Art Gallery GALLERY
(McIvor Rd; admission by donation; ⏰gallery 10.30am-5pm, gardens 8am-dusk) This excellent gallery in a 1925 Georgian-style manor contains works from many NZ artists. The landscaped gardens are studded with trees and trails, and include a children's playground and *wharepuni* (sleeping house). The gallery is 7km north of the city centre; follow North Rd then turn right into McIvor Rd.

Queens Park PARK

Wander around the half-wild, half-tamed Queens Park, with its trees, duck ponds, children's playground and Alice's castle.

Sleeping

Many places will store luggage for guests heading to Stewart Island. Motels cluster along Hwy 1 East (Tay St) and Hwy 6 North (North Rd).

TOP CHOICE **Bushy Point Fernbirds** HOMESTAY $$

(03-213 1302; www.fernbirds.co.nz; 197 Grant Rd; s/d incl breakfast $115/135) Two friendly corgis are among the hosts at this eco-aware homestay set on the edge of 4.5 hectares of private forest reserve and wetlands. Fernbirds is very popular with birding types, so booking ahead is essential. It's five minutes' drive from central Invercargill, and rates include a guided walk in the forest reserve.

Sparky's Backpackers HOSTEL $

(03-217 2905; www.sparkysbackpackers.co.nz; 271 Tay St; dm/d incl breakfast $25/60) Free breakfast, Sparky's chocolate cake and a genuine Southland welcome all feature at this quirky cross between a homestay and a hostel. The friendly owners were busy installing a new bathroom and an outdoor spa pool when we dropped by.

Victoria Railway Hotel HISTORIC HOTEL $$

(03-218 1281, 0800 777 557; www.hotelinvercargill.com; cnr Leven & Esk Sts; d $145-195) For a spot of 19th-century luxury, the plush rooms and swanky guests' areas in this grand old refurbished hotel fit the bill. The guests' dining room is elegant and the opulent house bar is crammed with South Island wines and local beers.

Living Space HOTEL $$

(03-211 3800; www.livingspace.net; 15 Tay St; d $75-129; @) Colourful, modern decor, ergonomically savvy design and relaxed service are showcased at this transformed 1907 warehouse. The studios are not huge, but feature self-contained kitchenettes and compact bathrooms.

Southern Comfort Backpackers HOSTEL $

(03-218 3838; 30 Thomson St; dm/s/d $28/65/66) Mellow, comfortable house with a TV-free lounge (hooray!), colourful rooms and a modern, well-equipped kitchen. Doubles are spacious and the lovely gardens are crammed with fresh herbs for cooking. Cash only.

388 Tay MOTEL $$

(0508 388 829, 03-217 3881; www.388taymotel.co.nz; 388 Tay St; d $120-160;) Modern and spacious units and a friendly welcome are standard at this well-run spot that's a standout along Invercargill's Tay St motel alley.

Tuatara Lodge HOSTEL $

(03-214 0954; www.tuataralodge.co.nz; 30-32 Dee St; dm $29, d $69-80; @) Rooms here are fairly basic, but they're clean and comfortable and it's the most central of Invercargill's budget accommodation. Staff are friendly and downstairs is a groovy traveller-focused cafe-bar. Transport to/from Bluff for Stewart Island stops just outside.

Invercargill Top 10 Holiday Park HOLIDAY PARK $

(0800 486 873, 03-215 9032; www.invercargilltop10.co.nz; 77 McIvor Rd; sites from $19, units $78-150; @) This quiet leafy place 6.5km north of town has private sites and good communal facilities. Modern, comfortable studios and self-contained cabins have en suites.

Eating

Duo RESTAURANT $$

(03-218 8322; 16 Kelvin St; lunch $16-22, dinner $32; 11.30am-2pm & 5.30pm-late) The elegant Duo has good-value lunch specials and a more expensive evening menu. Standouts include smoked salmon, herb-and-feta-crusted pork steaks and oven-baked blue cod. The wine list travels mainly to nearby Central Otago for some hard-to-find boutique tipples. Booking for dinner is recommended.

The Batch CAFE $$

(173 Spey St; snacks & mains $8-15) Lots of shared tables, a relaxed beachy ambience and top-notch coffee and smoothies add up to the cafe being regularly voted Southland's best. Delicious counter food includes bagels and brownies, and a smallish wine and beer list partners healthy lunch options. Open later on Friday nights, until 7.30pm.

Seriously Good Chocolate Company CAFE $

(147 Spey St; Mon-Fri) This sunny spot a short walk from central Invercargill specialises in individual artisan chocolates (around $1.50 each). Order a coffee and then abandon yourself to the difficult task of choosing flavours. The chilli and peanut cluster variations were both good enough for us to return a second day. Like it says on the tin... seriously good.

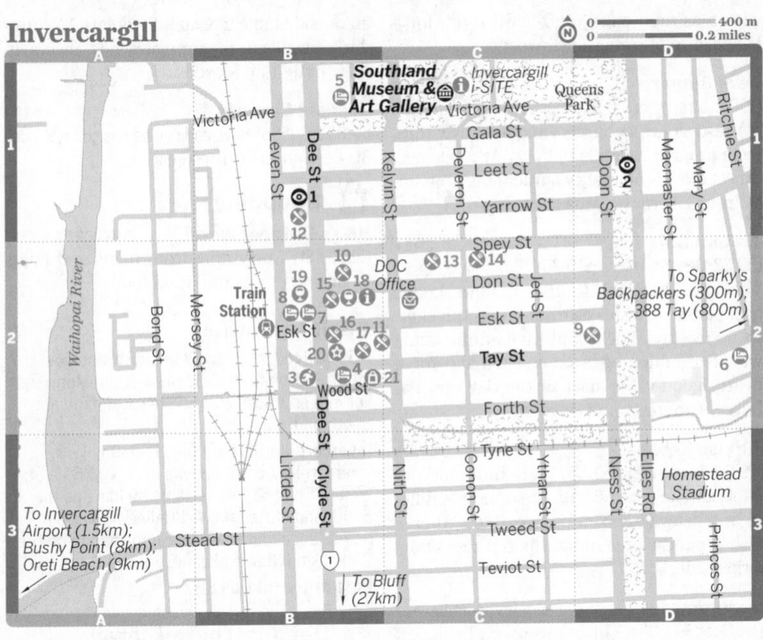

Invercargill

Top Sights
Southland Museum & Art Gallery ... C1

Sights
1 E Hayes & Sons ... B1
2 Water Tower ... D1

Activities, Courses & Tours
3 Invercargill Brewery ... B2

Sleeping
4 Living Space ... B2
5 Southern Comfort Backpackers ... B1
6 Sparky's Backpackers ... D2
7 Tuatara Lodge ... B2
8 Victoria Railway Hotel ... B2

Eating
9 Countdown ... D2
10 Devil Burger ... B2
11 Duo ... B2
12 Louie's Café ... B1
13 Seriously Good Chocolate Company ... C2
14 The Batch ... C2
15 Three Bean Café ... B2
Tuatara Café ... (see 7)
16 Turkish Kebabs ... B2
17 Zookeepers Cafe ... B2

Drinking
18 Kiln ... B2
19 Speight's Ale House ... B2

Entertainment
20 Reading Cinemas ... B2
Tillermans Music Lounge ... (see 10)

Shopping
21 H&J's Outdoor World ... B2

Zookeepers Cafe CAFE $$
(50 Tay St; meals $15-30) The Zookeepers is easily spotted by the giant corrugated-iron elephant on the roof. Staff are laid-back and friendly, and the meals are good value and tasty. Tuck into a warm balsamic beef salad or sip an Invercargill Brewery beer. Try the Wasp lager, a southern honey-infused spin on a traditional Pilsner.

Three Bean Café CAFE $
(73 Dee St; meals $12-16) Some of Invercargill's best coffee and casual eats are at this cosmopolitan main-drag cafe. Kick your day off

with a salmon bagel, and leave room for a baked slice of something sweet.

Devil Burger BURGERS $
(16 Don St; burgers $10-16, wraps $12-16; from 11am;) Tasty gourmet burgers and healthy wraps, including lots of vegie options. At weekends, expect crowds of hungry burger fans from upstairs at Tillermans Music Lounge.

Tuatara Café CAFE $
(30-32 Dee St; meals $10-20; 7am-late; @) The cafe attached to the Tuatara Lodge backpackers hostel is cool in a traveller-focused, dreadlocks-and-Kiwi dub kinda way. Scrambled eggs on toast make for a hearty good-value start to the day and the burgers are tasty and interesting.

Turkish Kebabs TURKISH $
(29 Esk St; from $13.50;) Tasty hummusy felafels and kebabs, all with the option of dine-in or takeaway. For indecisive diners, there's also Japanese and Indian food a few doors either side.

Countdown SUPERMARKET
(cnr Doon & Tay Sts) This is Invercargill's biggest supermarket.

Drinking & Entertainment

Louie's Café CAFE
(142 Dee St; Wed-Sat) This cosy cafe-bar specialises in tapas-style snacks ($12), and there's also a concise blackboard menu (mains $20 to $30). Relax near the fireside, tuck yourself away in various nooks and crannies, or spread out on a comfy padded sofa and enjoy the chilled-out music. There are occasional live gigs.

Tillermans Music Lounge LIVE MUSIC
(16 Don St; 9pm-late) Tillerman's is an alternative live-music/DJ venue, with live music ranging from local thrash bands to visiting rock or reggae talents. DJs spin mostly dub and house. Decrepit black couches and a battered old dance floor prove its credentials.

Kiln PUB
(7 Don St) Stylish bar with hanging lampshades, underlit bar and Great Aunt Edith's wallpaper. Easily the most civilised drinking option in town and surprisingly good food too. Try the parmesan-crusted blue cod with a Summer Ale.

Speight's Ale House PUB
(38 Dee St) Big-screen TVs for live sport, and Speight's brews south from Dunedin. Grab an outside table to watch Invercargill's after-dark cavalcade of annoying boy racers in their hotted-up Mazdas.

Reading Cinemas CINEMA
(03-211 1555; www.readingcinemas.co.nz; 29 Dee St) Discounts on Tuesdays.

Shopping

H&J's Outdoor World OUTDOOR EQUIPMENT
(32 Tay St) Everything from maps and boots to sleeping bags and dried food.

Information

DOC office (03-211 2400; www.doc.govt.nz; 7th fl, 33 Don St; 8.30am-4.30pm Mon-Fri) For info on tracks around Stewart Island and Southland.

Invercargill i-SITE (03-211 0895; www.invercargillnz.com; Queens Park, 108 Gala St; 8am-5pm; @) In the same building as the Southland Museum & Art Gallery. Bikes can be rented, and it's good for information on the Catlins and Stewart Island.

Post office (51 Don St)

Getting There & Away

Air

Air New Zealand (0800 737 000; www.airnewzealand.co.nz) flights link Invercargill to Christchurch (from $89, one hour) several times a day. **Stewart Island Flights** (03-218 9129; www.stewartislandflights.com) link Stewart Island and Invercargill (adult/child one-way $115/75, return $195/115, 20 minutes) three times a day. Ask about discounted standby fares.

Bus

Buses leave from the Invercargill i-SITE, where you can also book your tickets. Travel time to Dunedin is four hours, Te Anau three hours, Queenstown four hours, and Christchurch 10 hours. The Catlins Coaster (p627) and Bottom Bus (p619) also pass through Invercargill.

InterCity (www.intercity.co.nz) To Te Anau, Dunedin and Christchurch.

Atomic Shuttles (www.atomictravel.co.nz) To Dunedin and Christchurch.

Knightrider (www.knightrider.co.nz) Overnight to Dunedin and Christchurch; good to catch morning flights from either city.

Naked Bus (www.nakedbus.com) To Te Anau, Queenstown and Dunedin.

Tracknet (www.tracknet.net) To Te Anau and Queenstown.

Getting Around

Invercargill Airport (03-218 6920; www.invercargillairport.co.nz; 106 Airport Ave) is 3km west of central Invercargill. The door-to-door **Airport Shuttle** (☎03-214 3434) costs $12 from the city centre to the airport; more for residential pick-up. By taxi it's around $20; try **Blue Star Taxis** (☎03-218 6079) or **City Cabs** (☎03-214 4444).

Bluff

POP 2100

Bluff is Invercargill's port, 27km south of the city. The main reasons to come here are to catch the ferry to Stewart Island, pose for photos beside the **Stirling Point signpost**, or buy famous Bluff oysters. Also at Stirling Point is a huge chain-link sculpture by NZ artist Russell Beck. It symbolises the Maori legend where the South Island is the canoe of Maui and Stewart Island is the boat's anchor. At Stirling Point, the chain disappears into the ocean, and a companion sculpture on Stewart Island represents the other end of the anchor chain.

While Bluff isn't the South Island's southernmost point (that claim belongs to Slope Point in the Catlins), and even though Stewart Island and other dots of rock lie even further south, the phrase 'from Cape Reinga to Bluff' is oft-quoted to signify the entire length of NZ. NZ's main highway, SH1, terminates south of Bluff at Stirling Point, so it really does feel like the end of the country.

Kids will enjoy the small **Bluff Maritime Museum** (☎03-212 7534; 241 Foreshore Rd; adult/child $2/free; ⏲10am-4.30pm Mon-Fri, 1-5pm Sat & Sun) and clambering over a century-old oyster boat, while steam nerds will love the big old 600hp steam engine. There are interesting displays on Bluff's history complete the exhibition.

The **Bluff Oyster & Food Festival** (www.bluffoysterfest.co.nz) celebrates Bluff's most famous exports, and is held annually, usually in May. The oysters are in season from late March to late August. To buy fresh Bluff oysters, visit **Fowlers Oysters** (Ocean Beach Rd; ⏲9am-5pm Mar-Aug) on the way into town on the left.

Near the Four Square supermarket, **Stella's** (64 Gore St; ⏲6.30am-2pm) is your best bet for a coffee before braving the ferry crossing to Stewart Island. The seafood chowder and pies are pretty good too.

For more information, see www.bluff.co.nz.

Invercargill to Dunedin

Following SH1 is the most direct route between Invercargill and Dunedin. The pastoral scenery is pretty, but not as spectacular as the SH92 route via the Catlins. If you've got time, opt for the latter.

THE CATLINS

If you veer off SH1 and head for the coastal route between Invercargill and Dunedin (via SH92), you wind through the enchanting Catlins, a region that combines lush farmland, native forests and rugged bays. With bushwalks, wildlife-spotting opportunities and lonely beaches to explore, the Catlins is well worth a couple of days.

On a clear summer's day, surrounded by forest greens and ocean blues, there's nothing more beautiful than the Catlins coast. In the face of a sleety Antarctic southerly, it's a very different environment. Good luck.

The Catlins

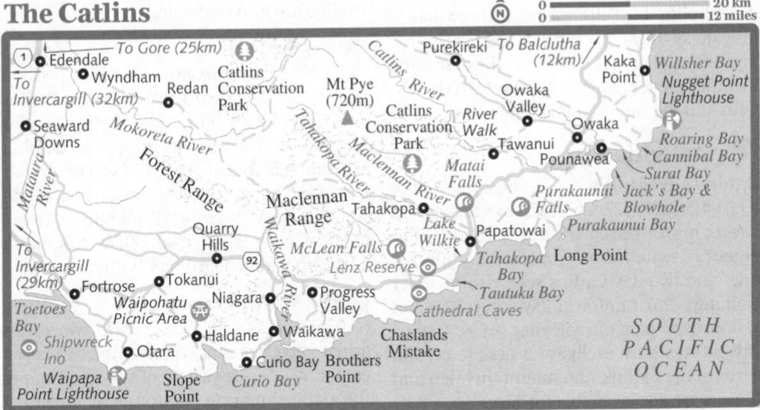

WORTH A TRIP

GORE

Around 66km northeast of Invercargill, Gore is the proud 'home of country music' in New Zealand, with the annual **Gold Guitar Week** (www.goldguitars.co.nz) in late May and early June ensuring all the town's accommodation is booked out for at least 10 days per year. For the other 355 days, good reasons to stop include a surprisingly cool art gallery, vintage biplanes and whisky tasting at the Hokonui Moonshine Museum. See www.gorenz.com for more local information.

The interesting **Hokonui Moonshine Museum** (www.hokonuiwhiskey.com; admission $5; 9am-4.30pm Mon-Fri, 10am-3.30pm Sat & Sun) and the **Gore Historical Museum** (admission by donation; 9am-4.30pm Mon-Fri, 10am-3.30pm Sat & Sun) share the same building and celebrate Gore's proud history of fishing, farming and illegal distilleries. Admission to the Moonshine Museum includes a wee dram of the local liquid gold.

The outstanding **Eastern Southland Gallery** (03-208 9907; 14 Hokonui Dr; admission by donation; 10am-4.30pm Mon-Fri, 1-4pm Sat & Sun), in Gore's century-old former public library, houses a hefty collection of NZ art including a large Ralph Hotere collection. The amazing John Money Collection combines indigenous folk art from West Africa and Australia with works by iconic New Zealand artist Rita Angus.

Croydon Aircraft Company (03-208 9755; www.croydonaircraft.com; SH94), 16km down the road to Queenstown, restores vintage aircraft and, for wannabe WWI flying aces, offers flights in a two-seater 1930s Tiger Moth biplane ($55/160 for 10/30 minutes) or other wee aircraft. There's also good eating at the **Moth** (www.themoth.co.nz; 1558a Waimea Hwy; lunch & pizza $11-24, 2-/3-course dinner $42/52; 10am-4pm Mon-Tue, 10am-late Wed-Sun) restaurant.

This route has many twists, turns and narrow sections, and while it's similar in distance, it's slower going than the inland route along SH1.

Flora & Fauna

The Catlins is a wonderful place for independent wildlife-watching. Fur seals and sea lions laze along the coast, while elephant seals breed at Nugget Point. In spring, keep your eyes peeled for southern right whales. Dolphins are also frequent visitors.

Unlike much of Southland, tall kahikatea, totara and rimu forests still exist in the Catlins. Prolific bird life includes the wonderfully noisy tui, and you'll also see kereru (NZ pigeons). Other sea, estuary and forest birds include the endangered yellow-eyed penguin and the rare mohua (yellowhead).

Activities

Catlins Adventures ADVENTURE TOUR
(03-415 8339, 027 416 8822; www.catlinsadventures.co.nz; per person 1/2 days $175/295) Energetic, switched-on operators offering one- and two-day Catlins scenic tours, river walking ($75), rainforest kayaking ($75) and yellow-eyed penguin viewing ($89). Catlins Adventures have exclusive access to certain areas of the Catlins, and mountain bikes and kayaks are also available for hire.

Catlins Wildlife Trackers WILDLIFE
(0800 228 5467, 03-415 8613; www.catlins-ecotours.co.nz) Papatowai-based Catlins Wildlife Trackers offer eco-centric guided walks and tours (three nights/two days $800), including all food, accommodation and transport. These conservation gurus have been running tours since 1990 and also manage Top Track, a 26km self-guided walk through beaches and a private forest; it costs $25 if you walk it in a 10-hour day, or $45 if you do it in two, including overnighting in a converted trolley bus. Guided trips focusing on wildlife are also available.

Catlins Surf School SURFING
(03-246 8552; www.catlins-surf.co.nz) Located in Porpoise Bay near Curio Bay, the Catlins Surf School runs 90-minute surfing lessons for $50. The occasional group of dolphin spectators is free of charge. If you're already confident on the waves, hire a board and wetsuit (very necessary) for three hours ($40). Owner Nick also offers tuition in stand-up paddleboarding (2½ hours, $75).

Catlins Marine Encounters BOAT TOUR
(03-929 6580, 027 212 1327; www.catlinsmarineencounters.co.nz) This Waikawa-based company offers a variety of ways to explore the Catlins' marine environment including

sea-mammal watching ($80), birdwatching and scenic harbour cruises ($45), and diving and fishing charters.

Catlins Horse Riding HORSE RIDING
(☎03-415 8368, 027 269 2904; www.catlinshorseriding.co.nz; 41 Newhaven Rd, Owaka; 1/2/3hr rides $40/70/90) the idiosyncratic coastline and landscapes on four legs with Catlins Horse Riding. Full-day rides including lunch are $180.

Tours

Bottom Bus TOUR
(☎03-477 9083; www.bottombus.co.nz; from $175) Does a regular loop from Queenstown to Dunedin, south through the Catlins to Invercargill, along the Southern Scenic Route to Te Anau, then back to Queenstown. It stops at all main points of interest, and you can hop off and catch the next bus coming through. There are lots of pass options. The Southlander pass ($375) lets you start anywhere on the loop and includes a Milford Sound cruise.

Catlins Coaster TOUR
(☎03-477 9083; www.catlinscoaster.co.nz; from $210) Run by Bottom Bus and offering day tours and trips through the Catlins from Dunedin and Invercargill. Check the website for details. Departures are more limited in winter.

Information

Contact the main **Catlins information centre** (☎03-415 8371; www.cluthacountry.co.nz; 20 Ryley St; ⊙9.30am-1pm & 1.30-4.30pm Mon-Fri, 10am-4pm Sat & Sun) in Owaka or the smaller **Waikawa visitors centre** (☎03-205 8006; waikawamuseum@hyper.net.nz; Main Rd; ⊙10am-5pm; @). The i-SITEs in Invercargill and Balclutha also have lots of Catlins information. Online, see www.catlins.org.nz and www.catlins-nz.com.

The Catlins has no banks and limited options for eating out or grocery shopping (except in Owaka). There's an ATM at the 4 Square supermarket in Owaka, and petrol stations (hours can be irregular) in Fortrose, Papatowai and Owaka. Stock up and fill up before you arrive.

Invercargill to Papatowai

Heading east and south from Invercargill, SH92 enters the Catlins region at Fortrose, from where the **Shipwreck Ino** is visible across the sandy harbour at low tide. Take the turn-off here towards Waipapa Point and use the coastal route via Haldane, Waikawa and Niagara (where you rejoin SH92). It's a slower, but more beautiful route, with lots to check out along the way. The **Waipapa Point lighthouse** dates from 1884, three years after a terrible maritime disaster when SS *Tararua* sank and 131 people drowned.

Turn off at Haldane and drive 5km to **Slope Point**, the South Island's southernmost point. A 20-minute walk across farmland leads to a stubby beacon and stubbier signpost atop a windswept spur with views up and down the coast. The track is closed in September and October for lambing.

Further east at **Curio Bay**, fossilised Jurassic-age trees are visible for four hours either side of low tide. The lookout is the place to be an hour or so before sunset, when you'll see yellow-eyed penguins waddling ashore. Just before Curio Bay, neighbouring **Porpoise Bay** has excellent accommodation and a beach that's safe for swimming. Blue penguins nest in the dunes and in summer Hector's dolphins come here to rear their young. Whales are occasional visitors, and fur seals and sea lions are often lounging on the rocks. It's also a good place to learn to surf.

A 4km drive past the McLean Falls Holiday Park, the walk to **McLean Falls** (40 minutes return) passes through tree ferns and rimu. Don't stop at the first falls – the real thing is a bit further on.

Cutting back into cliffs right on the beach, the huge, arched **Cathedral Caves** (www.cathedralcaves.co.nz; adult/child $5/1) are accessible only for two hours either side of low tide (tide timetables are posted on the website, at the highway turn-off and at visitor information centres). If you're happy to wade, you can walk in one entrance and out the other. From SH92 it's 2km to the car park, then a peaceful 15-minute forest walk down to the beach and a further 25 minutes to the caves.

Around 10km further east, an easy forest walk leads down to the dark peaty waters of Lake Wilkie (30 minutes return). A turn-off soon leads to secluded **Tahakopa Bay**. Just before the descent into Papatowai, stop at the **Florence Hill Lookout** with spectacular views of the sweeping arc of **Tautuku Bay**.

Papatowai provides a base for forays into the nearby forests. There's a handful of accommodation options and a general store selling petrol. There's also good picnicking at the mouth of the Tahakopa River.

Lost Gypsy Gallery (☎03-415 8908; SH92; ⊙11am-5pm Thu-Tue; 📶) occupies a roadside house-bus at Papatowai. Based on found objects, specialising in self-wound automata and things that go whirrr, this place is guaranteed to make you laugh. A fascinating gallery (admission $5, young children not allowed, sorry...) showcases some of artist Blair Sommerville's larger one-off pieces. We especially like the TV that runs on bicycle power. Blair's always up for a good chat, and there's also a funky coffee caravan and wi-fi.

Sleeping

SLOPE POINT

Slope Point Backpackers HOSTEL $
(03-246 8420; www.slopepoint.co.nz; 164 Slope Point Rd; sites per person from $12, dm $22-27, d $47, unit $87; wi-fi) Surrounded by trees, this rural property has modern dorms and rooms, along with a great-value self-contained unit. There's plenty of grass to pitch a tent or park a campervan, and the owners' children are always keen to show off the working farm. Board games, puzzles and loads of magazines take the place of TV.

Nadir Outpost GUESTHOUSE $
(03-246 8544; www.catlins-slopepoint.com; 174 Slope Point Rd; d $90) Nadir offers double rooms inside the owners' house, and a cosy, standalone cabin with kitchen facilities. There's a shop selling basic supplies and a forested area to pitch a tent ($12 per person) or park a van ($29 for two people). Meals are also available (breakfast $7 to $14, dinner $25).

CURIO BAY

Curio Bay Boutique Studios APARTMENT $$
(03-246 8797; www.curiobay.co.nz; 501 Curio Bay Rd; d $220) With big windows and an even bigger deck, these two plush beachside units are open to awesome sea views. Recline on the giant, rustic, timber-framed bed to feel like a king or queen. A splurgeworthy and romantic retreat if you're celebrating someone or something special.

Lazy Dolphin Lodge HOSTEL $
(03-246 8579; www.lazydolphinlodge.co.nz; 529 Curio Bay Rd; dm/d/tw $33/72/72; @ wi-fi) New owners have given this long-established place a renewed energy, and the views from the big lounge and deck towards the Porpoise Bay breakers are still among the South Island's finest. Other traveller-friendly benefits include private beach access and occasional sightings of seals and dolphins.

Curio Bay Holiday Park HOLIDAY PARK $
(03-246 8897; valwhyte@hotmail.com; 601 Curio Bay Rd; sites from $15) Very private campsites lost in a sea of tall flax make this a beautiful spot to camp. The camping ground nestles up to the small outcrop between Curio and Porpoise Bays, within easy walking distance to both. Guided nature walks are available.

Catlins Beach House RENTAL HOUSE $
(03-246 8340; www.catlinsbeachhouse.co.nz; 499 Curio Bay Rd; dm $25, d $70-95) This extremely comfortable house has a cosy woodburner for heating, a good kitchen, and a deck that opens onto a grassy lawn sloping down to the beach. Blue penguins nest hereabouts and can be heard waddling past making cute penguin sounds at night.

Catlins Surf Cottages RENTAL HOUSE $$
(03-246 8552; www.catlins-surf.co.nz; houses $110-190) A range of self-contained cottages and houses around Curio Bay can be rented from Catlins Surf. One-night rentals are fine, and it's a good option for travelling families or groups of three or four.

WAIKAWA

Penguin Paradise Holiday Lodge HOSTEL $
(03-246 8552; www.catlins-surf.co.nz; 612 Niagara-Waikawa Rd; dm/d/tw $25/56/56) Laid-back backpackers in a heritage cottage in Waikawa village near the estuary. Special combo deals ($70) of one night's accommodation and a 1½-hour surf lesson are also available.

Waikava Harbourview RENTAL HOUSE $$
(03-246 8866; www.southcatlins.co.nz; 14 Larne St; d $130-170) Waikava Harbourview is a four-bedroom house that's a good option for families or a group; up to 10 people can be accommodated. Opened in 2009, the newer one- and two-bedroom Harakeke and Toi Tois units are also good value.

MCLEAN FALLS

McLean Falls Holiday Park HOLIDAY PARK $
(03-415 8338; www.catlinscamping.com; SH92; sites per person $20, units $75-195; @ wi-fi) Just off the main road, McLean Falls Holiday Park has a number of Kiwiana-style cabins, newer chalets, and sites for vans and tents. The amenities blocks are spacious and very well maintained. The attached **Whistling Frog Café & Bar** (meals $10-30; 8.30am-9pm) does breakfast, lunch and dinner with a surprisingly cosmopolitan spin, and there's a good selection of South Island beer and wine.

PAPATOWAI

TOP CHOICE **Hilltop** LODGE $
(03-415 8028; www.hilltopcatlins.co.nz; 77 Tahakopa Valley Rd; dm $34, d $85-100) High on a hill

1.5km out of town, with native forest at the back door and surrounded by a sheep farm, this lovely old renovated pair of houses has spectacular views of the surrounding hills and the ocean. The en-suite double makes for a luxurious mini-splurge.

Catlins Wildlife Trackers COTTAGES $$
(☎0800 228 5467; www.catlins-ecotours.co.nz; d $145-170) This tour company offers a variety of accommodation around Papatowai, including the modern Pipipi eco-cottage, and four very comfortable, ecofriendly cottages (www.catlinsmohuapark.co.nz) on the edge of a native forest reserve.

Eating

You'll find roadside takeaways in Waikawa and Papatowai. The Papatoawi general store has a limited range of groceries.

TOP CHOICE **Niagara Falls Café** CAFE $$
(www.niagarafallscafe.co.nz; Main Rd; meals $13-24; ⌚8am-10pm; 📶🌶) Sharing a restored schoolhouse with a local art gallery, this is a friendly spot for a meal. Tuck into delicious, good-value cooking including steaks, blue cod and rack of lamb, or linger over coffee and home-cooked cakes and muffins. The beer and wine list is impressive, and the mighty falls themselves are nearby. Vegetarian and gluten-free options abound.

Papatowai to Balcutha

From Papatowai, follow the highway north to **Matai Falls** (a 30-minute return walk) on the Maclennan River, then head south-east on the signposted road to the tiered **Purakaunui Falls** (20 minutes return). Both falls are reached via cool, dark forest walks through totara and tree fern.

Continue along the gravel road from Purakaunui Falls to the 55m-deep **Jack's Blowhole**. In the middle of a sheep paddock 200m from the sea but connected by a subterranean cavern, this huge cauldron was named after Chief Tuhawaiki, nicknamed Bloody Jack for his cussin'. It's a fairly brisk 30-minute walk each way.

Owaka is the Catlins' main town (population a hefty 395), with a good information centre, a 4 Square grocery store – including an ATM – and a petrol station. An excellent **museum** (adult/child $5/free; ⌚9.30am-1pm & 1.30-4.30pm Mon-Fri, 10am-4pm Sat & Sun), attached to the information centre, has displays on local history. An attached theatrette shows interesting videos on the Catlins' deserved reputation as a shipwreck coast. Once you've stocked up or stopped for a meal, venture off to more remote, more attractive parts of the Catlins.

Pounawea, 4km east, is a beautiful little riverside town with some lovely places to stay. Across the inlet, **Surat Bay** is even quieter and also has accommodation. Sea lions are often seen on the beach between here and **Cannibal Bay**, a 30-minute beach walk away.

Heading north from Owaka, detour off SH92 to **Nugget Point**, stopping for the short walk out to the lighthouse at the end – the last 900m or so, with drops to the ocean on either side, is breathtaking, and the view of wave-thrashed vertical rock formations from the end is great, too. A spacious DOC viewing platform huddles around the lighthouse. Fur seals, sea lions and elephant seals occasionally bask together on the rocks down to your left, a rare and noisy coexistence. Yellow-eyed and blue penguins, shags and sooty shearwaters all breed here. Ten minutes' walk down from a car park is **Roaring Bay**, where a well-placed hide allows you to see yellow-eyed penguins coming ashore (best two hours before sunset). The best viewing is from a newly constructed hide. You should not use a flash when photographing the penguins. If you don't have your own transport, nightly **twilight tours** (☎0800 525 278; www.catlins.co.nz; per person $30) are run by the Nugget View and Kaka Point Motels.

From Nugget Point the road loops back through the little township of **Kaka Point**, which has a sandy, quiet beach and accommodation and is a nice spot for a meal. The road continues north from here to Balclutha.

Sleeping

OWAKA & PURAKAUNUI

DOC Camping Grounds CAMPSITE $
(www.doc.govt.nz; campsites $6) There are DOC camping grounds at Purakaunui Bay and inland at Tawanui.

POUNAWEA

Pounaewa Grove Motel MOTEL $$
(☎03-415 8339; www.pounaweagrove.co.nz; 5 Ocean Grove; d $120; 📶) Well managed by a friendly Kiwi–South African couple, these chic and stylish units are literally metres from the ocean. Flat-screen TVs, free wi-fi and modern bathrooms are thoroughly 21st century, but the enduring grandeur and energy of the Catlins coastline is on tap just outside. The motel is also the home base for the excellent Catlins Adventures (p626).

Pounawea Motor Camp HOLIDAY PARK $
(☎03-415 8483; www.catlins-nz.com/pounawea-motor-camp; Park Lane; sites from $28, units $45-80) Sitting right on the estuary and surrounded by native bush ringing with birdsong, this is a gem of a place to park your tent. Others think so too, and in the frenzied post-Christmas season you'll be sharing this beautiful spot with many Kiwi and international holidaymakers.

SURAT BAY

Newhaven Holiday Park HOLIDAY PARK $
(☎03-415 8834; www.newhavenholiday.com; Newhaven Rd; sites from $30, units $66-120; @📶) A few minutes' walk from the beach is this little camping area with modern cabins and facilities and three self-contained flats. Rent kayaks and bikes from Surat Bay Lodge, next door.

Surat Bay Lodge HOSTEL $
(☎03-415 8099; www.suratbay.co.nz; Surat Bay Rd; dm/d $29/68; @) Right beside the start of the track down to the beach, and next-door neighbours with the sea lions, this superbly located hostel has cosy, brightly decorated rooms and a friendly vibe. Rent a kayak ($12 to $40) or bike ($30 per day) and get exploring.

NUGGET & KAKA POINTS

Nugget Lodge LODGE $$
(☎03-412 8783; www.nuggetlodge.co.nz; Nugget Rd; d $165; 📶) Perched above the sea on the road south to the lighthouse, this pair of self-contained units has spectacular views up and down the coast. It's worth including their huge breakfast ($12.50 per person) with freshly baked bread and homemade muesli. If you're lucky you might spy a couple of resident sea lions lolling on the beach below you.

Nugget View & Kaka Point Motels MOTEL $$
(☎0800 525 278; www.catlins.co.nz; 11 Rata St; d $95-200; 📶) A veritable mini-village of motel options ranging from excellent-value older units through to more modern accommodation with private spa baths and verandahs. The friendly owners also operate one- and two-day tours of the Catlins, and twilight tours ($30 per person) to view Nugget Point and the penguin colony at Roaring Bay.

Kaka Point Camping Ground HOLIDAY PARK $
(☎03-412 8801; www.kakapointcamping.co.nz; 39 Tarata St; sites from $13.50, cabins per person $24; 📶) Cabins are basic but functional, and there is a lovely grassy, hedged area to pitch tents. There are bushwalks into the surrounding forest, and it's a short, though steep, stroll downhill to the beach and town.

Fernlea Backpackers HOSTEL $
(☎03-418 0117, 03-412 8834; Moana St; dm/d $25/55) Perched atop a hill, and a leafy, zigzag path above the street below, this tiny, basic bungalow is ultra-snug, with lovely sea views and basic facilities. Sometimes closed from May to September so phone ahead.

Eating

OWAKA

Catlins Cafe CAFE $$
(www.catlinscafe.co.nz; 3 Main Rd; mains $12-25; 📶) This super-cosy highway culinary diversion comes with loads of retro Kiwiana touches including comfy old sofas and rustic wooden furniture. The food's equally hearty and familiar from muesli and eggs Benedict for breakfast, through to top-notch burgers for lunch, and steak and blue cod for dinner. South Island wines and beers partner a serious approach to coffee.

Lumberjack Bar & Café CAFE $$
(3 Saunders St; mains $15-30; ⏲Tue-Sun) Park yourself at one of the Lumberjack's trademark rustic wooden tables and tuck into huge Catlins-sized meals including good burgers, steaks and seafood.

4 Square SUPERMARKET
(3 Ovenden St) Stock up for self-catering.

KAKA POINT

Point Café & Bar PUB $$
(58 Esplanade; bar menu $5-15, mains $27-30) Prop yourself at the driftwood bar for a cool beer, or grab a window seat for a sea view. Takeaways are also available at the attached store – grab a burger ($5) for the road.

Stewart Island

Travellers who undertake the short jaunt to Stewart Island will be rewarded with a warm welcome from both the local kiwi and the local Kiwis. New Zealand's 'third' island is a good place to spy the country's shy, feathered icon in the wild, and the close-knit community of Stewart Islanders (population 420) are relaxed hosts. If you're staying on the island for just a few days, don't be too surprised if most people quickly know who you are and where you came from – especially if you mix and mingle over a beer at NZ's southernmost pub, in the main settlement of Oban.

Once you've said g'day to the locals, there's plenty of active adventure on offer including kayaking and setting off on a rewarding tramp in Stewart Island's Rakiura National Park. With a worthwhile injection of effort, relative newcomers to tramping can easily complete one of NZ's Great Walks, and be surprised and entertained with an uninterrupted aria from native birds. And if a multiday tramp still sounds too intense, spying a kiwi in the wild can also be achieved with the straightforward combination of a short boat ride and an even shorter bush and beach walk.

History

Stewart Island's Maori name is Rakiura (Glowing Skies), and catch a glimpse of a spectacular blood-red sunset or the aurora australis and you'll quickly know why. According to myth, NZ was hauled up from the ocean by Maui, who said, 'Let us go out of sight of land, far out in the open sea, and when we have quite lost sight of land, then let the anchor be dropped.' The North Island was the fish that Maui caught, the South Island his canoe and Rakiura was the anchor – Te Punga o te Waka o Maui.

There is evidence that parts of Rakiura were occupied by moa hunters as early as the 13th century. The titi (muttonbird or sooty shearwater) on adjacent islands were an important seasonal food source for the southern Maori.

The first European visitor was Captain Cook, who sailed around the eastern, southern and western coasts in 1770 but couldn't figure out if it was an island or a peninsula. Deciding it was attached to the South Island, he called it South Cape. In 1809 the sealing vessel *Pegasus* circumnavigated Rakiura and named it after its first officer, William Stewart.

In June 1864 Stewart and the adjacent islets were bought from local Maori for £6000. Early industries were sealing, timber-milling, fish-curing and shipbuilding, with a short-lived gold rush towards the end of the 19th century. Today the island's economy is dependent on tourism and fishing, including crayfish (lobster), paua (abalone), salmon, mussels and cod.

Stewart Island (Rakiura)

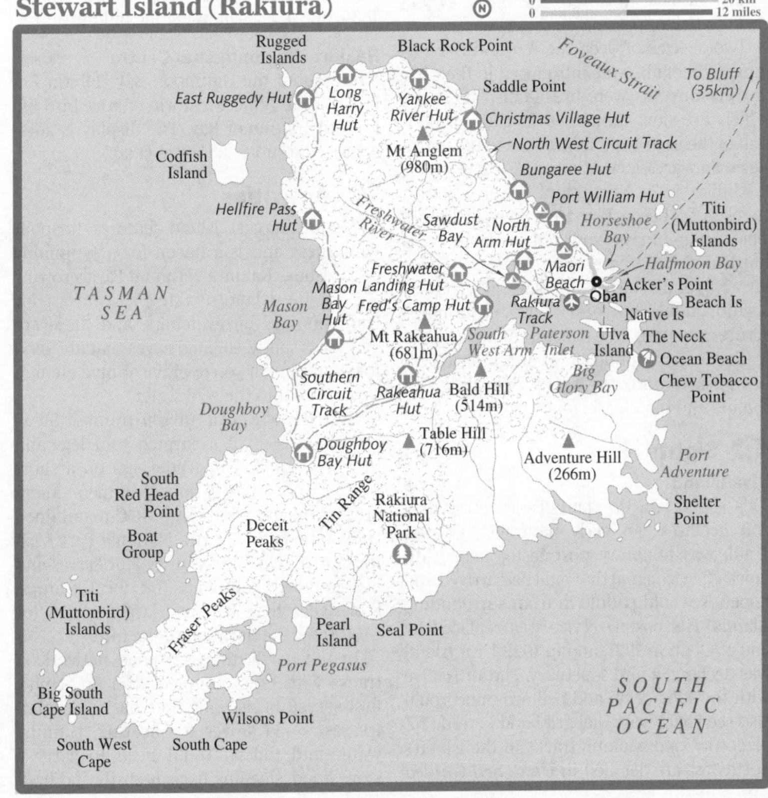

THE IMPORTANCE OF BEING PREPARED

Stewart Island's changeable weather can bring four seasons in one day. Frequent downpours create a misty, mysterious air and lots of mud, making boots and waterproof clothing mandatory. Make sure you're prepared for a variety of seasons. Nevertheless, the temperature is milder than you'd expect, with winter averaging around 10°C and summer 16.5°C.

Flora & Fauna

Nature has cranked the birdsong up to 11 here; you can't miss the tui, parakeets, kaka, bellbirds, fernbirds, robins and dotterels that constantly flap overhead and serenade you from gardens. You can also see kiwi and Fiordland crested, yellow-eyed and blue penguins. Ask locals about the evening parade of penguins on a small beach near the wharf. Don't feed any of the birds, as you run the risk of passing on diseases.

Two species of deer, the red and the Virginia (whitetail), were introduced in the early 20th century, as were brush-tailed possums, which are now numerous in the northern half of the island and destructive to the native bush. Stewart Island also has NZ fur seals.

Unlike NZ's North and South Islands, there is no beech forest on Stewart Island. The predominant lowland vegetation is hardwood but there are also lots of tree ferns, ground ferns and several types of orchid. Along the coast there's muttonbird scrub, grass tree, tree daisies, supplejack and leatherwood. Around the shores are clusters of bull kelp, fine red weeds, delicate green thallus and bladder ferns.

Sights

Ulva Island ISLAND

This island is a tiny paradise covering only 250 hectares. An early naturalist, Charles Traill, was honorary postmaster here. He'd hoist a flag to signal that mail had arrived and hopefuls would paddle in from surrounding islands. His postal service was replaced by one at Oban in 1921, and in 1922 Ulva Island was declared a bird sanctuary. The air is alive with the song of tui and bellbirds, and you'll also see kaka, weka, kakariki and kereru (NZ pigeon). Good walking tracks in the island's northwest are detailed in *Ulva: Self-Guided Tour* ($2), available from the DOC visitor centre. Popular routes include **Flagstaff Point Lookout** (20 minutes return) and **Boulder Beach** (1½ hours return). Many paths intersect amid beautiful stands of rimu, miro, totara and rata. During summer, water taxis go from Golden Bay wharf to Ulva Island. To get the most out of the island, consider going with a guide from Ruggedy Range Wilderness Experience or Ulva's Guided Walks.

Rakiura Museum MUSEUM

(Ayr St; adult/child $2/50c; 10am-1.30pm Mon-Sat, noon-2pm Sun) Models of various ferries from over the years, Maori artifacts, and exhibitions on whaling and early European settlement.

Presbyterian Church Hall CHURCH

(Kamahi Rd) The wooden Presbyterian Church Hall was relocated to Oban from a whaling base in Paterson Inlet in 1937.

Stone House HISTORIC BUILDING

At Harrold Bay, 2.5km southwest of Oban, is a stone house built by Lewis Acker around 1835, one of NZ's oldest stone buildings.

Rakiura Environmental Centre WILDLIFE

Learn about the Halfmoon Bay Habitat Rehabilitation Project restoring native bird life around Halfmoon Bay. The display is adjacent to the supermarket in Oban.

Activities

NZ's third-largest island features unspoilt wilderness and is a haven for a symphony of birdsong. Rakiura National Park protects 85% of the island, making it a mecca for trampers and birdwatchers, and there are countless sandy, isolated coves that are good for swimming if you're brave or mad enough to venture into the cool water.

Even if you're not a gung-ho tramper, Stewart Island is great to stretch your legs and immerse yourself in wilderness on a short tramp. For more serious trampers, there are excellent, multiday, DOC-maintained trails. The DOC Rakiura National Park Visitor Centre sells Backcountry Hut Passes and has detailed pamphlets on local tramps. Store gear here in small/large lockers for $10/20 for the duration of the hire.

In the north, there's a good network of tracks with huts occupied on a first-come, first-served basis. Each hut has foam mattresses, wood stoves for heating, running water and toilets. You'll need to carry a stove, food, sleeping bags, utensils and first-aid equipment. A tent can be useful over the busy summer holidays and Easter period. The southern part of the island is undeveloped and remote, and you shouldn't tramp on your own or go off the established tracks.

Day Walks TRAMPING

There are a number of short tramps, ranging from half an hour to seven hours; the majority are easily accessed from Halfmoon Bay. Pick up Day Walks ($2) from DOC Rakiura National Park Visitor Centre. The walk to **Observation Rock** (30 minutes return) has good views over Paterson Inlet. Continue past the old stone house at Harrold Bay to **Acker's Point Lighthouse** (three hours return), for good views of Foveaux Strait and the chance to see blue penguins and a colony of titi.

Rakiura Track TRAMPING

(www.doc.govt.nz) The 30km, three-day Rakiura Track is a well-defined, easy circuit starting and ending at Oban with copious bird life, beaches and lush bush en route. It requires a moderate level of fitness and is suitable for tramping year-round. The entire circuit is 37km in total (including the road sections) and showcases spectacular scenery. The circuit follows the open coast, climbs over a 250m-high forested ridge and traverses the sheltered shores of Paterson Inlet/Whaka a Te Wera. It passes sites of historical interest and introduces many of the common sea and forest birds of the island.

The Rakiura Track is one of NZ's Great Walks and bookings are required all year round to stay in the huts and at campsites. These must be made in advance, either online at www.doc.govt.nz or at the DOC Rakiura National Park Visitor Centre. There is a limit of two consecutive nights in any one hut.

Once an online booking has been received a confirmation letter may be printed from email. This is your ticket – read all the information contained within and bring a copy with you. All trampers are required to register their intentions at the visitor centre prior to departure for the Rakiura Track.

North West Circuit Track TRAMPING

(www.doc.govt.nz) Following the northern coast is the North West Circuit Track, a 125km trail taking 10 to 12 days. The 56km four-day **Southern Circuit Track** branches off the North West Circuit Track. Both tracks are suitable only for fit, well-equipped and experienced trampers. Mud is widespread and often deep and thick on the tracks, regardless of the season. Track times are an indication only, and extra time should be allowed in adverse conditions.

The North West Circuit Pass provides for a night in each of the backcountry huts. A Backcountry Hut Pass can be purchased for use in the huts; however, both the Port William and North Arm huts still need to be booked via the DOC website. The cost for these two huts is additional.

Bravo Adventure Cruises BIRDWATCHING

(☎03-219 1144; www.kiwispotting.co.nz) To see a kiwi in the wild, Bravo Adventure Cruises runs twilight tours ($140). In order to protect the kiwi, numbers are limited so make sure you book *well* ahead. Kiwi-spotting is also available with Ruggedy Range Wilderness Experience (p633).

Ruggedy Range Wilderness Experience TOURS, BIRDWATCHING

(☎0508 484 337, 03-219 1066; www.ruggedyrange.com; cnr Main Rd & Dundee St) Excellent guide Furhana Ahmad takes small groups on guided walks with an ecofriendly, conservation angle. A very popular excursion is the half-day trip to Ulva Island ($110); one- and two-night expeditions to see kiwi in the wild ($470 to $860) are also available. Ruggedy Range also specialises in the viewing of pelagic seabirds. Guided sea kayaking starts at $95, and you can also buy tramping and camping gear.

Rakiura Kayaks KAYAKING

(☎027 868 0318; www.rakiura.co.nz) Paterson Inlet consists of 100 sq km of sheltered, kayak-friendly waterways, with 20 islands, DOC huts and two navigable rivers. A popular trip is a paddle to Freshwater Landing (7km upriver from the inlet) followed by a three- to four-hour walk to Mason Bay to see kiwi in the wild. Rakiura Kayaks rents kayaks (half/full day $50/65) and also run guided paddles around the inlet ($65 to $105).

Ulva's Guided Walks WALKING TOUR

(☎03-219 1216; www.ulva.co.nz) Excellent three- to five-hour tours costing from $120 to $150 (transport included). Options include Ulva Island and Port William, a historic Maori and sealing site. Book at the Fernery (p636). If you're a mad-keen twitcher, see the website for the Birding Bonanza trip ($400) taking in everything avian.

Rakiura Charters FISHING

(☎03-219 1487, 0800 725 487; www.rakiuracharters.co.nz; adult/child from $100/70) Sightseeing and fishing outings on the *Rakiura Suzy*. Most popular is the half-day fishing cruise including a stop at the historic Whalers' Base. Multiday diving, fishing and hunting charters, and overnight trips are also available.

Stewart Island Experience GUIDED TOURS
(☎0800 000 511; www.stewartislandexperience.co.nz) Runs 2½-hour Paterson Inlet cruises (adult/child $85/22) via Ulva Island; 1½-hour minibus tours of Oban and the surrounding bays ($45/22); and 45-minute semisubmersible cruises ($85/42.50).

Stewart Island Spa DAY SPA
(☎03-219 1422; www.stewartislandspa.co.nz; Main Rd; treatments from $95; ⊙Dec-Mar) In a refurbished hilltop cottage, with options including crystal healing, a rainforest bath and a sauna and massage. Premium organic beauty products are used for all treatments. See Britt at the Kiwi-French Crepery for more information and bookings.

Sleeping

Finding accommodation can be difficult, especially in the low season when many places shut down. Booking ahead is recommended.

Self-contained rental houses offer good value, especially for families and groups. Note that many accommodation options have a two-night minimum stay or charge a surcharge for one night.

See www.stewartisland.co.nz for options.

Jo & Andy's B&B B&B $
(☎03-219 1230; jariksem@clear.net.nz; cnr Morris St & Main Rd; s $45-60, d & tw $90; @📶) An excellent option for budget travellers, this cosy blue home squeezes in twin, double and single rooms. A big breakfast of muesli, fruit and homemade bread prepares you for the most active of days. Jo and Andy are both great company, and there's hundreds of books if the weather packs up.

Observation Rock Lodge LODGE $$$
(☎03-219 1444, 027 444 1802; www.observationrocklodge.co.nz; 7 Leonard St; d from $195) Tucked away in native bush with views south to Golden Bay, this luxury lodge is run by the lovely Annett Eiselt from Perfect Dinner (p635). A sauna, hot tub and plenty of hidden sanctuaries around the bird-studded property add up to a relaxing island escape.

Greenvale B&B B&B $$$
(☎03-219 1357; www.greenvalestewartisland.co.nz; Elgin Tce; s/d $300/385; 📶) Just 50m from the sea, this modern home has stunning views over the strait. Both rooms have quality cotton bed linen and contemporary furnishings. It's a five-minute walk to Halfmoon Bay, and a two-second transition to the sunny deck.

Stewart Island Lodge LODGE $$$
(☎03-219 1085; www.stewartislandlodge.co.nz; Nichol Rd; d incl breakfast $390) This upmarket retreat with six rooms features king-size beds, a shared deck and a garden teeming with bird life. On a hill at the edge of town, the lodge commands magnificent views. Look forward to complimentary drinks and nibbles at 5pm every night.

Bunkers Backpackers HOSTEL $
(☎03-219 1160; www.bunkersbackpackers.co.nz; 13 Argyle St; dm/s/d $28/48/76; @📶) A renovated wooden villa houses Stewart Island's newest hostel. Shared areas are modern and sunny, and the rooms are spacious and spotless.

Pilgrim Cottage RENTAL HOUSE $$
(☎03-219 1144; www.kiwispotting.co.nz; 8 Horseshoe Bay Rd; d $140) This quaint, weatherboard cottage in a leafy oasis near town has wooden furnishings, a potbelly stove and a well-equipped kitchen. Expect lots of bird life.

Port of Call B&B B&B $$$
(☎03-219 1394; www.portofcall.co.nz; Leask Bay Rd; s/d incl breakfast $345/385) Take in ocean views, get cosy before an open fire, or explore an isolated beach. Port of Call is 1.5km southwest of Oban on the way to Acker's Point. It has a two-night minimum stay, and guided walks and water taxi trips can also be arranged.

Bay Motel MOTEL $$$
(☎03-219 1119; www.baymotel.co.nz; 9 Dundee St; d $165-185) Modern, comfortable units with lots of light and views over the harbour. Some units have big spa tubs, all rooms have full kitchens and two are wheelchair-accessible. When you've exhausted the island's bustling after-dark scene, Sky TV's on hand for on-tap entertainment.

Te Tahi Bed & Breakfast B&B $$$
(☎03-219 1487, 0800 725 487; www.rakiuracharters.co.nz; 14 Kaka Ridge Rd; d $200) A sunny conservatory immersed in verdant bush, ocean views and colourfully decorated bedrooms are the standouts at this friendly B&B just five minutes' walk from the bustling hub of Oban and Halfmoon Bay.

Kaka Retreat MOTEL $$$
(☎03-219 1252; www.kakaretreat.net; 7 & 9 Miro Cres; d from $260; @📶) These self-contained

SPOTTING A KIWI: A BRUSH WITH THE GODS

Considered the king of the forest by Maori, the kiwi has been around for 70 million years and is related to the now-extinct moa. Brown feathers camouflage the kiwi against its bush surroundings and a nocturnal lifestyle means spying a kiwi in the wild is a challenge. They're a smart wee bird – they even build their burrows a few months before moving in so newly grown vegetation can further increase their privacy.

Stewart Island is one of the few places on earth where you can spot a kiwi in the wild. As big as a barnyard chicken and numbering around 15,000 to 18,000 birds, the tokoeka (Stewart Island brown kiwi) is larger in size and population than other subspecies. They are also the only kiwi active during daylight hours. About two hours after sunrise and an hour before sunset, tokoeka forage for food in grassed areas, particularly on Mason Bay. Watch for white kiwi poo and telltale holes made by their long hunting beaks. When you spot one, keep silent, and stay still and well away. The birds' poor eyesight and single-mindedness in searching for food will often lead them to bump right into you.

The Stewart Island kiwi *(Apteryx australis lawryi)* is a distinct subspecies, with a larger beak and longer legs than its northern cousins. Kiwi are common over much of Stewart Island, particularly foraging around beaches for sandhoppers under washed-up kelp. Unusually, Stewart Island's kiwi are active during the day as well as at night – the birds are forced to forage for longer to attain breeding condition. Many trampers on the North West Circuit Track spot them. Because of Stewart Island's often-fickle weather, tours are sometimes cancelled, and you may need to spend a few nights on the island to finally see a kiwi.

studio units have luxury interiors and cosy verandah. With crisply modern decor and flash bathrooms, the superior units are among the island's best. An older-style family unit is good value for up to six people.

Stewart Island Backpackers HOSTEL **$**
(☎03-219 1114; www.stewartsislandbackpackers.com; cnr Dundee & Ayr Sts; dm/s/d $30/50/70) Friendly new management are breathing new life into this hostel. Recently renovated rooms are brightly painted, and many open onto a courtyard. There are only three beds per dorm, and table tennis and a shared barbecue keep things nicely social. There's an additional surcharge of $5 if you stay only one night, and tenting is $18 per person.

The Bach RENTAL HOUSE **$$$**
(☎03-219 1394; www.portofcall.co.nz; Leask Bay Rd; d $260) A modern self-contained studio unit, 1.5km southwest of Oban on the way to Acker's Point. It has a two-night minimum stay, and guided walks and water taxi trips can also be arranged.

Eating & Drinking

South Sea Hotel PUB **$$**
(26 Elgin Tce; mains $20-30; ⏲7am-9pm; 📶) This cafe-style spot does superb fish and robust seafood chowder. The attached pub is the town's main drinking hole, enlivened by occasional weekend bands and a loads-of-fun pub quiz that kicks off at 6.30pm on Sunday nights. Say hi to Vicky, quiz-mistress extraordinaire for us.

Perfect Dinner INTERNATIONAL **$$**
(☎027 444 1802, 03-219 1444; perfectdinner@observationrocklodge.co.nz; 3-course menu per person $89; ⏲Oct-May) Relocated from Germany, Annett Eiselt specialises in 'movable feasts'. She's available to provide three-course menus or gourmet platters ($69) wherever you desire on the island; at your accommodation, on a beach or somewhere else with equally terrific views. Produce is always seasonal, and ideally organic and sourced locally.

Kiwi-French Crepery CREPERIE **$$**
(Main Rd; crepes $13-28; ⏲9am-9pm) Savoury and sweet crepes are made to order in this cosy cafe, and the coffee is the best on the island. Try the chicken, pesto and camembert, or apple and cinnamon flavours. There's also regular soup specials, and owner Britt also sells gemstone jewellery and designs made from paua shells.

Church Hill Cafe, Bar & Restaurant RESTAURANT **$$$**
(☎03-219 1323; www.churchhillrestaurant.com; 36 Kamahi Rd; 2/3 courses $65/75; ⏲6pm-late) During summer this heritage villa's sunny deck provides hilltop views, and in cooler months you can get cosy inside beside the open fire. Regular highlights include manuka (tea

tree) smoked Stewart Island salmon, and old-fashioned dessert treats like apple and rhubarb crumble. It's essential to book for dinner, and by 5pm at the latest.

Kai Kart FISH & CHIPS $
(☎03-219 1225; Ayr St; meals $5-20; ⏲11.30am-2.30pm & 5-9pm Nov-Apr, reduced hours in winter) This caravan of cuisine serves up delicious blue cod, and the mussels with spicy satay sauce aren't far behind in the flavour stakes.

Ship to Shore SUPERMARKET $
(Elgin Tce; ⏲7.30am-7.30pm) Groceries and beer and wine, and sandwiches and baked goodies ($4 to $6) are also available.

Fishermen's Co-op SELF-CATERING $$
Fresh fish and crayfish from the main wharf.

Shopping

Glowing Sky CLOTHING
(www.glowingsky.co.nz; Elgin Tce; ⏲11am-3pm) Hand-printed T-shirts with Maori designs and NZ-made merino clothing.

Fernery ARTS & CRAFTS
(www.thefernerynz.com; Main Rd; ⏲10.30am-5pm Dec-Apr, to 2pm Oct-Nov) Crafts, paintings and island-themed books.

Information

There are no banks on Stewart Island. Credit cards are accepted for most activities but it's wise to bring enough cash for your stay. There's internet access, including wi-fi, at the South Sea Hotel, and most accommodation.

The Invercargill i-SITE has a wide range of information. Online, see www.stewartisland.co.nz.

DOC Rakiura National Park Visitor Centre (☎03-219 0002; www.doc.govt.nz; Main Rd; ⏲8am-5pm daily Jan-Mar, 8.30am-4.30pm Mon-Fri & 10am-2pm Sat-Sun Apr-late Oct, 8am-5pm Mon-Fri late Oct-Dec) Visit the free exhibition here to understand Stewart Island's flora and fauna. Backcountry Hut Passes and detailed maps of local tracks are also available. Please ensure if you are heading into the bush that you complete an intentions form to inform them of your whereabouts. Purchase books and cards with conservation themes, tramping supplies, and possum and merino clothing.

Post office (Elgin Tce) At Stewart Island Flights.

Ruggedy Range Birds & Forest Booking Office (☎0508 484 337, 03-219 1066; www.ruggedyrange.com; cnr Main Rd & Dundee St; ⏲7.30am-8pm Mon-Sun Sep-May, 8.30am-5.30pm Mon-Fri & 9.30am-2pm Sat & Sun Jun-Aug) Dedicated booking and information office for Ruggedy Range Wilderness Experience with birdwatching, tramping and water taxis on offer. Note that Ruggedy Range is not represented by other information centres on the island.

Stewart Island Experience (☎03-219 1456; www.stewartislandexperience.co.nz; 12 Elgin Tce; ⏲8.30am-6pm) In the big red building; books accommodation and activities. Also handles sightseeing tours and rents scooters, cars, fishing rods, dive gear and golf clubs.

Stewart Island Health Centre (☎03-219 1098; Argyle St; ⏲10am-12.30pm) 24-hour on-call service.

Getting There & Away

Air

Rakiura Helicopters (☎03-219 1155; www.rakiurahelicopters.co.nz; 151 Main Rd) This is the only helicopter company based on Stewart Island. It's available for transfers from Bluff ($250 per person), scenic flights ($50 to $785 per person) and charter flights for hunters and trampers.

Stewart Island Flights (☎03-218 9129; www.stewartislandflights.co.nz; Elgin Tce; adult/child one-way $115/75, return $195/115) Flies between the island and Invercargill three times daily. Phone ahead for good standby discounts.

Boat

Stewart Island Experience (☎03-212 7660, 0800 000 511; www.stewartislandexperience.co.nz; Main Wharf) The passenger-only ferry runs between Bluff and Oban (adult/child $69/34.50) around three times daily. Book a few days ahead in summer. The crossing takes one hour and can be a rough ride. The company also runs a shuttle between Bluff and Invercargill (adult/child $25/11) with pick-up and drop-off in Invercargill at the i-SITE, Tuatara Backpackers and Invercargill Airport. Cars and campervans can be stored in a secure car park at Bluff for an additional cost.

A shuttle also runs between Bluff and Queenstown (adult/child $69/34.50), and Bluff and Te Anau (adult/child $69/34.50) with pick-up and drop-off at the Real Journeys offices.

Getting Around

Water taxis offer pick-ups and drop-offs to remote parts of the island – a handy service for trampers. The taxis also service Ulva Island (return $25).

Stewart Island Water Taxi & Eco Guiding (☎03-219 1394)

Aihe Eco Charters & Water Taxi (☎03-219 1066; www.aihe.co.nz)

Sea View Water Taxi (☎03-219 1014; www.seaviewwatertaxi.co.nz)

Rakiura Helicopters can also provide remote access.

Rent a scooter (per half/full day $60/70) or a car (per half/full day $70/115) from Stewart Island Experience.

› Understand New Zealand

NEW ZEALAND TODAY 638

The Christchurch earthquake, the grounding of the MV *Rena*, the Rugby World Cup afterglow... Time for a Kiwi temperature check.

HISTORY 640

Tread a NZ timeline from Maori origins to Pakeha arrivals and recent ructions.

ENVIRONMENT 650

Get the low-down on the land, flora and fauna, national parks and environmental issues.

MAORI CULTURE 657

Read up on NZ's first people: history, religion, legends, traditions and the arts (and of course the *haka*).

THE KIWI PSYCHE 665

Global psychiatry: lie down on this couch NZ, and tell us all about yourself.

ARTS & MUSIC 670

The best Kiwi books, movies, TV, music and visual arts... This little nation punches well above its artistic weight.

population per sq km

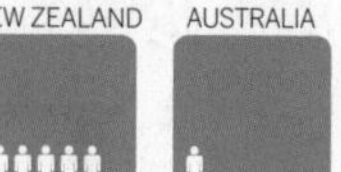

≈ 3 people

New Zealand Today

Shaky Isles

» Population: 4.4 million

» Area: 268,680 sq km (similar to Colorado, bigger than the UK)

» GDP growth: 1.1% (2011)

» Inflation: 1.8% (2011)

There's no denying it, New Zealand has had it tough over the last few years. It may be a long way away from just about everywhere but it is not immune to the vagaries of the global economy. In September 2010, just as the country was edging out of its worst recession in 30 years, a magnitude 7.1 earthquake struck near Christchurch, the nation's second-largest city. The damage was extensive but miraculously no life was lost, partly because the earthquake occurred in the early hours of the morning when people were in their beds (by way of comparison, Haiti's slightly smaller earthquake earlier that year killed more than 316,000 people).

While the clean-up was continuing on the East Coast, tragedy struck on the West Coast when an explosion occurred at the Pike River coalmine near Greymouth, sealing 29 men inside. All hope of rescue ended on 24 November when a second large explosion ripped through the mine.

Then in the early afternoon of 22 February 2011, a magnitude 6.3 earthquake struck Christchurch. This time the city wasn't so lucky and 185 people lost their lives. Canterbury has barely had a break since then, experiencing literally hundreds of aftershocks: a 6.3 earthquake killed an elderly man in June; a 5.8 rattled Christmas shoppers on 23 December; and a 5.5 got the new year off to a shaky start on 2 January 2012.

Just when it seemed that things couldn't get any worse, a fully loaded container ship, the MV *Rena*, hit the Astrolabe Reef in October 2011 and proceeded to leech heavy fuel oil into the Bay of Plenty, leading to NZ's worst environmental disaster. As we write, the recovery continues, with most of the fuel tanks drained and a substantial proportion of the containers removed.

You'll Need

» Travel insurance that covers you for high-risk activities

» Insect repellent to keep the sandflies at bay

» The ability to feign enthusiasm for rugby

» A bottomless appetite for Kiwi food and wine

Top Films

» *Lord of the Rings trilogy* (2001–03) Dir: Sir Peter Jackson

» *The Piano* (1993) Dir: Jane Campion

» *Whale Rider* (2002) Dir: Niki Caro

» *Once Were Warriors* (1994) Dir: Lee Tamahori

» *Boy* (2010) Dir: Taika Waititi

» *Sione's Wedding* (2006) Dir: Chris Graham

» *The Topp Twins: Untouchable Girls* (2009) Dir: Leanne Pooley

» *In My Father's Den* (2004) Dir: Brad McGann

» *Out of the Blue* (2006) Dir: Robert Sarkies

where they live

(% of New Zealanders)

if New Zealand were 100 people

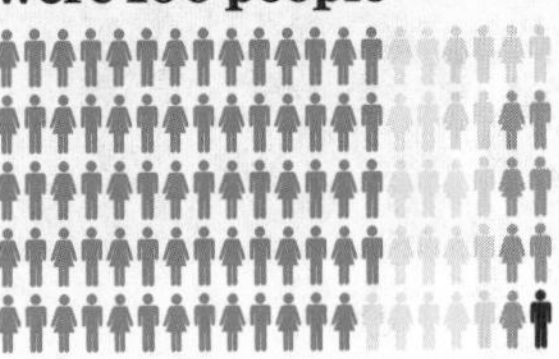

69 would be European
14 would be Maori
9 would be Asian
7 would be Pacific Islanders
1 would be Other

Pause, Engage

In the midst of all this doom and gloom, New Zealanders have soldiered on stoically, with the people of Christchurch proving remarkably resilient in the face of what is still an ongoing event.

Throughout September and October 2011, the influx of tourists for the Rugby World Cup provided a welcome distraction. Kiwis love sharing their spectacular country with visitors and in turn seeing it anew through foreign eyes. They never tire of being reminded of the rugged beauty of their beaches, mountains, fiords, glaciers, native forests and thermal regions. Although Christchurch missed out on hosting any games (its brand-new stadium, constructed for the event, lying in ruins), its rattled residents couldn't help but be cheered by the feel-good success of the tournament – and, of course, the national team's victory.

In the face of all that's occurred, you might be surprised by the extent to which the average Kiwi will genuinely want you to have a really, really good time during your stay. It's in these interactions with everyday, eager-to-please Kiwis that lasting memories are made. In the words of an enduring Maori proverb: *He aha te mea nui o te ao? He tangata! He tangata! He tangata!* (What is the most important thing in the world? It is people! It is people! It is people!).

» Unemployment: 6.5%

» Total number of snakes: 0

» Species of native mammals: 2 (both bats)

» Distance between North and South Islands: 23km

Faux Pas

» In Maori culture, sitting on a table is bad manners.

» Remove your shoes when entering a Maori meeting house or home.

» Don't call the fuzzy green fruit kiwis. In NZ they're kiwifruit; kiwi is a bird or a nationality.

Top Books

» *The Bone People* (1988) Keri Hulme

» *Mister Pip* (2007) Lloyd Jones

» *The Carpathians* (1988) Janet Frame

» *Bulibasha: King of the Gypsies* (1994) Witi Ihimaera

» *Live Bodies* (1998) Maurice Gee

» *Potiki* (1986) Patricia Grace

» *The House of Strife* (1993) Maurice Shadbolt

» *The Vintner's Luck* (2000) Elizabeth Knox

» *The 10pm Question* (2009) Kate de Goldi

History

James Belich
One of New Zealand's foremost modern historians, James Belich has written a number of books on NZ history and hosted the TV documentary series *The New Zealand Wars*.

New Zealand's history is not long, but it is fast. In less than a thousand years these islands have produced two new peoples: the Polynesian Maori and European New Zealanders. The latter are often known by their Maori name, 'Pakeha' (though not all like the term). NZ shares some of its history with the rest of Polynesia, and with other European settler societies, but has unique features as well. It is the similarities that make the differences so interesting, and vice versa.

Making Maori

Despite persistent myths, there is no doubt that the first settlers of NZ were the Polynesian forebears of today's Maori. Beyond that, there are a lot of question marks. Exactly where in east Polynesia did they come from – the Cook Islands, Tahiti, the Marquesas? When did they arrive? Did the first settlers come in one group or several? Some evidence, such as the diverse DNA of the Polynesian rats that accompanied the first settlers, suggests multiple founding voyages. On the other hand, only rats and dogs brought by the founders have survived, not the more valuable pigs and chickens. The survival of these cherished animals would have had high priority, and their failure to be successfully introduced suggests fewer voyages.

> *'Kaore e mau te rongo – ake, ake!'* (Peace never shall be made – never, never!) War chief Rewi Maniapoto in response to government troops at the battle of Orakau, 1864

NZ seems small compared with Australia, but it is bigger than Britain, and very much bigger than other Polynesian islands. Its regions vary wildly in environment and climate. Prime sites for first settlement were warm coastal gardens for the food plants brought from Polynesia (kumara or sweet potato, gourd, yam and taro); sources of workable stone

TIMELINE

AD 1000–1200

Possible date of the arrival of Maori in NZ. Solid archaeological evidence points to about AD 1200, but much earlier dates have been suggested for the first human impact on the environment.

1642

First European contact: Abel Tasman arrives on an expedition from the Dutch East Indies (Indonesia) to find the 'Great South Land'. His party leaves without landing, after a sea skirmish with Maori.

1769

European contact recommences with visits by James Cook and Jean de Surville. Despite some violence, both manage to communicate with Maori. This time NZ's link with the outside world proves permanent.

for knives and adzes; and areas with abundant big game. NZ has no native land mammals apart from a few species of bat, but 'big game' is no exaggeration: the islands were home to a dozen species of moa (a large flightless bird), the largest of which weighed up to 240kg, about twice the size of an ostrich. There were also other species of flightless birds and large sea mammals such as fur seals, all unaccustomed to being hunted. For people from small Pacific islands, this was like hitting the jackpot. The first settlers spread far and fast, from the top of the North Island to the bottom of the South Island within the first 100 years. High-protein diets are likely to have boosted population growth.

By about 1400, however, with big-game supply dwindling, Maori economics turned from big game to small game – forest birds and rats – and from hunting to gardening and fishing. A good living could still be made, but it required detailed local knowledge, steady effort and complex communal organisation, hence the rise of the Maori tribes. Competition for resources increased, conflict did likewise, and this led to the building of increasingly sophisticated fortifications, known as *pa*. Vestiges of *pa* earthworks can still be seen around the country (on the hilltops of Auckland, for example).

The Maori had no metals and no written language (and no alcoholic drinks or drugs). But their culture and spiritual life was rich and distinctive. Below Ranginui (sky father) and Papatuanuku (earth mother) were various gods of land, forest and sea, joined by deified ancestors over time. The mischievous demigod Maui was particularly important. In legend, he vanquished the sun and fished up the North Island before meeting his death between the thighs of the goddess Hine-nui-te-po in an attempt to conquer the human mortality embodied in her.Maori traditional performance art, the group singing and dancing known as *kapa haka,* has real power, even for modern audiences. Visual art, notably

For a thorough overview of NZ history from Gondwanaland to today, visit history-nz.org.

Rumours of late survivals of the giant moa bird abound, but none have been authenticated. So if you see a moa in your travels, photograph it – you have just made the greatest zoological discovery of the last 100 years.

THE MORIORI & THEIR MYTH

One of NZ's most persistent legends is that Maori found mainland NZ already occupied by a more peaceful and racially distinct Melanesian people, known as the Moriori, whom they exterminated. This myth has been regularly debunked by scholars since the 1920s, but somehow hangs on.

To complicate matters, there were real 'Moriori', and Maori did treat them badly. The real Moriori were the people of the Chatham Islands, a windswept group about 900km east of the mainland. They were, however, fully Polynesian, and descended from Maori – 'Moriori' was their version of the same word. Mainland Maori arrived in the Chathams in 1835, as a spin-off of the Musket Wars, killing some Moriori and enslaving the rest. But they did not exterminate them. The mainland Moriori remain a myth.

PAUL KENNEDY / LONELY PLANET IMAGES ©

» Statue of James Cook

1772

Marion du Fresne's French expedition arrives; it stays for some weeks at the Bay of Islands. Relations with Maori start well, but a breach of Maori *tapu* (sacred law) leads to violence.

1790s

Whaling ships and sealing gangs arrive in the country. Relations are established with Maori, with Europeans depending on the contact for essentials such as food, water and protection.

1818–36

Intertribal Maori 'Musket Wars' take place: tribes acquire muskets and win bloody victories against tribes without them. The war tapers off in 1836, probably due to the equal distribution of weapons.

woodcarving, is something special – 'like nothing but itself', in the words of 18th-century explorer-scientist Joseph Banks.

Enter Europe

NZ became an official British colony in 1840, but the first authenticated contact between Maori and the outside world took place almost two centuries earlier in 1642, in Golden Bay at the top of the South Island. Two Dutch ships sailed from Indonesia, to search for southern land and anything valuable it might contain. The commander, Abel Tasman, was instructed to pretend to any natives he might meet 'that you are by no means eager for precious metals, so as to leave them ignorant of the value of the same'.

Similarities in language between Maori and Tahitian indicate close contact in historical times. Maori is about as similar to Tahitian as Spanish is to French, despite the 4294km separating these island groups.

When Tasman's ships anchored in the bay, local Maori came out in their canoes to make the traditional challenge: friends or foes? Misunderstanding this, the Dutch challenged back, by blowing trumpets. When a boat was lowered to take a party between the two ships, it was attacked. Four crewmen were killed. Tasman sailed away and did not come back; nor did any other European for 127 years. But the Dutch did leave a name: 'Nieuw Zeeland' or 'New Sealand'.

Contact between Maori and Europeans was renewed in 1769, when English and French explorers arrived, under James Cook and Jean de Surville. Relations were more sympathetic, and exploration continued, motivated by science, profit and great power rivalry. Cook made two more visits between 1773 and 1777, and there were further French expeditions.

Unofficial visits, by whaling ships in the north and sealing gangs in the south, began in the 1790s. The first mission station was founded in 1814, in the Bay of Islands, and was followed by dozens of others: Anglican, Methodist and Catholic. Trade in flax and timber generated small European–Maori settlements by the 1820s. Surprisingly, the most numerous category of European visitor was probably American. New England whaling ships favoured the Bay of Islands for rest and recreation; 271 called there between 1833 and 1839 alone. To whalers, 'rest and recreation' meant sex and drink. Their favourite haunt, the little town of Kororareka (now Russell) was known to the missionaries as 'the hellhole of the Pacific'. New England visitors today might well have distant relatives among the local Maori.

The Ministry for Culture & Heritage's history website (www.nzhistory.net.nz) is an excellent source of info on NZ history.

One or two dozen bloody clashes dot the history of Maori–European contact before 1840 but, given the number of visits, interracial conflict was modest. Europeans needed Maori protection, food and labour, and Maori came to need European articles, especially muskets. Whaling stations and mission stations were linked to local Maori groups by intermarriage, which helped keep the peace. Most warfare was between

1837

Possums are introduced to New Zealand from Australia. Brilliant.

1840

Starting at Waitangi in the Bay of Islands on 6 February, around 500 chiefs countrywide sign the Treaty of Waitangi to 'settle' sovereignty once and for all. NZ becomes a nominal British colony.

1844

Young Ngapuhi chief Hone Heke challenges British sovereignty, first by cutting down the British flag at Kororareka (now Russell), then by sacking the town itself. The ensuing Northland war continues until 1846.

1858

The Waikato chief Te Wherowhero is installed as the first Maori King.

CAPTAIN JAMES COOK *TONY HORWITZ*

If aliens ever visit earth, they may wonder what to make of the countless obelisks, faded plaques and graffiti-covered statues of a stiff, wigged figure gazing out to sea from Alaska to Australia, from NZ to North Yorkshire, from Siberia to the South Pacific. James Cook (1728–79) explored more of the earth's surface than anyone in history, and it's impossible to travel the Pacific without encountering the captain's image and his controversial legacy in the lands he opened to the West.

For a man who travelled so widely, and rose to such fame, Cook came from an extremely pinched and provincial background. The son of a day labourer in rural Yorkshire, he was born in a mud cottage, had little schooling, and seemed destined for farm work – and for his family's grave plot in a village churchyard. Instead, Cook went to sea as a teenager, worked his way up from coal-ship servant to naval officer, and attracted notice for his exceptional charts of Canada. But Cook remained a little-known second lieutenant until, in 1768, the Royal Navy chose him to command a daring voyage to the South Seas.

In a converted coal ship called *Endeavour,* Cook sailed to Tahiti, and then became the first European to land at NZ and the east coast of Australia. Though the ship almost sank after striking the Great Barrier Reef, and 40% of the crew died from disease and accidents, the *Endeavour* limped home in 1771. On a return voyage (1772–75), Cook became the first navigator to pierce the Antarctic Circle and circle the globe near its southernmost latitude, demolishing the myth that a vast, populous and fertile continent surrounded the South Pole. Cook criss-crossed the Pacific from Easter Island to Melanesia, charting dozens of islands between. Though Maori killed and cooked 10 sailors, the captain remained sympathetic to islanders. 'Notwithstanding they are cannibals,' he wrote, 'they are naturally of a good disposition.'

On Cook's final voyage (1776–79), in search of a northwest passage between the Atlantic and Pacific, he became the first European to visit Hawaii, and coasted America from Oregon to Alaska. Forced back by Arctic pack ice, Cook returned to Hawaii, where he was killed during a skirmish with islanders who had initially greeted him as a Polynesian god. In a single decade of discovery, Cook had filled in the map of the Pacific and, as one French navigator put it, 'left his successors with little to do but admire his exploits'.

But Cook's travels also spurred colonisation of the Pacific, and within a few decades of his death, missionaries, whalers, traders and settlers began transforming (and often devastating) island cultures. As a result, many indigenous people now revile Cook as an imperialist villain who introduced disease, dispossession and other ills to the Pacific (hence the frequent vandalising of Cook monuments). However, as islanders revive traditional crafts and practices, from tattooing to *tapa* (traditional barkcloth), they have turned to the art and writing of Cook and his men as a resource for cultural renewal. For good and ill, a Yorkshire farm boy remains the single most significant figure in the shaping of the modern Pacific.

Tony Horwitz is a Pulitzer-winning reporter and nonfiction author. In researching Blue Latitudes (or Into the Blue), Tony travelled the Pacific – 'boldly going where Captain Cook has gone before'.

1860–69

First and Second Taranaki wars, starting with the controversial swindling of Maori land by the government at Waitara, and continuing with outrage over the confiscation of more land as a result.

1861

Gold discovered in Otago by Gabriel Read, an Australian prospector. As a result, the population of Otago climbs from less than 13,000 to over 30,000 in six months.

1863–64

Waikato Land War. Up to 5000 Maori resist an invasion mounted by 20,000 imperial, colonial and 'friendly' Maori troops. Despite surprising successes, Maori are defeated and much land is confiscated.

1868–72

East Coast war. Te Kooti, having led an escape from his prison on the Chatham Islands, leads a holy guerrilla war in the Urewera region. He finally retreats to establish the Ringatu Church.

Maori and Maori: the terrible intertribal 'Musket Wars' of 1818–36. Because Northland had the majority of early contact with Europe, its Ngapuhi tribe acquired muskets first. Under their great general Hongi Hika, Ngapuhi then raided south, winning bloody victories against tribes without muskets. Once they acquired muskets, these tribes saw off Ngapuhi, but also raided further south in their turn. The domino effect continued to the far south of the South Island in 1836. The missionaries claimed that the Musket Wars then tapered off through their influence, but the restoration of the balance of power through the equal distribution of muskets was probably more important.

Abel Tasman named NZ Statenland, assuming it was connected to Staten Island near Argentina. It was subsequently named after the province of Zeeland in Tasman's Holland.

Europe brought such things as pigs (at last) and potatoes, which benefited Maori, while muskets and diseases had the opposite effect. The negative effects have been exaggerated, however. Europeans expected peoples like the Maori to simply fade away at contact, and some early estimates of Maori population were overly high – up to one million. Current estimates are between 85,000 and 110,000 for 1769. The Musket Wars killed perhaps 20,000, and new diseases did considerable damage too (although NZ had the natural quarantine of distance: infected Europeans usually recovered or died during the long voyage, and smallpox, for example, which devastated native Americans, did not make it here). By 1840, the Maori had been reduced to about 70,000, a decline of at least 20%. Maori bent under the weight of European contact, but they certainly did not break.

Making Pakeha

By 1840, Maori tribes described local Europeans as 'their Pakeha', and valued the profit and prestige they brought. Maori wanted more of both, and concluded that accepting nominal British authority was the way to get them. At the same time, the British government was overcoming its reluctance to undertake potentially expensive intervention in NZ. It too was influenced by profit and prestige, but also by humanitarian considerations. It believed, wrongly but sincerely, that Maori could not handle the increasing scale of unofficial European contact. In 1840, the two peoples struck a deal, symbolised by the treaty first signed at Waitangi on 6 February that year. The Treaty of Waitangi now has a standing not dissimilar to that of the Constitution in the US, but is even more contested. The original problem was a discrepancy between British and Maori understandings of it. The English version promised Maori full equality as British subjects in return for complete rights of government. The Maori version also promised that Maori would retain their chieftainship, which implied local rights of government. The problem was not great at first, because the Maori version applied outside the small European settlements. But as those settlements grew, conflict brewed.

'God's own country, but the devil's own mess.' Prime Minister Richard (King Dick) Seddon, speaking on the source of NZ's self-proclaimed nickname 'Godzone'.

1886–87

Tuwharetoa tribe gifts the mountains of Ruapehu, Ngauruhoe and Tongariro to the government to establish the world's fourth national park.

JOHN ELK III / LONELY PLANET IMAGES ©

» Mt Ngauruhoe (p276), Tongariro National Park

1893

NZ becomes the first country in the world to grant the vote to women, following a campaign led by Kate Sheppard, who petitioned the government for years.

In 1840, there were only about 2000 Europeans in NZ, with the shanty town of Kororareka (now Russell) as the capital and biggest settlement. By 1850, six new settlements had been formed with 22,000 settlers between them. About half of these had arrived under the auspices of the New Zealand Company and its associates. The company was the brainchild of Edward Gibbon Wakefield, who also influenced the settlement of South Australia. Wakefield hoped to short-circuit the barbarous frontier phase of settlement with 'instant civilisation', but his success was limited. From the 1850s, his settlers, who included a high proportion of upper-middle-class gentlefolk, were swamped by succeeding waves of immigrants that continued to wash in until the 1880s. These people were part of the great British and Irish diaspora that also populated Australia and much of North America, but the NZ mix was distinctive. Lowland Scots settlers were more prominent in NZ than elsewhere, for example, with the possible exception of parts of Canada. NZ's Irish, even the Catholics, tended to come from the north of Ireland. NZ's English tended to come from the counties close to London. Small groups of Germans, Scandinavians and Chinese made their way in, though the last faced increasing racial prejudice from the 1880s, when the Pakeha population reached half a million.

Much of the mass immigration from the 1850s to the 1870s was assisted by the provincial and central governments, which also mounted large-scale public works schemes, especially in the 1870s under Julius Vogel. In 1876, Vogel abolished the provinces on the grounds that they were hampering his development efforts. The last imperial governor with substantial power was the talented but Machiavellian George Grey, who ended his second governorship in 1868. Thereafter, the governors (governors-general from 1917) were largely just nominal heads of state; the head of government, the premier or prime minister, had more power. The central government, originally weaker than the provincial governments, the imperial governor and the Maori tribes, eventually exceeded the power of all three.

The Maori tribes did not go down without a fight, however. Indeed, their resistance was one of the most formidable ever mounted against European expansion, comparable to that of the Sioux and Seminole in the US. The first clash took place in 1843 in the Wairau Valley, now a wine-growing district. A posse of settlers set out to enforce the myth of British control, but encountered the reality of Maori control. Twenty-two settlers were killed, including Wakefield's brother, Arthur, along with about six Maori. In 1845, more serious fighting broke out in the Bay of Islands, when Hone Heke sacked a British settlement. Heke and his ally Kawiti baffled three British punitive expeditions, using a modern variant of the traditional *pa* fortification. Vestiges of these innovative earthworks

Maurice Shadbolt's *Season of the Jew* (1987) is a semifictionalised story of bloody campaigns led by warrior Te Kooti against the British in Poverty Bay in the 1860s. Te Kooti and his followers compared themselves to the Israelites who were cast out of Egypt.

To find out more about the New Zealand Wars, visit www.newzealandwars.co.nz.

'I believe we were all glad to leave New Zealand. It is not a pleasant place. Amongst the natives there is absent that charming simplicity...and the greater part of the English are the very refuse of society.' Charles Darwin, referring to Kororareka (Russell), in 1860.

1901
NZ politely declines the invitation to join the new Commonwealth of Australia.

1908
NZ physicist Ernest Rutherford is awarded the Nobel Prize in chemistry for 'splitting the atom', investigating the disintegration of elements and the chemistry of radioactive substances.

1914–18
NZ's contribution to WWI is staggering for a country of just over one million people: about 100,000 NZ men serve overseas. Some 60,000 become casualties, mostly on the Western Front in France.

1931
Napier earthquake kills 131 people.

can still be seen at Ruapekapeka (south of Kawakawa). Governor Grey claimed victory in the north, but few were convinced at the time. Grey had more success in the south, where he arrested the formidable Ngati Toa chief Te Rauparaha, who until then wielded great influence on both sides of Cook Strait. Pakeha were able to swamp the few Maori living in the South Island, but the fighting of the 1840s confirmed that the North Island at that time comprised a European fringe around an independent Maori heartland.

The Six o'clock Swill referred to the frantic after-work drinking at pubs when men tried to drink as much as possible from 5.05pm until strict closing time at 6pm.

In the 1850s, settler population and aspirations grew, and fighting broke out again in 1860. The wars burned on sporadically until 1872 over much of the North Island. In the early years, a Maori nationalist organisation, the King Movement, was the backbone of resistance. In later years, some remarkable prophet-generals, notably Titokowaru and Te Kooti, took over. Most wars were small-scale, but the Waikato war of 1863–64 was not. This conflict, fought at the same time as the American Civil War, involved armoured steamships, ultramodern heavy artillery, telegraph and 10 proud British regular regiments. Despite the odds, the Maori won several battles, such as that at Gate Pa, near Tauranga, in 1864. But in the end they were ground down by European numbers and resources. Maori political, though not cultural, independence ebbed away in the last decades of the 19th century. It finally expired when police invaded its last sanctuary, the Urewera Mountains, in 1916.

Wellington-born Nancy Wake (codenamed 'The White Mouse') led a guerrilla attack against the Nazis with a 7000-strong army. She had the multiple honours of being the Gestapo's most-wanted person and being the most decorated Allied servicewoman of WWII.

Welfare & Warfare

From the 1850s to the 1880s, despite conflict with Maori, the Pakeha economy boomed on the back of wool exports, gold rushes and massive overseas borrowing for development. The crash came in the 1880s, when NZ experienced its Long Depression. In 1890, the Liberals came to power, and stayed there until 1912, helped by a recovering economy. The Liberals were NZ's first organised political party, and the first of several governments to give NZ a reputation as 'the world's social laboratory'. NZ became the first country in the world to give women the vote in 1893, and introduced old-age pensions in 1898. The Liberals also introduced a long-lasting system of industrial arbitration, but this was not enough to prevent bitter industrial unrest in 1912–13. This happened under the conservative 'Reform' government, which had replaced the Liberals in 1912. Reform remained in power until 1928, and later transformed itself into the National Party. Renewed depression struck in 1929, and the NZ experience of it was as grim as any. The derelict little farmhouses still seen in rural areas often date from this era.

1935–49

First Labour government in power, under Michael Savage. This government creates NZ's pioneering version of the welfare state, and also takes some independent initiatives in foreign policy.

1936

NZ aviatrix Jean Batten becomes the first aviator to fly solo from Britain to NZ.

1939–45

NZ troops back Britain and the Allied war effort during WWII; from 1942 a hundred thousand or so Americans arrive to protect NZ from the Japanese.

1948

Maurice Scheslinger invents the Buzzy Bee, NZ's most famous children's toy.

In 1935, a second reforming government took office: the First Labour government, led by Michael Joseph Savage, easily NZ's favourite Australian. For a time, the Labour government was considered the most socialist government outside Soviet Russia. But, when the chips were down in Europe in 1939, Labour had little hesitation in backing Britain.

NZ had also backed Britain in the Boer War (1899–1902) and WWI (1914–18), with dramatic losses in WWI in particular. You can count the cost in almost any little NZ town. A central square or park will contain a memorial lined with names – more for WWI than WWII. Even in WWII, however, NZ did its share of fighting: a hundred thousand or so New Zealanders fought in Europe and the Middle East. NZ, a peaceful-seeming country, has spent much of its history at war. In the 19th century it fought at home; in the 20th, overseas.

LAND WARS *ERROL HUNT*

Five separate major conflicts made up what are now collectively known as the New Zealand Wars (also referred to as the Land Wars or Maori Wars). Starting in Northland and moving throughout the North Island, the wars had many complex causes, but *whenua* (land) was the one common factor. In all five wars, Maori fought both for and against the government, on whose side stood the Imperial British Army, Australians and NZ's own Armed Constabulary. Land confiscations imposed on the Maori as punishment for involvement in these wars are still the source of conflict today, with the government struggling to finance compensation for what are now acknowledged to have been illegal seizures.

Northland war (1844–46) 'Hone Heke's War' began with the famous chopping of the flagpole at Kororareka (now Russell) and 'ended' at Ruapekapeka (south of Kawakawa). In many ways, this was almost a civil war between rival Ngapuhi factions, with the government taking one side against the other.

First Taranaki war (1860–61) Starting in Waitara, the first Taranaki war inflamed the passions of Maori across the North Island.

Waikato war (1863–64) The largest of the five wars. Predominantly involving Kingitanga, the Waikato war was caused in part by what the government saw as a challenge to sovereignty. However, it was land, again, that was the real reason for friction. Following defeats such as Rangiriri, the Waikato people were pushed entirely from their own lands, south into what became known as the King Country.

Second Taranaki war (1865–69) Caused by Maori resistance to land confiscations stemming from the first Taranaki war, this was perhaps the war in which the Maori came closest to victory, under the brilliant, one-eyed prophet-general Titokowaru. However, once he lost the respect of his warriors (probably through an indiscretion with the wife of one of his warriors), the war too was lost.

East Coast war (1868–72) Te Kooti's holy guerrilla war.

1953

New Zealander Edmund Hillary, with Tenzing Norgay, 'knocks the bastard off'; the pair become the first men to reach the summit of Mt Everest.

1973

Fledgling Kiwi prog-rockers Split Enz enter a TV talent quest… finishing second to last.

1974

Pacific Island migrants who have outstayed visas ('overstayers') are subjected to Dawn Raids by immigration police under Robert Muldoon and the National government. These raids continue until the early 1980s.

1981

Springbok rugby tour divides the nation. Many New Zealanders show a strong anti-apartheid stance by protesting the games. Others feel sport and politics shouldn't mix, and support the tour going ahead.

Better Britons?

British visitors have long found NZ hauntingly familiar. This is not simply a matter of the British and Irish origin of most Pakeha. It also stems from the tightening of NZ links with Britain from 1882, when refrigerated cargoes of food were first shipped to London. By the 1930s, giant ships carried frozen meat, cheese and butter, as well as wool, on regular voyages taking about five weeks one way. The NZ economy adapted to the feeding of London, and cultural links were also enhanced. NZ children studied British history and literature, not their own. NZ's leading scientists and writers, such as Ernest Rutherford and Katherine Mansfield, gravitated to Britain. This tight relationship has been described as 'recolonial', but it is a mistake to see NZ as an exploited colony. Average living standards in NZ were normally better than in Britain, as were the welfare and lower-level education systems. New Zealanders had access to British markets and culture, and they contributed their share to the latter as equals. The list of 'British' writers, academics, scientists, military leaders, publishers and the like who were actually New Zealanders is long. Indeed, New Zealanders, especially in war and sport, sometimes saw themselves as a superior version of the British – the Better Britons of the south. The NZ–London relationship was rather like that of the American Midwest and New York.

The Waitangi Treaty Grounds, where the Treaty of Waitangi was first signed in 1840, is now a tourist attraction for Kiwis and non-Kiwis alike. Each year on 6 February, Waitangi hosts treaty commemorations and protests

'Recolonial' NZ prided itself, with some justice, on its affluence, equality and social harmony. But it was also conformist, even puritanical. Until the 1950s, it was technically illegal for farmers to allow their cattle to mate in fields fronting public roads, for moral reasons. The 1953 American movie, *The Wild One,* was banned until 1977. Sunday newspapers were illegal until 1969, and full Sunday trading was not allowed until 1989. Licensed restaurants hardly existed in 1960, nor did supermarkets or TV. Notoriously, from 1917 to 1967, pubs were obliged to shut at 6pm. Yet the puritanical society of Better Britons was never the whole story. Opposition to Sunday trading stemmed, not so much from belief in the sanctity of the Sabbath, but from the belief that workers should have weekends too. Six o'clock closing was a standing joke in rural areas, notably the marvellously idiosyncratic region of the South Island's West Coast. There was always something of a Kiwi counterculture, even before imported countercultures took root from the 1960s.

There were also developments in cultural nationalism, beginning in the 1930s but really flowering from the 1970s. Writers, artists and filmmakers were by no means the only people who 'came out' in that era.

1985

Rainbow Warrior is sunk in Auckland Harbour by French government agents to prevent the Greenpeace protest ship from making its intended voyage to Moruroa, where the French are conducting nuclear tests.

JENNY & TONY ENDERBY / LONELY PLANET IMAGES ©

» Memorial to the sunken ship, *Rainbow Warrior* (p154)

1992

Government begins reparations for the Land Wars, and confirms Maori fishing rights in the 'Sealord deal'. Major settlements follow, including, in 1995, reparations for the Waikato land confiscations.

Coming In, Coming Out

The 'recolonial' system was shaken several times after 1935, but managed to survive until 1973, when Mother England ran off and joined the Franco-German commune now known as the EU. NZ was beginning to develop alternative markets to Britain, and alternative exports to wool, meat and dairy products. Wide-bodied jet aircraft were allowing the world and NZ to visit each other on an increasing scale. NZ had only 36,000 tourists in 1960, compared with more than two million a year now. Women were beginning to penetrate first the upper reaches of the workforce and then the political sphere. Gay people came out of the closet, despite vigorous efforts by moral conservatives to push them back in. University-educated youths were becoming more numerous and more assertive.

Scottish influence can still be felt in NZ, particularly in the south of the South Island. NZ has more Scottish pipe bands per capita than Scotland itself.

From 1945, Maori experienced both a population explosion and massive urbanisation. In 1936, Maori were 17% urban and 83% rural. Fifty years later, these proportions had reversed. The immigration gates, which until 1960 were pretty much labelled 'whites only', widened, first to allow in Pacific Islanders for their labour, and then to allow in (East) Asians for their money. These transitions would have generated major socioeconomic change whatever happened in politics. But most New Zealanders associate the country's recent 'Big Shift' with the politics of 1984.

In 1984, NZ's third great reforming government was elected – the Fourth Labour government, led nominally by David Lange and in fact by Roger Douglas, the Minister of Finance. This government adopted an antinuclear foreign policy, delighting the left, and a more-market economic policy, delighting the right. NZ's numerous economic controls were dismantled with breakneck speed. Middle NZ was uneasy about the antinuclear policy, which threatened NZ's ANZUS alliance with Australia and the US. But in 1985, French spies sank the antinuclear protest ship *Rainbow Warrior* in Auckland Harbour, killing one crewman. The lukewarm American condemnation of the French act brought middle NZ in behind the antinuclear policy, which became associated with national independence. Other New Zealanders were uneasy about the more-market economic policy, but failed to come up with a convincing alternative. Revelling in their new freedom, NZ investors engaged in a frenzy of speculation, and suffered even more than the rest of the world from the economic crash of 1987.

NZ's staunch antinuclear stance earned it the nickname 'The Mouse that Roared'.

The early 21st century is an interesting time for NZ. Food, wine, film and literature are flowering as never before, and the new ethnic mix is creating something very special in popular music. There are continuities, however – the pub, the sportsground, the quarter-acre section, the bush, the beach and the bach – and they too are part of the reason people like to come here. Realising that NZ has a great culture, and an intriguing history, as well as a great natural environment, will double the bang for your buck.

1995

Peter Blake and Russel Coults win the Americas Cup for NZ, sailing *Black Magic;* red socks become a matter of national pride.

2004

Maori TV begins broadcasting – for the first time, a channel committed to NZ content and the revitalisation of Maori language and culture hits the small screen.

2010

A cave-in at Pike River coalmine on the South Island's West Coast kills 29 miners.

2011

A severe earthquake strikes Christchurch, killing 185 people and badly damaging the central business district. NZ hosts (and wins!) the Rugby World Cup.

Environment

Vaughan Yarwood
Vaughan Yarwood is a historian and travel writer who is widely published in New Zealand and internationally. His most recent book is *The History Makers: Adventures in New Zealand Biography*.

The Land

New Zealand is a young country – its present shape is less than 10,000 years old. Having broken away from the supercontinent of Gondwanaland (which included Africa, Australia, Antarctica and South America) in a stately geological dance some 85 million years ago, it endured continual uplift and erosion, buckling and tearing, and the slow fall and rise of the sea as ice ages came and went. Straddling the boundary of two great colliding slabs of the earth's crust – the Pacific plate and the Indian/Australian plate – to this day NZ remains the plaything of nature's strongest forces.

The result is one of the most varied and spectacular series of landscapes in the world, ranging from snow-dusted mountains and drowned glacial valleys to rainforests, dunelands and an otherworldly volcanic plateau. It is a diversity of landforms you would expect to find across an entire continent rather than a small archipelago in the South Pacific.

Evidence of NZ's tumultuous past is everywhere. The South Island's mountainous spine – the 650km-long ranges of the Southern Alps – is a product of the clash of the two plates; the result of a process of rapid lifting that, if anything, is accelerating. Despite NZ's highest peak, Aoraki/Mt Cook, losing 10m from its summit overnight in a 1991 landslide, the Alps are on an express elevator that, without erosion and landslides, would see them 10 times their present height within a few million years.

On the North Island, the most impressive changes have been wrought by volcanoes. Auckland is built on an isthmus peppered by scoria cones, on many of which you can still see the earthworks of *pa* (fortified villages) built by early Maori. The city's biggest and most recent volcano, 600-year-old Rangitoto Island, is just a short ferry ride from the downtown wharves. Some 300km further south, the classically shaped cone of snowcapped Mt Taranaki/Egmont overlooks tranquil dairy pastures.

But the real volcanic heartland runs through the centre of the North Island, from the restless bulk of Mt Ruapehu in Tongariro National Park northeast through the Rotorua lake district out to NZ's most active volcano, White Island, in the Bay of Plenty. Called the Taupo Volcanic Zone, this great 250km-long rift valley – part of a volcano chain known as the 'Pacific Ring of Fire' – has been the seat of massive eruptions that have left their mark on the country physically and culturally.

Most spectacular were the eruptions that created Lake Taupo. Considered the world's most productive volcano in terms of the amount of material ejected, Taupo last erupted 1800 years ago in a display that was the most violent anywhere on the planet within the past 5000 years.

You can experience the aftermath of volcanic destruction on a smaller scale at Te Wairoa (the Buried Village), near Rotorua on the shores of Lake Tarawera. Here, partly excavated and open to the public, lie the remains of a 19th-century Maori village overwhelmed when nearby Mt Tarawera erupted without warning. The famous Pink and White Terraces (one of several claimants to the popular title 'eighth wonder of the world') were destroyed overnight by the same upheaval.

But when nature sweeps the board clean with one hand she often rebuilds with the other: Waimangu Valley, born of all that geothermal violence, is the place to go to experience the hot earth up close and personal amid geysers, silica pans, bubbling mud pools, and the world's biggest hot spring. Or you can wander around Rotorua's Whakarewarewa Thermal Village, where descendants of Maori displaced by the eruption live in the middle of steaming vents and prepare food for visitors in boiling pools.

A second by-product of movement along the tectonic plate boundary is seismic activity – earthquakes. Not for nothing has NZ been called 'the Shaky Isles'. Most quakes only rattle the glassware, but one was indirectly responsible for creating an internationally celebrated tourist attraction…

In 1931, an earthquake measuring 7.9 on the Richter scale levelled the Hawke's Bay city of Napier, causing huge damage and loss of life. Napier was rebuilt almost entirely in the then-fashionable art-deco architectural style, and walking its streets today you can relive its brash exuberance in what has become a mecca for lovers of art deco.

However, the North Island doesn't have a monopoly on earthquakes. In September 2010 Christchurch was rocked by a magnitude 7.1 earthquake. Less than six months later, in February 2011, a magnitude 6.3 quake destroyed much of the city's historic heart and claimed 185 lives, making it the country's second-deadliest natural disaster. NZ's second city continues to be jostled by aftershocks as it begins to build anew.

The South Island can also see some evidence of volcanism – if the remains of the old volcanoes of Banks Peninsula weren't there to repel the sea, the vast Canterbury Plains, built from alpine sediment washed down the rivers from the Alps, would have eroded away long ago.

But in the south it is the Southern Alps themselves that dominate, dictating settlement patterns, throwing down engineering challenges and offering outstanding recreational opportunities. The island's mountainous backbone also helps shape the weather, as it stands in the path of the prevailing westerly winds which roll in, moisture-laden, from the Tasman Sea. As a result bush-clad lower slopes of the western Southern Alps are among the wettest places on earth, with an annual precipitation of some 15,000mm. Having lost its moisture, the wind then blows dry across the eastern plains towards the Pacific coast.

The North Island has a more even rainfall and is spared the temperature extremes of the South – which can plunge when a wind blows in from Antarctica. The important thing to remember, especially if you are tramping at high altitude, is that NZ has a maritime climate. This means weather can change with lightning speed, catching out the unprepared.

NZ is one of the most spectacular places in the world to see geysers. Rotorua's short-lived Waimangu geyser, formed after the Mt Tarawera eruption, was once the world's largest, often gushing to a dizzying height of 400m.

GEYSERS

Wildlife

NZ may be relatively young, geologically speaking, but its plants and animals go back a long way. The tuatara, for instance, an ancient reptile unique to these islands, is a Gondwanaland survivor closely related to the dinosaurs, while many of the distinctive flightless birds (ratites) have distant African and South American cousins.

Due to its long isolation, the country is a veritable warehouse of unique and varied plants, most of which are found nowhere else. And with separation of the landmass occurring before mammals appeared on the scene, birds and insects have evolved in spectacular ways to fill the gaps.

ENVIRONMENTAL ISSUES IN AOTEAROA NEW ZEALAND

NANDOR TANCZOS

Aotearoa New Zealand likes to sell itself as clean and green. We have the NZ Forest Accord to protect native forests. National parks and reserves now cover a third of the country. Marine reserves continue to pop up around the coast. Our antinuclear legislation seems unassailable. A closer look, however, reveals a dirtier picture.

New Zealand is one of the highest per-capita emitters of greenhouse gases. We are one of the most inefficient users of energy in the developed world. Public transport is negligible in most places. Add the ongoing battle in many communities to stop the pumping of sewage and toxic waste into waterways, a conflict often spearheaded by *tangata whenua* (Maori), and the 'clean and green' label looks a bit tarnished.

One of our challenges is that our biggest polluting sector is also our biggest export earner. Pastoral farming causes half of our greenhouse-gas emissions. Clearing forests to grow cows and sheep has left many hillsides scoured by erosion. Grazing animals damage stream edges and lake margins and farm run-off has left many waterways unsafe for swimming or drinking. The worse culprit is dairy farming, and while regional councils and farming groups are fencing and planting stream banks to protect water quality, their efforts are outstripped by the sheer growth in dairying. Meanwhile governments are reluctant to take on the powerful farming lobby.

Our other major challenge is around mining and drilling. The state-owned company Solid Energy plans to expand coalmining on the West Coast and convert lignite (the dirtiest form of coal) into fertiliser and diesel. The government is also encouraging overseas companies to prospect for off-shore oil in what would be some of the deepest and most difficult waters for drilling in the world. Once again local *iwi* (tribes) such as Te Whanau a Apanui are in the front lines alongside environmental groups like Greenpeace, fighting to prevent the marine ecosystems of the East Coast being put at risk.

Despite these things, New Zealand has some good things going on. A high proportion of our energy is from renewable sources. Farm animals, except for pigs and chickens, are mostly grass fed and free range. We are getting better with waste minimisation and resource recovery. Like most countries, though, we need to make a stronger effort to develop not just sustainable, but regenerative economic systems.

Our biggest saving grace is our small population. As a result, Aotearoa is a place well worth visiting. This is a beautiful land with enormous geographical and ecological diversity. Our forests are unique and magnificent, and the bird species that evolved in response to an almost total lack of mammalian life are spectacular, although now reduced in numbers from introduced predators such as rats, stoats and hedgehogs.

Visitors who want to help protect our ecological integrity can make the biggest impact by asking questions of their hosts: every time you ask where the recycling centre is; every time you question wasteful energy use, car use and water use; every time you ask for organic or free-range food at a cafe or restaurant; you affect the person you talk to.

Aotearoa New Zealand has the potential to be a world leader in ecological wisdom. We have a strong tradition to draw from – the careful relationship of reciprocity that Maori developed with the natural world over the course of many, many generations. We live at the edge of the Pacific, on the Rim of Fire, a remnant of the ancient forests of Gondwanaland. We welcome conscious travellers.

Nandor Tanczos is a social ecologist based in Ngaruawahia. He was a Member of Parliament for the Green Party from 1999 to 2008.

The now extinct flightless moa, the largest of which grew to 3.5m tall and weighed over 200kg, browsed open grasslands much as cattle do today (skeletons can be seen at Auckland Museum), while the smaller kiwi still ekes out a nocturnal living rummaging among forest leaf litter for insects and worms much as small mammals do elsewhere. One of the country's most ferocious-looking insects, the mouse-sized giant weta, meanwhile, has taken on a scavenging role elsewhere filled by rodents.

As one of the last places on earth to be colonised by humans, NZ was for millennia a safe laboratory for such risky evolutionary strategies, but with the arrival first of Maori and soon after of Europeans, things went downhill fast.

Many endemic creatures, including moa and the huia, an exquisite songbird, were driven to extinction, and the vast forests were cleared for their timber and to make way for agriculture. Destruction of habitat and the introduction of exotic animals and plants have taken a terrible environmental toll and New Zealanders are now fighting a rearguard battle to save what remains.

Birds & Animals

The first Polynesian settlers found little in the way of land mammals – just two species of bat – but forests, plains and coasts alive with birds. Largely lacking the bright plumage found elsewhere, NZ's birds – like its endemic plants – have an understated beauty that does not shout for attention.

Among the most musical is the bellbird, common in both native and exotic forests everywhere except Northland, though like many birds it is more likely to be heard than seen. Its call is a series of liquid bell notes, most often sounded at dawn or dusk.

The tui, another nectar eater and the country's most beautiful songbird, is a great mimic, with an inventive repertoire that includes clicks, grunts and chuckles. Notable for the white throat feathers that stand out against its dark plumage, the tui often feeds on flax flowers in suburban gardens but is most at home in densely tangled forest ('bush' to New Zealanders).

B Heather and H Robertson's *Field Guide to the Birds of New Zealand* is a comprehensive guide for birdwatchers and a model of helpfulness for anyone even casually interested in the country's remarkable bird life.

Fantails are commonly encountered on forest trails, swooping and jinking to catch insects stirred up by passing hikers, while pukeko, elegant swamp-hens with blue plumage and bright-red beaks, are readily seen along wetland margins and even on the sides of roads nearby – be warned, they have little road sense.

If you spend any time in the South Island high country, you are likely to come up against the fearless and inquisitive kea – an uncharacteristically drab green parrot with bright-red underwings. Kea are common in the car parks of the Fox and Franz Josef Glaciers, where they hang out for food scraps or tear rubber from car windscreens.

Then there is the takahe, a rare flightless bird thought extinct until a small colony was discovered in 1948, and the equally flightless kiwi, NZ's national emblem and the nickname for New Zealanders themselves.

The kiwi has a round body covered in coarse feathers, strong legs and a long, distinctive bill with nostrils at the tip for sniffing out food. It is not easy to find them in the wild, but they can be seen in simulated environments at excellent nocturnal houses. One of the best is the Otorohanga Kiwi House, which also has other birds, including native falcons, moreporks (owls) and weka.

To get a feel for what the bush used to be like, take a trip to Tiritiri Matangi island. This regenerating island is an open sanctuary and one of the country's most successful exercises in community-assisted conservation.

BIRDWATCHING

The flightless kiwi is the species most sought after by birdwatchers. Sightings of the Stewart Island subspecies are common at all times of the year. Elsewhere, wild sightings of this increasingly rare nocturnal species are difficult, apart from in enclosures. Other birds that twitchers like to sight are the royal albatross, white heron, Fiordland crested penguin, yellow-eyed penguin, Australasian gannet and wrybill.

On the Coromandel Peninsula, the Firth of Thames (particularly Miranda) is a haven for migrating birds, while the Wharekawa Wildlife

KIWI SPOTTING

A threatened species, the kiwi is also nocturnal and difficult to see in the wild, although you can do this in Trounson Kauri Park in Northland, Okarito on the West Coast and on Stewart Island. They can, however, be observed in many artificially dark 'kiwi houses':

» Auckland Zoo (p73)
» Kiwi North (p131), Maunu
» Rainbow Springs Kiwi Wildlife Park (p304), Rotorua
» Otorohanga Kiwi House & Native Bird Park (p213)
» National Aquarium of New Zealand (p351), Napier
» Nga Manu Nature Reserve (p392), Waikanae
» Pukaha Mt Bruce National Wildlife Centre (p397), near Masterton
» Wellington Zoo (p373)
» West Coast Wildlife Centre (p469), Franz Josep
» Orana Wildlife Park (p485), Christchurch
» Willowbank Wildlife Reserve (p486), Christchurch
» Kiwi Birdlife Park (p569), Queenstown

Refuge at Opoutere Beach is a breeding ground of the endangered NZ dotterel. There's also a very accessible Australasian gannet colony at Muriwai, west of Auckland, and one in Hawke's Bay. There are popular trips to observe pelagic birds out of Kaikoura, and royal albatross viewing on the Otago Peninsula.

Two good guides are the revised *Field Guide to the Birds of New Zealand*, by Barrie Heather and Hugh Robertson, and *Birds of New Zealand: Locality Guide* by Stuart Chambers.

Nature Guide to the New Zealand Forest, by J Dawson and R Lucas, is a beautifully photographed foray into the world of NZ's forests. Far from being drab and colourless, these lush treasure houses are home to ancient species dating from the time of the dinosaurs. This guidebook will have you reaching for your boots.

MARINE MAMMAL-WATCHING

Kaikoura, on the northeast coast of the South Island, is NZ's nexus of marine mammal-watching. The main attraction here is whale-watching, but this is dependent on weather conditions, so don't expect to just be able to rock up and head straight out on a boat for a dream encounter. The sperm whale, the largest toothed whale, is pretty much a year-round resident, and depending on the season you may also see migrating humpback whales, pilot whales, blue whales and southern right whales. Other mammals – including fur seals and dusky dolphins – are seen year-round.

Kaikoura is also an outstanding place to swim with dolphins. Pods of up to 500 playful dusky dolphins can be seen on any given day. Dolphin swimming is common elsewhere in NZ, with the animals gathering off the North Island near Whakatane, Paihia, Tauranga, and in the Hauraki Gulf, and off Akaroa on the South Island's Banks Peninsula. Seal swimming is possible in Kaikoura and in the Abel Tasman National Park.

Swimming with sharks is also possible, though with a protective cage as a chaperone; you can do it in Gisborne.

Trees

No visitor to NZ (particularly Australians!) will go for long without hearing about the damage done to the bush by that bad-mannered Australian import, the brush-tailed possum. The long list of mammal pests introduced to NZ accidentally or for a variety of misguided reasons includes deer, rabbits, stoats, pigs and goats. But the most destructive by far is the possum, 70 million of which now chew through millions of tonnes of foliage a year despite the best efforts of the Department of Conservation (DOC) to control them.

Among favoured possum food are NZ's most colourful trees: the kowhai, a small-leaved tree growing to 11m, that in spring has drooping clusters of bright-yellow flowers (NZ's national flower); the pohutukawa, a beautiful coastal tree of the northern North Island which bursts into vivid red flower in December, earning the nickname 'Christmas tree'; and a similar crimson-flowered tree, the rata. Rata species are found on both

National Parks

TOWERING KAURI

When Chaucer was born this was a sturdy young tree. When Shakespeare was born it was 300 years old. It predates most of the great cathedrals of Europe. Its trunk is sky-rocket straight and sky-rocket bulky, limbless for half its height. Ferns sprout from its crevices. Its crown is an asymmetric mess, like an inverted root system. I lean against it, give it a slap. It's like slapping a building. This is a tree out of Tolkien. It's a kauri.

Joe Bennett (A Land of Two Halves) referring to the McKinney kauri in Northland.

islands; the northern rata starts life as a climber on a host tree (that it eventually chokes).

The few remaining pockets of mature centuries-old kauri are stately emblems of former days. Their vast hammered trunks and towering, epiphyte-festooned limbs, which dwarf every other tree in the forest, are reminders of why they were sought after in colonial days for spars and building timber. The best place to see the remaining giants is Northland's Waipoua Kauri Forest, home to three-quarters of the country's surviving kauri.

Now the pressure has been taken off kauri and other timber trees, including the distinctive rimu (red pine) and the long-lived totara (favoured for Maori war canoes), by one of the country's most successful imports – *Pinus radiata*. Pine was found to thrive in NZ, growing to maturity in just 35 years, and plantation forests are now widespread through the central North Island – the southern hemisphere's biggest, Kaingaroa Forest, lies southeast of Rotorua.

You won't get far into the bush without coming across one of its most prominent features – tree ferns. NZ is a land of ferns (more than 80 species) and most easily recognised are the mamaku (black tree fern) – which grows to 20m and can be seen in damp gullies throughout the country – and the 10m-high ponga (silver tree fern) with its distinctive white underside. The silver fern is equally at home as part of corporate logos and on the clothing of many of the country's top sportspeople.

> The icon in this book marks places that demonstrate a commitment to sustainability. Travellers seeking other sustainable tourism operators should look for operators accredited with Qualmark Green (www.qualmark.co.nz) or listed at Organic Explorer (www.organicexplorer.co.nz).

National Parks

A third of the country – more than 5 million hectares – is protected in environmentally important parks and reserves that embrace almost every conceivable landscape: from mangrove-fringed inlets in the north to the snow-topped volcanoes of the Central Plateau, and from the forested fastness of the Ureweras in the east to the Southern Alps' majestic mountains, glaciers and fiords. The 14 national parks, three marine parks and more than 30 marine reserves, along with numerous forest parks, offer huge scope for wilderness experiences, ranging from climbing, snow skiing and mountain biking to tramping, kayaking and trout fishing.

Three places are World Heritage areas: NZ's Subantarctic Islands, Tongariro National Park and Te Wahipounamu, an amalgam of several national parks in southwest NZ that boast the world's finest surviving Gondwanaland plants and animals in their natural habitats.

Access to the country's wild places is relatively straightforward, though huts on walking tracks require passes and may need to be booked in advance. In practical terms, there is little difference for travellers between a national park and a forest park, though dogs are not allowed in national parks without a permit. Camping is possible in all parks, but may be restricted to dedicated camping grounds – check first. Permits are required for hunting (game birds), and licences are needed for inland fishing (trout, salmon); both can be bought online at www.fishandgame.org.nz.

> The Department of Conservation website (www.doc.govt.nz) has useful information on the country's national parks, tracks and walkways. It also lists backcountry huts and campsites.

Maori Culture

John Huria

John Huria (Ngai Tahu, Muaupoko) has an editorial, research and writing background with a focus on Maori writing and culture. He was senior editor for Maori publishing company Huia (NZ) and now runs an editorial and publishing services company, Ahi Text Solutions Ltd (www.ahitextsolutions.co.nz).

'Maori' once just meant 'common' or 'everyday', but now it means...let's just begin by saying that there is a lot of 'then' and a lot of 'now' in the Maori world. Sometimes the cultural present follows on from the past quite seamlessly; sometimes things have changed hugely; sometimes we just want to look to the future.

Maori today are a diverse people. Some are engaged with traditional cultural networks and pursuits; others are occupied with adapting tradition and placing it into a dialogue with globalising culture. The Maori concept of *whanaungatanga* – family relationships – is important to the culture. And families spread out from the *whanau* (extended family) to the *hapu* (subtribe) and *iwi* (tribe) and even, in a sense, beyond the human world and into the natural and spiritual worlds.

Maori are New Zealand's *tangata whenua* (people of the land), and the Maori relationship with the land has developed over hundreds of years of occupation. Once a predominantly rural people, many Maori now live in urban centres, away from their traditional home base. But it's still common practice in formal settings to introduce oneself by referring to home: an ancestral mountain, river, sea or lake, or an ancestor. There's no place like home, but it's good to be away as well.

If you're looking for a Maori experience in NZ you'll find it – in performance, in conversation, in an art gallery, on a tour...

The best way to learn about the relationship between the land and the *tangata whenua* is to get out there and start talking with Maori.

Maori Then

Some three millennia ago people began moving eastward into the Pacific, sailing against the prevailing winds and currents (hard to go out, easier to return safely). Some stopped at Tonga and Samoa, and others settled the small central East Polynesian tropical islands.

The Maori colonisation of Aotearoa began from an original homeland known to Maori as Hawaiki. Skilled navigators and sailors travelled across the Pacific, using many navigational tools – currents, winds, stars, birds and wave patterns – to guide their large, double-hulled ocean-going craft to a new land. The first of many was the great navigator Kupe, who arrived, the story goes, chasing an octopus named Muturangi. But the distinction of giving NZ its well-known Maori name – Aotearoa – goes to his wife, Kuramarotini, who cried out, '*He ao, he ao tea, he ao tea roa!*' (A cloud, a white cloud, a long white cloud!).

Kupe and his crew journeyed around the land, and many places around Cook Strait (between the North and South Islands), and the Hokianga in Northland still bear the names that they gave them and the marks of his passage. Kupe returned to Hawaiki, leaving from (and naming) Northland's Hokianga. He gave other seafarers valuable navigational information. And then the great *waka* (ocean-going craft) began to arrive.

The *waka* that the first setters arrived on, and their landing places, are immortalised in tribal histories. Well-known *waka* include *Takitimu, Kurahaupo, Te Arawa, Mataatua, Tainui, Aotea* and *Tokomaru*. There are many others. Maori trace their genealogies back to those who arrived on the *waka* (and further back as well).

Arriving for the first time in NZ, two crew members of *Tainui* saw the red flowers of the pohutukawa tree, and they cast away their prized red feather ornaments, thinking that there were plenty to be had on shore.

What would it have been like making the transition from small tropical islands to a much larger, cooler land mass? Goodbye breadfruit, coconuts, paper mulberry; hello moa, fernroot, flax – and immense space (relatively speaking). NZ has over 15,000km of coastline. Rarotonga, by way of contrast, has a little over 30km. There was land, lots of it, and a flora and fauna that had developed more or less separately from the rest of the world for 80 million years. There was an untouched, massive fishery. There were great seaside mammalian convenience stores – seals and sea lions – as well as a fabulous array of birds.

The early settlers went on the move, pulled by love, by trade opportunities and greater resources; pushed by disputes and threats to security. When they settled, Maori established *mana whenua* (regional authority), whether by military campaigns, or by the peaceful methods of intermarriage and diplomacy. Looking over tribal history it's possible to see the many alliances, absorptions and extinctions that went on.

Histories were carried by the voice, in stories, songs and chants. Great stress was placed on accurate learning – after all, in an oral culture where people are the libraries, the past is always a generation or two away from oblivion.

Maori lived in *kainga,* small villages, which often had associated gardens. Housing was quite cosy by modern standards – often it was hard

HOW THE WORLD BEGAN

In the Maori story of creation, first there was the void, then the night, then Rangi-nui (sky father) and Papa-tu-a-nuku (earth mother) came into being, embracing with their children nurtured between them. But nurturing became something else. Their children were stifled in the darkness of their embrace. Unable to stretch out to their full dimensions and struggling to see clearly in the darkness, their children tried to separate them. Tawhiri-matea, the god of winds, raged against them; Tu-mata-uenga, the god of war, assaulted them. Each god child in turn tried to separate them, but still Rangi and Papa pressed against each other. And then Tane-mahuta, god of the great forests and of humanity, placed his feet against his father and his back against his mother and slowly, inexorably, began to move them apart. Then came the world of light, of demigods and humanity.

In this world of light Maui, the demigod ancestor, was cast out to sea at birth and was found floating in his mother's topknot. He was a shape-shifter, becoming a pigeon or a dog or an eel if it suited his purposes. He stole fire from the gods. Using his grandmother's jawbone, he bashed the sun so that it could only limp slowly across the sky, so that people would have enough time during the day to get things done (if only he would do it again!). Using the South Island as a canoe, he used the jawbone as a hook to fish up Te Ika a Maui (the fish of Maui) – the North Island. And, finally, he met his end trying to defeat death itself. The goddess of death, Hine Nui Te Po, had obsidian teeth in her vagina (obsidian is a volcanic glass that takes a razor edge when chipped). Maui attempted to reverse birth (and hence defeat death) by crawling into her birth canal to reach her heart as she slept. A small bird – a fantail – laughed at the absurd sight. Hine Nui Te Po awoke, and crushed Maui between her thighs. Death one, humanity nil.

to stand upright while inside. From time to time people would leave their home base and go to harvest seasonal foods. When peaceful life was interrupted by conflict, the people would withdraw to *pa,* fortified dwelling places.

And then Europeans began to arrive.

Maori Today

Today's culture is marked by new developments in the arts, business, sport and politics. Many historical grievances still stand, but some *iwi* (Ngai Tahu and Tainui, for example) have settled historical grievances and are major forces in the NZ economy. Maori have also addressed the decline in Maori language use by establishing *kohanga reo, kura kaupapa Maori* and *wananga* (Maori-medium preschools, schools and universities). There is now a generation of people who speak Maori as a first language. There is a network of Maori radio stations, and Maori TV is attracting a committed viewership. A recently revived Maori event is becoming more and more prominent – Matariki, or Maori New Year. The constellation Matariki is also known as Pleiades. It begins to rise above the horizon in late May or early June and its appearance traditionally signals a time for learning, planning and preparing as well as singing, dancing and celebrating. Watch out for talks and lectures, concerts, dinners, and even formal balls.

You can check out a map that shows *iwi* distribution and a good list of *iwi* (tribe) websites on Wikipedia (www.wikipedia.org).

Religion

Christian churches and denominations are important in the Maori world: televangelists, mainstream churches for regular and occasional worship, and two major Maori churches (Ringatu and Ratana) – we've got it all.

But in the (non–Judaeo Christian) beginning there were the *atua Maori,* the Maori gods, and for many Maori the gods are a vital and relevant force still. It is common to greet the earth mother and sky father when speaking formally at a *marae*. The gods are represented in art and carving, sung of in *waiata* (songs), invoked through *karakia* (prayer and incantation) when a meeting house is opened, when a *waka* is launched, even (more simply) when a meal is served. They are spoken of on the *marae* and in wider Maori contexts. The traditional Maori creation story is well known and widely celebrated.

The Arts

There are many collections of Maori *taonga* (treasures) around the country. Some of the largest and most comprehensive are at Wellington's Te Papa Museum and the Auckland Museum. Canterbury Museum in Christchurch also has a good collection, and Hokitika Museum has an exhibition showing the story of *pounamu* (nephrite jade, or greenstone).

You can stay up to date with what is happening in the Maori arts by reading *Mana* magazine (available from most newsagents), listening to *iwi* stations (www.irirangi.net) or weekly podcasts from Radio New Zealand (www.radionz.co.nz). Maori TV also has regular features on the Maori arts – check out www.maoritelevision.com.

Maori TV went to air in 2004, an emotional time for many Maori who could at last see their culture, their concerns and their language in a mass medium. Over 90% of content is NZ-made, and programs are in both Maori and English: they're subtitled and accessible to everyone. If you want to really get a feel for the rhythm and meter of spoken Maori from the comfort of your own chair, switch to Te Reo, a Maori-language-only channel.

TA MOKO

Ta moko is the Maori art of tattoo, traditionally worn by men on their faces, thighs and buttocks, and by women on their chins and lips. *Moko* were permanent grooves tapped into the skin using pigment (made from burnt caterpillar or kauri gum soot), and bone chisels: fine, sharp combs for broad work, and straight blades for detailed work. Museums in the major centres – Auckland, Wellington and Christchurch – all display traditional implements for *ta moko.*

The modern tattooist's gun is common now, but bone chisels are coming back into use for Maori who want to reconnect with tradition. Since the general renaissance in Maori culture in the 1960s, many artists have taken up *ta moko* and now many Maori wear *moko* with quiet pride and humility.

See Ngahuia Te Awekotuku's *Mau Moko: The World of Maori Tattoo* (2007) for the big picture, with powerful, beautiful images and an incisive commentary.

Can visitors get involved, or even get some work done? The term *kirituhi* (skin inscriptions) has arisen to describe Maori motif-inspired modern tattoos that non-Maori can wear.

CARVING

Traditional Maori carving, with its intricate detailing and curved lines, can transport the viewer. It's quite amazing to consider that it was done with stone tools, themselves painstakingly made, until the advent of iron (nails suddenly became very popular).

Some major traditional forms are *waka* (canoes), *pataka* (storage buildings), and *wharenui* (meeting houses). You can see sublime examples of traditional carving at Te Papa in Wellington, and at the following:

» Auckland Museum (p67) Maori Court

» Hell's Gate (p304) Carver in action every day; near Rotorua

» Otago Museum (p535) Nice old *waka* and *whare runanga* (meeting house) carvings, Dunedin

» Parihaka (p238) Historic site on Surf Highway 45, Taranaki

» Putiki Church (p242) Interior covered in carvings and *tukutuku* (wall panels), Whanganui

» Taupo Museum (p261) Carved meeting house

» Te Manawa (p252) Museum with a Maori focus, Palmerston North

» Waikato Museum (p196) Beautifully carved *waka taua* (war canoe), Hamilton

» Wairakei Terraces (p262) Carved meeting house, Taupo

» Waitangi Treaty Grounds (p146) *Whare runanga* and *waka taua*

» Whakarewarewa Thermal Village (p291) The 'living village' – carving, other arts, meeting house and performance, Rotorua

» Whanganui Regional Museum (p241) Wonderful carved *waka*, Whanganui

For information on Maori arts today, check out Toi Maori www.maoriart.org.nz.

The apex of carving today is the *whare whakairo* (carved meeting house). A commissioning group relates its history and ancestral stories to a carver, who then draws (sometimes quite loosely) on traditional motifs to interpret or embody the stories and ancestors in wood or composite fibreboard.

Rongomaraeroa Marae, by artist Cliff Whiting, at Te Papa in Wellington is a colourful example of a contemporary re-imagining of a traditional art form. The biggest change in carving (as with most traditional arts) has been in the use of new mediums and tools. Rangi Kipa uses a synthetic polymer called Corian to make his *hei tiki* (figure motif worn around the neck), the same stuff that is used to make kitchen benchtops. You can check out his gallery at www.rangikipa.com.

VISITING MARAE

As you travel around NZ, you will see many *marae* complexes. Often *marae* are owned by a descent group. They are also owned by urban Maori groups, schools, universities and church groups, and they should only be visited by arrangement with the owners. Some *marae* that may be visited include Huria Marae (p309) in Tauranga; Koriniti Marae (p251) on the Whanganui River Rd; Te Manuka Tutahi Marae (p322) in Wakatane; and Te Papa (p374) in Wellington.

Marae complexes include a *wharenui* (meeting house), which often embodies an ancestor. Its ridge is the backbone, the rafters are ribs, and it shelters the descendants. There is a clear space in front of the *wharenui* (ie the *marae atea*). Sometimes there are other buildings: a *wharekai* (dining hall); a toilet and shower block; perhaps even classrooms, play equipment and the like.

Hui (gatherings) are held at *marae*. Issues are discussed, classes conducted, milestones celebrated and the dead farewelled. *Te reo Maori* (the Maori language) is prominent, sometimes exclusively so.

Visitors sleep in the meeting house if a *hui* goes on for longer than a day. Mattresses are placed on the floor, someone may bring a guitar, and stories and jokes always go down well as the evening stretches out...

The Powhiri

If you visit a *marae* as part of an organised group, you'll be welcomed in a *powhiri* (formal welcome). The more common ones are outlined here.

There may be a *wero* (challenge). Using *taiaha* (quarter-staff) moves, a warrior will approach the visitors and place a baton on the ground for a visitor to pick up.

There is a *karanga* (ceremonial call). A woman from the host group calls to the visitors and a woman from the visitors responds. Their long, high, falling calls begin to overlap and interweave and the visiting group walks on to the *marae atea*.

It is then time for *whaikorero* (speechmaking). The hosts welcome the visitors, the visitors respond. Speeches are capped off by a *waiata* (song), and the visitors' speaker places *koha* (gift, usually an envelope of cash) on the *marae*. The hosts then invite the visitors to *hariru* (shake hands) and *hongi* (press foreheads together). Visitors and hosts are now united and will share light refreshments or a meal.

The Hongi

Press forehead and nose together firmly, shake hands, and perhaps offer a greeting such as *'Kia ora'* or *'Tena koe'*. Some prefer one press (for two or three seconds, or longer), others prefer two shorter (press, release, press). Men and women sometimes kiss on one cheek. Some people mistakenly think the *hongi* is a pressing of noses only (awkward to aim!) or the rubbing of noses (even more awkward).

Tapu

Tapu (spiritual restrictions) and *mana* (power and prestige) are taken seriously in the Maori world. Sit on chairs or seating provided (never on tables), and walk around people, not over them. The *powhiri* is *tapu,* and mixing food and *tapu* is right up there on the offence-o-meter. Do eat and drink when invited to do so by your hosts. You needn't worry about starvation: an important Maori value is *manaakitanga* (kindness).

Depending on the area, the *powhiri* has gender roles: women *karanga* (call), men *whaikorero* (orate); women lead the way on to the *marae,* men sit on the *paepae* (the speakers' bench at the front). In a modern context, the debate around these roles continues.

WEAVING

Weaving was an essential art that provided clothing, nets and cordage, footwear for rough country travel, mats to cover earthen floors, and *kete* (bags). Many woven items are beautiful as well as practical. Some were major works – *korowai* (cloaks) could take years to finish. Woven predominantly with flax and bird feathers, they are worn now on ceremonial occasions, a stunning sight.

Kupe's passage is marked around NZ: he left his sails (Nga Ra o Kupe) near Cape Palliser as triangular landforms; he named the two islands in Wellington Harbour Matiu and Makoro after his daughters; his blood stains the red rocks of Wellington's south coast.

Working with natural materials for the greater good of the people involved getting things right by maintaining the supply of raw material and ensuring that it worked as it was meant to. Protocols were necessary, and women were dedicated to weaving under the aegis of the gods. Today, tradition is greatly respected, but not all traditions are necessarily followed.

Flax was (and still is) the preferred medium for weaving. To get a strong fibre from flax leaves, weavers scraped away the leaves' flesh with a mussel shell, then pounded until it was soft, dyed it, then dried it. But contemporary weavers are using everything in their work: raffia, copper wire, rubber – even polar fleece and garden hoses!

The best place to experience weaving is to contact one of the many weavers running workshops. By learning the art, you'll appreciate the examples of weaving in museums even more. And if you want your own? Woven *kete* and backpacks have become fashion accessories and are on sale in most cities. Weaving is also found in dealer art galleries around the country.

HAKA

Experiencing *haka* can get the adrenaline flowing, as it did for one Pakeha observer in 1929 who thought of dark Satanic mills: 'They looked like fiends from hell wound up by machinery'. *Haka* can be awe-inspiring; they can also be uplifting. The *haka* is not only a war dance – it is used to welcome visitors, honour achievement, express identity or to put forth very strong opinions.

Maori legends are all around you as you tour NZ: Maui's *waka* became today's Southern Alps; a *taniwha* (aupernatural creature) formed Lake Waikaremoana in its death throes; and a rejected Mt Taranaki walked into exile from the central North Island mountain group, carving the Whanganui River.

Haka involve chanted words, vigorous body movements, and *pukana* (when performers distort their faces, eyes bulging with the whites showing, perhaps with tongue extended).

The well-known *haka* 'Ka Mate', performed by the All Blacks before rugby test matches, is credited to the cunning fighting chief Te Rauparaha. It celebrates his escape from death. Chased by enemies, he hid himself in a food pit. After they had left, a friendly chief named Te Whareangi (the 'hairy man' referred to in the *haka*), let him out; he climbed out into the sunshine and performed 'Ka Mate'.

You can experience *haka* at various cultural performances including at Mitai Maori Village (p294), Tamaki Maori Village (p294), Te Puia (p291) and Whakarewarewa Thermal Village (p291) in Rotorua; Ko Tane (p486) at Willowbank in Christchurch; Maori Tours (p420) in Kaikoura; and Myths & Legends Eco-tours (p404) in Picton.

But the best displays of *haka* are at the national Te Matatini National Kapa Haka Festival (p25), when NZ's top groups compete. It is held every two years, with the next festival in February 2013 to take place in Rotorua.

CONTEMPORARY VISUAL ART

A distinctive feature of Maori visual art is the tension between traditional Maori ideas and modern artistic mediums and trends. Shane Cotton produced a series of works that conversed with 19th-century painted meeting houses, which themselves departed from Maori carved houses. Kelcy Taratoa uses toys, superheroes and pop urban imagery alongside weaving and carving design.

Of course not all Maori artists use Maori motifs. Ralph Hotere is a major NZ artist who 'happens to be Maori' (his words), and his career-long exploration of black speaks more to modernism than the traditional *marae* context.

Contemporary Maori art is by no means only about painting. Many other artists use installations as the preferred medium – look out for work by Jacqueline Fraser and Peter Robinson.

There are some great permanent exhibitions of Maori visual arts in the major centres. Both the Auckland and Christchurch Art Galleries hold strong collections, as does Wellington's Te Papa.

See Hirini Moko Mead's *Tikanga Maori*, Pat and Hiwi Tauroa's *Visiting a Marae*, and Anne Salmond's *Hui* for detailed information on Maori customs.

CONTEMPORARY THEATRE

The 1970s saw the emergence of many Maori playwrights and plays, and theatre is a strong area of the Maori arts today. Maori theatre drew heavily on the traditions of the *marae*. Instead of dimming the lights and immediately beginning the performance, many Maori theatre groups began with a stylised *powhiri,* had space for audience members to respond to the play, and ended with a *karakia* or a farewell.

Taki Rua is an independent producer of Maori work for both children and adults and has been in existence for over 25 years. As well as staging its shows in the major centres, it tours most of its work – check out its website (www.takirua.co.nz) for the current offerings. Maori drama is also often showcased at the professional theatres in the main centres as well as the biennial New Zealand International Festival. Hone Kouka and Briar Grace-Smith (both have published playscripts available) have toured their works around NZ and to festivals in the UK.

Music plays an important role in traditional and contemporary Maori culture.

CONTEMPORARY DANCE

Contemporary Maori dance often takes its inspiration from *kapa haka* and traditional Maori imagery. The exploration of pre-European life also provides inspiration. For example, a Maori choreographer, Moss Patterson, used *kokowai* (a body-adorning paste made from reddish clay and shark oil) as the basis of his most recent piece of the same name.

NZ's leading specifically Maori dance company is the Atamira Dance Collective (www.atamiradance.co.nz), which has been producing critically acclaimed, beautiful and challenging work since 2000. If that sounds too earnest, another choreographer to watch out for is Mika Torotoro, who happily blends *kapa haka* (cultural dance), drag, opera, ballet and disco into his work. You can check out clips of his work at www.mika.co.nz.

MAORI FILM-MAKING

Although there had already been successful Maori documentaries (*Patu!* and the *Tangata Whenua* series are brilliant, and available from some urban video stores), it wasn't until 1987 that NZ had its first fiction feature-length movie by a Maori director with Barry Barclay's *Ngati*. Mereta Mita was the first Maori woman to direct a fiction feature, with *Mauri* (1988). Both Mita and Barclay had highly political aims and ways of working, which involved a lengthy pre-production phase, during which they would consult with and seek direction from their *kaumatua* (elders). Films with significant Maori participation or control include the harrowing *Once Were Warriors* and the uplifting *Whale Rider*. Oscar-shortlisted Taika Waititi, of Te Whanau-a-Apanui descent, wrote and directed *Eagle vs Shark*.

The New Zealand Film Archive (www.filmarchive.org.nz) is a great place to experience Maori film, with most showings being either free or relatively inexpensive. It has offices in Auckland and Wellington.

The first NZ hip-hop song to become a hit was Dalvanius Prime's 'Poi E', which was sung entirely in Maori by the Patea Maori Club. It was the highest-selling single of 1984 in NZ, outselling all international artists.

MAORI WRITING

There are many novels and collections of short stories by Maori writers, and personal taste will govern your choices. How about approaching Maori writing regionally? Read Patricia Grace *(Potiki, Cousins, Dogside Story, Tu)* around Wellington, and maybe Witi Ihimaera *(Pounamu, Pounamu, The Matriarch, Bulibasha, The Whale Rider)* on the North Island's East Coast. Keri Hulme *(The Bone People, Stonefish)* and the South Island go together like a mass of whitebait bound in a frying pan by a single egg (ie very well). Read Alan Duff *(Once Were Warriors)* anywhere, but only if you want to be saddened, even shocked. Definitely take James George *(Hummingbird, Ocean Roads)* with you to Auckland's West Coast beaches and Northland's Ninety Mile Beach. Paula Morris *(Queen of Beauty, Hibiscus Coast, Trendy but Casual)* and Kelly Ana Morey *(Bloom, Grace Is Gone)* – hmm, Auckland and beyond? If poetry appeals you can't go past the giant of Maori poetry in English, the late, lamented Hone Tuwhare *(Deep River Talk: Collected Poems)*. Famously sounding like he's at church and in the pub at the same time, you *can* take him anywhere.

The Kiwi Psyche

What Makes Kiwis Tick?

New Zealand is like that little guy at school when they're picking rugby teams – quietly waiting to be noticed, desperately wanting to be liked. Then, when he does get the nod, his sheer determination to prove himself propels him to score a completely unexpected try. When his teammates come to congratulate him he stares at the ground and mumbles, 'It was nothing, ay'.

While NZ is a proud little nation, Kiwis traditionally don't have time for show-offs. Jingoistic flag-waving is generally frowned upon. People who make an impression on the international stage are respected and admired, but flashy tall poppies have traditionally had their heads lopped off. This is perhaps a legacy of NZ's early egalitarian ideals – the ones that sought to avoid the worst injustices of the 'mother country' (Britain) by breaking up large land holdings and enthusiastically adopting a 'cradle to grave' welfare state. 'Just because someone's got a bigger car than me, or bigger guns, doesn't make them better' is the general Kiwi attitude.

People born in other countries make up 23% of NZ residents. Of these, the main regions of origin are the UK and Ireland (29%), the Pacific Islands (15%), Northeast Asia (15%) and Australia (7%).

NZ has rarely let its size get in the way of making a point on the international stage. A founding member of the League of Nations (the precursor to the UN), it ruffled feathers between the world wars by failing to blindly follow Britain's position. It was in the 1980s, however, that things got really interesting.

A Turbulent Decade

Modern Kiwi culture pivots on that decade. Firstly, the unquestioned primacy of rugby union as a source of social cohesion (which rivalled the country's commitment to the two world wars as a foundation of nation-building) was stripped away when tens of thousands of New Zealanders took to the streets to protest a tour by the South African rugby side in 1981. The protestors held that the politics of apartheid not only had a place in sport, they trumped it. The country was starkly divided; there were riots in paradise. The scar is still strong enough that most New Zealanders over the age of 40 will recognise the simple phrase 'The Tour' as referring to those events.

NZ is defined as a state in the Australian constitution. At the time of Australia's federation into one country it was hoped that NZ would join. On this side of the Tasman that idea proved as unpopular then as it does now.

The tour protests both harnessed and nourished a political and cultural renaissance among Maori that had already been rolling for a decade. Three years later, that renaissance found its mark when a reforming Labour government gave statutory teeth to the Waitangi Tribunal, an agency that has since guided a process of land return, compensation for past wrongs and interpretation of the Treaty of Waitangi – the 1840 pact between Maori and the Crown – as a living document.

At the same time antinuclear protests that had been rumbling for years gained momentum, with mass blockades of visiting US naval ships. In 1984 Prime Minister David Lange barred nuclear-powered or armed ships from entering NZ waters. The mouse had roared. As a result the US

'SO, WHAT DO YOU THINK OF NEW ZEALAND?' *RUSSELL BROWN*

That, by tradition, is the question that visitors are asked within an hour of disembarking in NZ. Sometimes they might be granted an entire day's research before being asked to pronounce, but asked they are. The question – composed equally of great pride and creeping doubt – is symbolic of the national consciousness.

When George Bernard Shaw visited for four weeks in 1934, he was deluged with what-do-you-think-of questions from newspaper reporters the length of the country. Although he never saw fit to write a word about NZ, his answers to those newspaper questions were collected and reprinted as *What I Saw in New Zealand: the Newspaper Utterances of George Bernard Shaw in New Zealand*. Yes, people really were that keen for vindication.

Other visitors were more willing to pronounce in print, including the British Liberal MP, David Goldblatt, who wrote an intriguing and prescient little book called *Democracy At Ease: a New Zealand Profile*. Goldblatt found New Zealanders a blithe people: kind, prosperous and fond of machines.

For the bon vivant Goldblatt, the attitude towards food and drink was all too telling. He found only 'the plain fare and even plainer fetch and carry of the normal feeding machine of this country' and shops catering 'in the same pedestrian fashion for a people never fastidious – the same again is the order of the day'.

Thus, a people with access to some of the best fresh ingredients on earth tended to boil everything to death. A nation strewn almost its entire length with excellent microclimates for viticulture produced only fortified plonk. Material comfort was valued, but was a plain thing indeed.

It took New Zealanders a quarter of a century more to shuck 'the same dull sandwiches', and embrace a national awareness – and, as Goldblatt correctly anticipated, it took 'hazards and misfortunes' to spur the 'divine discontent' for change.

But when it did happen, it really happened.

Russell Brown is a journalist and manager of the popular Public Address blog site (www.publicaddress.net).

threw NZ out of ANZUS, the country's main strategic military alliance, which also included Australia, declaring NZ 'a friend but not an ally'.

However, it was an event in the following year that completely changed the way NZ related to the world, when French government agents launched an attack in Auckland Harbour, sinking Greenpeace's antinuclear flagship *Rainbow Warrior* and killing one of its crew. Being bombed by a country that NZ had fought two world wars with – and the muted or nonexistent condemnation by other allies – left an indelible mark. It strengthened NZ's resolve to follow its own conscience in foreign policy, and in 1987 the New Zealand Nuclear Free Zone, Disarmament, and Arms Control Act became law.

> '...a sordid act of international state-backed terrorism...' – Prime Minister David Lange, describing the bombing of the *Rainbow Warrior* (1986)

From the Boer to Vietnam Wars, NZ had blithely trotted off at the behest of the UK or US. Not anymore, as is demonstrated by its lack of involvement in the invasion of Iraq. That's not to say that the country shirks its international obligations: NZ troops continue to be deployed in peacekeeping capacities throughout the world and are currently active in Afghanistan.

If that wasn't enough upheaval for one decade, 1986 saw another bitter battle split the community – this time over the decriminalisation of homosexuality. The debate was particularly rancorous, but the law that previously incarcerated consenting gay adults was repealed, paving the way for the generally accepting society that NZ is today. In 1999 Georgina Beyer, an openly transsexual former prostitute, would win a once-safe rural seat off a conservative incumbent – an unthinkable achievement in most of the world, let alone in the NZ of 13 years earlier.

Yet while the 1980s saw the country jump to the left on social issues, simultaneously economic reforms were carried out that were an extreme step to the right (to paraphrase one-time Hamiltonian Richard O'Brien's song 'The Time Warp'). The bloated public sector was slashed, any state assets that weren't bolted to the floor were sold off, regulation was removed from many sectors, trade barriers dismantled and the power of the unions greatly diminished.

If there is broad agreement that the economy had to be restructured, the reforms carried a heavy price. The old social guarantees are not as sure. New Zealanders work long hours for lower wages than their Australian cousins would ever tolerate. Compared with other Organisation for Economic Co-operation and Development (OECD) nations, NZ family incomes are low, child poverty rates are high and the gap between rich and poor is widening.

Yet there is a dynamism about NZ that was rare in the 'golden weather' years before the reforms. NZ farmers take on the world without the massive subsidies of yore, and Wellington's inner city – once virtually closed after dark by oppressive licensing laws – now thrives with great bars and restaurants.

Ironically, the person responsible for the nuclear age was a New Zealander. In 1917 Ernest Rutherford was the first to split the nucleus of an atom. His face appears on the $100 note.

As with the economic reforms, the 'Treaty process' of redress and reconciliation with Maori makes some New Zealanders uneasy, more in their uncertainty about its extent than that it has happened at all. The Maori population sat somewhere between 85,000 and 110,000 at the time of first European contact 200 years ago. Disease and warfare subsequently decimated the population, but a high birth rate now sees about 15% of New Zealanders (565,000 people) identify as Maori, and that proportion is likely to grow.

The implication of the Treaty is one of partnership between Maori and the British Crown, together forging a bicultural nation. After decades of attempted cultural assimilation it's now accepted in most quarters that the indigenous culture has a special and separate status within the country's ethnic mix. For example, Maori is an official language and there is a separate electoral roll granting Maori guaranteed parliamentary seats.

Yet room has had to be found for the many New Zealanders of neither British nor Maori heritage. In each new wave of immigration there has been a tendency to demonise before gradually accepting and celebrating what the new cultures have to offer. This happened with the Chinese in the mid-19th century, Croatians at the beginning of the 20th, Pacific Islanders in the 1970s and, most recently, the Chinese again in the 1990s. That said, NZ society is more integrated and accepting than most. People of all races are represented in all levels of society and race isn't an obstacle to achievement.

IT'S A WOMAN'S WORLD

New Zealand is justifiably proud of being the first country in the world to give women the vote (in 1893). Kate Sheppard, the hero of the women's suffrage movement, even features on the country's $10 bill. Despite that early achievement, the real role for women in public life was modest for many years. That can hardly be said now. Since 1997 the country has had two female prime ministers and for a time in 2000 every key constitutional position was held by a woman, including the prime minister, attorney general, chief justice, governor general and head of state – although New Zealanders can't take credit for choosing Betty Windsor for that last role. At the same time a Maori queen headed the Kingitanga (King Movement; see p213) and a woman led NZ's biggest listed corporation. Things have slipped a little since and only two of those roles are held by women – and, yes, one of those is filled by Queen Elizabeth II.

A SPORTING CHANCE

The arena where Kiwis have most sated their desperation for recognition on the world stage is sport. In 2011, NZ was ranked the third most successful sporting nation per capita in the world (behind only Jamaica and Norway). NZ's teams are the current world champions in Rugby Union and Rugby League, holding both the men's and women's world cup in each code.

For most of the 20th century, NZ's All Blacks dominated international rugby union, with one squad even dubbed 'The Invincibles'. Taking over this pastime of the British upper class did wonders for national identity and the game is now interwoven with NZ's history and culture. The 2011 Rugby World Cup victory did much to raise spirits after a year of tragedy and economic gloom.

For all rugby's influence on the culture, don't go to a game expecting to be caught up in an orgy of noise and cheering. Rugby crowds at Auckland's Eden Park are as restrained as their teams are cavalier, but they get noisier as you head south. In contrast, a home game for the NZ Warriors rugby league team at Auckland's Mt Smart Stadium is a thrilling spectacle, especially when the Polynesian drummers kick in.

Despite the everyman appeal of rugby union in NZ (unlike in the UK), rugby league retains the status of the working-class sport and support is strongest from Auckland's Maori, Polynesian and other immigrant communities. Still, taking the Rubgy League World Cup off the Australians – NZ's constant arch-rivals – brought a smile to the faces of even the staunchest supporters of the rival rugby code.

Netball is the leading sport for women and the one in which the national team, the Silver Ferns, perpetually vies for world supremacy with the Australians – one or other of the countries has taken the world championship at every contest (except for a three-way tie in 1979).

In 2010 the All Whites, NZ's national soccer (football) squad, competed in the FIFA World Cup for the second time ever, emerging with the totally unanticipated distinction of being the only unbeaten team in the competition. They didn't win any games either, but most Kiwis were overjoyed to have seen their first ever World Cup goals and three draws.

Other sports in which NZ punches above its weight include sailing, rowing, canoeing, equestrian, cycling and triathlon. The most Olympic medals NZ has won have been in athletics, particularly in track and field events. Cricket is the established summer team sport, although not one in which the Kiwis are currently setting the world alight.

If you truly want to discover the good, the bad and the ugly of the national psyche, the sporting field isn't a bad place to start.

For the younger generation, for whom the 1980s are prehistory, political apathy is the norm. Perhaps it's because a decade of progressive government has given them little to kick against – unlike those politicised by the anti–Iraq War movements elsewhere. Ironically, as NZ has finally achieved its own interesting, independent cultural sensibility, the country's youth seem more obsessed with US culture than ever. This is particularly true within the hip-hop scene, where a farcical identification with American gangsta culture has developed into a worrying youth gang problem.

For many, Sir Edmund Hillary, the first person to climb Mt Everest, was the consummate New Zealander: humble, practical and concerned for social justice. A public outpouring of grief followed his death in 2008.

A Long Way From Britain

Most Kiwis (except perhaps the farmers) would probably wish it rained a little less and they got paid a little more, but it sometimes takes a few years travelling on their 'Big OE' (Overseas Experience – a traditional rite of passage) before they realise how good they've got it. In a 2011 study of the quality of life in the world's major cities, Auckland was rated third and Wellington 13th.

Despite all the change, key elements of the NZ identity are an unbroken thread, and fortune is still a matter of economics rather than class. If you are well served in a restaurant or shop, it will be out of politeness or pride in the job, rather than servility.

In country areas and on bushwalks don't be surprised if you're given a cheery greeting from passers-by, especially in the South Island. In a legacy of the British past, politeness is generally regarded as one of the highest virtues. A 'please' and 'thank you' will get you a long way. The three great exceptions to this rule are: a) on the road, where genteel Dr Jekylls become raging Mr Hydes, especially if you have the misfortune of needing to change lanes in Auckland; b) if you don't speak English very well; and c) if you are Australian.

In 2009 and 2010 NZ topped the Global Peace Index, earning the distinction of being rated the world's most peaceful country. In 2011 it dropped to second place behind Iceland – something to do with all those *haka* performed during the Rugby World Cup, perhaps?

The latter two traits are the product of insularity and a smallness of world view that tends to disappear among Kiwis who have travelled (and luckily many do). The NZ/Australian rivalry is taken much more seriously on this side of the Tasman Sea. Although it's very unlikely that Kiwis will be rude outright, visiting Aussies must get pretty sick of the constant ribbing, much of it surprisingly ill-humoured. It's a sad truth that while most Australians would cheer on a NZ sports team if they were playing anyone other than their own, the opposite is true in NZ.

Number-Eight Wire

You might on your travels hear the phrase 'number-eight wire' and wonder what on earth it means. It's a catchphrase New Zealanders still repeat to themselves to encapsulate a national myth: that NZ's isolation and its pioneer stock created a culture in which ingenuity allowed problems to be solved and tools to be built from scratch. A NZ farmer, it was said, could solve pretty much any problem with a piece of number-eight wire (the gauge used for fencing on farms).

No matter where you are in NZ, you're never more than 128km from the sea.

It's actually largely true – NZ farms are full of NZ inventions. One reason big offshore film and TV producers bring their projects here – apart from the low wages and huge variety of locations – is that they like the can-do attitude and ability to work to a goal of NZ technical crews. Many more New Zealanders have worked as managers, roadies or chefs for famous recording artists (everyone from Led Zeppelin and U2 to Madonna) than have enjoyed the spotlight themselves. Which just goes to show that New Zealanders operate best at the intersection of practicality and creativity, with an endearing (and sometimes infuriating) humility to boot.

Arts & Music

It took a hundred years for post-colonial New Zealand to develop its own distinctive artistic identity. In the first half of the 20th century it was writers and visual artists who led the charge. By the 1970s, NZ pub rockers had conquered Australia, while in the 1980s, indie-music obsessives the world over hooked into Dunedin's weird and wonderful alternative scene. However, it took the success of the film industry in the 1990s to catapult the nation's creativity into the global consciousness.

Literature

A nationalist movement first arose in NZ literature in the 1930s, striving for an independent identity and challenging the notion of NZ simply being an annexe of the 'mother country'.

Katherine Mansfield's work began a NZ tradition in short fiction, and for years the standard was carried by novelist Janet Frame, whose dramatic life was depicted in Jane Campion's film of her autobiography, *An Angel at My Table*. Frame's novel *The Carpathians* (1989) won the Commonwealth Writers' Prize. A new era of international recognition began in 1985 when Keri Hulme's haunting *The Bone People* won the Booker Prize (the world is still waiting for the follow-up, *Bait*).

It wasn't until 2007 that another Kiwi looked likely to snag the Booker. Lloyd Jones' *Mister Pip* was pipped at the post, but the nomination rocketed his book up literature charts the world over; a film version is due in 2012.

Less recognised internationally, Maurice 'gee-I've-won-a-lot-of-awards' Gee has gained the nation's annual top fiction gong six times, most recently with *Blindsight* (2005) and *Live Bodies* (1998). His much-loved children's novel *Under the Mountain* (1979) was made into a seminal NZ TV series in 1981 and then a major motion picture in 2009. In 2004 the adaptation of another of his novels, *In My Father's Den* (1972), won major awards at international film festivals and is one of the country's highest grossing films. His latest novel is *Access Road* (2009).

Maurice is an auspicious name for NZ writers, with the late Maurice Shadbolt achieving much acclaim for his many novels, particularly those set during the NZ Wars. Try *Season of the Jew* (1987) or *The House of Strife* (1993).

MAORI VOICES IN PRINT

Some of the most interesting and enjoyable NZ fiction voices belong to Maori writers, with Booker-winner Keri Hulme leading the way. Witi Ihimaera's novels give a wonderful insight into small-town Maori life on the East Coast – especially *Bulibasha* (1994) and *The Whale Rider* (1987), which was made into an acclaimed film – while *Nights in the Gardens of Spain* (1996) casts a similar light on Auckland's gay scene. Patricia Grace's work is similarly filled with exquisitely told stories of rural *marae*-centred life: try *Mutuwhenua* (1978), *Potiki* (1986), *Dogside Story* (2001) or *Tu* (2004).

MIDDLE-EARTH TOURISM

If you are one of those travellers inspired to come down under by the scenery of the *LOTR* movies, you won't be disappointed. Jackson's decision to film in NZ wasn't mere patriotism. Nowhere else on earth will you find such wildly varied, unspoiled landscapes – not to mention poorly paid actors.

You will doubtless recognise some places from the films. For example, Hobbiton (near Matamata), Mt Doom (instantly recognisable as towering Ngauruhoe) or the Misty Mountains (the South Island's Southern Alps). The visitor information centres in Wellington, Twizel or Queenstown should be able to direct you to local *LOTR* sites of interest. If you're serious about finding the exact spots where scenes were filmed, buy a copy of Ian Brodie's nerdtastic *The Lord of the Rings: Location Guidebook*, which includes instructions, and even GPS coordinates, for finding all the important places.

Cinema & TV

If you first got interested in NZ by watching it on the silver screen, you're in good company. Sir Peter Jackson's NZ-made *Lord of the Rings* (*LOTR*) trilogy was the best thing to happen to NZ tourism since Captain Cook.

Yet NZ cinema is hardly ever easygoing. In his BBC-funded documentary, *Cinema of Unease,* NZ actor Sam Neill described the country's film industry as 'uniquely strange and dark', producing bleak, haunted work. One need only watch Lee Tamahore's harrowing *Once Were Warriors* (1994) to see what he means.

Other than 2003's winner *Return of the King*, *The Piano* is the only NZ movie to be nominated for a Best Picture Oscar. Jane Campion was the first Kiwi nominated as Best Director and Peter Jackson the first to win it.

The *Listener*'s film critic, Philip Matthews, makes a slightly more upbeat observation: 'Between (Niki Caro's) *Whale Rider,* (Christine Jeffs') *Rain* and *Lord of the Rings,* you can extract the qualities that our best films possess. Beyond slick technical accomplishment, all share a kind of land-mysticism, an innately supernatural sensibility'.

You could add to this list Jane Campion's *The Piano* (1993), Brad McGann's *In My Father's Den* (2004) and Jackson's *Heavenly Creatures* (1994) – all of which use magically lush scenery to couch disturbing violence. It's a land-mysticism constantly bordering on the creepy.

Even when Kiwis do humour it's as resolutely black as their rugby jerseys; check out Jackson's early splatter-fests and Taika Waititi's *Boy* (2010). Exporting NZ comedy hasn't been easy, yet the HBO-produced TV musical parody *Flight of the Conchords* – featuring a mumbling, bumbling Kiwi folk-singing duo trying to get a break in New York – has found surprising international success.

It's the Polynesian giggle-factor that seems likeliest to break down the bleak house of NZ cinema, with feel-good-through-and-through *Sione's Wedding* (2006) netting the second-biggest local takings of any NZ film.

The TV show *Popstars* originated in New Zealand, though the resulting group, True Bliss, was short-lived. The series concept was then picked up in Australia, the UK, and the US, inspiring the *Idol* series.

New Zealanders have gone from never seeing themselves in international cinema to having whole cloned armies of Temuera Morrisons invading the universe in *Star Wars.* Familiar faces such as Cliff Curtis and Karl Urban seem to constantly pop up playing Mexican or Russian gangsters in action movies. Many of them got their start in long-running soap opera *Shortland St* (7pm weekdays, TV2).

While the tourist industry waits for Jackson's *The Hobbit* (due late 2012), the NZ film industry has quietly continued producing well-crafted, affecting movies, such as *The Topp Twins: Untouchable Girls* (people's choice documentary winner at the Toronto and Melbourne film festivals, 2009).

Music

NZ music began with the *waiata* (singing) developed by Maori following their arrival in the country. The main musical instruments were wind instruments made of bone or wood, the most well known of which is the *nguru* (also known as the 'nose flute'), while percussion was provided by chest- and thigh-slapping. These days, the liveliest place to see Maori music being performed is at *kapa haka* competitions in which groups compete with their own routines of traditional song and dance. In a similar vein is the Pasifika Festival (p81) in Auckland, which has areas to represent each of the Pacific Islands. It is a great place to see both traditional and modern forms of Polynesian music, whether that means modern hip-hop beats or throbbing Cook Island drums, or island-style guitar, ukulele and slide guitar.

Gareth Shute

Gareth Shute wrote this music section. He is the author of four books, including *Hip Hop Music in Aotearoa* and *NZ Rock 1987–2007*. He is also a musician and has toured the UK, Europe and Australia as a member of The Ruby Suns and The Brunettes. He now plays in indie soul group The Cosbys.

Early European immigrants brought their own styles of music and gave birth to local variants during the early 1900s. In the 1950s Douglas Lilburn became one of the first internationally recognised NZ classical composers. More recently the country has produced a number of world-renowned musicians in this field, including opera singer Dame Kiri Te Kanawa, million-selling pop diva Hayley Westenra, composer John Psathas (who created music for the 2004 Olympic Games) and composer/percussionist Gareth Farr (who also performs in drag under the name Lilith). Each of the main universities in NZ has its own music school and these often have free concerts, which visitors can attend. Larger-scale performances are held in the Edge conglomerate of venues in Auckland and the Town Hall/Michael Fowler Centre in Wellington.

NZ also has a strong rock-music scene, its most acclaimed exports being the revered indie label Flying Nun and the music of the Finn Brothers. In 1981 Flying Nun was started by Christchurch record store owner Roger Shepherd (who sold it in the '90s, but bought back partial ownership in 2009). Many of the early groups came from Dunedin, where local musicians took the DIY attitude of punk but used it to produce a lo-fi indie-pop that received rave reviews from the likes of *NME* in the UK and *Rolling Stone* magazine in the US. Billboard even claimed in 1989: 'There doesn't seem to be anything on Flying Nun Records that is less than excellent.'

For indie rock fans, a great source of local information is www.cheeseontoast.co.nz, which lists gigs and has interviews/photographs of bands (both local and international). Local hip hop, pop, and rock is also discussed at www.thecorner.co.nz. One of the longest running local music websites is www.muzic.net.nz.

Many of the musicians from the Flying Nun scene still perform live to this day, including David Kilgour (from The Clean), Martin Phillipps (from The Chills), and Shayne Carter (from the Straitjacket Fits, now fronting Dimmer and The Adults). These days, the spirit of the scene is kept alive at Chick's Hotel (p545) in Port Chalmers (near Dunedin). The indie scene in NZ is being kept fresh by newer labels such as Lil Chief Records and Arch Hill Recordings. For more adventurous listeners, Bruce Russell continues to play in influential underground group The Dead C, and releases music through his Corpus Hermeticum label.

Since the millennium, the NZ music scene has developed a new vitality after the government convinced commercial radio stations to adopt a voluntary quota of 20% local music. This enabled commercially oriented musicians to develop solid careers. Rock groups such as Shihad, The Feelers and Op-shop have thrived in this environment, as have a set of soulful female solo artists (who all happen to have Maori heritage): Bic Runga, Anika Moa, and Brooke Fraser (daughter of All Black Bernie Fraser).

However, the genres of music that have been adopted most enthusiastically by Maori and Polynesian New Zealanders have been reggae (in the 1970s) and hip-hop (in the 1980s), which has led to distinct local forms. In Wellington, a thriving jazz scene took on a reggae influence to create a host of groups that blend dub, roots, and funky jazz – most notably Fat Freddy's Drop. Most of Wellington's music venues are located on Cuba St and immediate surrounds. The national public holiday, Waitangi Day, on 6 February, also happens to fall on the birthday of Bob Marley and annual reggae concerts are held on this day in Auckland and Wellington.

The local hip-hop scene has its heart in the suburbs of South Auckland, which have a high concentration of Maori and Pacific Island residents. This area is home to one of NZ's foremost hip-hop labels, Dawn Raid, which takes its name from the infamous early-morning house raids of the 1970s that police performed on Pacific Islanders suspected of outstaying their visas.

Dawn Raid's most successful artist is Savage, who sold a million copies of his single 'Swing' after it was featured in the movie *Knocked Up*. Within NZ, the most well-known hip-hop acts are Scribe, Che Fu, and Smashproof (whose song 'Brother' held number one on the NZ singles charts longer than any other local act).

Early in the new millennium, NZ also produced two internationally acclaimed garage rock acts: the Datsuns and the D4. In Auckland the main venues for rock music are the Kings Arms Tavern (p95) and Cassette Nine (p95), though two joint venues in St Kevins Arcade (off Karangahape Rd) are also popular – the Wine Cellar & Whammy Bar (p94). Wellington is rife with live music venues from Mighty Mighty (p383) to the San Francisco Bath House (p385), to Bodega (p385).

Dance music had its strongest following in Christchurch in the 1990s, spawning dub/electronica outfit Salmonella Dub and its offshoot act, Tiki Taane. Drum 'n' bass remains popular locally and has spawned internationally renowned acts such as Concord Dawn and Shapeshifter. Unfortunately the music scene in Christchurch was crippled by the

An up-to-date list of gigs in the main centres is listed at www.grooveguide.co.nz. Tickets for most events can be bought at: www.ticketek.co.nz, www.ticketmaster.co.nz, or, for smaller gigs, www.undertheradar.co.nz.

THE BROTHERS FINN

There are certain tunes that all Kiwis can sing along to, given a beer and the opportunity. A surprising proportion of these were written by Tim and Neil Finn, and many of their songs have gone on to be international hits.

Tim Finn first came to prominence in the 1970s group Split Enz. When the original guitarist quit, Neil flew over to join the band in the UK despite being only 15 at the time. Split Enz amassed a solid following in Australia, New Zealand and Canada before disbanding in 1985.

Neil then formed Crowded House with two Australian musicians (Paul Hester and Nick Seymour) and one of their early singles, 'Don't Dream It's Over', hit number two on the US charts. Tim later did a brief spell in the band, during which the brothers wrote 'Weather With You' – a song that reached number seven on the UK charts, pushing their album *Woodface* to gold sales. The original line-up of Crowded House played their final show in 1996 in front of 100,000 people on the steps of the Sydney Opera House (though Finn and Seymour reformed the group in 2007 and continue to tour and record occasionally). Tim and Neil have both released a number of solo albums, as well as releasing material together as the Finn Brothers.

More recently, Neil has also remained busy, organising a set of shows/releases under the name Seven Worlds Collide, which is a collaboration with well-known overseas musicians, including Jeff Tweedy (Wilco), Johnny Marr (The Smiths) and members of Radiohead. His latest band is the Pajama Club, a collaboration with wife Sharon and Auckland musicians Sean Donnelly and Alana Skyring.

Neil's son Liam also has a burgeoning solo career, which has seen him tour the US with Eddie Vedder and The Black Keys, as well as appearing on the David Letterman show. Both Tim and Neil were born in the small town of Te Awamutu and the local museum has a collection that documents their work.

earthquakes in late 2010 and early 2011. In the interim, a number of temporary spaces have opened up as gig venues; a full list of events can be found at www.christchurchmusic.org.nz. Further south, many local bands tour through Queenstown during the ski season, with the main venue being Dux De Lux (p586).

In summer, many of the beachfront towns throughout the country are visited by touring bands (winery shows are also popular). One venue of note in this respect is the Leigh Sawmill (p123) in Leigh (80km from Auckland).

A number of festivals take place over the summer months, including new year's celebration Rhythm & Vines and the Christian-rock festival Parachute (www.parachutemusic.com), held near Hamilton in January. Also recommended is the underground festival held early each year by A Low Hum (www.alowhum.com). Lovers of world music may enjoy the local version of Womad, which is held in New Plymouth and features both local and overseas acts that draw from traditional music forms.

Visual Arts

The NZ 'can do' attitude extends to the visual arts. If you're visiting a local's home don't be surprised to find one of the owner's paintings on the wall or one of their mate's sculptures in the back garden, pieced together out of bits of shell, driftwood and a length of the magical 'number-eight wire'.

This is symptomatic of a flourishing local art and crafts scene cultivated by lively tertiary courses churning out traditional carvers and weavers, jewellery makers, multimedia boffins, and moulders of metal and glass. The larger cities have excellent dealer galleries representing interesting local artists working across all media.

A wide range of cultural events is listed on www.eventfinder.co.nz. This is a good place to find out about concerts, classical music recitals and *kapa haka* performances. For more specific information on the NZ classical music scene, see www.sounz.org.nz.

Not all the best galleries are in Auckland or Wellington. The energetic Govett-Brewster Art Gallery (p227) – home to the legacy of sculptor and film-maker Len Lye – is worth a visit to New Plymouth in itself, and Gore's Eastern Southland Gallery has an important and growing collection.

Traditional Maori art has a distinctive visual style with well-developed motifs that have been embraced by NZ artists of every race. In the painting medium, these include the cool modernism of the work of Gordon Walters and the more controversial pop-art approach of Dick Frizzell's *Tiki* series. Likewise, Pacific Island themes are common, particularly in Auckland. An example is the work of Niuean-born Auckland-raised John Pule.

It should not be surprising that in a nation so defined by its natural environment, landscape painting constituted the first post-European body of art. John Gully and Petrus van der Velden were among those to arrive and paint memorable (if sometimes overdramatised) depictions of the land.

A little later, Charles Frederick Goldie painted a series of compelling, realist portraits of Maori, who were feared to be a dying race. Debate over the political propriety of Goldie's work raged for years, but its value is widely accepted now: not least because Maori themselves generally acknowledge and value them as ancestral representations.

From the 1930s NZ art took a more modern direction and produced some of the country's most celebrated artists including Rita Angus, Toss Woollaston and Colin McCahon. McCahon is widely regarded to have been the country's most important artist. His paintings might seem inscrutable, even forbidding, but even where McCahon lurched into Catholic mysticism or quoted screeds from the Bible, his spirituality was rooted in geography. His bleak, brooding landscapes evoke the sheer power of NZ's terrain.

Survival Guide

DIRECTORY A-Z 676
Accommodation 676
Business Hours 679
Children 679
Climate 679
Customs Regulations 680
Discount Cards 680
Electricity 680
Embassies & Consulates 680
Food & Drink 681
Gay & Lesbian Travellers 681
Health 682
Insurance 683
Internet Access 683
Maps 683
Money 684
Post 684
Public Holidays 685
Safe Travel 685
Shopping 685
Telephone 686
Time 686
Tourist Information 687
Travellers with Disabilities 687
Visas 687
Women Travellers 688
Work 688

TRANSPORT 690
GETTING THERE & AWAY 690
Entering the Country 690
Air 690
Sea 692
GETTING AROUND 692
Air 692
Bicycle 693
Boat 693
Bus 693
Car & Motorcycle 695
Hitching & Ride-Sharing 697
Local Transport 697
Train 698

LANGUAGE 699

Directory A–Z

Accommodation

Across New Zealand, you can bed down in historic guesthouses, facility-laden hotels, uniform motel units, beautifully situated campsites, and hostels that range in character from clean-living to tirelessly party-prone.

Accommodation listings are in order of authorial preference, based on our assessment of atmosphere, cleanliness, facilities, location and bang for your buck.

If you're travelling during peak tourist seasons, book your bed well in advance. Accommodation is most in demand (and at its priciest) during the summer holidays from Christmas to late January, at Easter and during winter in snowy resort towns like Queenstown.

Visitor information centres provide reams of local accommodation information, often in the form of folders detailing facilities and up-to-date prices; many can also make bookings on your behalf.

For online listings, visit **Automobile Association** (AA; www.aa.co.nz) and **Jasons** (www.jasons.com).

B&Bs

Bed and breakfast (B&B) accommodation is a growth industry in NZ, popping up in the middle of cities, in rural hamlets and on stretches of isolated coastline, with rooms on offer in everything from suburban bungalows to stately manors owned by one family for generations.

Breakfast may be 'continental' (cereal, toast and tea or coffee), 'hearty continental' (add yoghurt, fruit, home-baked bread or muffins), or a stomach-loading cooked meal including eggs, bacon and sausages. Some B&B hosts may also cook dinner for guests and advertise dinner, bed and breakfast (DB&B) packages.

B&B tariffs are typically in the $120 to $180 bracket (per double), though some places charge upwards of $300 per double. Some hosts continue to be cheeky-as-a-kea, charging hefty prices for what is, in essence, a bedroom in their home.

Online resources:

Bed & Breakfast Book (www.bnb.co.nz)

Bed and Breakfast Directory (www.bed-and-breakfast.co.nz)

Camping & Holiday Parks

Campers and campervan drivers alike converge upon NZ's hugely popular 'holiday parks', slumbering peacefully in powered and unpowered sites, cheap bunk rooms (dorm rooms), cabins and self-contained units that are often called motels or tourist flats. Well-equipped communal kitchens, dining areas and games and TV rooms often feature. In cities, holiday parks are usually a fair way from the action, but in smaller towns they can be impressively central or near lakes, beaches, rivers and forests.

The nightly cost of holiday-park camping is usually between $15 and $20 per adult, with children charged half-price; powered sites are a couple of dollars more. Cabin/unit accommodation normally ranges from $60 to $120 per double. Unless noted otherwise, the prices we've listed for campsites, campervan sites, huts and cabins are for two people. The 'big three' holiday park operators around NZ – Top 10, Kiwi Parks and Family Parks – all offer discount cards for loyal slumberers.

DOC CAMPSITES & FREEDOM CAMPING

A fantastic option for those in campervans are the 250-plus

> **BOOK YOUR STAY ONLINE**
>
> For more accommodation reviews by Lonely Planet authors, check out http://hotels.lonelyplanet.com. You'll find independent reviews, as well as recommendations on the best places to stay. Best of all, you can book online.

SLEEPING PRICE RANGES

The following price ranges refer to a double with en suite.

» **$ Budget** Less than $100

» **$$ Midrange** $100-180

» **$$$ Top end** More than $180

Price ranges generally increase by 20% to 25% in Auckland, Wellington and Christchurch. Here you can still find budget accommodation at up to $100 per double, but midrange stretches from $100 to $200, with top-end rooms more than $200.

vehicle-accessible 'Conservation Campsites' run by the **Department of Conservation** (DOC; www.doc.govt.nz), with fees ranging from free (basic toilets and fresh water) to $19 per adult (flush toilets and showers). DOC publishes free brochures with detailed descriptions and instructions to find every campsite (even GPS coordinates). Pick up copies from DOC offices before you hit the road, or visit the website.

DOC also looks after hundreds of 'Backcountry Huts', which can only be reached on foot. See the website for details.

Never just assume it's OK to camp somewhere. Always ask a local first. Check at the local i-SITE or DOC office, or with commercial camping grounds. If you are freedom camping (p695), treat the area with respect. Instant fines can be charged for camping in prohibited areas, or irresponsible disposal of waste. For more freedom camping info see, www.camping.org.nz.

Farmstays

Farmstays open the door on the agricultural side of NZ life, with visitors encouraged to get some dirt beneath their fingernails at orchards, and dairy, sheep and cattle farms. Costs can vary widely, with B&Bs generally ranging from $80 to $120. Some farms have separate cottages where you can fix your own food, while others offer low-cost, shared, backpacker-style accommodation.

Farm Helpers in NZ (FHINZ; www.fhinz.co.nz) produces a booklet ($25) that lists around 350 NZ farms providing lodging in exchange for four to six hours' work per day. **Rural Holidays NZ** (www.ruralholidays.co.nz) lists farmstays and homestays throughout the country on its website.

Hostels

NZ is packed to the rafters with backpacker hostels, both independent and part of large chains, ranging from small, homestay-style affairs with a handful of beds to refurbished hotels and towering modern structures in the big cities. Hostel bed prices listed throughout this book are nonmember rates, usually between $25 and $35 per night.

If you're a Kiwi travelling in your own country, be warned that some hostels only admit overseas travellers, typically inner-city places. If you encounter such discrimination, either try another hostel or insist that you're a genuine traveller and not a bedless neighbour.

Online, www.hostelworld.com is useful for pre-trip planning.

HOSTEL ORGANISATIONS

Budget Backpacker Hostels (BBH; www.bbh.co.nz) NZ's biggest hostel group, with around 300 hostels on its books, including homestays and farmstays. Membership costs $45 and entitles you to stay at member hostels at rates listed in the annual (free) *BBH Backpacker Accommodation* booklet. Nonmembers pay an extra $3 per night, though not all hostel owners charge the difference. Pick up a membership card from

PRACTICALITIES

» **News** Leaf through Auckland's *New Zealand Herald*, Wellington's *Dominion Post* or Christchurch's *The Press* newspapers, or check out www.stuff.co.nz.

» **TV** Watch one of the national government-owned TV stations (TV One, TV2, TVNZ 6, TVNZ 7, Maori TV and the 100% Maori language Te Reo) or the subscriber-only Sky TV (www.skytv.co.nz).

» **Radio** Tune in to Radio National for current affairs and Concert FM for classical and jazz (see www.radionz.co.nz for frequencies). Kiwi FM (www.kiwifm.co.nz) showcases NZ music; Radio Hauraki (www.hauraki.co.nz) cranks out classic rock (the national appetite for Fleetwood Mac is insatiable...).

» **DVDs** Kiwi DVDs are encoded for Region 4, which includes Mexico, South America, Central America, Australia, the Pacific and the Caribbean.

» **Electrical** To plug yourself into the electricity supply (230V AC, 50Hz), use a three-pin adaptor (the same as in Australia; different from British three-pin adaptors).

» **Weights & measures** NZ uses the metric system.

WWOOFING

If you don't mind getting your hands dirty, an economical way of travelling around NZ involves doing some voluntary work as a member of **Willing Workers on Organic Farms** (WWOOF; ☎03-544 9890; www.wwoof.co.nz). Membership of this popular, well-established international organisation scores you access to hundreds of organic and permaculture farms, market gardens and other environmentally sound cottage industries across the country. Down on the farm, in exchange for a hard day's work, owners provide food, accommodation and some hands-on organic farming experience. Contact farm owners a week or two beforehand to arrange your stay, as you would for a hotel or hostel – don't turn up unannounced!

A one-year online membership costs $40; an online membership and a farm-listing book, which is mailed to you, costs $50. You should be part of a Working Holiday Scheme when you visit NZ, as the immigration department considers WWOOFers to be working.

any member hostel, or have one mailed to you overseas for $50 (see the website for details).

YHA New Zealand (Youth Hostels Association; www.yha.co.nz) More than 50 hostels in prime NZ locations. The YHA is part of the **Hostelling International** (HI; www.hihostels.com) network, so if you're already an HI member in your own country, membership entitles you to use NZ hostels. If you don't already have a membership card from home, you can buy one at major NZ YHA hostels for $42 for 12 months, or book online and have your card mailed to you overseas for the same price. Hostels also take non-YHA members for an extra $3 per night. NZ YHA hostels also supply bed linen, so you don't need to bring a sleeping bag.

VIP Backpackers (www.vipbackpackers.com) International organisation affiliated with around 20 NZ hostels (not BBH or YHA), mainly in the cities and tourist hot-spots. For around $63 (including postage) you'll receive a 12-month membership entitling you to a $1 discount off nightly accommodation. You can join online, at VIP hostels or at larger agencies dealing in backpacker travel.

Nomads Backpackers (www.nomadsworld.com) Six franchisees throughout NZ: Auckland, Paihia, Rotorua, Taupo, Wellington and Queenstown. Membership costs AUD$37 for 12 months and like VIP offers NZ$1 off the cost of nightly accommodation. Join at participating hostels, backpacker travel agencies or online.

Base Backpackers (www.stayatbase.com) Chain with eight hostels around NZ. Expect clean dorms, girls-only areas and party opportunities aplenty. Offers a 10-night 'Base Jumping' accommodation card for $239, bookable online.

Pubs, Hotels & Motels

Pubs The least expensive form of NZ hotel accommodation is the humble pub. As is often the case elsewhere, some of NZ's old pubs are full of character (and characters), while others are grotty, ramshackle places that are best avoided, especially by women travelling solo. Also check whether there's a band cranking out the tunes the night you plan to be in town, as you could be in for a sleepless night. In the cheapest pubs, singles/doubles might cost as little as $30/60 (with a shared bathroom down the hall), though $50/80 is more common.

Hotels At the top end of the hotel scale are five-star international chains, resort complexes and architecturally splendorous boutique hotels, all of which charge a hefty premium for their mod cons, snappy service and/or historic opulence. We quote 'rack rates' (official advertised rates) for such places throughout this book, but discounts and special deals often mean you won't have to pay these prices.

Motels NZ's towns have a glut of nondescript, low-rise motels and 'motor lodges', charging between $80 and $180 for double rooms. These tend to be squat structures congregating just outside CBDs, or skulking by highways on the edge of towns. Most are modernish (though decor is often mired in the '90s) and have similar facilities, namely tea- and coffee-making equipment, fridge, and TV – prices vary with standard.

Rental Accommodation

The basic Kiwi holiday home is called a 'bach' (short for 'bachelor', as they were often used by single men as hunting and fishing hideouts); in Otago and Southland they're known as 'cribs'. These are simple self-contained cottages that can be rented in rural and coastal areas, often in isolated locations. Prices are typically $80 to $130 per night, which isn't bad for a whole house or self-contained bungalow.

For more upmarket holiday houses, the current trend is to throw rusticity to the wind and erect luxurious cottages on beautiful nature-surrounded plots. Expect to pay anything from $130 to $400 per double.

Online resources:

» www.holidayhomes.co.nz
» www.bookabach.co.nz
» www.holidayhouses.co.nz
» www.nzapartments.co.nz

Business Hours

Note that most attractions close on Christmas Day and Good Friday.

Shops & businesses 9am to 5.30pm Monday to Friday, and 9am to 12.30pm or 5pm Saturday. Late-night shopping (until 9pm) in larger cities on Thursday and/or Friday nights. Sunday trading in most big towns and cities.

Supermarkets 8am to 7pm, often 9pm or later in cities.

Banks 9.30am to 4.30pm Monday to Friday; some city branches also open Saturday mornings.

Post offices 8.30am to 5pm Monday to Friday; larger branches also 9.30am to 1pm Saturday. Postal desks in newsagencies open later.

Restaurants Food until 9pm, often until 11pm on Fridays and Saturdays.

Cafes 7am to 4pm or 5pm.

Pubs Noon until late; food from noon to 2pm and from 6pm to 8pm.

Climate

Auckland

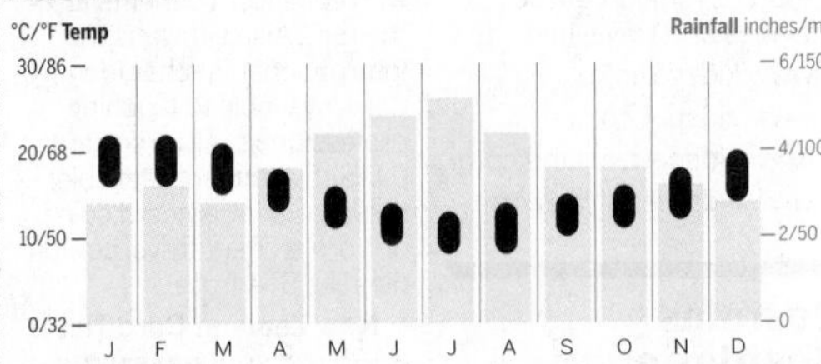

Christchurch

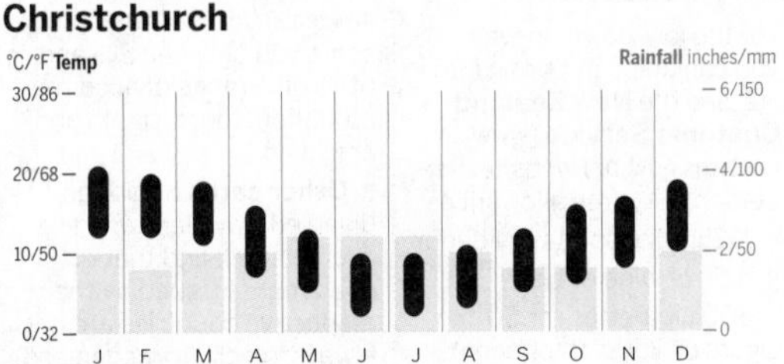

Queenstown

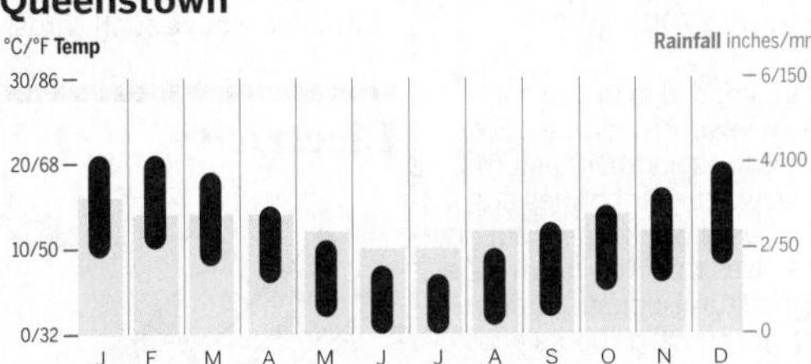

Children

Accommodation Many motels and holiday parks have playgrounds, games and DVDs, and occasionally fenced swimming pools and trampolines. Cots and highchairs aren't always available at budget and midrange accommodation, but top-end hotels supply them and often provide child-minding services. B&Bs aren't usually amenable to families – many promote themselves as kid-free. Hostels focusing on the backpacker demographic don't welcome kids either, but there are plenty of other hostels (including YHA hostels) that do.

Babysitting For specialised childcare, try www.rockmybaby.co.nz, or look under 'babysitters' and 'child care centres' in the *Yellow Pages* directory.

Car seats Some smaller car-hire companies don't provide baby seats – double-check that your company can supply the right-sized seat for your child, and that the seat will be properly fitted. Some companies may legally require you to fit the seat yourself.

Change rooms & breastfeeding Cities and most major towns have public rooms where parents can go to nurse a baby or change a nappy (diaper); check with the local visitor info centre or council, or ask a local.

Concessions Kids' and family rates are often available for accommodation, tours, entry fees, and air, bus and train transport, with discounts of as much as 50% off the adult rate. The definition of 'child' can vary from under 12 to under 18 years; toddlers (under four years old) usually get free admission and transport.

Eating out There are plenty of family-friendly restaurants in NZ with highchairs and kids' menus. Pubs often serve kids' meals and most cafes and restaurants (with the exception of upmarket eateries) can handle the idea of child-sized portions.

Health NZ's medical services and facilities are world-class, with goods like formula and disposable nappies widely available.

For helpful general tips, see Lonely Planet's *Travel with Children*. Handy online resources for kid-centric activities and travel info:

» www.kidzgo.co.nz
» www.kidspot.co.nz
» www.kidsnewzealand.com
» www.kidsfriendlynz.com

Customs Regulations

For the low-down on what you can and can't bring into NZ, see the **New Zealand Customs Service** (www.customs.govt.nz) website. Per-person duty-free allowances:

» 1125mL of spirits or liqueur
» 4.5L of wine or beer
» 200 cigarettes (or 50 cigars or 250g of tobacco)
» dutiable goods up to the value of $700.

It's a good idea to declare any unusual medicines. Biosecurity is another customs buzzword – authorities are serious about keeping out any diseases that may harm NZ's agricultural industry. Tramping gear such as boots and tents will be checked and may need to be cleaned before being allowed in. You must declare any plant or animal products (including anything made of wood), and food of any kind. You'll also come under greater scrutiny if you've arrived via Africa, Southeast Asia or South America. Weapons and firearms are either prohibited or require a permit and safety testing.

Discount Cards

» **International Student Identity Card** The internationally recognised ISIC is produced by the **International Student Travel Confederation** (ISTC; www.istc.org), and issued to full-time students aged 12 and over. It provides discounts on accommodation, transport and admission to attractions. The ISTC also produces the International Youth Travel Card, available to folks between 12 and 26 who are not full-time students, with equivalent benefits to the ISIC. Also similar is the International Teacher Identity Card, available to teaching professionals. All three cards (NZ$25 each) are available online at www.isiccard.co.nz, or from student travel companies like STA Travel.

» **New Zealand Card** This is a $35 discount **pass** (www.newzealandcard.com) that'll score you between 5% and 50% off a range of accommodation, tours, sights and activities.

» **Other cards** Senior and disabled travellers who live overseas will find that discount cards issued by their respective countries are not always 'officially' recognised in NZ, but that many places still acknowledge such cards.

Electricity

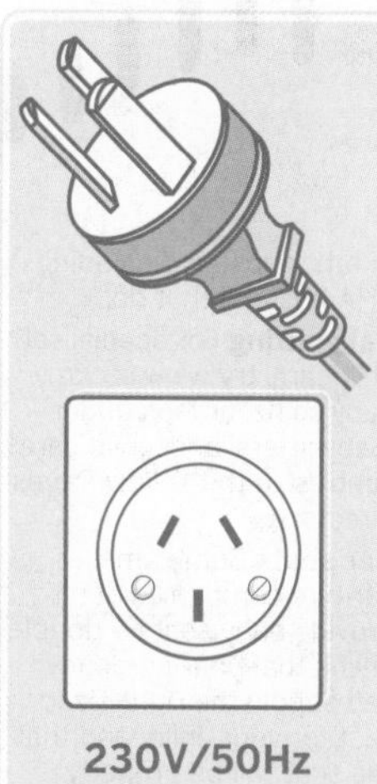

Embassies & Consulates

Most principal diplomatic representations to NZ are in Wellington, with a few in Auckland.

Remember that while in NZ you are bound by NZ laws. Your embassy will not be sympathetic if you end up in jail after committing a crime locally, even if such actions are legal in your own country.

In genuine emergencies you may get some assistance, but only if other channels have been exhausted. For example, if you need to get home urgently, a free ticket is unlikely as the embassy would expect you to have insurance. If you have all your money and documents stolen, it might assist with getting a new passport, but a loan for onward travel is out of the question.

Embassies, consulates and high commissions include the following:

Australia (☎04-473 6411; www.australia.org.nz; 72-76 Hobson St, Thorndon, Wellington)

Canada (☎04-473 9577; www.newzealand.gc.ca; L11, 125 The Terrace, Wellington)

China (☎04-472 1382; www.chinaembassy.org.nz; 2-6 Glenmore St, Kelburn, Wellington)

Fiji (☎04-473 5401; www.fiji.org.nz; 31 Pipitea St, Thorndon, Wellington)

France (☎04-384 2555; www.ambafrance-nz.org; 34-42 Manners St, Wellington)

Germany (☎04-473 6063; www.wellington.diplo.de; 90-92 Hobson St, Thorndon, Wellington)

Israel (☎04-439 9500; info@wellington.mfa.gov.il; L13, Bayley's Building, 36 Brandon St, Wellington)

Ireland (☎09-977 2252; www.ireland.co.nz; L7, Citigroup Bldg, 23 Customs St E, Auckland)

Japan (☎04-473 1540; www.nz.emb-japan.go.jp; L18, The Majestic Centre, 100 Willis St, Wellington)

Netherlands (☎04-471 6390; www.netherlandsembassy.co.nz; L10, PSIS House, cnr Featherston & Ballance Sts, Wellington)

UK (☎04-924 2888; www.britain.org.nz; 44 Hill St, Thorndon, Wellington)

USA (☎04-462 6000; http://wellington.usembassy.gov; 29 Fitzherbert Tce, Thorndon, Wellington)

Food & Drink

The NZ foodie scene once slavishly reflected Anglo-Saxon stodge, but nowadays the country's restaurants and cafes are adept at throwing together traditional staples (lamb, beef, venison, green-lipped mussels) with Asian, European and pan-Pacific flair.

Eateries themselves range from fry-'em-up fish-and-chip shops and pub bistros to cafes drowned in faux-European, grungy or retro stylings; to restaurant-bars with full à-la-carte service; to fine-dining establishments with linen so crisp you'll be afraid to prop your elbows on it. Listings are in order of authorial preference, based on our assessment of ambience, service, value and, of course, deliciousness. For online listings:

» www.dineout.co.nz

» www.menus.co.nz

On the liquid front, NZ wine is world class (especially sauvignon blanc and pinot noir), and you'll be hard-pressed to find a NZ town of any size without decent espresso. NZ microbrewed beers have also become mainstream.

EATING PRICE RANGES

The following price ranges refer to a main course.

» **$ Budget** Less than $15

» **$$ Midrange** $15 to $32

» **$$$ Top end** More than $35

Practicalities

Smoking Banned in all restaurants, pubs and bars.

Tipping Not mandatory, but feel free if you've had a happy culinary experience (about 10% of the bill).

Opening hours Restaurants to 9pm, often 11pm Friday and Saturday. Cafes 7am to 4pm or 5pm. Pub food noon to 2pm, and 6pm to 8pm.

Vegetarians & Vegans

Most large urban centres have at least one dedicated vegetarian cafe or restaurant. See the **New Zealand Vegetarian Society** (www.vegsoc.org.nz) restaurant guide for listings. Also look for the vegetarian icon in Eating listings in this book, as it indicates a good vegetarian selection.

Beyond this, almost all restaurants and cafes offer vegetarian menu choices (although sometimes only one or two). Many eateries also provide gluten-free and vegan options. Always check that stocks and sauces are vegetarian too.

TO MARKET, TO MARKET

There are more than 50 farmers markets held around NZ. Most happen on weekends and are happy local affairs where visitors will meet local producers and find fresh regional produce. Mobile coffee is usually present, and tastings are offered by enterprising and innovative stall holders.

Always take a bag to carry purchases, as many of the sustainably minded markets ban the use of plastic bags. And arrive as early as possible – the best produce sells out quickly.

Check out www.farmersmarkets.org.nz for dates and times of farmers markets throughout NZ.

Gay & Lesbian Travellers

The gay and lesbian tourism industry in NZ isn't as high-profile as it is in neighbouring Australia, but homosexual communities are prominent in the main cities of Auckland and Wellington, with myriad support organisations across both islands. NZ has relatively progressive laws protecting the rights of gays and lesbians; the legal minimum age for sex between consenting persons is 16. Generally speaking, Kiwis are fairly relaxed and accepting about homosexuality, but that's not to say that homophobia doesn't exist.

Resources

There are loads of websites dedicated to gay and lesbian travellers. **Gay Tourism New Zealand** (www.gaytourismnewzealand.com) is a good starting point, with links to various sites. Other worthwhile queer websites include the following:

» www.gaynz.com

» www.gaynz.net.nz

» www.lesbian.net.nz

» www.gaystay.co.nz

Check out the nationwide magazine *express* (www.gayexpress.co.nz) every second Wednesday for the latest happenings, reviews and listings on the NZ gay scene.

Festivals & Events

Big Gay Out (www.biggayout.co.nz) Free festival (food, drink, entertainment) held every February in Auckland.

Gay Ski Week (www.gayskiweeknz.com) Annual Queenstown snow-fest in August/September.

Out Takes (www.outtakes.org.nz) G&L film festival staged in Auckland, Wellington and Christchurch in June.

Health

New Zealand is one of the healthiest countries in the world in which to travel. Diseases such as malaria and typhoid are unheard of, and the absence of poisonous snakes or other dangerous animals makes this a very safe region to get off the beaten track and out into the beautiful countryside.

Before You Go

MEDICATIONS

Bring medications in their original, clearly labelled containers. A signed and dated letter from your physician describing your medical conditions and medications, including generic names, is also a good idea. If carrying syringes or needles, be sure to have a physician's letter documenting their medical necessity.

VACCINATIONS

NZ has no vaccination requirements for any traveller, but the World Health Organization recommends that all travellers should be covered for diphtheria, tetanus, measles, mumps, rubella, chickenpox and polio, as well as hepatitis B, regardless of their destination. Ask your doctor for an International Certificate of Vaccination (or 'the yellow booklet'), which will list all the vaccinations you've received.

INSURANCE

If your current health insurance doesn't cover you for medical expenses incurred overseas, you should think about getting extra insurance – check out www.lonelyplanet.com for more information. Find out in advance if your insurance plan will make payments directly to providers or reimburse you at a later date for overseas health expenditures. (In many countries doctors expect payment in cash.)

In New Zealand

AVAILABILITY & COST OF HEALTH CARE

Health insurance is essential for all travellers. While health care in NZ is of a high standard and not overly expensive by international standards, considerable costs can be built up and repatriation can be extremely expensive.

NZ does not have a government-funded system of public hospitals. All travellers are, however, covered for medical care resulting from accidents that occur while in NZ (eg motor-vehicle accidents, adventure-activity accidents) by the Accident Compensation Corporation (ACC). Costs incurred due to treatment of a medical illness that occurs while in NZ will only be covered by travel insurance. For more details, see www.moh.govt.nz and www.acc.co.nz.

The 24-hour, free-call **Healthline** (☎0800 611 116; www.healthline.govt.nz) offers health advice throughout NZ.

PHARMACEUTICAL SUPPLIES

Over-the-counter medications are widely available in NZ through private chemists. These include painkillers, antihistamines for allergies, and skin-care products.

Some medications that are available over the counter in other countries are only available by a prescription obtained from a general practitioner. These include the oral contraceptive pill, most medications for asthma and all antibiotics. If you take medication on a regular basis, bring an adequate supply and ensure you have details of the generic name, as brand names differ between countries. The majority of medications in use outside the region are available.

INFECTIOUS DISEASES

The giardia parasite is widespread in the waterways of NZ. Drinking untreated water from streams and lakes is not recommended. Using water filters and boiling or treating water with iodine are effective ways of preventing the disease. Symptoms consist of intermittent bad-smelling diarrhoea, abdominal bloating and wind. Effective treatment is available (tinidazole or metronidazole).

ENVIRONMENTAL HAZARDS

Hypothermia This is a significant risk, especially during the winter months or year-round in the mountains of the North Island and all of the South Island. Mountain ranges and/or strong winds produce a high chill factor, which can result in hypothermia, even in moderately cool temperatures. Early signs include the inability to perform fine movements (such as doing up buttons), shivering and a bad case of the 'umbles' (fumbles, mumbles, grumbles, stumbles). The key element of treatment are changing the environment to one where heat loss is minimised: changing out of wet clothing, adding dry clothes with wind- and waterproof layers, adding insulation and providing fuel (water and carbohydrates) to allow shivering to build the internal temperature. In severe hypothermia, shivering actually stops; this is a medical emergency requiring rapid evacuation in addition to the above measures.

Surf Beaches & Drowning NZ has exceptional surf beaches. The power of the surf can fluctuate as a result of the varying slope of the seabed at many beaches. Check with local surf lifesaving organisations before entering the surf and be aware of your own limitations and expertise.

Insurance

A watertight travel-insurance policy covering theft, loss and medical problems is essential. Some policies specifically exclude designated 'dangerous activities' such as scuba diving, parasailing, bungy jumping, white-water rafting, motorcycling, skiing and even tramping. If you plan on doing any of these things (a distinct possibility in NZ), make sure the policy you choose covers you fully.

You may prefer a policy that pays doctors or hospitals directly rather than you having to pay on the spot and claim later. If you have to claim later, make sure you keep all documentation. Some policies ask you to call back (reverse charges) to a centre in your home country where an immediate assessment of your problem is made. Check that the policy covers ambulances and emergency medical evacuations by air.

It's worth mentioning that under NZ law, you cannot sue for personal injury (other than exemplary damages). Instead, the country's **Accident Compensation Corporation** (ACC; www.acc.co.nz) administers an accident compensation scheme that provides accident insurance for NZ residents and visitors to the country, regardless of fault. This scheme, however, does not cancel out the necessity for your own comprehensive travel-insurance policy, as it doesn't cover you for such things as loss of income or treatment in your home country or ongoing illness.

Worldwide cover for travellers from over 44 countries is available online at www.lonelyplanet.com/bookings/insurance.do.

Internet Access

Getting online in NZ is easy in all but the most remote locales.

Internet Cafes

Internet cafes in the bigger urban centres or tourist areas are usually brimming with high-speed terminals. Facilities are a lot more haphazard in small, out-of-the-way towns, where a so-called internet cafe could turn out to be a single terminal in the corner of a DVD store.

Most hostels make an effort to hook you up, with internet access sometimes free for guests. Many public libraries have free internet access too, but there can be a limited number of terminals.

Internet access at cafes ranges anywhere from $4 to $6 per hour. There's often a minimum period of access, usually 10 or 15 minutes.

Wireless Access & Internet Service Providers

Increasingly, you'll be able to find wi-fi access around the country, from hotel rooms to pub beer gardens to hostel dining rooms. Usually you have to be a guest or customer to access the internet at these locations – you'll be issued with a code, a wink and a secret handshake to enable you to get online. Sometimes it's free; sometimes there's a charge.

The country's main telecommunications company is **Telecom New Zealand** (www.telecom.co.nz), which has wireless hot spots around the country. If you have a wi-fi-enabled device, you can purchase a Telecom wireless prepaid card from participating hot spots. Alternatively, you can purchase a prepaid number from the login page and any wireless hotspot using your credit card. See the website for hot spot listings.

If you've brought your palmtop or notebook computer, you might consider buying a prepay USB modem (aka a 'dongle') with a local SIM card: both Telecom and **Vodafone** (www.vodarent.co.nz) sell these from around $100. If you want to get connected via a local internet service provider (ISP), there are plenty of options, though some companies limit their dial-up areas to major cities or particular regions. ISPs include the following:

Clearnet (☎0508 888 800; www.clearnet.co.nz)

Earthlight (☎03-479 0303; www.earthlight.co.nz)

Freenet (☎0800 645 000; www.freenet.co.nz)

Slingshot (☎0800 892 000; www.slingshot.co.nz)

Maps

The **Automobile Association** (AA; ☎0800 500 444; www.aa.co.nz/travel) produces excellent city, town, regional, island and highway maps, available from its local offices. The AA also produces a detailed *New Zealand Road Atlas*. Other reliable countrywide atlases, available from visitor information centres and bookshops, are published by Hema, KiwiMaps and Wises.

Land Information New Zealand (LINZ; www.linz.govt.nz) publishes several exhaustive map series, including street, country and holiday maps, national park and forest park maps, and topographical trampers' maps. Scan the larger bookshops, or try the nearest DOC office or visitor information centre for topo maps.

Online, log onto **AA SmartMap** (www.aamaps.co.nz) or **Yellow Maps** (www.maps.yellowpages.co.nz) to pinpoint exact addresses in NZ cities and towns.

Money

ATMs & Eftpos

Branches of the country's major banks, including the Bank of New Zealand, ANZ, Westpac and ASB, have 24-hour ATMs that accept cards from other banks and provide access to overseas accounts. You won't find ATMs everywhere, but they're widespread across both islands.

Many NZ businesses use electronic funds transfer at point of sale (Eftpos), a convenient service that allows you to use your bank card (credit or debit) to pay directly for services or purchases, and often withdraw cash as well. Eftpos is available practically everywhere, even in places where it's a long way between banks. Just like an ATM, you need to know your personal identification number (PIN) to use it.

Bank Accounts

We've heard mixed reports on how easy it is for non-residents to open a bank account in NZ. Some sources say it's as simple as flashing a few pieces of ID, providing a temporary postal address (or your permanent address) and then waiting a few days while your request is processed. Other sources say that many banks won't allow visitors to open an account with them unless they're planning to stay in NZ for at least six months, or unless the application is accompanied by some proof of employment. Bank websites are also rather vague on the services offered to short-term visitors. If you think you'll need to open an account, do your homework before you arrive in the country and be prepared to shop around to get the best deal.

Credit & Debit Cards

Perhaps the safest place to keep your NZ travelling money is inside a plastic card! The most flexible option is to carry both a credit and a debit card.

CREDIT CARDS

Credit cards (Visa, Master Card etc) are widely accepted for everything from a hostel bed to a bungy jump. Credit cards are pretty much essential if you want to hire a car. They can also be used for over-the-counter cash advances at banks and from ATMs, depending on the card, but be aware that such transactions incur charges. Charge cards such as Diners Club and Amex are not as widely accepted.

DEBIT CARDS

Apart from losing them, the obvious danger with credit cards is maxing out your limit and going home to a steaming pile of debt. A safer option is a debit card, with which you can draw money directly from your home bank account using ATMs, banks or Eftpos machines. Any card connected to the international banking network (Cirrus, Maestro, Visa Plus and Eurocard) should work, provided you know your PIN. Fees for using your card at a foreign bank or ATM vary depending on your home bank; ask before you leave. Companies such as Travelex offer debit cards (Travelex calls them Cash Passport cards) with set withdrawal fees and a balance you can top-up from your personal bank account while on the road – nice one!

Currency

NZ's currency is the NZ dollar, comprising 100 cents. There are 10c, 20c, 50c, $1 and $2 coins, and $5, $10, $20, $50 and $100 notes. Prices are often still marked in single cents and then rounded to the nearest 10c when you hand over your money.

Moneychangers

Changing foreign currency or travellers cheques is usually no problem at banks throughout NZ or at licensed moneychangers such as Travelex in the major cities. Moneychangers can be found in all major tourist areas, cities and airports.

Taxes & Refunds

The Goods and Services Tax (GST) is a flat 15% tax on all domestic goods and services. Prices in this book include GST. There's no GST refund available when you leave NZ.

Tipping

Tipping is completely optional in NZ – the total at the bottom of a restaurant bill is all you need to pay (note that sometimes there's an additional service charge). That said, it's totally acceptable to reward good service – between 5% and 10% of the bill is fine.

Travellers Cheques

Amex, Travelex and other international brands of travellers cheques are a bit old-fashioned these days, but they're easily exchanged at banks and moneychangers. Present your passport for identification when cashing them; shop around for the best rates/lowest fees.

Post

The services offered by **New Zealand Post** (☎0800 501 501; www.nzpost.co.nz) are reliable and reasonably inexpensive. Within NZ, standard postage is 60c for regular letters and postcards, and $1.20 for larger letters.

International destinations are divided into two zones: Australia and the South Pacific, and the rest of the world. The standard rate for postcards is $1.90 worldwide, and for regular letters $1.90 to Australia and the South Pacific and $2.40 elsewhere. Express rates are also available. Check out the incredibly precise calculator on the website for more details, including info on parcels.

Public Holidays

NZ's main public holidays:

New Year 1 and 2 January
Waitangi Day 6 February
Easter Good Friday and Easter Monday; March/April
Anzac Day 25 April
Queen's Birthday First Monday in June
Labour Day Fourth Monday in October
Christmas Day 25 December
Boxing Day 26 December

In addition, each NZ province has its own anniversary-day holiday. The dates of these provincial holidays vary – when these dates fall on Friday to Sunday, they're usually observed the following Monday; if they fall on Tuesday to Thursday, they're held on the preceding Monday.

Provincial anniversary holidays:

Southland 17 January
Wellington 22 January
Auckland 29 January
Northland 29 January
Nelson 1 February
Otago 23 March
Taranaki 31 March
South Canterbury 25 September
Hawke's Bay 1 November
Marlborough 1 November
Chatham Islands 30 November
Westland 1 December
Canterbury 16 December

School holidays

The Christmas holiday season, from mid-December to late January, is part of the summer school vacation. It's the time you'll most likely to find transport and accommodation booked out, and long, grumpy queues at tourist attractions. There are three shorter school-holiday periods during the year: from mid- to late April, early to mid-July, and mid-September to early October. For exact dates see the **Ministry of Education** (www.minedu.govt.nz) website.

Safe Travel

Although it's no more dangerous than other developed countries, violent crime does happen in NZ, so it's worth taking sensible precautions on the streets at night or if staying in remote areas. Gang culture permeates some parts of the country; give any black-jacketed, insignia-wearing groups a wide berth.

Theft from cars is a problem around NZ – travellers are viewed as easy marks. Avoid leaving valuables in vehicles, no matter where they're parked; you're tempting fate at tourist parking areas and trailhead car parks.

Don't underestimate the dangers posed by NZ's unpredictable, ever-changing climate, especially in high-altitude areas. Hypothermia is a real risk.

NZ has been spared the proliferation of venomous creatures found in neighbouring Australia (spiders, snakes, jellyfish...). Sharks patrol NZ waters, but rarely nibble on humans. Much greater ocean hazards are rips and undertows, which can quickly drag swimmers out to sea: heed local warnings.

Kiwi roads are often made hazardous by speeding locals, wide-cornering campervans and traffic-ignorant sheep. Set yourself a reasonable itinerary and keep your eyes on the road. Cyclists take care: motorists can't always overtake easily on skinny roads.

In the annoyances category, NZ's sandflies are a royal pain. Lather yourself with insect repellent in coastal areas.

Shopping

NZ isn't one of those countries where it's necessary to buy a T-shirt to help you remember your visit, but there are some unique locally crafted items you might consider.

Clothing

Auckland, Wellington and Christchurch boast fashion-conscious boutiques ablaze with the sartorial flair of NZ designers. Check out www.fashionz.co.nz for up-to-date information. Keep an eye out for labels such as Zambesi, Kate Sylvester, Karen Walker, Trelise Cooper, NOM D and Little Brother.

From the backs of NZ sheep come sheepskin products such as footwear (including the much-loved ugg boot) and beautiful woollen jumpers (jerseys or sweaters) made from hand-spun, hand-dyed wool. Other knitted knick-knacks include hats, gloves and scarves.

Long woollen Swanndri jackets, shirts and pullovers are so ridiculously practical, they're almost the national garment in country areas. Most common are the red-and-black or blue-and-black plaid ones; pick up 'Swannies' in outdoor-gear shops.

Maori Art

Maori *whakairo rakau* (woodcarving) features intricate forms like leaping dolphins, as well as highly detailed traditional carvings. You'll pay a premium for high-quality work; avoid the poor examples in Auckland souvenir shops.

Maori artisans have always made bone carvings in the shape of humans and animals, but nowadays they cater to the tourist industry. Bone fish-hook pendants, carved in traditional Maori and modernised styles, are most common, worn on a leather string around the neck.

Paua

Abalone shell, called paua in NZ, is carved into some beautiful ornaments and jewellery and is often used as an inlay in Maori carvings. Be aware that it's illegal to take natural paua shells out of the country – only processed ornaments can be taken with you.

Pounamu

Maoris consider *pounamu* (greenstone, or jade or nephrite) to be a culturally invaluable raw material. It's found predominantly on the west coast of the South Island – Maoris called the island Te Wahi Pounamu (The Place of Greenstone) or Te Wai Pounamu (The Water of Greenstone).

One of the most popular Maori *pounamu* motifs is the *hei tiki*, the name of which literally means 'hanging human form'. They are tiny, stylised Maori figures worn on a leather string or chain around the neck. They've got great *mana* (power), but they also serve as fertility symbols.

The best place to buy *pounamu* is Hokitika, which is strewn with jade workshops and gift shops. Rotorua also has its fair share of *pounamu* crafts.

Traditionally, *pounamu* is bought as a gift for another person, not for yourself. Ask a few questions to ensure you're buying from a local operator who crafts local stone, not an offshore company selling imported (usually Chinese or European) jade.

Telephone

Telecom New Zealand (www.telecom.co.nz) The country's key domestic player, with a stake in the local mobile (cell) market.

Vodafone (www.vodafone.co.nz) Alternative mobile network option.

International Calls

Payphones allow international calls, but the cost and international dialling code for calls will vary depending on which provider you're using. International calls from NZ are relatively inexpensive and subject to specials that reduce the rates even more, so it's worth shopping around – consult the Yellow Pages for providers.

To make international calls from NZ, you need to dial the international access code (☎00), the country code and the area code (without the initial 0). So for a London number, you'd dial ☎00-44-20, then the number.

If dialling NZ from overseas, the country code is ☎64, followed by the appropriate area code minus the initial zero.

Local Calls

Local calls from private phones are free! Local calls from payphones cost $1 for the first 15 minutes, and 20c per minute thereafter, though coin-operated payphones are scarce – you'll need a phonecard. Calls to mobile phones attract higher rates.

Long Distance Calls & Area Codes

NZ uses regional two-digit area codes for long-distance calls, which can be made from any payphone. If you're making a local call (ie to someone else in the same town), you don't need to dial the area code. But if you're dialling within a region (even if it's to a nearby town with the same area code), you do have to dial the area code.

Information & Toll-Free Calls

Numbers starting with ☎0900 are usually recorded information services, charging upwards of $1 per minute (more from mobiles); these numbers cannot be dialled from payphones.

Toll-free numbers in NZ have the prefix ☎0800 or ☎0508 and can be called free of charge from anywhere in the country, though they may not be accessible from certain areas or from mobile phones. Telephone numbers beginning with ☎0508, ☎0800 or ☎0900 cannot be dialled from outside NZ.

Mobile Phones

Local mobile phone numbers are preceded by the prefix ☎021, ☎022, ☎025 or ☎027. Mobile phone coverage is good in cities and towns and most parts of the North Island, but can be patchy away from urban centres on the South Island.

If you want to bring your own phone and use a prepaid service with a local SIM card, **Vodafone** (www.vodafone.co.nz) is a practical option. Any Vodafone shop (found in most major towns) will set you up with a SIM card and phone number (about $40); top-ups can be purchased at newsagencies, post offices and petrol stations practically anywhere.

Alternatively, if you don't bring your own phone from home, you can rent one from **Vodafone Rental** (www.vodarent.co.nz) priced from $5 per day (for which you'll also need a local SIM card), with pick-up and drop-off outlets at NZ's major airports. We've also had some positive feedback on **Phone Hire New Zealand** (www.phonehirenz.com), which hires out mobile phones, SIM cards, modems and GPS systems.

Phonecards

NZ has a wide range of phonecards available, which can be bought at hostels, newsagencies and post offices for a fixed dollar value (usually $5, $10, $20 and $50). These can be used with any public or private phone by dialling a toll-free access number and then the PIN number on the card. Shop around – rates vary from company to company.

Time

NZ is 12 hours ahead of GMT/UTC and two hours ahead of Australian Eastern Standard Time. The

Chathams are 45 minutes ahead of NZ's main islands.

In summer, NZ observes daylight-saving time, where clocks are wound forward by one hour on the last Sunday in September; clocks are wound back on the first Sunday of the following April.

Tourist Information

Local Tourist Offices

Almost every Kiwi city or town seems to have a visitor information centre. The bigger centres stand united within the outstanding **i-SITE** (www.newzealand.com/travel/i-sites) network, affiliated with Tourism New Zealand (the official national tourism body). i-SITEs have trained staff, information on local activities and attractions, and free brochures and maps. Staff can also book activities, transport and accommodation.

Bear in mind that many information centres only promote accommodation and tour operators who are paying members of the local tourist association, and that sometimes staff aren't supposed to recommend one activity or accommodation provider over another.

There's also a network of **Department Of Conservation** (DOC; www.doc.govt.nz) visitor centres to help you plan activities and make bookings. Visitor centres – in national parks, regional centres and major cities – usually also have displays on local lore, flora, fauna and biodiversity.

Tourist Offices Abroad

Tourism New Zealand (www.newzealand.com) has representatives in various countries around the world. A good place for pretrip research is the official website (emblazoned with the hugely successful 100% Pure New Zealand branding), which has information in several languages, including German and Japanese. Overseas offices:

Australia (☎0415-123 362; L12, 61 York St, Sydney)

UK & Europe (☎020-7930 1662; L7, New Zealand House, 80 Haymarket, London, UK)

USA & Canada (☎310-395 7480; Suite 300, 501 Santa Monica Blvd, Santa Monica, USA)

Travellers with Disabilities

Kiwi accommodation generally caters fairly well for travellers with disabilities, with a significant number of hostels, hotels, motels and B&Bs equipped with wheelchair-accessible rooms. Many tourist attractions similarly provide wheelchair access, with wheelchairs often available.

Tour operators with accessible vehicles operate from most major centres. Key cities are also serviced by 'kneeling' buses (buses that hydraulically stoop down to kerb level to allow easy access); taxi companies offer wheelchair-accessible vans. Large car-hire firms (Avis, Hertz etc) provide cars with hand controls at no extra charge (advance notice required). Mobility parking permits are available from branches of **CCS Disability Action** (☎0800 227 200, 04-384 5677; www.ccsdisabilityaction.org.nz) in the main centres.

For good general information, see NZ's disability information website **Weka** (www.weka.net.nz), which has categories including Transport and Travel.

Want to tackle a wilderness pathway? Pick up a copy of *Accessible Walks* by Anna and Andrew Jameson ($26), with first-hand descriptions of 100-plus South Island walks. It's available online at www.accessiblewalks.co.nz. If cold-weather activity is more your thing, see the **Adaptive Snow Sports NZ** (www.disabledsnowsports.org.nz) website.

Visas

Visa application forms are available from NZ diplomatic missions overseas, travel agents and **Immigration New Zealand** (☎0508 558 855, 09-914 4100; www.immigration.govt.nz). Immigration New Zealand has over a dozen offices overseas; consult the website.

Visitor's Visa

Citizens of Australia don't need a visa to visit NZ and can stay indefinitely (provided they have no criminal convictions). UK citizens don't need a visa either and can stay in the country for up to six months.

Citizens of another 56 countries that have visa-waiver agreements with NZ don't need a visa for stays of up to three months, provided they have an onward ticket and sufficient funds to support their stay: see the website for details. Nations in this group include Canada, France, Germany, Ireland, Japan, the Netherlands and the USA.

Citizens of other countries must obtain a visa before entering NZ. Visas come with three months' standard validity and cost $110 if processed in Australia or certain South Pacific countries (eg Samoa, Fiji), or around $140 if processed elsewhere in the world.

A visitor's visa can be extended for stays of up to nine months within one 18-month period, or to a maximum of 12 months in the country. Applications are assessed on a case-by-case basis; visitors will need to meet criteria such as proof of ongoing financial self-support.

Apply for extensions at any Immigration New Zealand office – see the website for locations.

Work Visa & Working Holiday Scheme

WORK VISA

It's illegal for foreign nationals to work in NZ on a visitor's visa, except for Australians who can legally gain work without a visa or permit. If you're visiting NZ to find work, or you already have an employment offer, you'll need to apply for a work visa, which translates into a work permit once you arrive and is valid for up to three years. You can apply for a work permit after you're in NZ, but its validity will be backdated to when you entered the country. The fee for a work visa ranges from NZ$200 to NZ$310, depending on where and how it's processed (paper or online) and the type of application.

WORKING HOLIDAY SCHEME

Eligible travellers who are only interested in short-term employment to supplement their travels can take part in one of NZ's working-holiday schemes (WHS). Under these schemes citizens aged 18 to 30 years from 36 countries – including Canada, France, Germany, Ireland, Japan, Malaysia, the Netherlands, Scandinavian countries, the UK and the USA – can apply for a visa. For most nationalities the visa is valid for 12 months. It's only issued to those seeking a genuine working holiday, not permanent work, so you're not supposed to work for one employer for more than three months.

Most WHS-eligible nationals must apply for this visa from within their own country; residents of some countries can apply online. Applicants must have an onward ticket, a passport valid for at least three months from the date they will leave NZ and evidence of at least NZ$4200 in accessible funds. The application fee is NZ$140 regardless of where you apply, and isn't refunded if your application is declined.

The rules vary for different nationalities, so make sure you read up on the specifics of your country's agreement with NZ at www.immigration.govt.nz/migrant/stream/work/workingholiday.

Women Travellers

NZ is generally a very safe place for women travellers, although the usual sensible precautions apply: avoid walking alone late at night and never hitchhike alone. If you're out on the town, always keep enough money aside for a taxi back to your accommodation. Lone women should also be wary of staying in basic pub accommodation unless it looks safe and well managed. Sexual harassment is not a widely reported problem in NZ, but of course it does happen.

See www.womentravel.co.nz for more information.

Work

If you arrive in NZ on a visitor's visa, you're not allowed to work for pay. If you're caught breaching this (or any other) visa condition, you could be booted back to where you came from.

If you have been approved for a WHS visa, look into the possibilities for temporary employment. There's plenty of casual work around, mainly in agriculture (fruit picking, farming, wineries), hospitality or ski resorts. Office-based work can be found in IT, banking, finance and telemarketing. Register with a local office-work agency to get started.

Seasonal fruit picking, pruning and harvesting is prime short-term work for visitors. More than 300 sq km of apples, kiwifruit and other fruit and veg are harvested from December to May. Rates are around $10 to $15 an hour for physically taxing toil – turnover of workers is high. You're usually paid by how much you pick (per bin, bucket or kilogram). Prime North Island picking locations include the Bay of Islands (Kerikeri and Paihia), rural Auckland, Tauranga, Gisborne and Hawke's Bay (Napier and Hastings); on the South Island try Nelson (Tapawera and Golden Bay), Marlborough (around Blenheim) and Central Otago (Alexandra and Roxburgh).

Winter work at ski resorts and their service towns includes bartending, waiting, cleaning, ski-tow operation and, if you're properly qualified, ski or snowboard instructing.

VOLUNTOURISM

NZ presents a swathe of active, outdoorsy volunteer opportunities for travellers to get some dirt under their fingernails and participate in conservation programs. Programs can include anything from tree-planting and weed removal to track construction, habitat conservation and fencing. Ask about local opportunities at any regional i-SITE visitor information centre, or check out www.conservationvolunteers.org.nz and www.doc.govt.nz/getting-involved, both of which allow you to browse for opportunities by region.

Resources

Backpacker publications, hostel managers and other travellers are the best sources of info on local work possibilities. **Base Backpackers** (www.stayatbase.com/work) runs an employment service via its website, while the Notice Boards page on **Budget Backpacker Hostels** (BBH; www.bbh.co.nz) lists job vacancies in BBH hostels and a few other possibilities.

Kiwi Careers (www.kiwicareers.govt.nz) lists professional opportunities in various fields (agriculture, creative, health, teaching, volunteer work and recruitment), while **Seek** (www.seek.co.nz) is one of the biggest NZ job-search networks, with thousands of jobs listed.

Check ski-resort websites for work opportunities in the snow, and in the fruit-picking/horticultural realm, try the following websites:

- www.seasonalwork.co.nz
- www.seasonaljobs.co.nz
- www.picknz.co.nz
- www.pickingjobs.com

Income Tax

Death and taxes – no escape! For most travellers, Kiwi dollars earned in NZ will be subject to income tax, deducted from payments by employers – a process called Pay As You Earn (PAYE). Standard NZ income tax rates are 12.5% for annual salaries up to $14,000, then 19.5% up to $48,000, 32% up to $70,000, then 35% for higher incomes. A NZ Accident Compensation Corporation (ACC) scheme levy (2%) will also be deducted from your pay packet. Note that these rates tend to change slightly year to year.

If you visit NZ and work for a short time (eg on a working holiday scheme), you may qualify for a tax refund when you leave. Complete a *Refund Application – People Leaving New Zealand IR50* form and submit it with your tax return, along with proof of departure (eg air-ticket copies) to the **Inland Revenue Department** (www.ird.govt.nz). For more info, see the IRD website, or contact the **Inland Revenue Non-Resident Centre** (☎03-951 2020; nonres@ird.govt.nz; Private Bag 1932).

IRD Number

Travellers undertaking paid work in NZ must obtain an IRD number. Download the *IRD Number Application – Individual IR595* form from the **Inland Revenue Department** (www.ird.govt.nz) website. IRD numbers normally take eight to 10 working days to be issued.

Transport

GETTING THERE & AWAY

Flights, tours and rail tickets can be booked online at lonelyplanet.com/bookings.

Entering the Country

Disembarkation in New Zealand is generally a straightforward affair, with only the usual customs declarations to endure and the uncool scramble at the luggage carousel. Recent global instability has resulted in increased security in NZ airports, in both domestic and international terminals, and you may find customs procedures more time-consuming. One procedure has the Orwellian title Advance Passenger Screening, a system whereby documents that used to be checked after you touched down in NZ (passport, visa etc) are now checked before you board your flight – make sure all your documentation is in order so that your check-in is stress-free.

Passport

There are no restrictions when it comes to foreign citizens entering NZ. If you have a current passport and visa (or don't require one), you should be fine.

Air

There's a number of competing airlines servicing NZ and a wide variety of fares to choose from if you're flying in from Asia, Europe or North America, though ultimately you'll still pay a lot for a flight unless you jet in from Australia. NZ's inordinate popularity and abundance of year-round activities mean that almost any time of year airports can be swarming with inbound tourists – if you want to fly at a particularly popular time of year (eg over the Christmas period), book well in advance.

High season for flights into NZ is summer (December to February), with slightly less of a premium on fares over the shoulder months (October/November and March/April). The low season generally tallies with the winter months (June to August), though this is still a busy time for airlines ferrying ski bunnies and powder hounds.

Airports & Airlines

A number of NZ airports handle international flights, with Auckland receiving most traffic:

Auckland International Airport (AKL; ☎09-275 0789, 0800 247 767; www.aucklandairport.co.nz; Ray Emery Dr)

Christchurch Airport (CHC; ☎03-358 5029; www.christchurchairport.co.nz; Memorial Ave)

Dunedin Airport (DUD; ☎03-486 2879; www.dnairport.co.nz; Miller Rd)

Hamilton International Airport (HIA; ☎07-848 9027; www.hamiltonairport.co.nz; Airport Rd)

Queenstown Airport (ZQN; ☎03-450 9031; www.queenstownairport.co.nz; Sir Henry Wigley Dr)

Wellington Airport (WLG; ☎04-385 5100; www.wellington-airport.co.nz; Stewart Duff Dr)

Rotorua International Airport (☎07-345 8800; www.rotorua-airport.co.nz)

DEPARTURE TAX

An international departure tax of NZ$25 applies when leaving NZ at all airports except Auckland, Christchurch and Dunedin, payable by anyone aged 12 and over (NZ$10 for children aged two to 11, free for those under two years of age). The tax is not included in the price of airline tickets, but must be paid separately at the airport before you board your flight (via credit card or cash). Departing Auckland, Christchurch and Dunedin, a NZ$12.50 Passenger Service Charge (PSC) applies, which is included in your ticket price.

CLIMATE CHANGE & TRAVEL

Every form of transport that relies on carbon-based fuel generates CO_2, the main cause of human-induced climate change. Modern travel is dependent on aeroplanes, which might use less fuel per kilometre per person than most cars but travel much greater distances. The altitude at which aircraft emit gases (including CO_2) and particles also contributes to their climate change impact. Many websites offer 'carbon calculators' that allow people to estimate the carbon emissions generated by their journey and, for those who wish to do so, to offset the impact of the greenhouse gases emitted with contributions to portfolios of climate-friendly initiatives throughout the world. Lonely Planet offsets the carbon footprint of all staff and author travel.

AIRLINES FLYING TO & FROM NEW ZEALAND

Winging-in from Australia, Virgin Australia, Qantas and Air New Zealand are the key players. Air New Zealand also flies in from North America, but you can also head south with Air Canada and American Airlines. From Europe, the options are a little broader, with British Airways, Lufthansa and Virgin Atlantic entering the fray, and several others stopping in NZ on broader round-the-world routes.

NZ's own overseas carrier is Air New Zealand, which flies to runways across Europe, North America, eastern Asia and the Pacific. Airlines that connect NZ with international destinations include the following (note that 0800 and 0508 phone numbers mentioned here are for dialling from within NZ only):

Aerolineas Argentinas (AR; ☎09-379 3675; www.aerolineas.com.ar)

Aircalin (SB; ☎09-977 2238; www.aircalin.com)

Air Canada (AC; ☎09-969 7470; www.aircanada.com)

Air China (CA; ☎09-379 7696; www.airchina.com.cn)

Air New Zealand (NZ; ☎09-357 3000, 0800 737 000; www.airnewzealand.co.nz)

Air Pacific (FJ; ☎09-379 2404, 0800 800 178; www.airpacific.com)

Air Tahiti Nui (YN; ☎09-308 3360; www.airtahitinui.com.au)

Air Vanuatu (NF; ☎09-373 3435; www.airvanuatu.com)

American Airlines (AA; ☎09-912 8814, 0800 445 442; www.aa.com)

British Airways (BA; ☎09-966 9777; www.britishairways.com)

Cathay Pacific (CX; ☎09-379 0861, 0800 800 454; www.cathaypacific.com)

China Airlines (CI; ☎09-308 3364; www.china-airlines.com)

China Southern (CZ; ☎09-302 0666; www.flychinasouthern.com)

Emirates (EK; ☎09-968 2208, 0508 364 728; www.emirates.com)

Etihad Airways (EY; ☎09-977 2207; www.etihadairways.com)

Japan Airlines (JL; ☎0800 525 747; www.jal.com)

Jetstar (JQ; ☎0800 800 995; www.jetstar.com)

Korean Air (KE; ☎09-914 2000; www.koreanair.com)

LAN (LA; ☎09-308 3352; www.lan.com)

Lufthansa (LH; ☎09-303 1529; www.lufthansa.com)

Malaysia Airlines (MH; ☎09-379 3743, 0800 777 747; www.malaysiaairlines.com)

Qantas (QF; ☎09-357 8900, 0800 808 767; www.qantas.com.au)

Singapore Airlines (SQ; ☎09-379 3209, 0800 808 909; www.singaporeair.com)

South African Airways (SA; ☎09-977 2237; www.flysaa.com)

Thai Airways International (TG; ☎09-377 3886; www.thaiairways.com)

Virgin Atlantic (VS; ☎09-308 3377; www.virginatlantic.com)

Virgin Australia (DJ; ☎0800 670 000; www.virginaustralia.com)

Virgin Samoa (☎0800 670 000; www.virginaustralia.com)

Tickets

Automated online ticket sales work well if you're doing a simple one-way or return trip on specified dates, but are no substitute for a travel agent with the low-down on special deals, strategies for avoiding layovers and other useful advice.

ROUND-THE-WORLD (RTW) TICKETS

If you're flying to New Zealand from the other side of the world, RTW tickets can be bargains. They're generally put together by the big airline alliances, and give you a limited period (usually a year) in which to circumnavigate the globe. You can go anywhere the participating airlines go, as long as you stay within the prescribed kilometre extents or number of stops and don't backtrack when flying between continents. Ticket providers include the following:

Oneworld (www.oneworld.com)

Skyteam (www.skyteam.com)

Star Alliance (www.staralliance.com)

CIRCLE PACIFIC TICKETS

A Circle Pacific ticket is similar to a RTW ticket but covers a more limited region, using a combination of airlines to connect Australia, NZ, North America and Asia, with stopover options in the Pacific islands. As with RTW tickets, there are restrictions on how many stopovers you can take.

ONLINE TICKET SALES

For online ticket bookings, including RTW fares, start with the following websites:

AirTreks (www.airtreks.com) A US company with some tasty round-the-world fares.

Cheap Flights (www.cheapflights.com) Global sites (US, Australia/NZ, Spain, Germany, UK/Ireland, France, Canada and Italy) with specials, destination information and flight searches.

Cheapest Flights (www.cheapestflights.co.uk) Cheap worldwide flights from the UK; get in early for the bargains.

Co-operative Travel (www.co-operativetravel.co.uk) International site for affordable holiday packages.

Expedia (www.expedia.com) Microsoft's travel site; good for USA-related flights.

Flight Centre International (www.flightcentre.com) Respected operator handling direct flights, with sites for NZ, Australia, the UK, the USA, Canada and South Africa.

Roundtheworldflights.com (www.roundtheworldflights.com) Build your own adventure from the UK with up to six stops, including Asia, Australia, NZ and the USA. Good rates in the NZ winter.

STA Travel (www.statravel.com) The full package: flights (including RTW), tours, accommodation and insurance.

Travel Online (www.travelonline.co.nz) Good place to check worldwide flights from NZ.

Travel.com.au (www.travel.com.au) Solid Australian site; look up fares and flights to/from the country.

Travelocity (www.travelocity.com) Global site that allows you to search fares from/to practically anywhere.

Sea

It's possible (though by no means easy or safe) to make your way between NZ and Australia, and some smaller Pacific islands, by hitching rides or crewing on yachts. Try asking around at harbours, marinas, and yacht and sailing clubs. Popular yachting harbours in NZ include the Bay of Islands and Whangarei (both in Northland), Auckland and Wellington. March and April are the best months to look for boats heading to Australia. From Fiji, October to November is a peak departure season to beat the cyclones that soon follow in that neck of the woods.

There are no passenger liners operating to/from NZ, and finding a berth on a cargo ship (much less enjoying the experience) is no easy task.

GETTING AROUND

Air

Those who have limited time to get between NZ's attractions can make the most of a widespread network of intra- and inter-island flights.

Airlines in New Zealand

The country's major domestic carrier, Air New Zealand, has an aerial network covering most of the country. Australia-based Jetstar also flies between main urban areas. Between them, these two airlines service the main routes and carry the vast majority of domestic passengers in NZ. Beyond this, several small-scale regional operators provide essential transport services to outlying islands such as Great Barrier Island in the Hauraki Gulf, Stewart Island and the Chathams.

Operators include the following:

Air Chathams (☎03-305 0209; www.airchathams.co.nz) Services to the remote Chatham Islands from Wellington, Christchurch, Auckland and Napier.

Air Fiordland (☎0800 107 505, 03-249 6720; www.airfiordland.com) Services around Milford Sound, Te Anau and Queenstown.

Air New Zealand (NZ; ☎09-357 3000, 0800 737 000; www.airnewzealand.co.nz) Offers flights between 30-plus domestic destinations.

Air West Coast (☎03-738 0524, 0800 247 937; www.airwestcoast.co.nz) Operates charter and scenic flights ex-Greymouth, winging over the West Coast glaciers and Aoraki/Mt Cook, and stopping in Milford Sound, Queenstown and Christchurch.

Air2there.com (☎04-904 5130, 0800 777 000; www.air2there.com) Connects destinations across Cook Strait, including Paraparaumu, Wellington, Nelson and Blenheim.

Fly My Sky (☎09-256 7025; www.flymysky.co.nz) At least three flights daily from Auckland to Great Barrier Island.

Golden Bay Air (☎03-525 8725, 0800 588 885; www.goldenbayair.co.nz) Flies regularly between Wellington and Takaka in Golden Bay. Also connects to Karamea for Heaphy Track trampers.

Great Barrier Airlines (☎09-275 9120, 0800 900 600; www.greatbarrierairlines.co.nz) Plies the skies over Great Barrier Island, Auckland and Whangarei.

Jetstar (JQ; ☎0800 800 995; www.jetstar.com) Joins the

dots between key tourism centres: Auckland, Wellington, Christchurch, Dunedin and Queenstown (and flies Queenstown to Sydney).

Salt Air (☎09-402 8338, 0800 472 582; www.saltair.co.nz) Flies to Kerikeri from Whangarei and Auckland's North Shore.

Soundsair (☎0800 505 005, 03-520 3080; www.soundsair.co.nz) Numerous flights each day between Picton and Wellington, with connections to Blenheim and Nelson.

Stewart Island Flights (☎03-218 9129; www.stewartislandflights.com) Flies between Invercargill and Stewart Island.

Sunair (☎07-575 7799, 0800 786 247; www.sunair.co.nz) Flies to Whitianga from Auckland, Great Barrier Island, Hamilton, Rotorua and Tauranga. Other North Island routes too.

Air Passes

With discounting being the norm these days, and a number of budget airlines now serving the trans-Tasman route as well as the Pacific islands, the value of air passes isn't as red-hot as in the past.

From Los Angeles return, **Air New Zealand** (NZ; ☎09-357 3000, 0800 737 000; www.airnewzealand.co.nz) offers the Explore New Zealand Airpass, which includes a stop in either Wellington, Queenstown or Christchurch plus three other domestic NZ destinations. Prices at the time of research started at around US$1150.

Star Alliance (www.staralliance.com) offers the coupon-based South Pacific Airpass, valid for selected journeys within NZ, and between NZ, Australia and several Pacific islands, including Fiji, New Caledonia, Tonga, the Cook Islands and Samoa. Passes are available to nonresidents of these countries, must be issued outside NZ in conjunction with Star Alliance international tickets, and are valid for three months. A typical Sydney–Christchurch–Wellington–Auckland–Nadi pass cost NZ$1050 at the time of research.

Bicycle

Touring cyclists proliferate in NZ, particularly over summer. NZ is clean, green and relatively uncrowded, and has lots of cheap accommodation (including camping) and abundant fresh water. The roads are generally in good nick, and the climate is generally not too hot or cold. Road traffic is the biggest danger: trucks overtaking too close to cyclists are a particular threat. Bikes and cycling gear (to rent or buy) are readily available in the main centres, as are bicycle repair shops.

By law all cyclists must wear an approved safety helmet (or risk a fine); it's also vital to have good reflective safety clothing. Cyclists who use public transport will find that major bus lines and trains only take bicycles on a 'space available' basis and charge up to $10. Some of the smaller shuttle bus companies, on the other hand, make sure they have storage space for bikes, which they carry for a surcharge.

If importing your own bike or transporting it by plane within NZ, check with the relevant airline for costs and the degree of dismantling and packing required.

See www.nzta.govt.nz/traffic/ways/bike for more bike safety and legal tips.

Hire

The rates offered by most outfits for renting road or mountain bikes range from $10 to $20 per hour and $30 to $50 per day. Longer-term rentals are often available by negotiation.

Boat

NZ may be an island nation but there's virtually no long-distance water transport around the country. Obvious exceptions include the boat services between Auckland and various islands in the Hauraki Gulf, the inter-island ferries that chug across Cook Strait between Wellington and Picton, and the passenger ferry that negotiates Foveaux Strait between Bluff and the town of Oban on Stewart Island.

Bus

Bus travel in NZ is relatively easy and well organised, with services transporting you to the far reaches of both islands (including the start/end of various walking tracks), but it can be expensive, tedious and time-consuming.

NZ's dominant bus company is **InterCity** (☎09-583 5780; www.intercity.co.nz), which also has an extra-comfort travel and sightseeing arm called **Newmans**

NGA HAERENGA, NEW ZEALAND CYCLE TRAIL

The **Nga Haerenga, New Zealand Cycle Trail** (www.nzcycletrail.com) is a major nationwide project that has been in motion since 2009, expanding and improving NZ's extant network of bike trails. Funded to the tune of around $46 million, the project currently has 18 'Great Rides' under construction across both islands, most of which are already open to cyclists in some capacity. See the website for info and updates.

Coach Lines (☎09-583 5780; www.newmanscoach.co.nz). InterCity can drive you to just about anywhere on the North and South Islands. **Naked Bus** (☎0900 625 33; www.nakedbus.com) is the main competition, a budget operator with fares as low as $1 (!).

Seat Classes

There are no allocated economy or luxury classes on NZ buses; smoking is a no-no.

Reservations

Over summer, school holidays and public holidays, book well in advance on popular routes. At other times a day or two ahead is usually fine. The best prices are generally available online, booked a few weeks in advance.

Bus Passes

If you're covering a lot of ground, both **InterCity** (☎09-583 5780, 0800 222 146; www.intercity.co.nz) and **Naked Bus** (☎0900 625 33; www.nakedbus.com) offer bus passes that can be cheaper than paying as you go, but they do of course lock you into using their respective networks. InterCity also offers a 15% discount for YHA, BBH and VIP backpacker members. All the following passes are valid for 12 months.

Backpacker Buses also offers fixed-itinerary bus-pass options for dorm dwellers.

NATIONWIDE PASSES

Flexipass A hop-on, hop-off InterCity pass, allowing travel to pretty much anywhere in NZ, in any direction. The pass is purchased in blocks of travel time: minimum 15 hours ($117), maximum 60 hours ($449). The average cost of each block becomes cheaper the more hours you buy. You can top up the pass if you need more time.

Flexitrips An InterCity bus-pass system whereby you purchase a specific number of bus trips (eg Auckland to Tauranga would count as one trip) in blocks of five, with or without the north–south ferry trip included. Five/15/30 trips including the ferry cost $210/383/550 (subtract $54 if you don't need the ferry).

Aotearoa Adventurer, **Kiwi Explorer**, **Kia Ora New Zealand** and **Tiki Tour New Zealand** Hop-on, hop-off, fixed-itinerary nationwide passes offered by InterCity. These passes link up tourist hot spots and range in price from $645 to $1219. See www.travelpass.co.nz for details.

Naked Passport A Naked Bus **pass** (www.nakedpassport.com) that allows you to buy trips in blocks of five, which you can add to any time, and book each trip as needed. Five/15/30 trips cost $157/330/497. An unlimited pass costs $597 – great value if you're travelling NZ for many moons.

NORTH ISLAND PASSES

InterCity also offers 13 hop-on, hop-off, fixed-itinerary North Island bus passes, ranging from short $43 runs between Rotorua and Taupo, to $249 trips from Auckland to Wellington via the big sights in between. See www.travelpass.co.nz for details.

SOUTH ISLAND PASSES

On the South Island, InterCity offers 11 hop-on, hop-off, fixed-itinerary passes, ranging from $43 trips between Christchurch and Kaikoura, to $583 loops around the whole island. See www.travelpass.co.nz for details.

Shuttle Buses

Other than InterCity and Naked Bus, regional shuttle-bus operators include the following:

Abel Tasman Coachlines (☎03-548 0285; www.abeltasmantravel.co.nz) Traverses the tarmac between Nelson, Motueka, Golden Bay, and Kahurangi and Abel Tasman National Parks.

Alpine Scenic Tours (☎07-378 7412; www.alpinescenictours.co.nz) Has services around Taupo and into Tongariro National Park, plus the ski fields around Mt Ruapehu and Mt Tongariro.

Atomic Shuttles (☎03-349 0697; www.atomictravel.co.nz) Has services throughout the South Island, including to Christchurch, Dunedin, Invercargill, Picton, Nelson, Greymouth/Hokitika, Te Anau and Queenstown/Wanaka

Cook Connection (☎0800 266 526; www.cookconnect.co.nz) Triangulates between Mt Cook, Twizel and Lake Tekapo.

Dalroy Express (☎06-759-0197, 0508 465 622; www.dalroytours.co.nz) Operates a daily service between Auckland and New Plymouth via Hamilton, extending to Hawera Monday to Friday. Also runs from Auckland to Pahia, and from Hamilton to Rotorua and Taupo.

East West Coaches (☎03-789 6251, 0800 142 622; eastwestcoaches@xtra.co.nz) Offers a service between Christchurch and Westport via Reefton.

Hanmer Connection (☎0800 242 663; www.atsnz.com) Twice-daily services between Hanmer Springs and Christchurch.

Go Kiwi Shuttles (☎07-866 0336; www.go-kiwi.co.nz) Links Auckland with Whitianga on the Coromandel Peninsula daily, with extensions to Rotorua in summer.

Knightrider (☎03-342 8055, 0800 317 057; www.knightrider.co.nz) Runs a nocturnal service from Christchurch to Dunedin return. David Hasselhoff nowhere to be seen...

Southern Link Travel (☎0508 458 835; www.southernlinkkbus.co.nz) Roams across most of the South Island, taking in Christchurch, Nelson, Picton, Greymouth, Queenstown and Dunedin, among others.

Topline Tours (☎03-249 8059; www.toplinetours.co.nz) Connects Te Anau and Queenstown.

Tracknet (☎03-249 7777, 0800 483 262; www.tracknet.net) Daily track transport (Milford, Routeburn, Hollyford, Kepler etc) between Queenstown, Te Anau, Milford Sound, Invercargill, Fiordland and the West Coast.

Waitomo Wanderer (☎03-477 9083, 0800 000 4321; www.travelheadfirst.com) Does a loop from Rotorua or Taupo to Waitomo.

West Coast Shuttle (☎03-768 0028; www.westcoastshuttle.co.nz) Daily bus from Greymouth to Christchurch and back.

Backpacker Buses

If you feel like clocking up some kilometres with like-minded fellow travellers, the following operators run fixed-itinerary bus tours, nationwide or on the North or South Island. Accommodation and hop-on/hop-off flexibility are often included.

Adventure Tours New Zealand (☎09-526 2149; www.adventuretours.com.au)

Flying Kiwi (☎03-547 0171, 0800 693 296; www.flyingkiwi.com)

Kiwi Experience (☎09-336 4286; www.kiwiexperience.com)

Haka Tours (☎03-980 4252; www.hakatours.com)

Magic Travellers Network (☎09-358 5600; www.magicbus.co.nz)

Stray Travel (☎09-526 2140; www.straytravel.com)

Car & Motorcycle

The best way to explore NZ in depth is to have your own wheels. It's easy to hire cars and campervans at good rates; alternatively, consider buying your own vehicle.

FREEDOM CAMPING

NZ is so photogenic, it's tempting to just pull off the road at a gorgeous viewpoint and camp the night. But never just assume it's OK to camp somewhere: always ask a local or check with the local i-SITE, DOC office or commercial campground. If you are freedom camping, treat the area with respect – if your van doesn't have toilet facilities, find a public loo. Legislation allows for $200 instant fines for camping in prohibited areas, or improper disposal of waste (in cases where dumping waste could damage the environment, fees are up to $10,000). See www.camping.org.nz for more freedom camping tips, and www.tourism.govt.nz for info on where to find dump stations.

Automobile Association (AA)

NZ's **Automobile Association** (AA; ☎0800 500 444; www.aa.co.nz/travel) provides emergency breakdown services, maps and accommodation guides (from holiday parks to motels and B&Bs).

Members of overseas automobile associations should bring their membership cards – many of these bodies have reciprocal agreements with the AA.

Driving Licences

International visitors to NZ can use their home country's driving licence – if your licence isn't in English, it's a good idea to carry a certified translation with you. Alternatively, use an International Driving Permit (IDP), which will usually be issued on the spot (valid for 12 months) by your home country's automobile association.

Fuel

Fuel (petrol, aka gasoline) is available from service stations across NZ. LPG (gas) is not always stocked by rural suppliers; if you're on gas, it's safer to have dual-fuel capability. Aside from remote locations like Milford Sound and Mt Cook, petrol prices don't vary much from place to place (very democratic): per-litre costs at the time of research were around $2.10.

Hire

CAMPERVAN

Check your rear-view mirror on any far-flung NZ road and you'll probably see a shiny white campervan (aka mobile home, motor home, RV) packed with liberated travellers, mountain bikes and portable barbecues cruising along behind you.

Most towns of any size have a campground or holiday park with powered sites for around $35 per night. There are also 250-plus vehicle-accessible **Department of Conservation** (DOC; www.doc.govt.nz) campsites around NZ, ranging in price from free to $19 per adult: check the website.

You can hire campervans from dozens of companies, prices varying with season, vehicle size and length of rental.

A small van for two people typically has a minikitchen and foldout dining table, the latter transforming into a double bed when dinner is done and dusted. Larger 'superior' two-berth vans include shower and toilet. Four- to six-berth campervans are the size of trucks (and similarly sluggish) and, besides the extra space, usually contain a toilet and shower.

Over summer, rates offered by the main rental firms for two-/four-/six-berth vans start at around

$160/260/300 per day, dropping to as low as $45/60/90 in winter for month-long rentals.

Major operators include the following:

Apollo (09-889 2976, 0800 113 131; www.apollocamperco.nz)

Britz (09-255 3910, 0800 831 900; www.britz.co.nz)

Kea (09-448 8800, 0800 520 052; www.keacampers.com)

Maui (09-255 3910, 0800 651 080; www.maui.co.nz)

Pacific Horizon (09-257 4331; www.pacifichorizon.co.nz)

United Campervans (09-275 9919; www.unitedcampervans.co.nz)

BACKPACKER VAN RENTALS

Budget players in the campervan industry offer slick deals and funky, well-kitted-out vehicles for backpackers. Rates are competitive (from $35 per day May to September; from $80 per day December to February). Operators include the following:

Backpacker Campervans (0800 422 267; www.backpackercampervans.co.nz) Reliable operator, affiliated with Britz and Maui.

Backpacker Sleeper Vans (03-359 4731, 0800 325 939; www.sleepervans.co.nz) The name says it all.

Escape Rentals (0800 216 171; www.escaperentals.co.nz) Loud, original paintwork, plus DVDs, TVs and outdoor barbecues for hire.

Hippie Camper (0800 113 131; www.hippiecamper.co.nz) Think Combi vans for the new millenium.

Jucy (0800 399 736; www.jucy.co.nz)

Spaceships (09-526 2130, 0800 772 237; www.spaceshipsrentals.co.nz) The customised 'Swiss Army Knife of campervans', with extras including DVD and CD players, roof racks and solar showers.

Wicked Campers (09-634 2994, 0800 246 870; www.wicked-campers.co.nz) Spray-painted vans bedecked with everything/everyone from Mr Spock to Sly Stone.

CAR

Competition between car-rental companies in NZ is torrid, particularly in the big cities and Picton. Remember that if you want to travel far, you need unlimited kilometres. Some (but not all) companies require drivers to be at least 21 years old – ask around.

Most car-hire firms suggest (or insist) that you don't take their vehicles between islands on the Cook Strait ferries. Instead, you leave your car at either Wellington or Picton terminal and pick up another car once you've crossed the strait. This saves you paying to transport a vehicle on the ferries, and is a pain-free exercise.

INTERNATIONAL RENTAL COMPANIES

The big multinational companies have offices in most major cities, towns and airports. Firms sometimes offer one-way rentals (eg collect a car in Auckland, leave it in Wellington), but there are often restrictions and fees. On the other hand, an operator in Christchurch may need to get a vehicle back to Auckland and will offer an amazing one-way deal (sometimes free!).

The major companies offer a choice of either unlimited kilometres, or 100km (or so) per day free, plus so many cents per subsequent kilometre. Daily rates in main cities typically start at around $40 per day for a compact, late-model, Japanese car, and around $75 for medium-sized cars (including GST, unlimited kilometres and insurance).

Avis (09-526-2847, 0800 655 111; www.avis.co.nz)

Budget (09-529 7784, 0800 283 438; www.budget.co.nz)

Europcar (03-357 0920, 0800 800 115; www.europcar.co.nz)

Hertz (03-520 3044, 0800 654 321; www.hertz.co.nz)

Thrifty (03-359 2720, 0800 737 070; www.thrifty.co.nz)

LOCAL RENTAL COMPANIES

Local rental firms dapple the *Yellow Pages*. These are almost always cheaper than the big boys – sometimes half the price – but the cheap rates may come with serious restrictions: vehicles are often older, and with less formality sometimes comes a less protective legal structure for renters.

Rentals from local firms start at around $30 per day for the smallest option. It's obviously cheaper if you rent for a week or more, and there are often low-season and weekend discounts.

Affordable and independent operators with national networks include the following:

a2b Car Rentals (0800 666 703; www.a2b-carrentals.co.nz)

Ace Rental Cars (09-303 3112, 0800 502 277; www.acerentalcars.co.nz)

Apex Rentals (03-379 6897, 0800 939 597; www.apexrentals.co.nz)

Ezy Rentals (09-374 4360, 0800 399 736; www.ezy.co.nz)

Go Rentals (09-525 7321, 0800 467 368; www.gorentals.co.nz)

Omega Rental Cars (09-377 5573, 0800 525 210; www.omegarentalcars.com)

Pegasus Rental Cars (03-548 2852, 0800 803 580; www.rentalcars.co.nz)

MOTORCYCLE

Born to be wild? NZ has great terrain for motorcycle touring, despite the fickle weather in some regions. Most of the country's motorcycle-hire shops are in Auckland and Christchurch, where you can hire anything from a little 50cc moped (aka nifty-fifty) to a throbbing 750cc touring motorcycle and beyond. Recommended operators (who also run guided tours) with rates from $80 to $345 per day:

New Zealand Motorcycle Rentals & Tours (☎09-486 2472; www.nzbike.com)

Te Waipounamu Motorcycle Tours (☎03-377 3211; www.motorcycle-hire.co.nz)

Insurance

Rather than risk paying out wads of cash if you have an accident, you can take out your own comprehensive insurance policy, or (the usual option) pay an additional fee per day to the rental company to reduce your excess. This brings the amount you must pay in the event of an accident down from around $1500 or $2000 to around $200 or $300. Smaller operators offering cheap rates often have a compulsory insurance excess, taken as a credit-card bond, of around $900.

Most insurance agreements won't cover the cost of damage to glass (including the windscreen) or tyres, and insurance coverage is often invalidated on beaches and certain rough (4WD) unsealed roads – read the fine print.

Purchase

Buying a car then selling it at the end of your travels can be one of the cheapest and best ways to see NZ. Auckland is the easiest place to buy a car, followed by Christchurch: scour the hostel notice boards. **Turners Auctions** (☎03-343 9850, 09-525 1920; www.turners.co.nz) is NZ's biggest car-auction operator, with 10 locations.

LEGALITIES

Make sure your prospective vehicle has a Warrant of Fitness (WoF) and registration valid for a reasonable period: see the **Land Transport New Zealand** (www.landtransport.govt.nz) website for details.

Buyers should also take out third-party insurance, covering the cost of repairs to another vehicle in an accident that is your fault: try the **Automobile Association** (AA; ☎0800 500 444; www.aa.co.nz/travel). NZ's no-fault Accident Compensation Corporation scheme covers personal injury, but make sure you have travel insurance too.

Various car-inspection companies inspect cars for around $150; find them at car auctions, or they will come to you. Try **Vehicle Inspection New Zealand** (VINZ; ☎09-573 3230, 0800 468 469; www.vinz.co.nz) or the AA.

Before you buy it's wise to confirm ownership of the vehicle, and find out if there's anything dodgy about the car (eg stolen, or outstanding debts). The AA's **LemonCheck** (☎09-414 6665, 0800 536 662; www.lemoncheck.co.nz) offers this service.

BUY-BACK DEALS

You can avoid the hassle of buying/selling a vehicle privately by entering into a buy-back arrangement with a dealer. Predictably, dealers often find sneaky ways of knocking down the return-sale price, which may be 50% less than what you paid. Hiring or buying and selling a vehicle yourself (if you have the time) is usually a better bet.

Road Hazards

Kiwi traffic is usually pretty light, but it's easy to get stuck behind a slow-moving truck or campervan – pack plenty of patience. There are also lots of slow wiggly roads, one-way bridges and plenty of gravel roads, all of which require a more cautious driving approach. And watch out for sheep!

Road Rules

Kiwis drive on the left-hand side of the road; cars are right-hand drive. Give way to the right at intersections.

At single-lane bridges (of which there are a surprisingly large number), a smaller red arrow pointing in your direction of travel means that *you* give way.

Speed limits on the open road are generally 100km/h; in built-up areas the limit is usually 50km/h. Speed cameras and radars are used extensively.

All vehicle occupants must wear a seatbelt or risk a fine. Small children must be belted into approved safety seats.

Always carry your licence when driving. Drink-driving is a serious offence and remains a significant problem in NZ, despite widespread campaigns and severe penalties. The legal blood alcohol limit is 0.08% for drivers over 20, and 0% (zero!) for those under 20.

Hitching & Ride-Sharing

NZ is no longer immune from the perils of solo hitching (especially for women). Those who decide to hitch are taking a small but potentially serious risk. That said, it's not unusual to see hitchhikers along country roads.

Alternatively, check hostel notice boards for ride-share opportunities, or have a look at www.carpoolnz.org or www.nationalcarshare.co.nz.

Local Transport

Bus, Train & Tram

NZ's larger cities have extensive bus services but, with a few honourable exceptions, they are mainly daytime, weekday operations; weekend services can be infrequent or nonexistent. Negotiating inner-city Auckland is made easier by the Link and free City Circuit buses. Hamilton also has a free city-centre loop bus; Christchurch has a free city shuttle service and the historic tramway (closed post-earthquake at the time of research).

Most main cities have late-night buses on boozy Friday and Saturday nights.

The only city with a decent train service is Wellington, which has five suburban routes.

Taxi

The main cities have plenty of taxis and even small towns may have a local service.

Train

NZ train travel is about the journey, not about getting anywhere in a hurry. **Tranz Scenic** (☎04-495 0775, 0800 872 467; www.tranzscenic.co.nz) operates four routes:

Overlander Between Auckland and Wellington.

TranzCoastal Between Christchurch and Picton.

TranzAlpine Over the Southern Alps between Christchurch and Greymouth.

Capital Connection Weekday commuter service between Palmerston North and Wellington.

Reservations can be made through Tranz Scenic directly, or at most train stations (notably *not* at Palmerston North or Hamilton), travel agents and visitor info centres. Discounts on the *TranzCoastal* and *TranzAlpine* apply for children and seniors (30% off) and backpacker cardholders (20% off).

Train Passes

Tranz Scenic's **Scenic Rail Pass** (www.tranzscenic.co.nz) allows unlimited travel on all of its rail services, including passage on the Wellington–Picton Interislander ferry. A two-week pass costs $528/402 per adult/child. There's also a seven-day *TranzAlpine* and *Coastal Pacific* pass for $307/215.

WANT MORE?

For in-depth language information and handy phrases, check out Lonely Planet's *South Pacific Phrasebook*. You'll find it at **shop.lonelyplanet.com**, or you can buy Lonely Planet's iPhone phrasebooks at the Apple App Store.

New Zealand has three official languages: English, Maori and NZ sign language. Although English is what you'll usually hear, Maori has been making a comeback. You can use English to speak to anyone in New Zealand, but there are some occasions when knowing a small amount of Maori is useful, such as when visiting a *marae,* where often only Maori is spoken. Some knowledge of Maori will also help you interpret the many Maori place names you'll come across.

KIWI ENGLISH

Like the people of other English-speaking countries in the world, New Zealanders have their own, unique way of speaking the language. The flattening of vowels is the most distinctive feature of Kiwi pronunciation. For example, in Kiwi English, 'fish and chips' sounds more like 'fush and chups'. On the North Island sentences often have 'eh!' attached to the end. In the far south a rolled 'r' is common, which is a holdover from that region's Scottish heritage – it's especially noticeable in Southland.

MAORI

The Maori have a vividly chronicled history, recorded in songs and chants that dramatically recall the migration to New Zealand from Polynesia as well as other important events. Early missionaries were the first to record the language in a written form using only 15 letters of the English alphabet.

Maori is closely related to other Polynesian languages such as Hawaiian, Tahitian and Cook Islands Maori. In fact, New Zealand Maori and Hawaiian are quite similar, even though more than 7000km separates Honolulu and Auckland.

The Maori language was never dead – it was always used in Maori ceremonies – but over time familiarity with it was definitely on the decline. Fortunately, recent years have seen a revival of interest in it, and this forms an integral part of the renaissance of *Maoritanga* (Maori culture). Many Maori people who had heard the language spoken on the *marae* for years but had not used it in their day-to-day lives, are now studying it and speaking it fluently. Maori is taught in schools throughout New Zealand, some TV programs and news reports are broadcast in it, and many English place names are being renamed in Maori. Even government departments have been given Maori names: for example, the Inland Revenue Department is also known as Te Tari Taake (the last word is actually *take,* which means 'levy', but the department has chosen to stress the long 'a' by spelling it 'aa').

In many places, Maori have come together to provide instruction in their language and culture to young children; the idea is for them to grow up speaking both Maori and English, and to develop a familiarity with Maori tradition. It's a matter of some pride to have fluency in the language. On some *marae* only Maori can be spoken.

Pronunciation

Maori is a fluid, poetic language and surprisingly easy to pronounce once you remember to split each word (some can be amazingly long) into separate syllables. Each syllable ends in a vowel. There are no 'silent' letters.

Most consonants in Maori – *h, k, m, n, p, t* and *w* – are pronounced much the same as in English. The Maori *r* is a flapped sound (not rolled) with the tongue near the front of the mouth. It's closer to the English 'l' in pronunciation.

The *ng* is pronounced as in the English words 'singing' or 'running', and can be used at the beginning of words as well as at the end. To practise, just say 'ing' over and over, then isolate the 'ng' part of it.

The letters *wh*, when occuring together, are generally pronounced as a soft English 'f'. This pronunciation is used in many place names in New Zealand, such as Whakatane, Whangaroa and Whakapapa (all pronounced as if they begin with a soft 'f'). There is some local variation: in the region around the Whanganui River, for example, *wh* is pronounced as in the English word 'when'.

The correct pronunciation of the vowels is very important. The examples below are a rough guideline – it helps to listen carefully to someone who speaks the language well. Each vowel has both a long and a short sound, with long vowels often denoted by a line over the letter or a double vowel. We have not indicated long and short vowel forms in this book.

Vowels

a	as in 'large', with no 'r' sound
e	as in 'get'
i	as in 'marine'
o	as in 'pork'
u	as the 'oo' in 'moon'

Vowel Combinations

ae, ai	as the 'y' in 'sky'
ao, au	as the 'ow' in 'how'
ea	as in 'bear'
ei	as in 'vein'
eo	as 'eh-oh'
eu	as 'eh-oo'
ia	as in the name 'Ian'
ie	as the 'ye' in 'yet'
io	as the 'ye o' in 'ye old'
iu	as the 'ue' in 'cue'
oa	as in 'roar'
oe	as in 'toe'
oi	as in 'toil'
ou	as the 'ow' in 'how'
ua	as the 'ewe' in 'fewer'

Greetings & Small Talk

Maori greetings are becoming increasingly popular – don't be surprised if you're greeted with *Kia ora*.

Welcome!	*Haere mai!*
Hello./Good luck./ Good health.	*Kia ora.*
Hello. (to one person)	*Tena koe.*
Hello. (to two people)	*Tena korua.*
Hello. (to three or more people)	*Tena koutou.*
Goodbye. (to person staying)	*E noho ra.*
Goodbye. (to person leaving)	*Haere ra.*
How are you? (to one person)	*Kei te pehea koe?*
How are you? (to two people)	*Kei te pehea korua?*
How are you? (to three or more people)	*Kei te pehea koutou?*
Very well, thanks./ That's fine.	*Kei te pai.*

Maori Geographical Terms

The following words form part of many Maori place names in New Zealand, and help you understand the meaning of these place names. For example: Waikaremoana is the Sea *(moana)* of Rippling *(kare)* Waters *(wai)*, and Rotorua means the Second *(rua)* Lake *(roto)*.

a – of
ana – cave
ara – way, path or road
awa – river or valley
heke – descend
hiku – end; tail
hine – girl; daughter
ika – fish
iti – small
kahurangi – treasured possession; special greenstone
kai – food
kainga – village
kaka – parrot
kare – rippling
kati – shut or close
koura – crayfish
makariri – cold
manga – stream or tributary
manu – bird

maunga – mountain
moana – sea or lake
moko – tattoo
motu – island
mutu – finished; ended; over
nga – the (plural)
noa – ordinary; not *tapu*
nui – big or great
nuku – distance
o – of, place of…
one – beach, sand or mud
pa – fortified village
papa – large blue-grey mudstone
pipi – common edible bivalve
pohatu – stone
poto – short
pouri – sad; dark; gloomy
puke – hill
puna – spring; hole; fountain
rangi – sky; heavens
raro – north
rei – cherished possession
roa – long
roto – lake
rua – hole in the ground; two
runga – above
tahuna – beach; sandbank
tane – man
tangata – people
tapu – sacred, forbidden or taboo
tata – close to; dash against; twin islands
tawaha – entrance or opening
tawahi – the other side (of a river or lake)
te – the (singular)
tonga – south
ure – male genitals
uru – west
waha – broken
wahine – woman
wai – water
waingaro – lost; waters that disappear in certain seasons
waka – canoe
wera – burnt or warm; floating
wero – challenge
whaka... – to act as ...
whanau – family
whanga – harbour, bay or inlet
whare – house
whenua – land or country
whiti – east

Here are some more place names composed of words in the list:

Aramoana – Sea *(moana)* Path *(ara)*
Awaroa – Long *(roa)* River *(awa)*
Kaitangata – Eat *(kai)* People *(tangata)*
Maunganui – Great *(nui)* Mountain *(maunga)*
Opouri – Place of *(o)* Sadness *(pouri)*
Te Araroa – The *(te)* Long *(roa)* Path *(ara)*
Te Puke – The *(te)* Hill *(puke)*
Urewera – Burnt *(wera)* Penis *(ure)*
Waimakariri – Cold *(makariri)* Water *(wai)*
Wainui – Great *(nui)* Waters *(wai)*
Whakatane – To Act *(whaka)* as a Man *(tane)*
Whangarei – Cherished *(rei)* Harbour *(whanga)*

GLOSSARY

Following is a list of abbreviations, 'Kiwi English', Maori, and slang terms used in this book and which you may hear in New Zealand.

All Blacks – NZ's revered national rugby union team
ANZAC – Australia and New Zealand Army Corps
Aoraki – *Maori* name for Mt Cook, meaning 'Cloud Piercer'
Aotearoa – *Maori* name for NZ, most often translated as 'Land of the Long White Cloud'
aroha – love

B&B – 'bed and breakfast' accommodation
bach – holiday home (pronounced 'batch'); see also crib
black-water rafting – rafting or tubing underground in a cave
boozer – public bar
bro – literally 'brother'; usually meaning mate
BYO – 'bring your own' (usually applies to alcohol at a restaurant or cafe)
choice/chur – fantastic; great
crib – the name for a bach in Otago and Southland

DB&B – 'dinner, bed and breakfast' accommodation
DOC – Department of Conservation (or Te Papa Atawhai); government department that administers national parks, tracks and huts

eh? – roughly translates as 'don't you agree?'

farmstay – accommodation on a Kiwi farm

football – rugby, either union or league; occasionally soccer

Great Walks – a set of nine popular tramping tracks within NZ

greenstone – jade; *pounamu*

gumboots – rubber boots or Wellingtons; originated from diggers on the gum-fields

Hawaiki –an original homeland of the *Maori*

haka – any dance, but usually a war dance

hangi – oven whereby food is steamed in baskets over embers in a hole; a *Maori* feast

hapu – subtribe or smaller tribal grouping

hei tiki – carved, stylised human figure worn around the neck; also called a *tiki*

homestay – accommodation in a family house

hongi – *Maori* greeting; the pressing of foreheads and noses, and sharing of life breath

hui – gathering; meeting

i-SITE – information centre

iwi – large tribal grouping with common lineage back to the original migration from Hawaiki; people; tribe

jandals – a contraction of Japanese sandals; flip-flops; thongs; usually rubber footwear

jersey – jumper, usually woollen; the shirt worn by rugby players

kauri – native pine

kia ora – hello

Kiwi – A New Zealander; an adjective to mean anything relating to NZ

kiwi – flightless, nocturnal brown bird with a long beak

Kiwiana – things uniquely connected to NZ life and culture, especially from bygone years

kiwifruit – small, succulent fruit with fuzzy brown skin and juicy green flesh; aka Chinese gooseberry or zespri

kumara – Polynesian sweet potato, a *Maori* staple food

Kupe – early Polynesian navigator from *Hawaiki*, credited with the discovery of the islands that are now NZ

mana – spiritual quality of a person or object; authority or prestige

Maori – indigenous people of NZ

Maoritanga – things *Maori*, ie *Maori* culture

marae – the sacred ground in front of the *Maori* meeting house; more commonly used to refer to the entire complex of buildings

Maui – a figure in *Maori* (Polynesian) mythology

mauri – life force/principle

moa – large, extinct flightless bird

moko – tattoo; usually refers to facial tattoos

nga – the (plural); see also *te*

ngai/ngati – literally, 'the people of' or 'the descendants of'; tribe (pronounced 'kai' on the South Island)

NZ – the universal term for New Zealand; pronounced 'en zed'

pa – fortified *Maori* village, usually on a hilltop

Pacific Rim – modern NZ cuisine; local produce cooked with imported styles

Pakeha – *Maori* for a white or European person

Pasifika – Pacific Island culture

paua – abalone; iridescent paua shell is often used in jewellery

pavlova – meringue cake topped with cream and kiwifruit

PI – Pacific Islander

poi – ball of woven flax

pounamu – *Maori* name for *greenstone*

powhiri – traditional *Maori* welcome onto a marae

rip – dangerously strong current running away from the shore at a beach

Roaring Forties – the ocean between 40° and 50° south, known for very strong winds

silver fern – the symbol worn by the *All Blacks* and other national sportsfolk on their jerseys; the national netball team is called the Silver Ferns

sweet, sweet as – all-purpose term like choice; fantastic, great

tapu – a strong force in *Maori* life, with numerous meanings; in its simplest form it means sacred, forbidden, taboo

te – the (singular); see also *nga*

te reo – literally 'the language'; the *Maori* language

tiki – short for *hei tiki*

tiki tour – scenic tour

tramp – bushwalk; trek; hike

tuatara – prehistoric reptile dating back to the age of dinosaurs

tui – native parson bird

wahine – woman

wai – water

wairua – spirit

Waitangi – short way of referring to the Treaty of Waitangi

waka – canoe

Warriors – NZ's popular rugby league club, affiliated with Australia's NRL

Wellywood – Wellington, because of its thriving film industry

zorbing – rolling down a hill inside an inflatable plastic ball

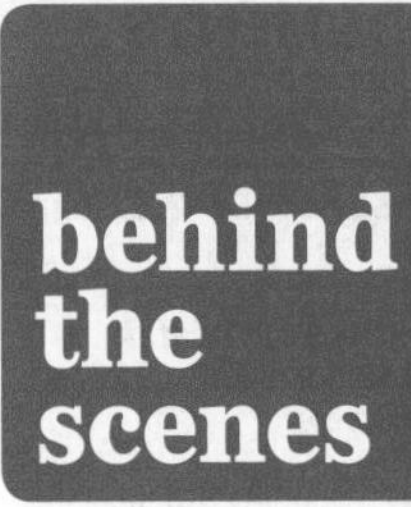

SEND US YOUR FEEDBACK

We love to hear from travellers – your comments keep us on our toes and help make our books better. Our well-travelled team reads every word on what you loved or loathed about this book. Although we cannot reply individually to postal submissions, we always guarantee that your feedback goes straight to the appropriate authors, in time for the next edition. Each person who sends us information is thanked in the next edition – the most useful submissions are rewarded with a selection of digital PDF chapters.

Visit **lonelyplanet.com/contact** to submit your updates and suggestions or to ask for help. Our award-winning website also features inspirational travel stories, news and discussions.

Note: We may edit, reproduce and incorporate your comments in Lonely Planet products such as guidebooks, websites and digital products, so let us know if you don't want your comments reproduced or your name acknowledged. For a copy of our privacy policy visit lonelyplanet.com/privacy.

OUR READERS

Many thanks to the travellers who used the last edition and wrote to us with helpful hints, useful advice and interesting anecdotes:

A Shaughan Anderson, Jen Andrews **B** Beverly Bacon, Geoff Barnes, Yvonne Bischofberger, Prue Blake, Steve Brightwell **C** David Carroll, Des Casey, Brendon Clough, Karen Connor, Barbara Curtis **D** Mike Davies, Bob Dickson, Petrina Dodd, Jake Downing, Cecile Dransart **E** Sarah Ensor, Megan Etherington, Rebecca Evans **F** Nick Fisentzidis **G** Jack Grinsted **H** Meirene Hardy-Birch, Jo Heaton, Tess Hellebrekers, Katrina Henderson, Claudia Hill **J** Cheryl Jensen, Trevor Johnston **K** Michelle Kinney, Chiharu Kitai, Lisa Knights **L** Glenda Lee, Ali Lemer, Gerard Long **M** Jo Mackie, Liz Maire, Erin McManus, Diana Morris, David Mules **N** Jane Nethercote **O** Helen Ough Dealy **P** Petrina Page, Diana Parr, Trent Paton, Ainsley Pope **S** Margret Sando, Sonya Sawyers, Elena Sedouch, Jan Simmons, Rajneel Singh, Rebecca Skinner, Kerryn Smith, Nyia Strachan **T** Elise Thomas, Sarah Thompson **V** Kaja Vetter **W** John Wotherspoon

AUTHOR THANKS

Charles Rawlings-Way

Thanks to the many generous, knowledgeable and quietly self-assured Kiwis I met on the road, especially the i-SITE staff in Palmerston North, Hamilton, Waitomo and New Plymouth. Thanks to Errol Hunt for the gig, and the everimpressive Lonely Planet production staff (including the Lords of SPP). Humongous gratitude to my tireless, witty and professional co-authors: Sarah, Brett, Peter and Lee. Thanks also to Warren for Wellington, and to Meg, Ione and Remy for holding the fort while I was away.

Brett Atkinson

Thanks to all the i-SITE and DOC staff I tapped for vital information. In Christchurch, special thanks to Kelly Wilkes, Sam Johnson, Monique Devereux, Roger Sutton, and Jeff and Naomi Peters. Cheers to Richard Emerson in Dunedin, and to Scott Kennedy and Tony Moore in Queenstown. At Lonely Planet, it's always great to work with Errol Hunt and the NZ author crew, ably assisted this time around by Jani Patokallio. Final thanks to Carol back at Casa Loma in Auckland.

Sarah Bennett & Lee Slater

Thanks to everyone who helped us on the road, including RTO and i-SITE staff, tourism operators and travellers. Many thanks DOC, especially Penny McIntosh, Katrina Henderson and Diana Parr. Big ups to everyone in-house at Lonely Planet, and to Team NZ, including Errol, Peter, Brett, Charles, Sarah Ewing, and by proxy Arnott Potter at CPP. To all who provided a park for our camper, a fridge for the flagon, and even turkey for thanksgiving: arohanui, e hoa ma, especially the Bennetts, Parsons, Pauls, Betzy Iannuzzi and John Kelly.

Peter Dragicevich

If I were to thank everyone who helped me eat and drink my way around Auckland it would be a very long list indeed. Particular thanks go to Shenita Prasad and Tania Wong for their help in the Coromandel, and to Joanne Cole in Northland. Extra special thanks are due to my trusty Bay of Islands sidekick Matt Swaine, Taupo font-of-all-knowledge Donna Jarden, and to Tony Dragicevich and Debbie Debono for the writing retreat.

ACKNOWLEDGMENTS

Climate map data adapted from Peel MC, Finlayson BL & McMahon TA (2007) 'Updated World Map of the Köppen-Geiger Climate Classification', *Hydrology and Earth System Sciences*, 11, 163344.

Cover photograph: Lush hills in front of Mt Taranaki (Egmont National Park), New Zealand, Jami Tarris/Corbis

Many of the images in this guide are available for licensing from Lonely Planet Images: www.lonelyplanetimages.com.

THIS BOOK

Lonely Planet founder Tony Wheeler wrote the first edition of Lonely Planet's *New Zealand* way back in the days of flares and sandals, in 1977, and in the 35 years since then a small army of authors have scoured the roads and trails of Aotearoa putting together ever-better guidebooks. This 16th edition was researched and written by Charles Rawlings-Way, Brett Atkinson, Sarah Bennett, Peter Dragicevich and Lee Slater. This guidebook was commissioned in Lonely Planet's Melbourne office, and produced by the following:

Commissioning Editor Errol Hunt

Coordinating Editors Dianne Schallmeiner, Gina Tsarouhas

Coordinating Cartographer Diana Von Holdt

Coordinating Layout Designer Jessica Rose

Managing Editors Barbara Delissen, Bruce Evans, Annelies Mertens

Managing Cartographers David Connolly, Amanda Sierp

Managing Layout Designer Chris Girdler

Assisting Editors Carolyn Bain, Elin Berglund, Carolyn Boicos, Samantha Forge, Cathryn Game, Lauren Hunt, Kim Hutchins, Kate James, Pat Kinsella, Helen Koehne, Kate Mathews, Mardi O'Connor, Charlotte Orr, Erin Richards, Gabrielle Stefanos, Simon Williamson

Assisting Cartographers Xavier Di Toro, Mick Garrett, Corey Hutchison, Jennifer Johnston

Cover Research Naomi Parker

Internal Image Research Rebecca Skinner

Language Content Branislava Vladisavljevic

Thanks to Anita Banh, Imogen Bannister, Daniel Corbett, Laura Crawford, Ryan Evans, Larissa Frost, Paul Iacono, Alison Lyall, Ross Macaw, Erin McManus, Anna Metcalfe, Virginia Moreno, Andy Neilson, Susan Paterson, Anthony Phelan, Martine Power, Kirsten Rawlings, Carlos Solarte, Gerard Walker

index

4WD tours 159, 411, 531, 576-7, 591, 599

A

Abel Tasman Coast Track 38, 437-8, **13**
Abel Tasman National Park 12, 435, 437-40, **437**
accommodation 676-9, *see also individual locations*
activities 35-53, *see also individual activities & locations*
adventure & amusement parks
  aMAZEme 304
  Cardrona Adventure Park 604
  Fyffe View Ranch Adventure Park 417
  Puzzling World 595
  Rainbow's End 75
  Spookers 74
  Waimarino Adventure Park 310
Aoraki/Mt Cook National Park 528-32, 613, **529**
aerial sightseeing, *see* scenic flights
Ahipara 160-2
air travel
  to/from Auckland 98
  to/from New Zealand 690-2
  to/from Wellington 387
  within New Zealand 692-3
airlines 691, 692-3
airports 690
Akaroa 17, 503-10, **507**
albatross 419, 420, 547, 548, 549
aMAZEme 304
amusement parks, *see* adventure & amusement parks
Anaura Bay 337
animals 653-4, *see also* birdwatching, *individual species,* zoos & wildlife parks
aquariums
  Eco World Aquarium 400-1
  Kelly Tarlton's 71-2
  Marine Studies Centre 548
  Milford Discovery Centre 616

000 Map pages
000 Photo pages

  National Aquarium of New Zealand 351
  Tongariro National Trout Centre 273
Aratiatia Rapids 262
archaeological sites, *see* historic sites
architecture 56, 63, 350-1
area codes 19, 220, 686
Arrow River 591
Arrowtown 587-91, **589**
art galleries, *see* galleries
Arthur's Pass 515-16
arts 659-64, 670-4
arts festivals
  Art Deco Weekend 353
  Christchurch Arts Festival 492
  Fringe NZ 25-6, 375
  International Film Festival 375
  Nelson Arts Festival 426
  New Zealand Comedy Festival 375
  New Zealand International Arts Festival 25, 375
  New Zealand International Comedy Festival 26, 81
  New Zealand International Film Festival 27, 81, 375
  NZ Body Painting Festival 268
  Oamaru Victorian Heritage Celebrations 29, 562
  Pohutukawa Festival 29
  Reel Earth Environmental Film Festival 253
  Sculpture on the Gulf 105
  Splore 26, 81
  Taranaki International Arts Festival 28, 230
  Wanaka Fest 599
  Wanganui Festival of Glass 243
  Wanganui Literary Festival 243
  World Buskers Festival 25, 492
  World of WearableArt Award Show 29, 375, 427
astronomy tours 524, 529, 607
Atene 249
ATMs 684
Auckland 6, 62-100, **61**, **64**, **68-9**, **72**, **76**, **78**, **82-3**, **86**, 7
  accommodation 60, 82-8
  activities 75-9
  children, travel with 77
  climate 60
  drinking 92-4
  entertainment 94-6
  festivals 80-2
  food 60, 62, 88-92
  highlights 61, 80
  internet access 97
  internet resources 62
  itineraries 33, 63
  shopping 96-7
  sights 62-75
  tourist information 97
  travel seasons 60
  travel to/from 98-9
  travel within 99-100
  walking tour 66, **66**
Automobile Association 676, 695

B

baches 101
Backcountry Hut Pass 40
backcountry huts 40
Ball, Murray 337
ballooning, *see* hot-air ballooning
Banks Peninsula 17, 503-10
Barrytown 457
Batten, Jean 646
Bay of Islands 10, 138-53, **126-7**, **138**,
  accommodation 125
  climate 125
  food 125
  high lights 126
  internet resources 128
  travel seasons 125
Bay of Plenty 308-30, **289**, 11
  accommodation 288
  climate 288
  highlights 289, 295
  travel seasons 288
B&Bs 676
beaches 24
  Auckland region 74, 115, 117, 124
  Bay of Islands 135
  Bay of Plenty 322, 327, 328
  Baylys Beach 167
  Christchurch 487
  Coromandel Peninsula 169, 181, 183, 183-4, 184-5, 186, 187-9
  East Coast 335
  Golden Bay 442, 443
  Great Barrier Island 109-13
  Hot Water Beach 184-5, 261
  Kapiti Coast 389-91, 392
  Lake Taupo 261
  Moeraki 566
  Muriwai Beach 117
  Nelson region 435
  Ninety Mile Beach 158-60
  Northland 157, 158, 167
  Ruapuke Beach 204
  safety 682-3
  Taranaki 228, 234, 238
  Te Henga (Bethells Beach) 116
  Tunnel Beach 537
  Waiheke Island 103
  Waikato 194-5, 203, 204
  West Coast 476
Beehive 370
beer, *see* breweries
bicycle travel, *see* cycling

Big Carrot 284
birdwatching 653-4, *see also individual birds*, zoos & wildlife parks
  hides 174, 526
Blackball 458
black-water rafting, *see* caves & caving, rafting
Blenheim 411-16
blokarting 319
Bluff 625
boat travel, *see also* boat trips
  to/from New Zealand 692
  to/from Wellington 387
  within New Zealand 693
boat trips, *see also* canoeing & kayaking, jetboating, rafting, sailing
  Auckland region 65, 80, 123
  Bay of Islands 139-41, 155
  Bay of Plenty 299, 305, 324
  Catlins, the 626-7
  Christchurch 490
  Coromandel Peninsula 182
  Doubtful Sound 618, 619
  Fiordland 617
  Hawke Bay 352
  King Country 212, 220
  Lake Taupo region 264, 266, 272, 274
  Lake Tekapo 524
  Marlborough Sounds 404, 405
  Milford Sound 616
  Queenstown 577-8
  Waikato 197, 201
  Wanaka 599
  Whakaari (White Island) 327
  Whangaui region 242
bone carving 201, 425, 464, 490
books, *see also* literature
  birdwatching 653
  culture 660, 663
  history 645
  regional topics 62, 128, 172, 194, 226, 260, 290, 335, 366, 400, 448, 482, 569, 536
  tramping 36
Brain Watkins House 309
Bream Bay 129-30
breweries
  Auckland region 117, 123
  Dunedin 537, 543
  Gisborne 340
  Greymouth 459
  Nelson region 429, 432
  Southland 621
  Taranaki 234
  Wanaka 595
  West Coast 450
Bridge to Nowhere 248, 249, **32**
budgeting 18
Buller Gorge 448, **52**
bungy jumping 47
  Auckland 75, 76
  Canterbury 512
  Central Plateau 287
  Lake Taupo region 267
  Queenstown 570-1
  Rotorua 294
Buried Village 305
bus travel
  to/from Auckland 98
  to/from Wellington 387-8
  tours 80
  within New Zealand 693-5
bushwalking, *see* Great Walks, tramping, walks
business hours 679
Butler, Samuel 522

C

Cambridge 206-9
camping 40, 336, 676-7, 693
Campion, Jane 671
canoeing & kayaking 51-3
  Abel Tasman National Park 438, 439
  Aoraki/Mt Cook National Park 530
  Auckland 76-7, 77
  Auckland region 120
  Banks Peninsula 506
  Bay of Islands 139, 150, 154
  Bay of Plenty 297, 299, 310, 316, 327
  Catlins, the 626
  Coromandel Peninsula 177, 184
  Doubtful Sound 618
  Fiordland 609-10, 617
  Franz Josef Glacier 472
  Golden Bay 442
  Hawke's Bay 352
  Lake Taupo region 265, 274
  Marlborough region 404, 405, 419
  Milford Sound 615, 616
  Nelson region 426
  Northland 132, 157
  Otago Peninsula 548
  Pororari River 456
  Queenstown region 592
  sporting events 449, 461
  Stewart Island 633
  Taranaki 229
  Waiheke Island 104
  Waikato 197, 198, 201
  Waioeka River 328
  Wanaka 597
  Wellington 373
  Whanganui National Park 248-9,
  Whanganui River 282, 284
Canterbury 510-32, **481**
  accommodation 480
  climate 480
  food 480
  highlights 481, 483
  internet resources 482, 500
  travel seasons 480
canyoning
  Coromandel Peninsula 175
  Queenstown 573
  Waitakere Ranges 115
  Wanaka 597
Cape Egmont Lighthouse 239
Cape Foulwind 450
Cape Kidnappers 361-2
Cape Palliser 394-5
Cape Reinga 158-60
Cape Runaway 335
car travel 19, 695-7
  maps 683
Cardrona 604
Carter Observatory 367
carvings 261, 660, **3**, *see also* bone carving
Caspian terns 444
Castle Hill 514
Cathedral Cove 183-4, **24**
cathedrals, *see* churches & cathedrals
Catlins, the 625-36, **625**
caves & caving 48
  Abbey Caves 131
  Aranui Cave 215
  Cathedral Caves 627
  Cave Stream Scenic Reserve 514
  Cavern Creek Caves 453
  Clifden (Waiau) Caves 619
  Crazy Paving & Box Canyon Caves 453
  Fox River Tourist Cave 455-6
  Glowworm Cave 215
  Harwood's Hole 440
  Honeycomb Hill Caves & Arch 453
  Kawiti Glowworm Caves 142
  King Country 215-16
  Muriwai's Cave 322
  Ngarua Caves 440
  Nikau Cave 195
  Nile River Caves 450
  Piripiri Caves Scenic Reserve 218
  Rawhiti Cave 440-1
  Ruakuri Cave 215
  Ruatapu Cave 272
  Te Anau Glowworm Caves 607
  Waitomo Caves 10, 214-18, **214**, **11**
cell phones 19, 686
Central Plateau 275-87, **259**
  accommodation 258
  climate 258
  food 258, 260
  highlights 259, 261
  internet resources 260
  travel seasons 258

Charleston 455
children, travel with 679-80
  Auckland 77
  Christchurch 491
  Queenstown 580
  Wellington 376
Christchurch 482-502, **484**, **488-9**
  accommodation 480, 492-5
  activities 487-90
  children, travel with 491
  drinking 482, 498-9
  entertainment 499-500
  festivals 491-2
  food 480, 482, 495-8
  highlights 481, 483
  internet resources 482, 500
  itineraries 487
  shopping 500
  sights 482-7
  tourist information 500-1
  tours 491
  travel to/from 501
  travel within 501-2
churches & cathedrals
  cardboard cathedral 484
  ChristChurch Cathedral 483-4
  Church of the Good Shepherd 524
  Holy Trinity Cathedral 67
  St Faith's Anglican Church 294
  St Patrick's Cathedral 64-5
  St Paul's Church 147
cinema 671
Clarence River 417
Clifden Suspension Bridge 619
climate 18, 35, 679, *see also individual regions*
climate change 691
climbing 274, 282, 316, 373, *see also* rock climbing
Colac Bay 620
Collingwood 443-4
conservation, *see* environmental issues, parks & reserves, zoos & wildlife parks
consulates 680-1
cooking courses 506
Cook, James 416, 640, 643
  monument 339, **641**
Cook Observatory 338
Copland Valley 477
Coroglen 183
Coromandel Peninsula 169-90, **170-1**
  accommodation 169
  climate 169
  food 172

000 Map pages
000 Photo pages

  highlights 170-1, 172
  internet resources 172
  travel seasons 169
Coromandel Town 176-9
Coronet Peak 24, 45, **15**
courses
  bone carving 425
  cooking 506
  mountaineering 530
  ropes 118, 182, 267
Crater Lake 280
crayfish 420
credit cards 684
Croydon Aircraft Company 626
cruises, *see* boat trips, sailing
culture 639, 649, 665, 669
  books 660, 663
  Maori people 13, 22, 26, 657-64, **27**
  Pacific Islander people 26, 81, 97, **27**
  tours 79, 132-3, 141, 147, 159, 164, 268, 272, 291, 294, 298, 341, 357, 374, 401, 420
Curio Bay 627
currency 18
customs regulations 680
cycling 48-50, 693
  Auckland region 118
  Bay of Islands 139
  Bay of Plenty 295-6, 311
  Canterbury 512
  Central Plateau 284
  Christchurch 487
  Coromandel Peninsula 174, 175, 179
  cycle touring 50
  East Coast 341
  Fox Glacier 474
  Franz Josef Glacier 470
  Golden Bay 440, 441
  Great Barrier Island 111
  Hawke's Bay 352
  Hokitika 463
  Kahurangi National Park 445
  Lake Taupo region 267
  Little River Rail Trail 492
  Makara Peak 373-4
  Marlborough Sounds 404
  Martinborough 392-3
  Minaret Burn Track 597
  Nelson region 425, 426, 441
  Nga Haerenga, New Zealand Cycle Trail 250, 693
  Otago Central Rail Trail 15, **15**
  Queenstown 575
  Ruapehu Whanganui Trails 285
  sporting events 29, 268, 461, 579
  Tongariro Forest 278
  Tongariro National Park 282
  Tongariro River Trail 273
  Victoria Forest Park 457
  Waikato 207
  Wanaka 598

D

dance 663
dangers, *see* safety
Dargaville 167-8
Darwin, Charles 645
Days Bay 373
Dean Forest 619
Denniston Plateau 452
Department of Conservation 677, 687, 695
disabilities, travellers with 626, 687
distilleries 561, *see also* breweries
Divide, the 612
diving 51
  Auckland 76
  Bay of Islands 138-9
  Bay of Plenty 310, 315, 324, 327
  Coromandel Peninsula 181, 184, 185
  East Coast 338
  Great Barrier Island 109-11
  Marlborough region 417
  Marlborough Sounds 404, 405
  Milford Sound 616
  Northland 136, 157
  Poor Knights Islands 136
  shark-cage dives 338, 341
dolphin spotting 654, **17**
  Auckland 75
  Banks Peninsula 506
  Bay of Islands 140, 141
  Bay of Plenty 310, 324, 327
  Catlins, the 626
  Kaikoura 418, 419
  Marlborough Sounds 404
  Te Waewae Bay 620
Doubtful Sound 618-19
Doubtless Bay 156-7
Dowse, The 371
drinking 23, 681, *see also* breweries, distilleries, wineries
driving, *see* car travel
Driving Creek Railway & Potteries 177
driving licences 695
Dundle Hill 216
Dunedin 535-47, **538**
  accommodation 533, 539-41
  activities 537-9
  climate 533
  drinking 543-4
  entertainment 544-5
  food 533, 541-3
  highlights 534, 535
  internet resources 536
  shopping 545
  sights 535-7
  tourist information 545

tours 537-9
travel seasons 533
travel to/from 546
travel within 546-7
Durie Hill Elevator 241-2
D'Urville Island 404
DVDs 677

E

earthquakes 486, 638, 645, 649, 651
East Cape 334-46
East Coast 331-63, **332-3**
accommodation 331
climate 331
food 335
highlights 332-3, 334
internet resources 335
travel seasons 331
Eastwoodhill Arboretum 339
economy 639, 646, 649, 667
electricity 677, 680
Elephant Rocks 564
Ellery Lake 478
embassies 680-1
emergencies 19
environmental issues 652
Cape Reinga 159
climate change 691
fishing 155
Lake Tasman 532
Maungatautari Ecological Island 207
MV *Rena* 315
One Tree Hill (Maungakiekie) 75
etiquette 661
events, *see* festivals & events, sporting events
exchange rates 19
extreme sports 21, *see also individual sports*

F

Fairlie 523
Farewell Spit 444
farmstays 677
festivals, *see also* arts festivals, food & wine festivals, *individual locations*, music festivals, sporting events
beer 375
comedy 25, 26, 27, 81, 311, 375
Festival of Lights 25, 82, 229
film 27, 81, 253, 375
flowers 230, 357, 520
gay & lesbian travellers 81, 681-2
literature 243
Maori culture 25, 26, 81, 212, 375
Pacific Island culture 26, 81, **27**
Pohutukawa Festival 29, 172
Waitangi Day 25, 142, 673, 685
film 367, 638, 663
festivals 27, 81, 253, 375
film locations 80, 209, 374, 385, 440, 514, 526, 564, 621, 671
Finn brothers 205, 673
Fiordland 607-19, **606**, **17**
accommodation 605
activities 605
climate 605
highlights 606
travel seasons 605
fishing 656
Bay of Plenty 298, 310
Coromandel Peninsula 177, 185
environmental issues 155
Great Barrier Island 109-11
King Country 212
Manapouri 617
Marlborough region 420
Mt Cook Salmon Farm 522
Queenstown 575
Stewart Island 633-4
Taupo region 266, 274
Wanaka 598
West Coast 467
flightseeing, *see* scenic flights
food 23, 681, *see also* food & wine festivals, *individual locations*
food & wine festivals
Bluff Oyster & Food Festival 625
Carrot Carnival 283
Devonport Food & Wine Festival 81
French Fest Akaroa 506
Gibbston Harvest Festival 578
Gisborne Food & Wine Festival 341
Kaikoura Seafest 29, 420
Kawhia Traditional Maori Kai Festival 212
Manawatu Wine & Food Festival 253
Marlborough Wine Festival 25, 411
Oamaru Wine & Food Festival 561
Toast Martinborough 29, 394
Waipara Wine & Food Festival 510
Wairarapa Wines Harvest Festival 394
Wellington on a Plate 375
Wildfoods Festival 26, 465
football 668
Footrot Flats 337
Forgotten World Hwy 220, 237
Fort Taiaroa 547
fortified villages
Kaikoura 416
Kororipo Pa 150
Motuhora (Whale Island) 327
Opapake Pa 216
Operiki Pa 248
Otatara Pa 351
Papaka Pa 323
Puketapou 323
Rangikapiti Pa Historic Reserve 156
Ruapekapeka Pa Historic Reserve 144
Ngati Hei 180
Soundshell 297
Te Hana Te Ao Marama 122
Toi's Pa 295
Whanganui National Park 246
Whangarei 132
Four Sisters 166
Fox Glacier 474-7, **475**
Frame, Janet 559, 670
Franz Josef Glacier 469-74, **470**, **10**
freedom camping 336, 695
French Pass 404

G

galleries, *see also* museums
Academy Galleries 367
Aigantighe Art Gallery 518
Anderson Park Art Gallery 621
Andris Apse Wilderness Gallery 468
Auckland Art Gallery 62-3
Christchurch Art Gallery 485
Chronicle Glass Studio 241
Dowse, The 371
Eastern Southland Gallery 626
Govett-Brewster Art Gallery 227
Hokitika Craft Gallery 463
Jagosi Jade 463-4
New Zealand Portrait Gallery 367
Shark Nett Gallery 410
Steampunk HQ 20, 560
Suter 423
Te Waipounamu Maori Heritage Centre 463
Tectonic Jade 463
Wallace Arts Centre 20, 74
Wellington City Gallery 367
gannets 117, 118, 324, 361, 362, 444
gardens, *see also* parks & reserves
Auckland Botanic Gardens 74
Butterfly & Orchid Garden 174
Christchurch Botanic Gardens 482
Connells Bay 104
Dead Dog Bay 104
Eastwoodhill Arboretum 339
Giant's House 504
Glenfalloch Woodland Garden 547-8
Miyazu Japanese Garden 424
Parnell Rose Gardens 71
Pukeiti Rhododendron Garden 234
Pukekura Park 226-7
Rapaura Water Gardens 176
Rose Garden 205
Trevor Griffiths Rose Garden 519
Waihi Waterlily Gardens 188
Wellington Botanic Gardens 371
Zealandia Sculpture Garden 121

gay travellers 81, 93, 681-2
geography 639, 650-1
geology 526, 532, 650-1
Geraldine 521-2
geysers 210, 262, 272, 291, 307
Giant's House 504
Gibbston Valley 585
Gillespie Pass 603
Gisborne 338-43, **340**
glaciers 10, 469-77, 528, **470**, **475**, **10**
Glenorchy 591-3
gliding 267, 565, *see also* hang gliding, paragliding
glowworms 216, 217, 450, 463, 607
gold panning 467, 588, 597
Golden Bay 440-4
golf 267, 298, 390, 588, 598
Gore 626
Graham, Stanley 465
Gravity Canyon 287
Great Barrier Island 109-13, **110**
Great Walks 37-8, **37**
  Abel Tasman Coast Track 38, 437-8, **13**
  Heaphy Track 14, 38, 444-5, 453-4, **14**
  Kepler Track 607-9, **609**
  Lake Waikaremoana Track 38, 345-6, **345**, **39**
  Milford Track 38, 613-14, **614**, **39**
  Rakiura Track 38, 633
  Routeburn Track 593, **594**
  Tongariro Northern Circuit 278
  Whanganui Journey 248, 249-50
Greymouth 455, 459-63, **460**
Greytown 395-6
gumdigging 159, 167

H

Haast region 477-9
Hahei 183-4
haka 662, **27**
Hamilton 195-201, **196**
hang gliding 425, 565, 573
Hanmer Springs 510-13, **511**
Hapuawhenua viaduct 284
Hari Hari 467-8
Harwood's Hole 440
Hastings 356-61, **357**
Hauraki Gulf 6, 100-13, **6**
Havelock 409
Hawea 604
Hawera 240
Hawke's Bay 347-63, **348**
health 682-3
Heaphy Track 14, 38, 444-5, 453-4, **14**
Hector 452
Helensville 118
heliskiing 45, 516, 530, 578
Hells Gate 304-5
Hermitage 528-9
herons 73, 468
hiking, *see* Great Walks, tramping, walks
Hillary, Edmund 529, 647, 668
Hinemoa 296, 299
historic sites, *see also* fortified villages
  Arrowtown Chinese Settlement 588
  baches 101
  Buried Village 305
  Christchurch Arts Centre 483
  Fort Taiaroa 547
  Hukutaia Domain 328
  Kororipo Pa 150
  Monmouth Redoubt 308-9
  Orakau 206
  Puketapu 322
  Rangikapiti Pa Historic Reserve 156
  Ruapekapeka Pa Historic Reserve 144
  Stony Batter Historic Reserve 104
  Te Hana Te Ao Marama 122
  Te Papaka 322
  Waitangi Treaty Grounds 146, 648
history 21, 640-9
  books 645
  European settlement 642-6
  internet resources 641, 642
  Land Wars 647
  Maori people 73, 212, 213, 238, 278, 296, 324, 347, 640-2
  Musket Wars 641, 644
  WWI 645
  WWII 646, 647
hitching 697
Hokianga Harbour 162-5
Hokitika 463-7, **464**
holidays 685
Hollyford Valley 613
Homer Tunnel 613
Hone Heke 144, 642
Horeke 163
horse trekking 48
hostels 677-8
hot springs
  Athenree Hot Springs 188
  Bay of Plenty 304-5
  Craters of the Moon 262
  Great Barrier Island 111
  Hanmer Springs Thermal Pools 511
  Hinemoa 299
  Lake Tekapo 524
  Lost Spring 181
  Mangatutu Hot Pools 363
  Maruia Springs 514
  Miranda Hot Springs 173
  Morere Hot Springs 344
  Motuhora (Whale Island) 327
  Ngawha Springs Pools 163
  Opal Hot Springs 209
  Parakai Springs 118
  Polynesian Spa 297
  Taranaki Thermal Spas 228-9
  Te Puia Hot Springs 211
  Te Whakarewarewa 291
  Tokaanu Thermal Pools 273
  Wairakei Terraces & Thermal Health Spa 262
  Waiwera Thermal Resort 120
hot-air ballooning
  Auckland 77
  Canterbury 516
  East Coast 357
  Queenstown 576
  sporting events 198
  Waikato 198
hotels 678
Hukutaia Domain 328
Hurworth Cottage 234
hypothermia 682

I

ice skating 576
immigration 647, 667, 687, 690
Inglewood 237
insurance
  car 697
  health 682
  travel 683
International Antarctic Centre 484-5
internet access 683
internet resources 19
  accommodation 656, 676
  air tickets 691-2, 693
  arts 674
  Auckland region 62
  Bay of Islands 128
  Canterbury 482, 500
  Central Plateau 260
  Christchurch 482, 500
  Coromandel Peninsula 172
  Dunedin 536
  East Coast 335
  food 681
  gay & lesbian travellers 681
  health 682
  history 641, 642
  King Country 194
  Maori people 129
  Marlborough region 400
  music 672, 673
  Nelson region 400
  Northland 128
  Queenstown 569
  sustainable travel 656

000 Map pages
000 Photo pages

Taranaki 226
tramping 36
Waikato 194
Wellington 366
West Coast 448
Whanganui region 226
Invercargill 621-5, **623**
i-SITE 687
itineraries 30-4
Auckland 63
Christchurch 487
Queenstown 571, 573
Rotorua 291
Wellington 367, 375

J

Jack's Blowhole 629
Jackson Bay 478
Jackson, Peter 385, 671
Jagosi Jade 463-4
jetboating 48
Auckland 77
Bay of Islands 141
Bay of Plenty 295, 321
Buller Gorge 449
Coromandel Peninsula 184
Dart River 592
East Coast 335
Fiordland 609-10
Haast River 478
Hawke Bay 352
King Country 221
Lake Taupo region 263, 272
Makaora 603
Motu River 329
Queenstown 571
Southern Scenic Route 620
Waiau Gorge 512
Waikato 207
Wanaka 597
Whanganui National Park 249
Whanganui region 252

K

Kai Iwi Lakes 166
Kaikoura 9, 416-23, **418**, **9**
Kaitaia 160
Kaiteriteri 435-6
Kapiti Coast 389-91
Karamea 452-5
Karangahake Gorge 189
Karekare 115
Karikari Peninsula 157-8
Katikati 320-1
kauri 656
Kauri Coast 165-8
Kawakawa 142
Kawau Island 108-9
Kaweka Ranges 363
Kawhia 211-12
kea 469
Kenepuru 409-11
Kepler Track 607-9, **609**
Kerikeri 150-3, **151**
King Country 211-22, **192-3**
accommodation 191
climate 191
highlights 192, 195
internet resources 194
travel seasons 191
Kingitanga 213, 667
Kingston Flyer, The 569
kiteboarding 48
Auckland 117
Karikari Peninsula 157
Nelson region 425
Waikato 203
kiwifruit 320
kiwis 131, 150-1, 207, 213, 304, 392, 469, 569, 635, 654
Knights Point 477
Kohukohu 162
Kororipo Pa 150
kotuku 468
Kowhitirangi 465
Kumeu 116-17

L

Lake Brunner 459
Lake Ferry 394-5
Lake Kaniere 465
Lake Karapiro 207
Lake Mahinapua 467
Lake Matheson 476
Lake Moeraki 477
Lake Ohau Forest 527-8
Lake Pukaki 526
Lake Rotokura 286
Lake Rotorua 29, **306**
Lake Surprise 284
Lake Sylvan 592
Lake Tarawera 305, **306**
Lake Tasman 532
Lake Taupo 260-75
Lake Tekapo 524-6
Lake Tutira 347
Lake Waikareiti 346
Lake Waikaremoana 344
Lake Waikaremoana Track 38, 345-6, **345**, **39**
Lake Wakatipu 593-5, **16**
Land Wars 647
languages 18, 699-703
Larnach Castle 547
Leigh 123
lesbian travellers 81, 93, 681-2
Lewis Pass 513-14
literature 664, 670, *see also* books
festivals 243
Lord of the Rings 440, 671
luging 295, 417, 556, 569, 575
Lyttelton 502-3

M

Mahia Peninsula 344
Makarora 603-4
Maketu 321
Manapouri 617-18
Manawatu Gorge 257
Mangakino 272
Mangapurua Trig 250
Mangawhai 128-9
Mansfield, Katherine 370, 670
Manu Bay 204
Maori people 13, 657-64, **27**
carvings 261, 660, **3**
festivals 25, 26, 81, 212, 375
fortified villages 122, 132, 144, 150, 156, 180, 216, 246, 248, 295, 297, 323, 327, 351, 416
history 73, 212, 213, 238, 278, 296, 324, 347, 640-2
internet resources 129
politics 73
regional highlights 22, 80, 129, 172, 195, 227, 261, 295, 334, 371, 401, 449, 483, 535, 569
religion 659
tours 79, 132-3, 133, 141, 147, 159, 164, 268, 272, 291, 294, 298, 341, 357, 374, 401, 420
Maori War & Early Settlers Cemetery 195
maps 36, 683
marae 661
Hinemahuru marae 335
Huria Marae 309
Kahungunu Marae 344
Koriniti Marae 251
Maketu Marae 212
Maniaroa Marae 220
Motuti Marae 162
Taane-nui-a-Rangi Marae 344
Te Manuka Tutahi Marae 20, 322
Turangawaewae Marae 195
Marahau 436-7
marine reserves, *see* parks & reserves
Marine Studies Centre 548
markets 24, 67, 201, 500, 681
Marlborough region 400-23, **399**, **412**
accommodation 398
climate 398
food 398, 400
highlights 399, 401
internet resources 400
travel seasons 398

Marlborough Sounds 404-5, **406**
Martinborough 392-3, **28**
Masterton 396-7
Matakana (Auckland region) 122-3
Matakana Island (Bay of Islands) 319
Matakohe 168
Matamata 209-10
Matauri Bay 154
Matiu-Somes Island 373
Maungakiekie (One Tree Hill) 74, 75
Maungatautari Ecological Island 207
Maungawhau (Mt Eden) 67
measures 677
medical services 682
Medieval Mosaic 521
Methven 516-18
microbreweries, *see* breweries
Middle-earth 374, 671
Mikhail Lermontov 404
Milford Sound 16, 615-17, **17**
Milford Track 38, 613-14, **614**, **39**
Miranda 173
Mitai Maori Village 294
Mitimiti 162
moa 261, 320, 440, 443, 641, 652, 653
mobile phones 19, 686
Moeraki Boulders 566
Mohaka viaduct 347
Mokau 220
Mokena Geyser 210
Mokoia Island 292
Molesworth Station 511
money 18, 19, 680, 684
Monmouth Redoubt 308-9
monuments
  Big Carrot 284
  Big Shearer statue 219
  Cook Monument 339, **641**
  Pohaturoa 322
  Rainbow Warrior 154, 648, 649, 666, **648**
  statue of Wairaka 324
  Stonehenge Aotearoa 396
  Te Tauihu Turanga Whakamana 339
Moriori people 641
motels 678
motorcycle travel 695-7
  maps 683
  sporting events 243, 621
  tours 80, 188
Motu River 329
Motueka 432-5, **433**
Motuhora (Whale Island) 327
Motuihe Island 101
Motuora Island 108

000 Map pages
000 Photo pages

Motutapu Island 100-1
mountain biking, *see* cycling
mountaineering 50
  Canterbury 529-30
  Dunedin 537
  Queenstown region 574, 593
  Taranaki 235
  Wanaka 598
Mt Cook Salmon Farm 522
Mt Eden (Maungawhau) 67
Mt Hikurangi 337
Mt Holdsworth–Jumbo Circuit 40
Mt Karioi 204
Mt Lyford 512
Mt Maunganui 315-19, **316**
Mt Ngauruhoe 276, **644**
Mt Pirongia 204-5
Mt Pureora 272
Mt Ruapehu 276
Mt Somers 518
Mt Taranaki 234-7, **32**
Mt Te Aroha 210
Mt Titiraupenga 272
Mt Tongariro 276
Mt Tutoko 613
Mt Victoria 73
Murchison 448-50
museums 22, *see also* galleries
  Auckland Museum 67
  Bluff Maritime Museum 625
  Cable Car Museum 371
  Canterbury Museum 483
  Cobblestones Village Museum 395
  East Coast Museum of Technology & Transpor 339
  Edwin Fox Maritime Museum 400
  Gumdiggers Park 159
  KD's Elvis Presley Museum 240
  Medieval Mosaic 521
  MOTAT 73
  Mount Surf Museum 316
  Museum of Wellington City & Sea 367
  National Army Museum 286
  Navy Museum (Auckland) 73
  New Zealand Rugby Museum 20, 252
  Omaka Aviation Heritage Centre 411
  Omaka Classic Cars 411
  Otago Museum 535
  Petone Settlers Museum 371
  Puke Ariki 226
  Rotorua Museum 20
  School of Mines & Mineralogical Museum 174
  Sir Edmund Hillary Alpine Centre 529
  Southward Car Museum 390
  Tairawhiti Museum 338
  Taranaki Aviation, Transport & Technology Museum 234
  Taranaki Pioneer Village 237-8
  Taupo Museum 261
  Te Ana Maori Rock Art Centre 518
  Te Papa 374, **22**
  Tramway Museum 389-90
  Vanished World Centre 564
  Vintage Car & Machinery Museum 521
  Volcanic Activity Centre 263
  Voyager – New Zealand Maritime Museum 65
  Waitomo Caves Discovery Centre 215
  Wanaka Transport & Toy Museum 595
  Warbirds & Wheels 595
  Weta Cave 370
  Whanganui Riverboat Centre 241
music 663, 672-4
music festivals
  Auckland region 81, 105
  Coromandel Peninsula 182
  Country Rock Festival 142
  Garden City SummerTimes 492
  Gold Guitar Week 626
  International Jazz & Blues Festival 253
  Jazz & Blues Festival 28, 142
  National Jazz Festival 311
  Nelson Jazz & Blues Festival 26, 426
  New Zealand Gold Guitar Awards 27
  Rhythm & Vines 29
  Rippon Festival 599
  WOMAD 26, 229
  World Buskers Festival 25
Musket Wars 641, 644
MV *Rena* 315, 638

N

Napier 348-56, **350**
National Aquarium of New Zealand 351
National Library of New Zealand 370-1
National Park Village 282-3
national parks & reserves, *see* parks & reserves
Nelson 423-30, **424**
Nelson region 423-45, **399**
  accommodation 398
  climate 398
  food 398
  highlights 399, 401
  internet resources 400
  travel seasons 398
netball 668
New Plymouth 226-33, **228**
New Zealand basics 18-19
news 677
Ngai Tahu people 483
Ngakawau 453
Nga-Tapuwae-o-te-Mangai 158
Ngati Tarara people 161
Ngati Tuwharetoa people 261
Ngati Whatua people 73

Ngatoro-i-rangi 278
Northland 125-37, **126-7**
accommodation 125
climate 125
food 125, 128
highlights 126, 129
internet resources 128
travel seasons 125
number-eight wire 669

O

Oakura 238-9
Oamaru 559-64, **560**
Ohakune 283-6
Ohinemutu 293-4
Ohope 327-8
Okarito Lagoon 468
Omahuta Forest 153
Omaka Aviation Heritage Centre 411
Omaka Classic Cars 411
Omaperer 164-5
Omarama 564-6
Omeka 158
One Tree Hill (Maungakiekie) 74, 75
Oparara Valley 453
opening hours 679
Operiki Pa 248
Opononi 164-5
Opotiki 328-30, 335
Opoutere 186
Opunake 239-40
Orakau 206
Orakei Korako 272
Orewa 119-20
Orokonui Ecosanctuary 536
Otago 15, 551-66, **534**
accommodation 533
climate 533
food 533
highlights 534, 535
travel seasons 533
Otago Peninsula 14, 545, 547-51, **548-9**, **14**
Otari-Wilton's Bush 371
Otatara Pa 351
Otorohanga 212-14
Owaka 629
Owhango 221-2

P

pa, *see* fortified villages
Paaku 185
Pacific Islander people 26, 81, 97, **27**
Paekakariki 389-90
Paeroa 190
Paihia 146-50, **146**
Pakiri 124
Palmerston North 252-6, **253**
Pancake Rocks 455
Papamoa 319
Paradise Valley Springs 304
paragliding 48, 295, 356, 425, 573, 574, 598
Paraparaumu 390-1
parasailing 139, 267, 295
Parihaka 238
parks & reserves 656, **655**
Abel Tasman National Park 12, 435, 437-40, **437**
AH Reed Memorial Kauri Park 131
Aoraki/Mt Cook National Park 528-32, 613, **529**
Canaan Downs Scenic Reserve 440
Coromandel Forest Park 177
Craigieburn Forest Park 514
Egmont National Park 234-7
Fiordland National Park 605, 613
Goat Island Marine Reserve 123
Kahurangi National Park 444-5
Kaimai Mamaku Forest Park 310
Kapiti Island 391
Long Bay Regional Park 118
Mahurangi Regional Park 121
Mangapohue Natural Bridge Scenic Reserve 218
McLaren Falls Park 310
Mt Alta Conservation Area 597
Mt Aspiring National Park 597, 603, 613
Mt Taranaki (Egmont National Park) 234-7
Nelson Lakes National Park 430-1
Nga Manu Nature Reserve 392
One Tree Hill (Maungakiekie) 74-5
Paparoa National Park 455-6
Pirongia Forest Park 204-5
Pisa Conservation Area 604
Pohatu Nature Reserve 505
Poor Knights Islands 136
Puke Ariki Landing 227
Pureora Forest Park 272
Rakiura National Park 631, 632
Rangikapiti Pa Historic Reserve 156
Rotokura Ecological Reserve 286
Ruapekapeka Pa Historic Reserve 144
Scandrett Regional Park 121
Shakespear Regional Park 119
Sugar Loaf Islands Marine Park 227
Tararua Forest Park 397
Tawharanui Regional Park 122
Te Tapuwae o Rongokako Marine Reserve 338
Te Urewera National Park 344-7, **39**
Te Whanganui-A-Hei Marine Reserve 182
Tongariro National Park 44-5, 275-82, **277**, **12**, **644**
Trounson Kauri Park 166
Victoria Forest Park 457
Wairere Boulders Nature Park 163
Westland Tai Poutini National Park 469, 613
Whakanewha Regional Park 104
Whanganui National Park 246-52, **247**
Whirinaki Forest Park 308
passports 687, 690
paua 685-6
Pauanui 185-6
Peel Forest 522-3
Pelennor battlefield 526
Pelorus Sounds 409-11
penguins 653
blue penguins 166, 324, 373, 401, 550, 560, 562, 627, 629, 632, 633
yellow-eyed penguins 547, 548-9, 550, 560, 562, 566, 626, 627, 629, 632
phonecards 686
Picton 400-7, **402**
Piha 115-16
Pike River coalmine disaster 638, 649
planning 638, *see also individual regions*
budgeting 677
itineraries 30-4
New Zealand's regions 54-7
repeat visitors 20
tramping 35-41
travel seasons 18
weather 35
plants 651-2, **28**,
Pohara 442-3
Pohaturoa 322
Pohutu 291
politics 73, 646, 649, 665-8
Poor Knights Islands 135-7
population 638, 639, 665, 667
Port Chalmers 545
Port Waikato 194-5
postal services 684
Pouakai Circuit 40
pounamu 686
Pouto Point 168
Prince of Wales' Feathers 291
public holidays 685
pubs 678
Puhoi 120-1
Puke Ariki 226
Puke Ariki Landing 227
Puketapu 322
Puketi Forest 153
Puketui Valley 186
Punakaiki 455
Putangirua Pinnacles 394

Q

quad-biking 118, 161, 163, 268, 280, 472, 512
Queenstown 16, 568-87, **570**, **572**, **576**
  accommodation 567, 579-82
  activities 570-6
  children, travel with 580
  climate 567
  drinking 584-5
  entertainment 585-6
  festivals 578-9
  food 567, 582-4
  highlights 568, 569
  internet resources 569
  itineraries 571, 573
  shopping 586-7
  sights 569-70
  tourist information 586-7
  travel seasons 567
  travel to/from 587
  travel within 587

R

Rabbit Island 432
radio 677
rafting 51-3
  Buller Gorge 448, **52**
  Canterbury 512, 523
  Clarence River 417
  East Cape 335
  Franz Josef Glacier 472
  King Country 215-16, 216
  Lake Taupo region 265
  Mohaka River 363
  Motu River 329
  Nelson region 426
  Nile River Caves 450
  Peel Forest 523
  Queenstown 571-3
  Rangitata River 522, 523
  Rotorua 296
  sporting events 449
  Tongariro River 273-4
  Wairoa River 309
  Wanaka 597
  Whanganui River 284
  Whataroa River 472
Raglan 201-3, **202**
railways
  Driving Creek Railway & Potteries 177
  Goldfields Railway 188
  Kingston Flyer, The 569
  Rain Forest Express 114
  Raurimu Spiral 221
  Taieri Gorge Railway 546
  Thames Small Gauge Railway 174
  TranzAlpine 17, 462, **17**
  Waitakere Tramline Society 114
Rainbow Warrior 154, 648, 649, 666, **648**
Rain Forest Express 114
Rakiura, *see* Stewart Island
Rakiura Track 38, 633
Rangiaowhia 206
Rangikapiti Pa Historic Reserve 156
Rangipo Desert 286
Rangirii 195
Rangitata River 522, 523
Rangitoto Island 100-1
Raurimu Spiral 221
Rawene 163-4
Rawhiti 137
Redwoods Whakarewarewa Forest 305
Reefton 457-8
Rees Valley 592
religion 659
Remarkables,the 45, **16**
rental accommodation 678-9
responsible travel, *see* sustainable travel
ride-sharing 697
river sledging, *see* rafting
Riverton 620-1
Roaring Bay 629
rock climbing 50-1
  Dunedin 537
  Hamilton 197
  Queenstown 574
  Rotorua 295
  Waikato 197-8, 206
  Waitomo Caves 216
  Wanaka 598
rock paintings 518, 564
rocksliding 341
ropes courses 118, 182, 267
Rotoroa Island 108
Rotorua 8, 290-304, **292**, **306**
  accommodation 299-301
  activities 294-8
  drinking 302
  entertainment 302
  food 290, 301-2
  highlights 289
  itineraries 291
  shopping 303
  sights 291-4
  tourist information 303
  travel to/from 303
  travel within 303-4
Routeburn Track 593, **594**
Ruahine Ranges 363
Ruapehu Whanganui Trails 285
rugby 12, 375, 424, 668, **12**
Russell 142-6, **143**
Rutherford, Ernest 483, 645, 667

S

safety 685
  beaches 682-3
  Hot Water Beach 185
  mountaineering 529-30
  tramping 36, 280
sailing
  Abel Tasman National Park 438
  Auckland region 65, 75
  Banks Peninsula 506
  Bay of Islands 139, 140, 141
  Bay of Plenty 310
  Coromandel Peninsula 177
  Lake Taupo region 265
  Nelson region 426
  Rotorua 298-9
  sporting events 142
sandboarding 164
scenic flights
  Aoraki/Mt Cook National Park 530
  Bay of Islands 141
  Bay of Plenty 298, 311, 324, 327
  Canterbury 524, 526
  Central Plateau 280, 284
  Christchurch 490
  Fiordland 610, 613, 612
  Fox Glacier 475, 476
  Franz Josef Glacier 471
  Golden Bay 441
  Gore 626
  Hokitika 465
  Lake Taupo region 268
  Makarora 603
  Marlborough region 405, 419
  Nelson region 433
  Queenstown 576
  Taranaki 235
  Wanaka 598, 599
  Wellington 374
  Whanganui region 242
scuba diving, *see* diving
sea kayaking, *see* canoeing & kayaking
sea lions 549, 550, 626
seals 394, 417, 419, 438, 450, 477, 548-9, 549, 626, 654
senior travellers 680
sheep-shearing 219, 311, 396, 417
Ship Creek 477
Shipwreck Ino 627
shopping 685-6, *see also individual locations*
Sir Edmund Hillary Alpine Centre 529
skiing & snowboarding 15, 24, 42-6, **44**
  Aoraki/Mt Cook National Park 530
  Auckland region 119

000 Map pages
000 Photo pages

Canterbury 516, 524
Central Plateau 276-7, 278
Hanmer Springs Ski Field 512
heliskiing 45, 516, 530, 578
Lake Taupo region 267
Mt Lyford Ski Field 512
Queenstown 578
sporting events 578-9
Taranaki 235-6
Sky Tower 63
skydiving 51
Auckland 76
Bay of Islands 139
Bay of Plenty 295, 310-11
Canterbury 516
Fox Glacier 475
Franz Josef Glacier 472
Glenorchy 592
Lake Taupo region 266
Marlborough region 417
Nelson region 433
Northland 132
Queenstown 574
Waikato 209
Wanaka 598
Skydome Observatory 167
smoking regulations 681
Snell, Peter 240
snorkelling, *see* diving
snowboarding, *see* skiing & snowboarding
soccer 668
Soundshell 297
Southern Scenic Route 619-21
Southland 621-5, **606**
accommodation 605
activities 605
climate 605
highlights 606
travel seasons 605
special events, *see* festivals & events, sporting events
spelunking, *see* caves & caving
sporting events
100K Flyer 268
Auckland Anniversary Day Regatta 80
Auckland Cup Week 81
Auckland International Boat Show 29
Balloons Over Waikato 198
BikeFest & Lake Taupo Cycle Challenge 29, 268
Buller Festival 449
Burt Munro Challenge 621
Coast to Coast 461
Day-Night Thriller 268
Epic Swim 268
Golden Shears 396
Great Lake Relay 268
Hamilton 400 198
Ironman New Zealand 268
Lake Taupo Cycle Challenge 29
motor racing 267
New Zealand International Sevens 26, 375
NZ Masters Games 243
Opotiki Rodeo 329
Point Sheep Shearing Show 417
Queenstown Bike Festival 579
Queenstown Winter Festival 578-9
rafting 449
rodeo 329
Running of the Sheep 219
Russell Birdman 28, 142
sailing 142
September.Cemetery Circuit Motorcycle Race 243
sheep-shearing championships 219
skiing & snowboarding 578-9
Tall Ship Race 142
Warbirds over Wanaka 599
Weekend Coastal Classic 142
sports 668, *see also* sporting events
Stardome Observatory 74
Steampunk HQ 560
Stewart Island 630-6, **631**
Stonehenge Aotearoa 396
Stratford 237-8
Sumner 496
surfing 53, *see also* beaches
Surville Cliffs 158
sustainable travel 128, 172, 194, 226, 260, 290, 335, 400, 482, 536
air travel 691
internet resources 656
tramping 41
Suter 423

T

Taihape 287
Tainui waka 212
Tairua 185-6
Takaka 440-2
Takiroa Maori Rock Art Site 564
Tama Lakes 280
Tamaki Maori Village 294
Tane Mahuta 166
Tangi te Korowhiti 212
Taranaki 223-40, **224-5**
accommodation 223
climate 223, 235
highlights 224, 226
internet resources 226
travel seasons 223
Tasman, Abel 640
Tasman Glacier 528
tattooing 660
Taumarunui 220-1
Taumatawhakatangihangakoauauotamateaturipukakapikimaungahoronukupokaiwhenuakitanatahu 362
Taupiri 197
Taupo 260-71, **262**, **264**
Tauranga 308-15
Tauranga Bay 154
Tauranga Bridge 335
Tawarau Forest 218
tax 684, 689, 690
Te Ana Maori Rock Art Centre 518
Te Anau 607-12, **608**
Te Araroa 40
Te Aroha 210-11
Te Awamutu 205-6
Te Hana Te Ao Marama 122
Te Henga 116
Te Henga (Bethells Beach) 116
Te Kaha 335
Te Kooti 347
Te Kuiti 219-20
Te Matua Ngahere 166
Te Papa 374
Te Papaka 322
Te Puia 291
Te Puke 321-2
Te Toto Gorge 204
Te Urewera National Park 344-7, **39**
Te Waewae Bay 620
Te Wahipounamu Southwest New Zealand World Heritage Area 613
Te Waikoropupu Springs 440
Te Waipounamu Maori Heritage Centre 463
Te Whakarewarewa 291
Te Wherowhero 642
Tectonic Jade 463
telephone services 19, 686
Thames 173-6, **174**
theatre 663
theme parks, *see* adventure & amusement parks
thermal spas, *see* hot springs
Tikitere 304-5
Timaru 518-21, **519**
time 686-7
tipping 681, 684
Tiritiri Matangi Island 108
Titirangi 113-14
Toanui viaduct 284
Toast Martinborough 375
Tokaanu Thermal Pools 273
Tokomaru Bay 336, 337
Tongariro Alpine Crossing 12, 40, 278-9, 282, **12**
Tongariro National Park 44-5, 275-82, **277**, **12**, **644**
Tongariro National Trout Centre 273

Tongariro Northern Circuit 278
Toroa 324
tourist information 687
tours
  4WD 159, 411, 531, 576-7, 591, 599
  astronomy 524, 529, 607
  cultural 79, 132-3, 141, 147, 159, 164, 268, 272, 291, 294, 298, 341, 357, 374, 401, 420
  food & wine 79, 105, 141, 311, 357, 374, 491, 539, 575, 578, 599
  motorcycle travel 80, 188
  walking 66, 79, 80
  wildlife 548-9
train travel 698, *see also* railways
  to/from Auckland 99
  to/from Wellington 388
tramping 22, 35-41, *see also* Great Walks, walks
  accommodation 40
  hut passes 281
  internet resources 36
  safety 36, 280
  sustainable travel 41
TranzAlpine railway 17, 462, **17**
travellers cheques 684
travel to/from New Zealand 690-2
travel within New Zealand 692-8
Treaty of Waitangi 146, 642, 644, 648, 665
trees 654-6
trekking, *see* Great Walks, tramping, walks
TSS *Earnslaw* 577-8
Tuatapere 619-20
Tuhua (Mayor Island) 319
tui 607, 626, 632, 653
Tupare 234
Turangi 273-5, **273**
Tutanekai 296
Tutukaka Coast 135-7
TV 671, 677
Twizel 526-7

U

Ulva Island 632
Underwater Observatory 570
unemployment 639
Urupukapuka Island 150, **11**

V

vacations 685
Vanished World Centre 564
vegetarian travellers 681
visas 19, 687-8
visual arts 663, 664, 674
volcanoes 651
  Auckland 71
  Hells Gate 304-5
  Motuhora (Whale Island) 327
  Mt Eden (Maungawhau) 67
  Mt Ngauruhoe 276, **644**
  Mt Ruapehu 276
  Mt Taranaki 234 , **32**
  Mt Tongariro 276
  Mt Victoria 73
  Rangitoto Island 100-1
  Tikitere 304-5
  Waimangu Volcanic Valley 307
  Wai-O-Tapu Thermal Wonderland 307, **8**
  Whakaari (White Island) 326-7
volunteering 688

W

waders 173, 444
Waiheke Island 103-8, **102**, **6**
Waihi 187-9
Waikanae 392
Waikato 194-211, **192-3**
  accommodation 191
  climate 191
  food 194
  highlights 192, 195
  internet resources 194
  travel seasons 191
Waikato River 196-7, **52**
Waikite Valley 307
Waimangaroa 452
Waioeka Gorge 335
Waioeka River 328
Wai-O-Tapu Thermal Wonderland 307, **8**
Waiouru 286
Waipapa Point 627
Waipara Valley 510
Waipoua Forest 165-6
Waipu 129-30
Wairakei 261-2, **264**
Wairarapa 391-7
Waireinga 204
Waitakere Tramline Society 114
Waitaki Valley 564-6
Waitangi 146-50
Waitangi Treaty Grounds 648
Waitomo Caves 10, 214-18, **214**, **11**
Waiwera 120
Wake, Nancy 646
wakeboarding 272
walks, *see also individual locations*, Great Walks, tramping
  Aoraki/Mt Cook National Park 530
  Banks Peninsula Track 505
  Bay of Plenty 310, 322
  Big Tree Walk 522
  Bridge to Nowhere 248, 249, **32**
  Cape Reinga Coastal Walkway 158
  Caples Track 594, **594**
  Charming Creek Walkway 453
  Coast to Coast Walkway 77-9
  Coromandel Peninsula 187
  East Coast 363
  Fiordland 613, 617
  Fox Glacier 474
  Franz Josef Glacier 470-1
  Gillespie Pass 603
  Great Barrier Island 111
  Greenstone Track 594, **594**
  Hillary Trail 114
  Kahurangi National Park 445
  Mangapurua/Kaiwhakauka Track 250
  Marlborough Sounds 404
  Matemateaonga Track 250
  Minaret Burn Track 597
  Mt Somers Subalpine Walkway 518
  Mt Taranaki (Egmont National Park) 235
  Nelson Lakes National Park 430
  Northern Tarawera Track 297
  North West Circuit Track 633
  Otago 537
  Queen Charlotte Track 40, 407-9
  Rainbow Mountain Track 297
  Rees-Dart Track 594
  Rob Roy Valley Track 597
  Round the Mountain Track 279
  Rotorua 297
  Ruapani Track 346
  Silica Rapids Track 280
  Southern Circuit Track 633
  Tama Lakes Track 280
  Tasman Glacier 530
  Tongariro Alpine Crossing 12, 40, 278-9, 282, **12**
  Tongariro River Trail 273
  Tuatapere Hump Ridge Track 40, 619-20
  Waikato River Trails 207
  Waipu Coastal Trail 130
  Wairakau Stream Track 155
  Wairake Track 204
  Wangapeka Track 445
  West Coast 453
  West Matukituki Valley 597
  Wharekirauponga walk 187
  Wilkin Valley Track 603
Wanaka 595-603, **568**, **596**, **2-3**, **43**
  accommodation 567
  climate 567

000 Map pages
000 Photo pages

food 567
highlights 568
travel seasons 567
Wanganui, *see* Whanganui
Warbirds & Wheels 595
Warkworth 121-2
waterfalls
Aratiatia Rapids 262
Bridal Veil Falls 204
Dawson Falls 235
Devils Punchbowl Waterfall 515
Fantail Falls 479
Haruru Falls 147
Huka Falls 261-2
Karekare Falls 115
Marokopa Falls 218
McLean Falls 627
Okere Falls 297
Rainbow Falls 151
Rere Falls 341
Sutherland Falls 614
Taranaki Falls 280
Tarawera Falls 297
Te Reinga Falls 344
Thunder Creek 479
Waiau Falls 180
Wainui Falls 442
Waireinga 204
Wairere Falls 209, 322
Waitonga Falls 284
Wentworh Falls 187
Whangarei Falls 131
Wharepuke Falls 151
Whirinaki Waterfalls 308
weather 18, 679, *see also individual regions*
weaving 662
websites, *see* internet resources
weights 677
Wellington 8, 366-89, **365**, **368-9**, **378-9**, **9**
accommodation 364, 375-9
activities 373-4
children, travel with 376
climate 364
drinking 383-4
entertainment 384-6
festivals 374-5
food 364, 379-83
highlights 365, 371
internet access 386
internet resources 366, 387
itineraries 367, 375
shopping 386
sights 367-73
tourist information 387
travel seasons 364
travel to/from 387-8
travel within 388-9
walking tour 372
Wellywood 385
West Coast 446-79, **447**
accommodation 446
climate 446
highlights 447, 449
internet resources 448
travel seasons 446
West Matukituki Valley 597
Westport 450-2
Whakaari (White Island) 326-7
Whakamaru 272
Whakatane 322-6, **323**
Whale Bay 204
whale-watching 9, 654
Auckland 75
Bay of Plenty 324
Catlins, the 626
Marlborough region 417-19
Te Waewae Bay 620
Whangamata 186-7
Whangamomona 237
Whanganui 240-6, **242**
Whanganui Journey 248, 249-50
Whanganui region, **224-5**
accommodation 223
highlights 224, 227
internet resources 226
travel seasons 223
Whangarei 130-5, **132**
Whangaroa Harbour 155
Wharepapa South 206
Whenuakite 183
white-water rafting, *see* caves & caving, rafting
Whitianga 180-3, **181**
wildlife, *see* animals, birdwatching, plants, zoos & wildlife parks
windsurfing 181, 203, 310, 374
wine 681
wineries 23, *see also* food & wine festivals
Auckland region 79, 98, 117
Bay of Islands 152
Bay of Plenty 309, 320
Coromandel Peninsula 189
Gibbston Valley 585
Gisborne 339
Hawke's Bay 348, 357, 360
Marlborough region 414-15, **412**
Nelson region 431, 432
Northland 160
Queenstown 578
tours 79, 105, 141, 311, 357, 491, 539, 575, 578, 599
Waiheke Island 103-4
Waipara Valley 510
Wairarapa 391-2, 394-5, **28**
Wingspan Birds of Prey Trust 304
women in New Zealand 644, 667
women travellers 688
work 688-9
world's second-longest place name 362
world's steepest residential street 536
WWI 645
WWII 646, 647
WWOOFing 678

Y

yachting, *see* boat trips, sailing
Yakas 166

Z

ziplining 575, 580
zoos & wildlife parks
Altura Gardens & Wildlife Park 215
Aroha Island 150-1
Auckland Zoo 73
Blue-Penguin Colony 560
DOC Te Anau Wildlife Centre 607
Farewell Spit 444
Hamilton Zoo 197
International Antarctic Centre 484-5
Katikati Bird Gardens 320
Kiwi Birdlife Park 569
Kotuku Sanctuary 468
Lake Tutira 347
Marshalls Animal Park 310
Miranda Shorebird Centre 173
Native Bird Recovery Centre 131
Nga Manu Nature Reserve 392
Orana Wildlife Park 485
Orokonui Ecosanctuary 536
Otorohanga Kiwi House & Native Bird Park 213
Owlcatraz 256
Paradise Valley Springs 304
Point Kean Seal Colony 417
Pukaha Mt Bruce National Wildlife Centre 397
Rainbow Springs Kiwi Wildlife Park 304
Royal Albatross Centre 547
Staglands Wildlife Reserve 373
Tauranga Bay Seal Colony 450
Wai Ariki Farm Park 512
Wellington Zoo 373
West Coast Wildlife Centre 20, 469
Willowbank Wildlife Reserve 486
Wingspan Birds of Prey Trust 304
Yellow-Eyed Penguin Conservation Reserve 547
Zealandia 373
zorbing 295

how to use this book

These symbols will help you find the listings you want:

- Sights
- Beaches
- Activities
- Courses
- Tours
- Festivals & Events
- Sleeping
- Eating
- Drinking
- Entertainment
- Shopping
- Information/ Transport

These symbols give you the vital information for each listing:

- Telephone Numbers
- Opening Hours
- Parking
- Nonsmoking
- Air-Conditioning
- Internet Access
- Wi-Fi Access
- Swimming Pool
- Vegetarian Selection
- English-Language Menu
- Family-Friendly
- Pet-Friendly
- Bus
- Ferry
- Metro
- Subway
- London Tube
- Tram
- Train

Reviews are organised by author preference.

Look out for these icons:

- TOP CHOICE — Our author's recommendation
- FREE — No payment required
- A green or sustainable option

Our authors have nominated these places as demonstrating a strong commitment to sustainability – for example by supporting local communities and producers, operating in an environmentally friendly way, or supporting conservation projects.

Map Legend

Sights
- Beach
- Buddhist
- Castle
- Christian
- Hindu
- Islamic
- Jewish
- Monument
- Museum/Gallery
- Ruin
- Winery/Vineyard
- Zoo
- Other Sight

Activities, Courses & Tours
- Diving/Snorkelling
- Canoeing/Kayaking
- Skiing
- Surfing
- Swimming/Pool
- Walking
- Windsurfing
- Other Activity/ Course/Tour

Sleeping
- Sleeping
- Camping

Eating
- Eating

Drinking
- Drinking
- Cafe

Entertainment
- Entertainment

Shopping
- Shopping

Information
- Post Office
- Tourist Information

Transport
- Airport
- Border Crossing
- Bus
- Cable Car/ Funicular
- Cycling
- Ferry
- Metro
- Monorail
- Parking
- S-Bahn
- Taxi
- Train/Railway
- Tram
- Tube Station
- U-Bahn
- Other Transport

Routes
- Tollway
- Freeway
- Primary
- Secondary
- Tertiary
- Lane
- Unsealed Road
- Plaza/Mall
- Steps
- Tunnel
- Pedestrian Overpass
- Walking Tour
- Walking Tour Detour
- Path

Boundaries
- International
- State/Province
- Disputed
- Regional/Suburb
- Marine Park
- Cliff
- Wall

Population
- Capital (National)
- Capital (State/Province)
- City/Large Town
- Town/Village

Geographic
- Hut/Shelter
- Lighthouse
- Lookout
- Mountain/Volcano
- Oasis
- Park
- Pass
- Picnic Area
- Waterfall

Hydrography
- River/Creek
- Intermittent River
- Swamp/Mangrove
- Reef
- Canal
- Water
- Dry/Salt/ Intermittent Lake
- Glacier

Areas
- Beach/Desert
- Cemetery (Christian)
- Cemetery (Other)
- Park/Forest
- Sportsground
- Sight (Building)
- Top Sight (Building)

Contributing Authors

Professor James Belich wrote the History chapter (p640). James is one of NZ's pre-eminent historians and the award-winning author of *The New Zealand Wars, Making Peoples* and *Paradise Reforged*. He has also worked in TV – *New Zealand Wars* was screened in NZ in 1998.

Tony Horwitz wrote the Captain James Cook boxed text (p643) in the History chapter. Tony is a Pulitzer-winning reporter and nonfiction author. His fascination with James Cook, and with travel, took him around NZ, Australia and the Pacific while researching *Blue Latitudes* (alternatively titled *Into the Blue*), part biography of Cook and part travelogue.

John Huria (Ngai Tahu, Muaupoko) wrote the Maori Culture chapter (p657). John has an editorial, research and writing background with a focus on Maori writing and culture. He was senior editor for Maori publishing company Huia and now runs an editorial and publishing services company, Ahi Text Solutions Ltd (www.ahitextsolutions.co.nz).

Josh Kronfeld wrote the Surfing in New Zealand boxed text (p53) in the Extreme New Zealand chapter. Josh is an ex–All Black flanker, whose passion for surfing NZ's beaches is legendary and who found travelling for rugby a way to surf other great breaks around the world.

Gareth Shute wrote the Music section (p672) in the Arts & Music chapter. Gareth is the author of four books, including *Hip Hop Music in Aotearoa* and *NZ Rock 1987–2007*. He is also a musician and has toured the UK, Europe and Australia as a member of The Ruby Suns and The Brunettes. He now plays in indie soul group The Cosbys.

Nandor Tanczos wrote the Environmental Issues in Aotearoa New Zealand boxed text (p652) in the Environment chapter. NZ's first Rastafarian Member of Parliament (NZ Greens Party), and the first to enter parliament in dreadlocks and a hemp suit, he was also the Green Party's spokesperson on constitutional issues and the environment from 1999 to 2008.

Vaughan Yarwood wrote the Environment chapter (p650). Vaughan is an Auckland-based writer whose most recent book is *The History Makers: Adventures in New Zealand Biography*. Earlier work includes *The Best of New Zealand, a Collection of Essays on NZ Life and Culture by Prominent Kiwis,* which he edited, and the regional history *Between Coasts: from Kaipara to Kawau*. He has written widely for NZ and international publications and is the former associate editor of *New Zealand Geographic,* for which he continues to write.

Thanks to Dr David Millar for his help with the Health content, Grace Hoet for her contribution to the Maori Culture chapter, and all the NZ regional tourism organisations for their help with pre-research briefings.

OUR STORY

A beat-up old car, a few dollars in the pocket and a sense of adventure. In 1972 that's all Tony and Maureen Wheeler needed for the trip of a lifetime – across Europe and Asia overland to Australia. It took several months, and at the end – broke but inspired – they sat at their kitchen table writing and stapling together their first travel guide, *Across Asia on the Cheap*. Within a week they'd sold 1500 copies. Lonely Planet was born.

Today, Lonely Planet has offices in Melbourne, London and Oakland, with more than 600 staff and writers. We share Tony's belief that 'a great guidebook should do three things: inform, educate and amuse'.

OUR WRITERS

Charles Rawlings-Way

Coordinating author; Plan Your Trip, Waikato & the King Country, Taranaki & Whanganui, Rotorua & the Bay of Plenty, Survival Guide English by birth, Australian by chance, All Blacks fan by choice: Charles' early understanding of Aotearoa was less than comprehensive (sheep, mountains, sheep on mountains...). He realised there was more to it when a wandering uncle returned with a faux-jade *tiki* in 1981. Mt Taranaki's snowy summit, Raglan's point breaks and Whanganui's raffish charm have enthralled. He's once again smitten with NZ's phantasmal landscapes, disarming locals and determination to sculpt its own political and indigenous destiny.

Brett Atkinson

Christchurch & Canterbury, Dunedin & Otago, Queenstown & Wanaka, Fiordland & Southland On his third research trip to the 'mainland', Brett explored Maori rock art, stayed in a historic cottage in the Gibbston Valley, and negotiated a penny-farthing bicycle around Oamaru. Two weeks researching earthquake-damaged Christchurch left him even more impressed with the resilience and determination of the people of Canterbury. Brett has covered ten countries for Lonely Planet, and more than 40 countries as a freelance travel and food writer. See also www.brett-atkinson.net.

Sarah Bennett & Lee Slater

The East Coast, Wellington Region, Marlborough & Nelson, The West Coast Raised at the top of the South, Sarah migrated to Wellington at 16 and has lived there ever since, except for various travels and a stint in London working at Lonely Planet's UK office. During research, she strives to find fault, particularly in relation to baked goods and beer selection. Sarah is joined in this endless quest by her husband and co-writer, Lee. English by birth and now a naturalised New Zealander, Lee's first career as an engineer has seen him travel extensively around Europe, the Middle East, North Africa and the Caucasus. Sarah and Lee are co-authors of *Let's Go Camping* and *The New Zealand Tramper's Handbook*. They are also freelance feature writers for newspapers and magazines, including the *Dominion Post* and *Wilderness*.

Peter Dragicevich

Auckland, Bay of Islands & Northland, Coromandel Peninsula, Taupo & the Central Plateau, New Zealand Today, The Kiwi Psyche, Arts & Music After nearly a decade working for off-shore publishing companies, Peter's life has come full circle, returning to West Auckland where he was raised. As Managing Editor of Auckland-based *Express* newspaper he spent much of the '90s writing about the local arts, club and bar scenes. This is the third edition of the *New Zealand* guide he's worked on and, after dozens of Lonely Planet assignments, it remains his favourite gig.

OVER PAGE MORE WRITERS

Published by Lonely Planet Publications Pty Ltd
ABN 36 005 607 983
16th edition – September 2012
ISBN 978 1 74220 017 0

10 9 8 7 6 5 4 3 2 1
Printed in China

Bestselling guide to New Zealand – source: Nielsen BookScan, Australia, UK and USA, March 2011 to February 2012